The Pacific Islands

THE PACIFIC ISLANDS

Environment and Society

REVISED EDITION

Moshe Rapaport

 UNIVERSITY OF HAWAI'I PRESS | HONOLULU

18 17 16 15 14 13   6 5 4 3 2 1

Library of Congress Cataloging-in-Publication Data
The Pacific islands : environment and society / [edited by] Moshe Rapaport.
— Revised edition.
    pages cm
 Originally published in 1999 by Bess Press.
 Includes bibliographical references and index.
 ISBN 978-0-8248-3586-6 (pbk. : alk. paper)
 1. Human geography—Islands of the Pacific. 2. Human ecology—Islands of
the Pacific. 3. Environmental protection—Islands of the Pacific. 4. Islands
of the Pacific—Geography. 5. Islands of the Pacific—Social life and customs.
6. Islands of the Pacific—History. I. Rapaport, Moshe.
 GF851.P33 2013
 304.20995—dc23
                                2012033129

Designed by Mardee Melton
Printed by Sheridan Books, Inc.

CONTENTS

List of Tables vii
Preface ix

The Physical Environment

1. Climate
   Andrew P. Sturman and Hamish A. McGowan 1
2. Oceanography
   Lynne D. Talley, Gerard J. Fryer, and Rick Lumpkin . . . 19
3. Geology
   *David M. Kennedy, Gerard J. Fryer, and
   Patricia Fryer.* 34
4. Geomorphology
   Patrick D. Nunn 45
5. Soils
   R. John Morrison 59
6. Water
   Derrick Depledge and James P. Terry 70

The Living Environment

7. Biogeography
   Brenden S. Holland and E. Alison Kay 83
8. Terrestrial Ecosystems
   *Harley I. Manner, Dieter Mueller-Dombois, and
   Moshe Rapaport.* 95
9. Aquatic Ecosystems
   Stephen G. Nelson. 109

History

10. The Precontact Period
    Frank R. Thomas 125
11. The Postcontact Period
    David A. Chappell 138
12. Changing Patterns of Power
    Terence Wesley-Smith 147

Culture

13. Language
    Andrew Pawley 159
14. Social Relations
    Lamont Lindstrom 172
15. Gender
    Julie Cupples and Nancy McDowell 182
16. Tenure
    Ron Crocombe 192

17. Law
    Richard Scaglion. 202
18. Religion
    John Barker 214
19. Literature
    Selina Tusitala Marsh 225
20. Art
    Caroline Vercoe 236
21. Music and Dance Performance
    Paul Wolffram 248

Population

22. Demography
    Jean Louis Rallu and Dennis Ahlburg. 263
23. Mobility to Migration
    John Connell and Moshe Rapaport. 275
24. Health
    Annette Sachs Robertson 287
25. Education
    Ron Crocombe. 299
26. Urban Challenges
    Donovan Storey and John Connell 310

Economy

27. Pacific Island Economies
    Geoff Bertram 325
28. Agriculture
    Harley I. Manner and Randolph R. Thaman 341
29. Logging
    Colin Filer. 355
30. Ocean Resources
    Vina Ram-Bidesi 364
31. Mining
    Glenn Banks 379
32. Tourism
    Simon Milne 392
33. Communications
    Michael R. Ogden 401
34. Development Prospects
    Donovan Storey and David Abbott 417

Atlas 423
Island Gazetteer 431
List of Contributors 439
Index 443

LIST OF TABLES

Table 1.1   Conditions Favorable or Necessary for Tropical Cyclone Genesis 5

Table 4.1   Geologic Time Scale Since the Cretaceous 47

Table 4.2   Classification of Pacific Islands Used as a Basis for Systematic Landscape Description 49

Table 4.3   Sediment Yields of Rivers in Papua New Guinea . . 51

Table 4.4   Selected Rates of Recession and Progradation on Pacific Island Coasts 53

Table 4.5   Rates of Lateral Inundation for Selected Island Groups in the South Pacific 54

Table 4.6   Selected Rates of Uplift and Subsidence for Pacific Islands. 54

Table 5.1   Average Rainfall Data for Suva and Nadi, Fiji Islands. 60

Table 5.2   Extent of Acid Soils in Some Pacific Island Countries 64

Table 5.3   Topsoil and Subsoil Nutrient Data for Two Fiji Pedons 66

Table 5.4   Changes in Soil Properties with Time for a Sugar Cane Farm, Seaqaqa, Vanua Levu, Fiji 67

Table 6.1   Long-Term Averages of Monthly Rainfall for Three Capital Cities in the Tropical Pacific Islands 71

Table 6.2   Largest Rivers on Selected Islands in the Tropical Pacific 71

Table 6.3   Domestic Water Consumption in Some Pacific Countries 73

Table 6.4   Typical Analyses for Freshwater Resources in the Pacific 76

Table 8.1   Classification of Pacific Island Terrestrial Ecosystems 106

Table 9.1   Number of Fish Species in Various Trophic Categories in the Purari River, Papua New Guinea 110

Table 9.2   Primary Productivity Rates in the Ocean 112

Table 9.3   Benefits and Costs of Symbiosis Between Corals and Zooxanthellae 113

Table 9.4   Comparison of Some of the Major Aquatic Ecosystems of the Pacific Island Region 119

App. 9.1   Taxonomic Relationships of Some Common Aquatic Invertebrates 119

Table 10.1   Major Pacific Island Plant Foods 127

Table 11.1   Political Status of Pacific Island Groups 144

Table 13.1   Approximate Number of Indigenous Languages and Unrelated Families in Pacific Regions. 160

Table 13.2   Some Austronesian Cognate Sets. 161

Table 13.3   Some Cognate Sets of the Trans–New Guinea Family 163

Table 13.4   Some Proto-Oceanic Terms for Canoe Parts and Seafaring 168

Table 13.5   Some Proto-Oceanic Terms for Horticulture and Food Plants 168

App. 17.1   Customary Law in the Pacific Islands 211

Table 22.1   Demographic Indicators for Pacific Island Countries and Territories 264

Table 22.2   Proportion of Population by Large Age Groups and Dependency Ratio 272

Table 23.1   Population Growth and Migration Rates, Pacific Islands. 279

Table 23.2   Pacific Island First-Generation Migrant Diasporas 280

Table 24.1 Demographic Estimates for Pacific Island
          Populations 290

Table 24.2 Infant and Child Health and Access Statistics
          in Selected Pacific Island Countries 293

Table 24.3 Maternal Health Statistics for Selected
          Pacific Islands. 294

Table 25.1 Percentage of Female Students at USP
          by Country 306

Table 26.1 Urbanization in the Pacific Islands. 311

Table 27.1 Background Data on Twenty-Seven Pacific
          Economies 326

Table 27.2 Per Capita GDP/GNI by Political Status 327

Table 27.3 Financing of the Current Account in
          Thirteen Pacific Island Economies 331

Table 27.4 Pacific Island First-Generation Migrant
          Diasporas 336

Table 28.1 Pacific Island Agricultural and Marine Exports . . 348

Table 29.1 Contribution of Logging to Deforestation
          in PNG 359

Table 30.1 The Relative Importance of Coastal Fisheries
          in the Pacific Islands. 366

Table 30.2 Annual Volume and Value of Commercial
          and Subsistence Coastal Fisheries 367

Table 30.3 Tuna Catch by Gear Type in Western and
          Central Pacific Fisheries Region 370

Table 30.4 Tuna Catch by Species in Western and
          Central Pacific Region 370

Table 30.5 Tuna Catch by Flagged Vessels in the Western
          and Central Pacific Ocean 371

Table 30.6 Cultivation of Aquaculture Commodities
          in the Pacific Islands Region 374

Table 31.1 Comparative Mineral Production Statistics
          for Selected Countries 381

Table 31.2 Mining's Contribution to Some Pacific Island
          Economies 382

Table 32.1 Background Data on Pacific Island Tourism . . . 393

Table 32.2 Solomon Islands Arrival Statistics 397

Table 33.1 Trans-Pacific Communication Cables 403

Table 33.2 Satellite Communications Infrastructure 404

Table 33.3 Pacific Islands Fixed-Line and Mobile
          Telephones 407

Table 33.4 Pacific Islands Internet and Broadband 409

Table 34.1 Poverty Head Counts in the Pacific 419

Table 34.2 Selected Human Development
          Index Trends 420

PREFACE

The Study of Regions

The study of regions is one of the oldest and most fundamental themes of scholarly inquiry and has long engaged academic interest alongside systematic approaches to scientific understanding. While populations and land areas of the Pacific Islands are relatively small, this vast archipelagic world is in many ways unique and offers special opportunities for regional study. Courses focusing on the Pacific Islands are offered at many universities, and Pacific Island Studies programs have been established. There is currently a vital need for a basic reference on Pacific Islands environment and society, which this book aims to fill.

The revaluation of place in the social sciences and humanities offers a contemporary rationale for the study of regions. As political boundaries have become permeable to economic, demographic, and cultural flows, distant places and regions come increasingly into view. Yet local institutions and cultures endure, providing the reassurances of stability, tradition, authenticity, and care. Modernization, long seen as transcending place and region, is conditioned by locale (Daniels 1992). Even in Hawai'i and New Zealand (sometimes considered part of the Pacific Rim) there is keen awareness of the historical and current linkages with other parts of the Pacific Islands region.

Regions are at best models of the real world. This is particularly so for the Pacific Islands, which range from far-flung coral atolls to large islands with fast-flowing rivers and high mountain ranges; from cultures where traditional chiefs still hold power to those where indigenous languages have become endangered. The boundaries of regions are notoriously difficult to define. Yet like all models, regions allow useful generalizations. Like other forms of education, regional awareness is an essential mode of dispelling ignorance, misunderstanding, mistrust, and conflict (Johnston 1990).

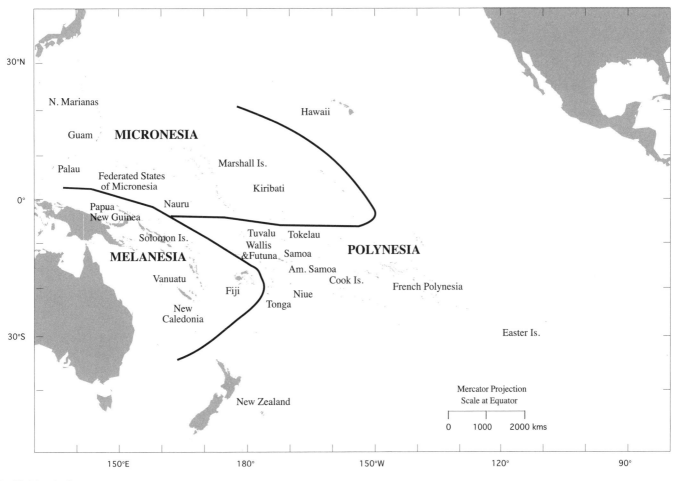

Pacific Island culture areas.

Rationales for Pacific Island regional study have been discussed by Wesley-Smith (1995). The diversity, isolation, and small-scale dimensions of islands and island populations present laboratory-like opportunities for research on general questions about nature and society. Information from the Pacific has sparked debate and rethinking on topics ranging from evolution to philosophy and culture. National interest has been an important factor in launching and funding regional studies programs. Regional study can also provide a venue for reorienting education to become more attuned to local needs and local empowerment.

The relation between researcher and researched, and the ethics thereof, has been the subject of heated debate and was a key question in the *Native Pacific Cultural Studies on the Edge* symposium (Diaz and Kauanui 2001). The case has been made for a moratorium on any ethnographic studies by non-native scholars (Trask 1991; Hereniko 2000). Teaiwa (in press) cautions against a "war-cry for ownership of knowledge and resources that can block critical investigation—even by indigenous people" and suggests that the critical question may be "not who does the work, but how it is done."

The status of New Zealand and Hawai'i as "First World societies," as well as New Zealand's location outside the tropics, have often led to the exclusion of these island groups from the field of Pacific Island Studies. Some studies of the Pacific Islands exclude New Guinea or New Zealand since major portions of these islands were rifted from continents. These islands are included in this volume as they do have much in common with other Pacific Island groups, and the ecological and socioeconomic contrasts relative to smaller, tropical islands enriches the comparative analysis of the region.

Organization and Scope

To address the need for a regional study, overviews of key topics in Pacific environment and society have been presented in this volume. While no rigid style was imposed, authors were requested to address issues of theory, historical change, and regional variability. To give priority to explanation, the chapters are organized by subject, covering both the natural environment and human society. References to particular locations are made where necessary for explanation and example and to illustrate intraregional variation, as deemed appropriate for the respective topics.

The book opens with the Physical Environment (chapters 1 through 6), which provides the foundation for the Living Environment (chapters 7 through 9). Coverage of society begins with History (chapters 10 through 12), followed by selected aspects of Culture (chapters 13 through 21). This sequence provides a broad basis for the subsequent focus on Population (chapters 22 through 26) and Economy (chapters 27 through 34). Interdisciplinary connections are present throughout, and a certain degree of overlap was unavoidable. Thus the chapter on politics is placed in accordance with its strong historical emphasis, but it could alternatively have been grouped elsewhere.

Within the book's geographic scope are the island groups of Melanesia, Micronesia, and Polynesia (Clark 2003). While there are cultural affinities between the Pacific Islands and Southeast Asia, the latter region has experienced two millennia of powerful influences from Asian civilizations. In the Pacific, distance and other factors (such as disease in lowland New Guinea) permitted society to develop in relative isolation from Asia, fostering a largely independent historical trajectory. Within the region, environmental and cultural differences are considerable, yet the Pacific Islands have much in common; they are joined, rather than divided, by the world's largest ocean (Hau'ofa 1993).

The study of the Pacific Islands region draws on the work of many academic disciplines, and the selection of authors has not been constrained within a narrow disciplinary or ideological framework. Authors include natural scientists, social scientists, and humanists who have devoted their research and careers to the Pacific Islands region and who have experience, including fieldwork, and knowledge of the relevant literature. Several authors are of indigenous descent or affiliation. Most are faculty members at Pacific Island universities and long-term residents of the region. All chapters were reviewed by competent scholars in the appropriate fields.

Themes

Among the chapters, emphases differ considerably depending on the subject and the interests and areas of expertise of the authors. Nonetheless, it is possible to briefly present four key themes tying together the diverse chapters in this volume. These include environmental process (chapters 1 through 9), social change (chapters 10 through 21), population-resource relations (chapters 22 through 34), and the Pacific Islands as a region (a theme implicit in this project as a whole).

Environmental process. Island groups as diverse as New Guinea, Hawai'i, Niue, and Tokelau are products of plate tectonic activity. Prevailing pressure and wind systems influence ocean currents and rainfall, which in turn affect landforms, biota, and the feasibility of human settlement. Having evolved in isolation, island ecosystems were severely affected by the arrival and proliferation of human settlers. This disturbance is exacerbated today by increasing overexploitation, soil erosion, exotic introductions, species extinctions, and pollution.

Social change. Factors of size and distance left island societies vulnerable to colonial intervention. Traditional systems of leadership, social organization, and beliefs have changed significantly since contact. Island societies have adapted and have been able to benefit from modern technologies and cultural offerings. Concurrently, there is a desire to maintain and revive indigenous identity and the arts. Systems of tenure, law, and governance introduced during the colonial period are being re-evaluated today.

Population-resource relations. Relative to continents, the Pacific Islands are remote, fragmented, and resource-poor. Population growth remains high, straining the capacity of governments to provide jobs and services. Subsistence horticulture and fisheries are losing ground. Sources of economic output include agriculture, fisheries and aquaculture, mining, tourism, and offshore fisheries licensing and other schemes. The emerging communications industry holds promise. Yet island communities remain dependent on foreign aid and migrate in large numbers to Pacific Rim countries.

The Pacific Islands as region. The Pacific Island region is the world's largest grouping of islands, spanning a third of the Earth's surface. Both physical environments and ecosystems have striking similarities across the region. Island societies have common roots and historical experiences, and they share many cultural features. Regionalism persists today through transnational networks of kin; a plethora of regional organizations; a literary and artistic renaissance; a close-knit academic community; and related identities, cultures, and destinies.

New in the Second Edition

The second edition of this book includes new chapters on gender, music and dance, logging, and development. The chapters on education, urbanization, health, ocean resources, and tourism have been replaced under new authorship. Additional collaborators have joined the chapters on geology, water, biogeography, art, and migration. Sadly, two of the contributors, Alison Kay and Ron Crocombe, are deceased and not able to view their chapter updates in print. Fortunately, Brenden Holland was able to work with Alison Kay's chapter and undertake an excellent and thorough updating.

Acknowledgments

Sincere thanks are due to the numerous reviewers, of which the following can be named: Tim Adams, Tim Bayliss-Smith, Chuck Birkeland, David Chappell, Bill Clarke, John Connell, John Culliney, Bryce Decker, Derrick Depledge, Sitaleki Finau, Michael Hamnett, Alison Kay, Kimberlee Kihleng, Robert Kiste, Stephen Levine, Nancy Lewis, Jim Mak, Harley Manner, Michael McCarthy, Steve Montgomery, John Morrison, Patrick Nunn, Wali Osman, Jim Parrish, Andrew Pawley, Karen Peacock, Jean-Louis Rallu, Rick Scaglion, Mary Spencer, Matthew Spriggs, Dick Stroup, Frank Thomas, Garry Trompf, and Terence Wesley-Smith.

For photos, thanks are due to Wendy Arbeit, Glenn Banks, John Barker, Honolulu Academy of Arts, Lamont Lindstrom, Harley Manner, Len Mason, Father Bernie Miller, Dieter Mueller-Dombois, Patrick Nunn, Michael Ogden, Vina Ram-Bidesi, Rick Scaglion, Donovan Storey, Andrew Sturman, Caroline Vercoe, Deborah Waite, Paul Williams, Paul Wolffram, Don and Carolyn Yacoe.

With hundreds of graphics and numerous collaborating authors, publishing this volume might have seemed daunting, but the University of Hawai'i Press was thankfully willing to take up the challenge. Thanks are particularly due to Keith Leber, who provided support with format and content revisions, and guided the project through the review process and subsequent corrections. Thanks are also due to support by UH Press director William Hamilton; executive editor Patricia Crosby; Nadine Little, who replaced Keith as acquisitions editor; managing editor Ann Ludeman, copy editor Drew Bryan, proofreaders Stuart Robson and Wendy Bolton, and design and production specialists Julie Chun and Mardee Melton.

I dedicate this book to Bryce and Shirley Decker.

BIBLIOGRAPHY

Clark, G. 2003. Dumont d'Urville's Oceania. *Journal of Pacific History* 38(2): 155–161.

Daniels, S. 1992. Place and the geographical imagination. *Geography* 77(4): 310–322.

Diaz, V. M., and J. K. Kauanui. 2001. Native Pacific cultural studies on the edge. *The Contemporary Pacific* 13(2): 315–342.

Hau'ofa, E. 1993. A new Oceania: Rediscovering our sea of islands. In *A new Oceania: Rediscovering our sea of islands,* ed. E. Waddell, V. Naidu, and E. Hau'ofa, 2–16. Suva: School of Social and Economic Development, University of the South Pacific.

Hereniko, V. 2000. Indigenous knowledge and academic imperialism. In *Remembrance of Pacific pasts: An invitation to remake history,* ed. R. Borofsky, 78–91. Honolulu: University of Hawai'i Press.

Johnston, R. J. 1990. The challenge of regional geography: Some proposals for research frontiers. In *Regional geography: Current developments and future prospects,* ed. R. J. Johnston, J. Hauer, and G. A. Hoekveld, 122–139. London: Routledge.

Teaiwa, T. (in press). For or before an Asia-Pacific studies agenda? Specifying Pacific Studies. In *Changing places: Critical perspectives and pedagogies in Asia-Pacific studies,* ed. T. Wesley-Smith and J. Goss, 171–193. Honolulu: University of Hawai'i Press.

Trask, H. K. 1991. Natives and and anthropologists: The colonial struggle. *The Contemporary Pacific* 3(1): 159–177.

Wesley-Smith, T. 1995. Rethinking Pacific Islands studies. *Pacific Studies* 18(2): 115–136.

The Physical Environment

The Pacific Islands were created through the cumulative action of volcanism, tectonism, and reef growth over millions of years. At the same time, many of the dramatic landscapes visible today—steep cliffs, deeply dissected valleys, sprawling coastal plains, and even reef *motu*—owe their existence in large extent to erosion induced by climatic and oceanographic forces. This section describes the physical environment of the Pacific Islands, with chapters on climate, oceanography, geology, geomorphology, soils, and water.

Climate

Andrew P. Sturman and Hamish A. McGowan

1

The islands of the Pacific Ocean experience a diverse variety of weather and climate (aggregate weather) due to their wide-ranging geographic locations, which encompass midlatitude to equatorial settings. Because Pacific islands are surrounded by vast areas of ocean, their climates are strongly influenced by maritime processes. Atmospheric circulation systems, terrain, and surface vegetation cover, however, frequently modify the maritime air masses that pass over islands. This results in distinct microclimates.

The main climate-related concerns for many Pacific Island nations are providing adequate water supplies and minimizing exposure to atmospheric hazards at a time of uncertain future climate change. The nature of atmospheric circulation in the Pacific region is such that there is considerable temporal and spatial variability. Some regions experience drought at the same time that others are flooded. The sustainability of many island societies is marginal, so such problems can place significant pressure on community viability.

Because of the immense diversity of atmospheric processes observed in the Pacific Basin, this chapter focuses only on some of the principal atmospheric phenomena relevant to the region. Local examples of these features are provided and their significance discussed. Observed and predicted climate change and variability are also reviewed. The major impacts of weather and climate on natural and human environments are also summarized. For additional information, the reader is referred to the bibliography at the end of the chapter.

Global Atmospheric Circulation and the Pacific Islands

The Importance of the Global Energy Balance

The driving force for weather and climate processes originates with incoming solar radiation. It is the uneven distribution of this energy across the globe that results in the Earth's atmospheric circulation (Sturman and Tapper 2006). The central part of the Pacific region receives a net radiation surplus of more than 80 W/m² (watts per square meter), while areas north and south of about 40° latitude experience a net deficit of energy (Figure 1.1). The surplus in the tropics results in high air and sea surface temperatures, causing rapid evaporation of water into the atmosphere.

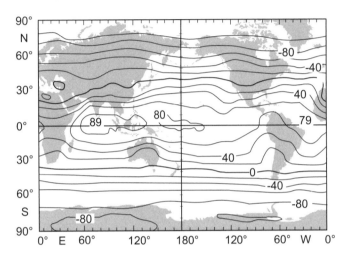

Figure 1.1. *Global distribution of net all-wave radiation, measured at the top of the atmosphere (W/m²) (modified after Peixoto and Oort 1992).*

Global and Regional Circulation Systems

The atmospheric circulation (assisted by the oceanic circulation) serves to transport surplus energy from the tropics toward the high-latitude region of deficit (Sturman and Tapper 2006). The broad features of the global atmospheric circulation are represented schematically in Figure 1.2. Strong rising motion (convection) is characteristic of the Intertropical Convergence Zone (ITCZ), where the northeast and southeast trade winds meet. Subtropical anticyclones (high-pressure zones of descending air) are located poleward of the trade-wind belt. This completes the Hadley cell, linking the tropics with the midlatitudes (Figure 1.3).

The westerly wind belt lies farther poleward, where outflow from the anticyclones meets cold air from the poles, turning toward the east as they meet. For both the westerlies and the trade winds, east-west movement is due to the Coriolis effect (deflection caused by the Earth's rotation). The southern hemisphere westerlies are much stronger and more enduring than those to the north, where the major continental landmasses disrupt the westerly airflow (Figure 1.4).

Seasonal changes in pressure distribution are considerably greater over the North than the South Pacific (Figure 1.4). During January an area of low pressure known as the Aleutian low

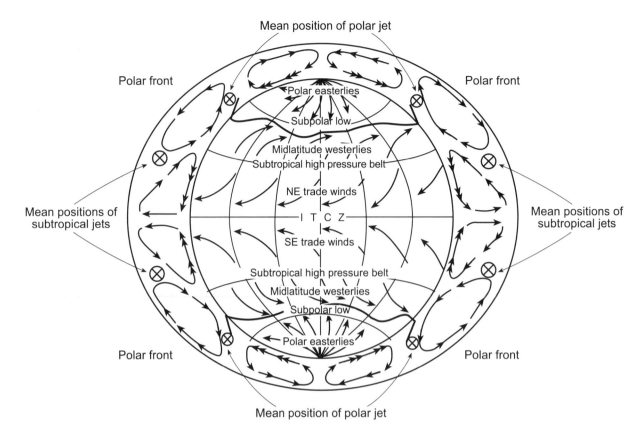

Figure 1.2. *Schematic representation of the global atmospheric circulation (modified after Miller and Anthes 1985).*

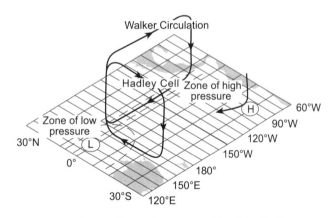

Figure 1.3. *Circulation cells over the central and South Pacific (from Sturman and Tapper 2006).*

dominates the northern section of the North Pacific, while the subtropical high is reduced in intensity. In contrast, the pressure pattern over the South Pacific retains a more zonal structure throughout the year, though the climate zones shift northward and southward with the seasons.

Another extensive feature driving Pacific pressure and wind systems is the Walker circulation. This is a primarily west-east-oriented cell, with rising motion over the Indonesia region (known as the maritime continent) and subsidence over the southeast Pacific (Figure 1.3). This circulation cell provides the easterly component of the trade winds and is closely linked to oceanic circulation.

Fluctuations in the intensity of the Walker Cell contribute to the El Niño-Southern Oscillation (ENSO) phenomenon discussed later (Sturman and Tapper 2006).

The ITCZ dominates atmospheric circulation of the central Pacific, but it moves north and south seasonally, particularly over the western Pacific (Figure 1.5). The intensity of convection along the ITCZ varies, with major activity occurring over Indonesia. A smaller center of action occurs over equatorial South America. In the narrow intermediate zone, there is a lessening of convective activity from December to February. This general pattern of convective activity results in cloudiness and precipitation over the western section of the ITCZ, where it merges with the South Pacific Convergence Zone (SPCZ) (Figure 1.5).

The SPCZ is a zone of cloudiness and precipitation occurring where southeast trade winds meet southerly flow from the New Zealand region (Vincent 1994). This is also a region where tropical cyclones frequently originate. Sea-surface temperature patterns are thought to play a part in its development, although the mechanisms are not fully understood. The SPCZ shows an increase in strength when it moves southward in the southern hemisphere summer (December–March). At this time, cross-equatorial flow appears to increase low-level convergence. The north-south movement of the SPCZ and changes in its intensity combine to produce seasonal changes in rainfall that vary over the different island groups of the South Pacific (Terry 2007).

Monsoons have traditionally been defined as reversals of wind direction resulting from seasonal heating and cooling of major

(a)

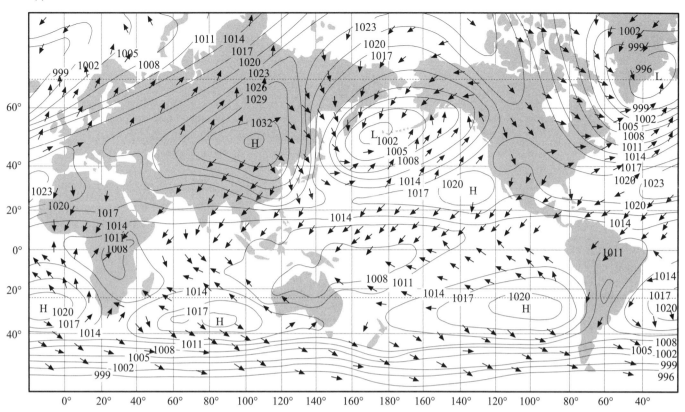

(b)

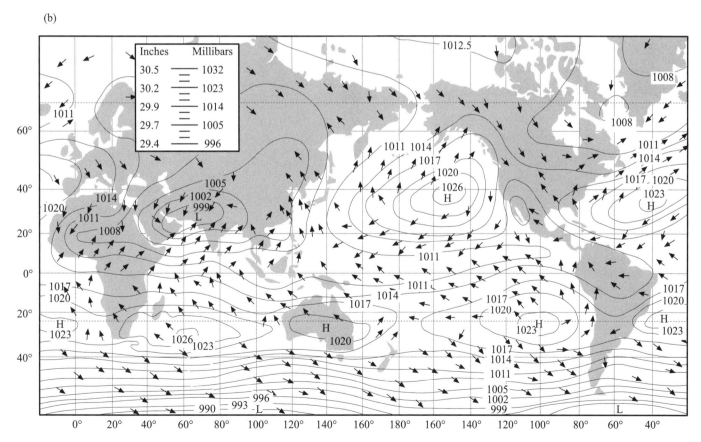

Figure 1.4. Mean sea-level pressure distribution (mb) and simplified wind field for the globe in (a) January and (b) July (Strahler and Strahler 1978).

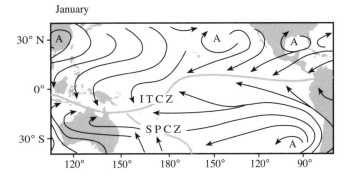

January

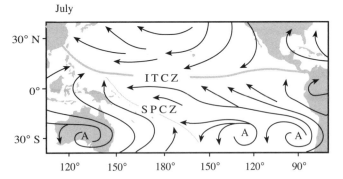

July

Figure 1.5. *Mean position of the Intertropical Convergence Zone (ITCZ) and South Pacific Convergence Zone (SPCZ) during January and July, showing the near-surface airflow. A represents an anticyclonic center (modified after Hastenrath 1988 and Thompson 1987).*

continental areas. There is sometimes confusion in the literature, however, as the movement of convergence zones across the Pacific during the year generally produces seasonal variations in the influence of different wind regimes. For example, movement of the SPCZ results in seasonal variations in the airflow and precipitation regime of the islands of Samoa, but this is not considered a true monsoonal regime.

Monsoons (see Ramage 1971) occur along the margins of the Asian continent, over the western central Pacific, and over northern Australia. The development of heat lows over Australia during the southern summer encourages a southward movement of the ITCZ. As a result, the northeast trade winds are drawn southward across the equator. South of the equator, the winds are deflected by the Earth's rotation, resulting in a northwest monsoonal flow (Figure 1.5).

Similarly, in the northern summer (June–August), the southeast trade winds are drawn northward across the equator by the powerful heat low in central Asia. Deflected to the right by the Earth's rotation, the winds shift to carry air northeastward across Southeast Asia and the Southern Marianas. The resulting monsoon winds then encounter the northeasterly trade wind flow from the central North Pacific along a section of the ITCZ (Figure 1.5). This convergence of wind streams causes a high frequency of tropical cyclones in the Guam region (Ding Yihui 1994).

Synoptic-Scale Weather Systems

Synoptic (large-scale) weather systems include anticyclones, midlatitude depressions, and tropical cyclones. These phenomena range in size from approximately 10^4 to 10^7 km^2 and generally prevail for several days to a week or more; they largely determine the observed daily weather (Sturman and Tapper 2006). Smaller-scale structures such as ridges of high pressure, troughs of low pressure, and fronts are frequently associated with these systems. In this section we discuss the synoptic-scale weather systems that most commonly affect the Pacific Islands.

Subtropical and Blocking Anticyclones

Subtropical anticyclones are regions of high pressure with descending and diverging air near the surface. They rotate counterclockwise in the southern hemisphere and clockwise in the northern hemisphere and are the driving force of the trade winds. They generally occur around 30° latitude over the North and South Pacific and are characterized by clear weather. Subsidence produces warming due to compression, which acts as a lid on the lower atmosphere (preventing convection, condensation, and precipitation) called a temperature inversion. This can be seen in Figure 1.6, which shows fair-weather cumulus with flattened tops where they reach the inversion layer.

Figure 1.6. *Fair-weather cumulus with flattened tops indicating the presence of a subsidence inversion (photo APS).*

The anticyclone over the North Pacific shows a strong annual variation in intensity, with a maximum in July (Figure 1.4). The strongest anticyclones are at the eastern side of the Pacific. Thus, the temperature inversion tends to be stronger and at a lower elevation over the eastern subtropical Pacific, declining in strength and lifting toward the western equatorial region (Figure 1.7). The trade-wind belts equatorward of these anticyclones have steady winds, with little variation in temperature and humidity. Daily variations do occur, however, in convective cloud and rainfall.

In the New Zealand region to the south, high-pressure ridges separate low-pressure troughs (often containing fronts) in the westerly wind belt (Figure 1.8). Following the passage of a frontal trough, subsiding air associated with the following ridge suppresses convective activity, resulting in fair-weather cumulus (Figure 1.6). Several days of fine settled weather are then usually experienced. In certain locations, local circulations, such as sea/land breezes and valley/mountain winds, may then develop (discussed later).

Anticyclones can develop poleward of the subtropical high-pressure regions and become almost stationary. These blocking

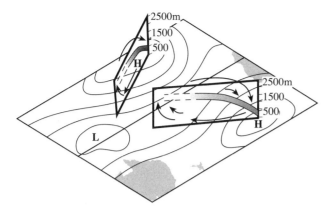

Figure 1.7. Schematic representation of the link between subsidence in the subtropical anticyclones and the development of temperature inversions in the trade wind belts north and south of the equator. The two cross sections illustrate the circulation of air across the northern and southern Pacific (using arrows), and the changing strength and height of the subsidence inversions (the shaded bands).

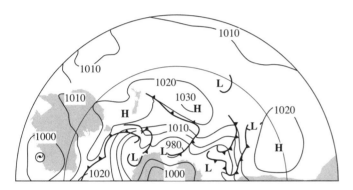

Figure 1.8. Typical pattern of alternating high-pressure ridges extending from the subtropical anticyclones and low-pressure disturbances embedded in the southern hemisphere westerlies (after Streten and Zillman 1984).

anticyclones cause a temporary halt to the normal eastward progression of weather systems in midlatitudes (Sturman and Tapper 2006). Two favored locations for anticyclonic blocking are east of New Zealand and in the northwestern Pacific. Blocking anticyclones to the east of New Zealand typically bring northeasterly winds and widespread stratiform cloud cover (called anticyclonic gloom) over east coastal regions.

Tropical Low-Pressure Systems

The most severe weather experienced in the tropical Pacific is associated with tropical cyclones (also called hurricanes or typhoons). These are intense, nonfrontal low-pressure systems occurring over tropical or subtropical waters (Holland 1993). Intense solar radiation over the oceans causes warm, humid air to converge and rise. When this produces meso-scale convective systems (storms), air rushing into the base of the convective clouds over thousands of square kilometers may start to rotate due to the Earth's rotation. As this rising air reaches the tropopause (12 to 15 km), it spirals outward, resulting in a spiral shape (Figure 1.9). A well-defined eye (10 to 50 km in diameter) may be seen near the center, characterized by gentle descent of air, clear skies, and light winds at the surface.

Figure 1.9. Satellite image of tropical cyclone Ingrid, off the coast of northern Queensland in Australia on March 8, 2005 (image obtained from the MODIS satellite).

At maturity, these weather systems can produce wind speeds in excess of 300 km/hr, torrential rain, storm surges, and large sea swells. The extreme wind speeds cause havoc on atolls and low-lying coastal areas. The powerful winds destroy crops and homes and often combine with heavy rainfall and high seas to produce severe flooding. Tropical cyclones occur primarily during summer, but they may occur at other times under favorable meteorological and oceanic conditions. Pielke (1990) outlined five conditions favorable or necessary for tropical cyclone formation. These are listed in Table 1.1.

Table 1.1

Conditions Favorable or Necessary for Tropical Cyclone Genesis

1. Sea surface temperatures higher than 26°C.
2. Little change of wind speed and direction with height through the troposphere, so that heat energy remains concentrated.
3. An existing tropical disturbance of some sort at the surface (e.g., an easterly wave or large convective complex).
4. Unstable thermal structure, enhancing deep vertical development (i.e., no trade wind inversion).
5. Location poleward of about 4° to 5° from the equator, where the Coriolis force equals zero.

Source: Modified from Pielke 1990.

In the southern summer, tropical cyclones typically originate in a region extending from the northeastern coast of Australia into the SPCZ (5°S and 20°S). They generally track westward (Sturman and Tapper 2006) before often veering toward the midlatitudes, becoming subtropical depressions, with their motion influenced by strong westerly flow (as shown in Figure 1.10a). As they move poleward, they become progressively weaker and develop cold cores in response to colder sea-surface temperatures.

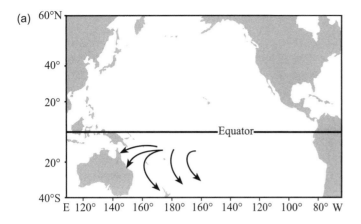

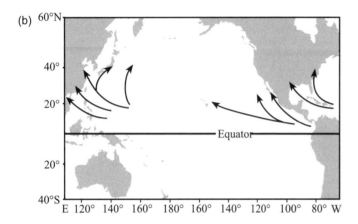

Figure 1.10. *Schematic representation of tropical cyclone tracks over the Pacific in (a) February and (b) August (adapted from Gray 1975).*

Figure 1.11 presents the monthly occurrence of tropical cyclones in the South Pacific region, while Figure 1.12 illustrates the interannual variation over the summer periods of 1969 to 2006. The main season between January and March is evident, although there is significant variability between years in the total number recorded, which is often related to ENSO.

In the northern summer the most active region for tropical cyclone formation is the northwestern Pacific (Figure 1.10b), where monsoonal southwesterlies encounter easterly trade winds. The main cyclone season is between July and November (Figure 1.13). In this region, tropical cyclones are usually referred to as typhoons, or supertyphoons when sustained wind speeds exceed 240 km/hr. For example, on the island of Guam the Joint Typhoon Warning Center names on average twenty-eight tropical cyclones annually, of which four typically reach supertyphoon status (Joint Typhoon Warning Center 1993). In comparison, the average annual occurrence of tropical cyclones in the southwest Pacific and eastern North Pacific is of the order of eleven and fifteen respectively, based on ten seasons between 1992 and 2001 (Murnane 2004).

Tropical cyclones form off the west coast of Mexico from May to November and typically move westward and sometimes northward toward Baja California (Figure 1.10b). Cyclones are much rarer in the vicinity of the Hawaiian Islands, with one to two cyclones every ten years (Martyn 1992).

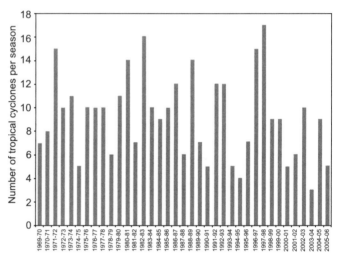

Figure 1.12. *Variation in tropical cyclone occurrence in the South Pacific over the summer seasons from 1969–1970 to 2005–2006 (after Terry 2007).*

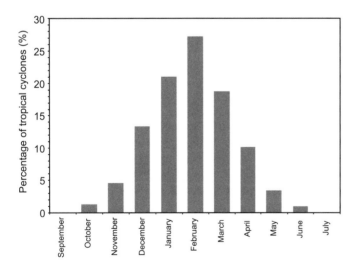

Figure 1.11. *Monthly variation of the frequency of tropical cyclones in the South Pacific over the period from 1970 to 2006 (after Terry 2007).*

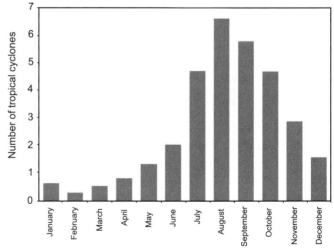

Figure 1.13. *Monthly variation of the frequency of tropical cyclones in the Northwest Pacific over the period 1959 to 2001 (after Chan 2004).*

Other low-pressure systems in the central part of the region include tropical and subtropical depressions. These features are much less intense than tropical cyclones, but they are still important features of the region. Tropical depressions have reduced wind rotation due to close proximity to the equator, and they are relatively weak. As they move away from the equator they may intensify to become tropical cyclones. Subtropical depressions can develop farther poleward in such areas as the southern Coral Sea, affecting New Zealand weather as they drift downwind to the east.

Over the North Pacific, the major region for the development of such low-pressure systems is over and southeast of Japan. Explosive development of subtropical depressions sometimes occurs north of Hawai'i at around 35° to 45° N (Gyakum et al. 1989), bringing intense rainfall known as Kona storms (Carlquist 1980), particularly during the winter season. Kona storms have the greatest concentration within a southwest-to-northeast-oriented band from west of Hawai'i to 40° N and 140° W and tend to travel to the northeast. Their development may occur due to a range of factors but most commonly they are associated with cold fronts and the movement of an upper-level disturbance of extratropical origin into the subtropics (Otkin and Martin 2004). A small number of such depressions may also form along the coast of California and Mexico. There is also some suggestion that upper tropospheric disturbances control the development of these weather systems (Schroeder 1993).

Midlatitude Low-Pressure Systems

Midlatitude weather systems affect only the New Zealand section of the Pacific Islands, and so will be dealt with only briefly. More details can be found in Sturman and Tapper (2006). The most significant feature of this region is the strong westerly wind belt, which produces rapid west to east movement of alternating lows and highs and their associated troughs and ridges. This region is one of rapid weather changes due to strong air mass interaction and the development of fronts. Low-pressure systems develop poleward of the subtropical anticyclones, and the frontal extensions periodically affect weather in New Zealand and (less frequently) Hawai'i.

Typical midlatitude low-pressure systems affecting New Zealand include Southern Ocean lows that frequently develop south of the country, particularly in winter, and move rapidly from west to east through the region (Figure 1.14a). In contrast, Tasman Sea lows develop off the coast of southeastern Australia and move more slowly eastward across central and northern New Zealand (Figure 1.14b). These low-pressure systems are responsible for the rapid weather changes experienced in this part of the Pacific.

Anticyclones also influence the New Zealand region by reducing the changeable nature of the weather. They move more slowly than the low-pressure systems and are normally associated with dry, sunny weather. Typically, subtropical anticyclones tend to occur over the northern part of the New Zealand region (as shown in Figure 1.14a), but they may extend farther south, resulting in blocking of the west-east movement of Southern Ocean lows (Figure 1.15).

Local Island Weather

On individual islands and parts of islands, synoptic-scale weather and climate are modified by local geographic factors. Specifically, the levels of temperature, wind, precipitation, and cloud cover of particular places are determined by the interaction of maritime air masses with local topography. Readers are also referred to Schroeder (1993), who provides a more detailed case study of the weather and climate of the islands of Hawai'i.

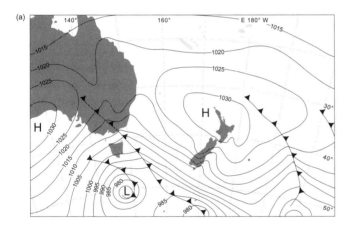

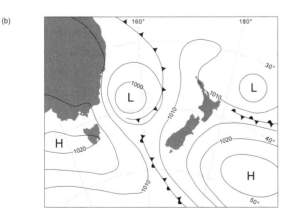

Figure 1.14. (a) Southern Ocean and (b) Tasman Sea low-pressure systems in the New Zealand region (after Sturman and Tapper 2006).

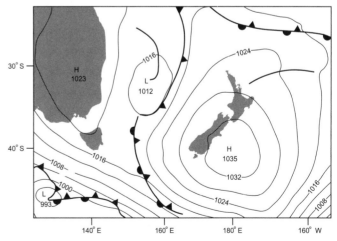

Figure 1.15. Blocking anticyclone off the east coast of New Zealand (after Sturman and Tapper 2006).

Local Winds

Islands have both dynamic and thermal effects on airflow. For example, interaction between thermally induced local winds, easterly trade winds, and local topography causes flow splitting of the easterly trade winds as they pass around the island of Hawaiʻi (Figure 1.16). Downslope (katabatic) winds develop just prior to sunset on leeward slopes as a result of surface cooling and spread to other slopes during the night. Cessation of the nocturnal wind regime starts one to two hours after sunrise with the onset of upslope (anabatic) winds (Schroeder 1993).

Observations from Papua New Guinea indicate that local sea breezes may travel as far as 150 km inland across coastal plains and may continue well after sunset at inland sites. The sea breeze front can bring showers and thunderstorms at inland sites later in the afternoon and early evening. Sea breezes also contribute to thunderstorm development over tropical islands. Sea breeze convergence is a common phenomenon leading to convective development over Auckland, New Zealand, as illustrated in Figure 1.17.

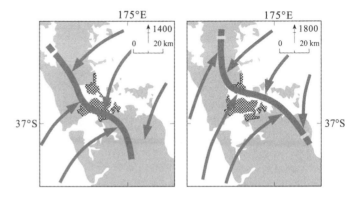

Figure 1.17. *The convergence of sea breezes from opposing coasts over Auckland, New Zealand, at 2 p.m. and 6 p.m. (after McKendry 1989, with kind permission from Kluwer Academic Publishers).*

Orographic Effects

Orographic (mountain)-induced precipitation is especially important in the larger Pacific islands, such as Hawaiʻi and New Zealand. But even relatively small hills only 50 m or so above the surrounding terrain have been observed to increase precipitation by 25 to 50 percent (Holgate 1973, Browning, Pardoe, and Hill 1975). Moist air meeting an obstacle is forced to rise, creating a feeder cloud (Figure 1.18a). Continued arrival of warm, moisture-laden air on windward slopes quickly leads to coalescence of condensed droplets and intense precipitation.

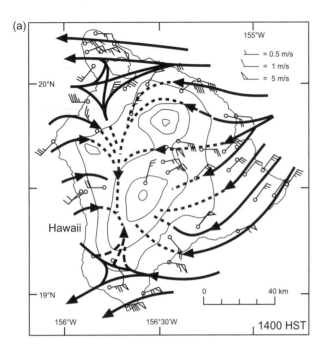

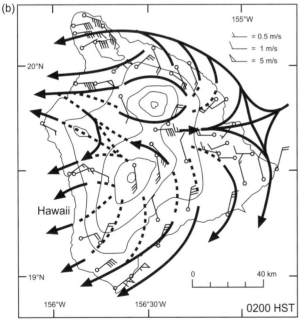

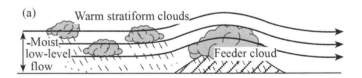

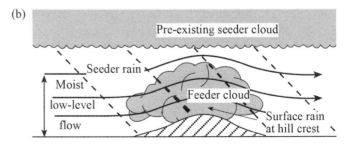

Figure 1.16. *Interaction of the prevailing northeast trades with thermally developed (a) daytime sea breeze and anabatic flow and (b) nocturnal land breeze and katabatic flow over the island of Hawaiʻi (after Chen and Nash 1994).*

Figure 1.18. *Effects of a hill or island obstacle on precipitation development, (a) the development of a feeder cloud and (b) the seeder-feeder mechanism (after Browning 1979).*

If a seeder cloud is present at higher levels as a result of large-scale vertical motion, precipitation falling from this cloud will coalesce with droplets in the feeder cloud, thereby enhancing rainfall (Figure 1.18b). Such orographic enhancement of cyclonic precipitation occurs in South Island, New Zealand, producing a pronounced west-to-east precipitation gradient. Immediately upwind of the Southern Alps, annual rainfall of more than 10,000 mm can occur, while to the east of the mountains values drop to less than 600 mm (Figure 1.19).

In the Hawaiian Islands, maximum annual rainfall (up to 7,000 mm) corresponds to areas of persistent orographic lifting of the northeast trade winds on windward slopes. The lowest annual rainfall totals on the island of Hawai'i are recorded over leeward slopes in an area of rain shadow (as low as 500 mm) along the Kona Coast, and high above the trade-wind inversion (as low as 250 mm) (Chen and Nash 1994; Juvik and Nullet 1994). These patterns are complicated by the diurnal fluctuations discussed above (upslope/downslope and onshore/offshore breezes).

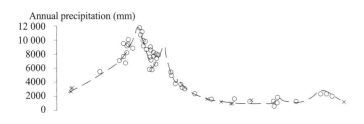

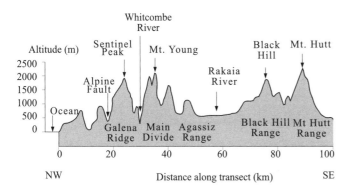

Figure 1.19. Precipitation transect over the Southern Alps of New Zealand (after Griffiths and McSaveney 1983).

On the islands of Savai'i and 'Upolu (Samoa), orographic enhancement of precipitation occurs in response to the seasonal oscillation in the region's wind regime. During the southern summer the SPCZ is situated poleward of the islands, and moist equatorial northeasterlies dominate (Figure 1.20a). During the southern winter the SPCZ moves equatorward of the islands. The islands are then affected by drier southeasterlies in close proximity to subtropical anticyclones (Figure 1.20b).

The orographic effect is also evident in the pattern of annual precipitation on Viti Levu, the main island of Fiji, where the influence of the southeast trade winds is apparent (Figure 1.21). The southeasterly winds cause lifting and rainfall enhancement on the upstream side of the island, with drier areas to the west and northwest.

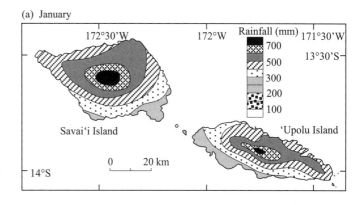

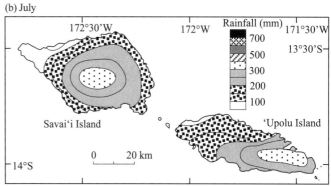

Figure 1.20. Monthly mean precipitation (mm) over Western Samoa for (a) January and (b) July, showing both seasonal and orographic influences (after Tualevao 1991).

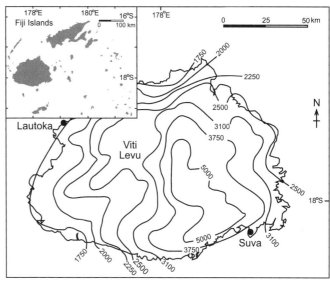

Figure 1.21. Annual precipitation (mm) over Viti Levu (after Terry 2007).

Thunderstorm Development

Thunderstorms are characterized by the development of cumulus and then cumulonimbus clouds, heavy rain, and strong winds (Figure 1.22). In the tropics, these storms are usually triggered by intense surface heating during daytime, initiating convection over land. Sea breezes may subsequently converge over the island,

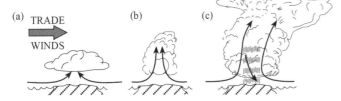

Figure 1.22. *Schematic illustration of island thunderstorm development. Convergence of sea breezes produces initial cumulus development during late morning (a), which is followed soon after by cumulus congestus (b) and a fully developed cumulonimbus by early afternoon (c).*

Figure 1.23. *Mature thunderstorm cell with well-defined anvil cloud. (photo APS).*

generally from midafternoon to late evening. In midlatitudes, thunderstorms may also be associated with frontal disturbances and orographic forcing, for example over the Southern Alps of New Zealand (Figure 1.23).

Precipitation during thunderstorms is linked to downdrafts, which may exhibit mean velocities between 5 to 8 m/s, with gusts exceeding 20 m/s (Cotton and Anthes 1989). Such gusts can cause damage to crops and homes and present a hazard to aircraft operations at and near airports. Thunderstorms are also often associated with tornadoes and lightning. On average at least twenty tornadoes are reported in New Zealand each year (Tomlinson and Nicol 1976). Tornadoes are much less common in other Pacific islands (Omolayo 1991).

Where local winds converge with the trade winds, as on the east coast of Hawai'i's Big Island, complex rainfall patterns result (Chen and Nash 1994). During nighttime, katabatic winds converge with the northeast trade winds, resulting in a nocturnal rainfall peak. During the day, anabatic winds contribute to rainfall over the ridgetops. In Papua New Guinea, offshore convergence of katabatic drainage flows with southeasterly trade winds (May to October) or equatorial westerlies (December to March) results in heavy rainfall (McAlpine, Keig, and Falls 1983).

Snowfall

Snowfall is frequently recorded in the Southern Alps of New Zealand, where annual snow accumulation may exceed 4,000 mm water equivalent. Snowfall may reach sea level in other parts of South

Island, although in general the transient winter snow line averages 1,000 m in southern New Zealand and 1,500 m on North Island mountains (Fitzharris, Owens, and Chinn 1992). Snow also falls on the high mountains of New Guinea, even near the equator. In this region, the snow line is above approximately 4,500 m. In the Star Mountains of West Papua,[1] extensive snowfields and glaciers exist. These are now under threat from rising global air temperatures.

Vog

Vog is a volcanic smog formed, under the influence of sunlight, by gases emitted from volcanoes, which mix with moisture and oxygen as they are transported downwind. It is an acidic mixture of gases and aerosols that occurs quite frequently on the island of Hawai'i as a result of emissions from the Kilauea volcano, and it is considered a serious local health hazard. The trade winds carry the vog from the eastern side of Hawai'i toward the south and southwest. The local sea breezes described earlier, however, can move the vog back onshore on the western side of the island. Figure 1.24 is a NOAA15 satellite image showing the plume of gases and light ash west of Kilauea volcano, on the Big Island of Hawai'i.

Figure 1.24. *MODIS satellite image (December 3, 2008) showing the plume of gases and light ash (vog) west of Kilauea volcano, on the Big Island of Hawai'i. Source: http://earthobservatory.nasa.gov/IOTD/view.php?id=36089.*

Regional Climate Patterns

The distribution of Köppen-Geiger climate types provides a general overview of climate in the Pacific Island region (Figure 1.25).

The dominant climatic influence is the latitudinal difference in solar radiation and air temperature, with maximum air temperatures of greater than 28°C over the equatorial region. Seasonal variation in temperature becomes significant only with distance from the equator. The latitudinal gradient is disturbed by the ocean circulation, particularly along the eastern edge of the Pacific, due to cool ocean currents. Westward ocean currents and trade winds result in the accumulation of warmer air over the western central Pacific (Figure 1.26).

The spatial pattern of precipitation is more complex than that of air temperature, as a result of the dependence on rising motion within the atmosphere. Island rainfall is strongly affected by the location of convergence zones such as the ITCZ and SPCZ,

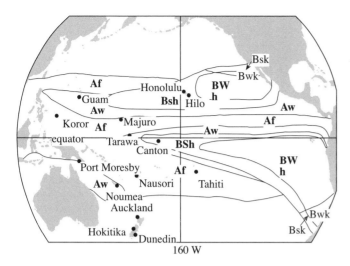

Figure 1.25. *Classification of climate types across the Pacific (after Thomas 1963). The types are defined using the Köppen-Geiger method, which is based on temperature and rainfall. Minor topographically induced variations are not included. The classification codes are: A = tropical (hot) and wet enough for tall trees: Af = rain all year; Aw = dry season in winter; B = dry (hot or cold); BS = steppe-like climate; BSh = hot; BSk = cold; BW = desert; BWh = hot; BWk = cold. New Zealand would be classified as type Cfb (mild humid, warm summers).*

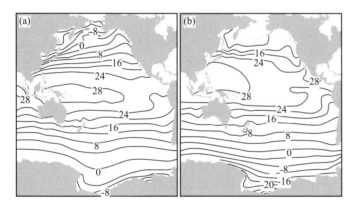

Figure 1.26. *Distribution of mean air temperature (°C) over the Pacific Ocean during (a) February and (b) August (after Martyn 1992).*

sea-surface temperatures, the passage of midlatitude troughs, depressions and their associated frontal systems, and the interaction of maritime air masses with island topography.

Figure 1.27 shows a region of maximum precipitation of more than 3,000 mm annually slightly north of the equator. The shape of this region reflects the merging of the ITCZ and SPCZ over the western central Pacific. The areas of least precipitation occur over the high-pressure, eastern side of the North and South Pacific, with minimum values below 200 mm annually. The remainder of the Pacific Ocean receives between about 500 and 2,000 mm annually.

Some tropical islands, such as Fiji and the Cook Islands, experience distinct wet and dry seasons as a result of changes in the location and intensity of convection associated with the convergence zones. Seasonal variability is particularly evident over the islands of the central South Pacific (Figure 1.28), where a relatively strong SPCZ results in heavy summer rainfall. A similar increase in rainfall occurs over the western North Pacific during summertime, when the ITCZ moves poleward. Some islands, such as Tuvalu and

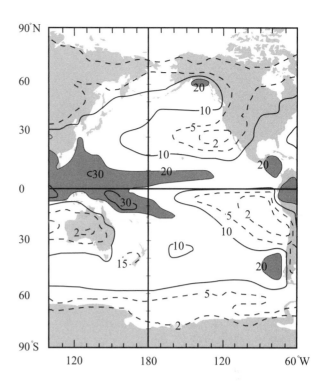

Figure 1.27. *Distribution of annual mean precipitation (X 100 mm) over the Pacific Ocean (after Peixoto and Oort 1992).*

Kiribati, have two wet seasons as convergence zones migrate back and forth over them. At higher latitudes, fronts are responsible for the majority of annual precipitation totals.

Climate graphs (Figure 1.29) provide further illustration of the main climate regimes. Temperature follows obvious latitudinal effects, with warm, almost constant monthly averages observed at sites located close to the equator. The most extreme annual temperature variations are observed in New Zealand, while other sites lie somewhere in between. There is a clear seasonal cycle in rainfall. In the tropical South Pacific, peak rainfall occurs between January and April; north of the equator, peak values occur between July and October.

Island topography plays an important part in the nature of these rainfall variations, as illustrated by the two stations (Honolulu and Hilo) on Hawai'i. Similar differences in rainfall are illustrated between stations on either side of the Southern Alps of New Zealand (Hokitika and Dunedin). The pattern is made a little complicated by time lag differences between some sites. Canton Island provides an example of a hot, dry site dominated by the stable trade wind regime.

The pattern of precipitation is related to that of cloud cover, with satellite imagery showing a relationship with the ITCZ and SPCZ (Figure 1.30). This relationship is not always clear, however, as some relatively dry areas may be dominated by clouds as well, such as the cold current regions over the eastern Pacific.

Climate Change and Variability

Earlier sections have already identified some sources of climate variability experienced across this sector of the globe. This section will focus on long-term climate change and variability.

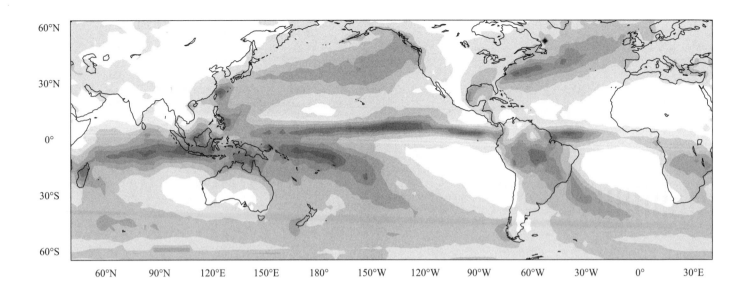

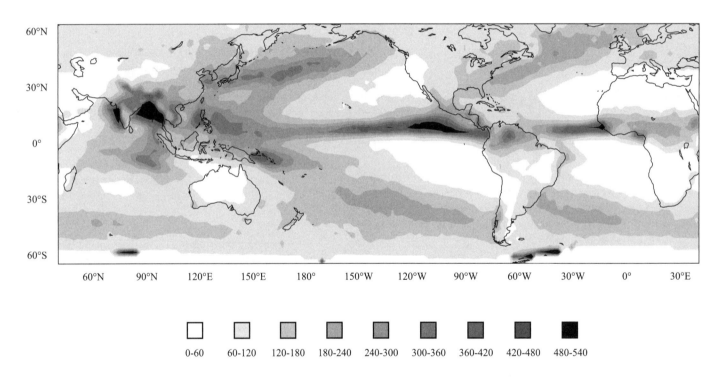

Figure 1.28. Mean monthly precipitation (mm) over the western South Pacific in (a) January and (b) July (after Wallace, Mitchell, and Lau 1995).

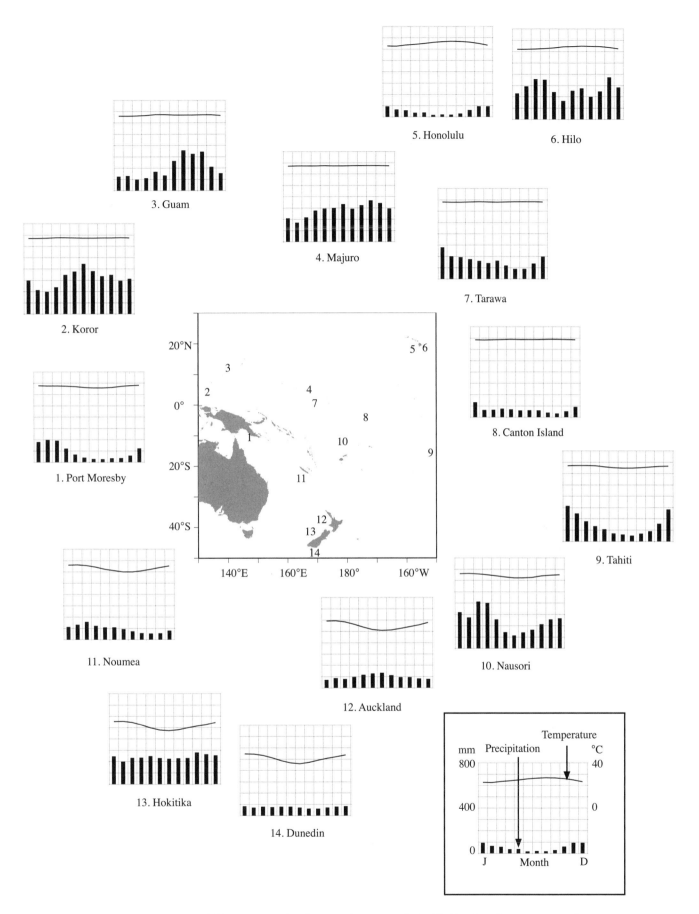

Figure 1.29. Graphs of temperature and rainfall for representative climate stations across the Pacific (data from Hoare 1996–1998).

El Niño–Southern Oscillation (ENSO)

The El Niño–Southern Oscillation (ENSO) phenomenon refers to periodic alterations in ocean-atmosphere circulation of the Pacific. It has significant effects on the weather and climate of this region, as well as on many other parts of the globe. The Southern Oscillation is represented by fluctuations in the intensity of the Walker circulation, which are caused by changes in the pressure gradient between the anticyclone in the eastern South Pacific and the equatorial trough (Figures 1.3 and 1.31). When the La Niña predominates, strong trade winds drag warm surface water across the ocean toward the western central Pacific. At the same time, cooler water upwells along the coast of South America (Figure 1.32).

During El Niño events, ocean and atmospheric circulations slow down. Trade wind effects on ocean surface temperatures are reduced, affecting regional sea level (Figure 1.33) as well as water

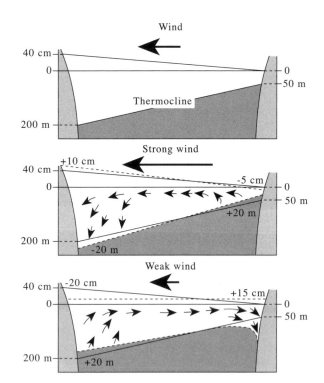

Figure 1.32. *Link between surface wind and ocean circulation during changes in phase of the Walker circulation (after World Meteorological Organization 1984).*

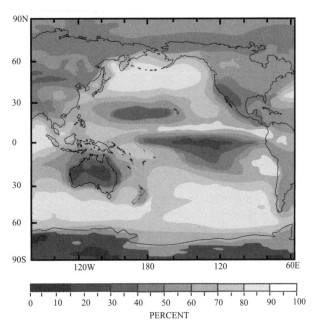

Figure 1.30. *Mean satellite-derived cloud amount over the Pacific Ocean, based on two years of data (after Rossow 1993).*

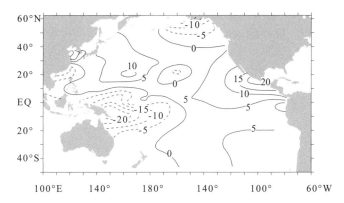

Figure 1.33. *Height anomalies (cm) of the ocean surface over the Pacific Ocean during the 1986–1987 El Niño (after World Meteorological Organization 1987).*

temperatures (Figure 1.34). The latter determine the productivity of the fisheries of areas such as the Peruvian coast (where the term El Niño originated). El Niño is also of global significance, with parts of the world as distant as Europe and the Antarctic experiencing a recognizable ENSO influence.

The pressure difference measured between Tahiti and Darwin is used to monitor the strength of the Walker circulation and indicate La Niña (positive pressure gradient anomaly) and El Niño events (negative pressure gradient anomaly). The Southern Oscillation Index (SOI) is derived from this pressure difference (Sturman and Tapper 2006). Variations in this phenomenon have a periodicity of between two and ten years, although since the late 1970s there has been a tendency for more frequent El Niño events (Trenberth and Hoar 1996) (Figure 1.35).

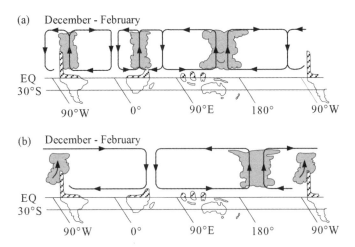

Figure 1.31. *(a) Typical Walker circulation and (b) its breakdown during El Niño events (after World Meteorological Organization 1984).*

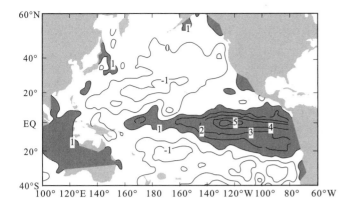

Figure 1.34. *Sea-surface temperature anomalies (°C) over the central Pacific Ocean during the 1982–1983 El Niño event (after World Meteorological Organization 1984). Warming greater than one degree is indicated by shading.*

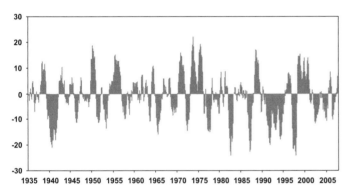

Figure 1.35. *Variations in the Southern Oscillation Index 1935 to 2007.*

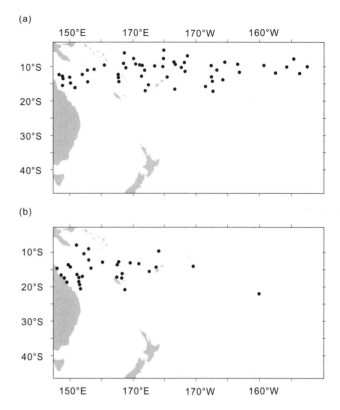

Figure 1.36. *Points of origin of southwest Pacific tropical cyclones during (a) El Niño and (b) La Niña situations (after Hastings 1990).*

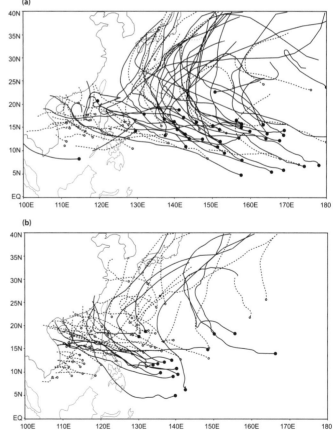

Figure 1.37. *Points of origin and tracks of Northwest Pacific tropical cyclones during (a) El Niño and (b) La Niña situations (after Chan 2004).*

Several climate features of the Pacific are affected by these ENSO events (Ropelewski and Halpert 1987). During El Niño, the normally wet western Pacific experiences drought conditions, a consequence of relatively higher pressures. Conversely, in the eastern Pacific the normal anticyclone is weakened, displacing the SPCZ to the north and east. Islands directly under the SPCZ during normal years will experience less rainfall during El Niño events, with drought conditions if the events persist; the reverse is true for islands lying at the margins of the SPCZ (Mullan 1992).

Farther from the equator, the Hawaiian Islands experience below normal rainfall in the winter and spring of the year following an El Niño (Schroeder 1993, Chu 1995). In the New Zealand region, the El Niño situation results in an increase in southwesterly flow. This interacts with orography to produce enhanced precipitation over the south and west of the country, with a decrease to the north and east (Gordon 1985, 1986).

During El Niño years, the SPCZ migrates north and east of its normal position, in parallel with a pool of warm water (that otherwise accumulates over the western central Pacific). As a result, a much larger region of the South Pacific is susceptible to tropical cyclone hazards (Figure 1.36). In the western North Pacific, the number of tropical cyclones tends to decrease in the year following an El Niño event, while during El Niño events tropical cyclones tend to last longer. It has also been found that cyclones originate farther east in this region when the SOI is negative (El Niño) and farther west when it is positive (La Niña) (Chan 2004), as shown in Figure 1.37.

Volcanic Eruptions

Volcanic eruptions can eject huge quantities of ash and gaseous sulfur into the atmosphere. Suspended particulates from such eruptions reduce radiation receipts. They may also act as condensation nuclei for rainfall. The most recent volcanic eruption to affect climate in the Pacific region (and globally) was the eruption of Mount Pinatubo. The June 1991 eruptions lowered mean global temperatures following the eruption by several tenths of a degree (Parker et al. 1996) due to increased atmospheric turbidity.

Similar observations have been made following the eruptions of El Chichón (April 1982) and Krakatau (August 1883). Recent evidence suggests that these and similar large volcanic eruptions may trigger temperature fluctuations in the stratosphere that in turn may affect stratospheric circulation patterns (Parker et al. 1996). These may manifest themselves in tropospheric weather and climate anomalies, such as below- or above-average surface temperatures.

The Enhanced Greenhouse Effect and Global Warming

Greenhouse gas emissions could have a profound impact on Pacific Island nations. Of particular concern are emissions of CO_2 from the combustion of carbon-based fuels and the continued destruction of tropical rain forests, which appear to be causing enhancement of the greenhouse effect and global warming. Temperatures in the Pacific are likely to increase more slowly than for continental areas of the globe because of the moderating influence of the oceans. Model predictions suggest that temperature and precipitation changes will be variable across the region (Christensen et al. 2007), as suggested by the predicted changes in precipitation over the central section of the Pacific Ocean illustrated in Figure 1.38. Results indicate a trend toward increasing precipitation over a large area of the tropical Pacific, extending along the equator. However, two regions of decreasing precipitation on either side of the wetter region were also indicated over eastern regions, while other areas show seasonal variability in predicted precipitation change (Christensen et al. 2007).

There is a tendency for climate model predictions to show stronger warming in the equatorial Pacific for the period 2080–2099

and less warming over the southern Pacific, with an annual increase of 1.8°C (Christensen et al. 2007). Temperature predictions for the North Pacific also tend to be less than the global average.

Other possible impacts include an increase in the frequency of droughts and floods. The potential impact of climate change on the occurrence of tropical cyclones is uncertain, although there is some suggestion that they will become more intense (Christensen et al. 2007). One possible effect is an alteration of present tropical cyclone paths due to modification of large-scale circulation patterns. For example, a greater expanse of warm sea-surface temperatures, particularly in subtropical regions, may result in tropical cyclones reaching midlatitude areas more frequently.

The Amazon, the Congo, and the maritime continent centered on Indonesia are the three main regions of convection on the globe. There is concern that deforestation in these areas may cause serious climate change, resulting from impacts on the large-scale global circulation. Global circulation models (GCMs) have been used to predict future climatic conditions in these regions, and they suggest that deforestation will increase local air temperature by approximately 2°C and reduce rainfall and evaporation by 20 to 30 percent (Eltahir 1996).

In general, large areas of tropical rain forest, such as in West Papua and Papua New Guinea, contribute strongly to large-scale atmospheric circulation, as they trigger and enhance vertical air motion. Their removal may not only significantly modify local weather and climate as already outlined, but potentially weaken these circulations, thereby possibly affecting the weather and climate of the Pacific Basin.

Global warming is also predicted to result in a sea-level rise of between 23 and 47 cm in the Pacific region by 2100, although this rise is unlikely to be uniform (Christensen et al. 2007). A sea-level rise at the top end of this range could accelerate coastal erosion and inundation of coastal lowlands, particularly in the Pacific, where a large proportion of the population lives close to the sea. The impact on coral atolls and their inhabitants would be especially dramatic. Climate change is also likely to affect water resources through changes in rainfall patterns and incursion of saltwater. In the tropical Pacific over the past one hundred years, ocean surface temperatures and island air temperatures have increased by 0.6 to 1°C, while change in sea level has been variable since the 1990s (Renowden

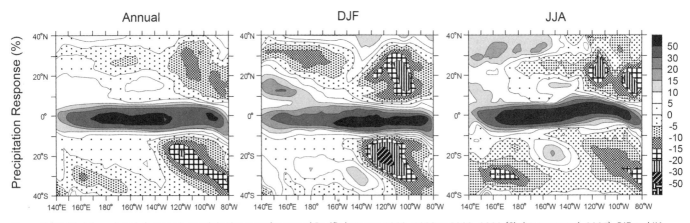

Figure 1.38. *Model predicted changes in precipitation over the central Pacific between 1980–1999 to 2080–2099 (Christensen et al. 2007). DJF and JJA represent December-January-February and June-July-August, respectively.*

2007). Tuvalu (2.9 mm/yr), Kiribati (5.8 mm/yr), Nauru (6.7 mm/yr), and the Cook Islands (0.8 mm/yr) have experienced rising sea level, although this is partly due to prolonged El Niño. The impact of global warming on Pacific coral reefs is made complex by intense ENSO events, such as in 1997–1998 and 2001–2002, when record high sea-surface temperatures caused die-off (Renowden 2007). The effects of changing sea level on coral depend on how fast the sea level rises, while increased acidity due to greater absorption of CO_2 could interfere with the construction of coral skeletons.

Summary

The weather and climate of the Pacific Island region have a significant impact on the lives of the people living there. As discussed in this chapter, the atmosphere provides a number of hazards, due to such extreme events as localized thunderstorms, tropical cyclones, floods, and droughts. Through development of knowledge about this region, it is possible to improve the accuracy of forecasts of these phenomena and therefore to reduce possible impacts on human activity.

In the long term, there is concern about possible impacts of global warming on the frequency and intensity of atmospheric hazards, as well as sea-level rise. Interannual and decadal-scale climate fluctuations also create problems for the local inhabitants, as seen with the Southern Oscillation. In this case, the complex interaction of atmospheric and oceanic circulation can lead to floods, drought, and reduction in the viability of fisheries.

Although the island peoples have traditionally operated a subsistence economy based on a plentiful supply of the basic necessities of life, it is apparent from contemporary knowledge of weather and climate that they have always had to respond to fluctuations and trends in atmospheric conditions. If the predicted effects of global warming come about, many island communities may well be unable to adapt. The response to changing conditions should be based on knowledge, in conjunction with careful planning and environmental management, to ensure sustainability into the future.

The extensive nature of the region, however, and the fact that it is sparsely inhabited and mostly ocean has meant that knowledge of weather and climate processes in the Pacific Island region is far from complete. A good understanding has been obtained of the general circulation, but more knowledge is required of local and regional variability and its causes.

NOTE

1. The western half of the island of New Guinea, which includes Indonesia's Papua Province and West Papua Province (formerly called Irian Jaya Province).

BIBLIOGRAPHY

Browning, K. A. 1979. Structure, mechanism and prediction of orographically enhanced rain in Britain. *Global Atmospheric Research Programme,* Series, No. 23, 88–114. Geneva: World Meteorological Organisation.

Browning, K. A., C. W. Pardoe, and F. F. Hill. 1975. The nature of orographic rain at wintertime cold fronts. *Quarterly Journal of the Royal Meteorological Society* 101: 435–452.

Carlquist, S. 1980. *Hawaii: a natural history: geology, climate, native flora and fauna above the shoreline.* Lawai, Kaua'i, Hawai'i: Pacific Tropical Botanical Garden.

Chan, J. C. L. 2004. Variations in the activity of tropical cyclones over the western North Pacific. In *Hurricanes and typhoons: past, present, and future,* ed. R. J. Murnane and Kam-biu Liu, 269–296. New York: Columbia University Press.

Chen, Y., and A. J. Nash. 1994. Diurnal variation of surface airflow and rainfall frequencies on the island of Hawaii. *Monthly Weather Review* 122: 34–56.

Christensen, J. H., B. Hewitson, A. Busuioc, A. Chen, X. Gao, I. Held, R. Jones, R. K. Kolli, W.-T. Kwon, R. Laprise, V. Magaña Rueda, L. Mearns, C. G. Menéndez, J. Räisänen, A. Rinke, A. Sarr, and P. Whetton, 2007. Regional climate projections. In *Climate change 2007: The physical science basis. Contribution of Working Group I to the Fourth Assessment Report of the Intergovernmental Panel on Climate Change,* ed. S. Solomon, D. Qin, M. Manning, Z. Chen, M. Marquis, K. B. Averyt, M. Tignor, and H. L. Miller. Cambridge and New York: Cambridge University Press.

Chu, P-S. 1995. Hawaii rainfall anomalies and El Niño. *Journal of Climate* 8: 1697–1703.

Cotton, W. R., and R. A. Anthes. 1989. *Storm and cloud dynamics.* San Diego: Academic Press.

Ding Yihui. 1994. *Monsoons over China.* Dordrecht: Kluwer Academic.

Eltahir, E. A. B. 1996. Role of vegetation in sustaining large-scale atmospheric circulations in the tropics. *Journal of Geophysical Research* 101: 4255–4268.

Fitzharris, B., I. Owens, and T. Chinn. 1992. Snow and glacier hydrology. In *Waters of New Zealand,* ed. M. P. Mosley, 75–94. Christchurch: The Caxton Press.

Gordon, N. D. 1985. The Southern Oscillation: A New Zealand perspective. *Journal of the Royal Society of New Zealand* 15: 137–155.

———. 1986. The Southern Oscillation and New Zealand weather. *Monthly Weather Review* 114: 371–387.

Gray, W. M. 1975. *Tropical cyclone genesis.* Atmospheric Science Paper 234. Fort Collins, Colo.: Colorado State University.

Griffiths, G. A., and M. J. McSaveney. 1983. Distribution of mean annual precipitation across some steepland regions of New Zealand. *New Zealand Journal of Science* 26: 197–209.

Gyakum, J. R., J. R. Anderson, R. H. Grumm, and E. L. Gruner. 1989. North Pacific cold season surface cyclone activity: 1975–1983. *Monthly Weather Review* 117: 1141–1155.

Hastenrath, S. 1988. *Climate and circulation of the tropics.* Dordrecht: Reidel.

Hastings, P. A. 1990. Southern Oscillation influences on tropical cyclone activity in the Australian/south-west Pacific region. *International Journal of Climatology* 10: 291–298.

Holgate, H. T. D. 1973. Rainfall forecasting for river authorities. *Meteorological Magazine* 102: 33–38.

Holland, G. J. 1993. *Ready Reckoner*—Chapter 9, Global Guide to Tropical Cyclone Forecasting, WMO/TC–No. 560, Report No. TCP–31. Geneva: World Meteorological Organisation.

Joint Typhoon Warning Center 1993. *Distribution of western North Pacific tropical cyclones.* 1993 Annual Tropical Cyclone Report, NTIS AD A235097, JTWC.

Juvik, J. O., and D. Nullet. 1994. A climate transect through tropical montane rain forest in Hawaii. *Journal of Applied Meteorology* 33: 1304–1312.

Lander, M. A. 1994. An exploratory analysis of the relationship between tropical storm formation in the western North Pacific and ENSO. *Monthly Weather Review* 122: 636–651.

Martyn, D. 1992. *Climates of the world.* Developments in Atmospheric Science 18. Amsterdam and New York: Elsevier.

McAlpine, J. R., G. Keig, and R. Falls. 1983. *Climate of Papua New Guinea.* Canberra: Australian National University Press.

McKendry, I. G. 1989. Numerical simulation of sea breezes over the Auckland region, New Zealand—air quality implications. *Boundary-layer Meteorology* 9: 7–22.

Miller, A., and R. A. Anthes. 1985. *Meteorology.* Columbus, Ohio: Merrill.

Mullan, A. B. 1992. Atmospheric circulation processes and features in the tropical Southwest Pacific. *Weather and Climate* 12: 59–72.

Murnane, R. J. 2004. The importance of best-track data for understanding the past, present, and future of hurricanes and typhoons. In *Hurricanes and typhoons: past, present, and future,* ed. Murnane, R. J. and Kam-biu Liu, 249–266. New York: Columbia University Press.

Omolayo, A. S. 1991. Forecasting freak winds in Fiji. *Proceedings of the Conference: South Pacific Environments; Interactions With Weather and Climate,* September 2–7, 1991, ed. John E. Hay, 143–144. Auckland: University of Auckland.

Otkin, J. A., and J. E. Martin. 2004. A synoptic climatology of the subtropical kona storm. *Monthly Weather Review* 132: 1502–1517.

Parker, D. E., H. Wilson, P. D. Jones, J. R. Christy, and C. K. Folland. 1996. The impact of Mount Pinatubo on world-wide temperatures. *International Journal of Climatology* 16: 487–497.

Peixoto, J. P., and A. H. Oort. 1992. *Physics of climate.* New York: American Institute of Physics.

Pielke, R. A. 1990. *The hurricane.* London: Routledge.

Ramage, C. S. 1971. *Monsoon meteorology.* New York and London: Academic Press.

Renowden, G. 2007. *Hot topic: Global warming and the future of New Zealand.* AUT Media.

Revell, C. G. 1981. *Tropical cyclones in the southwest Pacific, November 1969 to April 1979.* Miscellaneous Publication 170, Wellington: New Zealand Meteorological Service.

Ropelewski, C. F., and M. S. Halpert. 1987. Global and regional scale precipitation patterns associated with the El Niño/Southern Oscillation. *Monthly Weather Review* 115: 1606–1626.

Rossow, W. B. 1993. Clouds. In *Atlas of satellite observations related to global change,* ed. R. J. Gurney, J. L. Foster, and C. L. Parkinson, 141–163. Cambridge: Cambridge University Press.

Schroeder, T. 1993. Climate controls. In *Prevailing trade winds: Climate and weather in Hawai'i,* ed. M. Sanderson, 12–72. Honolulu: University of Hawai'i Press.

Strahler, A. N., and A. H. Strahler. 1978. *Modern physical geography.* John Wiley: New York.

Streten, N. A., and J. W. Zillman. 1984. Climate of the South Pacific Ocean. In *Climates of the oceans,* ed. H. van Loon. World Survey of Climatology, Amsterdam: Elsevier.

Sturman, A. P., and N. J. Tapper. 2006. *The weather and climate of Australia and New Zealand.* Melbourne: Oxford University Press.

Taylor, R. C. 1973. *An atlas of Pacific islands rainfall data.* Hawai'i Institute of Geophysics. 25 HIG-73-9, Honolulu: University of Hawai'i.

Terry, J. P. 2007. *Tropical cyclones: Climatology and impacts in the South Pacific.* New York: Springer.

Thomas, W. L. 1963. The variety of physical environments among Pacific Islands. In *Man's place in the island ecosystem: A symposium,* ed. F. R. Fosberg, 7–37. Honolulu: Bishop Museum Press.

Thompson, C. S. 1987. *The climate and weather of Tuvalu.* Miscellaneous Publication 188(6), Wellington: New Zealand Meteorological Service.

Thompson, C., S. Ready, and X. Zheng. 1992. *Tropical cyclones in the Southwest Pacific: November 1979 to May 1989.* Wellington: New Zealand Meteorological Service.

Tomlinson, A. I., and B. Nicol. 1976. *Tornado reports in New Zealand: 1961–1975.* Technical Note 229, Wellington: New Zealand Meteorological Service.

Trenberth, K. E. 1991. General characteristics of El Niño-Southern Oscillation. In *Teleconnections linking worldwide climate anomalies,* ed. M. H. Glantz, R. W. Katz, and N. Nicholls. Cambridge: Cambridge University Press.

Trenberth, K. E., and T. J. Hoar. 1996. The 1990–1995 El Niño-Southern Oscillation event: Longest on record. *Geophysical Research Letters* 23: 57–60.

Tualevao, P. N. 1991. The climate and weather system of W. Samoa. *Proceedings of the Conference: South Pacific Environments; Interactions With Weather and Climate,* September 2–7, 1991, ed. John E. Hay, 166–175. Auckland: University of Auckland.

Vincent, D. G. 1994. The South Pacific convergence zone (SPCZ): A review. *Monthly Weather Review* 122: 1949–1970.

Wallace, J. M., T. P. Mitchell, and A. R.H. Lau. 1995. Legates/MSU precipitation climatology. http://tao.atmos.washington.edu/legates_msu.

Warrick, R. A., C. Le Provost, M. F. Meier, J. Oerlemans, and P. L. Woodworth. 1996. Changes in sea level. In *Climate change 1995: The science of climate change,* ed. J. T. Houghton, L. G. Meira Filho, B. A. Callander, N. Harris, A. Kattenberg, and K. Maskell, 363–405. Cambridge: Cambridge University Press.

World Meteorological Organisation. 1984. *The global climate system— a critical review of the climate system during 1982–84.* Geneva: World Climate Data Program.

———. 1987. *Climate system monitoring.* Monthly Bulletin, No. 1987–8, August, World Geneva: Climate Program.

Oceanography

Lynne D. Talley, Gerard J. Fryer, and Rick Lumpkin

2

This is a brief introduction to the physical oceanography of the Pacific Islands region, the circulation, tsunamis, waves, sea level, temperature and salinity distributions, and the forces that create these. Since the tropical Pacific contains most of the island groups, and since the dynamics and properties of the tropical oceans differ from those at higher latitudes, this chapter primarily concerns tropical oceanography; but New Zealand is also briefly discussed.

The tropical Pacific is usually considered to lie between the astronomically defined tropics: the Tropic of Cancer (23.5°N) and the Tropic of Capricorn (23.5°S). There are other useful definitions of the tropics, based on how far the effect of the equator extends to the north and south in the atmosphere—approximately 20°. Within the ocean itself, the currents within 15° to 20° of the equator are oriented much more east-west than the currents at higher latitudes.

The tropics are a region of excess heating from the sun and of towering cloud convection and rainfall in narrow latitudinal bands. Compared with areas at higher latitudes, the frequency of storms and the average strength of the winds are low. Because these conditions affect the average height of surface waves, the wave climate of the tropics is relatively mild. Tsunamis, however, can pose an important danger, particularly in certain locations.

The tropical Pacific is the center of the global climate phenomenon known as the El Niño–Southern Oscillation, with quasi-cycles every three to seven years. During an El Niño event, the easterly trade winds weaken in the tropical Pacific and warm water builds up across the equatorial Pacific. This further changes the weather patterns in the atmosphere above, and the changes are propagated enormous distances around the globe.

Surface Waves, Tides, and Tsunamis

The ocean is constantly moving. Surface waves are what catch our eyes; they are created by wind blowing over the sea surface either nearby (small or choppy waves) or far away (long ocean swell). We are also usually aware of the daily or twice daily cycle of tides, as beaches and reefs are successively covered and exposed. At times of the year when tides are very high and storms create large surface waves, storm surges can become a problem in low-lying coastal areas. Once in a long while, residents of coastal areas might be affected by a large and long-period wave called a tsunami,

generated by an earthquake either nearby or very far away. These three types of waves, which have periods of minutes to hours, are described in this section.

Surface Waves

The wave climate of the Pacific Islands region is dominated by long-period swell reaching the area from distant storms, by relatively low amplitude, short-period waves generated by more local winds, and by the occasional bursts of energy associated with intense local storms.

Waves are characterized by their wavelength (distance between crests or troughs), their period (time between successive passage of a crest past a fixed point), and their height (crest to trough). Each type of wave can also be characterized by its restoring force. For surface waves, the restoring force to perturbations in sea-surface height is gravity, and so the waves are sometimes referred to as surface gravity waves. (For the very small "capillary" waves, the restoring force is the surface tension.)

Surface waves are mostly created by wind blowing across the sea surface. (The exceptions are the tides and tsunamis, which are described in the following sections.) If the wind persists, longer and longer waves are generated. The wave heights build proportionally to the strength and duration of the wind. Local waves forced by the wind travel in the direction of the wind. The period of a wave is the time between the passing of successive crests. For wind-generated waves, periods are on the order of seconds for the shortest waves to many minutes for the longest waves.

A large storm generates surface waves moving in all different directions under the storm. These travel away from the storm location, so if the storm is localized, waves will radiate outward from the storm area. The longer the waves, the faster they travel. Short waves are damped out much more rapidly by friction than are long waves. Long waves generated by storms at high latitudes, such as in the Gulf of Alaska, or far south in the Antarctic (or generated by earthquakes), can travel clear across the Pacific without much attenuation.

Typically the sea state (field of waves) is a jumble of waves of many different wavelengths, moving in many directions since the wind forcing them can be in many different directions. In the tropical Pacific, the wave field can be thought of as a superposition of waves forced by the local trade winds—the "trade wind sea"—and waves forced by distant storms. The trade wind sea is of small amplitude and is choppy since it is produced locally by winds that shift. The long-period swell from faraway storms is of relatively low amplitude in the open ocean and much more unidirectional than the trade wind sea.

The height of waves is now measured by various satellite sensors. A measure commonly used is significant wave height, which is the average height of the highest one-third of the waves, where the height is measured from trough to crest. NASA, NOAA, the JMA, CNES, and other operational organizations routinely produce maps of significant wave height from satellite altimetry and wave buoy information. The altimeter measures the height of the sea surface, although the significant wave height is usually constructed from the properties of the radar pulse. Maps and information are readily available online, both for previous years and also in near real time. Monthly analyses for the globe show that the average wave height in the tropical Pacific is typically less than 3 m, regardless of season, whereas wave height at high latitudes in the winter hemisphere typically reaches 3 to 6 m due to large storms (Figure 2.1).

As waves reach the shallow waters of a reef and island, they increase in amplitude and eventually break. The short-period trade wind sea produces relatively small surf height because of its short wavelengths. Large surf is produced by the long-period swell from distant storms, associated with correspondingly longer wavelength. The north shores of Pacific islands receive this long-period swell in the northern hemisphere winter, and the south shores in the southern hemisphere winter. Wave heights of 6 m in the surf zone are not uncommon. Surf in the winter swell on the north shore of O'ahu occasionally reaches over 15 m (Flament et al. 1997).

Because most Pacific islands are small and rise steeply from the sea floor, there is little shelf area that can affect the progress of the long waves. (Continental shelves typically refract waves.) Thus the waves impinge directly on the shore or reef and do not wrap around the islands.

Breaking waves contain a lot of energy, some of which goes into production of local currents—first into longshore currents and then into rip currents that carry water back out to sea. Breaking waves produce most of the circulation in the surface zone and in lagoons inside reefs.

Tides

Tides are produced by the gravitational attraction between the Earth and the moon and sun. Since the orbits of these bodies are regular, tides are regular and are the only part of the ocean's motion that can be exactly predicted. A full description of the tidal

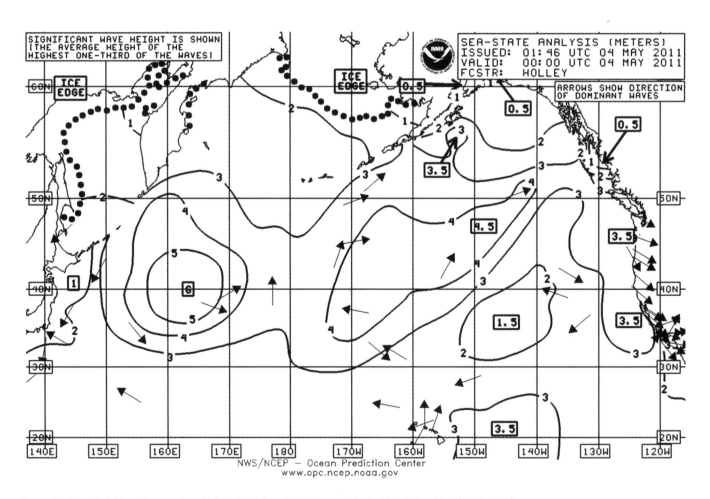

Figure 2.1. Wave heights on January 1 and July 1, 2008, from NOAA Wavewatch III's historical archive (NOAA 2008).

potential is beyond the scope of this text; the reader is referred to texts such as Knauss (1997) or Neshyba (1987).

The complete tide is a composite of the moon (lunar) and sun (solar) tides. The gravitational attraction between the Earth and moon (and to a lesser degree the sun) creates bulges of water on opposite sides of the Earth. On the side facing the moon, the gravitational attraction is largest and this creates one bulge. On the opposite side of the Earth, the gravitational attraction between the water and the moon is the smallest, which creates the bulge outward away from the moon. Since the Earth rotates daily, a point on the Earth passes through these bulges twice a day, resulting in semidiurnal (twice daily) components to the tide at each location. Because the moon does not generally lie over the equator, one of the bulges at a given point on the Earth is larger than on the other, which lends a diurnal (daily) component to the tide.

A modulation of the tidal range results from the relative positions of the moon and the sun: when the moon is new or full, the moon and the sun act together to produce larger spring tides; when the moon is in its first or last quarter, smaller neap tides occur. The cycle of spring to neap tides and back is half the twenty-seven-day period of the moon's revolution around the Earth and is known as the fortnightly cycle. The combination of diurnal, semidiurnal, and fortnightly cycles dominates variations in sea level throughout the islands.

The geometry of the oceans—the basin shape, local coastline, bays, and even harbor geometry—has a major effect on the local behavior of the tides. On scales of oceanic basins, tides exist as very long waves propagating in patterns determined by their period and the geometry of the basin. The tidal amplitude is very low in the central Pacific, but is higher in the tropical region of Australia, New Guinea, and Indonesia, as well as far to the north in the Gulf of Alaska and subpolar region.

Lines along which high tide occurs at the same time (called phase lines, shown as contours in Figure 2.2) converge at several points, called amphidromes, where the tidal range is zero. For the M2 tide, which is the principal lunar semidiurnal tide, there are several amphidromes in the Pacific: one in the eastern North Pacific, one in the eastern equatorial Pacific, one near Tahiti, and one in the eastern South Pacific, plus a series of more complicated amphidromes in the western tropical Pacific. Phase lines rotate counterclockwise around the amphidromes in the North Pacific

and clockwise around the ones in the South Pacific. For example, at the Hawaiian Islands, the offshore diurnal tide reaches the island of Hawai'i first and then sweeps across Maui, O'ahu, and finally Kaua'i. Local bathymetry affects the ranges and phases of the tides along the shore as the tidal waves wrap around the islands. For example, high tide at Hale'iwa on the north shore of O'ahu occurs more than an hour before high tide at Honolulu Harbor.

Tidal currents are associated with tidal variations of sea level, and near the shore they are often stronger than the large-scale circulation. Complete mapping of tidal currents requires direct measurements. As an example, in Hawai'i (Figure 2.3), the semidiurnal and diurnal tidal currents tend to be aligned with the shoreline. Due to high variability of tidal currents around the islands, however, this statistical picture may not correspond to the flow at a particular time: tidal currents cannot be predicted as precisely as tidal sea-level changes. Strong swirls often result from tidal currents flowing around points and headlands, and they present hazards to divers.

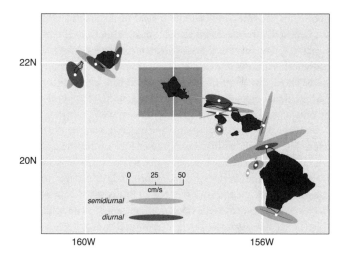

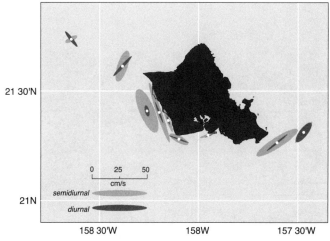

Figure 2.3. Tidal currents (cm/sec) at semidiurnal (gray) and diurnal (black) periods for the Hawaiian Islands. The major axes of the ellipses show the most probable orientation and strength of tidal currents. Data were taken variously from 1960 to 1995 and were provided by the University of Hawai'i, Hawai'i Institute of Geophysics; National Ocean Data Center, NOAA; and Science Applications International Corporation (after Flament et al. 1997).

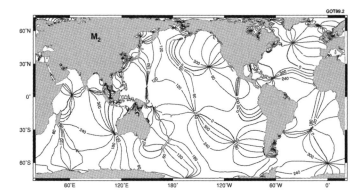

Figure 2.2. Map of the phase lag of the M2 tide relative to Greenwich. A phase of, say, 180 means that high tide occurs twelve hours past Greenwich mean time (Ray 1999).

Tsunamis

When the seafloor is raised (or lowered) suddenly during a shallow earthquake, water is raised with it, producing a mound of excess water at the sea surface. Gravity collapses the mound, producing a series of waves: a tsunami. Tsunamis are gravity waves, just like those generated by the wind, but their period is much longer, on the order of ten to sixty minutes. While earthquakes are the most common cause of tsunamis, the waves can be generated by any phenomenon that rapidly changes the shape of the sea surface over a large area: a volcanic eruption, landslide, or even meteorite impact. Since the largest shallow earthquakes occur in the subduction zones that ring the Pacific, and since these same subduction zones are dotted with volcanoes, the tsunami hazard throughout the tropical Pacific is high.

In the open ocean, the wavelength of a tsunami may be as much as two hundred kilometers, many times greater than the ocean depth, which is on the order of several kilometers. This huge wavelength means that the entire water column, from surface to bottom, is set into motion. For typical ocean depths of 5 km, a tsunami will advance at up to 650 km/hr, about the speed of a jet aircraft. A tsunami can therefore travel from one side of the Pacific to the other in less than a day. The speed decreases rapidly as the water shoals: in 15 m of water the speed of a tsunami (or of any wave with a long enough wavelength to feel the ocean bottom) will be only 45 km/hr.

As the tsunami slows in shoaling water, its wavelength is shortened. Just as with ordinary surf, the energy of the waves must be contained in a smaller volume of water, so the waves grow in height. Even though the wavelength has shortened, a tsunami will typically have a wavelength in excess of 10 km when it comes ashore. Each wave therefore floods the land (Figure 2.4) as a rapidly rising tide (hence the common English term tidal wave), lasting for several minutes, posing serious danger to some areas. The individual waves are typically from ten to thirty minutes apart, so the danger period can last for hours.

Run-up (maximum height the tsunami reaches on shore) can vary dramatically depending on seafloor topography. Small islands with steep slopes experience little run-up; wave heights there are only slightly greater than on the open ocean (around 1 m). For this reason the smaller Polynesian islands with steepsided fringing or barrier reefs are only at moderate hazard from tsunamis. Such is not the case for the Hawaiian Islands or the Marquesas, however. Both of these island chains are almost devoid of barrier reefs and have broad bays exposed to the open ocean. Hilo Bay at the island of Hawai'i and Tahauku Bay at Hiva Oa are especially vulnerable. During a tsunami from the eastern Aleutians in 1946, run-up exceeded 8 m at Hilo and 10 m at Tahauku; fifty-nine people were killed in Hilo, two in Tahauku (Shepard, Macdonald, and Cox 1950; Talandier 1993). Similarly, any gap in a reef puts the adjacent shoreline at risk. The tsunami from the Suva earthquake of 1953 did little damage because of Fiji's extensive offshore reefs. Two villages on Viti Levu located opposite gaps in the reef, however, were extensively damaged and five people were drowned (Singh 1991).

Tsunamis are generated by shallow earthquakes all around the Pacific, but those from earthquakes in the tropical Pacific tend to be modest in size. While such tsunamis may be devastating locally, they decay rapidly with distance and are not usually observed more than a few hundred kilometers from their sources. That is not the case with tsunamis generated by great earthquakes in the North Pacific or along the Pacific coast of South America. About half a dozen times a century a tsunami from one of these locations sweeps across the entire Pacific, is reflected from distant shores, and sets the entire ocean oscillating for days. The tsunami from the magnitude 9.5 Chile earthquake of 1960 (Figure 2.5) caused death and destruction throughout the Pacific: Hawai'i, Samoa, and Easter Island all recorded run-ups exceeding 4 m; sixty-one people were killed in Hawai'i, two hundred in Japan. A similar tsunami in 1868 from northern Chile caused extensive damage in the Austral Islands, Hawai'i, Samoa, and New Zealand. There were several deaths in the Chatham Islands (Iida, Cox, and Pararas-Carayannis 1967).

Figure 2.4. Aftermath of a tidal wave or a tsunami from the Aleutian Islands running ashore on the island of O'ahu, Hawai'i, in 1957. Run-up here is about 2 m (NOAA photo).

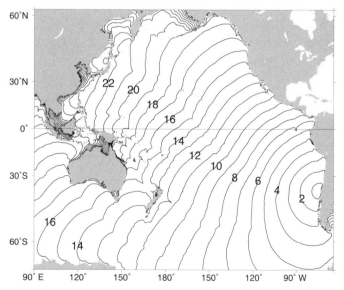

Figure 2.5. Travel times (hours) for the tsunami resulting from the magnitude 9.5 Chile earthquake of 1960.

A tsunami from a local earthquake may reach a nearby shore in less than ten minutes, making warning a difficult task, though in this case the shaking of the ground provides its own warning. For tsunamis from more distant sources, however, accurate warnings of a tsunami's arrival time are possible because tsunamis travel at a known speed. The current international tsunami warning system has twenty-six member nations that coordinate their warning activities through the Pacific Tsunami Warning Center (PTWC), operated in Hawai'i by the National Oceanic and Atmospheric Administration (NOAA). The Hawai'i center uses data from the global seismic network to identify and characterize potential tsunamigenic earthquakes, then verifies if a tsunami has been generated by querying tide gauge stations near the source. While the system is far from perfect (about half the warnings are false alarms), performance is constantly improving and there have been no missed warnings. Real-time information about earthquakes that could result in tsunamis is available on the PTWC website (http://www.ptwc.weather.gov/). The PTWC was, in the absence of a warning system for the Indian Ocean, the main supplier of information to the nations around the Indian Ocean for the very destructive Sumatra earthquake of 2004. The PTWC tracks possible tsunamis in the Indian Ocean and Caribbean Sea while international warning systems for these regions are being developed.

Temperature and Salinity Distribution in the Tropical Pacific

The temperature of the sea has a large effect on local climate (and what can grow in the water and on nearby land), on fog and precipitation, on hurricanes, and so on. The salt in seawater is what most obviously distinguishes it from fresh water and affects the ecology of coastal lagoons, tidal flats, and river mouths. Variations in salt content have a more indirect influence on climate than does temperature, for instance by affecting how deeply the surface layer of the ocean can mix and hence affecting the temperature at the sea surface.

Temperature

Ocean surface temperature globally is dominated by excess heating in the tropics compared with higher latitudes, resulting mainly from higher radiation from the sun in the tropics. This leads to a sea-surface temperature difference from equator to pole of about 30°C (Figure 2.6). In the tropics, including the tropical Pacific, the maximum sea-surface temperature is around 28°C and can rise to at most 30°C. This is considerably cooler than the maximum temperatures of about 50°C regularly found over land. It is hypothesized that the main regulation on the maximum ocean temperature is through cloud formation. Cloud formation increases dramatically when the sea-surface temperature is greater than about 27.5°C (Graham and Barnett 1987). The increased cloudiness increases the albedo (reflectivity of the Earth's atmosphere to space), which reduces the solar radiation reaching the sea surface (Ramanathan and Collins 1993), and thus keeps the surface temperature from rising much more.

The sea-surface temperature is not uniformly high in the tropical Pacific. A large warm pool is found in the central and western

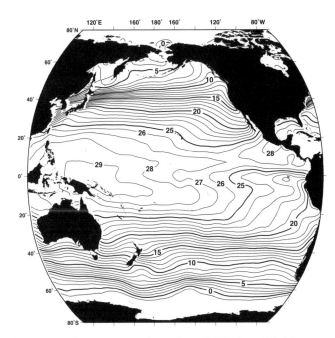

Figure 2.6. Surface temperature (annual mean) (°C). The gridded data are freely available from the National Oceanic and Atmospheric Administration atlas (Levitus and Boyer 1994a).

Pacific (Figure 2.6) and extends into the eastern and central Indian Ocean. Surface water in the eastern equatorial Pacific is several degrees cooler than in the west. The vertical thermal structure of the upper ocean is responsible for these differences. In the western Pacific, the surface layer, which is fairly well mixed, is approximately 100 m thick and warmer than about 28°C. Just below this surface layer, the temperature goes rapidly downward; this is called the thermocline.

In the central and eastern Pacific, the surface layer is shallower, and so colder water and the thermocline are found closer to the surface. Upwelling in the eastern Pacific (caused by offshore and off-equatorial currents) draws this cooler water to the surface, creating the equatorial cold tongue at the sea surface. Upwelling of cold water at the equator is apparent in sections crossing the equator (Figure 2.7). Upwelling in the western Pacific is weaker than in the east and draws up only warm water, and so an equivalent cold tongue along the equator is absent.

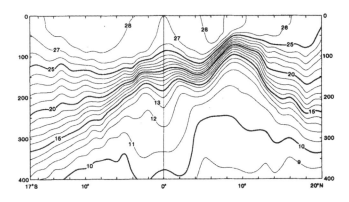

Figure 2.7. Mean subsurface temperature computed from forty-three separate cross sections at 150°W to 158°W, collected over a period of seventeen months in 1979 and 1980 (Wyrtki and Kilonsky 1984).

Upwelling is common along the west coast of South America, off Ecuador and Peru, and along the west coast of Central and North America. As a result of both the upwelling and the eastern boundary currents that flow toward the equator in these regions, sea-surface temperatures are relatively low along these coasts. The winds that create upwelling are strongest in the area just west of Costa Rica. Here the thermocline is lifted to within 10 m of the sea surface, in a feature called the Costa Rica Dome (Hofmann, Busalacchi, and O'Brien 1981).

Below the sea surface, temperature decreases to the ocean bottom (Figure 2.8). The most rapid change is in the upper 500 m, in the thermocline. Changes are more gradual below this. Temperature reaches about 1.2°C in the abyssal tropical Pacific. The initial temperature and salinity of all ocean water is set at the sea surface. The sea-surface temperature distribution (Figure 2.6) shows that water colder than about 18°C comes from latitudes higher than about 30°, hence outside the tropics. Waters of about 4° to 6°C come from latitudes of about 40° to 45° in both hemispheres. The coldest waters flow northward from the Antarctic region. These southern hemisphere waters, which fill the Pacific below 1,000 to 1,500 meters, are part of a circulation that extends through all of the oceans.

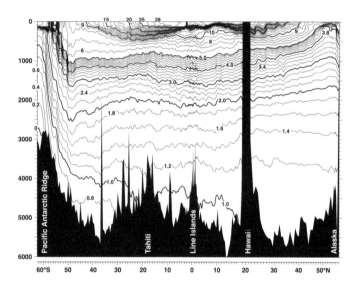

Figure 2.8. Vertical section of potential temperature (°C) from 150°W from data collected from 1987 to 1993 (after World Ocean Circulation Experiment Pacific Ocean Atlas, Talley 2007). Potential temperature is the temperature a parcel of water would have if moved to the sea surface with no change in heat content, and is lower than measured temperature since temperature increases when water is compressed due to the high pressure in the ocean.

The deepest waters come from the Weddell and Ross Seas of the Antarctic and the Greenland Sea just north of the North Atlantic. The North Pacific does not produce any of this deep water, and so its deep waters have traveled a long distance from their sea-surface origin. These deep waters have spent about five hundred years making the journey to the deep North Pacific (and slightly less time to the deep tropical Pacific). Waters that have been far from sea-surface forcing (heating/cooling and evaporation/precipitation) for a long time are fairly uniform because they mix with each other. Thus the deep Pacific contains a large amount of water in a very narrow range of temperature and salinity.

Salinity

Seawater density depends on temperature (warm water is less dense) and the amount of material dissolved in the water. The latter is mostly what is referred to as sea salt and is a combination of various salts. The total amount of salt in the world ocean is constant on all but the longest geological time scales. The total amount of fresh water in the ocean, however, is not constant; it is affected by evaporation, precipitation, runoff, and lockup of water in ice on land and on the sea. Hence salinity, which is more or less the grams of salts dissolved in a kilogram of seawater, varies as a result of surface freshwater inputs and exports.

The total range of salinity in most areas of the ocean is small enough that temperature actually contributes more to seawater density differences, but salinity differences are significant. For instance, if saltier water lies above fresher water, then the temperature difference between the two must be large enough to ensure stability (light water over dense water).

Surface salinity in the Pacific (Figure 2.9) shows clearly the net result of the atmospheric circulation described in chapter 1. Cloud formation and high precipitation occur in regions of rising, humid air, which are associated with low atmospheric pressure at the sea surface, such as in the Intertropical Convergence Zone (ITCZ) at 5° to 10°N, and in the subpolar regions poleward of 40° latitude. Surface salinity is low where precipitation is high. Evaporation and hence surface salinity are high where the air is dry; these are regions of atmospheric divergence (high-pressure zones at the surface).

Because temperature dominates the vertical density differences in most of the ocean (especially in the tropics), it decreases downward almost everywhere. The salinity distribution is more complex, with regions of salty water lying over fresher water and

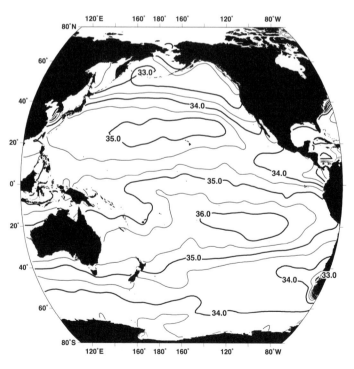

Figure 2.9. Surface salinity (annual mean). Data sources as in 2.4 (Levitus and Boyer 1994b). Note: Salinity units are equivalent to parts per thousand.

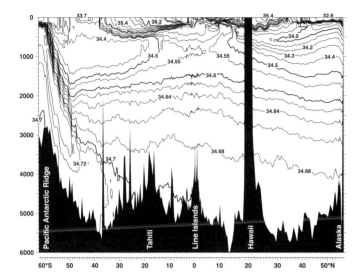

Figure 2.10. *Vertical section of salinity along 150°W. Data sources are the same as for 2.8.*

vice versa (Figure 2.10). Such salinity inversions are common. The high salinity in surface evaporation regions extends down to the thermocline. Below the high-salinity surface water is a layer of low-salinity intermediate water that extends from the rainy subpolar latitudes in the south and north toward the equator. Below this, the deep Pacific is filled with relatively more saline waters originating from the deep waters around Antarctica and from the Atlantic.

Along the equator, surface salinity is lowest in the western Pacific, where normally there is much more rainfall than in the central and eastern equatorial Pacific. The freshest surface water in the western equatorial Pacific actually extends only partway down into the vertically uniform, warm surface layer, with salinity increasing strongly downward midway within this uniform temperature layer. A relatively sharp front separates the fresh western equatorial surface water from the more saline central Pacific surface water. During periods such as El Niño, when the trade winds slacken (see page 14), the western low-salinity warm water floods eastward toward the central Pacific along the equator (Roemmich, Morris, and Young 1994).

Biological productivity in the sunlit surface layer of the ocean (the euphotic zone, about 100 m deep) relies on a continual supply of nitrate, phosphate, dissolved silica, and other nutrients. These are regenerated at depth as the decaying plants and animals and fecal pellets fall through the water column, with some portions, especially of the silica-bearing hard parts, reaching the ocean bottom. Thus nutrients are severely depleted in the surface layer, where they are used almost as quickly as they appear. Nutrients are found in abundance below the surface layer, especially where waters have been separated from the sea surface for a long time.

Nutrients reach the euphotic zone through upwelling, and so upwelling regions have slightly higher nutrient content and much higher biological productivity than downwelling regions (see below). The most productive regions occur where upwelling is vigorous and where the nutrient-rich thermocline is near the sea surface. Near-surface nutrients in the Pacific are high in the equatorial and eastern tropical Pacific, where upwelling is high, and low in the subtropical downwelling regions poleward of about 20° latitude.

Ocean Circulation in the Tropical Pacific

Aside from the waves, tides, and tsunamis discussed above, the ocean also has large-scale current movements that vary slowly over weeks to months, years, and many decades, or not at all (the mean circulation). These affect navigation. Currents are also important in moving water from one place to another, which redistributes heat, salt, and nutrients.

Surface Circulation

The Pacific sea-surface circulation (Figure 2.11) consists of two large subtropical gyres centered at 30°N and 30°S, which rotate clockwise in the northern hemisphere and counterclockwise in the southern hemisphere, a subpolar gyre centered at about 50°N and rotating counterclockwise, a major eastward flow that circles Antarctica called the Antarctic Circumpolar Current, and complicated but predominantly east-west ("zonal") currents in the tropics between the gyres. Surface flow is westward between 30°S and 5°N (the South Equatorial Current). Between 5°N and 10°N lies a strong eastward flow (the North Equatorial Countercurrent), corresponding to the climatic ITCZ. The westward flow between 10°N and 30°N is called the North Equatorial Current. The South Pacific Convergence Zone, fluctuating in strength seasonally in the southern hemisphere, creates an occasional appearance of a South Equatorial Countercurrent, which is more pronounced in the western South Pacific than in the east.

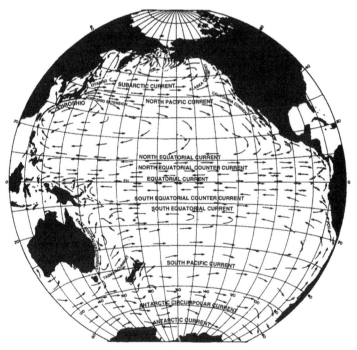

Figure 2.11. *Schematic of the surface circulation of the Pacific during the northern summer (after Tabata 1975). Abbreviations: EU (equatorial undercurrent), PCU (Peru-Chile undercurrent).*

In the western tropical Pacific, the circulation is dominated by strong currents that abut the western ocean boundary (Figure 2.12), but it is made complicated by the many islands and deep

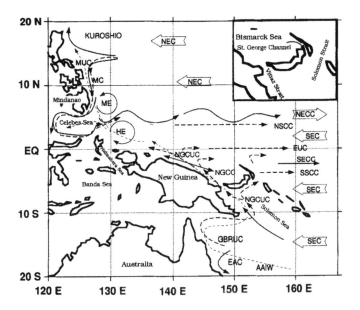

Figure 2.12. Schematic of the surface circulation of the western tropical Pacific (Fine et al. 1994). Surface current abbreviations (solid arrows): NEC (North Equatorial Current), NECC (North Equatorial Countercurrent), SEC (South Equatorial Current), MC (Mindanao Current), NGCC (New Guinea Coastal Current), EAC (East Australian Current), ME (Mindanao Eddy), HE (Halmahera Eddy). Subsurface current abbreviations (dashed arrows): MUC (Mindanao Undercurrent), NGCUC (New Guinea Coastal Undercurrent), NSCC (North Subsurface Countercurrent), EUC (Equatorial Undercurrent), SSCC (South Subsurface Countercurrent). The light dashed boundary shows the limit of the AAIW (Antarctic/Intermediate Water), which is the low-salinity subsurface layer seen at about 700–800 m depth in 2.10.

ridges. Australia forms the largest single part of the boundary. In the North Pacific, the North Equatorial Current reaches the western boundary at Mindanao in the Philippines and then splits northward (Kuroshio) and southward (Mindanao Current). The Kuroshio is one of the strongest currents in the world, similar to the Gulf Stream in speed and volume. It affects climate in Japan through its warmth and fisheries off Japan through both its warmth and relative lack of nutrients. The Mindanao Current separates from the coast of Mindanao around 5°N, flowing eastward into the North Equatorial Countercurrent and westward into the Celebes Sea. Eddies (circulations of about 50 to 200 km that are often variable over a period of weeks to months) are usually found east of Mindanao and east of Halmahera. The water entering the Celebes Sea forms the beginning of flow westward through the complex of Indonesian islands, threading through to Java and into the Indian Ocean.

In the South Pacific, the broad, westward-flowing South Equatorial Current reaches the western boundary through a complex of islands. The northern portion forms a northward-flowing western boundary current along New Guinea, called the New Guinea Coastal Undercurrent (Lindstrom et al. 1987; Tsuchiya et al. 1989). This flows northward to the equator. A portion of it turns eastward along the equator and forms part of the eastward-flowing subsurface Equatorial Undercurrent. A portion may continue slightly northward, joined by the westward flow just north of the equator, and then turns eastward, joining the separated Mindanao Current, into the North Equatorial Countercurrent.

The remainder of the westward-flowing South Equatorial Current flows north of Fiji into the Coral Sea and reaches the western boundary at Australia. Here it turns southward into the East Australian Current, which is the western boundary current, and then flows southward to the latitude of the northern tip of New Zealand. At this point, the current meanders a great deal and some portion of it separates and flows eastward across the Tasman Sea as the Tasman Front, and then along the northeastern boundary of New Zealand as the North Cape Current. The broad flow between New Zealand and Fiji is also eastward.

The large-scale surface flow is affected mainly by the larger landmasses, and less so by the small islands dotting the tropical and South Pacific. Intermediate and abyssal flows, however, are strongly affected by the ridges in which the small islands are embedded, as described next.

Subsurface Equatorial Circulation

The currents below the sea surface seem of less immediate importance to humans than are the surface currents, as they do not affect sailing or have an obvious effect on local sea-surface conditions such as temperature. The surface and deeper flows, however, are strongly coupled to each other. Successful models of the ocean circulation must include the flow below the surface, all the way down to the ocean bottom, where undersea rises and mountains strongly steer the bottom currents.

In most places of the world ocean, the currents vary gradually from surface to bottom. They are usually strongest at the surface, where they are closest to the wind, and gradually blend into the circulation of the abyss. However, within 5° latitude of the equator, the subsurface currents are much more complicated (Figure 2.13). Between 50 m and 250 m depth lies the strong eastward-flowing Equatorial Undercurrent. The undercurrent was originally discovered by Townsend Cromwell during a research expedition in the 1950s when the drogue deployed at that depth moved strongly eastward while the surface current was westward (Cromwell, Montgomery, and Stroup 1954). In speed, the Equatorial Undercurrent matches the strongest currents in the world (>100 cm/sec or 1 km/day), but it is vertically very thin (about 200 m thick), in contrast with other major currents such as the Kuroshio, Gulf Stream, and Antarctic Circumpolar Current, which reach to the ocean bottom.

Below the undercurrent, and flanking it on either side of the equator, lie the North and South Subsurface Countercurrents, flowing eastward (centered at around 4° on either side of the equator and from around 200 m depth downward). Directly beneath the Equatorial Undercurrent lies a weaker westward flow, which extends to about 1,000 m depth. Below this there is a regime of the so-called stacked jets, with many reversals in current direction, extending to the ocean bottom, and with vertical extent increasing toward the bottom (Firing 1989). Between 2° and 5° latitude, the vertical structure may show only a reversal or two. Farther away from the equator, the surface circulation extends to depths of 1,000 to 2,500 m, with much weaker flow below dominated by bottom topography.

The most general characteristic of circulation in the tropical Pacific is its exaggerated east-west nature compared with flow poleward of 20° latitude in both hemispheres, where gyres that

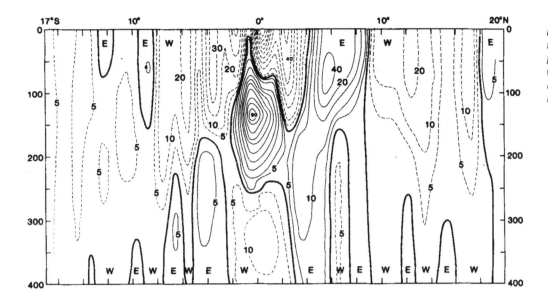

Figure 2.13. East-west currents in the central Pacific. Numbers are flows in cm/sec. These velocities were computed from the same locations as in 2.5 (Wyrtki and Kilonsky 1984).

also include more north-south flow are the norm. This zonality is characteristic of the tropical circulation in the Atlantic and Indian Oceans as well.

Deep Circulation

With increasing depth, the surface circulation weakens and shifts latitude. In the tropics, the surface circulation signatures disappear by about 500 to 1,000 m depth. Flow beneath this is predominantly zonal (east-west), with slight north-south movement. Various analyses show counterclockwise circulation north of the equator and clockwise circulation south of the equator, in elongated cells between the equator and about 10° latitude. (See Reid 1997 for an analysis of the whole of the deep circulation.) The deepest circulation is affected by the topography of the ridges and basins. Overall, there is net northward flow in a deep western boundary current, which enters the Pacific from the Antarctic east of New Zealand and passes through a deep gap near Samoa called the Samoan Passage. It moves on northward to the equator, crossing it in the western Pacific. North of the equator, a portion branches eastward to pass south of the Hawaiian Islands, and the other portion continues northward. The northward flow appears to move westward near the Kuroshio and then northward along the western boundary to the subpolar Pacific. Return flow to the south probably occurs along the East Pacific Rise in the eastern Pacific and then westward along the equator (Johnson and Toole 1993; Firing 1989).

Circulation Near Islands and Island Groups

Local circulation near islands and island chains can be affected by eddies generated by the ocean currents moving past the islands. Large island groups and especially the ridges upon which they sit also affect the large-scale ocean circulation. An example is flow near the Hawaiian Islands, which forms a ridge for deep flow. On the north side of the Hawaiian Islands, large-scale currents or large eddies (time-dependent currents of possibly smaller spatial extent) are sometimes found along the ridge (Talley and deSzoeke 1986). An eddy is often generated at the passage between the islands of

Maui and Hawai'i. Southwest of the ridge, in the lee of the flow of the westward ocean currents, eddy activity is reduced.

Forcing of the Circulation

All movements of ocean water must be generated by some force. Surface waves are created by the wind's blowing over the sea surface and catching on smaller waves to make larger ones. Tides are created by the gravitational pull between the Earth and the moon and sun. Tsunamis are created by undersea earthquakes. Ocean currents and large eddies are created by the wind's acting much more indirectly than for surface waves, and also by heating/cooling and precipitation/evaporation, which can cause the water to overturn. The upper ocean circulation in the tropical Pacific is driven mostly by the stress from the wind. The prevailing winds in the tropical Pacific are the trades or easterlies, which blow from east to west. Together with the westerlies of higher latitudes, these force the large subtropical gyres. The dominant influence of these gyres on the tropics is the broad-scale westward flow mentioned above, called the North Equatorial Current (north of 10°N) and the South Equatorial Current (from 5°N southward). We divide the wind forcing of the tropics into two regimes: off the equator and on the equator. The difference between these two is due to the Coriolis effect (deflection by the Earth's rotation), which is important at all latitudes except on and very close to the equator.

Good explanations of Ekman and geostrophic flows and the forcing that creates the gyres (see below) can be found in texts such as Tomczak and Godfrey (1994), Knauss (1997), Stewart (2005), and Talley et al. (2011).

Forcing of Nonequatorial Flows

Winds push on the very top of the ocean and move the water through frictional stress. Because of the Coriolis effect, the water flows in a very thin layer (around 1 m thick) off to the right of the wind in the northern hemisphere and to the left in the southern hemisphere. This thin layer then pushes on a thin water layer below it through friction, and so on, each slightly more to the right

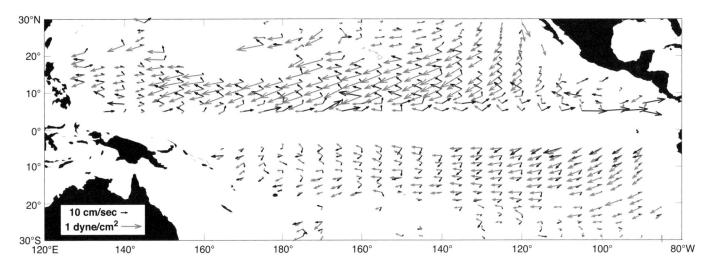

Figure 2.14. *Annual average surface wind stress (gray arrows in stress/unit area) and the average near-surface flow (black arrows in cm/sec) that arises directly in response to the winds. The surface wind stress acts on just the very surface of the ocean. This force is transmitted frictionally into the surface layer, and the direction of the stress turns with depth due to the rotation of the Earth. The direct stress disappears at only about 50 m depth. The resulting flow in the top 50 m or so of the ocean is to the right of the surface wind in the northern hemisphere and left in the southern hemisphere and is called Ekman transport. The black arrows in the figure are the average velocity based on hundreds of satellite-tracked surface drifters after the average flow resulting from the ocean's pressure field (geostrophic flow) is subtracted (arrows do not appear near the equator because the Ekman effect is very weak there, as discussed in the text) (after Ralph and Niiler 1999).*

than the layer above it (in the northern hemisphere). The overall flow due to the frictional stress dies out at about 20 to 100 m below the sea surface. The overall effect of the wind on this total layer is to drive a net flow of water exactly to the right of the wind in the northern hemisphere and exactly to the left in the southern hemisphere; this is called the Ekman transport (Figure 2.14). This 20- to 100-meter-deep frictional layer is referred to as the Ekman layer.

At all depths, from the very surface to the bottom, there is geostrophic flow, which is driven by horizontal pressure differences and deflected by the Coriolis force. The resulting geostrophic flow is always at exactly right angles to the pressure difference—to the right in the northern hemisphere and to the left in the southern hemisphere. The geostrophic flow at the sea surface is due to small but large-scale and long-lasting differences in sea-surface height, generally less than a meter, which produce horizontal differences in pressure in the water. The largest height differences, stable for long periods of time, drive the fastest currents such as the Kuroshio in the Pacific and the Gulf Stream in the Atlantic. Where these flows are most vigorous, they can reach to great depth and even to the ocean bottom.

The complete surface layer transport (Figure 2.15) is the sum of the geostrophic and Ekman components. Below the sea-surface Ekman layer, flow is solely geostrophic except in a frictional layer within 100 m of the ocean bottom.

The horizontal pressure difference ("gradient") that results in geostrophic flow can be created in two ways: (1) through heating/cooling and evaporation/precipitation (buoyancy forcing) and (2) indirectly by the winds via the Ekman layer. Buoyancy forcing, however, is weak compared with indirect wind forcing. How do the winds produce the horizontal pressure difference that drives geostrophic flow? Where Ekman transport converges, downwelling occurs. The ocean responds with slow equatorward geostrophic

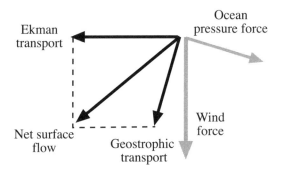

Figure 2.15. *Forces and flow in the ocean's surface layer, after Tomczak and Godfrey (1994). Transport is the total flow within the surface layer, which is about 50 m thick. Ekman transport is exactly to the right of the wind. Geostrophic flow is exactly to the right of the pressure difference. Net transport is the sum of the two.*

flow between the sea surface and about 2,000 m depth, creating heightened pressure in the western Pacific (subtropical gyres). Where Ekman transport diverges, upwelling occurs. The result is a slow poleward flow, with associated low pressure (subpolar gyre). This dynamical mechanism, called Sverdrup balance, is described in the textbooks referenced above.

As an example, at subtropical latitudes, westerly winds occur north of 30°N and trade winds occur south of 30°N. The resulting Ekman layer is convergent, resulting in downwelling all the way across the subtropical Pacific between about 15°N and 40°N. The ocean then flows slowly southward in this whole region, with fast northward return flow in the Kuroshio. The Kuroshio connects to the interior (central Pacific) flow through eastward flow (North Pacific Current), and the interior flow connects back to the Kuroshio through westward flow (North Equatorial Current). This creates the familiar large clockwise "gyre" in the midlatitude North Pacific.

The variation in trade wind strength due to the ITCZ between 5°N and 10°N leads to a permanent Ekman divergence and upwelling there. This off-equatorial upwelling results in slow northward flow in this narrow latitude range, which is returned southward by the Mindanao Current. This creates a counterclockwise circulation that is very narrow from north to south but extends all the way across the Pacific in the east-west direction. The southern part of the westward-flowing North Equatorial Current is part of this gyre. The swift eastward flow of the North Equatorial Countercurrent is also part of this gyre.

Forcing at the Equator

Directly on the equator, the effect of the Earth's rotation on the circulation vanishes, and so these concepts of geostrophic and Ekman flow do not apply. At the equator, the easterly trade winds push the surface water directly from east to west. This water piles up gently in the western Pacific (0.5 meters higher there than in the eastern Pacific). Because it is higher in the west than in the east, there is a pressure difference that causes the flow just beneath the surface layer to be eastward. This strong eastward flow is the Equatorial Undercurrent. The alternating eastward and westward jets found below the Equatorial Undercurrent on the equator die out about 2° latitude from the equator; the cause of the alternating jets has not been clearly identified.

Upwelling occurs at the equator due to poleward Ekman transport on either side of the equator, which is a consequence of the easterly trade winds. Along the equator just below the surface, waters in the east are colder than in the west, partly a result of the rising of the Equatorial Undercurrent from west to east. Upwelling in the eastern Pacific thus accesses much cooler water than in the western Pacific, and as a result the surface waters in the east along the equator are colder than in the west. However, even in the eastern Pacific, trade winds have seasonal changes. Equatorial upwelling is weaker in the northern winter and spring, giving rise to mini-El Niño conditions (see below) each year in the eastern equatorial Pacific.

Response to Changing Winds in the Tropics

When the trade winds weaken or even reverse, the flow of water westward at the equator weakens or reverses and upwelling weakens or stops. Surface waters in the eastern Pacific warm significantly since upwelling is no longer bringing the cool waters to the surface. The deep warm pool in the western Pacific thins as its water "sloshes" eastward along the equator in the absence of the trade winds that maintain the warm pool.

Heating/Cooling and Evaporation/Precipitation

Ocean water density is a function of temperature and salinity and so can be changed through heating/cooling and evaporation/precipitation. The resulting density changes can drive circulation. The effects of temperature and salinity on density and circulation, though, are much smaller than the effect of the wind. Temperature- and salinity-driven density changes, caused mainly by fluxes at the sea surface, are the only means of forcing circulation where the

indirect effect of wind forcing vanishes, as in the ocean deeper than about 2,000 m (except beneath very strong surface currents such as the Kuroshio). In the upper ocean, even though density fluxes do not greatly change the flow, they do have a major effect on ocean properties and on the overlying atmosphere, which is heated from below by the ocean.

The total surface heat flux into the ocean averaged over all seasons (Figure 2.16) shows the greatest heating along the equator and in the western warm pool region around Indonesia. The units of heating are watts/m², or energy flux per unit area. (1 watt = 1 joule/sec, where a joule is the mks unit for energy.) In the subtropics, where the western boundary currents bring warm water to midlatitudes, there is strong cooling, especially in the northern hemisphere. In order to maintain a fairly steady distribution of temperature, the ocean must transport heat from the areas where it gains heat to the areas where it loses it.

In the western warm pool region and all along the ITCZ there is major convection in the atmosphere, creating towering clouds. Precipitation in these regions creates pools of freshened surface waters, which can be seen in the large-scale surface salinity pattern as an east-west band of fresher water stretching all the way across the Pacific. In the midlatitude dry regions, excess evaporation under the atmospheric high-pressure cells creates high-salinity surface water. These waters can be traced by their salinity as they move to below the sea surface and are carried far by the ocean currents.

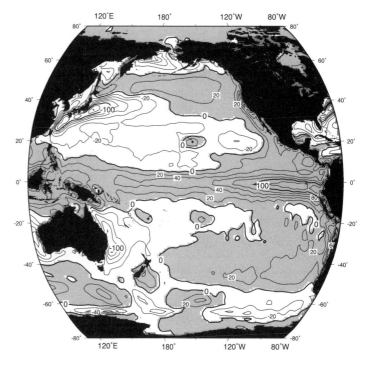

Figure 2.16. *Annual mean heat flux from the atmosphere to the ocean, using fluxes from the Southampton Oceanography Centre climatology (Grist and Josey 2003). Units are watts/m², which is energy flux per unit area. Positive numbers indicate that the ocean is being heated. Contour intervals are 20 W/m². Contributing to the heat flux, in order of relative importance, are the incoming radiation from the sun, loss of heat due to energy used in evaporation, loss of heat due to blackbody radiation, and loss of heat due to the difference in temperature between the sea surface and the overlying air.*

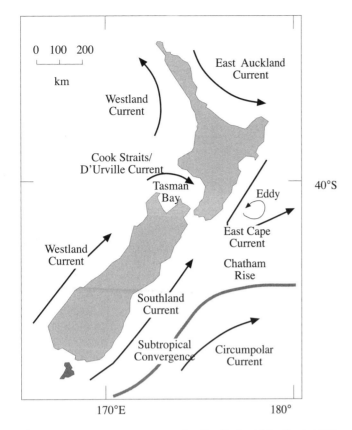

Figure 2.17. *Ocean currents surrounding New Zealand (after Heath 1985).*

Oceanography of New Zealand

New Zealand extends over some fifteen degrees of latitude into subtropical and midlatitude waters of the South Pacific. Its islands are large and have extensive embayments. Its surrounding oceans differ substantively from that of islands in the tropical Pacific in terms of currents, temperature, and salinity, discussed briefly here. For additional information, readers are referred to Heath (1985).

Bottom depths around New Zealand are relatively shallow, interrupting and diverting the eastward-flowing branch of the East Australian Current that crosses the Tasman Sea in the Tasman Front (Figure 2.17).

Surface temperature and salinity vary with latitude, ranging from 25°C and 35.8 in the north to 10°C and 34.5 in the south. Seasonal ranges of 6 to 7 °C and 0.3 to 0.4 occur for temperature and salinity, respectively. Subtropical and sub-Antarctic waters occur at the surface. The line along which the two water masses meet, south and east of New Zealand, is known as the Subtropical Convergence or Subtropical Front. Beneath the surface, with increasing depth, occur the Antarctic Intermediate Water (low salinity), Pacific Deep Water (low oxygen), and Antarctic Bottom Water (low temperature, higher salinity, higher oxygen).

Localized circulations occur in the many embayments of New Zealand, reflecting the input of different currents as well as freshwater runoff. Considerable variability in surface circulation is caused by prevailing winds. Between October and March, northerly winds are dominant, and surface circulation is mainly toward the head of the bay. Between April and August, southerly winds are dominant, and surface circulation is out of the bay.

El Niño–Southern Oscillation

Large changes in climate occur in the tropical Pacific over the course of three to seven years, as described in chapter 1. This phenomenon, known as the El Niño–Southern Oscillation (ENSO), is a coupled interaction between the atmosphere and ocean. Its effects reach far beyond the tropical Pacific through connections in the far-ranging atmospheric circulation.

The events that form a typical ENSO cycle were described by Rasmusson and Carpenter (1982). A Report to the Nation (NOAA OGP 1994) provides an excellent summary, as does the National Oceanic and Atmospheric Administration's website for El Niño (See McPhaden 1997).

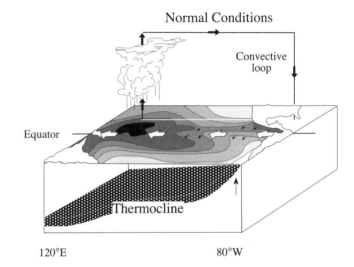

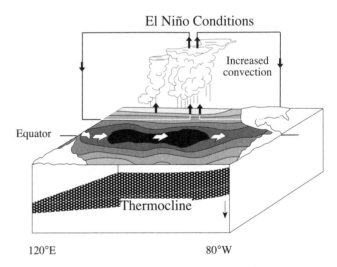

Figure 2.18. *Schematic of the relations between the ocean's temperature structure, surface winds (broad open arrows), ocean upwelling (small black arrows), atmospheric convection (up and down black arrows and dashed cells) and cloud patterns in the tropical Pacific during normal conditions and during an El Niño. (This figure is from the TAO Project Office, Dr. Michael J. McPhaden, director, and is available on the El Niño theme page of the NOAA/Pacific Marine Environmental Laboratory— http://www.pmel.noaa.gov/tao/elnino/nino-home.html, where one can find much more information about El Niño including current conditions and links to forecasts.) (Note: Horizontal scale in thousands of km; vertical scale in hundreds of m.)*

During an El Niño event (Figure 2.18), the normal easterly trade winds slacken, as indicated by a decrease in the atmospheric pressure difference between the central and western Pacific. Weakened trade winds result in reduced westward flow at the equator, which leads to a draining of the western warm pool toward the east. Equatorial ocean upwelling is reduced, which results in warmer sea-surface temperatures in the eastern Pacific. As the western warm pool cools slightly and the central and the eastern equatorial Pacific warm, the strength of the trade winds is further reduced. The large atmospheric convection cell over Indonesia moves eastward. This results in drought in the western Pacific (including Indonesia and Australia) and increased rainfall in the central and eastern Pacific (notably at Christmas Island, the Galapagos, and Ecuador).

The warm water in the eastern Pacific spreads to the eastern boundary and splits to flow north and south there. Upwelling off northern Peru might weaken or just draw on the warm, nutrient-poor equatorial water. The result is a decline in production in this important fisheries area. If the El Niño is particularly strong, its effect in the ocean can reach as far north as the California coast.

The opposite phase of the El Niño is called La Niña, characterized by especially strong trade winds, a well-developed warm pool in the western Pacific, and cold water at the equator in the central and eastern Pacific. During La Niña cold events there is strong rainfall in the western Pacific, little rainfall in the eastern Pacific, and major fisheries production in the eastern boundary region.

ENSO affects midlatitudes through "teleconnections" in the atmosphere. Changes in the western tropical Pacific reach far to the northeast and southeast through the atmosphere and directly affect climate in the coastal regions of the United States and South America.

El Niño warm events occur irregularly, but generally every three to seven years. Major progress was made during the 1990s toward predicting an El Niño event up to about one year in advance because the sequence of events in an El Niño event is often similar. Thus detection of early signs of El Niño, such as the appearance of warm water in the eastern tropical Pacific or the reversal of trade winds in the western tropical Pacific, can allow prediction of changes in rainfall and air temperature later in the year. A major observing and modeling network is now in place to continually monitor ocean and atmosphere conditions in the tropical Pacific to assist in diagnosing and forecasting El Niño (see McPhaden 1997).

The strength of El Niño varies greatly over an even more irregular time scale of ten to more than thirty years. For instance, El Niños in the 1940s were strong, followed by several decades of weak events, then followed by very strong El Niños again in the 1980s and 1990s. The events of 1982–1983 and 1997–1998 were the largest ever recorded. Long records of El Niños have been extracted from the reasonably long atmospheric pressure records at Tahiti and Darwin, Australia, and from growth and properties of the annual accretions in coral heads in the tropical Pacific. This so-called decadal modulation of El Niño continues to be much less well understood than El Niño itself, but it may be related to a Pacific Decadal Oscillation (Zhang, Wallace, and Battisti 1997).

Sea Level

Sea-level changes, especially along low-lying shorelines and islands, are increasingly of interest, as climate change gradually warms the oceans, melts land-fast ice, and raises sea level overall. Recent well-publicized increases in inundation and concerns about the future for low-lying islands such as Kiribati and the Tuvalu Islands in the tropical Pacific make this an important topic for this chapter.

Within the tropical Pacific region, sea level has strong inter-annual variations due to ENSO. During El Niño warm events, sea level is lower than normal in the western tropical Pacific and higher in the east. The surface height changes can be up to 15 cm higher and 15 cm lower (total amplitude of 30 cm or so). If climate change were to result in a change in frequency, duration, or amplitude of El Niño or La Niña events, there would be an associated sea-level trend in the tropical Pacific. Variations in the Asian-Australian monsoon and the Pacific Decadal Oscillation also affect tropical Pacific sea level (see Church, White, and Hunter 2006).

Apart from its variability due to tides, winds, and changing currents, as well as short-lived events such as storm surges and tsunamis, sea level is mainly a function of the amount of water in the ocean and water temperature. The main contributions to sea-level change due to anthropogenic forcing (global warming) are therefore melting of land-fast ice and glaciers, which simply adds volume, and thermal expansion due to warming. (Melting of sea ice does not change sea level, since sea ice is already floating isostatically in the ocean.) For thermal expansion, a change of 1°C in a layer of 100 m thickness results in a thickness increase of about 20 mm. Sea-level trends are reported in mm/year; the maximum trends in any regions are on the order of 15 mm/yr, which corresponds to one meter in 65 years. A trend of 3 mm/yr corresponds to one meter over 350 years.

Mean sea level for the entire ocean increased by 1.7 mm/yr during the twentieth century (17 cm over 100 years) (Bindoff et al. 2007). About half of this was due to melting of land-fast ice and glaciers and half was due to warming of the upper ocean.

While overall sea level has clearly been rising, averaged over the globe, sea level has risen in some regions and fallen in others. The geographic variation in sea-level change has been constructed for the decades since 1950 and is most accurate for the period of satellite altimetry, starting in 1993. Maps showing the global distribution of sea-level change for both of these periods have quite different implications for the tropical Pacific (Bindoff et al. 2007). The fifty-year trend suggests a relatively uniform increase in sea level throughout the Pacific, on the order of 3 mm/year. The trend since 1993, however, is dominated by ENSO (trend from El Niño to La Niña), yielding an increasing sea-level trend in the western tropical Pacific and decreasing in the eastern Pacific.

Tide gauge records at islands and along coastlines provide the best long records of sea-level change. Analysis of twelve records, of twenty-four to fifty-two years in length, located throughout the western tropical Pacific was carried out by Church, White, and Hunter (2006); they showed trends of 2 to 3 mm/yr increase at a number of locations. Because of reports of increasing flooding at Funafuti, Church, White, and Hunter focused on the record there since 1977, reconstructing subsidence of the tide gauge itself and confirming the estimate of a rise of 2 mm/year. Thus this is about equivalent to the global mean increase in sea level, and over one hundred years is added on to the ENSO signal, which is about the same size.

What lies ahead? Because it is well understood that current levels of anthropogenic forcing will not be changing soon, and because even a complete cessation of anthropogenic forcing would still result in climate changes over hundreds of years until the system reaches equilibrium, it is important to attempt to predict the sea-level changes expected for the future. The conservative prediction from the Intergovernmental Panel on Climate Change (IPCC 2007) is for an increase of 20 to 40 cm by the end of the twenty-first century. Note that this change is somewhat larger than the three-to-seven-year El Niño signal.

Acknowledgment

We are grateful for the extensive review of this chapter by Dick Stroup, respected colleague and friend, who died shortly before the first edition went to press. Dick's professional and personal contributions to ocean science were wide-ranging, and he is missed.

BIBLIOGRAPHY

Bindoff, N. L., J. Willebrand, V. Artale, A. Cazenave, J. Gregory, S. Gulev, K. Hanawa, C. Le Quéré, S. Levitus, Y. Nojiri, C. K. Shum, L. D. Talley, and A. Unnikrishnan. 2007. Observations: Oceanic climate change and sea level. In *Climate change 2007: The physical science basis. Contribution of Working Group I to the Fourth Assessment Report of the Intergovernmental Panel Climate Change,* ed. S. Solomon, D. Qin, M. Manning, Z. Chen, M. Marquis, K. B. Averyt, M. Tignor, and H. L. Miller. Cambridge and New York: Cambridge University Press.

Church, J. A., N. J. White, and J. R. Hunter. 2006. Sea-level rise at tropical Pacific and Indian Ocean islands. *Global Planet. Change* 53: 155–168.

Cromwell, T., R. B. Montgomery, and E. D. Stroup. 1954. Equatorial Undercurrent in the Pacific Ocean revealed by new methods. *Science* 119: 648–649.

Fine, R. A., R. Lukas, F. M. Bingham, M. J. Warner, and R. H. Gammon. 1994. The western equatorial Pacific: A water mass crossroads. *Journal of Geophysical Research* 99: 25063–25080.

Firing, E. 1989. Mean zonal currents below 1500 m near the equator 159W. *Journal of Geophysical Research* 94: 2023–2028.

Flament, P., S. Kennan, R. Lumpkin, M. Sawyer, and E. D. Stroup. 1997. The ocean atlas of Hawai'i. Copyrighted website: http://radlab.soest .hawaii.edu/atlas/.

Graham, N. E., and T. P. Barnett. 1987. Sea surface temperature, surface wind divergence, and convection over tropical oceans. *Science* 238: 657–659.

Grist, J. P., and S. A. Josey. 2003. Inverse analysis adjustment of the SOC air-sea flux climatology using ocean heat transport constraints, *J. Climate,* 20: 3274–3295.

Heath, R. A. 1985. A review of the physical oceanography of the seas around New Zealand—1982. *New Zealand Journal of Marine and Freshwater Research* 19: 79–124.

Hofmann, E. E., A. J. Busalacchi, and J. J. O'Brien. 1981. Wind generation of the Costa Rica dome. *Science* 214: 552–554.

Iida, K., D. C. Cox, and G. Pararas-Carayannis. 1967. *Preliminary catalog of tsunamis occurring in the Pacific Ocean.* Hawaii Institute of Geophysics Pub. HIG-67-10, Honolulu: University of Hawai'i.

IPCC. 2007. Summary for Policymakers. In *Climate change 2007: The physical science basis. Contribution of Working Group I to the Fourth Assessment Report of the Intergovernmental Panel on Climate Change,* ed. S. Solomon, D. Qin, M. Manning, Z. Chen, M. Marquis, K. B. Averyt, M. Tignor, and H. L. Miller. Cambridge and New York: Cambridge University Press.

Johnson, G. C., and J. M. Toole. 1993. Flow of deep and bottom waters in the Pacific at 10°N. *Deep-Sea Research* 40: 371–394.

Knauss, J. A. 1960. Measurements of the Cromwell Current. *Deep-Sea Research* 6: 265–286.

———. 1997. *Introduction to physical oceanography.* 2nd ed. Upper Saddle River, N.J.: Prentice-Hall.

Levitus, S., and T. P. Boyer. 1994a. *World ocean atlas. Vol. 4, Temperature.* Silver Spring, Md.: National Oceanographic and Atmospheric Administration, 129.

———. 1994b. *World ocean atlas. Vol. 3, Salinity.* Silver Spring, Md.: National Oceanographic and Atmospheric Administration, 111.

Lindstrom, E., R. Lukas, R. Fine, E. Firing, S. Godfrey, G. Meyers, and M. Tsuchiya. 1987. The western equatorial Pacific Ocean circulation study. *Nature* 330: 533–537.

Marchuk, G. I., and B. A. Kagan. 1983. *Dynamics of ocean tides.* Dordrecht: Kluwer.

McPhaden, M. J. 2013. El Niño theme page. http://www.pmel.noaa.gov/ tao/elnino/nino-home.html.

NOAA OGP (National Oceanographic and Atmospheric Administration, Office of Global Programs). 1994. NOAA/OGP/UCAR El Niño and climate prediction. Reports to the Nation on our Changing Planet. http://www.pmel.noaa.gov/tao/elnino/report/el-nino-report.html.

NOAA (National Oceanographic and Atmospheric Administration). 2008. NOAA Wavewatch III's Historical Archive. http://polar.ncep .noaa.gov/waves/historic.html.

Neshyba, S. 1987. *Oceanography: Perspectives on a fluid Earth.* New York: John Wiley and Sons.

Ralph, E. A., and P. P. Niiler. 1999. Wind-driven currents in the tropical Pacific. *Journal of Physical Oceanography* 29: 2121–2129.

Ramanathan, V., and W. Collins. 1993. A thermostat in the tropics. *Nature* 361: 410–411.

Rasmusson, E. M., and T. H. Carpenter. 1982. Variations in tropical sea surface temperature and surface wind fields associated with the Southern Oscillation/El Niño. *Monthly Weather Review* 110: 354–384.

Ray, R. D. 1999. A global ocean tide model from TOPEX/POSEIDON altimetry: GOT99.s. NASA/TM-1999-209478, 58.

Reid, J. L. 1997. On the total geostrophic circulation of the Pacific Ocean: Flow patterns, tracers and transports. *Progress in Oceanography* 39: 263–352.

Roemmich, D., M. Y. Morris, and W. R. Young. 1994. Equatorial fresh jets. *Journal of Physical Oceanography* 24: 540–558.

Shepard, F. P., G. A. Macdonald, and D. C. Cox. 1950. The tsunami of April 1, 1946. *Bulletin of the Scripps Institution of Oceanography of the University of California* 5: 391–470.

Singh, R. 1991. Tsunamis in Fiji and their effects. In *Workshop on coastal processes in the South Pacific Island Nations,* SOPAC (U.N. South Pacific Applied Geoscience Commission) Technical Bulletin 7: 107–120.

Stewart, R. H. 2005. Introduction to physical oceanography. http:// oceanworld.tamu.edu/resources/ocng_textbook/contents.html

Tabata, S. 1975. The general circulation of the Pacific Ocean and a brief account of the oceanographic structure of the North Pacific Ocean. Part I—circulation and volume transports. *Atmosphere* 13: 133–168.

Talandier, J. 1993. Le volcanisme et la sismicit. In *Atlas de la Polynesie Française.* Paris: ORSTOM (Inst. français de recherche scientifique pour le developpement en cooperation, Dept. en Territoires d'Outre-Mer), maps 26–27.

Talley, L. D. 2003. Shallow, intermediate and deep overturning components of the global heat budget. *Journal of Physical Oceanography* 33: 530–560.

———. 2007. *Hydrographic atlas of the World Ocean Circulation Experiment (WOCE). Volume 2: Pacific Ocean.* Edited by M. Sparrow, P. Chapman, and J. Gould. Southampton, U.K.: International WOCE Project Office. http://www.pord.ucsd.edu/whp_atlas/pacific_index .html

Talley, L. D., and R. A. deSzoeke. 1986. Spatial fluctuations north of the Hawaiian Ridge. *Journal of Physical Oceanography* 16: 981–984.

Talley, L. D., G. L. Pickard, W. J. Emery, and J. H. Swift. 2011. *Descriptive physical oceanography: An introduction.* 6th ed. Boston: Elsevier.

Tomczak, M., and J. S. Godfrey. 1994. *Regional oceanography: An introduction.* Oxford: Pergamon Press.

Tsuchiya, M. 1968. Upper waters of the intertropical Pacific Ocean. In *The Johns Hopkins Oceanographic Studies,* vol. 4, 50. Baltimore: The Johns Hopkins Press.

Tsuchiya, M., R. Lukas, R. A. Fine, E. Firing, and E. Lindstrom. 1989. Source waters of the Pacific Equatorial Undercurrent. *Progress in Oceanography* 23: 101–147.

Wyrtki, K., and B. Kilonsky. 1984. Mean water and current structure during the Hawaii-to-Tahiti shuttle experiment. *Journal of Physical Oceanography* 14: 242–254.

Zhang, Y., J. M. Wallace, and D. S. Battisti. 1997. ENSO-like interdecadal variability: 1900–93. *Journal of Climate* 10: 1004–1020.

Geology

David M. Kennedy, Gerard J. Fryer, and Patricia Fryer

3

The geological evolution of the Pacific Basin is founded in the processes that drive plate tectonics. Almost the entire ocean is floored by the Pacific Plate, which is in constant northwestward motion, driven by plumes deep within the Earth's mantle. At its northern, northeastern, and western boundaries the plate is subducted into the mantle, while new crust is created on its southern and southeastern sides at the spreading ridges of the East Pacific Rise (Figure 3.1). The resulting melting of the crust that occurs as it descends into the mantle at subduction zones leads to highly explosive volcanoes, which form arcs parallel with the ocean trenches that mark

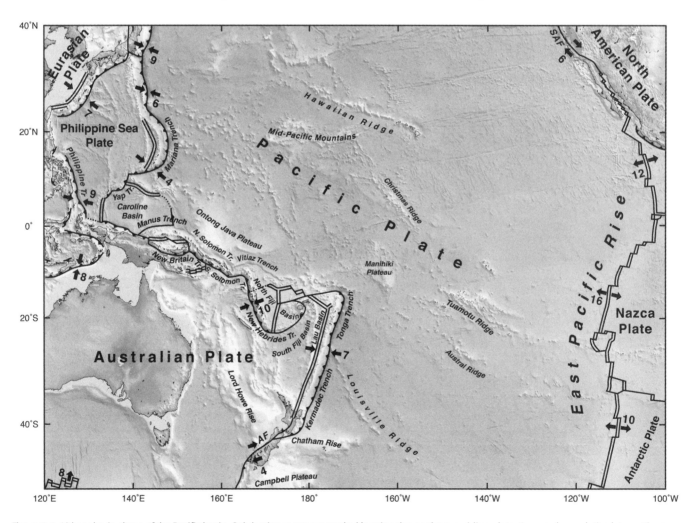

Figure 3.1. *Lithospheric plates of the Pacific basin. Subduction zones are marked by triangles on the overriding plate. Arrows show relative late motions across plate boundaries. Relative plate speeds are given in centimeters per year. SAF is the San Andreas Fault; AF is the Alpine Fault. Western Pacific plate margins are taken from Scheibner et al. (1991).*

the plate's edge. Often fragments of continental crust get caught in these convergent zones, causing major deformation of their form and complex geology such as found in New Caledonia or New Zealand. In the center of the plate, stationary plumes of hot mantle material, termed hot spots, are found, which cause further volcanism. These intraplate volcanoes have a much lower silica content than those found on the plate's edge and therefore are significantly less explosive. Dozens of island chains in the middle of the Pacific derive from such volcanic activity. The islands of the Pacific are therefore highly complex, with each displaying different geological forms related to the variety of tectonic and volcanic processes that formed them.

Plate Tectonics

Many Pacific Island chains show a clear age progression: young, volcanically active islands at the southerly end of the chain and old, extinct, and eroded islands to the north. J. Tuzo Wilson (1963) first showed that the age progressions mean that the seafloor is moving over stationary, episodically erupting hot spots. The idea of a horizontally moving seafloor, together with the much older observation that the continents themselves move (Wegener 1929), led to the realization that continents and seafloor together are carried along passively as part of the brittle outer layer of the Earth, termed the lithosphere.

The lithosphere is organized into eight major plates and several smaller ones that together cover the Earth. The Pacific Plate dominates the region with the smaller Nazca and Cocos Plates occurring along its South and Central American boundaries respectively. In the west the Philippine Plate is found while on its southwestern boundary the Pacific Plate collides with the Indo-Australian Plate. Several smaller areas of plate movement occur related to shearing along the plate margins with a small spreading ridge occurring at the Gorda Plate in North America. However, the complex interactions along the boundaries are best represented around Fiji, where evidence of counterclockwise rotation of the islands appears to occur. This has led to suggestions that Fiji occurs on its own "microplate" (Nunn 1998). The variety of island and continental forms that occur around the edge of the Pacific Ocean all directly relate to the type of plate interactions that occur. This gives rise to the term "Pacific rim of fire" to describe the volcanic activity along its margins.

The Pacific Plate contains some of the oldest oceanic crust on Earth with new crustal material still being formed along the spreading ridges of the East Pacific Rise, at rates of up to 210 mm/yr (Wilson 1996) (Figure 3.1). Here hot, upwelling rock from deep in the mantle begins to melt. The melt, called magma, inflates the ridges, stretching the lithosphere until it breaks in a long, narrow fissure. Lava erupts at the seafloor and forms vertical dikes (thin sheets of solidified magma) beneath the surface. As the seafloor is rafted away to either side, the underlying magma chamber is cut off, to be replaced by a new magma chamber. The surface lavas, the dikes, and the old, frozen magma chambers together form the oceanic crust, which is about 5 km thick. As the seafloor spreads and cools, the underlying upper mantle also cools and becomes stiffer. This causes the lithosphere to thicken with age from only a few kilometers at the ridge to about 70 km beneath old seafloor.

Lithospheric spreading at one location requires convergence elsewhere. Where plates converge, the lithosphere either sinks beneath an overriding plate or is compressed and uplifted to form mountain ranges (Figure 3.2). The plate-to-plate interactions in convergence zones cause earthquakes and feed the volcanoes that make up island arcs, such as found in Tonga. This process is particularly noticeable below the North Island of New Zealand, where explosive volcanism is found at Mount Ruapehu and Lake Taupo (Figure 3.3a, b). Mount Ruapehu's most recent significant eruption occurred in 1995, with small steam explosions occurring more regularly, the most recent in 2007 which caused a lahar to flow down several rivers 115 km to the ocean. The largest eruption from Lake Taupo, the Orunanui eruption of 26.5 Ka (thousands of years ago), was one of the largest volcanic eruptions documented in the past 250,000 years and generated fall deposits and associated volcanic lithologies equivalent to 530 km³ of magma (Wilson 2001). Mapping of seismic activity below the North Island also reveals the morphology of the plate subduction, with earthquake depths increasing to 300 to 700 km depth 350 km away from the initial point of subduction (Figure 3.4).

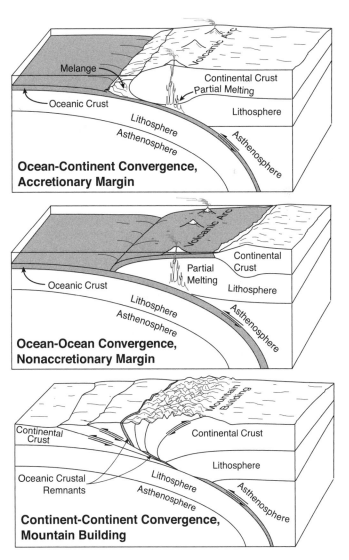

Figure 3.2. *Sketch of three different types of convergent plate boundaries: ocean-continent, ocean-ocean, and continent-continent.*

Figure 3.3. *The highly explosive Andestitic/Rhyolitic volcanoes of (a) Mount Ruapehu, New Zealand, and (b) Lake Taupo with Mount Ruapehu in the background. Typical hot spot volcanoes of (c) Mauna Loa, Hawai'i, still currently active, (d) Lord Howe Island, last active around 6 Ma, and (e) Diamond Head, Hawai'i. (f) Uplifted coral terraces of Niue.*

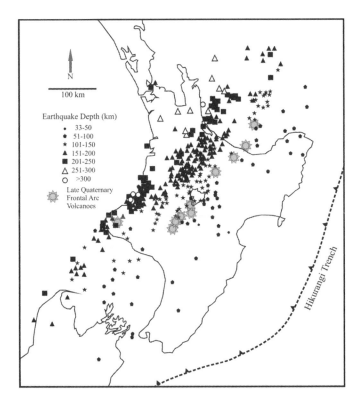

Figure 3.4. Depth of deep earthquakes (>30 km depth) beneath northern New Zealand. The increased depth toward the west delineates the position of the Pacific as it is subducted into the mantle (modified from Kamp 1992).

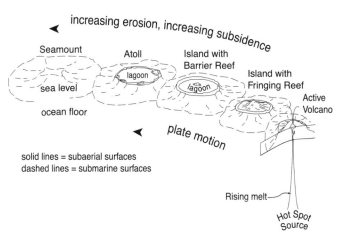

Figure 3.5. A schematic cross section of an oceanic lithospheric plate showing how plumes of rising melt feed hot spots. Volcanoes formed above the hot spot are rafted away in the direction of plate movement and thus increase in age with distance from the hot spot.

This process of subduction also draws down the seafloor to form deep ocean trenches. The sinking lithosphere forms the downwelling limb of a mantle convection cell; the upwelling limbs provide the source material for seafloor spreading. Where plates neither converge nor diverge, but simply slide past each other, the boundary between the two plates is a transform fault, which may stretch for hundreds of kilometers. California's San Andreas Fault is the best-known example, and the Alpine Fault of New Zealand is of comparable size. The most recent movement along the latter fault occurred in 1855 with a magnitude (MM) 8+ earthquake causing lateral displacement of up to 18.7 m (mean 15.5 ± 1.6 m) (Little and Rogers 2005).

Hot Spots and Linear Island Chains

Mantle rock rising beneath a midocean ridge does so as a vertical sheet, but the source rock for hot spots rises in confined plumes. There are generally considered to be fourteen hot spots in the Pacific. The plumes are thought to form over topographic irregularities at the core-mantle boundary, which concentrate heat, making the overlying mantle hotter than adjacent rock. Clouard and Bonneville (2001), however, analyzed the ages of 266 islands and seamounts related to Pacific hot spots back to 145 Ma (millions of years) and concluded that only four, Easter Island, Louisville on the Ontong Java Plateau, the Marquesas, and Hawai'i were true deep-mantle plumes, with the rest related to more shallow mantle processes. It is therefore likely that no single process causes hot spots and that shallow tectonic processes may be as important as

deeper ones (Peive 2007). Regardless of its origin, as hot rock rises buoyantly through the mantle, and as the plume rises to depths <70 km, it begins to melt. Less than 5 percent of the upwelling rock is melted, but this is enough to provide the source magma from which to build island chains (Figure 3.5) such as the Hawaiian Islands.

The composition of the magmas formed depends on the composition and degree of melting of the source rock. When mantle rock is partially melted, the resulting magma is basaltic. Basalt is the most common rock type in the Pacific basin. It is a dark gray to black rock with a low silica (SiO_2) content and a low content of volatile (low melting point) compounds such as water and carbon dioxide (Macdonald, Abbott, and Peterson 1983).

The first lava from a hot spot will be erupted on the seafloor. The surface of lava that erupts underwater is rapidly chilled to form a glassy skin. This skin swells and splits to release more lava, which in turn chills over. This is a repetitive process, and when these underwater lava forms are exposed in cross-section, they look like a stack of pillows and so are called pillow lavas. A pile of pillow lavas is weak, however, so gravity begins to pull the growing volcano apart. Tension produces radial cracks, called rifts. Once rifts form, magma is diverted from summit eruptions and instead is injected through rifts to feed flank eruptions. The magma left in a rift solidifies to form a dike. Rift zones expand and are filled repeatedly as new pulses of magma rise into the volcano. Eventually, the rift becomes a zone several kilometers wide underlain by solid dike rock. The dike complexes are more competent than the intervening rubbly flanks of pillow lava and thus act as buttresses, imparting localized internal strength to the seamount. Many seamounts on the Pacific Ocean floor are star shaped, with arms extending along the rift zones. Collapsed flanks, composed of piles of talus (mainly pillow lava fragments), lie between the arms.

As the seamount approaches sea level, pressure is reduced, and steam boiling off the hot lava expands explosively. Sea-water becomes involved in the eruption, and explosions shoot volcanic ash into the atmosphere. Falling ash is swept away by waves and currents, but eventually the volcano breaches the surface. Once a solid surface has formed above sea level, fluid lava flows predominate. The low silica, low gas content, and high temperature of basaltic lavas gives them low viscosity, which results in relatively gentle eruptions with very little ash. Repeated gentle eruptions and thin lava flows form broad, convex shield volcanoes. The entire process, from initial eruption at the seafloor to formation of an island shield volcano, takes at least a million years.

The net result of these eruptions are islands that rise, such as on Mauna Loa, Hawai'i, to over 9,000 km from the seafloor (Figure 3.3c). As volcanic activity is concentrated in their center, stress is placed on the outside of the volcanic edifice, which may collapse catastrophically. Sonar mapping of the seafloor around the Hawaiian Islands shows slide deposits extending two hundred kilometers from the islands (Moore et al. 1989) (Figure 3.6). A large tsunami would likely result from such an event, and deposits on O'ahu have been ascribed to such an event, known as the Lanai Tsunami, that occurred possibly around 220 Ka, although significant controversy exists around the origin of this deposit (Felton 2002). Smaller collapses of the basaltic cliffs occur on centennial scales, with one in 1975 thought to cause a 14.6 m high tsunami on the Halape–Apua Point coast of the island of Hawai'i (Goff et al. 2007). Similar evidence for large-scale slope failure is found around most volcanic islands.

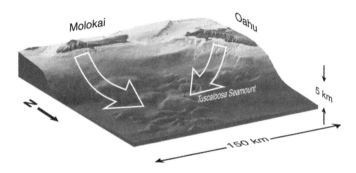

Figure 3.6. *Landslide paths in the Hawaiian Islands. The hummocky terrain of the sea bottom north of Moloka'i is characteristic of a landslide deposit. The entire north flank of Moloka'i has collapsed into the sea, as has the northwest flank of the Ko'olau Volcano of O'ahu. Tuscaloosa Seamount is a piece of the Ko'olau Volcano that slid more than 70 km from its original location. These landslides are the largest known landslides.*

Such landslides, together with the slow, continuous erosion by surf, rain, and wind, whittle away at the island. As long as the island is fed by the hot spot, volcanism will counter the erosion. Inevitably, however, seafloor spreading carries the island away from its source. Volcanism declines, then stops, and erosion reduces the island to sea level. Thus, in a midocean chain of islands, the degree of erosion correlates with distance from the active hot spot. The subsequent morphology an island develops after volcanism ceases will depend on whether it occurs within the tropics or not. Those islands in the tropics will develop coral reefs around their edges which provide a degree of protection from marine erosion, while those at higher latitudes are exposed to the full erosive capacity of the sea.

Coral reefs will initially establish around an island as a fringing reef (Kennedy and Woodroffe 2002). Due to the weight of the island mass upon the crust, the volcano begins to sink as the crust flexes below the island. Coral growth is, however, maintained at the surface in much the same location as the initial fringing reef. Continued vertical coral growth as the central island sinks leads to the development of a barrier reef and finally a coral atoll when the central volcanic mass sinks below the ocean surface (Figure 3.7a). This gradual development was first described by Charles Darwin in the 1840s, although it was only with the advent of deep drilling on the islands, initially by Edgeworth David in 1890–1910, and later in the 1940s (e.g., Emery 1948), that this theory was conclusively proven. Eventually, if coral growth is unable to be maintained the island will sink below the surface and a flat-topped submarine mountain known as a guyot is formed. The point that this occurs is known as the Darwin Point (Grigg 1982).

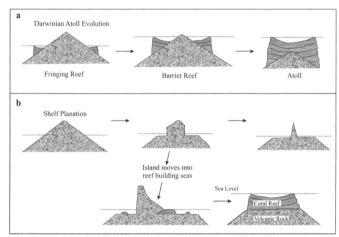

Figure 3.7. *(a) Classic Darwinian evolution of a coral atoll. As the central island mass sinks, coral growth is maintained at the surface, transforming a fringing reef to a barrier reef and finally an atoll. (b) In seas too cold for coral reefs, islands tend to be eroded, forming a planated surface. If they then move into reef building seas these surfaces become the foundation for coral reef growth (modified from Woodroffe et al. 2006).*

When islands form outside of tropical seas, erosion dominates. Islands in these locations are often characterized by vertical basaltic cliffs with shelves found below sea level. Lord Howe Island (Figure 3.3d) and Balls Pyramid in the Tasman Sea, southwest Pacific are classic examples of these islands. Both have vertical cliffs that rise to more than 500 m in height, almost 1 km high on Lord Howe, with a broad shelf an average of 50 m deep extending tens of kilometers from their base (Kennedy et al. 2002). It is thought that these horizontal surfaces form due to rates of erosion and subsequent reduction in weight of the volcanic edifice, balancing the sinking process as the islands move away from the hot spot (Nakada 1986). In the case of Lord Howe Island the volcanic edifice is also buttressed by a drowned section of continental crust, formed during the creation of the Tasman Sea in the final phase of the breakup of Gondwana, which inhibits subsidence.

The evolution of these hot-spot islands will therefore be dependent on where in the Pacific they develop. As the Pacific Plate is steadily moving north, those islands at the northern edge of the tropics are approaching the Darwin Point, while those at the southern margins are just entering reef-building seas. These islands at the southern margin may therefore be expected to eventually create new atolls that will drift farther north. Such a progression can be observed in the Tasman Sea between Lord Howe Island and Balls Pyramid, which have only just entered reef-building seas, to the atolls of Elizabeth and Middleton reefs some 200 km farther north (Woodroffe et al. 2005; Woodroffe et al. 2006) (Figure 3.7b).

Some intraplate island groups (notably the Cook Islands) appear not to show a clear age progression and thus have cast doubt on the hot-spot hypothesis. Wessel and Kroenke (1997), however, have demonstrated that confusing age progressions result from changes over geological time in Pacific plate motion (so that the islands trail off from the hot spot in varying directions). Moreover, episodic rejuvenation of volcanism can result as islands rise over adjacent hot-spot arches. Thus, superficial lava flows on the more distant, older islands may yield younger geological dates than islands closer to the hot spot.

The gradual sinking of an island caused by its weight upon the lithosphere can also affect other islands in the immediate region. The sagging creates a moat ("deep") around the volcano on the seafloor, forming a broad arch in the surrounding lithosphere (Figure 3.8). Because the currently active volcanoes are least eroded, they form the most concentrated load. As each island in turn is rafted away from the hot spot, it rises over the arch formed by the new volcanic center before settling back into a slow subsidence. Rising over the arch puts the island in tension, which may trigger a post-erosional rejuvenation of volcanism. Post-erosional features are scattered small cones of cinder and ash or small shield volcanoes. Diamond Head on the Hawaiian island of O'ahu is a typical example (Figure 3.3e).

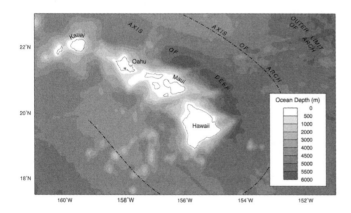

Figure 3.8. *Bathymetric map of the Hawaiian Islands showing the Hawaiian Ridge, Deep, and Arch.*

Once an island has ceased to be eruptive, it may also pass the arch formed by an adjacent island. Henderson Atoll in the eastern Pacific is an example of this, currently being uplifted as it passes over the bulge created by the high island of Pitcairn Island (Anderson et al. 2008; Duncan et al. 1974). This process of uplifting formerly subsiding atolls is particularly noticeable in areas where the Pacific Plate flexes before it is subducted at convergent margins. Niue is a classic example of this, with several coral terraces occurring above

sea level and the former atoll lagoon now found at an elevation of more than 60 m (Figure 3.3f). The Loyalty Islands have also been uplifted in this way by upwarping of the North Loyalty Basin prior to its subduction into the New Hebrides Trench (Milsom 2003).

Using terraces as a sole indicator of tectonic uplift can be problematic, as sea-level movements during the Quaternary (see Table 4.1) also form such features. During the last glacial maximum around 20 Ka, sea level was around 120 m below present and has been 5 to 8 m above present during the last interglacial period at around 125 Ka. Many raised coral features on islands reveal higher sea levels such as on Christmas Island, Kiribati, or on Tongatapu Island, Tonga. Where eustatic fluctuations are coupled with vertical tectonic movement, flights of terraces can be formed. The Huon Peninsula in Papua New Guinea is a classic example of this and is the key site for understanding Quaternary sea-level fluctuations (Chappell and Polach 1991). On subsiding islands such as Hawai'i drowned coral reefs around 220 Ka in age are found at 400 m depth (Webster et al. 2007) with others descending to 4 km depth. The relationship between the age of terraces and uplift can be difficult to predict, although mathematical modeling suggests that on rising coasts high-sea-level terraces tend to be preserved and vice versa for subsiding settings (Trenhaile 2002).

Islands at Spreading Centers

Young seafloor is hot, buoyant, and shallower than the surrounding seafloor, which is why divergent plate boundaries (also called spreading centers) form ridges. Sometimes a spreading center, or a volcano that first grew at a spreading center, breaches the sea surface to form an island. This can happen either because a nearby hot spot has fed additional magma to the spreading center, or because the spreading center itself is in shallower than normal water. In the Pacific, only Easter Island is associated with a true midocean ridge spreading center, the East Pacific Rise (Figure 3.1).

Not all divergent plate boundaries occur in the middle of large ocean basins. There is also spreading going on in several of the shallower seas around the western margin of the Pacific. Islands formed in such an environment include the Niua Group (Tonga), Tikopia (Solomon Islands), and the Witu Islands (Papua New Guinea).

Volcanism at spreading centers is responsible for rich ore deposits. Circulation of heated sea-water into fissures leaches out metals (e.g., copper, zinc, and lead), which are deposited at nearby hot springs. Most such deposits lie at water depths greater than 2 km and cannot be mined economically. Sometimes, however, a spreading center is carried into a subduction zone and caught up in a collision between a subducting landmass and the island arc. Fragments of the spreading center may then be scraped off and upthrust onto land, taking the ore deposits with them. The metal deposits of New Britain (Papua New Guinea) and Malaita (Solomon Islands) were formed in this way.

Island Arcs

The Pacific Plate is being subducted all along its western boundary. The subduction zones tend to establish themselves in broad, sweeping curves, so island chains formed along these zones are called island arcs. Island arc volcanism is driven by magma generation related to the subduction. If the subducting lithospheric plate has an abundant sediment cover, this may be scraped off and incorporated onto the overriding plate as a wedge termed a melange (Figure 3.2). The wedge may build up so much that it produces a ridge that dominates the forearc, the region between the island arc and the trench axis. If the forearc is uplifted by tectonic forces, the ridge may be lifted above the surface to form islands. Examples of such islands include Guam (Reagan et al. 2008) and Yap (Kobayashi 2004).

To explain how the island arc itself forms, it is necessary to consider the origin of island arc magma. Earthquake studies and seismic imaging show that the subducting plate penetrates to depths of 700 km or more. As the lithosphere subducts into the mantle, increases in pressure and temperature drive off water and carbon dioxide. The presence of these volatiles lowers the melting point of the overlying mantle to a point that magma is produced. This then rises, because it is less dense than the surrounding solid mantle, and the resultant volcanism at the seafloor builds a volcanic arc above the subduction zone. The islands that make up the Mariana arc, for example, are the summits of active volcanoes that formed on the seafloor about 100 km above the top of the subducting Pacific Plate. Like midoceanic hot-spot volcanoes, these islands can be unstable and can catastrophically collapse and cause a tsunami, such as occurred in 1888 when c. 5 km^3 of Ritter Island in the Marianas fell into the sea (Silver et al. 2005).

Along a volcanic arc, volcanoes are spaced roughly every 50 km. This characteristic spacing seems to be controlled by how much melt it takes to sustain a conduit from the melt zone. Melting begins where the subducting slab reaches a depth of 100 km, so, as already pointed out for the Marianas, volcanoes grow above that point. Since volcanoes grow directly above the melt zone, the distance of the volcanic arc from the trench axis depends on the dip of the subducting plate (Gill 1981). If the plate dips steeply, as it does beneath the Bismarck Archipelago, the arc is close to the trench—in the Bismarcks the distance is only 50 km. More typical are the Marianas, where the volcanic arc is 200 km from the trench axis (corresponding to a dip on the subducting plate of 30°). The shallowest dips of all occur below western South America; in Chile the arc-trench distance is 500 km.

Magma formed above subducting plates is most commonly of basaltic composition, at least initially. The magma of island arcs can also be andesitic, which has a higher silica and more volatile content than basalt. Andesite is a medium gray to green rock often containing visible white to light gray crystals (e.g., Macdonald, Abbott, and Peterson 1983). It can form either by incorporation of crustal materials into basaltic magma or by the cooling and partial crystallization of basaltic magma in a magma chamber. In partial crystallization the early-formed crystals settle out from the magma, leaving a melt with a different composition (more andesitic) than the parent basaltic magma. Andesitic lavas are chiefly found landward of the trenches that mark the circum-Pacific subduction zones. For this reason, the ring of volcanoes that encircles the Pacific is sometimes called the "Andesite Line" (Sugisaki 1972). Volumetrically, andesites make up only a small proportion of island arcs, but that proportion is commonly exposed at the summits of the volcanoes. Subduction zones sometimes generate rhyolite, magmas with silica and volatile contents that are even higher than andesite. These are pink or light gray and often have visible quartz crystals.

Magma formation in island arcs is another process that concentrates metal-bearing minerals to potential ore status. Metals are concentrated in fluids associated with the late stages of crystallization of magmas, especially andesitic and rhyolitic magmas. If these late-stage magmas crystallize underground and subsequently undergo partial melting, the new magmas may have an even greater concentration of ore minerals and metals. Repeated episodes of magma generation in arc environments can produce exceptionally rich ore-bearing deposits, such as the copper ores of Bougainville Island.

Island arc volcanoes are composed of lava flows interlayered between deposits of ash or coarser volcanoclastic material (tephra). Alternating lavas and volcanic debris layers permit the volcano to build up steep slopes (around 35°), forming a stratovolcano or composite cone. Eruptions are often explosive, a characteristic of andesitic and rhyolitic volcanoes. These eruptive explosions occur because the magma is highly charged with gases and because the higher silica content results in higher viscosity. Gases dissolved in magma come out of solution as the magma rises and pressure decreases. Higher viscosity makes the rising magma more resistant to the expansion of gas bubbles. If the amount of expanding gas is great enough, it can blow the magma apart very near the surface, hurling gas and fragmented rock debris high into the atmosphere.

If subduction occurs at a constant rate and in a constant direction, volcanoes tend to form a single arc above the magma source. Such simple geometry is easily disrupted. When a large, buoyant object, such as a continental fragment or an ancient island arc (both less dense than oceanic lithosphere), is rafted into the subduction zone, subduction may be blocked. If convergence between the plates continues, a new subduction zone must form away from the obstruction. Further, any change in motion at one margin of plate will affect all other margins. Such changes influence the location and nature of volcanism above the subduction zone.

The Vanuatu (New Hebrides) island arc, for example, has experienced a complex sequence of volcanic successions and structural disturbances in response to changes in the direction of subduction. Vanuatu consists of three separate volcanic arcs that lie parallel to one another (Figure 3.9). The western volcanic belt is the oldest (Kroenke 1984). Volcanic centers on these islands were active from about 15 to 11 Ma, during a period in which the oceanic plate to the east of the chain was being subducted toward the west. At the end of this period subduction stopped, cutting off the magma supply to the volcanoes. A new subduction zone formed to accommodate continued convergence between the plates, but the new subduction was in the opposite direction.

The plate to the west of the islands began subducting eastward beneath the Western Belt. This subduction uplifted and deformed the Western Belt and induced extension of seafloor east of it. By about 8 Ma, the eastward subduction had generated enough magma to form a new volcanic chain: the Eastern Belt. About 5 Ma the eastward-dipping, downgoing plate adopted a steeper angle of subduction. The locus of active volcanism, following its magma source, migrated westward to its present position and formed yet another chain of volcanoes, the currently active Central Chain (Figure 3.10).

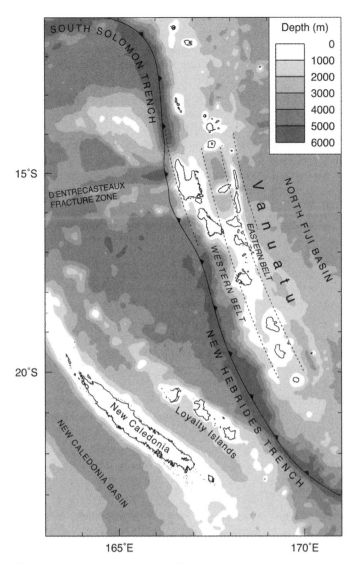

Figure 3.9. *Regional structure map of the Vanuatu island arc.*

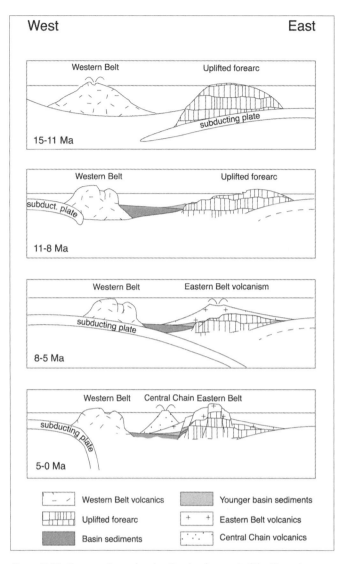

Figure 3.10. *Cross sections showing the development of the Vanuatu arc as a consequence of reversals in direction of subduction (redrawn after Nunn 1994).*

Marginal Seas and Backarc Basins

Around its western margin, the Pacific proper is separated from adjacent continents by marginal basins (seas). Marginal basins separate islands made of continental rocks from their parent continents; backarc basins form on the overriding-plate side of island arcs. The Tasman Sea between Australia and New Zealand is an excellent example of this type of tectonic setting (Figure 3.1). This area represents the final stage of breakup of the supercontinent of Gondwana, with the opening of the Tasman Sea occurring during the Late Cretaceous (c. 85 Ma). Running the length of the Tasman Sea, and in its center for most of its length, is the Lord Howe Rise, which connects to New Zealand at its southern margin. This rise is composed of a thin fragment of continental crust that detached from the Australian continent during the earliest stage of rifting (Stagg et al. 2002; Exon et al. 2007). Most active seafloor spreading occurred between 60 and 80 Ma (Willcox et al. 1980), but some debate still exists on whether this occurred in association with a convergent margin along the Pacific Plate. Muller et al. (2007)

suggested through mathematical modeling that this is unlikely between 48 and 74 Ma, an inference that is supported by a lack of island arc volcanics of this age along the rise. Associated with the creation of this rise are a number of sedimentary and structural basins that owe their origin to the same rifting processes that initially broke up the continental landmass. Similar marginal seas are also found in the South China Sea and the Sea of Japan on the northwestern margins of the Pacific.

Backarc basins, on the other hand, form from rifting and spreading behind island arcs, phenomena that are driven by subduction. The origin of the driving forces that initiate and sustain backarc basins is a matter of some debate. Karig (1971) suggested that rising diapirs (plumes) of mantle material behind subducting plates provide the extensional forces necessary for the formation of backarc basins. Moberly (1972) suggested that subducting plates "roll back" toward the ocean basins from which they come and in so doing drag the subduction systems oceanward. Such trench rollback and the associated migration of the outer edge of the overriding plate produce tension forces sufficient to cause backarc extension.

Backarc basins follow a two-stage evolution of rifting and spreading (Fryer 1995). Along the island arc, volcanic eruptions and intrusions build up a thick, brittle crust. The crust is weak, so any tension in the overriding plate will cause it to rift along the line of active volcanoes. Magma rises up to seal the rifts and build new lithosphere, but this is still the weakest region of the overriding plate. With repeated rifting and sealing, the new lithosphere grows, separating the still-active line of arc volcanoes from the remnant arc, the ridge that was cleaved off from the volcanic arc by the initial rifting.

During the initial stage of extension, lava erupted in the rifts may be of virtually any composition, from basaltic through rhyolitic (Fryer et al. 1990). In the initial stages, volcanism occurs over a broad region of the backarc basin. Eventually the extension in the backarc region widens the basin sufficiently so that seafloor spreading, like that at midocean ridges, becomes the mechanism by which the backarc basin grows. These processes may occur repeatedly, producing a series of island arcs, backarc basins, and remnant arcs. For example the Mariana convergent margin (Fryer 1996) began subducting prior to 50 Ma with a rifting event splitting the volcanic arc between 31 and 15 Ma, isolating the Palau-Kyushu Ridge and producing the central Parece Vela Basin until spreading ceased at 17 to 15 Ma. A second phase of rifting began about 10 Ma, separating an active volcanic arc from what was to become another remnant arc, the West Mariana Ridge. Extension of the Mariana Trough over the last 6 to 8 Ma contributed to the increasingly bow-like shape of the arc as the rifting and seafloor spreading continued to separate the active Mariana Ridge from the extinct West Mariana Ridge (Figure 3.11).

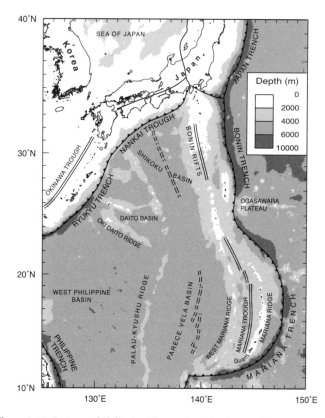

Figure 3.11. *Features of Philippine Plate region. Margins are denoted as in 3.1. Dashed double lines are relict spreading centers.*

Continental Islands

The large islands of the southwest Pacific (New Guinea, New Caledonia, Fiji, and New Zealand) are fragments of the ancient southern continent Gondwana, together with island arc accretions. The geology of these islands is complicated by extensive faulting, metamorphism, and magmatic intrusion. Much of the old geology has been further obscured by more recent volcanism. Nevertheless, guided by plate tectonics, a coherent story of how these islands evolved is beginning to emerge (Coleman 1997). The discussion here will focus on New Zealand (Figure 3.12), and will necessarily be brief.

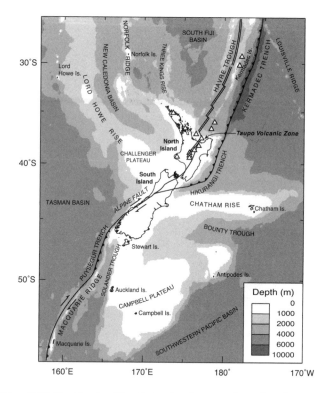

Figure 3.12. *The islands of New Zealand and surrounding submarine features. Volcanoes active within the last one thousand years are marked by white triangles.*

The oldest rocks in New Zealand date from the Cambrian (475–600 Ma) when it was part of an island arc forming offshore of the supercontinent of Gondwana. During the early Permian (c. 270 Ma) to the end of the Jurassic (130 Ma) it was welded onto Gondwana, where it remained until seafloor spreading created the Tasman Sea during the Mid-Cretaceous (c. 100 Ma). The suite of rocks that therefore separated from Gondwana is dominated by the Torlesse Super Group of clay-rich sandstones called greywacke, which are compressed and heated and turned into schist (often rich in the mineral mica) in the southern margin, overlying and intruded by a suite of volcanic lithologies (Kamp 1992).

Since separation, the geological evolution of New Zealand has been characterized by faulting as its continental crust is sheared across a subduction zone. The Hikurangi Trough to the northeast marks the western subduction of the Pacific Plate below the Indo-Australian Plate; on the southwestern margin, however, the subduction direction is reversed and the Pacific Plate overrides the

Indo-Australian Plate (Figure 3.10). In addition the islands have moved over some mantle hot spots. Much of the geology encountered therefore shares an origin with many of the islands of the Pacific.

Continual rifting, related to volcanic arc volcanism, occurs in the center of the North Island extending in an axis along the center of the island and paralleling the subduction zone. The subducting plate is estimated to be at around 65 km depth below the explosive volcanic centers of Mount Ruapehu and Lake Taupo (Reyners et al. 2006) (Figure 3.3a, b). This andesitic-rhyolitic volcanism extends north through the volcanic lakes of Rotoura and offshore toward Tonga. In addition, the North Island contains basaltic volcanoes similar to midocean hot spots. The largest city in New Zealand, Auckland, sits in the middle of one of these fields, with forty-eight eruption centers being found, the earliest eruption occurring around 140 Ka, and the most recent about 600 years ago on Rangitoto Island (Edbrooke 2001). In addition, large shield volcanoes of Tertiary age occur along the eastern margin of the South Island forming Banks and Otago Peninsulas.

The processes of plate convergence have also led to the development of a large accretionary wedge along the eastern North Island, as well as uplift of depositional basins on its western side. The Wanganui Basin sequence in the latter area contains an extensive suite of deep and shallow marine sequences, which represents some of the world's best-preserved eustatic sedimentary sequences for this period (Naish 2005). On the eastern margin of New Zealand, an accretionary wedge of deep marine mudstones and shallow marine carbonates are found, most dating from the Late Cretaceous (c. 70 Ma) to Pliocene (2–5 Ma) (Lee and Begg 2002) (Figure 3.13a). Similar marine sediment, scraped off the top of the subducting plate surface, is found on the east coast of the South Island (Rattenbury, Townsend, and Johnson 2006).

While subduction occurs to the north and south of New Zealand, the central part is composed of a transverse plate margin. As the North Island moved northward it was rotated counterclockwise and stretched out along the Alpine Fault (Figure 3.13b). This fault is predominantly strike-slip and has moved a total of 450 km in the last 27 Ma. There is also a small component of convergence, which causes uplift that forms the Southern Alps. These mountains, among the highest in the Pacific Islands region, have reached 3,700 m and continue to rise today.

Conclusion

The Pacific region displays each of the major processes of plate tectonics: hot-spot volcanism, divergent and convergent plate margin processes, and transform fault motion. All of the plate boundaries throughout the Pacific shift through time, adjusting to changes in plate motion. Such changes will continue. The modern southwest Pacific is a clutter of rifted continental fragments, abandoned island arcs, and shallow oceanic plateaus. This material is so resistant to subduction that a future adjustment in plate motions is inevitable. That adjustment may already be happening. A diffuse band of earthquakes has developed on the Pacific plate between Yap and Samoa, far north of the current subduction zones that stretch from New Guinea to Tonga (Kroenke and Walker 1986). Nearby, a bathymetric deep has developed on the seafloor. This may mark the birthplace of the Pacific's newest subduction zone, the Micronesian Trench.

Figure 3.13. (a) Alternating shallower water limestones (ridge crest) and deepwater mudstones at Te Mata Peak, Hawke's Bay. These sequences characterize the accretionary wedge along the eastern coast of New Zealand (photo courtesy of Cliff Atkins). (b) The Wellington Fault, part of the larger Alpine Fault System, running through Wellington. The fault trace is at the base of the steep hillslope on the left-hand side of the harbor.

BIBLIOGRAPHY

Andersen, M. B., C. H. Stirling, E.-K. Potter, A. N. Halliday, S. G. Blake, M. T. McCulloch, B. F. Ayling, and M. O'Leary. 2008. High-precision U-series measurements of more than 500,000 year old fossil corals. *Earth and Planetary Science Letters* 265: 229–245.

Chappell, J., and H. Polach. 1991. Post-glacial sea-level rise from a coral record at Huon Peninsula, Papua New Guinea. *Nature* 349: 147–149.

Clouard, V., and A. Bonneville. 2001. How many hotspots are fed by deep-mantle plumes? *Geology* 29: 695–698.

Coleman, P. J. 1997. Australia and the Melanesian arcs: A review of tectonic settings. *Journal of Australian Geology and Geophysics* 17: 113–125.

Darwin, C. R. 1860. *A naturalist's voyage (journal of research into the natural history and geology of the countries visited during the voyage of HMS 'Beagle' round the world).* London: Henry.

Duncan, R. A., I. McDougal, R. M. Carter, and D. S. Coombs. 1974. Pitcairn Island—another Pacific hot spot. *Nature* 251: 679–682.

Edbrooke, S. W. 2001. *Geology of the Auckland Area. 1:250000 Geological map 3.* Institute of Geological and Nuclear Sciences Ltd, Lower Hutt.

Emery, K. O. 1948. Submarine geology of Bikini Atoll. *Bulletin of the Geological Society of America* 59: 855–860.

Exon, N. F., Y. Lafoy, P. J. Hill, G. R. Dickens, and I. Pecher. 2007. Geology and petroleum potential of the Fairway basin in the Tasman Sea. *Australian Journal of Earth Sciences* 54: 629–645.

Felton, E. A. 2002. Sedimentology of rocky shorelines: 1. A review of the problem, with analytical methods, and insights gained from the Hulopoe Gravel and the modern rocky shoreline of Lanai, Hawaii. *Sedimentary Geology* 152: 221–245.

Fryer, P. 1995. Geology of the Mariana Trough. In *Backarc basins; tectonics and magmatism,* ed. B. Taylor, 237–279. New York: Plenum Press.

———. 1996. Tectonic evolution of the Mariana convergent margin. *Reviews of Geophysics* 34: 89–125.

Fryer, P., B. Taylor, C. Langmuir, and A. Hochstaedter. 1990. Petrology and geochemistry of lavas from the Sumisu and Torishima backarc rifts. *Earth and Planetary Science Letters* 100: 161–178.

Gill, J. B. 1981. *Orogenic andesites.* Berlin-Heidelberg: Springer-Verlag.

Goff, J., W. C. Dudley, M. J. Maintenon, G. Cain, and J. P. Coney. 2007. The largest local tsunami in 20th century Hawaii. *Marine Geology* 226: 65–79.

Grigg, R. W. 1982. Darwin Point: A threshold for atoll formation. *Coral Reefs* 1: 29–34.

Kamp, P. J. J. 1992. Tectonic architecture of New Zealand. In *Landforms of New Zealand* (2nd ed.), ed. J. M. Soons and M. J. Selby, 1–30. Auckland: Longman Paul.

Karig, D. E. 1971. Origin and development of marginal basins in the western Pacific. *Journal of Geophysical Research* 76: 2452–2561.

Kennedy, D. M., and C. D. Woodroffe. 2002. Fringing reef growth and morphology: A review. *Earth Science Reviews* 57: 255–277.

Kennedy, D. M., C. D. Woodroffe, B. G. Jones, M. E. Dickson, and C. V. G. Phipps. 2002. Carbonate sedimentation on subtropical shelves around Lord Howe Island and Balls Pyramid, Southwest Pacific. *Marine Geology* 188: 333–349.

Kobayashi, K. 2004. Origin of the Palau and Yap trench-arc systems. *Geophysical Journal International* 157: 1303–1315.

Kroenke, L. W. 1984. Cenozoic tectonic development of the Southwest Pacific. U.N. ESCAP, CCOP/SOPAC Technical Bulletin 6.

Kroenke, L. W., and D. A. Walker. 1986. Evidence for the formation of a new trench in the western Pacific. *Eos, Transactions of the American Geophysical Union* 67: 145–146.

Lee, J. M., and J. G. Begg. 2002. *Geology of the Wairarapa.* 1:250000 geological map series, no. 11. Institute of Geological and Nuclear Sciences Ltd, Lower Hutt.

Little T. A., and D. W. Rogers. 2005. Wairarapa Fault rupture—vertical deformation in 1855 and a history of similar events from Turakirae Head. In *The 1855 Wairarapa earthquake symposium—proceedings volume,* ed. J. Townend, R. Langridge, and A. Jones, 11–20. Greater Wellington Regional Council, Wellington.

Macdonald, G. A., A. T. Abbott, and F. L. Peterson. 1983. *Volcanoes in the sea: The geology of Hawaii,* 2nd ed. Honolulu: University of Hawai'i Press.

Milsom, J. 2003. Forearc ophiolites: A view from the western Pacific. *Geological Society Special Publications* 218: 507–515.

Moberly, R. 1972. Origin of lithosphere behind island arcs, with reference to the western Pacific. In *Studies in Earth and space sciences,* ed. R. Shagam et al., 35–55. *Geological Society of America Memoir 132.* Boulder, Colo.: Geological Society of America.

Moore, J. G., D. A. Clague, R. T. Holcomb, P. W. Lipman, W. R. Normark, and M. E. Torresan. 1989. Prodigious submarine landslides on the Hawaiian Ridge. *Journal of Geophysical Research* 94: 17465–17484.

Muller, R. D., K. Gohl, S. C. Cande, A. Goncharov, and A. V. Golynsky. 2007. Eocene to Miocene geometry of the West Antarctic Rift System. *Australian Journal of Earth Sciences* 54: 1033–1045.

Naish, T. R. 2005. New Zealand's shallow-marine record of Pliocene-Pleistocene global sea-level and climate change. *Journal of the Royal Society of New Zealand* 35: 1–8.

Nakada, M. 1986. Holocene sea levels in oceanic islands: Implications for the rheological structure of the earth's mantle. *Tectonophysics* 121: 263–276.

Nunn, P. D. 1998. *Pacific Island landscapes.* Institute of Pacific Studies, University of the South Pacific, Fiji.

Peive, A. A. 2007. Linear volcanic chains in oceans; possible formation mechanisms. *Geotectonics* 41: 281–295.

Rattenbury, M. S., D. B. Townsend, and M. R. Johnston. 2006. *Geology of the Kaikoura area.* 1:250000 Geological Map No. 13. Institute of Geological and Nuclear Sciences Ltd, Lower Hutt.

Reagan, M. K., B. B. Hanan, M. T. Heizler, B. S. Hartman, and R. Hicky-Vargas. 2008. Petrogenesis of volcanic rocks from Saipan and Rota, Mariana Islands, and implications for the evolution of nascent island arcs. *Journal of Petrology* 49: 441–464.

Reyners, M., D. Eberhart-Phillips, G. Stuart, and Y. Nishimura. 2006. Imaging subduction from the trench to 300 km depth beneath the central North Island, New Zealand, with Vp and Vp/Vs. *Geophysical Journal International* 165: 565–583.

Silver, E., S. Day, S. Ward, G. Hoffmann, P. Llanes, A. Lyons, N. W. Driscoll, R. Perembo, S. John, S. Saunders, F. Taranu, L. Anton, I. Abiari, B. Applegate, J. Engels, J. Smith, and J. Tagliodes. 2005. Island arc debris avalanches and tsunami generation. *Eos, Transactions of the American Geophysical Union* 86: 485–489.

Stagg, H. M. J., M. B. Alcock, I. Borissova, and A. M. J. Moore. 2002. *Geological framework of the southern Lord Howe Rise and adjacent areas.* Geoscience Australia Record 2002/25, Canberra.

Sugisaki, R. 1972. Tectonic aspects of andesite line. *Nature* 240: 109–111.

Trenhaile, A. S. 2002. Modeling the development of marine terraces on tectonically mobile rock coasts. *Marine Geology* 185: 341–361.

Webster, J. M., L. M. Wallace, D. A. Clague, and J. C. Braga. 2007. Numerical modeling of the growth and drowning of Hawaiian coral reefs during the last two glacial cycles (0–250 kyr). *Geochemistry, Geophysics, Geosystems* 8: Q03011.

Wegener, A. 1929. Die Entstehung der Kontinente und Ozeane, 4th ed. (rev.). Translated by J. Biram, 1967. *The origin of continents and oceans.* London: Methuen.

Wessel, P., and L. W. Kroenke. 1997. A geometric technique for relocating hotspots and refining absolute plate motions. *Nature* 387: 365–369.

Willcox, J. B., P. A. Symonds, K. Hinz, and D. Bennett. 1980. Lord Howe Rise Tasman Sea—Preliminary geophysical results and petroleum prospects. *BMR Journal of Australian Geology and Geophysics* 5: 225–236.

Wilson, C. J. N. 2001. The 26.5 ka Oruanui eruption, New Zealand: An introduction and overview. *Journal of Volcanology and Geothermal Research* 112: 133–174.

Wilson, D. S. 1996. Fastest known spreading on the Miocene Cocos–Pacific plate boundary. *Geophysical Research Letters* 23: 3003–3006.

Wilson, J. T. 1963. Evidence from islands on the spreading of ocean floors. *Nature* 197: 536–538.

Woodroffe, C. D., M. E. Dickson, B. Brooke, and D. M. Kennedy. 2005. Episodes of reef growth at Lord Howe Island, the southernmost limit in the southwestern Pacific. *Earth and Planetary Science Letters* 49: 222–237.

Woodroffe, C. D., D. M. Kennedy, B. P. Brooke, and M. E. Dickson. 2006. Geomorphological evolution of Lord Howe Island and carbonate production at the latitudinal limit to reef growth. *Journal of Coastal Research* 22: 188–201.

Geomorphology

Patrick D. Nunn

The Pacific Islands region extends over 130° of longitude and 70° of latitude. Some islands are more than 100,000 km² in size; others are miniscule. Some islands are pieces of ancient continent, hundreds of millions of years old; other islands are still growing, and periodic volcanic eruptions give subaerial landforms little chance to develop. Some tropical islands are so high they have ice caps; others are so low they can barely be seen on approach by sea. Some islands are rain-soaked; others sometimes go for years without rain.

Prevailing climatic and geological controls produce seemingly infinite permutations and militate against sweeping generalizations. Yet generalize we must to get some appreciation of Pacific Islands landscapes. This chapter begins by looking in detail at the principal causes of landscape diversity in the Pacific Islands, along with some pertinent examples. This is followed by a systematic account of landscapes on distinct island types. The chapter concludes with a discussion of rates of change and two key issues in Pacific Islands landscape study.

Controls on Landform Development

Climate and geology are the principal controls on global landform development. Climatic and oceanographic controls, particularly precipitation, are important causes of landform variation throughout the Pacific Islands. Geological controls are also important, but less so relative to continents because of the more restricted range of geologic structures and histories on islands (Nunn 1987). Many Pacific islands are seismically and volcanically active. In these cases, vertical tectonics (land-level movements) may overwhelm the influence of other factors in landscape evolution.

Long-term changes of climate and sea level (Figure 4.1) have also brought about changes in landforms on certain Pacific islands. Some landforms are relict in character, formed in the past when conditions were significantly different. On some islands, people have been the principal agents of landscape change, often blithely unaware of the long-term effects of their actions.

Climatic and Oceanographic Controls

Climate in the Pacific varies mostly with latitude. Islands nearest the equator are generally hotter and wetter and experience more

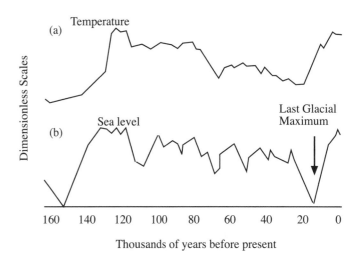

Figure 4.1. Changes in temperature and sea level during the past 150,000 years (after Nunn 1997). Temperature changes are derived from oxygen-isotope analyses of marine microrganisms; sea-level changes are from studies of emerged reefs on the Huon Peninsula, Papua New Guinea.

tropical cyclones (hurricanes, typhoons) than those farther from the equator. Changing amounts of solar radiation in the course of a year are responsible for significant seasonal variations of temperature and rainfall. On Tarawa, Kiribati, twice-yearly crossings by the Intertropical Convergence Zone (ITCZ) produce two peaks in precipitation. Geomorphic processes on such islands are affected by periodic changes in rainfall and water-table level. For example, it is possible that seasonal shifts in the relative amounts of fresh and saline groundwater in the intertidal zone are important in beachrock formation (Schmalz 1971).

Various aspects of climate also act as limiting factors in the development of particular landforms. Amphitheater-headed valleys, for example, can develop only on those high parts of volcanic islands where annual precipitation exceeds 2,000 mm (Nunn 1994a). The development of phosphate rock on many Pacific reef islands is one reason why they have survived so long. Phosphate rock of this kind requires deposition of guano and low annual precipitation levels to prevent its decomposition and leaching (Stoddart and Scoffin 1983).

In some of the westernmost Pacific islands, the reversal of winds associated with the Asian and Austral monsoons brings large amounts of orographic moisture to opposing sides of islands during summer and winter. Landform development on both sides may be similar, though during any season a different set of climatic processes dominates. The aridity of Easter Island is associated with the stationary high-pressure cell in the eastern Pacific. This has given rise to a set of semiarid landforms quite different from those of the nearest islands in French Polynesia, 2,400 km to the west.

The ocean circulation of the Pacific is dominated by two large gyres. The gyre in the North Pacific involves clockwise movement of water; that in the South Pacific involves counterclockwise movement. The impact of ocean currents on landform development is well represented by the presence of coral at unusually high latitudes in the western Pacific, where warm equatorial water is driven poleward.

A final consideration involves the gross distribution of islands within the Pacific. Most islands are within or just outside the tropics; there is a conspicuous paucity of islands in temperate and high latitudes. One reason for this is that the ocean water in these areas is too cool for coral growth. When an island drifts into these areas and sinks, it disappears. Yet an island that sinks within the coral seas will often develop a capping of coral reef and thus retain expression at the ocean surface.

An example is provided by the northern volcanoes in the Hawai'i–Emperor Island seamount chain. When the islands initially subsided beneath sea level, they were in warmer waters and developed a reef capping. The northwest drift of the Pacific Plate, however, has moved these islands into cooler waters. Subsequently, the islands along with the reef caps disappeared beneath the ocean surface, forming a chain of guyots.

The Lau Islands of eastern Fiji lie centrally within the coral seas. When the original volcanic islands (on which the modern islands are founded) sank, they developed either a reef cap or a reef fringe. Subject to uplift some two million years ago, these islands now appear as raised limestone islands. Where reefs have risen around a central volcanic core, a *makatea* island has been created.

Topographic and Geologic Controls

On account of their small sizes and locations within a persistent wind belt, many Pacific islands have well-defined windward and leeward sides, with marked differences in mean annual precipitation, vegetation, landforms, and landforming processes. Examples abound in the trade-wind belts, particularly in the South Pacific.

The large island of Viti Levu in Fiji lies in the path of the southeast trade winds all year (although cyclonic precipitation, generally in short bursts, commonly affects the entire island during the southern summer). Typical annual precipitation inland from the coast varies from 4,000 mm on the southeast side to 1,500 mm on the northwest side (see Table 5.1).

The southeast (windward) side of Viti Levu has a thick covering of regolith, or weathered rock (a consequence of high rainfall and chemical weathering). Much of the terrain is still forested, with sinuous streams following narrow valleys. The northwest (leeward) side of Viti Levu is covered largely by grasslands, probably established during the aridity associated with the Last Glacial Maximum

17 Ka (thousands of years ago), a view supported by recent empirical studies (Kumar et al. 2006). There is little regolith, and soil has accumulated mainly in valley bottoms.

Farther south, the influence of topography on climate and landform development is illustrated by South Island, New Zealand. The Southern Alps, which fringe the island's west coast, lie in the paths of the prevailing westerlies all year. The western slopes are wet, forested, and characterized by short, swift rivers and a narrow, discontinuous coastal plain. The eastern slopes are much drier, generally lacking in forest cover, with plains built largely from glaciofluvial (glacial melt) outwash, and crossed by long, wide rivers.

Volcanic and Tectonic Controls

Many Pacific islands are volcanically active, ranging from the large shield volcanoes on the island of Hawai'i to the many stratovolcanoes along the Pacific Rim such as Anatahan (Marianas) or the underwater Fonuafo'ou (Tonga). Particularly in the case of volcanoes that have become dormant or extinct in the last few hundred thousand years, much of the original volcanic shape may remain (Figure 4.2). In recently active volcanoes, cinder cones and other eruptive features may also be preserved.

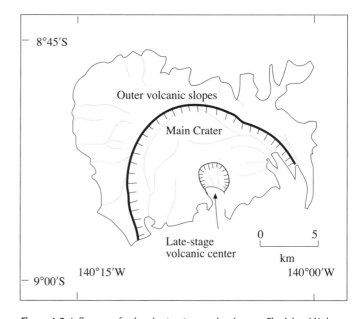

Figure 4.2. Influence of volcanic structure on landscape. The island Nuku Hiva in the Marquesas group (after Brousse et al. 1978 and Thomas 1990). Most of the island is formed from the slopes of the original volcano. The south central part is a caldera in which a late-stage volcano formed.

Most young volcanoes are radially drained. Slopes soon become deeply dissected, particularly where volcanic (rather than sedimentary) material makes up a large part of the surface. Amphitheater-headed valleys develop in the wetter, usually higher, parts. Where the walls of these valleys intersect, sharp, serrate ridges may form. Isolated, triangular-shaped parts of the original volcanic slopes, known as planezes, may remain. Volcanic sediments transported from upland ranges are important components of lowland landscapes, and have been so for much of the past few million years (Table 4.1).

Table 4.1

Geologic Time Scale Since the Cretaceous, Showing the Neogene Subperiod

Period	Subperiod	Epoch	Millions of years ago
Quaternary	Neogene	Holocene	.01–present
		Pleistocene	1.8–.01
Tertiary			24–.18
	Paleogene		66.4–24
Cretaceous			144–66.4

Such processes and landscapes cannot occur without significant precipitation. The need for moisture to produce alluvial sediments on volcanic islands is exemplified by arid Pinzón Island in the Galapagos group, where there has been a lack of significant erosion or soil development in the past several hundred thousand years (Baitis and Lindstrom 1980).

Islands in the western Pacific (where the oldest and largest island groups are located) are subject to plate boundary tectonic processes, resulting in uplift and subsidence. Uplift and subsidence also occur near midplate islands, where volcanic loading has caused a moat-and-arch formation. Several examples of raised reefs occur in the Southern Cook Islands as a consequence of loading by the high island, Rarotonga (McNutt and Menard 1978).

Most inhabited islands in Tonga are emerged limestone islands, marking the rising edge of the Australian Plate (Figure 4.3). Linear ridges mark old reef barriers, and residual hills mark old patch reefs. Successive uplifts during the Holocene (10 Ka to the present) elevated the *Porolithon onkodes* algal ridge on Tongatapu (Nunn 1993).

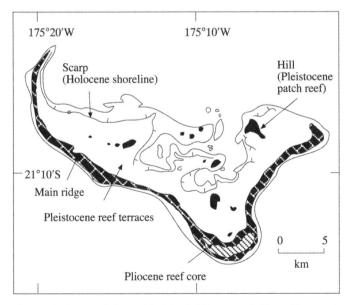

Figure 4.3. *Geomorphology of the island of Tongatapu in Tonga (Nunn and Finau 1995). Most landforms are from Roy (1990).*

Karst (eroded limestone) landscapes form when emerged reef is subjected to solution processes, characterized by dolines (depressions), with conical hills and steep pinnacles. The types of karst landscapes that develop on emerged reef surfaces of various ages were described for parts of Vanuatu by Strecker, Bloom, and Lecolle (1987). Raised limestone islands are often rich in phosphate (valued for fertilizer), and decades of mining activities have resulted in dramatic alterations to the landscape.

Uplift outside the coral seas often also produces staircases of emerged shoreline indicators, but these are commonly less easy to interpret than their counterparts within the coral seas, as residual deposits are often absent. Good examples are provided in various parts of New Zealand, where most landforms manifest the effects of emergence (Pillans 1986).

Subsidence may occur as a consequence of midplate volcanic loading, Pacific Plate drift, and tectonic instability at plate margins. Landforms produced by subsidence, such as embayments, may be visible along the coasts of Pacific islands. Embayments along the south coast of Vava‘u, Tonga, provide a good example (Figure 4.4). Subsidence occurs on many Hawaiian islands, but the coast lacks embayment except where the shoreline is sufficiently dissected.

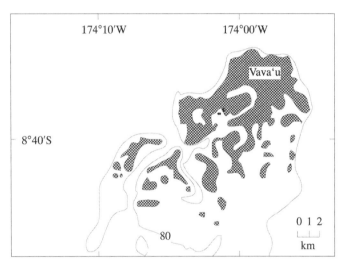

Figure 4.4. *Map of the Vava‘u island group on the Tonga frontal arc (Nunn 1994a). The insular shelf is delimited by the 50-m isobath. The form of the island group suggests increasing submergence from north to south.*

Environmental Change

Explaining Pacific island geomorphology requires some understanding of the environmental conditions that prevailed at the time island landforms first began evolving.

The tropical Pacific is known to have been drier around the Last Glacial Maximum. Yet islands in Hawai‘i received heavy rainfall, at least on their windward sides, creating a degree of dissection that is anomalous under present climate conditions (Gavenda 1992). In other parts of the Pacific, lowland sediment bodies began accumulating around the end of the Last Glacial Maximum, when precipitation exceeded present levels.

Vegetation is one of the most sensitive indicators of environmental change and also affects the types and rates of geomorphic processes. An example is provided by the past thirty thousand years of vegetation change in the New Guinea Highlands (Flenley 1979). A site 3,000 m above sea level would have lain above the forest limit until (about) 28 Ka, below it until 26 Ka, above it during the Last Glacial Maximum, and below it again following deglaciation (15–10 Ka).

The caldera Rano Kao on Easter Island is filled with erosional sediment, but it is uncertain whether this sediment accumulated under the present short-grass vegetation or under forest (long since removed). Pollen analyses suggest the latter option. The grassland is probably a recent phenomenon on Easter Island (with dry forest dominant previously), occurring some time after human settlement (Flenley and King 1984).

Sea-level changes have left a profound imprint on many Pacific coasts. Sea level rose from a low of -130 m at 17 Ka during the Last Glacial Maximum (about twenty-two thousand to eighteen thousand years ago) to a high of +1.5 m at 4 Ka (Pirazzoli and Montaggioni 1988; Jones 1992; Kayanne et al. 1993; Nunn 1995). Early Holocene sea-level rise inundated the lower parts of valleys that had existed during the Last Glacial (about ninety thousand to ten thousand years ago). Subsequently, falling sea levels led to the emergence of coastal plains that were ideal for human settlement (Figure 4.5).

Figure 4.5. Part of the north coast of the island of Tahiti, French Polynesia (Davis 1928).

Human Impacts

Humans have profoundly influenced the landscapes of most Pacific islands, but the precise extent of this influence, particularly with regard to pre-European populations, is the subject of debate (Nunn 1992, 1994b, 2001). There is a widely held belief that rapid and profound changes to Pacific Island environments took place following their first sustained occupation by humans (Kirch and Hunt 1997). While this seems applicable on some islands, it is clearly not applicable to others where, particularly since high-resolution paleoclimate records have become available, there appear to be more plausible explanations involving nonhuman changes (Nunn 2004, 2007a).

Undoubted effects of humans include the deliberate reshaping of the landscape, ranging from the reclamation of nearshore areas for coastal development to the removal of hills for roadways. More than a thousand years ago, artificial islands were constructed in the Langa Langa lagoon off Malaita in Solomon Islands for habitation sites. Reclaimed lands form the basis of much of downtown Honolulu and Waikīkī Beach, on Oʻahu, Hawaiʻi.

Mining has also been a major cause of landscape change. Extreme examples come from the island arcs of the western Pacific, rich in mineral ores. The effects of indiscriminate extraction of ore and mining waste disposal on Bougainville, Papua New Guinea (closed since 1989 after protests from local people), were detailed by Brown (1974). The effects of mining waste on estuaries and as a cause of recent shoreline progradation (extension) in New Caledonia were described by Bird, Dubois, and Iltis (1984).

Deforestation is a major contributor to landscape change in many parts of the Pacific. A tripling in volume of log exports from Papua New Guinea between 1979 and 1988 indicates the extent of the contemporary problem. Demand for hardwoods has led to rapidly increasing pressure on governments and landowners to sell this valuable resource.

Deforestation exposes the ground to direct impact by rain, which, in the tropical Pacific, is sometimes torrential. The result, particularly on steep slopes, is soil erosion by sheet wash, rilling, and eventually gullying. Many Pacific Island gullies are cut in regolith; the soil was lost long ago (Figure 4.6). On temperate Pacific islands, the effects of deforestation are also severe. In the Wairarapa area of North Island, New Zealand, as many as ninety soil slips per km^2 have been recorded on areas cleared of forest for sheep grazing (Glasby 1986).

Figure 4.6. Roadcut in regolith, Nuku-Lutu road, central Viti Levu Island, Fiji. Regolith forms in the humid tropics under rain forest and is rapidly eroded when exposed. Rilling and gullying are already affecting this outcrop, which is prone to failure as long as it remains exposed (photo PDN).

Forest clearance and other types of land-use changes have profoundly altered Pacific Island landscapes. Many river channels have become filled with sediment, and channel capacity has been reduced. Such rivers thus flood frequently and intensely (compare Figures 4.7 and 4.8). Many river terraces, favored for planting crops, have become flood-prone and can no longer be used. This has forced farmers onto steeper slopes, exacerbating the problems associated with lowland flooding (Figure 4.9).

Figure 4.7. The former bridge at Matainasau, central Viti Levu Island, Fiji, was built to ensure that the transinsular road would remain open even when the river flooded. This view is from downstream (photo PDN).

Figure 4.8. Flooding associated with tropical cyclone Kina in 1993 washed the Matainasau bridge away (see 4.7) and moved most of the boulders on the floodplain several kilometers downstream. The remains of the bridge are viewed from upstream (photo PDN).

Figure 4.9. Prices much higher than those that could be obtained on the open market are presently guaranteed for Fiji sugar under the Lome Convention. This has encouraged farmers to plant cane on steep slopes where such practices cannot be sustained for long and will lead to land degradation if continued. This view is of cane fields near Talekosovi, northern Viti Levu island (photo PDN).

Other human impacts are impossible to catalog meaningfully in a short space. Many modern human impacts are plainly evident, but controversy often attends the cause(s) of longer-term landscape changes following human settlement. The debate has become polarized between those who attribute the majority of landscape changes within this period to human actions and those who regard these changes as primarily the consequence of natural fluctuations in climate, sea level, and geomorphic processes.

Pacific Island Landscapes

Given the principal controls on landform development discussed above, the potential for landscape variability within the Pacific region is considerable. Pacific islands a thousand kilometers apart may have similar assemblages of landforms because of similarity in climate and geotectonic character. Conversely, on large, complex islands such as New Guinea and others in the western Pacific, landform type may exhibit considerable variability between islands within a short distance.

To accommodate these variations within a rational framework, several categories are defined in Table 4.2 and used as a basis for landscape description in the remainder of this section. There is clearly scope for overlap, but this need not be a problem as the categorization is intended only as an arbitrary device to facilitate landscape description.

Table 4.2

Classification of Pacific Islands Used as a Basis for Systematic Landscape Description

Type
Volcanic midplate islands
Volcanic plate margin islands
Continental islands
Limestone islands
Atolls
Islands of mixed lithology

Volcanic Midplate Islands

Most small, remote islands in the Pacific are volcanic in origin. They may be products of intraplate island-forming processes, such as are taking place at the southeast ends of many hot-spot chains. Examples include the Hawaiian, Samoan, and Society island chains (Duncan and Clague 1985).

Many of these islands formed from single volcanoes, so, depending on the time elapsed since the last major eruption, their landscapes exhibit a set of landforms that vary only slightly with latitude and altitude. Young islands of this kind commonly develop radial drainage, sometimes manifested as parasol ribbing in its initial stages, progressing to gullied slopes (Figure 4.10). Capture of adjacent streams by headward erosion of others leads to a less regular drainage pattern, often characterized by isolation of planezes.

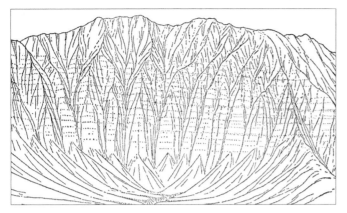

Figure 4.10. *Sketch of the Pali, northeast Oʻahu, Hawaiʻi (Davis 1928). Note the steep gullied slopes with the fans at their foot. The river channel is cut into sediments derived from the cliffs.*

Amphitheater-headed valleys are characteristic of midocean volcanic islands of the Pacific, though they are also found in islands at convergent margins. These occur mostly on igneous rocks where annual rainfall exceeds 2,000 mm and where elevation exceeds 500 m. Such valleys are typically narrow in their middle sections but open upstream into large amphitheaters surrounded by near-vertical slopes.

Early studies of such valleys demonstrated that they developed by parallel retreat of the surrounding walls (Figure 4.11). Scott and Street (1976) showed that this was accomplished by periodic soil avalanching during heavy rain. More recent work has shown that seepage of water from the base of these slopes carries sediment away, resulting in steep valley sides (Onda 1994). Resistant dike rock remains near vertical at valley heads, as in the Pali (Cliffs), on Oʻahu, Hawaiʻi (see Figure 4.10).

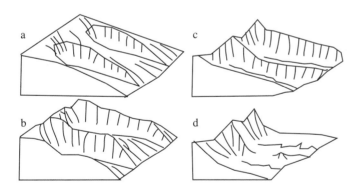

Figure 4.11. *Stages in the formation of amphitheater-headed valleys in Hawaiʻi (after Nunn 1994a and sources therein): (a) Orographic precipitation carves deep valleys, (b) valleys widen, (c), valley sides are lowered and breached, (d) only the steep headwall remains.*

An important control on islands that owe their origin to hotspot volcanism is the progressive subsidence of the islands as they move away from the fixed hot spot. Subsidence affects gross form in a regular manner. This was realized by some of the earliest scientists to work in the Pacific (Dana 1890) and has been quantified for the Society Islands (Morhange 1992).

Volcanic Plate Margin Islands

Island arcs of the western Pacific, such as those in Solomon Islands and the Bismarck Archipelago, have been influenced by their geographic location near continents (altering climate patterns) and along plate boundaries (intensifying tectonic activity).

Monsoon winds, related to summer heating on continental landmasses, bring heavy rainfall in some areas. Erosion of sediment from uplands has created extensive lowlands, especially along the coast. Lowland sediment bodies are moved in floods, often as mudflows or debris flows. Upland slopes are also prone to fail when their sediment cover becomes saturated.

Intense seismic and tectonic activity is present in island arcs. Earthquakes often trigger landslides and are a significant geomorphic agent in such settings (Peart 1991). Uplift is common, signaled by raised reefs surrounding many islands (Figure 4.12).

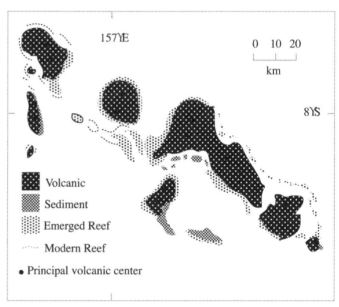

Figure 4.12. *Emerged coral reefs in Solomon Islands (after Nunn 1994a).*

Some islands in the western Pacific are being uplifted so rapidly that the land surface is unable to reach an equilibrium condition with respect to landforming processes. Upland erosion is thereby catalyzed, and catastrophic processes tend to be significant agents of denudation. Thus, the denudation rate of the island of Taiwan is among the highest in the world (Li 1976).

Continental Islands

Fragments of Gondwana exist in New Guinea, New Zealand, and New Caledonia. The landforms of such continental islands are old and highly diverse in comparison to those on other Pacific islands. Even in tectonically active New Zealand, erosion surfaces of Late Cretaceous age are found (Pillans et al. 1992).

New Zealand has been much modified by glaciation. Substantial shifts in geomorphic process regime (alternating between glaciation and stream erosion) have thus occurred over past geological history. Conversely, in tropical New Guinea, which was affected to a lesser extent by Quaternary climate changes, glaciation was limited to a narrow band of high-altitude landscapes.

Sediment yields from some rivers in Papua New Guinea (Table 4.3) are among the highest in the world, reflecting the high rainfall (which can reach 10,000 mm annually in the headwaters of the Fly River) (Pickup, Higgins, and Warner 1980), its intensity, the structure and lithology of the bedrock being eroded, and uplift.

Table 4.3

Sediment Yields of Rivers in Papua New Guinea

Station	Catchment area (km²)	Runoff (mm/year)	Vegetation cover (%)	Suspended sediment yield (m³/km²/year)
Ok Ningi	4.56	7208	95	2980–4050
Ok Tedi	420	5695	95	1720–2960
Ok Menga	240	6660	95	370–460
Alice	3900	5870	95	300–560
Fly at Kiunga	6300	5360	95	260–350
Aure	4360	2220	95	4190
Purari at Wabo	26300	2830	95	790
Ei Creek	16.25	2625	85	36.3

Source: Douglas and Spencer 1985 and sources therein.

On both New Guinea and New Zealand, a great range of karst landforms is found (Figure 4.13). When karst geomorphologists first began working in Papua New Guinea, they found such an extraordinary array of landforms that existing terminology proved inadequate to describe them (Williams 1972). It is the older, often larger-scale features that are distinctive relative to other Pacific Island karst landscapes.

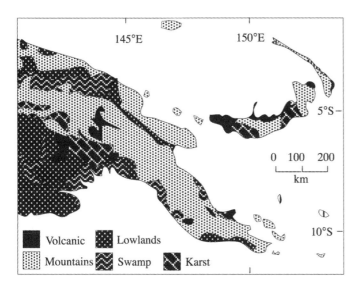

Figure 4.13. *Landforms of Papua New Guinea (after Löffler 1982).*

By virtue of their plate-boundary locations, such continental islands are sites of considerable tectonic activity, which tends to obscure the effects of other landscape processes.

Limestone Islands

Limestone islands are formed when reefs or other carbonate bodies emerge above sea level. They most commonly occur in the tropical Pacific. For an island to have emerged more than a few meters since the start of the Quaternary, that island must have been uplifted. Many such places are close to convergent plate boundaries. Limestone islands also occur away from plate boundaries, as when lithospheric loading (at a growing hot-spot volcano) causes compensatory uplift of a surrounding arch (Nunn 1994a).

Most karst on uplifted Pacific islands has formed on Quaternary reef limestones and consequently does not display many landforms associated with older limestones. Such landforms range from shallow solution dolines to more extensively hollowed karren forms. Karren karst is exposed on the islands of Niue (Schofield 1959) and Henderson (Paulay and Spencer 1988) and may become filled with phosphate, as on Nauru and Banaba Island in Kiribati (Hill and Jacobson 1989).

There has been much debate over the origins of high limestone islands, such as in Tonga and Lau (eastern Fiji). Based on the characteristic rim-and-basin morphology, Davis (1928) regarded these islands as emerged atolls. Later investigators (Hoffmeister and Ladd 1935, Ladd and Hoffmeister 1945, Nunn 1996) found that in situ corals were absent from their rims, suggesting that rim-and-basin morphology is more likely due to subaerial solution of an emerged limestone bank (Figure 4.14).

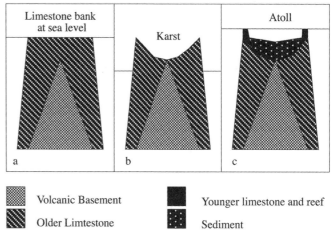

Figure 4.14. *How atolls might form from a limestone bank (after Nunn 1994a). (a) Limestone bank exists at sea level, (b) sea level falls and a saucer shape develops through rainwater solution, (c) sea level rises. Reef grows along rim, but is stifled by sediment in the center of the lagoon.*

Other islands in the Pacific are undoubtedly emerged atolls. Makatea, in the Tuamotu group, provides an example of a raised atoll related to lithospheric loading by the nearby Mehetia-Tahiti complex. Dating of exposed reefs indicates that emergence began in the late Tertiary, followed by the accumulation of phosphates. Uplift has continued subsequently, though there is some debate about the details of the geological history (Montaggioni 1985; Nunn 1994a).

Atolls

Within the coral seas, islands that subside beneath the ocean surface commonly retain terrestrial expression on account of coral reef growing upward from the flanks of sinking islands. A ring reef (or an atoll reef) is so formed. A late Holocene fall of sea level in the Pacific of around 1 to 2 m caused emergence and lateral outgrowth of many such reefs (Nunn 1994a, 1995). Carbonate sediments derived from surrounding reef slopes were washed onto reef surfaces, particularly during storms, forming islets around the cores of emerged reef. These islets are where most people live today in Kiribati, the Marshall Islands, Tokelau, Tuvalu, and other atoll groups (Figure 4.15).

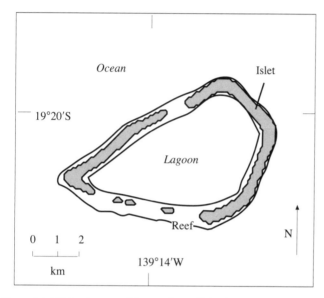

Figure 4.15. *Vairaatea, one of the smaller atolls in the Tuamotus, French Polynesia.*

Reef islets of this kind have been classified as cays and *motu* (Nunn 1994a). Cays are superficial and ephemeral, often forming or disappearing during large storms. *Motu* are formed in part of more consolidated materials (beach rock or phosphate rock), which protect their windward coasts from wave attack and ensure that their unconsolidated sediment cores endure longer than those of cays, which lack such protection.

Reef islet landforms in Tuvalu were found to differ depending on whether the islet had formed on an atoll reef or a table reef (lacking a central lagoon). The difference is manifested by the proportion of reef platform occupied by *motu*. *Motu* are many and occupy 8 to 23 percent of the atoll reefs. Conversely, there is usually only a single *motu* on a table reef, occupying 77 percent of the available space in the case of Niutao (McLean and Hosking 1991).

Along most ocean-facing coasts, sediment ridges are found. Those on the windward sides are generally coarser and more abrupt in form than those to leeward. Lagoon-facing shorelines also have ridges, but these tend to be more subdued because of lower wave energy. On the lagoon side, inlets known as barachois are often present (Nunn 1994a). These represent stages in the lagoonward extension of an atoll islet (Figure 4.16). Subsequent solution produces depressions in which ponds may form.

Figure 4.16. *Lagoonward extension of islets in the Tuamotus, French Polynesia (photo MR).*

Islands of Mixed Lithology

The most distinctive Pacific islands with a mixed lithology are of the *makatea* type, characterized by a volcanic interior fringed by uplifted reef limestone (Figures 4.17 and 4.18). The best examples of such islands occur in the Southern Cook group, raised as a result of lithospheric loading by the nearby high island, Rarotonga. Makatea Island in the Tuamotus differs from the islands in the Southern Cooks in that it lacks an emerged central volcanic core.

Typical *makatea* islands have a beveled volcanic core dissected by steep-sided, radial valleys. Transported regolith and soil fills the valley floors and the swampy depressions just landward of the contact between volcanics and limestone. Such depressions are prized for growing root crops, commonly taro (Figure 4.19). The elevated limestone walls are marked by basal epiphreatic (water-table) caves. Abandoned epiphreatic caves higher up mark relative standstills in the emergence process.

Other Pacific islands with a mixed lithology are usually comparatively large and formed by a variety of processes, commonly

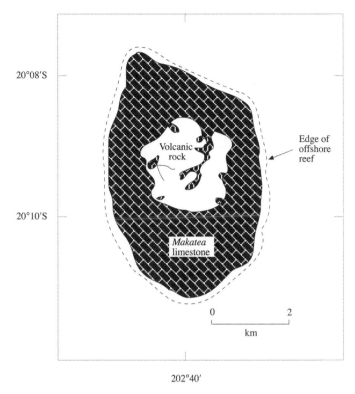

Figure 4.17. Mauke, a makatea *island in the Southern Cook group.*

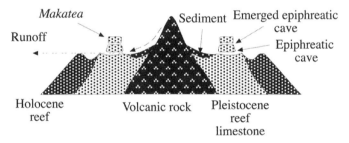

Figure 4.18. *Diagrammatic section across a* makatea *island.*

Figure 4.19. *Swamp depression with taro and other crops growing at the edge of the volcanics, Atiu, the Cook Islands (photo MR).*

associated with convergent plate boundaries. Good examples are found in Fiji, as in parts of the island of Viti Levu. Variations in landform type attributable to lithology, while recognizable, are largely obscured by differences associated with climate (Wright 1973, Nunn 1998).

Rates of Change

Comparatively little work has been done on the rates of landform change in the Pacific Islands. This is largely because most researchers have been based outside the region and have been unable to visit it regularly, and also because such measurements have not been a common priority. Yet knowledge of the rates at which landforms evolve is an essential prerequisite to understanding the relationship between process and form on Pacific islands. Three examples of the types of rates available are given in the following sections.

Coastal Change

Few Pacific Island coasts can be considered stable on a scale of hundreds of years. Within the past century, many coasts have either receded, prograded, or alternated between the two. Selected rates of recession and progradation are listed in Table 4.4.

Table 4.4

Selected Rates of Recession and Progradation on Pacific Island Coasts

Site	Rate (cm/year)	Source
RECESSION		
Easter Island (cliffs)	10	Paskoff 1978
Hawai'i—Waimea Bay, O'ahu (beach)	125	Campbell and Hwang 1982
New Zealand—Ngapotiki	346	Gibb 1978
PROGRADATION		
New Zealand—Tauranga Harbour	500	Healy 1977

In those parts of the Pacific Islands where systematic observations have not been made for long, the best record of coastal change comes from oral evidence from elderly, long-term residents of long-established coastal settlements. Using such data, rates of lateral inundation (encroachment of the sea on the land) were recorded for selected island countries (Table 4.5).

The existence of coral reefs off many Pacific coasts reduces the potential for their mechanical erosion by wave attack. On such coasts, most of the erosion is achieved by corrosion (chemical action), particularly along limestone coasts. In such places, groundwater often reaches nearshore waters through underwater springs, marking the seaward edge of a freshwater lens. The ferocity of wave attack along many reefless coasts in the Pacific Islands is manifest. For example, in Kaua'i (Hawai'i) and many of the islands in the

Geomorphology ■ 53

Table 4.5

Rates of Lateral Inundation for Selected Island Groups in the South Pacific

Island/Group	Number of stable sites studied	Rate of lateral inundation (cm/year)
Cook Islands	2	8.4
Fiji	16	15
Hawai'i*	1	125
Samoa	4	51.42[†]
Solomon Islands	20	10.8
Tonga	4	10
Tuvalu	1	18
Vanuatu	1	7.8

Source: Nunn 1990.

* Data from Waimea Bay on O'ahu (Campbell and Hwang 1982), regarded as the only stable island in the group (Moore 1970).

† This figure is greatly influenced by the high rate for Satalo on 'Upolu Island.

Marquesas (French Polynesia), offshore reef development is often poor or absent. This is testimony to the rapidity of lateral cutback of cliffs and the consequent impotence of subaerial denudation to reduce cliff-slope angle.

Denudation

Selected denudation rates are given below. This is one aspect of geomorphology that has received little attention in the Pacific Islands, so no coherent synthesis can yet be made.

Rates of surface lowering for various Hawaiian islands range from 0.04 to 0.19 mm/year (Li 1988). Contrast these values with those for the Ok Ningi in the New Guinea Highlands, where the ground surface is being lowered at 3 to 4 mm/year (Pickup, Higgins, and Warner 1980). The difference is explicable not only by climate but by process. In New Guinea mass wasting is a dominant agent of erosion. In Hawai'i, erosion is related mainly to chemical weathering.

A study of monzonite (a form of granite) cliff retreat in the high interior of Viti Levu Island, Fiji, was made by Nunn (1998). The area is subject to significant wet-dry seasonal conditions that drive processes of water erosion, such as sheet wash and basal undermining at springs. Combined with the effects of gravity, this causes scarp retreat. The maximum rate of scarp retreat was 2.46 mm/year.

On some Philippine islands under primary forest, around 3 tons/ha/year are lost through erosion, loss from open grasslands is 84 tons/ha/year, and overgrazed areas lose 250 tons/ha/year (Myers 1988). Commercial agriculture elsewhere has produced similar rates. Sugar cane planted on 18° to 22° slopes in Fiji were associated with a soil loss equivalent to 90 tons/ha/year (Clarke and Morrison

1987). Such rates greatly exceed the tropical soil-loss tolerance level of 13.5 tons/ha/year (Hudson 1971) and will inevitably lead to land degradation if unchecked.

Tectonic Change

Tectonic changes in the Pacific Islands include uplift and subsidence. These processes may operate aseismically (nonseismically), usually as long-term unidirectional movements upward or downward. They may also operate coseismically (earthquake-induced) as abrupt movements in one direction, commonly followed by a slower movement in the opposing direction (Nunn 1994a). Both types of movement are common on islands close to convergent plate boundaries in the Pacific (Berryman, Ota, and Hull 1992).

Representative rates of these movements from Pacific islands are listed in Table 4.6. The potential influence of these for landform evolution is clearly great.

Table 4.6

Selected Rates of Uplift and Subsidence for Pacific Islands

Island	Rate (mm/yr)
1. Aseismic uplift	
Anaa Atoll, Tuamotus	0.1
Hateruma, Ryukyu Is.	0.1–0.3
Huon Peninsula, Papua New Guinea	3.3
Maré, Loyalty Islands, New Caledonia	1.6–1.9
North Island (axial ranges), New Zealand	4.0
2. Aseismic subsidence	
Eniwetak, Marshall Islands	0.1–0.2
Hawai'i Island, Hawai'i	4.4
Moruroa, Tuamotus	0.12
North Island, New Zealand	0.1
3. Coseismic uplift	
Guadalcanal, Solomon Islands (1961)	1.5
Malakula, Vanuatu (1965)	1.2
Montague Island, Alaska (1964)	11.3
New Zealand (1929)	4.5
Vatulele Island, Fiji (Quaternary)	1.79
4. Coseismic subsidence	
Kodiak Island, Alaska (1964)	2.3

Source: After Nunn 1994a and sources therein.

Critical Issues in Landscape Study

Two major issues affecting the study of geomorphology in the Pacific Islands at present are, first, whether landscape change is primarily catastrophic or gradual in nature and, second, whether or not humans have played the principal role in postsettlement landscape change on Pacific islands. These issues are discussed below.

Catastrophic Versus Gradual Change

For more than 150 years, geomorphologists have argued about whether the landscape change that occurs during high-magnitude, low-frequency (catastrophic) events is more significant in landform evolution compared with the gradual change that occurs at most other times. The prevailing wisdom at present appears to favor the gradualist view, but this perhaps reflects the fact that few geomorphologists work and reside in the tropics, where floods, hurricanes, earthquakes, and volcanic activity are especially common. There is a clear case for catastrophism (Baker 1998).

An area of focus in this debate concerns the role of periodic storms in the long-term growth of atoll islets. From work in Ontong Java, Bayliss-Smith (1988) suggested that catastrophic storms, although often causing much erosion, have generally maintained atoll islets by simultaneously supplying coral debris to atoll reefs. According to Bayliss-Smith, the high frequency of mid-Holocene tropical cyclones allowed reef islets to maintain a steady state, but a recent decline in tropical cyclone frequency was causing the destruction of islets (Figure 4.20).

Other work has distinguished storms that either largely remove material from atoll reefs or cause it to accumulate (Blumenstock 1961; Bourrouilh-Le Jan and Talandier 1985). It is unclear precisely what causes particular effects to occur. An example of a landform constructed by hurricanes is provided in Figure 4.21.

Some catastrophic events occur so infrequently that they can hardly be thought to interfere with normal long-term landform evolution (Nunn 2009). Tsunami waves, which could have been caused by giant landslides or meteor impact, may have reached several hundred meters in height. The Hulopo'e Gravel on Lāna'i, Hawai'i, 326 m above sea level, is believed to have been deposited by such a wave 105 Ka (Moore and Moore 1984). Waves generated by that event may also have deposited gravels in Samoa, Fiji, and along the New South Wales coast of Australia (Nunn 1998; Young and Bryant 1992).

The 2004 Indian Ocean tsunami has had a profound influence on the gradualist-catastrophist debate, with many geomorphologists working on oceanic-fringe landscapes now more open to accepting the role of episodic catastrophes in shaping these. The Lāna'i gravel debate exemplifies this, with some recent work denying their origin as a result of giant-wave deposition (Keating and Helsley 2002) having been superseded by more recent research (Webster, Clague, and Braga 2007).

Human or Nonhuman Impacts

The debate over human versus natural environmental changes in Pacific Island postsettlement history has been outlined above. Further development of this debate will require considerably more data concerning early human-environment interactions in the region. The presence of charcoal in heavily impacted areas is often used as evidence of human causation although it is clear that natural vegetation can burn regularly in the absence of humans (Nunn 2001).

On some islands, there is a proven coincidence between early human settlement and the first appearance of charcoal (Stevenson and Dodson 1995); but on other islands, there is not (Pillans et al. 1992). Yet a causal association has rarely been questioned (Nunn

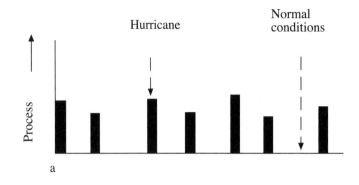

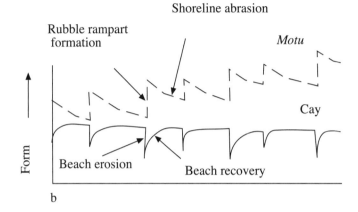

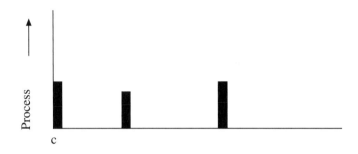

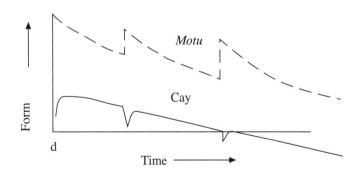

Figure 4.20. Possible role of tropical cyclones in reef-island geomorphology at two times during the Holocene on Ontong Java, Solomon Islands (after Bayliss-Smith 1988). (a) Mid-Holocene conditions with frequent storms, high wave energy, and reef productivity, (b) Mid-Holocene landforms: cays are in a steady state; motu are growing, (c) Late Holocene conditions with less frequent storms, lower wave energy, and reef productivity, (d) Late Holocene landforms: cays are intermittent or disappearing; motu are being eroded.

Figure 4.21. *Rubble rampart on Fakaofo Atoll, Tokelau, built through hurricane action (photo MR).*

defensive locations such as inland caves and mountaintops. This is a clear example of how climate change caused environmental change, which in turn produced profound and enduring societal changes.

Conclusion

The landforms of Pacific islands pose exciting new challenges for the next generation of geomorphologists. Many existing explanations of landform evolution in the Pacific have been uncritically transferred from continental areas, where different conditions prevail. In the next few decades, recognition of the unique character of Pacific island landforms will lead to critical re-evaluation of these explanations and to the development of more effective environmental management in the region.

1994b). Some studies have suggested that the earliest Holocene charcoal is an indicator of the earliest human presence (Kirch and Ellison 1994; Nunn 2004), even though archaeological evidence places this much later (Spriggs and Anderson 1993).

An important question is whether the earliest settlers sought to conserve or to radically modify the new island environments they settled. Support for the conservation argument comes from studies of traditional horticulture (Zan and Hunter-Anderson 1987) and re-evaluations of the role of people in landscape change (Athens and Ward 1993; Nunn 2007b; Nunn et al. 2007).

The importance of these debates for geomorphology is evident. According to one scenario, the landscape was rapidly and abruptly altered only when the first people arrived, but would otherwise have been more resilient. Conversely, if the landscape was already changing due to falling temperatures, falling sea levels, and changing rainfall levels, for instance, humans may only have marginally altered the rates of pre-existing processes. This is not only a question that pertains to the time of earliest human settlement of the Pacific Islands but also for most of their subsequent human occupation. In the past, it was usual for those trying to interpret cultural histories of the Pacific Islands to attribute most environmental and societal changes to human (internal societal) causes, such as population growth. But in truth there is often little (if any) independent and verifiable evidence for population growth, for example, as a cause of premodern environmental or societal changes in the Pacific Islands. This "cultural-determinist" view, while still widespread, is threatened by an opposing "environmental-determinist" view, which is bolstered by independently derived observations of past climates in the Pacific and their changes (Nunn 2003, 2007b; Nunn et al. 2007).

A well-studied example is that of the "AD 1300 Event," a period of rapid cooling and sea-level fall that occurred throughout the Pacific from about 1250 CE until 1350 CE (Nunn 2000, 2007a, 2007b). The sea-level fall converted many island coasts from saltwater (sea) embayments to brackish-water lakes or wetlands, and also depleted nearshore marine resources to such a great extent that there was an almost instant response from coastal peoples throughout the Pacific Islands. On most islands, conflict erupted—a result of fierce competition for the depleted food resource—and coastal settlements were abandoned in favor of those in fortifiable/

BIBLIOGRAPHY

Athens, J. S., and J. V. Ward. 1993. Environmental change and prehistoric Polynesian settlement in Hawai'i. *Asian Perspectives* 32: 205–223.

Baitis, H. W., and M. M. Lindstrom. 1980. Geology, petrography, and petrology of Pinzón Island, Galápagos archipelago. *Contributions to Mineralogy and Petrology* 72: 367–386.

Baker, V. R. 1998. Catastrophism and uniformitarianism: Logical roots and current relevance in geology. In *Lyell: The Past is the Key to the Present,* ed. D. J. Blundell and A. C. Scott, 171–182. Special Publication of the Geological Society of London, London.

Bayliss-Smith, T. 1988. The role of hurricanes in the development of reef islands, Ontong Java atoll, Solomon Islands. *The Geographical Journal* 54: 377–391.

Berryman, K. R., Y. Ota, and A. G. Hull. 1992. Holocene coastal evolution under the influence of episodic tectonic uplift: Examples from New Zealand and Japan. *Quaternary International* 15/16: 31–45.

Bird, E. C. F., J. P. Dubois, and J. A. Iltis. 1984. *The impacts of opencast mining on the rivers and coasts of New Caledonia.* Tokyo: United Nations University.

Blumenstock, D. I. 1961. A report on typhoon effects upon Jaluit Atoll. *Atoll Research Bulletin* 75: 1–105.

Bourrouilh-Le Jan, F. G., and J. Talandier. 1985. Sédimentation et fracturation de haute énergie en milieu récifal: tsunamis, ouragans et cyclones et leurs effets sur la sédimentologie et la géomorphologie d'un atoll: motu et hoa, à Rangiroa, Tuamotu, Paçifique SE. *Marine Geology* 67: 263–333.

Brousse, R., J.-P. Chevalier, M. Denizot, and B. Salvat. 1978. Etude géomorphologique des Iles Marquises. *Cahiers du Pacifique* 21: 9–74.

Brown, M. J. F. 1974. A development consequence: Disposal of mining waste on Bougainville, Papua New Guinea. *Geoforum* 8: 19–27.

Campbell, J. F., and D. J. Hwang. 1982. Beach erosion at Waimea Bay, O'ahu, Hawai'i. *Pacific Science* 36: 35–43.

Clarke, W. C., and J. Morrison. 1987. Land mismanagement and the development imperative in Fiji. In *Land degradation and society,* ed. P. Blaikie and H. Brookfield, 76–85. New York: Methuen.

Dana, J. D. 1890. *Characteristics of volcanoes.* New York: Dodd, Mead.

Davis, W. M. 1928. *The coral reef problem.* Washington: American Geographical Society (Special Publication 9).

Douglas, I., and T. Spencer. 1985. Present-day processes as a key to the effects of environmental change. In *Environmental change and tropical geomorphology,* ed. I. Douglas and T. Spencer, 39–73. London: George, Allen and Unwin.

Duncan, R. A., and D. A. Clague. 1985. Pacific plate motions recorded by linear volcanic chains. In *The ocean basins and margins, Vol. 7A, the Pacific,* ed. A. E. M. Nairn, F. G. Stehli, and S. Uyeda, 89–121. New York: Plenum Press.

Fairbridge, R. W., and H. B. Stewart. 1960. Alexa Bank, a drowned atoll on the Melanesian border plateau. *Deep-Sea Research* 7: 100–116.

Flenley, J. R. 1979. *The equatorial rain forest: A geological history.* London: Butterworths.

Flenley, J. R., and S. M. King. 1984. Late Quaternary pollen records from Easter Island. *Nature* 307: 47–50.

Gavenda, R. T. 1992. Hawaiian Quaternary paleoenvironments: A review of the geological, pedological, and botanical evidence. *Pacific Science* 46: 295–307.

Gibb, J. G. 1978. Rates of coastal erosion and accretion in New Zealand. *New Zealand Journal of Marine and Freshwater Research* 12: 429–450.

Glasby, G. P. 1986. Modification of the environment in New Zealand. *Ambio* 5: 267–271.

Healy, T. R. 1977. Progradation at the entrance to Tauranga Harbour, Bay of Plenty. *New Zealand Geographer* 33: 90–91.

Hill, P. J., and G. Jacobson. 1989. Structure and evolution of Nauru Island, central Pacific Ocean. *Australian Journal of Earth Science* 36: 365–381.

Hoffmeister, J. E., and H. S. Ladd. 1935. Foundations of atolls: A discussion. *Journal of Geology* 43: 653–665.

Hudson, N. W. 1971. *Soil conservation.* London: Batsford.

Jones, A. T. 1992. *Holocene coral reef on Kauai, Hawaii: Evidence for a sea-level highstand in the central Pacific.* Society for Sedimentary Geology, Special Publication 48: 267–271.

Kayanne, H., T. Ishii, E. Matsumoto, and N. Yonekura. 1993. Late Holocene sea-level change on Rota and Guam, Mariana Islands, and its constraint on geophysical predictions. *Quaternary Research* 40: 189–200.

Keating, B. H., and C. E. Helsley. 2002. The ancient shorelines of Lanai, Hawaii, revisited. *Sedimentary Geology* 150: 3–15.

Kirch, P. V., and J. Ellison. 1994. Palaeoenvironmental evidence for human colonization of remote Oceanic islands. *Antiquity* 68: 310–321.

Kirch, P. V., and T. L. Hunt, eds. 1997. *Historical ecology in the Pacific Islands.* New Haven, Conn.: Yale University Press.

Kumar, R., P. D. Nunn, J. E. Field, and A. de Biran. 2006. Human responses to climate change around AD 1300: A case study of the Sigatoka Valley, Viti Levu Island, Fiji. *Quaternary International* 151: 133–143.

Ladd, H. S., and J. E. Hoffmeister. 1945. *Geology of Lau, Fiji.* B. P. Bishop Museum, Bulletin 181.

Li, Y. H., 1976. Denudation of Taiwan Island since the Pliocene epoch. *Geology* 4: 105–107.

———. 1988. Denudation rates of the Hawaiian Islands by rivers and groundwaters. *Pacific Science* 42: 253–266.

Löffler, E. 1977. *Geomorphology of Papua New Guinea.* Canberra: Australian National University.

———. 1982. Landforms. In *Papua New Guinea atlas: A nation in transition,* ed. D. King and S. Ranck, 82–83. Port Moresby: University of Papua New Guinea.

McLean, R. F., and P. L. Hosking. 1991. Geomorphology of reef islands and atoll *motu* in Tuvalu. *South Pacific Journal of Natural Science* 11: 167–189.

McNutt, M., and H. W. Menard. 1978. Lithospheric flexure and uplifted atolls. *Journal of Geophysical Research* 83: 1206–1212.

Montaggioni, L. F. 1985. Makatea island, Tuamotu archipelago. *Proceedings of the 5th International Coral Reef Congress* 1: 103–158.

Moore, J. G. 1970. Relationship between subsidence and volcanic load, Hawaii. *Bulletin Volcanologique* 34: 562–575.

Moore, J. G., and G. W. Moore. 1984. Deposit from a giant wave on the island of Lanai, Hawaii. *Science* 226: 1312–1315.

Morhange, C. 1992. Essai de quantification de l'évolution géomorphologique d'un archipel volcanique tropical né d'un point chaud: le cas des iles de la Société en Polynésie française. *Zeitschrift für Geomorphologie* 36: 307–324.

Myers, N. 1988. Environmental degradation and some economic consequences in the Philippines. *Environmental Conservation* 15: 205–214.

Nunn, P. D. 1987. Small islands and geomorphology: Review and prospect in the context of historical geomorphology. *Transactions of the Institute of British Geographers,* New Series 12: 227–239.

———. 1990. Recent coastline changes and their implications for future changes in the Cook Islands, Fiji, Kiribati, the Solomon Islands, Tonga, Tuvalu, Vanuatu and Western Samoa. In *Implications of expected climate changes in the South Pacific region: An overview,* ed. J. C. Pernetta and P. J. Hughes, 149–160. UNEP Regional Seas Reports and Studies 128.

———. 1992. *Keimami sa vakila na liga ni Kalou (Feeling the hand of God): Human and nonhuman impacts on Pacific Island environments,* 2nd rev. ed. East-West Center, Occasional Paper.

———. 1993. The role of Porolithon algal-ridge growth in the development of the windward coast of Tongatapu island, Tonga, South Pacific. *Earth-Surface Processes and Landforms* 18: 427–439.

———. 1994a. *Oceanic islands.* Oxford: Blackwell.

———. 1994b. Beyond the native lands: Human history and environmental change in the Pacific Basin. In *The margin fades: Geographical itineraries in a world of islands,* ed. E. Waddell and P. D. Nunn, 5–27. Suva: Institute of Pacific Studies, University of the South Pacific.

———. 1995. Holocene sea-level changes in the south and west Pacific. *Journal of Coastal Research,* Special Issue 17: 311–319.

———. 1996. *Emerged shorelines of the Lau Islands.* Fiji Mineral Resources Department, Memoir.

———. 1997. *Keimami sa vakila na liga ni kalou (Feeling the hand of God): Human and nonhuman impacts on Pacific Island environments,* 3rd ed. Suva: University of the South Pacific, School of Social and Economic Development.

———. 1998. *Pacific Island landscapes.* Suva: Institute of Pacific Studies, University of the South Pacific.

———. 1999. *Environmental Change in the Pacific Basin: Chronologies, causes, consequences.* London: Wiley.

———. 2000. Environmental catastrophe in the Pacific Islands about AD 1300. *Geoarchaeology* 15: 715–740.

———. 2001. Ecological crises or marginal disruptions: The effects of the first humans on Pacific Islands. *New Zealand Geographer* 57: 11–20.

———. 2003. Revising ideas about environmental determinism: Human-environment relations in the Pacific Islands. *Asia-Pacific Viewpoint* 44: 63–72.

———. 2004. Through a mist on the ocean: Human understanding of island environments. *Tijdschrift voor Economische en Sociale Geografie* 95: 311–325.

———. 2007a. *Climate, environment and society in the Pacific during the last millennium.* Amsterdam: Elsevier.

———. 2007b. The AD 1300 Event in the Pacific Basin: Overview and teleconnections. *The Geographical Review* 97: 1–23.

———. 2009. *Vanished islands and hidden continents of the Pacific.* Honolulu: University of Hawai'i Press.

Nunn, P. D., and F. T. Finau. 1995. Late Holocene emergence history of Tongatapu Island, South Pacific. *Zeitschrift für Geomorphologie* NF 39: 69–95.

Nunn, P. D., R. Hunter-Anderson, M. T. Carson, F. Thomas, S. Ulm, and M. Rowland. 2007. Times of plenty, times of less: Chronologies of last-millennium societal disruption in the Pacific Basin. *Human Ecology: An Interdisciplinary Journal* 35: 385–402.

Ollier, C. D., and C. F. Pain. 1978. Geomorphology and tectonics of Woodlark Island, Papua New Guinea. *Zeitschrift für Geomorphologie* NF 22: 20–22.

Onda, Y. 1994. Seepage erosion and its implication to the formation of amphitheatre valley heads: A case study at Obara, Japan. *Earth Surface Processes and Landforms* 19: 627–640.

Paskoff, R. 1978. Aspects géomorphologiques de l'île de Pacques. *Bulletin de l'Association Géographique du France* 452: 142–157.

Paulay, G., and T. Spencer. 1988. Geomorphology, palaeoenvironments and faunal turnover, Henderson Island, S.E. Polynesia. *Proceedings of the 6th International Coral Reef Symposium* 3: 461–466.

Peart, M. 1991. The Kaiapit landslide: Events and mechanisms. *Quarterly Journal of Engineering Geology* 24: 399–411.

Pickup, G., R. J. Higgins, and R. F. Warner. 1980. Erosion and sediment yield in the Fly River drainage basins, Papua New Guinea. *Publications of the International Association of Hydrological Sciences* 132: 438–456.

Pillans, B. 1986. A late Quaternary uplift map for North Island, New Zealand. *Royal Society of New Zealand, Bulletin* 24: 409–417.

Pillans, B., W. A. Pullar, M. J. Selby, and J. M. Soons. 1992. The age and development of the New Zealand landscape. In *Landforms of New Zealand,* 2nd ed., ed. J. M. Soon and M. J. Selby. Auckland: Longman Paul.

Pirazzoli, P. A., and L. F. Montaggioni. 1988. Holocene sea-level changes in French Polynesia. *Palaeogeography, Palaeoclimatology, Palaeoecology* 68: 153–175.

Roy, P. S. 1990. The morphology and surface geology of the islands of Tongatapu and Vava'u, Kingdom of Tonga. United Nations ESCAP, CCOP/SOPAC Technical Report 62.

Schmalz, R. F. 1971. Beachrock formation on Eniwetok Atoll. In *Carbonate cement,* ed. O. P. Bricker, 17–24. Johns Hopkins University, Studies in Geology.

Schofield, J. C. 1959. *The geology and hydrology of Niue Island, South Pacific.* Wellington: New Zealand Geological Survey (Bulletin 62).

Scott, G. A. J., and J. M. Street. 1976. The role of chemical weathering in the formation of Hawaiian amphitheatre-headed valleys. *Zeitschrift für Geomorphologie,* NF 20: 171–189.

Spriggs, M., and A. Anderson. 1993. Late colonization of East Polynesia. *Antiquity* 67: 200–217.

Stevenson, J., and J. R. Dodson. 1995. Palaeoenvironmental evidence for human settlement of New Caledonia. *Archaeology in Oceania* 30: 36–41.

Stoddart, D. R., and T. P. Scoffin. 1983. Phosphate rock on coral reef islands. In *Chemical sediments and geomorphology,* ed. A. S. Goudie and K. Pye, 369–400. London: Academic Press.

Stoddart, D. R., C. D. Woodroffe, and T. Spencer. 1990. Mauke, Mitiaro and Atiu: geomorphology of makatea islands in the southern Cooks. *Atoll Research Bulletin* 341.

Strecker, M., A. L. Bloom, and J. Lecolle. 1987. Time span for karst development on Quaternary coral limestones: Santo Island, Vanuatu. In *Processus et mesure de l'érosion,* ed. A. Godard and A. Rapp, 369–386. Paris: Editions du Centre National de la Recherche Scientifique.

Thomas, N. 1990. *Marquesan societies.* New York: Oxford University Press.

Webster, J. M., D. A. Clague, and J. C. Braga. 2007. Support for the giant wave hypothesis: Evidence from submerged terraces off Lanai, Hawaii. *International Journal of Earth Sciences* 96: 517–524.

Williams, P. W. 1972. Morphometric analysis of polygonal karst in New Guinea. *Geological Society of America, Bulletin* 83: 761–796.

Wright, L. W. 1973. Landforms of the Yavuna granite area, Viti Levu, Fiji: A morphometric study. *Journal of Tropical Geography* 37: 74–80.

Young, R. W., and E. A. Bryant. 1992. Catastrophic wave erosion on the southeast coast of Australia: Impact of the Lanai tsunamis ca. 105 ka? *Geology* 20: 199–202.

Zan, Y., and R. L. Hunter-Anderson. 1987. On the origins of the Micronesian "savannahs": An anthropological perspective. In *Proceedings of the Third international Soil Management Workshop for the Management and Utilization of Acid Soils in Micronesia, February 2–6, 1987, Republic of Palau,* ed. J. L. Demeterio and B. DeGuzman, 18–27. Agricultural Experiment Station, College of Agriculture and Life Sciences, University of Guam.

Soils

R. John Morrison

5

Soils are one of the major resources of Pacific Islanders. Despite the islanders' dependence on the marine environment, soils are the source of a major proportion of the food, building materials, clothing, and medicines. The islands vary enormously in size, geomorphology, and geology, with a resultant diversity in soils. From the small atolls to the large continental islands, traditional technologies have been developed to effectively utilize this invaluable resource (Morrison et al. 1994). Many Pacific Island groups earn significant portions of their foreign exchange earnings through the export of agricultural and forest products (Browne 2006).

The Pacific Islands region covers a vast area extending from the Northern Marianas and Hawai'i in the north to French Polynesia and New Zealand in the south. This encompasses at least twenty-five countries and territories. Given the space limitations on this chapter, it is impossible to adequately discuss separately the soils of each of these island groups. The emphasis will, therefore, be on the factors and processes controlling the soil patterns in the region and issues relating to soil management, including erosion.

One of the difficulties encountered when discussing Pacific Island soils is classification, as important changes have taken place over the past fifty years. In the past thirty years or so, the system of soil classification most widely used in the Pacific Islands has been Soil Taxonomy (Soil Survey Staff 1975, 1999). This system is commonly used throughout the world and is continually being modified as new information or better criteria for grouping soils become available. In this chapter, all soils are classified in accordance with the criteria of Soil Taxonomy.

Soil Distribution—Some General Comments

A review of the information available on Pacific Island soils (Morrison and Leslie 1982; Leslie 1984a; Asghar, Davidson, and Morrison 1988) shows that Inceptisols are the most abundant soils. There are also significant areas of Mollisols, Alfisols, Ultisols, Oxisols, Andisols, and Entisols, and smaller areas of other soils.

Inceptisols ("young soils") have discernible signs of genesis, but without major diagnostic features. These soils occur in a wide range of landform situations and parent materials, including highly resistant parent material and recent volcanic ash deposits. Their

characteristics vary significantly, from shallow to deep profiles, and from very sandy to clay-rich soils.

Mollisols ("soft soils") have a thick, dark, organic-rich, base-rich A horizon (the "topsoil"). These exceptionally fertile "prairie" soils develop through extension of grass roots into the ground and reworking of the soil by earthworms, ants, rodents, and other subsurface animal life. These soils are more common in the region than would be expected from a purely climatic and topographic basis.

Alfisols are base-rich, with an argillic (clay-enriched) B horizon. These soils are highly fertile, with adequate supplies of necessary minerals, clays, and nutrients. They are found in humid conditions, in areas where base-rich materials have weathered in a relatively stable landform position. They are found in small areas in several island groups and more widely in New Zealand.

Ultisols ("ultimate soils") are base-poor, with an argillic B horizon. These highly weathered soils, usually dominated by red and yellow colors, are found mainly in stable landscapes in the older parts of large islands. The bulk of the nutrients is often in the surface layer, and productivity diminishes with use. The problem can be alleviated by the application of fertilizers, but these soils must be protected from erosion if fertility is to be maintained.

Oxisols ("oxide soils") are deep, highly weathered, oxide-rich, red, base-poor soils. These soils have undergone desilication and ferritization (accumulation of iron oxyhydroxides) and are found in stable landform positions on older islands. They are usually free-draining and have good structural characteristics. Here too, fertility declines rapidly after a few seasons of use, when nutrients held mainly in topsoils become exhausted.

Andisols ("dark soils") are relatively young, derived mainly from volcanic ash, with a high content of allophane (a short-range-order clay mineral). These soils are found in Fiji, Hawai'i, New Zealand, Papua New Guinea, Samoa, Solomon Islands, and Vanuatu, derived from basaltic or andesitic ash. The areal extent is not great, but where they do occur, they are important agricultural soils.

Entisols are very young and lack well-developed horizons. These are dominant in atolls, on a base of coral sand, rubble, or reef limestone, and in coastal and riverine areas on larger islands. These soils, occurring in relatively flat terrain, are important for agriculture, even if they do have limitations due to their youth (e.g., sandiness, low water retention, flood hazard).

Vertisols ("inverted soils") are self-churning soils, usually dominated by expanding clays (smectites). These soils are found in limited areas on the larger islands where a significant dry season occurs.

Histosols ("organic soils") are dominated by organic materials. They are found where hydrological conditions allow the buildup of organic matter, as in swampy coastal alluvial plains, upland depressions, and calderas. Where they have been drained they have considerable agricultural significance.

Other soils uncommonly found include Spodosols and Aridisols. Spodosols ("ashy soils") are characterized by leaching of organic matter, iron, and aluminum from the upper soil layers. These soils are present in Hawai'i, New Caledonia, and Fiji, but are generally rare. Aridisols ("arid soils") are found in areas with dry climates. In the Pacific Islands they occur in very limited areas, such as rain shadow locations in Hawai'i.

The Pacific Islands region is generally wet, with few very dry zones. Soils are either udic (dry less than ninety days in any year), perudic (moist continually), or ustic (dry for ninety or more days in most years, but moist for more than half the year). Soils on windward coasts of the larger islands usually have udic or perudic moisture regimes; ustic soils are found in leeward rain shadow areas. On atolls, rainfall is often irregular, and the classic definition of soil moisture regimes holds little meaning.

Temperature regimes are generally either isohyperthermic (average soil temperature greater than 22°C) or isothermic (average temperature of 15° to 22°C, in both cases with minimal seasonal variation). At the highest elevations, above 3,000 m (or at lower elevations in New Zealand), cooler temperatures are found. The isohyperthermic/isothermic elevational boundary varies with latitude, but for most of the region the boundary lies at around 500 to 700 m above sea level.

Mineral components of Pacific soils commonly include clay aluminosilicates (kaolinite, halloysite, and smectite), aluminum and iron oxyhydroxides (gibbsite and goethite), and carbonates (calcite). On Niue and Nauru, soils may be dominated by phosphate minerals. There are significant areas of young volcanic ash soils dominated by the short-range-order (transient) minerals allophane, imogolite, or ferrihydrite, for example, in northern Vanuatu, in Taveuni, Fiji, in the Santa Cruz group in Solomon Islands, and in Savai'i, Samoa.

The soil profile observed at any given location is the result of all the pedogenetic processes operating. The nature and extent of the processes occurring are determined by a number of soil-forming factors, which are discussed below.

Factors of Soil Formation

Climate

Climate is perhaps the most important factor in soil formation (providing sufficient time is available), as it determines, to a marked degree, the extent of weathering, the vegetation cover, and hydrological patterns.

Climate includes rainfall and temperature components and has varied over geological time. For the Pacific Islands, formation of most soils has taken place during the Quaternary (the last two million years), although older soils are found. While world climate has varied during the Quaternary (Dodson 1992), the Pacific Islands have generally been relatively wet and warm throughout this period.

Factors influencing soil temperature in the Pacific Islands include elevation and aspect. The drop in temperature with elevation varies with distance from the equator, but averages about 1°C for each 100-m rise in elevation. Most locations in the Pacific Islands have a relatively high mean annual temperature, with minimal seasonal variation. Consequently, the water percolating the soil is always warm (around 25°C), leading to relatively rapid weathering, vegetation growth, and microbiological activity.

Two rainfall parameters are important: mean annual rainfall and temporal distribution. Definition of the dry season is a problem, but it usually includes the months in which the soil has a water deficit (in which evapotranspiration exceeds rainfall). The principal effects of rainfall relate to leaching, determined by the volume of water passing through the profile. In the large Pacific islands, there is often a marked difference in rainfall between windward and leeward sides (see Table 5.1), leading to significant soil differences.

Table 5.1

Average Rainfall Data (mm) for Suva (Windward Side) and Nadi (Leeward Side), Fiji Islands

	J	F	M	A	M	J	J	A	S	O	N	D	YEAR
Suva	324	315	383	385	254	172	147	140	209	220	266	272	3087
Nadi	293	293	358	185	84	71	48	61	87	95	142	175	1892

Source: Fiji Meteorological Service, Information Sheets 21, 53, 71.

Climate affects organic matter content, base saturation, profile depth, texture, and clay mineral synthesis (Young 1976; Buol, Hole, and McCracken 1980). Topsoil organic matter (and associated nitrogen content) increases with increasing rainfall and with a fall in temperature (which retards decomposition). Increased rainfall tends to decrease pH, base saturation, and the silt-to-clay ratio. High temperature and rainfall cause leaching and result in desilication and ferritization. Gibbsite is found where temperature and leaching are high throughout the year; smectites (expanding clays), occur where the profile dries out seasonally.

Parent Material

The parent material of soils may consist of solid rock, regolith, volcanic ash, alluvial deposits, beach sands, or a previous soil profile. Three main attributes of parent materials influencing pedogenesis are the degree of consolidation, grain size, and mineral composition.

Pedogenesis can usually be evaluated once the initial state can be identified. This is one of the most important problems in soil development studies, as the parent material can be identified only by inference. It is not sufficient to dig through the soil to reach rock unaltered by weathering and assume this is the parent material. Such an assumption would be incorrect when the soil is derived from a thin superficial drift deposit, or from rocks higher up the slope, or when the underlying rock is nonhomogeneous.

The common parent materials in the Pacific Islands are volcanic basalts (as in Samoa) or andesites (Chioseul, Solomon Islands); volcanic ash and scoria (a porous volcanic rock, heavier than pumice) (Taveuni, Fiji); weathered uplifted mantle material (New Caledonia); carbonates (Funafuti, Tuvalu); sediments derived from volcanics (north Guadalcanal, Solomon Islands); sediments of mixed origin (Muri series, Rarotonga, the Cook Islands); uplifted marine sediments (southeast Viti Levu, Fiji); phosphates (Nauru); or decomposed organic matter (Kuk, Papua New Guinea).

The highly active tectonic nature of the region has led to interesting situations. In Tongatapu (Tonga), the island is covered with soils derived from andesitic tephra (Cowie 1980). These soils overlie a raised coral platform. The tephra varies in depth from about 5 m in the west to just over 1 m in the east, suggesting an origin in the volcanic islands to the west of Tongatapu. Two distinct tephra deposits have been recognized, the older (approximately 20,000 years old) giving rise to yellowish brown clays and the younger (less than 5,000 years old) giving rise to reddish brown clays and clay loams (soils of balanced texture).

The influence of volcanic ash on Pacific Islands soils cannot be overemphasized. Even in islands where ash is not a major soil parent material, ash additions from the numerous active volcanoes in the region have occurred in many locations. Even on atolls, the influence of pumice and scoria transported by sea has been recognized as important, with atoll residents collecting the washed-up material and adding it to their most productive garden soils.

Interesting parent material investigations have been conducted on Niue. Initially, interest was aroused by the radioactivity in the soils, detected by Fieldes in 1955 (Marsden, Ferguson, and Fieldes 1958). The exact source of the radiation has been the subject of considerable debate for more than forty years. The problem relates not to identifying the isotopes responsible, but to determining how they got there. For example, ^{230}Th and ^{231}Pa are present in relatively large amounts, but the parent isotopes ^{235}U, ^{238}U, and ^{240}U occur in only very small quantities.

The favored explanation at present (Whitehead et al. 1992) is that after the formation of weathered soils on the surface of the island, it was submerged for a period during a high-sea-level event. During the submergence, gibbsite- and goethite-rich soils adsorbed elements from seawater, including uranium. Upon re-emergence, the uranium daughter products accumulated, followed by leaching of uranium. The soils of Niue represent one of the most unique geochemical situations encountered in Pacific Island soils.

Relief and Landform

The major influence here is that of slope. Slope effects can be observed in the depth of the profile; the wetness, color, thickness and organic matter content of the surface horizon; the base saturation; and the presence and nature of pans (highly compacted layers). Relief has a direct effect on climate: precipitation through orographic uplift, and temperature through aspect (slope in relation to the sun). Relief also affects hydrology and vegetation.

Two very different classes of islands are present: atolls and other limestone islands with low relief (although raised coral islands have small areas of very steep slopes resulting from uplift), and volcanic and continental islands with steep, mountainous country deeply

incised by rivers and streams. In Fiji, steepland (slopes greater than 18°) covers 68 percent of the land surface, and rolling country (slopes 3° to 18°) 21 percent, with areas of low relief (less than 3°) representing only 11 percent. A similar picture is found in Samoa and many other high-island groups.

Relatively dry, oxidized (redder) soils are found in low-relief upper slope positions; wetter, grayer soils are found in toeslopes. In steep positions, soils are generally shallow, but there is significant variability in the region. In younger islands dominated by volcanic flows (e.g., Upolu, Samoa), soils are generally very shallow and stony, often occurring in patches on the slope where eroded material accumulates. In older islands (New Caledonia), or where volcanic ash is dominant (Taveuni, Fiji), weathering has proceeded to much greater depth, and the profiles on slopes greater than 20° can often be more than 1 m deep.

Hydrology

In some cases, soil materials are saturated with water for long enough that all the oxygen in the profile is removed and long enough for reducing (deoxygenated or anaerobic) conditions to prevail. The consequences include soils that are characterized by gray colors (due to Fe^{2+} species) or (when the soils are saturated for long periods but dry out long enough to allow some oxidation of iron to occur) extensive mottling (multiple colors). If the soils are saturated almost all the time ("gley soils"), organic matter decomposition is severely inhibited due to lack of oxygen, and Histosols may develop.

The main cause of wetness is impeded drainage. This is often caused by the presence of groundwater near the surface, but can be related to other landscape features. A typical situation is found at the bottom of slopes, where downward water slows and moves into the soil surface. If the profile at this point contains a layer that impedes drainage, the surface layers can become saturated for quite long periods, leading to reducing conditions. Decay is then inhibited and organic material accumulates. This is most prominent in the upper layers of the profile, giving rise to a surface water gley or pseudogley. A classic example occurs at Koronovia in Fiji (Leslie 1984b).

Soils showing a marked influence of wetness occur in coasts, lowlands, and poorly drained uplands. Reducing conditions generally occur in mangrove areas, as the soils are subject to water immersion and major surface additions of organic matter. These areas have often been cleared, particularly in backswamp locations, to facilitate intensive agriculture. This has resulted in acid sulfate soils (e.g., at Dreketi and Bua, on Vanua Levu, Fiji), and subsequent agricultural developments have proved either technically or economically unviable (Lal 1990).

Vegetation

As the main contributor of organic material, vegetation is one of the most important formative agents of soil. Vegetation is in turn dependent largely on climate.

Apart from the atolls, forests were probably the dominant vegetation on most islands prior to human contact. Palynological (pollen) studies (see Southern 1986) indicate that in some islands, grasslands developed during drier climates in the late Quaternary.

In some locations, grassland establishment coincided with the arrival of the first human settlers. Most grasslands are found where a marked dry season occurs and where fire may have a significant effect (such as North Guadalcanal, Solomon Islands, and Southern Highlands, Papua New Guinea).

Even after grasslands have become established, the effects of burning can be a significant factor in soil transformation. In the Guadalcanal Plains, for example, regular burning, with the loss of organic matter, has contributed to soils deficient in sulfur (Chase and Widdowson 1983). On other islands, the soils of areas that have burned regularly have been found to be lower in organic matter and nitrogen than comparable soils with lower frequency of burning (Morrison, Naidu, and Singh 1987).

On atolls, soils with undisturbed vegetation cover often have a well-developed, organic-rich A horizon. Disturbance of the native vegetation leads to a rapid reduction in the organic matter content and thinning of the A horizon (Morrison and Seru 1986). A special situation of vegetation influence on atolls is the Jemo series, identified by Fosberg (1954, 1957) in the Marshall Islands. This unique soil, with layered phosphatic material in the B horizon, appears to form under exclusively Pisonia vegetation, with the acidic decomposing organic matter combining with guano and coral limestone to produce the phosphate layers.

Time

Most Pacific islands are relatively young in geological terms, with the period of soil formation restricted to the Quaternary. Some very young parent materials are known. These include volcanic ash in Savai'i, Samoa, and Taveuni, Fiji, that is less than a thousand years old; recent alluvium deposits in the deltas of some of the major rivers; and coral sand deposited in coastal areas. Older soils and parent materials have been identified in Fiji, New Caledonia, and Solomon Islands, and Tertiary limestone has been identified on numerous raised islands (Guam, Niue, and Vatu Vara in Fiji).

Given the climate of the region, the rates of weathering and soil formation are relatively fast, with significant profile development occurring in one thousand years or less in some locations. Identification of chronosequences to facilitate studies on soil formation rates has proved difficult in the Pacific Islands, but attempts have been made to examine age sequences in a few locations. One of the best has been in Samoa, where the parent materials are dominantly basaltic lava flows.

The work of Wright (1963) and Schroth (1971) has shown that recent (less than three hundred years ago) flows have very weakly developed stony soils, while flows dating from 150 Ka have profiles of up to 60 cm deep with significant clay contents and base saturation. Flows dating from the Tertiary (2 to 2.5 Ma) have deep, oxidic profiles and are base-poor. This picture is clouded by the influence of ash additions to the soil surface during each period of volcanic activity.

An unusual chronosequence has been provided by the phosphate rock mining activities on Nauru. Mining left behind phosphate materials in which soil formation occurred. As the dates of mining were accurately known, it was possible to examine the rate of soil development through the accumulation of carbon and nitrogen (Figure 5.1; Manner and Morrison 1991).

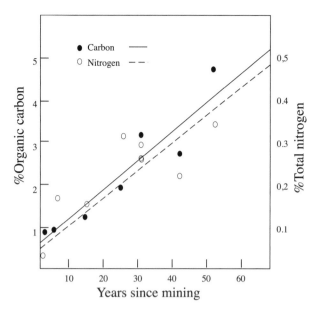

Figure 5.1. *The rate of soil development on Nauru as shown by the accumulation of carbon and nitrogen (Manner and Morrison 1991).*

On older, stable landforms, where the processes of weathering and pedogenesis have been operating for long periods, Oxisols and other oxic soils tend to dominate. This has been observed in Fiji (Morrison et al. 1987), Guam (Young 1988), New Caledonia (Latham, Quantin, and Aubert 1978), Palau (Smith 1983), and Solomon Islands (Wall and Hansell 1976).

Human Beings

The role of human beings in soil genesis has been recognized in many locations. In the Pacific Islands, these effects manifest themselves through the impacts caused by slope modification, as in terraces for yam and taro production (Kuhlken 1994; Roe 1989) and vegetation change associated with fire and erosion. Other human-related effects that have been observed are the effects of drainage (discussed above) and intensive grazing, particularly of goats on very small islands. The extent of such impacts varies enormously in the region, from small terraces to major areas of vegetation change on some islands.

Processes of Soil Formation

The processes of soil formation are summarized in Figure 5.2 (modified from Simonson 1959). The processes are not unique to the Pacific Islands, but some processes are of greater importance due to the prevailing environmental conditions. The dominant climatic conditions in the region (high temperatures and rainfall) are especially conducive to high weathering rates. The generally wet conditions mean that chemical weathering is dominant, with primary minerals being rapidly attacked. In addition, the relatively high temperatures contribute to the high weathering rates because:

(a) ionization of water increases with temperature, making it more corrosive;

(b) the solubility of most substances in water increases with temperature;

(c) reactions (such as solution) proceed more rapidly with increasing temperature;

(d) water viscosity decreases with increasing temperature, and water penetrates farther into the rock or soil.

In the Pacific Islands, the dominant soil-forming processes are associated with organic matter additions, humification (organic matter decomposition and incorporation), mineral transformations, and water movement through the profile. Organic matter production is generally high, leading to the depositing of significant litter on the soil surface, where decomposition soon ensues. Organic matter turnover is usually quite rapid, unless some feature of the vegetation or the location (wetness, elevation, aspect) leads to accumulation.

Water movements through the profile lead to eluviation (removal of materials from upper layers), illuviation (deposition of material in lower layers), leaching of weathering products, and the availability of water for mineral transformation reactions. Desilication is common in soils derived from aluminosilicate parent materials, with the accumulation of aluminum and iron oxyhydroxides increasing with time. Evidence of illuviation (such as clay "skins" on the surface of soil structural units) is common in Pacific soils derived from volcanic materials in stable landform positions.

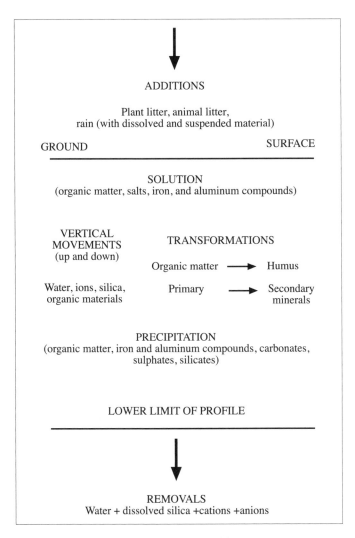

Figure 5.2. *Diagrammatic representation of soil-forming processes.*

Spodic horizons (caused by the movement of aluminum, iron, and organic matter down the profile in solution) are rare, as the necessary conditions of vegetation, water, and parent material occur infrequently. Water movements in profiles are such that the accumulation of carbonate or soluble salts in soils is extremely rare.

Soils Use and Management

The major factors affecting use are soil properties (for example, depth, slope, drainage, nutrient status), climate, and proximity to potential markets. The proximity of markets is particularly important for food crops, which are grown close to many urban centers for local sale. Export-oriented crops (sugar, cocoa, coffee, tea, and oil palm) are often grown at distances from markets in areas with suitable climate and soils, with the exception of fresh fruit, such as, papaya, which is exported by air and therefore grown relatively close to the points of export.

For the larger islands (>1000 km²), climate differences between the windward and leeward sides of the islands are often very important (see Table 5.1). Crops adapted to a period of water stress in their life cycle are grown predominantly on the drier sides of the islands, while drought-sensitive crops are grown on the windward sides. Thus sugar and oil palm are usually found on deep soils in areas with a marked dry season (Viti Levu, Fiji, and Guadalcanal, Solomon Islands, respectively), while taro, rice, and cocoa are found in wetter areas. For the smaller islands, the climate effects are less marked, and on the atolls, there is effectively no rainfall variation.

In the larger islands, there are extensive areas of acid soils (in this context, acid soils are considered as soils with pH in water (1:1) of less than 5.5 and where the exchange complex has significant levels of aluminum present) (Table 5.2). The main factor contributing to this extensive area of acid soils in the region is the hot and wet climate (high rates of weathering and leaching). Some human activities (land clearance and burning) lead to more acid soils while others (mulching, addition of coral sand) may help to maintain the fertility and reduce the rate of acidification.

Overall, Pacific Island acid soils are generally underutilized. Many countries could significantly increase their agricultural production with the development of appropriate management strategies. Factors to be considered in this context include the use of lime and fertilizers, the introduction or development of acid-tolerant crops, including tree crops, the more efficient use of available water, and the provision of a guaranteed market for the increased production (Morrison, Naidu, and Singh 1988; Morrison et al. 1989).

On atolls, soil properties are largely dominated by the calcareous nature of the parent material, even where this has been covered with volcanic ash or other materials. The soils tend to be shallow, alkaline, and coarse-textured, having carbonatic mineralogy with a very low silica content. Fertility can be high in undisturbed soils under natural vegetation, but can decrease dramatically as a result of inappropriate cultivation techniques (land clearance and fire).

As for all tropical soils, organic matter in coralline soils performs an important role in the concentration and cycling of plant nutrients. Since Pacific Island carbonate soils are frequently sandy and excessively well drained, organic matter has a second key role—that of moisture retention. The moisture retention in the absence of organic matter is very low (see Figure 5.3). The total amount

Table 5.2

Extent of Acid Soils in Some Pacific Island Countries

Country/ Territory	Aerial extent of acid soils %	Comments
American Samoa	20–40	Volcanic soils (Mollisols and Andisols)
Cook Islands	40–60	Volcanic soils
Fed. States of Micronesia	60–80	Volcanic soils and soils derived from continental type rocks
Fiji	40–50	Derived from volcanics and associated sediments
French Polynesia	60–70	Volcanic soils
Guam	20–25	Often steepland soils
New Caledonia	40–50	Derived from metamorphic rocks, volcanic rocks, including ultramafics
Northern Marianas	20–40	Volcanic soils
Palau	80	Volcanic soils
Papua New Guinea	8–15	Mainly wet lowland soils
Samoa	10–20	Volcanic (basaltic soils)
Solomon Islands	40–50	Volcanic soils
Tonga	5–10	Volcanic soils
Vanuatu	30–50	Volcanic soils
Wallis and Futuna	70–80	Volcanic soils

of water retained in the soil profile often remains low, and plants are subject to water stress unless the rainfall is high and relatively constant, or unless the local groundwater can be tapped.

Soils derived from carbonate materials have a wide range of uses despite their limitations. Such materials are the only soils in several island groups (Tuvalu, Tokelau) and are common soils in other groups (the Cook Islands, French Polynesia). Inhabitants of these islands have developed agricultural practices to produce a wide range of crops on such soils. These include coconuts, pandanus, breadfruit, citrus, and vegetables, with the specific practices and crops dependent on local factors, including the rainfall pattern. The use of mulches and pits dug down to the water table are among the practices utilized to achieve significant production (Small 1972; Chase 1992).

Soil Erosion

In many Pacific islands, environmental conditions (heavy rain, steep slopes) indicate a high potential for soil erosion. Despite the obvious evidence of erosion in rivers (sediment loads) and on the land surface (rills and gullies) there is remarkably little experimental data on erosion rates. There is a dearth of measurements from erosion plots and only a limited amount of information from other techniques, e.g., erosion stakes, sediment loads.

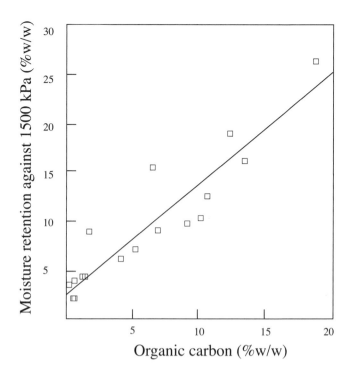

Figure 5.3. *The variation in moisture retention with organic matter content for some Tarawa soils. 1.5 MPa is the maximum suction force plants can exert (Morrison and Seru 1986).*

In Fiji, Glatthaar (1988) and Liedtke (1989) measured soil losses of 22 to 80 t/ha/yr on slopes of 5° to 29° in a sugar cane growing area north of Nadi. In the Waimanu catchment (in southeastern Viti Levu, Fiji), erosion was about 53 t/ha/yr. Landslides are clearly visible on steep slopes of the larger islands. A major rainstorm in April 1986 caused some 620 landslides in the Waimanu catchment alone, corresponding to a soil movement of 92 t/ha/yr or 3.5 mm over the whole catchment. Field observations of soil loss in Fiji using erosion stakes or profile reference points were reported by Clarke and Morrison (1987), who calculated soil losses of 90 to 300 t/ha/yr for areas where forest or indigenous grassland were converted to intensive sugar cane production.

The factors contributing to soil erosion are rainfall (erosivity), soils (erodibility), topography, vegetative cover, and erosion control practices. Erosivity (the ability of the rain to cause erosion) is closely related to rainfall intensity. In the Pacific Islands, rainfall intensity data are very limited. Calculation of erosion index (EI) values (see Hudson 1981) is possible for only a few locations. Examination of rainfall data for Fiji led to the following EI values (Ambika Prasad and J. Morrison, unpublished results):

Suva (Laucala Bay)	1,210
Nadi (Airport)	930 (utilizing all rains over 10 mm/hr)
Sigatoka	817

The limited rainfall intensity information suggests that EI values are >500/yr for most of the region. These EI values are extremely high when compared with figures of 100 to 500 throughout the major agricultural areas of the world.

Wischmeier and Mannering (1969) describe erodibility of a soil as "a complex property dependent both on its infiltration capacity and on its capacity to resist detachment and transport by rainfall and runoff." Erodibility is therefore dependent on properties such as particle size distribution, organic matter content, presence of structure-cementing agents (such as iron and aluminum oxyhydroxides), the nature of the clay minerals, and ion chemical balance. These five properties largely determine the stability of soil aggregates. Bulk density, a measure of soil compactness (g/cm^3), and air-filled pore space determine the infiltration characteristics.

Much of the regional landscape is dominated by steep, mountainous country, deeply incised by rivers and streams. Since much of the surface runoff following heavy rain is over steep slopes, the erosivity of the water is markedly increased. Steep slopes lead to frequent landslides following heavy rain. On several sites where indirect studies of erosion have taken place, the rates have been much lower than expected based on site characteristics. One explanation may be very high water infiltration rates, such as those observed by Willatt, Suqa, and Limalevu (1995). On a Typic Humitropept (an Inceptisol) having slopes up to 30°, infiltration rates having an arithmetic mean >200 mm/h were measured, with only 14 mm runoff out of 1,300 mm of rainfall.

Vegetative cover is an important factor in erosion control since this intercepts much of the rainfall and reduces the energy of its impact on the soil surface. Vegetation has the added advantage (over other types of soil cover) that it is rooted in the soil, and the roots help to keep the soil in place. In the Pacific Islands, plant growth is rapid due to the abundant rain and tropical temperatures. It is unusual for bare soil surfaces to remain so for any length of time under natural conditions. However, the harvesting of crops, the clearing of land for agriculture, logging, and certain construction activities all lead to extensive removal of the vegetative cover on the soil, contributing to erosion.

Erosion-control measures include biological methods involving maximum cover of the soil surface (mulch, cover crops, and mixed cropping), and mechanical measures (terracing). Biological methods are usually more efficient than mechanical, and the mechanical methods can lead to even greater problems if not properly designed and executed. The use of buffer strips involving vetiver grass or pineapples or legume trees, and tillage along the contour, have proved very effective erosion-control measures in the region.

A major problem encountered in assessing soil erosion in the Pacific Islands is the absence of data on erosion rates under "natural" conditions. This is understandable given the difficulties in locating suitable situations and attempting to carry out appropriate experiments in such isolated locations. Without such information, conclusions about the impact of people on the rates of erosion must obviously be speculative.

Suspended Sediment Loads in Rivers

Another method of examining erosion rates is by studying the movement of suspended sediment in rivers. A survey of sediment loads carried by rivers to the coastal zone in Oceania has been made using available (both published and unpublished) data (Asquith, Kooge, and Morrison 1994). The method of calculating sediment yield selected was that of Fournier (1960). The results of the sediment yield calculations for the South Pacific islands indicate a total regional annual sediment load in rivers of 2.49 x 10^9 t (with Papua New Guinea producing 2.02 x 10^9 t/yr of this total).

The sediment yield estimate of approximately 2.5 x 10^9 t/yr is not unrealistic in the light of the global sediment budgets/flux calculations of Walling and Webb (1987), Milliman and Mead (1983), and Milliman (1990a, b). Milliman (1990b) noted that global fluvial sediment flux estimated by the Fournier method was 32 to 51 x 10^9 t/yr. While this estimate is probably high (current opinion puts the value at more like 15 x 10^9 t/yr), there is a general consensus in the literature that the contribution from Oceania represents a considerable proportion of the global value. Milliman (1990b) noted that Southern Asia and Oceania (in this definition including Island Southeast Asia and New Zealand) contribute more than 70 percent of the world's sediment flux, with Oceania discharging 3 x 10^9 t/yr of sediment to the ocean (Figure 5.4). This is close to the value obtained independently by Asquith et al. (1994).

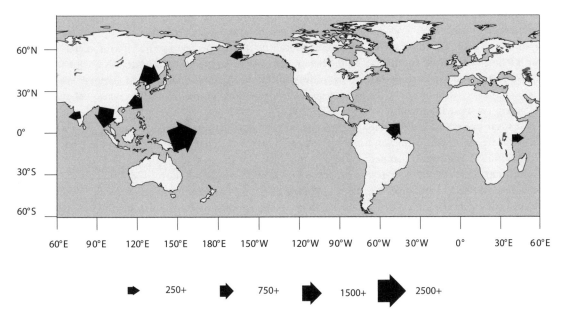

Figure 5.4. Outflow of sediment from the world's major rivers; numbers are in millions of tons/year (after Milliman 1990b).

Nutrient Losses via Soil Erosion

In addition to the physical damage brought about by soil erosion, the transported materials, being derived mainly from topsoils, carry with them significant quantities of valuable plant nutrients. This is particularly important in the Pacific Islands, where, for many soils, the surface layer represents the "richest" part of the whole profile. This is well illustrated for two Fiji soils by the data in Table 5.3.

Table 5.3

Topsoil and Subsoil Nutrient Data for Two Fiji Pedons

Soil	Depth (cm)	%C	%N	Ext. P mg/kg	Exch K	Cations Ca	(cmol/kg) Mg
SQ2	0–15	6.67	0.41	42	0.26	3.00	1.27
	15–50	0.76	0.07	8	0.03	0.16	0.05
KBA-S	0–10	8.00	0.51	28	0.25	3.90	1.84
	10–34	2.78	0.19	15	0.09	0.38	0.28

Source: Data from Morrison et al. 1987b.

This transport of nutrients represents two environmental hazards: the loss of valuable plant growth resources, which is detrimental for agriculture, and the movement of nutrients in the coastal zone, where they may contribute to eutrophication (nutrient overload) and related problems. Nutrient loss contributes to the generally low agricultural yields noted in the region (Morrison, Naidu, and Singh 1987) and the increased agricultural use of marginal land, which further exacerbates the erosion/sedimentation problem (Morrison et al. 1990).

Impacts of Intensive Agriculture on Soils

With rising populations and costs of imported foodstuffs, there is an increasing requirement for greater food production in the Pacific Islands. This, in turn, will occur with greater intensification of agriculture and is likely to have significant impacts on soils in the absence of good soil management. Limited information is available on the impacts of intensive agriculture on Pacific Island soils. One study has examined changes in soils following intensive sugar cane cultivation in Fiji over a twenty-five-year period (Morrison and Masilaca 1989; Morrison, Gawander, and Ram 2005).

Sugar cane has been planted in Fiji for more than a hundred years. Attractive markets and good sugar prices in the 1970s led to expansion onto virgin land to enhance sugar production and increase national foreign exchange earnings. The largest planned expansion occurred on the island of Vanua Levu, including a new production area in the Seaqaqa region (located around 16°31'S, 179°07'E) producing about 300,000 tons of sugar cane from approximately 6,000 ha of land under cane. Prior to sugar cane cultivation, the Seaqaqa area was dominated by *talasiga* (literally "sunburned" land) grasslands (consisting of *Sporobolus* and *Pennisetum* grasses with *Dicranopteris* and *Pteridium* ferns) or poor secondary forest of *Acacia, Syzygium,* and *Fagraea* spp. The introduction of sugar cane onto virgin land in Seaqaqa provided an opportunity to study the changes in important soil chemical and physical properties over time with intensive crop cultivation.

This study was conducted on a typical sugar cane farm located on rolling terrain. Prior to "natural" vegetation removal and land disturbance or planting of sugar cane, a soil survey was carried out, and an area of approximately 0.2 ha was selected for the detailed study. The soil was classified as a Typic Haplustox, clayey, oxidic, isohyperthermic (Soil Survey Staff 1975)—a deep, well-drained, moderately structured, oxide-rich, nutrient-poor soil. The site was located on a slightly convex 8° slope 60 m long, with a southeast aspect. Soil samples were collected from three depths (0 to 20, 30 to 40, and 70 to 80 cm) prior to sugar cane planting and at regular time intervals thereafter, and analyzed for parameters including pH, organic carbon content, total nitrogen, ion exchange properties, bulk density, and water retention capacity (full details of methods are given in Morrison, Gawander, and Ram 2005).

Results of the analyses of the topsoil samples are summarized in Table 5.4. The pH of the soil samples decreased (from 5.5 to 4.4) with increasing period of cultivation and this may be attributed to the effect of various changes. The observed pH decrease could be due to the combination of the decrease in organic matter content, addition of N fertilizers, and removal of bases (Ca, Mg, K) in harvested cane. There was a marked decrease in the organic carbon content of soils within the first eighteen months of cultivation. Following this initial decline, the organic carbon content stabilized at about 70 percent of its original value for the next three years. The decline in organic matter content of the soils may be attributed to the increased mixing (with subsoil materials) and aeration of soils enhancing mineralization of labile organic matter.

Cation Exchange Capacity (CEC) values varied over the study period in the range from 13.7 to 22.6 cmol/kg. Initially there was a decrease with time after cultivation in line with falls in organic matter. The values then increased and decreased over time, but showed no significant correlations with other soil parameters. There was a marked increase in bulk density after one year, possibly due to impact of tractors and harvest operations and mixing of topsoil and subsoil material during land preparation. The upper B horizon was quite compact and had a bulk density of about 1.1, whereas the topsoil bulk density was 0.89 (Table 5.4). Land preparation and cultivation led to a breakdown in soil structure, and there was a gradual removal of topsoil (during harvesting and by erosion after harvesting before new growth covered the soil surface) over the years due to cultivation. All these factors contributed to the increase in bulk density by 29 percent within the first fourteen years of cultivation (1978–1992).

The water retention against 1500 kPa suction was included in the study to monitor the changes in the clay content and surface area of the soils. The values showed a gradual increase with time (Table 5.4). There were significant drops recorded for the samples taken in the 65 and 164 months of the study period and may have been due to some irreversible dehydration during prolonged periods of moisture deficit. There had been almost eighteen months of high moisture deficit during the period from March 1983 to October 1984, but the moisture stress in 1991 to 1992 was less marked.

Given the decrease in CEC and the increasing acidification of soils, it is not surprising that the exchangeable calcium (Ca) and magnesium (Mg) values decreased markedly (Figure 5.5) with

Table 5.4

Changes in Soil Properties with Time (1978–2002) for a Sugar Cane Farm, Seaqaqa, Vanua Levu, Fiji

Depth	Date	Time	pH	Org C	Total N	BD	15 Bar	CEC/pH7	Exch Ca	Exch Mg	Exch K	Exch H+Al	Exch Ca+Mg
(cm)		(mths)	(H₂O)	%	%	g/cc	Water %	cmol/kg	cmol/kg	cmol/kg	cmol/kg	cmol/kg	cmol/kg
0–15	Mar-78	0	5.50	5.59	0.46	0.89	14.6	19.00	3.10	1.10	0.20	0.40	4.40
	Aug-78	1	5.00	4.95	0.32	1.02	14.3	14.40	3.40	0.60	<0.1	0.20	4.00
	Feb-80	19	5.00	4.15	0.28	1.08	15.5	13.70	2.30	0.20	<0.1	0.30	2.50
	Dec-80	29	5.10	4.23	0.26	1.04	16.1	20.60	2.40	0.20	0.22	<0.1	2.60
	Dec-81	41	4.90	4.32	0.28	1.10	16.4	21.90	2.10	0.30	0.21	0.20	2.40
	Dec-82	53	5.00	3.67	0.29	1.11	17.3	14.20	1.80	0.26	0.28	<0.1	2.06
	Dec-83	65	4.80	4.06	0.22	1.09	13.6	14.60	1.10	0.14	0.14	<0.1	1.24
	Mar-92	164	5.20	3.14	0.24	1.15	14.0	17.30	0.49	0.79	0.17	0.40	1.28
	Sep-92	170	5.20	3.09	0.23	nd	21.2	22.60	1.30	0.21	0.08	<0.1	1.51
	Sep-93	182	4.80	2.20	nd	nd	nd	19.20	0.64	0.29	<0.1	<0.1	0.93
	Apr-95	201	nd	2.67	0.23	nd	17.7	17.00	1.15	0.32	0.08	0.36	1.47
	Apr-97	225	4.40	3.56	0.22	nd	24.7	19.60	0.82	0.10	0.08	0.23	0.92
	Apr-02	285	4.75	4.30	nd	nd	nd	19.08	0.77	0.11	nd	nd	0.88
30–40	Apr-78	0	5.70	1.91	0.15	1.07	17.7	7.50	0.50	0.20	<0.1	0.20	1.30
	Dec-83	65	5.80	2.22	0.12	nd	14.0	9.70	0.56	0.07	0.04	<0.1	0.63
	Mar-92	164	5.30	1.28	0.07	nd	15.3	11.70	0.34	0.60	0.16	0.20	0.94
	Sep-93	182	4.90	1.74	nd	nd	nd	12.00	0.27	0.11	<0.1	<0.1	0.38
	Apr-95	201	nd	1.92	0.16	nd	14.9	13.30	0.72	0.07	0.03	0.10	0.79
	Apr-97	225	4.40	2.38	0.12	nd	21.0	15.20	0.34	0.06	0.04	<0.1	0.40
	Apr-02	285	4.58	2.10	nd	nd	nd	8.32	0.64	0.06	nd	nd	0.70
70–80	Apr-78	0	5.50	0.67	0.06	1.13	15.5	5.50	0.50	0.20	<0.1	0.10	0.70
	Dec-83	65	5.90	0.90	0.08	nd	13.6	6.00	0.28	0.02	0.02	<0.1	0.30
	Mar-92	164	5.90	0.77	0.05	nd	14.8	5.10	0.09	0.17	0.13	0.15	0.26
	Sep-93	182	5.00	0.81	nd	nd	nd	5.10	<0.1	<0.1	<0.1	<0.1	<0.2
	Apr-95	201	nd	0.98	0.07	nd	19.1	10.30	0.10	0.02	0.03	<0.1	0.12
	Apr-97	225	5.10	0.89	0.03	nd	18.6	10.60	0.16	0.04	0.08	<0	0.20
	Apr-02	285	5.02	1.40	nd	nd	nd	6.94	0.37	0.05	nd	nd	0.42

increasing period of cultivation. This decrease in the concentrations of exchangeable bases in soils may be attributed to a number of factors, including the decrease in the capacity of the soil to retain cations (CEC), the low usage of phosphorus fertilizers (superphosphate is the main source for Ca), erosion, and crop removal. Analysis of fertilizer inputs and crop removals indicated that it is likely that in most years more bases were removed in harvesting than were added in fertilizers.

The results from the analyses of the subsurface soil samples are also shown in Table 5.4. Several points are worthy of discussion. The 70 to 80 cm samples data indicated very marginal change over

the twenty-five years of the study period. There was no significant change (p<0.01) in organic carbon and total nitrogen contents. The pH values remained relatively unchanged for the first fifteen years, but showed some decline in the last ten years of the study, possibly due to long-term decline in bases. The drop in concentrations of exchangeable bases may be attributed to the decline in potassium (K) and Ca fertilizer usage and uptake by the deep roots of the sugar cane.

In the 30 to 40 cm layer, the pH values declined over the study period. The organic carbon content increased initially together with the CEC, while the concentrations of bases declined substantially

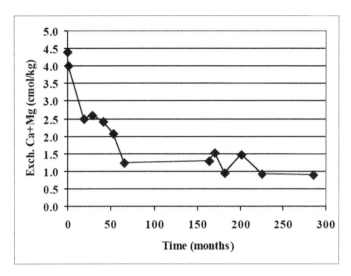

Figure 5.5. *Exchangeable Ca+Mg changes over time for a soil under sugar cane cultivation at Seaqaqa, Vanua Levu, Fiji.*

during the same period. The increased organic carbon was probably due to two factors. First, cultivation, that is, tree removal, ripping, and rotovating during land preparation, would have caused the movement of some topsoil material down in the profile, even to a depth of 30 to 40 cm. Second, the roots of sugar cane, which are capable of going down to a depth of 2 m in soils, may have facilitated further accumulation of organic material at depth, either by root development and die-back or even by illuviation.

The cane farm in this study has been under continuous production for almost twenty-five years, and the yields have been reasonably stable as a result of good farm management practices. It is not uncommon to see farms in the Seaqaqa area fallowed for one or two seasons following low production. This in itself is not a bad practice, but when the farm is to be replanted it is usually noted that the weeds are removed by bulldozing which removes the best part of the surface soil. No such activity occurred at this site. For a rainfed farm on an Oxisol, the cane yields were reasonable (averaging about 55 t/ha/yr) in view of the fact that fertilizer use has declined. This indicates that fertilizer use can be decreased provided good farm management practices are used to sustain cane yields and soil fertility.

This study indicates that long-term intensive sugar cane cultivation leads to marked changes in the topsoil properties. The significant changes may be attributed to decreases in organic matter and to increased bulk density. In the 30 to 40 cm horizon, increased organic carbon and CEC values were observed, while at the 70 to 80 cm level, no significant changes were observed in most parameters. Similar observations have been made at other sites in the Seaqaqa area. The decline in the organic matter content and the associated decrease in CEC and increase in bulk density are not only detrimental to sugar cane growth but also increase soil degradation in the cane-growing belt. This would result in declining yields over the long term. It is essential that initiatives be taken to ensure that further decline in soil quality does not occur following the changes resulting from initial clearance and land preparation activities. The data trends indicate that insufficient quantities of bases (Ca, Mg, K) are being added, in most years, to compensate for crop removal and

leaching. This is a critical factor in maintaining the productivity and sustainability of soils that have low natural levels of bases. It is expected that many similar changes occur with intensive production of other crops in the Pacific Islands.

Conclusion

Soils represent one of the major natural resources of the Pacific Islands. We are fortunate that for many islands, good information on soils is available. In some cases, adequate information is not yet available. Given the fragile nature of Pacific Island environments (small islands separated by substantial stretches of ocean), it is imperative that good soil management be practiced if local inhabitants are to sustain production of food and forest products. The small size of many of the islands is an environmental hazard in this context. Mistakes in environmental management may be extremely difficult to rectify, at least in the short term. Recognizing the importance of soils and the development of national sustainable land-use plans is essential for the future well-being of Pacific Islanders.

BIBLIOGRAPHY

Asghar, M., T. J. Davidson, and R. J. Morrison, eds. 1988. *Soil taxonomy and fertility in the South Pacific.* Apia: University of the South Pacific.

Asquith F., M. Kooge, and R. J. Morrison. 1994. *Transportation of sediments via rivers to the ocean and the role of sediments as pollutants in the South Pacific.* Reports and Studies No. 72. Apia: South Pacific Regional Environment Programme.

Browne, C. 2006. *Pacific island economies.* New York: International Monetary Fund.

Buol, S. W., F. D. Hole, and R. J. McCracken. 1980. *Soil genesis and classification,* 2nd ed. Ames: Iowa State University Press.

Chase, L. D. C., and J. P. Widdowson. 1983. Sulphur in the agriculture of Pacific high islands. In *Sulphur in S.E. Asian and S. Pacific agriculture,* ed. G. Blair and R. A. Till, 206–217. Armidale, N.S.W.: University of New England Press.

Chase, R. C., ed. 1992. *Review of agricultural development in the atolls.* Apia: University of the South Pacific.

Clarke, W. C., and R. J. Morrison. 1987. Land mismanagement and the development imperative in Fiji. In *Land degradation and society,* ed. H. C. Brookfield and P. M. Blaikie, 176–185. London: Methuen.

Cowie, J. D. 1980. Soils from andesitic tephra and their variability, Tongatapu, Kingdom of Tonga. *Australian Journal of Soil Research* 18: 273–284.

Dodson, J. 1992. *The naive lands: Prehistory and environmental change in Australia and the Southwest Pacific.* Melbourne: Longman Cheshire.

Fiji Meteorological Service. n.d. *Information sheets 21, 153, 171.* Nadi.

Food and Agriculture Organization, United Nations. 1990. *Soil map of the world.* Paris: UNESCO.

Fosberg, F. R. 1954. Soils of the Northern Marshall atolls, with special reference to the Jemo series. *Soil Science* 78: 99–107.

———. 1957. Description and occurrence of atoll phosphate rock in Micronesia. *American Journal of Science* 225: 584–592.

Fournier, F. 1960. *Climat et erosion: La relation entre l'erosion du sol l'eau et les precipitations atmospheriques.* Paris: Presses Universitaires de France.

Glatthaar, D. 1988. The sediment load of the Waimanu River southeastern Viti Levu, Fiji. In *Report about two research projects in the Republic of Fiji,* ed. H. Liedtke and D. Glatthaar, 52–75. Sponsored by the German Research Foundation. Bochum: Geographical Institute, Ruhr University.

Hudson, N. 1981. *Soil conservation*. Ithaca, N.Y.: Cornell University Press.

Kuhlken, R. 1994. *Tuatua ni Nakavadra:* A Fijian irrigated taro agro-system. In *The science of Pacific Island peoples.* Vol. 2, *Land use and agriculture,* ed. R. J. Morrison, P. Geraghty, and L. Crowl, 51–62. Suva: Institute of Pacific Studies, University of the South Pacific.

Lal, P. N. 1990. *Conservation or conversion of mangroves in Fiji.* Occasional Paper No. 11. Honolulu: Environment and Policy Institute, East-West Center.

Latham, M., P. Quantin, and G. Aubert. 1978. Étude des sols de la Nouvelle-Caledonie. Paris: ORSTOM.

Leslie, D. M. 1984a. A proposal for an Oceania Benchmark Sites Network for Agrotechnology Transfer OBSNAT. Proceedings of the International Symposium on Minimum Data Sets for Agrotechnology Transfer, March 1983, 33–54. ICRISAT Centre, India.

———. 1984b. *Soils of the Koronivia Agricultural Research Station, Viti Levu, Fiji.* New Zealand Soil Survey Report, 75, Soil Bureau, DSIR, Lower Hutt.

Liedtke, H. 1989. Soil erosion and soil removal in Fiji. *Applied Geography and Development* 33: 68–92.

Manner, H. I., and R. J. Morrison. 1991. A temporal sequence chronosequence of soil carbon and nitrogen development after phosphate mining on Nauru Island. *Pacific Science* 45: 400–404.

Marsden E., G. J. Fergusson, and M. Fieldes. 1958. Notes on the radioactivity of soils with application to Niue Island. Proceedings of the Second International Conference on the Peaceful Uses of Atomic Energy, Geneva 18, 514.

Milliman, J. D. 1990a. *Discharge of fluvial sediment to the oceans: Global, temporal and anthropogenic implications.* Washington D.C.: NAS/NRC Press.

———. 1990b. Fluvial sediment in coastal seas: Flux and fate. *Nature and Resources* 26(4): 12–21.

Milliman, J. D., and R. H. Meade. 1983. World-wide delivery of river sediment to the oceans. *Journal of Geology* 91:1–21.

Morrison, R. J. 1991. Some Andosols from Savai'i, Western Samoa. *Soil Science Society of America Proceedings* J. 55: 159–164.

Morrison, R. J., W. C. Clarke, N. Buresova, and L. Limalevu. 1990. Erosion and sedimentation in Fiji: An overview. In *Research needs and applications to reduce erosion and sedimentation in tropical steeplands,* ed. R. R. Ziemer, C. L. O'Loughlin, and L. S. Hamilton, 14–23. Wallingford: IAHS Publication No. 192.

Morrison, R. J., J. S. Gawander, and A. N. Ram. 2005. Changes in the properties of a Fijian Oxisol over 25 years of sugarcane cultivation. In *Proceedings International Society of Sugar Cane Technologists XXV Congress,* ed. D. M. Hogarth, vol. 2, 139–146, Guatemala: ISSCT.

Morrison, R. J., P. Geraghty, and L. Crowl, eds. 1994. *The science of Pacific Island peoples.* Vol. 2, *Land use and agriculture.* Suva: Institute of Pacific Studies, University of the South Pacific.

Morrison, R. J., and D. M. Leslie, eds. 1982. *Proceedings of the South Pacific Regional Forum on Soil Taxonomy.* Institute of Natural Resources, University of the South Pacific.

Morrison, R. J., and A. S. Masilaca. 1989. Changes in the properties of a Fijian Oxisol following sugarcane cultivation. In *Soil management and smallholder development in the Pacific Islands,* ed. E. Pushparajah and C. R. Elliot, 271–281. Bangkok: IBSRAM.

Morrison, R. J., R. Naidu, P. Gangaiya, and Yee Wah Sing. 1989. Amelioration of acid soils in Fiji. In *Soil management and smallholder development in the Pacific Islands,* ed. E. Pushparajah and C. R. Elliot, 255–270. Bangkok: IBSRAM.

Morrison, R. J., R. Naidu, S. Naidu, and R. A. Prasad. 1987. *Classification of some reference soils from Viti Levu and Vanua Levu, Fiji.* INR Environmental Studies Report No. 38, University of the South Pacific.

Morrison R. J., R. Naidu, and U. Singh. 1987. Sulphur in the agriculture of Papua New Guinea and the South Pacific Islands. In *Fertilizer sulphur requirements and sources in developing countries of Asia and the Pacific,* 57–66. Bangkok: FADINAP/FAO/Sulphur Institute/ACIAR.

———. 1988. Acid soils of Fiji. In *Management and utilization of acid Soils of Oceania,* ed. J. L. Demeterio and B. DeGuzman, 83–103. Mangilao: University of Guam.

Morrison, R. J., and V. B. Seru. 1986. *Soils of Abatao Islet, Tarawa, Kiribati.* Envir. Studies Report 27. Suva: Institute of Natural Resources, University of the South Pacific.

New Zealand Soil Bureau. 1979. *Soils of the Cook Islands: An introduction.* Wellington: New Zealand Ministry of Foreign Affairs.

Roe, D. 1989. The Kolevu terraced taro system, west Guadalcanal. In *Soil management and smallholder development in the Pacific Islands,* ed. E. Pushparajah and C. R. Elliot, 205–212. Bangkok: IBSRAM.

Schroth, C. L. 1971. Soil sequences of Western Samoa. *Pacific Science* 25: 291–300.

Simonson, R. W. 1959. Outline of a generalised theory of soil genesis. *Soil Science Society of America Proceedings* 23: 152–156.

Small, C. A. 1972. *Atoll agriculture.* Tarawa: Agriculture Department, Gilbert and Ellis Islands Government.

Smith, C. W. 1983. *Soil survey of the islands of Palau, Republic of Palau.* Washington, D.C.: U.S. Dept. of Agric. Soil Conservation Service.

Soil Survey Staff. 1975. *Soil taxonomy: A basic system of soil classification for making and interpreting soil surveys.* Washington, D.C.: U.S. Dept. of Agric. Handbook No. 436, U.S. Gov. Printing Office.

Soil Survey Staff. 1999. *Soil taxonomy: A basic system of soil classification for making and interpreting soil surveys.* 2nd ed., Washington, D.C.: U.S. Dept. of Agric. Handbook No. 436, U.S. Gov. Printing Office.

Southern, W. 1986. The late Quaternary environmental history of Fiji. PhD thesis. Canberra: Australian National University.

Wall, J. R. D., and J. R. F. Hansell. 1976. *Land resources of the Solomon Islands.* Vol. 8, *Outer Islands.* Surbiton: Land Resources Division UK.

Walling, D. E., and B. W. Webb. 1987. Material transport by the world's rivers: Evolving perspectives. In *Water for the future: Hydrology in perspective.* Proceedings of the Rome Symposium, April 1987. Wallingford: IAHS Publ. No. 164.

Whitehead, N. E., R. G. Ditchburn, W. J. McCabe, and P. Rankin. 1992. A new model for the origin of the anomalous radioactivity in Niue Island South Pacific soils. *Chemical Geology, Isotope Geoscience Section* 94: 247–260.

Willatt, S. T., J. Q. Suqa, and L. Limalevu. 1995. Water infiltration and implications for soil erosion: A case study at Waibau, Viti Levu, Fiji. *South Pacific Journal of Natural Science* 14: 43–54.

Wischmeier, W. H., and J. V. Mannering. 1969. Relation of soil properties to its erodibility. *Soil Science Society of America Proceedings* 33: 131–137.

Wright, A. C. S. 1963. *Soils and land use of Western Samoa.* Wellington: New Zealand Soil Bureau Bull. 22.

Young, A. 1976. *Tropical soils and soil survey.* Cambridge: Cambridge University Press.

Young, F. J. 1988. *Soil survey of the Territory of Guam.* Washington, D.C.: United States Department of Agriculture Soil Conservation Service.

Water

Derrick Depledge and James P. Terry

6

A supply of fresh water is a prerequisite to any settlement. The needs of the people who first came to the Pacific were met by pre-existing supplies, which they either could see or knew where to find. The technology was simple and adequate, perhaps using lengths of bamboo or locally made clay pots as containers for collection and storage.

Rainfall was collected from the trunk of a tree using a thick bush rope. Groundwater was collected from hand-dug wells, usually shallow, but sometimes reaching considerable depth. Cave pools and coastal springs were also utilized where available. The location of a village was often dictated by the presence of freshwater springs or the proximity of a stream.

With the arrival of the Europeans, water resource development progressed and benefited from the new technologies and materials available to the particular nation involved over the period of colonization. Those Pacific Island groups with continuing dependence still have ongoing support and sometimes the latest technology from the affiliated country.

Improvements in water supply included the development of previously unknown groundwater resources, the ability to transport and distribute water to consumers, the ability to treat and disinfect surface water that was previously not used or was used with subsequent adverse effects on health and well-being, the availability of large containers, such as tanks and cisterns, and the construction of large dams to store water.

The development of water resources for domestic purposes in the Pacific as well as for other human activities, including agriculture and industry, which are growing in scale, increasingly requires consideration of the effect on the existing ecosystems and the environment in general.

The scattered nature of settlement in the islands of the Pacific has led to a system of land tenure, which is seen to include the water that flows over or under the ground. Access to stream or spring flow may be possible only with the permission of and payment to local landowners. The concept of ownership of water by the state is not widely accepted in the Pacific, although in some countries legislation allows the government to control the allocation of resources.

Modern development of adequate supplies of fresh potable water resources involves some considerable expense. The motto of the (Western) Samoa Water Board is "Water, a Gift from God."

Simple messages such as this, although probably meeting the early missionaries' purpose of giving the people a reason to look after their water supply, now obstructs, to some extent, the need to put a value and a cost on the supply of water and to finance the production of clean water and maintenance of supply systems by charging consumers. A 1988 estimate of the value of water resources in New Zealand, for example, including water for supply, hydropower, recreation, freshwater fisheries, gravel replenishment, and waste disposal, was almost NZ$2.5 billion (Mosley 1988).

Available Water Resources

Rainfall

Water is taken from every phase of the water cycle. The primary source of fresh water over the Pacific Ocean is from the atmosphere in the form of precipitation. This is used directly or feeds the surface and underground freshwater resources. Most Pacific islands exist as small landmasses in a predominantly oceanic region. The airstreams approaching most coastlines have often traversed large tracts of water and are moisture laden. Mean relative humidity and annual rainfall are, therefore, generally high throughout the Pacific, but the rainfall is variable both spatially and temporally.

Spatially, rainfall available as a water resource is affected by the presence or absence of high ground, the seasonal movement and location of the intertropical and South Pacific convergence zones, and the passage of cyclones and troughs of low pressure associated with depressions.

Temporally, rainfall has daily, seasonal, and secular variations that, although predictable to some extent from mean values (e.g. Table 6.1), can never be anticipated sufficiently to prevent drought or flooding from causing some degree of physical hardship. The pattern of late afternoon rain in the tropical areas, rainy seasons, and yearly variations related to global climatic changes such as the El Niño–Southern Oscillation all affect the availability of rainwater as a resource.

Effective rainfall, that is, the rainfall contributing to runoff (surface water) and to the groundwater reserves, is limited by the amount of evaporation that occurs and transpiration by plants. These processes remove particularly large volumes in the tropical

Table 6.1

Long-Term Averages of Monthly Rainfall for Three Capital Cities in the Tropical Pacific Islands

	Jan.	Feb.	Mar.	Apr.	May	Jun.	Jul.	Aug.	Sep.	Oct.	Nov.	Dec.	Year
Rainfall in millimeters													
Suva, 18°09'S 178°27'E (1942–2002 data)													
	343	293	373	366	245	168	142	148	191	206	254	269	2998
'Alofi, 19°03'S 169°55'W (1910–1998 data)													
	271	248	280	200	129	83	99	96	106	132	142	200	1992
Majuro, 7°05'N 171°23'E (1974–2003 data)													
	213	177	213	276	288	296	314	292	325	364	335	289	3380

Source: Fiji, Niue, and RMI Meteorological Services.

Note: Suva City (Fiji) is located at 6 m elevation on the southeast windward coast of Viti Levu, a high volcanic island; 'Alofi (Niue) is situated 23 m above sea level on a raised limestone island; Majuro (Marshall Islands) is a low-lying atoll.

and subtropical areas of the Pacific and reduce the available water resources. Average annual values for potential evapotranspiration in the tropical Pacific are in the region of 1,700 to 1,800 mm (Nullet 1987).

The South Pacific is also thought to be one of the regions in the world most likely to be especially affected by climate change, according to the Intergovernmental Panel on Climate Change (NIWA 2007). Projected rainfall change of between ±14 to 15 percent by the year 2100 and an increase in frequency of heavy rainfall events is forecast at this stage.

Surface Water

Surface water is found in rivers and other channels, lakes, reservoirs, and wetlands. It is found where there is sufficient rainfall or groundwater discharge to provide the resource and where soils and the underlying geological materials are relatively impermeable. Countries with large landmasses, such as Papua New Guinea (PNG) and New Zealand, have large catchment areas and often long rivers with high mean flows. The three largest rivers in PNG, the Sepik, Fly, and Purari, have a combined catchment area of over 200,000 km², over one-third the area of the whole country (Piliwas 1996). Rivers in New Zealand have smaller but substantial catchment areas (the Clutha, 21,000 km²) and length (the Waikato, 425 km²). Flows can be high, with an estimated total annual discharge for New Zealand rivers of about 415 km³/yr. The Clutha in the South Island of New Zealand has a mean discharge of 563 m³/s (Mosley 1995).

Other high islands in the Pacific have small catchment areas (Table 6.2), where permeability is low, often with rapid runoff characteristics, given to flash flooding on occasions. The average catchment area on Oʻahu in Hawaiʻi, for example, is only 2.6 km² (Peterson 1991).

Perennial and ephemeral streams are also found on smaller islands where conditions are favorable. The island of ʻEua in Tonga,

Table 6.2

Largest Rivers on Selected Islands in the Tropical Pacific

Island	Country	Largest river	Approximate basin area (km²)
Viti Levu	Fiji	Rewa	2918
Malaita	Solomon Islands	Wairaha	486
Grande Terre	New Caledonia	Yate	437
Guadalcanal	Solomon Islands	Lungga	394
Espiritu Santo	Vanuatu	Jourdain	369
Vanua Levu	Fiji	Dreketi	317
Savaiʻi	Samoa	Sili	51
Upolu	Samoa	Vaisigano	33

for example, has constantly flowing water fed from inland cave systems, and there are numerous spring-fed streams on the higher islands of Vanuatu and Solomon Islands.

Lakes vary in size from the large volcanic, glacial, and man-made lakes of New Zealand to small depressions on islands such as Mitiaro in the Cook Islands, containing shallow and sometimes brackish water reserves.

Because the residence time of water on the Earth's surface is small compared to that of groundwater, surface water resources, particularly rivers and streams, respond more rapidly to variations in the local rainfall pattern and are therefore more limited in their availability.

Groundwater

Groundwater is found throughout the Pacific, with only the smallest islands not having a usable freshwater lens perched above saline water. Available storage ranges from thin fragile lenses, perhaps 1 to 2 m thick, to large aquifers in limestone, volcanic, or sedimentary sequences on larger islands. On small islands, demand may exceed limited reserves. On Tarawa Atoll in Kiribati, the extremely high population density in the main administrative center on the small islet of Betio—approximately 15,000 people/km²—means that the groundwater lens is unable to meet water demands. Water must be piped from larger aquifers on Bonriki and Buota islands, which lie more than 30 km away in the southeast of the atoll (White, Falkland, and Scott 1999). In contrast, some islands have abundant groundwater resources; for example the 1,800 or so inhabitants of the elevated coral atoll of Niue have water reticulated to all their houses on the island from a lens (Figure 6.1), which has a maximum thickness, estimated from electrical resistivity soundings, of 50 to 170 m (Jacobson and Hill 1980).

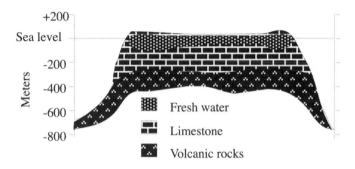

Figure 6.1. Water sources on Niue (after Falkland 1991).

Groundwater, with a global average residence time of about 1,400 years, is less affected by the temporal and secular variations of rainfall than is surface water. By comparison, the global average residence time for water in rivers is twelve days and in lakes 1.2 years. Small island groundwater lenses, however, may have comparatively small residence times. Typical atoll islets rise little more than 2 to 3 m above sea level; generally consist of coral sands and gravels, in which the freshwater lenses are found, overlying a solid limestone formation; and have limited width and area (Figure 6.2).

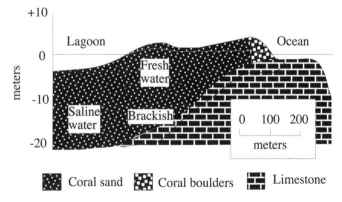

Figure 6.2. Water sources on Tarawa, Kiribati (after Falkland 1991).

Groundwater on these atolls is particularly liable to be affected by climate changes caused by any global warming. Apart from reductions in recharge from any decreases in rainfall, there are the threats imposed by any sea-level rise and possible inundation

from storm surges associated with any increase in the occurrence of cyclone formation. Cyclone Percy in February 2005 serves to illustrate. The storm inundated Pukapuka Atoll in the Northern Cook Islands. For at least a year after the event, the groundwater lens on the atoll's main southern island experienced salination by a downward-percolating layer of seawater (Terry and Falkland 2010).

Atolls are highly responsive to the capricious nature of rainfall. Exploitable water resources may be as low as 20 percent of the mean annual recharge to the lenses (Anthony 1991). Moreover, vegetation, and coconut trees in particular, act as phreatophytes and are known to consume large quantities of water directly from the shallow groundwater table by transpiration. Stem flow measurements on mature coconut trees on the island of Bonriki in Tarawa, Kiribati, indicate that 100 to 150 liters may be used by a single tree each day (White 1996).

There is a clear distinction between the water-bearing strata on small islands and those on the larger and higher islands. Larger islands can have high-yielding and extensive aquifers in limestone, volcanic, or sedimentary rock sequences (Figure 6.3). Limestone formations are often uplifted reefs that have been subjected to karstification, giving them a secondary porosity that renders them highly permeable. Volcanic sequences forming aquifers may consist of in situ lava flows, perhaps faulted and intruded by dikes, and reworked volcanic material in bedded horizons. Alluvial plains of varying permeability are found in many of the larger islands of the Pacific. They consist of sand and gravel with finer materials derived from adjacent mountain chains or other high ground.

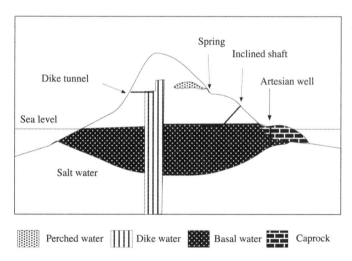

Figure 6.3. Water sources on a high island.

At locations adjacent to plate margins, and where recent volcanic activity has taken place, thermal groundwater is often found, either rising from depth or being heated from the elevated ground temperatures in the area. In particular these thermal areas are found adjacent to the Australian-Indian/Pacific plate boundary. There are two main groups of geothermal waters, the low-temperature waters (20° to 100°C), associated with active faulting, and the high-temperature waters (>100°C), associated with areas of active volcanism (Hunt and Bibby 1992).

Water-Related Hazards

River Floods

Intense rainfalls produced by tropical storms can generate rapid and large responses in Pacific Island streams and rivers. Maximum channel capacities are often exceeded by peak discharges, which frequently leads to floodplain inundation. Many of the worst flood events are caused by tropical cyclones. Analysis of hydrological records for the Tontouta River in New Caledonia showed that 65 percent of the largest historical flows were caused by cyclones and 75 percent of cyclone-induced floods were overbank events. In Solomon Islands, Cyclone Namu in May 1986 resulted in the worst catastrophe of recent times. Parts of Guadalcanal recorded cumulative storm precipitation totaling 874 mm. Swollen rivers on the Guadalcanal Plains burst their banks, claiming at least one hundred lives (Trustrum, Whitehouse, and Blaschke 1989). As well as the immediate fatalities, such river floods cause lasting repercussions that small-island economies can ill-afford, through the destruction of homes and infrastructure, disease outbreaks, and damage to crops that forces up local food prices and reduces national export revenue.

Droughts

Most Pacific islands suffer from periodic droughts, often associated with ENSO-driven rainfall variability. Although on many islands insufficient data exist to evaluate typical baseline drought conditions, the 1997–1998 drought in Fiji might be indicative of the type of droughts likely to be experienced in the future (Bettencourt et al. 2002). This event caused damages of US$140 to 166 million in crops, water supply, livestock, and nutritional deficiencies (Stratus Consulting 2000). On those islands with surface water (often used for both urban supply intake and domestic purposes in rural areas), low streamflow levels during dry spells are normally a better indication of actual water resource availability than at-a-point rainfall data. This is because discharge reflects (antecedent) precipitation over the wider catchment and incorporates the influence of local physiographic, geological, and hydrometeorological characteristics. In the Ba River of Fiji, it has been shown that average stream baseflows bear a close relationship with lagged Southern Oscillation Index (SOI) values, indicating the influence of the Southern Oscillation on seasonal stream hydrology (Terry 2005).

Water Use

Domestic Use

The demand for water in the Pacific varies greatly. There are urban areas, particularly in those countries consisting of small atolls, where population densities are as high as 10,000 people per km². But despite the trend toward urban migration and unlike the world as a whole, the Pacific requires much of its domestic water in a rural setting. PNG has a large population for a Pacific country, but the land area is so great that the overall density of population is only around 8 per km², which is just below the average density for the whole of the Pacific.

Urban usage ranges in value from lows of 20 to 40 liters per capita per day (lpcd) in Tarawa, Kiribati, to more than 1,200 lpcd in Rarotonga and 1,090 lpcd in Tahiti. Table 6.3 shows the wide range of consumption per capita throughout the region. It should be noted, by contrast, that European targets for domestic water consumption are now set at 120 lpcd.

Table 6.3

Domestic Water Consumption in Some Pacific Countries

Location	Water use (lpcd)
Aitutaki, Cook Islands	150–200
Rarotonga, Cook Islands	1200
Fiji	100–200
Kiribati	30–100
Marshall Islands	100
Nauru	40
Niue	350 (est.)
Palau	150 (SW Islands)
Samoa	230 (Samoa Water Authority)
Solomon Islands	150 (urban areas)
Tonga	170 (urban area)
Tuvalu	<50

Source: SOPAC Water and Sanitation Section n.d.

Agricultural and Industrial Use

Agriculture and industry are major contributors to the New Zealand economy. Irrigation alone consumes about 1.1 km³ each year (Mosley 1995), while many of the dairy factories scattered throughout the two main islands use volumes in excess of 1,500 m³ daily. Industrial uses can also be high. The aluminum smelter in Southland, New Zealand, consumes 4,500 m³ per day from groundwater resources derived from the underlying gravels. New Zealand Steel in the North Island uses 1,700 m³ per day. On a lesser scale, in Fiji there are more than 1,000 ha of rice with facilities for irrigation (Raj 1996).

On the main island of Viti Levu there are three storage reservoirs for irrigation water with capacities ranging from 1 to 3 million m³; 65 km of canals deliver water to farms; 300 ha are used for sprinkler irrigation of vegetable crops. In Hawai'i, storage of water for agriculture is particularly difficult because of the highly permeable volcanic rocks and soils. Water is therefore transported via a network of ditches and tunnels from wet mountainous areas to the drier lowlands for irrigation of crops such as sugar cane. In 1985, 85 percent of all water use in Hawai'i was for agriculture, mostly irrigation (Department of Land and Natural Resources 1987). In Guam, 3.5 percent of the public water supply is used for irrigation annually.

Stock usage can be high in countries with intensive grazing, such as New Zealand. Free-ranging herds, such as those providing meat for the beef industry in Vanuatu, use less water. In Samoa stock consume an estimated total of about 100 m³ a day. Agricultural water use in rural areas or outer islands in the Pacific varies greatly depending on available resources. In the village, the animals such as pigs, goats, and chickens belonging to a household can create a demand of perhaps an additional 0.5 persons.

Other Uses

Hydropower is being developed throughout the Pacific, providing 80 percent of the requirements in New Zealand and providing substantial contributions to the power needs of Samoa, PNG, French Polynesia, Hawai'i, and Fiji. This is not strictly a consumptive use but affects stretches of rivers where diversion or damming occurs.

On the higher islands, fast-flowing perennial rivers have been harnessed for hydroelectric power. Schemes ranging from small micro-hydroelectric power to large-scale power stations have been built in the Pacific.

Also on the larger islands, lakes and rivers are used for recreational purposes, including boating, swimming, fishing, and other aquatic sports. Artificially created lakes, associated with hydropower development, are also used in this way. For example, Lake Karapiro in New Zealand has an international rowing course and is used for many boating activities.

Water is used extensively for the disposal of wastes, both in a liquid and a solid form. Rivers, in particular, are the recipients of much of the municipal, sometimes treated effluent from sewage disposal systems.

Technologies for Water Supply

Conventional Technology, Rainwater

To collect rainwater a catchment is required and some form of storage must be constructed. On a household scale, tanks are built to collect the rain from roofs, provided the roofs are of suitable material, such as galvanized iron, aluminum, or clay or cement tiles. Tanks in the Pacific are made of ferrocement, steel, timber, fiberglass, and heavy-duty polyethylene. Water quality is generally good provided adequate precautions are taken to keep roofs clean and prevent access to the tanks by insects and small animals. In the Pacific, rainwater collection ranges from the simple catchment from house roofs into small containers or tanks to large-scale catchments directing flow to a reservoir or storage tank. This last method can be illustrated by the use of the thirty hectares of the airport runway in Majuro in the Marshall Islands, which provides an average of almost 800,000 m³/year to the water supply for Majuro, assuming that 20 percent of the rainfall is lost to evaporation (Doig 1996). Adjacent reservoirs can store about 57,000 m³ of raw water and 7,600 m³ of treated water.

Conventional Technology, Surface Water

Water resources from rivers, streams, and lakes are used throughout the Pacific, specifically on the higher islands. Water may either be impounded behind a dam to create storage or be taken directly from a stream or other intake. In Rarotonga in the Cook Islands, an average of 1,200 m³ per day is taken from twelve filtered or open intakes from the radial streams that flow from the central high area of the island. Eighty-six percent of the population of Fiji receives on average 167,000 m³/day of reticulated water, mainly derived from surface water sources. Ninety-five percent of the reticulated supply in French Polynesia is obtained from river sources.

Small gravity-fed systems, consisting of an intake, a supply line, and either a storage tank or standpipes in the villages, have been installed in many Pacific Island countries, such as Vanuatu, to provide water to one or more villages. These may suffer from intermittent supply, especially during the dry season, and siltation during heavy rains. The major advantage of gravity systems is the economy of operation and maintenance.

Conventional Technology, Groundwater

The use of groundwater varies from individual household wells to major supplies from large aquifers supplying major cities, such as Christchurch in New Zealand (Figure 6.4).

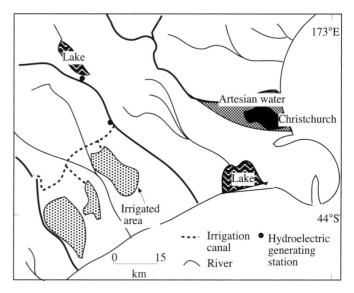

Figure 6.4. Water resources in Christchurch, New Zealand (after Soons 1972).

The simple, shallow hand-dug well on a small island is usually something of a health hazard because of its open condition and the proximity of sanitation facilities or the existence of free-ranging stock. Major improvements have been made by providing a cover, generally a concrete slab, over open wells and installing a hand pump to replace the rope and bucket previously used (Mourits and Depledge 1995). Various projects are under way in such countries as Solomon Islands and Vanuatu to provide hand-pumped wells in the villages.

In some locations major projects have been undertaken to relocate wells away from villages and sources of pollution, such as in the outer islands of the Gilbert Group in Kiribati. Here, a UN project has used diaphragm pumps, placed in the villages to pump water from wells located at safe distances of up to 750 m from the dwellings. Beyond 750 m, electric pumps are used, with solar energy as the motive power (Metutera 1996).

Where there is a high demand on the shallow groundwater of small islands, recent projects have used infiltration galleries with horizontal, shallow perforated pipes feeding a central well to skim the fresh water from the lenses (Figure 6.5). The galleries use

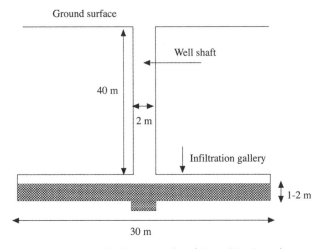

Figure 6.5. *Diagram of infiltration gallery (after Falkland 1991).*

helical rotor pumps to maintain a small and steady extraction of the water resource, limiting the drawdown and thus avoiding localized saltwater intrusion (Falkland 1991). Examples of such galleries in the Pacific can be found in Majuro, the Marshall Islands, Tarawa, Kiribati, and Aitutaki in the Cook Islands.

On Christmas Island (Kiritimati), new gallery installations provide fresh water to the increasing populations of the four villages there. These are pumped using solar pumps and windmills, although the latter have been extracting water at a rate that has caused sand infiltration, reducing the life of the pump cylinders (Falkland A. pers. comm.).

Groundwater resources from volcanic sequences, such as those found in Hawai'i and French Polynesia, can provide high quantities of water from confined conditions. In Tahiti, wells drilled at the base of slopes yield up to 100 liters/second with little drawdown (Guillen 1996). In Hawai'i, high-yielding aquifers are located behind dikes and fault structures and are often tapped by horizontal wells or tunnels (Peterson 1991). Basal volcanic sequences around the Hawaiian Islands provide the bulk of the groundwater from skimming tunnels (Maui Tunnels), which are similar to infiltration galleries but on a larger scale.

Groundwater supplies from limestone aquifers for urban areas such as Port Vila in Vanuatu and Honiara in Solomon Islands are generally of good quantity and quality, requiring minimal treatment.

Thermal groundwater is used in the Pacific for cooking, heating, bathing, and recreation. The hot springs of Rotorua in New Zealand are a typical example. Villages adjacent to dormant or active volcanoes, such as Savo in Solomon Islands and Yasur in Tanna, Vanuatu, utilize thermal groundwater.

Unconventional Technology, Importation

Importation of water is practiced in Fiji during dry spells. Water is barged to outer islands or tankered to water-short villages on the main islands by the Public Works Department. This places a large demand on the national budget, with annual costs sometimes exceeding FJ$1 million (UNDHA 1994).

In Nauru, where most of the island has been exploited for phosphate mining, rendering groundwater unsuitable for use,

water supply from roof catchments has been supplemented by importing water originally using the return trips of the ships used to export the ore.

Unconventional Technology, Desalination

With the end of mining approaching, the Nauru government installed a desalination plant to provide fresh water for the island nation. This consisted of a plant using a distillation process and waste heat from the power station. A period of drought at the end of the millennium resulted in plant failure with limited production available since.

Desalination technology has also been used on a small scale in other countries of the Pacific. These include the Marshall Islands (Ebeye), where a multiple-effect distillation plant is currently providing 450 m^3/day, and Tuvalu (Funafuti), where a small reverse osmosis plant with an installed capacity of 15 m^3/day is used as a standby for the hospital.

Other Unconventional Technology

To conserve valuable freshwater supplies, salt water has been used for firefighting and sewage disposal systems at some locations, such as Tarawa in Kiribati and Majuro and Ebeye in the Marshall Islands. A total of 189 lpcd of seawater are used in the two urban centers of the Marshalls. In the outer islands people often use seawater for washing to conserve their freshwater supplies.

In the urban context, demand management and other water conservation techniques are used to reduce the amount of water required. Various actions are used in the Pacific to promote economy of water use, including metering of all consumers, education in the need to economize on water, promotion of efficient plumbing and sanitary fittings, reduction of unaccounted-for water by leak detection and system rehabilitation (Goodwin 1996), and adjustment of tariffs to reflect true costs and to penalize extravagant use.

In French Polynesia the introduction of a payment system for water reduced consumption to 25 percent of the previous usage. A 43 percent reduction in consumption was reported in Honiara, Solomon Islands, following the introduction of metering. Similarly, in Pohnpei in the Federated States of Micronesia, a 25 percent reduction in consumption followed metering and a revised pricing structure for water supply. In American Samoa, metering reduced consumption from a maximum of 570 lpcd to an average of 230 lpcd.

Water Quality

Natural Water Quality

Water, being the "universal solvent," is affected by the medium over which or through which it passes. Rainwater is generally low (<10 mg/l) in dissolved solids, although usually a little acidic. Surface waters and groundwater have chemical compositions that reflect their origin. Typical analyses from the Pacific are shown in Table 6.4. As well as picking up harmless elements from the environment, water, in all phases of its natural cycle, also picks up contaminants, both natural and man-made (Gangaiya and Morrison 1988).

Table 6.4

Typical Analyses for Freshwater Resources in the Pacific (mg/kg except for pH and conductivity)

	Niue Ground water	Nauru Rain water	Kiribati Ground water	Vanuatu Thermal spring	Vanuatu River water
conductivity (mS/cm)	321	21	575	nr	350
pH	7.7	6.5	8.4	7	7.25
TDS (total dissolved solids)	17	10	nr	nr	190
chloride	10	1	17	10,700	48
sulfate	4	0.3	6.2	170	2
carbonate	nr	<0.5	6	nr	nr
bicarbonate	163	9	346	nr	78
potassium	2	nr	0.31	200	7
magnesium	9	0.6	23	38	2
sodium	6	1	9.5	4,740	15
calcium	44	1	83	2,560	24

Source: SOPAC Water and Sanitation section n.d.
NR: Not recorded

Rainfall in places like Hawai'i can be affected by the gaseous emissions from volcanoes, causing the phenomenon of "acid rain," which can leach roof materials and cause metals such as lead to accumulate in the water stored in tanks. Similarly, ash and other particles emitted from volcanoes in New Zealand have affected water supplies in areas surrounding eruptions. In PNG, Rabaul's water supply was destroyed by falling ash from the 1994 eruption.

In the context of small atoll islands and in coastal regions, groundwater supplies can be affected by saline intrusion if the resource is overpumped.

Man-Made Contamination of Water Supplies

A growing waste stream threatens many water supplies, people's health, and the often fragile ecosystems of the Pacific. A range of pollutants affects water resources. These are derived partly from industrial and agricultural sources, but mostly from urban development and other nuclear settlements (Morrison, Gangaiya, and Koshy 1996). In fact, humans have always used water deliberately as a waste-transporting agency. The Pacific, as elsewhere, has many examples of polluted water resources.

Mining is a major potential polluter of surface waterways in the Pacific. Heavy metals used in processing ore, as well as sediment from the catchment disturbance caused by excavation, roading, and tailings dam construction, are a threat to rivers that take the mine discharges in such countries as New Zealand, PNG, and Fiji.

Similarly, forestry operations can be a cause of serious degradation of catchments in the tropical and subtropical countries (Bruijnzeel and Critchley 1994). The high and intense rainfalls experienced in many areas can lead to rapid soil stripping following clear felling of rain forests if codes of practice are not followed diligently. The resulting sedimentation of rivers accompanying deforestation can destroy natural water habitats not only in streams but beyond the river mouth onto reefs and coastal areas. Samoa, the Federated States of Micronesia, and most Melanesian countries have all experienced this type of pollution of their water resources (Asquith, Kooge, and Morrison 1994).

Agricultural use of fertilizers, herbicides, fungicides, and pesticides, except in New Zealand, is not yet widespread (Morrison, Gangaiya, and Koshy 1996). The growing of crops such as squash pumpkins in Tonga and Vanuatu and sugar cane in Fiji and Hawai'i is leading to an increased use of these possible water pollutants, but no major problems have been detected to date, largely because small amounts of insecticides and fungicides are being used and they are generally the type that break down rapidly on contact with the soil.

Industry is also limited in the Pacific Island nations, except for New Zealand. The large-scale freezing works (abattoirs), pulp and processing mills, refineries, smelters, and other industrial developments found in New Zealand are rare elsewhere in the Pacific. A nickel smelter in Noumea, New Caledonia, sugar refineries on the main islands of Fiji, and major mining operations in PNG are exceptions.

In both the urban and rural areas of the Pacific there is the problem of liquid and solid waste disposal from domestic sources. Failure to deal with these adequately can have disastrous effects on water supplies from both a health and an environmental point of view (Morrison 1997).

Water-borne diseases spread by fecally contaminated water include the viral diseases infectious hepatitis and poliomyelitis and the bacterial diseases cholera, typhoid, and bacillary dysentery. Diarrheal diseases caused by both viruses and bacteria contribute to the deaths of many children each year in places such as Kiribati (Saito 1995) and throughout the Pacific. Disease-causing biological agents (pathogens) affect the health and well-being of many adults as well, reducing their income-generating capacity and effectiveness in the workplace. They have a large and significant impact on morbidity and mortality rates in the Pacific.

Where water-flushed toilets exist, large quantities of water often may be needed. Pour-flush toilets require a reliable supply. For other sanitation types, water is still needed for hand washing if good hygiene is practiced. Most sanitation facilities have the potential to contaminate water supplies. On small islands, where groundwater is a major source, the ability of effluent from latrines to penetrate to the water table can pollute the groundwater supply and can lead to the spread of disease (Dillon 1996).

Universal access to a safe water supply, coupled with the availability of sanitary means of excreta disposal, would bring about a marked increase in the standard of living and economic well-being of many in the Pacific region. In Honiara in Solomon Islands in 1993, for example, each child under one year of age suffered an average of four incidents of infectious diseases including skin diseases, yaws, red eye, and fever (Solomon Islands Government 1993a).

High infant mortality rates in some locations, and the presence of malaria and other vector-transmitted illnesses throughout a large part of Melanesia, are a real concern in the region. Open tanks, uncovered containers, and other standing water, particularly during rainy seasons, provide breeding grounds for the mosquito larvae that transmit malaria and other diseases such as dengue fever to humans. In PNG in 1990 the infant mortality rate was 57.5 per 1,000 live births, down from 93 in 1975 (Berhane 1994). In the same year the Kiribati infant mortality rate was 65. Poor sanitation and inadequate supplies of clean water are major factors in the prevalence of water-related diseases. In 1992 in Solomon Islands, 440 malaria cases per 1,000 persons were reported (Solomon Islands Government 1993b). Regular typhoid epidemics have occurred in periurban areas of Port Moresby and other towns in PNG.

Remedial and Preventive Measures

Where required, most Pacific reticulated urban water supplies are disinfected by the use of chlorine, either in gas or liquid form. This is generally effective in eliminating bacterial contamination.

Water extracted for supply from waterways may also be discolored from time to time by sediment, particularly during heavy rain periods, and may require sedimentation and/or filtration treatment. Sophisticated treatment plants to deal with the suspended and soluble solids are operated in such places as Auckland in New Zealand to provide a clean potable water supply for the city. Simpler treatment facilities are found in smaller urban areas of the Pacific such as 'Apia in Samoa, where a series of slow sand filters and sedimentation tanks are used.

In the village or rural situation, particularly where the population is increasing, there is a need for improved health and hygiene education related to the processes of water supply, waste disposal, and food preparation. The location of latrines at some distance and downstream from shallow wells would reduce the risk to health from waterborne diseases.

In some of the developing countries of the Pacific, waterless toilets, either ventilated improved pit (VIP), or composting types, have been tried. The composting zero-discharge toilets do not contribute effluent to the ground, which results in unpolluted groundwater supplies (Crennan 1996). The composting toilet trials on Christmas Island (Kiritimati) (Figure 6.6), however, are being suspended at the request of the Kiribati government.

There is little legislation in many of the Pacific Island countries regarding the protection of the water supply. Only in New Zealand, Hawai'i, and some of the French and American territories are protection zones in evidence. Guam, for example, has an Environmental Protection Agency that administers wellhead protection zones around the one hundred wells that supply most of the island, and a designated groundwater management and protection zone. Elsewhere, land tenure problems often preclude any national resolution to protect water resources. Zones have been proposed for the water supply catchment for Port Vila in Vanuatu (Depledge 1994), but they do not have the backing of legislation.

Many rivers, lakes, and wetlands in New Zealand have been preserved from development through water conservation orders. Some are in national parks and are regarded as having recreational value.

Assessment of Future Needs, Availability, and Threats to Supply

Growing Populations and Urbanization

Fewer than eight million people live in the developing island nations of the Pacific. Growth rates are locally high and are increasing regionally at rates ranging from zero in Samoa to 3.6 percent in Solomon Islands (World Bank 1990). The population may double in the next twenty-five years (East-West Center 2001). Much migration from the small island nations to the larger and more affluent neighbors such as New Zealand and Australia accounts for the low growth rates of such places as Samoa and Tonga. There is also migration from the rural areas and from the outer islands to urban centers. The major problems arise in the periurban areas, where squatter settlements develop without the aid of the amenities of the urban area proper, such as power reticulation and a safe water supply.

Urban water supply continues to be a problem for many countries because of the increasing pressure population growth puts on the resources. Aging infrastructures with a high percentage of leakage also contributes to the problem. Semiprivatization, practiced in such places as Vanuatu, New Caledonia, and French Polynesia, appears to be partially successful in providing adequate supplies (Alla 1994). Other countries, less convinced that such an important resource should be dealt with by a private company, have opted for some form of corporatization, removing political interference from the water supply operation and giving the organization some form of autonomy, as in the (Western) Samoa Water Authority, the Tonga Water Board, and the Solomon Islands Water Authority.

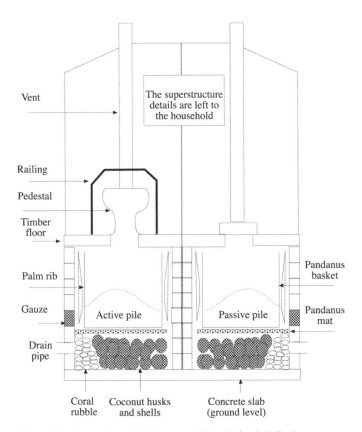

Vent

Railing

Pedestal

Timber floor

Palm rib

Gauze

Drain pipe

The superstructure details are left to the household

Active pile

Passive pile

Pandanus basket

Pandanus mat

Coral rubble

Coconut husks and shells

Concrete slab (ground level)

Figure 6.6. Composting toilet diagram, Kiritimati Island, Kiribati.

Industrial and Agricultural Growth

In the world as a whole, agriculture, particularly in the form of irrigation, accounts for a major part of the water usage. In the Pacific, apart from New Zealand and some small areas in a few of the high-island countries, irrigation is little practiced. This may change in the future with the introduction of lucrative food crops such as squash pumpkins for Asian markets.

Water demand is likely to increase with the independence of many nations and their drive toward self-sufficiency. Tourism and small industries—especially agro-industries such as sugar, oil, and copra—will create demands. Tourism is becoming a major income earner for many nations and is having a marked effect on the availability of resources. In places such as French Polynesia, Vanuatu, Tonga, and Fiji, there has been an increase in the numbers of tourists arriving, and the diversion of available water to resort activities has led to a decline in the amount of water available for local use.

Mining activities and logging of the high-value hardwoods of the Pacific tropical forests are likely to expand in the Melanesian countries. There is a clear need to introduce enforceable environmental legislation in these countries as soon as possible.

Environmental Needs and Ecosystems

Land-based activities on the often small habitable landmasses of the Pacific affect both the fragile freshwater resources and the coastal and marine ecosystems surrounding the land. A growing population rate, together with the displacement of traditional land practices by introduced agriculture, mining, and forestry developments, is seriously stressing the freshwater resources and the land and marine resources. River systems and even shallow groundwater reservoirs receiving pollutants in turn pass these on to the marine environment by the natural gravitation of fresh water to the sea. Thus we have a growing concern for the nearshore waters of many Pacific Island nations and for the reefs that receive much sediment and sometimes toxic wastes via inland waterways from mining, forestry, and other land disturbances. Sewage is a major contributor to pollution in the Pacific. This pollution affects both fresh water and marine waters adjacent to the coast. The septic tanks used extensively in Port Vila, Vanuatu, contribute many nutrients and even microorganisms to the underlying groundwater, the harbor, and lagoons.

Integrated Water Resources Management

The supply of unpolluted fresh water in the twenty-first century continues to be a major concern for small-island developing states in the Pacific. Apart from the existing needs and concerns for fresh water of the various sectors noted above, the South Pacific has been identified by the IPCC as being one of the four regions of the world to be especially affected by climate change (NIWA 2007). Although current predictions of global warming and climate change remain speculative, the temperature increases and rate of increase in the twentieth century for the region (IPCC 2001) indicate that freshwater resources may be affected, particularly by any sea-level rise, changes in rainfall patterns, and possibly by changes in the incidence and/or intensity of storms in the Pacific (Burns 2000). There is a need to continue close monitoring of the needs, use, and availability of the resource.

Yet hindrances to effective water governance often exist because of competing activities in watersheds such as urban and rural water supplies, commercial forestry, tourist developments, and subsistence agriculture. There is also the problem of overlapping responsibilities of various government agencies and existing legislation. In Fiji, for example, several legislative acts have a bearing on water resource availability, use, and management, including the Rivers and Streams Ordinance, the Irrigation Act, and the Drainage Act. Water management may be further complicated by the disconnectedness between traditional community values and national administration practices. All of the above combine to present many challenges to good water governance at different scales and across various sectors.

To bring together the diverse activities being undertaken by the various sectors dealing with the fragile freshwater resources in the Pacific, some regional and international agencies have developed a Regional Action Plan (RAP) to coordinate the activities of the organizations involved in water resources (ADB and SOPAC 2002). This plan was presented to the 3rd World Water Forum held in Kyoto, Japan, in 2003.

Subsequent meetings and discussions have led to the commencement of an Integrated Water Resources Management plan (IWRM) for Pacific Island countries (SOPAC 2007). These plans, advocated by the United Nations to accelerate achievement of the Millennium Goals in Water and Sanitation, are already under way. Based on the original RAP, the initial stages, consisting of plans for fourteen of the participating countries, were undertaken during 2006–2007.

Another step in this process has been the establishment of a regional training center for IWRM at the University of the South Pacific, which is the main provider of tertiary education to twelve island nations. A "Water Virtual Learning Center" was established in 2005 at the university campus in Fiji, with UN assistance, to provide professional training in "Pacific-customized" IWRM to scientists and policy makers, with the aim of improving sustainable water-resource-management practices.

The objective of IWRMs is to bring together the often competing demands on limited water and land resources from economic, environmental, and public health sectors. These have been mentioned earlier in this chapter, but the fourteen individual country plans already completed have confirmed that serious threats to the Pacific Island countries' management of their resources will come from rapid population growth, continuing urban migration, deforestation changes to catchments, poor waste management leading to pollution, and the increasing challenges posed by possible climate change.

Water Politics in Hawai'i

A recent dispute over water diversion on O'ahu illustrates some of the political, economic, and environmental issues relevant to water allocation in Hawai'i. The Waiāhole ditch is a tunnel extending 43 km through O'ahu's main mountain range, channeling water from dikes in the windward side of the island to the dry leeward side.

It was built in 1916 by a coalition of sugar planters, pumping an average 107,000 m³/d for irrigation in leeward O'ahu.

In the early 1990s, declines in the profitability of agriculture led the Oahu Sugar Company (largest user of the Waiāhole ditch) to transfer its operations to the Philippines, where labor prices were lower. Thirty-six thousand hectares were released from sugar production, and up to 83,000 m³/d of ditch water was dumped into leeward gulches. Leeward landowners, farmers, resorts, the state Department of Agriculture, the Honolulu Board of Water Supply, and the U.S. Navy favored continuing the diversion. Waiāhole taro farmers, Native Hawaiian groups, and environmentalists demanded return of water to the windward side.

Those demanding windward restoration argued that the ditch violated traditional Hawaiian water rights, lowered windward stream levels, promoted root rot on windward taro (which requires cool water flow), and endangered native aquatic species in windward streams and Kāne'ohe Bay (formerly an important estuarine fish nursery). They maintained that leeward needs could be served through groundwater. Leeward interests argued that water was needed for agriculture, residential, and commercial development, golf courses, aquifer recharge, and urban growth, and that groundwater was too expensive or insufficient.

Hearings by the state Water Use Commission, which controls water use in Hawai'i, began in November 1995. In December 1997, the commission issued its decision (Kreifels 1997). It allocated continued leeward diversion of 53,000 m³/d for use in agriculture, golf courses, and other uses and returned 49,000 m³/d to the windward side to raise stream levels and for use by windward farmers (the latter included 7,500 m³/d as a possible future reserve for leeward agricultural expansion). The issue remains in dispute, but the decision has set an important precedent.

Conclusion

Pacific Island water use reflects the still-developing nature of the area, with water supply technology ranging from the primitive to the most modern. Each has its merits and its drawbacks. The real need for individual communities, large and small, is an appropriate technology that is also affordable and sustainable. While meeting the basic needs for human beings, that is, for drinking, cooking and washing, it must also meet the requirements of maintaining hygiene. The future will also bring an increasing demand from the agricultural, industrial, forestry, tourism, and other economic sectors. The vital contribution of clean fresh water to the environmental and ecological stability of the Pacific will also take on an increasing importance. Added to the conflicting demands on the resources, there is the uncertainty and variability of water supply arising from the spatially and temporally limited supplies and the threat of global warming and climate change.

BIBLIOGRAPHY

ADB and SOPAC. 2002. *Pacific Regional Action Plan on Sustainable Water Management, Suva, Fiji,* Misc Report 547, SOPAC, Suva, Fiji.

Alla, P. 1994. Public/private partnership—an optional way of delivering a better service in the water industry. In *Pacific water sector planning, research and training,* 121–124. Honiara: UNESCO/SOPAC/UNDDSMS.

Anthony, S. S. 1991. Case study 7: Majuro Atoll. In *Hydrology and water resources of small islands: A practical guide,* ed. A. Falkland, 368–374. Paris: UNESCO/IHP.

Asquith, F., M. Kooge, and R. J. Morrison. 1994. *Transportation of sediments via rivers to the ocean and the role of sediments as pollutants in the South Pacific.* Reports and Studies No. 72. Apia: South Pacific Regional Environment Programme.

Berhane, D. 1994. Position and issues paper, country background. PNG: Water and Sanitation Committee, PNG.

Bettencourt, S., J. Campbell, N. de Wet, A. Falkland, J. Feresi, R. Jones, P. Kench, G. Kenny, W. King, P. Lehodey, L. Limalevu, R. Raucher, T. Taeuea, J. Terry, N. Teutabo, and R. Warrick. 2002. The impacts of climate change in Pacific Island economies: Policy and development implications. *Asia Pacific Journal on Environment and Development* 9: 142–165.

Bruijnzeel, L. A., and W. R. S. Critchley. 1994. *Environmental impacts of logging moist tropical forests.* Paris: UNESCO/IHP Humid Tropics Programme Series No. 7.

Burns, W. C. G. 2000. The impact of climate change on Pacific Island developing countries in the 21st century. In *Climate change in the South Pacific: Impacts and responses in Australia, New Zealand and small island states,* ed. A. Gillespie and W. C. G. Burns, 233–251. Dordrecht: Kluwer Academic.

Convard, N. 1993. *Land-based pollutants inventory for the South Pacific region.* Apia: SPREP Report and Study Series No. 68.

Crennan, L. 1996. Case study 4: Composting toilet trial in Kiritimati, Kiribati. In *Technologies for augmenting freshwater resources in small island developing states.* Suva: UNEP/SOPAC.

Department of Land and Natural Resources. 1987. Water use 1985. Unpublished data, Dept. of Land and Natural Resources, Hawai'i.

Depledge, D. 1994. *The urban water resources of Port Vila, Vanuatu.* Vila Hydrogeological Report, Dept. of Geology, Mines and Water Resources.

———. 1996. *Water resources development and management in the Pacific Region.* Keynote presentation, ADB Regional Consultation Workshop, Manila.

Dillon, P. 1996. *Groundwater pollution by sanitation on tropical islands.* A UNESCO/IHP Study. CSIRO Groundwater Studies Report No. 6.

Doig, K. 1996. *Republic of Marshall Islands water and sanitation action plan.* Suva: SOPAC Tech Report 236.

Duncan, M. J. 1992. Flow regimes of New Zealand rivers. In *Waters of New Zealand,* ed. M. P. Mosley, 13–27. Christchurch: NZ Hydrological Society.

East-West Center 2001. Pacific Island regional assessment of the consequences of climate variability and change. Honolulu: East-West Center.

Falkland, A. 1991. *Hydrology and water resources of small islands: A practical guide.* Paris: UNESCO Studies and Reports in Hydrology No. 49.

———. 1999. Impacts of climate change on water resources of Pacific islands. PACCLIM Workshop, Modelling the Effects of Climate Change and Sea Level Rise in Pacific Island Countries, New Zealand.

Gangaiya, P., and R. J. Morrison. 1987. Natural waters in the South Pacific Islands. In *Chemistry serves the South Pacific,* ed. J. Bonato et al., 160–168. Suva: Institute of Pacific Studies, University of the South Pacific.

Goodwin, R. 1996. *A programme of action for the sustainable development of water resources in Micronesia.* Keynote Address, Water Resources Management in the Pacific Rim Conference, Guam.

Guillen, J. 1996. Augmenting freshwater resources in small islands: French Polynesia. In Proceedings of workshop on maximising and augmenting freshwater resources in small islands, SOPAC, Fiji, Feb. 6–8, 1996.

Hunt, T. M., and H. M. Bibby. 1992. Geothermal hydrology. In *Waters of New Zealand,* ed. M. P. Mosley, 147–166. Christchurch: NZ Hydrological Society.

IPCC (Intergovernmental Panel on Climate Change). 2001. *Working Group II to the Third Assessment Report, Climate Change 2001: Impacts, adaptation, and vulnerability.* Cambridge: Cambridge University Press.

Jacobson, G., and P. J. Hill. 1980. Hydrogeology of a raised coral atoll—Niue Island, South Pacific Ocean. *BMR Journal of Geology and Geophysics* 5: 271–278.

Kreifels, S. 1997. A state commission decision on Waiahole Ditch will divert millions of gallons. *Honolulu Star-Bulletin,* December 24, 1997.

Metutera, T. 1996. Case study 1: Augmenting freshwater resources in Kiribati. In *Technologies for augmenting freshwater resources in small island developing states.* Suva: UNEP/SOPAC.

Morrison, R. J., ed. 1997. *Waste management in small island developing states in the South Pacific.* 2 vols. Bangkok: UNEP.

Morrison, R. J., P. Gangaiya, and K. Koshy. 1996. Contaminated soils in the South Pacific Islands. In *Contaminants and the soil environment in the Australasia-Pacific region,* ed. R. Naidu et al., 659–670. Amsterdam: Kluwer Academic Publisher.

Mosley, M. P. 1988. *Climate change impacts—the water industry.* Chapter 20. Wellington: New Zealand Ministry for the Environment.

———. 1995. Flow regimes in New Zealand. In *Rivers and people in Southeast Asia and the Pacific—partnership for the 21st century.* Paris: UNESCO/IHP.

Mourits, L., and D. Depledge. 1995. *Handpumps in the S Pacific—a review.* Suva: SOPAC Technical Report No 224.

NIWA. 2007. Climate change: The Intergovernmental Panel on Climate Change 4th Assessment Report—the South Pacific. *Island Climate Update 80,* May 2007.

Nullet, D. 1987. Water balance of Pacific atolls. *Water Resources Bulletin* 23: 1125–1132.

Peterson, F. L. 1991. Case study 6: Hawaiian Islands. In *Hydrology and water resources of small islands: A practical guide,* ed. A. Falkland, 362–367. Paris: UNESCO/IHP.

Piliwas, L. 1996. *Papua New Guinea country paper.* Regional Consultation Workshop, Asian Development Bank, Manila, May 10–14, 1996.

Raj, R. 1996. *Fiji country paper.* Regional Consultation Workshop, Asian Development Bank, Manila, May 10–14, 1996.

Saito, S. 1995. *Knowledge, attitudes and practices research on diarrhoeal diseases.* Tarawa: Kiribati Child Survival Project.

Solomon Islands Government. 1993a. *Incidence rate of disease in 1993 per 1,000 persons.* Honiara: Statistics Unit, Ministry of Health and Medical Services.

Solomon Islands Government. 1993b. *The national antimalaria plan of operation, 1994–1998.* Honiara: Ministry of Health and Medical Services National Antimalarial Programme, December 1993.

Soons, J. M. 1972. *Modern geography: Water, with reference to Australia and New Zealand.* Auckland: Reed Education.

SOPAC. 2007. Integrated water resources management in Pacific Island countries, a synopsis. GWP Consultants, SOPAC Secretariat, Suva.

Stratus Consulting. 2000. Economic implications of climate change in two Pacific Island country locations. Case illustration of Tarawa, Kiribati and Viti Levu. Report prepared under subcontract to the Center for International Climate and Environmental Research, Oslo, Norway for the World Bank, Stratus Consulting, Boulder, Colorado.

Terry, J. 2005. Hazard warning! Hydrological responses in the Fiji Islands to climate variability and severe meteorological events. In *Regional hydrological impacts of climatic change—hydroclimatic variability,* ed. S. Franks, T. Wagener, E. Bøgh, H. V. Gupta, L. Bastidas, C. Nobre, and C. de Oliveira Galvão, 33–41. International Association of Hydrological Sciences, Publication 296.

Terry, J. P., and A. C. Falkland. 2010. Responses of atoll freshwater lenses to storm-surge overwash in the Northern Cook Islands. *Hydrogeology Journal* 18: 749–759.

Trustrum, N. A., I. E. Whitehouse, and P. M. Blaschke. 1989. Flood and Landslide Hazard, Northern Guadalcanal, Solomon Islands. Department of Scientific and Industrial Research, New Zealand. Unpublished report for United Nations Technical Cooperation for Development, New York, 6/89 SOI/87/001.43.

UNDHA. 1994. Assessment of drought problems in Fiji. *Water Resources Journal* 30(12): 94–105.

White, I. 1996. Personal communication, Water Research Foundation of Australia, Australian National University.

White, I., A. Falkland, and D. Scott. 1999. *Droughts in small coral islands: Case study, South Tarawa, Kiribati.* UNESCO IHP-V, Technical Documents in Hydrology, No. 26. Paris: UNESCO.

World Bank. 1990. *Social indicators of development.* Washington, D.C.: World Bank.

The Living Environment

The Pacific Islands are home to diverse ecosystems—strand communities on shoreline plains and atolls, montane forests cloaking the interior of high islands, and marine ecosystems extending offshore. Island flora and fauna are distinctive, with high rates of endemism, taxonomic disharmony, and vulnerability to invasion and extinction. Biotic distributions vary considerably in accordance with geotectonic history, ease of dispersal, habitat availability, and human interference. This section explains how Pacific Island biota have spread and evolved, then describes the principal ecosystems.

Biogeography

Brenden S. Holland and E. Alison Kay

7

Biogeography is the scientific discipline that seeks to understand the distribution of animal and plant life on earth. As a fundamentally integrative, multidisciplinary field, biogeography has both historical and predictive powers. Such varied fields as climatology, ecology, geology, phylogenetics, and physiology contribute to our understanding of why species naturally occur where they do, providing the most complete picture obtainable of how and where biodiversity is generated as well as how and where it is lost. In recent decades it has become evident that if we are to understand the patterns of natural distributions of organisms on earth, we need to begin to elucidate the processes driving these patterns. Islands have played and continue to play key roles in revealing the mechanisms that influence species diversity and distributions. The biotas of the thirty thousand islands of the Pacific (Spiess 2007), more islands than are found in the Indian and Atlantic Oceans combined, have been central to biogeography since the eighteenth century when Captain Cook and his ships' companies began the exploration of the Pacific, returning to Europe with specimens of strange and previously unknown organisms. A century later, the inferences made independently by Charles Darwin and Alfred Russell Wallace greatly heightened scientific interest in the unique flora and fauna of islands. Ultimately these insights sparked the birth of island biogeography, an important field that focuses on the natural history, biodiversity, and conservation of life on islands.

Today Pacific Island biogeography continues to contribute in major ways to our understanding of biodiversity. The birds of New Guinea served as model organisms for Mayr's (1942) groundbreaking definition of allopatric speciation. The ants of Melanesia were key players in Wilson's *Taxon Cycle* (1961) and MacArthur and Wilson's *Theory of Island Biogeography* (1967). The finches of the Galápagos (Grant 1986) and the Hawaiian honeycreepers (Freed, Conant, and Fleisher 1987), spiders (Gillespie 2004), moths (Rubinoff 2008), and silverswords (Baldwin and Sanderson 1998) provide classic examples of adaptive radiations. Pacific Island tree snails are important to ongoing biodiversity research and to concepts of speciation without adaptive radiation and insular endemism (Gulick 1890; Clarke and Murray 1969; Holland and Hadfield 2002, 2004; Lee et al. 2007; Cowie and Holland 2008). In addition to dozens of studies focusing on Pacific Island biogeography published in recent years, important compilations of studies and reviews include the seminal book *Hawaiian Biogeography: Evolution on a Hot Spot Archipelago* (Wagner and Funk 1995) and more recently a special issue of the *Philosophical Transactions of the Royal Society* (Trewick and Cowie 2008), commemorating the 150th anniversary of Darwin's publication of *On the Origin of Species* and the bicentennial of his birth. These works showcase recent molecular approaches to biogeographic studies of terrestrial Pacific Island radiations.

Although we are still addressing some of the same questions the pioneers in the field of Pacific Island biogeography posed starting in the late eighteenth century, thanks to new sets of powerful molecular tools the field has been reinvigorated and a number of these fundamental questions are beginning to yield answers: How do animals and plants arrive on islands? Why are island species so different from their continental ancestors? How do a few colonizing species diversify into dozens over time? What is the pace of speciation on islands versus continental environments?

In this chapter, trends in island distribution patterns and some of the mechanisms that explain these observations are discussed and distinguished, to highlight differences in pattern and process among insular island biotas and those of the continents, both terrestrial and marine.

Recent commentaries (e.g., Cowie and Holland 2006; Trewick, Paterson, and Campbell 2007) have highlighted the need for a shift toward more integrated studies if hypotheses about the evolution of island biotas are to be adequately addressed. The application of molecular approaches to biogeography has enhanced our ability to understand patterns in biodiversity and diversification. With increasing confidence and precision, biologists can explore topics such as relative roles of vicariance and dispersal in island species diversification, and geographic sources, pathways, and timing of island colonization events. A molecular approach enables researchers to delineate precisely and quantitatively the spatial extent of endemic species distributions, species boundaries, and hierarchical systematic relationships among lineages from proximate islands, distant islands, and continents and islands. Importantly, molecular phylogenetics has enabled testing of evolutionary hypotheses including those that were first stimulated by observations of the island faunas. We conclude the chapter with a brief discussion of human impacts and conservation considerations. The tremendous number of recent studies employing a DNA approach to island biogeography demonstrates that there is great potential in the use of molecular systematics to underpin the study of adaptation and diversification during evolution, and it shows that the field is a youthful one with much work yet to be done.

Patterns

Island Biota

It has been clear for centuries that distributions of animals and plants on islands are not random. As explorer-naturalists from Europe traversed the oceans in wooden sailing vessels, they began to recognize certain consistencies in some of the peculiarities. Forster's (1996) observations on Cook's second voyage of 1772–1775 in the Pacific are especially perceptive: "The countries of the South Sea . . . contain a considerable variety of animals, though they are confined to a few classes only," and to Forster's apparent delight, "this happy country is free from all noxious and trouble-some insects; no wasps, nor mosquitoes." Such observations hint at what we now refer to as the "disharmonic" nature of island biotas. Because the processes of dispersal, colonization, establishment, persistence, and extinction are highly selective, island assemblages have systematic compositions often lacking in whole categories of taxa relative to continental communities. Biogeographers refer to "filters" of varying strengths, where the degree of geographic isolation (i.e., distance from potential colonization source)—coupled

with an interplay of island age, area, habitat complexity, latitude, and maximum elevation, together with dispersal ability and reproductive potential of the species in question—determine filter strength in precluding arrival of certain organisms. For example, groups that have relatively good dispersal and establishment ability tend to be represented even on geologically young, remote islands. Groups including birds, bats, flying insects, spiders, snails, ferns, plant species with wind or ocean dispersal and or sticky spores and seeds, or those that are consumed and transported in the guts of birds, are frequently represented in isolated oceanic island communities. Missing, however, are poorly dispersing groups such as large grazing mammals, nonvolant medium and small mammals, reptiles, amphibians, and freshwater species (Figure 7.1).

Long before plate tectonic theory had been formulated, nearly a century before side-scan sonar had been developed, refined, and applied to mapping seafloor topography, a number of Darwin and Wallace's contemporaries proposed that oceanic island chains are merely remnant mountain peaks of a past continent that has since subsided and eroded from view beneath the swells of the Pacific Ocean. Referred to as the "South Pacific Continent" or "Mid-Pacific Continent" hypothesis, and based on the absence of certain vertebrates such as reptiles and mammals and in some cases on the physical similarity in taxa on widespread islands, a number of versions of the theory were proposed by several naturalists including Hutton (1896), Baur (1897), Pilsbry (1900), and others. Examining the very same disharmonic distributions on Pacific islands,

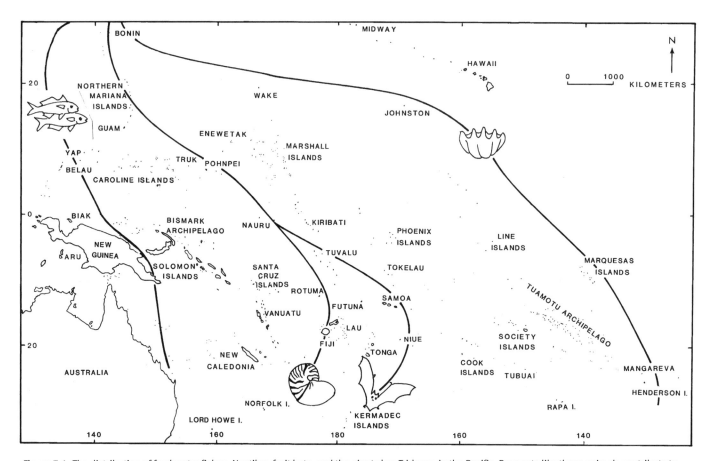

Figure 7.1. The distribution of freshwater fishes, Nautilus, fruit bats, and the giant clam Tridacna in the Pacific. Dropouts like these animals contribute to species attenuation west to east across the Pacific.

however, Wallace correctly concluded in 1882 that the Polynesian fauna have been forever insular and "have derived their constituents by over-sea drift and by wind or by birds carrying animals or their eggs" (Wallace 1876). Meanwhile Darwin, likewise convinced that oceanic islands had been populated by long-distance dispersal, had been quietly conducting experiments and testing sea survival of various plant seeds, frog eggs, and land snails, to address the question of how species are transported across great swaths of open ocean. Today, of course, high-resolution digital imaging of seafloor topography and well-developed geophysical models of plate tectonic motion reveal that the isolated oceanic islands of the Pacific arose in place as a result of volcanic forces, and that the endemic lineages are derived from ancestors that arrived via long-distance oceanic dispersal (de Quieroz 2005; Cowie and Holland 2006).

However, in some cases, long-standing assumptions of island biogeography are being challenged by molecular data, for example, the idea that amphibians are unable to cross marine barriers, as noted by Darwin in *On the Origin of Species* (1859). While it may appear to be common sense that organisms such as frogs, newts, and toads are poor oceanic dispersers due to a physiological inability to tolerate salt, two frog species found in the Comoros archipelago 300 km from Madagascar have recently been shown using DNA analyses to be endemic island frogs and to be derived from two independent colonization events (Vences et al. 2003). To paraphrase Darwin (1859) himself: Given enough time, many things that seem unlikely can occur.

The Cook ships returned to England in 1780 with bird skins, land snails, and pressed plants, the first of countless curious specimens that were to be described from the Pacific Islands during the ensuing two hundred years. There were massive araucarias and kauris on the continental islands of New Zealand and New Guinea, and breadfruit, palms, *Pandanus,* and climbing vines such as *Freycinetia* on oceanic islands. Among the strangest birds in the world were the flightless moa, the legendary giant ratite of New Zealand that turned out not only to be real, but enormous as well, attaining a height of 3.6 m and 250 kg; at least four species of flightless Hawaiian goose-like birds that were the ecological equivalents of the giant Galápagos and Indian Ocean island tortoises, and also had evolved to fill ecological niches left vacant by the absence of grazing mammals; the kagu in New Caledonia, small birds with a bark like a dog; megapodes on Vanuatu and in Palau, fowl-like birds that deposit their eggs in soil, in hot volcanic ash piles, and under heaps of decaying leaves; and in Samoa, tooth-billed pigeons with powerful curved bills. Butterflies from New Guinea were described as "bird-winged," the achatinelline tree snails from Hawai'i as "gem-like" (Figure 7.2).

Among endemic Pacific Island radiations is an array of remarkable features attributed to otherwise familiar flora and fauna. In Hawai'i, raspberries lack thorns, and mints have lost their characteristic fragrance; on Rarotonga, *Fitchia,* a relative of the sunflower, is a woody tree (Carlquist 1965). In the Galápagos, one of the two species of iguanas is marine and dives under the breaking Pacific surf to feed on seaweeds. In both the Galápagos and Hawai'i, finchlike birds behave like woodpeckers, while others have bills adapted for crushing seeds. Flightless birds evolved multiple times on islands across the Pacific, tiny predatory caterpillars roam Hawai'i's

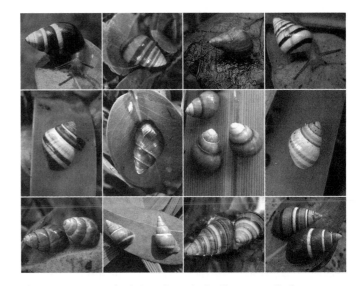

Figure 7.2. Extant endemic Hawaiian achatinelline tree snails, from upper left to right: Achatinella sowerbyana, *O'ahu;* Achatinella livida, *O'ahu;* Partulina crocea, *Maui;* Achatinella fulgens, *O'ahu;* Achatinella fuscobasis, *O'ahu;* Achatinella lila, *O'ahu;* Achatinella livida, *O'ahu;* Achatinella fuscobasis, *O'ahu;* Achatinella decipiens, *O'ahu;* Partulina tappaniana, *Maui;* Achatinella mustelina, *O'ahu;* Partulina redfieldi, *Moloka'i (photos BSH).*

rain forests, some ambush and devour drosophilid flies (Montgomery 1983), while others prey on tiny endemic snails by spinning silk holdfasts to secure the shell in place while the caterpillar consumes the soft body parts (Rubinoff and Haines 2005). The youngest and highest Hawaiian Island, Hawai'i, has an endemic insect at the treeless 4,200 m (13,796 ft.) summit of the Mauna Kea volcano, the wekiu bug, a flightless hemipteran that routinely endures huge thermal fluctuations, including subfreezing nights, and feeds on dead insects blown upslope and deposited amidst the barren lava and ash flows (Ashlock and Gagné 1983). The remarkable freshwater biotas consisting of fishes, crustaceans, and gastropods on oceanic islands are descendants of marine ancestors.

Genera on high islands have a disproportionately large number of species (Zimmerman 1942). In Hawai'i, more than 90 percent of the insects are endemic; the extremely diverse fly genus *Drosophila,* a group with about a thousand species (O'Grady and DeSalle 2008), is rivaled only by the moth genus *Hyposmocoma* (Rubinoff 2008) in species richness. The average number of species per genus in Hawaiian insects is 9.8 (range 1–218) (Zimmerman 1948). In Tahiti and Samoa, where more than 90 percent of the land snails are endemic, there are ten to twenty species per genus (Kay 1995). It was once said that each valley and ridge in Hawai'i had its own species of land snail (Emerson 1941); Garrett (1887) wrote of Society Island tree snails as "rare and peculiar to one valley in Tahiti," and molecular studies are confirming the high species diversity of these oceanic archipelagoes (Holland and Hadfield 2004; Lee et al. 2007; Lee et al. 2008).

The Pacific Marine Biota

On Cook's second voyage into the Pacific, Forster (1996) commented on "difficulties in the collection" of marine organisms, "not only from our very short stay in many places, but . . . because we were obliged . . . to depend upon the natives . . . there being no expert fishermen on board." Nevertheless, he noted that "The South Sea is rich in fish, and has a great variety of species." R. B. Hinds (1844), on the *Sulphur*, remarked that in the ocean, "large and important groups of mollusks are entirely absent," that the marine shells attenuated in species numbers from west to east across the Pacific, and that marine mollusks seemed to have their origins to the west.

These early reports are confirmed by modern observations. The focus of marine species diversity lies to the west, in New Guinea, Indonesia, the Philippines, and Southeast Asia; diversity decreases with increasing latitude and distance to the east: "to move inwards from the Cook Islands to Tonga is to move . . . from bare, barren reef flats to communities of seagrasses and mangroves, abundant ophiuroids (sea stars) and probably twice as many genera of reef building corals" (Stoddart 1976). Among the mollusks, the abalones (Haliotidae), vase shells (Vasidae), and giant clams (Tridacnidae) occur as far east as the Marshall and Society Islands but are not in Hawai'i. Numbers of species attenuate, from 70 cowrie species in the Philippines to 55 on Guam and 30 in Hawai'i (Kay 1984), and from 300 coral species in Indonesia to 50 in Hawai'i (Veron 1995). In the inshore fish fauna, the numbers range from 1,357 species for Palau and Yap, 844 for the Marianas, 800 for the Marshalls, and 536 for the Hawaiian Islands (Randall 1992).

Distribution patterns of Pacific marine biota generally follow those of the terrestrial taxa with three exceptions: there is relatively lower marine endemism; there are no endemic families or genera (only endemic species); and the number of species per genus is lower than for terrestrial lineages. Pickering (1854), of the United States Exploring Expedition in Hawai'i in 1841, may have been the first to document the relatively lower marine versus terrestrial

endemism when he remarked that "the marine shells inhabiting the . . . Hawaiian group . . . are in general very widely diffused," but "each separate island of the Hawaiian group contains land-shells . . . that are not found on the neighboring islands, nor in any part of the whole globe." In Hawai'i, more than 99 percent of land snail species are endemic, there is an endemic family, the Amastridae, and many endemic genera, averaging forty species per genus. In the marine mollusks, about 26 percent of the species are endemic, but again endemism is at the species level only (Kay 1984), and there are typically no more than two or three endemic species in a genus (Kay and Palumbi 1987). Endemism in marine species in the Society Islands is similar to that in Hawai'i (Kay 1984), but there is virtually no marine endemism in the Line Islands (Kay and Switzer 1974), Marshalls (Kay and Johnson 1987), or Marianas (Vermeij, Kay, and Eldredge 1983).

Process

Distribution Patterns Explained

Because all Pacific oceanic islands originate as volcanoes and begin their existence devoid of life, every animal and plant on these islands is descended from an ancestral lineage that arrived via dispersal, in some cases by a dispersal event that was by necessity long-distance, especially for isolated island archipelagoes such as the Hawaiian Islands (Cowie and Holland 2006). Indeed Price and Clague (2002) used geological modeling to argue that at the time of the formation of the oldest high Hawaiian Island, Kaua'i, about five million years ago, the archipelago was made up of low, widespread islands unsuitable for upper-elevation cloud forest terrestrial taxa. Thus colonization of Kaua'i from older islands is not

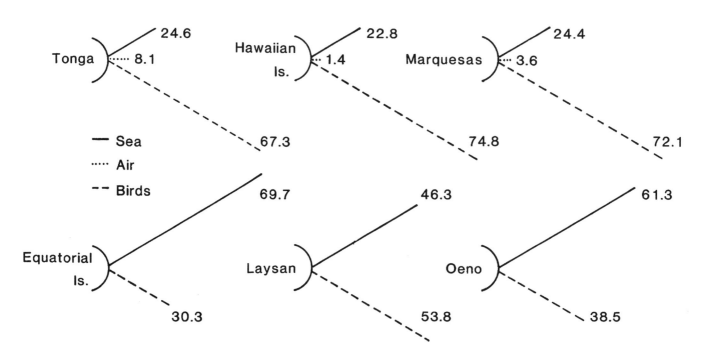

Figure 7.3. *Diagrams of modes of seed dispersal for some Pacific islands. Percentages calculated from the number of immigrants thought to account for the contemporary native species for each dispersal mode. Adapted from Carlquist (1967).*

likely, and therefore most of the extant Hawaiian radiations arrived via long-distance colonization events. A summary of molecular lineage age estimates suggests that 80 percent of these studies found that ages of the most recent common ancestors were no older than Kaua'i, implying that Kaua'i or a younger island was the island origin of most Hawaiian lineages.

The efficacy of various modes of dispersal is highly variable (Figure 7.3). Predictably, the first organisms to arrive on oceanic islands are generally plants with barbed or sticky seeds carried by bats and birds, and, as Gressitt and Yoshimoto (1963) demonstrated by sampling the jet stream high over the Pacific, small insects, spiders, and spores. Representatives of seventy-three insect families were collected in that aerial plankton; 53 percent of those families are reported in a recent survey of Henderson Island (Benton 1995), where moths and flies make up 50 percent of the insect fauna. Fourteen percent of the global fern genera are found in the Marquesas and Hawai'i (Wagner 1991). Land snails are also excellent dispersers, as evidenced by their presence and diversity in even the most remote oceanic islands. For example, the Hawaiian Islands have roughly 750 valid land snail species in fifteen families, and 99 percent of these species are endemic (Cowie, Evenhuis, and Christensen 1995). Species richness of the Hawaiian Islands rivals that of all of North America.

The role of dispersal in the distribution of marine organisms in the Pacific is similarly demonstrable: pumice and other lightweight materials raft young corals in the open ocean (Jokiel 1984); long-lived molluskan larvae have been collected from the open ocean in the central Pacific (Scheltema 1986); experiments with coral planulae indicate that some species are viable in the plankton for at least three months (Richmond 1982). The records of pelagic duration of larval fishes of thirty-five days in the central Pacific in contrast to forty-five days in the Hawaiian Islands (Brothers and Thresher 1985) are also evidence for the importance of larval dispersal. Planktonic larvae must remain competent, that is, able to successfully settle and metamorphose, for periods sufficient to allow dispersal and distant recruitment, and, as with terrestrial organisms, poorly dispersing marine species such as baler shells (*Melo*), abalone (*Haliotis*), and anemone fishes are absent. Others—wrasses (Labridae), moray eels (Muraenidae), cowries (Cypraeidae), and cone shells (Conidae)—are overly rich; for example in the cone shells, genus *Conus* spp., more than 60 percent of the five hundred global species occur from Hawai'i to the Indo-Pacific (Duda and Kohn 2005), but only three of these span the region from Hawai'i to the eastern Pacific.

The expanse of open ocean (5,000 to 7,000 km) that separates the tropical west coast of America from the Indo-West Pacific, referred to as the east Pacific barrier, is often cited as the major reason for the relatively few fishes, mollusks, and corals with Indo-West Pacific affinities that occur along the western coast of tropical America (Grigg and Hey 1992): 54 trans-Pacific shore fish species (Rosenblatt and Waples 1986), 61 species of marine mollusks (Emerson 1991), and 56 coral species (Veron 1995). That this segment of the Pacific acts as a substantial dispersal barrier to eastward movement of shallow water marine species is contradicted by the analyses of eleven trans-Pacific fishes. Their genetic composition is compatible with the notion that the fishes are either recently dispersed or the results of continuing gene flow from the Indo-Pacific

(Rosenblatt and Waples 1986). Clearly inshore demersal reef fishes and benthic shallow water invertebrates, however, have life histories that are more strongly impacted by the east Pacific barrier than do pelagic fish and invertebrate species, where ranges can be enormous, and there is recent remarkable molecular evidence for panmixia (random mating) and gene flow spanning ocean basins and beyond.

Distance and chance, both factors in long-distance dispersal, take a toll; a minute fraction of dispersal events are successful, and a very few ancestors account for a plethora of species on oceanic islands. A single colonization accounts for the 72 species of partulid land snails (Crampton 1925) of Tahiti, 99 species of achatinelline tree snails of Hawai'i (Cowie, Evenhuis, and Christensen 1995; Holland and Hadfield 2004), more than five hundred species of *Drosophila* in the Hawaiian Islands (Kaneshiro 1988), and hundreds of species of the endemic Hawaiian moth genus *Hyposmocoma* (Rubinoff 2008). Sixteen successful colonizations resulted in more than 80 species of land snails in the Galápagos (Peck 1991), and 270 to 282 successful colonizations gave rise to the Hawaiian angiosperm flora of 956 species (Wagner 1991). In effect, thousands of species of plants, birds, insects, spiders, and land snails, many of them endemic to a single island, or to a ridge or a valley on an island, arose in situ by autochthonous phyletic speciation following a single colonization event.

Simple calculations can be instructive in terms of inferring speciation rates over time in different lineages. For example, the estimated maximum lineage age of the achatinelline tree snails of the Hawaiian Islands is the age of O'ahu, approximately 3.7 million years (Holland and Hadfield 2004), and given the total number of species of 99 (Cowie, Evenhuis, and Christensen 1995), we estimate approximately 27 species arose per million years in this Hawaiian lineage.

Given that few individuals arrived by chance, the result is initial persistence of small populations sequestered by isolation, where arriving gene pools are likely only partial representations of ancestral genetic compositions, resulting in unique allelic combinations and extreme founder effects. Given high-island habitats, speciation is fueled by mosaic environments, characterized by microclimates, mountainous valleys, extreme rain gradients, *kīpuka,* lava tubes, and individual islands themselves, each presenting potential gene flow barriers and novel opportunities for niche partitioning and availability. But there are no barriers to natural adaptive "experiments" in form, function, and ecology on islands. Continental climax communities with suites of competitors and enemies confining species within particular biological niches have been left behind. Genetic variants that may have had little chance of surviving in the old environment survive and become fixed as new niches are invaded and adaption to a variety of novel ecological settings proceeds. As the descendants of one ancestral stock after another move into available niches, the landscape is filled by animals and plants doing things very differently from continental ancestors.

Changes in ancestral habits, from insect to bird pollination, from shrub to woody tree, from insectivore to woodpecking in a bird, from feeding on the yeasts of decaying fruits to predation on spiders in *Drosophila,* from herbivory to feeding on snails, and from terrestrial to freshwater lifestyle in caterpillars, are all examples of adaptive shifts. Such dramatic shifts allow the occupation of niches that were previously vacant and the use of previously untapped resources. Where there were no large herbivores, tortoises filled the niche in the Galápagos, and geese and the *moa-nalo*, heavy-bodied flightless derivatives of ducks, once filled the niche in Hawai'i (Olson 1991).

If the descendants of a single immigrant ancestor have undergone multiple adaptive shifts, the evolutionary result can be an adaptive radiation. The primary examples of adaptive radiation in the Pacific occur most noticeably on islands at the edge of the dispersal range. In the Galápagos Islands, thirteen finches and in the Hawaiian Islands more than fifty honeycreepers evolved a range of feeding habits such as seed cracking, woodpecking, cactus eating, and honey sucking, otherwise empty niches. Twenty-eight endemic Hawaiian species of what was a North American tarweed range in form from low-growing tufts of greenery on bare lava on the slopes of the volcano at 75 m to the majestic silverswords of Haleakalā and Mauna Kea at elevations of 4,000 m (Carr 1987).

Speciation Rates on Islands

Islands are frequently termed "natural laboratories" for biology and are useful in helping to understand lineage ages and rates of speciation. The general approach relies on the idea that given geological ages of islands, the maximum possible ages of single island endemics are the age of the island. Today we can use DNA markers to confirm evolutionary relationships, determine "polarity" within radiations, define endemic lineages, and infer the number of colonizing lineages per island. Given the number of colonizations, the age of the lineage, and the number of species, we can estimate colonization rates as well as speciation rates. For example, as mentioned earlier, the Hawaiian snail fauna consists of approximately 750 species, and these species arose via an estimated thirty different colonization events. Given the age of the oldest high island, Kaua'i, 5.1 million years, we can estimate that there has been one successful land snail colonization event each 170,000 years in the Hawaiian Islands. Timelines for many radiations have been estimated from the ages of islands. On Rapa (Austral Islands), five million years old, 67 species of flightless weevils (beetle subgroup *Miocalles*) and

45 achatinellid and 24 endodontoid land snail species have evolved (Paulay 1985; Solem 1982). On Tahiti (Society Islands), about one million years old, there are 70 species of endemic beetles (*Mecyclothorax*) (Perrault 1987). Twenty-five of the 26 species of picturewing *Drosophila* (Carson 1983) and 19 of the 42 species of amber snails in the genus *Succinea* (Cowie, Evenhuis, and Christensen 1995; Rundell, Holland, and Cowie 2004) evolved on the island of Hawai'i in less than 500,000 years. On Henderson Island, which is 285,000 years old, there are an endemic flightless rail and a fruit dove that coevolved with 20 fruit species in that brief period of time (Diamond 1995). It has long been assumed that each endemic group (genus, subfamily, or family) of oceanic island species has resulted from in situ speciation from a single ancestral taxon (Zimmerman 1948). Although this assumption has rarely been tested, recent molecular studies have begun to reveal surprising results contradicting this long-standing assumption, with evidence for multiple Hawaiian colonizations for what had been previously considered single lineages of snails, spiders, crane flies, and birds (Cowie and Holland 2008).

Plate tectonics and the sequential formation of islands provide an additional dimension to the remarkable patterns observed in insular evolution. Each oceanic island in the linear, chronological series of volcanoes formed as the Pacific Plate passes over the hot spot is colonized by founders from the preceding volcano, and speciation ensues. The process repeats as new islands form, and it ultimately results in a succession of single-island endemic species with the sister species of each taxon on a neighbor island, the basal taxa on older islands (Funk and Wagner 1995), and the younger lineage components on the more recent islands (Figures 7.4 and 7.5). This pattern, of older lineage components within a radiation occupying older islands is termed the "Progression Rule" of biogeography.

Patterns of marine endemism on islands generally reflect high dispersal of immigrants: 20 to 30 percent endemism for marine mollusks and fishes in the Hawaiian and the Society Islands and the near absence of species and genus level endemism in marine mollusks (Kay 1984) and shore fishes (Randall 1992; Springer 1982) of the central Pacific. Nor are there radiations in the sea comparable with the adaptive suites of moths, birds, snails, or the silversword alliance on land. Species-to-genus ratios are of the order of 1–2 to 1 among the corals (Jokiel 1987), other marine invertebrates (Kay and Palumbi 1987), and fishes (Hourigan and Reese 1987), far below the >10–20 to 1 ratios in the terrestrial biota. Recent molecular investigations, however, are beginning to confirm endemism and investigate origins, evolutionary history, and population structure of marine island species (Bird et al. 2007), as well as geographic source and systematic identity of introduced marine taxa (Holland 2000; Holland et al. 2004).

Fossil records in the Pacific also provide evidence for a scenario of dispersal, immigration, and recolonization in marine habitats. Reef-associated limestone from the Eocene in the various islands records the time current atolls stood above the sea as high islands. Above Eocene fossil reefs are Miocene marine mollusks, which were associated with seagrass beds and mangrove swamps, now absent on these atolls, and above the Miocene reefs are shells of the Pleistocene age, which may have arrived only a few thousand years ago (Kay and Johnson 1987). Fossil corals dredged from the Emperor Seamounts document the occurrence of reef corals in the

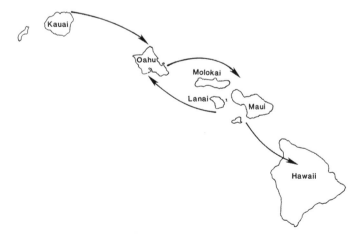

Figure 7.4. Interisland dispersal events in the Hawaiian Islands, showing founder species dispersing from older islands to the younger islands, with an occasional "backward" jump.

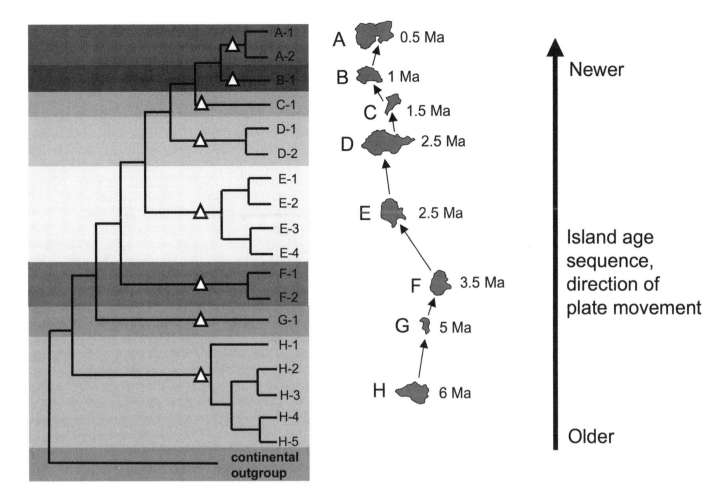

Figure 7.5. *Each island that makes up a volcanic archipelago forms sequentially as the tectonic plate the islands occupy moves across a stationary hot spot, a breach in the earth's crust through which molten lava flows to the surface, in this case the seafloor. This map depicts a hypothetical oceanic island chain (Ma = mega annum, or million years, white triangles represent monophyletic island clades or branches), an associated cladogram depicts a biogeographic pattern that is frequently observed to varying degrees, termed the progression rule (Hennig 1966; Wagner and Funk 1995). According to the progression rule as it applies to island radiations, initial colonization occurs on the oldest island, and subsequent lineage-splitting events are driven by dispersal and colonization followed by isolation and allopatric diversification, as newer islands emerge. The result is that older components of endemic lineages are often found on older islands. This pattern can be used as a framework within which biogeographers study island phylogenies, which are often more complex and may involve diversification within islands, back colonizations from newer to older islands, and dispersal pathways that skip over islands. A second biogeographic hypothesis represented is the center of origin (Hennig 1966) idea, which assumes that the clade within the lineage that is oldest will have the highest diversity, shown in clade H, taxa 1–5.*

Hawaiian Archipelago thirty-four million years ago in the early Oligocene (Grigg 1988). Since the Oligocene extinction, recolonization and changes in coral species composition have occurred in Hawai'i. Miocene corals of Midway differ from those of the Oligocene in the Emperor Seamounts, and the corals of the Hawaiian Islands today are different again from those on Midway's Miocene reefs.

The fossil reefs of Mauke and Niue (Paulay 1990), all now above sea level, also represent episodes of extinction and recolonization, but reflect cycles of sea-level change over periods of six to eight thousand years during the Cenozoic, when large areas of shallow shelf environments were stranded during Ice Age sea-level regressions. One-third of Pacific inner reef bivalves may have become extinct during the sea-level changes, and the modern fauna is interpreted as resulting from post-Pleistocene recolonization, when rising seas flooded inner reef habitats (Paulay 1990).

Both the recent and fossil patterns of endemism are explained if the ocean is considered an open system in which animals and plants come and go, with regular gene flow by dispersal, where isolation may be less likely than on land, and marine habitats, rather than being filled by speciation in situ as they are in the forests of remote high islands, are filled by dispersal and recruitment via "island hopping" from other archipelagoes. Marine endemics generally result from single immigration and speciation events, mainly derived from Indo–West Pacific ancestors (Kay and Palumbi 1987).

Dispersal and Vicariance: Insular Speciation and Continental Islands

Darwin, Wallace, and many other "fathers" of biogeography supported the plausibility of oceanic dispersal, and there was general acceptance of it until the 1960s and 1970s, when two developments sparked a revolution in historical biogeography: plate tectonic theory and cladistic methods. Between the 1970s and the advent of molecular techniques, there was a relatively widespread perception that dispersal was an unscientific and untestable biogeographic explanation (Cowie and Holland 2006). Today however, the importance of dispersal in oceanic island biogeography has been soundly confirmed, in the words of de Quieroz "resurrected," not as the only factor driving fragmented distributions, but instead as a critical partner to vicariance in shaping diverse island biotas (de Quieroz 2005). The tremendous diversity of oceanic island land snails and other organisms is fundamentally dependent on dispersal, and the effects of dispersal are evident both on a small intra-archipelago scale and on a larger ocean-wide scale.

Although clearly a fundamentally important force in the biology and diversification of island species, dispersal alone does not account for all distribution patterns in the Pacific. Unique elements in the biotas of New Zealand, New Caledonia, New Guinea, and Fiji—the tuatara (*Sphenodon*), a small, lizard-like reptile in New Zealand that has been extinct elsewhere in the world for sixty million years, the Antarctic beeches and araucaria pines in New Caledonia that co-occur only in a few parts of Australasia and South America, and iguanas in Fiji that are otherwise restricted to the Americas and Madagascar—are not readily explained by dispersal theory. Nor does dispersal theory alone explain the hundreds of species of drosophilid flies and land snails, traceable to only a few dispersing ancestors on Pacific islands. Explanations for these patterns are the domain of island vicariance, whereby patterns originate largely as the result of geological forces: on a global scale, the movement of tectonic plates and their associated continental landmasses; on islands, in terms of uplift, island formation and fragmentation, subsidence and erosion, and the myriad of events that form the rugged topography and dynamic geological mosaic of mature high islands. Vicariance theory requires dispersal in the early history of the taxon before the imposition of the barriers, the subsequent disruption of once continuous ranges of species by abiotic factors, followed by speciation. Through the use of molecular tools, detailed patterns that support either vicariance, dispersal, or a combination of the two as the dominant forces can be revealed (Cowie and Holland 2006; Holland and Cowie 2007).

Origins of the Insular Biotas

The pattern of the Western relationships of the biota of the Pacific Islands remarked on by the early explorer-naturalists is generally acknowledged by botanists, zoologists, and marine biologists, excepting the American biota of the Galápagos and American elements such as the iguanids in Fiji and birds and silverswords in Hawai'i. The Western relationships are, however, complex. Much of the biota of New Zealand and New Caledonia, the kauris and araucarias, the amphibians and reptiles, and flightless birds such as the moa and the kagu, is a reflection of ancient Gondwanaland origins. Other elements of Pacific Island floras and faunas are more recent derivatives of the Oriental and Papuan regions, their ancestors found in Southeast Asia and Australasia.

Among the Pacific archipelagoes, the Hawaiian Islands are at once the most remote and the best studied. Recent scientific publications show that monophyly and a single geographic origin of

Hawaiian radiations have been confirmed, including achatinelline tree snails, drepanidine honeycreepers, drosophilid flies, *Havaika* spiders, *Hylaeus* bees, and *Laupala* crickets. Other radiations are derived from multiple colonizations: *Tetragnatha* and *Theridion* spiders, succineid snails, possibly *Dicranomyia* crane flies, and *Porzana* rails (see Cowie and Holland 2008). Geographic origins of many invertebrate groups remain obscure, largely because of challenges related to sampling all potential source regions. Those of vertebrates are better understood, probably because lineages have not radiated as extensively as invertebrates have, species richness is far lower, and morphology allows identification of source regions. Most birds, and the bat, have New World origins. Within the archipelago, most radiations follow, to some degree, a progression rule pattern, diversifying as they colonize newer from older islands sequentially, although speciation often also occurs within islands. Most invertebrates are single-island endemics. However, among multi-island species studied, complex patterns of diversification are exhibited, reflecting enhanced dispersal potential (succineids, *Dicranomyia*). Instances of Hawaiian taxa colonizing other regions are being revealed (*Scaptomyza* flies, succineids) (Cowie and Holland 2008).

The marine biota with its diversity center in the Indo-Malayan Archipelago is representative of the Indo–West Pacific. But whereas terrestrial biologists do not argue about the nature of presumed source areas, marine biologists ask a fundamental question: Is the Indo-Malayan Archipelago (in its widest sense) a center of origin for the Pacific Islands, or did their ancestors speciate in the central Pacific and accumulate in the Indo-Malayan center of diversity secondarily? Biogeographer Ekman (1953) referred to the Indo-Malayan region as "the centre and focus from which the others recruited the main contingent of its fauna." His thesis was based on the notion that a high diversity center would pour out species that were dispersed eastward. The American geologist Ladd (1960) proposed the opposite scenario: speciation occurred in the islands of the central Pacific, and prevailing winds and currents carried species westward into the East Indies. Ladd and others who support his argument for the Indo-Malayan Archipelago as a center of accumulation find the oldest representatives of seagrasses, mangroves, corals, marine mollusks, and barnacles (McCoy and Heck 1976; Kay 1990; Newman 1986) in the central Pacific rather than in the Indo-Malayan Archipelago.

Alternative explanations have been proposed to explain the center of diversity. Rosen (1984) suggests a "diversity pump," with alternating speciation on outlying islands feeding a center and speciation within the center, both fueled by vicariance associated with geotectonic and glacio-eustatic events. Pandolfi's (1992) hypothesis involves displacement of whole faunas by plate tectonic movement, emergence of land barriers during the Miocene collision of Gondwana-Australia and Southeast Asia, and the Plio-Pleistocene sea-level fluctuations producing land barriers and fragmented island areas.

Human Impacts

In terms of negative impacts of human habitation, anthropogenic introduction of alien species is among the most devastating. Deleterious effects of biological introductions impinge upon commerce, human health, the natural environment, and biodiversity (Pimentel et al. 2001). In the United States alone, annual financial burdens associated with alien species have been estimated at US$120 to 137 billion (Pimentel, Zuniga, and Morrison 2005). Combining data for the United States, United Kingdom, Australia, South Africa, India, and Brazil led to an estimate of the cost of damage in these six countries of US$314 billion per year (Pimentel et al. 2001). Nowhere are the effects of invasive species more directly evident than on islands.

The Pacific Islands described by the naturalist-explorers of the late eighteenth century were not the pristine islands of dreams, but islands that had been inhabited, in some cases densely, and intensively cultivated for three millennia. Forster (1996) vividly describes the stamp of human settlement in the Society Islands in 1774: "the plains . . . give greater room for cultivation than mountainous exposures [but] the remotest extremities of the vallies [are] covered with plantations"; in the Marquesas "the variety of plants is not . . . so great, owing to the room which the plantations take up in the woods themselves." Notes of early twentieth-century expedition scientists further suggest that even these remotest of island habitats were extensively altered long ago, for example in the Marquesas: "The native flora below 1000 ft has been replaced in large measure by immigrants, and to a considerable extent up to 2,500 feet" (Adamson 1939). Thus in general, since most native island fauna are dependent to varying degrees on the presence of native flora, intact island ecosystems presently tend to be restricted to upper elevations of high islands, since these areas harbor the only remaining native forest in virtually all Pacific Island groups.

The purposeful introduction of cultivated plants and livestock, as well as the unintentional release of stowaway rats and weeds in prehistoric years, are major means by which organisms reached remote islands. As human populations burgeoned, native island vegetation was displaced, but both intentional and accidental introductions of animals and plants continue today. Due to faster transportation and global economic markets, modern introductions far outnumber the cultigens and stowaways of the prehistoric Pacific.

The discovery of prehistoric bird bones from archaeological sites throughout the Pacific suggests the immensity of change in Pacific Island biotas since humans arrived three thousand years ago. From 1985 to 1995, Steadman (1995) estimates ten species or populations lost on each of approximately eight hundred major oceanic islands of the Pacific, for a total loss of eight thousand species or populations. Extinctions attributable to Western impact continue today. Garrett (1887) writes of collecting "several thousand specimens" of Tahitian land snails. Almost fifty years after Garrett's death, malacologists wrote "of not finding any live specimens of the critical species reported" (Cooke 1935). And one hundred years later, the predatory land snail *Euglandina rosea* virtually extirpated the entire remaining partulid snail fauna of Moorea (Society Islands) within ten years of its introduction (Murray et al. 1988). In the Hawaiian Islands all but perhaps ten of the forty-one species of the tree snail *Achatinella* known in 1900 are extinct on O'ahu (Holland and Hadfield 2004). Scientists predict that the Hawaiian monk seal may be extinct within a few decades; 70 percent of the endemic birds are extinct, and perhaps 90 percent of the lands snails are gone. On Guam, the brown tree snake has virtually extirpated the native birds (Savidge 1987). Throughout the Pacific,

fruit bats and pigeons have been hunted to the point of extinction (Wiles, Engring, and Falanruw 1991).

Due to overharvesting, pollution, and habitat destruction, coastal marine populations have disappeared, or been substantially reduced, often to the point of ecological extinction. Numbers of two species of sea turtles in American Samoa, the green turtle *Chelonia mydas* and the hawksbill *Eretmochelys imbricata,* have declined significantly from historic levels because of habitat loss and subsistence harvests (Tuato'o-Bartley, Morrell, and Craig 1993).

Much of the prehistoric bird extinction was human-induced (Steadman 1997), due to consumption of birds and eggs by humans, and due to the introduction of rats, pigs, dogs, and ants, and later cats and the Indian mongoose. Predation, however, was but one cause. Cultivation of the agricultural landscape meant the removal of native vegetation and forest cover, resulting in displacement of native birds and insects, slope erosion, and deposition of enormous amounts of terrigenous sediment on lowlands and reef flats (J. Allen 1997; M. S. Allen 1997).

Theoretically, an island population should remain stable, changing only in composition as one species is extinguished and another takes its place, that is, by turnover. Steadman (1985) estimated a prehuman turnover rate of zero to three vertebrates in approximately four thousand years on five islands in the Galápagos and twenty-one to twenty-four populations of vertebrates lost in the two centuries since people arrived on those same islands. If those estimates are correct, human-related extinctions are roughly two orders of magnitude greater than prehuman extinction in the Galápagos.

Extinctions in the Pacific, except for those associated with geotectonic and sea-level changes, appear to be largely human induced. In prehistoric time, land and seabirds were hunted to extinction; other extinctions resulted as the landscapes were altered for agriculture, forests were burned, and trees were harvested. Invasive animals and plants, both prehistoric and recent, continue to decimate sensitive native biotas, with additive impacts. Extinction of the terrestrial biota of oceanic islands has enormous biogeographical implication as fossils indicate that prehistoric distribution patterns were far more extensive than today. Conversely, biogeographic data, especially that generated using molecular approaches, has enormous utility in designing and establishing effective conservation policies and programs that can ensure the long-term persistence of the diverse, threatened fauna of the islands of the Pacific.

BIBLIOGRAPHY

Adamson, A. M. 1939. Review of the fauna of the Marquesas Islands and discussion of its origin. Pacific Entomological Survey Publication 10, Bulletin 159, Bishop Museum, Honolulu.

Allen, J. 1997. Pre-contact landscape transformation and cultural change in windward O'ahu. In *Historical ecology in the Pacific Islands,* ed. P. V. Kirch and T. L. Hunt, 230–247. New Haven, Conn.: Yale University Press.

Allen, M. S. 1997. Coastal morphogenesis, climatic trends, and Cook Island prehistory. In *Historical ecology in the Pacific Islands,* ed. P. V. Kirch and T. L. Hunt, 124–146. New Haven, Conn.: Yale University Press.

Ashlock, P. D., and W. C. Gagné. 1983. A remarkable new micropterous /Nysius /species from the aeolian zone of Mauna Kea, Hawai'i

Island (Hemiptera: Heteroptera: Lygaeidae). *International Journal of Entomology* 25(1): 47–55.

Baldwin, B. G., and M. J. Sanderson. 1998. Age and rate of diversification of the Hawaiian silversword alliance (Compositae). *Proceedings of the National Academy of Sciences USA* 95: 9402–9406.

Baur, G. 1897. New observations on the origin of the Galápagos Islands, with remarks on the geological age of the Pacific Ocean. *American Naturalist* 31(368): 661–680.

Benton, T. G. 1995. Biodiversity and biogeography of Henderson Island's insects. *Biological Journal of the Linnean Society* 56: 245–259.

Bird, C. E., B. S. Holland, B. W. Bowen, and R. J. Toonen. 2007. Contrasting phylogeography in three endemic Hawaiian limpets (*Cellana* spp.) with similar life histories. *Molecular Ecology* 16(15): 3173–3187.

Brothers, E. G., and R. E. Thresher. 1985. Pelagic duration, dispersal and the distribution of Indo-Pacific coral reef fishes. In *The ecology of deep and shallow coral reefs,* vol. 2, ed. M. Reaka, 53–59. NOAA Symposium Series Undersea Res., Washington, D.C.: U.S. Department of Commerce.

Carlquist, S. 1965. *Island life.* New York: The Natural History Press.

Carr, G. D. 1987. Beggar's ticks and tarweeds: Masters of adaptive radiation. *Trends in Evolution and Ecology* 2: 192–195.

Carson, H. 1983. Chromosomal sequences and interisland colonizations in Hawaiian *Drosophila*. *Genetics* 103: 465–482.

Clarke, B., and J. Murray. 1969. Ecological genetics and speciation in land snails of the genus *Partula*. *Biological Journal of the Linnean Society* 1: 31–42.

Cooke, C. M., Jr. 1935. In H. E. Gregory, report of the director for 1934. *Bishop Museum Bulletin* 133: 36–55.

Cowie, R. H., N. L. Evenhuis, and C. C. Christensen. 1995. *Catalog of the native land and freshwater molluscs of the Hawaiian Islands.* Leiden: Backhuys Publishers.

Cowie, R. H., and B. S. Holland. 2006. Dispersal is fundamental to evolution on oceanic islands. Guest editorial, *Journal of Biogeography* 33(2): 193–198.

———. 2008. Molecular biogeography and diversification of the endemic terrestrial fauna of the Hawaiian Islands. *Philosophical Transactions of the Royal Society of London B* 363(1508): 3363–3376.

Crampton, H. E. 1925. Contemporaneous organic differentiation in the species of *Partula* living in Moorea, Society Islands. *American Naturalist* 59: 5–35.

Darwin, C. R. 1859. *On the origin of species by means of natural selection, or the preservation of favoured races in the struggle for life.* London: John Murray.

de Queiroz, A. 2005. The resurrection of oceanic dispersal. *Trends in Ecology and Evolution* 20: 68–73.

Diamond, J. M. 1995. Introduction to the exploration of Henderson Island. *Biological Journal of the Linnean Society* 56: 1–5.

Duda, T. F., and A. J. Kohn. 2005. Species level phylogeography and evolutionary history of the hyperdiverse marine gastropod genus *Conus*. *Molecular Phylogenetics and Evolution* 34(2): 257–272.

Ekman, S. 1953. *Zoogeography of the sea.* London: Sidgwick and Jackson.

Emerson, O. P. 1941. Punahou under Daniel Dole. In *Punahou: 1841–1941,* ed. M. C. Alexander and C. P. Dodge. Berkeley: University of California Press.

Emerson, W. K. 1991. First records for *Cymatium mundum* (Gould) in the eastern Pacific Ocean, with comments on the zoogeography of the tropical trans-Pacific tonnacean and non-tonnacean prosobranch gastropods with Indo-Pacific faunal affinities in West American waters. *The Nautilus* 105: 62–80.

Forster, J. R. 1996. In *Observations made during a voyage round the world, on physical geography, natural history, and ethic philosophy,* ed. N. Thomas, H. Guest, and M. Dettelbach. Honolulu: University of Hawai'i Press.

Freed, L. A., S. Conant, and R. C. Fleisher. 1987. Evolutionary ecology and radiation of Hawaiian passerine birds. *Trends in Ecology and Evolution* 2: 196–203.

Funk, V. A., and W. L. Wagner. 1995. Biogeography of seven ancient Hawaiian plant lineages. In *Hawaiian biogeography: Evolution on a hot spot archipelago,* ed. W. L. Wagner and V. A. Funk, 160–194. Washington, D.C.: Smithsonian Institution Press.

Garrett, A. 1887. On the terrestrial molluscs of the Viti Islands. Part 1. *Proceedings of the Zoological Society of London* 1887: 164–189.

Gillespie, R. G. 2004. Community assembly through adaptive radiation in Hawaiian spiders. *Science* 303: 356–359.

Grant, P. 1986. *Ecology and evolution of Darwin's finches.* Princeton, N.J.: Princeton University Press.

Gressitt, J. L., and C. M. Yoshimoto. 1963. Dispersal of animals in the Pacific. In *Pacific Basin biogeography: A symposium,* ed. J. L. Gressitt, 283–292. Honolulu: Bishop Museum Press.

Grigg, R. W. 1988. Paleoceanography of coral reefs in the Hawaiian-Emperor chain. *Science* 240: 1737–1743.

Grigg, R. W., and R. Hey. 1992. Paleoceanography of the tropical Eastern Pacific Ocean. *Science* 255: 172–178.

Gulick, J. T. 1890. Divergent evolution through cumulative segregation. *Journal of the Linnean Society of London Zoology* 20: 189–274.

Hennig, W. 1966. *Phylogenetic systematics.* Urbana: University of Illinois Press.

Hinds, R. B. 1844. *The zoology of the voyage of H.M.S. "Sulphur" under the Command of Captain Sir Edward Belcher . . . during the years 1836–1842.* London: Smith Elder and Co.

Holland, B. S. 2000. Genetics of marine bioinvasions. *Hydrobiologia* 420: 63–71.

Holland, B. S., and R. H. Cowie. 2007. A geographic mosaic of passive dispersal: Population structure in the endemic Hawaiian amber snail *Succinea caduca* (Mighels 1845). *Molecular Ecology* 16(12): 2422–2435.

Holland, B. S., M. N. Dawson, G. L. Crow, and D. K. Hofmann. 2004. Global phylogeography of *Cassiopea* (Scyphozoa: Rhizostomeae): Molecular evidence for cryptic species and multiple invasions of the Hawaiian Islands. *Marine Biology* 145: 1119–1128.

Holland, B. S., and M. G. Hadfield. 2002. Islands within an island: Phylogeography and conservation genetics of the endangered Hawaiian tree snail *Achatinella mustelina*. *Molecular Ecology* 11(3): 365–376.

———. 2004. Origin and diversification of the endemic Hawaiian tree snails (Achatinellinae: Achatinellidae) based on molecular evidence. *Molecular Phylogenetics and Evolution* 32(2): 588–600.

Hourigan, T., and E. Reese. 1987. Mid-ocean isolation and the evolution of Hawaiian reef fishes. *Trends in Ecology and Evolution* 2: 187–191.

Hutton, F. W. 1896. Theoretical explanations of the distribution of southern faunas. *Proceedings of the Linnean Society of New South Wales* 21 (1896): 36–47.

Jokiel, P. L. 1984. Long-distance dispersal of reef corals by rafting. *Coral Reefs* 3: 113–116.

———. 1987. Ecology, biogeography and evolution of corals in Hawai'i. *Trends in Ecology and Evolution* 2: 179–182.

Kaneshiro, K. 1988. Speciation in the Hawaiian *Drosophila*. *BioScience* 38: 258–263.

Kay, E. A. 1984. Patterns of speciation in the Indo-West Pacific. In *Biogeography of the tropical Pacific,* ed. F. J. Radovsky, P. H. Raven, and S. H. Sohmer. Bishop Museum Special Publication 72: 33–44.

———. 1990. The Cypraeidae of the Indo-Pacific: Cenozoic fossil history and biogeography. *Bulletin of Marine Science* 47: 23–34.

———. 1995. Diversification and differentiation: Two evolutionary patterns in the molluscan fauna of Pacific islands with consequences for conservation. In *Biodiversity and conservation in the mollusca,* ed. A. C. van Bruggen, S. M. Wells, and Th. C. M. Kemperman, 37–53. Leiden: Backhuys Publishers.

Kay, E. A., and S. Johnson. 1987. Mollusca of Enewetak Atoll. In *The natural history of Enewetak*, vol. 1, ed. M. Devaney, E. S. Reese, B. L. Burch, and P. Helfrich, 105–146. Office of Scientific and Technical Information, U.S. Dept. of Energy.

Kay, E. A., and S. R. Palumbi. 1987. Endemism and evolution in Hawaiian marine invertebrates. *Trends in Ecology and Evolution* 2: 183–186.

Kay, E. A., and M. F. Switzer. 1974. Molluscan distribution patterns in Fanning Island lagoon and a comparison of the mollusks of the lagoon and seaward reefs. *Pacific Science* 28: 275–295.

Ladd, H. S. 1960. Origin of Pacific Island molluscan fauna. *American Journal of Science* 258A: 310–315.

Lee, T., J. Burch, Y. Jung, T. Coote, P. Pearce-Kelly, D. Ó Foighil. 2007. Tahitian tree snail mitochondrial clades survived recent mass extirpation. *Current Biology* 17(13): 502–503.

Lee, T., J.-Y. Meyer, J. B. Burch, P. Pearce-Kelly, and D. Ó Foighil. 2008. Not completely lost: Two partulid tree snail species persist on the highest peak of Raiatea, French Polynesia. *Oryx* 42: 615–619.

MacArthur, R. H., and E. O. Wilson. 1967. *The theory of island biogeography*. Princeton, N.J.: Princeton University Press.

Mayr, E. 1942. *Systematics and the origin of species*. New York: Columbia University Press.

McCoy, E. D., and K. L. Heck. 1976. Biogeography of corals, seagrasses, and mangroves: An alternative to the center of origin concept. *Systematic Zoology* 25: 201–210.

Montgomery, S. L. 1983. Carnivorous caterpillars: The behavior, biogeography and conservation of *Euplithecia* (Lepidoptera: Geometridae) in the Hawaiian Islands. *Geojournal* 76: 549–556.

Murray, J. E., E. Murray, M. S. Johnson, and B. Clarke, 1988. The extinction of *Partula* on Moorea. *Pacific Science* 42: 150–153.

Newman, W. A. 1986. Origin of the Hawaiian marine fauna: Dispersal and vicariance as indicated by barnacles and other organisms. In *Crustacean biogeography,* ed. R. H. Gore and K. L. Heck, 21–49. Rotterdam: A. A. Balkema.

O'Grady, P., and R. DeSalle. 2008. Out of Hawaii: The origin and biogeography of the genus *Scaptomyza* (Diptera: Drosophilidae). *Biology Letters* 4: 195–199.

Olson, S. 1991. Patterns of avian diversity and radiation in the Pacific as seen through the fossil record. In *The unity of evolutionary biology: Proceedings of the Fourth International Congress of Systematics and Evolutionary Biology,* vol. 1, ed. E. C. Dudley, 314–318. Portland, Ore.: Dioscorides Press.

Pandolfi, J. M. 1992. Successive isolation rather than evolutionary centres for the origination of Indo-Pacific reef corals. *Journal of Biogeography* 19: 593–609.

Paulay, G. 1985. Adaptive radiation on an isolated oceanic island: The Cryptorhynchinae (Curculionidae) of Rapa revisited. *Biological Journal of the Linnean Society* 26: 95–187.

———. 1990. Effect of Late Cenozoic sea level fluctuations on the bivalve faunas of tropical oceanic islands. *Paleobiology* 16: 413–434.

Peck, S. B. 1991. The Galápagos Archipelago, Ecuador: With an emphasis on terrestrial invertebrates, especially insects; and an outline for research. In *The unity of evolutionary biology: Proceedings of the Fourth International Congress on Systematic and Evolutionary Biology,* vol. 1, ed. E. C. Dudley, 1319–1336. Portland, Ore.: Dioscorides Press.

Perrault, G. G. 1987. Microendemisme et speciation de genre *Mecyclothorax* (Coleoptera-Carabidae Psydrini) et Tahiti (Polynesie Francaise). *Bulletin de la Societe de Zoologie de France* 112: 419–427.

Pickering, C. 1854. *The geographic distribution of animals and plants.* Boston: Little Brown and Co.

Pilsbry, H. A. 1900. The genesis of mid-pacific faunas. *Proceedings of the Academy of Natural Science, Philadelphia* 52: 568–581.

Pimentel D., S. McNair, J. Janecka, J. Wightman, C. Simmonds, C. O'Connell, E. Wong, L. Russel, J. Zern, T. Aquino, and T. Tsomondo. 2001. Economic and environmental threats of alien plant, animal, and microbe invasions. *Agricultural Ecosystems and Environment* 84: 1–20.

Pimentel D., R. Zuniga, and D. Morrison. 2005. Update on the environmental and economic costs associated with alien-invasive species in the United States. *Ecological Economics* 52: 273–288.

Price, J. P., and D. A. Clague. 2002. How old is the Hawaiian biota? Geology and phylogeny suggest recent divergence. *Proceedings of the Royal Society of London B* 269: 2429—2435.

Randall, J. E. 1992. *Endemism of fishes in Oceania.* UNEP: Coastal resources and systems of the Pacific Basin: Investigation and steps toward protective management. UNEP Regional Seas Reports and Studies No. 147.

Richmond, R. 1982. Energetic considerations in the dispersal of *Pocillopora damicornis* (Linnaeus) planulae. *Proceedings of the Fourth International Coral Reef Symposium* 2: 153–156.

Rosen, B. R. 1984. Reef coral biogeography and climate through the Late Cenozoic: Just islands in the sun or a critical pattern of islands? In *Fossils and Climate,* ed. P. J. Brenchley, 201–262. Chichester: Wiley.

Rosenblatt, R. H., and R. S. Waples. 1986. A genetic comparison of allopatric populations of shore fish species from the Eastern and Central Pacific Ocean: Dispersal or vicariance. *Copeia* 2: 275–284.

Rubinoff, D. 2008. Phylogeography and ecology of an endemic radiation of Hawaiian aquatic case-bearing moths (Hyposmocoma: Cosmopterigidae). *Philosophical Transactions of the Royal Society B* 363: 3459–3465.

Rubinoff, D., and W. P. Haines. 2005. Web-spinning caterpillar stalks snails. *Science* 309(5734): 575.

Rundell, R. J., B. S. Holland, and R. H. Cowie. 2004. Molecular phylogeny and biogeography of endemic Hawaiian succineid land snails (Pulmonata: Gastropoda). *Molecular Phylogenetics and Evolution* 31: 246–255.

Savidge, J. A. 1987. Extinction of an island forest avifauna by an introduced snake. *Ecology* 68: 660–668.

Scheltema, R. S. 1986. Long-distance dispersal by planktonic larvae of shoalwater benthic invertebrates among Central Pacific islands. *Bulletin of Marine Science* 39: 241–256.

Solem, A. G. 1982. *Endodontoid land snails in the Pacific Islands* (Mollusca: Pulmonata: Signwrethra). Part II. Families Punctidae and Charopidae, Zoogeography. Chicago: Field Museum of Natural History.

Spiess, F. N. 2007. Pacific Ocean. In Microsoft Encarta online encyclopedia. See http://www.msnencarta.com/encyclopedia_761564220/Pacific_Ocean.html.

Springer, V. G. 1982. Pacific Plate biogeography with special reference to shore fishes. *Smithsonian Contributions to Zoology* 376: 1–182.

Steadman, D. W. 1985. Fossil birds from Mangaia, Southern Cook Islands. *Bulletin of the British Ornithological Club* 105: 58–66.

———. 1995. Prehistoric extinctions of Pacific Island birds: Biodiversity meets zooarchaeology. *Science* 267: 1123–1131.

———. 1997. Extinctions of Polynesian birds: Reciprocal impacts of birds and people. In *Historical ecology in the Pacific Islands,* ed. P. V. Kirch and T. L. Hunt, 51–79. New Haven, Conn.: Yale University Press.

Stoddart, D. R. 1976. Continuity and crisis in the reef community. *Micronesica* 12: 1–9.

Trewick, S. A., A. M. Paterson, and H. J. Campbell. 2007. Hello New Zealand. *Journal of Biogeography* 34: 1–6.

Trewick, S. A., and R. H. Cowie, eds. 2008. Evolution on Pacific islands: Darwin's legacy. *Philosophical Transactions of the Royal Society B* 363(1508): 3287–3465.

Tuato'o-Bartley, N., T. E. Morrell, and P. Craig. 1993. Status of sea turtles in American Samoa in 1991. *Pacific Science* 47: 215–221.

Vences, M., D. R. Vieites, F. Glaw, H. Brinkmann, J. Kosuch, M. Veith, and A. Meyer. 2003. Multiple overseas dispersal in amphibians. *Proceedings of the Royal Society of London, Series B* 270: 2435–2442.

Vermeij, G. J., E. A. Kay, and L. G. Eldredge. 1983. Molluscs of the Northern Mariana Islands, with special reference to the selectivity of oceanic dispersal barriers. *Micronesica* 19: 27–55.

Veron, J. E. N. 1995. *Corals in space and time. The biogeography and evolution of the* Scleractinia. Townsville: University of New South Wales Press.

Wagner, W. L. 1991. Evolution of waif floras: A comparison of the Hawaiian and Marquesan Archipelagos. In *The unity of evolutionary biology, proceedings of the Fourth International Congress of Systematics and Evolutionary Biology,* vol. 1, ed. E. C. Dudley, 267–284. Portland, Ore.: Dioscorides Press.

Wagner, W. L., and V. A. Funk. 1995. *Hawaiian biogeography.* Washington, D.C.: Smithsonian Institution Press.

Wallace, A. R. 1876. *The geographical distribution of animals.* 2 vols. London: MacMillan.

Wiles, G. J., J. Engring, and M. V. C. Falanruw. 1991. Population status and natural history of *Pteropus mariannus* on Ulithi Atoll, Caroline Islands. *Pacific Science* 45: 76–84.

Wilson, E. O. 1961. The nature of the taxon cycle in the Melanesian ant fauna. *American Naturalist* 95: 169–193.

Zimmerman, E. C. 1942. Distribution and origin of some eastern oceanic insects. *American Naturalist* 76: 280–307.

———. 1948. *Insects of Hawaii,* vol. 1. Honolulu: University of Hawaiʻi Press.

Terrestrial Ecosystems

Harley I. Manner, Dieter Mueller-Dombois, and Moshe Rapaport

8

Prior to European contact, virtually all Pacific Islanders lived in rural locations, dependent on the natural environment for basic subsistence needs. This dependence inevitably resulted in large-scale ecosystem conversion. Today, the pace and intensity of exploitation have accelerated. Areas under primary forest, comprising many rare, endemic species of plants and animals, are covered by secondary forest, savannas, agriculture, and urban development. The study of terrestrial ecosystems and their modification has thus become a critical issue in the Pacific Islands. Vegetation is used as the principal biological component by which terrestrial ecosystems are recognized.

Strand and Atolls

The strand is that portion of the beach or coastline of volcanic rock or coral limestone located adjacent to the seashore but above the high-tide line (Fosberg 1960). The vegetation of the strand is a relatively narrow band of halophytic (salt-tolerant) herbs, shrubs, and tree species, often characterized by fleshy leaves with a salty sap, as well as by stunted and prostrate growth forms along windswept coasts (Figure 8.1). These species are well adapted to the harsh conditions of physical disturbance, salinity, drought, desiccation, and rocky, calcareous soils. Most strand species are widespread and indigenous to the tropical and subtropical Pacific Islands. Given the large number of atolls in the Pacific and the high ratio of coastline to land area, this ecosystem is one of the most common in the region.

Atoll ecosystems are strand-like in character and support the relatively few species tolerant of salinity (Figure 8.2). The individual *motu* on an atoll do not always support all species found throughout the atoll. The *motu* often support only fragmental communities consisting of very few species. But most are indigenous.

Figure 8.1. Strand vegetation on a Micronesian atoll (photo HIM).

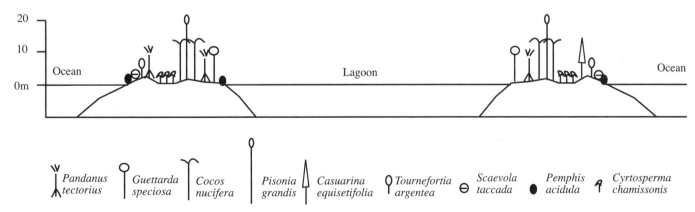

Figure 8.2. Profile diagram of vegetation on a coral atoll, showing depressions used for growing Cyrtosperma chamissonis.

On large *motu* exceeding a few hectares, natural vegetation tends to be more luxuriant, particularly where the freshwater lens is better developed. Large *motu* usually contain several phreatophytic (reliant on groundwater) species in their interior. Such islets commonly display a zonation of vegetation that coincides with the availability of fresh groundwater. The following zones may be present:

1. A sparse halophytic cover of vines, grasses, and sedges on the upper foreshore of windward coasts. One of the most widespread plant species is the prostrate vine *Ipomoea pescaprae* (beach morning glory). Also found here are some grasses and shrubs (particularly *Scaevola taccada*). The small tree or arborescent shrub *Pemphis acidula* commonly forms thickets on limestone rock along atoll beaches.
2. A halophytic low forest fringe. This is often dominated by *Tournefortia argentea* (the tree heliotrope) and typically occurs on the beach crest.
3. Littoral forest composed of halophytic, low-statured species. This may include *Pandanus tectorius* and *Casuarina equisetifolia* (ironwood), now mostly displaced by coconut plantations.
4. Mixed forests composed of several phreatophytic species. They may form two layers, with *Pisonia grandis* or *Calophyllum inophyllum* in the upper canopy and *Guettarda speciosa* in a lower subcanopy. Here too, the indigenous species have now become largely displaced.
5. Central depression with marsh or swamp forest vegetation. On the larger islets, these depressions have usually been excavated and enlarged for the cultivation of *Cyrtosperma chamissonis* (swamp taro) and *Colocasia esculenta* (taro). Some depressions may be saline and consequently contain mangroves.
6. Halophytic forest on lagoon shore beaches. Mangroves, including *Bruguiera gymnorrhyza* and *Rhizophora* spp., sometimes form small stands fringing lagoon shores.

On smaller *motu* this zonation is often reduced or absent. The vegetation then is composed only of low-lying shrubs, grasses, and sedges (Stoddart 1975). On dry atolls, even where large *motu* are present, the vegetation is likewise restricted and dominated by only a few salt-tolerant and drought-resistant species, often forming monospecific communities (Mueller-Dombois and Fosberg 1998). On Taongi Atoll in the Northern Marshall Islands, the forest and scrub vegetation is dominated by *Tournefortia argentea*. In the Phoenix Islands, pure stands of *Cordia subcordata* can be found (Hatheway 1955). In moister atolls of the Southern Marshall Islands, *Pisonia grandis* grows in species-pure dense stands, often accompanied by the presence and smell of guano (Hatheway 1953). These stands of *Pisonia* were formerly widespread features of atolls. Their monodominance as forest species may be related to the harsh, salty atoll environment and the very small total number of plant species available, as well as to their dispersal by seabirds. *Pisonia* fruits are sticky and become attached to birds' feathers and feet.

Rainfall has a pronounced effect on species numbers in atoll ecosystems. For example, Canton Island in the Phoenix group, with only 500 mm of rainfall per year, supports only fourteen species of vascular plants, while Arno Atoll in the central Marshalls, with more than 4,000 mm, supports about ten times as many (Wiens 1962).

Mangroves

Mangrove ecosystems are a naturally occurring group of taxonomically unrelated trees and shrubs that grow in the tidal zones of wind-protected deltas, estuaries, and other muddy seashores of the tropics (Ellison 1991). Mangroves are obligatory halophytes and exist only in habitats that are periodically inundated by seawater (Figure 8.3). They are best developed on leeward and protected coastlines and are virtually absent from wind-exposed sandy coasts and headlands where there is an active surf (Hosokawa, Tagawa, and Chapman 1977). The distribution of mangrove species is influenced by a number of factors, including frequency and duration of seawater flooding, consistency of the soil, the degree of fresh water at river mouths, and the concentration of brackish water (Walter 1971). At the seaward edge, mangroves are represented by very few species, in many cases by only one species. Inland, where fresh water dominates, the variety is greater, but only in areas of high species diversity.

Figure 8.3. *Mangrove forest of* Bruguiera gymnorrhiza *in a "mangrove depression" on Puluwat Atoll (photo HIM).*

Mangrove species can be divided into two major centers of diversity with little overlap: a western hemispheric group consisting of eight species and an eastern hemispheric group of forty species (Tomlinson 1986). Almost all mangrove species in the Pacific Islands belong to the eastern hemispheric group, with a center of diversity between 135°E and 150°E. Mangrove ecosystems are best developed in the western Pacific islands of Palau, Papua New Guinea, and Solomon Islands, and least developed in Polynesia, with Samoa (four species) representing its easternmost extension (Tomlinson 1986; Woodroffe 1987). One species is found as far north as southern Kyushu (31°N) in Japan (Hosokawa, Tagawa, and Chapman 1977) and as far south as Victoria, Australia, at 38°S latitude (Tomlinson 1986). Likewise, the only mangrove species in New Zealand, *Avicennia resinifera*, extends as far south as 38°S (Wardle 1991). *Rhizopora mangle*, from Central America, has a disjunct distribution in the Pacific. Ellison (1991) has suggested that the distribution pattern of *R. mangle* is the result of subsidence of atolls in the central and eastern Pacific, which causes local extinctions.

In Pohnpei, a mangrove species (*Gynotroches axillaris*) is, surprisingly, found growing at 700 m elevation near the dwarf cloud forest on Mount Nanalaud. Mangrove ecosystems also occur in the Central and Eastern Caroline atolls. In the Marshall Islands, mangrove species can be found in clear water in what has been called "mangrove depressions" (Fosberg 1947). These depressions, some of which are abandoned taro pits (Fosberg 1960: 13), are rock lined and relatively mud free. Similar kinds of mangrove depressions can be found in Nauru and Puluwat Atoll. Elsewhere in the Caroline Islands, small areas of mangroves grow in sheltered lagoonal areas on Losap, Mokil, Woleai, and Western Kiribati.

The soils of mangrove ecosystems are often soft, muddy, shallow, anaerobic, acid sulfate clays. In order to survive in such soils, mangrove trees have specialized root systems. These include aerial roots, prop roots, buttress roots, and pneumatophores (breathing roots), root structures that allow for the exchange of gaseous oxygen. These root systems are also effective sediment and litter traps that allow for the succession of mangroves farther offshore and high rates of biological productivity. Mangrove ecosystems also provide protection of coastlines and shore areas from wind and wave action. They are critical habitats for larval and juvenile fishes, crabs, and other faunistic life forms.

Natural mangrove sites in the western Pacific have become increasingly endangered by coastal and urban development. Conversely, mangrove species were introduced into Hawai'i for sediment control in 1902, but are now considered pests, displacing native coastal biota in several sheltered lagoon areas.

Freshwater Wetlands

Marshes and swamps are freshwater wetlands, where the water table fluctuates near or above the land surface, or where the soil surface is permanently saturated (Figure 8.4). Marshes can be considered early successional stages dominated by herbaceous vegetation. Under natural conditions marshes can develop into swamps (freshwater wetlands with forest development). Since these ecosystems are associated with impeded drainage, they occur in depressions or low-lying areas adjacent to rivers and streams, at the edges of lakes and volcanic craters, and in coastal lowlands where the sediment accumulation impedes the flow of fresh water to the ocean. Typical tree cover includes *Barringtonia asiatica* and *Hibiscus tiliaceus* (Stemmermann 1981). Wetlands can also form in locations where artesian springs break the land surface.

Because they are important habitats for waterfowl, such wetlands are now often protected from development, but they have been much modified by human settlement. Pacific Islanders have traditionally used many of these wetlands for the cultivation of *Colocasia esculenta* and *Cyrtosperma chamissonis*, converting entire watershed basins for this purpose. Thus in Hawai'i, few wetlands remained in a pristine form by the time of European contact. Colonial settlement brought further changes, as streams were intensively channeled with concrete plumes, and low-lying coastal wetlands were permanently drained to accommodate expansion of coastal and urban settlement.

There are many types of freshwater swamp ecosystems. Fosberg (1960) lists several types of grass and sedge marshes in Micronesia, the most prominent of which is the tall cane-like grass

Figure 8.4. Nipa palm (Nypa fruticans), Talafofo River, Guam. The leaves of the Nipa palm were once used for thatch. This mangrove species grows typically at the fresh-water end of the brackish-to-fresh water gradient in estuaries. Nipa palm was introduced from the Philippine Islands but is naturalized in some rivers on the southeastern end of the island (photo HIM).

Phragmites karka. This species, along with *Saccharum spontaneum*, forms extensive grasslands along the intermittently flooded lowlands of Papua New Guinea. It is found between sea level and 2,000 m elevation but is less extensively distributed in the other islands of Melanesia. These swampy grasslands occur in poorly drained areas and are maintained by periodic fires. One of the interesting grass species is *Leersia hexandra*, the principal component of "floating islands" in Papua New Guinea rivers and lakes (Leach and Osborne 1985).

The *Metroxylon sago* palm swamp forest is exploited for starch by coastal and riverine peoples in Papua New Guinea, Vanuatu, and Solomon Islands. In Solomon Islands and Fiji, related species are *M. salomonense* and *M. vitiense,* respectively. In Papua New Guinea, sago starch is an important item of barter between sago producers and fisherfolk from the coast and offshore islands (Lea and Irwin 1967). While these palm swamp forests are natural in origin, many are tended in the sense that trees and the undergrowth are weeded and individual trees are transplanted. Another related species is *Metroxylon amicarum*, the ivory nut palm. In the high islands of Pohnpei and Kosrae are small patches of these palms within the rain forest. Also notable are peat swamps dominated by *Pandanus* spp. in Fiji and Papua New Guinea, and niaouli (*Melaleuca quinquenervia*) swamps and wetland savannas in New Caledonia.

Lowland Rain Forests

Primary rain forest was originally the principal lowland ecosystem landward of the strand on most Pacific high islands (Figure 8.5). Lowland rain forests are generally found on the windward sides of islands where the monthly rainfall exceeds 100 mm and there is no deficiency in soil moisture. In many Pacific islands, these primary forests have been replaced by secondary forests, scrub, savannas, and urban development. However, significant stands of tall, majestic rain forest still remain in the lowlands of Papua New Guinea and Solomon Islands, due to the more extensive areas covered and (with the presence of malaria) relatively sparse human populations.

lianas (woody vines); and tall trees with plank buttresses and aerial roots. A groundcover may be absent because most sunlight is intercepted by the tree canopy. The tallest trees exceed 37 m in height (Lea and Irwin 1967; Brookfield with Hart 1971). Rates of organic matter decomposition and nutrient cycling are rapid because of high temperatures and humidities. Tropical rain forests are one of the world's most productive ecosystems because of their almost year-round growth activity. The total aboveground plant biomass in a lowland tropical rain forest can be more than 400 metric tons per hectare (1975).

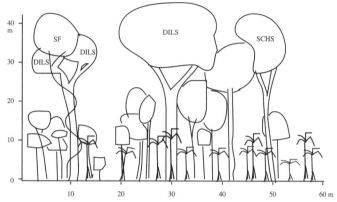

Figure 8.6. *Profile diagram for a diverse, mixed species lowland rain forest in Kolombagara, Solomon Islands, dominated by the shade bearers* Dillenia salomonensis *(DILS) and* Schizomeria serata *(SCHS), and including a strangling fig (SF) and the palm* Physokenta insolita *(after Whitmore 1974).*

Lowland rain forests are rich in species composition. It is not uncommon to find between eighty and one hundred species of trees per hectare in a tropical lowland rain forest (Brookfield with Hart 1971). The richness of tree species in such a diverse forest usually leaves room for only a few individuals of a particular species per unit area. On tropical islands, the lowland rain forest is less diverse in plant and animal life forms and species relative to the continental tropics and often has smaller-sized populations, but more individuals per species may be accommodated on a given area.

Montane Rain Forests

With increasing altitude, the tropical lowland rain forest gives way to a simpler structured, less speciose, montane rain forest. Upland species gradually replace lowland forest species. Trees with buttresses disappear, and tree ferns often become dominant in the undergrowth. At these higher elevations, orographically uplifted air cools to the condensation point, resulting in cloudiness and frequent, heavy rainfall. Solar radiation is reduced as a consequence. These forests, rich in endemics, are found at elevations varying from 600 to 2,000 m on most high islands. Certain tree families, such as Myrtaceae (myrtle family), Rubiaceae (coffee family), and Rutaceae (citrus family), are usually well represented.

In New Guinea, montane forest consists of two main types: mixed broadleaved forests, some with tall, emerged araucariads, and monodominant forests of southern hemisphere oaks (*Castanopsis*), beech (*Nothofagus*), pines (*Araucaria*), or podocarps.

Figure 8.5. *Typical rain forest at 300 m on Viti Levu, Fiji. These forests are species-rich and contain many endemic plants (photo HIM).*

Latitude and elevation are also important in the distribution of rain forests. At low latitudes in the equatorial tropics (0° to 10° latitude), the tropical lowland rain forest may range from sea level to 1,000 m. In the subequatorial tropics (10° to 23° latitude), lowland rain forests are usually restricted to lower elevations (below 600 m) and the windward side of islands (Brookfield with Hart 1971). Lowland rain forests in the Hawaiian Islands (20°N) are likewise restricted to elevations below 600 m (Mueller-Dombois and Bridges 1981b). At the fringes of the tropical belt, subtropical rain forests can be found in the Bonins, Lord Howe, Norfolk Island, and the Kermadecs (Mueller-Dombois and Fosberg 1998).

Primary lowland rain forests are typically multilayered, have closed canopies, and are composed mainly of broadleafed evergreen trees (Figure 8.6). Exceptions are found in Eastern Melanesia (Vanuatu, Fiji, New Caledonia) and on Norfolk Island, where southern hemisphere conifers (mostly araucariads and podocarps) are prominent members of tropical and subtropical lowland rain forests. Additional life forms of the tropical rain forest are epiphytic ferns and orchids; tall, herbaceous monocots (bananas, gingers);

The upper canopy of the broadleaf forests can reach 30 m; that of the conifer forests can be twice that height. In Fiji, Vanuatu, and New Caledonia, conifers—particularly *Araucaria* species—are important forest components; *Agathis* and *Podocarpus* spp. are present as well. *Nothofagus* forests occur in Papua New Guinea, New Zealand, and New Caledonia.

A subtype of montane rain forest is the cloud forest (Hamilton, Juvik, and Scatena 1995). Clouds moving as fog near ground and through the canopy of such forests precipitate on leaves, branches, and all cooled surfaces including the epiphytes, which serve as condensation surfaces. The resulting drip adds considerable quantities of water to the root system. Soils under cloud forests are often waterlogged or boggy. The vegetation is then characterized by short, gnarled, or stunted trees covered with mosses, liverworts, ferns, and orchids (Figure 8.7). On very porous substrates, such as on young volcanic islands, however, cloud forest trees may be as tall as those in less cloud-frequented areas.

Figure 8.7. Boggy cloud forest at 700 m, Pohnpei. Most trees are stunted, standing only 3 m tall because of high cloud cover and saturated soil. The endemic palm Clinostigma ponapensis *is shown here as on the few tall-growing trees (photo HIM).*

In Papua New Guinea montane rain forest is generally found near and above 2,000 m, as the landmass of this large island results in an upward shift of ecological zonation (also called the Massenerhebung's effect). In contrast, on other, smaller high islands in the tropical Pacific, montane rain forest occurs at lower elevations, usually above 500 m. In Pohnpei, montane rain forest starts below 700 m. Small areas of this forest type are also found on Kolombangara, Solomon Islands, at 300 to 400 m (Brookfield with Hart 1971). On Oʻahu these forests occur upward of 460 m elevation, depending on their topographic position relative to cloud frequency (Ripperton and Hosaka 1942). Gagné and Cuddihy (1990) report that they found cloud forests at 1,200 to 2,000 m elevation on Maui, Molokaʻi, and Hawaiʻi.

Bogs may also occur in these cool and moist montane forests. They occur in areas of impeded drainage, generally on flat to gently sloping topography underlain by impervious substrates. These bogs are generally highly oligotrophic (nutrient poor, oxygen starved, and acidic). The accumulation of humus and peat from dead biotic material is often considerable, because of the slow rates of organic matter decomposition. Bog vegetation is dominated by hummock-forming grasses, sedges (especially *Oreobolus* spp.), and

ferns. Shrubs and even stunted trees may also be present, particularly in drier areas. Many of the species in these bogs are endemics. Specialized species found in the montane bogs of Hawaiʻi include dwarf *Metrosideros*, bog greensword (*Argyroxiphium*), *Cheirodendron,* and various lobelias (Campanulaceae).

Due to the rugged prevailing conditions, montane forests have experienced less modification than adjacent lowland areas in most parts of the Pacific and provide refugia for many native biota no longer present elsewhere. With the notable exception of highland valleys in Papua New Guinea (densely populated and intensely cultivated for millennia), montane habitats experienced relatively minimal disturbance by indigenous Pacific Islanders. Following European settlement, montane forest has become increasingly displaced by forest clearance, conversion to pasture, and the introduction of species such as guava (*Psidium cattleianum*), exotic birds (displacing pollinators of endemic plants), and European pigs (with a greater tendency to establish feral populations as compared with indigenous pre-European introductions).

Leeward Ecosystems

On the leeward sides of high islands in the trade wind zones, rainfall is much reduced because of the rain shadow effect (Figure 8.8). Compressional warming of winds downslope can produce an additional desiccation effect. A wide range of community types has been noted for leeward areas, including dry forests, shrublands, and grasslands (Gagné and Cuddihy 1990). These dry seasonal forests usually have open canopies and contain species that can tolerate several months of drought. Trees and shrubs in such ecosystems are usually scattered in savanna-like formations, but sometimes form thickets. The height of the canopy is lower than that of forests at comparable elevations on the windward side. In Hawaiʻi, remnant dry forests are quite rich, containing at least thirty tree species, adapted to drought through small leaves (as in *Diospyros* and *Santalum* spp.) or deciduous habit (such as *Erythrina sandwicensis*) (Mueller-Dombois and Fosberg 1998). Most of the natural vegetation on leeward coasts and lower mountain slopes, however, has been destroyed by clearance, conversion to agriculture and pasture, and introduced herbivores, and the land is currently covered by introduced grasses, shrubs, and trees.

Figure 8.8. Dry, leeward scrub on Oʻahu, Hawaiʻi. Valley and upper slopes in the background are enclosed in cloud (photo MR).

Secondary Forests

Secondary forests and related biota are found in most parts of Oceania where disturbed indigenous forests have been allowed to regenerate after cessation of frequent perturbations (Figure 8.9). This process of secondary forest development may be defined as a succession involving mostly fast-growing, short-lived trees that invade following a disturbance of a large area when rainfall is adequate and soil nutrient conditions are still favorable for tree growth and forest formation. Secondary forests follow abandoned farmlands, waste places, logged forests, and areas of shifting cultivation whenever fallow lengths (resting times) are long enough to allow for the return of forest (Clarke 1966; Manner 1981; Fosberg 1960). Secondary forests are thus successional stages that have not yet advanced to primary forest redevelopment. Notably absent are the shade-adapted trees (sciophytes) that characterize primary forests.

For much of Melanesia, where former garden sites are abandoned to fallow for six years or more, the succeeding vegetation is a secondary forest (Manner 1981). If population pressure on land results in shorter fallow, or if areas under fallow are subjected to fire, the succession is curtailed to a bush fallow. With more frequent disturbance by fire, an anthropogenic grassland will follow, even in rain forest environments (Mueller-Dombois 1981a). In the northern limestone plateau of Guam, secondary vegetation consists mainly of shrubs because of short fallow periods, which interrupt the forest succession. Also in Guam, *Leucaena leucocephala* has formed persistent low-stature forests on slopes underlain by limestone. This provides a prominent example of a formerly mixed species habitat reoccupied by an aggressive species with a tendency to form monodominant stands.

In contrast to primary forest formation, the development of secondary forests is quite rapid. Secondary forests can reach a height of 12 m in three years because of favorable light conditions and their very soft wood (Walter 1971). Unlike primary successions, where species turnovers are often associated with modifications of soils and microclimate (Whittaker 1975), secondary succession is driven more strongly by differential rates of growth and survival of the mostly shade-intolerant pioneer species (Manner 1981).

Secondary forest tree species are shorter-lived, and the height of the canopy they form is typically lower and less variable than that of the primary forest. Often, the leaves of secondary forest species are lighter in color than those of primary forest species.

The early stages of secondary succession are characterized by an abundance of weedy annuals, grasses, ferns, and shrubs, as well as vines (e.g. *Merremia* in Melanesia), many of which are heliophytes (sun-loving species). As succession proceeds, the fast-growing secondary trees are displaced by the more shade-tolerant species. Eventually, the secondary forest species give way to the longer-lived and taller primary forest species. Frequent perturbations (including forest clearance and introduction of such species as *Passiflora mollissima* in Hawai'i and *Miconia calvescens* in Tahiti, as well as feral fauna), however, can easily shift the balance between these two broad ecological groups of species.

Savannas, Grasslands, and Shrublands

In Pacific islands with volcanic soils, fern and grass savannas occupy extensive areas in both humid tropical rain forest and seasonally drier climates (Figure 8.10). Savannas in the arid areas of the southern coast of Papua New Guinea and those on the flooded lower reaches of the Snake, Markham, and Sepik rivers (Brookfield with Hart 1971; Haantjens, Mabbutt, and Pullen 1965) are believed to be natural in origin. By contrast, in many areas where slash-and-burn agriculture is practiced, there is evidence that repeated human-set fires are responsible for arresting vegetation recovery in the savanna stage (Clarke 1966; Street 1966; Nunn 1994). The conversion of forest to savanna ecosystems is accompanied by a sharp drop in biological diversity. Soils under anthropogenic savannas are chemically and physically degraded forest soils (Street 1966; Brookfield with Hart 1971; Manner 1981).

There are many types of savannas in the Pacific found under a wide range of climates and edaphic (soil-controlled) conditions. In New Caledonia, the *niaouli* (*Melaleuca quinquenervia*), or paperbark tree, savanna is extensive in its distribution throughout the leeward lowlands (Gillison 1983). In the dry, hot savannas of southern Papua New Guinea, woody species display adaptations to fire and

*Figure 8.9. Secondary forest in a Micronesian rain forest gap. Identifiable components are the kochop palm (*Clinostigma ponapensis*) and tree ferns. The gap is dominated by heliophytes (photo HIM).*

Figure 8.10. Savanna and ravine forest with coconuts, in southern Guam. These savannas are frequently burned, and as a result the ravine forests have been greatly reduced in area. Remnant ravine forests have been increasingly displaced by coconuts, breadfruit, and other cultivated species (photo HIM).

drought. These adaptations include small- to medium-sized trees with root suckering; thickened and waxy cuticles; seed adapted to fire or heat shock; thick and deeply fissured bark; or highly inflammable bark consisting of paper-thin laminations (which serve to clear old growth and promote reproduction). On the floodplains of the Ramu, Snake, and Sepik rivers, there are tall grasslands of many species. A unique savanna is found in the Markham and Ramu floodplains, where *Cycas media* is the arboreal component. These fire-adapted tree savannas and low-lying floodplain savannas appear to be of natural origins.

Some savannas previously thought to be anthropogenic may also be natural. Recent palynological evidence in Fiji suggests that the *talasiqa* savannas on the leeward sides of Viti Levu, Vanua Levu, and Lakeba Island predated the arrivals of humans (Latham 1983). Zan and Hunter-Anderson (1987), citing the presence of endemic plant species in Micronesian savannas, suggest that these may have originated during a period of aridity predating the arrival of humans. However, there is evidence that human-set fires are responsible for the maintenance and spread of the Micronesian savannas. The presence of endemic species does not preclude an anthropogenic origin, as these endemics may have invaded the savannas after they were formed (Fosberg 1960). When protected from fire, such savannas are usually invaded by a secondary growth of trees, often by ironwood trees (*Casuarina equisetifolia*) as the first pioneers (Mueller-Dombois and Fosberg 1998).

For Guam, palynological evidence by Athens and Ward (2004) strongly supports an anthropogenic origin of savannas. Their pollen and sediment core analyses dating back from 9,300 years to the present indicated forested conditions during the early Holocene. The appearance of charcoal particles in the cores, suggesting human colonization, appear at 4300 cal BP (calibrated years before present), followed by the appearance of *Lycopodium* and *Gleichenia* ferns around 3900 cal BP. Other forms of disturbance, grasses and charcoal, which signal the demise of the forests and the development of the present savannas in southern Guam, become dominant in quantity at 2900 cal BP.

High-Altitude Ecosystems

High-altitude ecosystems are found at elevations above the inversion in Papua New Guinea, Hawai'i, and Maui. Above the inversion layer, usually coinciding with the orographically formed upper cloud layers, precipitation decreases and the air becomes progressively drier and cooler (Figure 8.11).

In Hawai'i, an inversion may occur between 1,200 and 2,000 m, depending on slope position relative to the incoming trade winds. Where the inversion occurs near the lower level of 1,200 m, and where the trade winds have already lost some of their moisture on the wet slopes, a mesophytic (moderately wet) mountain parkland can be encountered. These are typically characterized by *Acacia koa* tree colonies in a matrix of grassland and scrub. At higher elevations, another legume tree, *Sophora chrysophylla*, often along with *Myosporum sandwicensis*, becomes more common. At 2,000 m, mountain parkland merges with subalpine vegetation, characterized by tussock grasses (such as *Deschampsia*, with a tufted growth form, usually golden-yellow in color), scattered *Sophora*, and shrubs.

*Figure 8.11. Alpine desert in the crater of Haleakala, Maui. At between 2,500 and 3,000 m, this area lies above the inversion layer and is the habitat of the endemic silversword (*Argyroxiphium sandwicense*) (photo HIM).*

On Mauna Loa, in Hawai'i Volcanoes National Park, Mueller-Dombois and Bridges (1981) identified the following successive upslope ecosystems: a subalpine open *Metrosideros* scrub forest with scattered trees (2,040 to 2,380 m); a treeline of open *Metrosideros* scrub with scattered trees (up to 2,590 m); an alpine scrub desert dominated by the heath shrubs *Vaccinium* and *Styphelia* (up to 3,080 m); a *Rhacomitrium* moss desert (up to 3,350 m); and above that a lava stone desert up to the summit at 4,208 m. The summit area is often covered with snow during several winter months.

In Papua New Guinea, which lies within 10° of the equator, subalpine vegetation occurs at higher elevations (3,500 to 4,000 m). Tussock grasslands can be found at high-elevation intermontane basins and valleys in Papua New Guinea, notably in areas of waterlogged soils (Smith 1975). Such tussocks are interspersed with patches of small trees and shrubs. Also present at these high elevations are savannas with scattered tree ferns, and grasslands dominated by bamboos. Above 4,100 m, woody shrubs become increasingly scarce, and short grasses predominate. A tundra zone is reached at about 4,300 m, characterized by a sparse growth of lichens, mosses, and hardy grasses.

Because of their cold climate, remote location, and lack of suitability for agriculture or pasture development, high-altitude ecosystems have been less affected by human perturbation, much more so than montane forests. In spite of this protection, though, displacement by introduced biota poses an important potential threat to native species.

High-Latitude Ecosystems

New Zealand, in southern Polynesia, represents the most isolated continental island group in the Pacific. In aggregate size, New Zealand is comparable to New Guinea. It represents an ancient fragment of the former Gondwana continent and was historically always positioned at higher latitudes (the "Roaring Forties"), in a much cooler environment than elsewhere in the Pacific Islands region. New Zealand's landmass extends more than 1,500 km through three latitudinal climatic zones: warm temperate (most of the North Island), cool temperate (southern half of the South Island), and central temperate (Wardle 1991). At the vertical scale, New Zealand has a range of altitudinal ecosystems comparable to that of the tropical high islands of New Guinea and Hawai'i, but with a biota adapted to the cooler climates.

Due to colder temperatures and lack of surrounding coral reefs, New Zealand's coastal ecosystems lack the characteristic plant assemblages so common in the tropical and subtropical Pacific Islands. A mangrove species (*Avicennia marina*), however, is found on the North Island, varying in size with latitude (ranging from 10 m high at the far north to less than a meter tall at the limits of its distribution, around 38°S). Extensive sand dunes exist inland of the coastal strand, anchored by the sedge *Desmoschoenus spiralis* and sand grass *Spinifex hirsutus*. On rocky beaches and cliffs, succulents are commonly found, adapted to conditions of salt spray. Farther inland, coastal forest begins, including *Metrosideros excelsa* and *M. umbellata,* varying in their distribution with latitude.

The western portions of both main islands lie in the path of the prevailing winds (westerlies), and annual precipitation exceeds 1,000 mm, increasing along a southward gradient. Lowlands in the warm-temperate zone contain many Malesian (Island Southeast Asian) rain forest elements. Central temperate lowlands have elements in common with the montane environment of the warm temperate zone on the North Island, including several *Nothofagus* species. Cool temperate lowlands in the south contain floristic elements of central subalpine zones, such as New Zealand's mountain beech (*N. solandri var. cliffortioides*) as well as heath and cushion shrubs. In the extreme south, alpine tussock grasses form the native lowland vegetation.

New Zealand is famous as the center of diversity for the southern hemisphere gymnosperm (conifer) family Podocarpaceae. Podocarp species once dominated lowland rain forests, though these have been reduced to remnants. The podocarps occur as towering emergents over lower canopies of angiosperm (flowering plant) hardwoods with tropical relationships. The angiosperm flora is diverse and includes several *Metrosideros* species (*M. excelsa, M. robusta,* and *M. umbellata*), roughly coinciding in their distribution with the three latitudinal temperate zones. A native palm (*Rhapalostylis sapida*) and several tree ferns (*Cyathea* spp.) occur in association with podocarp-angiosperm forests. Remnant stands of giant kauri (*Agathis australis*) still survive in the North Island, and pollen records indicate that various *Araucaria* spp. were also once present.

Because of its age, large size, and many habitats, New Zealand is worthy of particular attention by those interested in Pacific Island ecosystem studies. But a recent government report (1997) draws attention to the declining state of New Zealand's natural biota. According to the report, 85 percent of the lowland forests and wetlands have vanished since the 1200s, when the islands were first settled by Polynesians. An estimated one thousand living species are threatened with extinction, including the kiwi bird, now a national icon. Of ninety-three birds known to have evolved and existed only in New Zealand, forty-three are now extinct and thirty-seven are in danger of extinction, due to habitat modification and alien introductions.

For further discussion of New Zealand's terrestrial ecosystems, readers are referred to Enting and Molloy (1982), Gunson (1983), Fleet (1986), and Wardle (1991).

Ultramafic Maquis

One of the most distinctive ecosystems in the Pacific Islands is the New Caledonian maquis, found in the southern massif, and a few smaller outcroppings of peridotite (exposed mantle rock) and serpentine (metamorphosed peridotite) on New Caledonia, comprising about a third of the island. The substrate rock and soils are poor in phosphorus, potassium, and calcium (normally necessary for plant survival and growth), but with relatively high concentrations of nickel, magnesium, chromium, cobalt, and other metals. This substrate was deposited in the early Tertiary with the overthrusting of a thick layer of oceanic crust atop a distant fragment of Gondwana (Morat et al. 1981).

Over the past sixty million years, a specialized biotic community has developed, capable of withstanding an edaphic environment that is toxic to most plant biota (Figure 8.12). The maquis community is made up of many ancient Gondwana relicts, which have adapted to the otherwise toxic substrate. Variations in rock and soil mineral composition and isolation of ultramafic fragments in distant parts of the island have led to an extraordinary degree of speciation: at least 1,031 species are native species (more than half the total number of species in New Caledonia), 91 percent of which are endemic (Morat 1993).

Figure 8.12. Agathis ovata *growing in ultramafic maquis, New Caledonia (photo DMD).*

The name "maquis" derives from certain apparent similarities with the Mediterranean maquis. New Caledonia maquis is found in a variety of climatic conditions, from sea level to the highest mountains (1,600 m), from less than 900 mm of rainfall annually to over 4 m. The typical vegetation consists of stunted trees (generally up to 2.5 m, though higher in some areas) with tough, waxy leaves, often sparsely grouped in rosettes at the end of branches, amidst a variety of sedges, ferns, and herbs, with emergent southern pines (*Araucaria* spp.) and kauris (*Agathis* spp.). The families Myrtaceae, Rutaceae, Rubiaceae, and Proteaceae are well represented. Spines, succulents, and grasses are absent (Jaffré 1980; Mueller-Dombois and Fosberg 1998).

Growth is remarkably slow in the New Caledonian maquis vegetation, an effect that persists to some extent even if the species are planted in a more fertile environment. There is an exuberant production of flowers, but seeds seldom make it to maturity due to slow growth, recurrent dry periods, and insect predation, and young plants are seldom seen in the maquis. Interestingly, even when a significant perturbation occurs, such as a forest fire, replacement by other species does not occur, apparently because few other species can thrive given the high concentrations of heavy metals. Instead, the original community structure slowly re-establishes itself (Jaffré 1980).

Recent Volcanic Ecosystems

Volcanic activity on the island of Hawai'i offers insights into the dynamics of primary succession (Figure 8.13). Every few years, new land surfaces are created by lava flows. As lava flows toward the sea, older flows and the vegetation on them are destroyed, while others are left intact, sometimes only in the form of pockets or *kīpuka* (islands of older vegetation) surrounded by more recent volcanic substrate and biota. Various studies conducted in *Metrosideros polymorpha*–dominated forests suggest that this primary successional process is quite predictable within the rain forest environment (Mueller-Dombois 1987).

The initial colonizers of new lava surfaces are blue-green algae. Then ferns and mosses assemble in the fissures. Four to five years later, the lava surfaces are covered by lichens, while *M. polymorpha*

Figure 8.13. *Lava flow with young, developing forest of* Metrosideros polymorpha, *one hundred years old, near Kilauea, Hawai'i Island (photo DMD).*

seedlings begin to spread across the new lava flows. This stage is associated with invasion of mainly native pioneer shrubs, such as *Dubautia scabra* and *Vaccinium reticulatum,* and scattered tall ferns of *Sadleria cystheoides.* After 50 to 200 years, the club moss *Lycopodium cernuum* and the tall sedge *Machaerina angustifolia* may form a closed groundcover. During this time *Metrosideros* individuals develop from seedlings into saplings. Between 50 and 200 years of substrate age, the sapling stands may be from 3 to 8 m tall. After 150 to 250 years, there is a higher, denser canopy of *Metrosideros,* with an undergrowth of *Cibotium* tree ferns, native rain forest shrubs, and other subcanopy species (Mueller-Dombois 1987, Mueller-Dombois and Loope 1990).

This sequence of development is estimated to take as long as 400 years (Atkinson 1970) on lava flows, or 200 to 300 years on volcanic ash. It may be followed by a synchronous stand-level dieback of the senescing (advanced aging) *Metrosideros* canopy cohort. Dieback may then be triggered by a climatic instability, resulting in physiological shock (this affects even younger trees, but the latter survive, while the old ones succumb). *Metrosideros* then can be expected to regenerate into a new forest, as other native species are not able to become successional dominants. However, invasion by alien heliophytes is entirely possible at this stage if such alien pioneer species are in the neighborhood of dieback stands. In the 1930s, a forest dieback area on Maui was partly replanted with alien species for watershed protection. One of the planted species, *Melaleuca quinquenervia,* is actively invading the remaining area and spreading over partially recovered *Metrosideros* scrub on waterlogged ground (Mueller-Dombois 1987).

Other recent volcanic ecosystems in the Pacific Islands occur in the Northern Marianas, Tonga, Vanuatu, Papua New Guinea, New Zealand, and the Galápagos Islands (Mueller-Dombois and Fosberg 1998).

Limestone Forest and Scrub

Raised limestone islands occur widely across the Pacific, the consequence of reef uplift and accretion at plate boundaries or volcanic loading by midplate islands. Some islands (Nauru) are formed entirely of limestone; in other locations (Mangaia), a limestone *makatea* wall surrounds a volcanic core. In a third variant (parts of Papua New Guinea), pockets of limestone exist on continental or volcanic substrates. The limestone substrate is porous, alkaline (pH 7.5 or above, compared to 6 or below for volcanic substrates), and usually with thin soils. In some areas, extensive solution by water has led to extensive dissection, leaving a rocky, pit-and-pinnacle topography known as karst (*feo* or *makatea* in Polynesia), with almost no soil. Enormous deposits of phosphate rock occur on raised limestone islands.

The vegetation on raised limestone islands may be considered a modified strand type, with transitional stages to a diverse, species-rich forest. In level areas with accumulated soils and adequate rainfall, and where elevation ensures minimal salinity, the forest resembles that of adjacent volcanic or continental islands, but often with many strand species or derivatives. In the southern Marianas, the genera *Ficus* (including banyans), *Pandanus, Artocarpus,* and many others are common, along with a scrubby undergrowth of smaller trees and shrubs, and (with adequate moisture) a thick epiphyte cover, especially ferns (*Asplenium nidus* and other species) (Mueller-Dombois and Fosberg 1998). In Micronesia, such limestone forests can still be found in the southern Marianas, the Palau Rock Islands, and Fais. Only remnants remain on Nauru and Banaba (Kiribati), both stripped during past phosphate mining.

Northern Guam, composed of raised limestone, contrasts sharply with volcanic southern Guam. Much of the limestone plateau (mostly a U.S. military base) is still wooded, with a mixture of *Artocarpus, Ficus, Pandanus,* and other species. In contrast, the southern, volcanic portion of the island is covered by a savanna dominated by tall swordgrass (*Miscanthus*), with forest remaining mainly in ravines and steep slopes. Elsewhere as well, savannas do not occur on elevated limestone islands. Two explanations have been suggested by Mueller-Dombois and Fosberg (1998): (1) volcanic soils are more easily invaded by grasses following fires and agricultural clearing; and (2) volcanic terrain tends to be more hilly, and thus more subject to erosion and replacement by grasses.

Limestone forests in Melanesia are exceptionally diverse, probably a consequence of high rainfall, superimposed layers of volcanic ash, and proximity to biotic source areas. For example, the raised limestone island of Pio (off San Cristobal in the Solomons) is covered by a tropical rain forest with emergents reaching 40 m high, with buttress and stilt roots, abundant lianas (vines) up to half a meter in diameter, epiphytic ferns, orchids, and strangler figs (Voronov et al. 1994). Similarly, vast karst areas in the Bismarcks and main island of Papua New Guinea are covered with the same mixed-species lowland rain forest present on adjacent volcanic and continental substrates, though in low-rainfall locales *Casuarina papuana* often dominates (Pajimans 1975).

Limestone forest on the Loyalty Islands and Isle de Pins contains many of the trees present in rain forests of the main island of New Caledonia (*Intsia, Albizia, Canarium,* and others), with a canopy reaching 20 m, including emergent banyans and *Araucaria columnaris* trees. However, other gymnosperms are absent, and the forest is less luxuriant in diversity than the main island.

Limestone forests on Tonga, enriched by a meter or more of volcanic ash deposits, are much degraded, but remnants still exist on some islands, with canopies of up to 30 m high, dominated by

Figure 8.14. *Limestone forest with* Casuarina equisetifolia *and other species on the outer edge of the* makatea *of Atiu, Cook Islands, with an understory of* Scaevola *and* Pemphis *(photo MR).*

Calophyllum neo-ebudicum, Elaeocarpus tonganus, and a variety of other species (Drake et al. 1993). Inner portions of the *makatea* walls surrounding the Southern Cook Islands (Figure 8.14) contain low, species-rich forests, locally dominated by *Barringtonia asiatica, Pandanus tectorius,* and *Elaeocarpus tonganus.* Makatea, in the Tuamotus (devastated by phosphate mining), once had extensive limestone plateau forests composed of *Pandanus tectorius, Ficus prolixa, Guettarda speciosa, Pritchardia vuyltekeana* (an endemic palm), and other species. Farther east, on Henderson Island, a similar limestone forest still survives.

Endemic plant species are rarely found in most limestone islands of the Pacific. None, for example, are found in Nauru. In Palau's limestone forests in the Ngerukuid Preserve, however, three endemic species, *Hydriastele plalaunsis, Sterculia palauensis,* and *Timonus subauritus* constituted 11 percent of the measured trees (Kitalong 2008). A survey of Babeldaob Island in 2004–2005 found eighteen endemic species restricted to southeast Babeldaob, of which seven were only found in the limestone forests located there (Kitalong 2008).

Fauna in Ecosystems

Because of their mobility, many animal species range widely across different ecosystems. Moreover, zoogeographical syntheses are lacking for the Pacific Islands as a whole. Nevertheless, some preliminary generalizations will be offered, primarily concerning native birds and mammals. In most cases, birds are the most visible faunal element of the region's terrestrial ecosystems. As with plants, native animal distributions drop sharply with distance from New Guinea. Mammals are limited almost entirely to New Guinea and (to a much lesser extent) some former land-bridge islands. In the more distant Pacific, terrestrial mammals are represented only by bats (rats are thought to have been introduced by humans).

A variety of seabirds frequent strand and atoll ecosystems, particularly in areas where human disturbance is minimal and where natural vegetation is relatively intact. Many species spend most of their life in the open sea, visiting land only when nesting. Other seabirds, such as fairy terns, noddies, frigate birds, and tropic birds, prefer more sheltered waters for feeding and are often found along some shore areas. A wide variety of migrating shorebirds, or waders (plovers, sandpipers, and other species) is found in the Pacific, often arriving suddenly after storms (Pratt, Bruner, and Berrett 1985).

Mangroves attract large populations of some birds, for example, the cicada bird and the mangrove flycatcher. Some birds, like the Fiji population of little heron, are virtually restricted to mangroves. There are freshwater wetlands in the coastal lowlands of most Pacific islands with dependent birds highly vulnerable to ecosystems disturbance. Today some of the most significant wetlands in the Pacific are man-modified ponds (including taro pond fields) and reservoirs. These habitats are essential for the survival of ducks, coots, gallinules, stilts, herons, and other species.

Grasslands and savannas provide an important habitat for native birds (for example, rails, hawks, and owls) and mammals (wallabies, spiny anteaters, and rodents in southern New Guinea). Such habitats have become increasingly disturbed; thus exotic birds (such as skylarks and meadowlarks) often predominate. However, some native species have adapted to exotic biota (such as the golden white-eye in *Leucaena* and *Algoroba* stands in Micronesia). A few native birds (such as the lesser golden plover) thrive even in city parks in the urban Pacific (Pratt, Bruner, and Berrett 1985). Similarly, some mammals (especially fruit-eating bats) exist and thrive even in disturbed habitats.

Lowland and montane forests are the most important habitat for Pacific Island land birds. New Guinea, with its extensive area, diverse habitats, and proximity to continents, has an exceptionally rich assortment of forest birds (Beehler, Pratt, and Zimmerman 1986). The spectacularly colored bird of paradise and hut-constructing bower birds of New Guinea's rain forests have long served as models for evolutionary studies. Hawai'i's honeycreepers show remarkable adaptations to different forest habitats and feeding niches through changes in coloration and beak structure. Some birds appear to have coevolved with particular plant species and remain mutually interdependent.

Studies in New Guinea have shown that altitudinal zonation exists in many forest bird species (Figure 8.15). Fruit pigeons, crowned pigeons, several kingfisher genera, and certain lories, parrots, and birds of paradise species are found almost entirely in lowland forests; other species (some honeyeaters, astrapias, bowerbirds, and the six-wired birds of paradise, for example) are restricted to upland regions. Diversity begins to decline at high elevations (above 1,500 m in New Guinea) as a consequence of reduced land area, cooler temperatures, higher incidence of cloud and fog, lower plant productivity and diversity, and lower canopy height and structural diversity (Beehler, Pratt, and Zimmerman 1986).

The greatest diversity of native mammals occurs in New Guinea, particularly in its montane forests (Flannery 1995a, 1995b). Mammals native to New Guinea include marsupials (kangaroos, cuscuses, bandicoots, possums, quolls, and related species), monotremes (spiny anteaters), and murids (rats and mice). Beyond the adjacent land bridge islands, bats (including frugivorous, nectivorous, and insectivorous species) are the only native mammalian fauna currently present. Most mammals (with the notable exception of murids and bats in Hawai'i and New Zealand) are of Australian origins.

Monotremes evolved well before the time New Zealand and New Caledonia split off from Australia (around 80 Ma), but they became extinct in both areas soon afterward. In New Zealand, periodic underwater submergence apparently selected for species that can fly between islands. Birds thus become "the ecological equivalents of giraffes, kangaroos, sheep, striped possums, long-beaked echidnas and tigers" (Flannery 1995c), including twelve species of moa. The moa, in turn, may have selected for the divaricating growth habit of many New Zealand plants (where the plant exterior is protected by tough, leafless twigs).

Flannery (1995c) suggests that in New Caledonia the challenge was the toxic soils that developed after the oceanic overthrust (formerly more extensive in area), selecting for energy-conservative species, such as reptiles. These then underwent an extraordinary adaptive radiation equivalent to that of birds in New Zealand. They included crocodiles, horned turtles, and goannas (relatives of the Komodo dragons). All these (like most of the large birds of New Zealand) became extinct shortly after the arrival of human colonists. Today, New Caledonia's native reptile population consists solely of geckos and skinks.

Conclusion

Figure 8.16 shows an idealized high island with its natural ecosystems in summary form. From the top down, they include high-altitude ecosystems (restricted to the tallest islands), followed by montane rain forest (present on most of the Pacific high islands), and lowland and coastal ecosystems (found even on islands less than 500 m in elevation). We would suggest, following Mueller-Dombois and Fosberg (1998), that altitudinal range (as a surrogate for climate) can be considered a key unifying principle in the study and classification of Pacific Island terrestrial ecosystems or biomes. Physiognomy, structure, and functions of distant islands are often remarkably alike in similar topographic/climatic zones, even though considerable variability exists at the local level.

We have shown that other natural controls also play important roles in shaping Pacific Island ecosystems, including proximity to

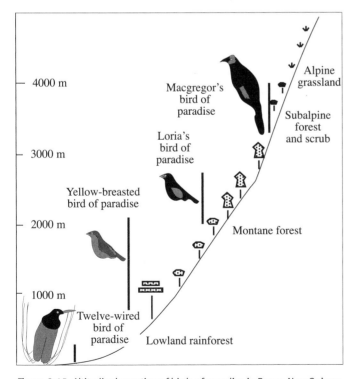

Figure 8.15. Altitudinal zonation of birds of paradise in Papua New Guinea (after Keast 1996).

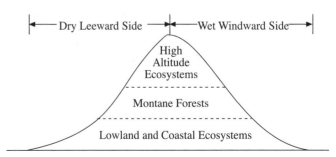

Figure 8.16. Ecosystem zonation in an idealized high island (after Mueller-Dombois and Bridges 1981).

the ocean, streamflow, and substrate (Table 8.1). These controls exert their influence by specific stresses on component plant and animal biota. Thus, only salt-adapted species survive on coral atolls and high island coastal ecosystems. Mangrove, swamp, and bog species must be adapted to prolonged immersion in standing water. A specialized suite of biota exists on recently cooled lava flows, and yet another highly specialized suite has evolved to withstand the toxic heavy metals present in ultramafic rock substrates.

Table 8.1

Classification of Pacific Island Terrestrial Ecosystems

Control	Ecosystem type	Characteristic stress
Oceanic	Strand and atoll	Waves, salt spray, salt inundation
	Mangroves	Tidal currents
Fluvial	Wetlands	Stream flow
Climatic/ Topographic	Lowland rain forests	Shade
	Montane rain forests	Cold, relief, thin soils
	Leeward ecosystems	Aridity
	Secondary forest and scrub	Fire, degraded soils
	Savannas	Fire, degraded soils
	High altitude	Cold, wind
	High latitude	Cold, seasonal changes
Edaphic	Ultramafic maquis	Toxicity
	Recent volcanic ecosystems	Porosity, thin soils
	Limestone forest and scrub	Porosity, alkalinity

Since their arrival, humans have made use of natural ecosystems in the Pacific Islands. Many ecosystems have been altered, some purposefully and irrevocably by exploitive practices, such as the release of mammalian herbivores (Cuddihy and Stone 1990; Stone, Smith, and Tunison 1992). Most changes reflect a tragedy of the commons (Hardin 1968) and have occurred in the name of progress and civilization. New species are constantly being introduced into the islands, ostensibly to improve the quality of life for humans. In spite of efforts to control importation, pest organisms, such as the brown tree snake on Guam, are often accidentally introduced and become invasive. Aggressive alien plant species with new strategies (such as seed dispersal by alien birds or feral pigs) may outcompete native key species, thereby disrupting natural ecosystems. For example, in Palau, the introduced trees *Falcataria moluccana* and *Adenanthera pavonina* and the vine *Merremia peltata* are considered invasive and threats to native forests, while the greater sulfur-crested cockatoo, *Cacatua galerita,* is decimating the endemic palm, *Hydriastele palauensis* (Kitalong 2008)

Active vegetation management has become a necessary task in these island ecosystems, where their natural maintenance mechanisms have been compromised. The success of controlling alien species through ecosystem management has varied, but there is guarded optimism (Stone, Smith, and Tunison 1992). Ecosystem change will continue to rise as human populations increase and make further demands on the remaining natural ecosystem (Figures 8.17 and 8.18). Not all the indigenous biota of the islands, however, are weak competitors. In the absence of adverse human disturbances, there is a chance that many of the native species that are the key ecosystem builders may survive. Much depends on human attitudes, environmental policy, and adequate resource management. The integration of traditional leadership and knowledge with governmental support for community-based management of resources may be an effective strategy for biotic conservation and reducing human disturbance of natural ecosystems.

Pohnpei Island can serve as a case study for such efforts. The upland forest serves as the major watershed for the island and is the main habitat for 24 species of birds, of which five are endemic, and 264 species of plants, of which 111 are endemic (Raynor 1994; Raynor and Kostka 2003). At least 29 terrestrial snails are endemic to the island and found mainly in the upland forests (Merlin and Raynor 2005). This forest was reduced from 40 percent of the total land area in 1975 to 15 percent in 1995 because of homesteading, road development, commercial cultivation of *sakau* (*Piper methysticum*), and other human activities and introductions (Merlin and Raynor 2005). This disturbance of the island's primary forest has been labeled the most significant environmental disaster since the island's settlement more than 2,500 years ago (Merlin and Raynor 2005).

Efforts to restrict development and use of the forest during the 1970s and 1980s through legislation were failures because of the pressures of population growth, expansion of the cash economy, changes to the land tenure system, and the like. In 1996, the Pohnpei State Government, in conjunction with the Nature Conservancy (and more recently, the Conservation Society of Pohnpei) launched the Pohnpei Community Resource Management Program, a strategy that recognizes the key role of traditional leadership structures and locally based communities in managing natural environments. This program has resulted in the establishment of conservation reserves

Figure 8.17. Succession on phosphate-mined areas of Nauru Island. The site was mined during the 1950s. The successional development is slow. The dominant shrub here (1981) was Scaevola taccada (photo HIM).

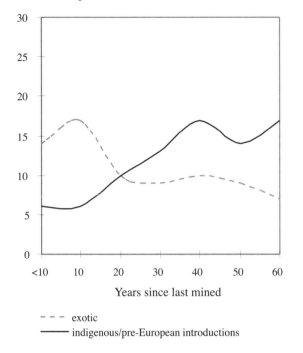

Number of species

<10   10   20   30   40   50   60

Years since last mined

– – – exotic
——— indigenous/pre-European introductions

Figure 8.18. Successional changes following mining on Nauru (after Manner et al. 1985). The most important tree species in revegetated areas included Calophyllum inophyllum, Ficus prolixa, Morinda citrifolia, *and* Guettarda speciosa.

and reduction of forest clearance for agriculture. Similar programs are found in Fiji (Aalbersberg, Tawake, and Parras 2005), Solomon Islands (Wein and Chatterton 2005), Palau (Palau Conservation Society 2003), and Papua New Guinea (Ross and Dabek 2006).

We suggest that for the purpose of biological conservation on islands, where humans determine the doom or survival of indigenous ecosystems to a much greater degree than elsewhere, research efforts with high conservation value be increased (Mueller-Dombois 1981b). Research results in knowledge and understanding. Such research has been fostered by the Pacific Asia Biodiversity Transect Network (PABITRA) in Fiji, Samoa, and Palau (Mueller-Dombois 2008). The PABITRA projects which involve capacity building of island scientists emphasize the long-term monitoring of natural and humanized ecosystems. With this work comes an awareness of the value of the naturally evolved biodiversity as a self-functioning resource in the dynamics of native ecosystems.

BIBLIOGRAPHY

Aalbersberg, B., A. Tawake, and T. Parras. 2005. Village by village: Recovering Fiji's coastal fisheries. In *World resources 2005: The wealth of the poor—managing ecosystems to fight poverty,* Chapter 5. Turning natural assets into wealth: Case studies, 144–151. World Resources Institute (WRI) in collaboration with United Nations Development Programme, United Nations Environment Programme, and World Bank.

Athens, J. S., and J. V. Ward. 2004. Holocene vegetation, savanna origins and human settlement of Guam. *Records of the Australian Museum,* Supplement 29: 15–30.

Atkinson, I. A. E. 1970. Successional trends in the coastal and lowland forest of Mauna Loa and Kilauea volcanoes, Hawaii. *Pacific Science* 24: 387–400.

Beehler, B. M., T. K. Pratt, and D. A. Zimmerman. 1986. *Birds of New Guinea.* Princeton, N.J.: Princeton University Press.

Brookfield, H. C., with D. Hart. 1971. *Melanesia: A geographical interpretation of an island world.* London: Methuen.

Clarke, W. C. 1966. From extensive to intensive shifting cultivation: An example from central New Guinea. *Ethnology* 5: 347–359.

———. 1977. The structure of permanence: The relevance of subsistence communities for world ecosystem management. In *Subsistence and survival: Rural ecology in the Pacific,* ed. T. Bayliss-Smith and R. Feachem, 364–384. London: Academic Press.

Cuddihy, L. W., and C. P. Stone. 1990. *Alteration of native Hawaiian vegetation, effects of humans, their activities and introductions.* Honolulu: Cooperative National Park Resources Studies Unit, University of Hawai'i.

Drake, D. R., W. A. Whistler, T. J. Motley, and C. T. Smeda. 1996. Rain forest vegetation of 'Eua Island, Kingdom of Tonga. *New Zealand Journal of Botany* 34: 65–77.

Ellison, J. C. 1991. The Pacific paleogeography of Rhizophora mangle L. (Rhizophoraceae). *Botanical Journal of the Linnean Society* 105: 271–284.

Enting, B., and L. Molloy. 1982. *The ancient islands: New Zealand's natural environments.* Wellington: Port Nicholson Press.

Flannery, T. 1995a. *Mammals of New Guinea.* Ithaca, N.Y.: Cornell University Press.

———. 1995b. *Mammals of the south-west Pacific and Moluccan Islands.* Ithaca, N.Y.: Cornell University Press.

———. 1995c. *The future eaters: An ecological history of the Australasian lands and people.* New York: Brazillier.

Fleet, H. 1986. *The concise natural history of New Zealand.* Singapore: Heinemann.

Fosberg, F. R. 1947. Micronesian mangroves. *Journal of the New York Botanical Garden* 48: 128–138.

———. 1960. The vegetation of Micronesia. 1. General descriptions, the vegetation of the Marianas Islands, and a detailed consideration of the vegetation of Guam. *Bulletin of the American Museum of Natural History* 119(1): 1–76 and plates 1–40.

Gagné, W. L., and L. W. Cuddihy. 1990. Vegetation. In *Manual of the flowering plants of Hawaii,* ed. D. R. Wagner et al., vol. 1, 45–114. Honolulu: Bishop Museum Press.

Gillison, A. N. 1983. Tropical savannas of Australia and the Southwest Pacific. In *Ecosystems of the world.* Vol. 13, *Tropical savannas,* ed. F. Bourliere, 183–243. Amsterdam: Elsevier Scientific Publishing Co.

Government of New Zealand. 1997. *State of New Zealand's environment 1997.* Wellington: Government Printing Office.

Gunson, D. 1983. *Collins guide to the New Zealand seashore.* Auckland: Collins.

Haantjens, H. A., J. A. Mabbutt, and R. Pullen. 1965. Environmental influences in anthropogenic grasslands in the Sepik plains, New Guinea. *Pacific Viewpoint* 6: 215–219.

Hamilton, L. S., J. O. Juvik, and P. N. Scatena, eds. 1995. Tropical montane cloud forests. *Ecological Studies Series,* vol. 110. New York: Springer-Verlag.

Hardin, G. 1968. The tragedy of the commons. *Science* 162: 1243–1248.

Hatheway, W. H. 1953. The land vegetation of Arno Atoll, Marshall Islands. *Atoll Research Bulletin* 16: 1–68.

———. 1955. The natural vegetation of Canton Island, an Equatorial Pacific atoll. *Atoll Research Bulletin* 43: 1–8.

Hosokawa, T., H. Tagawa, and V. J. Chapman. 1977. Mangals of Micronesia, Taiwan, Japan, the Philippines and Oceania. In *Wet coastal ecosystems,* ed. V. J. Chapman, 271–291. Amsterdam: Elsevier Scientific Publishing Co.

Jaffré, T. 1980. *Etude écologique du peuplement végétal des sols dérivés de roches ultrabasiques en Nouvelle-Calédonie.* Paris: ORSTOM.

Keast, A. 1996. Avian geography: New Guinea to the eastern Pacific. In *The origin and evolution of Pacific Island biotas, New Guinea to Eastern Polynesia: Patterns and processes,* ed. A. Keast and S. E. Miller, 373–398. Amsterdam: SPB Academic Publishing Company.

Kitalong, A. H. 2008. Forests of Palau: A long term perspective. *Micronesica* 40(1/2): 8–30.

Latham, M. 1983. Origin of the talasiga formation. In *The eastern islands of Fiji: A study of the natural environment, its use and man's influence on its evolution,* ed. M. Latham and H. C. Brookfield, 129–141. General Report No 3, UNESCO/UNFPA Man and the Biosphere Project. Paris: ORSTOM.

Lea, D. A. M., and P. G. Irwin. 1967. *New Guinea: The territory and its people.* Melbourne: Oxford University Press.

Leach, G. J., and P. L. Osborne. 1985. *Freshwater plants of Papua New Guinea.* Port Moresby: University of Papua New Guinea Press.

Manner, H. I. 1981. Ecological succession in new and old swiddens of montane Papua New Guinea. *Human Ecology* 9(3): 359–377.

Manner, H. I., R. R. Thaman, and D. C. Hassall. 1985. Plant succession after phosphate mining on Nauru. *Australian Geographer* 17: 185–195.

Merlin, M., and W(B). Raynor. 2005. Kava cultivation, native species conservation, and integrated watershed resource management on Pohnpei Island. *Pacific Science* 59(2): 241–260.

Morat, P., T. Jaffré, J. M. Veillon, and H. S. MacKee. 1981. Végétation. *Atlas de la Nouvelle-Calédonie* 28. Paris: ORSTOM.

Morat, P. 1993. Our knowledge of the flora of New Caledonia: Endemism and diversity in relation to vegetation types and substrates. *Biodiversity Letters* 1: 72–81.

Mueller-Dombois, D. 1981a. Fire in tropical ecosystems. In *Fire regimes and ecological properties,* ed. H. A. Mooney, T. M. Bonnickson, N. L. Christensen, I. E. Lotan, and W. A. Reiners, 137–176. USDA Forest Service General Technical Report WO-2b.

———. 1981b. Understanding Hawaiian forest ecosystems: The key to biological conservation. In *Island ecosystems: Biological organization in selected Hawaiian communities,* ed. D. Mueller-Dombois, K. W. Bridges, and H. L. Carson, 502–520. US/IBP Synthesis Series 15. Stroudsburg, Pa.: Hutchinson Ross Publishing Company.

———. 1987. Forest dynamics in Hawaii. *Trends in Ecology and Evolution* 2(7): 216–220.

———. 2008. The evolution of the Pacific-Asia Biodiversity Transect Network in the Pacific Science Association. *Micronesica* 40(1/2): 1–7.

Mueller-Dombois, D., and K. W. Bridges. 1981. Introduction. In *Island ecosystems: Biological organization in selected Hawaiian communities,* ed. D. Mueller-Dombois, K. W. Bridges, and H. L. Carson, 35–76. US/IBP Synthesis Series 15. Stroudsburg, Pa.: Hutchinson Ross Publishing Company.

Mueller-Dombois, D., and F. R. Fosberg. 1998. Vegetation of the tropical Pacific Islands. *Ecological Studies* 32.

Mueller-Dombois, D., and L. L. Loope. 1990. Some unique ecological aspects of oceanic island ecosystems. *Monographs on Systematic Botany of the Missouri Botanical Gardens* 32: 21–27.

Mueller-Dombois, D., et al. 1981. Altitudinal distribution of organisms along an island mountain transect. In *Island ecosystems: Biological organization in selected Hawaiian communities,* ed. D. Mueller-Dombois, K. W. Bridges, and H. L. Carson, 77–180. US/IBP Synthesis Series 15. Stroudsburg, Pa.: Hutchinson Ross Publishing Company.

Nunn, P. D. 1994. *Oceanic islands.* Oxford: Blackwell Publishers.

Pajimans, K. 1975. *Explanatory notes to the vegetation map of Papua New Guinea.* Land Research Series no. 35. Melbourne, Australia: CSIRO (Commonwealth Scientific and Industrial Research Organization).

Palau Conservation Society. 2003. *History, culture, tradition, environment: Annual report.* Koror, Palau: Palau Conservation Society.

Pratt, H. D., P. L. Bruner, and D. G. Berrett. 1985. *The birds of Hawaii and the tropical Pacific.* Princeton, N.J.: Princeton University Press.

Raynor, B. 1994. Resource management in upland forests of Pohnpei: Past practices and future possibilities. *Isla: A Journal of Micronesian Studies* 2(1): 47–66.

Raynor, B., and M. Kostka. 2003. Back to the future: Using traditional knowledge to strengthen biodiversity conservation in Pohnpei, Federated States of Micronesia. *Ethnobotany Research & Applications* 1: 70–79.

Ripperton, J. C., and E. Y. Hosaka. 1942. Vegetation zones of Hawaii. *Hawaii Agricultural Experiment Station Bulletin* No. 89. Honolulu.

Ross, T., and L. Dabek. 2006. The tree kangaroo conservation program—community-based conservation on the Huon Peninsula, Papua New Guinea. *Conservation Evidence* 3: 47–48.

Schmid, M. 1989. The forests in the tropical Pacific archipelagoes. In *Tropical rain forest ecosystems: Biogeographical and ecological studies,* ed. H. Leith and M. J. A. Werger, 283–301. Ecosystems of the World 14B. Amsterdam: Elsevier Scientific Publishing Co.

Smith, J. B. 1975. Mountain grasslands of New Guinea. *Journal of Biogeography* 2: 27–44.

Stemmermann, L. 1981. *A guide to Pacific wetland plants.* Honolulu: U.S. Army Corps of Engineers.

Stoddart, D. R. 1975. Vegetation and floristics of the Aitutaki *motus.* Atoll Research Bulletin 190: 87–116.

Stone, C. P., C. W. Smith, and J. T. Tunison. 1992. *Alien plant invasions in native ecosystems of Hawaii: Management and research.* University of Hawaiʻi in cooperation with the National Park Resources Studies Unit. Honolulu: University of Hawaiʻi Press.

Street, J. M. 1966. Grasslands on the highland fringe in New Guinea: Localisation, origin, effects on soil composition. *Capricornia* 3: 9–12.

Thorne, R. F. 1963. Biotic distribution patterns in the tropical Pacific. In *Pacific basin biogeography: A symposium,* ed. J. L. Gressitt, 311–350. Tenth Pacific Science Congress, Honolulu (1961). Honolulu: Bishop Museum Press.

Tomlinson, P. B. 1986. *The botany of mangroves.* Cambridge: Cambridge University Press.

Voronov, A. G., Y. G. Puzachenko, V. N. Sozinov, G. M. Ignatiev, and V. S. Skulkin. 1994. General characteristics of the islands and their vegetation. In *The ecosystems of small islands in the Southwest Pacific (the sixth expedition of the SS "Callisto"),* ed. J. C. Pernetta and H. I. Manner, 46–106. UNEP Regional Seas Reports and Studies N. 151 and SPREP Reports and Studies No. 63.

Walter, H. 1971. *Ecology of tropical and subtropical vegetation.* Translated by D. Mueller-Dombois. Edited by J. H. Burnett. Edinburgh: Oliver and Boyd.

Wardle, P. 1991. *Vegetation of New Zealand.* Cambridge: Cambridge University Press.

Whitmore, T. C. 1974. *Change with time and the role of cyclones in tropical rain forest on Kolomobangara, Solomon Islands.* Commonwealth Forestry Institute Paper no. 46. Oxford: Holywell.

Whittaker, R. H. 1975. *Communities and ecosystems.* Heidelberg: Springer Verlag.

Wein, L., and P. Chatterton. 2005. *A forest strategy for the Solomon Islands, 2006–2011.* Honiara, Solomon Islands: World Wildlife Fund, Solomon Islands.

Wiens, H. J. 1962. *Atoll environment and ecology.* New Haven, Conn.: Yale University Press.

Woodroffe, C. D. 1987. Pacific Island mangroves: Distribution and environmental settings. *Pacific Science* 41: 166–185.

Zan, Y., and R. L. Hunter-Anderson. 1987. On the origins of the Micronesian "savannahs": An anthropological perspective. In *Proceedings of the third international soil management workshop for the management and utilization of acid soils in Micronesia, February 2–6, 1987, Republic of Palau,* ed. J. L. Demeterio and B. DeGuzman, 18–27. Agricultural Experiment Station, College of Agriculture and Life Sciences, University of Guam.

Aquatic Ecosystems

Stephen G. Nelson

9

The vast area of the Pacific Islands region is largely underwater and is blessed with a diverse array of interesting and valuable aquatic ecosystems, including those of inland fresh waters, mangroves, seagrass meadows, coral reefs, kelp beds, continental shelves, seafloor slopes, the open ocean, and the deep sea. The focus in this chapter is primarily on the structure and function of these ecosystems, comparing their biotic assemblages, their trophic structures, and the sources and fates of organic materials and nutrients within. Every ecosystem relies on such processes. The inputs upon which consumers and decomposers depend must either come from primary producers (photosynthetic or chemosynthetic) or be imported from other ecosystems. Examination of these processes provides a useful means of comparing different types of ecosystems. Many aspects of these ecosystems, however, are poorly known, and given the breadth of the subject matter, it is difficult to provide depth of coverage for all the topics considered. With those cautions, I will attempt to provide an overview of some of the major aquatic ecosystems in the region.

Inland Fresh Waters

The numbers and kinds of species found in Pacific Island fresh waters (Figures 9.1 and 9.2) vary considerably, depending on the dominant food sources and the physical characteristics of their environments. For example, the number of aquatic species usually increases from headwaters to estuaries, where fresh water and seawater mix (Maciolek and Timbol 1981). Diversity also decreases from the west to the east in Oceania (Fitzsimmons, Nishimoto, and Devick 1996). Island size and geographic isolation also affect the species composition of these ecosystems. Most Pacific Island streams have few species relative to the streams and large rivers of New Guinea (Allen 1991). Also, tropical and temperate inland aquatic ecosystems differ considerably. For example, New Zealand has a distinctive freshwater biota, which differs considerably from those in the tropical Pacific.

There are, however, striking similarities among the biotic assemblages of tropical Pacific Island streams. This is the case because relatively few taxonomic groups of organisms have the dispersal abilities and life-history characteristics necessary for traversing oceanic expanses and successfully establishing in insular fresh

Figure 9.1. The Ngermeskang River, Palau.

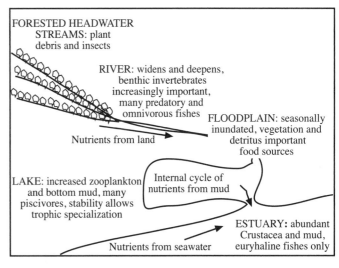

Figure 9.2. Tropical freshwater ecosystems (after Lowe-McConnell 1977).

waters (Ryan 1991; Fitzsimmons, Nishimoto, and Devick 1996). There are approximately thirty families of fishes occurring frequently in freshwater streams of the tropical Pacific (Parham 2005). Prominent groups include gobies, flagtails, and eels (Maciolek and Ford 1987; Nelson et al. 1997; Donaldson and Myers 2002; Fitzsimmons, Parham, and Nishimoto 2002). Among the tropical oceanic islands of the Pacific, diversity of freshwater fishes decreases from west to east with approximately thirty-eight species inhabiting the freshwater habitats of the Micronesian Islands and only five species in Hawaiʻi (Fitzsimmons, Parham, and Nishimoto 2002; McDowall 2003). Stream invertebrates include shrimps, crabs, snails, bivalves, sponges, and even a species of nudibranch. Many of these fishes and macroinvertebrates (other than insects) are diadromous—spending a stage of their life cycle in fresh water and another stage in the ocean. A few species, such as thiarid snails, spend their entire lives in fresh water.

In these stream ecosystems, primary producers are mainly attached algae, filaments, mats, and gelatinous colonies, which grow on exposed surfaces of rock and submerged roots (Sherwood 2006). Additional organic input is derived from leaf fall, detritus, and other materials derived from the terrestrial communities within the watershed. Nitrogen, phosphorus, and other nutrients run into the stream from the soil. Atmospheric nitrogen becomes available through fixation by blue-green algae. Nutrients regenerated by fishes and shrimps may also be important to the primary producers, especially during periods of low stream flow.

In the streams of tropical islands, herbivores are numerous. Epilithic (stone-attached) algal films and filamentous macroalgae are consumed by gobies, snails, and others. Mountain gobies (*Stiphodon* spp.) are the most abundant of herbivorous fishes in many of these streams. These gobies feed on algal films of bedrock, boulder, or cobble. Some fishes feed on filamentous algae and larval aquatic insects, while others feed on shrimps, snails, or small fishes. Other organisms, such as some aquatic snails, rely mainly on terrestrial organic inputs. Decapod crustaceans are also important and prominent consumers of the inland aquatic fauna of the Pacific Islands (Buden et al. 2001; Crowl et al. 2001; Leberer and Nelson 2001; Larned et al. 2003). Atyid shrimps, such as those in the genera *Atyopsis, Atyoida,* and *Caridina,* are sediment and filter feeders, removing particulate matter with brush-like appendages. These feeding activities result in the removal of sediment from rock surfaces, which allows increased growth of algae on the cleared surfaces (Pringle et al. 1993). Detrital processing by these freshwater shrimp increases the concentrations of organic particulate matter and nutrients in streams (Crowl et al. 2001). The larger Palaemonid shrimps, such as species in the genus *Macrobrachium,* are omnivorous, feeding on plant materials, algae, and invertebrates. Both kinds of shrimp are found at high densities throughout island streams in the tropical Pacific and are responsible for most of the secondary productivity (Bright 1982).

The most extensive inland aquatic habitats in the Pacific Islands are the great rivers and swamplands of Papua New Guinea. The Sepik and the Fly are among the world's most powerful rivers in terms of annual water flow. The rivers wind gradually to the sea, often changing course, leaving a trace of lagoons, oxbow lakes, and vast swamplands—which convert into grasslands during the winter dry season. Large chunks of this vegetation are periodically

torn off the Sepik banks, drifting off as floating islands, often with trees and animals aboard (Wheeler 1988). As lakes in the Fly River system refill, grasses (*Echinochola praestans* and *Leersia hexandra*) and floating aquatic plants form rafts that can, at times, cover over 90 percent of the surface area (Swales et al. 1999).

Here as well, most inland aquatic fauna have marine affinities. The fauna is diverse, with numerous endemics. Native species include more than two hundred frogs, nine turtles, six eels, several snakes, and two crocodiles (Keast 1996; Swales et al. 1999). Catfishes (Ariidae and Plotosidae) are well represented, with twenty-eight recorded species. New Guinea's freshwater fishes (329 species) are large, with more than half growing longer than 30 cm; the few small species (such as gobies) are found mainly in small side streams (Lowe-McConnell 1987; Coates 1993). The flood plains of the Fly River alone provide habitats for sixty-six fish species from thirty-three families (Swales et al. 1999), with most areas dominated by eighteen species of catfishes in the families Arridandae (eleven species) and Plotodidae (seven species). In these flood plains, pelagic shoals of herring (*Nematalosa* spp.) are often abundant, particularly in the oxbow lakes. The Sepik-Ramu river system of New Guinea has fewer fish species, all either amphidromous or freshwater species derived from marine ancestors (Dudgeon and Smith 2006). A rich variety of food sources is exploited, depending on the zone (Table 9.1).

Table 9.1

Number of Fish Species in Various Trophic Categories in the Purari River, Papua New Guinea

Feeding mode	Small creeks	River	Delta (upper)	Delta (lower)
Detritivores	4	8	4	9
Fructivores	0	3	2	3
Other plant eaters	0	3	0	2
Insectivores	4	5	3	4
Molluscivores	0	0	4	4
Prawn eaters	0	12	14	20
Crab eaters	0	0	0	11
Piscivores	1	6	7	15
Omnivores	0	3	2	2

Source: After Lowe-McConnell 1987 and sources therein.

The consumers of New Zealand's stream ecosystems differ considerably from those of tropical Pacific islands. Here, few species are herbivores (Huryn 1996). Insects are more important in aquatic food webs than is the case on tropical islands. Invertebrate fauna include many aquatic insects, two types of crayfish, atyid shrimps, and snails. An extensive study of the Waipara River found fifty-seven species of stream invertebrates (Suren and Jowett 2006). There, ostracods constituted 25 percent of the invertebrate fauna, and other common species were larval elmid beetles and chironomids, oligochaetes, and hydrobid snails. Fishes include galaxids, smelts, eleotrids, graylings, a lamprey, and freshwater eels (McDowall 1990).

Inland aquatic ecosystems are highly vulnerable to human activities. Because removal of vegetation increases sediment loads, reduces the input of organic materials, increases stream temperatures, and alters water levels, construction near streams must include precautions to ensure that exposed sediment is not washed into the water. Irrigation runoff may contain herbicides, pesticides, and overly high nutrient levels. Dams can block migrations of diadromous species and, through flow changes, alter the distributions of aquatic organisms (Concepcion and Nelson 1999). Development of areas near island streams often alters the habitats, making them more vulnerable to invasions of introduced species. For example, of twenty-six fish species collected from Hawaiian streams, sixteen were non-native (Brasher et al. 2006), with the more developed sites at lower elevation being the most affected. Of special concern is the impact of species introductions. Many introduced species have become established in Pacific Island fresh waters; these have often had detrimental effects on the indigenous fauna. There are only a few cases in which the introductions are considered to have been of benefit, and some have resulted in complete disaster. On Nauru, for example, introduced tilapia have made it impossible to continue the traditional culture of milkfish, which now must be imported from Guam or Kiribati (Nelson and Eldredge 1991). In New Zealand, introduced aquatic plants have become a major nuisance (McDowall 1990), and in New Guinea introduced fishes such as climbing perch and walking catfish are increasing in abundance and causing concern for native species in floodplain habitats (Swales et al. 1999; Storey et al. 2002).

Mangrove Ecosystems (Mangals)

Of the various nearshore ecosystems on Pacific Islands (Figure 9.3), mangroves rise highest above sea level, forming dense forests in estuaries and flooded shores of the tropics and subtropics (Hosakawa, Tagawa, and Chapman 1977; Ewel, Hauff, and Cole 2003), and they extend as far south as the North Island of New Zealand (Figure 9.4). Mangrove ecosystems are the tropical counterparts of temperate salt marshes. They are important ecologically in trapping both sediment and nutrients and in providing habitat for diverse assemblages of fishes and invertebrates. Aerial roots (Figures 9.4 and 9.5) serve to trap sediment and fine organic materials. Nutrients are also brought in through tidal action. The rates of nitrogen fixation in the sediments of mangrove swamps are high (ranging from 0.03 to 2.8 g/m²/year) (Howarth, Marino, and Lane 1988).

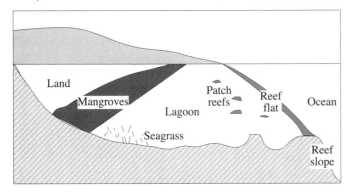

Figure 9.3. Nearshore ecosystems in the tropical Pacific.

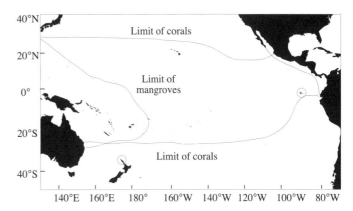

Figure 9.4. Limits for the distribution of mangroves and coral in the Pacific Islands (after Kay 1980 and Nunn 1994). Outlier populations of mangroves are shown in northern New Zealand and the Galapagos.

Figure 9.5. Mangrove ecosystem, Micronesia.

Mangals have provided numerous valuable resources to Pacific Islanders for generations. For example, archaeological studies in the Mariana Islands, where mangroves occupy only a small portion of the coastline, revealed that the first people to arrive, several thousand years ago, relied heavily on clams (*Anadara antiquata*) harvested from mangrove habitats, along with other marine sources, for sustenance. In later periods, around 1000 CE, harvests shifted to smaller bivalves and reef gastropods, a change in resource use attributed to the reduction of mangrove habitats from sea-level rise (Amesbury 2007). Today, among the most important cultural resources in the region are the mangrove crabs *Scylla* spp., large portunid crabs that are highly valued throughout the Pacific Islands. For example, on the island of Kosrae, mangrove crabs (*Scylla serrata*), which are harvested for family feasts, as gifts, for export, and for sale to local hotels, are suffering population declines as a result of overharvesting (Bonine et al. 2008).

Efforts to manage, protect, and restore mangrove habitats and resources are ongoing in many of the Pacific Islands, but the situation in the Hawaiian Islands is much different. Because of their geographic isolation, there are no native mangrove trees in Hawai'i. Propagules of the red mangrove (*Rhizpophora mangle*), however, were introduced on the island of Moloka'i in 1920 to stabilize soil erosion. The introduction was too successful, and today the spread of this mangrove is the cause of concern, as it is considered invasive (Chimmer et al. 2006). Unwanted expansion of mangrove habitat in New Zealand is a result of increases in sedimentation and nutrient inputs from inland development (Lovelock et al. 2007).

Although mangrove trees are very productive, their leaves are rich in tannins, which inhibit consumption by terrestrial insects and other consumers. The palatability of the leaves is also decreased because of high cellulose and fiber and low nitrogen content. Much of the organic input from mangrove trees requires microbial enrichment and decomposition before it can be of use to aquatic consumers. Microbial activity reduces the carbon-nitrogen ratio from one-third to one-half of that of newly fallen leaves in about eight months, increasing the protein content and nutritional value (Twilley, Lugo, and Patterson-Zucca 1986). This decomposition of organic material is facilitated by the activities of burrowing marine organisms, since material decomposes more rapidly when buried. Decomposition is also facilitated by the high sulfate content of mangrove sediments (Lugo, Brown, and Brown 1988).

Microbial activity is also important in converting dissolved organic matter (DOM) released from decaying vegetation and living plants into particulate organic matter (POM), needed by filter-feeding organisms and detritivores (Mann 1988). Some of the DOM is taken up by bacteria, which form aggregates that can be colonized by other microorganisms. Some aggregates sink to the bottom and are consumed by a variety of crustaceans, including amphipods, isopods, copepods, and shrimps (Camilleri and Ribi 1986).

Consumers are abundant and diverse in mangrove ecosystems. Because the finer organic particles are easily suspended in the water column by tidal action, and because the mangrove roots provide surfaces for attachment, mangroves have an abundance of oysters, shrimps, crabs, and other invertebrates. Oysters often cover the submerged roots of mangrove trees (Braley 1982). Mud crabs, fiddler crabs, and penaeid shrimps are often prominent. Numerous fishes are present, including mudskippers (small gobies) and rabbitfishes.

Mangroves are vulnerable to many of the same anthropogenic disturbances as the inland waters. For example, on Guam, an oil spill from an upstream refinery killed a large portion of the already limited number of mangroves. Replanting of seedlings has restored the mangrove community, although it will be some time before the ecosystem recovers completely. The health of mangroves is dependent on frequent flushing from tidal action, and barriers to tidal flow will result in death of the affected trees. On Babeldaup in the Palau Islands, construction of a shrimp pond resulted in destruction of a large section of mangrove, both from clearing during pond construction and from the subsequent disturbance of tidal flow. The destruction of mangroves and other coastal ecosystems in areas converted to shrimp farms is a significant environmental problem throughout the tropics (Lockwood 1997). This concern was expressed clearly in 1996 by a group of twenty-one nongovernmental organizations calling for a global moratorium on expansion of shrimp farming until the criteria of sustainability could be met. It has been estimated that about 50 percent of mangrove ecosystems have been transformed or destroyed by human activity (Vitousek et al. 1997).

Seagrass Meadows

Along shores protected from wave action, seagrasses flourish and form meadows, a source of food and shelter to a wide variety of marine organisms (Brouns and Heijs 1991). Seagrasses grow in soft sediments and stabilize them (Figure 9.6). Like mangroves, seagrasses evolved from terrestrial plants and have roots that extract nutrients from the sediments in which they grow. Seagrasses provide a habitat for numerous species of marine invertebrates, fishes, and algae. Unlike coral reefs and mangroves, seagrasses are present in both tropical and temperate coastal areas. There are numerous genera of seagrasses throughout the tropical Pacific islands, including *Halophila, Syringodium, Thallasia, Cymodocea,* and *Halodule* (Skelton and South 2006).

Figure 9.6. Seagrass meadow, Micronesia.

Tropical seagrasses have high rates of primary production (Table 9.2). But since they evolved from terrestrial plants, their blades have a high content of indigestible cellulose and fiber. Nonetheless, seagrasses provide food for herbivorous fishes, urchins, shrimps, sea turtles, and dugongs (Stevenson 1988; Andre, Gyuris, and Lawler 2005; Aragones et al. 2006). Dugong browsing on seagrasses can result in cleared strips within the beds (Donning 1981). Early insights into the importance of herbivory in seagrass meadows came from halos, or bare areas around rocks or other shelters in the seagrass meadows, created and maintained by herbivorous fishes and sea urchins. Rabbitfishes and parrotfishes also frequently

Table 9.2

Primary Productivity Rates in the Ocean

Location	Average productivity (gC/m²/yr.)*
Open ocean (tropical)	40
Open ocean (temperate)	120
Continental shelf	200
Upwelling zones	300
Seagrasses (temperate)	600
Mangroves	800
Coral reefs	1000
Kelp beds	1000
Seagrasses (tropical)	1500

Source: After Sumich 1988; Barnes and Hughes 1982.
*Average figures from various studies; much higher maxima frequently occur.

feed on seagrass. Biomass retained in seagrass meadows is eventually broken down by bacteria and other microoganisms. Some seagrasses contain secondary metabolites that deter herbivorous fishes (Paul, Nelson, and Sanger 1990), and seagrass blades resistant to herbivores and decomposers can end up being exported to other ecosystems. For example, there are even reports of undecomposed seagrass blades in deep-sea environments (Phillips and Menez 1988). The organic material is either retained within the bed or exported to other coastal environments.

These ecosystems are often threatened by human activities. Those that are particularly likely to adversely affect seagrasses include dredging and filling associated with coastal development, sewage discharge, thermal pollution, and agricultural runoff. Increased nutrient input to seagrass meadows may result in increased productivity but a decrease in species diversity, as some seagrass species are better able to use the increased nutrients than others (Vitousek et al. 1997). In some areas, seagrass habitats have also been altered because of the overfishing of sea turtles (Stevenson 1988).

Coral Reefs

Coral reefs are massive biogeological structures characterized by high productivity in areas of low dissolved nutrient concentrations, and by great species diversity among most taxonomic groups, including fishes, invertebrates, algae, and others (Figure 9.7).

The physical structures that constitute the reef framework are composed primarily of calcium carbonate, deposited by reef-building (hermatypic) corals and calcareous algae. Reef-building corals are colonial animals that are able to grow rapidly with the aid of dinoflagellates (single-celled algae) in the genus *Synbiodinium*. All reef-building corals are dependent on these endosymbionts, known as zooxanthellae, which photosynthesize and translocate nutrients to their host and assist in the deposition of calcium carbonate needed in reef formation (Muller-Parker and D'Elia 1997). The zooxanthellae benefit from receiving nitrogen, excreted as ammonium by the coral polyps (Table 9.3).

Figure 9.7. Coral reef, Palau.

Table 9.3

Benefits and Costs of Symbiosis Between Corals and Zooxanthellae

Benefits	Costs
A. Coral	
Supply of carbon	Regulation of algal growth
Increased growth and reproduction	High oxygen tension
Facilitation of calcification	Rejection of excess algae
Conservation of nutrients	Affected by algal disease
Sequestration of toxins by algae	
B. Zooxanthellae	
Supply of carbon dioxide	Translocation of carbon
Maintenance in photic zone	Low growth rates
Uniform environment	Subject to expulsion by host
Protection from grazers	Losses by predators of coral
High population density enabled	

Source: After Muller-Parker and D'Elia 1997.

The number of symbioses between autotrophic organisms and invertebrates is a striking feature of coral reefs. There is diversity and zonation within species (Rowan and Knowlton 1995; Rowan et al. 1997) and among reef organisms. Marine invertebrates in at least five phyla have symbiotic associations with dinoflagellates of the genus *Symbiodinium* (Stat, Carter, and Hoegh-Guldberg 2006). For example, giant clams (*Tridacna* spp.) also have symbiotic zooxanthellae in their tissues, and many species of ascidians (filter-feeding sea squirts) contain symbiotic algae of the genus *Prochloron*. Many sponges, and some other organisms, contain symbiotic cyanobacteria. It is these symbioses that allow the high productivity of reef ecosystems to be sustained.

Exogenous sources of nutrients are in relatively short supply in most coral reef ecosystems, especially on atolls (Hatcher 1997). Rates of nitrogen fixation by benthic (bottom-dwelling) bacteria and cyanobacteria, however, are high, contributing significantly to coral reef nitrogen budgets (Yamamuro, Kayanne, and Minagawa 1995). Nutrients are also brought in from the open ocean. Even though tropical oceanic waters are low in dissolved nutrients, attached algae and autotrophic symbionts are able to rapidly take up available nutrients. Near schools of fish, ammonium concentrations may be elevated, and coral reef algae can rapidly exploit even brief pulses of nutrients (Nelson 1985). Fishes that feed in the water column and then take shelter in the reef transport materials and nutrients from pelagic (open sea) ecosystems to coral reefs. On high islands, nutrient inputs from terrestrial runoff are important. Downwelling is another source of nutrients on some islands. In the northern portion of Guam, which is a raised limestone plateau, the freshwater lens has a relatively high content of nitrate, and seeps provide nutrients that are important to coral reefs. Endo-upwelling may be another source of nutrients on atolls (Figure 9.8).

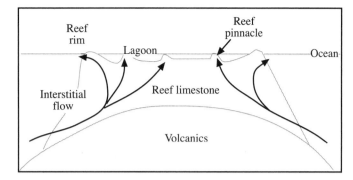

Figure 9.8. *Idealized section through an atoll showing endo-upwelling (after Rougerie and Wauthy 1993). Deep interstitial nutrient-rich water is warmed by geothermal heat, causing it to rise and exit through cracks in the reef rim and lagoon bottom, facilitating growth of coral pinnacles (patch reefs) and the surrounding reef endo-upwelling is also hypothesized to have contributed to phosphate depositions in raised limestone islands.*

Because of these numerous sources of nutrients, some feel that coral reef productivity is limited by the surface area available to primary producers (rather than being limited by nutrients) (Long-hurst and Pauly 1987). Raising nutrient inputs results in increases in biomass of benthic algae (Hatcher 1997), which can block coral recruitment. The major primary producers in reef ecosystems are attached macroalgae and symbiotic microalgae. Schools of herbivorous surgeonfishes, parrotfishes, and rabbitfishes roam the reefs, browsing or grazing on any sprig of macroalgae not defended by calcification or secondary metabolites (Paul 1992). Sea turtles, such as the green sea turtle *Chelonia mydas,* are large herbivores that feed on a variety of seaweeds on coral reefs (Kolinski et al. 2006). Thus, the standing crops of macroalgae are usually low, except in areas that are less accessible to herbivorous fishes, such as on shallow reef flats or near river mouths. Some species of damselfish defend patches of algae from other herbivores and remove unwanted algae (Lassuy 1980).

There are many kinds of consumers in coral reef ecosystems. Butterfly fishes, triggerfishes, corallivorous marine snails, and starfishes feed directly on coral polyps. Other fishes harvest the zooplankton that feed on particulate matter. Invertebrate herbivores, particularly sea urchins, also have significant roles in the functioning of coral reef ecosystems (Carpenter 1997). The corals themselves are consumers, obtaining nutrition from capturing planktonic (floating) organisms and from the uptake of dissolved organic matter. The result is a highly efficient use of energy and nutrients (Figure 9.9). Organic material falling into bottom sediment is consumed by invertebrates and reef fish (Nelson and Wilkins 1988). Sea cucumbers feed on sediments, selectively ingesting nutrient-rich particles. These organisms can be abundant in some reef habitats, especially in shallow lagoons or reef flats. Sediment-feeding surgeonfish (such as *Ctenochaetus striatus*) are often numerous in coral reef habitats.

While utilization of nutrients and energy in coral reef ecosystems is highly efficient, export of materials to surrounding ecosystems also occurs. Some of this is from predation by pelagic fishes. Most of the export is in the form of particulate organic matter that is carried out to sea by currents. This particulate organic matter consists largely of mucus secreted by corals. Loss of biomass from

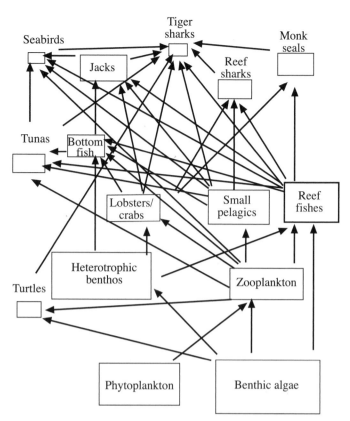

Figure 9.9. *Representation of the food web on French Frigate Shoals, Northwest Hawaiian Islands (after Polovina 1984). The area of each box is proportional to the logarithm of the biomass of each group.*

macroalgae and other organisms also occurs in association with tropical storms, which are frequent and often severe in some areas.

Coral reefs are extensive and most diverse in the western Pacific, with more than four hundred species recorded, whereas fewer than one hundred occur in eastern Polynesia (Paulay 1997). Postulated explanations include differences in oceanographic conditions (cooler waters in the eastern Pacific due to cold currents and upwelling) and geotectonic factors (warm, shallow seas in Southeast Asia; difficulty dispersing against prevailing easterly currents; and closure of Central America during the Pliocene 5 to 2 Ma, severing the connection with Caribbean corals).

The lack of coral reefs in temperate latitudes has been attributed to lethal effects of low temperature, competition by macroalgae (such as kelp), and the costs of calcification. The deposition of calcium carbonate requires the release of carbon dioxide from solution, as shown:

$$Ca^{++} + 2HCO_3^- \rightarrow CO_2 + H_2O + CaCO_3$$

In cool, temperate waters, CO_2 tends to remain in solution (as with a carbonated beverage), and the above reaction becomes energetically costly. In tropical waters, CO_2 (used in photosynthesis by zooxanthellae) tends to come out of solution, and $CaCO_3$ (used for the reef framework) is deposited (Hallock 1997).

Over geological time, reef (and other) limestones have effectively tied up a significant portion of atmospheric CO_2, making the Earth a livable planet. (Had this not occurred, atmospheric temperatures would have risen dramatically, due to the sun's natural aging and increasing luminosity.) The evolution of efficient photosynthetic mechanisms in algae and terrestrial plants has had a similar beneficial function. Humans, however, are upsetting this balance by burning vast amounts of fossil fuels and damaging coral reefs (Hallock 1997, Hoegh-Guldberg et al. 2007).

While natural events such as typhoons, earthquakes, outbreaks of the crown-of-thorns starfish, and sea-level fluctuations can have substantial effects on reefs, the impacts of human activities are the major threat to these ecosystems. Coral reefs throughout the world are being degraded at an alarming rate, leading to economic, ecological, and cultural losses (Birkeland 2004; Richmond et al. 2007). The rapid, global increase in atmospheric carbon dioxide and accompanying global warming is among the most ominous threats to coral reef ecosystems. The associated warming of the oceans can cause stress to corals, as it is well documented that increases in temperature of only 1 or 2 degrees C can result in the symbiotic zooxanthellae being ejected, resulting in coral bleaching. In addition, approximately 25 percent of the increase in atmospheric carbon dioxide enters the ocean resulting in acidification and reduction of carbonate concentration, which is needed for corals and other calcifying organisms (Langdon et al. 2003; Hoegh-Guldberg et al. 2007). Another serious threat to the coral reefs around high islands is increased sedimentation resulting from unwise management of island watersheds (Richmond et al. 2007). Other forms of human disturbances include reef mining, land clearing, sewage discharge, thermal discharge from power plants, overfishing, and anchor damage. One sign of stress in corals is bleaching, the loss of zooxanthellae or their pigments related to elevated temperatures and exposure to ultraviolet or intense visible irradiance, causing oxidative stress and inhibiting photosynthesis (Lesser 1996).

Kelp Ecosystems

The temperate nearshore waters of New Zealand have extensive areas of hard substrate ("rocky reefs"), providing a rich benthic environment. Nutrient concentrations around New Zealand coasts are higher than in the tropical Pacific and support a large biomass of macroalgae and phytoplankton. The macroalgal flora of New Zealand is diverse, with approximately seventy-seven known species (Hurd et al. 2004). Algae growth in temperate waters is also facilitated because specialized fish herbivores are rare, relative to the tropics (Paulay 1997). Competition can be severe and space availability becomes limiting for benthic algae and dependent organisms.

The shorelines here are often dominated by various kelp (large brown algae) species attached to rocky substrates (Figure 9.10). Kelp occurs in dense stands subtidally, often forming a closed canopy over smaller algae. The giant kelp *Macrocystis pyrifrea*, suspended by air bladders at the base of each leaf, forms undersea "forests" reaching up to 30 m in height and occupying as much as 10 m² of space per individual in sheltered locations on the South Island (Schiel, Andrew, and Foster 1995).

As is characteristic of temperate rocky shores, conspicuous zonation is found in the macroalgae of New Zealand. Schiel (1988, 1994) described an upper zone dominated by *Carpophyllum* spp. (bladder kelp); an intermediate zone with abundant sea urchins but few macroalgae; and a deep zone (>10 m) of monospecific stands of *Ecklonia radiata* (Figure 9.11) or stands of *E. radiata* mixed with

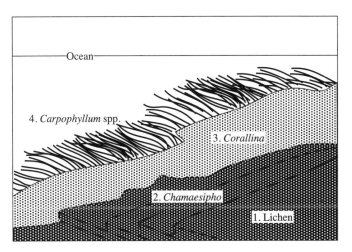

Figure 9.10. *Shoreline zonation in northeast New Zealand (after Morton and Miller 1968). From top down, the following are shown: a lichen-encrusted platform, oyster ledges, a coralline algae ledge, and fringing, subtidal kelp.*

a. Northern New Zealand

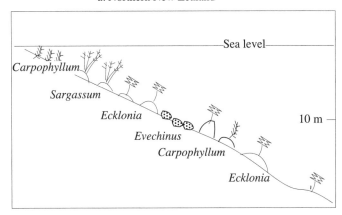

b. Southern New Zealand

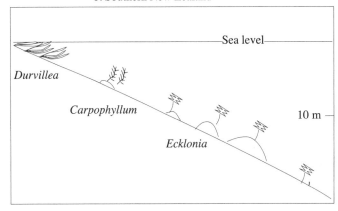

Figure 9.11. *Schematic representation of depth distribution of prominent kelp species in New Zealand (after Schiel 1988).*

other canopy-forming macroalgae (Goodsell et al. 2004). In southern New Zealand, *Carpophyllum* spp. are replaced by *Durvillea antarctica* (bull kelp) at the uppermost level.

Primary productivity is high in kelp ecosystems. Some of this productivity is exported to adjacent ecosystems, as is evident by the piles of drift algae occurring on beaches, particularly following storms. The remaining productivity is stored in the biomass of the algal beds or consumed by herbivores.

Invertebrate consumers are abundant along the shores of New Zealand, while there are few herbivorous fishes. Sea urchins (*Evecinus cloroticus*) and abalone (locally called paua) (*Haliotis* spp.) are important herbivores in kelp beds (Schiel, Andrew, and Foster 1995). Small herbivores include shrimps, crabs, marine snails, and amphipods. Some herbivores harvest phytoplankton. A conspicuous example of these are the mussels, filter feeders that often form dense beds. Various fishes and marine mammals feed on the abundant invertebrates or smaller fishes. New Zealand is also the home of several species of diving birds, including penguins.

Kelp ecosystems are highly vulnerable to human activities and particularly to overfishing. Pollution, such as that resulting from the thermal discharges of power plants and oil spills, can cause much damage to shoreline ecosystems. New Zealand's concern over the potential for radioactive pollution by other countries engaged in the transportation or detonation of nuclear materials within the Pacific Ocean region has been clearly articulated and has led to some highly visible political clashes over the years (notably with France and the United States, though these disputes have become less strident in recent years).

Continental Shelf, Seamount, Deep Coral, and Slope Ecosystems

On many Pacific islands, the seafloor slopes sharply downward to several km depth. But at two locations—New Guinea and New Zealand—the seafloor slopes gradually down to around 200 m depth (the continental shelf) prior to dropping steeply to the ocean floor (Figure 9.12). Large portions of these waters (the neritic marine province) are sufficiently shallow for sunlight to penetrate, supporting phytoplankton and benthic algae. Neritic ecosystems receive abundant nutrients from adjacent landmasses. The waters are also well mixed through wind, tidal action, and, in some locations, upwelling (Barnes and Hughes 1982; Longhurst and Pauly 1987). In these areas, the discharge of organic material and nutrients has a large effect on coastal ecosystems.

Thus, primary productivity and respiration are relatively high above continental shelves. In the Gulf of Papua, benthic respiration

was estimated to be over 300 mgCm^{-2} with pelagic respiration at nearly 900 mgCm^{-2} (McKinnon, Carleton, and Duggan 2007). That study also estimated that primary productivity rates were approximately 600 mgCm^{-2} in areas affected by the river plume and approximately 150 mgCm^{-2} at offshore stations. The interactions between neritic waters and benthos are numerous. Approximately 20 percent of the primary productivity is consumed by pelagic herbivores; the remainder sinks to the bottom, enriching the sediments and providing nutrition for detrital feeders and decomposers. Benthic organisms often spend a portion of their lives as larvae in the pelagic zone (as many as 80 percent of the macrobenthic invertebrates in tropical waters), taking advantage of the rich phytoplankton production (Barnes and Hughes 1982).

Consumers of shelf benthos include clams, oysters, worms, crabs, lobsters, starfishes, sea urchins, sponges, and fishes. Fishes, along with squid, are abundant in neritic ecosystems and are the targets of commercial fisheries, particularly in New Zealand. Fish communities differ depending on the dominant substrate. For example, groupers (Serranidae) and snappers (Lutjanidae) are found in rocky areas, while threadfins (Polynemidae) and grunts (Pomadasyidae) are found in muddy or sandy areas (Longhurst and Pauly 1987). Surface waters are home to large schools of sardines (Clupeidae) and anchovies (Engraulidae). These are, in turn, hunted by mackerels, tunas, and sharks. Temperate waters have a less diverse shelf fauna, but with many species akin to tropical groups.

Slope fauna (below 200 m depth) are more widely distributed (antitropically and circumglobally), relative to shelf species, owing to the homogenous environment. In New Zealand, common species include orange roughy (*Noplostethus atlanticus*), hoki (*Macruronus novazelandiae*), deep-sea dories (*Allocyttus* spp., *Pseudocyttus maculatus*), and ling eel (*Genypterus blacodes*). With increasing depth, fish have larger eyes and heads, smaller abdomens, and other adaptations to poor light and dispersed food sources. Evidence elsewhere suggests that slope fauna decrease in abundance and diversity with increasing depth, although narrow strata of high diversity may occur at midslope levels (around 500 m) (Ward and Blaber 1994). Many of the commercially valuable deepwater fishes are long-lived and slow-growing, making populations of these fishes susceptible to overfishing (Fry, Brewer, and Venables 2006).

Seamounts are major features of the seafloor in the Pacific Island region. These are isolated submerged volcanoes, most of which are inactive, that rise thousands of meters above the seafloor (Koslow 2007). Seamounts intensify currents flowing past them and create localized areas of upwelling of nutrient-rich waters and increasing primary productivity in the waters above. The increased current flows combined with the steepness of the seamounts are not conducive to sediment accumulation, and the result is increased bare rock habitat suitable for colonization by numerous suspension-feeding invertebrates, including deepwater corals. Seamounts are hot spots of diversity in the region. Richer de Forges, Koslow, and Poore (2000) collected more than 850 species, about a third of which were new to science, from twenty-four seamounts sampled in the southwest Pacific. Large groups of benthoplegic fishes are associated with seamounts and some of these populations are exploited as fishery resources.

There are also coral ecosystems in deeper waters around the Pacific Islands, and these are perhaps best known around the

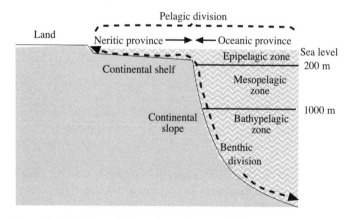

Figure 9.12. Divisions of the marine environment (after Lowe-McConnell 1977).

Hawaiian Islands (Grigg 1965; Parrish and Baco 2007). These include species in several orders of the class Anthozoa, including stony coral, black corals, gold corals, gorgonians, soft corals, and Pennatulacean corals. In addition, there are at least four species of stylasterids (class Hydrozoa). Ecosystems in which deep corals are predominant range in depth from around 30 m to over 2,000 m. These corals do not form reefs, but they are important components of ecologically important communities that include numerous species of fish (Parrish and Boland 2004) and invertebrates. Deep corals are also an important economic resource, as some species are harvested and used in making jewelry (Grigg 2001).

Continental shelves and slopes are subject to damage by oil spills, sewage and thermal discharges, and overfishing. Dams block nutrients from entering the neritic zone, resulting in a potential decline in fisheries. Intense commercial fishing affects continental shelf ecosystems by removing substantial amounts of biomass. Enormous amounts of nontarget species (including 90 percent of shrimp trawl catch) are discarded every year from commercial marine fisheries (Vitousek et al. 1997; Mangel, Hofman, and Twiss 1993). Trawls, by dragging along the bottom, also damage the habitats of other species.

In recent decades, the New Zealand fisheries industry has increasingly turned to the deep waters at the edge of the continental shelf (the continental slope), trawling at bottom and midlevel waters down to 1,000 m. Dense concentrations of commercially important fish exist at these depths, yielding a fish catch of several hundred tons annually, unmatched elsewhere in the Pacific Islands. Many of these species (such as the orange roughy) are long-lived, with up to one-hundred-year life spans and relatively low recruitment rates. Following intense exploitation, stocks are likely to drop sharply and may have difficulty recovering.

Pelagic Ecosystems

The ocean is divided vertically into pelagic and benthic components (the water column and the seafloor, respectively). The pelagic division in turn includes an epipelagic zone (0 to 200 m), a mesopelagic zone (200 to 1,000 m), and a bathopelagic zone (below 1,000 m). Sharp gradations of illumination and temperature occur with depth in the epipelagic zone. Diurnal and (in temperate waters) seasonal changes are also marked. Below this, the mesopelagic zone has very little light, a very gradual temperature gradient, and little seasonal variation. Oxygen may be depleted, but there are often high concentrations of phosphates and nitrates. The bathypelagic zone below is characterized by continuous darkness, low temperatures, and high pressures (Lowe-McConnell 1977).

Tropical ocean waters are generally nutrient-poor, since nutrient upwelling is less common than in temperate regions. There is an upwelling zone in the eastern Pacific, but this extends westward only as a narrow strip along the equator. Near New Guinea and New Zealand, productivity is raised because of the discharge of groundwater and rivers from large adjacent landmasses. With the above exceptions, however, waters of the open ocean are low in nutrients and primary productivity (Figure 9.13).

Primary production occurs only in the photic (or euphotic) layer, where light penetrates sufficiently for photosynthesis to occur.

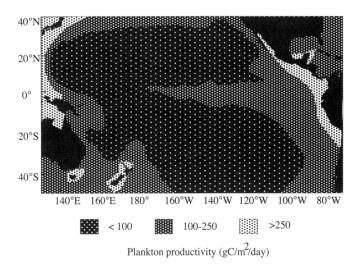

Plankton productivity (gC/m^2/day)

Figure 9.13. Phytoplankton productivity in the Pacific Ocean (after Barnes and Hughes 1982 and sources therein).

This layer extends to a maximum of 250 m under conditions of full sunlight and clear water. Primary production is accomplished mainly by phytoplankton, which are carried in the water column but slowly sink to the depths below. The picoplankton (primarily photosynthetic bacteria) are also a significant source of primary production, especially in nutrient-poor waters. Phytoplankton and picoplankton are so efficient at taking up nutrients that in some areas the dissolved nitrogen is not easily detectable. Nitrogen and phosphate are regenerated by zooplankton, driving photosynthesis and stimulating the growth of the primary producers. Another source of nutrients in oceanic waters is dissolved organic matter (Tanoue, Ishii, and Midorikawa 1996).

Phytoplankton are consumed by herbivorous copepods and other organisms. The copepods are in turn consumed by pelagic jellyfish, larval fish, larval crabs and lobsters, predatory copepods, and other zooplankton. Most marine fish larvae from the tropics feed on copepods, although there is specialization in some groups. For example, chaetodontids (butterfly fishes) feed only on chaetognaths (arrow worms) and acanthurids (surgeonfishes) feed primarily on appendicularids (Sampey et al. 2007). The smaller consumers are preyed upon by larger fish and other components of the nekton (active swimmers, as differentiated from the floating plankton).

At the top of the food chain are large nekton, including predatory sharks, tunas, billfishes, and marine mammals. Most of these species feed on fishes, crustaceans, and cephalopods. Others have more restricted diets. One such specialized feeder is the dolphin fish (*Coryphaena* spp.), which preys on flying fish (Longhurst and Pauly 1987). The billfishes, such as marlins, are deep-diving, aggressive feeders, with a diet consisting largely of other fishes. Because these nekton are large and highly mobile, they can seek out food-rich patches even in waters of low productivity. Not all large nekton feed on large prey, however. The huge whale shark, which grows to more than 17 m in length, feeds by filtering very small zooplankton from the water column. Another large filter-feeding shark is the megamouth (*Megachasma pelagius*), which supports its 4.5-m-long body by capturing zooplankton on tiny teeth and cartilagenous filters (Longhurst and Pauly 1987).

Nekton productivity is proportional to primary productivity, but at a much attenuated level. Secondary productivity diminishes by roughly an order of magnitude at each additional level in the trophic chain, often represented as an energy pyramid. There are energy losses at each level, resulting from unconsumed individuals (which eventually input to decomposers) and energy lost through metabolic activity. Thus, productivity (and biomass) of top predators is only a fraction of that of herbivorous species (Barnes and Hughes 1982).

Most of the organic material produced in the epipelagic zone of the open sea is consumed there. The remaining 20 percent sinks to the depths below and enters the mesopelagic zone. Here, low light levels make vision possible to suitably adapted organisms but will not support photosynthesis. There is no primary production, and organic inputs are derived from above. Inhabiting this zone are numerous fishes and shrimps. Most of these species do not wait for organic material to fall from above, but make nocturnal migrations into epipelagic areas to forage. Most theories advanced to explain these daily vertical migrations assume that the main benefit is increased foraging success in the upper waters. But warmer temperatures and higher dissolved oxygen levels may be more important in explaining this phenomenon (Williamson et al. 1996). Whatever the cause of this migration, the result is the transport of organic materials and nutrients from the shallower areas into the mesopelagic. Materials not consumed in the mesopelagic zone sink into the deep sea.

Deep-Sea Ecosystems

Deep-sea ecosystems are oligotrophic, having relatively few available food sources. Most organic particles are consumed and mineralized at much lesser depths (Figure 9.14). The amount of organic matter that reaches the ocean floor depends partly on the productivity of the surface water above it, but depth is a major factor (Hobbie 1988). A particle may take months to sink to the bottom, and only around 3 percent of the particulate organic matter produced in the euphotic zone ever reaches the deep sea (Jannasch and Taylor 1984). The deep sea is thus low in productivity. Exceptions occur

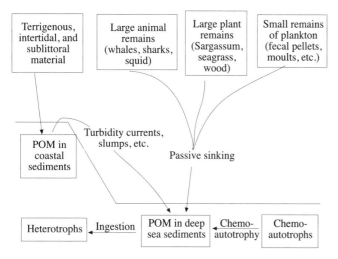

Figure 9.14. Conceptual model of the potential sources, transport, and sinks for organic matter to the deep sea (after Gage and Tyler 1991 and sources therein).

where the carcasses of large fishes or whales sink to the bottom, and at hydrothermal vents, as discussed below.

Deep-sea organisms have a variety of adaptations that allow them to survive the severe physical and biological conditions. Light does not penetrate beyond the photic zone, so the only light available is that which is produced by the organisms themselves (bioluminescence) or from the glow of fissures and vents in the ocean floor. Many deep-sea fishes, shrimps, and squids have photophores, special organs in the skin for producing light, which aid in species recognition, provide camouflage, and possibly serve in communication.

Deep-sea organisms must also contend with high pressure and low temperature, and the enzymes of their metabolic systems have become adapted to these conditions. There is a general decrease in metabolic rate among fishes and invertebrates as depth increases. The decreased metabolic rate is largely the result of the reduced activity levels of deep-sea organisms. Reduced levels of activity are presumably an adaptation to the limited and unpredictable supplies of food, conditions that may favor sit-and-wait strategies over active foraging (Somero, Dahlhoff, and Gibbs 1991; Koslow 2007).

Hydrothermal vents occur at areas of seafloor spreading or near areas of subduction, such as the Marianas Trough (Hessler and Lonsdale 1991) and midoceanic ridges (Koslow 2007). Other hydrothermal vents are located near the Caroline Islands, New Guinea, and New Zealand. In such locations, organisms are exposed to warm waters laden with metals and hydrogen sulfide. These waters would be toxic to most marine organisms, but resident species have evolved physiologically (Hessler and Lonsdale 1991), enabling them to survive and flourish. Warm, chemical-rich water emitted from the vents allows chemosynthesis by thermophilic bacteria. Bacteria, in turn, support abundant consumer populations (Van Dover and Fry 1994), which include large clams and tube-dwelling pogonophoran worms. The large pogonophorans, which grow to two meters in length and are found in abundance at hydrothermal vents, do not have mouths. The discovery of this anatomical feature led to questions as to the sources of pogonophoran nutrition, and it has since been documented that these animals, and many other deep-sea organisms, are hosts to symbiotic chemosynthetic bacteria (Haygood 1996; Koslow 2007), which provide nutrients. The rapidly growing tubeworms have a specialized feeding structure, the trophosome, which contains dense populations of chemosynthetic bacteria (Robinson and McCavanaugh 1995).

Other communities of organisms that depend on chemosynthesis are found on the seafloor in areas of cold seeps (Koslow 2007). These are areas where sulfides, methane, or other hydrocarbons seep from the sediments. These areas are primarily along the edges of continents where sediments are rich in organic material. The communities associated with these seeps include large vesicomyid clams, mussels, tubeworms, and polychaetes, which form localized, dense clumps on the seafloor. The species found at these seeps mostly differ from those of the warm-water vent communities, although they share a dependence on symbiotic, chemosynthetic bacteria. Cold seeps are more stable than hydrothermal vents and persist for hundreds or even thousands of years. This allows the development of greater diversity and results in selection favoring longevity (Berquist, Williams, and Fisher 1999) instead of rapid growth.

Conclusion

In this review, I have attempted to cover some of the major aquatic ecosystems of the Pacific Island region. Some of their features are summarized in Table 9.4. The aquatic ecosystems of the Pacific Islands region are diverse and of great practical significance and economic value and immeasurable aesthetic value. Their complexity and vulnerability to human activities, on both local and global scales, are now being more fully appreciated (Vitousek et al. 1997), but they are still poorly understood. A greater understanding of the structure and function of these ecosystems will occupy ecologists for decades to come. The endeavors of these scientists will be crucial for resource management in the future (De Leo and Levin 1997). In the meantime, we should be careful in our stewardship of these ecosystems. We must ensure that they remain valuable sources of fascination and practical benefits to the generations that follow.

Table 9.4

Comparison of Some of the Major Aquatic Ecosystems of the Pacific Island Region

Ecosystem	Input	Primary production	Consumers
Fresh waters	Leaf fall, nutrient run-off from adjacent terrestrial ecosystems	Mostly from attached algae	Fishes, shrimps, snails, eels
Mangroves	Organic materials and nutrients from rivers and the sea	Leaf production from mangrove trees, estuarine and marine algae	Fishes, shrimps, crabs, and other invertebrates
Seagrass meadows	Nutrients from rivers, sea, and sediments	Seagrasses; benthic marine algae	Fishes, shrimps, crabs, and other invertebrates, dugongs
Coral reefs	Nutrients from the rivers and the sea, nitrogen fixation, regeneration by marine organisms	Symbiotic algae; benthic marine algae, phytoplankton	Reef fishes; invertebrates; marine turtles, sea snakes
Kelp	Nutrients from the rivers and the sea, nitrogen fixation, regeneration by marine organisms	Macroalgae and other algae, phytoplankton	Invertebrates; fish
Continental shelf, terrestrial runoff, regeneration by marine organism	Nitrogen fixation	Photosynthetic picoplankton, phytoplankton, benthic marine algae	Zooplankton, fishes, invertebrates, and marine mammals
Open-ocean, euphotic zone	Nitrogen fixation; regeneration by marine organism	Photosynthetic picoplankton, phytoplankton	Zooplankton, pelagic fishes, invertebrates, and marine mammals
Deep sea	Nutrients and organic materials from zones above	Symbiotic chemo-synthetic bacteria	Slow moving fishes, benthic invertebrates

Appendix 9.1.

Taxonomic Relationships of Some Common Aquatic Invertebrates

Phylum	Class	Freshwater species	Marine species
Arthropoda	Crustacea	Crabs, shrimps, crayfishes	Crabs, lobsters, shrimps, amphipods, copepods, barnacles
Mollusca	Gastropoda	Snails	Snails, sea slugs
	Bivalvia	Clams	Oysters, clams
	Cephalopoda		Squids, octopi
Annelida	Polychaeta	Worms	Bristle worms
Echinodermata	Holothuridea		Sea cucumbers
	Echinoidea		Sea urchins
	Asteroidea		Starfishes; brittle stars
Coelenterata	Anthozoa		Corals, sea anemones
	Scyphozoa		Jellyfishes
Chordata	Ascidiacea		Sea squirts
Poriphera		Sponge (rare)	Sponges

BIBLIOGRAPHY

Allen, G. R. 1991. *Field guide to the freshwater fishes of New Guinea.* Publication No. 9 of the Christensen Research Institute.

Amesbury, J. R. 2007. Mollusk collecting and environmental change during the prehistoric period in the Mariana Islands. *Coral Reefs* 26: 947–958.

Andre, J., E. Gyuris, and I. R. Lawler. 2005. Comparison of the diets of sympatric dugongs and green turtles on the Orman Reefs, Torres Strait, Australia. *Wildlife Research* 32: 53–62.

Aragones, L.V., I. R. Lawler, W. J. Foley, and H. Marsh. 2006. Dugong grazing and turtle cropping: Grazing optimization in tropical seagrass systems? *Oecologia* 149: 635–647.

Barnes, R. S. K., and R. N. Hughes. 1982. *An introduction to marine ecology.* London: Blackwell.

Berquist, D. C., F. M. Williams, and C. R. Fisher. 1999. Longevity record for deep-sea invertebrate. *Nature* 403: 499–500.

Birkeland, C. 2004. Ratcheting down the coral reefs. *BioScience* 54: 1021–1027.

Bonine, K. M., E. P. Bjorkstedt, K. C. Ewel, and M. Palik. 2008. Population characteristic of the mangrove crab *Scylla seratta* (Decapoda: Portunidae) in Kosrae, Federated States of Micronesia: Effects of harvest and implications for management. *Pacific Science* 62: 1–19.

Braley, R. D. 1982. Reproductive periodicity in the indigenous oyster *Saccostrea cucullata* in Sasa Bay, Apra Harbor, Guam. *Marine Biology* 69: 165–173.

Brasher, A. M. D., C. D. Luton, S. L. Goodbred, and R. H. Wolff. 2006. Invasion patterns along elevation and urbanization gradients in Hawaiian streams. *Transactions of the American Fisheries Society* 135: 1109–1129.

Bright, G. 1982. Secondary benthic productivity in a tropical island stream. *Limnology and Oceanography* 27: 472–480.

Brouns, J., and F. Heijs. 1991. Seagrass ecosystems in the tropical west Pacific. In *Ecosystems of the World 24. Intertidal and littoral ecosystems,* ed. A. C. Mathieson and P. H. Nienhuis, 371–390. New York: Elsevier.

Buden, D. W., D. B. Lynch, J. W. Short, and T. Leberer. 2001. Decapod crustaceans of the headwater streams of Pohnpei: Eastern Caroline Islands, Federated States of Micronesia. *Pacific Science* 55: 257–265.

Camilleri, J. C., and G. Ribi. 1986. Leaching of dissolved organic carbon (DOC) from dead leaves, formation of flakes from DOC, and feeding on flakes by crustaceans in mangroves. *Marine Biology* 91: 337–344.

Carpenter, R. C. 1997. Invertebrate predators and grazers. In *Life and death of coral reefs,* ed. C. E. Birkeland, 98–229. New York: Chapman and Hall.

Chimmer, R. A., B. Fry, M. Y. Kaneshiro, and N. Cormier. 2006. Current and historical expansion of introduced mangroves on Oʻahu, Hawaiʻi. *Pacific Science* 60: 377–383.

Coates, D. 1993. Fish ecology and management of the Sepik-Ramu, New Guinea, a large contemporary tropical river basin. *Environmental Biology of Fishes* 38: 345–368.

Concepcion, G., and S. G. Nelson. 1999. Effects of a dam and reservoir on the distributions and densities of macrofauna in tropical streams of Guam (Mariana Islands). *Journal of Freshwater Ecology* 14: 447–454.

Crowl, T. A., W. H. McDowell, A. P. Covich, and S. L. Johnson. 2001. Freshwater shrimp effects on detrital processing and nutrients in a tropical headwater stream. *Ecology* 82: 775–783.

De Leo, G. A., and S. Levin. 1997. The multifaceted aspects of ecosystem integrity. *Conservation Ecology* (online) 1(1): 3. http://www.consecology.org/voll/issl/art3.

Donaldson, T. J., and R. Myers. 2002. Insular freshwater fish faunas of Micronesia: Patterns of species richness and similarity. *Environmental Biology of Fishes* 65: 139–149.

Donning, D. P. 1981. Sea cows and sea grasses. *Palaeobiology* 7: 417–420.

Dudgeon, D., and R. E. W. Smith. 2006. Exotic species, fisheries and conservation of freshwater diversity in tropical Asia: The case of the Sepik River, Papua New Guinea. *Aquatic Conservation: Marine and Freshwater Ecosystems* 16: 203–215.

Ewel, K. C., R. D. Hauff, and T. G. Cole. 2003. Analysing mangrove forest structure and species distribution on a Pacific island. *Phytocoenologia* 33: 251–266.

Fitzsimmons, J. M., R. T. Nishimoto, and W. S. Devick. 1996. Maintaining biodiversity in freshwater ecosystems on oceanic islands of the tropical pacific. *Chinese Biodiversity* 4: 23–27.

Fitzsimmons, J. M., J. Parham, and R. T. Nishimoto. 2002. Similarities in behavioral ecology among amphidromous and catadroumous fishes on the islands of Hawaiʻi and Guam. *Environmental Biology of Fishes* 65: 123–129.

Ford, J. I., and R. A. Kinzie III. 1982. Life crawls upstream. *Natural History* 91(12): 60–67.

Fry, G. C., D. T. Brewer, and W. N. Venables. 2006. Vulnerability of deepwater, demersal fishes to overfishing: Evidence from a study around a tropical volcanic seamount in Papua New Guinea. *Fisheries Research* 181: 126–141.

Gage, J. D., and P. A. Tyler. 1991. *Deep-sea biology: A natural history of organisms at the deep-sea floor.* Cambridge: Cambridge University Press.

Goodsell, P. J., M. J. Fowler-Walker, B. M. Gillanders, and S. D. Connell. 2004. Variations in the configuration of algae in subtidal forests: Implications for invertebrate assemblages. *Austral Ecology* 29: 350–357.

Grigg, R.W. 1965. Ecological studies of black coral in Hawaii. *Pacific Science* 19: 244–260.

———. 2001. Black coral: History of a sustainable fishery in Hawaii. *Pacific Science* 55: 291–299.

Hallock, P. 1997. Reefs and reef limestones in earth history. In *Life and death of coral reefs,* ed. C. E. Birkeland, 13–42. New York: Chapman and Hall.

Hatcher, B. G. 1997. Organic production and decomposition. In *Life and death of coral reefs,* ed. C. E. Birkeland, 140–174. New York: Chapman and Hall.

Haygood, M. G. 1996. The potential role of functional differences between Rubisco forms in governing expression in chemoautotrophic symbioses. *Limnology and Oceanography* 41: 370–371.

Hessler, R. R., and P. F. Lonsdale. 1991. Biogeography of the Mariana Trough hydrothermal vents. In *Marine biology, its accomplishment and future prospect,* ed. J. Mauchline and T. Nemoto, 65–182. Tokyo: University of Tokyo Press; Amsterdam: Elsevier Science Publishers.

Hobbie, J. E. 1988. A comparison of the ecology of planktonic bacteria in fresh and salt water. *Limnology and Oceanography* 33: 750–764.

Hoegh-Guldberg, O., P. J. Mumby, A. J. Hooten, R. S. Steneck, P. Greenfield, E. Gomez, C. D. Harvell, P. F. Sale, A. J. Edwards, K. Caldeira, N. Knowlten, C. M. Eakin, R. Iglesias-Prieto, N. Muthiga, R. H. Bradbury, A. Dubi, and M. E. Hatziolos. 2007. Coral reefs under rapid climate change and ocean acidification. *Science* 318: 1737–1742.

Hosakawa, T., H. Tagawa, and V. J. Chapman. 1977. Mangals of Micronesia, Taiwan, Japan, the Philippines, and Oceania. In *Ecosystems of the world 1. Wet coastal ecosystems,* ed. V. J. Chapman, 271–291. New York: Elsevier Science Publishers.

Howarth, R. W., R. Marino, and J. Lane. 1988. Nitrogen fixation in freshwater, estuarine, and marine ecosystems: 1. Rates and importance. *Limnology and Oceanography* 33: 669–687.

Hurd, C. L, W. A. Nelson, R. Falshaw, and K. Neill. 2004. History, current status, and future of marine algal research in New Zealand: Taxonomy, ecology, physiology and human uses. *Phycological Research* 52: 80–106.

Huryn, A. D. 1996. An appraisal of the Allen paradox in a New Zealand trout stream. *Limnology and Oceanography* 4: 243–252.

Jannasch, H. W., and C. D. Taylor. 1984. Deep-sea microbiology. *Annual Review of Microbiology* 38: 487–514.

Kay, E. A. 1980. *Little worlds of the Pacific: An essay on Pacific basin biogeography.* University of Hawai'i, Harold L. Lyon Lectures 9: 1–40.

Keast, A. 1996. Pacific biogeography: Patterns and processes. In *The origin and evolution of Pacific Island biotas,* ed. A. Keast and S. E. Miller, 477–512. Amsterdam: SPB Academic Publishing.

Kolinski, S. P., R. K. Hoeke, S. R. Holzwarth, L. I. Ilo, E. F. Fox, R. C. O'Conner, and P. S. Vroom. 2006. Nearshore distribution and an abundance estimate for green sea turtles, Chelonia mydas, at Rota Island, Commonwealth of the Northern Mariana Islands. *Pacific Science* 60: 509–522.

Koslow, T. 2007. *The silent deep. The discovery, ecology, and conservation of the deep sea.* Chicago: University of Chicago Press.

Langdon, C., W. S. Broecker, D. E. Hammond, E. Glenn, K. Fitzsimmons, S. G. Nelson, T. H. Peng, I. Hajdas, and G. Bonani. 2003. The effect of elevated CO_2 on the community metabolism of an experimental coral reef. *Global Biogeochemical Cycles* 17(1): Article number 1011.

Larned, S. T., R. A. Kinzie III, A. P. Covich, and C. T. Chong. 2003. Detritus processing by endemic and non-native Hawaiian stream invertebrates: A microcosm study of species-specific effects. *Archives fur Hydrobiolige* 156: 241–254.

Lassuy, D. R. 1980. Effects of "farming" behavior by Eupomacentrus lividus and Hemiglyphidodon plagiometopon on algal community structure. *Bulletin of Marine Science* 30: 304–312.

Leberer, T., and S. G. Nelson. 2001. Factors affecting the distribution of atyid shrimp in two tropical insular rivers. *Pacific Science* 55: 389–398.

Lesser, M. P. 1996. Elevated temperature and ultraviolet radiation cause oxidative stress and inhibit photosynthesis in symbiotic dinoflagellates. *Limnology and Oceanography* 41: 272–283.

Lockwood, G. 1997. World shrimp production with environmental and social accountability: A perspective and a proposal. *World Aquaculture* 28: 52–55.

Longhurst, A. R., and D. Pauly. 1987. *Ecology of tropical oceans.* San Diego: Academic Press.

Lovelock, C. E., I. C. Feller, J. Ellis, A. M. Schwarz, N. Hancock, P. Nicolls, and B. Sorrel. 2007. Mangrove growth in New Zealand estuaries: The role of nutrient enrichment at sites with contrasting rates of sedimentation. *Oecologia* 153: 633–641.

Lowe-McConnell, R. H. 1977. *Ecology of fishes in tropical waters.* Institute of Biology, Studies in Biology no. 76. London: Edward Arnold.

———. 1987. *Ecological studies in tropical fish communities.* Cambridge: Cambridge University Press.

Lugo, A. E., S. Brown, and M. M. Brown. 1988. Forested wetlands in freshwater and salt-water environments. *Limnology and Oceanography* 33: 894–909.

Maciolek, J. A., and J. I. Ford. 1987. Macrofauna and environment of the Nanpil-Kiepw River, Ponape, Eastern Caroline Islands. *Bulletin of Marine Science* 41: 623–632.

Maciolek, J. A., and A. S. Timbol. 1981. Environmental features and macrofauna of Kahana estuary, Oahu, Hawaii. *Bulletin of Marine Science* 31: 712–722.

Mangel, M., R. S. Hofman, and J. R. Twiss, Jr. 1993. Sustainability and ecological research. *Ecological Applications* 3: 573–575.

Mann, K. 1988. Production and use of detritus in various freshwater, estuarine, and coastal marine ecosystems. *Limnology and Oceanography* 33: 910–930.

McDowall, R. M. 1990. Freshwater fishes and fisheries of New Zealand—the angler's Eldorado. *Reviews in Aquatic Sciences* 2: 281–341.

———. 2003. Hawaiian biogeography and the islands' freshwater fish fauna. *Journal of Biogeography* 30: 703–710.

McKinnon, A. D., J. H. Carleton, and S. Duggan. 2007. Pelagic production and respiration in the Gulf of Papua during May 2004. *Continental Shelf Research* 27: 1643–1655.

Morton, J., and M. Miller. 1968. *The New Zealand sea shore.* London-Auckland: Collins.

Muller-Parker, G., and C. F. D'Elia. 1997. Interactions between corals and their symbiotic algae. In *Life and death of coral reefs,* ed. C. E. Birkeland, 96–113. New York: Chapman and Hall.

Nelson, S. G. 1985. Immediate enhancement of photosynthesis by marine macrophytes in reponse to ammonia enrichment. *Proceedings of the Fifth International Coral Reef Congress, Tahiti,* vol. 5: 65–70.

Nelson, S. G., and L. G. Eldredge. 1991. Distribution and status of introduced cichlid fishes of the genera Oreochromis and Tilapia in the islands of the South Pacific and Micronesia. *Asian Fisheries Science* 4: 11–22.

Nelson, S. G., J. E. Parham, R. B. Tibbatts, F. A. Camacho, T. Leberer, and B. D. Smith. 1997. Distributions and microhabitats of the amphidromous gobies in streams of Micronesia. *Micronesica* 30: 83–91.

Nelson, S. G., and S. deC. Wilkins. 1988. Sediment processing by the surgeonfish Ctenochaetus striatus at Moorea, French Polynesia. *Journal of Fisheries Biology* 32: 817–824.

Nunn, Patrick D. 1994. *Oceanic islands.* Oxford: Blackwell.

Odum, H. T., B. J. Copeland, and E. A. McMahan. 1974. *Coastal ecological systems of the United States,* vol. 1. Washington, D.C.: The Conservation Foundation in cooperation with National Oceanic and Atmospheric Administration, Office of Coastal Environment.

Parham, J. E. 2005. Survey techniques for freshwater streams on Oceanic islands: Important design considerations for the PABITRA project. *Pacific Science* 59: 283–291.

Parrish, F. A., and A. R. Baco. 2007. State of U.S. deep coral ecosystems in the Western. Pacific region: Hawaii and the United States Pacific Islands. In *The state of deep coral ecosystems of the United States,* ed. S. E. Lumsden, T. F. Hourigan, A. W. Bruckner, and G. Dor, 155–194. Silver Springs, Md.: NOAA Technical Memorandum CRCP-3.

Parrish, F. A., and R. C. Boland. 2004. Habitat and reef-fish assemblages of band summits in the Northwest Hawaiian Islands. *Marine Biology* 144: 1065–1073.

Paul, V. J. 1992. Seaweed chemical defenses on coral reefs. In *Ecological roles of marine natural products,* ed. V. J. Paul, 24–50. Ithaca, N.Y., and New York: Comstock Publishing Associates.

Paul, V. J., S. G. Nelson, and H. R. Sanger. 1990. Feeding preferences of adult and juvenile rabbitfish Siganus argenteus in relation to chemical defenses of tropical seaweeds. *Marine Ecology Progress Series* 60: 23–34.

Paulay, G. 1997. Diversity and distribution of reef organisms. In *Life and death of coral reefs,* ed. C. Birkeland, 298–353. New York: Chapman and Hall.

Phillips, R. C., and E. G. Menez. 1988. *Seagrasses.* Smithsonian Contributions to the Marine Sciences 94. Washington, D.C.: Smithsonian Institution Press.

Polovina, J. J. 1984. Model of a coral reef ecosystem I. The ECOPATH model and its application to French Frigate Shoals. *Coral Reefs* 3: 1–11.

Pringle, C. M., G. A. Blake, A. P. Covich, K. M. Buzby, and A. Finley. 1993. Effects of omnivorous shrimp in a montane tropical stream: Sediment removal, disturbance of sessile invertebrates and enhancement of understory algal biomass. *Oecologia* 93: 1–11.

Richer de Forges, B., J. A. Koslow, and G. C. B. Poore. 2000. Diversity and endemism of the benthic seamount fauna of the southwest Pacific. *Nature* 405: 944–947.

Richmond, R. H., T. Rongo, Y. Golbuu, S. Victor, N. Idechong, G. Davis, W. Kostka, L. Neth, M. Hamnett, and E. Wolanski. 2007. Watersheds and coral reefs: Conservation science, policy, and implementation. *Bioscience* 57: 598–607.

Robinson, J. J., and C. M. McCavanaugh. 1995. Expression of form I and form II Rubisco in chemoautotrophic symbioses: Implications for the interpretation of stable carbon isotope values. *Limnology and Oceanography* 40: 1496–1502.

Rougerie, F., and B. Wauthy. 1993. The endo-upwelling concept: From geothermal convection to reef construction. *Coral Reefs* 12: 19–30.

Rowan, R., and N. Knowlton. 1995. *Intraspecific diversity and ecological zonation in coral-algal symbiosis.* Proceedings of the National Academy of Science 92: 2850–2853.

Rowan, R., N. Knowlton, A. Baker, and J. Jara. 1997. Landscape ecology of algal symbionts creates variation in episodes of coral bleaching. *Nature* 388: 265–269.

Ryan, P. A. 1991. The success of the Gobiidae in tropical Pacific insular streams. *New Zealand Journal of Marine and Freshwater Research.* 18: 25–30.

Sampey, A., A. D. Mckinnon, M. G. Meekan, and M. I. McCormick. 2007. Glimpse into guts: Overview of the feeding of larvae of tropical shorefishes. *Marine Ecology Progress Series* 339: 243–257.

Schiel, D. R. 1988. Algal interactions on shallow subtidal reefs in northern New Zealand: A review. *New Zealand Journal of Marine and Freshwater Research* 22: 481–489.

———. 1994. Kelp communities. In *Marine biology,* ed. L. S. Hammond and R. N. Synnot, 345–361. Sydney: Longman Cheshire.

Schiel, D. R., N. L. Andrew, and M. S. Foster. 1995. The structure of subtidal algal and invertebrate assemblages at the Chatham Islands, New Zealand. *Marine Biology* 123: 355–367.

Sherwood, A. R. 2006. Stream macroalgae of the Hawaiian Islands: A floristic survey. *Pacific Science* 60: 191–205.

Skelton, P. A., and G. R. South. 2006. Seagrass biodiversity of the Fiji and Samoa islands, South Pacific. *New Zealand Journal of Marine and Freshwater Research* 40: 345–356.

Somero, G. N., E. Dahlhoff, and A. Gibbs. 1991. Biochemical adaptations of deep-sea animals: Insights into biogeography and ecological energetics. In *Marine biology, its accomplishment and future prospect,* ed. J. Mauchline and T. Nemoto, 39–57. Tokyo: University of Tokyo Press; Amsterdam: Elsevier Science Publishers.

Stat, M., C. D. Carter, and O. Hoegh-Guldberg. 2006. The evolutionary history of Symbiodinium and scleractinian hosts—Symbiosis, diversity, and the effect of climate change. *Perspectives in Plant Ecology, Evolution, and Systematics* 8: 23–43.

Stevenson, J. C. 1988. Comparative ecology of submerged grass beds in freshwater, estuarine, and marine environments. *Limnology and Oceanography* 33: 867–893.

Storey, A. W., I. D. Roderick, R. E. W. Smith, and A. Y. Maie. 2002. Spread of the introduced climbing perch (*Anabas testudineus*) in the Fly River System, Papua New Guinea, with comments on possible ecological effects. *International Journal of Ecology and Environmental Sciences* 28: 103–114.

Sumich, J. L. 1988. *An introduction to the biology of marine life.* Dubuque, Iowa: William Brown Publishers.

Suren, A. M., and I. G. Jowett. 2006. Effects of floods versus low flows on invertebrates in a New Zealand gravel-bed river. *Freshwater Biology* 51: 2207–2227.

Swales, S., A. W. Storey, I. D. Roderick, and B. S. Figa. 1999. Fishes of floodplain habitats of the Fly River system, Papua New Guinea, and changes associated with El Niño droughts and algal blooms. *Environmental Biology of Fishes* 54: 389–404.

Tanoue, E., M. Ishii, and T. Midorikawa. 1996. Discrete dissolved and particulate proteins in oceanic waters. *Limnology and Oceanography* 41: 1334–1343.

Twilley, R. R., A. E. Lugo, and C. Patterson-Zucca. 1986. Litter production and turnover in basin mangrove forests in southwest Florida. *Ecology* 67: 670–683.

Van Dover, C. L., and B. Fry. 1994. Microorganisms as food resources of deep-sea hydrothermal vents. *Limnology and Oceanography* 39: 51–70.

Vitousek, P. M., H. A. Mooney, J. Lubchenco, and J. M. Milillo. 1997. Human domination of earth's ecosystems. *Science* 277: 494–499.

Ward, T. J., and S. J. M. Blaber. 1994. Continental shelves and slopes. In *Marine biology,* ed. L. S. Hammond and R. N. Synnot, 333–344. Sydney: Longman Cheshire.

Wheeler, T. 1988. *Papua New Guinea: A travel survival kit.* Footscray, Vic.: Lonely Planet Publications.

Williamson, C. E., R. W. Sanders, R. E. Moeller, and P. L. Stutsman. 1996. Utilization of subsurface food resources for zooplankton reproduction: Implications for diel vertical migration theory. *Limnology and Oceanography* 41: 224–233.

Yamamuro, M., H. Kayanne, and M. Minagawa. 1995. Carbon and nitrogen stable isotopes of primary producers in coral reef ecosystems. *Limnology and Oceanography* 40: 617–621.

History

Pacific Islanders have had varying experiences under colonialism. The impact was especially profound in land-rich islands amenable to agricultural settlement. In the worst situations, islanders have become outnumbered, deprived of their land, marginalized, or assimilated into the dominant society. Fewer settlers arrived on very small islands, but traditional sociopolitical, economic, and religious systems have been severely challenged. This section explores Pacific Islands history, with chapters on prehistory, the postcontact period, and politics.

The Precontact Period

Frank R. Thomas

10

As the pace of European exploration of the Pacific quickened in the second half of the eighteenth century, an increasing number of insular societies were drawn into the various processes of culture contact, often with disastrous consequences. Thus ended what may be considered the prehistory of an area, archipelago, or specific island and the beginning of the historic period. The history of the region is of course known to us from the written sources left by a variety of individuals (explorers, traders, missionaries) who interacted with Pacific Islanders. The former were also responsible for providing the outside world with the first accounts on the origin of Oceania's inhabitants.

Prehistory, as defined by most contemporary scholars, draws on several disciplines, including but not limited to linguistics, biological anthropology, the study of oral tradition, and archaeology. As Chappell (chapter 11, this volume) points out, these approaches may also provide important information on the recent past and offer alternative perspectives on the nature of early Western and Pacific Islander encounters. Clearly, no single approach for understanding the past can claim supremacy. Conflict between disciplines may be a source of healthy skepticism that allows us to look at our methods and theories in a more critical way.

This chapter attempts to present a synthetic view of the Pacific Islands before European contact by examining data gathered from a range of disciplines and by showing how various methods and theories have led to explanations or interpretations. Several themes, reflecting the diversity and unity of recent investigations in the region, are addressed. They include (1) origins and direction of settlement, (2) subsistence strategies, (3) long-distance exchange, (4) demography, (5) sociopolitical evolution, (6) warfare, and (7) human impact on island ecosystems. For a detailed treatment of these topics, the reader is referred to Kirch (2000).

The review relies largely on Western scientific approaches. This is not to deny the importance of indigenous perspectives and understanding. Much of what we claim to know about the past is firmly embedded in the present. This should always be borne in mind, as the past and the present are, and always will be, contested between members of different cultural associations and even among so-called homogenous groups. While conflicts over the ownership and control of cultural resources and interpretation of the past are not expected to be resolved anytime soon, there is much room for dialogue between indigenous voices and outsiders.

Origins and Direction of Settlement

Pleistocene Occupation of Greater Australia and Beyond

The settlement of the Pacific may be divided into two broad phases: (1) a Pleistocene (the world's most recent period of repeated glaciations from about 1.8 million to 10,000 years ago) occupation of Sahulland (also called Sahul—Greater Australia, including New Guinea) and islands of Near Oceania (Bismarck to Solomon archipelagoes) and (2) a mid-Holocene colonization past the main Solomon Islands into Remote Oceania (Figure 10.1) (Green 1991).

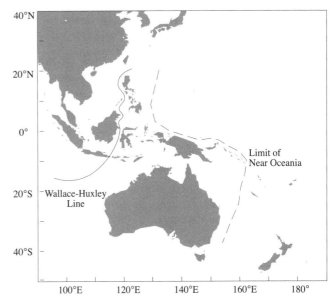

Figure 10.1. *Significant biogeographical boundaries in the southwest Pacific (after Bellwood 1993).*

East of the Wallace-Huxley Line lies Wallacea, which comprises the islands between the continental shelves of Sundaland (mainland Southeast Asia, western Indonesia, and the adjacent continental shelf) and Sahulland. Dispersal into Wallacea from Sundaland (where human antiquity is presumed to be greater in view of the presence of the premodern hominid *Homo erectus* in Java and possibly from the island of Flores in Wallacea) could only be accomplished by crossing stretches of open ocean (even at lowest sea level), although from this region to San Cristobal at the end of the Solomons chain, most islands are intervisible.

It is reasonable to assume that with falling sea level, the frequency of successful voyaging and colonization would have been high. But also, with rising postglacial seas, marine resources gained in importance for some populations, promoting seafaring skills. There are few reliably dated Pleistocene sites in Wallacea. On Flores, a hominid believed to be related to *Homo erectus* may have lived between 94,000 and 12,000 years ago (Morwood et al. 2004; Morwood et al. 2005). On Sulawesi, evidence of occupation may stretch as far back as 30,000 BP ("Before Present," or prior to 1950 CE, from which radiocarbon dates are measured) (Clark 1991). In the northern Moluccas, coastal caves were definitely occupied by 33,000 BP (Bellwood 1997).

Sites dating between 30,000 and 20,000 BP are known throughout Australia, as are some even older sites (up to 60,000 BP), according to luminescence techniques (Lilley 2006; Smith and Sharp 1993). Australia's cultural evolution appeared to have had only minor influence on subsequent developments elsewhere in the Pacific. The northern part of Sahulland, however, presented greater opportunities for economic transformations, setting the stage for expansion farther east.

In the New Guinea Highlands, Kosipe and Nombe are the two oldest known sites, having been occupied by at least 25,000 BP (Allen 1993). The Huon Peninsula in northeastern New Guinea yielded waisted axes dating back more than 40,000 years (Groube et al. 1986). Several cave, rock shelter, and open-air Pleistocene sites, associated with the local exploitation of chert (a flintlike quartz) and obsidian (volcanic glass), are known east of New Guinea (Figure 10.2). They include sites on New Britain, New Ireland, Manus (Admiralty Islands), and Buka (northern Solomons). Evidence of cultural activities in the region stretches between 39,500 and 35,500 BP (Leavesley 2006).

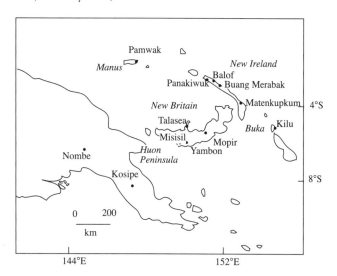

Figure 10.2. *Pleistocene sites in the southwest Pacific (after Gosden 1993).*

The Holocene and the Lapita Phenomenon

As the glaciers retreated worldwide and sea levels rose and then stabilized, important cultural transformations were under way. Probably the most notable change involved the first attempts at plant domestication, which would later have tremendous impacts on human demography and social evolution. By the early Holocene, New Guinea and most if not all the islands of Near Oceania displayed rich cultural, linguistic, and human biological diversity.

Suddenly (within a few centuries), a well-marked cultural horizon appeared from the Bismarcks to Samoa (Figure 10.3). On present evidence, this Lapita horizon was the first to have reached the islands of Remote Oceania (Green 1979). The most diagnostic trait associated with this horizon consists of a distinctive dentate-stamped pottery style, Lapita, named after a site on the west coast of New Caledonia and related to earlier findings on the northeastern tip of New Britain. This pottery is known from various localities as far away as Samoa. Because of the absence of pre-Lapita occupation in Remote Oceania, it has been suggested that further expansion into the Pacific required substantial improvements in navigational skills and technology, not available to Pleistocene and early Holocene seafarers, even at times of lower sea level (Irwin 1992: 43; but see Nunn [1993: 20] for the opposing viewpoint).

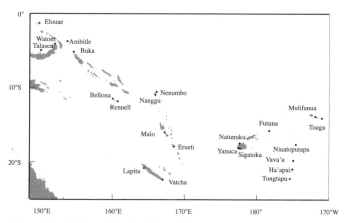

Figure 10.3. *Major Lapita sites (after Bellwood 1993).*

Alternatively, factors of biogeography (limited plant and animal resources on more distant islands) rather than limitations in seafaring technology could effectively have prevented early settlement of Santa Cruz, Vanuatu, and New Caledonia unless "an economy based on cultivation or at least a developed form of wild plant-food production involving transportation of many useful plant species" was already established (Spriggs 1993b: 141).

Lapita may be looked at in terms of continuities and discontinuities with the preceding period. Continuities include the expansion of an exchange system identified archaeologically in the form of obsidian and a trend toward increasing exploitation of marine resources (Spriggs 1993a). At Kuk, in the New Guinea Highlands, there is evidence for a well-developed pre-Lapita agricultural system 6,000 years ago where taro and possibly *Australimusa* bananas were grown (Golson 1977). The notion that Lapita colonists carried cultigens and agricultural techniques from Southeast Asia has been modified by genetic research showing that some of these cultigens are native to wider areas, including New Guinea (Table 10.1) (Denham, Haberle, and Lentfer 2004; Yen 1985). A regional interactive model and mutual transformations of practice before, during, and after the presumed appearance of Lapita have been proposed for understanding the development of agriculture and arboriculture in New Guinea (Denham 2004).

Table 10.1

Major Pacific Island Plant Foods

Species	Origin
Trees and shrubs	
Artocarpus altilis (breadfruit)	New Guinea
Cocos nucifera (coconut)	Indo-Pacific
Metroxylon spp. (sago)	New Guinea
Musa sapientum (banana)	Southeast Asia
Musa troglodytarum (Australimusa banana)	New Guinea
Pandanus tectorius	Indo-Pacific
Piper methysticum (kava)	Melanesia
Syzigium maaccense (mountain apple)	Southeast Asia
Tubers	
Alocasia macrorrhiza	Southeast Asia
Colocasia esculenta (taro)	Southeast Asia
Cyrtorsperma chamissonis (swamp taro)	Southeast Asia
Dioscorea spp. (yam)	Southeast Asia
Ipomoea batatas (sweet potato)*	Americas
Tacca leotopetaloides (arrowroot)	Southeast Asia
Other plants	
Oriza sativa (rice)–Marianas only*	Southeast Asia
Saccharum officinarum (sugar cane)	New Guinea

* Use uncertain prior to European contact

Perhaps the most compelling piece of evidence in favor of discontinuity is the sudden appearance of a highly decorated ceramic style in the Bismarcks and the almost instantaneous (in archaeological terms) spread of Lapita east to Santa Cruz (Solomon Islands), Bourewa (Fiji), Niuatoputapu (Tonga), and Toʻaga (Manuʻa, American Samoa), by at least 3200 BP and covering a distance greater than 3,500 km within a span of a few generations (Kirch et al. 1990; Nunn et al. 2004). Although the "high" islands of the Marianas, Palau, and Yap in western Micronesia have a settlement history comparable in length to the earliest Lapita sites in Near Oceania and the western fringes of Remote Oceania, there is at present no convincing evidence of contemporary occupation on the string of atolls stretching across the Caroline Islands (Clark et al. 2006; Rainbird 2004).

Other elements that seem to be associated with the initial appearance of Lapita include a distinctive adz kit; shell ornaments; animal husbandry of pig, dog, and chicken; the first evidence of plant domestication as revealed by macrofossils; a new settlement pattern of stilt houses over lagoons or on small offshore islands; and the expansion in the distribution of New Britain and Admiralty

(Lou) Island obsidian westward to Sabah (Borneo) and eastward to Fiji (Nunn 2007b; Spriggs 1993a).

In sum, Lapita emerges as a blend of both external and indigenous elements. The linguistic evidence supports the view that there was a movement of people from island Southeast Asia into the Bismarcks and beyond (Bellwood 1993). Likewise, groups that carried ceramic technology expanded from other areas of Southeast Asia to settle the Marianas and Palau. Language remains one of the most powerful links between Oceanian and Southeast Asian populations (Pawley and Ross 1993). In Near Oceania, the new migrants found previously established populations who spoke non-Austronesian languages, presumably the descendants of the first Pleistocene inhabitants, and interacted with them to produce the rich linguistic, biological, and cultural types found in the region today (Gibbons 1994; Kayser et al. 2006).

Small, founding populations who ventured farther into the eastern Pacific underwent a series of genetic changes (Houghton 1996; Serjeantson and Gao 1995). There is, however, clear evidence for a genetic trail leading back into Southeast Asia (Pietrusewsky 1994; Serjeantson and Hill 1989).

Toward the Sunrise and the Margins

The rapid spread of Lapita from the Bismarcks to the Fiji-Tonga-Samoa area is in marked contrast to the colonization history of the rest of Polynesia and eastern Micronesia. The so-called "long pause" on the order of perhaps a thousand years along the western margins of Polynesia has intrigued archaeologists. While some radiocarbon dates and environmental proxies, such as charcoal influxes in sediment cores, suggest settlement of the remote eastern Pacific in the first few centuries CE or perhaps earlier (Hunt and Holsen 1991; Kirch 1984: 267, 1997b; Sutton 1987), critics point out the unreliability of the dated samples or their precise association with human activities (Anderson 1996; Hunt and Lipo 2006; Spriggs and Anderson 1993). On the other hand, some of these early dates might represent failed isolated settlements.

Irwin (1992: 71–74) argues there was no navigational threshold compelling people to pause in Western Polynesia, and that a distinction should be made between voyages of exploration and those carried out for the purpose of actual colonization. He further states that the apparent dearth of evidence for early settlement in the regions east of western Polynesia and north of eastern Melanesia could relate to sampling error and low archaeological visibility, for example the intervening atolls would have presented ecological factors to filter out pottery making. Subsidence of Pacific Plate islands, together with coastal progradation from land clearing and deposition of upslope sediments later in time, are some of the processes that would hinder the discovery of early human settlements in coastal environments.

Dickinson (2003) has reviewed the evidence for mid- to late-Holocene high sea-level stands and argued for the relatively late appearance of habitable islets on several of the atolls and table reefs, which might explain why the earliest indications of human occupation on some of the low coral islands do not seem to stretch back more than 2,000 years (Di Piazza 1999; Riley 1987; Weisler 1999). Even on islands exposing volcanic bedrock or uplifted limestone, coastal flats most suitable for habitation were largely submerged during high-stand conditions. Alternative hypotheses for the centuries-long pause in Western Polynesia prior to the colonization of Eastern Polynesia are presented by Kennett, Anderson, and Winterhalder (2006) and Anderson et al. (2006), who suggest that this chronological gap might relate to population infilling and the intensification of subsistence strategies, and the increasing difficulty of sailing against the prevailing southeast trades until El Niño events became more frequent and of greater intensity.

Terrell (1986: 86) suggests that in the process of expansion into the eastern Pacific, and before a successful landfall was made, "many human lives were lost at sea." Irwin (1992: 88–89), however, argues that these failures resulted in relatively few deaths, but were part of an exploring strategy of "upwind, uplatitude method of search and return."

Continued expansion toward the extremities of the "Polynesian Triangle" or "Marginal Polynesia" brought ancient voyagers to lands lying outside the tropics (e.g., Easter Island, New Zealand). The peculiar climate of those regions, the great distances separating the various archipelagoes, and the attendant reduction in the frequency of contacts, together with the challenges and opportunities offered by the new environments, contributed to further divergence among scattered communities.

It has been suggested that the relatively late settlement of the marginal East and South Polynesian islands (Anderson 2005) may have been facilitated by environmental conditions prevailing at the time, the Medieval Warm Period, bracketed between 750 and 1250 CE (Nunn 2007a: 59). The subsequent abandonment of the Line and Phoenix Islands, together with other localities such as Pitcairn, Henderson, Norfolk, and Nihoa and Necker in the Hawaiian Archipelago, the so-called "mystery" islands (Bellwood 1979: 352), has been correlated with the onset of increasing climatic instability during the mid-second millennium CE, interrupting long-distance exchanges and leading to declines in food resources, both terrestrial and marine, caused by falling sea level (Amesbury 2007; Anderson 2002; Nunn 2000, 2007a: 195; Nunn et al. 2007).

For many years, the only evidence for contact between Polynesia and South America was the presence of the sweet potato (*Ipomoea batatas*), introduced prior to European contact from South America, but presumably picked up by Polynesian navigators who then brought it back to the islands (Yen 1971). Questions remain as to the presumed South American origin of the Polynesian bottle gourd (*Lagenaria siceraria*) (Clarke et al. 2006). More recently, the coconut (*Cocos nucifera*), Polynesian chickens, sewn-plank boats, and composite bone fishhooks have been added to the list of plants, animals, and items of material culture that could have been carried from the Pacific Islands to the west coasts of North, Central, and South America in prehistoric times (Jones and Klar 2005; Storey et al. 2007; Ward and Brookfield 1992).

Subsistence Strategies

Terrestrial Resources and Production

In the vast territory stretching across the southern portion of Sahulland (Australia), cultural communities were able to disperse in their search for food. Indeed, the landscape provided an array of animal resources, while the coasts supplied fish and shellfish. Wild plants were also exploited, but true agriculture did not develop to an extent comparable to that of New Guinea.

Groube (1989) proposed a sequence for the emergence of food production in northern Sahulland. From initial forest foraging and hunting, people began to select and promote certain plants through minimal clearance and expansion of the forest fringes. As group territories stabilized, forest management led to permanent or semipermanent promoted stands (e.g., sago) in the wet forested regions, and the management of scattered natural stands in areas with a dry season. In the latter case, the system evolved into forest gardens. Between 10,000 and 5,000 years ago, intergroup competition and perhaps the introduced Asian pig may have played key roles in the development of this strategy. The final stage was achieved by the creation of fenced or ditched gardens to keep growing pig populations out of cultivated areas.

The presence of waisted axes in New Guinea and Australia by at least 40,000 years ago may provide indirect evidence of forest clearance associated with food plant promotion.

Carbonized particles from several New Guinea Highland sites, including the Baliem Valley (West Papua), Kosipe, and Telefomin, demonstrate that humans were actively manipulating the environment at different times during the last 30,000 years. The overall impact appeared to have been minimal, however, possibly due to low population densities in the late Pleistocene (Haberle 1993). It is not until 7000 BP that we begin to have clear evidence for human impact on the vegetation from the Baliem Valley.

Beyond Sahulland, evidence for late Pleistocene and early Holocene environmental and plant manipulation is scanty. Remains of *Canarium* nuts from Pamwak and Kilu may indicate deliberate planting, tending, and harvesting of these resources, which were possibly introduced from New Guinea, and could assist in modeling a pathway to agriculture based on energetically efficient arboriculture in the depauperate forests on the smaller islands (Spriggs 1993b). A successful colonizing strategy would also include the deliberate introduction of wild animals such the bandicoot (*Echymipera kalubu*) at Pamwak, cuscus (*Phalanger orientalis*), and wallaby (*Thylogale brunii*), whose remains have been found in New Ireland caves (Flannery and White 1991). Other introductions, particularly rat species, were more likely accidental by-products of human colonization of the islands.

In sum, one could interpret changes in the archaeological record after 20,000 BP as an attempt to mimic the greater biological diversity of New Guinea—in effect, bringing resources to people rather than moving people to resources. This was accompanied by the transfer of materials such as obsidian (Gosden 1993). According to Gosden, this new strategy may have started when growing populations restricted mobility. By the time humans penetrated into Remote Oceania, it would be fair to say that the Indo-Pacific tuber/root/tree crop complex (Table 10.1) had developed to a degree that enabled the biogeographically depauperate islands to support relatively large social units.

Coconuts and pandanus, being salt-tolerant, may have been established on coasts before the arrival of humans. The coconuts, whose floating ability has been documented, would have supported people in the face of scarce water resources. Coconuts and irrigated taro could be relied upon perennially and, together with breadfruit and pandanus, could be preserved (Alkire 1978: 30). In some instances, the absence of precontact dogs, pigs, and fowl indicate a lack of sufficient food or water (particularly on atolls) and competition with humans. Birds would have been relatively abundant, however, at least in the initial stages of human settlement.

At higher latitudes, a number of tropical crops simply could not thrive. In New Zealand, horticulture was dominated by the sweet potato, supplemented by yam, taro, gourd, and *Cordyline terminalis*. Because of a more benign climate, food production had achieved greater success on the North Island compared to the South Island. However, the long coastline and vast land area of both islands provided ample opportunities for a hunting-gathering-fishing economy that included the exploitation of fern root, large sea mammals, and gigantic flightless birds (Davidson 1983). Other islands lying outside the tropics such as the Kermadecs, Chathams, Norfolk, Rapa, and Easter would have posed similar challenges to the establishment of introduced crops and animals.

Data on prehistoric food production are varied and include both direct and indirect evidence such as food preparation tools; large-scale anthropogenic burning and concomitant erosion; anthropophilic land snails; the recovery of pig and chicken bones and their strong association with horticultural systems; pond fields and other forms of irrigation; garden soils under mounds; desiccated, waterlogged, and carbonized plants; and trace elements in bone.

Marine Exploitation

Fish and marine invertebrates constitute a significant portion of the protein diet of many Pacific Island societies (Figure 10.4). It is apparent from the archaeological record that the general patterns of marine resource exploitation, particularly nearshore faunas, extend far back into the prehistoric record (Butler 1988; Nagaoka 1988).

Figure 10.4. *Shell middens in the lagoon of Vairaatea, Tuamotus (photo MR).*

Environments characterized by broad reef flats led to the development of fishing gear and techniques quite distinct from those employed around islands lacking such features.

Intensification of Production

In his seminal work on subsistence agriculture, Barrau (1965) described two basic environments: "the wet and the dry." Taro fits into Barrau's first division, while yams, sweet potatoes, and a range of other crops belong in the second. Indigenous systems were of two types: extensive and intensive. The former characterized shifting cultivation, in which the garden plots were left fallow after cropping to allow for soil regeneration, while the latter featured changes in hydrologic and edaphic (soil-related) conditions to increase yields (Kirch 1979).

A good example of studies of agricultural intensification is provided by research in Hawai'i. Taro pondfields (Figure 10.5) were particularly numerous on windward sides of islands. Irrigation technology and coordinated water use were cited by Allen (1991) as having played crucial roles in fostering political complexity by producing large surpluses for the ruling classes to further

(a)

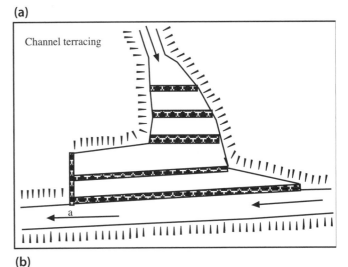

(b)

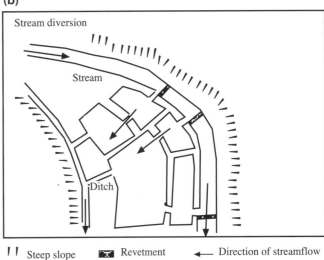

Figure 10.5. *Types of taro pondfields (after Kirch 1984). (a) Channel terracing. (b) Stream diversion.*

legitimize their position of authority. On Oʻahu, production of taro surpluses was achieved by 1400 CE, reflecting the centralized control of agriculture. It appears, however, that the most complex and militarily most powerful chiefdoms arose in dry, leeward sections (Kirch 1994: 318–319).

On leeward Maui and Hawaiʻi Island, sweet potatoes, sugar cane, gourds, and bananas were grown, perhaps as early as 1350 CE (Kirch 1985: 224–225, 230). At European contact, dense human populations inhabited leeward districts, including those on Oʻahu, where sweet potato and fishponds provided a suitable resource base (Thomas 1995). Indeed, the Hawaiian Islands offered a unique form of intensified use of certain marine resources achieved by the construction of fishponds to raise milkfish and mullet (Kirch 1985: 211–214).

Long-Distance Exchange

Pleistocene and Lapita Exchange Systems

The transfer of "small but continuous amounts" of obsidian is clearly attested in Pleistocene and early Holocene sites on both New Britain and New Ireland beginning at least 20,000 years ago (Allen 1993: 145). The wild animal transfers from New Guinea to the smaller islands may also have been incorporated in exchange networks.

With the appearance of Lapita, there was a corresponding expansion in trade, both geographically and in the quantity of material being moved. New Britain Talasea obsidian has been found as far away as the Reef Islands (2,000 km from the source) and Fiji, some 3,700 km distant (Kirch 1991:147). In the Reef–Santa Cruz Islands, evidence for imports also includes chert, oven stones, stone adzes, and ceramics over a period of seven hundred years. These findings suggest that trade may have been carried out through (1) direct access and local reciprocity at distances of less than 30 km; (2) one-stop reciprocity with groups 300 to 400 km distant; and (3) down-the-line exchange over greater distances (Green 1982). The Lapita system clearly differed from the more specialized and geographically constricted systems described ethnographically in the western Pacific (Malinowski 1932).

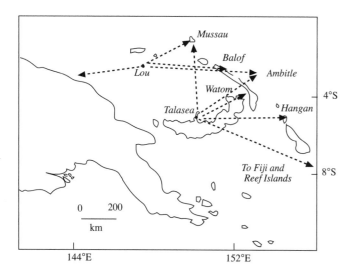

Figure 10.6. *Directions of obsidian exchange in the southwest Pacific (after Lacey 1982).*

Within the Bismarck Archipelago, recent investigations have documented the presence of both Talasea and Lou obsidian at a number of Lapita sites (Figure 10.6). Of particular interest are the changes in the frequency of materials over time. In the Mussau Islands, roughly equal amounts of Talasea and Lou obsidian give way to a dominance of Lou material. Watom Island shows the opposite trend, while sites in southwest New Britain have very occasional Lou pieces, yielding instead numerous Talasea and Mopir imports (Kirch 1991: 148).

Some Interaction Spheres within Remote Oceania

Kirch (1978) expressed the view that cultural adaptation in Remote Oceania must have evolved through a trajectory of increasing isolation. While this model may hold for specific localities such as the Hawaiian Archipelago, Easter Island, New Zealand, and in the "mystery" islands, there is no basis for concluding that such a process was under way in the Fiji/Tonga/Samoa region (Davidson 1977; Green 1981). Little is known about the intensity of trade between the island of Tongatapu and the northern Tongan outliers, Fiji, and Samoa prior to about five hundred years ago—after Lapita had long since disappeared. The ethnographic evidence shows that trade was entrenched within an intricate system of alliances, as reflected in the exchange of status items (Kirch 1984: 239, 322).

Farther out in the eastern Pacific, physical distance and perhaps the relatively greater physical uniformity of islands "offered fewer possibilities for development of distinctively localized production, and hence for complementary goods-focused exchange" (Oliver 1989: 564). Nevertheless, given recent conclusions regarding the nature of ancient navigation skills (Irwin 1992), it would seem reasonable to suggest the possibility of engaging in regular trade with mother communities after settlement (cf. Terrell, Hunt, and Gosden 1997). Where there is ethnographic evidence for extensive networks, such as between the Tuamotu and Society archipelagoes, Yap and Palau (as exemplified by limestone money), or Yap and coral islands to the east (the *sawai* system), there is good reason to use archaeology to trace the evolution of those systems (Fitzpatrick 2008).

As our knowledge improves, we can expect to fill some of the gaps in our understanding of exchange in the vast region of Remote Oceania. For example, recent geochemical studies have confirmed the transfer of basalt from Tutuila in American Samoa to Mangaia in the Southern Cooks from 1000–1500 CE (Weisler and Kirch 1996). Henderson, an elevated limestone island in the southeast Pacific that was uninhabited at European contact, yielded imported basalt, volcanic oven stones, volcanic glass, and pearlshell, suggesting an interaction sphere that included Pitcairn and Mangareva, ending about 1400–1450 CE (Weisler 1994).

Explaining Exchange

Exchange among insular communities undoubtedly provided several benefits, including access to resources that were either absent or in short supply as a result of geologic/biogeographic differences, access to resources subjected to environmental hazards, access to mates in situations of demographic instability, and access to certain "prestige" items to enhance the position of elites. Part of the success of the Lapita expansion into Remote Oceania could be attributed to the maintenance of ties with communities on the better-endowed islands of Near Oceania. This strategy was undoubtedly of great benefit in the initial stages of settlement before local resources could be properly assessed (cf. Kirch 1988).

Because of their overall marginality, atolls occupy a prominent position in discussions of exchanges (Williamson and Sabath 1984). Alkire (1978) described several examples of interisland ties in the form of clusters and complexes. One of the most celebrated cases of extensive networks was the *sawe,* which hierarchically linked Gagil District on Yap to outer atolls stretching for 1,000 km. As with several other atoll groups, populations in the Marshall Islands were linked by such intercommunity support networks, which were adaptive to latitudinal variation in rainfall that resulted in differential production of foodstuffs between the dry north and the wetter south, and to the risk of cyclone damage, prompting Marshallese chiefs to secure landholdings scattered over several islets of the same atoll, as well as land rights to resources on other atolls (Spennemann 2006).

Kirch (1991) commented on both the ceremonial and symbolic component of Lapita exchange based on his Mussau data. Elaborately decorated, labor-intensive ceramics were traded in high volumes and appear to have been exchanged for shell artifacts. The pottery did not show evidence of having been used in a utilitarian context, such as food preparation. The plainware ceramics, however, were locally manufactured and distributed apart from the decorated sherds, and thus may have functioned differently.

The general conclusion then would be that the production and exchange of decorated pots, shells, and perhaps other items were monitored by elites. In the western Pacific, the collapse of long-distance trade in prestige goods led to increasing trade density over a more restricted space and big-man competitive feasting at the local level. The same process of collapse may have been a factor in the development of theocratic feudalism in some eastern Pacific societies (Friedman 1981).

Demography

It has long been assumed that rapid population growth generally followed settlement of a pristine ecosystem (*r*-selection). Through time, the intrinsic growth would level off at or near carrying capacity because of increased mortality as density rises (Figure 10.7). Such growth is termed logistical or *K*-selected (Diamond 1977). On small, relatively impoverished islands, the need to devise strategies for managing population growth may have arisen quickly so as not to outstrip resources (Bayliss-Smith 1974). While warfare, human sacrifice, cannibalism, infanticide, and abortion may have contributed to population regulation, there were also nonviolent means such as moral restraint, ritual celibacy, prolonged lactation, adoption, and several other measures (Klee 1980). It may be, however, that in some instances underpopulation was a more serious threat to community survival than population pressure (McArthur, Saunders, and Tweedie 1976). In fact, relatively large families and clans would be necessary to ensure adequate levels of production.

Reliable estimates of population throughout the Pacific region at the time of European contact are hard to come by. However, precontact household and settlement archaeology combined with

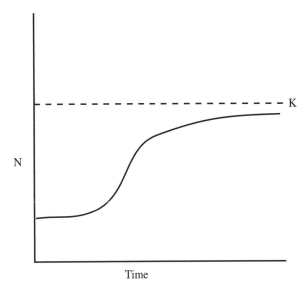

Figure 10.7. *Logistic growth curve (after Kirch 1984).*

measures of agricultural production are now offering new insights (Kirch and Rallu 2007). There is growing evidence that many island groups suffered dramatic declines in their population following initial contact with Europeans, although demographers, historians, and archaeologists alike concede that such decline varied in intensity from island to island and from place to place in larger landmasses. Differential population density at the time of contact may have set the stage for the subsequent impact of introduced diseases, with denser settlements suffering the greatest decline because of the higher risk of contagion.

Exchange may be examined as a response to risk and uncertainty affecting local resources. Sustained contacts would not only confer advantages in situations of environmental instability, but would also ensure the transfer of people to counter demographic instability, particularly during early stages of colonization (Hunt and Graves 1990). With the establishment of more stable demographic levels and a more secure subsistence base, the need to pursue long-distance voyaging perhaps would have diminished (Kirch 1990).

Warfare

Open conflicts and warfare may be linked to a variety of circumstances, including the notion that organized aggression may reflect ecological disequilibrium (Nunn 2007a: 153).

There appears to be a correlation between territoriality and densely distributed, predictable resources. This correlation can be attributed to the fact that maintaining exclusive access to such resources within an area outweighs the costs of defending them (Dyson-Hudson and Smith 1978). At the same time, such resources constitute the most attractive objects of competitive aggression. In such environments, one might expect to find organized groups bent on defending and acquiring territory.

Conflict over resources, including arable land, has left numerous traces in the archaeological record throughout the Pacific Islands. These comprise the actual weapons and fortified sites such as those found in Fiji, New Zealand's North Island, and Rapa

(Figure 10.8). Other indicators of aggressive behavior include mortuary remains showing death by violent means and wholesale destruction of property and religious sites such as the famous *moai* statues of Easter Island.

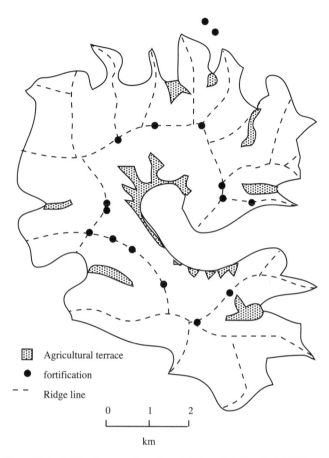

Figure 10.8. Fortifications on Rapa, French Polynesia (after Kirch 1984).

Conflict obviously cannot be reduced to underlying ecological principles of competition. Goldman's (1970) thesis that status rivalry had affected the history of all Polynesian societies (and by extension Proto-Oceanic communities) is instructive here. As Kirch writes:

> Population increase and land shortage did not cause endemic warfare in Polynesian islands; they provided a context and stimulus wherein *ariki* [chief] and *toa* [warrior], striving for domination over people and resources, created through conflict, alliance, subversion, and persuasion, social and political systems never before realized in Polynesia (1984: 216).

Sociopolitical Evolution

Kirch (1984) argued that chiefdoms tended to arise in large and densely settled, agrarian societies (Figure 10.9). Pressure on resources (see below) stimulated storage of foods, which enhanced the managerial role of the chief and allowed for surplus in time of abundance. Intensification of production is likely to have been stimulated by increasing population, but power struggles and

warfare were ancient features of Pacific Island cultures, and the development of hierarchies may also have occurred without population pressure. As Kirch argued:

> Chiefs and the kinship groups they headed took advantage of surplus production to continually renegotiate the relations of asymmetry, hierarchy, dominance, and hegemony both within and without the local group.... Hence the importance of social production to an understanding of the processes of agricultural innovation and intensification (1994: 313).

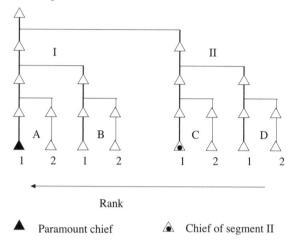

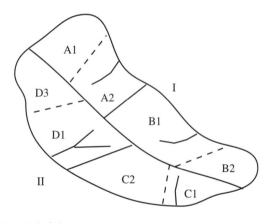

Figure 10.9. Apical clan segmentation, chiefly succession, and territorial fissioning in a hypothetical island (after Kirch 1984).

Green (1980) described the prehistory of Makaha Valley on Oʻahu to demonstrate increasing stratification in the area. The earliest settlement dates to about 1100 CE. Within one or two centuries, there is evidence of modification on the valley slopes for dryland farming and the appearance of temporary field shelters. Between 1400 and 1500 CE, permanent dwellings were built. Irrigation complexes increased the types of production, and a major religious temple (*heiau*) was built (correlating with chiefs who could extract a surplus and mobilize the labor). About 1650 CE, a Lono-class *heiau* was converted into a *luakini* temple (where human sacrifice was practiced). A large irrigation ditch indicates intensification of production.

Figure 10.10. Remants of marae *(precontact temple platforms) on Pukarua, Tuamotus (photo MR).*

Figure 10.11. Remains of Nan Madol, Pohnpei (photo LEM).

Figure 10.12. Latte post and capstone, Tinian, Northern Marianas (photo LEM).

By European contact, commoners had lost their genealogies and land and were organized under lateral kin relationships. The *ali'i* (chiefs) were divided into conical clans whose pinnacle was the paramount chief. Tribute was paid to the high chief and used for his organization of advisors and priests, and others who were his immediate support. Large quantities of food were allocated for the construction of irrigation systems, fishponds, temples, chiefs' tombs, and craft specialists (as in Tonga and Tahiti). Chiefs supported commoners through ritual and provision of subsistence in times of shortage. Hawaiian social organization pushed chiefdoms to their structural limit.

Human Impact on Island Ecosystems

Influence on Native Vegetation

Since the 1970s, archaeologists working in the Pacific, with support from environmental scientists, have contributed a great deal toward our understanding of the processes of landscape change coinciding with the arrival of early settlers and continuing throughout the prehistoric sequence, with implications for demographic change, agricultural intensification, and the development of social complexity. It can no longer be assumed that indigenous populations, unlike other cultural groups, had exerted only minimal influence on their physical surroundings. While the scale of environmental disturbance has accelerated with European intrusion, it is clear that indigenous societies impacted both terrestrial and marine environments, sometimes in very significant ways.

Data in support of prehistoric human-induced vegetation change in the Pacific come from a variety of sources. Two oceanic islands, which have become objects of extensive paleoenvironmental research, are briefly reviewed (for other examples, see Kirch [1984: 139–146]).

Pollen cores taken from volcanic crater lakes on Easter Island suggest a decline in forest cover in the last millennium, resulting in the grasslands that have characterized the island ever since. Trees would have been felled not only for the purpose of land clearance associated with agriculture and settlements, but also to provide the material needed to transport and raise the numerous megalithic statues. The construction and removal of the statues would have considerably disturbed the surrounding vegetation, causing an increase in soil erosion (Bahn and Flenley 1992). Recent work, however, suggests that prehistoric, human-induced ecological catastrophe and cultural collapse have been overrated (Hunt 2007).

Interdisciplinary work on Mangaia has documented the beginning of significant environmental changes by about 1000 BP, as evidenced by forest clearance and conversion into fernlands (Figure 10.13); burning, with corresponding increases in charcoal influx; increased soil erosion and alluvial deposition in valley bottoms; remains of domesticated plants and animals, as well as introduced rats and land snails; and avifaunal extinctions (Kirch 1997a).

Besides measuring the degree of environmental change, historical ecologists are also challenged in their ability to disentangle the effects of natural processes from those induced by humans (Kirch 1997b; Nunn et al. 2007). It is important to keep in mind the potential significance of natural phenomena—the effects of climate, sea level, and tectonic forces—to account for environmental

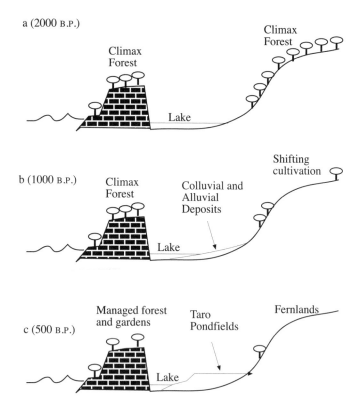

a (2000 B.P.)

Climax Forest

Climax Forest

Lake

b (1000 B.P.)

Climax Forest

Colluvial and Alluvial Deposits

Shifting cultivation

Lake

c (500 B.P.)

Managed forest and gardens

Taro Pondfields

Fernlands

Lake

Figure 10.13. *Forest clearance over time in Mangaia, Cook Islands (after Kirch 1997).*

change on many islands during their postsettlement history. According to Nunn (2007a), with the advent of the Medieval Warm Period, beginning about 1200 BP and lasting to 650 BP, much of the tropical Pacific was warmer and drier than at present, promoting erosion and fires. Forest clearance would have aggravated landscape instability. The Little Ice Age that followed may have put an end to successful long-distance voyaging as temperatures fell and storminess increased. Nunn's conclusions are being challenged by climatic data from the central Pacific (Allen 2006), which highlight the potential influence of climate variability, at a variety of scales, on Pacific peoples and the biota and landscapes with which they interacted.

Climate-related disruption of crop growing systems would have been an important source of social stress. In Fiji, beginning about 850 BP, there was a proliferation of fortified structures, which may have been related to changing climate (Nunn 2007a). The dry weather that followed this transitional period would also have created additional stresses. On Easter Island, reduction of trees to build canoes and statues, and perhaps the decline of navigational knowledge following the breakdown in long-distance voyaging, left no escape. Oral traditions and archaeological evidence indicate a period of warfare from 1300 to 1650 CE, coinciding with the Little Ice Age. Abandonment of some of the "mystery" islands might also be tied to the issue of climate change (McCall 1994).

Careful analysis and interpretation of the paleoenvironmental record should assist future researchers in their assessments of the relative contribution of humans and natural phenomena in bringing about environmental changes (cf. Haberle 1993).

Impacts on Native Fauna

Human disturbance of island vegetation resulted in the reduction or extinction of several bird species through habitat destruction or fragmentation. Direct predation was another cause for changes in faunal composition, as were the destructive activities of introduced rats (cf. Cassels [1984] for an overview). While every species is capable of withstanding certain levels of predation, some are more susceptible to overexploitation and extinction than others because of slow reproductive rates and few natural predators, resulting in restricted mobility and the lack of effective defensive mechanisms. Insular terrestrial fauna, such as flightless birds, are a case in point (Anderson 1989). Since the discovery of extinct New Zealand *moa* remains, the number of human-induced bird extinctions throughout the Pacific has expanded considerably (Steadman 1997). Large-bodied lizards, such as the extinct iguana from Lifuka, Tonga, also suffered at the hands of human predators.

Turtles were also greatly reduced following a period of intense exploitation coinciding with early human presence on several Pacific islands (Dye and Steadman 1990; Kirch 1984: 146–147). A number of studies have examined the long-term impacts of human exploitation and environmental change on fish, invertebrate, reptile, and sea mammal populations resulting in a decline in species diversity and reduction in average age and size (Allen 2003).

What is less clear, however, is the extent of human impact on the marine environment. Weisler (2001) presents evidence for local extinction of the Bullmouth helmet shell (*Cypraecassis rufa*) from Utrik Atoll in the Marshalls. However, contemporary observations on the presence or absence of marine organisms appear to be largely determined by chaotic or unpredictable recruiting events that shape the structure of reef assemblages over a particular time period (Sale 1980). In addition, by virtue of biological, ecological, and behavioral attributes, species display different degrees of resilience to human exploitation (Catterall and Poiner 1987; Poiner and Catterall 1988). The disappearance of two giant clam species, *Tridacna gigas* and *Hippopus hippopus,* from several island groups illustrates the fate of vulnerable organisms, even when using traditional gathering methods (Munro 1989). Yet with relatively low human population on most atolls and the presence of extensive lagoon and ocean reefs, marine resources would have generally remained unaffected by human activities.

Some observers have suggested that people living on atolls were more acutely aware of resource limitations than communities on larger continental or volcanic islands, and thus realized at an early stage the need to conserve existing resources (Akimichi 1986; Klee 1985; Zann 1985).

Conclusion

The prehistory of the Pacific Islands has been shown to be a complex mix of external influences and local processes of cultural change against the background of a dynamic environment in a variety of settings. Humans did not simply adapt to changing conditions; they also manipulated their social and natural environments, sometimes leading to their collapse. More often than not, however, challenges were overcome and opportunities seized, leading to what we may consider sustainable livelihoods.

Acknowledgments

I wish to thank M. Carson, P. Nunn, A. Pawley, M. Rapaport, M. Spriggs, and an anonymous reviewer for their comments and suggestions for improving this chapter.

BIBLIOGRAPHY

Akimichi, T. 1986. Conservation of the sea: Satawal, Micronesia. In *Traditional fishing in the Pacific: Ethnographical and archaeological papers from the 15th Pacific Science Congress,* ed. A. Anderson, 15–33. Honolulu: Pacific Anthropological Records No. 37, B. P. Bishop Museum.

Alkire, W. H. 1978. *Coral islanders.* Arlington Heights, Ill.: Ahm Publishing.

Allen, J. 1991. The role of agriculture in the evolution of the pre-contact Hawaiian state. *Asian Perspectives* 30: 117–132.

———. 1993. Notions of the Pleistocene in Greater Australia. In *A community of culture: People and prehistory of the Pacific,* ed. M. Spriggs, D. E. Yen, W. Ambrose, R. Jones, A. Thorne, and A. Andrews, 139–151. Canberra: Occasional Papers in Prehistory No. 21, Department of Prehistory, Research School of Pacific Studies.

———. 2002. Resolving long-term change in Polynesian marine fisheries. *Asian Perspectives* 41: 195–212.

———. 2003. Human impact on Pacific nearshore marine ecosystems. In *Pacific archaeology: Assessments and prospects,* ed. C. Sand, 317–325. Nouméa: Département d'Archéologie, Service des Musées et du Patrimoine de Nouvelle Calédonie.

———. 2006. New ideas about Late Holocene climate variability in the Central Pacific. *Current Anthropology* 47: 521–535.

Amesbury, J. R. 2007. Mollusk collecting and environmental change during the Prehistoric Period in the Mariana Islands. *Coral Reefs* 26: 947–958.

Anderson, A. 1989. Mechanics of overkill in the extinction of New Zealand moas. *Journal of Archaeological Science* 16: 137–151.

———. 1996. Adaptive voyaging and subsistence strategies in the early settlement of East Polynesia. In *Prehistoric Mongoloid dispersals,* ed. T. Akazawa and E. J. Szathmáry, 359–373. Oxford: Oxford University Press.

———. 2002. Faunal collapse, landscape change and settlement history in Remote Oceania. *World Archaeology* 33: 375–390.

———. 2005. Distance looks our way: Remoteness and isolation in Early East and South Polynesia. In *The Reñaca papers: VI International Conference on Easter Island and the Pacific,* ed. C. M. Stevenson, J. M. R. Aliaga, F. J. Morin, and N. Barbacci, 1–12. Los Osos, Calif.: Easter Island Foundation.

Anderson, A., J. Chappell, M. Cagan, and R. Grove. 2006. Prehistoric maritime migration in the Pacific Islands: An hypothesis of ENSO forcing. *The Holocene* 16: 1–6.

Bahn, P., and J. Flenley. 1992. *Easter Island, earth island.* London: Thames and Hudson.

Barnes, S. S. 2007. Barcoding fish: Prospects for a standardized DNA-based method of species-level identification for archaeological fish remains. *Hawaiian Archaeology* 11: 54–60.

Barrau, J. 1965. L'Humide et le sec: An essay on ethnological adaptation to contrastive environments in the Indo-Pacific area. *Journal of the Polynesian Society* 74: 329–346.

Bayliss-Smith, T. P. 1974. Constraints on population growth: The case of the Polynesian Outlier Atolls in the precontact period. *Human Ecology* 2: 259–295.

Bellwood, P. S. 1979. *Man's conquest of the Pacific: The prehistory of Southeast Asia and Oceania.* New York: Oxford University Press.

———. 1993. The origins of Pacific peoples. In *Culture contact in the Pacific: Essays on contact, encounter and response,* ed. M. Quanchi and R. Adams, 2–14. Cambridge: Cambridge University Press.

———. 1997. Ancient seafarers: New evidence of early Southeast Asian sea voyages. *Archaeology* 50(2): 20–22.

Butler, V. L. 1988. Lapita fishing strategies: The faunal evidence. In *Archaeology of the Lapita cultural complex: A critical review,* ed. P. V. Kirch and T. L. Hunt, 99–115. Seattle: Research Report No. 5, Thomas Burke Memorial Washington State Museum.

Cassels, R. 1984. Of New Zealand and other Pacific Islands. In *Quaternary extinctions: A prehistoric revolution,* ed. P. S. Martin and R. G. Klein, 741–761. Tucson: University of Arizona Press.

Catterall, C. P., and I. R. Poiner. 1987. The potential impact of human gathering on shellfish populations, with reference to some NE Australian Intertidal Flats. *Oikos* 50: 114–122.

Clark, G., A. Anderson, and D. Wright. 2006. Human colonization of the Palau Islands. *Journal of Island & Coastal Archaeology* 1: 215–232.

Clark, J. T. 1991. Early settlement in the Indo-Pacific. *Journal of Anthropological Archaeology* 10: 27–53.

Clarke, A. C., M. K. Burtenshaw, P. A. McLenachan, D. L. Erickson, and D. Penny. 2006. Reconstructing the origins and dispersal of the Polynesian bottle gourd (*Lagenaria siceraria*). *Molecular Biology and Evolution* 23: 893–900.

Davidson, J. M. 1977. Western Polynesia and Fiji: Prehistoric contact, diffusion and differentiation in adjacent archipelagoes. *World Archaeology* 9: 82–94.

———. 1983. Maori Prehistory: The state of the art. *Journal of the Polynesian Society* 92: 291–307.

Denham, T. 2004. The roots of agriculture and arboriculture in New Guinea: Looking beyond Austronesian expansion, Neolithic packages and indigenous Origins. *World Archaeology* 36: 610–620.

Denham, T., S. Haberle, and C. Lentfer. 2004. New evidence and revised interpretations of early agriculture in Highland New Guinea. *Antiquity* 78: 839–857.

Diamond, J. M. 1977. Colonization cycles in man and beast. *World Archaeology* 3: 249–261.

Dickinson, W. R. 2003. Impact of Mid-Holocene hydro-isostatic highstand in regional sea level on habitability of islands in Pacific Oceania. *Journal of Coastal Research* 19: 489–502.

Di Piazza, A. 1999. Te Bakoa site. Two old earth ovens from Nikunau Island (Republic of Kiribati). *Archaeology in Oceania* 34: 40–42.

Dye, T. S., and D. W. Steadman. 1990. Polynesian ancestors and their animal world. *American Scientist* 78(3): 207–215.

Dyson-Hudson, R., and E. A. Smith. 1978. Human territoriality: An ecological reassessment. *American Anthropologist* 80: 21–41.

Fitzpatrick, S. M. 2008. Maritime interregional interaction in Micronesia: Deciphering multi-group contacts and exchange systems through time. *Journal of Anthropological Archaeology* 27: 131–147.

Flannery, T. F., and J. P. White. 1991. Animal translocations: Zoogeography of New Ireland mammals. *National Geographic Research and Exploration* 7: 96–113.

Friedman, J. 1981. Notes on structure and history in Oceania. *Folk* 23: 275–295.

Gibbons, A. 1994. Genes point to a new identity for Pacific Pioneers. *Science* 263(5143): 32–33.

Goldman, I. 1970. *Ancient Polynesian society.* Chicago: University of Chicago Press.

Golson, J. 1977. No room at the top: Agricultural intensification in the New Guinea Highlands. In *Sunda and Sahul: Prehistoric studies in Southeast Asia, Melanesia and Australia,* ed. J. Allen, J. Golson, and R. Jones, 601–638. London: Academic Press.

Gosden, C. 1993. Understanding the settlement of the Pacific Islands in the Pleistocene. In *Sahul in review: Pleistocene archaeology in Australia, New Guinea and Island Melanesia,* ed. M. A. Smith, M. Spriggs, and B. Fankhauser, 131–136. Canberra: Occasional Papers in Prehistory No. 24, Department of Prehistory, Research School of Pacific Studies, Australian National University.

Green, R. C. 1979. Lapita. In *The prehistory of Polynesia,* ed. J. D. Jennings, 27–60. Cambridge, Mass.: Harvard University Press.

———. 1980. *Makaha before 1880 AD.* Honolulu: Pacific Anthropological Records No. 31, B. P. Bishop Museum.

———. 1981. Location of the Polynesian homeland: A continuing problem. In *Studies in Pacific languages & cultures: In honour of Bruce Biggs,* ed. J. Hollyman and A. Pawley, 133–158. Auckland: Linguistic Society of New Zealand.

———. 1982. Models for the Lapita cultural complex. *New Zealand Journal of Archaeology* 4: 6–19.

———. 1991. Near and Remote Oceania—Deestablishing "Melanesia" in culture history. In *Man and a half: Essays in Pacific anthropology and ethnobiology in honour of Ralph Bulmer,* ed. A. Pawley, 491–502. Auckland: Polynesian Society.

Groube, L. 1989. The taming of the rain forests: A model for Late Pleistocene forest exploitation in New Guinea. In *Foraging and farming: The evolution of plant exploitation,* ed. D. R. Harris and G. C. Hillman, 292–304. London: Unwin Hyman.

Groube, L., J. Chappell, J. Muke, and D. Price. 1986. A 40,000 year-old human occupation site at Huon Peninsula, Papua New Guinea. *Nature* 324: 453–455.

Haberle, S. 1993. Pleistocene vegetation change and early human occupation of a tropical mountainous environment. In *Sahul in review: Pleistocene archaeology in Australia, New Guinea and Island Melanesia,* ed. M. A. Smith, M. Spriggs, and B. Fankhauser, 109–122. Canberra: Occasional Papers in Prehistory No. 24, Department of Prehistory, Research School of Pacific Studies, Australian National University.

Houghton, P. 1996. *People of the great ocean: Aspects of human biology of the early Pacific.* Cambridge: Cambridge University Press.

Hunt, T. L. 2007. Rethinking Easter Island's ecological catastrophe. *Journal of Archaeological Science* 34: 485–502.

Hunt, T. L., and M. W. Graves. 1990. Some methodological issues of exchange in oceanic prehistory. *Asian Perspectives* 29: 107–115.

Hunt, T. L., and R. M. Holsen. 1991. An early radiocarbon chronology for the Hawaiian Islands: A preliminary analysis. *Asian Perspectives* 30: 147–161.

Hunt, T. L., and C. P. Lipo. 2006. Late colonization of Easter Island. *Science* 311(5766): 1603–1606.

Irwin, G. 1992. *The prehistoric exploration and colonisation of the Pacific.* Cambridge: Cambridge University Press.

Jones, S., and P. V. Kirch. 2007. Indigenous Hawaiian fishing practices in Kahikinui, Maui: A Zooarchaeological Approach. *Hawaiian Archaeology* 11: 39–53.

Jones, T. L., and K. A. Klar. 2005. Diffusionism reconsidered: Linguistic and archaeological evidence for prehistoric Polynesian contact with southern California. *American Antiquity* 70: 457–484.

Kayser, M., S. Brauer, R. Cordaux, A. Casto, O. Lao, L. A. Zhivotovsky, C. Moyse-Faurie, R. B. Rutledge, W. Schiefenhoevel, D. Gil, A. A. Lin, P. A. Underhill, P. J. Oefner, R. J. Trent, and M. Stoneking. 2006. Melanesian and Asian origins of Polynesians: mtDNA and Y chromosome gradients across the Pacific. *Molecular Biology and Evolution* 23: 2234–2244.

Kennett, D., A. Anderson, and B. Winterhalder. 2006. The ideal free distribution, food production, and the colonization of Oceania. In *Behavioral ecology and the transition to agriculture,* ed. D. Kennett and B. Winterhalder, 265–288. Berkeley: University of California Press.

Kirch P. V. 1978. The Lapitoid period in West Polynesia: Excavations and survey in Niuatoputapu, Tonga. *Journal of Field Archaeology* 5: 1–13.

———. 1979. Subsistence and ecology. In *The prehistory of Polynesia,* ed. J. D. Jennings, 286–307. Cambridge, Mass.: Harvard University Press.

———. 1984. *The evolution of the Polynesian chiefdoms.* Cambridge: Cambridge University Press.

———. 1985. *Feathered gods and fishhooks.* Honolulu: University of Hawai'i Press.

———. 1988. Long-distance exchange and island colonization: The Lapita case. *Norwegian Archaeological Review* 21: 103–117.

———. 1990. Specialization and exchange in the Lapita Complex of Oceania (1600–500 B.C.). *Asian Perspectives* 29: 117–133.

———. 1991. Prehistoric exchange in Western Melanesia. *Annual Review of Anthropology* 20: 141–165.

———. 1994. *The wet and the dry: Irrigation and agricultural intensification in Polynesia.* Chicago: University of Chicago Press.

———. 1997a. Changing landscapes and sociopolitical evolution In Mangaia, Central Polynesia. In *Historical ecology in the Pacific Islands: Prehistoric environmental and landscape change,* ed. P. V. Kirch and T. L. Hunt, 147–165. New Haven, Conn.: Yale University Press.

———. 1997b. Introduction: The environmental history of Oceanic Islands. In *Historical ecology in the Pacific Islands: Prehistoric environmental and landscape change,* ed. P. V. Kirch and T. L. Hunt, 1–21. New Haven, Conn.: Yale University Press.

———. 2000. *On the road of the winds: An archaeological history of the Pacific Islands before European contact.* Berkeley: University of California Press.

Kirch, P. V., T. L. Hunt, L. Nagaoka, and J. Tyler. 1990. An ancestral Polynesian occupation site at To'aga, Ofu Island, American Samoa. *Archaeology in Oceania* 25: 1–15.

Kirch, P. V., and J-L. Rallu, eds. 2007. *The growth and collapse of Pacific Island societies: Archaeological and demographic perspectives.* Honolulu: University of Hawai'i Press.

Klee, G. A. 1980. Oceania. In *World systems of traditional resource management,* ed. G. A. Klee, 245–282. New York: John Wiley and Sons.

———. 1985. Traditional marine resource management in the Pacific. In *Culture and conservation: The human dimension to environmental planning,* ed. J. A. McNeely and D. Pitt, 193–202. Dover, N.H.: Croom Helm.

Koch, G. 1986. *The material culture of Kiribati.* Suva: Institute of Pacific Studies, University of the South Pacific.

Lacey, R. 1982. Archaeology and early man. In *Atlas of Papua New Guinea,* ed. D. King and S. Ranch, 4–5. Port Moresby: University of Papua New Guinea.

Leavesley, M. 2006. Late Pleistocene complexities in the Bismarck Archipelago. In *Archaeology of Oceania: Australia and the Pacific Islands,* ed. I. Lilley, 189–204. Malden, Mass.: Blackwell.

Lilley, I. 2006. Archaeology in Oceania: Themes and issues. In *Archaeology of Oceania: Australia and the Pacific Islands,* ed. I. Lilley, 1–28. Malden, Mass.: Blackwell.

Malinowski, B. 1932. *Argonauts of the Western Pacific.* London: George Routledge & Sons.

McArthur, N., I. W. Saunders, and R. L. Tweedie. 1976. Small population isolates: A micro-simulation study. *Journal of the Polynesian Society* 85: 307–326.

McCall, G. 1994. Little Ice Age: Some proposals for Polynesia and Rapanui (Easter Island). *Journal de la Société des océanistes* 98: 99–104.

Morwood, M. J., P. Brown, Jatmiko, T. Sutikna, E. Wahyu Saptomo, K. E. Westaway, Rokus Awe Due, R. G. Roberts, T. Maeda, S. Wasisto, and T. Djubiantono. 2005. Further Evidence for small-bodied hominids from the Late Pleistocene of Flores, Indonesia. *Nature* 437: 1012–1017.

Morwood, M. J., R. P. Soejono, R. G. Roberts, T. Sutikna, C. S. M. Turney, K. E. Westaway, W. J. Rink, J. X. Zhao, G. D. van den Bergh, Rokus Awe Due, D. R. Hobbs, M. W. Moore, M. I. Bird, and L. K. Fifield. 2004. Archaeology and age of a new hominid from Flores in Eastern Indonesia. *Nature* 431: 1087–1091.

Munro, J. L. 1989. Fisheries for giant clams (Tridacnidae: Bivalvia) and prospects for stock enhancement. In *Marine invertebrate fisheries: Their assessment and management,* ed. J. F. Caddy, 541–558. New York: John Wiley & Sons.

Nagaoka, L. 1988. Lapita subsistence: The evidence of non-fish archaeofaunal remains. In *Archaeology of the Lapita cultural complex: A critical review,* ed. P. V. Kirch and T. L. Hunt, 117–133. Seattle: Research Report No. 5, Thomas Burke Memorial, Washington State Museum.

Nunn, P. D. 1993. Beyond the naive lands: Human history and environmental change in the Pacific Basin. In *The margin fades: Geographical itineraries in a world of islands,* ed. E. Waddell and P. D. Nunn, 5–27. Suva: Institute of Pacific Studies, University of the South Pacific.

———. 2000. Environmental catastrophe in the Pacific Islands around A.D. 1300. *Geoarchaeology* 15: 715–740.

———. 2007a. *Climate, environment and society in the Pacific during the last millennium.* Amsterdam: Elsevier.

———. 2007b. Echoes from a distance: Research into the Lapita occupation of the Rove Peninsula, Southwest Viti Levu, Fiji. In *Oceanic explorations: Lapita and Western Pacific settlement,* ed. S. Bedford, C. Sand, and S. P. Connaughton, 163–176. Canberra: Australian National University E Press.

Nunn, P. D., R. Hunter-Anderson, M. T. Carson, F. Thomas, S. Ulm, and M. J. Rowland. 2007. Times of plenty, times of less: Last-millennium societal disruption in the Pacific Basin. *Human Ecology* 35: 385–401.

Nunn, P. D., R. Kumar, S. Matararaba, T. Ishimura, J. Seeto, S. Rayawa, S. Kuruyawa, A. Nasila, B. Oloni, A. Rati ram, P. Saunivalu, P. Singh, and E. Tegu. 2004. Early Lapita settlement site at Bourewa, Southwest Viti Levu Island, Fiji. *Archaeology in Oceania* 39: 139–143.

Oliver, D. L. 1989. *Oceania: The native cultures of Australia and the Pacific Islands,* vol. I. Honolulu: University of Hawai'i Press.

Pawley, A., and M. Ross. 1993. Austronesian historical linguistics and culture history. *Annual Review of Anthropology* 22: 425–459.

Pietrusewsky, M. 1994. Pacific-Asian relationships: A physical anthropological perspective. *Oceanic Linguistics* 33: 407–429.

Poiner, I. R., and C. P. Catterall. 1988. The effects of traditional gathering on populations of the marine gastropod *Strombus luhuanus* linne [*sic*]1758, in Southern Papua New Guinea. *Oecologia* 76: 191–199.

Rainbird, P. 2004. *The archaeology of Micronesia.* Cambridge: Cambridge University Press.

Riley, T. J. 1987. Archaeological survey and testing, Majuro Atoll, Marshall Islands. In *Marshall Islands archaeology,* ed. T. Dye, 169–270. Honolulu: Pacific Anthropological Records No. 38, B. P. Bishop Museum.

Sale, P. F. 1980. Assemblages of fish on patch reefs—predictable or unpredictable? *Environmental Biology of Fishes* 5: 243–249.

Serjeantson, S. W., and X. Gao. 1995. *Homo sapiens* is an evolving species: Origins of the Austronesians. In *The Austronesians: Historical and comparative perspectives,* ed. P. Bellwood, J. J. Fox, and D. Tryon, 165–180. Canberra: Department of Anthropology, Research School of Pacific and Asian Studies, Australian National University.

Serjeantson, S. W., and A. V. S. Hill. 1989. The colonization of the Pacific: The genetic evidence. In *The colonization of the Pacific: A genetic trail,* ed. A. V. S. Hill and S. W. Serjeantson, 286–294. Oxford: Oxford University Press.

Smith, M. A., and N. D. Sharp. 1993. Pleistocene sites in Australia, New Guinea and Island Melanesia: Geographic and temporal structure of the archaeological record. In *Sahul in review: Pleistocene Archaeology in Australia, New Guinea and Island Melanesia,* ed. M. A. Smith, M. Spriggs, and B. Fankhauser, 37–59. Canberra: Occasional Papers in Prehistory No. 24, Department of Prehistory, Research School of Pacific Studies, Australian National University.

Spennemann, D. H. R. 2006. Freshwater lens, settlement patterns, resource use and connectivity in the Marshall Islands. *Transforming Cultures eJournal* 1(2): 44–63.

Spriggs, M. 1993a. Island Melanesia: The last 10,000 years. In *A community of culture: The people and prehistory of the Pacific,* ed.

M. Spriggs, D. E. Yen, W. Ambrose, R. Jones, A. Thorne, and A. Andrews, 187–205. Canberra: Occasional Papers in Prehistory No. 21, Department of Prehistory, Research School of Pacific Studies, Australian National University.

———. 1993b. Pleistocene agriculture in the Pacific: Why not? In *Sahul in Review: Pleistocene archaeology in Australia, New Guinea and Island Melanesia,* ed. M. A. Smith, M. Spriggs, and B. Fankhauser, 137–143. Canberra: Occasional Papers in Prehistory No. 24, Department of Anthropology, Research School of Pacific Studies, Australian National University.

Spriggs, M., and A. Anderson 1993. Late colonization of East Polynesia. *Antiquity* 67: 200–217.

Steadman, D. W. 1997. Extinctions of Polynesian birds: Reciprocal impacts of birds and people. In *Historical ecology in the Pacific Islands: Prehistoric environmental and landscape change,* ed. P. V. Kirch and T. L. Hunt, 51–79. New Haven, Conn.: Yale University Press.

Storey, A. A., J. M. Ramirez, D. Quiroz, D. V. Burley, D. J. Addison, R. Walter, A. J. Anderson, T. L. Hunt, J. S. Athens, L. Huynen, and E. A. Matisoo-Smith. 2007. Radiocarbon and DNA evidence for a pre-Columbian introduction of Polynesian chickens to Chile. *National Academy of Sciences of the USA* 104: 10335–10339.

Sutton, D. G. 1987. A paradigmatic shift in Polynesian prehistory: Implications for New Zealand. *New Zealand Journal of Archaeology* 9: 135–155.

Terrell, J. 1986. *Prehistory in the Pacific Islands: A study of variation in language, customs, and human biology.* Cambridge: Cambridge University Press.

Terrell, J. E., T. L. Hunt, and C. Gosden. 1997. The dimension of social life in the Pacific: Human diversity and myth of the primitive isolate. *Current Anthropology* 38: 155–195.

Thomas, F. R. 1995. Excavations at Maunalua Cave, Hawai'i Kai, O'ahu. *Hawaiian Archaeology* 4: 17–26.

———. 2007. The behavioral ecology of shellfish gathering in Western Kiribati, Micronesia. 1: Prey Choice. *Human Ecology* 35: 179–194.

Ward, R. G., and M. Brookfield. 1992. The dispersal of the coconut: Did it float or was it carried to Panama? *Journal of Biogeography* 19: 467–480.

Weisler, M. I. 1994. The settlement of Marginal Polynesia: New evidence from Henderson Island. *Journal of Field Archaeology* 21: 83–102.

———. 1999. The antiquity of aroid pit agriculture and significance of buried A horizons on Pacific Atolls. *Geoarchaeology* 14: 621–654.

———. 2001. Life on the edge: Prehistoric settlement and economy on Utirik Atoll, Northern Marshall Islands. *Archaeology in Oceania* 36: 109–133.

Weisler, M. I., and P. V. Kirch. 1996. Interisland and interarchipelago transfer of stone tools in prehistoric Polynesia. Washington, D.C.: Proceedings of the National Academy of Sciences of the United States of America 93: 1384–1385.

Williamson, I., and M. D. Sabath. 1984. Small population instability and island settlement patterns. *Human Ecology* 12: 21–34.

Yen, D. E. 1971. Construction of the hypothesis for distribution of the sweet potato. In *Man across the sea: Problem of pre-Columbian contacts,* ed. C. L. Riley, C. Kelley, C. W. Pennington, and R. Rands, 328–342. Austin: University of Texas Press.

———. 1985. Wild plants and domestication in Pacific Islands. In *Recent advances in Indo-Pacific prehistory,* ed. V. N. Misra and P. S. Bellwood, 315–329. Leiden: E. J. Brill.

Zann, L. P. 1985. Traditional management and conservation of fisheries in Kiribati and Tuvalu Atolls. In *The traditional knowledge and management of coastal systems in Asia and the Pacific,* ed. K. R. Ruddle and R. E. Johannes, 53–77. Jakarta: UNESCO/Regional Office for Science and Technology for Southeast Asia.

The Postcontact Period

David A. Chappell

11

This chapter traces historical changes in Oceania from early Euroamerican contacts through colonial rule into the post-1945 era of decolonization. The reader should be aware, however, that history is never separate from the present, because each generation reinterprets the past in light of its own priorities. The written history of the Pacific Islands was produced mainly by outsiders until very recently, and as an academic subject that is taught in universities the field really dates only to the 1950s. Foreign explorers, missionaries, traders, and colonial officials kept many records, but their accounts were often biased, privileging the "civilizing" influence of outsiders. Colonial historians tended to perpetuate these one-sided impressions, while critics stressed the negative effects of outsiders on indigenous societies, from deaths caused by introduced diseases to cultural losses when native peoples adopted Christianity or metal tools and weapons. For example, Alan Moorehead's *The Fatal Impact* describes the decline of native peoples and customs in Tahiti and Australia after contact.

This Eurocentric historiography of the islands began to change in the 1950s, when J. W. Davidson of the Australian National University recommended what came to be called an "island-centered" or "islander-oriented" approach. He and his followers urged scholars to do fieldwork, rather than simply researching in colonial archives, and to consider other sources of data, such as oral traditions, archeology, ethnobotany, linguistics, and anthropology. The goal was to focus on the historical interplay between indigenous and foreign actors to reveal participation by native peoples in making their own history (Howe 1984). Greg Dening (1980) and Marshall Sahlins (1985) blended histories of culture contact with anthropological data, creating "ethnographic history." Other scholars warned that a Euroamerican-dominated capitalist "world system" created economic exploitation and dependency (Howard and Durutalo 1987), and indigenous nationalists spoke of past and ongoing victimization by outsiders (Trask 1993; Walker 1990). As more Oceanians joined the ranks of academic historians, they added their voices to these debates (e.g. Meleisea 1987).

Early Interactions with Euroamericans

Before Ferdinand Magellan named and crossed the Pacific in 1520–1521, the ocean basin was divided into subregions by an equilibrium of disinterest. For thousands of years, sheer distance had limited contact between Oceania and the Pacific Rim to sporadic interaction with insular Southeast Asia and, probably, South America. Oceania was a self-contained, culturally diverse maritime world linked together by its own exchange networks and canoe migrations, but like the Americas it hovered just out of reach of global trends. In 1513, however, Portuguese and Spanish explorers arrived at the western and eastern shores of the Pacific, respectively, and soon other explorers began to cross Oceania on missions for the emerging world economy. European monarchs sought to bypass Middle Eastern middlemen and gain direct access to Asian spices and silks. In the process, Columbus stumbled upon the Americas, where Spain reaped a windfall of gold and silver by enslaving native peoples (Hezel 1983; Howe 1984).

Ferdinand Magellan, a Portuguese sailing for Spain, left Europe in 1519 with five ships to finish the job that Columbus had set out to do—reach Asia by sailing west. By the time the expedition rounded Cape Horn, the stormy tip of South America, the sea beyond looked relatively peaceful, hence the name "Pacific" (by a lucky coincidence, it was not hurricane season). Magellan next accomplished two things: his ships were the first known to have crossed the entire Pacific, and they did so without seeing anyone until they reached Guam. Unfortunately, the latter feat meant that his crews were starving and ill when they encountered the Chamorro people of the Marianas. Moreover, two systems of property were colliding: the Spanish believed in private ownership (and knew they were only halfway around the globe), while the Chamorros, like most Oceanians, emphasized communal property sharing and expected to assimilate new arrivals, including their material possessions. The Chamorros went out to the Spanish ships in sailing canoes to exchange gifts.

Antonio Pigafetta, Magellan's chronicler, wrote that they "boarded the ships and stole one thing after another, to such an extent that our men could not protect their belongings" (Paige 1969). Violence resulted, and Magellan labeled Guam the Island of Thieves, beginning a process of (mis)naming that would persist for centuries. He himself died in another conflict in the Philippines, but one of his ships managed to return home with enough cloves to make a profit, thus encouraging more Spanish adventures across the Pacific (Rogers 1995). These included three expeditions from Peru to Melanesia in search of ancient King Solomon's gold mines, but violence similar to that on Guam left only a few place names like "Solomon Islands" as a lasting legacy. More significant was the establishment of the first trans-Pacific shipping route; from the sixteenth to the eighteenth centuries, Spanish treasure galleons traded Mexican silver for Asian luxury goods at Manila. Yet they still missed most of the Pacific Islands, since they sailed by a northerly route (Howe 1984).

On Guam, however, Spanish priests arrived with an armed escort in 1668. Jesuit father Diego Luis de San Vitores set out to convert the Chamorros to Catholicism, baptizing young children he befriended by giving them sugar from his pockets. Some Chamorros, such as Kipuha (a statue of him stands in Hagåtña today), welcomed the Spanish, but others forcibly opposed the foreign intrusion. After San Vitores himself took up arms and was killed, fighting between pro-Spanish forces and rebels almost depopulated the Marianas. Combat deaths, relocation to Guam, and diseases reduced the epidemiologically vulnerable Chamorros by about 90 percent in a single generation (Rogers 1995). This holocaust would be repeated on other Pacific islands exposed to intensive foreign contact, just as it had occurred on the American mainland.

Meanwhile, British and French raiders attacked Spanish treasure ships in the Pacific as well as the Atlantic. The Dutch made brief excursions into the South Pacific in the 1600s but soon decided to devote their colonizing energies to spice-rich Southeast Asian islands. They left a few place names, like Tasmania and New Zealand, on maps.

Up to this time, European contacts with Pacific Islanders had been fleeting and tragic. Serious attempts at communication came only after a peace treaty between Britain and France in 1763 enabled their navies to explore Oceania more systematically. Expeditions carrying scientists and artists set out to test geographic theories that a Northwest Passage might link the Atlantic and the Pacific, or that a Terra Australis Incognita (unknown southern continent) was balancing the Eurasian landmass. The problem of obtaining adequate provisions of food and water still haunted ships until British explorer Samuel Wallis found Tahiti in 1767. Tahiti's reputation for hospitality, nurtured by the Pomare family, helped to foster a myth of the South Pacific as a paradise, where people never had to work hard, loved freely, and lacked the material greed of Western culture. In fact, that myth derived from a deliberate strategy devised by indigenous leaders. After their first violent encounter with Wallis, Tahitian elders sent young women out to the ships to offer sexual favors in return for such rare treasures as iron—at the unexpected price of venereal disease (Moorehead 1966).

When French explorer Louis Antoine de Bougainville arrived at Tahiti in 1768, he and his crew were entranced. He even took a man called Ahutoru to Paris as a specimen of a "noble savage." French Enlightenment writers like Denis Diderot lamented the fate of Tahitians now that European ships began to frequent the island, but the Pomares and other ambitious chiefs added foreign trade contacts to traditional power dynamics in their quest for supremacy. Pomare I presented himself as a king to James Cook and organized the sale of pork to feed the convicts in the new British colony of Australia (founded in 1788). Pomare II welcomed English Protestant missionaries in 1797, and by 1815 he had conquered Tahiti with their help as gunrunners—combining this assistance with shrewd political marriages with other chiefly families (Howarth 1985; Howe 1984). A similar process occurred in Hawai'i, where Kamehameha I united the islands using both indigenous alliances and trade contacts with foreigners who were buying local sandalwood or transshipping furs from Northwest America to China (Howe 1984).

Explorers paved the way for missionaries and traders by gathering information about resources in the Pacific basin. In 1789, HMS Bounty went to Tahiti to collect breadfruit trees to feed African slaves on Jamaica; despite the famous mutiny, William Bligh finally completed his task on a second voyage in 1792. The London Missionary Society arrived in 1797 with a Tahitian vocabulary compiled by a Bounty mutineer. On his third expedition to the Pacific, Cook purchased furs from Native Americans on the northwest coast, and after his death in Hawai'i, his crew sold those furs for a great profit in China. A New Englander from Cook's crew persuaded American ships to enter the trade. Some recruited Hawaiian sailors, one of whom was Henry Opukahaia, whose death in New England inspired the first American Protestant missionaries to come to Hawai'i in 1820. Those missionaries arrived just after Kamehameha's death, when American whaleships were beginning to hunt the Japan grounds and winter in Hawai'i. The native kapu (law) system had declined as foreigners and those who traded with them broke the rules, so the missionaries found Hawai'i ready to transform into a Christian state like Tahiti (Sahlins 1981). By 1850, the land systems in both kingdoms had been privatized, much to the disadvantage of most indigenous people (Scarr 1990; Newbury 1980).

In the early stages of the nineteenth century, a precarious balance existed between indigenous leaders and foreign traders and advisors. Beachcombers, who deserted from Euroamerican vessels or were shipwrecked, earned acceptance by offering linguistic and technical skills to chiefs while adopting local customs. Some were kidnapped, like Isaac Davis and John Young, whom Kamehameha I rewarded handsomely for their services. Those on Pohnpei acquired a monopoly over trade with ships, while other beachcombers died in local wars or left the islands to become tattooed carnival curiosities in Europe. Hundreds of indigenous islanders also played this role, as ships that recruited them as sailors dropped them off on any generic island before leaving the region. By 1846, there were four hundred Hawaiians in Tahiti and two hundred Tahitians in Hawai'i. As whaling ships developed seasonal circuits around the region, nearly every island traded with foreign vessels and sent out or received seamen. The Tuamotus sold pearls, and Micronesia exported tortoiseshell, copra, and bêche-de-mer. Fiji had both sandalwood and bêche-de-mer to offer, and New Caledonia and Vanuatu began to export sandalwood and receive missionaries by the 1840s (Howe 1984; Maude 1968).

Native teachers (indigenous missionaries) played a major role in the conversion of islanders to Christianity (Howe 1984). English and American missionaries pursued a "Polynesian strategy" by winning over the chiefs of Hawai'i, Tahiti, and Tonga so that the masses of commoners would follow. They then sent new converts westward to other islands, assuming that indigenous teachers would be able to communicate better and pave the way for white missionaries. Yet half the native teachers died prematurely. The farther west they went, the graver the risk for Polynesians: in Melanesia they encountered many different languages and customs, frequent warfare between small polities, and deadly malaria. Gradually, however,

Oceanians "indigenized" Christianity, sometimes blending it with their own beliefs. In Samoa, Siovili returned from travels overseas to create his own quasi-Christian church. Meanwhile, becoming a Protestant pastor was similar to being a *matai*, or titled chief. In 1850, Samoan teachers went on strike to demand equal pay with whites and succeeded (Howe 1984).

By the mid-1800s, the balance of contact increasingly tilted in favor of industrialized foreign powers. As Oceanians bought more imports, traders shrewdly sold manufactured goods on credit, adding interest until they could call on their country's warships to demand payment—or land. Like Guam, Tahiti, and Hawai'i, New Zealand became a focal point of Euroamerican expansion. The Maori had begun to grow potatoes and wheat and cut trees to sell to whalers and sealers from the British colony in Australia. Maori men worked on foreign ships, and English missionaries began to preach Christianity with help from Maori teachers. In 1820, Chief Hongi Hika visited London, where King George IV gave him a shotgun and a suit of armor that he used in wars against his old enemies. By 1840, British agents persuaded Maori chiefs to sign the Treaty of Waitangi, which was supposed to be a model arrangement that would protect Maori rights while allowing English colonists to settle in New Zealand. But the Maori version did not use "mana" to describe the "sovereignty" that the Maori chiefs ceded, and disputes over the treaty's meaning and over land sales led to wars. The Maori impressed the English with their military skills and in 1858 even elected their first king to unite their efforts, but they finally lost the wars and more than three million acres (Howe 1984; Walker 1990).

In the 1840s, France was competing with Britain for influence in the islands and began to seek secure "ports of call" for its ships. Using the pretext that Catholic missionaries had not been welcomed in Tahiti (where English Protestants had already converted most of the population), the French navy conquered the Society Islands and nearby archipelagoes beginning in 1842. France also established missionary control over Wallis and Futuna and in 1853 took New Caledonia, despite local resistance. In Tahiti and Wallis and Futuna the French allowed Polynesian rulers to retain symbolic authority, but in Melanesian New Caledonia, which had thirty indigenous language groups, they seized land and punished resisters by forcing them onto crowded reserves. By 1900, the Kanaks of New Caledonia retained only 10 percent of their land, they had to perform forced labor, and their chiefs were appointed by French police. Meanwhile, France brought twenty thousand convicts, as well as ranchers and coffee farmers, to New Caledonia between 1864 and 1894; descendants of those European migrants today make up one-third of the territory's population (Henningham 1992).

As foreign business expanded in Oceania, labor supply became a serious issue. During the sandalwood trade in Melanesia in the 1840s, it proved easier to control workers if they were removed from their home island so they would be at the mercy of their employers. By the 1860s, the blockade of southern cotton in the American Civil War caused a Pacific plantation boom, so recruiters sought workers mainly in populous Melanesia, where they already had sandalwood contacts. By the early 1900s, 120,000 Oceanian workers left their home islands on contract to plantations in Queensland (Australia) or islands like Fiji and Samoa. At first, ships often kidnapped laborers, a practice known as "blackbirding." In 1862–1864, for example, Peru seized 3,500 islanders from as far

west as the Gilbert Islands to work in mines and plantations; few of the captives returned home, and epidemics killed many of those left behind. Another notorious case was that of the *Carl*, an Australian-based vessel that lured canoes alongside and then kidnapped the islanders in 1871; when their captives tried to rebel, the crew fired into the hold and killed a hundred of them. Such incidents led to Australian attempts to regulate labor recruiting in the 1870s so that the process became more voluntary (Howe 1984; Maude 1981).

Labor migration and planter ambitions helped prepare the way for colonial rule. In 1877, Britain created the Western Pacific High Commission, which sent naval patrols to Melanesia not only to regulate labor recruiting but also to protect traders and missionaries. In 1887, France and England signed a joint naval agreement to patrol the New Hebrides, effectively transforming it into a labor reserve for New Caledonia and Australia. Native "passage-masters" gathered recruits before ships arrived, and returnees brought back trade boxes full of manufactured goods they could use to get married or pay debts. Asians also labored on plantations in Oceania, changing the demography of places like Hawai'i and Fiji. Sugar planters in Hawai'i benefited from the Mahele of 1848–1850, which privatized land, and pressure from creditors and planters forced Fijian chiefs to cede their sovereignty to Britain in 1874. Gov. Arthur Gordon set aside 83 percent of the land for Fijians, but imported indentured laborers from India to grow sugar cane. His dual policy would create an ethnic crisis in Fiji, which like New Caledonia became an ethnically bipolar society (Scarr 1990).

Colonialism and Resistance

By the 1880s, competition among imperial powers around the world was intensifying, partly for prestige and partly for strategic or economic gain. A scramble for colonial real estate began, usually rationalized by claims that Euroamericans would "civilize" the natives (or else prevail through Social Darwinian "survival of the fittest"). When foreign contact bolstered indigenous leaders, as in Hawai'i or Tahiti, they might be coopted or later overthrown, but trade could also destabilize indigenous societies. In Samoa, traders sold guns to opposite sides in local wars and then demanded land in payment for debts, while in parts of Melanesia, guns brought back by overseas laborers increased warfare to the point where local leaders sometimes asked to be "pacified." In 1887, King David Kalākaua of Hawai'i tried to forge a last-ditch alliance with High Chief Malietoa Laupepa of Samoa, but German warships prevented the pact. Not even the destruction of six foreign warships in 'Apia harbor by a hurricane could keep Samoa from being partitioned by Germany and the United States. Britain also partitioned New Guinea with the Dutch and Germans and attempted to share the New Hebrides with France in a problematic "condominium" arrangement. Because of its early base in Sydney, Britain and its settler surrogates (Australia and New Zealand) acquired a dozen colonies in the South Pacific (Howe, Kiste, and Lal 1994; Rodman and Cooper 1983).

The northern Pacific saw old and new imperial actors in competition. Spain laid claim to Micronesia because of its early bases in the Marianas and Philippines, but American missionaries and German copra traders were more active in the Carolines and Marshalls. In 1885, Germany annexed the Marshalls and Carolines. Spain protested, so Pope Leo XIII arbitrated, awarding the Carolines to Spain politically but permitting German traders and American missionaries to continue operating. Spain tried to establish a garrison on Pohnpei, but indigenous chiefs resisted so strongly that the Spanish hid in their fort and finally sold the Carolines to Germany in 1898. By that year, the upstart United States had defeated Spain in the Spanish-American War, seizing Guam and the Philippines. Meanwhile, American residents in Hawai'i had overthrown the monarchy of Queen Lili'uokalani in 1893, with intimidating support from the U.S. ambassador and warships in Honolulu Harbor. An American-dominated "republic" willingly ceded Hawai'i to the U.S. empire in 1898 as a strategic naval base from which to control Guam and the Philippines. Pago Pago Harbor in eastern Samoa was also annexed in 1899 (Hezel 1995; Hanlon 1988; Howe, Kiste, and Lal 1994).

By 1900, then, every island in Oceania had come under foreign colonial rule, through destabilization and cession or outright conquest. Even Easter Island was seized by the Chilean navy in 1888. When a treaty was signed, as the Berlin Convention of 1884–1885 required, it was usually misunderstood by the indigenous chiefs, who often regarded it as a friendship agreement or just another paper to sign for a passing warship. Warships had developed a habit of threatening islanders to pay their debts and often bombarded villages, as when a missionary had been chased off Tanna in 1865. But now the foreigners came to stay. Even inland New Guinea encountered patrols by Australians and Germans, who enforced their authority, collected taxes, recruited labor, and took land for plantations or gold mines. On small islands like Nauru and Banaba, British mining companies began to plunder the environment by digging up phosphate ore, using laborers from other islands or from Asia (Howe, Kiste, and Lal 1994; Hezel 1995).

Colonial rule was the most unequal form of contact with outsiders yet, since the indigenous peoples became subjects of distant governments and, in varying degrees, lost control of their own destiny. They would experience new economic activity, but the majority of profits usually went into other hands and left the islands. Whatever wages or rents remained perpetuated the consumption of imports, so economic dependency on outsiders only increased. The education provided by mission schools tended to produce clerks for the colonial administration, who in effect became collaborators in the redirection of their futures toward the capitalist world economy (Howard and Durutalo 1987). In some cases, the new rulers used indigenous elites to legitimize their policies, but there was a general colonization of native minds, as white mastas insisted on their own cultural superiority (Wolfers 1975; Lal 1992).

Nevertheless, Pacific Islanders tested the limits of colonial power in order to preserve a degree of sovereignty. Their resistance took a variety of forms, from armed force to alternative churches and economic cooperatives, to sly noncompliance. In 1900, Britain signed a Treaty of Friendship with King Taufa'ahau Tupou II of Tonga. This arrangement respected the 1875 monarchical constitution but stipulated that a British resident would give advice in all cabinet decisions. Would the advice have to be followed? Tupou II took a stand on the issue of the Tonga Ma'a Tonga Kautaha, a copra-marketing cooperative created in 1909 to bypass British traders, who charged Tongans twice as much as Europeans for their imports. Most Tongans joined the *kautaha* and began to transport their copra directly to Sydney for better prices, so the British traders complained. The British resident confiscated *kautaha* property on the charge of misappropriation of funds by its expatriate manager, but Tupou won his case in the court of the Western Pacific High Commission and had the resident recalled to London. In contrast, the Fijian Great Council of Chiefs cooperated with Britain, as in 1912, when Apolosi Nawai formed a cooperative called the Viti Kabani. His vociferous advocacy on behalf of his fellow *taukei* (commoners) against both chiefs and colonizers led to his being charged with embezzlement and sedition. Despite repeated arrests, he continued protesting—even creating his own church and calling himself king until he was finally deported for good (Hempenstall and Rutherford 1984).

Varying colonial contexts inspired different forms of resistance. The German governor of Western Samoa, Wilhelm Solf, closed down a native economic cooperative and deported chiefs who opposed his administration, but Albert Hahl of German New Guinea responded to revolts by trying to protect native lands while at the same time recruiting labor for planters. In 1910, Pohnpeians of Sokehs district took up arms against a brutal German governor, but warships soon defeated them. The rebel leaders were lined up and shot on the beach and their families deported to an outer island. In World War I, Germany lost its colonies to Japan north of the equator and to Britain, Australia, and New Zealand in the South Pacific. Palauans soon organized a protest against the Japanese: the Modekngei movement advocated a return to Palauan values and survived repression. In Western Samoa, a nonviolent Mau movement arose in 1926 in opposition to the heavy-handed policies of the New Zealand military governor. Despite a massacre of peaceful protestors in 'Apia in 1929, known as Black Saturday, the Mau was legalized in 1935 and won almost every seat in the subsequent Fono election (Hempenstall and Rutherford 1984; Meleisea 1987). American Samoa had its own Mau (Chappell 2000).

Melanesia, where colonizers tried to rule very diverse, small-scale societies, produced many examples of resistance. In 1927, Basiana, a *ramo* (bounty hunter) on Malaita in Solomon Islands, organized the ambush of British district officer William Bell, who had tried to collect taxes and confiscate firearms on his patrols. A destructive punitive raid by British militia and rival Solomon Islanders captured Basiana and hanged him (Keesing 1992). Two years later, police and boat operators in Rabaul (New Guinea) went on strike for better wages, but they put their trust in local missionaries, who refused to help. The Australian administration sentenced Sumsuma and other ringleaders to years of hard labor in the Wau goldfields (Gammage 1975). Perhaps the most imaginative protests came from so-called "cargo" movements led by local prophets, who often combined Christian rituals and indigenous beliefs in new churches that promised millennial change and material rewards. A so-called Vailala "madness" in Papua in 1919 was explained by a government anthropologist as a sign that modernization was causing mental breakdown among natives. Actually, Papuans were subtly mocking the Australians by shaking violently when near them. Some rocked in chairs on verandas, sipping drinks and commenting on how lazy white men were since they did no apparent work (Worsley 1968).

World War II was a turning point in Pacific history, as islanders encountered more destruction, larger numbers of outsiders, and more dramatic innovations than ever before. Apart from Pearl Harbor, most actual fighting occurred in the western Pacific, but even in the eastern islands, the United States established supply bases that had economic and cultural impacts on the indigenous peoples. In 1942, Japan advanced from its Micronesian bases as far south as New Guinea and Solomon Islands and began to bomb northern Australia. At the first warnings of Japanese invasion, most Europeans fled, leaving islanders to wonder what had happened to their much-vaunted superiority. Only a few coast watchers remained behind to report on troop movements, so islanders from Guam to Guadalcanal had to face a new invader alone. At times, relations with the Japanese were positive, but as the war continued, their demands grew more ruthless. Most of the people of Nauru were relocated to Chuuk as laborers, for example, and when food supplies became limited, Japanese troops generally considered natives expendable. The American liberation was destructive due to massive bombing and fighting from bunker to bunker. The United States paid $100 in compensation for each islander killed.

Oceanians played several roles in the war and gained new insights into the outside world. Many served as wage laborers at military bases, and in New Guinea, they carried supplies and wounded. The Australians gratefully nicknamed them "fuzzy wuzzy angels" and commemorated their services in song, but the carriers later complained they had not been compensated for their efforts. Other islanders fought as soldiers, notably the commandos recruited in Fiji at the request of Ratu Lala Sukuna, who like Maori leaders urged his people to prove their loyalty to Britain in order to gain political rewards later. Islander encounters with common soldiers from the United States and Australia were relatively egalitarian compared with previous race relations. Despite colonial orders not to share food or supplies with natives, the soldiers fraternized with them. Black American troops impressed the islanders because their segregation in supply services made them look like "big men" in charge of material wealth. On Malaita, U.S. troops also fueled local protest efforts by advising natives that the United States too had once been a British colony but had won its independence. This helped to inspire the Maasina Rule Movement, which set up local councils, customary courts, and cooperatives that defied the British. Because of exposure to greater quantities of imported goods, more "cargo" churches evolved, and islanders aspired to better wages and new dietary preferences like corned beef and Spam (White and Lindstrom 1989; Howe, Kiste, and Lal 1994; Keesing 1992).

Challenges of Decolonization

Despite United Nations support for self-determination after 1945, decolonization in the Pacific Islands is still far from complete, for strategic and economic reasons. World War II was followed by the Cold War, a global competition between the United States and the Soviet Union and their allies that divided the world into two rival camps. In the Pacific, the United States wanted to avoid another Pearl Harbor by maintaining advanced bases around communist powers in Asia. After taking over Micronesia from Japan, it acquired formal control over those islands from the United Nations (UN) in 1947 as a "strategic" Trust Territory. By 1952, the United States formed a defensive alliance with Australia and New Zealand called ANZUS, effectively denying the whole region to communist

intrusion. The United States and Britain also demonstrated their nuclear capabilities in more than seventy atomic tests, mainly in the Marshall Islands and the Australian desert between 1946 and 1962. Just as those tests came to an end, France began hundreds of nuclear experiments of its own in the Tuamotu atolls from 1966 to 1996 (Thompson 1994).

This legacy of nuclear testing in Oceania is a bitter one for many islanders. The people of Bikini in the Marshall Islands were exiled from their atoll in 1946 and have never been able to return to their radioactive homeland, except for a temporary sojourn in the 1970s. Despite monetary compensation from the United States, Marshallese still complain about ruined islands, leukemia, thyroid cancer, and "jellyfish" babies as a result of their being treated like "guinea pigs" by a colonial power. The residents of Kwajalein Atoll were evicted in 1951 in favor of U.S. military personnel, who continue to run missile tests there. French testing has aroused more protest because from 1966 to 1974 it occurred aboveground, in violation of the 1963 test ban treaty, and even after the tests were moved underground, questions remained about the safety of setting off atomic blasts in coral atolls. In 1985, self-governing Oceanian countries signed a treaty that created a South Pacific Nuclear Free Zone, banning all testing and storage of nuclear weapons. Only in 1996, after performing another series of hotly protested blasts, did France (along with the United States and Britain) sign the SPNFZ treaty (Firth 1987; *Pacific Islands Monthly,* May 1996). Perhaps "nuclear colonialism" is finally coming to an end.

Unlike the United States and France, Britain chose to scale back its colonial empire after India gained independence in 1947. The British withdrawal "east of Suez" spurred decolonization in Australian and New Zealand territories as well. The UN played a more active role in this process after its 1960 resolution that non–self-governing peoples should be offered three choices: independence, free association, or incorporation—i.e., equal rights within the colonizing country, such as Hawai'i's statehood in 1959 (Roff 1991). In 1962, Western Samoa was the first country to regain its independence, with the provision that only *matai* be allowed to vote or run for office. Nauru won control of its phosphate industry and became independent in 1968, and by 1980, Tonga, Fiji, Papua New Guinea, Solomon Islands, Kiribati, Tuvalu, and Vanuatu also voted for independence. Vanuatu (formerly New Hebrides) owed its sovereignty to British support, since co-administrator France actively opposed independence to protect planter interests. These new states formed the Pacific Forum in the 1970s to pool their resources and gain more regional clout. In the 1980s, three western Pacific states formed the Melanesian Spearhead with a similar purpose (Thompson 1994).

Nation building has been a challenge for many of these states, since their boundaries and government structures are legacies of colonialism. In culturally diverse Melanesia, national elites brought up through the colonial educational and administrative systems have tried to enforce unity and develop their considerable mineral resources. But secession movements on Bougainville in Papua New Guinea (PNG), the western Solomons, and on Santo and Tanna in Vanuatu have tested such visions. Some Melanesian leaders have tried to build consensus around *kastom* (custom), "Melanesian socialism," or the "Melanesian Way," but these concepts have not replaced local loyalties. Even the wealth from mining is limited by demands from multinational companies to keep wages, taxes, and environmental protection to a minimum or else they will relocate. Urban centers like Port Moresby face growing crime problems from unemployed migrants, and the vote-of-no-confidence system borrowed from Britain makes it hard for a coalition government to last very long. Half of PNG's parliament is voted out in every election (Wanek 1996).

Fiji became independent in 1970, after negotiations between Fijian and Indian leaders. Indians had organized labor unions and long pushed for elected representation, but Fijian chiefs had relied on British protection. In 1959, chiefs had broken up a multiethnic strike by urging their commoners not to listen to "sweet-talking" Indians, and in 1963, when Fijian commoners received the right to vote for the first time, they supported their chiefs instead of Indian opponents of the power elite. At independence, each ethnic group was guaranteed twenty-two seats in the lower house of Parliament, and Fijian land and customary rights could only be changed with approval by six of the eight high chiefs in the upper house. For seventeen years, an alliance led by Ratu Sir Kamasese Mara held power with votes from Fijians, Muslim Indians (who feared the Hindu majority), and other minorities. In 1987, however, a coalition of Hindu Indians and western and urban Fijians outvoted Mara's alliance. The new government of Timoci Bavadra, a western Fijian, was soon overthrown in a military coup by Sitiveni Rabuka, who is now Fiji's prime minister. Thousands of Indians have emigrated, but the constitution has gone through two revisions, first very pro-Fijian and then more moderate (Lal 1992; Dawn of a new era 1998). That first coup was followed by two more in 2000 and 2006, but what emerged were increasing divisions among Fijians based on regions, chiefdoms, and social class. The 2006 coup, for example, was led by the Fijian army commander against a Fijian prime minister, so the danger is that military coups might replace electoral politics in what was a democracy before 1987.

In countries where native sovereignty movements cannot play the military card, activists wage uphill struggles against immigrant power. In Hawai'i, Guam, and New Zealand, the indigenous peoples are minorities in their own islands and face what some call "ethnocide," or cultural assimilation by the majority. Since the 1970s, activists have revived their languages and cultures and have had limited success at recovering land. The U.S. Navy stopped bombing practice on Kaho'olawe, and the U.S. Congress admitted complicity in the overthrow of the Hawaiian monarchy; it also returned some military land on Guam to the local government, but it rejected a Guam Commonwealth proposal. A Waitangi Tribunal is slowly redressing Maori grievances about land, water, and fishing rights. France abolished forced labor and granted French citizenship in its Pacific territories in 1946, but it also jailed nationalist leaders in Tahiti and New Caledonia during unrest in the late 1950s. Nuclear testing in French Polynesia and French immigration to New Caledonia during a nickel boom stirred new protests, but aid money from Paris (and the loyalty of European settlers in New Caledonia) has kept nationalists from gaining a democratic majority. The 1980s were violent in New Caledonia, but accords reached in 1988 and 1998 postponed votes on independence in return for a gradual devolution of powers to the territory (Robie 1989; Henningham 1992; Chappell 1998). New Caledonia and French Polynesia now have increasing autonomy, but tension remains in the former between loyalist French, Asian, and Polynesian immigrants and the slightly outnumbered but pro-independence indigenous Kanak, and in the latter between indigenous factions who support either autonomy or full independence. France continues to pour in financial aid to enhance its prestige, though nickel mining in New Caledonia is bringing new development to the Kanak-ruled northern province.

Five resource-poor Pacific Island countries have chosen to decolonize by voting for free association, which allows self-government but also continued economic (and military) ties to the colonizing power. In the North Pacific, the Marshall Islands, the Federated States of Micronesia, and Palau have all signed a Compact of Free Association with the United States. They are self-governing members of the UN and the Pacific Forum but receive millions of dollars in "strategic rent" from the United States, which retains military options. Palau at first had an antinuclear clause in its constitution, but after years of economic pressure from the United States, it removed that and approved the compact. Micronesians are not U.S. citizens (except in the Northern Marianas, which became a Commonwealth), but as "habitual residents" they can migrate freely to the United States. In the South Pacific, the Cook Islands and Niue opted for free association with New Zealand, which grants them self-government at home but also New Zealand citizenship and subsidies. Most people in those two states have now moved to New Zealand for better jobs and schooling. Three very small island groups, Tokelau, Pitcairn, and Easter Island, remain dependencies of New Zealand, Britain, and Chile, respectively (Roff 1991; Hayes 1991). Table 11.1 shows the current political status of Pacific Island groups.

Economics has thus compromised sovereignty in Oceania. Today at least 500,000 anglophone islanders have migrated to the United States, Australia, and New Zealand, and within the French circuit, more than half of Wallis and Futuna's population has moved to mineral-rich New Caledonia for jobs. This process has received an acronym, MIRAB, for migration, remittances (money and goods sent home to families), aid, and bureaucracy (government salaries are often paid by foreign aid grants) (Bertram and Watters 1985). Returnees who have lived abroad and received Western educations sometimes challenge traditional elites and push for democratic reforms, as in Samoa and Tonga (Campbell 1992). Some observers see MIRAB as neocolonial dependency, while others regard it as the continuation of an ancient voyaging dynamic (Hayes 1991; Hau'ofa 1994). Small island countries can also benefit from the United Nations Law of the Sea, which grants exclusive economic zones for two hundred miles around their shores. The Pacific Forum, for example, has negotiated a collective tuna fishing agreement with the United States. Saipan, Fiji, and American Samoa are developing garment industries for export, sometimes importing outside workers from Asia, while Kiribati still sends laborers to the Nauru mines or foreign ships. Tuvalu lives mainly off stamp sales and a trust fund, and Hawai'i relies almost entirely on tourism (Fairbairn et al. 1991). In the so-called "Pacific century," Oceania is generally pursuing a path of interdependence. The question remains: What form should "development" take? MIRAB at least empowers indigenous families and governments to choose, but outside aid donors often prescribe top-down planning based on Western economic models and free trade policies to attract investors. Another approach to avoiding domination by multinational corporations would be to

Table 11.1

Political Status of Pacific Island Groups

Colonial power	Integrated	Dependent	Free association	Independent
UK and France				Vanuatu (1980)
United Kingdom		Pitcairn		New Zealand (1907) Fiji (1970) Tonga (1970) Tuvalu (1978) Solomon Is. (1978) Kiribati (1979)
France		French Polynesia New Caledonia Wallis and Futuna		
New Zealand		Tokelau	Cook Is. (1965) Niue (1974)	
Australia				Nauru (1968) Papua New Guinea (1975)
United States	Hawaii (1959)	American Samoa Guam N. Marianas* (1978)	Marshall Is. (1986) FSM (1986) Palau (1994)	
Chile		Easter Island		

* Commonwealth

ask the local people what kinds of change would respect their traditional values and protect their environments (Gegeo 1998; Hanlon 1998; Hviding 1996).

The Past as Prologue

The past five hundred years in the Pacific Islands have witnessed accelerating change. During the first half of that period, the impact of Euroamericans was minimal, except on Guam, which Spain colonized brutally. By the late 1700s, local chiefs began to exploit growing contacts with foreign explorers and traders to enhance their own status. In the mid-1800s, however, such interaction began to favor outside powers, who had industrialized, until by 1900 sovereignty itself was lost.

Imperialism has been studied from various angles, ranging from the industrialized "cores" of a global system to resistance and negotiation by indigenous peoples in the "periphery" (Doyle 1986). Despite the superficial transformations on political maps, colonialism in the Pacific Islands varied greatly from place to place. In the Marianas, Hawai'i, New Zealand, and New Caledonia, native people were marginalized and dispossessed of most of their lands, but in Fiji, Tonga, and Samoa, traditions survived more or less intact, as did their landownership systems. Nicholas Thomas has argued that colonialism was not really monolithic and should be studied as a series of projects undertaken by many actors, including missionaries, traders, planters, administrators, and anthropologists, who sometimes disagreed with each other. This plurality, when combined with the diversity of native societies and also differing strategic and economic values of the islands to outsiders, makes it difficult to assess the impact of foreign rule in a general way (Thomas 1994).

Recent studies of "subaltern" (colonized) peoples suggest that their quest for full independence is limited by subtle cultural, social, and economic changes that complicate their visions of the past and future (Prakash 1994). Hence the preference by many Pacific Islanders for integration into the former colonizing country as a commonwealth, state, or territory, or for the negotiated, relative autonomy of "free association," in order to end the inequality of colonial status without losing access to development aid. Postcoloniality is thus an elusive concept, even in supposedly sovereign countries. Robert Jackson has called many former colonies quasi-states, because their structures and borders are artificial colonial creations that exist mainly in international law and hence need ongoing subsidies and policing from abroad (Jackson 1990). The rebellion of Bougainville and frequent changes of government leadership in PNG have led some observers to call it a neocolonial state whose national elite is really replicating expatriate rule over diverse local "nations" (Wanek 1996).

Some outside security analysts have warned of an emerging "arc of instability" in the ethnically diverse countries of Melanesia. They invoke fears of possible "failed states" and potential havens for terrorism, pointing to the armed secession movements in Vanuatu and PNG, the recurring coups in Fiji, and also the civil war in Solomon Islands between Guadalcanal and Malaitan migrants in the early twenty-first century. Regional peacekeeping forces have intervened in both Bougainville and the Solomons, and even once-prosperous Nauru has faced bankruptcy as its phosphate mines run dry. Meanwhile, in Tonga and Samoa, challenges to chiefly leaders by urbanized or well-traveled indigenous critics have led to debates over who benefits from "traditionalism" (Lawson 1996). Epeli Hau'ofa of Tonga has accused Western-educated chiefs of manipulating traditions in a two-faced way to keep power for themselves while they actually adopt untraditional lifestyles (Hau'ofa 1987). But Europe itself went through centuries of trauma to create modern states, so why should the new states of Oceania be exempt from such challenging growing pains? Instead of blaming Pacific customs for these problems, more attention could be paid to the changes caused by colonialism and development projects that disrupt local traditions (Chappell 2005).

Modernity is a concept based on the assumption that constant change leads to progress, but every society has to struggle to decide what degree or kind or pace of change is best, so that it keeps its own identity. In September 2007 the UN finally passed a Declaration of the Rights of Indigenous Peoples to control their own resources and to self-determination, though pressures and temptations from the outside continue to test indigenous identities. Sovereign Nauru is so "hooked" on imports that the people are developing diabetes from eating too much junk food, while subaltern Maoris, Hawaiians, and Chamorros are relearning their own languages in schools to resist total assimilation. Global warming threatens the very existence of atoll populations, and irresponsible logging and mining projects damage the environments of large islands. Local councils and indigenous protest movements, however, have mobilized to make their voices heard with some success, as in the case of Kanak appeals to the European Union against mining pollution. Regional cooperation in the Pacific Forum or Melanesian Spearhead offers hope for small island states to band together in a competitive world arena, while out-migration is developing transnational networks through which Oceanians can explore new frontiers of opportunity and change. The quest for truly self-sustaining nation-states may be illusory, since even the United States is the largest debtor country on the planet right now, yet there remains considerable dynamism in Pacific societies, even if outsiders fail to recognize grassroots initiatives.

In fact, outsiders never have understood Oceania very well, from Magellan's violent encounter with Guam, to the myth of South Seas "paradise" invented by Tahitians (and perpetuated by modern tourism), to the ways that Oceanians "indigenized" Christianity and corned beef, to today's experiments in free association and migratory transnationalism. Cultures are never static. Despite all the tragic loss of life from alien diseases, colonial conquest, world wars, and nuclear testing, and other traumas such as foreign immigration, racial discrimination, and exploitative capitalism, Pacific Islanders are survivors. That is how they became Oceanians in the first place.

As Hau'ofa (1994) puts it,

> Oceania is vast, Oceania is expanding, Oceania is hospitable and generous, Oceania is humanity rising from the depths of brine and regions of fire deeper still. . . . We must not allow anyone to belittle us again, and take away our freedom.

BIBLIOGRAPHY

Bertram, I. G., and R. F. Watters. 1985. The Mirab economy in South Pacific microstates. *Pacific Viewpoint* 26(3): 497–519.

Campbell, I. C. 1992. *Island kingdom: Tonga, ancient and modern.* Christchurch: University of Canterbury Press.

Chappell, D. 1998. Finally, Wallisians get recognition. *Islands Business* 24: 9, 22–23.

——. 2000. The forgotten Mau: Anti-navy protest in American Samoa, 1920–1935. *Pacific Historical Review* 69(2): 217–260.

——. 2005. "Africanization" in the Pacific: Blaming others for disorder in the periphery? *Comparative Studies in Society and History* 47: 286–317.

Dawn of a new era. 1998. *Islands Business* 24: 9, 23.

Dening, G. 1980. *Islands and beaches.* Melbourne: Melbourne University Press.

Doyle, M. 1986. *Empires.* Ithaca, N.Y.: Cornell University Press.

Fairbairn, T. C., Morrison, R. Baker, and S. Groves. 1991. *The Pacific Islands: Politics, economics and international relations.* Honolulu: University of Hawai'i Press.

Firth, S. 1987. *Nuclear playground.* Honolulu: University of Hawai'i Press.

Gammage, B. 1975. The Rabaul strike 1929. *Journal of Pacific History* 10(3): 3–29.

Gegeo, D. 1998. Indigenous knowledge and empowerment: Rural development examined from within. *The Contemporary Pacific* 10(2): 289–315.

Hanlon, D. 1998. *Remaking Micronesia: Discourses over development in a Pacific territory, 1944–1982.* Honolulu: University of Hawai'i Press.

Hau'ofa, E. 1987. The new South Pacific society: Integration and independence. In *Class and culture in the South Pacific,* ed. A. Hooper, S. Britton, R. Crocombe, J. Huntsman, and C. Macpherson, 1–12. Suva: University of the South Pacific.

——. 1994. Our sea of islands. *The Contemporary Pacific* 6(1): 148–161.

Hayes, G. 1991. Migration, metascience, and development policy in Island Polynesia. *The Contemporary Pacific* 3(1): 1–58.

Hempenstall, P., and N. Rutherford. 1984. *Protest and dissent in the colonial Pacific.* Suva: University of the South Pacific.

Henningham, S. 1992. *France and the South Pacific.* Honolulu: University of Hawai'i Press.

Hezel, F. 1983. *The first taint of civilization: A history of the Caroline and Marshall Islands in precolonial days, 1521–1885.* Honolulu: University of Hawai'i Press.

——. 1995. *Strangers in their own land: A century of colonial rule in the Caroline and Marshall Islands.* Honolulu: University of Hawai'i Press.

Howard, M., and S. Durutalo. 1987. *The political economy of the Pacific Islands to 1945.* Townsville, Qld.: James Cook University Press.

Howarth, D. 1985. *Tahiti: A paradise lost.* New York: Penguin.

Howe, K. R. 1984. *Where the waves fall: A new South Sea Islands history from first settlement to colonial rule.* Honolulu: University of Hawai'i Press.

Howe, K. R., R. Kiste, and B. Lal. 1994. *Tides of history: The Pacific Islands in the twentieth century.* Honolulu: University of Hawai'i Press.

Hviding, E. 1996. *Guardians of Marovo Lagoon: Practice, place, and politics in maritime Melanesia.* Honolulu: University of Hawai'i Press.

Jackson, R. 1990. *Quasi-states: Sovereignty, international relations and the Third World.* New York: Cambridge University Press.

Keesing, R. 1992. *Custom and confrontation: The Kwaio struggle for cultural autonomy.* Chicago: University of Chicago Press.

Lal, B. 1992. *Broken waves: A history of the Fiji Islands in the twentieth century.* Honolulu: University of Hawai'i Press.

Lawson, S. 1996. *Tradition versus democracy in the South Pacific: Fiji, Tonga and Western Samoa.* New York: Cambridge University Press.

Maude, H. E. 1968. *Of islands and men.* Melbourne: Oxford University Press.

——. 1981. *Slavers in paradise.* Canberra: Australian National University Press.

Meleisea, M. 1987. *The making of modern Samoa.* Suva: University of the South Pacific.

Moorehead, A. 1966. *The fatal impact: An account of the invasion of the South Pacific, 1767–1840.* New York: Dell.

Newbury, C. 1980. *Tahiti nui: Change and survival in French Polynesia.* Honolulu: University of Hawai'i Press.

Pacific Islands Monthly.

Paige, P. S., ed. 1969. *The voyage of Magellan: The journal of Antonio Pigafetta.* Englewood Cliffs, N.J.: Prentice-Hall.

Prakash, G. 1994. Subaltern studies as postcolonial criticism. *American Historical Review* 99(5): 1475–1490.

Robie, D. 1989. *Blood on their banner: Nationalist struggles in the South Pacific.* London: Zed Books.

Rodman, M., and M. Cooper, eds. 1983. *The pacification of Melanesia.* New York: University Press of America.

Roff, S. 1991. *Overreaching in paradise: United States policy in Palau since 1945.* Juneau, Alaska: Denali Press.

Rogers, R. 1995. *Destiny's landfall: A history of Guam.* Honolulu: University of Hawai'i Press.

Sahlins, M. 1981. *Historical metaphors and mythical realities.* Ann Arbor: University of Michigan Press.

———. 1985. *Islands of history.* Chicago: University of Chicago Press.

Scarr, D. 1990. *The history of the Pacific Islands.* Melbourne: Macmillan.

Thomas, N. 1994. *Colonialism's culture.* Princeton, N.J.: Princeton University Press.

Thompson, R. 1994. *The Pacific Basin since 1945.* New York: Longmans.

Trask, H. K. 1993. *From a native daughter: Colonialism and sovereignty in Hawai'i.* Monroe, Maine: Common Courage Press.

Walker, R. 1990. *Ka whawhai tonu matou: Struggle without end.* Auckland: Penguin.

Wanek, A. 1996. *The state and its enemies in Papua New Guinea.* Richmond, UK: Curzon.

White, G., and L. Lindstrom, eds. 1989. *The Pacific theater: Island representations of World War II.* Honolulu: University of Hawai'i Press.

Wolfers, E. 1975. *Race relations and colonial rule in Papua New Guinea.* Sydney: University of Sydney Press.

Worsley, P. 1968. *The trumpet shall sound: A study of cargo cults in Melanesia.* New York: Schocken.

Changing Patterns of Power

Terence Wesley-Smith

12

The Leaders believe the Pacific can, should and will be a region of peace, harmony, security and economic prosperity, so that all its people can lead free and worthwhile lives.

—Auckland Declaration, April 6, 2004

Some commentators had already condemned the region to a dismal future when Pacific Island leaders crafted their optimistic prologue to the Pacific Plan for Strengthening Regional Cooperation and Integration in mid-2004. Citing tense civil-military relations in some island states, ethnic conflicts associated with natural resource exploitation, as well as ongoing issues of poor governance and corruption, Australian political scientist Ben Reilly suggested that the region was experiencing a process of "Africanisation":

> Taken together, these factors indicate a growing weakness of democracy and an increasing likelihood of further troubles in the region in the future. In particular, they indicate that some of the problems that have plagued states in sub-Saharan Africa may well be emerging in the South Pacific as well, creating enormous challenges both for the island states themselves and for regional powers such as Australia and New Zealand which aspire to influence regional developments (Reilly 2000: 263).

Few would deny that some Pacific Island countries face significant political challenges. Fiji has experienced four coups since 1987, the latest a military takeover in December 2006. Port Moresby–based professor of politics Allan Patience describes Papua New Guinea in terms of dysfunctional political institutions, collapsed essential services, gratuitous human rights violations, and "thousands of people suffering needlessly and dying prematurely" (Patience 2005: 1–2). By early 2003, after twenty-five years of independence, state institutions in Solomon Islands had effectively collapsed, and today the country remains under the control of the Australian-led Regional Assistance Mission to the Solomon Islands (RAMSI). Even usually stable Tonga experienced riots in late 2006 that left a good portion of urban Nuku'alofa in ruins.

Yet Reilly's analysis downplays the region's considerable diversity, focuses only on negative developments, and does not do justice to the complexities of either the Pacific or the African experience (Chappell 2005; Fraenkel 2004). At best, such accounts take too much for granted about island societies and the international politics of development. At worst, they are alarmist and feed into a history of Pacific doomsaying dating back to a series of influential publications in the early 1990s. A widely-discussed 1993 volume edited by Rodney Cole, for example, warned that a combination of slow economic growth, rapidly rising population, and shortsighted policy in the region could lead to catastrophe within a generation (Cole 1993). More recently, there has been talk of a Pacific "arc of instability," usually imagined to include West Papua, Papua New Guinea, Solomon Islands, and Fiji, as well as a new focus on "failed" and "failing" states in the region (see, for example, Wainwright 2003; Windybank 2003; Ayson 2007).

Such analyses matter because they are often motivated by and imbedded in the policy considerations that drive external interests in the region. As Greg Fry (1997) notes, doomsday accounts are usually accompanied by prescriptive messages promoting particular types of social, economic, and political change. This was certainly the case with Cole's *Pacific 2010*, which advocated market-friendly economic restructuring as a remedy for the perceived ills of the region. Reilly limits himself to a concluding call for "a major process of democratic renewal" in the islands. But the focus on growing regional instability speaks directly to the dominant concern of policy makers in the external states most active in the region, especially Australia, and his emphasis on democratic institutions supports an important dimension of their preferred solution. Not only do these explanatory paradigms inform policy toward the region, but they are linked directly to the continuation of diplomatic, financial, and technical support to aid-dependent island states. As Fry put it, a seemingly objective framework of ideas about the nature, dynamics, and desirability of social change such as those deployed by Reilly or Cole "has the potential to significantly affect the parameters within which future possibilities are worked out" (Fry 1997: 27).

As the doomsayers suggest, poor governance, corruption, and economic mismanagement may indeed contribute to the region's current woes, and attention to these issues is certainly warranted if regional leaders are to achieve a peaceful, secure, and prosperous future. Yet in order to fully understand the challenges facing Pacific Island nations today we first need to be aware of the fundamental forces structuring change in the region. For many generations island societies have been profoundly influenced by the ideas, values, and interests that animate the wider systems of politics and economics in which they now operate. We need to understand how the historical interaction of external and internal forces effectively created the taken-for-granted bounded political entities of today and produced the basic institutions of state governance now characterized as "failed" or "failing."

Pre-European Patterns of Power

We know much about the spatial and chronological dimensions of the human settlement of the Pacific Islands, but relatively little about the social and political characteristics of the early settlers (Kirch 2000). We assume that the earliest arrivals, who entered the Australia–New Guinea region from Southeast Asia at least fifty thousand years ago, were loosely organized, impermanent, and relatively unstratified bands of hunters and gatherers. It is unclear what structural changes, if any, occurred as these Papuan-speaking populations expanded over the main landmasses and occupied adjacent islands as far east as Solomon Islands over the next twenty thousand years or so. Since everybody had more-or-less equal access to the material necessities of life, there would have been few economic levers of control available to ambitious individuals. Power relations probably revolved around age and gender differences.

The potential for using economic means to exercise power would have expanded with the independent development of agriculture in one or more parts of the western Pacific some nine thousand years ago, and its spread and intensification over subsequent millennia. The ethnographic record for New Guinea and adjacent islands suggests a useful distinction between political systems in which men's power was based on their control of wealth and those in which it rested on the control of knowledge or ideas (Harrison 1993). Maurice Godelier, for example, proposed that the term "big man," first generalized for all of Melanesia by Marshall Sahlins in an influential article (Sahlins 1963), be reserved for those societies, mainly in Highland New Guinea, where wealth exchanges had become essential to social reproduction. He argued that other societies, where the available "points of power" were limited to ritualized activities, particularly male initiation, were better described as "great man" societies (Godelier 1991). Godelier's classificatory scheme implies some sort of evolutionary link between the two systems. There is little direct evidence, however, that big-man societies actually emerged over time from great-man societies, and even if they did the factors that might have propelled such a transition remain obscure. It was clearly not a universal process, since many different patterns of leadership and degrees of stratification were apparent among the thousands of Papuan-speaking societies by the time Europeans arrived. It is worth noting, however, the absence from these societies of concepts of genealogically based rankings of persons or descent groups.

The evolution of big-man societies is believed to have been fueled, or at least accelerated, by the "Ipomoean Revolution" (Golson and Gardner 1990). The introduction of the sweet potato permitted the accumulation of significant food surpluses, which could then be converted into pigs, making escalating exchanges more feasible.

Differences among Papuan-speaking groups were almost certainly less significant than differences between these groups and a second wave of migrants from Southeast Asia that arrived in coastal New Guinea and adjacent islands some 4,500 years ago. It seems likely that these early Austronesian-speaking groups brought an ideology of ascribed hierarchy with them, or at least developed it in the process of expansion. Certainly there is strong evidence of stratification among the Austronesian-speaking groups that began to expand rapidly from the Bismarck Archipelago, through Island Melanesia, and on into the uninhabited reaches of Western Polynesia about 3,500 years ago. According to Patrick Kirch (1984), these groups were rank-organized, with seniority based upon genealogical distance from a founding ancestor, and ruled by hereditary chiefs. These groups were, of course, the ancestors of the present-day Polynesians and of most Micronesian populations.

The degree to which such principles were elaborated and emphasized over time in particular Austronesian societies appears to be a product of a whole range of local environmental, social, and economic factors. Some societies in Polynesia, such as Pukapuka in the Cook Islands, remained relatively egalitarian, while others, such as Hawai'i, Tonga, and the Society Islands, developed elaborate, hierarchical, and centralized political systems. Still others, like Easter Island, may have been highly stratified at some point in their histories, but had returned to less elaborate forms of organization by the time Europeans arrived. In Micronesia, the highest degree of stratification occurred on Pohnpei and Yap in the Caroline Islands, with the Southern Gilbert Islands and Nauru among those places that had relatively egalitarian social and political structures when Europeans arrived. The general argument here is that Austronesian and non-Austronesian societies followed fundamentally different trajectories of political development in Oceania, with Austronesian societies producing many variations on the theme of genealogically based rank. Non-Austronesian societies were no less varied, but structures of power had more to do with individual control of strategic resources than with heredity.

The major problem with this conceptual scheme is, of course, that by no means all Austronesian-speaking groups in the southwestern part of the region had hereditary forms of leadership when Europeans arrived. Some analysts have argued that these Austronesian-speaking big-man or great-man societies had somehow "devolved" over time from earlier hierarchical forms. However, the situation can also be explained in terms of historical interaction between Austronesian interlopers and resident Papuan populations. Peter Bellwood, for example, suspects that a great part of the postulated deconstitution of chieftainship may instead be the result of the "strong influence and even cultural takeover by Papuan speakers of Austronesian social networks" (Bellwood 1990). In this process of "Papuanization," numerically superior resident groups might have adopted the language of the visitors in order to join their productive regional networks or colonizing expeditions. Both forms of leadership may have coexisted for a while, with the Papuan model eventually becoming dominant.

The Colonial State

Indigenous trajectories of political change were rudely interrupted by the arrival of Europeans into the region and the eventual establishment of colonial rule over all Pacific Island societies. Colonialism was everywhere a powerful force, but it was by no means a monolithic one. Its impact on a particular population depended upon a variety of factors, not least the length of the colonial experience. Spain established colonial rule in Guam and the rest of the Marianas as early as 1668, but most Pacific islands were not formally incorporated into foreign empires until the second half of the nineteenth century. Some Pacific populations, most notably in the Highlands of New Guinea, did not come under external government control until the second half of the twentieth century. One island group, Tonga, felt the pressure of external interests but managed to avoid direct colonial rule altogether. A significant number of Pacific Island places experienced a succession of at least two different colonial masters over the years, most notably as a result of the defeat of Germany in World War I and of Japan in World War II and the subsequent loss of their respective territories to other powers.

The process of political change precipitated by colonial rule took many different forms and can only be fully understood on a case-by-case basis. But for all Pacific places, colonization ultimately meant the establishment of that most fundamental unit of Western political organization, the state, a formal hierarchy of legislative, administrative, and judicial institutions designed to create and maintain order among a population occupying a particular territory defined by geographical boundaries.

The closest indigenous approximations to the Western state were the elaborate and stratified chiefdoms in the Austronesian-speaking societies of Polynesia and Micronesia. In Hawai'i, for example, Europeans found complex, hierarchical decision-making structures involving members of the chiefly class (ali'i), their stewards (konohiki), and a "considerable body of councilors, priests, executants, and other retainers who formed a 'court' of the paramount chief" (Kirch 1984). The boundaries of these polities expanded and contracted over time, but often incorporated whole islands. The political system in Tonga was even more elaborate, with dual paramount chiefs of the Tui Tonga and hau lines controlling the entire Tongan archipelago and beyond, ultimately extending their influence to Samoa and Eastern Fiji (Kirch 1984).

It is tempting to categorize these entities as pre- or protostates, suggesting that, given time, they would have evolved or developed into European-style states. The historical circumstances surrounding the evolution of states in Europe, however, were quite specific, especially in their economic dimensions, and there is no reason to believe that Pacific entities would have followed that particular trajectory rather than an almost infinite number of others. What we do know is that in the nineteenth century, chiefs in Hawai'i, Tahiti, and Tonga used their connections with European interlopers to expand these structures into full-blown states "complete with public governments and public law, monarchs and taxes, ministers and minions" (Sahlins 1963).

In some ways the more centralized, unified, and stratified Pacific polities were better placed to resist the colonial advance, but only the Tongan state survived for any length of time, and chiefly structures were more typically used to further colonial ends. Britain, for example, ruled Fiji by attaching itself to the top of a hierarchical network of chiefly power, and Spain, Germany, and Japan all attempted to use chiefly structures to govern their possessions in Micronesia. In other cases, the colonial power bypassed, and

eventually undermined, the chiefly establishment, as occurred in French Polynesia after the collapse of the Pomare dynasty, and in Hawai'i after the overthrow of the monarchy in 1893, as well as in the Cook Islands and northern and central parts of the Gilbert Islands.

Pacific Island places with smaller-scale, less permanent, and more diffuse big-man or great-man political systems were more difficult for colonial powers to govern effectively, as they provided more opportunities for the persistence of indigenous political institutions and practices. With no suitable pre-existing political structures to work through, colonial authorities in New Guinea, Solomon Islands, and New Hebrides (later Vanuatu) were forced to construct entirely new administrative units and institutions and create a new class of native officials to occupy their lower levels. Even by the end of the colonial era, state structures in these places tended to be rudimentary, fragmented, and inefficient.

European colonization forged political boundaries that were significantly different from pre-existing ones. In the vast majority of cases, colonial boundaries created much larger political units than before, bringing often disparate communities together for the first time. The colonial boundaries of French Polynesia, for example, joined five different archipelagoes whose inhabitants had few traditional cultural or political links, and each colonial entity in Melanesia encompassed literally hundreds of previously autonomous groups. While traditional political boundaries were often fluid and sometimes relatively open, colonial boundaries were usually clearly defined, permanent, and impermeable. The division of the Pacific Islands into colonial entities sent neighboring groups off on quite different trajectories of change.

The nature and extent of Western-style government structures established in a territory usually reflected the perceived interests of the colonial power. In extreme cases, such as Dutch New Guinea and British (later Australian) Papua before World War II, where the only significant interest was strategic control, a token government presence was sufficient. Subject populations living away from easily accessible coastal areas were often left largely to their own devices between the infrequent visits of government patrols. On the other hand, in settler colonies like New Zealand, Hawai'i, and New Caledonia, or resource-rich places like Nauru, indigenous populations were confronted with much more extensive, comprehensive, and intrusive government structures.

In most Pacific places before World War II, colonial government was largely about controlling native populations and regulating their activities to facilitate colonial interests. It involved varying degrees of violence, domination, exploitation, and racism (Hanlon 1994). Colonial policies were often justified as serving native interests as well, as part of some wider civilizing mission. Such ideas were, no doubt, sincerely held by principled colonial officials, but they rested squarely on European notions of racial and cultural superiority, progress, and manifest destiny. Some colonial officials, like Lt. Gov. Hubert Murray in Papua or Sir Arthur Gordon in Fiji, even placed native interests above foreign ones at times. But their ability to decide what was best for the native population, and which aspects of native life should and would be protected, reveals much about the essential nature of the colonial system (West 1968; Lal 1992).

Colonization took political power away from local Pacific Islands communities and put it in the hands of resident colonial officials and, ultimately, in the hands of decision makers in remote capitals in Europe, the United States, Australia, and New Zealand. The instrument of imperial control was the colonial state, which defined new, enduring territorial configurations and installed alien administrative mechanisms. The extent to which the lives of particular Pacific populations were affected by developments depended largely on which colonial jurisdiction they found themselves in and on the interests and policies of the administering power at the time. The persistence of indigenous political forms and structures may, in some cases, have resulted from local resistance or intrinsic qualities of those institutions, or both. But more often they endured because they were allowed or even encouraged to do so by the colonial power in furtherance of its own interests.

Power Returned, Power Retained

Europe's mighty global empires disintegrated in the second half of the twentieth century under nationalist pressures in the colonies that proved increasingly difficult to contain. The political face of the Pacific has been transformed over the past fifty years as well. Starting with Western Samoa (now Samoa) in 1962, nine island entities have achieved full independence, and most Pacific Islanders now live in independent states.[1] More than half of all island territories, however, have not acquired this status and retain constitutional or other significant links to the colonial power. The key question regarding which island colonies would become independent and which would remain dependent was not determined by the physical or economic characteristics of the colony or even the expressed desire of the people, although these factors were important in some cases. Instead, the critical variable was the interests of the colonial power.

Stewart Firth argued that "the greater the strategic value of a territory, the less likely that territory has been to proceed to sovereign status" (Firth 1989). This argument works well for the Pacific territories governed by the United States. According to Robert Kiste, from the beginning "American involvement in the Pacific Islands has predominantly been motivated by strategic and security concerns" (Kiste 1994). These considerations were certainly important in determining the political status of Hawai'i, the Northern Marianas, and (arguably) Guam, all of which became permanently integrated into the United States political system.[2] The Federated States of Micronesia, the Marshall Islands, and Palau are now self-governing nations, but their compacts of free association with the United States effectively trade control of military and security matters in return for massive financial subsidies from Washington and free movement to the United States.[3]

Nor has independence ever appeared to be a real option for those Pacific Islanders colonized by France, which remains determined to maintain a global presence (Aldrich 1989). In 1954 France unilaterally removed New Caledonia, French Polynesia, and Wallis and Futuna from the United Nations' list of non–self-governing territories on the grounds that they "enjoyed self-government within the French Republic" (Maclellan and Boengkih 1996). Since that time, France has consistently maintained that its Pacific territories are not colonies but integral parts of the French state. It has, however, been prepared to endorse new statuses for its dependencies from time to time. Perhaps the most dramatic shift came with the Matignon Accords, negotiated in the face of escalating political violence in New Caledonia in 1988. The agreement between representatives of the generally pro-independence Kanaks, the French state, and mainly non-Kanak residents intent on maintaining ties to France, provided for a referendum on independence to be held a decade later. In 1998, however, the parties instead signed the Noumea Accords, which accelerated the devolution of state power to the Noumea government and postponed the referendum on independence for at least a further fifteen years. Enhanced autonomy, coupled with massive injections of resources targeted at Kanak communities, appear to have taken the edge off demand for full independence. Meanwhile, French Polynesia has also achieved a significant degree of local political control since 1984 through a series of autonomy initiatives. Although recognized in 2006 as an associate member of the Pacific Islands Forum, a regional organization that limits participation to entities with a substantial degree of independence, French Polynesia (or Tahiti Nui) remains firmly under French sovereignty and heavily dependent on Paris for its economic needs.

On the other hand, independence was the only option presented to other Pacific Islanders. This was the case for residents in colonies of Great Britain, whose reduced capacity to maintain global interests dictated a deliberate policy of withdrawal from the region. Fiji, Solomon Islands, and the Gilbert and Ellice Islands Colony (which split into two independent entities, Kiribati and Tuvalu), were all granted full independence in the 1970s, with the New Hebrides (Vanuatu) eventually following suit in 1980, despite resistance from France, Britain's partner in the condominium government. This was a staged withdrawal, with local leaders exerting significant influence on events, especially in the final stages (Macdonald 1994). Nevertheless, for these people, as for the peoples of the American and French territories, the decolonization process was largely controlled by the colonial power and ultimately reflected its interests.

New Zealand was keen to withdraw from its island dependencies as well. The few economic and strategic benefits yielded by direct control of Western Samoa, the Cook Islands, Niue, and Tokelau were more than offset by the diplomatic costs of defying growing anticolonial sentiment in the international community. Its decolonization policy was shaped soon after the end of the Pacific War in response to nationalist demands in Western Samoa, when it was decided to prepare the territory for independence as soon as possible. The possibility of integration with New Zealand was effectively ruled out for the Cook Islands, and later for Niue and Tokelau, on constitutional grounds, even though this might well have been the preferred option for these Pacific Islanders. Eager to maintain their connections with and access to New Zealand, Cook Islanders (1965) and Niueans (1974) agreed to accept Wellington's preferred option, self-government in free association with New Zealand. These entities retain the option of withdrawing from the agreement at any time in favor of full independence (Wesley-Smith 1994). Despite concerted attempts by officials from New Zealand and the United Nations, Tokelau has so far refused to adopt a new "decolonized" status. UN-sponsored referenda in February 2006 and October 2007 narrowly failed to yield the two-thirds majority needed to approve free association status (Huntsman and Kalolo 2007).

Unlike New Zealand, Australia was in no hurry to decolonize its Pacific territories, where it had real interests at stake. But its best efforts to retain control of Nauru's lucrative phosphate resources were ultimately defeated by a combination of factors, including astute local leadership, pressure from the United Nations, and the disunity of Australia's partners in the trusteeship agreement, New Zealand and Great Britain. Australia recognized that the strategically important territories of Papua and New Guinea, which it administered together after World War II, would eventually achieve self-government, but it envisaged a long period of preparation. Mounting pressure from the United Nations in the 1960s, however, persuaded Australia to adopt an accelerated program of decolonization that resulted in independence in 1975. The option of integration into the Australian federation as a state, which would have addressed Australia's strategic concerns directly, was considered but quickly abandoned on the grounds that the overwhelmingly white Australian public would never accept large numbers of Melanesians in their midst.

The global decolonization movement liberated many Pacific Islanders from direct colonial rule, but left others dependent and dissatisfied. Dissidents in West Papua (earlier known as Irian Jaya), for example, a Dutch colony inhabited by more than a million Melanesians incorporated into Indonesia in 1962, continue to wage a sporadic guerrilla war against Indonesian sovereignty under the banner of the Organisasi Papua Merdeka (OPM), or Free Papua Movement (see, e.g., Elmslie 2002). In New Caledonia, the Front Liberation Nationale Kanak et Socialiste (FLNKS), although not as powerful as it once was, still spearheads the Kanak struggle for independence against the opposition of settlers, who represent a majority in the territory, as well as the French state. Meanwhile, indigenous minorities in other settler colonies, most notably New Zealand and Hawai'i, are also demanding redress of historical grievances and the right to sovereignty and self-determination.

Making States and Nations

It was perhaps inevitable that where political power was returned to Pacific Islanders it was returned in the form of a European-style nation-state. This was, after all, the fundamental unit in the existing global political system, from which all international status, legitimacy, and protection from external aggression would be derived. The process of decolonization itself was orchestrated in important ways by the United Nations, an international institution committed by its charter to preserving the notion of state sovereignty. Furthermore, the new leaders generally saw this as the appropriate instrument to achieve their goals. It is important to remember that what they had in mind was radical transformation of societies that in most cases had already been profoundly altered by the forces of capitalism and colonialism—a process that soon came to be known as "development." The "humpty-dumpty" of indigenous political and economic forms had long since fallen off the wall, and the challenge was to put the pieces together again in what were seen as new and progressive ways (Migdal 1988; Kelly and Kaplan 2001).

Nevertheless, it is difficult to overemphasize the significance of this turn of events. Putting the basic elements of the nation-state together in the Pacific and elsewhere in the developing world has been difficult, to say the least. Theorists usually distinguish between the state, an administrative-legal structure with sovereignty over citizens within a bounded territory, and the nation, a group of people who feel as if they belong together by virtue of some perceived shared cultural characteristics or common heritage. Ideally the boundaries of the two will coincide, and the process of political development in the developing world is often referred to as "nation building." This is misleading because usually both nation and state have to be created, and assembling viable state structures is almost always the first order of business. It is also misleading because this bland architectural metaphor masks the contested and often violent nature of the process.

In the previously colonized world, the perceived benefits of statehood may well be outweighed by the costs. These costs may be economic, for as Christopher Clapham points out, "states, with their extensive hierarchies and permanent employees are expensive to maintain" and the necessary resources have to be extracted from citizens in the form of taxes (Clapham 2003: 28). Or they might be social, as the state meets resistance from clan or tribal collectivities grounded in subsistence-based economies and animated by quite different cultural and political values. Historically, the process of state making, of accumulation of power in the hands of a central administrative apparatus, has almost always involved coercion and collective violence. This was certainly the case with the "organized crime" of state formation in Western Europe, which Charles Tilly notes "cost tremendously in death, suffering, loss of rights, and unwilling surrender of land, goods and labor" (Tilly 1985: 169–191).

Nor is it surprising that a strong sense of nationhood has been difficult to achieve in many parts of Oceania (see, e.g., Foster 1995; Otto and Thomas 1997). This is particularly the case in places like Papua New Guinea, Solomon Islands, and Vanuatu, where extreme cultural and linguistic fragmentation defies the creation of common identities, and in territories that have attracted significant numbers of permanent settlers from Europe or Asia. It is not easy to foster a sense of solidarity and common purpose between indigenous Fijians and the descendants of migrant workers from India, who until the 1980s constituted a majority of the population, especially considering the persistence of stark communal hierarchies established during a century of British rule. Nor is it easy to persuade fragmented Kanak tribal groups that they share a national identity with each other, let alone the settlers of European, Asian, and Polynesian origin who have been numerically and economically dominant in New Caledonia for many decades. But even in culturally homogenous places like Samoa, political life has long been focused at the local level, and the assertion of centralized state power alongside appeals to national identity are still regarded with suspicion.

Despite the imposed nature of the nation-making project, and the colonial nature of the territorial spaces in which it operates, there is no doubting the contemporary relevance of the nation-state in Oceania. It is a model to be emulated, resisted, or rejected, but rarely ignored (Foster 2002: 11).

State Success and State Stress

Given these inauspicious circumstances, the state-making project in Oceania has been remarkably successful. Most of the region's island entities have remained politically stable over the past five decades.

Not only has conflict been the exception rather than the rule, but where upheavals have occurred they have usually been short-lived. Even if recent crises in Papua New Guinea and Solomon Islands have proved more costly in human and material terms, they pale in comparison to the conflicts that characterize many other parts of the previously colonized world.

Perhaps the most important factor impacting the success or failure of state-building efforts in Oceania is the existing basis for statehood. In general, those places with hierarchical traditional political systems, culturally homogenous populations, and a colonial history that has supported such institutions, have weathered the traumas of state building better than places lacking such attributes. In Samoa, for example, successive colonial powers (Germany and New Zealand) worked through and thereby helped reinforce at least certain aspects of traditional political structures. Samoan nationalism was, in turn, forged in opposition to New Zealand's administration of the islands (Meleisea 1987, 1988). The Kingdom of Tonga also has a long history of grafting modern political institutions onto quasi-traditional ones. Here the essential ingredients of statehood had been in place since the nineteenth century, and when Tonga terminated its protectorate arrangement with Britain in 1970, a strong sense of Tongan national identity was already well established.

Both Samoa and Tonga have had to struggle with thorny political issues in recent decades, but these have involved the nature and operation of state institutions rather than the fundamentals of nation-statehood. In Samoa, the tension between centralized state institutions established at independence and local centers of power based on traditional chiefly *matai* titles was softened somewhat by limiting suffrage and parliamentary participation to holders of *matai* titles. Although the shift to universal suffrage in 1990, coupled with the recent proliferation of *matai* titles, represents a significant shift toward a more "modern," democratic form of politics, it has by no means resolved central-local tensions (Le Tagaloa 1992; Leiataua and Alailima 1994).

In Tonga a pro-democracy movement has argued that the present concentration of political power in the monarch and a handful of noble families is no longer appropriate, and it advocates a shift to more broadly based representative institutions (Campbell 1994). In 2006, frustration at the lack of action on a proposed reform initiative provoked a brief but destructive burst of violence from pro-democracy demonstrators in Nuku'alofa. Perhaps spurred by this alarming turn of events, George Tupou V promised to implement sweeping democratic reforms. In the elections of 2010, seventeen out of twenty-six representatives were designated as popularly elected seats (formerly only nine), fourteen of which were won by Tonga's pro-democracy party.

In some ways the colonial history of Fiji also appears to provide a promising foundation for state-building efforts. Here the British adapted existing chiefly structures of power to form a comprehensive system of native administration. Not only were some chiefly confederacies disadvantaged by this scheme, however, but the large number of plantation workers imported from India were subject to separate (and harsher) treatment under the colonial regime. These colonially reinforced communal asymmetries have proved difficult to overcome in postcolonial Fiji, as demonstrated by the military coups of 1987 and George Speight's so-called civilian coup of May 2000. Although ostensibly carried out to protect indigenous land and political rights in the face of an assertive Indo-Fijian population, these coups reflect as well serious tensions and rivalries within the indigenous Fijian community (see, e.g., Lal 1988; Scarr 1988; Robertson and Tamanisau 1988; Ravuvu 1991; Field, Baba, and Naboba-Baba 2005). In late 2006 coup leader Commodore Frank Bainimarama explicitly rejected the policies of the previous government of Laisania Qarase, which tended to favor indigenous interests and concerns, and promised a general "clean-up" of what he perceived to be an inefficient and corrupt state bureaucracy (Fraenkel 2007, 2008). Despite all this upheaval, however, it is worth noting that the struggle in Fiji is about control of the state rather than challenges to the institution of the state itself.

The thousands of small, autonomous, and culturally distinct societies thrown together to form Vanuatu, Solomon Islands, and Papua New Guinea have provided the most daunting conditions for would-be state builders. These are communities that survived for many thousands of years without anything resembling a state. These are places that were changed but hardly transformed during a colonial interlude that was both brief (effectively less than thirty years for the Highlands of Papua New Guinea) and superficial. As Sinclair Dinnen put it, in each of these countries "the entanglements of pre-colonial and colonial forces is implicated deeply in the challenges of the post-colonial present" (Dinnen 2004: 72).

The peculiar legacy of colonial rule in Vanuatu was parallel state administrative structures, one erected by the British and one by the French, which actively competed with each other for influence throughout the archipelago, especially in the run-up to independence. Although it was a relatively simple matter to merge these bureaucratic structures when the colonial powers finally withdrew, the legacy for national identity was much more profound and divisive. British support for and French opposition to independence served to further polarize national political communities already mobilized on either side of the francophone-anglophone divide.

The leadership crisis of the late 1980s shattered the hegemony of the Vanua'aku Pati and marked the decline of the anglophone-francophone politics forged in opposition to French policies in the late colonial period. In many ways, the new politics, built around smaller, more personalized and locally based political factions, better reflects the archipelago's extremely fragmented cultural landscape. This situation, however, is even more problematic than the earlier one because, in a sense, Vanuatu has been denationalized. Raised anew is the challenge of forging a viable Ni-Vanuatu identity out of myriad competing local and regional identities based on vernacular language and *kastam* (Van Trease 1995b, 1995c).

Like Vanuatu, neighboring Solomon Islands consists of a collection of small-scale traditional communities loosely tied together by emerging market forces, rudimentary state institutions, and, perhaps most important, church networks, none of which predate the colonial era. Unlike in Vanuatu, there was no oppositional external force, no common enemy, to help forge a unified identity among these disparate colonial subjects. Independence was given by the British, not wrested from them, and while it bequeathed common citizenship on all inhabitants of the colony, it did not bestow a coherent national identity. As Christine Jourdan points out, nationalism in Solomon Islands is essentially an urban phenomenon, created by those citizens "who have to shape a future for themselves away from custom and tradition," and encouraged by pragmatic state officials concerned "to hold the country together." It is transmitted to the hinterlands by educational institutions and is part of an emerging popular culture that incorporates elements of both tradition and modernity; it gains much of its strength from Pijin, a lingua franca that because of its relatively recent origin, belongs to no one and everyone at the same time (Jourdan 1995).

The postcolonial state lacks the coercive capacity of its colonial predecessor and has little economic hold over ordinary citizens, most of whom remain firmly attached to village economies that are still largely self-sufficient. Whatever legitimacy it enjoys must be earned through the provision of desired modern services such as health and education and by meeting the demands of rural people for development. This is a virtually impossible task, given the limited financial and other resources available to the state and the escalating claims on them by a rapidly growing population. In 1995, Ian Frazer noted that after two decades of independence, the Solomon Islands state was "no closer to the kind of legitimacy required for stability and unity in the future" (Frazer 1995).

In the late 1990s the inadequacies of state institutions became abundantly clear in the face of escalating conflict between indigenous residents of the main island of Guadalcanal and groups from other parts of the country, mainly Malaita, who had migrated to Honiara and surrounding areas in search of economic and other opportunities. Despite subsequent attempts to find a negotiated solution—most notably the October 2000 Townsville Peace Agreement—political and economic conditions in the country continued to deteriorate (Bennett 2002; Moore 2004; Kabutaulaka 2002; Fraenkel 2004). By 2003 routine functions of government had effectively ceased to operate and problems of crime and disorder were acute. In July of that year, the Australian-organized regional intervention force, RAMSI, arrived to restore order (Kabutaulaka 2005; Hameira 2007).

In many ways the problems of state making and nation making in Solomon Islands are mirrored on a much larger scale in its giant western neighbor, Papua New Guinea. As in Solomon Islands, the national state lacks both legitimacy and the resources to coerce recalcitrant citizens into submission. Attempts to win allegiance through the delivery of essential services and development projects to local constituencies have not proved particularly successful and may even have been counterproductive. The evidence suggests that state resources and the bureaucratic institutions that deliver them are often captured by local interests and made to serve quasi-traditional institutions and values rather than centralized, modern ones (Jacobsen 1995: 239). This process, a type of reverse colonization, attests to the resilience of indigenous ways of life and economy, but it reduces the effectiveness of the state and confounds its modernizing mission. Attempts to create a sense of nationhood, which must of necessity emphasize a common future rather than a common past for the country's diverse citizens, have met with some success in urban areas. But even in towns, local or ethnic identities remain important signifiers, and in some rural parts of the country there is little or no sense of belonging to the nation or identifying with its mission (see, e.g., Clark 1996).

The Bougainville crisis, which caused enormous suffering and at least ten thousand deaths, is the most troubling example so far of the hazards of state making in the Pacific Islands and of the destructive potential of development or modernizing processes generally. For nearly a decade, state officials were unable either to negotiate a settlement to the crisis or force compliance by military means. In a dramatic move to break the impasse before the 1997 general elections, the national government of Sir Julius Chan hired a foreign mercenary company, Sandline International, to spearhead a military operation designed to crush the rebel force and retake Panguna mine. The plan backfired when military commander Brig. Gen. Jerry Singirok broke ranks to publicly condemn the scheme and demand its revocation. He argued that the use of sophisticated counterinsurgency equipment would produce many casualties and implied that Prime Minister Chan and other senior officials were benefiting financially from the $36 million mercenary contract. In the face of a massive public outcry and clear signs that most of the military were sympathetic to Singirok's position, the Sandline initiative collapsed in disarray (Dorney 1998; O'Callaghan 1999).

And yet the inability of the Papua New Guinea state to impose a military solution to the Bougainville crisis left no option but a negotiated settlement. By 2001, a lengthy and comprehensive peace initiative brokered by New Zealand had yielded extraordinary results. The Bougainville Agreement allows Bougainville a considerable degree of autonomy under the terms of its own constitution and provides for a referendum on full independence from Papua New Guinea after a decade of self-government (Regan 2002). The situation is, of course, not without its problems. The whole peace-building initiative is still ultimately based upon Western-style institutions and it is not yet clear whether state- and nation-making efforts will prove any more successful in this culturally diverse island region than in other parts of Melanesia. Certainly, recent plans to revive the mining industry on Bougainville, albeit under local control and with new overseas partners, run the risk of producing the same tensions that led to the eruption of the Bougainville crisis two decades ago (Connell 2005).

The New Globalization

Decolonization efforts in the developing world since World War II have centered on the institutions of the nation-state, itself an artifact of an expansive nineteenth-century European colonialism. In the Pacific Islands, as elsewhere in the colonized world, liberation from colonialism has come to mean gaining control of a Western-style state structure and then creating a coherent national community out of the various groups enclosed by its boundaries. Some Pacific Island peoples have yet to achieve political independence, while those that have now realize that this is only the beginning of a long and often arduous process of state and nation building.

Recent global developments have made the process of making Pacific states and nations even more problematic. The Cold War masked the deepening realities of globalization, not least in the Pacific, where Western powers heavily subsidized state- and nation-making efforts essentially to counter an assumed "Soviet threat." Indeed, by the early 1980s per capita aid flows to the Pacific were among the highest in the world and these resource transfers came with few conditions attached. Since the collapse of the Soviet Union in 1989, however, Pacific Island states have operated in a much less forgiving international environment. Inspired by the neoliberal imperatives of the new globalization, aid donors and international financial institutions have made concerted efforts to persuade island leaders to implement comprehensive economic and political reforms (Firth 2006).

Oceania's reform agenda owes its immediate origins to two critical World Bank reports of the early 1990s and the urgings of influential analysts in Australia and New Zealand (World Bank 1991, 1993; Slatter 2006: 27). In 1994 Australia began to use its aid "as a carrot and stick to ensure Pacific Islands governments reduce the size of their civil services, privatize, [and] encourage private investment" (Firth 2000: 185). Since then all the major aid agencies and lending institutions active in the region, as well as the Pacific Islands Forum, have adopted this "reform speak" (Slatter 2006: 27). More recently the agenda has expanded to embrace "good governance," not only because of concerns about regional instability, but because qualities of accountability, efficiency, and transparency have come to be seen as prerequisites to successful economic reform. If it is not clear how these small and vulnerable economies will fare in the unforgiving world of free trade, it is abundantly clear that the required reforms are by their very nature disruptive of traditional economic and land use practices that have guaranteed the social integrity and subsistence security of island societies for centuries.

Australia's policy of "cooperative intervention" announced in June 2003 represented a further and dramatic shift in the expectations attached to statehood in Oceania and a renewed emphasis on "hands on" involvement in the internal affairs of Pacific Island states (Fry and Kabutaulaka 2008). The new policy, which yielded significant initiatives in Nauru, Papua New Guinea, and Solomon Islands, marked the return to prominence of security considerations in regional affairs, this time driven by concerns about global terrorism. Its architects drew heavily on ideas associated with the failed-state paradigm. An influential report released just prior to the RAMSI intervention, for example, described Solomon Islands as a "petri dish for transnational threats" and argued that the contagion could spread to other countries in the region (ASPI 2003: 13–14).

Increasing concern about "failed" and "failing" states raises difficult questions about state rehabilitation and reconstruction, questions that have become suddenly relevant in the Pacific with the RAMSI intervention. The problem is not necessarily with the post-conflict phase of intervention, and RAMSI successfully restored some semblance of law and order in Solomon Islands within six months of its arrival. Much more problematic is the second and ongoing phase, described as "working with Solomon Islanders to rebuild their political and security institutions, to ensure effective long-term service delivery, functioning democratic processes and a revived economy" (Wainwright 2003: 495). So far, the emphasis has been on strengthening some administrative aspects of central government, the management of public finances, and on finding ways to stimulate economic growth. While not denying the potential value of these centralized efforts, critics charge that they repeat some of the mistakes of the past. According to a 2006 report, the central challenge "is to build a bridge between state and society" and to improve conditions in the rural areas and outer islands where the bulk of the population actually lives (Oxfam 2006: 7).

The issue here is not really the availability of resources or administrative expertise. Institutional structures can be readily designed by consultants and established or re-established with the help of skilled and experienced expatriates. What is much more difficult for outsiders (or insiders for that matter) to change is the wider political culture in which Western-style state institutions must operate over the longer term. Competing economic formations, ideologies, and identities remain resilient in most Pacific places considered candidates for state failure. Universal "common-sense" ideas about society and government projected onto Solomon Islands or Papua New Guinea from global centers of power are highly unlikely to be internalized any time soon.

To have any measure of success, state-building activities will have to work with existing institutions and ideologies of governance. They will require much time, modest expectations, and perhaps even a willingness to redraw political boundaries. Above all these are tasks that can only be accomplished by islanders themselves. The alternative may be continuing external control, perhaps through some revived form of international trusteeship or system of mandates. Such a process, which some might describe as recolonization, should be quickly condemned as unacceptable—especially since the impulse to intervene and reform has more to do with the interests of external powers than the welfare of Pacific Islanders.

NOTES

This is a revised and updated version of my chapter in the first edition of this volume. It also draws on some materials previously published in Wesley-Smith 2006 and 2007.

1. The independent states are Samoa (1962), Nauru (1968), Fiji (1970), Tonga (1970), Papua New Guinea (1975), Solomon Islands (1978), Tuvalu (1978), Kiribati (1979), and Vanuatu (1980).

2. Hawai'i became the fiftieth state of the union in 1959. The Northern Mariana Islands achieved de facto commonwealth status in 1978, although the process was not legally complete until the official termination of the Trust Territory of the Pacific Islands in 1986. Guam remains on the United Nations list of territories yet to be decolonized, although its long-term affiliation with the United States seems likely.

3. Renegotiated compacts of free association with the Federated States of Micronesia and the Marshall Islands took effect in 2004 under financial terms that were less favorable to the island entities. Palau's compact is due to be reviewed in 2009.

BIBLIOGRAPHY

Aldrich, R. 1989. France in the South Pacific. In *No longer an American lake: Alliance problems in the South Pacific,* ed. J. Ravenhill, 76–105. Berkeley: Institute of International Studies, University of California at Berkeley.

ASPI (Australian Strategic Policy Institute). 2003. Our failing neighbour: Australia and the future of the Solomon Islands. An ASPI Policy Report. Sydney: ASPI.

Ayson, R. 2007. The "arc of instability" and Australia's strategic policy. *Australian Journal of International Affairs* 61(2): 215–231.

Bellwood, P. 1990. Hierarchy, founder ideology and Austronesian expansion. Paper presented at the Hierarchy, Ancestry and Alliance conference, Australian National University.

Bennett, J. 2002. Roots of conflict in Solomon Islands—though much is taken, much abides: Legacy of tradition and colonialism: State, society and governance in Melanesia. Discussion Paper #2002/5. Canberra: Australian National University.

Campbell, I. C. 1994. The doctrine of accountability and the unchanging locus of power in Tonga: Current developments in the Pacific. *The Journal of Pacific History* 29(1): 81–94.

Chappell, D. 2005. 'Africanization' in the Pacific: Blaming others for disorder in the periphery? *Comparative Studies in Society and History* 47(2): 286–317.

Clapham, C. 2003. Putting state collapse in context: History, politics and the genealogy of the concept. In *State failure, collapse and reconstruction,* ed. Jennifer Milliken. Malden, Mass.: Blackwell Publishing.

Clark, J. 1996. Imagining the state, or tribalism and the arts of memory in the Highlands of Papua New Guinea. In *Narratives of the nation in the South Pacific,* ed. T. Otto and N. Thomas, 65–90. Amsterdam: Harwood Academic Publishers.

Cole, R. V., ed. 1993. Pacific 2010: Challenging the future. Pacific Policy Paper #9. Canberra: National Centre for Development Studies, Australian National University.

Connell, J. 2005. Bougainville: The future of an island microstate. *The Journal of Pacific Studies* 28(2): 192–217.

Davidson, B. 1992. *The Black man's burden: Africa and the curse of the nation-state.* New York: Times Books.

Dinnen, S. 2004. The trouble with Melanesia. In *The eye of the cyclone—Issues in Pacific security,* ed. Ivan Molloy. Sippy Downs, Qld.: Pacific Islands Political Studies Association and University of the Sunshine Coast.

Dorney, S. 1998. *The Sandline affair: Politics and mercenaries in the Bougainville Crisis.* Sydney: ABC Books.

Elmslie, J. 2002. *Irian Jaya under the gun: Indonesian economic development versus West Papuan Nationalism.* Honolulu: University of Hawai'i Press.

Field, M., T. Baba, and U. Naboba-Baba. 2005. *Speight of violence: Inside Fiji's 2000 coup.* Canberra: Pandanus Books.

Firth, S. 1989. Sovereignty and independence in the contemporary Pacific. *The Contemporary Pacific* 1(1&2): 75–96.

———. 2000. The Pacific Islands and the globalization agenda. *The Contemporary Pacific* 12(1): 177–192.

———, ed. 2006. *Globalization and governance in the Pacific Islands.* Canberra: Australia National University E Press.

Foster, R. ed. 1995. *Nation making: Emergent identities in postcolonial Melanesia.* Ann Arbor: University of Michigan Press.

———. 2002. *Materializing the nation: Commodities, consumption, and media in Papua New Guinea.* Bloomington: Indiana University Press.

Fraenkel, J. 2004. *The manipulation of custom: From uprising to intervention in the Solomon Islands.* Christchurch: University of Canterbury Press.

———. 2007. The Fiji coup of December 2006: Who, what, where and why? In *From election to coup in Fiji,* ed. Jon Fraenkel and Stewart Firth, 420–449. Canberra: Australian National University E Press.

———. 2008. Fiji, issues and events, 2007. *The Contemporary Pacific* 20(2): 450–460.

Frazer, I. 1995. Decentralization and the postcolonial state in Solomon Islands. In *Lines across the sea: Colonial inheritance in the postcolonial Pacific,* ed. B. V. Lal and H. Nelson, 95–109. Brisbane: Pacific History Association.

Fry, G. 1997. Framing the islands: Knowledge and power in changing Australian images of the 'South Pacific.' *The Contemporary Pacific* 9(2): 305–344.

Fry, G., and T. Kabutaulaka, eds. 2008. *Intervention and state-building in the Pacific: The legitimacy of co-operative intervention.* Manchester: Manchester University Press.

Godelier, M. 1991. An unfinished attempt at reconstructing the social processes which may have prompted the transformation of great-man societies into big-man societies. In *Big-men and great-men: Personifications of power in Melanesia,* ed. M. Godelier and M. Strathern. Cambridge: Cambridge University Press.

Golson, J., and D. S. Gardner. 1990. Agriculture and sociopolitical organization in New Guinea highlands prehistory. *Annual Review of Anthropology* 19: 395–417.

Hameira, S. 2007. The trouble with RAMSI: Reexamining the roots of conflict in the Solomon Islands. *The Contemporary Pacific* 19(2): 409–441.

Hanlon, D. 1994. Patterns of colonial rule in Micronesia. In *Tides of history: The Pacific Islands in the Twentieth Century,* ed. K. R. Howe, R. C. Kiste, and B. V. Lal, 93–118. Honolulu: University of Hawai'i Press.

Harrison, S. 1993. The commerce of cultures in Melanesia. *Man* 28: 139–159.

Huntsman, J., with K. Kalolo. 2007. *The future of Tokelau: Decolonising agendas 1975–2006.* Auckland: Auckland University Press.

Jacobsen, Michael. 1995. Vanishing nations and the infiltration of nationalism: The case of Papua New Guinea. In *Nation making: Emergent identities in postcolonial Melanesia,* ed. R. J. Foster. Ann Arbor: University of Michigan Press.

Jourdan, C. 1995. Stepping stones to national consciousness: The Solomon Islands case. In *Nation making: Emergent identities in postcolonial Melanesia,* ed. R. J. Foster. Ann Arbor: University of Michigan Press.

Kabutaulaka, T. 2002. A weak state and the peace process in Solomon Islands. Honolulu: East-West Center Working Paper, Pacific Islands Development Series #14.

———. 2005. Australian foreign policy and the RAMSI intervention in Solomon Islands. *The Contemporary Pacific* 17(2): 283–308.

Kelly, J., and M. Kaplan. 2001. *Represented communities: Fiji and world decolonization.* Chicago and London: University of Chicago Press.

Kirch, P. 1984. *The evolution of Polynesian chiefdoms.* Cambridge: Cambridge University Press.

———. 2000. *On the road of the winds: An archaeological history of the Pacific Islands before European contact.* Berkeley: University of California Press.

Kiste, Robert C. 1994. United States. In *Tides of history: The Pacific Islands in the twentieth century,* ed. K. R. Howe, R. C. Kiste, and B. V. Lal, 227–257. Honolulu: University of Hawai'i Press.

Lal, B. V. 1988. *Power and prejudice: The making of the Fiji crisis.* Wellington: New Zealand Institute of International Affairs.

———. 1992. *Broken waves: A history of the Fiji Islands in the twentieth century.* Pacific Islands Monograph Series, No. 11. Honolulu: University of Hawai'i Press.

Le Tagaloa, A. F. 1992. The Samoan culture and government. In *Culture and democracy in the South Pacific,* ed. R. Crocombe et al., 117–137. Suva: Institute of Pacific Studies, University of the South Pacific.

Leiataua, V., and F. Alailima. 1994. Restructuring Samoa's chiefdom. In *New politics in the South Pacific,* ed. W. von Busch et al., 247–269. Rarotonga and Suva: Institute of Pacific Studies, University of the South Pacific, in association with the Pacific Islands Political Studies Association.

Macdonald, B. 1994. Britain. In *Tides of history: The Pacific Islands in the twentieth century,* ed. K. R. Howe, R. C. Kiste, and B. V. Lal, 170–194. Honolulu: University of Hawai'i Press.

Maclellan, N., and J. Boengkih. 1996. France's decolonisation process in New Caledonia: Conflict on the path to self-determination. Pacific Series Working Paper No. 1. Melbourne: Centre for Asia-Pacific Studies, Victoria University of Technology.

Meleisea, M. 1987. *The making of modern Samoa: Traditional authority and colonial administration in the history of Western Samoa.* Suva: Institute of Pacific Studies, University of the South Pacific.

———. 1988. *Change and adaptation in Western Samoa.* Christchurch: Macmillan Brown Centre for Pacific Studies, University of Canterbury.

Migdal, J. S. 1988. *Strong societies and weak states: State-society relations and state capabilities in the third world.* Princeton, N.J.: Princeton University Press.

Moore, C. 2004. *Happy isles in crisis: The historical causes for a failing state in Solomon Islands.* Canberra: Asia Pacific Press.

O'Callaghan, M.-L. 1999. *Enemies within: Papua New Guinea, Australia, and the Sandline crisis.* Netley: Doubleday.

Otto, T., and N. Thomas, eds. 1997. *Narratives of nation in the South Pacific.* Amsterdam: Harwood Academic Publishers.

Oxfam. 2006. *Bridging the gap between state and society: New directions for the Solomon Islands.* Honiara: Oxfam International.

Patience, A. 2005. *The ECP and Australia's middle power ambitions.* Canberra: Australia National University, State, Society and Governance in Melanesia Discussion Paper 2005/4.

Ravuvu, A. 1991. *The facade of democracy: Fijian struggles for political control, 1830–1987.* Suva: Reader Publishing House.

Regan, A. 2002. The Bougainville political settlement and prospects for sustainable peace. *Pacific Economic Bulletin* 17(1): 114–129.

Reilly, B. 2000. The Africanisation of the South Pacific. *Australian Journal of International Affairs* 54(3): 261–268.

Robertson, R. T., and A. Tamanisau. 1988. *Fiji—shattered coups.* Sydney: Pluto Press.

Sahlins, M. D. 1963. Poor man, rich man, big man, chief: Political types in Melanesia and Polynesia. *Comparative Studies in Society and History* 5(3): 285–303.

Scarr, D. 1988. *The politics of illusion: The military coups in Fiji.* Kensington: University of New South Wales Press.

Slatter, C. 2006. Treading water in rapids? Non-governmental organizations and resistance to neo-liberalism in Pacific Islands states. In *Globalization and governance in the Pacific Islands,* ed. S. Firth, 23–42. Canberra: Australia National University E Press.

Tilly, C. 1985. War making and state making as organized crime. In *Bringing the state back in,* ed. P. Evans, D. Rueschemeyer, and T. Skocpol, Cambridge: Cambridge University Press.

Van Trease, H. 1995a. The colonial origins of Vanuatu politics. In *Melanesian politics: Stael blong Vanuatu,* ed. H. Von Trease, 3–58. Christchurch and Suva: Macmillan Brown Centre for Pacific Studies, University of Canterbury and Institute for Pacific Studies, University of the South Pacific.

———. 1995b. Years of turmoil, 1987–91. In *Melanesian politics: Stael blong Vanuatu,* ed. H. Von Trease, 73–118. Christchurch and Suva: Macmillan Brown Centre for Pacific Studies, University of Canterbury and Institute for Pacific Studies, University of the South Pacific.

———. 1995c. The election. In *Melanesian politics: Stael blong Vanuatu,* ed. H. Von Trease, 119–158. Christchurch and Suva: Macmillan Brown Centre for Pacific Studies, University of Canterbury and Institute for Pacific Studies, University of the South Pacific.

Wainwright, E. 2003. Responding to state failure—The case of Australia and the Solomon Islands. *Australian Journal of International Affairs* 57(3): 485–498.

Wesley-Smith, T. 1994. Australia and New Zealand. In *Tides of history: The Pacific Islands in the twentieth century,* ed. K. R. Howe, R. C. Kiste, and B. V. Lal, 195–226. Honolulu: University of Hawai'i Press.

———. 2006. There goes the neighbourhood: The politics of failed states and regional intervention in the Pacific. In *Redefining the Pacific? Regionalism past, present, and future,* ed. J. Bryant-Tokalau and I. Frazer, 121–126. Aldershot: Ashgate Publishing.

———. 2007. The limits of self-determination in Oceania. *Social and Economic Studies* 56(1&2): 182–208.

West, F. J. 1968. *Hubert Murray: The Australian pro-consul.* Melbourne: Melbourne University Press.

Windybank, S. 2003. Will Papua New Guinea become a 'failed state'? *International Herald Tribune,* April 8.

World Bank. 1991. *Pacific Island economies: Toward higher growth in the 1990s.* Washington, D.C.: World Bank.

———. 1993. *Pacific Island economies: Toward effective and sustainable growth.* Vol. I: Overview. Washington D.C.: World Bank.

Culture

Pacific Island cultures are rich and diverse, ranging from the numerous ethnolinguistic groupings of Melanesia, to the spatially extended cultures of Micronesia, to the remarkably homogenous cultures characteristic of Polynesia. Traditional cultures have altered significantly following external contact, but they have remained resilient. Even where indigenous islanders are minorities, cultural revivals are currently under way. This section explores Pacific Island cultures, with chapters on language, social relations, gender, tenure, law, religion, literature, art, and music and dance.

Language

Andrew Pawley

13

The Pacific Islands constitute, by two different measures, the most linguistically diverse region in the world. One measure is language density.[1] Roughly 20 percent of the world's six to seven thousand languages are packed into this region, which contains less than 1 percent of the world's land mass and population. A second index refers to the number of different (maximal) language families, i.e., linguistic stocks not known to be related to each other, which have no known relatives outside the region. This is a measure of deep genealogical diversity and gives an indication of how long the families have been there. The 1,300 or so distinct languages[2] spoken by the indigenous peoples of the Pacific Islands divide into more than twenty unrelated families—a degree of deep diversity greater than that of either Africa (five families) or Europe (two families plus Basque and Maltese) before Columbus.[3] The fact that all but three of the Pacific Island language families are confined to Western Melanesia (New Guinea and the Bismarck and Solomons archipelagoes) indicates that Western Melanesia is a relic area where many ancient language families persist.

In the colonial period, further layers of complexity were added to this setting with the introduction of a number of European and Asian languages and the development of several widely used pidgin and creole languages. The present chapter seeks to place this formidable linguistic diversity in its geographical and historical contexts.

Can anything be learned about the geography of the Pacific by studying the languages of its peoples? The answer, surely, is yes. From careful study of their languages we can, at the very least, learn much about how different communities perceive their physical environments and how they order their social worlds. Languages can be thought of as codes for talking about and interpreting the world—indeed, as codes for constructing conceptual worlds. To learn a language is to learn, among other things, a vocabulary of concepts and a body of formulas for talking about different subject matters. In fact, a large part of becoming competent in any science or other field of conventional knowledge or belief is learning how its participants talk about their subject matter.

Traditional Pacific Island societies have developed rich and elaborate terminologies for certain aspects of their natural and man-made environments.[4] But more significant than the size of terminologies is their content and structure—the nature of the concepts and the way these are ordered. In recent years, for example, there has been extensive research comparing the way spatial

relations and directions are represented in different Pacific Island languages (Bennardo 2002). Many types of spatial coordinate systems can be distinguished, reflecting adaptations to different habitats (coral islands, volcanic islands, mountain valleys, etc.).

In any Pacific language, a good deal of the vocabulary speakers use for talking about their surroundings will translate readily into English and other languages and, to a much lesser extent, into the technical lexicons of scientists. But one also finds terms without close translation equivalents, and some of these reveal insights that have escaped Western ecologists. An example is the term *abn*, used by the Kalam people of the Schrader Ranges, Papua New Guinea. *Abn* are systems of natural tunnels or cavities, often extending into large galleries, that are present underneath the forest floor in certain places. Such underground tunnel systems occur above about 1,500 m on the wet slopes of the midmontane rain forest and are inhabited by many animals that the Kalam hunt. The ethnobiologist Ralph Bulmer glossed *abn* by a neologism, "undercroft (of the forest)," and comments:

> To ecologists these [spaces] are just part of the "litter layer." But to English-speakers who are not biologists, "litter" suggests loose leaves and compost, and gives no inkling of the complexities of this underground world. . . . The absence of a technical biological term for *abn* perhaps reflects the limited extent to which ecologists have focussed on genuinely primary forests, climax vegetation of a sufficient antiquity to create and sustain such subterranean tunnel systems. (Majnep and Bulmer 2007: 43)

After presenting some basic facts about the various languages and language families found in the Pacific, we ask what can be learned from comparative linguistics about the prehistory of the various cultures, economies, and ecological adaptations of Pacific societies.

The Language Families of the Pacific, Their Distribution and Internal Relationships

The distribution of Pacific Island languages and language families (stocks of languages sharing a common ancestor but having no well-established genetic relationship to other stocks) is compactly indicated in *Ethnologue* (Gordon 2005) and is mapped in detail in the two-volume *Language Atlas of the Pacific Area* (Wurm and Hattori 1981– 1983). The three-volume *Atlas of Languages of Intercultural Communication in the Pacific, Asia and the Americas* (Wurm, Mühlhäusler, and Tryon 1996) also treats nonindigenous languages.

When scanning the maps in these works one is overwhelmed by the dense concentration of languages in Melanesia (Table 13.1). The island of New Guinea is not much bigger than France, but linguistically speaking it is the equivalent of a continent, with more than nine hundred languages falling into numerous distinct families and isolates.[5] Another three hundred or so languages are spoken in Island Melanesia, from the Bismarck Archipelago to Vanuatu, and these belong to several different families.

Table 13.1

Approximate Number of Indigenous Languages and Unrelated Families in Pacific Regions

Region	Land area (sq. km)	Languages	Families
West Papua	415,000	248	4
Papua New Guinea mainland	406,650	728	15+
Admiralty Is.	2,098	29	1
New Britain and offshore islands	35,862	45	3+
New Ireland & Mussau	9,615	18	2
Bougainville	9,329	28	2
Solomon Islands	29,800	63	3
Vanuatu	12,190	112	1
New Caledonia & Loyalties	19,100	25	1
Fiji-Rotuma	18,270	3–6	1
Micronesia	3,750	11–17	1
Polynesian Triangle excluding NZ	25,050	15	1
New Zealand	268,500	1	1

Source: After Gordon 2005; Wurm and Hattori 1981–1983.

By contrast, the area made up of Micronesia, Fiji, and the Polynesian Triangle is relatively homogeneous, containing fewer than forty languages, all belonging to the Austronesian family. Whereas in Melanesia the norm is many languages per island group or large island, in the Polynesian Triangle and in Micronesia each well-defined island group generally has a single language.

Most Pacific Island languages have fewer than five thousand speakers. The largest indigenous language communities (figures are approximate and exclude emigrants) are Standard Fijian (480,000) and three Polynesian languages: Samoan (270,000), Tahitian (140,000), and Tongan (100,000), plus several in the Highlands of Papua New Guinea: Enga (170,000), Melpa (130,000), and in the highlands of West Papua: Western Dani (150,000), Grand Valley Dani (100,000), and Ekagi (100,000). The largest languages of Micronesia are Chamorro (spoken in the Marianas), with about 60,000 speakers and Kiribati, with about 70,000.

The position of many indigenous languages in the Pacific is being weakened by socioeconomic changes that favor the use of major world languages, chiefly English and French, and in parts of Melanesia the adoption of pidgins as a first language. Among the languages in decline are Chamorro, Hawaiian, Maori, and Tahitian. It is likely that many of the smaller Pacific Island languages will not survive the twenty-first century.

The Austronesian Family

Most of the language families present in Melanesia have no relatives outside this region. There is, however, one that is clearly intrusive. The vast Austronesian family (formerly often called "Malayo-Polynesian") is spread two-thirds of the way around the tropical world from Madagascar to Easter Island (Figure 13.1). In the Pacific, it extends from Taiwan and Hawai'i in the north to New Zealand in the south.

Recent estimates place the number of languages in the Austronesian family at around 1,200 (Gordon 2005; Tryon 1995), far ahead of any other generally accepted language family in the world except the African family sometimes called Niger-Congo. About 500 of the Austronesian languages are found in Melanesia, Micronesia, and Polynesia. The remainder lie farther west, in Indonesia excluding its New Guinea provinces (more than 400), Malaysia (108), and the Philippines (165), with smaller numbers in Taiwan (15, excluding several that recently became extinct), Vietnam (9), Thailand (1), and Madagascar (3).

It is easy to find cognates (words inherited from a common ancestor) between the most widely separated Austronesian languages. An asterisk before a form on Table 13.2 indicates that it is reconstructed, not directly attested.[6] This ease reflects the fact that the dispersal of the Austronesian-speaking peoples across the Indo-Malaysian archipelago and across Oceania was relatively recent, mainly taking place after 2000 BCE (see discussion later in this chapter).

Arriving at a reliable family tree for a large family of languages is usually much harder than merely establishing genetic relatedness. A family tree subgroups languages to show a putative sequence of branchings. The most reliable method of subgrouping is by shared innovations. To show that a family has subgroups A, B, and C, we must demonstrate that the members of each subgroup share a significant body of common changes to the protolanguage exclusive of the others. There is disagreement about the higher branches of Austronesian, but the classification in Figure 13.2 (a modified version of that developed by Blust 1978, 1982, 1993–1994, 1995a) has a fair degree of general acceptance.

It is a striking fact that all the Austronesian languages of Melanesia east of 136°E, plus the Polynesian languages and all the languages of Micronesia except Chamorro and Palauan (Belauan), fall

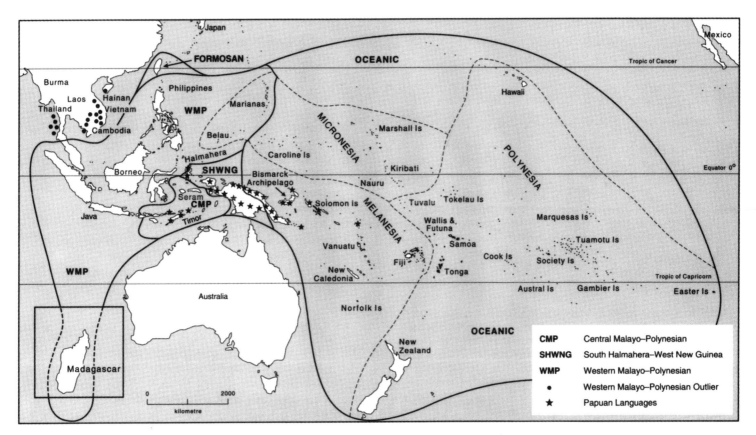

Figure 13.1. *Distribution of the Austronesian family and its major subgroups (Madagascar shown as inset).*

Table 13.2

Some Austronesian Cognate Sets

	"eye"	"liver"	"louse"	"rain"	"eight"
Proto Austronesian	*maCa	*qatay	*kutu	*qudaL	*walu
Paiwan (Taiwan)	maca	qatsay	kasiw	qudal	alu
Tagalog (Philippines)	mata	atay	kuto	ulan	walo
Toba Batak (Indonesia)	mata	ate-ate	hutu	udan	walu
Manam (Papua N. Guinea)	mata	—	kutu	ura	—
Kwaio (Solomons)	maa	l/ae/fou	'uu	uta	kwalu
Lolomatui (Vanuatu)	mata	ate	kutu	uhe	welu
Puluwat (Micronesia)	maah	ya/ya	uuw	wut	waluw
Bauan (Fiji)	mata	yate	kutu	uca	walu
Tongan (Polynesia)	mata	'ate	kutu	'uha	valu

into a single subgroup (probably a fourth-order subgroup) of Austronesian, known as "Oceanic."[7] The boundary between Oceanic and the rest of Austronesian runs through western New Guinea and curves northwest through Micronesia east of Belau and the Marianas. The closest relatives of Oceanic are the Austronesian languages of south Halmahera and Cenderawasih Bay, at the northwestern end of West Papua, which comprise the Halmahera–West New Guinea group (Blust 1978).

Because of the rapid initial spread of Oceanic languages (see below) and the formation of complex dialect networks in many

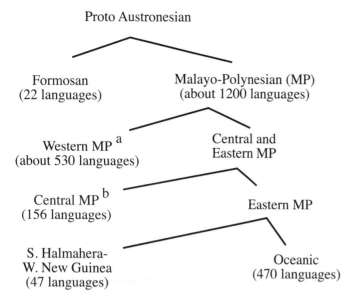

Figure 13.2. High-order subgroups (after Blust 1995). Notes: (a) Nine of the twenty-two recorded Formosan languages are now extinct. (b) Western Malay-Polynesian is a residual category comprising the Malayo-Polynesian languages of Madagascar, the Philippines, Malaysia, and Indonesia as far east as mid-Sumbawa and including Sulawesi. (c) Central Malay-Polynesian includes the languages of the islands of eastern Indonesia east of Sulawesi and mid-Sumbawa, excluding South Halmahera and the non-Austronesian languages of Timor and Halmahera. Some Central Malayo-Polynesian languages are spoken on the Bomberai Peninsula, on the Bird's Head of New Guinea.

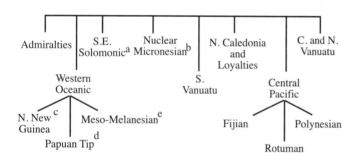

Figure 13.3. Major high-order subgroups of Oceanic. Notes: (a) Roughly Guadalcanal, Malaita, San Cristobal. (b) Languages of Micronesia excluding Chamorro, Belau, and Yapese. (c) From Sepik to Morobe. (d) Central, Milne Bay, and Northern Provinces of Papua. (e) Roughly New Britain from Willaumez Peninsula east, New Ireland, and W. Solomons.

regions, there are few well-marked high-order subgroups within Oceanic. Geraghty's (1983) study of the Fijian group illustrates the way innovations can spread unevenly across a dialect chain. Figure 13.3 shows a fairly conservative view of the high-order subgroups of Oceanic.[8]

Structural Characteristics of Oceanic Austronesian Languages

Four to five thousand years of diversification within the Austronesian family has produced a range of grammatical systems comparable in diversity to that exhibited across the Indo-European subgroups: Romance, Germanic, Slavic, etc. However, there are certain characteristics common to many Austronesian languages of the Oceanic subgroup. Among these are

- Words typically consisting of two or three open syllables (without consonant clusters or final consonants), e.g., Hawaiian *hale* 'house,' *lau* 'leaf,' *makani* 'wind,' *wahine* (woman).
- A distinction in first person plural pronouns between "we, excluding the addressee," and "we, including the addressee."
- The obligatory marking of nouns, when possessed by a pronoun, to distinguish kinds of possessive relationships: inalienable (body part and kinship terms), edible, drinkable, or general; e.g., Fijian *tama-na* (his father), *ke-na ika* (his fish [as food]), *me-na bia* (his beer [to drink]), *no-na vale* (his house [general]).
- Word order in which the verb precedes the direct object and the noun precedes its modifier (verb-final New Guinea languages, influenced by their Papuan neighbors, are an exception.)
- An elaborate transitivity system, in which transitive verbs are derived by a short or long transitive suffix (Proto-Oceanic *-i and *-akini) and the direct object slot may be filled by nominals standing for a wide range of semantic roles: undergoer, place, goal, stimulus, cause, concomitant, instrument, beneficiary.
- A number of other verb-deriving affixes (e.g., *paka-causative, *paRi- collective action or reciprocal relation, and *ta- spontaneous stative) and several affixes that derive nouns from verbs (*i- , *-in-, and *-ana).

For further comparative information on the structure and lexicon of Oceanic languages see Blust (2009), Clark (2009), Lynch (1998), Lynch, Ross, and Crowley (2002), Sebeok (1971), Ross (1988), Ross, Pawley, and Osmond (1998, 2003, 2008 , 2011), Tryon (1976, 1995), Tryon and Hackman (1983).

The Non-Austronesian or Papuan Families of Melanesia

Although they do not form an established genetic unit, the indigenous non-Austronesian languages of Melanesia are usually collectively referred to as "Papuan." Over the past fifty years there has been considerable debate over how many distinct Papuan families there are. The most reliable classification to date is that of Ross (2001, 2005). Ross compared 605 languages, using cognation in pronoun forms as the main (though not the sole) basis for recognizing families. He concluded that there are some twenty-three families that cannot on present evidence be related to each other, plus nine or ten isolates. For each of the larger families, he sought to determine a sequence of innovations in pronoun forms and categories that would yield subgroups. Ross' study indicates that the Papuan languages show less deep genetic diversity than was recognized by the contributors to Wurm (1975) and by Wurm and Hattori (1981–1983) but more than was proposed by Foley (1986).

In mainland New Guinea there are about seventeen distinct maximal families (often called "phyla") of Papuan languages plus several isolates (Figure 13.4). In Island Melanesia, in the region from New Britain to the Solomons, there are several more such families.

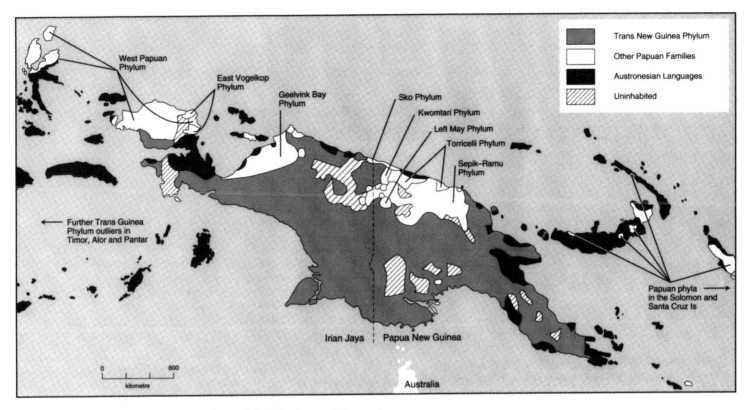

Figure 13.4. Papuan families of New Guinea and the Halmahera and Timor regions.

To the west of New Guinea, a number of non-Austronesian languages are spoken on Timor, Alor, and Pantar and on Halmahera.

One very large Papuan family has been identified. The Trans–New Guinea (TNG) family contains more than 400 of the 750 or so non-Austronesian languages of Melanesia (Wurm 1975; Pawley 2005a, 2005b, 2005c; Ross 2005), making it the third largest language family in the world (in number of members). The family completely dominates the central cordillera that runs the length of New Guinea, and it covers large parts of northern and southern New Guinea.

The precise membership and the subgrouping of the very diverse TNG family remain controversial. Only a small number of cognate sets—fewer than 200—have been securely identified as being shared by widespread subgroups of TNG (Table 13.3). These and certain nonlinguistic facts (see below) indicate that the family began to diversify many (perhaps seven to ten) millennia ago.

Table 13.3

Some Cognate Sets of the Trans–New Guinea Family

	"breast"	"eat"	"louse"	"name"
Proto TNG	*amu	*na	*niman	*ibi
Asmat (S. West Papua)	—	na-	—	yipi
Kati (W. PNG)	ane	—	im	—
Kiwai (SW coast, PNG)	amo	—	nimo	—
Kewa (W. Highlands, PNG)	—	na "food"	ibi	—
Kuman (C. Highlands, PNG)	aemu	—	numan	—
Kube (Morobe Prov., PNG)	namu	ne	imiŋ	—
Katiati (Madang Prov., PNG)	ama	—	ñima	nimbi
Aomie (Central Prov., PNG)	ame	—	ume	ihe

Structural Characteristics of Trans–New Guinea Languages

Although there is considerable variation in the grammatical typology of TNG languages, certain features are widespread (Foley 1986, 2000). These include the following, illustrated by examples from the Kalam language (see also the discussion in the section following this on Kalam language and the environment):

- Quite complex verb morphology, with suffixes on main verbs that mark the person and number of the actor or subject and mark tense, aspect, or mood.
- Word order in which the direct and indirect object precede the verb and a modifying clause precedes the noun it modifies, e.g., "I shot the pig that ate my sweet potatoes" is expressed in Kalam as "I pig the sweet potatoes my ate-it shot-I."
- Serial verb constructions, consisting of a string of consecutive bare verb stems that describe conventional sequences of actions in a highly analytic way, e.g., "to

taste" is expressed as "eat perceive," "to feel" as "touch perceive," and "to fetch" as "go get come."

- Small inventories of verb stems, compensated by use of standardized serial verb sequences and/or by phrasal verbs consisting of a nominal adjunct(s) + verb, e.g., "to see" is "eye perceive," "to hear" is "ear perceive," "to dream" is "sleep perceive."

- In sentences consisting of two or more clauses there is "switch-reference" and "relative tense" marking on nonfinal clauses. The verb in a nonfinal clause carries a suffix or suffixes that indicate (1) whether that verb has the same actor or subject (SS) as the verb in the final clause in the sentence or a different actor or subject (DS) and (2) whether the event denoted by the medial verb is prior to (PRIOR), simultaneous with (SIM), or future to (FUT) that of the final verb, as for example, the Kalam sentence:

Nad wog g-na-k-nŋ,	You work do-you-past-DS.SIM
cn kmap ag-ig,	we song utter-SS.SIM
amn-nu-k	go-we-past

"While you were working, we were going along singing."

Other (non–Trans–New Guinea) Papuan Families

The greatest concentration of non–Trans–New Guinea families (or phyla) and isolates is to be found on the northern side of the central cordillera of New Guinea, from the Bird's Head to the Sepik-Ramu Basin and especially in the Sepik region (Figure 13.4).

Claims have been made for a large Sepik-Ramu family, comprising some ninety languages spoken in the Sepik and Ramu basins. Foley (2005) and Ross (2005), however, reject these claims and divide the languages concerned into several groups, including a Lower Sepik family of six languages, very remotely related to a Lower Ramu family of twelve languages, a small Yuat family, spoken in the Yuat River region, and a very diverse Sepik family of some fifty languages, stretching from the western boundary of the Lower Sepik–Ramu family all the way to the West Papua border.

The Torricelli family consists of about forty-seven languages centered in the Torricelli and Prince Alexander Ranges between the Sepik River and the north coast and extending into northwest Madang Province. A second group of Torricelli languages lies to the west and south of the Murik Lakes, and a third, small group is spoken on the coast in northwest Madang Province, separated from its sisters by recently intrusive languages of the Ndu branch of the Sepik family.

Several smaller families have been identified, including Sko (spoken on and near the north coast around the PNG–West Papua border), Kwomtari (northwest part of Sandaun or West Sepik Province), Left May (south of Kwomtari around the May River, a tributary of the Sepik), and Amto-Musian (between Kwomtari and Left May).

At the western end of New Guinea there is the Geelvink Bay family, spoken on the coast of Cenderawasih (formerly Geelvink) Bay, the small East Bird's Head family, and the West Papuan family, which comprises about twenty-five languages spoken at the western end of New Guinea, on the northern part of the Bird's Head, on North Halmahera Island, and on Yapen Island.

In addition, there are a number of isolates—individual languages with no established relatives—scattered about New Guinea, especially in the Sepik area.

Although Austronesian languages now dominate Island Melanesia, several pockets of Papuan languages have survived in the western part of this region. New Britain contains two small families. There is an isolate on New Ireland, two small families in Bougainville, while the four Papuan languages in the Central Solomons represent an uncertain number of families (Ross 2001).[9]

On the Number and Size of Language Communities in Melanesia

It would be natural for the Eurocentric observer to ask: Why are there so many languages and language families in Melanesia? Why are the language communities so small? But a Melanesian might equally well ask: Why are there so few languages and language families in Europe? The fact is that in its linguistic diversity, Melanesia is not very different from North or South America up until the nineteenth century and from many areas of contemporary southern Asia, sub-Saharan Africa, Central America, and Amazonia. Before the rise of city-states and empires, political units everywhere were small, probably seldom larger than a collection of kinship groups or a village containing a few hundred or at most a few thousand people. No unit had the political and economic power to dominate a large area. Neighboring polities were often hostile. Given these severe limits on the size of sociopolitical groups, and given that all languages are constantly changing, the dispersal of a language community was bound to lead to linguistic fragmentation.

In the Pacific Islands, small polities and hostile neighbors were not the only constraints on the size of speech communities. In New Guinea and New Britain, in particular, rugged and heavily forested mountain ranges and extensive swamps imposed natural limits to communication. Substantial ocean gaps between islands everywhere provided natural points of linguistic fission. In Micronesia and Polynesia, the position of boundaries between languages and dialects correlates closely with the length of voyages by canoe (Marck 1986, 2001).

The larger territorial range and population size of most languages in Polynesia (one language per island group) and Micronesia compared with New Guinea and Island Melanesia (many languages per island group of comparable size) can be attributed to a combination of factors: (1) Eastern Polynesia and certain parts of Micronesia were settled by Austronesian speakers much later than most parts of Island Melanesia, so there has been less time for local diversification. (2) Unlike New Guinea and most of Island Melanesia, Polynesia and Micronesia were uninhabited before the arrival of Austronesian speakers. The founding colonizers of each island group, therefore, could occupy the whole region rather than being confined to residual pockets of territory around established communities. (3) Sailing skills were better developed or better maintained in Micronesia and Polynesia than in most parts of Melanesia. (4) The existence of powerful hereditary chieftainships within island groups such as Hawai'i, Tonga, and the Societies provided social and political bases for regular interisland voyaging.

European and Other Recently Arrived Languages

Coexisting with the indigenous languages in almost every part of the Pacific are languages that have been brought by European and Asian settlers in the last few centuries. French is the first language of most people in New Caledonia and many on Tahiti and is an important second language throughout French Polynesia (the Society Islands, Marquesas, the Tuamotus, etc.) and in Vanuatu. Distinctive varieties of French have developed in New Caledonia and the Society Islands.

English is the now the first language of most people in Hawai'i and New Zealand and is an important second language throughout the Pacific Islands except in the French-speaking regions. Highly distinctive varieties of English have developed in various Pacific Island regions (Burridge and Kortmann 2004), including Fiji (Mugler and Tent 2004; Tent and Mugler 2004), Pitcairn and Norfolk Island (Ingram and Mühlhäusler 2004; Mühlhäusler 2004), and Hawai'i (Sakoda and Siegel 2004a, 2004b), where there is a continuum between standard American English and Hawaiian Creole (aka Pidgin).

In Fiji, several Indian languages are spoken by descendants of indentured plantation workers who arrived in the late nineteenth and early twentieth centuries. Fiji Hindi, with more than 400,000 speakers, is the most important lingua franca among Fiji Indians (Barz and Siegel 1988). In Hawai'i, Japanese and a number of Chinese and Filipino languages are spoken by sizable subgroups of the community. Chinese languages are spoken by small populations of Chinese settlers in most Pacific nations. On Easter Island, Spanish coexists with the indigenous Polynesian language.

Recently Developed Languages: The Pidgins and Creoles

As contact between Europeans and Pacific peoples intensified in the nineteenth century, new languages began to be created to bridge the communication gap. The most important of these was nineteenth-century South Pacific Pidgin (Tryon and Charpentier 2004). This started as an unstable contact language (a "jargon") used by English speakers with Australian aborigines and later with Pacific Islanders. It did not become a fully functional language until the late nineteenth century when it came to be used in plantation contexts in the South Pacific as the main lingua franca among Melanesian workers who had no other common language. South Pacific Pidgin was then taken to various parts of Melanesia by repatriated plantation workers returning home. Strong regional variants developed. The best known of these are Tok Pisin (also called New Guinea Pidgin), Solomon Islands Pijin, and Bislama, spoken in Vanuatu.

Tok Pisin is the popular "grassroots" interethnic language of Papua New Guinea. It is spoken as a second language by perhaps five million people and is now the first language of many thousands of urban dwellers (Mühlhäusler 1979; Smith 2002). In the Solomons, Pijin (Jourdan 2002; Keesing 1988) and in Vanuatu, Bislama (Crowley 1990) play similar roles.

The Melanesian pidgins are mixed languages in that they use forms largely derived from English, but in many cases the meanings and pronunciations of these forms have been radically changed under the influence of indigenous (mainly Austronesian) languages. For example, the pronouns of Tok Pisin use elements taken from English that have been completely reworked to create a pronominal system with four persons and three numbers and no gender and case distinctions, identical in structure to that of many Oceanic languages. The singular pronouns are: *mi* (I/me), *yu* (you), *em* (he/him, she/her). The dual pronouns are *mitupela* (we/us two excluding the addressee), *yumi tupela* (we two including the addressee), *yutupela* or *tupela* (you two), and *tupela* (they/them two). The plural pronouns are *mipela* (we three or more excluding the addressee), *yumi* (we/us three or more including the addressee), *yupela* (you three or more), and *ol* (they three or more).

Hawaiian Pidgin, aka Hawaiian Creole (see above), has independent origins (Sakoda and Siegel 2003, 2004a, 2004b). This language developed in the plantations of Hawai'i in the late nineteenth century, initially in the interactions between indentured workers whose mother tongues were Portuguese and Cantonese and speakers of Hawaiian and English (and later, speakers of Japanese, Korean, and Philippine languages). In the twentieth century Hawaiian Pidgin became the first language of most people born in Hawai'i.

Historical Context

Reconstructions of human prehistory in the Pacific have relied chiefly on three disciplines: archaeology, historical linguistics, and biological anthropology. The archaeological record contains little direct evidence of perishable artifacts and the intangible elements of culture. In these matters historical linguistics can be a rich source of information. The central method of historical linguistics, however, tells detailed stories only in cases where language families show numerous cognate sets. The set of surviving cognates diminishes with time, so that after a few thousand years the evidence grows very thin.

Archaeological evidence (Thomas, this volume; O'Connell and Allen 2004) shows that humans reached the Australia–New Guinea continent upward of 40,000 years ago. By 40,000 years ago they had settled New Britain and New Ireland and by about 30,000 years ago they had reached Bougainville in the main Solomons group, separated from New Ireland by 180 km of ocean. By contrast, in the Pacific islands beyond the main Solomons group there are no archaeological sites known to be older than 1200 BCE. These remote islands evidently remained uninhabited by humans until the Austronesian diaspora.

We turn now to the question of whether historical linguistics can tell us anything about the prehistory of Melanesia during the tens of millennia before the arrival of the Austronesians.

Explaining the Diversity of Papuan Languages

The weight of the evidence suggests that most or all of the surviving Papuan families are the outcome of in situ diversification that began in Western Melanesia after humans arrived more than 40,000 years ago. With two trivial exceptions, none of the twenty or so Papuan families found in Western Melanesia have known relatives outside of this area. The exceptions are branches of the Trans–New Guinea and West Papuan families that came to be spoken in the Timor and Halmahera regions, respectively (Ross 2005). The lack of external relatives does not rule out the possibility of further population movements into New Guinea from Wallacea after initial colonization. (Indeed it would be surprising if there were none, although they need not have left surviving daughter languages.) What we know of the archaeology and population genetics of the Bismarcks and the Solomons indicates, however, that after initial settlement, the peoples of these two regions were largely isolated from New Guinea and from each other throughout the Pleistocene (Friedlaender 2007; Pawley et al. 2005; Spriggs 1997).

It may be that, ultimately, most of the contemporary Papuan language families of New Guinea, the Bismarcks, and the Solomons stem from a single ancestor. If that is so, evidence of common origin has almost completely faded. There are a few tantalizing lexical resemblances among certain non-TNG families of North New Guinea, and between certain of these and TNG (Reesink 2005). Such resemblances may be interpreted as due to chance or diffusion or as the faint signal of ancient common origin. Dunn, Reesink, and Terrill (2002) have made a statistical argument for greater-than-chance structural resemblances among the Papuan families of the Bismarcks and the Solomons, suggestive either of remote common origin or of diffusion.

As there was a land bridge connecting Australia and New Guinea as recently as about 8,000 years ago, one might expect to find traces of old connections between Australian languages and one or more Papuan families, but no solid evidence has been found (see Foley 1986 for some speculations).

The Puzzle of the Trans–New Guinea Family

Given that the norm in New Guinea is small Papuan families with small geographic ranges, it is paradoxical that this island is also home to the world's third most numerous language family, and one with an impressive geographic spread: the Trans–New Guinea family. When and where did the TNG expansion begin and what powered it?

By 10,000 to 7,000 years ago some societies in the Central Highlands of Papua New Guinea had begun to cultivate root crops (Denham et al. 2003; Denham 2005). It seems likely that the initial dispersal of TNG languages was linked to the appearance of these agricultural systems. There are several reasons for making this connection.

(i)   TNG is predominantly a family of the central cordillera that runs almost the full length of New Guinea. Most of the highlands valleys were heavily forested in the early Holocene and may have had no permanent populations, or only very small ones, before about 10,000 BP. However, during the late Pleistocene, from 30,000 years ago onward, when there were extensive subalpine grasslands in the highland valleys, hunter-gatherers made seasonal visits to hunt large animals and gather prized plant foods such as the nuts of the mountain pandanus (*Pandanus jiulianetti* + *P. brosimus*) (Evans and Mountain 2005). Many societies in the Central Highlands of Papua New Guinea still use a special "pandanus language," with a vocabulary completely different from ordinary speech, when gathering and cooking mountain pandanus nuts.

The wide use of such a ritual language implies a long-standing importance of these nuts as a food source.

It seems unlikely that the TNG family would have achieved its present dominance of the central highlands unless its speakers possessed some cultural advantages that enabled them to build up populations that could maintain year-round habitation of the major highland valleys and do so for many millennia.

(ii) The location is about right. The Central Highlands of Papua New Guinea, between the Strickland River and Morobe Province, is where we find the greatest concentration of high-order subgroups within TNG. Whether it was the *original* dispersal center is uncertain but it is safe to say that this was a very early area of TNG expansion.

(iii) The timing is about right. The TNG family looks to be somewhere between 7,000 and 10,000 years old. The lexical diversity of the TNG languages is much greater than that which differentiates the main branches of the Indo-European family, which probably broke up at least 5,000 to 6,000 years ago.

It would be nice to be able to support these arguments with Proto-TNG lexical reconstructions associated with agriculture, but as yet no historical linguist has undertaken a thorough, New Guinea–wide search for cognates in cultural domains. At present a term for "taro" (something like *ma) is about the only such reconstruction that can be tentatively attributed to early TNG because of its wide distribution. But as this term stands alone, instead of being embedded in a full terminology for parts of the plant and practices associated with its cultivation, diffusion cannot be ruled out.

The Austronesian Dispersal: Continuity and Change in Culture and Environment

We turn now to the history of the Austronesian family, which dominates the Pacific Islands outside of the New Guinea mainland. Where did the family originate? What factors enabled Austronesian languages to spread so widely? Was the dispersal everywhere associated with the gradual modification of an ancestral Austronesian material culture and social structure, or did the colonists often undergo rapid cultural change after settling in new environments and/or after coming into contact with alien peoples? Were Austronesian languages often adopted by other peoples with whom the colonists traded or intermarried?

The most economical hypothesis places the dispersal center of any language family in the region of its greatest genetic diversity, i.e., where its primary branches or subgroups come together. Although the recorded Austronesian languages of Taiwan number fewer than twenty, they appear to fall into several primary subgroups, coordinate with a single subgroup comprising the rest of Austronesian (Figure 13.3). The generally accepted Austronesian subgrouping strongly favors Taiwan as the location of Proto-Austronesian and the primary dispersal center of the entire family (Blust 1978, 1982, 1993, 1995a, 2009).

Proto-Oceanic, the stage immediately ancestral to almost all the Austronesian languages of the southwest and central Pacific, was probably located in the Bismarck Archipelago. A northwest

Melanesian location is indicated by the subgrouping pattern—the greatest diversity of high-order subgroups is in this area and the closest relatives of Oceanic are found at the western end of New Guinea (Blust 1978)—and by certain lexical reconstructions for fauna, which include names of animals confined to Western Melanesia and eastern Indonesia (Blust 1982), e.g., *kasuari (cassowary), *kadroRa (cuscus, phalanger), and *mwaja (bandicoot). A strong association can be made between the distinctive archaeological culture known as Lapita, which appears suddenly in the Bismarcks around 1400 BCE, and Proto-Oceanic (Green 2003; Kirch 1997, 2000; Spriggs 1997; Pawley 2007a).

The rake-like Oceanic family tree (Figure 13.3), with a scattering of high-order subgroups local to different parts of Melanesia, suggests that once Oceanic speakers began to move beyond the Bismarck Archipelago they quickly established colonies in various parts of the southwest Pacific. This view is reinforced by the archaeological evidence, which shows that bearers of the Lapita culture colonized the eastern Solomons, Vanuatu, New Caledonia, and Fiji between 1200 and 1000 BCE, reached Tonga by 950 BCE, and reached Samoa by 900–800 BCE (Green 2003). The Oceanic-speaking Lapita peoples were the first human settlers of each of these regions. Their rapid expansion eastward, however, was halted in western Polynesia. Here there was a pause of more than a millennium, marking the development of a distinctive Polynesian language and culture, before Oceanic speakers successfully colonized the major island groups lying far to the east of Samoa. The Societies, Cooks, Marquesas, and Hawai'i were not settled until well into the first millennium CE. New Zealand was reached only about 800 years ago.

The settlement history of Micronesia followed a different course (Rainbird 2004). In the second millennium BCE the Marianas and Palau, on the western margins of Micronesia, were colonized by speakers of Malayo-Polynesian languages, probably from the Philippines and/or eastern Indonesia. At around the same time, or soon after, Yap was settled by speakers of an Oceanic language, possibly from the Bismarck Archipelago (Ross 1996a). However, the central and eastern Carolines, and the Kiribati (Gilbert) and the Marshall Islands were probably not settled until some time in the first millennium BCE, by speakers of an Oceanic language, from which stem all the modern Micronesian languages other than Chamorro, Palauan, and Yapese.

What factors powered this remarkable diaspora of Austronesian-speaking peoples? Various commentators have argued that key elements must have been (1) possession of sophisticated watercraft and navigational abilities, allowing rapid dispersal across ocean gaps, and (2) an agricultural "package" involving crops and domestic animals, enabling Austronesian immigrants to dominate and marginalize or absorb nonfarming populations throughout Island Southeast Asia and to survive on islands with impoverished biota in the central Pacific.

In South China and Taiwan, sites with large, permanent villages, showing a range of ceramic vessels often with incised and stamped decorations and sometimes containing residues of grains, appear before 3000 BCE. These assemblages have forebears elsewhere on the East Asian mainland, especially on the coast of China south of the Yangzi. Sites with comparable features appear in the Philippines, Borneo, and Sulawesi only after about 2000 BCE

(Bellwood 1997). Before the arrival of Austronesian horticulturalists, the Philippines and much of the Indo-Malaysian archipelago were, presumably, occupied exclusively by foraging peoples or small-scale horticulturists.

In the mid–second millennium BCE, sites with a range of ceramic pots, jars, and bowls, some showing distinctive, elaborate, dentate-stamped and incised patterns and with an elaborate suite of shell artifacts, appear suddenly in the Bismarck Archipelago north of New Guinea. Some of these sites are associated with large villages having stilt houses. Within three or four centuries of its appearance in the Bismarcks, close relatives of this Lapita cultural complex, as it is known, turn up in various parts of the southwest Pacific, reaching 5,000 km eastward across as far as Fiji, Tonga, and Samoa (Kirch 1997, 2000; Thomas, this volume). Lapita sites east of the main Solomons chain show some differences, such as a shift from stilt houses to houses built on the ground and some reduction in variety and degree of decoration of ceramic vessels.

One point of dispute among archaeologists is whether the various elements attributed to the Lapita culture were (1) introduced as a complete package by Austronesian speakers coming from the west, (2) mainly the product of long periods of local development, or (3) the outcome of a mixture of introduced and local elements.

The linguistic evidence runs strongly against position (2). Lapita assemblages have a geographic distribution that strongly connects them to the Oceanic subgroup of Austronesian languages. And Oceanic languages show continuities in vocabulary, indicating that Proto-Oceanic speakers had an economy and technology similar to that attributed to the bearers of the Lapita culture. Furthermore, much of the Proto-Oceanic economic and technological vocabulary goes back at least to Proto–Malayo-Polynesian. It is hard to escape the conclusion that early Lapita was primarily an imported "Austronesian" culture. That does not, however, rule out the possibility that Lapita culture owed some elements to local innovation and to borrowing from "Papuan" speech communities. Subsequently, in some regions of Western Melanesia, Oceanic and Papuan-speaking communities had upward of 3,000 years of trade and intermarriage, often with far-reaching effects on their languages and cultures.

There is a large body of cognate vocabulary that yields lexical reconstructions (see note 5) bearing on questions of continuity and change in culture and environment associated with the Austronesian diaspora.[10] This material leaves little doubt that the Austronesian expansion into and across the Pacific was, for the most part, carried out by colonists who imported their culture with them and whose linguistic descendants, in many cases, maintained many features of the ancestral culture. Upward of thirty terms to do with seafaring can be reconstructed for Proto-Oceanic (Ross, Pawley, and Osmond 1998). These terms are continued in widely scattered daughter languages from New Guinea to Micronesia and Polynesia and most of them continue Proto–Malayo-Polynesian prototypes. Table 13.4 gives a sample.

A term for double canoe is not reconstructable for Proto-Oceanic, but is attributable to Proto-Polynesian, suggesting that the double canoe may have been developed by Oceanic speakers only after they moved into the central Pacific.

Lexical comparisons show that Proto-Austronesian speakers had a cluster of terms for rice and millet: *pajay (rice plant,

Table 13.4

Some Proto-Oceanic Terms for Canoe Parts and Seafaring

	Meaning
*waga	outrigger canoe (generic); large sailing canoe
*tola	kind of large canoe
*baban	plank; canoe plank or strake
*soka(r)	thwart
*(q)oRa	washstrake, probably topstrake
*pataR	platform (over hull and outrigger)
*saman	outrigger float
*kiajo	outrigger boom
*patoto	connective sticks attaching float to boom
*kata(q)e, *kate(q)a	free side of canoe, opposite the outrigger
*layaR	sail
*jila	boom or yard of (triangular) sail
*ŋuju	projecting headboard of prow
*pose	(canoe) paddle
*lima(s), nima(s)	bailer
*laŋon	rollers
*laŋon-i	place rollers under a boat
*ujan, *lujan	to load (a boat); cargo, freight
*quliŋ	to steer; rudder

Table 13.5

Some Proto-Oceanic Terms for Horticulture and Food Plants

	Meaning
*quma	garden, plantation
*poki	to clear ground for planting
*talo(s)	taro, *Colocasia esculenta*
*piRaq	elephant ear taro, *Alocasia macrorrhiza*
*bulaka	swamp taro, *Cyrtosperma chamissonis*
*qupi	greater yam, *Dioscorea alata*; yam (generic)
*up(e,a)	taro seedling
*pudi	banana, *Musa* cultivars
*joRaga	banana, *Australimusa* group
*topu	sugar cane, *Saccharum officinarum*
*laqia	ginger, *Zingiber officinale*
*kuluR	breadfruit, *Artocarpus altilis*
*Rabia	sago, *Metroxylon* spp., mainly *Metroxylon sagu*
*sag(u)	sago starch
*talise	Java almond, Indian almond, *Terminalia catappa*
*qipi	Tahitian chestnut, Pacific chestnut, *Inocarpus fagifer*
*[ka]ŋaRi	canarium almond, *Canarium* spp.
*kapika	Malay apple and rose apple, *Eugenia* spp.
*ñonum	*Morinda citrifolia*
*tawan	*Pometia pinnata*
*quRis	Polynesian plum, Tahitian apple, *Spondias cytherea*
*ñatu(q)	tree with avocado-like fruit and hardwood, *Burckella obovata*

paddy), *beRas (husked rice), *Semay (cooked rice), *ZaRami (rice straw), and *zawa (millet), as well as *qumah (garden, cultivated field) (Blust 1995b, 1995c, 2009). A group of terms for root crops are attributable to Proto–Malayo-Polynesian but not (on present evidence) to Proto-Austronesian: *tales (taro: Colocasia sp.), *qubi (yam: Dioscorea sp.), *biRaq (giant arum: Alocasia sp.). Whereas all the root crop terms persist in Proto-Oceanic, none of those for grain crops do, indicating that rice and millet were not part of the Proto-Oceanic economy. It it is likely that cereals were less suited than root and tree crops to the tropical environments encountered by the Austronesian colonists. Table 13.5 lists a selection of Proto-Oceanic terms having to do with horticulture and food plants, based on Ross (1996b; Ross, Pawley, and Osmond 2008).

Although they came to dominate the Philippines and Indonesia, Austronesian languages had much less impact in mainland New Guinea, where they are mainly confined to certain patches along the north coast and southeast Papua. This distribution suggests that some of the non-Austronesian peoples of the north coast were already practicing agriculture when the Austronesians arrived or at least had an economy capable of supporting high population densities. At any rate, they had the numbers and organization to hold their ground. There are abundant signs that the Austronesians at first had a similar, marginal distribution in Halmahera, Timor, New Britain, New Ireland, Bougainville, and the Solomons. In due course, however, a large part of these regions became Austronesian-speaking, though not without a good deal of linguistic and cultural exchange between immigrants and aboriginal populations (Dutton and Tryon 1994).

NOTES

1. I am indebted to Ann Chowning, Margaret Florey, Robin Hide, Malcolm Ross, Matthew Spriggs, and Gerard Ward for useful comments on the first draft. Research reported here on the Kalam language and ethnobiology was supported by grants from the Wenner Gren Foundation for Anthropological Research, the NZ University Grants Committee, and the Papua New Guinea Biological Foundation.

For present purposes the Pacific Islands are defined as consisting of Melanesia, Micronesia, and Polynesia, that is, "Oceania." It will be necessary however to touch on relationships with languages of contiguous regions. Within Melanesia a distinction is made between New Guinea and what is often termed "Island Melanesia."

2. These are fairly conservative estimates. Linguists usually regard two speech traditions as different languages if connected speech in the two is mutually unintelligible for most practical purposes. This criterion leaves a considerable residue of unclear cases, where a parent language has given rise to a chain of dialects that continue to diverge, as in the case of the Romance languages, where there is still some mutual intelligibility between Spanish, Portuguese, Catalan, Italian, Romansch, Sardinian, and others.

3. Two language families (like two people) are spoken of as "unrelated" if they are not known to share a common ancestor. It is not possible to prove that two languages are not, ultimately, genetically related; one can only show that there is no good evidence for positing a genetic connection. To establish that languages are related one must demonstrate that they share resemblances that must be attributed to direct inheritance rather than to other causes—borrowing, chance, or universal characteristics of human speech. Among the kinds of resemblances indicating common descent are systematic sound correspondences in words with related meanings.

4. We find striking differences between languages in the domains that are elaborated. It is common for small traditional societies to distinguish by name about one thousand different wild plants and for horticultural communities to name fifty or more varieties of a single plant species when it is a staple crop. The Kaluli of Papua New Guinea, who live surrounded by wet rain forest near Mount Bosavi, have more than ninety words for different kinds of noises made by water (S. Feld personal communication).

5. One way of measuring the linguistic diversity in a region is simply to count the number of different languages—comparable to reckoning diversity of fauna, say, by counting the number of species. But if all the languages—or bird species—of a region were to belong to a single family, the genetic diversity in these domains would be shallow no matter how large the number of languages or species. A measure of deep genetic diversity is the number of distinct genetic stocks

(language groups that have no established relationships to any other groups).

6. Linguistic "reconstructions" are elements (sounds, words, etc.) attributed to a prehistoric language on the basis of inference, as opposed to observation. For a reconstruction to be reliable it must be based on systematic agreements between elements in recorded languages, following the procedures of the genetic comparative method, which rests crucially on the principle of regularity of sound change. See also note 3.

7. The Oceanic group is defined by a number of common innovations in sound system and grammar. Evidence for Oceanic was first put forward by Dempwolff (1934–1938), and subsequent research (e.g., Ross 1988; Lynch, Ross, and Crowley 2002) has refined his arguments and generally strengthened the case.

8. This subgrouping is based on many sources, summarized in Lynch, Ross, and Crowley (2002) and Pawley and Ross (1995). Less conservative subgroupings would lump together certain of these subgroups.

9. In their atlas, Wurm and Hattori (1981–1983) lump all the Papuan languages from New Britain to the Solomons in an East Papuan phylum, together with Yeletne of Rossel Island. This highly speculative grouping has no solid support (Ross 2001, 2005). The non-Polynesian languages of the Reef Islands and Santa Cruz have sometimes been classified as Papuan but recent work has established that they are Oceanic (Ross and Næss 2007).

10. About 1,000 lexical reconstructions have been attributed to Proto-Austronesian and more than 4,000 to Proto–Malayo-Polynesian (Blust 1995c). The first four volumes of a six-volume treatment of Proto-Oceanic lexicon, containing about 2,000 cognate sets with commentary, have appeared (Ross, Pawley, and Osmond 1998, 2003, 2008, 2011). A Proto-Polynesian lexical file has grown to over 3,000 reconstructions (Biggs and Clark 2006). Extensive lexicons have also been reconstructed for Proto-Micronesian (Bender et al. 2003) and Proto–North and Central Vanuatu (Clark 2009).

BIBLIOGRAPHY

Barz, R. K., and J. Siegel. 1988. *Language transplanted—the development of overseas Hindi.* Wiesbaden: Harrassowitz.

Bellwood, P. 1996. The origins and spread of agriculture in the Indo-Pacific region. In *The origins and spread of agriculture and pastoralism in Eurasia,* ed. D. Harris, 465–498. London: UCL Press.

———. 1997. *Prehistory of the Indo-Malaysian Archipelago,* rev. ed. Honolulu: University of Hawaiʻi Press.

———. 2004. *The first farmers: The origins of agricultural societies.* London & New York: Wiley/Blackwell.

Bellwood, P., J. J. Fox, and D. Tryon, ed. 1995. *The Austronesians: Historical and comparative perspectives.* Canberra: Department of Anthropology, Research School of Pacific and Asian Studies, Australian National University.

Bender, B., F. Jackson, J. C. Marck, K. Regh, H-M. Sohn, S. Trussel, and J. Wang. 2003. Proto-Micronesian Reconstructions—I. *Oceanic Linguistics* 42(1): 1–110. Proto-Micronesian Reconstructions—II. *Oceanic Linguistics* 42(2): 271–358.

Bennardo, G., ed. 2002. *Representing space in Oceania: Culture in language and mind.* Canberra: Pacific Linguistics.

Biggs, B., and R. Clark. 2006. Proto-Polynesian lexical file (POLLEX). Computer file. Department of Maori Studies, University of Auckland.

Blust, R. A. 1978. Eastern Malayo-Polynesian: A subgrouping

argument. In *Second International Conference on Austronesian Linguistics: Proceedings,* ed. S. A. Wurm and L. Carrington, 181–234. Canberra: Pacific Linguistics.

———. 1982. The linguistic value of the Wallace Line. *Bijdragen tot de Taal-, Land en Volkenkunde* 138: 231–250.

———. 1993–94. Central and Central-Eastern Malayo-Polynesian. *Oceanic Linguistics* 32: 241–293.

———. 1995a. The position of the Formosan languages: Method and theory in Austronesian comparative linguistics. In *Papers for International Symposium on Austronesian Studies Relating to Taiwan,* ed. P. J-K. Li, C-H. Stang, and Y-K. Huang, 585–650. Taipei: Institute of Historical Philology, Academia Sinica.

———. 1995b. The prehistory of the Austronesian-speaking peoples: A view from language. *Journal of World Prehistory* 9(4): 453–510.

———. 1995c. Austronesian comparative dictionary. Computer file. Department of Linguistics, University of Hawai'i.

———. 2009. *The Austronesian languages.* Canberra: Pacific Linguistics.

Burridge, K., and B. Kortman, ed. 2004. *Varieties of English.* Vol. 3, *The Pacific and Asia.* Berlin: Mouton de Gruyter.

Clark, R. 1976. *Aspects of Proto-Polynesian syntax.* Auckland: Linguistic Society of New Zealand.

———. 2009. *Leo Tuai. A comparative lexical study of North and Central Vanuatu languages.* Canberra: Pacific Linguistics.

Crowley, T., 1990. *From Beach-la-Mar to Bislama: The development of the national language of Vanuatu.* Oxford: Oxford University Press.

Dempwolff, O. 1934–38. *Vergleichende Lautlehre des austronesichen Wortschatzes.* Vols. 1 (1934), 2 (1937), 3 (1938). Berlin: Dietrich Reimer.

Denham, T. 2005. Agricultural origins and the emergence of rectilinear ditch networks in the Highlands of New Guinea. In *Papuan pasts: Cultural, linguistic and biological histories of Papuan speaking peoples,* ed. A. Pawley, R. Attenborough, J. Golson, and R. Hide, 329–361. Canberra: Pacific Linguistics.

Denham, T., S. Haberle, C. Lentfer, R, Fullagar, J. Field, M. Therin, N. Porch, and B. Winsborough. 2003. Origins of agriculture at Kuk Swamp in the Highlands of New Guinea. *Science* 201: 189–193.

Dunn M., G. Reesink, and A. Terrill. 2002. The East Papuan languages: A preliminary typological appraisal. *Oceanic Linguistics* 41: 28–62.

Dutton, T. E., and D. T. Tryon, eds. 1994. *Language contact and change in the Austronesian world.* Berlin: Mouton de Gruyter.

Evans, Benjamin, and Mary-Jane Mountain. 2005. Pasin bilong tumbuna: Archaeological evidence for early human activity in the Highlands of Papua New Guinea. In *Papuan pasts: Cultural, linguistic and biological histories of Papuan-speaking peoples,* ed. A. Pawley, R. Attenborough, J. Golson, and R. Hide, 363–386. Canberra: Pacific Linguistics.

Foley, W. F. 1986. *Papuan languages.* Cambridge: Cambridge University Press.

———. 2000. The languages of the New Guinea area. *Annual Review of Anthropology* 29: 357–404.

———. 2005. Linguistic prehistory in the Sepik-Ramu basin. In *Papuan pasts: Cultural, linguistic and biological histories of Papuan-speaking peoples,* ed. A. Pawley, R. Attenborough, J. Golson, and R. Hide, 109–144. Canberra: Pacific Linguistics.

Friedlaender, Jonathan, ed. 2007. *Population genetics, linguistics, and culture history in the southwest Pacific: A synthesis.* New York: Oxford University Press.

Geraghty, P. 1983. *Topics in Fijian language history.* Oceanic Linguistics Special Publication 18. Honolulu: University of Hawai'i Press.

Green, R. C. 2003. The Lapita horizon and traditions: Signature for one set of oceanic migrations. In *Pacific archaeology: Assessments and prospects. Proceedings of the international conference for the 50th anniversary of the first Lapita conference (July 1952),* ed. C. Sand, 95–129. Les Cahiers de l'Archéologie en Nouvelle-Calédonie. Vol. 15. Noumea: New Caledonia Museum.

Gordon, Raymond. 2005. *Ethnologue: Languages of the world,* 15th ed. Dallas: SIL International.

Ingram, J., and P. Mühlhäusler. Norfolk Island-Pitcairn English: Phonetics and phonology. In *Varieties of English.* Vol. 3, *The Pacific and Asia,* ed. K. Burridge and B. Kortman, 267–291. Berlin: Mouton de Gruyter.

Jourdan, Christine. 2002. *Solomon Islands Pijin: A trilingual cultural dictionary.* Canberra: Pacific Linguistics.

Keesing, R. C. 1988. *Melanesian languages and the Oceanic substrate.* Stanford, Calif.: Stanford University Press.

Kirch, P. V. 1997. *The Lapita peoples.* Oxford: Blackwell.

———. 2000. *On the road of the winds: An archaeological history of the Pacific Islands before European contact.* Berkeley: University of California Press.

Lynch, John. 1998. *Pacific languages: An introduction.* Honolulu: University of Hawai'i Press.

Lynch, J., M. Ross, and T. Crowley, eds. 2002. *The Oceanic languages.* London: Curzon Press.

Majnep, I. S., and R. Bulmer. 2007. *Animals the ancestors hunted: An account of the wild mammals of the Kalam area, Papua New Guinea.* Adelaide: Crawford House.

Marck, J. 1986. Micronesian dialects and the overnight voyage. *Journal of the Polynesian Society* 95(2): 253–258.

———. 2001. *Polynesian language and culture history.* Canberra: Pacific Linguistics.

Mugler, F., and J. Tent, 2004. Fiji English: Morphology and syntax. In *Varieties of English.* Vol. 3, *The Pacific and Asia.* ed. K. Burridge and B. Kortman, 546–567. Berlin: Mouton de Gruyter.

Mühlhäusler, P. 1979. *Growth and structure of the lexicon of New Guinea Pidgin.* Canberra: Pacific Linguistics.

———. 2004. Norfolk Island-Pitcairn English (Pitkern Norfolk): Morphology and syntax. In *Varieties of English.* Vol. 3, *The Pacific and Asia,* ed. K. Burridge and B. Kortman, 568–582. Berlin: Mouton de Gruyter.

O'Connell, J., and J. Allen. 2004. Dating the colonization of Sahul (Pleistocene Australia–New Guinea): A review of recent research. *J. Archaeological Science* 31: 835–853.

Pawley, A. 2005a. The chequered career of the Trans New Guinea hypothesis: Recent research and its implications. In *Papuan pasts: Cultural, linguistic and biological histories of Papuan-speaking peoples,* ed. A. Pawley, R. Attenborough, J. Golson, and R. Hide, 67–107. Canberra: Pacific Linguistics.

———. 2005b. Papuan languages. In *Encyclopaedia of language and linguistics,* 2nd. ed., vol. 9, ed. K. Brown et al., 162–171. Oxford: Elsevier.

———. 2005c. The Trans New Guinea family. In *Encyclopaedia of language and linguistics,* 2nd ed., vol. 13, ed. K. Brown et al., 17–22. Oxford: Elsevier.

———. 2007a. The origins of early Lapita culture: The testimony of historical linguistics. In *Oceanic explorations: Lapita and western Pacific settlement,* ed. S. Bedford, C. Sand, and S. P. Connaughton, 7–49. Canberra: ANU E Press.

———. 2007b. Recent research on the historical relationships of the Papuan languages, or, What does linguistics say about the prehistory of Melanesia? In *Population genetics, linguistics, and culture history in the southwest Pacific: A synthesis,* ed. J. Friedlaender, 36–58. New York: Oxford University Press.

Pawley, A., R. Attenborough, J. Golson, and R. Hide. 2005. *Papuan pasts: Cultural, linguistic and biological histories of Papuan-speaking peoples.* Canberra: Pacific Linguistics.

Pawley, A., and M. Ross. 1995. The prehistory of the Oceanic languages: A current view. In *The Austronesians: Historical and comparative perspectives,* ed. P. Bellwood, J. Fox, and D. Tryon, 39–74. Department of Anthropology, Research School of Pacific and Asian Studies, Australian National University.

Powell, J. M. 1976. Ethnobotany. In *New Guinea vegetation*, ed. K. Paijmans, 106–183. Canberra: CSIRO.

Reesink, G. 2005. West Papuan languages: Roots and development. In *Papuan pasts: Cultural, linguistic and biological histories of Papuan speaking peoples*, ed. A. Pawley, R. Attenborough, J. Golson, and R. Hide, 185–219. Canberra: Pacific Linguistics.

Ross, M. D. 1988. *Proto Oceanic and the Austronesian languages of western Melanesia*. Canberra: Pacific Linguistics.

———. 1996a. Is Yapese Oceanic? In *Reconstruction, classification, description. Festschrift in honour of Isidore Dyen*. ed. B. Nothofer, 121–166. Hamburg: Verlag Meyer & Co.

———. 1996b. Reconstructing food plant terms and associated terminologies in Proto Oceanic. In *Oceanic Studies: Proceedings of the First International Conference on Oceanic Linguistics*, ed. J. Lynch and F. Pat, 165–223. Canberra: Pacific Linguistics.

———. 2001. Is there an East Papuan phylum? Evidence from pronouns. In *The boy from Bundaberg: Studies in Melanesian linguistics in honour of Tom Dutton*, ed. A. Pawley, M. Ross, and D. Tryon, 301–321. Canberra: Pacific Linguistics.

———. 2005. Pronouns as a preliminary diagnostic for grouping Papuan languages. In *Papuan pasts: Cultural, linguistic and biological histories of Papuan speaking peoples*, ed. A. Pawley, R. Attenborough, J. Golson, and R. Hide, 15–65. Canberra: Pacific Linguistics.

———. 2011. The lexicon of Proto Oceanic: The culture and environment of ancestral Oceanic society. Vol. 4, *Animals* Canberra: Pacific Linguistics.

Ross, M. D., and Å. Næss, 2007. An Oceanic origin for Äiwoo, the language of the Reef Islands? *Oceanic Linguistics* 46: 456–498.

Ross, M. D., A. Pawley, and M. Osmond, eds. 1998. *The lexicon of Proto Oceanic: The culture and environment of ancestral Oceanic society*. Vol. 1, *Material culture*. Canberra: Pacific Linguistics.

———. 2003. *The lexicon of Proto Oceanic: The culture and environment of ancestral Oceanic society*. Vol. 2, *The physical environment*. Canberra: Pacific Linguistics.

———. 2008. *The lexicon of Proto Oceanic: The culture and environment of ancestral Oceanic society*. Vol. 3, *Plants*. Canberra: Pacific Linguistics.

Sakoda, K., and J. Siegel. 2003. *Pidgin grammar: An introduction to the Creole language of Hawaiʻi*. Honolulu: Bess Press.

———. 2004a. Hawaiʻi Creole: Phonology. In *Varieties of English*. Vol. 3, *The Pacific and Asia*, ed. K. Burridge and B. Kortman, 210–233. Berlin: Mouton de Gruyter.

———. 2004b. Hawaiʻi Creole: Morphology and syntax. In *Varieties of English*. Vol. 3, *The Pacific and Asia*, ed. K. Burridge and B. Kortman, 524–545. Berlin: Mouton de Gruyter.

Sebeok, T. E., ed. 1971. *Current trends in linguistics*. Vol. 8, *Linguistics in Oceania*. The Hague: Mouton.

Smith, G. P. 2002. *Growing up with Tok Pisin. Contact, creolization and change in Papua New Guinea's national language*. London: Battlebridge.

Spriggs, M. 1997. *The Island Melanesians*. Oxford and Cambridge, Mass.: Blackwell.

Tent, J., and F. Mugler. 2004. Fiji English: Phonology. *Varieties of English*. Vol. 3, *The Pacific and Asia*. ed. K. Burridge and B. Kortman, 234–266. Berlin: Mouton de Gruyter.

Tryon, D. 1976. *New Hebrides languages: An internal classification*. Canberra: Pacific Linguistics.

———, ed. 1995. *Comparative Austronesian dictionary*. 5 vols. Berlin: Mouton de Gruyter.

Tryon, D., and J-M. Charpentier. 2004. *Pacific pidgins and creoles: Origins, growth and development*. Berlin: Mouton de Gruyter.

Tryon, D., and G. Hackman. 1983. *Solomon Islands languages: An internal classification*. Canberra: Pacific Linguistics.

Wurm, S. A., ed. 1975. *New Guinea area languages and linguistics*, vol. 1. Canberra: Pacific Linguistics.

Wurm, S. A., and S. Hattori, ed. 1981–1983. *Language atlas of the Pacific area*, vol. 1 (1981), vol. 2 (1983). Canberra: Pacific Linguistics.

Wurm, S. A., P. Mühlhäusler, and D. Tryon, eds. 1996. *Atlas of languages of intercultural communication in the Pacific, Asia and the Americas*. 3 vols. Berlin: Mouton de Gruyter.

Social Relations

Lamont Lindstrom

14

Alexander Selkirk, marooned in the Juan Fernandez Islands of the southeastern Pacific between 1704 and 1709, inspired one of literature's most enduring sociological horror stories. In *Robinson Crusoe,* Daniel Defoe retold Selkirk's castaway experience to explore the individual's relations with society. By the end of the story, after surviving several years of lonely and desperate isolation, Crusoe builds a new society on his desert island beginning with his Man Friday. Enduring debates about the "individual" and whether or not individuals can exist outside society, and also about humanity's growing estrangement from nature, have ensured the lasting popularity of Defoe's novel. These issues began to take on a particular urgency in Defoe's eighteenth century as capitalism, with its system of economic classes, was intensifying, reshaping long-standing social relational patterns.

Many early European explorers expected distant Pacific islands to be deserted like Crusoe's sanctuary. They were astonished to find them inhabited. We now know that apart from odd castaways like Selkirk, the human occupation of the Pacific Islands has been a social endeavor. Humans everywhere are social animals, but understandings of the person and the group differ from place to place and change from time to time. In the years since Defoe's fable, social theorists frequently have looked to the Pacific's many island societies as a laboratory in which to explore the diverse nature of personhood and sociability. They have also turned to Pacific societies to document connections between social structure, relational patterns, and environmental constraints.

Social Relation, Identity, Role

A variety of interests, both political and theoretical, including the colonialist imperatives of governance and control, have motivated European efforts to map out Pacific social orders. This ongoing concern to make sociological sense of the Pacific has informed Western debates about the definition and scope of personhood and society, and questions about how individuals fit into that larger social order. Over the past two centuries, Pacific cultures have provided data for alternative constructions of personhood and society that Western critics have used to either justify or to challenge their own social orders (Molloy 2008). The romantic South Seas or, alternatively, the savage South Seas both acquired their peculiar character in a contrastive relationship with a Europe imagined to be enervated and dreary or a Europe celebrated as admirably evolved and civilized.

Like those fabulous blind men who grasp different parts of the elephant, scholars have approached Pacific social orders at several different levels. For some, the basic unit of analysis is the individual and then his or her personal network of social relationships (see Hage and Harary 2007). Others start with the social relationship itself as the fundamental social unit—a dyad that relates two persons into larger groups and institutions. And still others begin with those larger groups (clans, lineages, villages, chiefdoms) and institutions (the economy, religion, moiety systems, and so forth) as their primary units of analysis. Whether focused at the level of person, relational dyad, or institution, a common conclusion is that Pacific Islanders remain, even today, less individualistic and more embedded within their social relationships and kin groups than are, say, most Americans, Europeans, or Australians.

Before surveying social relations in the Pacific, we should first recollect the standard sociological model of a relationship. This, simply, is a dyad comprising two endpoints (*social identities*) joined together by culturally organized exchange behavior (a *role*). This schema of *identity* and *role* attempts to capture the basics of how people relate in culturally patterned ways. Every social relation involves a pair of social identities, or capacities or positions, that people must assume in order to relate together in locally understandable ways. Important social identities are labeled, for example, some English examples from the United States include parent/child, brother/sister, teacher/student, chief/commoner, lover/lover, friend/friend. Children born into a society learn the inventory of locally recognized and named social identities (see Ochs 1988; Schieffelin 1990; Morton 1996).

Along with paired social identities, children also learn local expectations of the *roles,* or the appropriate behavior, or culturally scripted interaction, associated with related identities. The minimal shared expectations of roles must be met or a person's claim to the associated identity may be lost. If I do not treat my children right, my identity as a proper father may be impugned. If I behave unexpectedly, my identity claims may lose social legitimacy. "Treating someone right," or relating in general, always involves some form of exchange. Social interaction thus can be rephrased largely as exchange. For relationships to endure, the people in them must at least occasionally exchange something. And important relations—those beyond the casual or passing—require ongoing and repeated acts of exchange. When interaction ceases, relations fade away.

There are four basic sorts of relational exchange tokens: communications (words and nonverbal signals); acts of body contact such as petting, touching, kissing, blows, and beatings; things, goods, or material items, some of which are animate (pigs, for example, along with other animal and plant species are important Pacific exchange items); and, occasionally, other human beings. One's role comprises expectations about the exchange of these several sorts of tokens within a social relationship, given one's identity therein as, say, a "chief" or a "mother" or a "husband." Brothers, for instance, must give and receive from one another the locally expected sorts of words and things. If they do not, their brotherhood is no longer true or real.

During any one day, people take on many social identities, some simultaneously, as they engage in social relationships. Most relationships are context-dependent, associated with particular times and places. Risi, for example, who lives in Port Vila, Vanuatu, waking in the morning finds herself engaged mostly within child/parent kin relations. Walking to school highlights her friend/friend identities. Then, within the schoolroom context, her student/teacher relations come to the fore, interpolated with ongoing student/student, friend/friend, and perhaps girlfriend/boyfriend connections. After school, she takes on economic identities of coworker/coworker, clerk/customer, and employee/boss in the small trade store where she works. In the evening, she returns home and in this context her kin identities once again become predominant.

A few social identities—notably those of gender, age, race/ethnicity, and, notably in the Pacific, kin-group membership—are less tied to specific contexts. Instead, people carry these fundamental (although still culturally recognized) social capacities around within them throughout the day, wherever they are. Identities of kinship, age, and gender often influence the other social relations in which that person takes part, be these economic, political, or religious.

The diversity of cultures across the immense spread of the Pacific Ocean makes the attempt to generalize or summarize island social relations difficult. One can describe almost as many differences as commonalities among Pacific cultures. Life, and the social relations that structure it, on Oʻahu, Tanna, Fais, Viti Levu, and Guam differ in remarkable ways. Moreover, many of the sorts of social relations in which islanders now engage in the twenty-first century are unlike those their ancestors enjoyed in 1900 and before, and this is as true of isolated Anuta in Solomon Islands as it is of metropolitan Honolulu or Auckland (Feinberg 2004). Moreover, social relations in today's Pacific towns and cities, where people are more firmly tied into global networks, are no longer the same as those back in rural villages or outer-island hinterlands.

This chapter, which takes a rural ("traditional") rather than urban perspective, explores general features of Pacific social relationships. It reviews basic Pacific understandings of the person and the means by which islanders define, create, cultivate, and repair their social relations. In so doing, however, it inevitably must neglect much of the diversity and complexity of social life across the region as a whole.

Personhood

The tenor and organization of a social relationship obviously have much to do with the "persons" involved. And the Pacific person—at least in still traditionalist regions—may not be necessarily the same as the "individual," as this has developed in the West. Many have suggested, in fact, that the individual (as we know ourselves to be today) appeared fairly recently in European history, an artifact of modernity, of the Enlightenment, and of an industrialized, capitalist mode of production. Humans everywhere conceive of "persons." All languages have words for "me" and "you" and also various permutations of "he and/or she," "we," "you all," and "they." Everyone also has a notion of a self—some intellectual and emotional consciousness of being. But people may not conceive of their persons and their selves also as individualistic, at least not to the same degree.

Those of us who know ourselves as individuals have absorbed a set of values and expectations about that individuality (even if our life experiences and emotions do not always measure up to the ideal). The Western person (and self)—at least if this person is normal and "balanced"—should live within his or her skin. The person is bounded, autonomous, and unique. Individual identity does not spill over to incorporate other, also presumably autonomous, individuals. Nor does personal identity include parts of the landscape. Zen-like, oceanic experiences of satori, in which the boundaries of individual personality melt away and one becomes one with Nature, are seemingly only for mystics, the insane, and drug abusers. Furthermore, individuals should strive for a unified knowledge of self so that life gets read as a dramatic journey with a satisfactory beginning, middle, and end, and (if all goes well) a purpose as well. Our major individualist duty is to tend to, and to develop, ourselves—to become the best that we might be.

Those theorists who have concerned themselves with personhood here and there about the Pacific have argued that many islanders conceive of themselves—and therefore of their social relations in general—in less individualistic terms. In many island cultures, sense of self goes beyond the skin to incorporate other persons and also aspects of objects and landscape. Traditionally, some islanders may also have less coherent, less unified, and less singular conceptions of selves, as analyses of the person and its ontology in different Pacific cultures have suggested (see, for examples, accounts of Pacific ethnopsychologies in White and Kirkpatrick 1985).

Polysided Polynesians

The constitution of the Samoan person has been debated since the early work of Margaret Mead in the 1920s. Mead, like many American anthropologists of her day, was interested in the fit between personality and cultural patterns; see also Levy 1973. Bradd Shore (1982) has argued that Samoans expect people's behavior to reflect their multiple "sides" rather than some singular and integrated inner self. The Samoan person, like a prism, is faceted:

> While the European concept of the integrated, coherent, and "rounded" personality suggests the metaphor of a sphere, the most perfectly "integrated" of objects, the contrasting Samoan metaphor implicit in the Samoan conception of person is a many-faceted gem. (Shore 1982: 141)

The person differs depending on which facet of personality is turned to the fore—which side is then socially engaged. This gem metaphor emphasizes the several surfaces of personality rather than supposing some coherent inner depth where the truth, or authenticity, of a person might be sought.

Samoan personality facets include one's kinship and political identities and also a set of character traits. People may have complex and rapidly changeable characters as well as multiple social identities. Shore notes:

> Samoans on the whole do not focus on a temperamental or behavioral consistency within a person, although they may recognize one or more traits as strong within that person. The emphasis for evaluating people is not the consistency of behavior with behavior, or of trait with trait, but rather the appropriateness of a trait to a given situation. (1982: 140)

People do not conceive of an integrated, consistent self inhabiting a body over the long term. Promising, for instance, has different weight in Samoa than it does in the West insofar as there is no internally consistent person to guarantee that the promise will be fulfilled from one context to the next. Also, Samoans, like most Pacific Islanders, do not value privacy (or at least do not admit to liking to be alone, as this would be impolite and suspicious). Shore suggests that if left alone, people may lose grasp of who they are since their personality depends on and reflects their relations with others, rather than welling upward from a sense of having a coherent and enduring inner self that inhabits their bodies. It is commonplace that islanders almost everywhere fail to appreciate Western demands for individual privacy—time alone that helps shore up the boundaries of our personalities when these become frayed. Personal privacy, in the Pacific, menaces rather than protects the self, given its different constitution.

Melanesian Dividuals

Drawing partly on her research near Mount Hagen, in the Highlands of Papua New Guinea, Marilyn Strathern (1988; see also Read 1955) has suggested that Melanesians are "dividuals" rather than individuals. The latter term, from the Latin for "indivisible," clearly reflects Western notions of a bounded, unified, and autonomous self. Strathern proposed that Papua New Guineans instead know themselves to comprise divisible parts, each of which reflects their participation in various social relationships, particularly kin relations. She writes:

> A Melanesian model of the person would already incorporate the fact of connection or relation. The person is not axiomatically "an individual" who, as in Western formulations, derives an integrity from its position as somehow prior to society. (1988: 93)

Strathern argued that Papua New Guineans conceive of their bodies as a "microcosm of relations" (1988: 131; see also Lipuma 2001; Kuehling 2005). The body, too, and not just the self, is built up of different bits and pieces, the residue of past and present exchanges with others. People in a relationship exchange goods, and these "things are conceptualized as parts of persons" (1988: 178). I, as a person, include part of you—my mother—because of the direct impact your presence has had on me, and also because the food and other objects that you gave me have remained part of you even as I took them into my body.

A conception of dividuated persons whose parts are composed of personalized objects they receive from other dividuated persons obviously challenges the simple Western model of a social relationship. In this model, recall, two independent individuals exchange tokens (objects, words) that they believe to be alienable or disconnectable from the self. We might, however, still use the standard sociological model of two identities linked by exchange. But if Strathern is correct, this does not in Melanesia represent two autonomous individuals swapping alienable objects. Rather, the relational dyad comprises a side or part (or Samoan facet) of one person that incorporates—on the opposite side of the relationship—some part of another person as well as the inalienable items, words, and goods that flow within (and not between) this particular facet of joint personality.

Micronesian Insides

Islanders on Ifaluk, according to Catherine Lutz (1988), share the Samoan and New Guinean idea of the person as fundamentally social: "The person is first and foremost a social creature and only secondarily, and in a limited way, an autonomous individual" (1988: 81). The Ifaluk have weak notions of personal boundaries, for example, and "it is considered natural that one person's thought should influence another's" (1988: 88). A person's "internal processes are seen as acquiring their significance in relation to social processes" (1988: 96). Because Ifaluk boundaries between self and other are porous, people understand their feelings mostly to originate externally rather than to emerge from internal emotional processes: "their emotional lives are their social lives" (1988: 101). On Ifaluk, too, aspects of the Pacific self are located at least partly outside the body.

These analyses of Pacific understandings of the person as faceted, multiple, and not completely contained within the body help explain a number of other aspects of Pacific cultures. Some, for example, have noted difficulties in eliciting coherent life histories from islanders. If people do not conceive of themselves as an autonomous and unique personality, they may be unaccustomed to talking about themselves as if they have only one long life story. Only those who believe that they remain essentially the same through time and space—who imagine that they are engaged in some life journey that has a beginning, middle, and an end—may be used to telling coherent, developmental life stories. Moreover, in places such as Fiji, chiefs and important storytellers sometimes use the first-person pronoun "I" to recount what some ancestral namesake accomplished in the past (Lindstrom 1985). Here one's personality—at least in the ways people have of talking about this—can incorporate long-dead personages and historic feats.

Many islanders have several personal names, furthermore, that correspond to various facets of their personality. They may have various names simultaneously and they also may change their main name throughout their lives, as different aspects of their personality emerge or as they change character altogether. My Vanuatu friend Tihinei, for example, was first called by another name. Arguing over a boy, she accidentally killed a girl by knocking her down and smashing her head against a tree. After a lengthy dispute-settlement process, her father gave her to the family of the dead girl. She then took the name of her victim, Tihinei, to replace (or impersonate) the girl within her grieving family.

We can also understand in this way why many islanders believe that unbalanced or otherwise unsettled social relations can make them sick. Social discord, or social relationships gone bad, can lead to imbalance, or illness, in the body. Thinking and feeling—processes that we believe to occur within the body—in many island ethnopsychologies emanate from a person's network of relationships (which islanders might experience as part of the self). In most Pacific societies, there is little use for a language of individual creativity to explain the origins of new ideas. Rather, a rhetoric of supernatural inspiration or of learning from others is used to account for novelty. Knowledge comes from the dead, or from parents or elders, and not from one's own internal thought processes (Lindstrom 1990). Here, as with disease, islanders look beyond the body to assign responsibility and to explain novel ideas that we might see as originating from within individuals.

But one must resist the temptation to draw overly rigid oppositions between faceted, dividual islanders on the one hand, and unified, coherent Westerners on the other. Several excellent life histories of islanders have been compiled, for example, despite their supposed lack of coherent selves. These are people who can and do think of their lives as organized developmentally from time to time and event to event (see, e.g., Keesing 1978; A. Strathern 1979). Tihinei's new family, too, never completely accepted her as a replacement for their dead daughter. Nor did the first Tihinei's boyfriend welcome the new Tihinei's continuing amorous advances. Although Tihinei had acquired the social personality of her dead rival, her original personality—or perhaps even her individuality—was not forgotten.

Moreover, people everywhere today are engaged, to one degree or another, in global communicative and exchange networks that circulate notions of the autonomous and responsible individual (see Barker 2007a). Still, the image of the normally autonomous person in the West can also be a caricature. Many of our neighbors may be as many-sided as the ordinary Pacific person, as depicted in the above analyses.

In summary, the constitution and interplay of social relations depends on local understandings of the "person." The standard sociological model of a social relationship that comprises autonomous individuals who are linked by communication and exchange can distort Pacific notions of personhood and how persons relate themselves together into larger social units. Such units, in the islands, most commonly are kinship groups.

Kinship

Kin relations structure most islanders' everyday lives (Figure 14.1). Residence groups are based on kinship. Kinship determines the membership of economic enterprises as well as political and religious associations. Most people live, work, politic, and worship with kin, and these relations combine to define much of who they are. The extended family is common throughout the region, except among the most cosmopolitan. Even in urban centers, such as Papeete, Noumea, and 'Apia, and among those communities (e.g.,

the Hawaiians and New Zealand Maori) that are now encapsulated within settler states, kinship remains important. The Hawaiian 'ohana ("family") and the Maori whaanau ("family"), hapuu ("sub-tribe"), and iwi ("tribe") remain in various ways socially and symbolically powerful today.

Figure 14.1. Father and son construct a new house in Samaria village, Tanna, Vanuatu (photo LL).

Various descent and marriage patterns characterize Pacific societies today. Kinship structures before the colonial era may have been even more diverse. Monogamy and polygyny both were customary marriage practices in different island societies. Although monogamy has spread to become the standard marriage form, especially since most islanders today are Christian, polygyny also is not uncommon, especially in parts of Melanesia, where successful men occasionally may marry more than one wife. Jimmy Stephens, for instance, a political leader involved in the independence of Vanuatu, was partly renowned for the number of his wives.

All the major types of descent reckoning occur in one Pacific society or another. Recent comparative research, however, has suggested that speakers of Proto-Oceanic who settled much of the Pacific practiced matrilineal descent (Hage and Marke 2003). This original matriliny endures on some islands but elsewhere has transformed into other forms of descent, perhaps better to suit ecological conditions. Matrilineal rules of descent still determine kin-group membership in parts of Melanesia (e.g., northern Vanuatu, the Trobriand Islands, parts of Bougainville) and Micronesia (e.g., Pohnpei, Chuuk, Palau). In these societies children become members of their mother's (and mother's brothers') lineages and clans. Elsewhere, people today follow patrilineal or cognatic rules to define the bounds of their descent groups. In patrilineal systems, children share the father's kin-group affiliations. With cognatic (or "bilateral") descent rules, individuals may choose which of their various kin connections, through their mother's or father's side, to activate and therefore which local kin groups to join. Cognatic systems more flexibly distribute individuals among groups insofar as individuals can choose to join different groups of kin in order to access land and other resources. Such choice would be ecologically useful in redistributing an island's human population according to currently available resources.

Other traditional kin practices persist as well. In many Pacific societies, particularly in Polynesia, brother/sister ties are emphasized in one fashion or another. In some communities, as in Tonga and Fiji, older sisters command their brothers' respect (see, e.g., Chambers and Chambers 2001). These traditional sibling ties continue to affect contemporary political relations among the ruling families of Tonga and Fiji. Brothers and sisters, and in some places sons-in-law and mothers-in-law, must avoid certain topics of discussion (such as those involving sexuality and pregnancy) and sometimes avoid one another altogether. This ritual avoidance may relate to marriage practices: unless a sister marries into a certain kin group, her brother may be unable to marry a woman from that group. Ritualized "joking" relations sometimes parallel these avoidance relations. Men who stand next to each other in the kin category "brother-in-law," for instance, in some societies must joke around. Brother/brother relations, too, are politically and economically important throughout the Pacific (see Marshall 1983).

Whatever descent rule locally applies, kin groups such as extended families, clans, and lineages are significant units within the social fabric. In rural areas, people's land and sea rights continue to derive from their kin-group memberships (Hviding 1996; Feinberg 2004). Even in regions where land has been commodified or otherwise alienated from customary land-tenure systems, people may still assert rights to that property based on their kin identities. Traditional kinship relations, furthermore, still often shape a person's choice of whom to marry (see, e.g., Rio 2007). In urban areas, migrants typically employ kin connections to acquire places to live and also often employment. Neighborhoods and settlements of people all from the same region have emerged in or around most Pacific cities. Islanders prefer to live with kin, or at least with people from home areas. In Papua New Guinea, for example, the term "*wantok* ('same language') system" describes the ongoing resilience of rural kin and regional ties within urban areas and within the nation's political and economic organizations. In Vanuatu, the same tendency to import rural kinship relations and support systems into town has been called "islandism."

Relatedness

A person's membership in this or that kin group depends on local cultural notions of descent and relatedness. Although all island cultures recognize "blood" and other shared substances as meaningful for the creation of kin identities, these ideologies of shared substance may be less important than they are in the West (see Linnekin and Poyer 1990). Children also become related to parents through acts of exchange or environmental influence as much as by virtue of their birth. I may become a member of my father's lineage because people believe that I have inherited his blood, or bones, or some other natural substance from him. But I may also become a member of that group if he has nurtured me, or named me, or if I have grown up on his land. These acts of exchange, in fact, make me into his son as they make him my father.

It follows, then, that adoption and fosterage are common in almost all Pacific societies (see Brady 1976). The Hawaiian word for adopted child, *hanai,* comes from "feeding." An exchange of children among families functions to distribute people over sometimes limited landscapes. It also deepens political relations between relatives and neighbors who adopt or foster each other's children. Adoption is facilitated by cultural beliefs that nurture—not just nature—creates kinship. Pacific definitions of the person that incorporate one's social relations also come into play here. My identity—who I truly am—depends greatly on who has cared for me. I become not just what I have eaten, but also part of whoever has fed me, as they become part of me. People establish relations and create kinship through regular acts of sharing and exchange in addition to simpler facts of birth or marital alliance.

Exchange

Islanders create, maintain, and repair their social relations through acts of exchange. Exchange ceremonies, often keyed to important points in a person's life cycle, remark changing positions within a network of kin relations (Figures 14.2 and 14.3). The birth of a baby, the circumcision of a son, the first menstruation of a daughter, the marriage of a child, and the death of a parent all commonly demand the exchange of goods between at least two extended families. Some anthropologists have attempted to model Pacific social structures as the effect of concatenated individual acts of exchange (see, e.g., Schwimmer 1973; Schieffelin 1976).

Figure 14.2. Man killing a pig to be given to an exchange partner in Tanna's nakwiari *ritual dance cycle (photo LL).*

Figure 14.3. Rauaua wraps tuber pudding for baking in an earth oven; this is later given to guests at a funeral feast (photo LL).

Tokens of exchange everywhere in the Pacific include foodstuffs—here again is the symbolic connection between feeding and relatedness. The pig, especially, is a ubiquitous and valued exchange token in almost every Pacific society (except for those, like New Caledonia, that traditionally lacked pigs). Islanders, depending on local ecosystem, also exchange fish, fowl, turtles, dogs, cassowaries, flying foxes—the gamut of larger, available Oceanic animals, wild and domesticated. They also have elaborated a variety of other exchange tokens, ranging from the shell bead and red-feather "moneys" of Solomon Islands to the shell armbands and necklaces of the Trobriand Islands, whale teeth in Fiji, and the large stone disks of Yap. Cash, nowadays, is as common as pigs in lubricating social relations, as are various market commodities that people give one another alongside traditional exchange goods (see Akin and Robbins 1999).

Marriage brings into existence new, affinal relations of kinship between two families and is everywhere celebrated with exchange of goods. Marriage patterns differ, however, from urban areas—where men and women may choose whom to marry, and to marry in church—to rural areas, where traditional marital ritual may still obtain. In Vanuatu, for instance, courts recognize three sorts of marriage: civil, religious, and "customary." Even in urbanized areas, sometimes onerous exchanges of goods that anthropologists have called "bride price" or "bridewealth" remain common in many Pacific societies. In Port Moresby, for example, urbanites jokingly refer to young women as "Toyotas," since that is what their families will demand from prospective suitors. In some Melanesian cultures, like Tanna, people arrange "sister-exchange" marriages. A woman marries into one family, which then must provide a second woman in return (Figure 14.4).

Figure 14.4. Men from one family give one of their daughters to man from a second, who must provide a daughter in return (photo LL).

Islanders exchange goods to repair, as well as to create, social relations. When relations become "entangled" (see Watson-Gegeo and White 1990), people attempt to settle their disputes in formal or informal courts, or at village meetings where they talk out the problem. Among Hawaiians, for example, families in conflict may come together to "set things right" (ho'oponopono) by discussing the issue at hand. Pacific dispute-settlement procedures typically attempt restitution rather than punishment of guilty individuals. Tihinei, as noted above, took on the personality of her victim to restore a family's loss. This, too, speaks of people's concern to preserve the social fabric of relationships rather than the rights or responsibilities of autonomous individuals. Traditionally, where settlement procedures failed, kin and village groups might go to war. Given Pacific conceptions of the person as socially embedded, killing or injuring any relative of the wrongdoer could satisfy honor and balance affairs.

Where dispute-settlement works, however, both parties to a conflict exchange gifts (Figure 14.5), although one side may give more than the other. In Samoa, for example, if someone seriously offends another, to repair relations the chiefs from his or her family apologize (ifoga) by visiting the highest chief of the injured family. They humble themselves by sitting outside his house, their heads bowed and covered with fine woven mats. If the apology is accepted, they present fine mats and also money to the injured family (and may also receive food and small gifts in return). Exchange of this sort functions to restore social relations, just as other acts of exchange once brought these relationships into being and sustained them through time.

Figure 14.5. Man ritually breaks off a branch from a kava plant he is giving away as part of a dispute-settlement exchange (photo LL).

Violence

Compared with American or European norms, violence in the Pacific is modest. No Pacific society was in fact pacific, in that violence both within groups and between groups occurred traditionally. Wars of territorial aggression and violent chiefly competition for paramount status shaped the history of most Polynesian and Micronesian societies. In Melanesia, people also fought over land as well as exchange and marital imbalances and other sore points of conflict (see Gardner and Heider 1968; Knauft 1990).

Colonialization and missionization efforts dampened warfare for several generations throughout much of the Pacific. Recently, however, intergroup conflict has returned in new political form in a number of Pacific states. A rebellion on Bougainville during the 1980s and 1990s, for example, cost several thousand lives. Urban conflict in Honiara, the capital city of Solomon Islands, mostly between indigenous residents of Guadalcanal (where Honiara is located) and migrant families from Malaita Island, erupted in 1999. The Australian government, supported by military and police personnel from other Pacific states, sent in forces in 2003 to restore law and order (Fraenkel 2005). There has also been passing but still deadly violence in New Caledonia and French Polynesia associated with political efforts to acquire independence from France. Fears of potential violence between the indigenous and Indo-Fijian communities of Fiji also constrain politics in that state, which has suffered a series of coups, the most recent in 2006, to protect the political privileges of indigenous Fijians vis-à-vis the Indo-Fijian community (Fraenkel and Firth 2007). Violence has increased in urban areas, such as Port Moresby and other cities in Papua New Guinea, associated with the emergence of urban youth gangs (raskols, in Pidgin English) (Harris 1988). In Chuuk, too, fighting among young men, usually drunk, became a serious social problem in the 1970s (Marshall 1979).

Whereas intergroup violence declined during the twentieth century, intragroup violence—particularly domestic conflict—has increased in many Pacific societies. Recurrent domestic violence occurs in many island families between husbands and wives, between parents and children, and among siblings. "Many Pacific societies consider a certain level of family violence to be normal and acceptable" (Counts 1990). Patterns and frequencies of "normal" violence differ from society to society. In much of Melanesia, for example, parents strike children only reluctantly, and siblings observe rules that permit younger to strike older, but not vice versa. In some Polynesian societies, on the other hand, parents more freely discipline children with slaps and blows (see, for Samoa, Freeman 1983: 205).

Domestic violence has worsened in some Pacific towns and cities as migrant families live apart from their extended kin whose presence once would have provided various sorts of support and also restraints to keep violence from getting out of hand. Migrants to urban areas come under financial and interpersonal stress, some of which manifests itself in wife beating and child abuse. Alcohol use is commonly associated with domestic violence, especially since in many Pacific cultures, such as Palau, drunks are partially absolved of responsibility for their actions (Nero 1990). In Chuuk, alcohol-related violence between men and women and also between village youths became such a problem that women successfully campaigned for a prohibition on alcohol sales (Marshall and Marshall 1990).

Rates of violence directed against the self, including suicide, have also increased in the Pacific. In various island societies, different categories of people are more or less likely to kill themselves given the play of social forces and everyday stress. Throughout much of Melanesia, the typical suicide is a young woman. These women often endure painful pressure to marry against their will, and marriage pulls them into a series of new relationships with husband and his kin in which they are subordinated. Although people on Tanna, for example, aver that a woman has ultimate right to refuse any man that her parents have selected to become her husband, it may be very difficult for her to resist this choice. Some women attempt (and sometimes succeed) to kill themselves by climbing and jumping from trees to signal the seriousness of their opposition to an unwanted engagement.

In Micronesia and Polynesia, conversely, boys and young men are most likely to kill themselves. Typical mechanisms of suicide include hanging and drinking herbicide. Many of these boys and adolescents kill themselves "in a state of anger at having been scolded or punished by a parent or some other elder" (Freeman 1983: 220; see also Hezel, Rubinstein, and White 1985). Suicide patterns reflect local cultural concepts of power, shame, and compensation. "In different ways, all of these cultural conceptions are concerned with the dilemmas of anger and other intense emotions felt by persons in low status positions who have limited avenues for expressing these emotions and promoting moral claims" (White 1985: 12).

Equivalence and Hierarchy

Very few human relations are egalitarian. Most of the time people must deal with others who, in important ways, are not their equals, as often parents and children, men and women, and chiefs and followers do. Exchange patterns within such relationships work to sustain hierarchy and inequality. Unbalanced gift giving may strengthen the political capital of those who give vis-à-vis those who receive. Or it may mark the status of a chief and the duty of others to support the high-born.

In some parts of the Pacific, relations between adult men, and between kin groups, ideally are egalitarian. An ethos of economic and political equivalence characterizes many Melanesian societies. People strive to sustain balance in their exchange relationships. On Tanna, for example, to celebrate the successful circumcision of his son, a man will publicly present a heap of exchange goods (pigs, kava, mats, baskets, bark skirts, lengths of cloth, blankets) to one of his wife's brothers. He expects, eventually, to receive everything back when that brother-in-law gives him goods in return, celebrating the circumcision of one of his own sons. People nowadays write down exact numbers of exchanged objects to ensure a balanced exchange. If someone falls ill, people may suggest that he has left his exchange relationships unbalanced too long. Positive and negative reciprocity are equally important in the maintenance of relational equivalence. It is important to pay back gifts that one has received, but also to return injury for injury, insult for insult (see Trompf 1994; Barker 2007b).

Despite an ethos of interpersonal equivalence, leaders direct the affairs of Pacific villages, families, lineages, and clans. Contrasts between the chiefly systems of Polynesia and Micronesia and the more egalitarian political systems of Melanesia have often been noted. The position of chief is an ascribed status. Men, and in some cases women, from certain descent groups succeed to the position of chief because of their genealogical identity—they descend from other chiefs. Inherited chiefly status in Polynesia often comes with attributions of *mana*, or a personal power or efficacy that ordinary people lack. In some societies, such as Tonga, a single chiefly lineage sits atop the social pyramid. In others, a coterie of leading families controls the various districts of an island. In addition to chiefly and common lineages, a class described as "slaves" existed in some eastern Polynesian societies. Comparative theory has attempted to explain these hierarchical variations as caused by the distribution of environmental resources (Sahlins 1958) or as an evolutionary outcome of aristocratic status competitions (see Goldman 1970).

In much of Melanesia, on the other hand, leaders (or "big men," a term that Pacific Studies has borrowed from Melanesian Pidgin English) achieve their positions on the basis of individual abilities to organize economic exchange, settle disputes, demonstrate wisdom, and otherwise influence community opinion. The distinction between the Melanesian big man and the Polynesian and Micronesian chief is too simple in that it obscures the fact that chiefs also exist in various Melanesian societies and that Polynesian (and Micronesian) chiefly leadership is based on individual ability as well as genealogical position. In Samoa, for example, all families control chiefly (*matai*) titles that they bestow on those family members who promise to serve kin-group interests.

Class

Traditional hierarchies of chief and commoner or big man and follower are increasingly sliding into modern inequalities based on class. Whereas kinship once structured and colored political relationships between leaders and followers (the chief or big man leading his kin group), economic inequalities of class nowadays increasingly underlie political authority in the Pacific (see, e.g., Gewertz and Errington 1999; Strathern and Stewart 2000; Smith 2002). Many local leaders, in addition, today base their authority on the state rather than solely in custom (see White and Lindstrom 1997).

In some places, state constitutions have been designed that recognize traditional systems of hierarchy. In Samoa, for example, only *matai* (those with chiefly titles) may run for Parliament. Chiefly families are also very influential within the political systems of Tonga, the Cook Islands, and Fiji. But customary limitations on chiefly authority that once worked to mute social inequality have often broken down. In Tonga and also in the Marshall Islands (where chiefly control of land has provided certain families the lion's share of U.S. military land rents), for example, people today criticize chiefs who have taken advantage of their positions to enrich themselves, neglecting traditional social and economic responsibilities.

As Pacific Islanders have become engaged in the global marketplace, inequalities based on economic position have increased. Hierarchies of class now overlay those of kinship and status, especially in those states where some families are enriched by their control of land, forests, minerals, and other resources being exploited by multinational corporations (West 2006). Ben Finney undertook one of the first studies of class formation in two Tahitian communities in the early 1960s (Finney 1973b). He wrote then of "the emergence of a South Seas type of urban proletariat" that was appearing "virtually overnight" (1973b: 140). Since that time, urban migration has accelerated. Every Pacific state has at least one city—or a sizable town—that is the political, economic, and cultural focus of the nation (see, e.g., Connell and Lea 1995 for Polynesia; Haberkorn 1989 for Vanuatu). And islanders have also established settler communities in New Zealand, Australia, the United States, and beyond (see Small 1997; Marshall 2004).

Urbanization, wage labor opportunities, limited access to secondary education, and the growth of state bureaucracies have all accentuated class formation in many Pacific nations. Many families now depend on wage labor rather than on subsistence farming or gardening (Errington and Gewertz 2004). Labor unions have been established in most Pacific states, and workers—particularly government employees—have gone on strike in Solomon Islands, Vanuatu, and elsewhere (see Howard 1986).

The growing importance of class over kinship is not limited to urban areas. Finney (1973a) also studied local business entrepreneurs around the town of Goroka in the Papua New Guinea Highlands. In the 1960s, big men, or traditional village leaders, had begun to apply their organizational and managerial skills to create successful coffee plantations and trucking businesses. Twenty years later, he returned to study "a new elite of wealthy business leaders" (Finney 1987).

On Ambae Island, Vanuatu, similarly, "a category of relatively rich individuals is emerging . . . through inequalities of customary land distribution that allow a few large landholders to earn incomes at least four times as large as the average copra [dried coconut] producer. . . . The wealthy operate more and more as capitalists" (Rodman 1987: 162; see also Hooper 1987). Given the continuing importance of kin groups and other sorts of customary relationships, however, Western labels of class (bourgeois and proletarian, big and small peasants) hide much of the complexity of Pacific economic and political relationships (Gewertz and Errington 1999).

Ethnicity

We encounter familiar difficulties when we apply Western notions of "ethnicity" to Pacific Island societies. We typically base our definitions of ethnic identity in shared "blood" (or race), custom, language, and so forth. Linnekin and Poyer, however, exploring various Pacific understandings of identity, argue that in many Pacific societies, group identities, ethnic or otherwise, are less essentially part of one's nature but are based, rather, in a person's behavior (1990: 4–5; see Howard 1989; Crocombe 1993). According to Linnekin and Poyer, Pacific perceptions of personal and group identity admit that

> people can voluntarily shift their social identities, that a person can maintain more than one identity simultaneously, and that behavioral attributes—such as residence, language, dress, participation in exchanges—are not only significant markers but are also effective determinants of identity. (1990: 9)

Western notions of ethnicity, however, do inform identity and politics in Hawai'i (the most ethnically complex Pacific archipelago) and New Zealand, where individuals must define themselves in terms of powerful ethnic categories of Maori, (other) Pacific Islander, or pakeha (European) (see King 1991). And in contemporary Hawai'i, a second system of group identity that contrasts "local" with "nonlocal"—relying on behavioral attributes such as residence, language, and dress—overlaps understandings of ethnic identity as based in essential features of race or ancestry. Ethnic politics is also underway in other island states with European and Asian settler populations, notably New Caledonia, French Polynesia, Guam, and the Marianas (Ward 1992). People's uses of ethnic categories, however, are not necessarily identical with ways ethnicity gets constructed beyond the Pacific.

Fijian politics since independence have been shaped by a serious ethnic divide between indigenous Fijians and the Indo-Fijian community descended from laborers recruited by the British to work sugar cane plantations (Ewins 1992; Lal 2006). Others, however, have argued the greater significance of class over ethnicity in Fiji: The military restored ruling families (which were of both indigenous and Indo-Fijian ancestry) to a position of state domination (see, e.g., Howard 1991). In Papua New Guinea some have explained, and sometimes justified, the attempt by secessionists on Bougainville to achieve independence in ethnic terms. The "black skins" of Bougainville, in this rhetoric, differ ethnically from the "red skins" who inhabit the rest of the country (Nash and Ogan 1990; see also Larmour 1992).

As more people move to Pacific towns and cities and come to rely on wage labor rather than the land to eat, their identities are less and less defined by local kin-group memberships. Here, islanders are becoming more individualistic in the sense that they are now more money-oriented and less dependent or interested in their extended families. At the same time, they are reaching out beyond their traditional kin groups to join new communities and associations that are defined by shared economic position (class), or by broader identities of shared geographic origin, language, religion, and so on (ethnicity). Shared religious affiliation, in particular, is an increasingly important aspect of identity throughout most of the Pacific (see White 1991; Robbins 2004; Eriksen 2008). Creeping economic modernity, increasing individuality, and growing class and ethnic differentiation, however, do not necessarily anticipate an impending disintegration of kinship and other customary Pacific social relations.

Changing Relationships

Once-current theories that everyone in the world, eventually, as they develop economically and politically, will come to resemble Europeans and Americans are clearly wrong. Although nowadays global economic and communication systems move ideas, images, goods, and people around the world with increasing felicity, local cultural orders do manage to survive. If the world system did indeed result in nothing but cultural homogeneity, then Japan today would be no different from, say, Oklahoma. People, as active participants in these global networks, maintain significant ability to choose what to consume and what to refuse, what to listen to and what to tune out. Furthermore, they can decide to use products and ideas in novel ways that make sense of the global in local terms. The local, in this fashion, redirects and reshapes incoming social and cultural forces.

Undoubtedly, however, Pacific Islanders today are increasingly involved in global networks that are affecting the shape of their everyday social relationships. Selkirk, or his literary avatar Robinson Crusoe, was an eighteenth-century allegory. A castaway existence is no longer feasible or even creditable as a South Pacific romance. Even the few families surviving on isolated Pitcairn Island get mail and radio transmissions. People on Tanna, Aitutaki, and Easter Island, and in Honolulu, Los Angeles, and Sydney are increasingly interrelated.

New exchange flows, new identities of class and ethnicity, and new, perhaps, conceptions of responsible, autonomous, and coherent persons will no doubt have an increasing impact on island social relationships. Notably, debate is under way at the moment in many Pacific communities about the changing roles of women and men within island families (see Jolly and Macintyre 1989; Eriksen 2008), and also about proper relations between chiefs (and big men) and their onetime followers within island states. Social relations such as these are today increasingly unsettled and transformed by new global opportunities and challenges of economic and political development in the islands.

BIBLIOGRAPHY

Akin, D., and J. Robbins. 1999. *Money and modernity: State and local currencies in Melanesia.* Pittsburgh: University of Pittsburgh Press.

Barker, J. 2007a. *Ancestral lines: The Maisin of Papua New Guinea and the fate of the rainforest.* Peterborough, Ont.: Broadview Press.

———. 2007b. *The anthropology of morality in Melanesia and beyond.* London: Ashgate.

Brady, I. 1976. *Transactions in kinship: Adoption and fosterage in Oceania.* ASAO Monograph No. 4. Honolulu: University Press of Hawai'i.

Chambers, K., and A. Chambers. 2001. *Unity of heart: Culture and change in a Polynesian atoll society.* Prospect Heights, Ill.: Waveland Press.

Connell, J., and J. P. Lea. 1995. *Urbanisation in Polynesia.* Canberra: National Centre for Development Studies, Australian National University.

Counts, D. A. 1990. Introduction. Special issue: Domestic violence in Oceania. *Pacific Studies* 13(3): 1–5.

Crocombe, R. 1993. Ethnicity, identity and power in Oceania. In *Islands and enclaves,* ed. G. Trompf, 195–223. New Delhi: Sterling Publishers.

Eriksen, A. 2008. *Gender, Christianity and change in Vanuatu: An analysis of social movements in North Ambrym.* London: Ashgate.

Errington, F., and D. Gewertz. 2004. *Yali's question: Sugar, culture, and history.* Chicago: University of Chicago Press.

Ewins, R. 1992. *Colour, class, and custom: The literature of the 1987 Fiji coup. Regime change and regime maintenance in Asia and the Pacific, No. 9.* Canberra: Australian National University.

Feinberg, R. 2004. *Anuta: Polynesian lifeways for the twenty-first century,* 2nd ed. Long Grove, Ill.: Waveland Press.

Finney, B. R. 1973a. *Big-men and business: Entrepreneurship and economic growth in the New Guinea Highlands.* Honolulu: University Press of Hawai'i.

———. 1973b. *Polynesian peasants and proletarians.* Cambridge, Mass.: Schenkman Publishing Company.

———. 1987. *Business development in the Highlands of Papua New Guinea.* Pacific Islands Development Program Research Report, No. 6. Honolulu: East-West Center.

Fraenkel, J. 2005. *The manipulation of custom: From uprising to intervention in the Solomon Islands.* Wellington: Victoria University Press.

Fraenkel, J., and S. Firth. 2007. *From election to coup in Fiji: The 2006 campaign and its aftermath.* Canberra: Asia Pacific Press.

Freeman, D. 1983. *Margaret Mead and Samoa: The making and unmaking of an anthropological myth.* Cambridge, Mass.: Harvard University Press.

Gardner, R., and K. G. Heider. 1968. *Gardens of war: Life and death in the New Guinea stone age.* New York: Random House.

Gewertz, D., and F. Errington. 1999. *Emerging class in Papua New Guinea: The telling of difference.* Cambridge: Cambridge University Press.

Goldman, I. 1970. *Ancient Polynesian society.* Chicago: University of Chicago Press.

Haberkorn, G. 1989. *Port Vila: Transit station or final stop?* Pacific Research Monograph No. 21. Canberra: National Centre for Development Studies, Australian National University.

Hage, P., and F. Harary. 2007. *Island networks: Communication, kinship, and classification structures in Oceania.* Cambridge: Cambridge University Press.

Hage, P., and J. Marck. 2003. Matrilineality and the Melanesian origin of Polynesian Y chromosomes. *Current Anthropology* 44: S121–127.

Harris, B. M. 1988. *The rise of rascalism: Action and reaction in the evolution of rascal gangs.* IASER Discussion Paper No. 54. Port Moresby: Institute of Applied Social and Economic Research.

Hezel, F. X., D. H. Rubinstein, and G. M. White. 1985. *Culture, youth and suicide in the Pacific: Papers from an East-West Conference.* Honolulu: Center for Pacific Island Studies, University of Hawai'i.

Hooper, A., ed. 1987. *Class and culture in the South Pacific.* Auckland: Centre for Pacific Studies, University of Auckland; Suva: Institute of Pacific Studies, University of the South Pacific.

Howard, M. C. 1986. History and industrial relations in the South Pacific. *South Pacific Forum.* Special issue, Labour history in the South Pacific 3: 1–10.

———. 1989. Ethnicity and the state in the Pacific. In *Ethnicity and nation-building in the Pacific,* ed. M. C. Howard, 1–49. Tokyo: United National University Press.

———. 1991. *Fiji: Race and politics in an island state.* Vancouver: University of British Columbia Press.

Hviding, E. 1996. *Guardians of Morovo Lagoon: Practice, place, and politics in maritime Melanesia.* Honolulu: University of Hawai'i Press.

Jolly, M., and M. Macintyre. 1989. *Family and gender in the Pacific: Domestic contradictions and the colonial impact.* Cambridge: Cambridge University Press.

Keesing, R. M. 1978. *'Elota's story: The life and times of a Solomon Islands big man.* New York: St. Martin's Press.

King, M. 1991. *Pakeha: The quest for identity in New Zealand.* Auckland: Penguin Books.

Knauft, B. M. 1990. Melanesian warfare: A theoretical history. *Oceania* 60: 250–311.

Kuehling, S. 2005. *Dobu: Ethics of exchange on a Massim Island.* Honolulu: University of Hawai'i Press.

Lal, B. 2006. *Islands in turmoil: Elections and politics in Fiji.* Canberra: Asia Pacific Press.

Larmour, P. 1992. The politics of race and ethnicity: Theoretical perspectives on Papua New Guinea. *Pacific Studies* 15(2): 87–108.

Levy, R. I. 1973. *Tahitians: Mind and experience in the Society Islands.* Chicago: University of Chicago Press.

Lindstrom, L. 1985. Personal names and social reproduction on Tanna. *Journal of the Polynesian Society* 94: 27–45.

———. 1990. *Knowledge and power in a South Pacific society.* Washington, D.C.: Smithsonian Institution Press.

Linnekin, J., and L. Poyer. 1990. *Cultural identity and ethnicity in the Pacific.* Honolulu: University of Hawai'i Press.

Lipuma, E. 2001. *Encompassing others: The magic of modernity in Melanesia.* Ann Arbor: University of Michigan Press.

Lutz, C. A. 1988. *Unnatural emotions: Everyday sentiments on a Micronesian atoll and their challenge to Western theory.* Chicago: University of Chicago Press.

Marshall, M. 1979. *Weekend warriors: Alcohol in a Micronesian culture.* Palo Alto, Calif.: Mayfield Publishing Company.

———. 1983. *Siblingship in Oceania: Studies in the meaning of kin relations.* ASAO Monograph No. 8. Lanham, Md.: University Press of America.

———. 2004. *Namoluk: Beyond the reef.* Boulder, Colo.: Westview Press.

Marshall, M., and L. B. Marshall. 1990. *Silent voices speak: Women and prohibition in Truk.* Belmont, Calif.: Wadsworth Publishing Company.

Molloy, M. A. 2008. *On creating a usable culture: Margaret Mead and the emergence of American cosmopolitanism.* Honolulu: University of Hawai'i Press.

Morton, H. 1996. *Becoming Tongan: An ethnography of childhood.* Honolulu: University of Hawai'i Press.

Nash, J., and E. Ogan. 1990. The red and the black: Bougainvillean perceptions of other Papua New Guineans. *Pacific Studies* 13: 1–17.

Nero, K. L. 1990. The hidden pain: Drunkenness and domestic violence in Palau. Special issue: Domestic violence in Oceania. *Pacific Studies* 13: 63–92.

Ochs, E. 1988. *Culture and language development: Language acquisition and language socialization in a Samoan village.* Cambridge: Cambridge University Press.

Read, K. 1955. Morality and the concept of the person among the Gahuku-Gama. *Oceania* 54: 233–282.

Rio, K. 2007. *Power of perspective: Social ontology and agency on Ambrym island, Vanuatu.* Oxford: Berghahn Books.

Robbins, J. 2004. *Becoming sinners: Christianity and moral torment in a Papua New Guinea society.* Berkeley: University of California Press.

Rodman, M. C. 1987. *Masters of tradition: Consequences of customary land tenure in Longana, Vanuatu.* Vancouver: University of British Columbia Press.

Sahlins, M. 1958. *Social stratification in Polynesia.* Seattle: University of Washington Press.

Schieffelin, B. B. 1990. *The give and take of everyday life: Language socialization of Kaluli children.* Cambridge: Cambridge University Press.

Schieffelin, E. L. 1976. *The sorrow of the lonely and the burning of the dancers.* New York: St. Martin's Press.

Schwimmer, E. 1973. *Exchange in the social structure of the Orokaiva: Traditional and emergent ideologies in the Northern District of Papua.* London: C. Hurst.

Shore, B. 1982. *Sala'ilua: A Samoan mystery.* New York: Columbia University Press.

Small, C. 1997. *Voyages: From Tongan villages to American suburbs.* Ithaca, N.Y.: Cornell University Press.

Smith, M. F. 2002. *Village on the edge: Changing times in Papua New Guinea.* Honolulu: University of Hawai'i Press.

Strathern, A. 1979. *Ongka: A self-account by a New Guinea big-man.* London: Duckworth.

Strathern, A., and P. Stewart. 2000. *Arrow talk: Transaction, transition, and contradiction in New Guinea Highlands history.* Kent, Ohio: Kent State University Press.

Strathern, M. 1988. *The gender of the gift: Problems with women and problems with society in Melanesia.* Berkeley: University of California Press.

Trompf, G. W. 1994. *Payback: The logic of retribution in Melanesian religions.* Cambridge: Cambridge University Press.

Ward, A. 1992. The crisis of our times: Ethnic resurgence and the liberal ideal. *Journal of Pacific History* 27: 83–95.

Watson-Gegeo, K., and G. M. White. 1990. *Disentangling: Conflict discourse in Pacific societies.* Stanford, Calif.: Stanford University Press.

West, P. 2006. *Conservation is our government now: The politics of ecology in Papua New Guinea.* Durham, N.C.: Duke University Press.

White, G. M. 1985. Suicide and culture: Island views. In *Culture, youth and suicide in the Pacific: Papers from an East-West Center conference,* ed. F. X. Hezel, D. H. Rubinstein, and G. M. White, 1–14. Honolulu: Center for Pacific Island Studies, University of Hawai'i.

———. 1991. *Identity through history: Living stories in a Solomon Islands society.* Cambridge: Cambridge University Press.

White, G. M., and J. Kirkpatrick. 1985. *Person, self, and experience: Exploring Pacific ethnopsychologies.* Berkeley: University of California Press.

White, G. M., and L. Lindstrom 1997. *Chiefs today: Traditional Pacific leadership and the postcolonial state.* Stanford, Calif.: Stanford University Press.

Gender

Julie Cupples and Nancy McDowell

15

The Nature of Gender

If one were to examine the indices of ethnographies written before 1970 or so, there would probably be no entry for "gender." There might be one for "women" or "the sexes," but these entries would almost certainly not encompass what is meant today by "gender." All human groups recognize that people come in two basic models, male and female; gender, however, refers not to these specifically biological differences and capabilities but to what human creativity makes of them: cultures define and construct female and male beyond these observable biological contrasts. A sexual division of labor seems to be a genuine human universal, but there are few hard-and-fast rules as to which gender performs which tasks. Although it is true that women tend to be responsible for the domestic realm and men the public, there are almost always exceptions. What scholars designate as gender is a social construction through which people view the world and in terms of which they behave and interpret the behavior of others. Notions of gender permeate most aspects of any human life. Gender is intimately associated with concepts of person, and it is the basis for both the sexual division of labor and marriage and thus critical to both production and reproduction. As the foundation for the family and marriage, gender contrasts constitute the core upon which not only the next generation is built, but also the heart of extensive kinship systems, structures, and networks. In some places, everything—plants, animals, gods—have gender as well, and the entire cosmos is predicated on this distinction constructed by culture.

These concepts are not necessarily immutable but can be fluid and change over time, as is apparent in Pacific history. Because it is impossible to cover the nature of gender in the entire Pacific through time, our initial focus is on traditional notions and the early colonial period; more contemporary concerns are described in the latter half of this chapter as well as in other chapters of this volume.

Anthropological Perspectives

Early Seminal Work

The study of gender *as* gender is relatively recent in anthropology, probably originating in the 1970s. Until then, most ethnographers pretty much ignored what women did beyond their economic

tasks and occasionally their roles in the family and child rearing, and they certainly did not often seriously investigate what constituted the nature of female and male in conceptual systems. What men did—public ritual, economic exchange, and political activities—was described as "the culture" (see especially Ardener 1982; Strathern 1988; Strathern 1987). There were, however, a few critical exceptions to this tendency, and some of the most significant early work on gender was conducted in the Pacific region.

Mead's studies on Samoa (1928, 1930) and Papua New Guinea (PNG) (especially 1935) are pioneering works on the subject. Her first ethnographic work in the Pacific was in Samoa in 1925–1926, where she investigated the nature of adolescence. Her focus was on young girls and their experiences, and her conclusion was that adolescence need not be the period of rebellion and angst that it was in many if not most Western cultures.[1] In the process of doing this study, she noted significant amounts of information about gender and male-female relations (see Mead 1928, 1930).

It was a later work of Mead's, however, that became canonical in the field: in *Sex and Temperament in Three Primitive Societies* (1935), she reported the results of field investigations in three lowland societies in Papua New Guinea. Gender notions contrasted dramatically in these three places: among the Arapesh, both men and women were nurturing and mild, while among the Mundugumor both women and men were aggressive and assertive. The third society, the Tchambuli (today the Chambri), seemed to reverse 1930s middle-class American assumptions in that men, for example, were engaged in ritual and artistic production while women completed important economic transactions at the market.

Mead and other early investigators began with a focus on children and socialization—the provenience of women—but attention began to shift during the 1970s partly as a result of the feminist movement, and again the Pacific region played an important role. Marilyn Strathern's seminal work *Women in Between*, published in 1972, is among the first full-length treatments of women and their roles in the Papua New Guinea Highlands. Strathern focuses on the nature of women and their value among the people of Mount Hagen and stresses the distinction between "producers" and "transactors." Producers, including most women, were responsible for *producing* things (feeding pigs, growing sweet potatoes, etc.) while transactors, essentially men, were in charge of *transacting* and exchanging, processes central in the society. Men recognized that women were essential as producers and as the intermediaries between affines, but they excluded women from transactional occasions and political events. Women were able to exert informal influence away from the public realm.

Malinowski's works on the Trobriand Islands are early classics in anthropology, and they were frequently held up to students as models of relatively complete ethnographic descriptions. His description (1922) of the vast and complex interisland exchange network known as the *kula* was required reading. Although Malinowski had commented twice that women were important in mortuary rituals, he never expanded to say how or why. Annette Weiner returned later to the Trobriands and found something Malinowski had apparently missed or thought unimportant: that women had an elaborate and extensive set of exchanges that was just as central and intertwined with Trobriand cultural life as the *kula* network (Weiner 1976). By looking at Trobriand society through the lens provided by women, Weiner was able to offer a far more complete understanding of the culture than that of Malinowski's partial depiction.

These issues take us far from the concerns about the sexual division of labor and the "position of women" that early investigators comment upon,[2] but they do provide a context for looking at constructions of gender in the Pacific.

Melanesia

The Trobriands were and continue to be anomalous in Melanesia (along with Manam Island [Lutkehaus 1982]) in that there exist notions of hierarchy and rank much more reminiscent of Polynesia than Melanesia: the *relative* sexual freedom and absence of notions of pollution among Trobrianders is uncharacteristic of Melanesian societies. The New Guinea Highlands, in particular, offer a dramatically different picture of gender and gender relations that contrasts not only with the island peoples but also to some extent with many of the inhabitants of the lowlands of PNG. The highlands have long been known as an area in which male-female antagonism and opposition are one of the most striking characteristics of the societies; throughout most of the area, men believe that women are clearly inferior beings and that it is only natural that men dominate women. The result is a frequent residential segregation of the sexes, a relatively strict division of labor by sex, male appropriation of the labor and fertility of women, pervasive beliefs in the ability of women to pollute men through their bodily fluids (especially menstrual blood), the existence of ritual means to purify men and ensure the growth of boys, and ostentatious male ritual (especially at initiation). Men tended to do all the heavy gardening work as well as hunting and defense/warfare, while women did routine gardening chores and saw to the domestic realm.

The assertion that sexual opposition and antagonism characterize the highlands, while true, masks some diversity in systems of belief and behavior. One cannot say, for example, that women do not participate in exchange, for in Mendi they do (Lederman 1984), and Sexton (1984: 121) describes a fascinating development in the Chuave and Goroka Districts in the 1960s and 1970s in which women constructed an exchange system they called *wok meri* ("women's work"). Relatively small groups of women pooled their earnings and conducted exchanges with other *wok meri* groups, replicating bridewealth, birth, and marriage transactions; the pooled money was also a source of small loans for members.

Meggitt (1964) attempted to identify regularities within this highland diversity. He delineated three complexes of "social attitudes and practices" (206) apparent in the area. The first occurs in the Western Highlands and includes the Mae Enga. Here, men and women live separate lives. Females are considered to be wildly different from males, and all females past menarche are polluting and must be avoided because they are "intrinsically unclean" (208). Women are especially dangerous during their menstrual periods and thus must remain in seclusion; they are likewise dangerous during childbirth, and even the newborn is polluted for several months due to contact with the mother's intimate fluids. Because of the danger, men are ambivalent about sexual intercourse, and they copulate with their wives only to produce children (210).

The second nexus Meggitt isolates is among the Kuma of the Central Highlands. Although men and women sleep separately, women and sexuality are not as dangerous to men, and they do not fear pollution from women as Mae Enga men do. Premarital sexual relationships occur without condemnation, and married men indulge in extramarital affairs (to the consternation of their wives). This does not mean, however, that men and women have companionable relationships: "there exists . . . a deep-rooted antagonism between the sexes." (Meggitt 1964: 220). Although men believe themselves to be superior and dominant, women do not always submit as they should, and men continually worry that they will lose control. Meggitt reads "the position of women" as relatively high here.

Meggitt's third variant occurs in the Eastern Highlands; it is characterized by a mixture of the Mae and Kuma types. He believes that this merging supports his main thesis that where people marry their traditional enemies and where most adult women in a location are in-married from enemy groups, pollution notions will prevail as among the Mae Enga; where there is no "persisting animosity between affinally connected groups, there is also little or no fear of feminine pollution and sexuality," as among the Kuma (220). The existence of continual enmity or warfare, and its association with the need for male solidarity, exacerbated the dramatic separation between male and female in many areas throughout Melanesia (see Herdt 2006; Tuzin 2001).

Marriage is one of the primary contexts in which men and women interact as adults. In an early work tellingly titled *Pigs, Pearlshells, and Women: Marriage in the New Guinea Highlands* (1969), the editors, Glasse and Meggitt, focus on marriage as a transaction between kin groups such as (typically in the highlands) patrilineal clans or lineages. Such transactions characteristically involved bridewealth, that is, a transfer of material goods, particularly pigs and valuable items like shells and feathers, from the groom's kin to the bride's. Women rarely had much say in the choice of their partners, but then frequently young men did not either. Divorce was infrequent when bridewealth was large and a woman's natal kin did not demonstrate a strong continuing interest in her welfare. In some societies, the kin group attempted to spread marriages out among a variety of other groups, whereas elsewhere strong bonds would be created between two descent groups by frequent intermarriage over generations (Glasse and Meggitt 1969). In such ways marriages framed political alliances as well.

Most Melanesian societies, highlands and lowlands, had similar political organizations. They were egalitarian as far as individual men were concerned, and a man achieved status and position through a variety of means: leadership in warfare, oratory, feast giving, and participation in sometimes elaborate exchange networks. This "big man" political system rarely incorporated "big women," but women invariably exerted some informal influence. Occasionally, as producers women had a say in the disposition of their products, while in other places they did not. Women almost always had some power, some ability to act as their own agents, if only to leave and become prostitutes, as Wardlow (2006) describes for *pasinja meri* (passenger women, those who ride as passengers on the highlands highways) among the Huli or to commit "revenge suicide," as Counts (1984) describes among the Lusi in northwest New Britain.

Many of these highlands themes typify lowland Melanesia (including New Caledonia, Vanuatu, and Solomon Islands): a sexual division of labor, complex beliefs about the differential nature of woman and man, and to a lesser extent the idea that women can and do pollute men. But there exists here a much greater range of diversity; it is possible (if not always appropriate) to generalize about the highlands (e.g., a tendency to patrilineal descent), but it is much more difficult to do so in the lowlands. For example, a wide range of descent systems can be found here, including matrilineal, cognatic, and bilateral as well as patrilineal, and some unusual ones have been reported as well (e.g., Mead 1935; McDowell 1977, 1991; Thurnwald 1916). Marriage may occur by bridewealth, brideservice, sister exchange, and/or infant betrothal.

Elaborate and complex male initiation cycles and secret ritual knowledge assume a prominent role in some areas but not others. Some groups initiate girls, but of the nine societies included in a volume on *female* initiation in Melanesia (Lutkehaus and Roscoe 1995), eight of the societies are outside of the highlands, and the exception is the recent creation by highlands women of the *wok meri* cooperative (Sexton 1984). In a very few societies (e.g., Mundugumor [Mead 1935; McDowell 1991], Orokaiva [Chowning 1977: 61], and Nduindui [Chowning 1977: 61]), girls are sometimes initiated along with the boys. Women are not always completely excluded from ritual and ceremonial occasions in most of the lowlands; indeed, they sometimes take crucial roles as dancers or as the required audience for male performance, and occasionally gender itself is a significant focus in ritual (e.g., Bateson 1958).

The extent to which women actually knew the sacred secrets the men kept is a question of enduring interest. Sometimes the investigator "suspected" that women knew more than they should (e.g., Hogbin 1970), while other times fieldworkers (especially female fieldworkers) were able to discover the extent of women's knowledge (e.g., Mead 1935). The Ilahita Arapesh provide an illuminating example. Tuzin had studied the lowland Sepik village of Ilahita in 1969–1972 and published vivid descriptions of the men's cult and its secrets (1976, 1980). He returned in 1985–1986 to learn that the men had only the year before revealed all the secrets to the women. Although the men had expected the women to be shocked, they were not; they appeared to be indifferent to these wonderful secrets. Furthermore, they had pretty much known all along that there were no monsters that ate their sons during initiation (Tuzin 1997).

As noted above, the Trobriand Islands seem to be uncharacteristic of much of Melanesia, and the same is true of many of the islands in the Massim. Here women are more publicly valued, have more independence, are not as polluting as elsewhere; sexual relationships—both premarital and within marriage—are not dangerous but pleasurable. Lepowsky (1993) argues that the society on the island of Vanatinai is egalitarian and that there are "big women" here as well as "big men." Women fully participate in the exchange of *kula* valuables, and Lepowsky (211) notes that other groups in this area include women in the *kula* exchange network (e.g., Tubetube, Normandy Island, East Calvados). In a recent publication, Kuehling (2005) tells us that despite Malinowski's assertion to the contrary, women on Dobu do occasionally participate in the *kula* (but may be too "shy" to speak in the public context).

Polynesia and Micronesia

Although there are certainly some similarities, even a fleeting comparison of Melanesia with Polynesia reveals striking differences. And although Polynesian societies certainly differed from one another, the area exhibited far less internal diversity than did Melanesia. For example, there are about 1,100 distinct and mutually unintelligible languages spoken in Melanesia, while there are only 50 or so spoken in the relatively homogeneous area of Polynesia (Oliver 1989: 883, 1026). Oliver (883) comments that although atoll and volcanic islands provide different environmental opportunities and constraints, and thus employ varying subsistence techniques, overall, Polynesian societies "were all very much alike in some fundamental features of social structure, especially those having to do with kinship. This is perhaps not surprising in view of their history, namely, their common derivation from a historically interrelated cluster of communities . . . within a time frame of less than two millennia, and the subsequent isolation of most of them from cultural traditions markedly different from those they shared."

Two differences between most of Melanesia and Polynesia stand out: the relatively high position of women and the prevalence of a pronounced system of rank in Polynesia. Everywhere in Polynesia women were, if not equal to men, at least relatively autonomous agents in their own right and valued as such. For example, although Marquesan women were typically more nurturing than men, both genders were ideally independent and strong (Riley 2004: 638); women possessed significant amounts of domestic decision-making power despite the titular male head of household (Riley 642). Although early observers in Tahiti missed some of the subtle differences in power and some of the ways in which women were restricted, they remarked on the apparent equality between the sexes: "the early observers took note of women chiefs with effective political power, of women participating in sports (sometimes wrestling with men), of upper-class women dominating and sometimes beating their husbands, and of many women who were curious, active, independent, and seemingly very little under submission to their men. For purposes of political power, descent was reckoned in both the maternal and paternal lines, and, as indicated by the mention of female chiefs, a woman could sometimes find herself, because of her genealogical superiority and abilities, in a position of power" Levy (1973: 234). Oliver's (1989: 35) reading of the early sources confirms that "far from being oppressed chattel, precontact Tahitian women were socially valued and . . . they were major actors in social, economic, and political affairs." Levy (234) suggests that some of these early observations were the result of Western gender expectations: "some of the dimensions which, ideally, are supposed to characterize male/female differences in the West are not strongly marked [in Tahiti]. Men, for example, are not particularly more aggressive than women. Women do not seem to be much 'softer' or more 'maternal' than men; both men and women exhibit a certain coolness toward their children and their mates."

One source of the perception that men and women were not significantly unequal in traditional Polynesia might have been the relatively fluid nature of the sexual division of labor. There were tasks specifically assigned only to women and others assigned only to men, but in Polynesia there seems to have been more adaptability. In early Tahiti, for example, many important tasks were done by men or women (Levy 1973: 233), and the sexual division of labor was not especially rigid (Lockwood 1993: 21). Lockwood notes that both men and women had access to land through their kin groups, and neither "dominated control of means of production" (39). The domestic group shared and cooperated, and the contributions of both male and female were valued (39). Often, as Riley (2004: 639) notes for the Marquesas, there was recognition that both men and women produced and prepared food.

The relatively high position of women and the prevalence of a pronounced system of rank are related: in most Polynesia societies, rank overrode gender in that women of high rank were considered to be superior in some ways to men of low rank (women were not, however, quite the equals of men of the same rank). The behavior appropriate to high-ranking women was sometimes different from that of other women; in Samoa, for example, the *taupou* (usually the daughter of a high-ranking chief; Mageo [1998: 263] translates the term as "village princess") was expected to remain chaste and virginal until her marriage, but commoners and lower-ranking girls were freer to engage in sexual liaisons (Shankman 1996). High-ranking women were frequently exempt from some of the chores of domesticity and had public roles of religious and/or political importance. In some Polynesian systems, women could hold titles of their own and sometimes even perform public, "chiefly" roles. Certainly, most chiefs, priests, and religious practitioners were men, but Lockwood (1993: 38, 25) reports that some high-ranking women led groups into battle, and a woman, Pomare IV, ruled in Tahiti for fifty years. In the Marquesas, most chiefs, shamans, craft specialists, and warriors were men, but high-ranking women did sometimes occupy these positions (Riley 2004: 640). Linnekin (1990: 5) states that "the ideology of male dominance seems weakly developed in early Hawaii and it is well documented that chiefly women at least were autonomous political actors with considerable personal and spiritual power."

Reckoning descent in both mother's and father's line was typical of Polynesia; only three groups (Tikopia, Pukapuka, and Ontong Java) deviate from this norm (Oliver 1989: 938), and thus one could "inherit" rank from one's mother or father. Although Linton (1926: 154) claims that descent and primogeniture were central determinants of titles and chiefly roles, some Polynesian societies were more flexible with regard to supposedly inherited titles, and occasionally elements of achieved status were included in the system. Both ascription and achievement were relevant factors in traditional Marquesan chieftainship (Riley 2004: 635). Shankman (1996: 558) claims that "in Samoa, chieftainships combined achievement and ascription, placing greater emphasis on achievement than the more stratified islands of Hawaii and Tahiti. Samoa was a more 'open' system with an intense rivalry and competition for high-ranking titles in a political environment of shifting alliances and warfare."

There are outward similarities between Melanesian notions of pollution and Polynesian *mana* and *tapu,* but the resemblances are superficial and misleading. There is some evidence of menstrual taboos in traditional Tahiti, but Levy (1973: 37–38) notes that men occasionally helped clean up menstrual fluids—an act that would undoubtedly bring horror to the hearts of most Melanesian men. Women's activities were restricted in Tahiti in that they (except an occasional high-ranking woman) were kept away from the sacred *marae* area; whether women were perceived to be contaminating in any way is, however, uncertain (Lockwood 1993: 35–37).

Although there has been much published on just what "*mana*" means in various parts of Polynesia (see especially Shore 1989, but also Firth 1940, 1957), most agree that it refers to some kind of power or force that inheres in certain kinds of people—the high-ranking, the sacred, the set apart. Often, the firstborn child, male *or* female, possessed more *mana* (as in Tahiti [Lockwood 1993: 19]). Typically, *mana* went with rank, and high-ranking women could possess more *mana* than their younger brothers. Linton (1926: 154) says that "even the sacred chief of Tonga had to accord certain marks of respect to his elder sister." *Tapu* (taboo) refers to the idea that certain things should not be brought into conjunction with one another, particularly things or people who possess different amounts of *mana*. Those with great quantities of *mana,* such as the highest-ranking men and women, should be shown respect and not be touched, and in some places they were not allowed to touch the ground.

Sexual relations among many if not most Polynesian groups were relatively uninhibited and free, certainly if compared to Melanesian ones. Riley (2004: 642) reports that traditional Marquesans not only had a variety of partners before marriage, but also that sexuality was consciously taught. In Tahiti, sexual freedom (especially before marriage) was prized by both men and women (Lockwood 1993: 37–38). Marriage among higher-ranking people was not left to chance or choice; it was often part of the process of alliance making with other groups, but commoners and those of lower rank had more choice of partner. Polygyny was typically restricted to higher-ranking people; monogamy characterized commoners. Only on the Marquesas was polyandry present, and here there was still one "principal" husband (Linton 1926: 152–153; Thomas 1989).

Micronesia falls between the relatively homogeneous Polynesia and relatively heterogeneous Melanesia. There have been many attempts to impose some order on the variety of Micronesian societies. Oliver (1989: 957) astutely notes that the boundaries of the subareas are dependent on the criteria used to define them; for example using principal crops to define subareas of Micronesia would result in a different constellation than if one used social stratification or kinship. These different classifications of areas within Micronesia reveal the difficulty of generalizing about gender relations here. But some things do seem apparent. First, although matrilineal descent does not mean that women have the predominant positions of public power anywhere, there does tend to be a correlation between it and a stronger position and higher sense of autonomy and agency for women. Second, in societies in which ascribed status and rank are important, women of high rank will have more power than those of low rank and probably even more than men of lower rank, as they do in Polynesia. (Here, as in Polynesia, the ecological differences between low coral atolls and high volcanic islands are likely to be significant.)

Geographic Perspectives

The societies of the Pacific, like societies the world over, are gendered in culturally specific and dynamic ways. Commitment to gender equality across the region is uneven, with progress made in some areas and with significant challenges remaining in others. Moreover, what constitutes desirable gender objectives differs from one region, organization, and person to another. Since the 1980s, gender has been central to Pacific development initiatives, embodied in paradigms such as Women in Development (WID) and Gender and Development (GAD). WID emerged in the 1970s as an attempt to integrate women into development processes and overcome their exclusion. GAD emerged in the 1980s and has attempted to shift the focus from "women" to "gender," by attention to power relations between men and women and through an emphasis on empowerment, participation, and gender mainstreaming. Implementing gender-sensitive development policies is, however, a difficult thing to achieve. Both WID and GAD are valued for their success in putting gender on international development agendas, but they have been criticized for their tendency to homogenize and essentialize women, sometimes treating them problematically as victims of traditional cultural norms (Bhavnani, Foran, and Kurian 2003). In recent years, there has been a burgeoning geographic scholarship on gender in the Pacific, which has engaged with these problematics and has highlighted the geographically specific ways in which gender is operationalized and contested across specific Pacific societies and by women and men.

The following sections outline some of the key debates on gender in the Pacific, focusing on politics and governance, education and health care, violence and militarization, and environment and climate, considered by many scholars and development practitioners to be some of the most pressing issues currently facing the Pacific. Our attention to gender is organized thematically for ease of understanding, but it is important to recognize that these are not discrete or bounded themes but overlap with one another in many ways.

Gender, Politics, and Governance

One of the key barriers to greater gender equity in a society is the way formal political institutions tend to be dominated both by men and by masculinist forms of thinking. Gender mainstreaming aims to change this situation. Part of the solution is getting more women in positions of political leadership, but this alone is not sufficient. It is also important to change the cultures of polities, making them more responsive to gender. In New Zealand, gender inequality remains persistent even though women have managed to occupy a number of top positions in politics and business. At the start of the millennium, as Magee (2001) writes, women held the positions of prime minister, leader of the opposition, and chief justice, and a woman also headed Telecom, the country's largest company. In 1999, New Zealand elected its first ever female MP of Pacific Island descent. At the same time, women continue to earn less than men and do most of the country's unpaid work.

According to Gambaro (2006), the Pacific is one of the worst performing regions in the world with respect to the percentage of women holding national parliamentary seats. She states that women constitute only 3 percent of all Pacific members of parliament, and of the eleven countries in the world that have no female representation in their national parliaments, six are in the Pacific. Government commitment to promoting gender equality is improving but is still inadequate. Most of the studies carried out on gender in the region have been conducted by NGOs and community organizations outside of the government sector (Wallace 2000). There are however a number of initiatives in place to improve the situation. Since the mid-1990s, organizations such as CAPWIP (Center for Asia-Pacific Women and Politics) and WiPPac (Women in Politics Pacific Centre) have held conventions to train and promote women leaders, producing some quantitative gains (Wallace 2000). More recently, the Pacific Islands Forum Secretariat (Huffer et al. 2006) has explored some of the factors that constrain women's access to formal political spheres. This report indicates that despite significant educational and cultural barriers, Pacific women's traditional status as community leaders and decision makers enables some of them to enter the political field.

Throughout the Pacific, women are deploying a series of extragovernmental strategies to improve their ability to participate in decision-making structures, using a variety of official and informal political spaces. Some women have found international good governance frameworks promoted by the United Nations and transnational networks of NGOs as a means to access centers of decision making. Others, however, have formed grassroots organizations in their communities and in their churches. In parts of Melanesia, Christianity has become central to the promotion of gender equity in governance. While church-based organizations are controversial in the gender and development field, Douglas (2002) believes that given that churches are sites in which large numbers of Pacific women are mobilized, their potential for pursuing socially progressive or radical agendas should not be simply dismissed (see also Scheyvens 2003; Dickson-Waiko 2003). It is clear that church-based organizations are appealing sites for political mobilization because they enable women to participate in the development process and gain visibility in the public sphere; but because they are widely viewed as traditional and culturally acceptable, such participation is less likely to generate conflict. It is important however not to romanticize women's political involvement at a community level. While this work is valuable on a number of levels, it is unpaid and often does not involve men, and it can therefore add considerably to women's workloads. In effect, if community work is simply added onto other productive and reproductive tasks, which cannot be renegotiated, women can find themselves stretched to the breaking point.

Education and Health Care

Gender shapes our lives in many ways, influencing opportunities to get an education, earn a decent living, enjoy good health, or live free from violence. In this regard, health care and education are sectors that are crucial to addressing gender disparities. According to Keating (2007), boys outnumber girls at all levels of the education system throughout the Pacific, and this inequality increases with age. Some Pacific countries, especially in Polynesia and Micronesia, have made significant progress toward reducing or eliminating gender disparities in primary education. In Melanesia, there are many girls who are unable to complete their primary education (Lewis 1998; NZAID 2007). Postprimary educational opportunities, especially for women and girls, remain limited in many countries. While recent globalizing processes have created some employment opportunities for women in sectors such as tourism and garment manufacture, it is clear that educational disadvantages suffered as children limit women's income-earning capabilities in later life.

Many of the key health care challenges facing the Pacific have significant gender dimensions. In some countries, maternal mortality rates are high by international standards, especially in Papua New Guinea and Solomon Islands, access to reproductive and primary health care services is patchy and inadequate, and the region has seen the rates of both tuberculosis and HIV increase. Women are particularly affected by inadequate health care services because they usually have the main responsibility for caring for children, the elderly, the sick, and family members with disabilities.

The spread of HIV/AIDS is potentially one of the most serious health issues facing the Pacific. It threatens to undermine both development and the struggle for gender equality, especially in countries such as Papua New Guinea, where the disease is now widespread and has been declared a generalized epidemic, affecting almost 2 percent of the adult population (PNG National AIDS Council 2005). Solomon Islands, Tuvalu, Fiji, Kiribati, and the Cook Islands are also showing sharp increases in infection rates, due in part to seafaring traditions. As in other parts of the world, we can witness the feminization of the HIV/AIDS epidemic in the Pacific region as women become infected through heterosexual transmission in ever-greater numbers. The low status of women, which compromises their ability to get and use condoms, and their level of exposure to sexual violence makes them vulnerable to the epidemic. Gender inequality increases the spread of HIV, and the spread of HIV exacerbates gender inequality.

Gender-Based Violence and Militarization

Many Pacific women have become active in initiatives to address the gendered dimensions of violence and conflict. Gender-based violence is a serious problem in the Pacific and it includes both domestic violence and violence as a result of civil conflict. According to Keating (2007), violence against women is arguably the worst manifestation of gender inequality in the Pacific.

Gender-based violence affects both men and women. During violent conflicts, both men and women can end up being victims and suffering from conflict-related trauma, but the ways in which these processes play out is often differentiated by gender.

The Pacific has been a key site for nuclear testing and the establishment of U.S. military bases. Both Hawai'i and Guam have a strong U.S. military presence, which permeates the fabric of everyday life in several ways, which can be analyzed in terms of their implications for both gender and "race." Teaiwa (2000) has used the concept of "mili-tourism" to explore the gendered and racialized ways in which militarism and tourism have become intertwined. She argues that in the Western cultural imagination the Bikini atoll is constituted simultaneously as a site of nuclear destruction and erotic fantasy. Representations of the exoticized Pacific Island woman function to domesticate nuclear technology, obscuring its devastating consequences. Men too are affected by the gendered inequalities on which militarism depends. As Cachola et al. (2008) write, young men who live near U.S. bases in the Asia-Pacific region often understand masculinity in military terms.

One of the barriers to dealing with domestic abuse in the Pacific is that it has for a long time been viewed as a private issue, something many women tend to accept as a normal part of marriage and gender relations (Counts 1990; Toren 1994; Cribb and Barnett 1999). In rural villages in Western Samoa, as Cribb and Barnett (1999) write, there is no legal redress for battered women, but violence by men against women is considered to bring shame upon the whole family, which to some extent acts as a deterrent. In this context, extended family networks provide essential shelter and support for battered women.

Slowly, though, domestic violence is being reframed as both a development issue and a matter of public health, and it is receiving more attention. This reframing has resulted from UN initiatives such as CEDAW (Convention for the Elimination of All Forms of Discrimination against Women) and the work of individual women's organizations. All Pacific Island nations, with the exception of Tonga, Nauru, and Palau, have ratified CEDAW and as a result the legislative frameworks available to deal with domestic violence are being strengthened. Key women's organizations such as the Women's Refuge Movement in New Zealand or the Women's Crisis Centre in Fiji have played key roles in both helping individual women who have suffered domestic violence as well as raising public awareness of the issue.

While women are often victims of domestic abuse, many Pacific men and women have been caught up in civil conflict in their countries. The consequences of civil conflict are overwhelmingly negative for both men and women but often in different ways. In recent civil conflicts in Solomon Islands, Fiji, and Bougainville, rape and sexual assault have been systematically used as a weapon of war (Hakena 2000; Pollard 2000; Leslie and Boso 2003). Conflict can also intensify women's caregiving responsibilities if food provision or other economic or domestic activities become more difficult or if the conflict causes health care and education facilities to close. There is no doubt that gender-based violence of all kinds undermines women's ability to participate in the development process and maintain their productive or reproductive responsibilities, and it often results in poor health, low self-esteem, or feelings of guilt.

Men are also impacted by violence. In societies with long histories of marginalization generated by colonialism and struggles over land and resources, violent conflict is sometimes viewed as the only available political option. Prevailing expressions of masculinity, along with limited study and employment opportunities, often lead young men into violent organizations, such as gangs or military groups. In Solomon Islands, it was primarily young men from Guadalcanal who became part of the Guadalcanal Revolutionary Army and the Isatabu Freedom Fighters, who fought to displace non-indigenous mainly Malaitan settlers from Honiara. This forced a violent response from the Malaitans, who formed the Malaita Eagle Force (Leslie and Boso 2003). In New Zealand, many disaffected young (and not so young) men become part of violent and criminal cultures through gang membership. The members of high-profile gangs such as the Mongrel Mob and Black Power are predominantly male and of Maori and Pacific Island descent.

Dominant understandings of the relationship between gender and conflict have often simplistically assumed that men are more likely to be the perpetrators of violence and women the victims. Even when men are killed in battle, they are often viewed as heroes rather than victims. Similarly, women are often viewed in essentialist terms as being naturally more peace-loving than men. The gendered dynamics of conflict are, however, not so straightforward. Recent scholarship on the relationship between gender and conflict has questioned these binary understandings (see, for example, Cockburn 2001; Enloe 2000; Moser and Clark 2001). As Moser's (2007) work on Solomon Islands has indicated, while women continued to maintain traditional caregiving roles during the conflict, they also took on additional economic activities, often taking on men's work, especially when male family members were injured or killed. While some women worked hard to promote peace and reconciliation, others engaged in fighting or kept weapons at home. Conflict can further entrench gender inequalities or it can sometimes encourage women to take on new roles. In Solomon Islands, many women emerged from the conflict feeling empowered as they had gained new skills, while some men perceived a diminished status as leaders and breadwinners as a result of the conflict (Moser 2007). Moser cites a male research participant from Solomon Islands who believes that women have become more powerful since the armed conflict. Women often gain these skills through the roles they play as peace builders. Organizations such as Women for Peace in the Solomon Islands or Leitana Nehan Women's Development Agency in Bougainville have worked hard to tackle the consequences of gender-based violence and promote both reconciliation and a culture of peace in their respective countries (Hakena 2000; Leslie and Boso 2003; Moser 2007).

Gender is therefore central to making sense of civil conflicts, but we must pay closer attention to the geographically specific and complex ways the gendered dynamics of conflict unfold in a given context.

Pacific Masculinities

It is clear that the gendered dynamics of violence, conflict, and militarization in the Pacific cannot be understood without focusing on both men and women. The shift from women to gender in development theory and policy led to a greater degree of awareness of the need to include men in development. Given the ways women were often excluded from development priorities, much gender and development work has tended understandably to attempt to prioritize women's needs and interests. More recent concerns, however, have been expressed about men and masculinities. The tenth

triennial conference of Pacific women held in Nouméa, New Caledonia, in May 2007 highlighted the need to better engage with men and boys as advocates for gender equality. Scholars and practitioners have become aware that solutions to key social problems in the Pacific, such as domestic violence, civil conflict, and reproductive health, can only be found with the active support and involvement of both men and women.

As Cleaver (2001) notes, it is rare for men to be explicitly mentioned in gender and development policy documents. When men do appear, they are often framed as lazy, drunk, violent, or as an obstacle to women's development. This "women as victim, men as problem" approach to gender and development overlooks the ways men and women might work together for the good of their families and their communities (Cornwall 2000). It also overlooks the ways men might also experience gendered feelings of powerlessness and vulnerability (Cornwall 2000).

Pacific masculinities have become a key focus of academic scholarship in recent times. Scholars have been exploring the ways in which the colonial experience is central to the construction of indigenous masculinities across the Pacific (see, for example, Tengan 2002; Walker 2008). These constructions often have contradictory outcomes. Surfing in Hawai'i, for example, embodies indigenous revitalization and resistance to colonial domination but it also attracts the foreign tourist gaze, which perpetuates dominant neocolonial understandings of Hawaiian "beachboys" as soft and emasculated (Walker 2008). In both New Zealand and Fiji, rugby games are begun with indigenous war chants, constructing men in gendered and racialized terms as hypermasculine "warriors for the nation" (Teaiwa 2005). These cultural expressions should not be understood as precolonial indigenous traditions but as having emerged in the course of colonialism (Hokowhitu 2004, 2008; Tengan 2008).

New Zealand has been described by Phillips (1996) as a man's country because of the ways national identity has tended to coalesce around the male stereotype and male national icons. The dominant male stereotype, which comes together in the iconic image of the kiwi bloke, promotes notions of kiwi ingenuity and practicality, but it also involves social pressure to prove one's manhood on the rugby field, behind the steering wheel, and at the pub. These pressures, which contribute to New Zealand's high road death toll, rugby-related spinal and other injuries, and high levels of alcoholism, have a significant social cost for men and women (Phillips 1996; see also Law, Campbell, and Schick 1999). Southern rural masculinities continue to be highly effective in beer advertising (Law 2006), and the cultural legacy of the tough practical pioneer man who does not feel the cold affects our ability to deal with environmental problems such as air pollution (Cupples, Guyatt, and Pearce 2007). We can see therefore that while the kiwi bloke is a hegemonic stereotype to which not all New Zealand men conform (Law, Campbell, and Schick 1999), it is nonetheless a familiar one that continues to shape New Zealand society and culture in different ways.

Gender, Environment, and Climate Change

Climate change and related forms of environmental degradation are decisively reshaping the geographies of the Pacific. Sea-level rise is already producing damaging economic, social, and emotional effects in a number of islands of the Pacific, threatening homes, agriculture, and livelihoods. Large-scale logging and mining activities have also had devastating environmental consequences in some areas. Consequently, the Pacific has become central to global debates about environmental degradation and climate change. The ways these processes are gendered are however often less well understood. While climate change affects everybody who lives in the Pacific, it affects different people in different ways depending on their levels of vulnerability and resilience, their social position in society, and their dependence on environmental resources. Given that men and women often have different social and economic responsibilities and unequal access to land titles or environmental resources, it is clear that resource scarcity or degradation will affect them differently. In the Federated States of Micronesia, for example, men tend to concern themselves with ocean-related activities, while women are occupied in land-based or reef-based activities (Anderson 2002), and men and women often have quite distinct environmental knowledges (Scheyvens 1998). Across the Pacific, women are often more severely affected by environmental degradation because women are responsible for providing food, firewood, or water to the household. If these resources become scarce because of environmental change, women's workloads will increase, affecting their ability to engage in other productive activities and producing stress or ill health.

Although women are often more harmed than men by environmental change, women are often underrepresented in government and other environmental agencies. Consequently, women's particular needs and skills are often overlooked and women are deprived of input in resource-management decisions on which their lives and livelihoods depend. Large-scale logging in Solomon Islands and mining in Papua New Guinea has generated widespread environmental destruction and social decay (Scheyvens and Lagisa 1998). As Scheyvens and Lagisa have indicated, the economic benefits that have derived from these activities have disproportionately benefited men, while environmental destruction has disproportionately disadvantaged women. For example, in Lihir in PNG, all businesses created to service the mines have been registered in men's names, and women make up only 10 percent of the mining workforce. Women's workloads have also increased because men are no longer available to help with subsistence agriculture. They also often have little control over how men's cash earnings are spent and have therefore witnessed an increase in alcohol consumption by men. Membup and Macintyre (2000) describe how the sudden availability of cash as a result of mining employment in Lihir in Papua New Guinea led to "furious beer drinking" among male mining employees. In Solomon Islands, logging has ruined important trees and plants that women used as medicines or as construction materials and has polluted waterways on which women depend for fresh water or shellfish (Scheyvens and Lagisa 1998). These gender impacts are not, however, uniform. Not all women are disadvantaged in the same way, and some men too find themselves at a disadvantage. While men might not be as immediately affected by environmental degradation as women, they will begin to suffer in the long term as these problems deepen and escalate (Scheyvens and Lagisa 1998).

A recent body of scholarship, however, has documented the benefits to people, environments, and communities when a gender-sensitive approach to environmental management is taken. A high participation of women in Pacific Island drought task forces created during the 1997–1998 El Niño event led to much more effective local conservation and public health strategies at the community level, enabling communities to live more effectively with risk (Anderson 2002). Women are often active within the grassroots of environmental movements and are often at the forefront of such struggles to protect the environment. This is not because women are naturally or inherently more concerned than men about the environment, but rather because they depend more heavily on it to fulfill their gender roles or responsibilities. As Scheyvens (1998) writes, gender equity and environmental sustainability should be viewed as complementary goals. If gender equity concerns are disregarded, environmental management projects might well fail.

Conclusion

The challenges posed by endemic gender inequality in a context of rapid global change require flexible thinking. Dominant understandings of gender are being interrogated more than ever before. Gender is increasingly understood as a fluid and dynamic process with shifting and uncertain boundaries. The same can be said of academic disciplines. Once rooted in unifying concerns and methodologies, disciplines are now borrowing from each other more and more, and their boundaries are becoming more diffuse and fluid. Both geography and anthropology are disciplines that have served as intellectual justifications for colonialism, and both have been revolutionized by intellectual developments associated with postcolonialism, postmodernism, and poststructuralism. Fortunately, in many ways we are beginning to critically examine our colonial origins and forge in the process new anticolonial geographies and anthropologies. The diverse expressions of gender in the Pacific along with the gendered challenges faced by Pacific societies are fertile ground for developing more hybrid and more flexible scholarship and activism.

NOTES

1. Freeman (1983) disputes Mead's findings; for an excellent summary of this controversy, see Shankman (1996).

2. See M. Strathern's edited volume (1987) for a later consideration of issues of equality and inequality.

BIBLIOGRAPHY

Anderson, C. L. 2002. Gender matters: Implications for climate variability and climate change and for disaster management in the Pacific Islands. *Intercoast: International Newsletter of Coastal Management,* 24–25, 39.

Ardener, S., ed. 1982. *Perceiving women.* London: Malaby Press.

Bateson, G. 1958. *Naven: A survey of the problems suggested by a composite picture of the culture of a New Guinea tribe drawn from three points of view.* Stanford, Calif.: Stanford University Press.

Bhavnani, K., J. Foran, and P. A. Kurian. 2003. An introduction to women, culture and development. In *Feminist futures: Reimagining women, culture and development,* ed. K. Bhavnani, J. Foran, and P. A. Kurian, 1–39. London: Zed Books.

Blackwood, E., and S. E. Wieringa, eds. 1999. *Same-sex relations and female desires: Transgender practices across cultures.* New York: Columbia University Press.

Cachola, E., L. Festejo, A. Fukushima, G. Kirk, and S. Perez. 2008. Gender and U.S. bases in Asia-Pacific. *Foreign Policy In Focus,* March. Available at http://fpif.org/fpiftxt/5069. Accessed May 14, 2008.

Chowning, A. 1977. *An introduction to the peoples and cultures of Melanesia,* 2nd ed. Menlo Park, Calif: Cummings Publishing Company.

Cleaver, F. 2000. Do men matter? New horizons in gender and development. *ID21.* Available at http://www.id21.org/static/insights35editorial.htm. Accessed May 9, 2008.

Cockburn, C. 2001. The gendered dynamics of armed conflict and political violence. In *Victims, perpetrators or actors? Gender, armed conflict and political violence,* ed. C. O. N. Moser and F. C. Clark, 13–29. London: Zed Books.

Cornwall, A. 2000. Missing men? Reflections on men, masculinities and gender in GAD. *IDS Bulletin* 2: 18–25.

Counts, D. 1984. Revenge suicide by Lusi women: An expression of power. In *Rethinking women's roles: Perspectives from the Pacific,* ed. D. O'Brien and S. Tiffany, 71–93. Berkeley: University of California Press.

———. 1990. Domestic violence in Oceania. Special issue. *Pacific Studies* 3: 1–303.

Cribb, J., and R. Barnett. 1999. Being bashed: Western Samoan women's responses to domestic violence in Western Samoa and New Zealand. *Gender, Place & Culture* 6(1): 49–65.

Cupples, J., V. Guyatt, and J. Pearce. 2007. "Put on a jacket, you wuss": Cultural identities, home heating and air pollution in Christchurch, New Zealand. *Environment and Planning A:* 2883–2898.

Dickson-Waiko, A. 2003. The missing rib: Mobilizing church women for change in Papua New Guinea. *Oceania* (1/2): 98–119

Douglas, B. 2002. Why religion, race, and gender matter in Pacific politics. *Development Bulletin* 59: 11–14.

Enloe, C. 2000. *Maneuvers: The international politics of militarizing women's lives.* Berkeley and Los Angeles: University of California Press.

Firth, R. 1940. An analysis of mana: An empirical approach. *Journal of the Polynesian Society* 49: 483–510.

———. 1957. A note on descent groups in Polynesia. *Man* 57: 4–8.

Fisk, E. K., ed. *New Guinea on the threshold.* Canberra: Australian National University Press.

Freeman, D. 1983. *Margaret Mead and Samoa: The making and unmaking of an anthropological myth.* Cambridge, Mass.: Harvard University Press.

Gambaro, T. 2006. Opening speech: Symposium on the harmonisation of gender indicators. *Development Bulletin,* 4–6.

Glasse, R. M., and M. J. Meggitt, eds. 1969. *Pigs, pearlshells, and women: Marriage in the New Guinea Highlands.* Englewood Cliffs, N.J.: Prentice-Hall, Inc.

Hakena, H. 2000. Strengthening communities for peace in Bougainville. *Development Bulletin,* 16–19.

Herdt, G. 2006. *The Sambia: Ritual sexuality, and change in Papua New Guinea.* Belmont, Calif.: Thomson Wadsworth.

Hogbin, I. 1970. *The island of menstruating men.* Scranton, Pa.: Chandler Publishing.

Howard, A., and R. Borofsky, eds. *Developments in Polynesian ethnology.* Honolulu: University of Hawai'i Press.

Huffer, E., J. Fraenkel, F. Taomia, S. Saitala Kofe, O. Guttenbeil Likiliki, and A. Lauti. 2006. *A Woman's place is in the house—the House of Parliament.* Fiji: Pacific Islands Forum Secretariat.

Jolly, M., and M. Macintyre, eds. 1989. *Family and gender in the Pacific: Domestic contradictions and the colonial impact.* Cambridge: Cambridge University Press.

Keating, A. 2007. Gender in the Pacific Island states: Literature review and annotated bibliography. AusAID Gender Equality Thematic Group. Available at http://www.siyanda.org/docs/Keating_pacific_islands_bibliography.doc. Accessed May 9, 2008.

Kuehling, S. 2005. *Dobu: Ethics of exchange on a Massim Island, Papua New Guinea.* Honolulu: University of Hawai'i Press.

Law, R. 2006. Beer advertising, rurality and masculinity. In *Country boys: Masculinity and rural life,* ed. H. Campbell, M. Mayerfeld Bell, and M. Finney, 203–216. University Park: Pennsylvania State University Press.

Law, R., H. Campbell, and R. Schick. 1999. Introduction. In *Masculinities in Aotearoa New Zealand,* ed. R. Law, H. Campbell, and R. Schick. 13–35. Palmerston North: Dunmore Press.

Lederman, R. 1984. Who speaks here? Formality and the politics of gender in Mendi, Highland Papua New Guinea. In *Dangerous words: Language and politics in the Pacific,* ed. D. L. Brenneis and F. R. Myers, 85–107. New York: New York University Press.

Lepowsky, M. 1993. *Fruit of the motherland: Gender in an egalitarian society.* New York: Columbia University Press.

Leslie, H., and S. Boso. 2003. Gender related violence in the Solomon Islands: The work of local women's organisations. *Asia Pacific Viewpoint* 44(3): 325–333.

Levy, R. I. 1973. *Tahitians: Mind and experience in the Society Islands.* Chicago: University of Chicago Press.

Lewis, N. D. 1998. Intellectual intersections: Gender and health in the Pacific. *Social Science and Medicine* (6): 641–659.

Linnekin, J. 1990. *Sacred queens and women of consequence: Rank, gender, and colonialism in the Hawaiian Islands.* Ann Arbor: University of Michigan Press.

Linton, R. 1926. *Ethnology of Polynesia and Micronesia.* Chicago: Field Museum of Natural History.

Lockwood, V. S. 1993. *Tahitian transformation: Gender and capitalist development in a rural society.* Boulder, Colo.: Lynne Rienner Publishers.

Lutkehaus, N. C. 1982. Ambivalence, ambiguity, and the reproduction of gender hierarchy in Manam Society. *Social Analysis* 12: 36–51.

Lutkehaus, N. C., and P. B. Roscoe, eds. 1995. *Gender rituals: Female initiation in Melanesia.* New York: Routledge.

Magee, A. 2001. Women. *Asia Pacific Viewpoint* 42(1): 35–45.

Mageo, J. M. 1998. *Theorizing self in Samoa: Emotions, genders, and sexualities.* Ann Arbor: University of Michigan Press.

Malinowski, B. 1922. *Argonauts of the Western Pacific.* London: Routledge & Kegan Paul.

McDowell, N. 1977. The meaning of "rope" in a Yuat River village. *Ethnology* 16: 175–183.

———. 1991. *The Mundugumor: From the field notes of Margaret Mead and Reo Fortune.* Washington, D.C.: Smithsonian Institution Press.

Mead, M. 1928. *The coming of age in Samoa.* New York: William Morrow & Co.

———. 1930. *Social organization of Manu'a.* Honolulu: Bernice P. Bishop Museum Bulletin No. 76.

———. 1935. *Sex and temperament in three primitive societies.* New York: William Morrow & Co.

Meggitt, M. J. 1964. Male-female relationships in the Highlands of Australian New Guinea. In *New Guinea: The Central Highlands,* ed. J. Watson. *American Anthropologist* Special Publication 66(4), Part 2: 204–224.

Membup, J., and M. Macintyre. 2000. Petzstorme: A woman's organisation in the context of a PNG mining project. *Development Bulletin* 51: 55–57.

Moser, A. 2007. The peace and conflict gender analysis: UNIFEM's research in the Solomon Islands. *Gender and Development* 2: 231–239.

Moser, C. O. N., and F. C. Clark. 2001. Introduction. In *Victims, perpetrators or actors? Gender, armed conflict and political violence,* ed. C. O. N. Moser and F. C. Clark, 3–12. London: Zed Books.

NZAID. 2007. *Achieving gender equality and women's empowerment.*

Wellington: New Zealand's International Aid and Development Agency. Available at http://www.nzaid.govt.nz/library/docs/gender-doco.pdf. Accessed May 10, 2008.

O'Brien, D., and S. Tiffany, eds. 1984. *Rethinking women's roles: Perspectives from the Pacific.* Berkeley: University of California Press.

Oliver, D. L. 1989. *Oceania: The Native cultures of Australia and the Pacific Islands,* vols. 1 and 2. Honolulu: University of Hawai'i Press.

Phillips, J. 1996. *A man's country: The image of the pakeha male—a history.* Auckland: Penguin Books.

PNG National AIDS Council. 2005. *Papua New Guinea National Strategic Plan on HIV/AIDS 2006-2010.* Available at www.png_nsp_on_hiv_06-10.pdf. Accessed May 10, 2008.

Pollard, A. A. 2000. Resolving conflict in Solomon Islands: The women for peace approach. *Development Bulletin,* 50-54.

Riley, K. C. 2004. Marquesans. In *Encyclopedia of sex and gender: Men and women in the world's cultures.* Vols. 1 and 2, ed. C. R. Ember and M. Ember, 635-644. New York: Kluwer Academic/Plenum Publishers.

Scheyvens, R. 1998. Subtle strategies for women's empowerment. *Third World Planning Review* 20(3): 235-253.

———. 2003. Church women's groups and the empowerment of women in the Solomon Islands. *Oceania* 1/2: 24-43.

Scheyvens, R., and L. Lagisa. 1998. Women, disempowerment and resistance: An analysis of logging and mining activities in the Pacific. *Singapore Journal of Tropical Geography* 19(1): 51-70.

Sexton, L. D. 1984. Pigs, pearlshells, and 'women's work': Collective response to change in Highland Papua New Guinea. In *Rethinking women's roles: Perspectives from the Pacific,* ed. D. O'Brien and S. W. Tiffany. Berkeley: University of California Press.

Shankman, P. 1996. The history of Samoan sexual conduct and the Mead-Freeman controversy. *American Anthropologist* N.S. 98(3): 555-567.

Shore, B. 1989. *Mana* and *tapu.* In *Developments in Polynesian ethnology,* ed. A. Howard and R. Borofsky, 137-173. Honolulu: University of Hawai'i Press.

Strathern M. 1972. *Women in between: Female roles in a male world: Mount Hagen, New Guinea.* New York: Seminar Press.

———, ed. 1987. *Dealing with inequality: Analyzing gender relations in Melanesia and beyond.* Cambridge: Cambridge University Press.

———. 1988 *The gender of the gift: Problems with women and problems with society in Melanesia.* Berkeley: University of California Press.

Teaiwa, T. K. 2000. Bikinis and other s/pacific n/oceans. In *Voyaging in the contemporary Pacific,* ed. D. Hanlon and G. M. White, 91-112. Lanham, Md.: Rowman & Littlefield.

———. 2005. Articulated cultures: Militarism and masculinities in Fiji during the mid-1990s. *Fijian Studies* 3(2): 201-222.

Tengan, T. K. 2002. (En)gendering colonialism: Masculinities in Hawai'i and Aotearoa. *Cultural Values* 3: 239-246.

Thomas, N. 1989. Domestic structures and polyandry in the Marquesas Islands. In *Family and gender in the Pacific,* ed. M. Jolly and M. Macintyre, 65-83. Cambridge: Cambridge University Press.

Thurnwald, R. 1916. Banaro society. *Memoir of the American Anthropological Association* 3(4).

Toren, C. 1994. Transforming love: Representing Fijian hierarchy. In *Sex and violence: Issues in representation and experience,* ed. P. Harvey and P. Gow, 18-39. London: Routledge.

Tuzin, D. 1976. *The Ilahita Arapesh: Dimensions of unity.* Berkeley: University of California Press.

———. 1980. *The voice of the Tambaran: Truth and illusion in Ilahita Arapesh religion.* Berkeley: University of California Press.

———. 1997. *The cassowary's revenge: The life and death of masculinity in a New Guinea society.* Chicago: University of Chicago Press.

———. 2001. *Social complexity in the making: A case study among the Arapesh of New Guinea.* New York: Routledge.

Walker, I. H. 2008. Hui Nalu, beachboys, and the surfing boarder-lands of Hawai'i. *The Contemporary Pacific* 20(1): 89-114.

Wallace, H. 2000. Gender and the reform process in Vanuatu and the Solomon Islands. *Development Bulletin,* 23-25.

Wardlow, H. 2006. *Wayward women: Sexuality and agency in a New Guinea Society.* Berkeley: University of California Press.

Watson, J., ed. 1964. New Guinea: The Central Highlands. *American Anthropologist* Special Publication 66(4) Part 2.

Weiner, A. 1976. *Women of value, men of renown: New perspectives in Trobriand exchange.* Austin: University of Texas Press.

White, G. M., and J. Kirkpatrick, eds. 1985. *Person, self, and experience: Exploring Pacific ethnopsychology.* Berkeley: University of California Press.

Tenure

Ron Crocombe

16

Land and water tenures are shaped by the environment, by past experiences and present circumstances of the people who live by them, and by external forces. Tenure systems also influence ecology, society, and economy in a continuing process of interaction.

Tenures used to be guided only by diverse traditional customs and precedents. Today they are also covered by laws—lots of laws—of the fourteen independent nations and twelve dependent territories of the region. Foreign influences on tenures are more prominent than ever, coming now from the World Bank and Asian Development Bank, and from former colonial powers with continuing interests in the region (most strongly Australia), working both directly through their aid programs and indirectly through regional agencies that they fund and heavily influence.

The more intensively used and more valuable the unit of land or water, the more important law is likely to be; the smaller and poorer the unit, the more significant custom is likely to remain. Custom tends to be more important in rural communities, but at the national level and in situations of intense use and heavy investment, formal law is usually dominant. In practice, however, it is not a case of some areas being covered by law and others by custom, because most land and water is influenced by both in varying degrees.

Traditional Precedents

Pacific Island tenure systems were diverse, but shared some common elements. All evolved to facilitate allocation of rights of access for subsistence agriculture (the dominant food source in most places), seafoods (which were important in coastal areas and predominant in a few), and hunting and foraging (which was supplementary except in a few infertile pockets where it was the main food source).

Rights to land were in all cases multiple, conditional, and negotiable. What was owned was not the land or water so much as rights to it—rights vis-à-vis other people. No rights were absolute. Some rights to land and water were held by individuals, but there were many shades of difference between the rights of even close relatives. Rights of males differed from (and were generally superior to) those of females. Rights of older brothers, and cousins of more senior lines, were often superior to those of juniors. Resident rightholders took precedence, other things being equal, over non-residents. Labor strengthened rights, so those who worked the land

enhanced their claims over those of equal blood right who did not. And more forceful personalities and more persuasive arguments could tilt balances, for multiple principles could be called upon and given varying degrees of emphasis to benefit those relying on them.

No one person held all rights to any one plot of land (nor do people anywhere, incidentally, including in commercialized, industrialized societies). As well as interacting laterally with the rights of one's peers, individual rights were nested with those of extended families, lineages, clans, tribes—and now of course, of governments, banks, insurance systems, and other institutions including aid donors. Wives (or in some cases in-marrying husbands) held rights contingent on the marriage. The land rights of adoptees varied greatly even within communities, for much depended on the circumstances of the adoption and the relationship of the adopting parents and the adoptee. Refugees and others with special needs were often accommodated under negotiated arrangements, but the rights of refugees and adoptees were often vulnerable once the person who granted the rights died.

As Guiart (1996) observes, "there is no formal ownership of land in Western terms [but] systems regulating access to land for each individual in each generation." Tui Atua (2007) explains that relationship for Samoa. Day-to-day decisions were based on broad customary principles modified by pragmatism, as different customs could be used to justify different actions. For example, seniority might of itself give priority over juniors, but persons with outstanding records of military or community service might rate higher. As the Fijian anthropologist Nayacakalou (1992) pointed out, custom provided guidelines rather than rigid frameworks.

As there was no writing or mapping, rights and boundaries relied on memory. The memories of specialists in this art were at times prodigious. Although memory is selective and tends to deflect in the interest of the person remembering, it allows flexibility and adaptation. Tuimaleali'ifano's (1997) study of the competing and often radically different memories of Samoan experts in relation to the same land and chiefly titles—always deflected to the service of the "remembering" party—is an excellent example of a Pacific-wide (and humanity-wide) tendency.

Most land rights were transferred by inheritance from a parent or other close blood relative, but in the process many factors came into play. These included the needs of individuals, the harmony or conflict between potential heirs and heritors, the extent to which heirs had used that land, who provided for the elders in their declining years, what payments were made at funerary feasts (this was particularly important in some Vanuatu and Solomon Islands cultures), and other considerations.

Warfare was more important in transferring land rights than is often recognized. Wars were usually triggered by disputes over pigs or other property, over women, insults, or compensation. But as a consequence of war, land rights often changed hands. A New Zealand Maori proverb observed that the deaths of men were caused by land and women, and Ballard (1996) notes that although Papua New Guineans often deny that wars were fought over land, many resulted in land acquisition. He notes that Huli people deny they fought for land, but the oral history of three thousand plots there showed that wars "reconfigured the social landscape on a massive scale." Those who lose in such conquests seldom relinquish their claims to the land or their hope that eventually they will get it back. Examples could be presented from throughout the region.

Every household needed access to several kinds of land for different purposes, so soils and crops influenced tenures. Even on atolls, with their apparent uniformity, plots were usually narrow slices running from the lagoon to the ocean to give the holder access to different microenvironments. Most people have rights in more than one such "slice," because that facilitates exchange of use rights with others in a complex pattern of mutual obligation and reciprocity that broadens options and enhances social security (Clarke 1994; Crocombe 1968).

Rights in multiple plots of land were necessary because most crops required seven to fifteen years of fallow after harvest due to the leaching of soils by rain and heat and the rapid concentration of pests and weeds in gardens. Fallowing facilitates flexible allocation of land, adapted to the needs of those involved at the time the land is ready to plant again. But taro (*Colocasia*) and *puraka* (*Cyrtosperma*) can be grown continuously in fertile swamps, and thus rights to them were strictly defined. At the other extreme, medicinal plants, fibers, trees, birds, and animals were scattered in the wild and accessible to all members of the large community.

Climate was a vital determinant. Most plants brought by the Maori from tropical Polynesia to New Zealand would not grow, so they relied more on hunting and gathering, which necessitated rights to large areas being shared by many people.

Demography influenced tenures, with denser populations recognizing more precise and detailed rights than sparser populations, except when self-propagating species provided much of the diet (as in a few fertile and densely populated estuaries of coastal Papua). Likewise, the more labor needed for production, the more individualized the tenure tended to be, so the intensive cultivation and longer storage feasible for the staple yams on Tonga's rich soils led to a more individualized system, with households spread across the countryside. Samoa, on the other hand, with rocky soil that was difficult to cultivate, relied more on self-propagating breadfruit and bananas, which required minimal effort and facilitated village living and communal tenures.

For most of the region, about one-tenth of a hectare of land per person was needed under cultivation at a time, although this varied with soils and crops. Because of the long fallow, half to two hectares of gardening land per person (up to ten hectares per family) was needed in addition to land for hunting and foraging.

Traditional Rights to Water

Polynesians and Micronesians were among the world's most skilled mariners, navigators, and fishermen for many centuries. As might be expected among people who depended so heavily on the resources of the sea, their marine tenures were among the world's most complex and included different categories of rights (to reefs, shoals, passages, swamps, etc.) being held by communities, descent groups, and individuals; rights to use of surface waters being differentiated from those of bottom waters; rights to particular fish being separate from those of other fish and from the waters they swam in; and sometimes seasonal changes in rights. Some atoll cultures had rules for the allocation of rights to logs and other things that floated offshore or drifted on shore.

Culture, values, and knowledge should not be overlooked. Some Papua New Guinea people (such as the Koitabu) lived near the sea for centuries but made little use of it, while others (such as the Motu) who arrived later with intimate understanding of marine environments used it intensively. Similar juxtapositions of communities with skills to exploit different environments were common in Melanesia, often leading to trade between the two economies.

Where waters are extensive and foods plentiful, there will be little subdivision, with many rights being held by the community. Several communities may have rights of access through a reef passage, even though only the community where it is located will have rights to fish in it. Those who invest labor, such as in making fish weirs, will have stronger rights of use than those who do not (see, e.g., Atanraoi 1995; see D'Arcy 2006 for central Micronesia).

Salt water in lagoons, estuaries, and the open sea was usually a more important source of food and other resources than fresh water. The degree to which rights were divided by area varied enormously, with some cultures making detailed provision for individual rights to highly valued fishing sites. The number of persons sharing rights was generally larger the farther the site was from the village and the more difficult it was to mark. Thus open sea was often accessible to all whose community lands bordered it, whereas shallow waters and fringing reefs were more clearly demarcated.

Even far inland where fresh water is plentiful, customary rights to it are detailed (see, e.g., Pospisil 1965). The rights cover who may draw drinking water from where, who may bathe and where, who may catch fish and prawns and where and when, who may divert water for irrigation or other use, access rights, and so on.

External Influences

All the ancient systems have been radically modified, and today's customary tenures are very different from yesterday's. Yet elements of the ancient traditional systems outlined above are still evident—more markedly in isolated areas.

New technology, from steel tools to bulldozers, radically alters the amount of land one person can farm, and the terms of its tenures. High technology and a money economy lead to global markets and the attraction or seduction to turn Melanesian forests into Japanese toilet paper, the chiefly beverage kava (*Piper methysticum*) into an herbal medicine, coconut oil into "health" soap, and bêche-de-mer (trepang, or sea cucumber) into aphrodisiacs for the international market. The demand for imports leads Kanaks to grow coffee for

Europe, Tongans to replace yams for subsistence with pumpkins for Japan, and Micronesians to work in hotels rather than gardens.

New products require different land types. Coconuts had been grown in small quantities for subsistence, but commercial production requires larger areas. Most attempts to farm cattle have been abandoned, or reduced to a few, because farmers cannot get sufficiently exclusive rights to a large enough area to make it economical, and when they do they are often obliged to give the cattle away to provide feasts at community functions. Moreover, many Pacific people are averse to fences, which may imply mistrust. Many fences have been chopped down.

Central governments brought substantial change. Most Melanesian communities recognized no authority over more than a few hundred people, and few Polynesian communities contained more than a few thousand. In both cases, leaders at the top did not usually interfere in the day-to-day allocation of land rights. Change wrought by central governments is often thought to be due to their being colonial, but it is an inevitable by-product of technological development. The Kingdom of Tonga, which was never a colony, introduced the most extensive tenure reforms of any government in the region (Crocombe 1975a; Maude and Sevele 1987).

Another action of any national government is to stop warfare—or at least to try. No one doubts the virtue of stopping warfare, but it was done without adequate understanding of the longer-term function of warfare in adjusting land to population. So no adequate alternative access was provided for those who outgrew their former areas or whose needs changed due to cash cropping or other new uses.

Demography is closely related to tenure. Last century many Pacific populations were decimated by introduced diseases to which they had no immunity, by more lethal weapons, and by labor migration. This century, growing immunity and better medical services has led to booming populations, so in many situations there are five times as many people to be accommodated than the traditional tenures were designed for. The proud claim that every islander has customary rights to land is hollow when, as for a growing proportion, their rights are minuscule, fragmented, restricted, badly located relative to today's opportunities, or shared with hundreds of others.

Density of people per square kilometer of land ranges from only ten in Melanesia to 170 in Micronesia, but with great variations within both. Moreover, much of Melanesia is too mountainous for human habitation. But despite population increase, much land is used less and less effectively, as tenure problems and preference for urban occupations attract people away.

Moreover, the past twenty years has seen more immigration into the region than ever before, particularly Chinese and Filipino immigration throughout, but especially to the Marianas, Palau, Papua New Guinea, and Fiji. This too has implications for tenure.

Indigenous people no longer live where they used to. Whereas traditional systems evolved in a context where most people spent their whole lives in one locality, mobility has been growing for more than a century. The first change, in the 1800s, involved young men working on foreign ships, plantations, and mines, as missionaries, or in other capacities. New medical, educational, commercial, and religious services led to concentration in villages and towns of people who were formerly spread more evenly across the landscape.

This process continues, but tenure adaptations have in most cases been inadequate to accommodate them satisfactorily.

Motor transport and the abolition of warfare expanded the range over which rights could be effectively maintained. Traditionally, few people held rights more than five kilometers from home, and most considerably less. Now, in many islands (e.g., American Samoa, the Cook Islands, French Polynesia, Niue, and many outer islands of Fiji), most "owners" live on another island in that country, or abroad.

Risks and Benefits of Codification

Since customs are often disputed, does it help to codify them? Not necessarily, for codification changes custom by cementing it in place, whereas flexibility was one of its key elements. It would be impossible to implement a law that said, as customary systems provided, that rights fade over time to the extent they are not used and relative to the needs of others who use or want to use them more, that those who fulfill community obligations best usually receive stronger support for rights, and that good memory, persuasive power, and physical force enhance de facto land rights.

Land customs have been codified in a few places such as Kiribati and Tuvalu, where populations are small and the atolls relatively uniform. Each of those countries has one main language and similar land customs. More commonly, custom is not defined, and in cases of dispute, the courts decide what accords best with custom for that case. Most land courts of the region, however, have vastly more cases than they have the time or resources to resolve. Where judgments are given, many are ignored, as many governments lack the administrative capacity to enforce the decisions of their land courts.

In most of the rural Pacific the law states that custom shall prevail, but it is always with qualifications. Many customary systems accepted that serious offenders be killed, banished, deprived of land rights, or have their homes burned, their animals confiscated, or property destroyed. Most such actions are prohibited by law today. Even where custom has been completely replaced by law officially, custom often "invades" the law. Thus governments that nationalized all seawater are not always able to implement that law and will not force legal rights over the (legally former) customary owners who have votes in the next election.

Land Registration—When, What, and How?

Registration aims to define who owns what rights in order to resolve disputes as well as enhance stability, productivity, and environmental protection. These goals, however, will not necessarily be achieved. A major difference between most tenures in Europe and Asia today on the one hand, and traditional Pacific tenures on the other, leads to much misunderstanding. In customary Pacific tenures (as in earlier customary systems in Europe and Asia), land and water rights waxed and waned at different phases of life from birth through death in response to personal, family, and community needs, and to political and economic forces. This constant living process gave flexibility, which has negative attributes as well as positive. In capitalistic and communistic societies, on the other hand, rights are precisely defined in area and time. A seller's rights are extinguished, and the buyer acquires them in total. It is the same with gift or inheritance, or joining a commune. This was not so in Pacific societies, where one who gave, lent, or sold land rights to another did so as part of a continuing relationship. Rights were never fixed, but constantly strengthened or weakened, and the rights of those away too long faded out or were superseded.

Registration was resisted where people feared it might facilitate forced sale, but in most situations registration was welcomed in order to confirm one's rights, for land disputes were common.

When lands commissions were set up to register land, people usually insisted that they register the traditional boundaries recognized at that time for subsistence purposes. But the small, fragmented lots into which lands were divided for subsistence often differed in size, shape, and location from what would be best suited to the commercial farming or other occupations many of them were then going into.

In any case, registration is a long and expensive process. The governments of Fiji and the Cook Islands decided more than one hundred years ago to register all land, expecting it would take a few years, but neither has completed the process. The decision more than thirty years ago to register all land in Papua New Guinea has been followed by almost no progress, and Lakau (1995) is one of many who caution against hasty or extensive registration of customary land in rural Papua New Guinea. Public trust in the government is low, its funds and skills are limited, and change in rural communities is too complex for systems to keep up with in the present sociopolitical climate.

After registration, in most Pacific Island countries land rights can be acquired only by accident of birth—that is, by inheritance from parents. This is a poor basis for allocating what is in many cases their most valuable resource. Those who originate from isolated islands or remote areas find it difficult to get effective access to land near towns, ports, markets, or jobs. Likewise, many whose grandparents had adequate land but large families now have nominal rights to such infinitesimal plots, or share the rights with so many others, that the plots are of little but symbolic value. Traditional mechanisms of gift, permissive occupancy, adoption, voluntary reallocation, and warfare have not been adequately substituted for, even though a mobile population in a modern economy needs much more flexibility of land transfer.

Sale of land is prohibited in most Pacific Island countries, or if allowed is strictly controlled. This ensures that families do not lose their rights, but the prohibition should be adapted to current need. In the Cook Islands, Nauru, Niue, Tokelau, and Tonga, for example, it is against the law to sell land rights, even to close relatives. American Samoa allows sale between blood kin. In the Cook Islands, Nauru, and New Zealand, once a name is on the register it stays there, and those who by customary processes would have retained rights in some lands and dropped out of others remain in perpetuity—and their children and grandchildren ad infinitum.

Land rights were inherited primarily through the father but could be inherited through the mother. Rights through both were seldom activated for long. Once land is registered, however, no one wants to "fade out" of any plot, so tiny plots now have hundreds of legal owners. Many individuals in Nauru now "own" one thousandth or less of a share in a plot less than a hectare.

These problems are not caused by traditional systems, none of which enabled such ridiculous results. Partly they were caused by colonial governments that understood the way rights were acquired better than the way they withered if not activated. Even more, today they are caused by those who insist on every descendant inheriting a share of every piece. If land is registered and sale is forbidden (as in much of the region), and all offspring inherit equal rights from both parents, the number of "owners" in each plot more than doubles every generation. Many Polynesian and Micronesian people accept it as their established custom, which it is now, although it is very different from earlier traditions (see, e.g., Crocombe 1975b; Crocombe and Meleisea 1994; Crocombe, Tongia, and Araʻitia 2007; France 1969; Ward and Kingdon 1995; and many others).

In Fiji and Samoa freehold land may be sold, but freehold comprises only 4 percent of the area in each (it was 8 percent in Fiji until the government returned some land to indigenous ownership). In Kiribati, land may be sold to other I-Kiribati if the buyer can prove that he or she has no land on that island and needs it for housing or other approved purposes, and if the seller can prove that the land being sold is surplus to the requirements of the seller and his or her family. But the rule is often overlooked in Tarawa, where one-third of the national population lives and where some people are landless. In Papua New Guinea, land can be sold "in accordance with custom," which provides some flexibility but also leaves the process open to accumulation of large areas by entrepreneurs.

In most countries, land transfer is restricted to leasing, often subject to heavy restrictions. It is also cumbersome in situations such as in French Polynesia or the Cook Islands, where leasing a house site may require the approval of dozens or hundreds of individuals with rights in it.

Land Alienation

In Melanesian societies with complex monetary systems, land could be bought using traditional currency (see, e.g., Pospisil 1963), but where this occurred it was in a context of ongoing social relationships. Outright sale of land was unfamiliar to most Pacific peoples, and when European entrepreneurs purchased large tracts (most sales took place between 1840 and 1900), there was often misunderstanding on both sides about what rights changed hands and for how long. Europeans familiar with freehold thought they had bought all rights unconditionally, whereas many islanders thought equally genuinely that they had provided land to immigrants in need, with the customary understanding that it would revert to them if the "buyer" did not use it, and that they would receive periodic help and tribute from those to whom they supplied land.

In the early stages there were also many instances of cheating and fraud on both sides. The worst European speculators deceived Vanuatu people of enormous areas (Sope 1976; Van Trease 1987), and Samoans sold Europeans three times the total area of Samoa (Meleisea 1990; Schoeffel 1996). Some lands were taken by force by colonial governments, as in New Zealand (Kawharu 1977; Ward 1974), New Caledonia (Saussol 1979), and Hawaiʻi (Meller and Horwitz 1987), or by local chiefs, as in Tonga (Rutherford 1977), Fiji (Routledge 1985), and Kiribati (Namai et al. 1987).

Nevertheless, in the region as a whole, expatriates generally found plenty of people willing to sell their land. The view often heard today, that Pacific Islanders would never sell their lands, was not the case. They wanted money or things it would buy, but often also hoped that plantations or other facilities built on alienated land would facilitate employment, trade, roads, wharves, and even education or medical services. These hopes were often not realized, or inadequately achieved, and many regretted having sold. Foreign buyers, however, had little difficulty buying much more land throughout the region than they were ever able to use over the ensuing hundred years. Capital and labor were much harder to get than land. One of the few places where all alienated land was used was Micronesia from 1914 to 1945, when Japanese settlers outnumbered indigenous people (Peattie 1988; Yanaihara 1940).

Where land sale was stopped it was often due to the influence of missions, colonial governments, or local chiefs who had become aware of problems caused by alienation elsewhere. Because of the wars over land between Maori and Europeans in New Zealand, the United Kingdom forbade sale of land in Fiji and annulled most of the sales that had taken place before it became involved. The United Kingdom allowed New Zealand to administer the Cook Islands only on the condition that land sale was forbidden. Germany refused to recognize most land purchases by Europeans in Samoa before it took control.

Leasing therefore became the common way immigrants acquired land rights from about 1900 onward. It was better because the original owners earned rent and got the land back at the end of the lease—usually sixty-six or ninety-nine years. But the erosion of the fixed rents due to inflation and the massive rise in populations made leasing less popular. As a result, the worldwide trends for lease terms to be shorter, for rents to be reviewed regularly, and for benefits to be shared more widely (e.g., shares of turnover or profit, and participation in ownership and management of enterprises on leased land) are now apparent in the Pacific.

Much of the formerly alienated land has gone back to the descendants of its former owners. Vanuatu cancelled all freehold titles and declared all land to be owned by indigenous people under custom, though immigrants could lease lands they were actually farming (Alatoa et al. 1984; Arutangai 1987). Papua New Guinea and Solomon Islands adopted similar but less comprehensive policies. The pro-independence party in New Caledonia has a similar goal. The Fiji government recently decided to return about half of the land it then owned to indigenous ownership (land it had acquired because the land had been declared "ownerless," or because the owning clans had died out). This amounts to about 4 percent of the total land area of Fiji. All Japanese were repatriated from Micronesia after World War II, and most of the lands they occupied are now held by Micronesians. Kiribati bought back the alienated Line Islands. The government or individuals in Western Samoa acquired almost all foreign-owned land. Now very little land is owned by immigrants in the tropical South Pacific except in the French territories and West Papua, where massive immigration from Java and other parts of Indonesia has been accompanied by confiscation, intimidation, and forced sales, reinforced by the fact that the Indonesian government does not recognize indigenous rights except to land that is currently under cultivation.

Even where immigrants outnumbered indigenes, and where most of the land was alienated to Europeans or Asians (as in Guam, Hawai'i, the Northern Marianas, New Caledonia, New Zealand, Palau, and Pohnpei), large areas have been returned to indigenous ownership in recent years due to political and economic action. More is likely to return. The proportion of national income deriving from land is reducing, however, so some of the gains are more symbolic than real. And given current trends in the region, it will not be surprising if land that is acquired from Europeans will be controlled by new Asian investors within a generation or two.

One of the ironies is that where no land was ever alienated (as in Tonga, Niue, the Cook Islands, Wallis and Futuna, and with trivial exceptions Tokelau and Tuvalu), or where alienated land has long since been returned (as in Samoa), the desire of people to emigrate permanently is strong. To the maximum extent that they can gain access, the countries they want to settle in are those where most land was alienated and converted to tenures and uses that enabled those countries to generate vastly higher incomes. As a result, many more Polynesians now live in New Zealand, Australia, the United States, Chile, France, and elsewhere than in island Polynesia, and many Micronesians emigrate to the United States since access was granted in 1986. They have no qualms about buying freehold land where they settle.

Every nation wants (and has) roads, public buildings, port facilities, and airports. Many need space to resettle disadvantaged people. Moreover, every Pacific Islands government has a policy of attracting capital to generate income and employment. Hotels, factories, plantations, even the Japanese spaceport that was planned for Kiritimati Island (Kiribati), with leases negotiated, all need land, and they modify tenures in practice—even if there is no change in law or stated principle.

Public facilities necessitate acquiring rights from private interests. This does not mean that only one form of tenure is suitable for public lands, but some change to the former systems is inevitable. One might have assumed before independence that land acquisition in the public interest would be easier after independence, but it is harder due to growing populations, the increasing value of land, and a visible decline since the 1990s in public confidence in the elected governments.

Other intensive uses are beset by similar contentions. Disputes over the relative benefits to lessees and landowners have seen resorts, factories, and other enterprises burned or closed. Even tiny, isolated, government-owned telecommunications repeater stations on remote peaks that had never been used by anyone have amazingly high values attributed to them by a range of claimants, a range that gets wider as the payouts increase. Many national facilities in Papua New Guinea, including airports, have been seized, smashed, or threatened in the ongoing battle for more compensation.

In subsistence societies the needs of the community took precedence over those of individuals. The community is now the nation, and land rights increasingly need to be allocated according to public need. But cultural change takes place at different speeds, and land is always an area of cultural lag, so it may take time before the systems of land allocation catch up with the current needs of the people they are intended to serve.

The Continuing Evolution of Marine Tenures

Customary rights to coastal waters and tropical lagoons tended to shrink after contact with industrial technology. Reliance on the sea was reduced by population losses in the 1800s, the growth of paid employment, emigration, commercial agriculture, and imported proteins. Today, however, the sea is becoming more intensively used due to rising populations, new marine products (e.g., cultivated seaweed and shellfish, tropical fish for foreign aquariums, octopus exported to Japan), and tourist diving.

Many governments declared a century ago that all water, and land below high-water mark, were henceforth government property and available equally to everyone. In practice, however, customary rights usually continued to be recognized in varying degrees.

Even in countries where laws provide that coastal waters belong to the customary owners and that custom shall determine their use, much has changed. If what was a quiet village becomes a town and harbor, the water rights and practices are going to adapt, whatever the law or custom says. Likewise, when people who fished for subsistence begin fishing commercially, or when products formerly regarded as rubbish (such as sea cucumber) become commercial products, then the tenure of the water where these products are harvested may change in practice if not in principle.

Some governments are giving greater recognition to customary rights. Indigenous Fijians assert traditional claims to water vis-à-vis Indian and other immigrants. These claims were a significant factor in all four coups suffered by governments of Fiji between 1987 and 2006. Traditional rights were acknowledged by both the independent government since 1970 and the colonial government before that, but they were not implemented much in practice. Growing populations, more commercial fishing, and heightened ethnic tensions have led to closer definition and stricter enforcement of such rights. Likewise, in Manus (Papua New Guinea), increased population and commercialization, including tuna boats catching bait fish, have extended claims and intensified competition for coastal waters (Carrier 1983).

The technology for culturing pearls enhanced the value of suitable lagoons. Customary claims were reasserted or reinterpreted. Pearl farmers wanted exclusive rights to an area. As the best spaces filled up, competition became keener. And as some people were going to be rich, jealousy sharpened disputes over access, even though there was no precise customary precedent for commercial use of lagoon space. Many atoll people who worked in town now came, along with some who had never been on their "home" atoll (but whose forebears had come from there), to claim water for pearls and land for living. And some strangers from other islands arrived because in law the lagoon was public property for any citizen of the nation—not just the island (and in French Polynesia lagoon space is allocated by the government). Pearl farming has changed the de facto tenure and use of the lagoons and exacerbated disputes in the Tuamotu Islands (Rapaport 1996) and the northern Cook Islands (Newnham 1997), as well as generating enormous differences in incomes. It is likely to have similar effects in Tuvalu, Kiribati, the Marshall Islands, and other places that are beginning pearl culture. What to do about lagoon rights is constantly discussed, but progress in resolving the problems is slow.

More extensive use of reefs, particularly commercial use, naturally enhances claims to them. Outboard motors and new fishing technology, including refrigeration, extend the distance over which rights can be effectively exercised (and claimed or stretched!).

Catching octopus for export from the outer reefs of Tarawa and Maiana is a profitable new industry. It, and the commercial production of selected seaweeds, may lead to stronger assertions of traditional rights to reefs, and their more precise definition. Other new reef products being explored, and in some cases exploited, include pharmacological extracts from marine plants and animals. Tourism and sand for construction are leading to more disputes over rights between low- and high-tide marks and to beaches. For case studies on current directions in traditional marine tenures, see South et al. (1995).

The United Nations Law of the Sea (LOS) Convention arose out of disputes between nations of North and South America. Although the origin was incidental to the Pacific Islands, the islands are the greatest beneficiaries of the new regime. LOS recognizes a 12-nautical-mile territorial zone and a 188-nautical-mile exclusive economic zone (EEZ). This new marine tenure is the basis for the largest source of earnings (mainly from tuna and snapper) for Kiribati and Tuvalu, and for a potential bonanza for the Cook Islands, which has vast deposits of seabed minerals in its EEZ.

Although national governments control the EEZs, they may make concessions to component units. In the Federated States of Micronesia and Papua New Guinea, there are different formulae for marine rights to be shared between the national government and state or provincial governments. The United States has granted the economic benefits (not the sovereignty) from waters around Guam and the Northern Marianas to their local governments. And in some Pacific Island nations, the claims of local landowning communities to adjacent waters are recognized in varying degrees.

Beyond the EEZ lie the international waters, which are coming under increasing international control, including the International Seabed Authority, which leases mining rights to seabed minerals to member nations of the United Nations. The rights in the Clarion-Clipperton zone southeast of Hawai'i were the first to be so allocated.

The Influence of Fresh Water Sources on Tenure Forms

Crops like irrigated taro enabled higher productivity, denser populations, more elaborate social and leadership systems, and more complex rights to land and water. Where irrigated taro is the main starch food, the whole valley was the primary traditional political unit in which a chief or council of chiefs controlled people and water. Within the valley, smaller clans and families controlled the water they drew off for their taro. Watersheds were the main boundaries (in contrast to localities where irrigation is not used, where the watercourse rather than the watershed is often the boundary). Taro requires hard labor, so the right to it almost always lay with the household that did the work.

On atolls there are no valleys and no running water. Fresh water is scarce and therefore more valuable than on high islands, where it is generally plentiful. On atolls, access to water requires different technology and results in different patterns of social organization, even among atoll people who came from high-island origins (which most did).

The main root crop on many atolls (*Cyrtosperma*) required irrigation. Atolls often evolved more egalitarian leadership systems because there is no need for central control of water. Even more work is required than with taro on high islands, so the household that supplies the labor has strong rights to the land and the tubers. There are exceptions to these generalizations for other reasons, but it was commonly so.

Fresh water is obtained by digging down through the porous coral to the fresh water that floats on the salt, causing the salt water to sink in a curve, which is deepest at the center of the land on the islet. So land in the center is more fertile and more valuable than land at the edges. Digging wells for domestic water is hard work—and was even harder before the introduction of metal tools in the past century—so wells are valuable assets of those who dug them. It was harder still to dig pits to create gardens deep enough that tubers reach the freshwater lens. Because there is only sand and coral rock at that level, soil is created from leaves, food remains, and surface soil from elsewhere. Each tuber is cultivated by hand, with soil and mulch packed around it as it grows. This exceedingly hard work is reflected in the value of that crop and the concentration of rights to it in the planter.

Rights to the Bowels of the Earth, and Up to the Skies

Like subsistence agriculturalists everywhere, Pacific peoples seldom used more than a few centimeters of soil. There was surface mining of stone for tools, salt for cooking, and ochre for painting, but no awareness of the existence or value of gold, copper, nickel, and other minerals.

Colonial governments usually followed their metropolitan principle, which in many cases meant that minerals belonged to the state and that income should be used for public benefit. In practice, unfortunately, this benefit was often for the colonial public more than the indigenous public. Since independence, much of the income has been absorbed by the central bureaucracy rather than used for national development. Former or present landowners were usually compensated for disturbance, although France did not compensate for the nickel mines in New Caledonia, nor Indonesia for the gold and copper mines in West Papua, nor Japan for Angaur in Palau.

Independent governments followed the principle of national ownership of minerals. Responding to the public demand for employment and income, they increasingly sought investment, much of it foreign because of the low propensity to save in most Pacific communities. This national interest, however, conflicted with the interest of the landowners. The most spectacular case was Bougainville, where the civil war that raged for ten years from 1989 was triggered by the dispute between landowners and the national government over benefits from the copper mine—then the government's largest source of revenue. Smaller disturbances over the same issue have occurred at most mines, at the only producing oil fields, and at other developments. Consequently the Papua New Guinea government decided to give landowners much more of the benefit. That did not stop the trend, however, which applies whether the enterprise is owned nationally or from abroad. Where landowners see an opportunity for more benefits, they or their lawyers can build a sense of grievance and maximize claims. Some, like Donigi (1994), believe that all benefits belong to the traditional landowners and that governments have no right to them. The share for those who supply capital and expertise is also a matter of contention. But most elected governments consider that most of the massive benefits derived from such "unearned increment" should accrue to them to provide public services. The principle that all parties should benefit is generally accepted, but what constitutes a fair share is one of the most contentious issues in much of the region today (Larmour 1989).

The Fiji government had a long dispute with the United States because U.S. military aircraft flew through the Nadi Flight Information Zone, which includes not only Fiji but all airspace above a certain altitude over much of Tuvalu, Nauru, and Kiribati, east to Samoa and south to the New Zealand zone. The dispute was finally settled by giving Fiji additional aid. Since then the Small Islands States group (the Cook Islands, Kiribati, Nauru, Niue, and Tuvalu) has been investigating the possibility of charging aircraft (including all aircraft between Australia and New Zealand and the Americas) to fly through their airspace—in the way Japan pays Russia for the same privilege. Maori claimed to own all radio waves in New Zealand and demanded compensation for their use by broadcasters (the main one at the time was the government). The claim was rejected by the Supreme Court, but it is still being pursued.

The Land Rights of Women

In 90 percent of Melanesia, all of Polynesia, and part of Micronesia, tenure rights were inherited mainly through men. Even in the 10 percent of cultures where they were transmitted predominantly through women, land management was performed largely by men. The colonial governments were from patrilineal cultures of Europe, and Christianity is a male-dominated religion. When Japan, whose culture and religions were likewise patrilineal, was the colonial power in Micronesia, this further reduced traditional matrilineal principles there. In the part of Fiji (Bua) where matrilineal principles prevailed, the United Kingdom government absorbed them into the predominant patrilineal pattern. But even without pressure from governments or religions, commercial agriculture had a similar effect, so it became common for Tolai men in Papua New Guinea and Ifira men in Vanuatu to transfer lands they derived from their mothers, on which they had planted coffee, cocoa, or other commercial crops, to their sons rather than their sisters' sons as they would have under custom.

Change has been radical in some countries, minimal in others. Thus in Hawai'i, French Polynesia, the Cook Islands, Niue, and New Zealand, where land rights and chiefly titles were the prerogative of men, they are now just as commonly held by women. The change came about as a result not of policy or activism, but of largely imperceptible shifts in behavior in response to such technologically driven innovations as women gaining control of reproduction, labor-saving devices, and a related world ethos of equal education and opportunity. In Guam and the Northern Marianas, where the traditional matrilineal systems changed to patrilineal during Spanish, German, and Japanese colonial eras, now both sexes inherit equally. A trend toward greater equality in land rights is discernible in Kiribati and Samoa, but there is little sign of it in Tonga or most of Melanesia. Islamic influence from Indonesia in West Papua will reinforce patrilineal tendencies there.

The Future

Needs have changed radically, and some tenures have changed too, but in the Pacific as elsewhere, tenure change lags behind social and economic change. Resistance to conscious changes in land tenure is often reinforced by the assumption that the traditional system was God-given and should remain forever. Caution is compounded by the history of land alienation in some countries and by the insecurity of paid work, for alternative social security systems are minimal and jobs precarious. Nevertheless, amazing changes are acceptable, even insisted on (often reinterpreted as traditional) if people assume they will benefit from them.

Change cannot be achieved by laws or policies if there is strong resistance to them—as in the case of the Mau rebellion in Samoa (in response to attempts to individualize land), Fiji's ineffective provisions to cancel the rights of absentees (described above), and the short-term lease provisions in the Cook Islands, which aimed to boost productivity but which met with apathy.

Because changes in tenures lag behind other changes in society, increasing the mismatch between customary principles and current aspirations reinforces other motives, leading the more enterprising and innovative to seek livelihoods off the land. That tendency will remain. For those who stay on the land, the discrepancies themselves generate slow but imperceptible change (see, e.g., O'Meara 1990).

In Fiji, where 14,000 long-established Indian settlers lease farms from indigenous Fijians, conflict is high over rents and political issues. Some lessees have been harassed into abandoning the farms. Many have not been renewed at the end of their thirty-year terms, and many such farms have gone out of production, reducing productivity and national income.

Water rights are no less contentious. In New Zealand, some Maori claim 100 percent of the two-hundred-mile EEZ. In a recent settlement the government gave Maori claimants half of the national fishing quota. Other Maori claim all rivers, which are now public assets, as tribal property. If current experiments with wave energy and ocean thermal energy conversion succeed, they will have implications for tenure of suitable reefs throughout the region.

The only places in the world where comprehensive land reforms have been quickly implemented are those where someone holds absolute power (or close to it) and forces the changes. The only comprehensive reform in the Pacific was in Tonga, where a conquering warlord introduced a new system as part of a package designed to retain his power. It worked. His descendants still rule Tonga a century and a half later, though their powers are now much reduced. The Australian government in 2008 set aside US$50 million for land reform in the Pacific Islands, but how effectively that will be spent remains to be seen. (Their approach is set out in AusAID 2008.)

Radical change is not an option, but progressive, incremental improvements are feasible. Tenure change seldom takes place until the problems are acute, but in many islands they are. Even so, meeting the challenges head-on can lead to violent resistance and become counterproductive. De facto change often takes place long before de jure change is feasible. Tenures take longer to adjust than most aspects of life, so the tendency is to get on with other activities. Some improvements are taking place, but the Pacific will not be alone in the world if many rural communities become stagnant backwaters occupied by apathetic people, while more rapid adaptations take place in towns.

Author's Note

This chapter is a version, greatly shortened by the editor, of chapter 11 of *The South Pacific,* by Ron Crocombe (University of the South Pacific, 2008). Those interested in the original should refer to that source. Linda Crowl, Peter Larmour, and Howard Van Trease kindly made helpful comments on the draft, but they are not responsible for remaining errors and omissions.

Most geographical and anthropological studies in the Pacific include some information on land tenure. In addition, an extensive range of publications focuses on land tenure. For land tenure studies of the Pacific Islands region generally, see Acquaye et al. 1987; Bartlett et al. 1981; Crocombe 1991; Lundsgaarde 1974; Waigani Seminar 1971; and Ward and Kingdon 1995.

It is hard to know what to cite from the vast volume of published and unpublished material on land and water tenure systems in the region. Items included were determined as much on the basis of what was at hand at the time of writing as on an assessment of relative importance.

BIBLIOGRAPHY

Acquaye, E., et al. 1987. *Land tenure and rural productivity in the Pacific Islands.* Suva: University of the South Pacific.

Akimichi, T. 1991. Sea tenure and its transformation in the Lau of North Malaita, Solomon Islands. South Pacific Study. *Land tenure and rural productivity in the Pacific Islands* 12(1): 7–22.

Alatoa, H., et al. 1984. *Land tenure in Vanuatu.* Suva: University of the South Pacific.

Angleviel, F., et al. 1992. *Atlas de Nouvelle Caledonie.* Noumea: ORSTOM.

Arutangai, S. 1987. Vanuatu: Overcoming the colonial legacy. In *Land tenure in the Pacific,* ed. R. Crocombe, 261–302. Suva: University of the South Pacific.

Asghar, M. 1988. Land use in Western Samoa. In *Soil taxonomy and fertility in the South Pacific,* ed. M. Asghar, T. Davidson, and R. J. Morrison, 376–390. Apia, Western Samoa: University of the South Pacific.

Atanraoi, P. 1995. Seeking security and sustainability in a situation of high mobility. In *Customary land tenure and sustainable development,* ed. R. Crocombe, 55–74. Noumea: South Pacific Commission.

AusAID (Australian Aid for International Development). 2008. *Making land work.* Canberra: AusAID.

Ballard, C. 1996. *The politics of resource ownership in Papua New Guinea.* National Centre for Development Studies Seminar. Canberra: Australian National University.

Bartlett, A., et al. 1981. *Land, people and government: Public lands policy in the South Pacific.* Suva: University of the South Pacific.

Carrier, J. G. 1981. Ownership of productive resources on Ponam Island, Manus Province. *Journal de la Société des Océanistes* 37: 205–217.

———. 1983. Profitless property: Marine ownership and access to wealth on Ponam Island. *Ethnology* 22: 133–151.

Clarke, W. C. 1994. Traditional land use and agriculture in the Pacific Islands. In *The science of Pacific Island peoples,* vol. 2, ed. J. Morrison, P. Geraghty, and L. Crowl, 11–38. Suva: University of the South Pacific.

Crocombe, R. 1964, ed. *Land tenure in the Cook Islands.* Melbourne: Oxford University Press.

———. 1968. Observations on land tenure in Tarawa. *Micronesica* 4: 27–37.

———. 1975a. Land tenure in Tonga. In *Land and migration,* ed. S. H. Fonua, 43–61. Nuku'alofa: Tonga Council of Churches.

———. 1975b. Pre-contact traditional land tenure: The ideological base. *South Pacific Quarterly* 25(3): 13–19.

———, ed. 1981. *Land, people and government: Public lands policy in the Pacific Islands.* Suva: University of the South Pacific.

———, ed. 1991. *Land tenure in the Pacific.* Suva: University of the South Pacific.

Crocombe, R., and M. Meleisea, eds. 1994. *Land issues in the Pacific.* Christchurch: University of Canterbury Press.

Crocombe, R., M. Tongia, and T. Ara'itia, 2007. *Absentee land ownership in the Cook Islands: Social and economic consequences.* Canberra: AusAID.

D'Arcy, Paul, 2006. *The people of the sea: Environment, identity, and history in Oceania.* Honolulu: University of Hawai'i Press.

Decker, B. 1983. Land tenure. In *Atlas of Hawaii,* ed. R. W. Armstrong, 152. Honolulu: University of Hawai'i Press.

Donigi, P. 1994. *Indigenous or aboriginal rights to property: A Papua New Guinea perspective.* Port Moresby: University of Papua New Guinea Press.

Elders of Nukunonu. 1987. Customary principles in Nukunonu. *In Land tenure in the atolls,* ed. R. Crocombe, 110–113. Suva: University of the South Pacific.

EMPAT (Economic Management Policy Advisory Team). 1996. *Economic use of land in the FSM: A review and description of land tenure systems in the FSM.* Manila: Asian Development Bank Occasional Paper no. 6.

Falanruw, M. 1994. Traditional fishing in Yap. In *Science of Pacific Island peoples,* vol. 1, ed. R. J. Morrison, et al., 41–58. Suva: University of the South Pacific.

Fonua, P. 1991. Consequences of return migrants to a Tongan village. In *In search of a home,* ed. L. Mason and P. Hereniko, 3–23. Suva: University of the South Pacific.

France, P. 1969. *The charter of the land: Custom and colonization in Fiji.* Melbourne: Oxford University Press.

Guiart, J. 1996. Land tenure and hierarchies in eastern Melanesia. *Pacific Studies* 19(1): 1–29.

Hooper, A., and J. Huntsman. 1987. Tenure, society and economy. In *Land tenure in the atolls,* ed. R. Crocombe, 117–140. Suva: University of the South Pacific.

Hudson, R. 1996. Pitcairn Island lands. Unpublished report to Pitcairn Council.

Hviding, E. 1996. *Guardians of Marovo lagoon: Practice, place, and politics in maritime Melanesia.* Honolulu: University of Hawai'i Press.

Johannes, R. E. 1981. *Words of the lagoon: Fishing and marine lore in the Palau District of Micronesia.* Berkeley: University of California Press.

———. 1994. Pacific Islands people's science and marine resource management. In *Science of Pacific Island peoples,* ed. R. J. Morrison, et al. Suva: University of the South Pacific.

Kalauni, S., et al. 1977. *Land tenure in Niue.* Suva: University of the South Pacific.

Kamikamica, J. 1987. Making native land productive. In *Land tenure in the Pacific,* ed. R. Crocombe, 226–239. Suva: University of the South Pacific.

Kawharu, H. 1977. *Maori land tenure.* London: Oxford University Press.

Knudsen, K. 1964. *Titiana: A Gilbertese community in the Solomon Islands.* Eugene: University of Oregon Press.

Lakau, A. 1995. Options for the Pacific's most complex nation: Papua New Guinea. In *Customary land tenure and sustainable development,* ed. R. Crocombe, 95–118. Noumea: South Pacific Commission.

Larmour, P., ed. 1979. *Land in Solomon Islands.* Suva: University of the South Pacific.

———, ed. 1984. Alienated land and independence in Melanesia. *Pacific Studies* 8(1): 1–47.

———. 1989. Sharing the benefits: Customary landowners and natural resource projects in Melanesia. *Pacific Viewpoint* 30(1): 56–74.

———. 1991. *Customary land tenure: Registration and decentralization in Papua New Guinea.* Port Moresby: National Research Institute.

Lawrence, P., and I. Hogbin. 1967. *Studies in New Guinea land tenure.* Sydney: Sydney University Press.

Leupena, T., and K. Lutelu. 1987. Providing for the multitude. In *Land tenure in the atolls,* ed. R. Crocombe, 143–165. Suva: University of the South Pacific.

Lundsgaarde, H., ed. 1974. *Land tenure in Oceania.* Honolulu: University of Hawai'i Press.

Mason, L. 1987. Tenures from subsistence to star wars. In *Land tenure in the atolls,* ed. R. Crocombe, 3–27. Suva: University of the South Pacific.

Maude, A., and F. Sevele. 1987. Tonga: Equality overtaking privilege. In *Land tenure in the Pacific,* ed. R. Crocombe, 114–142. Suva: University of the South Pacific.

McPhetres, S. 1993. The history of land issues in the Commonwealth of the Northern Marianas. *Umanidat* 1(1): 14–19.

Meleisea, M. 1980. *O tama uli: Melanesians in Samoa.* Suva: South Pacific Social Sciences Association.

———. 1990. *The making of modern Samoa.* Suva: University of the South Pacific.

Meller, N., and R. Horwitz. 1987. Hawaii: Themes in land monopoly. In *Land tenure in the Pacific,* ed. R. Crocombe, 25–44. Suva: University of the South Pacific.

Namai, B., et al. 1987. The evolution of Kiribati land tenures. In *Land tenure in the atolls,* ed. R. Crocombe, 30–39. Suva: University of the South Pacific.

Nayacakalou, R. 1965. The bifurcation and amalgamation of Fijian lineages over a period of fifty years. *Proceedings of the Fiji Society for 1960 and 1961,* Suva, Fiji.

———. 1992. *Leadership in Fiji.* Suva: University of the South Pacific.

Newnham, R. T. 1996. Social impact of pearl culture on Manihiki. Manuscript, Rarotonga.

O'Meara, J. T. 1990. *Samoan planters: Tradition and economic development in Polynesia.* Fort Worth, Tex.: Holt, Rinehart and Winston.

Overton, J., ed. 1988. *Rural Fiji.* Suva: University of the South Pacific.

Panoff, M. 1964. *Les structures agraires en Polynesie Francaise.* Papeete: ORSTOM.

Peattie, M. 1988. *Nan'yō: The rise and fall of the Japanese in Micronesia 1885–1945.* Honolulu: University of Hawai'i Press.

Pospisil, L. 1963. *Kapauku Papuan economy.* New Haven, Conn.: Yale University Publications in Anthropology No. 67.

———. 1965. A formal analysis of substantive law: Kapauku Papuan laws of land tenure. *American Anthropologist* 67(5): 186–214.

Prasad, B., and C. Tisdell. 1996. Getting property rights "right": Land tenure in Fiji. *Pacific Economic Bulletin* 11(1): 31–46.

Rakoto, A. 1973. Can custom be custom-built? Cultural obstacles to Fijian commercial enterprise. *Pacific Perspective* 2(2): 32–35.

Rapaport, M. 1996. Between two laws: Tenure regimes in the Pearl Islands. *The Contemporary Pacific* 8(1): 33–49.

Ravault, F. 1980. Land problems in French Polynesia. *Pacific Perspective* 10(2): 31–65.

Rodman, M. 1987. *Masters of tradition: Consequences of customary land tenure in Longana, Vanuatu.* Vancouver: University of British Columbia Press.

Rogers, G., ed. 1986. *The fire has jumped.* Suva: University of the South Pacific.

Routledge, D. 1985. *Matanitu: The struggle for power in early Fiji.* Suva: University of the South Pacific.

Rutherford, N. 1977. *Friendly islands: A history of Tonga.* Melbourne: Oxford University Press.

Saussol, A. 1979. *L'Héritage: essai sur le problème foncier Mélanesien en Nouvelle Caledonie.* Paris: Société des Océanistes, Musée de l'Homme.

Schoeffel, P. 1996. *Sociocultural issues and economic development in the Pacific Islands.* Manila: Pacific Studies Series, Asian Development Bank.

Sope, B. 1976. *Land and politics in the New Hebrides.* Suva: South Pacific Social Sciences Association.

South, R. et al., eds. 1995. *Traditional marine tenure and the sustainable management of marine resources in Asia and the Pacific.* Suva: International Ocean Institute.

Tabira, N., et al. 1990. *Traditional fishing rights in Papua New Guinea.* Occasional Papers no. 20. Kagoshima, Japan: Kagoshima University Research Center for the South Pacific.

Tonkinson, R. 1968. *Maat village: A relocated community in the New Hebrides.* Eugene: University of Oregon Press.

Tui Atua Tupua Tamasese Taisi Efi. 2007. Samoan jurisprudence and the Samoan land and titles court. Public lecture, Centre for Pacific Studies, University of Auckland.

Tuimaleali'ifano, M. 1997. Fa'a Samoa: History and process of traditions. PhD thesis, University of the South Pacific, Suva.

Van Trease, H. 1987. *The politics of land in Vanuatu.* Suva: University of the South Pacific.

Waigani Seminar. 1971. Land tenure and indigenous group enterprise in Melanesia, collected papers of the Waigani Seminar (unpublished). Port Moresby: University of Papua New Guinea.

Waiko, J. 1995. *Land: Customary ownership versus state control in Papua New Guinea and Australia.* Sydney: University of New South Wales Centre for South Pacific Studies.

Ward, A. 1974. *A show of justice: Racial amalgamation in nineteenth century New Zealand.* Canberra: Australian National University Press.

———. 1982. *Land and politics in New Caledonia.* Canberra: Australian National University.

Ward, R. G., and E. Kingdon, eds. 1995. *Land, custom, and practice in the South Pacific.* Cambridge: Cambridge University Press.

Yanaihara, T. 1940. *Micronesia under the Japanese mandate.* Oxford: Oxford University Press.

Law

Richard Scaglion

17

One of the most striking characteristics of "law" in most contemporary Pacific Island nations is what legal scholars call "legal pluralism." Legal pluralism is the simultaneous existence of different types of legal systems within a single setting. In the contemporary Pacific, legal pluralism most often derives from legal heritages that combine "custom" law and "introduced" law in various ways. In any given country, however, there also can be multiple and sometimes contradictory forms of customary law, the simultaneous existence of which creates even more difficulties for Pacific nations as they struggle to create unified and equitable national legal systems.

In Papua New Guinea, there are upward of 850 distinct language groups (Grimes 1992: 877), each of which represents a different cultural group with its own customary legal system. The problems in reconciling these many different and sometimes conflicting systems of customary law have been profound. Vanuatu also has more than a hundred customary legal systems (Grimes 1992: 897), and in addition must reconcile all these with two very different introduced systems: British and French. Even where "custom law" is relatively homogeneous, colonial legacies can create problems in legal pluralism. American Samoa and Samoa, for instance, are separate countries with similar customary systems. But they must contend with very different introduced systems that in the former case stress the Constitution and laws of the United States, and in the latter the rules of English common law and equity as developed in English and New Zealand courts.

The existence and importance of legal pluralism in contemporary Pacific nations is a reflection of historical and ongoing tensions in island life: conflicts between customary ideas and Christian teachings; between traditional notions of group-based or corporate responsibility and introduced concepts of individual legal responsibility and rights; between customary approaches, in which disputes cannot be isolated from the broader social context, and introduced legal systems, in which courts attempt to deal with offenses as discrete occurrences; between the authority of local leaders and that of the regional and national courts and governments. Thus the story of contemporary legal institutions in the Pacific is very much a story of negotiation and reconciliation between and among competing models of law, authority, and morality.

This chapter briefly reviews the nature of indigenous Pacific legal systems, concentrating on the nature of authority and the processes of dispute management. I argue that there are two different basic models of indigenous law: one found in hierarchical societies, the other based on the dispute process of egalitarian societies. I then turn to an examination of how these two models condition the research paradigms social scientists have applied to studies of Pacific legal systems. Finally I examine the nature of legal pluralism in the contemporary Pacific, focusing on the dialectic between "traditional" and "introduced" legal systems, and consider the negotiation of various conflicting legal issues for contemporary island life.

Indigenous Legal Systems

The numerous and diverse peoples of the Pacific Islands, who arguably constitute nearly a quarter of all societies known to anthropologists, can be divided into two basic groups. The first group migrated to the Pacific Islands fifty thousand years or more ago, but inhabited only Australia, New Guinea, and a few nearby islands. The other group, the Austronesians, also settled parts of Melanesia, but alone colonized all the previously undiscovered areas of Micronesia and Polynesia within the past five thousand years or so (see Thomas, this volume). The Austronesian language family is one of the largest in the world, numbering around twelve hundred languages spread widely throughout Southeast Asia and the Pacific (see Pawley, this volume). During the past two thousand years, Austronesians have been the premier seafaring peoples in the world, discovering most of the far-flung islands of the vast Pacific Basin. Because of their presumably common background and relatively rapid dispersal throughout the Pacific Islands, the contemporary Austronesian peoples of the Pacific all have relatively similar languages and cultures.

In contrast to the Austronesians, the earlier Pacific migrants, who presumably did not speak Austronesian languages, today have very diverse cultures and languages. As a result, they constitute a group more because of a contrast with the Austronesians than because of any clearly distinguishing characteristics of their own. Because of this, they are often referred to simply as "Non-Austronesians." Despite their cultural diversity, however, a few generalizations can be made about the Non-Austronesian peoples of the Pacific. They were certainly less enthusiastic seafarers than were the Austronesians. Most groups lived in the interior of larger islands or on the Australian continent, practicing horticulturally based subsistence techniques or foraging, whereas the Austronesians were more likely to live in coastal areas and to combine fishing and maritime exploitation with horticultural techniques. The most important contrast for our purposes here, however, is that Austronesians tend to have hierarchically organized social structures, whereas Non-Austronesians almost uniformly have egalitarian social organizations based on reciprocal relationships. The result is widely different types of customary political and legal organizations (Scaglion 1996).

Contrasts are often drawn between the people and cultures of "Melanesia" on the one hand and "Polynesia" and "Micronesia" on the other. As we shall see, one such example is the classic contrast between the "Polynesian Chief" and the "Melanesian Big-Man" (Sahlins 1963) as models of indigenous political leadership. Such contrasts are often of limited utility because they do not pay adequate attention to the distinction between Austronesians and Non-Austronesians nor to the fact that both types of peoples live within the boundaries of "Melanesia." Hence, chiefly authority is strong among the Austronesian-speaking Trobriand Islanders of Papua New Guinea, but virtually nonexistent among the Non-Austronesian highlands tribes of the interior of this same country. Because of its cultural heterogeneity, Melanesia defies easy classification and thwarts a geographically based division between hierarchical and egalitarian systems of authority.

In order to better understand competing models of law in the contemporary Pacific, we must consider how different types of societies conceptualize authority and power. Legal scholars have long recognized that the presence or absence of legitimized power, or authority, in any given society is critical to an analysis of conflict resolution. Complex societies, having some form of centralized government, usually also have well-developed notions of authority. In socially stratified, hierarchical cultures, legal authorities can use their legitimate power to force compliance with rules or laws. Hopefully (but certainly not always), these laws reflect local notions of right and wrong and have been constructed for the greater good of society. Whether or not this is the case, legal systems in hierarchical societies give considerable "weight" to rules of behavior, thus privileging formalized laws and procedures.

It follows that legal scholars or social scientists who study complex societies gravitate toward research paradigms emphasizing formal "rules." In the egalitarian, decentralized tribal societies found in many parts of Melanesia, however, there are no formal legal authorities, and formal rules are much less important. Disputes between people are handled on a case-by-case basis, sometimes through consensus solutions based on notions of fairness or "equity," sometimes by various sorts of political maneuverings. Thus, scholars working in these types of societies often adopt a "processual" paradigm, focusing on the processes through which disputes actually become resolved. Studying the processes of dispute resolution rather than formal legal rules helps such researchers to better explain what goes on in acephalous societies.

As an example of these different approaches, we might profitably compare Riesenberg's (1968) study of the hierarchically organized (Austronesian) polity of Ponape (now Pohnpei, in the Federated States of Micronesia) with Koch's (1974) study of the Non-Austronesian Jalé people of Highland New Guinea. Riesenberg spends much time describing the formal structure of Pohnpeian society. He takes up the nature of promotion and succession; the types of titles and the honorific forms associated with them; the positions of Nahnmwarki and Nahnken, the two supreme chiefs of each tribe; the nature of political councils, courts, and trials; punishments meted out by chiefs; supernatural sanctions bolstering chiefly authority; and the prerogatives of chiefs. Only after the formal structure is described does he examine the nature of prestige competitions in which social statuses are contested. Although he sees rules as flexible, Riesenberg stresses that an understanding of formal rules is necessary for understanding the dialectic between rules and processes that together constitute Pohnpeian law:

> Thus, when an informant relates the theory of political advancement he is essentially giving the rules of descent-group seniority; but the case histories related in this work reveal how these rules must be accommodated and compromised in applying them to a complex political system. And it is the application of them and their delicate balancing against all the other principles previously mentioned that result in a flexible but stable and workable state. (Riesenberg 1968: 111)

Likewise, in examining social relations on the Polynesian island of Rapa, Hanson (1970) chose first to describe the rules or norms of behavior, which he likened to "maps," before describing how actual practice departs from this ideal set of rules:

> Norms governing many important social relationships in Rapa have been mapped out, but these provide only the bare outlines of expected behavior. They neither delineate each detail, nor are they observed with mechanical precision. Rapans adhere to them like a vessel to the shipping lanes in a broad swath of ocean, not like a train confined to its rails. In this and the following two chapters are numerous examples of how Rapans observe, bend, or controvert these norms. (Hansen 1970: 116)

In both cases, the researchers chose to focus on "rules" of behavior as a point of departure from which actual behavior was measured. In contrast is Koch (1974), who focuses on conflict resolution among the Non-Austronesian Jalé and a social context in which there are no legal norms at all:

> Jalé society lacks not only forensic institutions like courts and offices whose incumbents exercise a delegated judicial authority, but even more rudimentary institutions such as forums convened to discuss a dispute. Nor do the Jalé have positions of political leadership that empower their incumbents to exercise control over a local community and to adjudicate disputes among its members.
>
> Furthermore, although my own observations of behavior and informants' descriptions of customary modes of conduct could be collated in a catalog of rules, the Jalé themselves do not formulate any legal norms. Rather, they speak of their behavior either as "what we do," which describes a right and approved course of action, or as "what is not done," which refers to wrong and reprehensible conduct. (Koch 1974: 31)

In my own studies of the customary law of the Non-Austronesian Abelam peoples of the Sepik area of Papua New Guinea (Scaglion 1976, 1981), I found that Abelam also were disinterested in formulating or even discussing abstract "rules" of behavior:

> Most informants not only showed a distinct lack of interest in my attempts to formulate any general statements about traditional conflicts, but also displayed a frustrating refusal to make any definite statements about cases in the abstract. "Someone might do it that way," "someone would do that if he felt like it," were common responses to abstract hypothetical cases. Thus even abstract hypothetical cases had to be described using specific individuals and situations: "What if X's pig ruined six yams from Y's garden?" (Scaglion 1981: 30)

Perhaps the differences between these two basic models of dispute management—one rule-governed, one situation-specific—can best be illustrated by reference to actual "trouble cases," or instances of dispute. The first case I will examine involves a dispute over succession to a title on the hierarchically organized island of Pohnpei, as described by Riesenberg (1968: 19). As I mentioned previously, Riesenberg found it necessary to first explain the "rules" of succession (before showing how these rules were contested and manipulated). In Pohnpei society, there are two "lines" of chiefs, one headed by the Nahmwarki (which Riesenberg calls the "A-line") and one headed by the Nahnken (the "B-line"). The titles in the A-line are all ranked, and Riesenberg refers to them as A1 (the Nahmwarki himself), A2, A3, etc. The B-line is similarly organized. Ideally, the highest titles of the A-line are held by the senior males of a single "royal" clan, whereas the highest titles of the B-line are held by the senior males of another "noble" clan. Again ideally, male titleholders in the A-line marry B-line females and vice versa, thus assuring that all high chiefs would carry royal blood on one side and noble blood on the other. Ideally, rules of primogeniture apply. In fact, however, the system is even more complicated. Descent is matrilineal, and high-ranking men were often polygamous, having secondary wives from "commoner" clans. Therefore, they might have "commoner" sons older than their "noble" sons. Also, they often adopted children, who were distinguished from "real" children. Furthermore, all children born to the Nahmwarki or Nahnken before they ascended to their titles are called *tiekepe,* or "true" children, but those children born after they assumed their titles are called *ipwin pohn warawar,* or "born upon the ditch," referring to the chasm separating these men of greatest honor from all other people. Those "born upon the ditch" receive the greatest deference.

The above rules seem very complicated, and indeed they are. When a high chief dies, if the holder of the next highest title is a capable individual, an eldest son, born of both "royal" and "noble" blood, and "born upon the ditch," then the line of succession is usually clear. But this is rarely the case, and two or more individuals frequently have conflicting claims, which they pursue by stressing the importance of one rule over another. In the case that Riesenberg describes, the B2 titleholder wished to ascend to the B1 title upon the death of the titleholder. But there was contestation and conflict and a surprising outcome in which rules were manipulated. Riesenberg describes this as follows (see Figure 17.1):

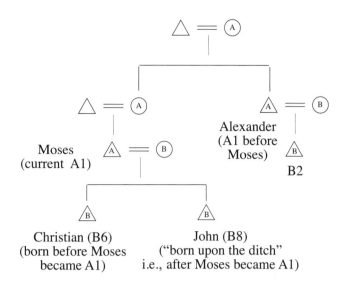

Figure 17.1. *Genealogy of contestants mentioned in text (based on data in Riesenberg 1968).*

The B1 of Madolenihmw, Sali by name, died in 1959 or 1960. The A1, Moses, had a son, John, who was Born Upon the Ditch. John, the 8th of his children, had the title of B8. Moses did not want to promote the B2 to B1 but wished instead to elevate his own oldest son, Christian, who was B6. . . . At the promotion feast Moses arose, with the traditional cup of kava, made a speech that dwelled on Ponapean customs concerning those Born Upon the Ditch, then called his son John up, gave him the cup, and proclaimed him B1. John, in his twenties, was a victim of tuberculosis (he died soon after). He made a speech that mentioned his own inadequacies, inexperience, and illness, then he called on his brother, Christian, gave him the cup, and said that Christian would be B1 instead of him. All of this had been rehearsed ahead of time. The A1 would have found it a delicate and difficult matter to promote the B6 to B1 ahead of the B2, but by using the device described here he got around the problem.

This case illustrates the centrality of rules in hierarchical societies: even when rules are broken, their breaking is most often framed and legitimized according to other rules. It can be contrasted with a trouble case that occurred among the egalitarian, Non-Austronesian Abelam people, which I witnessed in 1975 (adapted from Scaglion 1976: 94–95):

> Kaprélép and Paal, who lived in the same ceremonial group, were having affairs with each other's wives. Each knew, but for a time neither said anything. Finally one day they met and had some words. Kaprélép, who was especially angry, picked up a stone and hit Paal over the head, knocking him semiconscious. Paal's cousin (father's brother's son), who was in the same clan, but who had moved into a different ceremonial group from the disputants, happened to be nearby. He grabbed Kaprélép by the throat and began strangling him. Other bystanders pulled them apart.
>
> Nyamio, a big man from the ceremonial group of the disputants, heard the noise and set out to investigate. When

he arrived, he succeeded in calming down the disputants, including Paal, who had by then revived. They then had an informal meeting or "moot," attended by the many onlookers who had gathered. After much discussion, both principals agreed to end their affairs and forget the trouble. In order to formalize this mediated settlement, Nyamio suggested that they exchange shell rings in a formal, therapeutic ceremony of reconciliation called *ngwayé kundi.*

Later that day, Kaprélép and Paal each gave a shell ring to Nyamio, who held one in each hand. Each disputant held a small quantity of lime on the leaves of the *narandu* plant (a symbol of peace), and each smeared the lime on his counterpart's chest. Nyamio then chanted a special conciliatory *ngwayé kundi* song, after which he gave each man the other's shell ring, thus "killing" the trouble.

In our studies of customary law in the decentralized Jalé and Abelam societies, which lack formal "rules" of behavior, Koch and I focused on the actual processes of negotiation and mediation through which conflicts are managed (see, e.g., Scaglion 1983). We, like many other legal scholars who work in similar situations, were interested in how leaders like Nyamio, who did not actually possess legitimized authority, managed to sway people's opinions and settle disputes. Such leaders, called big men, achieve influence and exercise power through their individual accomplishments. Unlike the chiefs of many Pacific societies, whose power depends upon succession to ascribed, hereditary office, big men are free-enterprising individualists whose charisma and accomplishments earn them a following. In such societies, individual leaders rise and fall, and the social groups over which they have influence are likewise constantly shifting. However, big men rarely exercise influence beyond a small group of kin and supporters, and in these cultures there are no traditional forms of authority transcending the local level.

Reconciling Customary and Introduced Law at the National Level

Well before European contact, some Pacific societies were hierarchically organized whereas others were decentralized. Given these two different forms of political and judicial organization, what forms of law have emerged from the meeting of colonial and customary legal systems? When Pacific peoples came into contact with Europeans during the colonial era, European nations were all hierarchically organized. Where European powers came into contact with hierarchically organized, rule-oriented Pacific societies, customary and introduced legal models have shared certain basic characteristics. Colonial governments, recognizing the ascribed power of chiefs, often made efforts to co-opt, complement, or build upon existing legal authority. Introduced legal and political structures in such contexts (mainly in Micronesia and Polynesia) often reflected, or worked in concert with, traditional forms of authority in some fashion or another. Though power was often contested, because traditional and introduced structures were based on similarly hierarchical models, similar sets of expectations applied. Colonial powers often found it easier to try to modify existing systems rather than to attempt to replace them entirely.

Other Pacific societies (mostly in Melanesia), however, were acephalous, lacking in any forms of centralized authority recognizable to colonial governments. Traditional forms of conflict management in egalitarian societies, while effective in the smaller, more personal contexts in which they developed, were thought to be largely untenable in the colonial and postcolonial context of a developing nation-state. They were often regarded as "uncivilized" by colonial authorities, and efforts were made to replace indigenous legal systems or to supersede them with hierarchical models of law. Consequently, contemporary national law in these countries has tended to fit less comfortably with traditional forms than in contexts in which indigenous Pacific peoples employed hierarchical models. Although colonial authority has been contested in both contexts, the fields of contestation have varied.

Because of their structural similarity to European models of authority, Austronesian legal systems have been co-opted, modified, and/or changed by colonial administrations over a long period of time. Some Polynesian hierarchies took on British- or American-style governments well over one hundred years ago. While as of this writing Tonga remains a hereditary monarchy, today there is a constitution, formal written statutes passed by a legislative assembly, and a parliament, which is controlled by hereditary chiefs. In other Polynesian hierarchies, chiefs share influence with introduced forms of authority. The Territorial Council of Wallis and Futuna comprises the three traditional chiefs and three other members appointed by the chief administrator. In still other locations, traditional chiefs act in an advisory capacity. In the Cook Islands, the House of Ariki advises on matters related to custom; in the Republic of the Marshall Islands, the Council of Iroij may request consideration of statutes affecting customary law.

It took much longer for non-Austronesian, "egalitarian" methods of conflict resolution to be formally recognized and integrated into national legal systems. In Papua New Guinea, the first village courts, designed to apply local customary law, were established in 1975 (Figures 17.2 and 17.3). In contrast to this is the land and chiefly titles court of hierarchically organized Samoa, a court established by Germany nearly three-quarters of a century earlier, in 1903, to hear disputes related to *matai* (chiefly) titles and local land matters by applying local custom. Although the German colonial government in Samoa recognized and empowered local chiefs early, the German colonial government's reaction to local leadership in German New Guinea was quite different. Realizing that no one was really "in charge" at the local level, the colonial government attempted to establish local nontraditional authorities by setting up introduced titles of leadership (Luluai and Tultul) in village contexts. Not surprisingly, the authority of these "leaders" was generally not recognized by local people.

A comparison of legal development in Papua New Guinea and Samoa provides an interesting contrast. During the Australian colonial era, Papua New Guinea's formal court structure was established in much the same form as it exists today. The formal courts use the rules and procedures of introduced Western law, primarily by applying Australian law and British common law to given fact situations. There are few if any of the mediation and consensus settlement procedures that characterize much of Papuan customary law. At the top of the formal court structure is

Figure 17.2. Maprik courthouse, East Sepik Province, Papua New Guinea (photo RS).

Figure 17.3. Village court meeting, East Sepik Province, Papua New Guinea (photo RS).

the supreme court, which hears appeals from the national court. The national court has exclusive original jurisdiction over major criminal and civil matters. Each major region has a district court, with more limited civil and criminal trial jurisdiction, and several local courts, the lowest level of formal courts, originally designed to serve people at the local level.

Before the introduction of village courts, this formal court structure operated with little or no regard for local custom. Disputes within villages were usually handled in informal village meetings, or moots, as they had always been, and there was very little interaction between these traditional "remedy agents" and the introduced courts (Scaglion 1976). It has been only recently, in an attempt to better integrate customary and introduced law, that village courts were established by the *Village Courts Act 1973* (No. 12 of 1974). The primary function of a village court is to "ensure peace and harmony in the area for which it is established by mediating in and endeavoring to obtain just and amicable settlements of disputes" by applying local customs (s. 18). In this way, Papua New Guinea has been able to subsume its multiplicity of customary legal systems

into a single structure. Local leaders, serving as magistrates, can follow local procedures and apply local custom with the weight of law. Village court compromise solutions and decisions are recognized and usually upheld by the local courts.

In Samoa, where customary law has long been applied in courts, local leaders have had a far longer involvement in formal legal structures. The nearly one hundred-year-old land and titles court, for example, is often considered to be the most influential court in Samoa today. The court comprises Samoan judges (chiefs appointed for three-year terms) and assessors (senior chiefs appointed from a panel). The chief justice or a judge of the supreme court acts as president of the court and provides guidance on legal and procedural matters, but only rarely actually presides over hearings, where unwritten Samoan custom and usage are followed exclusively. The court holds three almost continuous and concurrent sittings: two on 'Upolu and one on Savai'i. The court has exclusive jurisdiction over matters involving *matai* (chiefly) titles and land matters. There is no provision for review. No decision can be challenged in any other court, nor can any other court hear matters of chiefly titles or land (Anesi and Enari 1988).

Today both Samoa and Papua New Guinea have what legal scholars would call "similar sources of law." Both countries have a constitution and recognize formal acts or statutes of a national parliament. Both recognize the laws and statutes of their pre-independence colonial powers (New Zealand and England in the case of Samoa; Australia and England in the case of Papua New Guinea) that were in force before independence (1962 for Samoa, 1975 for PNG), to the extent these are not inconsistent with statute or inappropriate to the circumstances of the country. Both recognize local custom and usage within certain limits, and both recognize the principles and rules of English common law and equity that are not in conflict with any of the above sources of law.

Yet even in Samoa, tensions between introduced and customary law exist, and the relative influence of each continues to be negotiated. Surprisingly, the Samoan Fono, or village council, perhaps the most institutionalized local, customary law court in the Pacific Islands today, has only recently (Village Fono Act, 1991) been recognized by law. As Sapolu (1988) points out, there has been a gradual erosion of the influence of the Fono. Although the constitution expressly recognizes Samoan custom and usage as applied to local government, it also vests judicial power in the formal courts: the court of appeal, supreme court, magistrates' courts, and the land and titles court. Thus, to the extent that formal courts apply case-law decisions derived from other common law countries, and the parliament passes statutes adopted from or modeled upon Western law, it is likely that the Fono's influence will continue to decline.

Papua New Guinea and Samoa are both independent countries that have never had large numbers of outside settlers. But in many industrialized Pacific locales, such as Australia, Hawai'i, and New Zealand, the descendants of outside settlers today outnumber indigenous Pacific Islanders. Accommodating the needs of these diverse populations through legal pluralism has been yet another challenge in the contemporary Pacific. An innovative experiment in reconciling the legal systems of the indigenous New Zealanders (Maori) with the descendants of the mostly British settlers (pakeha, or white New Zealanders) is the Waitangi Tribunal. The tribunal was established in New Zealand (Aotearoa) in 1975 by the Treaty of Waitangi Act, the object of which was "to provide for the observance and confirmation of the principles of the Treaty of Waitangi" (Ward 1991: 98).

The Treaty of Waitangi itself was signed in 1840 by the first British governor and some five hundred Maori chiefs. But the intentions of the signers, and the interpretation of the treaty itself, have been highly controversial virtually from the outset, owing largely to the existence of both English and Maori-language versions of the treaty. The first major area of controversy is over the parties involved in the treaty: do "the Maori" constitute a singular collectivity or are they separate ethnic groups and therefore multiple treaty partners? Maori activists seeking coequal power with pakeha prefer the former formulation. An alternative interpretation regards treaty agreements as having been made with a number of separate groups. Article 1 of the English version, for example, states that "The Chiefs of the Confederation of the United Tribes of New Zealand, and the separate and independent Chiefs who have not become members of the Confederation" cede to the Queen of England "all the rights and powers of Sovereignty" that the "Confederation or the Individual Chiefs" exercise over their respective territories, suggesting an agreement with separate groups.

Even more controversial is the meaning of the "sovereignty" that the Maori chiefs ceded to the British in 1840. In the Maori-language version, the chiefs agreed to give up *kawanatanga*. This is a neologism derived from the transliteration of *kawana* (governor) and the critical idea of "authority," the importance of which I have described at length earlier in this chapter. The new word implied some sort of novel, national, overarching authority, which the Maori chiefs no doubt thought would help protect their chieftainships and land. The chiefs (*rangatira*) expressly did NOT give up either their own *rangatiratanga* or their *mana*, words denoting chiefly authority. Article 2 in the English version seems to concede this, confirming the chiefs and tribes in "the full exclusive and undisturbed, possession of their Lands and Estates, Forests, Fisheries and other properties" so long as they wished to retain them. The Maori version, however, seems to go even further than this, confirming for the chiefs and the people the *tino rangatiratanga* of their lands and their *taonga* (a broad term meaning "valued possessions"). Whatever the Maori understanding(s) of the agreement may have been, and before the interior or southern chiefs had even signed the treaty, the British declared sovereignty over the entire North Island by cession, and the South Island and Stewart Island by right of discovery (Ward 1991: 91). It quickly became clear that, to the British, "sovereignty" meant something much more sweeping than the Maori chiefs ever imagined *kawanatanga* might encompass.

Today the Waitangi Tribunal, chaired by the chief judge of the Maori land court and comprising a bicultural and interdisciplinary membership, has broad powers to interpret the treaty. The tribunal can review and make recommendations on any act, regulation, policy, or practice of the Crown that a Maori complainant feels has injured his or her rights under the treaty. It can also, by its own initiative, challenge any law it deems likely to breach the treaty. In certain cases it is empowered to make "binding recommendations," although it has not yet done so (Durie 1996). The tribunal has made wide-ranging recommendations on issues ranging from industrial pollution of rivers to the status of the Maori language as a *taonga*, or valued thing.

According to the chairman of the tribunal, Chief Judge Edward Taihakurei Durie (1996), contemporary claims involve "resource management policies, the impact of development works, Maori language, land administration, Maori participation in economic development, judicial systems, administrative structures, Maori land law, the alienation of state assets by the Crown, education, immigration, the status accorded Maori women, intellectual property rights, cultural maintenance, fishing, hunting, foraging, and a range of laws and regulations." Not everyone, however, views the tribunal in a positive light. Critics point to the slowness of the tribunal process, the failure of Maori to regain surplus Crown land, and the negative impact of economic reforms on Maori communities as evidence of its lack of effectiveness. Some see the very existence of the tribunal as an agency of suppression of the Maori people. Whether or not this is the case, the tribunal has had some successes in reconciling the customary practices of the Maori people with the authority of the modern nation-state.

Although specific details vary greatly, most contemporary Pacific Island nations currently have some form of "custom" law existing side by side with "introduced" law (Appendix 17.1; Powles and Pulea 1988). Most often, customary law governs land and sometimes succession, local government, and marriage and divorce. Introduced law typically governs criminal matters, cash-oriented economic transactions, and the activities of the central government. Yet the spheres of customary and introduced law often overlap and intersect, leaving quite a bit of room for legal maneuvering, as the cases of Papua New Guinea, Samoa, and New Zealand all suggest.

Negotiating Law in the Local Context

What is "authority"? What is "custom law"? Such terms are not easy to define. In the discussions above, I have for analytic purposes drawn sharp contrasts between chiefs and big men, between hierarchical and egalitarian societies. Such simplistic dichotomies, however, do not adequately convey the complexity and richness of the legal process in any given local situation. The authority of chiefs is often questioned, negotiated, and limited. Big men sometimes exercise considerable influence and can wield a certain amount of power. Although I have argued that rules are more formally inscribed in hierarchical societies, egalitarian tribal societies do not lack notions of morality and fairness. Many egalitarian societies have quite complicated normative orders, which play important parts in shaping how cases actually get resolved. Furthermore, while many legal scholars believe that the rules of law in complex societies are clear and predictable and determine the outcomes of cases, legal realists and legal anthropologists see "law" as much less certain, with rules that are highly variable, sometimes vague, and often contested and manipulated.

A brief examination of the nature of leadership in the contemporary Pacific will serve as an example. Feinberg and Watson-Gegeo's volume titled *Leadership and Change in the Western Pacific* (1996) suggests that chiefs and big men may not really be so different after all, since "prevalent stereotypes of ascribed leadership markedly fail to reflect the actual processes and struggles of political life" (Whitehouse 1996: 393). Chiefly authority emerges as amorphous and fluid, no easier to pin down or clearly describe than are more decentralized forms of leadership. Niko Besnier's article "Authority and Egalitarianism: Discourses of Leadership on Nukulaelae Atoll" describes how "Nukulaelae people reminisce longingly about the days when any command issued by a chief or the council would be cheerfully complied with by everyone" (1996: 103). Such a "discourse of nostalgia," however, is in dialectic opposition to a "discourse of egalitarianism," which surfaces in the manipulation of symbolic tools associated with counterhegemonic action, such as ridicule, gossip, contempt, and spoofing. Ironically, leaders are reproached for being leaders because they are too "bossy" and set themselves above others. One of the most common ways Nukulaelae leaders negotiate their difficult position is by not presenting themselves as speaking or acting on their own behalf. Rather, they present themselves as the *sui*, or representative of a group, thus being "noble," and placing the concerns of the group above their own selfish priorities. In so doing, they emerge as persons worthy and deserving of positions of leadership.

Such strategies are not really different from those used by big men in egalitarian societies. In one conflict case I recorded (adapted from Scaglion 1976: 158–159), Abelam big men acted in comparable fashion:

> Kwumun had land near another village. One day he discovered one of his pigs speared to death, lying putrefied on the other village's land adjacent to his own. After bringing a few men to see the pig, he buried it, and went to see Nyamio, his group's leading big-man, to discuss the problem. Together with some big-men who would act as representatives of the adjoining village, Nyamio arranged for a "moot" (informal village meeting for the purposes of conflict resolution) to be held in Kwumun's hamlet the next week in order to discuss the problem with all principals to the dispute.
>
> In what was widely perceived to be a power play by Kwumun's antagonists, the visiting delegation, which was expected to arrive in the morning, did not come until 12:30 p.m. When all were finally seated, Kwumun stated his case. Why had his pig been killed? Had it ruined any gardens? If so, why hadn't he been told? His speech was answered by a big-man representing the other group, who stated that the two men who speared the pig had gone to a nearby village and he wasn't sure why they had done it. Nyamio then countered with a speech designed to embarrass the opposing big-men. What kind of big-men were they anyway, if the young men didn't even listen to them? Couldn't they control their followers? After this, a few other speeches were given, but the absence of the principals made settlement impossible.
>
> Another moot was set for the next week at the other village, so that the principals would be more likely to be present. When the morning of the scheduled day dawned, a heavy rain the previous night had made the paths slippery, and Kwumun's group decided not to go. Nyamio sent word that the other group's big-men should settle the case by themselves, and, if acceptable, he and the others would abide by their decision.
>
> About a week later, word was returned that the two guilty men refused to admit killing the pig, but everyone knew they had done it. The big-men, acting as representatives of their group, proposed that a piglet would be designated and raised for Kwumun. Members of their group would all contribute a little, and when the piglet reached the size of the slaughtered pig, it would be given to Kwumun, who was satisfied with this resolution.

This case demonstrates not only the importance of corporate responsibility above individual liability, but also the use of the same sorts of discursive strategies contrasting authority and egalitarianism that were described by Besnier. Nyamio, in an attempt to discredit the big men from the rival village, stressed their lack of authority. If they had power, they should be able to control their followers. If they couldn't, they were ineffective leaders. His rivals, on the other hand, played on the egalitarian principle, portraying themselves merely as representatives of their group. By putting aside their own self-interests and agreeing to make restitution to preserve the honor of the group, they reinforced their legitimacy as leaders in the eyes of their followers.

The power of local people to manipulate, contest, and redefine various aspects of law has not always been recognized by social scientists. Scholars have often seen "law" in colonial contexts as a vehicle for encoding and perpetuating power relationships. Even in postcolonial situations, asymmetrical power relationships have often been stressed, particularly in situations where traditional chiefs attempt to maintain power or where emerging elites attempt to exercise it. Consideration of the politics of dominance and resistance and the articulation between national and local legal systems has led some researchers to take what Galanter (1981: 1) has called a "legal centralism" perspective, also called the "command" model of law (cf. Kidder 1979). In this approach, law is regarded as an instrument of domination by a ruling class over an essentially powerless peasantry (see, e.g., Fitzpatrick 1980). Thus aliwala (1982: 191), in an analysis of Papua New Guinea's village courts, sees these local-level courts as bringing about "greater involvement and control by the state and a degree of authoritarianism on the part of court officials. The result is relatively alienated dispute settlement with relatively little scope for community involvement and party consensus." But other researchers in Papua New Guinea take a "legal interactionism" approach, which sees local people not so much as an oppressed peasantry, but rather as local innovators with the agency to affect their own affairs. Examples of studies supporting this perspective include Strathern (1972), Westermark (1978), Scaglion (1979, 1990), Rodman and Rodman (1984), Rodman (1985), and Zorn (1990). These studies demonstrate how Pacific Islanders consciously and creatively affect local-level legal development.

Perhaps the most dramatic example of this is Rodman's (1985) study of legal innovation in Ambae, Vanuatu. When the national government effectively withdrew from participation in local legal affairs at the end of the colonial era, local people, particularly in the district of Longana, employed this context for legal innovation. In a conscious and systematic manner, they codified a specific and detailed set of laws for themselves. While this case is unusual, local people throughout the Pacific continually shape their own legal destinies in less dramatic ways. In a study of changing patterns in village court use in a rural area of Papua New Guinea

(Scaglion 1990), I noticed that the proportion of women plaintiffs had increased dramatically. It seemed that rather than submitting disputes to a little-understood, introduced court, or attempting to have them settled in the male-dominated forum of village politics, women were increasingly choosing a forum in which local custom was recognized, but where changing social patterns and women's rights were also being acknowledged. A wider study of conflict cases throughout rural Papua New Guinea (Scaglion and Whittingham 1985) found that village courts were the single most successful remedy agent in resolving women's grievances. By channeling disputes to the remedy agent of their choice, Papua New Guinean women have made progress toward achieving some measure of legal equality with men. Zorn (1990) reports similar findings in her analysis of village courts in an urban context, examining how magistrates innovatively interpret law to respond to changing social circumstances.

Clearly, national governments, ruling elites, and the relatively powerless all seek to further their own ends. Increasingly, discourses of cultural authenticity and indigenous rights frame these efforts. Studies of interactive legal pluralism thus fit broadly within a growing awareness of the "politics of culture" in the Pacific Islands (cf. Feinberg 1995). Increasingly, culture itself is seen as an entity that can be self-consciously manipulated to suit individual and group interests. Keesing and Tonkinson's (1982) volume on reinventing traditional culture in Island Melanesia demonstrated the power of *kastom* as a symbol of identity, the indigenous past(s) constructed in the present for political purposes (see also Hanson's controversial 1989 article on Maori custom). Because custom is fluid and difficult to codify, it can be interpreted and used for various purposes: to justify certain practices or actions, to shape and reshape cultural identities, and to redefine and recreate the past to suit contemporary political agendas (White and Lindstrom 1993). Studies of language use within disputing contexts in the Pacific also reinforce this position (see, e.g., Brenneis and Myers 1984; Watson-Gegeo and White 1990; Goldman 1983; Brison 1992; Duranti 1994).

Global Transformations

As we have seen, customary law can be quite flexible, and, in general, it has been appropriate for the small face-to-face contexts in which it developed. But is customary law adequate for coping with the demands of modern nation-states in a globalizing world? Contemporary Pacific states must cope with problems of immigration and emigration, tourism, intermarriages with outsiders, diasporas of their citizens living abroad, remittance economies, international trade and banking, multinational corporations, contracts, intellectual property rights, and a host of other issues that result from changing social conditions. Should Pacific Island nations merely adopt the legal systems received from colonial governments to deal with these new problems? To what extent can—or should—customary law be considered when dealing with contemporary issues?

An interesting example of how customary law fails to fit changing socioeconomic circumstances is the so-called "Nagol jump" case of Vanuatu. The Nagol jump or "land dive" is a well-known custom of southern Pentecost island sometimes considered to be the forerunner of contemporary bungee jumping. Each year when a rich yam harvest signals that the liana vines have the right qualities for the jump, men build towers of up to one hundred feet tall, tie vines to their ankles, and leap from specially constructed platforms, ideally brushing their heads against the ground just as the vines break their fall.

The land dive has become known worldwide and is now a significant tourist attraction that generates considerable cash income. The legal case *In re the Nagol Jump, Assal and Vatu v. The Council of Chiefs of Santo and Santo Regional Council* (1992 Vanuatu Supreme Court 5) involved intellectual property rights ownership and the legality of "moving" the land dive from its traditional location on Pentecost to the neighboring island of Santo to take advantage of an additional tourism market. Certain groups, believing they were denied their fair share on Pentecost, planned to stage a dive on Santo, arguing that they were being denied their constitutional rights of freedom of expression, assembly and association, movement, and equal treatment under the law. The defendants argued that customary procedures had to be followed before moving the jump, which must include securing the approval of both the area chiefs and the National Council of Chiefs. The facts of the matter were contentious and complex, and, recognizing that no provision of the introduced law applied to the case, the chief justice attempted to forge a compromise. Without necessarily stating that the dive could never be moved, he directed that it be returned to Pentecost. He ordered that if any custom owner should choose to perform the dive on Pentecost outside of the traditional villages from which it originates, then all the custom owners and their clan should share equally in the responsibility for the dive and in the profits. On the rare occasions when the dive would leave Pentecost, majority consent of the custom owners and local chiefs should be first obtained, with the final decision resting with the National Council of Chiefs, and that the custom owners all should be invited to participate and share in the profits. Thus the court extended customary practice in the face of changing socioeconomic circumstances.

In the land dive case, because no rule of introduced law applied, the chief justice reluctantly considered and extended customary law, preserving its spirit and broadening its application. But this is the exception rather than the rule. Being more familiar with introduced law, justices in Pacific Island nations have generally avoided considering customary law whenever possible. Most often, clashes of customary and introduced laws are resolved in favor of the introduced law, changing the very nature of custom. An example is the case of *Noel v. Toto* (1995 Vanuatu Supreme Court 3, discussed in Brown 2005: 97–98 and 210–212), which pitted customary notions of collective rights to land in Vanuatu with introduced Western concepts of individual landownership and gender equality. A dispute arose in a family that had traditionally observed patrilineal inheritance and control over land. The uncontested head of the family in land matters, both in custom and as adjudicated by the courts, was one Crero Toto (then deceased). The land in dispute was called Champagne Beach, a lovely stretch that attracted tourists and generated considerable cash income. Noel, the applicant in the dispute, was the son of Crero's daughter Julie (then also deceased). Noel claimed a share of the income generated by the land by rights of descent through the female line. But under traditional rules of descent and landownership and use, Noel belonged to the lineage of his father, and would not have shared in the land of Crero's patrilineage.

It appeared to the court that conflicting principles of customary and introduced law were at issue in this case. On the one hand, the constitution guaranteed equal rights for women. On the other, Article 74 affirmed that rules of custom shall form the basis of ownership and use of land in Vanuatu. Justice Kent opted to recognize Western values over traditional ones. He affirmed:

> It is clear that it was the intention of the Constitution to guarantee equal rights for women. . . . The evidence before me suggests that custom, with respect to land rights does not give the same right to women as it does to men. . . . The custom therefore discriminates against women on the grounds of sex. (Brown 2005: 97–98)

Acknowledging the conflict with Article 74, he stated:

> This may mean that in determining land rights in the future, there will be a change in the basis of determining land ownership. This does not mean that land ownership will be decided otherwise than in accordance with custom. Custom law must provide the basis for determining ownership, subject to the limitation that any rule of custom which discriminates against women cannot be applied. General principles of land ownership will not be changed. (Brown 2005: 98)

There is no doubt that his decision did in fact weaken traditional local principles of landownership, moving them away from patrilineal patterns toward bilateral ones. But were traditional and introduced legal principles really in conflict in this case? In many patrilineal systems, Julie's children, both male and female, would have shared equally in the land of her husband, just as she shared equally with her brothers in the land of Crero Toto, her father. It is also true, however, that under customary law, neither Julie *nor* her brothers would have shared in the land of their mother, just as Noel *and* his sisters would not have shared in the land of *their* mother (Julie). It could therefore be argued that the same customary rules applied equally to both males and females in this unilineal kinship system (albeit differently from the conventions of bilateral kinship) and therefore not necessarily contrary to the gender equality provisions of the constitution.

But Justice Kent did observe a key dimension of this case:

> The intrusion of money into the area of custom raises new considerations however. Custom is sometimes said to be something that has existed from time immemorial. The use and distribution of money by custom owners could not be said to be something that has given rise to a custom from time immemorial. Accordingly, I think it is open to the Supreme Court to establish some principles with regard to the use of money, but that must be done by reference in some way to custom rules. (Brown 2005: 211)

This opens the door to preserving traditional rights in landownership while at the same time bringing the distribution of nontraditional cash proceeds from that land that result from changing economic circumstances more in line with introduced law.

Changing economies in the Pacific Islands frequently precipitate disputes, which the formal legal system typically resolves in favor of Western patterns, as happened in the case of *Noel v. Toto* in Vanuatu cited above. The net result, for better or worse, characteristically moves Pacific economic and social organizations away from traditional configurations. The same often happens in family law, with, for example, monogamous patterns typically favored over polygamous ones. But interestingly, in Solomon Islands, in certain segments of family law, case law has tended to work in the opposite direction, recognizing less formal marriage patterns that would not be recognized in the West in order to protect the legitimacy of children and the rights of women. A complicated case that tested the difficulty of proving a traditional marriage in law and uncovered the complexities of "islander" identity and immigration is *Edwards v. Edwards* (1996 Solomon Islands High Court 75; Brown 2005: 110–111). Veronica Edwards believed she was the lawful widow of one Victor Edwards, having been married under Kiribati custom. She therefore applied to the high court to be the coadministratrix with the respondent, Carol Edwards, who was the daughter of Victor from his first marriage that had ended in divorce. Carol argued that even if the marriage of her father (Victor) with Veronica could be established as valid under Kiribati custom, it should not be recognized by the courts of Solomon Islands, which should only recognize the customary law of the indigenous people of Solomon Islands. In his decision, the judge gave a rare acknowledgment to customary law, stating that "the definition of 'customary law' should not be read restrictively, but rather should be seen as remedial in its application and given a fair, wide and liberal interpretation." He upheld the validity of the marriage based partly on that fact that a food party or feast that traditionally marked a marriage in Kiribati custom had been held, and that the couple had had four children between 1985 and 1991. Here, then, is an example of a case in which customary law was not only upheld by the state courts, but actually given a progressive interpretation.

A related case in Solomon Islands was *Rebitai v. Chow and Others* (2001 Solomon Islands High Court 85). The facts of the case were complicated, but the case centered on the question of how customary marriage should be defined. The plaintiff was an indigenous islander and the defendant was of Chinese descent born in Solomon Islands. The defendant, Francis Chow, wanted to withdraw from his long-term relationship with the plaintiff without legal consequences, claiming that as a person of Chinese descent, he could not marry in custom, and that in any case the requirements of custom had not been observed, which his expert witness claimed included such things as obtaining permission for the marriage, payment of bride price, and holding a marriage feast. The plaintiff admitted that no bride price had been paid and no customary ceremony had been held, but maintained that the marriage was nevertheless valid because their relationship was accepted by her family and the community at large based on their living together for twenty-four years and having children and grandchildren. Her expert witness stated that although payment of bride price and exchange of goods and food took place in the past, in modern times the critical factor was acceptance by the community. The judge found nothing barring non-islanders from entering into customary marriages and upheld the validity of the marriage, wanting to protect the children from dislocation of their traditional land rights. Thus, once again in Solomon Islands, in the area of family law, customary law was interpreted broadly.

The cases reviewed in this section give just a taste of the complex issues that Pacific Islanders face in reconciling customary law and introduced law in a rapidly globalizing world. They suggest that customary principles can be used as the basis for innovative legislation, but they also underline the complexity of such efforts. Entire ethnographic descriptions have been written detailing the multiple issues that arise as a result of such changing circumstances as Christian conversion (Robbins 2004), pollution from mining activities (Kirsch 2006), the establishment of an ecological preserve on traditional land (West 2006), and the effects of widespread commercial logging (Barker 2008). Pacific Islanders must choose among competing models of law, authority, and morality on a daily basis. Legal pluralism can provide the means for reconciling traditional and global life as Pacific peoples seek to maintain what is good about customary law and to merge it with introduced law with the goal of crafting legal systems that meet both the demands of the modern state in a contemporary world and the needs of ordinary people affected by global processes. But much work remains.

Appendix 17.1

Customary Law in the Pacific Islands

Political entity	Legally recognized aspects of customary law	Role of traditional leaders in administration of justice
American Samoa	Customs of the Samoan people that are not in conflict with the laws of American Samoa or the U.S. are recognized (Am. Sam. Code Annotated, S. 1.02); mainly in relation to land, chiefly titles, and local government.	The Senate consists of *matai* (chiefs). Associate judges are *matai*, and village courts administer customary law, presided over by a *matai* (associate judge).
Australia	Customs of the aboriginal and Torres Strait Island people are recognized in limited areas. Land rights of aboriginal peoples are recognized.	In the Torres Straits, Queensland's Community Services (Torres Strait) Act 1984 (as amended 1986) empowers island courts to hear matters of custom.
Cook Islands	The ancient custom and usage of the people of the Cook Islands is recognized in relation to customary land (Cook Islands Act 1915 [NZ], S. 422, S. 446).	The House of Ariki (chiefs) acts in an advisory capacity in relation to custom.
Federated States of Micronesia	Micronesian customs and traditions are recognized (Constitution of the F.S.M., art. XI, S. 11).	Local-level litigation (in local languages) takes place in village courts presided over by justices chosen for respect and knowledge of custom.
Fiji	Customs of the indigenous people of Fiji relating to the holding of customary land and aspects of chiefly authority and local government are recognized.	The Council of Chiefs has privileged representation in the Senate.
Guam	The customary law of Chamorros (indigenous people of Guam) is not recognized.	
Hawai'i	Local customary law, with particular regard to property rights, is recognized.	
Kiribati	Local custom of the people of Kiribati, particularly in relation to land, marriage, and adoption, to the extent that it is not inconsistent with natural justice, equity, and good conscience, or any statute, is recognized (Magistrates' Courts Ordinance, S. 42).	Magistrates' courts are presided over by individuals with knowledge of local custom.
Marshall Islands, Republic of	Customary law of the Marshall Islands, particularly in relation to land, marriage, and the holding of chiefly titles, is recognized.	A council of twelve Iroij (chiefs) is selected by custom. The council may request reconsideration of statutes affecting customary law. Chiefs also resolve local disputes and maintain order according to custom.
Nauru	The institutions, customs, and usages of the Nauruan people are recognized in relation to land, personal property, and succession.	
New Caledonia	Customs and usages of the Kanak people that relate to civil matters (such as land, succession, marriage and divorce, and adoption) are recognized for French citizens of ethnic Melanesian origin (unless expressly renounced).	

Political entity	Legally recognized aspects of customary law	Role of traditional leaders in administration of justice
New Zealand	Customs of the Maori people in regard to land matters are recognized.	The Maori land court has jurisdiction over Maori land; it appeals to the Maori appellate court. Maori wardens have local disciplinary and welfare responsibilities. The Waitangi Tribunal hears matters related to the treaty.
Niue	The customs and usages of the people of Niue in relation to land and fishing rights are recognized.	
Norfolk Island	Customary law is not recognized except by specific statute.	
Northern Mariana Islands	The customs of the indigenous people (Chamorro and Carolinian), particularly in relation to domestic relations, land tenure, wills, and traditional methods of healing, are recognized.	
Palau	The traditional laws of Palau are recognized; in cases of conflict, statutes prevail only to the extent that they do not conflict with the underlying principles of traditional law (Constitution, art. V, S. 2).	A Council of Chiefs advises the president on traditional laws and customs.
Papua New Guinea	The customs of the people are recognized to the extent they do not conflict with constitutional law or statute and are not repugnant to the general principles of humanity.	Village courts, presided over by groups of magistrates who are local leaders knowledgeable in customary law, exercise limited primary jurisdiction in most local matters.
Pitcairn	Customary law is not formally recognized.	
Samoa	Samoan custom and usage are recognized in relation to the holding of *matai* (chiefly titles), customary land, and the rules of village government.	Laws are made by a Parliament comprising mostly *matai*. Local justice is administered in Village Fonos (councils), which have become institutionalized.
Solomon Islands	The rules of customary law prevailing in specific areas of Solomon Islands are recognized subject only to the Constitution and statutes of Parliament.	Local courts in areas defined by language and custom have unlimited jurisdiction in customary law.
Tokelau	In principle, custom is almost totally overridden by specific legislation except in land matters.	In practice, village daily life is ruled by custom.
Tonga	As an independent monarchy, the King of Tonga is the highest traditional leader, and the Constitution and statutes of the Legislative Assembly reflect customary law.	Parliament is controlled by hereditary chiefs.
Torres Strait Islands	See Australia	See Australia
Tuvalu	Recognized are principles expressing Tuvalu values, culture and tradition as set out in the Preamble to the Constitution of 1986 and adopted as the basic law of Tuvalu; with regard to land, succession, and adoption, Tuvalu custom and tradition are largely codified in the Lands Ordinance and Lands Code 1956.	Island Councils receive bills "for consideration and comment" between sessions of Parliament.
Vanuatu	The customary law of the people of Vanuatu is recognized, especially custom in relation to the ownership and use of land and to institutions and procedures for resolving disputes concerning ownership.	A National Council of Chiefs is advisory, has certain powers of appointment, and is consulted on national land law. Custom chiefs are represented on regional councils and island courts.
Wallis and Futuna	The customs of the people of Wallis and Futuna that do not contradict general legal principles are recognized, especially in relation to property held in accordance with custom (Law 61.814 arts. 3 and 4).	The Territorial Council, comprising the three traditional chiefs of Wallis and Futuna, and three members appointed by the chief administrator, advise and review bills. At the local level, assessors of the court of first instance are locally born and generally have knowledge of local custom.

BIBLIOGRAPHY

Anesi, T., and A. F. Enari. 1988. The land and chiefly titles court of Western Samoa. In *Pacific courts and legal systems,* ed. G. Powles and M. Pulea, 107–111. Suva: University of the South Pacific.

Barker, J. 2008. *Ancestral lines: The Maisin of Papua New Guinea and the fate of the rainforest.* Peterborough, Ont.: Broadview Press.

Besnier, N. 1996. Authority and egalitarianism: Discourses of leadership on Nukulaelae Atoll. In *Leadership and change in the Western Pacific,* ed. R. Feinberg and K. A. Watson-Gegeo, 93–128. London: Athlone.

Brenneis, D., and F. R. Myers. 1984 (1991). *Dangerous words: Language and politics in the Pacific.* Prospect Heights, Ill.: Waveland Press.

Brison, K. J. 1992. *Just talk: Gossip, meetings, and power in a Papua New Guinea village.* Berkeley: University of California Press.

Brown, K. 2005. *Reconciling customary law and received law in Melanesia: The post-independence experience in Solomon Islands and Vanuatu.* Darwin, N.T.: Charles Darwin University Press.

Duranti, A. 1994. *From grammar to politics: Linguistic anthropology in a Western Samoan village.* Berkeley: University of California Press.

Durie, E. T. 1996. Speech delivered at a conference on Indigenous peoples: Rights, lands, resources, autonomy at the Vancouver Trade and Convention Centre, British Columbia, March 20–26.

Feinberg, R., ed. 1995. The politics of culture in the Pacific Islands. Special issue of *Ethnology* 34(2 and 3).

Feinberg, R., and K. A. Watson-Gegeo, eds. 1996. *Leadership and change in the Western Pacific: Essays presented to Sir Raymond Firth on the occasion of his ninetieth birthday.* London: Athlone, London School of Economics Monographs on Social Anthropology No. 66.

Fitzpatrick, P. 1980. *Law and state in Papua New Guinea.* New York: Academic Press.

Galanter, M. 1981. Justice in many rooms: Courts, private ordering and indigenous law. *Journal of Legal Pluralism* 19: 1–47.

Goldman, L. 1983. *Talk never dies: The language of Huli disputes.* London: Tavistock.

Grimes, B. F., ed. 1992. *Ethnologue: Languages of the world,* 12th ed. Dallas: Summer Institute of Linguistics.

Hanson, F. A. 1970. *Rapan lifeways: Society and history on a Polynesian island.* Boston: Little, Brown and Co.

———. 1989. The making of the Maori: Culture invention and its logic. *American Anthropologist* 91: 890–902.

Keesing, R., and R. Tonkinson, eds. 1982. Reinventing traditional culture: The politics of custom in Island Melanesia. Special issue of *Mankind* 13.

Kidder, R. L. 1979. Toward an integrated theory of imposed law. In *The imposition of law,* ed. S. Burman and B. Harrell-Bond, 289–306. New York: Academic Press.

Kirsch, S. 2006. *Reverse anthropology: Indigenous analysis of social and environmental relations in New Guinea.* Stanford, Calif.: Stanford University Press.

Koch, K. F. 1974. *War and peace in Jalémó: The management of conflict in Highland New Guinea.* Cambridge, Mass.: Harvard University Press.

Paliwala, A. 1982. Law and order in the village: The village courts. In *Law and social change in Papua New Guinea,* ed. D. Weisbrot, A. Paliwala, and A. Sawyer, 191–217. Sydney: Butterworths.

Powles, G., and M. Pulea. 1988. *Pacific courts and legal systems.* Suva: University of the South Pacific.

Riesenberg, S. H. 1968. *The native polity of Ponape.* Smithsonian Contributions to Anthropology 10. Washington: Smithsonian Institution Press.

Robbins, J. 2004. *Becoming sinners: Christianity and moral torment in a Papua New Guinea society.* Berkeley and Los Angeles: University of California Press.

Rodman, W. L. 1985. A law unto themselves: Legal innovation in Ambae, Vanuatu. *American Ethnologist* 12: 603–624.

Rodman, W. L., and M. C. Rodman. 1984. Rethinking kastom: On the politics of place naming in Vanuatu. *Oceania* 55: 242–251.

Sahlins, M. 1963. Poor man, rich man, big-man, chief: Political types in Melanesia and Polynesia. *Comparative Studies in Society and History* 5: 285–303.

Sapolu, F. 1988. Adjudicators in Western Samoa. In *Pacific courts and legal systems,* ed. G. Powles and M. Pulea, 60–64. Suva: University of the South Pacific.

Scaglion, R. 1976. Seasonal patterns in western Abelam conflict management practices. PhD thesis, University of Pittsburgh.

———. 1979. Formal and informal operations of a village court in Maprik. *Melanesian Law Journal* 7: 116–129.

———. 1981. Samukundi Abelam conflict management: Implications for legal planning in Papua New Guinea. *Oceania* 52: 28–38.

———. 1983. The effects of mediation styles on successful dispute resolution: The Abelam Case. *Windsor Yearbook of Access to Justice* 3: 256–269.

———. 1990. Legal adaptation in a Papua New Guinea Village Court. *Ethnology* 29: 17–33.

———. 1996. Chiefly models in Papua New Guinea. *The Contemporary Pacific* 8: 1–31.

Scaglion, R., and R. Whittingham. 1985. Female plaintiffs and sex-related disputes in rural Papua New Guinea. In *Domestic violence in Papua New Guinea,* ed. S. Toft, 120–133. Port Moresby: Papua New Guinea Law Reform Commission, Monograph No. 3.

Strathern, M. 1972. *Official and unofficial courts: Legal assumptions and expectations in a Highlands community.* New Guinea Research Unit Bulletin No. 47. Canberra: Australian National University.

Ward, A. 1991. Interpreting the Treaty of Waitangi: The Maori resurgence and race relations in New Zealand. *The Contemporary Pacific* 3: 85–113.

Watson-Gegeo, K. A., and G. M. White, eds. 1990. *Disentangling: Conflict discourse in Pacific societies.* Stanford, Calif.: Stanford University Press.

West, P. 2006. *Conservation is our government now: The politics of ecology in Papua New Guinea.* Durham, N.C., and London: Duke University Press.

Westermark, G. 1978. Village courts in question: The nature of court procedure. *Melanesian Law Journal* 6: 79–96.

White, G. M., and L. Lindstrom. 1993. Custom today. Special issue of *Anthropological Forum* 6(4).

Whitehouse, H. 1996. From possession to apotheosis: Transformation and disguise in the leadership of a cargo movement. In *Leadership and change in the Western Pacific,* ed. R. Feinberg and K. A. Watson-Gegeo, 376–397. London: Athlone.

Zorn, J. G. 1990. Customary law in the Papua New Guinea village courts. *The Contemporary Pacific* 2: 279–311.

Religion

John Barker

18

What is "Oceanic religion"? Until recently many scholars restricted the term to the religions of Pacific Islanders as they existed before extensive European contact. They wrote of mission Christianity as an intrusive force and sought to explain a variety of postcontact religious movements as indigenous responses to colonialism. Today, with Christianity entrenched across the region, a sharp distinction between indigenous and foreign religions is no longer viable.

For most Pacific Islanders, the religion of the present is a complex and ever-changing mix of local and imported elements. In some cases, especially where missionaries have only recently been at work, the "traditional" and "Christian" may be readily distinguished (Knauft 2002; Robbins 2004). More often one encounters situations such as on Ujelang in the Marshall Islands (Carucci 1997). The people of this isolated atoll dedicate four months each year to competitive singing, dances and games, and feasts. The ritual season climaxes on December 25 and the first Sunday of the new year. On these days the community lavishes food upon their minister, whom they expect, as with the chiefs of old, to keep some for his own use and redistribute the rest among the congregation. Laurence Carucci shows that the Ujelang way of celebrating Christmas parallels pre-Christian rituals meant to assure prosperity. But this Christmas celebration also incorporates and speaks to the Ujelang people's experience of successive colonial regimes, of displacements during the Second World War and nuclear testing years, of a commitment to Congregational Christianity, and of a desire to be culturally distinct within Micronesia. Christmas on Ujelang turns out to be about a lot of things.

Such mixings and fusions are common across the Pacific Islands (Figure 18.1). On the surface at least they reflect the inroads made by Western ideas and practices upon Oceanic cultures. At a deeper level, however, they are the living productions of a profoundly experiential and flexible appreciation of the spiritual that long predates the exploration and conquest of the region by Europeans. Spectacular instances of religious transformation in indigenous religious practices are well known. Many New Guinea people, for instance, traded magic, mythologies, and even whole ritual complexes with their neighbors (Harrison 1993). From premissionary Hawai'i we have the fascinating example of Queen Ka'ahumanu, who in 1819 instigated the overthrow of the elaborate system of ritual prohibitions that had previously separated men from women, nobles from commoners (Howe 1984: 163–168).

Early observers often portrayed islanders as slaves to unchanging customs. This stereotype suited the colonial project (see Thomas 1994). More careful historical and ethnographic work, however, has revealed the highly innovative, often performative quality of Oceanic religions (e.g., Schieffelin 1976; Wagner 1972). Paradoxically, this very openness has allowed many aspects of older indigenous religions to continue into the present, insinuated into Christian forms and more visibly syncretic religious movements such as the famed Melanesian "cargo cults."

There is no aspect of Oceania more difficult to generalize about than religion. In part, this has to do with the cultural diversity, the mix of historical influences, and the inventiveness of local religious expressions across the region. But it also has to do with the extraordinary attention outsiders have paid to Oceanic religion over the years. Turn to any standard regional bibliography and you will find hundreds of articles and books dealing with religion (e.g., Fry and Maurico 1987; Haynes and Wuerch 1995; Taylor 1965). There is a staggering amount of detailed information on virtually every aspect of religion from every corner of this vast region, yet there have been few published overviews of religion in Oceania. The most comprehensive is an essay by Garry Trompf, the pre-eminent scholar of Oceanic religions today, which surveys traditional religions, "cults of intrusion," and Christianity and provides a useful annotated bibliography (Swain and Trompf 1995). Excellent entries on Micronesian, Melanesian, Polynesian, and Oceanic religions, as well as a historic overview of religious scholarship in the region, can be found in Mircea Eliade's *Encyclopedia of Religion* (Eliade 1987). John Garrett (1982, 1992, 1997) has written the most comprehensive history of missionary efforts and the establishment of national churches. Manfred Ernst (1994,

Figure 18.1. *Atiu island woman, dancing in church during New Year celebration (photo MR).*

2006) and his colleagues have provided comprehensive surveys of organized religion on a country-by-country basis. Several fine surveys of millenarian movements exist, mostly focused upon Melanesian cargo cults (Burridge 1969; Worsley 1968). Finally, mention should be made of Trompf's important surveys of Melanesian religion in general (1991) and the theme of moral retribution ("payback") in particular (1994). Such studies are extremely helpful. Still, given the enormous richness of the materials available, the paucity of studies of religion above the level of local culture is striking.

I do not attempt a comprehensive account of Oceanic religion here. Instead, I confine myself to some general observations and themes, although along different lines than those pursued by Trompf (Swain and Trompf 1995). For convenience, I define three roughly distinguished historical contexts: indigenous religions as they existed around the time of contact with Europeans; religious practices and beliefs after contact, particularly as influenced by Christian missionaries and indigenous religious leaders; and the contemporary situation, simultaneously marked by a renewal of ancient religious forms and a new wave of Christian missionary efforts. Readers should be aware that this is at best a useful fiction. Oceanic peoples experienced European contact in vastly different circumstances over a time period ranging from the sixteenth century to the late 1960s. Further, indigenous peoples in settler colonies like New Zealand, Hawai'i, and New Caledonia had a markedly different and generally more brutal experience of colonialism than people elsewhere who remained majorities in possession of their own lands. Finally, the religious expressions described here under the three "periods" may all be witnessed today, often in the same places.

Oceanic Religions at Contact

In this section and the next I use the "ethnographic past" voice to indicate that much of what I'm describing is based upon studies of pre-Christian societies. As I have already noted, however, many aspects of "traditional" religions continue into the present.

Different as the religious systems were, most elaborated a few basic themes:

Intimacy of the Spiritual World

Everywhere in Oceania people lived in intimate proximity to spiritual influences and entities (Figure 18.2). No one has described the "enchantment" of the Oceanic landscape with greater elegance than the missionary-ethnographer Maurice Leenhardt, who studied the relationships between myth and the land in New Caledonia (Leenhardt 1979). His observations are broadly applicable. The Maisin people of Oro Province in Papua New Guinea, with whom I have worked, sacrificed to the ancestors whenever they started new gardens; walked quietly around certain pools, glades, and swamps, the continuing residences of the heroes of their myths; told of encounters with monsters in the deep forest; and manipulated certain foods and materials to attain or avoid spiritual powers (Barker 2007). This is not to say that Maisin, any more than other Oceanic people, walked in fear of ghosts, sprites, and things that go bump in the night. The numinous was an expected part of everyday life—not good or bad, but simply an unavoidable reality. One day when

walking to a remote garden, I observed to a Maisin friend that we had come a long way from other people. He replied flatly that we were hardly alone; we were entirely surrounded by spirits. And so we were.

Figure 18.2. In the Tuamotus, interatoll voyages always begin with a prayer (photo MR).

In Polynesia and eastern Melanesia spiritual intimacy was conveyed most powerfully in the related concepts of *mana* and *tabu*. *Mana* can be understood as the manifestation of godly power in this life. Entities that generate or that order may be described as having or enacting *mana*. In Polynesia, *mana* proclaimed itself in images of abundance, of which perhaps the most spectacular were the chiefs themselves, whose "beauty" was marked by bright costumes, brilliant rituals, generous gifts to the people, and often marked corpulence (Shore 1989: 138–139). People throughout the region associated "chiefly" with agricultural fecundity in a wide variety of ways. In Tikopia, as elsewhere, a chief received the first fruits of gardens in community ceremonies and enjoyed precedence in eating as he was "terrestrial agent for the god—bestowing food, and hence 'owner' of all resources" (Firth 1936: 482). A person, thing, or place manifesting *mana* was surrounded and constrained by ritual prohibitions (*tabu*), meant to prevent contagion from (and to) less sacred entities. By virtue of their godly *mana*, chiefs not only proclaimed *tabu*s over resources, such as coconuts, but they also were *tabu* themselves to less sacred persons. Hawaiian chiefs, for instance, maintained an elaborate system of food and etiquette restrictions meant to protect their *mana* from the deleterious effects of commoners and members of the other gender.

There was no clear line between the spiritual and human in indigenous religions. Those engaging or encountering spiritual powers took on aspects of the spiritual themselves. In Melanesian societies, those wishing to use magic for hunting, gardening, healing, or attacking enemies had to prepare by avoiding foods and substances that might "cool" their bodies and undergoing disciplines to "heat" themselves up. Once prepared, they themselves became spiritually dangerous to others. Since serious illness or accidents in most places were understood to have spiritual causes, humans—acting as sorcerers and witches—were widely believed to have the ability to bring illness, accidents, and death to others (Fortune 1932). The sorcerer's power, however, was not entirely willful. In the southern Papuan society of Mekeo and elsewhere, one could get very sick merely by approaching a sorcerer without proper precautions. The sorcerer, witch, shaman, and magician acted as visible entry points for spiritual power in human society: power that as humans they could influence but not completely control. The greatest sorcerers/healers in Mekeo were called "men of sadness," in part because of the toll that constant engagement in the spiritual took upon their social relations and their bodies. They were simultaneously terrifying and tragic (Stephen 1995; cf. Young 1983).

The Autonomy of Spirits

Early missionaries sometimes accused Oceanic peoples of "worshiping" spirits and gods. Everywhere, however, attitudes toward spiritual beings were far more ambivalent than this would suggest. On the Micronesian atoll of Ifaluk, people openly spoke of their hate for and fear of the ghosts that bedeviled their lives (Spiro 1952). In communities on Manus Island in Papua New Guinea, "Sir Ghost," the spirit of a recently departed father, maintained a brooding watch over the economic activities of every household (Fortune 1936). In Hawai'i, commoners welcomed the annual return of Lono with orgiastic rites, only to witness the slaying of the god by their human king (Sahlins 1985). In these different cases we witness a desire to influence spiritual entities that are recognized as having powers beyond human understanding or control.

Students of Oceanic religion distinguish between varieties of spiritual entities. We can roughly arrange these into a continuum ranging from those closest to those furthest away from living humans roughly as follows: ghosts, ancestral spirits, nonhuman spirits, culture heroes, gods. In many places, ghosts would hang around villages following a death, both helping and hurting individuals and households. Among the Maisin, for instance, a recently deceased father might visit a daughter in a dream to advise her of a good place to plant a garden or to request a certain name for a baby, but the same ghost feeling lonely might just as easily take the soul of a newborn. Ancestral spirits or gods could be just as capricious and unpredictable, but because they had far greater power than ghosts, they had to be appealed to in larger communal ceremonies. Given the common experiences of violence and uncertainty of health and food in many areas, many communal rituals were directed at the fickle deities influencing war and fertility (Mageo and Howard 1996).

Scholars have long noticed the general correspondence between social organization and cosmology. In the hierarchically organized societies of Polynesia, religious worldviews were "vertically" oriented, focused upon deities who created the world and founded the chiefly lines of descent (Swain and Trompf 1995). Trompf cautions us not to draw too strong a contrast with the small-scale societies elsewhere in the Pacific, noting the presence of high gods in several Melanesian and Micronesian communities. Still, in general, Melanesian cosmologies tended to have a more "lateral" emphasis, in which ancestral and nonhuman spiritual forces occupied the near landscape rather than the sky or distant horizon.

The Transformative Power of Ritual

Ritual can be defined as a set of formalized behaviors that, when used properly, harness spiritual power in such a way as to bring about a transformation in the empirical world. Ritual is thus often provisional—open to modification and experimentation.

Magic and sacrifices were probably the most common rituals carried out in daily life. Islanders gathered special substances and chanted incantations to aid the growth of food in the gardens, to strengthen the abilities of dogs to track game, to attract fish into nets, and to undertake a wide variety of other necessary subsistence activities (Malinowski 1954). In most places, people also made use of magic to deal with the uncertainties of romances and conflicts. In colonial times, Melanesians adapted magic to aid and protect their teams during soccer or cricket matches. Everywhere, islanders made sacrifices of food and wealth to spirits and gods, mirroring the exchanges that guided human morality. In giving tribute to their chiefs, Polynesians gave to the gods. In turn, the gods, through the chief, ideally redistributed the blessings of the land and sea back to the people, thus assuring bounty in the coming months (Firth 1970; Williamson 1933).

The most common communal rituals in villages centered on transformations in the life cycle: birth, sexual maturity, marriage, and death. Such occasions were often marked by massive feasts and exchanges as well as spectacular ceremonials (Figure 18.3). Weddings between aristocratic families in Tonga, for instance, occasioned huge celebrations during which meters upon meters of decorated bark cloths (tapa) were presented as gifts. In Melanesia, life transition ceremonies called for years of careful planning on the part of ambitious leaders: the planting of special gardens, the raising of suitably fat village pigs, the careful cultivation of allies who might be induced to make contributions. The elaborate male initiation ceremonies among the Ilahita Arapesh in the Sepik region, to take one example, thus also presented an opportunity for not-so-covert competition between political rivals (Tuzin 1980). The "secular" politics of ritual, however, should not blind us to their religious aspects. The beautiful mourning and memorial ceremonies performed for years after the death of important women and men in parts of New Britain and New Ireland, for instance, served to revitalize the people's connections with the ancestors by giving them a physical form among the living (Küchler 2002). One would first hear the unearthly "voices" of the ancestors from the bush before their eruption into the village clearing in the form of elaborate masked dancers. The death feasts were a communal sacrifice to the ancestors, assuring not only the safe passage of the recently deceased into the spiritual world but also the continuing reproduction and prosperity of human society (Errington 1974).

The work of spiritual transformation was often hard and dangerous. Public rituals could require huge outlays of labor, food, and wealth; last for weeks or months at a time; and impress observers

Figure 18.3. Traditional dancing by Maisin youth, Papua New Guinea. The distinctive decorations worn by the dancers are believed to have been set at the time of creation. Each clan has its own distinct tapa cloth designs and arrangements of shells and feathers. As they dance, the Maisin see and merge with their ancestors, bringing mythic memory to life (photo JB).

and participants alike with spectacular art and performances. Much of the Oceanic art in museums today provides exquisite testimony to the creative forces of island rituals. What such art cannot reveal is how islanders themselves became physically transformed in the larger public spectacles, particularly initiations and rites connected to the fostering of male aggressiveness and warfare. In various parts of Melanesia, young boys underwent terrifying hazing; permanently incised their bodies with exquisite tattoos and raised lacerations; ingested the semen of senior males to promote growth; or, most notoriously, consumed portions of the bodies of diseased relations or murdered enemies, seeking to imbibe something of their spiritual essence (Bateson 1958; Herdt 1984; Zegwaard 1959). The stakes involved in rituals of fertility, manhood, or warfare could be extraordinarily high. Failure could bring the wrath of gods and ancestral spirits upon a people, leading to famine, dissension, or massacre at the hands of enemies (e.g., Keesing 1992).

Rituals are the most visible and ordered of religious phenomena. For that reason, scholars have long been interested in their more general social functions in traditional societies. In the Trobriand Islands of Papua New Guinea, to take a well-studied example, Annette Weiner (1976) has argued that the elaborate exchanges of male and female wealth in mortuary ceremonies served to reproduce kin groups and gender distinctions over time, giving that society a marked cultural stability. In ancient Tahiti, on the other hand, virtually every kin, occupational, and political group "had its own more or less distinctive set of spirit tutelars, and a specific place, a *marae,* for interacting with them" (Oliver 1989: 907). In effect, Tahitian commoners typically owed allegiance both to the spirits of their natal kin groups and to the gods of their chief. The ornate rituals at chiefly *marae*s secured a chief's following while virtually guaranteeing conflict as he fought to gain other chiefs' congregations. Such contests were thus at once secular and religious. Priests and others who had special knowledge of the invisible world of the spirits and gods wielded extraordinary power.

Some students have looked for even wider functions. One of the best-known studies of ritual from Oceania is Roy Rappaport's (1984) *Pigs for the Ancestors.* Drawing on meticulous ethnographic detail, Rappaport argued that warfare and peacemaking rituals among the Maring of Papua New Guinea, at which large numbers of pigs were slaughtered and eaten, formed a cycle that kept the human population in balance with the carrying capacity of their mountain environment. The argument was provocative and remains controversial. Still, no one would disagree with Rappaport's primary insight: religion, including ritual, formed part of the fabric of traditional Oceanic societies. As such, it should be viewed as an integral component of a total ecological system.

Power and Knowledge

Religious attitudes are fostered not only in practices but also through what people know and imagine (Herdt and Stephen 1989). Knowledge of the spiritual was stored and passed on to new generations in a variety of forms and media. These included narratives (mythologies, legends, entertaining tales), songs and chants, magical incantations, and prayers. Corresponding to Western notions of literature, such forms were relatively easy to record and thus occupy a large part of the published works on Oceanic religions. In recent years, scholars have worked hard to understand this material in terms of the cultures that produced it (e.g., LeRoy 1985; Valeri 1985). But many religious narratives, such as the powerful Maori creation stories of Rangi (heaven) and Papa (earth), have a universal appeal and through the work of popular writers like Joseph Campbell have become widely known. The Papua New Guinea scholar John Waiko (1981) reminds us that knowledge of the spiritual was not confined to linear forms in traditional societies, but conveyed through all the senses (Gell 1993). It became manifest in material culture, in rituals, in the experience of mishaps, and in the very geography of one's surroundings. Some of the most innovative work on Oceanic religion today explores the myriad ways such knowledge was created, communicated, and remembered (Barth 1975; Battaglia 1990; Biersack 1996).

In a classic article on the Baloma spirits of the Trobriand Islands, Bronislaw Malinowski (1954) observed that knowledge of the spiritual was not distributed evenly. People differed in what they knew. Just as important, only a few people developed specialized esoteric knowledge. As Lamont Lindstrom (1990) shows in an important study of the Tanna Islanders of Vanuatu, the lineaments of knowledge and power often run in parallel courses. The small-scale societies of Melanesia are famed for the relative weakness of leaders, particularly compared with the ranked and sometimes stratified societies that formed in parts of Micronesia and Polynesia. Melanesians almost universally embraced ethics based upon the common practice of reciprocal exchange (Mauss 1990 [1925]). Anthropologists have sometimes called Melanesian societies "egalitarian," a confusing description that obscures the fierce competitive spirit and resulting inequalities that characterized much of the region. In the never-ending game of exchanges, the man or woman who gardens better, gives away more food, speaks eloquently, fights fiercely, or, especially, possesses esoteric knowledge gains important advantages. At the same time, he or she becomes vulnerable to the attacks of competitors. Sorcerers and witches were the great levelers in Melanesian societies, since they tended to attack individuals who stood out from others in possessions or abilities (Fortune 1932). In some places, however, leaders known to be sorcerers achieved almost despotic power through terror (Young 1983).

The elaborate male initiation rites carried out in many Melanesian societies also often involved secret knowledge, sometimes revealed to initiates only after they had passed through six or seven stages and had become old men themselves (Barth 1975; Tuzin 1980). The male cults ordered members into ranks based on their degree of initiation. They also articulated a sharp distinction between male and female. There has been much discussion among scholars, however, as to whether the gender distinction is best understood as a straightforward expression of male domination or of gender complementarity (Bonnemère 2004; Errington and Gewertz 1987). The lineaments of power were even more overt in the ranked societies of Polynesia and high-island Micronesia. Here priestly specialization, which reached its climax in the temple complexes of Tahiti and Hawai'i, reinforced an essentialized difference between the aristocratic elite and everyone else (Goldman 1970).

Religious assumptions did not merely reinforce political structures in Oceania; they formed one set of elements in ever-shifting political arrangements, constantly subject to modification. Not only might the whims of the gods change during a war, new gods or spiritual forces might reveal themselves. This explains why the arrival of Europeans in the Pacific Islands simultaneously posed a political and a religious challenge to Oceanic peoples. The Hawaiians identified Captain Cook with their god Lono, but in a new guise signaling unpredictable consequences (Sahlins 1985). Some interior peoples of New Guinea had myths warning of spirits that would enter the land from the south and bring about the destruction of the world; when the first colonial patrol emerged out of the rain forest in the 1930s, these people faced the stark choice of beating back these harbingers of doom or fleeing (Schieffelin and Crittenden 1991). For their part, a large contingent of Europeans—the Christian missionaries—were indeed committed to bringing a new religious "truth" to the islanders, one they hoped would displace indigenous understandings of the spiritual. They did not entirely succeed, but their efforts changed the religious lives of Oceanic peoples forever.

Mission Christianity and Postcontact Religious Movements

Apart from early Spanish missionary efforts in Guam and some of the Carolines, the mission era began in 1797 when the newly formed London Missionary Society sent a shipload of lay missionaries to Tahiti (Gunson 1978). Over the course of the next century, virtually all the major denominations of Western Europe and its settler colonies staked claims in the Pacific Islands. Roman Catholic and Protestant orders competed to win souls, but for the most part the Protestants respected each other's zones of influence, resulting in a geography of denominational affiliations that is reflected in the national churches of today. Missionaries were among the first whites to settle in the islands, often years before colonial powers took control.

As they became familiar with local political alignments and learned the vernacular, missionaries became brokers manipulated by the factions struggling to control the islands. In Tahiti, Tonga, and Fiji, newly converted chiefs found their alliances with the newcomers useful in conquering their rivals and unifying the islands for the first time (Barker 2005). After the colonial powers took over, the missionaries continued to play the role of broker. In most places, they provided the basic social services of schooling and medicine. Colonial administrators, always stretched for resources, regarded missions as a necessary if not always entirely reliable part of the apparatus needed to control and "civilize" native populations (Thomas 1994). And, indeed, missions were instrumental not only in teaching native populations the "three Rs" but, at a more fundamental level, familiarizing them with Western notions of time, space, and authority (Knauft 2002; Smith 1982).

A small number of Europeans directed and consolidated mission work in most places. The main bearers of the new religion, however, were almost always Pacific Island converts. In 1821, John Williams of the London Missionary Society began the "native agency," a small group of trusted converts who were sent out to settle in non-Christian areas, often at great risk to their own lives. Over the succeeding decades of the nineteenth and early twentieth centuries, Tongans preached the gospel to Fijians, Samoans found converts in Tuvalu, and Hawaiians spread American Congregationalism across central Micronesia (Lange 2005). In a massive effort, hundreds of Polynesian and eastern Melanesian missionaries introduced Christianity in the small coastal communities of Papua New Guinea under the banners of a half-dozen denominations. Many of these dedicated men and women were buried there, victims of disease, poor nutrition, and sometimes violence (Crocombe and Crocombe 1982).

As each new mission base was consolidated, another army of indigenous teachers, evangelists, and clergy set out for the next village, valley, or island. Most New Guinea Highlanders thus heard of Christianity from coastal converts who settled among them (Radford 1987). The ever-growing mission networks created a conduit for the diffusion of plants, domesticated animals, technologies, and cultural practices from the central Pacific to the peripheries (Latukefu 1978). It is not correct, then, to see conversion in Oceania simply as an encounter between indigenous and Western cultures. Almost everywhere, islanders acted as mediators, reinterpreting Christianity according to local cultural orientations and values (Brock 2005). The type of Christianity taught by hierarchically oriented Polynesian missionaries in Papua New Guinea thus differed profoundly from the styles adopted by their Melanesian brethren and often clashed with the wishes of their European supervisors (Wetherell 1978, 1980, 1989).

Compared with other mission fields, Christianity spread across Oceania with amazing rapidity. This is not to say, however, that the path of conversion was necessarily easy or smooth. Depending upon their theological and cultural backgrounds, missionaries found much to object to. There was universal condemnation of cannibalism, head-hunting, human sacrifice, and other ritual expressions of warrior cultures. Missionaries also frowned upon polygyny, sorcery, and many of the more elaborate rituals that they tended to see as expressions of "idolatry." Particularly before the establishment of colonial control over the islands, however, missionaries had limited abilities to do much more than condemn. The effective agents of change were often the core group of first converts. In many parts of Polynesia, the arrival of missionaries coincided with massive social and political turmoil, wars, and loss of population through introduced diseases. Such disasters weakened faith in the traditional deities while strengthening the position of those chiefs who aligned themselves with the new Christian god (Barker 2005).

In many places converts used their intimate knowledge of local beliefs to stage power encounters to demonstrate the superior power of the Christian god over ancestral spirits (Tippett 1967; Tuzin 1997). Converts desecrated ancestral shrines in parts of Solomon Islands, gathered and destroyed magical materials in public bonfires in Papuan villages, and broke into men's cult houses to reveal sacred masks and carvings to uninitiated boys and women (Burt 1994). The extraordinary firsthand account of the conversion of the Cook Islands written by the evangelist Maretu in 1871 reveals the importance of confrontation, coercion, and fear in the missionary campaign (Crocombe 1983). One should not paint too negative a picture, however. Missionaries also found much to admire in Oceanic cultures, which they compared favorably to the social ills of Europe (Thomas 1994); the early island proselytizers won over many converts through persuasion and dedication and are remembered fondly today; and, finally, for many, Christianity presented some protection from the more oppressive demands of indigenous religion and the disruptions of colonial change.

Even where new Christians cast off the visible signs of the old religion, there were continuities as they translated their new faith into culturally familiar terms. Thus Samoans and Tongans transformed the theologically egalitarian Congregationalist and Methodist missions into vehicles of hierarchy in which the pastor assumed the exalted place of the old chiefs and priests. Congregations showered their pastors with lavish gifts as a visible token of their devotion to God (Roach 1987). In Melanesia and Micronesia, people identified local sacred sites with biblical events—as Eden, the site of Christ's crucifixion, or Jerusalem. The old ancestral and bush spirits lived on in the guise of "devils"; Mary and other Christian figures come to people in dreams to warn of future events and to heal sickness; and even God could be reconfigured as a kind of super sorcerer (Barker 1990, 1992; Boutilier, Hughes, and Tiffany 1978).

On the mission and colonial frontiers, and often beyond them, indigenous prophets inspired independent religious movements that often merged aspects of indigenous religions with elements of Christianity and Western practices in response to the various crises brought on by contact. In New Zealand, conflicts between Maori and the growing white population, especially over the expropriation of land, led certain prophets to reject missionary readings of the Bible in favor of interpretations more in accord with their own epistemology and experience. Te Ua Haumene gained the first large following. Inspired by the angel Gabriel, Te Ua taught that the Maori were the true chosen people of Jehovah, whom they could call upon to defeat the Europeans. Many of his followers believed that the prophet's rituals and spells would grant them immunity from European bullets, a belief they put into practice (with disastrous results in the Maori Wars of 1864–1865). Te Ua's Pai Marire ("good and peaceful") movement inspired the later King movement and the Ringatu Church (Clark 1975). Since Te Ua's day, Maori prophets have continued to inspire new movements and churches, the most important being the Ratana church, begun in the 1920s. Strongly separatist, such movements and churches have drawn upon Maori culture and distinct readings of the Bible, framing the political and social challenges Maori face in religious terms (Sinclair 1990).

Similar if less enduring religious movements occurred in Tahiti, Samoa, Fiji, and elsewhere. They were almost always countered by colonialist reprisals. Missionaries and government officials usually regarded independent religious movements as retrograde descents into "superstition," as forms of collective "madness" and, worst, serious challenges to their own authority. In an important study of the Fijian prophet Navosavakadua, of the 1880s "Tuka Cult," Martha Kaplan (1995) directs our attention to the roles colonialists played in the shaping of religious movements. In the case of the Tuka movement, the prophet and his followers developed their message and actions partly in the face of unrelenting hostility on the part of the colonial authorities and their chiefly allies. More important over the long term, the authorities committed their reified understanding of the Tuka cult to the official record. The definition served to legitimize the temporary removal of Navosavakadua's followers to a distant island and close surveillance of their activities after their return. It also led scholars to misread the Tuka as an early form of a cargo cult.

The reality that religious movements emerged and dissolved along the colonial frontier, pushed and pulled by a multitude of different influences, challenges any easy interpretation. At the same time, it adds to their exotic and dramatic appeal. This is especially apparent with the famed "cargo cults" of Melanesia. Early in the twentieth century, colonial observers reported strange ritual movements among some coastal New Guineans. The best known was the "Vailala Madness," so described by the Papuan government anthropologist F. E. Williams (1923), who investigated several religious movements in the region. In the Gulf of Papua, prophets convinced large numbers of people that their ancestors could be induced to return to life if the proper preparations were made. They would come in ships bearing vast quantities of the material goods—"cargo"—enjoyed by European colonialists. To hasten the event, villagers performed rituals mimicking European actions. They held marching drills, erected "radio masts" to receive messages from the ancestors, and constructed wharves. Williams attributed such behavior to an awe of the "superior" culture of the Europeans. He was far more concerned that adherents fell into ecstatic trances, writhing on the ground and shouting out apparently meaningless words. In his view, this was nothing less than mass psychosis.

The "Madness" was suppressed, but reports of apparently similar "cults" continued to be filed in succeeding years. Cargo figured in only a minor way in several of these, notably the "Taro cult" in Papua and Maasina Rule in Solomon Islands (Laracy 1983; Williams 1928). With the end of World War II and the expulsion of Japanese forces from northern Melanesia, religious movements like that at Vailala broke out in several widespread regions and on a much greater scale. It was around this time that some unknown resident invented the memorable phrase "cargo cult," which quickly entered into common parlance (Lindstrom 1993). The most important movements centered on the prophets Yali in Madang, Paliau on Manus Island, and Yaliwan in the East Sepik—all in Papua New Guinea—and the mysterious figure of Jon Frum on Tanna Island in Vanuatu. These and other movements received considerable attention, not least from the postwar generation of anthropologists who made them into their special study.

No subject in Oceanic religion has attracted as much attention and exercised as many intellectual muscles as the cargo cults. Most administrators thought that the cults reflected an ignorance of the workings of the capitalist economy and would fade as education and experience improved. Anthropologists detected in the patterns of the movements deeper inherent rationalities. Peter Worsley (1968) saw the cults as, in part, protests against European hegemony that in some cases, notably Maasina Rule, functioned to draw people from different cultural and linguistic backgrounds into emergent nationalist movements. In a superbly detailed study of Yali, Peter Lawrence (1964) argued that the cults should be understood as modern expressions of a traditional ideology that would remain convincing to Melanesians until the rural economy underwent serious change. Kenelm Burridge (1960), writing about the same area, understood cargoism in more religious terms, as a redemptive quest to re-establish the moral reciprocities between white men and Melanesians that, according to indigenous myths, existed at the beginning of time. Developing an earlier line of argument advanced by V. Lanternari (1963), Andrew Lattas (1998) has analyzed cargo narratives as symbolic representations of the experience of oppression, while Trompf (1994) has argued that the movements should be understood as native reprisals against colonial domination.

Even as cargo cult studies proliferated at a pace with the "cults" themselves, scholars began to express some doubt about the concept. Some worry about its empirical fitness: many different kinds of religious movements, some of which have little explicitly to do with cargo, get lumped into the category; there is also a tendency to see every local economic endeavor, from trade stores to regional cooperative societies, as a nascent cargo cult. Others consider the term itself a slander demeaning Melanesian peoples. The most serious challenge to cargo cult studies comes from a book by Lamont Lindstrom (1993), which convincingly illustrates the ways Western obsessions and desires about commodities, mixed with assumptions about cultural "others," have insinuated themselves into discussions about cargoism. Whatever we might choose to call them, religious movements continue to emerge in Melanesia. Cargo cults and other variants of indigenous religious movements will continue to challenge understanding for the foreseeable future (e.g., Harkin 2004; Jebens 2004).

Oceanic Religion Today

By 1960, when the Pacific Islands were in the early stages of decolonization, Christianity had become the "traditional" religion of most islanders. In Polynesia and the longer-contacted areas of Micronesia and Melanesia, churches formed the social and often political center of village life, while in many places missions operated most of the schools and medical facilities. The Protestant churches were in an advanced stage of localization as islander clergy rose through the ranks and metropolitan mission societies devolved authority to the emerging national churches (Figure 18.4). Localization of the Roman Catholic Church has proceeded much more slowly due to the difficulty of finding clergy willing to dedicate themselves to lifelong celibacy and the authority structure of the church itself. Even here, however, the ranks of indigenous clergy

Figure 18.4. Minister of Congregationalist Church, Atiu, Cook Islands (photos MR).

have gradually increased and those of religious orders even faster. By the early 1960s, the attitudes of the mission churches toward indigenous culture had softened markedly from the early days. This was mainly a long-term local evolution, the product of a century or more of accommodations to indigenous customs and orientations. A change was more dramatically signaled by policies adopted by the international missions and churches, most notably the embrace of the doctrine of "inculturation" by the Roman Catholic Church in the wake of the Vatican II Council. Experiments incorporating indigenous art, music, and architectural forms into Christian worship began, while students at island theological colleges were encouraged to seek out the resonances between Pacific and Christian religious ideas in their theses. The more daring clergy even talked about reviving pre-Christian rituals that had been banned by their predecessors as "heathenish," much to the confusion of their older parishioners (Arbuckle 1978).

In terms of church membership, the Pacific Islands today are among the most thoroughly Christianized regions of the world. The surveys conducted by Manfred Ernst (1994, 2006) and his colleagues suggest that well over 90 percent of indigenous Pacific Island populations formally belong to a church. Even in Papua New Guinea, long considered the stronghold of traditional religion given its remarkable cultural diversity and remoteness of many of its communities, the official rate of church membership according to the 2000 census is a staggering 96 percent (Gibbs 2006: 98). The religious scene today, however, is far more diverse than it was forty years ago. While a solid majority of islanders belong to one or another of the "mainline" churches—the descendants of the early missions—a growing number have been joining a diverse group of rival denominations. Some of the most popular have had a long history in the region but only recently enjoyed exponential growth, notably the Church of Jesus Christ of Latter-day Saints (Mormons), the Seventh-day Adventist Church, and the Assemblies of God. They have been joined by a large assortment of mainly conservative Evangelical, Fundamentalist, and Pentecostal sects, most of them very small, which have swept through the region, forming a new wave of missionary outreach. The theological particulars of these groups vary immensely, but they mostly share a strongly individualist ethic, a personal commitment to their faith and church, and an abiding suspicion if not outright hostility toward a wide array of indigenous customs deemed "un-Christian" (Jebens 2005; Jorgensen 2005; Robbins 2004).

Alternatives to institutional Christianity exist, although they occupy a tiny part of the religious spectrum among indigenous islanders. Small populations of traditionalists as yet unreached by or resistant to missionaries continue to exist in remote parts of Melanesia (Keesing 1992). A few local religious movements in Melanesia have evolved into more stable associations, which along with the much larger Maori churches form some of the few stable indigenous religious organizations in the region. By far the most internationally famous is the John Frum Movement—a long-lasting "cargo cult" with about eight thousand adherents on the island of Tanna in Vanuatu. It is regularly visited by tourists and journalists and was recently featured in a tongue-in-cheek documentary in which several members visit Britain, commenting upon strange customs of its natives, and meet with Prince Philip, whom they regard as a son of God (Adams 2007). Small congregations of the Bahá'í faith exist in most Pacific countries. Despite the presence of large numbers of Muslim migrants in the Indonesian province of West Papua and Hindu and Muslim Indians in Fiji (descendants of laborers brought to that country during the colonial period), the indigenous populations remain overwhelmingly Christian. Mosques have recently been built in Papua New Guinea and Vanuatu, although to date they draw most of their followers from the immigrant Asian population.

Secularism has also made inroads on Christianity across the region, reflected not so much in the numbers of declared atheists and agnostics as shifting government policies and public attitudes. With the significant exception of Indonesia—which recognizes six official religions (including Protestantism and Catholicism but not indigenous "animist" religions)—Pacific Island nations officially accept the principle of freedom of religion. Some leaders of the mainline churches have called for restrictions on the activities of their "Third Wave" rivals, but most islanders appear to have become tolerant of growing denominational diversity, and such proposals have not gotten far. The scope of church involvement in public life has also become more restricted over time. Where they don't run schools outright, governments set most of the educational curricula and have assumed much of the responsibility for health care, areas largely left to the missions during the colonial period. Perhaps most important, islanders are becoming increasingly exposed to people holding different religious views or no religion at all. This has long been the case in places like Hawai'i or New Zealand, but is also true for the massive numbers of islanders who have migrated to urban centers or abroad in recent decades and even for rural populations as radio, television, and Internet networks expand. The same globalizing forces that have enabled "Third Wave" evangelism in the region may also work to undermine the overall force of religion in people's lives simply by presenting them with more options and, as important, a means to escape the hold of long-established local churches.

Despite such changes, Christianity has a much more profound presence and influence than in most Western countries. In many rural areas, church services and offices are closely aligned with customary leadership and associated rituals (Toren 2006). In Samoa, for instance, ministers of the mainline churches receive similar formal greetings and regular gifts from villagers as traditional chiefs. The authority of Anglican priests and bishops in Solomon Islands rests as much on their embodiment of *mana* as on their knowledge of the Scriptures (White 1991). In rural and urban areas alike, churches provide for much of civil society in Pacific Island nations. Beyond generally well-attended church services, the larger public festivals tend to occur on the major days of the church calendar such as Christmas, Easter, or the anniversary of the arrival of the first missionaries (Errington and Gewertz 1994). The churches have spawned a huge number of voluntary organizations, devoted to both devotional and social causes. The most popular are church women's associations, which engage in activities such as organizing church festivals, fundraising in support of local church and social projects, and campaigns against alcohol and drug abuse (Douglas 2003). At the national and regional levels, the churches have also sponsored a wide range of nongovernmental organizations focused upon a variety of social and political causes including social justice, sustainable development and environmental conservation, and health policies in the areas of sexually transmitted diseases. Finally, at the regional and global level, churches often provide a link to the home islands for the massive numbers of islanders who have left their homes and settled permanently in New Zealand, Hawai'i and the U.S. mainland, and elsewhere (Allen 2001).

Not surprising in this environment, political appeals to Christian identity are common. Long God Yumi Stanap ("in God we stand") is the official motto of Vanuatu, matching Samoa's Fa'avae i le Atua Samoa ("God be the foundation of Samoa"), and Papua New Guinea's constitutional recognition of "Christian principles that are ours now." Indigenous clergy have frequently played prominent roles in nationalist struggles. Walter Lini, the first prime minister of Vanuatu, was an Anglican priest; Jean-Marie Tjibaou, a charismatic leader of the Kanak independence movement in New Caledonia before his assassination in 1989, was a former Catholic priest; and church leaders in the Indonesian province of West Papua play a delicate but key role mediating between the state and a largely resistant indigenous population (Rutherford 2006). In Melanesian countries especially, Christian values along with promises of economic development provide politicians with a means to appeal across multiple linguistic and cultural boundaries. Such appeals, however, can be as divisive as unifying. Church authorities occasionally intrude directly into politics, but sectarian rivalries mainly take shape in contests between political candidates during elections and in debates on legislation and policies. In recent elections in Papua New Guinea, for instance, many candidates have appealed to "Christian" values to advance positions reflecting the preferences of their own denominations such as laws banning missionaries from rival groups, state funding of approved churches, and restrictions on the distribution of birth control devices and education (Gibbs 2004).

While open sectarian conflict is rare, religious loyalties may inflame ethnic, nationalist, and other tensions. Thus the long-established minority community of Muslim Papuans on the far west coast of Indonesian New Guinea find themselves squeezed between loyalty to their religion and the increasingly Christian identity of the nationalist movement in West Papua (Jaap Timmer, personal communication). In Fiji, the churches have become entangled in often bitter struggles between indigenous nationalists and the descendants of Indian indentured laborers, most of whom are Hindu, Sikh, or Muslim. Given the strong association of Christianity with indigenous Fijian culture and identity, it is not surprising that many—probably most—indigenous Fijians conflate their religious identity with a desire to remain the dominant political force in the country. At the extreme edge of opinion, one finds nationalists who regard Fiji as a Christian nation and call for the expulsion of Indo-Fijians. In the face of such sentiments, however, prominent religious leaders from both ethnic communities have called for understanding and reconciliation, and this is also the official stance of the government (Hock 2006; Newland 2006).

From the time of earliest human settlement, Oceania has been a meeting place for cultures. As this chapter demonstrates, religious insights and experiences formed an essential part of indigenous life in the past and will continue to form a key lens through which Pacific peoples understand and shape their destiny for the foreseeable future. Research on religion has always held a fundamental priority in Oceanic studies, resulting in a massive database of ethnographic, historical, literary, and artistic productions. Oceanic religious experience has been too complex and diverse to be accommodated within a single academic discipline. Anthropology, history, psychology, missiology, religious studies, and geography, among others, have all made their contributions. Much of this material, in the form of books, films, and recordings, has made its way back into Pacific communities, where it is adding yet another dimension to religious understandings and creativity. Ironically, the work of outside scholars has dominated discussions of Oceanic religions, often drowning out the voices of the people themselves. As Pacific Islanders, scholars and laypeople alike, reappropriate their religious traditions, we can look forward to the emergence of new insights into the spiritual dimensions of human existence. The literature on Oceanic religion has reached that point of richness where one can begin to appreciate how much more there is to learn.

BIBLIOGRAPHY

Adams, G. 2007. Strange island: Pacific tribesmen come to study Britain. *The Independent,* http://news.independent.co.uk/uk/this_britain/article2932252.ece. Accessed January 3, 2008.

Allen, L. 2001. Participation as resistance: The role of Pentecostal Christianity in maintaining identity for Marshallese migrants living in the midwestern United States. *Journal of Ritual Studies* 15: 55–61.

Arbuckle, G. A. 1978. The impact of Vatican II on the Marists in Oceania. In *Mission, church and sect in Oceania,* ed. J. A. Boutilier, D. T. Hughes, and S. W. Tiffany, 275–299. Ann Arbor: University of Michigan Press.

Barker, J., ed. 1990. *Christianity in Oceania: Ethnographic perspectives.* Asao monograph no. 12. Lanham, Md.: University Press of America.

———. 1992. Christianity in western Melanesian ethnography. In *History and tradition in Melanesian anthropology,* ed. J. Carrier, 144–173. Berkeley: University of California Press.

———. 2005. Where the missionary frontier ran ahead of empire. In *Missions and empire,* ed. N. Etherington, 86–106. Oxford: Oxford University Press.

———. 2007. *Ancestral lines: The Maisin of Papua New Guinea and the fate of the rainforest.* Peterborough, Ont.: Broadview.

Barth, F. 1975. *Ritual and knowledge among the Baktamin of New Guinea.* New Haven, Conn.: Yale University Press.

Bateson, G. 1958. *Naven.* Stanford, Calif.: Stanford University Press.

Battaglia, D. 1990. *On the bones of the serpent: Person, memory, and mortality in Sabarl Island society.* Chicago: University of Chicago Press.

Biersack, A. 1996. Word made flesh: Religion, the economy, and the body in the Papua New Guinea Highlands. *History of Religions* 36: 85–111.

Bonnemère, P. 2004. *Women as unseen characters: Male ritual in Papua New Guinea.* Philadelphia: University of Pennsylvania Press.

Boutilier, J. A., D. T. Hughes, and S. W. Tiffany, eds. 1978. *Mission, church, and sect in Oceania.* Ann Arbor: University of Michigan Press.

Brock, P. 2005. New Christians as evangelists. In *Missions and empire,* ed. N. Etherington, 132–153. Oxford: Oxford University Press.

Burridge, K. 1960. *Mambu: A study of Melanesian cargo movements and their social and ideological background.* New York: Harper and Row.

———. 1969. *New heaven, new earth: A study of millenarian activities.* New York: Schocken.

Burt, B. 1994. *Tradition & Christianity: The colonial transformation of a Solomon Island society.* London: Harwood.

Carucci, L. M. 1997. *Nuclear nativity: Rituals of renewal and empowerment in the Marshall Islands.* DeKalb: Northern Illinois University Press.

Clark, P. 1975. *'Hauhau': The Pai Marire search for Maori identity.* Auckland: Auckland University Press.

Crocombe, M. 1983. *Cannibals and converts: Radical change in the Cook Islands.* Suva: Institute of Pacific Studies, University of the South Pacific.

Crocombe, R., and M. Crocombe, eds. 1982. *Polynesian missions in Melanesia.* Suva: Institute of Pacific Studies, University of the South Pacific.

Douglas, B., ed. 2003. *Women's groups and everyday modernity in Melanesia.* Oceania 74(1&2).

Eliade, M., ed. 1987. *Encyclopedia of religion.* New York: Macmillan.

Ernst, M. 1994. *Winds of change: Rapidly growing religious groups in the Pacific Islands.* Suva: Pacific Conference of Churches.

———, ed. 2006. *Globalization and the re-shaping of Christianity in the Pacific Islands.* Suva: Pacific Theological College.

Errington, F. K. 1974. *Karavar. Masks and power in a Melanesian ritual.* Ithaca, N.Y.: Cornell University Press.

Errington, F., and D. Gewertz. 1987. *Cultural alternatives and a feminist anthropology: An analysis of culturally constructed gender interests in Papua New Guinea.* Cambridge: Cambridge University Press.

———. 1994. From darkness to light in the George Brown jubilee: The invention of nontradition and the inscription of a national history in East New Britain. *American Ethnologist* 21: 104–122.

Firth, R. 1936. *We the Tikopia: A sociological study of kinship in primitive Polynesia.* London: Allen and Unwin.

———. 1970. *Rank and religion in Tikopia.* London: George Allen and Unwin.

Fortune, R. F. 1932. *Sorcerers of Dobu.* London: Routledge and Kegan Paul.

———. 1936. *Manus religion: An ethnological study of the Manus natives of the Admiralty Islands.* Philadelphia: American Philosophical Society.

Fry, G. W., and R. Maurico. 1987. *Pacific basin and Oceania.* Oxford: Clio.

Garrett, J. 1982. *To live among the stars: Christian origins in Oceania.* Geneva: World Council of Churches.

———. 1992. *Footsteps in the sea: Christianity in Oceania to World War II.* Suva: Institute of Pacific Studies.

———. 1997. *Where nets were cast: Christianity in Oceania since World War II.* Suva and Geneva: Institute of Pacific Studies, University of the South Pacific in association with the World Council of Churches.

Gell, A. 1993. *Wrapping in images: Tattooing in Polynesia.* Oxford: Oxford University Press.

Gibbs, P. 2004. Politics, religion, and the churches: The 2002 election in Papua New Guinea. *SSGM Working Papers,* http://rspas.anu.edu.au/papers/Melanesia/working_papers/04_02wp_Gibbs.pdf. Accessed January 10, 2008.

———. 2006. Papua New Guinea. In *Globalization and the re-shaping of Christianity in the Pacific Islands,* ed. M. Ernst, 81–158. Suva: Pacific Theological College.

Goldman, I. 1970. *Ancient Polynesian society.* Chicago: University of Chicago Press.

Gunson, N. 1978. *Messengers of grace: Evangelical missionaries in the South Seas, 1797–1860.* Melbourne: Melbourne University Press.

Harkin, M. E., ed. 2004. *Reassessing revitalization movements: Perspectives from North America and the Pacific Islands.* Lincoln: University of Nebraska Press.

Harrison, S. 1993. The commerce of cultures in Melanesia. *Man* 28: 139–158.

Haynes, D. E., and W. L. Wuerch. 1995. *Micronesian religion and lore: A guide to sources, 1526–1990.* Westport, Conn.: Greenwood Press.

Herdt, G. H., ed. 1984. *Rituals of manhood: Male initiation in Papua New Guinea.* Berkeley: University of California Press.

Herdt, G., and M. Stephen, eds. 1989. *The religious imagination in New Guinea.* New Brunswick, N.J.: Rutgers University Press.

Hock, K. 2006. Non-Christian religions in Fiji. In *Globalization and the re-shaping of Christianity in the Pacific Islands,* ed. M. Ernst, 390–439. Suva: Pacific Theological College.

Howe, K. R. 1984. *Where the waves fall: A new South Sea Islands history from first settlement to colonial rule.* Honolulu: University of Hawai'i Press.

Jebens, H., ed. 2004. *Cargo, cult, and culture critique.* Honolulu: University of Hawai'i Press.

———. 2005. *Pathways to heaven: Contesting mainline and fundamentalist Christianity in Papua New Guinea.* Oxford: Berghahn.

Jorgensen, D. 2005. Third wave evangelism and the politics of the global in Papua New Guinea: Spiritual warfare and the recreation of place in Telefolmin. *Oceania* 75: 444–461.

Kaplan, M. 1995. *Neither cargo nor cult: Ritual politics and the colonial imagination in Fiji.* Durham, N.C.: Duke University Press.

Keesing, R. M. 1992. *Custom and confrontation: The Kwaio struggle for cultural autonomy.* Chicago: University of Chicago Press.

Knauft, B. M. 2002. *Exchanging the past: A rainforest world of before & after.* Chicago: University of Chicago Press.

Küchler, S. 2002. *Malanggan: Art, memory and sacrifice.* Oxford: Berg.

Lange, R. 2005. *Island ministers: Indigenous leadership in nineteenth century Pacific Islands Christianity.* Canberra: Pandanus Books.

Lanternari, V. 1963. *The religions of the oppressed: A study of modern messianic cults.* New York: New American Library.

Laracy, H. 1983. *Pacific protest. The Maasina Rule movement. Solomon islands, 1944–1952.* Suva: Institute of Pacific Studies, University of the South Pacific.

Lattas, A. 1998. *Cultures of secrecy: Reinventing race in Bush Kaliai cargo cults.* Madison: University of Wisconsin Press.

Latukefu, S. 1978. The impact of South Sea Islands missionaries on Melanesia. In *Mission, church, and sect in Oceania,* ed. J. A. Boutilier, D. T. Hughes, and S. W. Tiffany, 91–108. Ann Arbor: University of Michigan Press.

Lawrence, P. 1964. *Road belong cargo: A study of the cargo movement in the southern Madang District, New Guinea.* Melbourne: Melbourne University Press.

Leenhardt, M. 1979. *Do kamo.* New York: Antheneum.

LeRoy, J. 1985. *Fabricated world.* Vancouver: University of British Columbia Press.

Lindstrom, L. 1990. *Knowledge and power in a South Pacific society.* Washington, D.C.: Smithsonian Institution Press.

———. 1993. *Cargo cult: Strange stories of desire from Melanesia and beyond.* Honolulu: University of Hawai'i Press.

Mageo, J. M., and A. Howard, eds. 1996. *Spirits in culture, history, and mind.* New York and London: Routledge.

Malinowski, B. 1954. *Science, magic and religion.* Garden City, N.Y.: Doubleday.

Mauss, M. 1990 [1925]. *The gift: The form and reason of exchange in primitive and archaic societies.* London: Routledge.

Newland, L. 2006. Fiji. In *Globalization and the re-shaping of Christianity in the Pacific Islands,* ed. M. Ernst, 317–389. Suva: Pacific Theological College.

Oliver, D. L. 1989. *Oceania: The native cultures of Australia and the Pacific Islands.* Honolulu: University of Hawai'i Press.

Radford, R. 1987. *Highlanders and foreigners in the upper Ramu: The Kainantu area 1919–1942.* Melbourne: Melbourne University Press.

Rappaport, R. A. 1984. *Pigs for the ancestors: Ritual in the ecology of a New Guinea people.* New Haven, Conn.: Yale University Press.

Roach, E. 1987. From English mission to Samoan congregation. PhD thesis, Columbia University.

Robbins, J. 2004. *Becoming sinners: Christianity and moral torment in a Papua New Guinea society.* Berkeley: University of California Press.

Rutherford, D. 2006. Nationalism and millenarianism in West Papua: Institutional power, interpretive practice, and the pursuit of Christian truth. In *The limits of meaning: Case studies in the anthropology of Christianity,* eds. M. Engelke and M. Tomlinson, 105–128. Oxford: Berghahn.

Sahlins, M. 1985. *Islands of history.* Chicago: University of Chicago Press.

Schieffelin, E. L. 1976. *The sorrow of the lonely and the burning of the dancers.* New York: St. Martin's Press.

Schieffelin, E. L., and R. Crittenden. 1991. *Like people you see in a dream: First contact in six Papuan societies.* Stanford, Calif.: Stanford University Press.

Shore, B. 1989. Mana and tapu. In *Developments in Polynesian ethnology,* ed. A. Howard and R. Borofsky, 137–173. Honolulu: University of Hawai'i Press.

Sinclair, K. P. 1990. The Maori tradition of prophecy: Religion, history, and politics in New Zealand. In *Contemporary Pacific societies,* ed. V. S. Lockwood, T. G. Harding, and B. J. Wallace, 321–334. Englewood Cliffs, N.J.: Prentice Hall.

Smith, M. F. 1982. Bloody time and bloody scarcity: Capitalism, authority, and the transformation of temporal experience in a Papua New Guinea village. *American Ethnologist* 9: 503–518.

Spiro, M. E. 1952. Ghosts, Ifaluk, and teleological functionalism. *American Anthropologist* 54: 497–503.

Stephen, M. 1995. *A'aisa's gifts: A study of magic and the self.* Berkeley: University of California Press.

Swain, T., and G. Trompf. 1995. *The religions of Oceania.* London: Routledge.

Taylor, C. R. H. 1965. *A Pacific bibliography.* London: Oxford University Press.

Thomas, N. 1994. *Colonialism's culture: Anthropology, travel and government.* Princeton, N.J.: Princeton University Press.

Tippett, A. R. 1967. *Solomon Island Christianity. A study in growth and obstruction.* London: Lutterworth.

Toren, C. 2006. The effectiveness of ritual. In *The anthropology of Christianity,* ed. F. Cannell, 185–210. Durham, N.C.: Duke University Press.

Trompf, G. W. 1991. *Melanesian religion.* Cambridge: Cambridge University Press.

———. 1994. *Payback: The logic of retribution in Melanesian religions.* Cambridge: Cambridge University Press.

Tuzin, D. F. 1980. *The voice of the Tambaran: Truth and illusion in Ilahita Arapesh religion.* Berkeley: University of California Press.

———. 1997. *The cassowary's revenge: The life and death of masculinity in a New Guinea society.* Chicago: University of Chicago Press.

Valeri, V. 1985. *Kingship and sacrifice: Ritual and society in ancient Hawaii.* Chicago: University of Chicago Press.

Wagner, R. 1972. *Habu: The innovation of meaning in Daribi religion.* Chicago: University of Chicago Press.

Waiko, J. D. 1981. Binandere oral tradition: Sources and problems. In *Oral traditions in Melanesia,* ed. D. Denoon and R. Lacey, 11–30. Port Moresby: University of Papua New Guinea and the Institute of Papua New Guinea Studies.

Weiner, A. B. 1976. *Women of value, men of renown: New perspectives on Trobriand exchange.* Austin: University of Texas Press.

Wetherell, D. 1978. From Fiji to Papua: The work of the 'Vakavuvuli.' *Journal of Pacific History* 13: 153–172.

———. 1980. Pioneers and patriarchs: Samoans in a nonconformist mission district in Papua, 1890–1917. *Journal of Pacific History* 15: 130–154.

———. 1989. 'The bridegroom cometh': The lives and deaths of Queensland Melanesians in New Guinea, 1893–1956. *Pacific Studies* 12: 53–90.

White, G. M. 1991. *Identity through history: Living stories in a Solomon Islands society.* Cambridge: University of Cambridge Press.

Williams, F. E. 1923. *The Vailala Madness and the destruction of native ceremonies in the Gulf Division.* Port Moresby: Government Printer.

———. 1928. *Orokaiva magic.* Oxford: Oxford University Press.

Williamson, R. W. 1933. *The religious and cosmic beliefs of central Polynesia.* Cambridge: Cambridge University Press.

Worsley, P. 1968. *The trumpet shall sound: A study of "cargo cults" in Melanesia.* New York: Schocken Books.

Young, M. 1983. *Magicians of manumanua.* Berkeley: University of California Press.

Zegwaard, G. A. 1959. Headhunting practices of the Asmat of West New Guinea. *American Anthropologist* 61: 1020–1041.

Literature

Selina Tusitala Marsh

19

This chapter examines the terrain of Pacific literature published in English by its indigenous peoples. With a few outliers, like Cook Islander Florence Johnny Frisbie's *Miss Ulysses of Pukapuka* (1948), this is a "land" barely four decades old, with its genesis occurring in the late 1960s. The broad aesthetic foundation of this terrain is deeply embedded in oral traditions, a field still in development in terms of adequately critiquing literature simultaneously engaged in the rich orature of its cultures. This chapter, however, confines itself to examining major critical, thematic, and aesthetic developments in Pacific literature and argues that writings once read reductively as sociological or anthropological texts to support essentialist assumptions about cultures from the outside, can and should be read holistically in their geographical, historical, social, and political contexts if they are to be fully and critically engaged with. It is not my intention to produce an annotated bibliography, but selective texts indicative of developments in the field will be examined.

"Pacific" Criticism

The geographic outlay of the region commonly known as the Pacific, or Oceania (using Hau'ofa's [Waddell, Naidu, and Hau'ofa 1993] development of Wendt's [1976b] notion of Oceania), is examined in detail throughout this book. But in terms of popular conceptions surrounding what constitutes the Pacific in the study of its literatures, it is informative to examine the seminal critical texts produced in particular periods of its development and how they have shaped ideas and definitions about the region.

In 1980, Subramani's landmark critical text *South Pacific literature: From myth to fabulation* focused critical attention on the eleven English-speaking Commonwealth countries served by the University of the South Pacific (the Cook Islands, Fiji, Kiribati, Nauru, Niue, Solomon Islands, Tokelau, Tonga, Tuvalu, Samoa, and Vanuatu), one of two of the first universities established in the Pacific (the other being Papua New Guinea). He demarcates the region according to its colonial centers: Papua New Guinea; New Caledonia and French Polynesia; the "American Pacific" with Guam, the Marshall Islands, Federated States of Micronesia, Palau, Northern Marianas, American Samoa, Hawai'i; Rapanui, colony of Chile and the only Spanish-speaking Polynesians; Australia (Aborigine) and New Zealand (Maori); and the South Pacific. Due to the comparatively high production of indigenous literature in

the South Pacific, it gained prominence over other areas in the field and was the first to produce a critical text from inside the region. Despite the regional specificity of the title, an unintended effect of Subramani's critical companion was to further make the term "Pacific literature" synonymous with "Anglophone South Pacific literature," leading, albeit inadvertently, to further marginalization of literature from other geographical regions in varying degrees.

Of course, all these regions have their own unique historical and geographical complexities that made access to the study and dissemination of their literatures problematic for the majority of Pacific peoples in Anglophone centers of learning (the context of this chapter). Pacific Francophone literature has only recently been translated for general distribution among Anglophone readers. In 2004, New Caledonia's leading Kanak writer, Dewe Gorode, had a collection of short stories, *The Kanak apple season,* translated into English. This was followed by a translation of her poetry collection, *Sharing as custom provides,* in 2005. In 2005 the exquisitely produced *Vārua tupu: New writing from French Polynesia* was published in *Manoa: A Pacific Journal* by the University of Hawai'i Press. The first of its kind, it brings indigenous francophone literature from Tahiti and French Polynesia to the English-speaking world in an eclectic mix of fiction, poetry, memoir, art, and photography. Tahitian women writers have also sought wider readership with Tahiti's first Mā'ohi novel, Chantal Spitz's *L'Ile de rêves écrasés* (1991), recently translated into the novel *Island of shattered dreams* in 2007. Alongside the award-winning trilogy of now Australian-based Célestine Hitiura Vaite—*Breadfruit* (2000, 2006), *Frangipani* (2004), *Tiare* (2006)—these two have inscribed Tahitian women writers on the literary map. Vaite's fiction enjoys global distribution, a testament not only to some savvy marketing but to its ability to culturally cross over into a mainstream, Anglophone readership. Meanwhile critical texts like Robert Nicole's *The word, the pen, and the pistol: Literature and power in Tahiti* (2001) offer an examination into the relationship between history, power, knowledge, and literature in the colonial and postcolonial contexts of Tahiti. Such texts foster a critical discourse around indigenous worldviews and frameworks useful in informing the reading of such texts.

As is true elsewhere, the development of writing centered around the establishment of higher institutions of learning. Notably, the University of Papua New Guinea (UPNG) and the University of the South Pacific in Suva (and to a lesser degree, its eleven extension centers throughout the South Pacific) were the hubs of literary production and dissemination from the late 1960s. At UPNG, Ulli Beier was instrumental in establishing and editing several influential literary journals including *Kovave* (1969–1974), later replaced by *Papua New Guinea writing,* the *Papua Pocket Series,* and the anthology *Voices of Independence* (1980). The journals *Gigibori, Ondobondo,* and *Bikmaus* also helped to foster writing, as did a national writing competition in 1981, from which a selection of entries in the 1981 national annual literature competition edited by Kathy Kituai and John Kolia was published in 1982. For more about these early years of literary and artistic development, see Beier's *Decolonising the mind: The impact of the university on culture and identity in Papua New Guinea, 1971–1974* (2005).

Literary activity in the region during the 1960s and 1970s paralleled its political activity. Alan Natachee, considered Papua's first poet laureate, was the first to publish poetry throughout the 1960s, Vincent Eri's *Crocodile* (1970) was PNG's first novel, and Albert Maori Kiki's *Ten thousand years in a lifetime* (1968) was the first published autobiography. Writing competitions maintained the impetus, and three collections of student poetry were published between 1973 and 1976. Nora Vagi Brash and John Kolia in particular wrote numerous plays for stage and radio between 1971 and 1981. The late 1980s saw several anthologies capturing the wealth of production, Papiya Chakravarti's *Papua New Guinea literature in English: A bibliography, 1974–1985* in 1986, and Ganga Powell's *Through Melanesian eyes: An anthology of Papua New Guinean writing* in 1987. Established fiction writer Russel Soaba's *Maiba* (1985) and writer and literary critic Regis Stella have also been important in the literary scene (see, for example, *Melanesian Passages* (2004) by Stella and Lynda Aniburi Maeniani). Later the field widened enough to enable specialized anthologies like Adeola James' *PNG women writers: An anthology* in 1996. The steady production of writing continues to depend predominantly upon the patronage of universities and government departments. Steven Winduo, who has two collections of poetry in English and Tok Pisin, *Lomo'ha I am, in spirit's voice I call* (1991) and *Hembemba: Rivers of the forest* (2000), is an important figure in the literary scene. He is the founding editor of *Savanna flames: A Papua New Guinea journal of literature, language, and culture* (still in circulation today and the main vehicle for creative publication) and is currently director of the Melanesian and Pacific Studies (MAPS) Centre at UPNG (with its own publishing program) and chair of the National Literature Board. Arguing that the millennium has brought another literary renaissance, Winduo has been instrumental in ensuring that the board, alongside the National Cultural Commission, plays a major role fostering a resurgence of interest. In 2007 a national writing competition was held in which more than three hundred entries were submitted. It was also the first year the University of Papua New Guinea held its own writers' workshop in Port Moresby attended by more than eighty aspiring and established writers (Nalu).

By comparison, Goetzfridt's annotated bibliography on literature in the Pacific Islands until 1994 (1995) omits the French and Spanish colonies (while including Australia and New Zealand) and has few entries for literature produced by the indigenous peoples of American Samoa, Micronesia, and Hawai'i. An exception seems to be the 1991 establishment of the literary journal *Storyboard: A journal of Pacific imagery,* published from the Department of English and Applied Linguistics at the University of Guam. It has begun to feature the work of new Micronesian writers north of the equator. But hands-on research within the area may also reveal some surprising results. In islands where the politics of publication often exclude the indigenous population, self-publication may be an option. For example, during a morning spent at Emalus Campus of the University of the South Pacific at Port Vila, I came across several self-published books that have eluded electronic detection, like Hermana Ramarui's *Palauan Perspectives* (1984), the first collection of Palauan poetry I'd come across apart from Valentine Sengebau's *Microchild: An anthology of poetry,* published in 2004 (Northern Mariana Islands Council for the Humanities) and Mildred Sope's *A questioning mind* (1987).

Additionally, the dispersal of students from these regions to larger island metropoles with a more developed publishing infrastructure that can specifically cater to marginalized voices has produced many firsts. Of note is Pohnpeian poet Emelihter Kihleng's first collection of poetry written in English, *My urohs* (2008), published by Kahuãomanoa Press, an independent press based in Hawai'i dedicated to providing a forum for new and student writers. Hawai'i is a meeting point for many North Pacific students, writers, and academics attending universities and/or sponsored by major organizations like the East-West Center at the University of Hawai'i at Manoa, which is committed to nurturing East-West contacts across disciplines.

Any discussion of the development of Hawaiian literature itself, however, necessarily considers questions surrounding terminology and definition that are prefaced by wider arguments surrounding ongoing colonization and social histories of displacement, indentured labor, and migration that affect identity. In this ongoing colonial context, where America, Japan, and other foreign interests continue their military and touristic endeavors, exactly who and what is Hawaiian, local, kama'aina, Kanaka Maoli, or haole is fiercely debated. In mainstream criticism and literary production, the phrase "Hawaiian writer" has come to refer to any literature written by anyone resident in Hawai'i. From the late 1970s, the rise of noncommercial presses successfully operating without affiliation to a college or university gave space for grassroots voices to sound out a Hawai'i-centric local sensibility that has risen, in large part, from the Asian indentured laborer communities from the early nineteenth century. One of the longest-running publishing houses, Bamboo Ridge, was founded by Darrell Lum and Eric Chock in 1978. *Bamboo Ridge: A Hawaii writer's quarterly,* edited by Lum and Chock, helped launch the careers of many successful Hawai'i-based writers, including popular third-generation Japanese American author Lois-Ann Yamanaka (1996).

But many Native Hawaiians have sought to distinguish their voices from what they consider melting pot, assimilationist projects and policies that threaten their unique status as Kanaka Maoli. In 1999 the publication of *'Õiwi: A native Hawaiian journal,* published by nonprofit Kuleana 'Õiwi Press, signaled a landmark development in indigenous publication. *'Õiwi* builds upon the strong literary tradition established by the long history of Kanaka Maoli literacy.

The emergence of specialist publishers in the Pacific has been an important development in terms of establishing and developing creative writing in book culture. Worthy of mention include Vanuatu's Black Stone Publications and Samoa's Niu Leaf Publications, which cater to local needs while managing some international presence. The infrastructure is usually small and vulnerable, as they are dependent upon one or two individuals (the late Grace Mera Molisa and Momoe Malietoa Von Reiche respectively). Pacific-based publishers with a more developed infrastructure are often affiliated with universities and educational institutions and include Mana Publications, Institute of Pacific Studies (Fiji), Pacific Writers Forum (Fiji), The Oceania Centre for Arts and Culture (Fiji), The University of Hawai'i Press, Pandanus Books (Research School for Pacific Asian Studies, Australian National University), Centre for Pacific Studies (University of Auckland), and various University of the South Pacific Centre presses. A few, like Huia Publishers in New Zealand, are able to remain specialized in mainstream publishing.

There are also several journals of note produced by tertiary institutions. The University of Hawai'i Press publishes *Manoa*, a biannual journal publishing critical and creative writing from America, Asia, and the Pacific with select issues focusing on the Pacific (see, for example, volume 5(1), 1993), while its Pacific Islands Monograph Series provides an important publishing outlet for Pacific-based research. The University of Hawai'i Press's Talanoa: Contemporary Pacific Literature series has reprinted key canonical texts by Albert Wendt, Patricia Grace, Hone Tuwhare, Alan Duff, Witi Ihimaera, Epeli Hau'ofa, John Kneubuhl, and Victoria Kneubuhl, which has made them available to contemporary audiences and accessible to the North American market. In conjunction with the Center for Pacific Islands Studies, UH Press also publishes *The Contemporary Pacific,* a biannual journal with critical writings covering social sciences and humanities developments in the Pacific region. Island-based journals like Fiji's *Dreadlocks* series (*Dreadlocks indentured, Dreadlocks interrupted*) are beginning to enjoy a higher profile throughout the region and beyond.

What must not be overlooked are the all-important school journals, which are vehicles for mass publication and which now provide important archival sources for early poetry. For example, Vanuatu's national library in Port Vila holds numerous publications including *The Gong: Magazine* produced by the pupils of British Secondary School, published from 1971 onward; *Rorgarea Form Three: Magazine* produced by the pupils of British Secondary School; *Onesua magazine*; and a beautiful, colored, digitally produced magazine, *Malapoa College: Literary supplement.*

To return to regional definitions of the Pacific literature, Paul Sharrad defines Pacific literature as that which comes from the indigenous populations of Oceania: from Guam in the north to New Zealand in the south; PNG in the west to French Polynesia and Rapanui in the east. He excludes Aboriginal writing from Australia, arguing that its outlook is more "continental" than "oceanic," but he acknowledges important commonalities due to their indigenous status and ongoing colonial subjugation (2003). While pointing out that the geographical biases in literary reception and criticism of Pacific literature favors the South, he concedes that it is the most logical emphasis, covering the most prolific areas around Polynesia and Melanesia. As a formal area of study, the strongest critical and creative production of Pacific literature covers the Anglophone southwest of Oceania, centered around the critical and creative organizations based around the University of Papua New Guinea and the University of the South Pacific, Fiji.

Sharrad's biography, *Albert Wendt and Pacific literature: Circling the void* (2003), is at the same time an in-depth critical assessment of Pacific literature through the lens of the work of its most prolific author. For other critical surveys of the development of Pacific literature in this region, see Va'ai's *Literary representations in western Polynesia: Colonialism and indigeneity* (1999), Keown's *Pacific Islands writing* (2007), and the three major anthologies of Pacific literature (with the last focusing solely on poetry) edited by Albert Wendt, *Lali* (1980), *Nuanua: Pacific writings in English since 1980* (1995), and *Whetu moana: Contemporary Polynesian poems in English* (2003), also edited by Reina Whaitiri and Robert Sullivan. Another landmark development was the 1994 conference in Hawai'i titled Theorizing Pacific Literature: Inside Out. Although not the first conference to theorize about Pacific literature, it was one of the first international conferences to consciously do so "from the inside out," enabling a significant number of Pacific Island writers and scholars to participate. The subsequent publication, *Inside out: Literature, cultural politics, and identity in the New Pacific* (1999), demonstrated the growth of interest in culturally, politically, and historically contextualized critical frameworks within which to view this literature.

The remainder of this chapter focuses on this remarkable writing, mainly from the South Pacific region. To give some insight into the creative energies it peruses, it will delve selectively into writing that highlights hallmark themes and aesthetic issues in the development of Pacific literature and its criticism.

Mana: The Beginning

There is a difference between literature "on" the Pacific and literature "of" the Pacific. Before the 1960s, most writing on or about the Pacific and its peoples was written by nonindigenous authors. Such writings and imaginings played a significant part in the ideological colonization of the Pacific by the Western world. Since the mid-1970s, an increasing number of critics have documented how Maori and Pacific Islanders were contained, categorized, and to a certain extent controlled through various stereotypes (see Wendt 1976a, 1980, 1995; Subramani 1975, 1978, 1985, 1989; Grace and Ihimaera 1978; Sharrad 1993a; Pearson 1968, 1984; Sinclair 1992; and Krauth 1978). From early first-contact voyage accounts (Cook, Bougainville, Byron, Carteret, Wallis, and, as Pearson [1984] points out, through the bias of editors like Hawkesworth), to missionary writings like that of Vicesimus Knox, who wrote the influential "On the Savage Manner of South Sea Islanders and the Best Means of Improving Them" (Subramani 1985), to the literature and art produced by canonical masters of the West (Herman Melville, Robert Louis Stevenson, Somerset Maugham, James Michener, Jack London, and artist Paul Gauguin), racist and stereotypical constructions of islanders were formed and perpetrated. In these texts Pacific Islanders are either exoticized, as seen in the stereotypes of the noble savage and golden people, or demonized, as in the stereotypes of children of nature or black devils (Wendt 1976a), or simply part of a passive backdrop to European action. In his seminal essay "Towards a new Oceania," Wendt (1976a) argues that these reflected changing trends in European thought rather than actual Pacific realities. Often, literature on the Pacific revealed what Said called the orientalizing eye/I, where, according to the norms and categories of knowledge of the West, indigenous peoples are constructed as different, as the exotic Other (Said 1979). African American feminist critic bell hooks notes that many Western ideologies have enough influence to penetrate our self-perceptions: "They had the power to make us see and experience ourselves as 'Other'" (hooks 1992). An ocean away, Wendt acknowledges this forced "otherness" and subsequent self-alienation in terms of language: "To some extent, I am still a stereotyped tourist wandering through the stereotyped tropical paradises, a cliché viewing the South Seas through a screen of clichés" (Wendt 1976a). Sinavaiana describes the Americanization of eastern Samoa as another "rudely imposed story about who we are." But the story remains unfinished. She notes:

> Having internalized the dynamics of this embattled plot—as have all colonized peoples—I now look for words that can reconcile the combatants. I look for stories that can cut through the veils of shadow that flutter across our faces, threatening to smother the spirit, to extinguish the breath. (Sinavaiana 1995)

Said (1994) argues that "[t]he power to narrate or to block other narratives from forming or emerging is very important to culture and imperialism, and constitutes one of the main connections between them." Unblocking our stories is one of the many ways of exposing, exploring, and deconstructing the various ideological colonizations of the mind. Writing and storytelling are an integral part of "decolonizing the mind" (Thiongo 1986).

Polemic in tone, didactic in nature, and indicative of early postcolonial literature elsewhere, first-wave writing from the Pacific reacted against the negative influence of colonialism. Eurocentric ideologies inherent in colonial education and religion were often the subject of derision, as demonstrated by Ruperake Petaia's satirical poem "Kidnapped" (Petaia 1980: 10):

> I was six when
> Mama was careless
> she sent me to school
> alone
> five days a week
>
> One day I was
> kidnapped by a band
> of Western philosophers
> armed with glossy-pictured
> textbooks and
> registered reputations . . .
>
> . . . Each three-month term
> they sent threats to
> my Mama and Papa
>
> Mama and Papa loved
> their son and
> paid ransom fees
> each time
> Mama and Papa grew
> poorer and poorer
> and my kidnappers grew
> richer and richer
> I grew whiter and whiter . . .

The ability of the empire to write back (a play on words by Salman Rushdie; see introduction to Ashcroft, Griffiths, and Tiffin 1989) enabled the voicing of a Pacific consciousness in the public literary realm. Literature "of" the Pacific not only allowed a critiquing of literature on the Pacific, but aided in creating and affirming indigenous cultural production. Gramsci defines "hegemony" as a consensual domination through the influence of ideas and institutions (see also Said 1994). The majority of English departments (the institution) in the Pacific, and literature (the medium of ideas) being taught within these departments, generally continue to affirm Eurocentric hegemony. Despite being superseded by the United States and Russia in international political and economic power, Britain remains the center of cultural production within Commonwealth countries (see Ashcroft, Griffiths, and Tiffin 1989).

Destabilizing that Eurocentric canon in the Pacific is as vital today as it was thirty years ago. Today, Pacific children are still being colonized through a Eurocentric education that has little relevance to their lives. In "Reality," a poem by Tongan poet and scholar Konai Helu Thaman, a young boy has achieved success in Western education, yet upon returning to his island, discovers that the books and blackboards have little use. The last stanza compares images of Western education with decay, in contrast with "Pacificness" and growth:

> I see my teacher
> Sitting on a sterile rock
> Near the beach
> Selling green coconuts
> What do I do now?
> An old man close-by whispers,
> "Come fishing with me today
> For you have a lot to learn yet." (Thaman 1987)

Trained as a teacher, Thaman relates how she felt she was part of the conspiracy of colonialism while teaching Tongan children English realities:

> I know Shakespeare was/is a great writer . . . and Wordsworth too—but can you tell me why 13-year-old Tongan children should memorize "Daffodils" when they do not even have any idea what daffodils are, or look like? (Hereniko 1992)

Thaman saw it as her responsibility as an educator to place culturally relevant and affirming material into the hands of Tongan schoolchildren—thus beginning her career as one of the most prolific and well-read poets in the Pacific. Wordsworth's "Daffodils" is again used as a kind of postcolonial trope almost two decades later in the works of Sia Figiel in her novella *Girl in the moon circle* (1996) and her collaborative spoken word compact disc with Teresia Teaiwa, *Terenesia* ("Daffodils: The native version"). From Thaman to Figiel, writers have rejected the exclusive primacy of a Eurocentric canon and, like Pulitzer Prize winner Toni Morrison, have written what they wanted to read.

The core group of catalyst organizations involved in the dissemination of critical and creative works in the Pacific are centralized in Fiji: The South Pacific Creative Arts Society (SPCAS), The Institute of Pacific Studies, and The Pacific Writer's Forum. The South Pacific Association of Commonwealth Literatures and Languages is an important organization that usually changes its presidency every three to six years. When it has been in the South Pacific (Fiji, Papua New Guinea, Samoa), Pacific literature has flourished under this additional forum for publication and critical discussion. It is the role played by SPCAS, however, that is frequently found at the hub of any discussion surrounding the genesis of Pacific literature.

Initially established as the Writers Society in Fiji in 1972 by New Zealander Ken Arvidson with the involvement of Ron and Marjorie Crocombe and Albert Wendt, the society became the South Pacific Creative Arts Society in 1973. Based at the University of the South Pacific in Suva, Fiji, the society consisted of volunteers, among whom were now notable and influential authors Joe Nabola, Raymond Pillai, Howard Van Trease (Vanuatu Center), and Konai Helu Thaman. In 1973, Cook Islander Marjorie Tuainekore Crocombe proudly launched *Mana*, the society's four-page literary section in the *Pacific Islands Monthly*. Due to overwhelming response from the public, it became independent and was launched as a literary biennial in English in 1976. It was the Pacific's first international literary publication and continues to be instrumental in fostering and disseminating writing in and beyond the Pacific. To this day it plays a central part in fostering and disseminating indigenous Pacific voices. For example, in 2000 a special issue of *Mana* focused on the Cook Islands. Edited by two established local writers, Jean Tekura Mason and Vaine Rasmussen, it showcases song, chant, story, essay, and poetry from the year 2000 with new writers appearing alongside the work of published poets (Audrey Brown). Rasmussen's second collection of poetry, *Te-ava ora*, was published by *Mana* (Suva) in 1999 while Mason's first collection, *Tattoo = tatau*, was published in 2001.

As founding editor in its first edition, Marjorie Crocombe wrote:

> The canoe is afloat. The flow of creativity in poetry, drama, storywriting, as well as other forms of creative expression from painting to wood sculpture has expanded enormously (in Oceania). Hidden talents are being developed, ideas are being expressed, confidence is growing, and the volume and quality increase all the time. (introduction)

By 1974, the literary canoe was indeed afloat. As waves of change in power and technology beat upon island shores, increasingly indigenous writers emerging from a Western education began voyaging in their literary canoes and increasingly gained shoreline access. This was quite a feat considering that Pacific literature is comparatively young, having arisen from one of the last regions in the world to receive literacy. Prior to 1960 there was a virtual absence of published fiction.

By 1975 the University of the South Pacific had employed Wendt, who began organizing and teaching courses in creative writing at the English Department. The various creative writing courses coupled with access to a publishing outlet provided the necessary stimulus for the growth of Pacific creative writing in significant ways.

Political upheaval and the politics of decolonization predominated during the late 1960s and 1970s in the Pacific. Indigenous peoples began entering educational and political structures previously dominated by colonials. Indeed, colonizing powers seeking to divest themselves of regions now actively fighting for independence began grooming individuals to take over via educational scholarships to New Zealand and Australia. Crocombe observes the effects on literature:

> People all over the Pacific were wanting to express themselves and to have their thoughts communicated to others in their own countries and through the Pacific—even beyond it if there was an interest (Crocombe 1973).

As the globe continued to shrink, anticolonial struggles for self-determination by indigenous peoples the world over provided sources of inspiration, strength, and comradeship. Tertiary institutions established in the islands typically became the centers in mediating anticolonial consciousness. Universities were also the largest facilitators of writing in English. These institutions enabled a fertile milieu in which people gathered, shared, and developed ideas about the decolonization movements occurring throughout the Pacific. Notably, the universities of Papua New Guinea and the South Pacific in Fiji became two of the most influential centers of political thought and change. These institutions produced and consumed much Pacific writing—fiction and nonfiction.

In 1980 Wendt gathered together representative poems, short stories, and excerpts of novels and edited *Lali: A Pacific anthology*, the first collection of Pacific literature written in English. A *lali* is a hollowed-out log, beaten with one (or two) heavy sticks, used to gather, summon, and inform people of impending events. This collection contains some of the first "drum beats" of voices sounding out through the Pacific to the Pacific—calling islanders to listen to and read the writings of their own people. Acknowledging that many of the works published were the first works of the writers, Wendt stated his intention to "capture the essence and spirit of the beginnings of our literature before it ages, divides, branches into more 'sophisticated' journeys and forms and techniques." The literary beginnings of the Pacific possessed the "raw power of innocent anger, joy, and lament" (Wendt 1980). The writing addressed what Wendt called the *aitu* (evil spirits) of colonialism: racism, oppression, corruption, and societal changes wrought by rapid modernization.

Fervent excitement, expectation, and hope surrounded this first wave of literature. First-wave writing was, not surprisingly, characterized by its tendency to vilify "the colonizer," reacting against a history of domination replete with racist stereotypes that aimed to pacify indigenous voices. According to Subramani (1985), this reaction formed "an inner dialectic of the new literature." As evidenced in other writings that emerged out of similar colonial contexts, early Pacific literature was typically "nationalistic, angry, protesting, lamenting a huge loss" (Wendt 1995). Albert Leomala's poem "Kros" is often used to best exemplify this stage. From the then New Hebrides (an independent Vanuatu from 1980), Leomala challenges the power of the English language and the ideological weight it has bandied about by prioritizing Pidgin, the local common creole used among Ni-Vanuatu. In "Kros" he uses it to protest missionization in a bare, direct, and confrontational manner:

> *Kros mi no wandem yu* (Cross I hate you
> *Yu kilim mi* You are killing me
> *Yu sakem aot ol* You are destroying
> *We blong mi* My traditions
> *Mi no wandem yu Kros.* I hate you Cross.) (Wendt 1980)

Colonial and indigenous people were often seen in "irreconcilable opposition." As a result, much of the fiction from the Pacific Islands espoused unwavering "political and social commitment, with a heavily tragic, pessimistic vision of our times." Writing vented individual political awakening and assertion against colonial domination and exploitation. Other poetry attempted to reconstruct past losses and is thus "a fabulous storehouse of anthropology, sociology, art, religion, history, dance and music" (Wendt 1995).

A lull occurred in the middle of the 1970s. Wendt points out that the fledgling writers who began the literary movement were also the urban educated of the islands. These people became the new leaders in government, education, and business, rapidly filling positions of authority and power in their growing and independent island nations. As such, the demands of either attaining self-determination or administering it quickly consumed their time and focus. Some authors wrote later through a different outlet (Beier 1980). Others never wrote again (Wendt 1980).

Ironically, some writers became the embodiment of the type of colonialism they had earlier rejected and protested in their writing. Despite colonial administrators giving way to "native sons," the structure of oppressive power relations remained the same. In many situations, the process of colonialism merely saw a change of skin color of those in power. To borrow an image from Fanon, although the new civil servants had black skins, many continued to wear white masks (Fanon 1968). For many, independence held a "false gleam"—a common metaphor of postcolonial writers like Achebe (1958) and Thiongo (1986). Neocolonialism became the subject of derision in much writing, captured by Thaman's widely published poem "Uncivil Servants":

> Many of my friends
> Are civil servants
> With uncivil thoughts . . .
>
> But they cannot erase my existence
> For my plight chimes with the hour
> And my blood they drink at cocktail parties
> Always full of smiling false faces
> Behind which lies authority and private interests.
> (Thaman 1980)

Samoan poet and artist Momoe Malietoa Von Reiche personifies the town while metaphorically connecting human obesity with internal corruption and material consumption in her poem "This Town." The experts—both indigenous and foreign—work to the detriment of her people:

> This town is puffing with faalavelaves,
> Panting with a brain overload of
> Experts and crooked lawyers,
> Wheezing with conniving politicians and
> Gregarious customs officers.
> This town is going to die suddenly
> Of constipation.
> (Von Reiche 1988)

Two years later Maori produced their own anthology with *Into the world of light: An anthology of Maori writing* (Ihimaera and Long 1982), which surveyed literature from the previous ten years. Maori writing began to flourish from 1970, a decade during which Maori were published in all the literary genres (see Ihimaera and Long 1982). Like Hawaiians, Maori, despite being Tangata Whenua, found themselves a minority in their own country, forming 10 percent of the total New Zealand population by 1960 (Ihimaera and Long 1982). Like the Hawaiians, they refused to be marginalized. While mourning the losses of the past, Maori literature centered on reclaiming traditional stories and critiquing Maori/pakeha race relations and conflicts. In the realms of creative writing, they have actively contended with life-changing events, voicing their grief, anger, protest, endurance, strength, *mana,* and *aroha* in response to colonization and its resultant eviction from the *whenua*—and consequently from their traditional ways of life—and the move to modernization, its dependence upon a cash economy, and the subsequent rural-to-urban drift for Maori in search of paid employment.

Literature is one way of processing the past, asserting identity, and validating experiences that were previously denigrated. The noticeable absence of a glossary in this anthology indicated that despite popular opinion, New Zealand was not a monolingual, monocultural society. Maori literature, and its steady growth, argued for the need to reconsider New Zealand's national identity as bilingual and bicultural. Maori fought alongside Europeans in the World Wars—if they were considered good enough to fight for the "mother country" of England, then they should be considered equal to Europeans in all fields of life. Rowley Habib's Maori Battalion war poetry carries the subtext that the indomitable Maori spirit will fight until victory is won and justice is served, both on and off the battlefields. "Ka whawhai tonu, ake, ake, ake" is commonly used as a refrain in contemporary Maori protest movements. Nga Pitiroirangi's "Orakau" reads

> Again the storming of the troops of the palisades.
> Again the repulse.
> Again the storming.
> And yet again the repulse. Wave upon wave.
> Through a day and a night and another day . . .
>
> And the women and children in battle.
> Again the use of sticks for bullets.
> And still the invaders come
> Their numbers seem limitless.
> For every man who falls two move up to take his place.
> They seem indestructible.
> The spirit of the defenders fails.
>
> Yet through the ordeal, the sinking morale
> These words are still able to be uttered.
> 'Friend, this is the word of the Maori.
> Ka whawhai tonu, ake, ake, ake.'
> We will fight forever and ever and ever.
> (Ihimaera and Long 1982)

What is commonly considered a second wave of writing is captured in Wendt's second anthology, *Nuanua: Pacific writing in English since 1980,* published in 1995. The *nuanua* (rainbow) imagery symbolizes the diversity of cultures and languages, of fauna and flora found in Polynesia, Melanesia and Micronesia . . . also . . . the richness and variety of our literatures, both oral and written. (Wendt 1995)

Issues surrounding colonization and decolonization still thematically predominated the writing, undoubtedly a reflection on their impact in people's lives. Wendt writes:

Colonialism, racism, modernization, and their effects on us remain major preoccupations in our literature. A sense of profound loss still pervades that writing. At the same time in those countries struggling for their independence the writing is full of anger and hope. (Wendt 1995)

Subthemes included loss of pride and self-esteem, loss of traditional skills due to urbanization, alienation from a Westernized society, the effects of modernity and materialism on local cultures, corruption of indigenous elite, discussion surrounding identity politics, and internal forms of oppression within society.

Writers tended to veer away from vilifying colonists or attacking simplified power oppositions and turned criticism inward. Hereniko observes "more experimentation in language as writers become confident enough to speak in their own unique voices, sometimes critically about their own cultures or leaders" (Goetzfridt 1995: foreword). Writing that critiqued patriarchy and women's disempowerment also surfaced (Marsh 2004). Jully Makini (Sipolo) from Solomon Islands and Molisa from Vanuatu became two leading Melanesian poets who critiqued the position of women within their own societies and also, for the first time in this medium, publicly proffered "a woman's views" (Sipolo 1981). They challenged the uncritical use of "tradition" and argued that custom was being used as a cultural bulwark to keep women from becoming empowered in rapidly modernizing societies. Molisa critiques *kastom* (Vanuatu-specific customs) and argues that it is often used as a patriarchal tool to keep women (and other less privileged groups) oppressed. Her often quoted poem "Custom" notes:

> *Inadvertently*
> *misappropriating*
> *"Custom"*
> *misapplied*
> *bastardised*
> *murdered*
> *a Frankenstein*
> *corpse*
> *conveniently*
> *recalled*
> *to intimidate*
> *women*
> *the timid*
> *the ignorant*
> *the weak. (Molisa 1983)*

Molisa's deliberate use of the English word "custom"—as opposed to its Vanuatu dialect *kastom*—subtly critiques the seemingly sanctified belief that all *kastom* stems from unadulterated, untainted, pure forms of tradition. Using the word "custom"

signifies the modern influence and manipulation inherent in the shaping of seemingly traditional belief systems.

In her second collection of poetry, *Colonised people* (1987), Molisa parallels the oppressive power relations behind colonialism with that of patriarchy and sexism. Molisa states in the introduction:

In a state of oppression Women are multiply oppressed compared with Men. Such is clear in Vanuatu. Vanuatu is now free of foreign colonial domination but NiVanuatu Women are still colonised.

With stronger, more confident developments in theme came increasingly indigenous shifts in literary style. Despite the anger voiced in blatant antiwhite, anti-Western, anticolonial, anti-Christian content in the first wave, Hereniko notes the irony in the use of structures and forms used to express this anger, which in some ways worked against itself (Goetzfridt 1995: foreword). Wendt (1995) observes the commonly used modernist style of writing imitating the realist mode adopted by English canonical writers such as Eliot, Yeats, and Pound. He describes the style as containing "deliberate ambiguity and complexity, irony, unified structures and characterization, the search for originality and uniqueness, and the concealment of artifice in the hope of transcending time and place." It became apparent that decolonization was a journey, not a destination. Writers like Molisa and Makini continue to lead the way for others to use creative writing as a vehicle for voicing other forms of internal oppressions.

Recent Pacific literature leans toward more personal explorations of the Pacific psyche. Increasingly, contemporary writing focuses on a pan-Pacific identity brought about by frequent physical and educational mobility, rapid urbanization, and the influx of modern technology. For example, Fijian Joseph Veramu's novel *Moving through the streets* (1994) allows a creative glimpse into the lives of youth in the rapidly urbanized and intensely integrated city of Suva.

A strong current of writing is being produced by the Pacific diaspora. Established Indo-Fijian writers Satendra Nandan, Subramani, Mohit Prasad, and Vijay Mishra have written of diaspora and the *girmit* (Indian migrant laborer) experience, some, as in Nandan's case, since 1976 (*Faces in a village,* the first book of poetry in English to be published in Fiji). For urban second- and third-generation Pacific Islanders a common focus is the exploration of multicultural identities. Of Banaban, Gilbertese, and African American descent, Teresia Kieuea Teaiwa states in her collection *Searching for Nei Nimʾanoa* (1995) that her poetry is a means through which she navigates her way through life with "the joys and pains of a mixed cultural identity and a feminine gender" (Teaiwa 1995). Niuean-born John Puhiatau Pule's *Shark that ate the sun* (1992) weaves song, legend, chant, myth, and poetry—in prose and epistolary form in both English and Niuean—in his tale of a Niuean family's migrant experience in New Zealand. Samoan-born, New Zealand–educated performance poet and author Sia Figiel's novel *Where we once belonged* (1996) lyrically examines Samoan life and transforming identities through the eyes of a young adolescent girl. Figiel's novel won the 1997 Booker Prize for First Book in the Asia/Pacific region and was a finalist for the Commonwealth Writers Prize, evidence of her ability to culturally cross over and produce culture-specific works grounded in universal themes. Figiel's novel was recently adapted for the stage (by Dave Armstrong, directed by

Colin McColl and Dave Fane) and premiered in Wellington, New Zealand, in 2008 to critical acclaim. Tongan and New Zealander poet Karlo Mila's first poetry collection, *Dream fish floating* (2005), was propelled into New Zealand mainstream literary consciousness when it won a national prize for Best First Book. Several of her poems have been featured in the national secondary school exam in 2006-2007. Her second collection, *A well written body* (2008), is a collaborative project with artist Delicia Sampero. In 2008, a nine-poet Pasifika performance show called *Polynation* traveled from New Zealand to premiere at the Queensland Poetry Festival—the first show of its kind. There is evidence everywhere that indigenous writers are not content to be confined to the cultural margins in New Zealand or anywhere else.

Recent developments in Melanesian writing has seen several exciting "firsts." In 2008 *Tôghàn*, the first novel written (in French) by Ni-Vanuatu Marcel Meltherorong was published by Alliance Francaise of Vanuatu. Hopefully this significant voice will be translated into English soon. If the reception of *Vārua Tupu* is anything to go by, the demand by Anglophone readers for Francophone literature remains strong. Poetry remains the leading genre for publication within the Pacific. Makini published her third collection of poetry, *Flotsam and jetsam,* in 2007 while Thaman has published her fifth, *Songs of love* (1999).

Anthologies are beginning to capture the eclectic cultural mixes now demographically significant in urban centers from Suva to Auckland. Writers' collectives such as Fiji's Niu Wave Writers Collective published the popular anthology *Niu waves* (2001), which includes an essay on the genesis of the collective and how it was formed by a small group of dedicated poets reading at Trapps, a local bar in Suva. Tipping their hat to the collective, a collection of fiction and poetry titled *Niu voices: Contemporary Pacific fiction volume 1* was published in New Zealand in 2006. These writers were selected from a national writing competition for Pacific Islanders sponsored by Huia Publishers (New Zealand's only Maori-owned mainstream publishing house) and *SPACIFIK* magazine (a contemporary magazine aimed at Maori and Pacific communities). *Niu voices* is indicative of Huia Publishers' recent moves to broaden their focus on Maori writing—undoubtedly helped by Mila's national award in 2005. But mainstream publishers have long realized the value of indigenous writers who are able to cross over into a mainstream readership. For example, Reed Publishers (now Raupo) in Auckland has long been the publishers for leading Maori author Witi Ihimaera. In a recent project, Ihimaera edited and selected fiction for *Get on the waka: Best recent Maori fiction* (2007), a volume showcasing the work of established Maori authors since 2000. In a sweeping gesture that started in Fiji and traverses the Pacific, the anthology *Writing the Pacific* (2007) suggests further crossing of cultural and geographically imposed boundaries.

From Fiji's intimate, personal weekly readings based in a local bar, to New Zealand's nationally advertised writing competitions, to the collation of previously published writers, to the inclusive sweeping of the region for both new and established writers, it is clear that the process of anthologizing aptly caters to the unique, geographical and sociocultural-political terrain within the Pacific, between each island, within each island, within each cultural group, and within each relationship formed between writer and publisher.

In addition to this overview is the brief consideration of filmic

texts. Film and literature have stories at their heart. Maori filmmaker Merata Mita views film, more so than literature, as a natural progression from oral storytelling:

> History contains stories and therefore stories are very important. It doesn't surprise me that there's a reaching towards film and video which is strongly a visual kind of storytelling from a people who have strong oral traditions. I mean, we didn't go in for writing. We had carefully coded inscriptions that became carving or koro patterns which the keepers of that knowledge would decipher. (Mita 1996)

Dynamic Samoan-born, New Zealand–bred filmmaker Sima Urale has gained international recognition for her work. Like Pule, she also explores the experience of a Polynesian family that has migrated to New Zealand. Urale privileges the view of the child in *O tamaiti* (The children) (1996). The film, with its sharp black-and-white images, relies heavily on visual and aural effects rather than on dialogue. In silence, Urale gives voice to the voiceless. Her acclaimed docudrama *Velvet dreams* (2005) inverts the anthropological lens and creatively examines Western fetishistic consumerism of an exoticized Pacific. The mainstream film hit *A Samoan wedding* (2006) was written and performed by the Auckland-based comedy troupe The Naked Samoans. Its New Zealand release title, *Sione's wedding,* was considered too ethnic-specific for an overseas market. It succeeded in both the difficult genre of comedy and in overseas distribution, but it also received criticism within the Samoan community around issues of representation. The particular brand of comedy performed by The Naked Samoans (often risqué) has gained a foothold in the overseas market—as proven by their commercially successful adult cartoon series *bro'Town* (www.brotown.co.nz/index.html). But so has the phenomenally popular Samoan comic duo Laughing Samoans (Tofiga Fepulea'i and Eteuati Ete), who specifically cater to a local, island-style sense of humor (www.laughingsamoans.com).

The Pacific Islands Film Festival, organized by Pacific Islanders in Communications and based in Hawai'i, holds annual film festivals that showcase films by indigenous people. Increasing numbers of Pacific Islanders are writing, directing, and producing their own stories on film and video. The organization grows stronger every year. The crossover between film and theater is becoming increasingly common. For example, Fijian playwright Larry Thomas has made several successful films (1999, 2002, 2004a, 2004b) as has Hereniko (2004).

Similarly, locally run theater has grown. Kumu Kahua Theatre was founded in 1971 and remains committed to producing plays about life in Hawai'i, by Hawai'i's playwrights, for Hawai'i's people. Victoria Kneubuhl, of Hawaiian/Samoan descent, has had many of her plays produced by Kumu Kahua, which also boasts a one-hundred-seat theater. Another long-running theater group has been Vanuatu's Wan Smol Bag Theatre, established in 1989. Taking full advantage of the strength of orality and performance as a central mode of entertainment and communication in Vanuatu, the immensely popular theater engages in "entertainment education," drama created to convey issues central to the health and vitality of a growing nation (half the population is under twenty-nine years of age). Topics such as AIDS, teenage pregnancies, and environmental concerns are dramatized (and now frequently filmed for DVD) and followed by an informative discussion with the audience. Working in conjunction with nongovernmental and donor organizations, Wan Smol Bag is largely coordinated by scriptwriter and actor Jo Dorras (see www.wan-smolbag-theatre.org).

The growing productivity of Auckland's Pacific Theatre (founded by Justine Simei-Barton), and Christchurch's Pacific Underground Theatre in New Zealand has ensured a Pacific presence in the past decade in Auckland theater. Rarely does a theatrical season pass without the staging of a play or plays by Pacific playwrights, including the work of Nina Nawalowalo, Jason Greenwood, David Fane, Oscar Kightley, The Naked Samoans, Makerita Urale, Dianna Fuemana, Leilani Unasa, Fiona Truelove, Sia Figiel, Victor Rodger, or the Black Friars (www.blackfriarscompany.blogspot.com), to name a few. The existence of national funding bodies such as Creative New Zealand, with a dedicated Pacific Committee, has been instrumental in fostering the Pacific arts scene.

As access to the Internet increases, the future holds endless possibilities. There are literary websites designed and coordinated by Pacific peoples ranging from promoting global multicultural writing (see, for example, Samoan poet Doug Poole's global poetry site, Blackmail Press at www.nzpoetsonline) to specifically Pacific poetry. In 2006 Pasifika Poetry Web (www.nzepc.auckland.ac/pasifika) was established in coordination with the New Zealand Electronic Poetry Centre. It is the only website of its kind dedicated to audio, text, and audiovisual reproduction of Pasifika poetry. Poems, alongside contextual interviews with poets, are used as teaching resources at the University of Auckland and among secondary schools. Pasifika Poetry Web uses available technology to embrace Pacific epistemologies. Knowing by doing, seeing, hearing, and performing, the site takes poetry "off the page" and onto the screen where performance poets like Samoan and New Zealand writer Tusiata Avia's multimodal work can be more fully realized. Her work reflects other exciting developments of urban-based diasporic Pacific writers whose cutting-edge contemporary work is characterized by the fusion of genres such as poetry, dance, song, chant, and drama. SistaNative (www.sistanative.com) and Latai Taumoepeau are Tongan sisters and artists who are based in and perform throughout Australia. While unpublished per se, they have a huge presence on the Internet, where their performance poetry and dance is posted. The advent of sites like Facebook, MySpace, YouTube, and Bebo have created another dimension to Pacific literary creativity and public access to these texts. Here writers can post writings and performances for free downloading. Whereas an enduring public voice was largely the domain of print media and endorsed by a book culture, here publication in public space has shifted from the hands of publishers into those of creators. This forum increasingly suits writers who feel marginalized from the politics of mainstream publication.

In one of the first Pacific literature course books within the Pacific, Subramani, teaching at the University of the South Pacific in Fiji at the time, addressed the sometimes antagonistic diverse demographic within Fiji's borders by writing:

Reading imaginative literature is one of the ways of breaking geographical and cultural barriers and participating in the larger universe and understanding the human condition (1994).

Pacific literature offers a bridge on which to cross into other geographical and cultural borders. This was argued by Wendt, who has often promoted the idea that Pacific literature should be read side by side with texts of history and other disciplines, not to seek anthropological truth, but to catch a glimpse of some of the humanity of the object—thus seeing it as subject. Breaking down strict demarcations allows insight into the imagination, experience, and emotional reality of a place through some of its people. Such an exercise would render a whole and more informed understanding of the people and places of the Pacific. For literature—song, chant, dance, oratory, proverb, myth, legend, poetry, short story, novel, theater, autobiography, biomythography, and film—is embedded with the histories, values, epistemologies, and humors of a people.

Hence, the importance of anthologies in the Pacific. The pivotal role of editors and anthologists like Wendt, Crocombe, Cliff Benson, Larry Thomas, and Witi Ihimaera, to name a few, has allowed creative, diverse, established, and developing collective voices to cross over into each other's literary borders and meet in a communal space.

If creative writing is visualized as a metaphorical map tracing spiritual and cultural landscapes, the reader, alongside the author, can explore the peaks and valleys of the human experience. Insight takes place from the emotional truths as well as the scientific ones—each shedding light on the other. We come to know a little more about other people and ultimately about ourselves as we continue to express, to examine. This visualization is, thus, an open invitation for ongoing dialogue:

> Therefore,
> friend,
> before the wind shakes
> and the sky gathers
> let us sit a moment
> by the hum's edge
> and the fringe of light,
> the quiet water under
> the bullfrog's assertion
> where the finger of water
> points into silence.
>
> There our words
> will find the delicate filaments
> that anchor brain to belly or heart,
> words to tease other words
> and words
> that bear unseen
> the source
> which we must touch
> to see.
> ("Invitation," Pio Manoa, in Wendt 1995)

BIBLIOGRAPHY

Achebe, C. 1958. *Things fall apart*. London: Heinemann.
———. 1986. *Arrow of God*. New York: Anchor Books.
Ashcroft, B., G. Griffiths, and H. Tiffin. 1989. *The empire writes back: Theory and practice in post-colonial literatures*. London and New York: Routledge.

Beckwith, M. W. 1981. *The Kumulipo: A Hawaiian creation chant.* Honolulu: University of Hawai'i Press.

Beier, U., ed. 1980. *Voices of independence: New black writing from Papua New Guinea.* New York: St. Martin's Press.

———. 2005. *Decolonising the mind: The impact of the university on culture and identity in Papua New Guinea, 1971–1974.* Canberra: Pandanus Books and Research School of Pacific and Asian Studies, Australian National University.

Crocombe, M. T. 1973. Pacific personality. Samoa's Albert Wendt, poet and author. *Mana: A South Pacific Journal of Language and Literature* 1: 45–47.

———. 1976. Introduction. *Mana: A South Pacific Journal of Language and Literature* 1: 1.

Fanon, F. 1968. *Black skins, white masks.* London: MacGibbon and Kee.

Figiel, S. 1996. *Where we once belonged.* Auckland: Pasifika Press.

———. 1996. *Girl in the moon circle.* Suva, Fiji: Mana Publications.

Goetzfridt, N. 1995. *Indigenous literature of Oceania: A survey of criticism and interpretation.* Westport, Conn.: Greenwood Press.

Gorode, Dewe. 2004. *The Kanak apple season: Selected short fiction of Dewe Gorode.* Translated and edited by P. Brown. Canberra: Pandanus Books.

———. 2004. *Sharing as custom provides: Selected poems.* Translated and edited by R. Ramsay and D. Walker. Canberra: Pandanus Books.

Grace, P. 1978. *Mutuwhenua: The moon sleeps.* Auckland: Longman Paul.

———. 1986. *Potiki.* Auckland: Viking.

Grace, P., and W. Ihimaera. 1978. The Maori in literature. In *Tihe Maori ora: Aspects of Maoritanga,* ed. M. King, 80–85. Wellington: Methuen.

Guralnik, D. B., ed. 1984. *Webster's new world dictionary of the American language.* New York: Warner Books and Simon & Schuster.

Hamasaki, R. 1994. Mountains in the sea: The emergence of contemporary Hawaiian poetry in English. In *Hawaii literature conference: Reader's guide,* ed. Lorna Hershinow. Honolulu: Hawaii Literary Arts Council.

Hawkins, J. M. 1988. *The Oxford paperback dictionary,* 3rd ed. Oxford: Oxford University Press.

Hereniko, V. 1992. Interview with Konai Helu Thaman. *Mana: A South Pacific Journal of Language and Literature* 9: 2.

———. 1995. *Indigenous knowledge and academic imperialism.* Unpublished paper presented at Contested Ground: Pacific History Conference, Honolulu, Hawai'i.

———. 2004. *The land has eyes.* Written and directed by Vilsoni Hereniko. Northcote, Vic.: Umbrella Entertainment: Te Maka Productions.

Hereniko, V., and S. Schwarz. 1994. *Talking chief: The role of the critic in a colonized Pacific.* Unpublished paper.

hooks, bell. 1984. *Feminist theory: From margin to center.* Boston: South End Press.

———. 1992. *Black looks: Race and representation.* Boston: South End Press.

Ihimaera, W., ed. 1992. *Te Ao marama: Contemporary Maori writing.* Auckland: Reed.

Ihimaera, W., and D. S. Long, eds. 1982. *Into the world of light: An anthology of Maori writing.* Auckland: Heinemann.

James, A. 1996. *PNG women writers: An anthology.* Melbourne: Longman Australia.

Keown, M. 2007. *Pacific Islands writing: The postcolonial literature of Aotearoa/New Zealand and Oceania.* Oxford: Oxford University Press.

Kituai, K., and J. Kolia., eds. 1981. *A selection of entries in the 1981 national annual literature competition.* Port Moresby: Institute of Papua New Guinea Studies.

Krauth, N. 1978. Politics and identity in Papua New Guinean literature. *Mana: A South Pacific Journal of Language and Literature* 2(2): 45–48.

Manoa, P. 1995. Invitation. In *Nuanua: Pacific writing in English since 1980,* ed. Albert Wendt, 73. Auckland: University of Auckland Press.

Marsh, S. T. 2004. *Ancient banyans, flying foxes, white ginger: Five Pacific women poets.* PhD thesis, University of Auckland.

Mita, M. 1996. Issues of cultural diversity. Pacific Island Images Film Festival, Pacific Islanders in Communication, University of Hawai'i at Mānoa Art Auditorium, August 2, 1996.

Molisa, G. M. 1983. *Black stone: Poems.* Suva: Mana.

———. 1989a. *Black stone II: Poems.* Port Vila, Vanuatu: Black Stone Publications; Vanuatu USP Centre.

———. 1989b. *Colonised people: Poems.* Port Vila, Vanuatu: Black Stone Publications.

Nalu, M. 2008. PNG literature undergoing renaissance. *The National,* www.thenational.com.pg/011207/w3.htm. Accessed March 31, 2008.

Nicole, R., ed. 2001. *Niu waves: Contemporary writing from the Pacific.* Suva: Pacific Writing Forum; Oceania Centre for Arts and Culture.

———. 2001. *The word, the pen, and the pistol: Literature and power in Tahiti.* Albany: State University of New York Press.

Orbell, M. 1995. *The illustrated encyclopedia of Maori myth and legend.* Christchurch: Canterbury University Press.

Pearson, B. 1968. The Maori and literature 1938–65. In *The Maori people in the nineteen-sixties: A symposium,* ed. E. Schwimmer, 217–256. New York: Academic Press.

———. 1984. *Rifled sanctuaries: Some views of the Pacific Islands in Western literature.* Macmillan Brown Lectures 1982. Auckland: University of Auckland Press.

Petaia, R. 1980. *Blue rain: Poems by Ruperake Petaia of Western Samoa.* Apia, Western Samoa: University of South Pacific Centre, Western Samoa, Mana Publications.

Powell, G. 1987. *Through Melanesian eyes: An anthology of Papua New Guinean writing.* South Melbourne: Macmillan.

Pule, J. P. 1992. *The shark that ate the sun: ko e ma'go ne kai e la'.* Auckland: Penguin Books.

Saaga, E., C. Sinavaiana, and J. Enright. 1990. *Three Tutuila poets.* Pago Pago, American Samoa: Le Siuleo o Samoa.

Said, E. 1979. *Orientalism.* New York: Vintage Books.

———. 1994. *Culture and imperialism.* New York: Vintage Books.

Sharrad, P. 1993a. A rhetoric of sentiment: Thoughts on Maori writing with reference to the short stories of Witi Ihimaera. In *New Zealand literature today,* ed. R. K. Dhawan and W. Tonetto, 60–72. New Delhi: Indian Society for Commonwealth Studies.

———, ed. 1993b. *Readings in Pacific literature.* Wollongong: New Literatures Research Centre.

———. 2003. *Albert Wendt and Pacific literature: Circling the void.* Manchester: Manchester University Press; Auckland: Auckland University Press.

Sinavaiana, C. 1995. Storytelling as healing. Summer Institute for Pacific Women. Unpublished paper.

Sinclair, K. 1992. Maori literature: Protest and affirmation. *Pacific Studies* 15(4): 283–309.

Sipolo, J. 1981. *Civilized girl: Poems.* Suva: South Pacific Creative Arts Society.

———. 1986. *Praying parents: A second collection of poems.* Honiara, Solomon Islands: Aruligo Book Centre.

Soaba, R. 1985. *Maiba.* Washington, D.C.: Three Continents Press.

Stella, R., and Lynda Aniburi Maeniani. 2004. *Melanesian passages.* Papua New Guinea: Melanesian and Pacific Studies, University of Papua New Guinea.

Subramani. 1975. Review of best stories of the South Seas. *Journal of the Polynesian Society* 84(4): 523–536.

———. 1978. Images of Fiji in literature. In *South Pacific images,* ed. C. Tiffin, 43–52. St. Lucia: University of Queensland Press.

———. 1985. *South Pacific literature: From myth to fabulation.* Suva: University of the South Pacific.

———. 1989. Indo-Fijian writing. *Ethnies* 4: 41–47.

———. 1992. *South Pacific literature: From myth to fabulation,* rev. ed. Suva: University of the South Pacific.

———. 1994. LL102 Pacific literature in English: Introduction and assignments. Semester 2, 1994. Suva, Fiji: Department of Literature and Language, School of Humanities, The University of the South Pacific.

Sullivan, R. 2006. *Savaiki regained: Alistair Te Ariki Campbell's poetics.* MA thesis. University of Auckland.

Teaiwa, T. 1995. *Searching for Nei Nim'anoa.* Suva, Fiji: Mana Publications.

Teaiwa, T., and S. Figiel. 2000. *Terenesia: Amplified poetry and songs.* Hawai'i Dub Machine. Honolulu: 'Elepaio Press.

Thaman, K. H. 1987. *Hingano: Selected poems, 1966–1986.* Suva, Fiji: Mana Publications.

———. 1980. *You, the choice of my parents.* Suva, Fiji: Mana Publications.

———. 1999. *Songs of love: New and selected poems 1974–1999.* Suva, Fiji: Mana Publications.

Thiongo, N. 1986. *Decolonising the mind: The politics of language in African literature.* London: J. Currey; Portsmouth, N.H.: Heinemann.

Thomas, L. 1999. *Compassionate exile.* Produced and directed by Bob Madey and Larry Thomas. Suva, Fiji: University of the South Pacific.

———. 2002. *A race for rights.* Produced and directed by Larry Thomas. Suva, Fiji: University of the South Pacific.

———. 2004a. *Bitter sweet hope.* Produced and directed by Larry Thomas. Suva, Fiji: Regional Media Centre, Secretariat of the Pacific Community.

———. 2004b. *Outcasts = les exclus.* Larry Thomas; traduction de Sonia Lacabanne; mise en scène, Isabelle de Haas; photographies Éric Dell'Erba Exclus Nouméa, Nouvelle-Calédonie: Agence de développement de la culture kanak; Éditions Grain de Sable.

Tiffen, C., ed. 1978. *South Pacific images.* Brisbane: South Pacific Association for Commonwealth Literature and Language Studies.

Trask, H. 1994. *Light in the crevice never seen.* Corvallis, Ore.: Calyx Books.

Urale, M. 1996. *O tamaiti* (The children). Paewai Productions, New Zealand Film Commission.

———. 2005. *Velvet dreams.* Produced by Vincent Burke, Clifton May. Top Shelf Productions.

Va'ai, S. 1999. *Literary representations in Western Polynesia: Colonialism and indigeneity.* Apia: National University of Samoa, 338–350.

Von Reiche, M. M. 1988. *Tai: Heart of a tree: A collection of poems.* Auckland: New Women's Press.

Waddell, E., Vijay Naidu, Epeli Hau'ofa, eds. 1993. *Oceania: Rediscovering our sea of islands.* Suva, Fiji: School of Social and Economic Development, The University of the South Pacific in association with Beake House.

Webb, J., and K. Nandan. 2007. *Writing the Pacific: An anthology.* Suva: Pacific Writers Forum.

Wendt, A. 1976a. *Inside us the dead: Poems, 1961–1974.* Auckland: Longman Paul.

———. 1976b. Towards a new Oceania. *Mana: A South Pacific Journal of Language and Literature* 1(1): 49–60.

———. 1980. *Lali: A Pacific anthology.* Auckland: Longman Paul.

———. ed. 1995. *Nuanua: Pacific writing in English since 1980.* Auckland: Auckland University Press.

Wendt, A., R. Whaitiri, and R. Sullivan, eds. 2003. *Whetu moana: Contemporary Polynesian poems in English.* Auckland: Auckland University Press.

Yamanaka, L. *Wild meat and the bully burgers.* San Diego: Harcourt, Brace & Company, 1996.

Art

Caroline Vercoe

20

Pacific art practice encompasses a rich and varied body of objects, dance forms, song, performance, adornment both permanent and temporary, and oral histories. Distinctive yet diverse, it emerges as a vital and important expression and vessel of cultural knowledge, memory, emotion, and experience. Prior to Western contact and subsequent colonization, what we call art today played an essential role within Pacific cultures. This chapter discusses a range of art forms produced in the Pacific in relation to a number of themes. They include gender and the impact and legacy of colonial contact, the role of art as a visual symbol of rank and authority, and the idea that Pacific art forms embody material wealth. I will also discuss a number of contemporary gallery-based Pacific artists who draw on traditionally conceived art forms and incorporate materials, objects, and technologies from their urban environments.

Recent scholarship has offered new and alternative interpretations of Pacific material culture. As the disciplines of history, anthropology, and art history have become increasingly reflexive, there has been a revision of entrenched viewpoints regarding indigenous creative practice. The social history of art is increasingly being focused on, and a more complex appreciation is being afforded to the roles that gender, intercultural contact, and migration have and are playing in relation to the development and maintenance of Pacific art forms. This revisionist practice is seen in the work of writers such as Vilsoni Hereniko, Ngahuia Te Awekotuku, and Albert Wendt. It can also be heard in the writings of historian Greg Dening and his innovative notion of history as performance, and in anthropologist Adrienne Kaeppler and her work on the interrelationship between Tongan dance and *ngatu* (decorated bark cloth), which highlights the way they reflect wider social and cultural roles. Archaeologists Kirch and Green (2001: 5–6) have called for their discipline to be acknowledged in terms of the development of a more multifaceted account of the emergence and growth of Pacific culture. "Only when archaeologists, valued interpreters of their unique historical 'texts,'" they write, "are accorded seats in the same seminar room, will historical anthropology truly be able to encompass the *longe duree* of nonliterate societies."

The assumption that Pacific visual creative practice is art has become a norm and the debates about the term "art" and its relevance or existence in Pacific and other indigenous cultures that occurred in the 1980s and 1990s have waned. Steven Hooper (2006:

28) makes the point that "[i]rrespective of the epithet, the word art is now firmly established, intended not so much to appropriate objects into European systems of classification, but to honour [Pacific] skills and creativity in the same way that 'art traditions' from all over the world are now honoured and valued." Increasingly, too, Pacific scholars are focusing on the roles that traditional art forms play in the twenty-first century, their role in island-based as well as migrant contexts, and in the work of contemporary gallery-based artists.

In general, Pacific art practice tends to be discussed in terms of the geographic constructs of Polynesia, Melanesia, and Micronesia. Fiji, on the cusp of Melanesia and Polynesia, has historical ancestral connections with Tonga and Samoa, in particular the eastern group of Lau which has strong artistic affinities with Tonga. In 1521, the Portuguese explorer Ferdinand Magellan named the vast expanse of ocean, home of a myriad of islands, the Pacific, due to its peaceful and tranquil nature. While the fifteenth and sixteenth centuries saw Spain and Portugal emerge as colonial superpowers, their focus was on Central and South America; their goal to find El Dorado, gold, and the conversion of pagans to Catholicism. The Pacific did not lure these conquistadors.[1] Perhaps its great expanse of ocean dotted with hundreds of islands did not hold the promise of vast wealth. From the late eighteenth century, however, the Pacific region was very much on the minds of foreign powers. The Enlightenment philosophies of Rousseau and Diderot in Europe played an important role in the way the Pacific was conceived and imagined by Europeans. Often cast as simultaneously alluring, friendly, and exotic, while also fearsome and primitive, the Pacific of early images and journals seemed to cast a certain spell on foreign visitors.

Along with the settlement and development of industries and the claiming and subsequent colonization of various island groups by imperial powers came an intense focus on and collection of objects, coined "artificial curiosities." This Eurocentric mindset influenced the way objects were collected. In keeping with the mediums afforded fine arts status in Western cultures, carved forms (with their stylistic affinities to sculptural practice) were collected in volume compared to the fiber-based material culture largely produced by women. Collectors tended to favor carved objects produced by men because they were seen to be more visually spectacular, and collectors felt that forms produced by women were largely utilitarian or craft (Thomas 1995). Of the tapa cloth that was collected, much was cut into small pieces and pasted into books that resemble samplers of embroidery or quilting types. This practice meant that knowledge of the relevant sizes of the various pieces was lost and that their context was irrevocably changed in relation to their social and cultural uses.

The Pacific, or Oceania, remains a contested site in relation to ongoing attempts to classify and imagine this vast area of islands and ocean. It has been broadly labeled in three groups: Melanesia, derived from the French Melanesie, meaning "black islands," named by Dumont d'Urville during his 1832 voyage; Polynesia, meaning "many islands"; and Micronesia, meaning "small islands," both derived from Greek vernacular. Pacific cultures revolved around well-developed, complex political and social systems. Unlike the effects of colonization, the exchange and intermarriage that went on between different island groups did not result in homogenization, for cultures retained their distinctive identities.

Around six thousand years ago, Austronesian settlers from Southeast Asia arrived in the Pacific, bringing with them Lapita culture. Along with a variety of implements, tools, and animals, they also introduced a distinctive pottery-making tradition, shards of which have been found on islands around the Pacific including Papua New Guinea, Solomon Islands, New Caledonia, Tonga, Samoa, and Fiji. While a number of art forms such as *tatau* (tattoo), *lalava* (lashing), and tapa (decorated bark cloth) bear strong resemblances to the distinctive graphic form of Lapita pottery, Deborah Waite (1999: 246) urges caution in ascribing too close a link. She argues that "design-making in the Lapita tradition died out centuries before it recurred in various historic arts." Lapita traditions were not the first creative forms produced within the Pacific. Figurative and abstract designs, including images of hands, faces, and animals, have been found on rock formations as well as carvings in stone and objects.

Lapita designs, however, have inspired new generations of Pacific artists, including contemporary painters and sculptors who have drawn on its rich cultural heritage. In particular, the extensive navigational expertise of the Lapita people has provided artistic points of departure, a means of identification, and a vehicle to explore contemporary themes of Pacific migration and travel. Samoan artist Fatu Feu'u's painting *Nuanua Malama. Light of the Rainbow* (1988) employs Lapita symbols to illustrate a continuum of Pacific migration. He deploys the distinctive symbols as part of a sweeping rainbow that arches down the canvas to form a series of patterned forms, referencing part of the highly distinctive Samoan *pe'a tatau*, worn by men and bearing close visual affinities with Lapita designs. In doing this Feu'u makes a tangible connection between ancient migration into the Pacific and contemporary migration patterns around and beyond it. Pacific people remain highly mobile, and it is often the performance and practice of traditional art forms in new homelands that enables strong links to cultural identities to be maintained.

Pacific art forms differ markedly from the Western fine arts tradition. Western fine art objects are generally made to be displayed in art galleries or museums. They are seldom touched or worn. The majority of art forms produced within the Pacific, however, are made specifically to be functional within particular ceremonies, events, or performances. They play a crucial role in the maintenance and reinforcement of concepts and principles central to Pacific life. Prior to the nineteenth century, histories, ancestral lineages, and creation narratives were stored in chant, song, and dance forms as well as manifested in visual objects, or symbolized in dynamic patterns and motifs. The performance and display of them was a vital means of teaching histories and maintaining their awareness and importance. Highlighting the value of textile arts in Tongan culture, in particular the *kie hingoa* (named fine mat), Queen Salote has said,

> Each line of kings had its own ceremonial mats which were carefully preserved from generation to generation. In fact, our history is written, not in our books, but in our mats. . . . The *ta'ovala* I wore when I met Queen Elizabeth on Her Majesty's arrival in Tonga was 600 years old. Worshipped in the 13th century as a symbol of the ancient gods, the mat belonged to the chiefly family of Malupo on the island of 'Uiha. (Bain 1967: 77)

These forms are not made for permanent display and measures are not always taken to ensure their conservation or immortality in physical terms. The appreciation of an object or performance as having creative or artistic value is often intricately linked to its function. A good example of this is body adornment, which plays a key role in a wide array of ceremonies, celebrations, and rituals throughout the Pacific. Marriages, births, and deaths, along with ceremonies relating to religious practice and the conferring of titles, require the production of a range of material objects such as fine mats, tapa, quilts and a variety of forms of body adornment. These occasions are often accompanied by dance, song and speeches, and the gifting of food, reflecting a wide range of different yet complementary forms of creative expression.

In Tonga, valuables made for ceremonial purposes are called *koloa*. They comprise an important and highly visual form of material wealth. Textile *koloa*, including fine mats (Figure 20.1), *ngatu* (decorated bark cloth), and quilts, are produced by women who as producers of this wealth are afforded a high social status. Other art forms are also valued in relation to their significance within particular occasions. Richard Moyle (1988: 200) has described Samoan dance as "essentially a group expression of social values." Adrienne Kaeppler (1993: 9) echoes this sentiment in relation to Tongan dance. "Dance may be considered art, work, ritual, ceremony or entertainment or any combination of these depending on the culture or society that produces it. Dance is one of the surface manifestations of the deep structure of a society, which can be communicated by dancing oneself or by observing dance." Highlighting the importance of the *lakalaka* dance in Tongan culture, in particular one performed on the occasion of the coronation of King Taufa'ahau Tupou IV in 1967, Kaeppler (1993: 32) writes,

> Lakalaka is the contemporary formal dance type in which the performers, in effect, deliver a speech in unison, dramatizing their speech with actions. . . . The speech poetry pays allegiance to the King, tells his genealogy and deeds, refers to events or places that the performing village is known for, and upholds the present social order of Tonga. A *lakalaka* is performed by "all" the adult men and women of the village serving as a force of communal arousal and pride.

The reciprocal exchange of objects and food in relation to ceremonial and ritual occasions is widely practiced in the Pacific. In New Ireland, funerary rites and subsequent memorial festivities can take place over several months to a year after the funeral. They adhere to a number of defined stages that involve feasting, the production of ornate carved images and masks known as *malagan* (Figures 20.2 and 20.3), elaborate dances, and performances. Functioning on a number of levels, they commemorate the dead and enact a means of transitioning them from the living world as well as paying homage to their ancestors. The term *malagan* also refers to the wider ceremonial context, which features elaborate ceremonies that involve the wider community.

> *Malagan* festivities are occasions for the expression of solidarity with the moiety and clan. They contribute to the maintenance of the existing economic structure, social prestige, and traditional ideology. Furthermore, practically every kind of northern New Ireland art is attached in some way to the mortuary rites. The social, economic, and aesthetic centrality of these rites is thus established. (Lincoln 1987: 31)

Prior to the nineteenth century, throughout the Pacific, inter-island contact and trade was common, and there was a rich history of relationships between particular groups. Marriage, warfare, and trading created a dynamic context for intercultural exchange. The importance of exchange—the act of giving—was an essential and integral part of forming political alliances. The production of material goods was necessary to facilitate reciprocal gifting and to maintain trade-related ties. In Western Polynesia, there was a lively relationship between the island groups of Samoa, Tonga, and Fiji. Samoan and Tongan parties would journey to Fiji to trade fine mats and tapa cloth for coveted red feathers. A Samoan proverbial expression refers to the two sons of the Uimanu'a who went to Fiji to get *'ula* for their father. 'Ula are the feathers that embodied much cultural significance as both a form of adornment and as part of the valuable *'ie toga* (fine mats). The proverb *'Ua maua 'ula futi-futi* (To have nothing but shredded feathers) relates to one who is careless and wasteful and is derived from the story of the two sons aforementioned, who on their return from Fiji to Samoa plucked the feathers to pieces and the pieces were carried away by the wind (Schultz 1965: 69). Fijians in turn placed great value (as did their Tongan neighbors) on Samoan *'ie toga* (fine mats). White nautilus shells used in head adornments were often traded from Tonga. In 1830, John Williams writes that Samoans

> also make a small kind of mat which they weave with a remarkably fine thread from a species of the Palm leaf. These mats are much sought after by the Togataboons, who come from Tonga in their canoes to purchase them a distance of six or seven hundred miles as an article of dress for the Tonga chiefs. Seven large canoes had visited the Samoas from Tonga just before our arrival to purchase the above articles. (Moyle 1984: 48)

By the mid-nineteenth century, however, colonial settlement had halted these relationships and mass-produced materials and objects, including mirrors, beads, shell, and fabric along with metal implements and nails were quickly assimilated into the production and design aesthetic of many art forms. So popular was the demand for blue beads that John Williams in 1830 commented, "A single row of blue beads presented to the person in whose hands a captive falls will generally be the means of saving his life" (Moyle 1984: 244–245). While missionary activity drastically impacted the practice of *tatau* (tattoo), dance, and the production of carvings, which were central to indigenous religious belief systems, many forms were maintained. Often, however, their significance changed to reflect new influences and experiences. Carved objects made for religious worship were an obvious target for missionaries, who saw them as pagan and heathen, and the symbolic desecration of them was common practice throughout the Pacific as a highly visible sign of one's successful conversion to the new religion. Williams describes one such event, which took place in Rarotonga in 1837.

> A day or two afterwards, they requested us to take our seat outside the door; and on doing so, we observed a large concourse of people coming toward us, bearing heavy burdens. They walked in procession, and dropped at our feet 14 immense idols, the smallest of which was about 5 yards in length. Near the wood were red feathers and a string of small pieces of polished pearl shells, which were said to be the manava or soul of the god. Some of the idols were torn to pieces before our eyes; others were reserved to decorate the rafters of the chapel we proposed to erect; and one was kept to be sent to England, which is now in the missionary museum. (Moyle 1984)

The introduction of previously scarce and by implication highly revered items such as shells (Figure 20.4) and feathers on a mass scale significantly affected the way they functioned and the enabling role they played in terms of their meaning within the prevailing social order. Discussing the impact of cash and mass influx of shells to Mount Hagen society in the Western Highlands of Papua New Guinea, Andrew Strathern (1979: 533) writes, "Europeans from the 1930's onwards brought shells in, and offered them, outside of *moka* or bridewealth, to all those who could supply in return produce, pigs, or labour. . . . At once, a market was created which threatened to turn upside-down the big-men's monopoly." He argues, though, that these changes have worked to transform existing economic and cultural economies rather that signaling their demise.

> In harnessing cash to the structure of *moka* partnerships, today's big-men have clearly repeated the manoeuvres of their predecessors thirty years ago, when Europeans brought in large quantities of shells from the coastal sites where they are found. By letting cash into bridewealth payments, for example, they redefine cash as a "basic valuable," which every man needs, while at the same time stipulating that pigs also must continue to be paid; and pigs have to be produced by domestic labour in the same way as before. (Strathern 1979: 536)

All societies invest art with social meaning. Body adornment represents a rich and diverse context for creative expression. The way the body is dressed and adorned therefore can embody cultural and spiritual significance. In Pacific culture, where the appreciation and awareness of a thing as art depends to a considerable extent on its significance within the context of a certain event, the importance of presentation within the overall structure becomes paramount.

Figure 20.1. Women dressed in fine mats for funeral, Nukualofa, Tonga (photo WA).

Figure 20.2. Malagan figure, Northern New Ireland (photo HAA).

Figure 20.3. Leader of malagan wearing kapkap mask accompanied by two malagan dancers, Kaviang, New Ireland (photo DCY).

Figure 20.4. Initiated men presenting shell currency to Dukduk, Tubuan, and Maus masks, Kabilomo, Duke of York Islands (photo DCY).

Figure 20.5. Men's nighttime fire dance, Baining, Gaulim, New Britain (photo FBM).

Unlike Polynesia and Micronesia, Melanesia is a site of rich mask-making traditions. They play a crucial role in performances and dance (Figure 20.5). Intimately associated with the veneration of particular religious or ancestral figures or within initiation rituals, they take a range of stylistic forms, including figurative facial representations, animals such as the crocodile, bird, and snake, and more abstract and stylized designs. Often constructed from embellished tapa cloth over a wooden frame, masks also feature human hair, feathers, coconut shell, shell, beads, and seeds among other things. In the Asmat region, part of the Papuan Province of Indonesia, mask ceremonies continue to play a vital role in cultural life. Eric Kjellgren (2007: 30) describes their ongoing importance,

> The Spirits of the recently dead (ndat) lie at the core of Asmat religion and are central to the theme of Asmat art. . . . Almost all Asmat subgroups celebrate the mask feast, a sequence of rituals that culminates when the dead, embodied by performers in dramatic full-length fibre body masks with rustling skirts of sago-palm leaves, emerge from the forest to visit the living. . . . Although performance of the mask feast had all but ceased by the early 1960s, the ceremony was revived in the early 1980s and continues to be performed today.

Pacific societies generally were highly stratified in terms of the prevailing social order. Those of very high rank could often trace their ancestral lineage to the gods. Religious beliefs often revolved around ancestral or progenitor figures. In Polynesia, principal deities presided over particular domains in the natural environment, and they were afforded allegiance by those who worked in their realm. Linguistic variations of Tangaroa/Tangaloa, Ku/Tu, and Lono/Rongo, among others, were revered, and creation narratives were intimately associated with these deities. In Aotearoa/New Zealand, carving was introduced into the human realm from the underwater realm, where Tangaroa reigned supreme. The most prominent of these narratives features an ancient chief named Rua. Manuruhi, Rua's son, offends Tangaroa, who kidnaps him, transforms him into the shape of a bird, renders him mute, and sets him up as a *tekoteko* carving on his house, named Huiteananui, beneath the ocean. Rua pursues Tangaroa and finds Manuruhi affixed to his home, surrounded by other carvings that to his surprise are talking to each other. He recognizes his son through his intense stare. Rua reclaims him and in revenge sets Tangaroa's house alight, taking with him some of the carvings from the porch. Back in the human world, these carved forms became the templates for the first carvings, but unfortunately they did not have the power of speech.[2] Sidney Moko Mead (1984: 69) elaborates,

> Tangaroa thus provides an ideal for human carvers to emulate—the suggestion of movement in the figures, and the suggestion of speech or of talk. The fact that human carvers could not make their *poupou* really talk was "explained" in the myth as being the result of Ruatepupuke's fire. Nonetheless, good creators could make their *poupou* "talk" in a different way, in a silent language that could be understood by those observant people who understood the artistic code of communication. It could be said that the moment in the myth when Ruatepupuke looked up and saw his son Manuruhi trying desperately to speak to him is remembered in all carvings that show an open mouth "struggling to speak."

This communicative dynamic that Mead describes is further elaborated by the use of *paua* shells, taken from Tangaroa's realm, which are often used to represent the eyes of carved figures.

Thomas (1995: 155) suggests an intrinsic link between materials used in a range of art forms and creation narratives,

> For the people of the Society Islands feathers were associated directly with origins and divine fecundity. The first being, Ta'aroa, had long existed in an absolute void, but after an eternity broke out through his shell to differentiate the heavens and the earth, light and darkness and a succession of foundations for the rock and earth. . . . Ta'aroa created other gods and shook off the red and yellow feathers that had initially covered his body: these "became tress, plantain clusters, and verdure upon the land." . . . Although certain plants and crops were identified with other particular deities, plant life in general is thus a transmutation of Ta'aroa's feathers.

Thomas' commentary highlights the crucial relationship between the environment and cultural practice and belief systems. In keeping with the idea that highly ranked people could occupy godlike status, carved objects were also often adorned in a similar way to people. The interrelationship between the human world and the realm of the gods and ancestors was often mediated through the ritualized use of objects such as carved forms, kites, masks, and highly revered materials taken from the natural environment. These forms functioned within highly regulated and often complex rituals and ceremonies that could also involve the offering of gifts and sacrifices. Social distinctions in relation to status and rank were manifest visibly in a variety of sophisticated and elaborate forms of adornment. One's rank could be visually identified by distinctive forms of body adornment and clothing, some of which could only be worn by those of appropriate rank. Throughout the Pacific, adornment functions as a visible signifier of a range of meanings. Given that many Pacific societies were highly regulated, in particular Micronesia and the Hawaiian and Society Island groups, body adornment (both temporary and permanent) formed a key site of its articulation (Thomas 1995: 152).

In Hawai'i *ahu ula* (finely made feathered cloaks), comprising thousands of feathers and sometimes taking months or years to complete, were made to be worn by individuals of chiefly rank. Bird catchers and feather workers belonged to a specialist feather guild, who were affiliated to the deity Kuhuluhulumanu. As with prestige fine mats, cloaks were often named and carried immense symbolic value. As in Tahiti, yellow and red feathers garnered the most value and featured in cloaks, deity figures, and temple forms. In Tahiti, Aotearoa/New Zealand, and Hawai'i, feathered cloaks were produced by a process of attaching the feathers to a backing fiber. In all three groups, elaborate feathered cloaks featured as markers of chiefly rank. Te Rangi Hiroa (Peter Buck) insists however that each group developed its own distinctive production technique. The abundance and variety of bird life in Hawai'i meant that a highly specialized industry developed in relation to the collection and processing of feathers. He explains that red feathers from the *'i'iwi* featured in garments, along with those of a darker red hue taken from the *'apapane*. Highly prized yellow feathers came from the *'o'o* and the *mamo*. "These birds" he writes, "were caught in the moulting season, the yellow feathers were plucked out, and the birds set free to grow another crop for the next season. The *'i'iwi* and the *'apapane*, on the other hand, had so many red feathers that they would not have survived plucking, so they were killed and eaten" (Te Rangi Hiroa 1957: 218–219).

Helmets known as *mahiole* were also produced in Hawai'i, with different styles made to denote the relevant rank and status of the wearer. Feathered *mahiole* were worn as regalia for high chiefs and kings, while those made of human hair or in a distinctive mushroom form were worn by warriors and lesser-ranking chiefs (Te Rangi Hiroa 1957: 231). The crested form of the *mahiole* has strong stylistic affinities with effigies of the war god Ku, a figurative god form made up of feathers, shell, teeth, and sometimes human hair. This stylistic interface between different art forms testifies to the holistic role that art played and the way indigenous belief systems pivoted around genealogical connections between the human and spirit or deity world (Figure 20.6).

Just as in Tonga and Samoa, where fine mats are seen to contain histories and genealogies, high-ranking *kula* shells are revered in a similar way in the Massim region of Papua New Guinea. Expert sailors make long-distance voyages in outrigger canoes required by the *kula* interisland trading system. The maintenance and exchange of *kula* shells also reflect the way culturally significant objects are valued not only in relation to their material form, but also in terms of their capacity to reflect enhanced status onto the current owner through its association with those who have owned it in the past. Like many Pacific cultures that have a rich maritime history, canoes are highly embellished with carvings as well as other adornment forms. Shirley Campbell (2002: 193) explains its significance,

> The art of *kula* is a dynamic medium of communication in which the associated systems of meaning are integrated with others to reflect Vakutan spheres of social experience. Rituals connected to the garden, those employed in fishing, in marriage, conception and childbirth encode information that formulates a Vakutan worldview. . . . In seeking to understand the meanings operating within different contexts of communication we begin to understand the complexity with which ideologies are constructed and reinforced. We cannot hope to understand what the graphic forms used to embellish canoe prow and splashboards mean without also seeking to understand the art of doing *kula*. Likewise, the rituals of *kula*, the transactions and the tensions associated with it, can only be fully understood when the meanings encoded within the carvings have also been investigated.

The Massim region is known for its prolific and highly accomplished carving tradition. As early as 1895, local carvers had realized the lucrative value of their carvings in the eyes of Western visitors. Campbell (2002: 45) states that this interest sparked an increase in the production of carved forms. "As the demand increased," she writes, "particularly in the late 1950s through to the early 1970s, the carving community multiplied and with it the level of production was augmented to satisfy this new and lucrative market." Many of the carvings were made specifically with the tourist or collector in mind. Other consequences of this development were that some regions not formally known for carving began the practice, and a greater number of men became carvers, especially in those areas that tourists regularly visited. But in other areas, master carvers continued to be trained and to produce works specifically for ceremonial and ritualistic purposes, for exchange and gifting, and for local use (Figure 20.7). Works made as part of *kula* cultural practice feature ornate prow works, patterns carved directly onto the canoes in which the voyages take place, and elaborately carved boards that function as splash boards. Geometric designs are juxtaposed with animal forms that include bats, birds, insects, and shellfish as well as mythical creatures. Chants and incantations often accompany the production of specific forms. Some are associated with certain colors, which like other areas of the Pacific afford symbolic value.

Throughout the Pacific, gender plays a decisive role in relation to art making. A term that is commonly used interchangeably with sex, gender has been increasingly theorized in a much more complex way. Gender is now seen to be integrally concerned with the ways people develop their sense of self as male or female in relation

Figure 20.6. War club, Marquesas Islands (photo HAA).

Figure 20.7. Prow of war canoe, New Georgia Island, Solomon Islands National Museum (photo DW).

to their prevailing social, religious, and cultural experiences, as opposed to purely their biological sex. Femininity and masculinity within gender studies is seen as socially constructed, leading a number to argue that individuals perform their gender.[3] Increasingly, scholars working in non-Western societies have pointed out that gender is not simply a question of relations between and among men and women. More broadly construed, explorations of gender address the notion that relations between the men and women are integrally linked with wider aspects of culture. Introducing a volume of essays examining female roles as well as the use of spiritual images of women in male rituals in Papua New Guinea, Pascale Bonnemere argues that "male initiations do not concern exclusively boys or even men, as earlier works, whether they were psychologically oriented or used a male-domination model, tended to conclude. Although these two aspects (male ontology and reproduction of a power hierarchy between the genders) are present, they do not exhaust the subject" (Bonnemere 2004: 11). He goes on to suggest that there often exist complementary ritualized practices carried out by women that run in tandem with particular phases of male initiations.

Gender also has implications in relation to the division of labor. Within the Pacific, art production tends to be gender specific. Men tend to work with hard materials such as wood, bone, and stone, and women tend to work with soft materials including flax, fiber, and fabric. Jehanne Teilhet (1983: 49) suggests that originally

there were no distinctions in relation to the value ascribed to various materials, but that over time precedence was given to forms traditionally produced by men. She argues that gender divisions in relation to art practice may not be wholly related to the materials used, but also to the tools employed to create the works.

> In traditional cultures, men have controlled women's use of materials by not allowing them to use the tools necessary to work hard materials. In Polynesia, the artists' tools are somewhat animistic; they are thought to possess intelligence, given their own names and in some cases even their own genealogy. A tool can accrue prestige, power and sanctity, for it is the conscious, conjoined efforts of tools and men that create carvings. Carving is a religious act. In Hawaii, the artist consecrated his tools by a sacrifice and a chant to ensure that sufficient *mana* was contained in them, consequently ensuring the efficacy of the image, "the house of the god."

Ritualized activities also accompanied the production of art forms by women. Discussing the process of Maori weaving, Mick Pendergrast (1987: 13) states, "Ritual prohibitions are observed and great respect is shown for the material throughout all stages, from planting through to harvesting and the preparation of the fibre. These continue with the artistic designing of the work and the weaving itself. The spiritual essence, or *mauri*, contained in all living things and natural objects is acknowledged, protected and retained through all processes and into the completed *kakahu* [cloak]." In Samoa, prior to the introduction of manufactured dyes, the process of making *lama,* a black pigment made from the kernel of the candlenut that is used to design *siapo* (Samoan decorated bark cloth), also involved ritualized elements.

Prior to the introduction of fabric into the Pacific in the nineteenth century, bark cloth, made from the processed inner bast of the paper mulberry tree, brought into the Pacific by the Lapita people, was used for a wide range of utilitarian, clothing, and ceremonial uses. In Western Polynesia, in particular the island groups of Tonga, Samoa, and Fiji, where the tree grows well, tapa making continues today. Tongan women in particular are prolific producers of *ngatu*. In Tonga, *ngatu* continues to be made on a large scale due to the requirements of the monarchy, reflecting its ongoing importance. *Ngatu* designs also functioned to reflect the prevailing social system. From the early 1900s, figurative motifs including crowns, crests, and other forms of royal regalia became incorporated into the overall design. Historical events have also been commemorated on *ngatu*. These include the appearance of Halley's Comet over Tonga in 1910 and the installation of electric lighting in the streets of Nukualofa (Neich and Pendergrast 1987: 13). While the process of making the cloth is relatively generic across the Pacific, designs and motifs vary markedly.

In Samoa and Tonga, designs are often applied either by a freehand painting technique or through a process of rubbing and highlighting. The overall design tends to conform to a grid pattern, with motifs often taken from nature, including flower, shell, seeds, and fruit, pared down to stylized pattern forms. In Fiji, designs applied to *masi* (Fijian decorated bark cloth) are characterized by graphic, geometric forms that are applied using stencils and fine lines applied with a bamboo pen. In the Lau group, bark cloth known as *Gatu vakaviti,* translated as Tongan cloth in the style of Fiji, is decorated using rubbed designs and shares strong affinities with its Tongan neighbors. Both Fiji and Hawai'i are known for their innovative approaches in the decoration of bark cloth. Brightly colored bark cloth features in both island groups. In Fiji *masi kuvui* is produced through a smoking process, in which the cloth is hung over a frame. In Hawai'i, the abundance of plant life meant that a range of colored dyes including red, yellow, purple, and blue could be made. Hawaiian *kapa* (decorated bark cloth) designs were applied using a variety of methods, including bamboo stamps, ruling, and freehand. Figurative elements are not characteristic, unlike in many other areas of the Pacific. While relatively few pieces remain today, they reflect a highly innovative and complex approach in relation to the overall design aesthetic. These innovations include a distinctive watermark pattern that was imprinted into the cloth itself, leaving a tactile and patterned surface, and the perfuming of *kapa,* either by adding plant-derived scent to the dye or by laying scented material within the layers of the cloth itself (Krauss 1993: 70). In Niue, few examples of *hiapo* (decorated bark cloth) remain. Those that do, however, are thought to have been made around the 1880s. They feature highly intricate and detailed hand-painted designs that include a range of plant life and a distinctive circular composition. Images of ships and women dressed in European clothing are also featured, reflecting colonial arrival and settlement. Bark cloth is also made in Melanesia. The Oro Province of Papua New Guinea is known for its tapa making, which continues to be done for ceremonial purposes as well as for the tourist market. As previously discussed, there is also a rich tradition of tapa mask making in Melanesia.

In Eastern Polynesia and Hawai'i, it is thought that missionary women introduced sewing and embroidery to women of high rank around the 1830s. By the late nineteenth century, quilt making had come to take the place of tapa making as women turned to this new form. As early as 1858, documentation exists stating that patchwork quilts were featured in a wedding ceremony in Tahiti (Hammond 1986: 30). Known as *tivaevae* in the Cook Islands, *tifaifai* in the Society Islands, and *kapa* in Hawai'i (interestingly the same name that is given to decorated bark cloth), appliqué and patchwork quilts function as treasured items of exchange and gifting on important occasions and as a highly visual sign of cultural identity. Increasingly, quilts are also being made by migrant Pacific communities in New Zealand, Australia, and the United States as a means of continuing cultural practice and as a form of gifting.

Tatau (tattoo) traditions within the Pacific also reflect the way gender relations play out in the wider social and cultural system. It also represents an important and highly visual form of adornment and signifier of cultural heritage and identity. In *Wrapping in Images,* Alfred Gell (1993: 1) maintains that *tatau* in Polynesia played a crucial role in politics, warfare, and religion, to the extent that "the description of tattooing practices becomes, inevitably, a description of the wider institutional forms within which tattooing is embedded."

In many Pacific societies, *tatau* played an important role in marking transitional periods of a person's life. The pain endured in the process of receiving *tatau* or other permanent forms of body adornment such as scarification is often seen as an integral part of the overall process. For many it is conceived of in symbolic terms—once one has experienced this, one will be better equipped to cope with life's challenges and traumas. In Samoa for instance, one reason men receive a more elaborate tattoo (*pe'a*) as opposed to women (*malu*) is because women experience the pain of childbirth.

Prior to the arrival of missionaries and colonial settlement in the Pacific, permanent forms of body adornment were widely worn by both men and women. European voyagers became fascinated by the *tatau* traditions they saw. They feature in the earliest images sketched by voyaging artists. Captain Cook recorded a version of the word tattoo in 1769 while in the Marquesas, and it is generally thought that the term is derived from the Polynesian *tatau*. Although dramatically affected by colonization, *tatau* traditions in Eastern Polynesia, in particular in the Society Islands and the Marquesas, were widely practiced. Gell maintains that "all-over tattooing," that is, tattooing from head to toe, is a development unique to these two island groups. He states:

> But it was not just the uncommonly complete coverage of the body surface by tattoos which distinguishes the Marquesan style; no less remarkable was the large number and individual complexity of the motifs employed. . . . Von den Steinen (1925) enumerates no less that 174 individually named motifs still recognized by his Marquesan informants in 1891—half a century after tattooing had been officially forbidden by the French colonial authorities. (Gell 1993, 163)

Tattoo functioned in a range of ways. It provided a highly visible indication of one's social rank and cultural group, it reflected an individual's status within initiation contexts, it functioned as a form of adornment, enhancing one's beauty as well as a fearsome presence in times of warfare. It also functioned as a symbol of mourning and loss. In the 1820s, the missionary William Ellis described seeing Queen Kamamalu "receiving a tattoo on her tongue as an expression of grief for her recently deceased mother in law. When Ellis mentioned to her how painful the practice must be, she replied, '*He eha nui no, he nui roa ra ku'u aroha*' ('Great pain indeed, greater is my affection.')" (Kwiatkowski 1966: 45). In Samoa and Aotearoa/New Zealand, *tatau* traditions remain strong and there has been a revival of *tatau* in a number of Pacific Island groups. The Samoan master *tufunga ta tatau* Paulo Sulu'ape has stated that the significance of the *pe'a* (Samoan *tatau* worn by men) marks his transition into adulthood as well as his capacity to serve the chiefs in all manner of food, kava, and social events. This service element is a crucial part of the commitment of the individual and his decision to have a *pe'a* (Adams et al. 2010).

Pacific artists are also developing a strong profile within art gallery contexts. In Aotearoa/New Zealand, Australia, and Hawai'i, where there is an established gallery system, Pacific artists have attained significant local and international profiles. Contemporary Maori artists have a relatively long history of gallery-based art practice. In the 1950s, the first Maori artists trained in art schools. Artists like Selwyn Muru, Arnold Wilson, and Fred Graham explored their Maori heritage and cultural forms in tandem with their increasing interest in European modernist traditions. Wilson's *Tane Mahuta II* (1954) is a carving named after the god of the forest rendered in a style that evokes the simplicity of prevailing modernist sculptors Henry Moore and Barbara Hepworth. Pacific Islands migration to Aotearoa/New Zealand began in earnest after World War II. By the late 1980s, Samoan Fatu Feu'u (Figure 20.8), Niuean John Pule, and Tongan Filipe Tohi were establishing profiles within the New Zealand art community. Their art practice reflected a blend of influences relating to both their islands and migrant homes. The mid-1990s has seen the emergence of a number of New Zealand–born Pacific artists, many of whom graduated from art schools, exhibiting regularly in dealer galleries. For many, their experience of the islands is often filtered by stories told to them by parents and grandparents, as they may not have spent any considerable time in the islands of their heritage. Issues of cultural identity, then, can become a complex negotiation between a number of different countries and cultural backgrounds (Vercoe 2004: 91).

More and more, Pacific communities in New Zealand are falling outside of conventional "immigrant" categories. More Cook Islanders, for instance, reside in New Zealand than in the Cook Islands and more Niueans live in New Zealand than in Niue. Of a local population of less than 1,500 in Niue, Niueans in New Zealand number over 20,000 (Sissons 2005: 113). Issues of belonging become an increasing priority. As first and second generations of Pacific artists born in New Zealand engage with issues of cultural identity, memory and notions of belonging emerge as key points of departure. Like many urban Maori artists who may not have much firsthand knowledge of their tribal homelands, parents, grandparents, and extended family members often become crucial vehicles and arbiters of cultural knowledge and identity. The telling of

Figure 20.8. *Nuanua Malama/Light of the Rainbow, Fatu Feu'u, 1988 (photo CV).*

stories and recounting of memories for many becomes important in relation to the awareness of and identification with their cultural and geographic heritages.[4]

Maori artist Brett Graham has created a body of work that firmly situates his practice within the wider Pacific. His carved works in particular draw on a range of Polynesian sculptural styles. In doing this, he makes tangible links between his own heritage and other Polynesian cultures and islands. Many of his titles and concepts are informed by Polynesian concepts and histories—Lapita culture, navigation, and colonial legacies. His sculptural practice does not characteristically reference the distinctive curvilinear style that characterizes "traditional" Maori carving. He has instead chosen to look further back, to a period of Maori carving that Sydney Moko Mead describes as *Te Tipunga* (the Growth) (1200–1500). This period predates the development of the cursive style. *Kahukura* (1995) takes the form of a sweeping arc. Conceived as an homage to Maori weaver Rangimarie Hetet, who had recently died, the work evokes a monumental cloak. *Kaiwhakatere* (the Navigator) (2000) tells a narrative of migration and arrival at Aotearoa. Comprising three parts, representing a bird's head, a canoe, and an altar, it highlights the rich navigational heritage of Maori, their voyage across the ocean, and their arrival and settlement. More recently Graham has developed his sculptural practice to incorporate multimedia elements.

Digital video artist Rachel Rakena explores her Maori identity as well as notions of memory and histories. *Mihi Aroha* (2002), a tribute to her recently deceased mother, took the form of a *whare*, or house structure. Against the translucent walls and ceiling were projected e-mail messages the artist had received, streaming down the structure to resemble tears. Rakena has made a number of works that explore the capacity of the Internet to maintain cultural ties when one is far from home, to essentially form another community. Submerged figures swimming under the water also feature in a number of her works. They speak of a more fluid and poetic notion of identity, which like the Internet is not defined by particular geographies or places.

Maori, Niuean, Samoan artist Janet Lilo's art practice also engages with the Internet, in particular the site YouTube and social networking sites Bebo and Facebook. In her Top 16 (2007–2010)

Figure 20.9. *TOP 16, Installation Detail, Janet Lilo, 1988 (photo CV).*

installations (Figure 20.9), a number of television monitors are featured, which screen a variety of Pacific youth singing along to hiphop music and talking about their experiences and the importance of hip-hop culture to them, in an often frank, personal, and candid way. Dispersed around the walls above the monitors are a myriad of profile shots taken from Facebook and Bebo personal pages. Her work highlights the increasing importance that social Internet networks play in the lives of young people, pointing to the agency of digital mediums to transform and reshape cultural expression.

New Zealand–born Samoan Edith Amituanai's work speaks of narratives of belonging and home. Like Lilo, she does not attempt to locate her identity within a wider Pacific land and seascape, but rather focuses on what is distinctive and familiar within her domestic space (Figure 20.10). As a first-generation, New Zealand–born Samoan artist, her photography references "home" in its most intimate sense. Amituanai has developed a number of series of photographs that depict the homes of her family and friends. These interior domestic portraits reflect the ways her family and others in her community have established a sense of home that retains its "island" identity but is also very much a part of New Zealand culture. This locating of one's identity within domestic spaces highlights the value of memory, relationships, and the performative agency of cultural practice that enables the continuation and maintenance of distinctive identities within migration contexts.

Figure 20.10. *The Manu Lounge, Edith Amituanai, 2006 (photo CV).*

The Red Wave Collective is based at the Oceania Centre for the Arts and Culture at the University of the South Pacific in Fiji. Founded by the Tongan scholar Epeli Hau'ofa, this collective of artists explores Hau'ofa's vision of an Oceanic identity that looks within instead of toward the West for artistic vision and inspiration. Tongan artist Lingikoni Vaka'uta represents Pacific mythological narratives in his paintings. His *Legend of Maui Slowing the Sun* (2006) features both figurative and abstract elements. It draws on a range of Pacific art forms including tapa cloth designs, carving styles, shields, and *tatau*. His fluid and organic forms present a dynamic enactment of Maui's feat that seems to position him in a kind of supernatural realm. Fijian artist William Bakalevu's paintings also evoke ancient narratives. His *Legend of Mount Uluiqalau* (2005) references the legend, with sweeping colorful forms, as well as the tradition of weaving. The figurative composition is set in a central panel of the work, between two painted panels that resemble a woven background. The Red Wave Collective reflects a strong commitment to the articulation of Pacific stories and narratives, stressing a vital continuum in relation to their relevance to the artists' lives.

While gallery-based artistic practice has emerged relatively recently in Papua New Guinea, a number of Melanesian artists have established a presence in the international art world. Mathias Kauage's paintings speak of the changing experiences and transitions faced by communities in Papua New Guinea. Susan Cochrane (2007: 119) describes his work as defining his generation. A prolific artist, Kauage's paintings emerging in the 1980s addressed a range of issues including the changing role of women in society and the impact of technology in his area. His works often feature planes, helicopters, cars and trucks, and the commemoration of political figures. *Helicopter* (1982) reflects his characteristic blending of Western and Melanesian references. It features a woman with ceremonial markings seated in a helicopter, its form made up of a range of stylized and colorful patterns.

In Hawai'i, contemporary gallery-based practice, like in other areas of the Pacific, often draws on traditional forms, but also engages with prevailing social and political issues. In 1959, Hawai'i became a state of the United States of America. Formally annexed to the United States, it has experienced a long history of colonial settlement. Carver Rocky K. Jensen has created a body of work that draws on traditional Hawaiian forms. While many of the forms he draws on, including the tiki, have been co-opted by the tourist industry, his knowledge of Hawaiian culture infuses into his works a significance that highlights their importance to Hawaiians in the present. A number of contemporary artists engage with political concerns, dealing with issues of land and ownership and with the importance of maintaining their native language and voice, and they reflect on the impact of mass tourism on their cultural practice. Malia Kane Kuahiwinui's *Aia no ke ola i ka waha; aia no ka make i ka waka* (1997), a mixed media work on acetate, reflects on the legacy of legislation banning native languages. The work features a collage of newspaper articles written in both Hawaiian and English, superimposed over historical photographs of Native Hawaiians, some of whose faces have been obscured. Chuck Kawai'olu Souza's work also engages with the legacy of colonialism in Hawai'i. His *E Ho'okani no i ka waha; aia no ka make i ka waha* (1997) takes the form of a drum made of wire and plastic wrap, inscribed with

text in Hawaiian and English, including the words "resist," "doubt," "and hopeless." Evoking the sounds of a drum call to action, these artists' works appeal to their viewers to be aware of the position of Native Hawaiians and of the importance of valuing their heritage and importance as the indigenous people of Hawai'i.

The term Pacific art evokes a wide and varied range of forms of creative expression, spanning a number of media, expanding and challenging conventional definitions of what art can be. It embodies a diversity of cultural forms of expression and reflects changes and developments in the face of colonial settlement and transition. While some forms ceased to be produced as societies changed and adjusted, others were maintained and many developed in new ways, reflecting the innovation and resilience of Pacific cultural heritage. Today, artistic creative expression remains a vital part of the lives of Pacific communities both in the Islands and in migrant contexts. It provides important and ongoing points of identification, as well as new points of departure as artists continue to develop and explore their heritage and identities.

NOTES

1. While Mendaña made excursions into the Pacific in the sixteenth century, he did not complete comprehensive cartographies or make significant inroads. See Vercoe 2004.

2. For a more detailed account of this narrative see Mead 1984: 64–69.

3. See Beauvoir 1972; Butler 1995.

4. The past decade has seen a number of international exhibitions of art from the Pacific. They include Paradise Now? (2004), at the Asia Society Museum in New York; Pasifika Styles (2006–2008), at the Museum of Archeology and Anthropology at Cambridge University; and Datelines: Contemporary Art from the Pacific (2007), at the Galerie der Stadt Sindelfingen in Germany. See Vercoe 2009.

BIBLIOGRAPHY

Adams, M., S. Mallon, P. W. Brunt, and N. Thomas. 2010. *Tatau: Samoan tattoo, New Zealand art, global culture.* Wellington: Te Papa Press.

Anderson, J., ed. 2009. *Crossing cultures: Conflict, migration and convergence.* Melbourne: The Miegunyah Press.

Bain, K. 1967. *The friendly islanders: A story of Queen Salote and her people.* London: Hodder & Stoughton.

Beauvoir, S. de. 1972. *The second sex.* Translated by H. M. Parshley. Harmondsworth: Penguin.

Bonnemere, P., ed. 2004. *Women as unseen characters: Male ritual in Papua New Guinea.* Philadelphia: University of Pennsylvania Press.

Butler, J. 1995. *Gender trouble: Feminism and the subversion of identity.* New York: Routledge.

Campbell, S. F. 2002. *The art of Kula.* Oxford: Berg.

Chiu, M., ed. 2004. The many faces of paradise in *Paradise Now? In Contemporary art from the Pacific.* New York: Asia Society.

Cochrane, S. 2007. *Art and life in Melanesia.* Newcastle: Cambridge Scholars Press.

Gell, A. 1993. *Wrapping in images: Tattooing in Polynesia.* Oxford: Clarendon Press.

Hammond, J. D. 1986. *Tifaifai and quilts of Polynesia.* Honolulu: University of Hawai'i Press.

Hooper, S. 2006. *Pacific encounters: Art and divinity in Polynesia 1760–1860.* Wellington: Te Papa Press.

Kaeppler, A. 1993. *Poetry in motion: Studies of Tongan dance.* Tonga: Vava'u Press.

Kirch, P. V., and R. C. Green. 2001. *Hawaiki, ancestral Polynesia: An essay in historical anthropology.* Cambridge: Cambridge University Press.

Kjellgren, E. 2007. *Oceania: Art of the Pacific Islands in the Metropolitan Museum of Art.* New Haven, Conn.: Yale University Press.

Krauss, B. H. 1993. *Plants in Hawaiian culture.* Honolulu: University of Hawai'i Press.

Kwiatkowski, P. F. 1996. *The Hawaiian tattoo.* Kohala, Hawai'i: Holona, Inc.

Lincoln, L. 1987. *Assemblage of spirits: Idea and image in New Ireland.* New York: George Braziller.

Mallon, S., and P. F. Pereira, eds. 2002. *Pacific Art Niu Sila: The Pacific dimension of contemporary New Zealand Arts.* Wellington: Te Papa Press.

Mead, S. M., ed. 1984. *Te Maori: Maori art from New Zealand Collections.* New York: Abrams in association with the American Federation of Arts.

Mead, S. M., and B. Kernot, eds. 1983. *Art and artists of Oceania.* Palmerston North: Dunmore Press.

Moyle, R. 1984. *The Samoan journals of John Williams. 1830 and 1832.* Canberra: Australian National University Press.

———. 1988. *Traditional Samoan music.* Auckland: Auckland University Press.

Neich, R., and M. Pendergrast. 1997. *Pacific tapa.* Auckland: David Bateman.

Pendergrast, M. 1987. *Te Aho Tapu the sacred thread: Traditional Maori weaving.* Auckland: Reed Publishing.

Rapaport, M., ed. 1999. *The Pacific Islands: Environment & society.* Honolulu: Bess Press.

Schultz, E. 1965. *Proverbial expressions of the Samoans.* Translated by Brother Herman. Wellington: Polynesian Society.

Sissons, J. 2005. *First peoples: Indigenous cultures and their futures.* London: Reaktion Books.

Strathern, A. 1979. Gender, ideology and money in Mount Hagan. *Man* 14(3) (September).

Te Rangi Hiroa (Peter H. Buck). 1957. *Arts and crafts of Hawaii: Clothing.* Honolulu: Bishop Museum Press.

Teilhet, Jehanne. 1983. *Paradise reviewed: An interpretation of Gauguin's Polynesian symbolism.* Ann Arbor, Mich.: UMI Research Press.

Thomas, N. 1995. *Oceanic Art.* London: Thames and Hudson.

Vercoe, C. 2004. The many faces of paradise. In *Paradise Now? Contemporary art from the Pacific,* 34–47. New York: Asia Society.

———. 2009. Belonging and homelands: Negotiating identity in Aotearoa/New Zealand. In *Crossing cultures: Conflict, migration and convergence,* ed. Jaynie Anderson, 799–802. Melbourne: Miegunyah Press.

Waite, D. 1999. Art. In *The Pacific Islands: Environment & society,* ed. M. Rapaport. Honolulu: Bess Press.

Wedde, I., ed. 1994. *Fomison: What shall we tell them?* Wellington: City Gallery.

Music and Dance Performance

Paul Wolffram

21

Music and dance performance have come to be understood as key components of Pacific identity and fundamental elements of Pacific life and culture. Oceanic performance contexts vary widely. They include ritual undertakings, political and religious processes, and occasions of informal celebration. They may variously involve soloists, large or small ensembles of men and women, or spiritual entities; and performances often include vocals, instrumentation, costume, and accoutrements in combination with choreographed movement. Often the performance of music and dance is based on a poetic text—which may be a form of oratory or incantation or may make reference to legends or historic or contemporary events. Today, Pacific music and dance consist of both traditional and modern forms that are in a constant state of change and development.

Across the three broad regional divisions of Melanesia, Micronesia, and Polynesia comparable distinctions may be observed. For example, dance movements are predominantly in the vertical plane in Melanesia. Dancers move with a clearly articulated bobbing motion, and the movement of a dance troupe, from one area to another, is common. In contrast, Polynesian troupes tend to be stationary during performance, and dance actions occur with broad emphasis on horizontal movement, typically smooth-flowing actions of the arms, hands, and hips. In Micronesia dancers are also likely to be stationary but in contrast to Melanesia and Polynesia the movements may be more exact and sharp, the fingers, hands, hips, and arms of Micronesian dancers moving with practiced precision.

While some islands and geographical regions have received considerable attention from researchers and scholars, there are still many music, dance, and performance cultures that remain to be sufficiently described. Since the 1700s missionaries, explorers, and civil servants have produced descriptions of Pacific music and dance in an effort to comprehend and control Pacific people. Early accounts of Pacific music and dance attempted to grasp the musical and movement systems of Oceania in European terms and they were often abstracted from their performance context. The processes and methodologies employed by outsiders attempting to come to terms with Pacific music and dance have varied greatly across the decades. A gradual shift toward long-term ethnographic observation and, in more modern times, increasing participation in performance has accompanied a rising interest in comprehending music and dance performance systems from a local perspective. In

addition there are increasing numbers of Pacific peoples engaged in the production of academic and general accounts of the region's music and dance practices.

From prehistorical times the societies of the Pacific, including their cultural and artistic dimensions, have continually been in the process of augmentation and change. The determining factors of cultural change have included war, migration, famine, population growth, disease, and in more recent years environmental challenges brought about by climate change as well as political and economic forces (see Fitzpatrick 2001). While some of these factors are perceived to be the result of external dynamics and processes, others can be attributed to local activities and determinants. In the realm of Pacific music and dance, researchers have increasingly adopted a constructionist approach that credits Pacific people with artistic and aesthetic autonomy. Rather than being seen as at the mercy of external pressures or as passive victims of globalization, Pacific people are now more commonly perceived as actively engaged in appropriation, creative development, and change, and as always having been so. Pacific societies are now understood as active reproducers of ritual processes rather than passive inheritants of tradition (see Jolly 1992; Miller 1994). Whether the music and dance performance practices are internally devised, adopted from neighboring Oceanic groups, or appropriated from global media sources, performance continues to play a central role in expressing local identities and creating Pacific societies.

History and Environment

Little is known about the first people who are understood to have entered the Pacific from Southeast Asia about fifty thousand years ago (Meyer 1995: 13). No real evidence of their music and dance performance practices is available to us. Over time and as a result of the great distances of ocean that separate many island groups, the cultures of Oceanic peoples diversified. The societies that developed in Melanesia, Micronesia, and Polynesia share some fundamental similarities, but within each region there are elements that are not consistent in the wider area.

Environmental factors have had a profound influence on life in the Pacific. The vastness and riches of the Pacific Ocean have played an important role in the development of cultural life, just as the cultures of densely forested and landlocked communities of

Highland Papua New Guinea and West Papua are also intimately related to their physical environment (see Feld 1990). Both the Pacific Ocean and the rugged geography of larger Pacific islands have ensured isolation for many communities and led to the development of intensely local forms of music and dance. For others, the ocean has been a means of transport and has provided the opportunity for communities to travel vast distances for economic, social, and cultural exchange (McLean 1999: 9). In Melanesia, exchange networks existed along the north coast of the mainland of Papua New Guinea, between the islands of the Kula ring and between New Ireland and its northern outliers (see Damon and Wagner 1989; Foster 1995). Among the Polynesian islands vast journeys were made between island groups such as Tonga and Samoa and between eastern Polynesia and Aotearoa (McLean 1999: 7–9). In the Micronesian "Yap Empire" journeys were made to the high islands to maintain political ties and provide assistance following devastating storms that destroyed food sources (Lingenfelter 1975). During these interisland encounters groups were able to learn new music and dance forms from one another and enlarge their repertoires with new sounds, costumes designs, and movement motifs.

Perhaps nowhere can the influence of the environment be seen and heard as strongly as in the lyrics of Pacific song. Songs about fish, birds, and other environmental resources of the sea and land abound in the Pacific. Some of these songs seem to have originated as incantations, used to draw a fish into a net or onto a hook, as in this Tokelauan example:

Tuia ko te atu: *The bonito is hooked:*
Te tiuvaka e!   *O the swordfish!*

Here a fisherman succeeds in hooking a bonito, but before he can bring the fish in, a swordfish impales it. The song's short format is a distilled version of a topic that captures the essence of an event and encourages contemplation or reflection. In this case, the two lines of this epigrammatic song contain both the joy and excitement of a catch and the despair of losing it moments later. In a more general sense the song reflects man's reliance on nature and subservience to the natural order (Thomas, Tuia, and Huntsman 1990: 30–31). In many Melanesian songs a short text makes reference to places or geographical and environmental features. In the island region of Papua New Guinea songs frequently include the names of distinctive geological formations or large stones that are associated with "place spirits" who are believed to inhabit these objects and places. The inclusion of "place spirit" names in a song text may variously link the song with a specific clan or simply generate associations in the audience to spiritual power and prestige.

In the highland region of Papua New Guinea, among the Kaluli people all melodies are perceived as being derived from birds. The Kaluli see all melodic sound structures as "natural" and a product of the environment. The "culture" found inside the melody in the text is crafted for aesthetic appeal in relation to the melodic form. Many Kaluli terms used to describe musical patterns and styles are drawn from the environment. One of the most common is the metaphoric use of waterfalls to describe many different aspects of song form, performance, and the relationship between singing parts (Feld 1990: 165–174). During *gisaro* ceremonies, held in Kaluli long houses, the texts of songs performed with dances make reference to local places and landmarks in order to generate nostalgia

and ultimately move the audience to tears (Schieffelin 1976: 179):

A kalo bird at Dubia Ridge is calling juu . . . juu.
The kalo calling there is calling you.
Go see the Walaegomono pool,
Go see the fruited gala sago.

The song continues in the same fashion listing various trees, streams, and ridges and describes their destruction through strong winds. The song deliberately creates associations in the audience with emptiness and loss. The places and objects listed in *gisaro* are often deliberately selected for their relationship with deceased community members. The listing of places and landmarks in these songs often evokes strong emotions that may compel audience members to ritualistically burn performers (Schieffelin 1976: 179–180). In *gisaro* and in many aspects of Kaluli music and dance the relationship between people and their rain forest environment is explicitly evoked. Kaluli society, culture, and environment are fundamentally bound as one.

In his work on the Tikopia, a Polynesian population in Solomon Islands, Raymond Firth has noted that composers make extensive reference to the natural environment as reflections on the human condition. Use of poetic images from nature are common in Tikopian songs of voyaging, in which storm clouds and high seas are employed as images of danger and uncertainty (Firth 1990: 33–34). In Micronesia and Polynesia songs often lament the loss of husbands, fathers, and brothers on fishing expeditions or exploratory voyages. Canoes are frequently used in Polynesian song as representations and metaphors of history, travel, and human mastery of or subjection to natural elements. In this example, a *haka* from Aotearoa, performed to welcome visitors onto a *marae* (temple), the visitors are identified with their ancestral canoe (McLean and Orbell 1975: 32):

Leader: Aa, tooia mai	Aa, haul up
Chorus: Te waka!	The canoe!
Leader: Ki te urunga	To its rest
Chorus: Te waka!	The canoe!
Leader: Kit e moenga	To its bed
Chorus: Te waka!	The canoe!
All: Kit e takotoranga I takoto ai te waka!	To the place where it will lie the canoe!

Pacific cultures have traditionally relied on readily available materials sourced from the natural environment for the construction of musical instruments, costume, and accoutrements. In some Melanesian societies rare and unusual costume features such as exotic bird feathers or shells help dancers to stand out from their fellow performers. Great value may be placed on these objects, and dangerous journeys might be undertaken to acquire them. In many Polynesian societies costumes are uniform and a certain aesthetic quality of material is what determines its selection. The use of shiny and glossy pandanus and cordyline leaves is common in many Polynesian dance troupes. Polynesian groups living outside their Pacific home substitute other cheap and readily available materials, such as plastic bags, that have the same aesthetic qualities. This tradition continues in the Pacific among modern genres such as Pacific hip-hop. Patriq Futialo, aka Tha Feelstyle, is a New

Zealand–based hip-hop artist of Samoan ancestry who performs in both English and Samoan. The image on the inside cover of his debut album *Break it to pieces* (2004) shows Futialo in a matching dark pinstripe suit and tie and wearing dark glasses and a fedora hat. The image is almost entirely hip-hop right down to the thick gold "bling" (jewelry) he wears around his neck. Except in this case that "bling" has been constructed from gold candy wrappers tied end to end. The image combines the traditional with the modern, in a graceful subversion of hip-hop culture and a loving reference to his Samoan heritage (Figure 21.1).

Figure 21.1. Tha Feelstyle: Inside cover "Break it to pieces."

Musical Instruments

The range of instruments in the Pacific at the time of European contact was not extensive when compared to other regions of the world, but the instruments often played an important part in Pacific societies. The elaborate carvings on the exterior surface of many instruments and ritualized practices that were a part of their construction point toward their value and esteem within many Oceanic cultures (see Flintoff 2004; Fischer 1986). In many Pacific societies, especially in Melanesia and Polynesia, instruments were associated with high-ranking individuals such as Polynesian chiefs or were perceived to be the "voice" of spiritual entities. As a result of these associations many instruments were regarded with respect and wonder and were often revered or feared (see Messner 1983; Wassman 1991; McLean 1999: 347–365).

All instruments of Oceanic origin were made of natural material locally obtained, or in some cases procured through trade networks. The nature and availability of resources with which to construct instruments varies greatly—for example in Aotearoa, New Zealand, where bamboo was not available as a medium for the construction of pipes and flutes. For the Polyneisan people who made their way to Aotearoa and became what are now known as the Maori, bones and wood carefully drilled were employed as substitutes (see McLean 1996; Flintoff 2004). In the highland region of Papua New Guinea shell and crustacean claws were imported

via trade networks from the coastal areas for use as items of personal decoration, as currency, and as musical instruments. In many Micronesian islands resources such as hard wood and animal skins were rare and therefore directly affected the types of instruments constructed in this region.

The majority of traditional instruments in the Pacific were membranophones (skin drums) and idiophones (struck instruments) with some aerophones (wind instruments) and relatively few chordophones (string instruments). The two principal skin drums used in Oceania are cylindrical wooden drums with a single head constructed from lizard, snake, or sometimes fish skin. In Polynesia, particularly eastern Polynesia, skin drums were used on *marae* grounds as part of ceremonies to address and honor gods. The instruments were highly venerated and only used on special occasions. When introduced into Hawai'i, the drum kept its exclusive status and was used to announce the arrival of the king. Smaller *pahu* (drum) are still used in Hawaiian *hula* performances. Use of the drums generally known as the *kundu,* or hourglass drum, is widely spread in Melanesia and parts of Micronesia. *Kundu* are used in conjunction with singing and dance, and sometimes as signaling devices (Figure 21.2). In general the drums produce a single note and are designed for volume and rhythmic purposes rather than as pitched drums. These drums range in size from small enough to carry and play while dancing to four to five feet long (see Fischer 1986).

Slit drums or slit gongs are also common in the Pacific. Slit drums may be constructed from a branch or a section of tree hollowed out lengthwise like a canoe. These idiophones are played with one or two short sticks or, as is common in parts of Melanesia, jolted with the end of a wooden staff or pole (Figure 21.3). The instruments are used to accompany music and dance performances and as signaling devices to communicate at times detailed information across vast distances (Pongiura 1995: 110–120). Slit drums vary in size from half a meter long in the Cook Islands to the size of a fully grown tree in Ambrym Vanuatu and Aotearoa (Fischer 1986: 166; McLean 1996: 169).

Bamboo pipes (stamping tubes) are used to accompany dance in several parts of Melanesia and Polynesia. Different lengths of bamboo, sometimes three feet in length, are held vertically and struck against the ground or stones with the closed end down

Figure 21.2. Men from the New Ireland Lak region of PNG beat kundu *(photo PW).*

Figure 21.3. *Sanguma band playing PNG* garamut *(slit drum) (photo GH).*

(Figure 21.4). Other idiophones, such as calabashes struck with the hand, are widely used in *hula* accompaniment in Hawai'i, and various kinds of rattles and tapping sticks are found in many forms across Oceania. To make the rhythm of dance movements audible, objects such as seashells, coconut shells, and animal or fish teeth are strung together and worn on the body. Sometimes costumes generate an aural dimension to the dance, like the full body spirit figures of New Ireland and New Britain or the reed skirts worn by Maori performers.

Figure 21.4. *Solomon Islands bamboo band (photo GH).*

In Oceania, nose flutes and both end-blown and side-blown flutes are played. In parts of Papua New Guinea some bamboo flutes are important objects in male secret societies (Figures 21.5 and 21.6). Bundles of bamboo flutes and racks of panpipes are prevalent in Solomon Islands and other parts of Melanesia. The Maori have flutes made of elaborately carved wood and bone. The jaw harp is found in various forms throughout the Pacific and is most often a personal musical instrument, used for amusement (Figure 21.7). The bullroarer is also found in various forms in all regions of the Pacific, where it is often associated with secret activities, arcane knowledge, or as a "spirit voice." Stringed instruments (chordophones) were scarce in the precontact Pacific. Only a few forms of the musical bow are known from Hawai'i, Guam, and the Marquesas Islands.

Melanesia has the largest inventory of instrument types, with most of them being on the island of New Guinea, which includes Papua New Guinea and West Papua (Irian Jaya) (McLean 1994). Of the instrument types documented in Melanesia, most are still in use in at least one community. Polynesia has significantly fewer instruments than Melanesia, and the majority of the instruments in the region are in the two large Polynesian countries of Hawai'i and Aotearoa. Many traditional Hawaiian instruments are still played on a regular basis as part of the traditional performing arts culture that has been growing in Hawai'i since the early 1970s (Stillman 1998). In Aotearoa New Zealand, the traditional instruments of the Maori have, in the past twenty years, enjoyed a remarkable revival in which a playing tradition and knowledge base has been re-established. Today in Aotearoa, the construction of instruments such as *koauau, nguru,* and *putorino* has been revitalized and continues to grow along with their playing techniques (see Flintoff 2004). Since the mid-1990s the use of these instruments with *kapa haka* (traditional performance) groups and other Maori performers has become widespread (Figures 21.8 and 21.9). Micronesia has the smallest inventory of traditional instruments and today there are very few that are used on a

Figure 21.5. *Tongan nose flute (photo PW).*

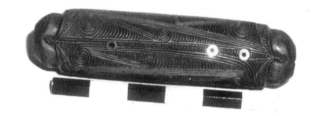

Figure 21.6. *Maori* koauau *flute (photo PW).*

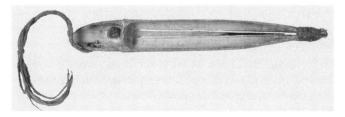

Figure 21.7. *Melanesian jaw harp (photo PW).*

Figure 21.8. Maori putorino
(photo PW).

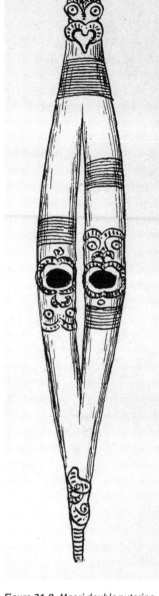

Figure 21.9. Maori double putorino
(photo PW).

Figure 21.10. Banaban stick dance: Te Karanga (photo JC).

regular basis. Bamboo or wooden sticks are still used during some dance performances as concussion sticks. These six-foot poles are used betweens pairs of dancers who beat rapid rhythms in combination with quick movements designed to enhance the rhythm of the vocal parts (Figure 21.10).

Dance and Performance

Like language, dance is a system of knowledge, a way to account for time, space, and place. Dance can reflect status and gender; it is used to enhance texts and the message contained within the performance. Dance involves participants in a structured system of moving, breathing, and being as one with other dancers or alone with the music. As indicated above, dance is usually part of a wider activity that provides the performance with meaning and context, while it also delivers these things back to the participants and audience. Like language in the Pacific, dance is preserved in memory along with the knowledge and aesthetics that combine to deliver culturally constructed meaning through movement instead of words.

Dance in Oceania has been interpreted in a variety of ways. Early encounters described by European missionaries, traders, and anthropologists range from condemnation of the primitive displays of sexuality to fascination, intrigue, and a genuine curiosity about the nature of the movements and gestures. The methods of description and analysis of dance practices in the Pacific vary considerably, and even today detailed analysis of structure, genre, kinemic, and morphokinemic aspects of Oceanic dance is rare. Many anthropological and ethnomusicological accounts provide some details of dance from which it is possible to gain a limited understanding of the dance practices in the region. Increasingly, film and video recordings make the dance traditions of many Pacific societies more visible, but with the exception of a few exemplary studies, few in-depth accounts and explanations of Pacific dance exist.

As described above, there are three main traditions that correspond with the three cultural and geographical divisions of the Pacific. Smith and Kaeppler describe one found in New Guinea and Island Melanesia in which the legs and body are used. The second tradition, found in Polynesia, uses the hands and arms to "illustrate" the meaning of the poetic lyrical elements. In the third tradition, in Micronesia, dance movements are understood to "decorate" the poetry. Increasingly these distinctions have been seen to be eroding as a result of ongoing and more regular exchanges between the people of these three regions (Smith and Kaeppler 1980: 59). Events such as sports, religious exchanges, and festivals provide Pacific people with the opportunity to view and interact with the dance and cultural traditions of other regions. While cultural exchanges continue to inform and inspire change, it is unlikely that regional distinctions will entirely disappear.

Often, music and dance are only two features of many that make up a "performance" occasion, and their abstraction or conceptual separation from other actions that take place may be inconceivable from an emic point of view.

Melanesian Dance

Melanesian dance is often part of a long and complex ceremonial cycle. The fundamental basis of dance in Melanesia, as described by many scholars, is rhythm. In traditional dance systems, especially in New Guinea, dance is predominantly a male activity. The emphasis was, and to a large extent remains, on participation as part of a group rather than individual display and virtuosity. Many New Guinea dance groups arrange themselves in two parallel lines that face each other, or in large circles. In both arrangements the location of the audience is not specified and the dance troupe may move from one area to another through the course of the performance.

The pared-down nature of highland dance movements accommodates the elaborate and often cumbersome headdress and costume features that are important features of the "display" element in these societies (Figure 21.11). The dominant movement is a bobbing of the entire body actuated in the dancer's knees, ankles, and hips, while the upper body inclines slightly forward. A leader will set this pattern of movement in motion until the entire troupe moves as one with each up-and-down movement coinciding with the beat.

All this emphasis on vertical movement in combination with costume and rhythm is a manifestation of social and cultural views in which men are seen to rise and fall and all people and communities are believed to each have access to greater and lesser things according to conceptual principles surrounding the natural order and the ebb and flow of life (see Brennan 1970; Brown 1978).

In the island region of Papua New Guinea spectacular dance displays are held at important stages of the extensive mortuary rites, where the combination of costume and movement reaffirms social

Figure 21.11. *Enga Highlands dancers (photo GH).*

Figure 21.12. *Lak men's dance (photo PW).*

Figure 21.13. *Lak Nataka-Tubuan dance (photo PW).*

values (Figures 21.12 and 21.13). Large-scale community dances performed by separate groups of males and females mark the end of mourning observances and the "replacement" of deceased community leaders by new ritual hosts. The dances held on these occasions are typically conducted in grid patterns in which each member performs synchronized movements against a strong rhythmic accompaniment provided by a separate group of *kundu* and small bamboo slit-gong players who also sing. The dancers, who are often costumed in uniform colors and materials, articulate the rhythmic patterns provided by the accompanying group with rapid movements of the hands, arms, and upper body. As in the mainland of Papua New Guinea a strong vertical movement motif pervades the performance (see Lulungan 1983; Errington 1974; Hesse and Aerts 1996).

Polynesian Dance

In Polynesia, dance is often broadly described as a visual extension of poetry. Dance in many Polynesian societies provides the means to interpret the poetry of the lyrics on a deeper level. Often the poetic texts are deliberately veiled or indirect and the dance movements that accompany the song performance provide a means of deciphering masked and implied meanings. Composers in Polynesia are highly skilled and often revered individuals in the multifaceted production of poetry, choreography, and music. The hands and arms provide the majority of interpretive movements that draw on and extend a highly developed literary tradition that includes set movements and relates to specific metaphors and concealed meanings. Texts often refer to genealogical lines and myths, and audiences need to be informed about the traditions and histories involved with each performance group in order to fully engage with the performances.

Kaeppler has shown that Polynesian music and dance has considerable variety between and within communities and societies. This variety and complexity has gone largely unrecognized due to European emphasis on melodic and harmonic dimensions of performance. The result has led to simplistic categorization of Polynesian music and dance practices into "indigenous" and "acculturated" based on the rhythmic and tonal elements that are apparent to outside observers (Kaeppler 1998a: 311–317). For many Polynesian societies music is only realized in performance with choreographed movements that illuminate the "meaning" of the music (Figures 21.14 and 21.15).

In the Eastern Polynesian islands of Tahiti, group dancing is a combined display of skill, physical beauty, and endurance in which tightly synchronized movements are delivered in large-scale displays of costume, music, and coordinated movement. Tahitian

Figure 21.14. Tongan lakalaka *(photo PW).*

Figure 21.15. Tongan dance with paddles (photo PW).

dance, or *ori Tahiti,* may include sections of improvised couples dancing within a larger group performance. The *ra'atira* (dance teacher) choreographs the movements and directs performers during rehearsal sessions. The colorful costumes worn by Tahitian dancers may also involve large and elaborate headdresses that can extend to two or three feet above the performer's head.

In the Tokelau Islands, situated north of Samoa in the western Pacific, the *fatele* is the pre-eminent dance of the people. The *fatele* is performed in the context of celebration and an atmosphere of relaxed competitiveness in which two groups at either end of a house face each other. While the elders oversee the proceedings, all others present take part in the alternating performances. While one group sits and watches, the other performs, and the roles are then reversed. As the evening progresses the atmosphere of the performance is built through the selection of songs by each group, including the performance of new compositions and much-loved older songs. Humor, and the "fit" or appropriateness of one song in answer to another, adds to the enjoyment of the performances. The "winner" of the night is not formally judged but generally conceded to the group whose choice of song and superior display of dance and costume give them the upper hand (see Thomas 1996).

Micronesian Dance

Micronesia is a diverse region stretching over a vast ocean area from the Palau group in the west to the Line Islands in the east and encompassing at least twelve mutually unintelligible languages. Diversity in the physique, cultures, and social and political aspects of Micronesians is attributed to the different routes and periods of migration from Southeast Asia. The dance of Micronesia similarly features great variation. Like the other regions of the Pacific, the environmental features of the Micronesian islands have contributed significantly to the music and dance practices of the region. Many Micronesian societies have a long history of open-ocean voyaging that can be seen in features of the dance, such as the close attention paid to the movements of birds or the creeping movements of the constellations across the night sky. Similarly the tiny atoll environments of the Micronesian region may be reflected in the careful and economic use of gestures in a performance space or the egalitarian approaches to social organization, as seen in performance groups that allow each performer enough time to proudly display himself or herself to the community. Micronesian dance is like Polynesian dance in that they both accompany poetry, but Micronesian dance differs in an important way. Movements in Micronesia decorate the poetry rather than illustrate the words as is often the case in Polynesia. Micronesian dance movements and gestures may have associated meaning, but it tends to be metaphorical and express a theme or concept rather than disclose a definite set of meanings. Traditionally dance movements of the region are actuated in the wrists and hands, fingers, arms, head, and eyes.

In the Yap Islands of western Micronesia, part of the Federated States of Micronesia, dances occur in both seated and standing positions. In *par-nga-but* performances, seated dancers are arranged in lines and costumed in grass skirts and in arm and head decorations fashioned from coconut palm leaves and flowers. Movements of the upper body, arms, and hands relate to the text of the songs, which usually concern well-known events and people.

Figure 21.16. Banaban traditional action song (photo JC).

In the Republic of Kiribati in eastern Micronesia, many old dances are still performed (Figure 21.16). Dance in Kiribati is traditionally performed by groups who share ancestral relations. The elaborate displays of skills and compositional prowess shown in performance were considered valuable clan knowledge. Competition remains an important part of Kiribati performance, and even on occasions where no outward competition is evident, a fierce competitive streak underlies most performances. Dance competitions are judged by the precision of movements and accuracy of gesture along with the appeal of the choreography to the audience, the attractiveness of the dancers, and the overall excitement generated in the audience during the performance.

Dance in many parts of Kiribati generates an ecstatic state of joy in performers and audience members. Expressed in the term *angin tem air* ("the power of the dance"), the dance performance is specifically designed to heighten tension and expectation in an effort to build the dramatic presence of the performance. The result as experienced by the performers is typically labored breathing, crying, trembling, and screaming. While those in the accompanying performance group may also experience an ecstatic state evidenced by increased tempo, increased dynamics of vocalization, and moving with greater force. The ecstatic experience is produced by the dance in the context of the event and in combination with physiological factors, which relate to social identity, sexuality, and shyness. I-Kiribati believe that spirits move through people during such moments and that this is the power of the dance (Smith 1998: 712–721).

Traditional Music

As outlined at the beginning of this chapter, in many traditional Pacific societies music or organized sound was often accompanied by dance, but it was also performed in a variety of contexts and occasions where choreography for display or communication was not present. The term "music" is used here to indicate an organized and structured framework of sounds that exists within a formal cultural aesthetic. It can variously include sounds that may and may not conform to a Western understanding of the term "music." These organized and structured frameworks rely on their formal cultural aesthetic values to carry meaning and convey it to others who work within the same system of knowledge. Consequently, they relate to wider cultural, social, and political features of the society and rely on the imaginations and cognitive processes of other cultural insiders to render them comprehensible. In short, musical meaning or understanding of musical aesthetics is often dependent on a thorough comprehension of the society of which it is a part.

The voice dominated as the primary musical instrument in precontact Pacific societies. The majority of traditional singing was chant-like in its use of relatively few pitches, and it employed a limited compass, as described in early accounts by Cook and other explorers (see Kaeppler 1998b: 14–22). This does not imply that the music was simple. The range of pitches used may have been perceived by the local performers as less important to the music than the manner of singing, enunciation, use of trills, plays on vowels, sliding pitches, and shifting tempo, as well as extramusical sounds such as calls and shouts or body percussion. The lyrics or poetry of songs are of great importance to many Pacific societies. The words are at times given privilege over all other musical aspects because they are where the emphasis and importance of the performance resides. In other Oceanic communities movement and its coordination with rhythm provides the focus for performers and audiences, and the lyrics or vocal parts are used simply to complement and enhance rhythmic aspects.

Although chant and chant-like vocal lines were dominant, two- and three-part singing was extant in several precontact Pacific cultures. In most cases one part repeats a single pitch while the other part rises and falls above it, for example in Tokelau a song form called *hiva hahaka* (see Thomas 1996). In Tonga, three-part harmony was part of the repertoire, and various forms of polyphony were employed (Linkels 1992: 38). Singing in parallel seconds is quite common in parts of the Pacific, where it results in heterophony, intentional simultaneous performance of two slightly variant versions of the same melody. Responsorial singing practices are not as common as they are in Africa but there are instances of this type of musical arrangement in the Pacific, with "overlapping" lines in which the second part comes in singing the same line as the first before the first has finished.

The contexts that formed the venues for musical performance in precontact Oceania were as diverse as the musical practices that took place there. In Polynesia, music was performed in honor and in recognition of the community leaders who usually attained their chiefly office through genealogical lines. In this sense, music and dance were performed in support of the sociopolitical structure and reinforced Polynesian notions of prestige and *mana*. Songs were also used to gently criticize the status quo and therefore helped to bring about social change, even in hierarchical societies like Tonga (see Pond 1995). The words of songs were, and are still, composed by specialists in the arts of poetry, movement, and music. In Micronesia, even more so than in other Pacific societies, the ocean has played a dominant part in the day-to-day lives of the inhabitants of these often tiny islands. Music was performed as part of religious ceremonies for the gods of the sea, storms, and wind. In some Micronesian islands, songs were used for medicinal purposes or to steady and guide the hand of a tattooist. Arrivals and departures were always significant moments in the lives of Micronesians and were celebrated with performances that included singing, dancing, and feasting. Musical performance traditions also surrounded births and deaths and were used to ensure fertility. Melanesian

Figure 21.17. *Sepik long flute players (photo GH).*

musical performance contexts were largely based around exchanges that mark current, potential, renewed, or recently severed relationships. The occasions that led to a performance included warfare or crisis events, rituals that marked entry into secret societies or the advancement within age grades, funeral and mortuary rites, and rites associated with leadership and social organization, like the construction of sacred houses (Figure 21.17).

There are significant differences between the musical systems of the three regions of Melanesia, Micronesia, and Polynesia, and even within these three large regions there exists considerable variation.

On the broadest level singing styles can be said to parallel linguistic patterns, and in Melanesia, where there are more than eight hundred distinct languages, the musical systems are just as diverse. A wide spectrum of musical forms are present in Melanesia "with only one or as many as six notes: with small intervals or with large intervals; with a small range or a large range; with level, arching, undulating, descending or even triadic (including yodeling) contours; with syllabic or melismatic text settings; with isometric or hetrometric rhythm; with repeated motif, responsorial, verse-refrain or progressive forms; and with casual or prescribed polyphony" (Smith and Kaeppler 1980: 63). In Polynesia, where languages are more similar, McLean has described at least three broad singing styles, two solo and one multipart, which often coexist (McLean 1999: 413–415). One of the solo styles is an unpitched "*sprechgesang,*" in which syllables provide the rhythmic determination. Used for the duration of a song or as a section within pitched songs, they often contain important text, and their accurate delivery is the focus rather than the pitches employed. The second dominant solo style of Polynesia contains more melodic variation and sustained tones and features greater metric organization and a level or arching contour of phrasing. The multipart style of singing may include a drone part or moving parallel motion parts, often with two or three separated vocal parts. While these three styles dominate Polynesian singing there are also responsorial forms, and in the majority of multipart singing forms of the region there is a built-in tonic drone that is especially noticeable when the tonic is in the middle of the range of the song. In Micronesia, again paralleling the linguistic patterns, vocal styles are heterogeneous. Multipart singing with a drone is a significant feature, and parallelism exists in several Micronesian societies.

Voice timbre and styles of vocal production have developed regional and local distinctions in numerous parts of the Pacific. In many parts of Melanesia and in both Eastern and Western Polynesia, a nasal vocal quality is widely reported. Early European accounts complained of strident and shrill tones in wide areas of French Polynesia and the Samoan Islands. Singing in traditional styles of the Pacific is often considered harsh to Western ears, as many societies in Melanesia and Tonga perceive forceful vocal attack and substantial volume as indicators of musical quality. Falsetto singing is a feature of several societies in Papua New Guinea and Solomon Islands and is also reported in the traditional music of Bellona (Rossen 1987: 312), the Marquesas Islands (Craig 1980: 23), and Tonga (Moyal 1993: 398).

Much has changed in Oceania with the arrival of non-Pacific people. New forms of religion, economics, communication, and cultures have brought with them novel singing techniques and musical structures. As the presence of European, American, and Asian people grew through the colonial period, the influence of foreign musical, dance, and performance practices also expanded. While much has changed and music and dance practices continue to evolve, numerous aspects of traditional Pacific music and performance remain. Traditional musical practices continue to inform individual and collective identity while they help to maintain unique Pacific perspectives of the world.

Modern Music

Modern musical practices of the Pacific region are significantly different from the music of precontact Oceanic societies. The introduction of multipart triadic harmony in the form of religious hymns by missionaries to most Pacific islands by the late nineteenth and early twentieth centuries had a profound impact. This was followed by brass bands and stringed instruments in the form of guitars and ukuleles, which opened up new forms of production and broadened the musical horizon. Many of these introduced musical forms, genres, and instruments have undergone a process of indigenization, and instruments such as the ukulele and styles like "string band" have come to be perceived as essentially Pacific in nature. Since the 1960s and increasingly across the Pacific, people have looked back to earlier musical practices and traditions for their unique identity. These traditional, indigenous, and evolving music forms mix the old with the modern to create a new popular Pacific music.

As noted above, it is difficult to overestimate the impact of hymns on the musical life of Pacific people. Hymn singing ushered in a new world of sounds and concepts including harmony, a chromatic scale, keys, and the concepts of major and minor, as well as new timbre and voice qualities. For some Pacific peoples the notion of singing as a large group without choreographed or associated movements was initially perceived as peculiar. Many of these novel introductions accompanied the teaching and learning of hymn songs. Why hymns were so quickly taken up and the styles and musical concepts of hymnody so rapidly adopted can be attributed to the association of hymns with Western material goods, but also to the novelty of these new sounds for Oceanic peoples. Vocal music already occupied a privileged position in many Pacific societies, and singing was and continues to be perceived as a powerful form of communication. In the majority of precontact Pacific societies it seems that music was related to magic and spiritual efficacy; it was the vehicle for history and knowledge and was perceived as a sacred and spiritual activity. When European forms of harmony and styles of part singing were introduced, in some societies, especially in Melanesia, it was understood as a new and powerful form of magic.

In 1875 the Reverend George Brown and his Fijian missionary assistants sailed into the Saint George Channel between New Ireland and New Britain. The ship arrived in Port Hunter off the largest island in the Duke of York group. The following day, Sunday, August 15, 1875, a service was held on the decks of the ship, and the sound of harmonized Christian hymns was heard for the first time in the New Guinea islands. According to accounts of that day, hundreds of men and women listened to the strange singing as they watched from the shore (Threlfall 1975: 31). On hearing hymn singing for the first time, the inhabitants of the Duke of York Islands were immediately intrigued by the sound:

> We sat just under yon coconut palm, and we awaited developments. Soon the worshippers began to sing, and we said to one another, "That is a fine incantation of theirs!" That was the beginning of our acquaintance with the *Lotu* [church/religion]. (*Australasian Methodist Missionary Review,* July 5, 1909: 14)

The local perception was of hymns as "incantations" or magical recitations. The ritualistic aspects of the church services, including the prayer and song, caused the church music to be perceived as a magical charm. The strong association between the hymn singing and the church's power would have been immediately evident to the people of the Duke of York Islands. From an indigenous point of view the church has several features in common with local magic and religious practices like the region's secret male societies. Soon after witnessing the church service, the community leaders in the Duke of Yorks arranged to purchase the church, and the new vocal sounds associated with it, from the missionaries in exchange for local shell currency. Missionaries across the Pacific were quick to understand the powers of attraction that the hymns seemed to have and took advantage of this by putting emphasis on the translation of hymns into local languages or the teaching of English so that the message of the hymns would be carried through the music. This account from the Duke of York Islands was repeated in many Pacific islands throughout the nineteenth and twentieth centuries.

Modern hymn singing continues to play an important role in Pacific life, and hymns can be heard in most Pacific communities several times a week. In French Polynesia and the Cook Islands, hymns have been indigenized and are known respectively as *himene* and *imene*. *Himene* are formal choral Tahitian songs of a religious nature and based in verse and harmonic structure on Protestant hymns (see McLean 1999: 33–46). *Imene tuki* are traditional hymns unaccompanied and noted for a drop in pitch at the end of phrases, and sometimes the addition of rhythmic nonsensical syllables. *Imene tuki* emerged out of the Cook Islands Protestantism established in the 1820s. Hymn singing continues to play an important part in the predominant denomination of the Cook Islands, the "Cook Islands Christian Church." Most *imene tuki* were translations of English evangelical hymns. Over the years many more Cook Island Maori hymns have been composed by local ministers, and today hymns may be composed by any member of the congregation.

The *tuki* "rhythmic grunts" of the men occur near the ends of phrases and are combined with *pe'e,* "traditional chanting." Modern *imene* may contain up to seven separate vocal parts and result in a distinctive sound that is unique to the Cook Islands (Lloyd 1994).

In the mid-nineteenth century, when European colonial intervention in the Pacific was well-established, brass bands were at the height of their popularity in Britain, Germany, and other parts of Europe. The introduction of four-part harmony to the Pacific by missionaries no doubt set the stage for the local appreciation of brass bands. The association of brass bands with military and economic power undoubtedly played a part in local interest in brass groups. Another aspect of the brass band that may have been appealing to Pacific communities was the communal nature of these large ensembles. Like dance troupes, brass bands perform in lines and grids, and the collective display aspect of brass bands that marched and played in unison was attractive. Brass band performance groups became well-established among Maori communities in New Zealand, in Papua New Guinea associated with the police, and in Hawai'i, where they were linked with the royal court and came to be known as the king's musicians.

Arguably nowhere in the Pacific have brass bands enjoyed more popularity than in Tonga. In Tongan society, brass bands hold a special place in the hearts of the people, and there are hundreds of them. There are many community bands and nearly every church and school has at least one brass band. Among the most prestigious are the Royal Corps of Musicians and the Tongan Police Band. Tongan churches have no organs, so their choirs are often accompanied by brass bands. Missionaries and secondary school principals introduced the first brass bands. The British education system served as a model for these schools and for many other structures that were to be adopted by Tongan people, including laws and the institutions of royalty (Linkels 1992: 97). Today brass bands have been institutionalized as part of Tonga's society. The bands perform on a wide variety of occasions, in church services on Sunday or at sporting events during halftime, and they perform the national anthem when the king pays a visit somewhere. In many cases the local compositions and arrangements contain a middle section that is sung, in which only the drummers and the tuba player continue to play while the other musicians vocalize. Tongans take great pride and pleasure in their brass bands, and according to some local musicians the success of brass bands in Tonga is related to their ability to produce loud music, which fits with traditional Tongan ideals in which performances should be full of emotion and delivered loudly (Aldred 1997: 221–226).

Pacific string bands employ unique combinations of instrumentation and a variety of tunings that have originated in the Pacific region and remain an important part of modern Pacific music. The development and spread of this musical form across Oceania has had a profound impact on local music and musical practices of the region. Early Pacific music on stringed instruments occurred in Hawai'i, where it is believed the Portuguese *bra-guin-ha* was transformed into the ukulele, and Spanish guitars were transformed into Hawaiian guitars. What evolved from this combination of instruments and sung poetry in the late nineteenth century became know as Hawaiian music. Some believe that from Hawai'i this concept traveled throughout Polynesia to other areas of Oceania in the early and mid-twentieth century, while others describe a simultaneous evolution in other Pacific nations independent of Hawaiian music (Kaeppler 1998a: 137). What is clear today is that this combination of ukulele, guitars, single string bass, local percussion instruments, and indigenous poetic forms has proliferated throughout the region. In each island area, string band music is transformed by the indigenous music system into which it is incorporated. In many areas string band music is associated with local, cultural, ethnic, and national identities.

In Papua New Guinea string band music is produced in ensembles that include guitars, ukuleles, local percussive instruments such as *kundu* drums (hourglass membranophones), and predominantly male vocalists (see Crowdy 2005). Vocal lines blend in interlocking and overlapping polyphonies that frequently employ tight harmonies and are often in sync with the strongly metric guitar or ukulele strums (Feld 1988: 96). Guitars were introduced to Papua New Guinea in large numbers by servicemen during World War II. One explanation of the prolific adoption of string band music in Melanesia is that where linguistic and cultural groups were unable to comprehend the music of their neighbors, string-band music formed a musical lingua franca (see Webb 1993). Papua New Guinea string bands developed into regional styles through the 1960s and 1970s that reflected local musical traits including melodic, textual, rhythmic, and vocal timbre. With independence in 1975, a proliferation of songs, mostly in Tok Pisin, exhorted communities to cooperate and band together as a nation and as a people, fostering a national identity. String bands came to symbolize modernity and the progressive aspects of Papua New Guinean society, but with the rise of power bands (electrified popular music ensembles) in urban areas during the 1970s and 1980s, string bands came to be seen by city and town dwellers as outmoded and old-fashioned. Power bands, catering to disco venues, hotel audiences, and all-night dancing parties, performed a mostly foreign lineup of cover songs to audiences of young unmarried men and women (see Webb 1993; Crowdy 2005). In more recent years string bands have enjoyed a period of resurgence. Many musicians and cultural commentators have come to understand string band music as a truly local musical form, one that accommodates indigenous languages, musical styles and aesthetics, and Tok Pisin (PNG's lingua franca) into an authentically local popular music.

Several other introduced musical genres that have become important in many Pacific cultures during the past thirty years include reggae and hip-hop. Reggae and hip-hop, perhaps more so than any other genres in the second half of the twentieth century, have been appropriated and indigenized by Pacific peoples. Reggae continues to enjoy huge popularity among Hawaiian, New Zealand, Samoan, New Caledonian, and many other Pacific people, and hip-hop culture is expanding its influence in large and small Pacific islands. The popularity and the appropriation of both reggae and hip-hop has been attributed to the perceived associations between Caribbean and African American peoples, and Pacific Island youth (see Henderson 2007; Zemke-White 2001; Imada 2006; Weintraub 1998). Reggae in the Pacific has for many artists come to represent a struggle for political, cultural, and economic freedom, a class-based struggle, and for some a racial struggle between indigenous inhabitants and others, as in Hawai'i, New Zealand, and New Caledonia. Hip-hop has also been associated with resistance struggles and indigenous severity in several Pacific nations (Mitchell 1996: 214).

Jawaiian music, a mixture of Caribbean and Hawaiian sounds, came about in the late 1980s and early 1990s as a result of indigenous and local Hawaiian youth interest in reggae. Andrew Weintraub cites the factors involved in the development of Jawaiian as the worldwide popularity of reggae; a desire for a musical relationship with Jamaicans, who are perceived as having a shared history of oppression; and perceived similarities of lifestyle in both island groups (Weintraub 1998: 79). Jawaiian music dominated Hawaiian radio play through most of the late 1990s and continues to enjoy popular support. The music has come to reflect "local" (a group that includes indigenous and non-indigenous people who identify as being Hawaiian) ideas and is seen as representing Hawaiian youth identities. The music often has a political message that reflects "local" concerns, including landownership and the reclamation of indigenous lands (Stillman 1998: 95–99).

In New Caledonia *kaneka,* a musical form closely associated with the Kanak independence struggle, draws on local musical traits and reggae influences in what has been a conscious process of indigenization. In the late 1980s Kanak musicians began to research their traditional rhythmic, textual, and melodic forms to establish a basis on which to construct a popular music that would be rooted in indigenous Kanak forms but remain accessible and relevant to youth of New Caledonia. A key element in the evolution of *kaneka* was the recognition and appropriation of a New Caledonian pan-regional rhythmic style of a crotchet followed by a quaver, this became a pan-Kanak rhythmic base for *kaneka* (Goldsworthy 1998: 47). Performance of *kaneka* in modern New Caledonia is both a statement of sociopolitical allegiance to the movement for independence and an onomatopoeic reference to the basic percussive beat upon which most *kaneka* music is based.

Maori rap group Upper Hutt Posse, in Aotearoa New Zealand, were early Pacific adopters of rap music and the trappings of what was to become known as hip-hop culture. As early as 1985 Upper Hutt Posse were performing in a mixture of Maori and English languages. Like other Pacific hip-hop artists that were to follow, including Sudden Rush in Hawai'i, Upper Hutt Posse's rap was politically motivated (Imada 2006). It forcefully protests the inequalities of Maori people living in urban environments. The group continues to perform and has produced eleven albums, with an increasing number of songs in Te Reo (Maori language) with lyrics that reflect Maori concerns about the survival of Te Reo, environment, Maori people, and culture. Many songs utilize *tauonga pouru* (traditional Maori instruments), *karanga* (calls or chants), in combination with hip-hop, reggae, funk and bass rhythms, and rock and blues guitar riffs (Mitchell 1996). For much of the 1980s and 1990s hip-hop music produced by Maori and Pacific Island people was centered around diasporic communities in the west coast of the United States, in Australia, and in New Zealand where there are large concentrations of Pacific peoples. In more recent years hip-hop performers in Samoa, Fiji, Tonga, and other islands without large numbers of people living in other countries around the Pacific Rim have seen the rise of hip-hop music among urban youth in and around their towns and cities. The accessibility of production equipment including turntables, samplers, and microphones, combined with affordable digital technologies such as computers and access to the Internet, has contributed to the widespread production of hip-hop among Pacific Island youth.

BIBLIOGRAPHY

Aldred, H. M. 1997. *Ifi palasa: Brass bands in Tonga*. Masters thesis, Victoria University of Wellington, Wellington, New Zealand.

Brennan, P. W. 1970. Enga referential symbolism: Verbal and visual. In *exploring Enga culture: Studies in missionary anthropology*. Second anthropological conference of the New Guinea Lutheran mission, ed. Paul W. Brennan, 17–50. Wapenamanda: New Guinea Lutheran Mission.

Brown, P. 1978. *Highland peoples of New Guinea*. Cambridge: Cambridge University Press.

Craig, R. D., ed. 1980. *The Marquesas Islands: Their descriptions and early history by reverend Robert Thompson (1816–1851)*, 2nd ed. Laie: Institute for Polynesian Studies.

Crowdy, D. 2005. *Guitar style, open tunings, and stringband music in Papua New Guinea*. Boroko, Papua New Guinea: Institute of Papua New Guinea Studies.

Damon, F. H., and R. Wagner, eds. 1989. *Death rituals and life in the societies of the Kula ring*. DeKalb, Ill.: Northern Illinois University Press.

Errington, F. K. 1974. *Karavar: Masks and power in Melanesian ritual*. London: Cornell University Press.

Feld, S. 1988. Aesthetics as iconicity of style, or lift-up-over sounding: Getting into the Kaluli groove. *Yearbook for traditional music* 20(1): 74–113.

———. 1990. *Sound and sentiment: Birds, weeping, poetics, and song in Kaluli expression*. Philadelphia: University of Pennsylvania Press.

Firth, R. 1990. *Tikopia songs: Poetic and musical art of a Polynesian people of the Solomon Islands*. Cambridge: Cambridge University Press.

Fischer, H. 1986. *Sound producing instruments in Oceania: Construction and playing technique—distribution and function*. Boroko: Institute of Papua New Guinea Studies.

Fitzpatrick, J. M., ed. 2001. *Endangered peoples of Oceania: Struggles to survive and thrive*. Westport, Conn.: Greenwood Press.

Flintoff, B. 2004. *Taonga puoro: Singing treasures, the musical instruments of the Maori*. Nelson, N.Z.: Craig Potton Publishing.

Foster, R. J. 1995. *Social reproduction and history in Melanesia: Mortuary ritual, gift exchange, and custom in the Tanga Islands*. Cambridge: Cambridge University Press.

Goldsworthy, D. 1998. Indigenization and socio-political identity in Kaneka music of New Caledonia. In *Sound alliances: Indigenous peoples, cultural politics and popular music in the Pacific*. London: Cassell.

Henderson, A. K. 2007. *Gifted flows: Engaging narratives of hip hop and Samoan diaspora*. PhD thesis, University of California, Santa Cruz.

Hesse, K., and T. Aerts. 1996. *Baining life and lore*, 2nd ed. Port Moresby: University of Papua New Guinea Press.

Imada, A. L. 2006. Head rush: Hip hop and a Hawaiian nation on the rise. In *The vinyl ain't final: Hip hop and the globalization of black popular culture*, ed. Dipannita Basu and Sidney J. Lemelle, 85–99. London: Pluto.

Jolly, M. 1992. Specters of inauthenticity. *Contemporary Pacific* 4(1): 49–72.

Kaeppler, A. 1998a. Understanding dance. In *The Garland encyclopaedia of world music volume 9: Australia and the Pacific Islands*. New York: Garland Publishing Inc.

———. 1998b. Encounters with the other. In *The Garland encyclopaedia of world music volume 9: Australia and the Pacific Islands*. New York: Garland Publishing Inc.

Lingenfelter, S. G. 1975. *Yap political leadership and cultural change in an island society*. Honolulu: University Press of Hawai'i.

Linkels, A. 1992. *Sounds of change in Tonga: Dance, music and cultural dynamics in a Polynesian kingdom*. Nuku'alofa, Tonga: Taulua Press.

Lloyd, R. 1994. *The Cook Island imene reo metua and imene tuki*. Masters thesis, University of New England, Armidale, N.S.W., Australia.

Lulungan, T. 1983. Tolai music. In *Bikmaus: The journal of Papua New Guinea affairs, ideas and the arts* 4(3): 24–32.

McLean, M. 1994. *Diffusion of musical instruments and their relation to language migration in New Guinea*. Port Moresby, Papua New Guinea: Cultural Studies Division, National Research Institute.

———. 1996. *Maori music*. Auckland: Auckland University Press.

———. 1999. *Weavers of song: Polynesian music and dance*. Auckland: Auckland University Press.

McLean, M., and M. Orbell. 1975. *Traditional songs of the Maori*. Auckland: Auckland University Press.

Messner, G. F. 1983. The friction block lounuat of New Ireland: Its use and socio-cultural embodiment. In *Bikmaus: The journal of Papua New Guinea affairs, ideas and the arts* 4(3).

Meyer, A. J. P. 1995. *Oceanic art*. Germany: Konemann Verlagsgesellschaft.

Miller, D. 1994. *Modernity: An ethnographic approach*. Oxford: Berg.

Mitchell, T. 1996. *Popular music and local identity: Rock, pop and rap in Europe and Oceania*. New York: Leicester University Press.

Moyal, R. M. 1993. Drone, melody and decoration—paradigm lost. *Ethnomusicology* 37(3): 387–405.

Pond, W. 1995. *Faiva: Trails of skill: The song and dance of Tongan politics, 1773–1993*. PhD thesis, Victoria University of Wellington.

Pongiura, S. P. W. 1995. Garamut communication of the Yangoru. *Occasional Papers in Pacific Ethnomusicology* 4. Auckland: University of Auckland.

Rossen, Jane Mink. 1987. *Songs of Bellona Island*. 2 vols. *Acta Ethnomusicologica Dancia*, 4. Copenhagen: Forlaget Kragen.

Schieffelin, Edward L. 1976. *The sorrow of the lonely and the burning of the dancers*. New York: St. Martin's Press.

Smith, B. 1998. The music and dance of Micronesia. In *The Garland encyclopaedia of world music volume 9: Australia and the Pacific Islands*, New York: Garland Publishing Inc.

Smith, B., and A. Kaeppler. 1980. Pacific Islands: Introduction. In *The new Groves dictionary of music and musicians*, ed. S. Sadie. London: Macmillan.

Stillman, A. 1998. Hula hits, local music and local charts: Some dynamics of popular Hawaiian music. In *Sound alliances: Indigenous people, cultural politics, and popular music in the Pacific*, ed. Philip Hayward. London: Cassell.

Thomas, A, I. Tuia, and J. Huntsman. 1990. *Songs and stories of Tokelau: An introduction to the cultural heritage*. Wellington: Victoria University Press.

Thomas, A. 1996. *New song and dance from the central Pacific: Creating and performing the Fatele of Tokelau in the islands and New Zealand*. Stuyvesant, N.Y.: Pendragon Press.

Threlfall, N. 1975. *One hundred years in the islands: The Methodist/United Church in the New Guinea Islands Region 1875–1975*. Rabaul, Papua New Guinea: Trinity Press.

Wassmann, J. 1991. *The song to the flying fox*. Boroko, Papua New Guinea: National Research Institute.

Webb, M. 1993. *Lokal musik: Lingua franca song and identity in Papua New Guinea*. Boroko, Papua New Guinea: National Research Institute.

Weintraub, A. N. 1998. Jawaiian music and local cultural identity in Hawai'i. In *Sound alliances: Indigenous peoples, cultural politics and popular music in the Pacific*, ed. Philip Hayward. London: Cassell.

Zemke-White, K. 2001. Rap music and Pacific identity in Aotearoa: Popular music and the politics of oppression. In *Tangata o te moana nui: The evolving identities of Pacific peoples in Aotearoa/New Zealand*, ed. Cluny MacPherson, Paul Spoonley, and Melani Anae, 228–242. Palmerston North: Dunmore Press.

Population

Population growth—rapid in independent countries, slow or even negative in dependent entities and urbanized societies—is a critical concern in the contemporary Pacific. Burgeoning towns and cities are dealing with unemployment, housing shortages, and social malaise. Demands for education, health services, and gender equality are increasing, yet the relevance of existing programs has been questioned. These issues are explored in this section, with chapters on demography, mobility, health, education, and urbanization.

Demography
A Slow or Stalled Demographic Transition Affecting Development

Jean Louis Rallu and Dennis Ahlburg

22

Unlike Asia, where population aging is the dominant population issue, population growth and issues related to a large youthful population remain a major concern in Pacific Island countries (PICs). The experience of PICs seems to indicate that rapid growth in some countries and mass emigration in others, and associated high dependency ratios, hinder development. Many countries experienced higher population than economic growth in the 1990s and early 2000s, and evidence of increasing poverty has emerged— a lack of opportunity and low and unstable income (Abbott and Pollard 2004) rather than extreme income poverty and hunger witnessed in developing countries in other regions of the world.

Although the Pacific is varied, economic, demographic, and social progress has been slow everywhere, whether it is fertility reduction, life expectancy increase, job creation, or progress toward achieving the MDGs (Millennium Development Goals), a series of UN demographic, social, health, economic, and environmental targets linked to economic and human development.

This chapter will consider recent demographic trends in the Pacific in the fields of fertility, mortality, migration, age structure, and population and development. A brief review of MDG attainment will provide a general view of development progress in the region, helping define major issues.[1]

Population Trends and Age Structures

Fertility

In Polynesia, after rapid decline in the late 1960s and 1970s, fertility transition stalled in the 1980s, with TFR[2] between 3.5 and 4.5 (Rallu and Ahlburg 1999), and the situation has not changed much since then (see Figure 22.1). TFRs have recently risen to 2.9 and 3.9 in the Cook Islands and Tuvalu, countries that appeared to be headed toward replacement fertility.

In the high-population-density atoll countries of Micronesia, latecomers to the fertility transition such as RMI (Republic of the Marshall Islands) experienced rapid decline in fertility in the second half of the 1980s and the early 1990s, but TFR stabilized around 4.5 according to 1999 census and 2007 DHS (Demographic and Health Survey) data. FSM (Federated States of Micronesia) has also shown declining though still high fertility with a TFR of 3.4. Kiribati's fertility development is more complex. Kiribati

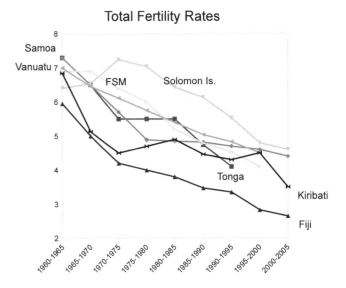

Figure 22.1. Total fertility rate in selected Pacific Island countries, 1960–2005.

experienced early fertility decline to 4.5 in 1970–1975 but this was short-lived because the Catholic Church opposed the government's family planning policy and TFR increased to 4.9 in the late 1970s and fluctuated around 4.5. A new period of decline was observed beginning in the late 1990s and by 2005 the TFR was 3.5. Palau is the only PIC to have completed the fertility transition with the TFR reaching 2.0 in 1995–2000 and remaining below replacement level, 1.94, in 2000–2005.

In Melanesia, Fiji has seen further fertility decline from 3.1 in 1996 to 2.7 in 2003–2004. The decline is mostly due to changes in Indian fertility, with TFR falling below replacement in 1998 and reaching 1.9 in 2003–2004; it was even lower (1.7) after the 2000 coup. Fijian TFR is much higher and stagnating around 3.3 in 1999–2004 after a drop from 3.6 in 1996–1998.[3] For other Melanesian countries (or Western Melanesia[4]), vital registration is incomplete and we must rely on indirect estimates based on census data that are sometimes questionable. Based on 1999 and 2000 censuses, TFR was 4.8 in Solomon Islands and Vanuatu, and 4.6 in PNG. Because the total growth rate of population exceeds the natural rate

Table 22.1

Demographic Indicators for Pacific Island Countries and Territories

	Mid-2011 population (thousands)	Land area (km²)	Population density (per km²)	Urban population (percentage urban)	Crude birth rate (per thousand)	Crude death rate (per thousand)
Melanesia						
Fiji	852	18,272	47	52	20.8	8.5
New Caledonia	252	19,103	13	67	15.4	5.7
Papua New Guinea	7,014	462,243	15	13	29.8	7.5
Solomon Is.	552	28,370	19	19	31.3	5.6
Vanuatu	246	12,190	20	26	29.2	4.8
Micronesia						
FSM	102	701	146	23	24.6	6.0
Guam	192	541	355	93	17.9	5.6
Kiribati	103	811	127	44	27.8	8.3
Marshall Is.	55	181	304	72	31.1	5.8
Nauru	10	21	476	100	29.7	8.9
Northern Marianas	64	457	140	91	18.3	3.0
Palau	21	444	47	84	13.6	7.7
Polynesia						
American Samoa	67	200	335	93	23.5	4.5
Cook Is.	15.5	237	65	76	16.8	7.3
French Polynesia	274	3,521	78	57	16.7	5.4
Niue	1.5	259	4	38	14.8	9.7
Samoa	184	2,935	63	22	24.4	5.4
Tokelau	1.1	12	100		31.0	7.0
Tonga	105	650	162	34*	26.5	6.1
Tuvalu	11	26	374	51	22.9	9.0
Wallis and Futuna	14.2	142	100	na	19.4	5.9
New Zealand	4,405	270,692	16	86	14.3	6.7
Hawai'i[†]	1,375	16,637	83	70	14.6	7.4

Sources: Population, growth, birth and death rates, life expectancy, total fertility rate, teenage fertility rate, urban population, life expectancy, infant mortality rate: UNESCAP 2011 datasheet; national census and DHS reports (various years). Urban growth rate: UNDESA World Urbanization Prospects 2009, for years 2005–2010.

Rate of natural increase (percent)	Total fertility rate (per woman)	Specific fertility rate ages 15–19 (per thousand)	Total growth rate (percent)	Net migration rate (percent)	Urban growth rate (percent)	Life expectancy at birth M/F (years)	Infant mortality rate (per thousand)
1.2	2.6	37	0.5	-0.7	1.5	67/72	17
1.0	2.1	20	1.3	0.3	2.6	73/80	5
2.2	3.9	63	2.2	0.0	2.3	61/65	46
2.6	4.1	66	2.6	0.0	4.3	66/69	37
2.4	3.8	52	2.4	0.0	4.3	69/73	25
1.9	3.4	51	0.4	-1.5	0.6	68/70	32
1.2	2.4	50	2.7	1.5	1.3	74/79	8
2.0	3.5	75	1.8	-0.2	1.7	59/63	52
2.5	4.4	127	0.7	-1.8	2.7	64/68	21
2.1	3.3	78	2.1	0.0	0.3	55/57	46
1.5	1.6	69	-0.1	-1.6	2.1	74/77	5
0.6	2.0	29	0.6	0.0	1.8	66/72	20
1.9	4.0	54	1.2	-0.7	2.1	69/76	11
1.0	2.5	62	0.3	-0.7	2.0	70/76	12
1.1	2.1	49	1.1	0.0	1.7	73/78	7
0.5	2.6	28	-2.3	-2.8	-1.4	67/76	8
1.9	3.8	26	0.4	-1.5	1.3	70/76	21
2.4	4.9	43	-0.9	-3.3	na	68/71	33
2.0	3.9	19	0.5	-1.5	0.7	70/75	21
1.4	3.7	44	0.5	-0.9	1.4	62/65	31
1.4	2.2	12	0.8	-0.6	na	74	6
0.8	2.1	22	0.9	0.1	1.0	79/83	6
0.7	2.2	20	1.2	0.5	na	78/83	6.5

* Greater Nukuʻalofa is considered urban; Nukuʻalofa represents 23.2% of total population in 2006 with growth rate of 0.5% over 1996–2006; growth rate of suburban area is 1.7%.

† Except population and density, data for Hawaiʻi relate to years 2006–2007, based on data from US Census Bureau and State of Hawaiʻi.

of growth and migration is small, it seems likely that TFR in these countries is underestimated. For example, with only slight emigration to New Caledonia, Vanuatu had an estimated total growth rate of 2.6 percent and an estimated natural growth rate[5] of 2.2 percent in the period from 1989 to 1999. Data from the 1999 census of Solomon Islands showed a growth rate of 3.0 percent while the census estimate of natural growth is 2.7 percent. It is thought that the TFR declined in PNG and Vanuatu in the early part of the current decade, while Solomon Islands probably experienced an increase during the 1999–2000 crisis that disrupted health services. The 2007 DHS revealed little change in TFR from 4.8 in 1997–2001 to 4.6 in 2002–2006.

French territories have nearly achieved the fertility transition, with TFR of 2.1 in New Caledonia in 2005 and in French Polynesia in 2006, and 2.2 in Wallis and Futuna in 2004–2006. In New Caledonia, even the predominantly Melanesian North Province showed a TFR of 2.07, while the Loyalty Islands have higher fertility (2.65). In the U.S. territories, the NMI (Northern Mariana Islands) have the lowest TFR (1.6).[6] In Guam, the TFR has fallen from 3.8 in 1995 to 2.6 in 2007. Declines have also been observed in American Samoa, but the TRF is still high at 3.1. The cost of raising large families in the relatively more developed economies of U.S. and French territories may be a reason for more rapid fertility decline.

Teenage pregnancies are a concern in many PICs, with recent increases linked to urbanization and associated behavior changes. Extramarital births indicate that unprotected premarital sex is not uncommon, but little is known of its frequency or the number of partners, both of which elevate the risk of HIV infection. Data reported in Ahlburg and Larson (1995) indicate that in NMI teenagers are sexually active, that condom use is less than 20 percent, and that in Fiji and Vanuatu survey respondents believed that a large majority of the population was sexually active before marriage. Also of concern is the frequency of extramarital sex. In Fiji and Vanuatu surveys show that extramarital sex is believed to be very common. In PNG data indicate that 23 percent of currently married men, 6 percent of currently married women, 33 percent of never-married men, and 12 percent of never-married women age fifteen to forty-nine years reported having nonregular sex in the last twelve months (that is, sex with a person who is not a regular partner or a spouse) (Ahlburg and Larsen 1995). Individuals with a high rate of change of sex partners play a disproportionate role in the spread of HIV and other sexually transmitted diseases.

Contraceptive prevalence rates (CPR) are low in PICs, with only the Cook Islands, FSM, and recently Fiji having rates above 45 percent, while rates in Tonga, Niue, and RMI are between 35 and 40 percent. In these countries rates have sometimes plateaued or reversed direction.[7] CPR was between 10 and 20 percent in Western Melanesia, Kiribati, and Tonga. Recent surveys, however, have shown increases in Vanuatu (37 percent) and Solomon Islands (34 percent), but the figure for Vanuatu is questionable. Data on unmet contraceptive need available from recent DHS[8] show that teenagers have higher unmet need in RMI but data are not reliable for Solomon Islands. High teenage fertility, sometimes used as a proxy for unmet need, is consistent with low contraceptive prevalence among teenagers. Possible explanations for high teenage fertility are the traditional position of churches on modern contraception, the lack of information and reluctance of teenagers to visit health centers about sexual and reproductive health, because of social disapproval of extramarital births. Youth-friendly sexual and reproductive health services need to be developed to reduce teenage pregnancies and risks of HIV transmission.

In summary, with relatively few exceptions, most PICs have TFR between 3.0 and 4.0. Among populations that were the most advanced in the fertility transition, TFR has stabilized above 3.0 for indigenous Fijians and increased in the Cook Islands and Tuvalu.

Mortality

With civil and health registration systems being more incomplete for deaths than births in most PICs, life expectancy estimates are mostly indirect estimates based on census data. Bias may be important in countries characterized by high migration,[9] and an estimated rapid increase in life expectancy to above 70 years in Polynesia (Table 22.1) would need to be assessed from other data sources. In Micronesia, life expectancy remains low in Kiribati (61 years), but higher in RMI (66) and FSM (67). Life expectancy increase has been negligible from the mid-1990s in these three countries. Mortality has been increasing in Nauru, with life expectancy of only 56 years due to lifestyle diseases. Palau has higher life expectancy, 69 years, but it has not shown any progress since 1995.

Estimates for Western Melanesia must be viewed with caution because age remains imprecisely estimated for older adults, with biases varying by gender. The female population is particularly underenumerated above the age of 40, resulting in sex ratios around 123 males per 100 females at ages 60 and over in Vanuatu, Solomon Islands, and PNG. However, despite data problems, it is clear that life expectancy is low in PNG while Vanuatu and most of Solomon Islands have unexpectedly high estimated life expectancy. Life expectancy appears to be stagnant in Fiji around 67 to 68 years.

More reliable estimates are available for infant mortality.[10] There is substantial progress in infant mortality reduction in some PICs, notably in Polynesian countries: the Cook Islands, Tonga, and Samoa, as well as in Fiji and Palau, with IMRs between 10 and 20 per 1,000. Infant mortality is much higher in Kiribati (52), RMI (33), FSM (40), and Nauru (42), and higher still in PNG and Solomon Islands, with IMRs around 65 per 1,000 in the late 1990s; the low figure from the 2007 DHS in Solomon Islands is questionable. In Vanuatu, the estimated IMR is around 25 per 1,000. RMI and Kiribati show stagnation at rather high levels, respectively around 30 per 1,000 and 50 per 1,000, while Fiji, the Cook Islands, and Palau show very slow progress but at much lower levels: between 10 per 1,000 and 18 per 1,000. High infant mortality is often associated with lack of health services, particularly with low access to ante- and postnatal care in rural areas. These shortages mostly affect Western Melanesia and remote islands of the poorer PICs. Stagnation at moderate levels is linked with lack of modern infrastructure and low levels of qualifications among health personnel that may be related to brain drain in emigration countries. Altogether, the attainment of MDG goal 4 (reduction of child mortality by two-thirds between 1990 and 2015) is unlikely to be met at the current pace of improvement in Melanesia, Kiribati, FSM, and Nauru, while RMI is nearly on track. Countries that had low IMR in 1990—Fiji, Palau, the Cook Islands, and Tonga—will have difficulty reaching the goal as it implies rates below 10 per 1,000, which are linked with a high quality of health services. Thus, only Samoa and possibly RMI and Vanuatu are likely to reach the goal, at levels between 12 and 20 per 1,000.

Stagnating life expectancy is due to noncommunicable or life-style diseases that increase adult mortality in Polynesia and Micronesia, and increasingly in Melanesia, and it has erased progress in infant mortality when it has occurred. Most PICs, particularly in Polynesia and Micronesia, have dual mortality patterns: high frequency of communicable and noncommunicable diseases.

A major issue regarding life expectancy is linked to the spread of HIV. The number of HIV infections is growing steadily, and while the number of AIDS cases is relatively small, it too is growing. If underreporting is similar to that in other developing countries, the actual number of HIV infections and AIDS cases may be ten or more times the number reported. Without changes in behaviors that place people at risk of infection, the potential exists for sero-prevalence rates[11] on the order of 2 to 5 percent of the population. Such rates of infection would considerably increase mortality and would slow but not reverse population growth (Ahlburg, Larson, and Brown 1998). PNG is already well on the path to an African-type pandemic, with a reported incidence rate of 1.6 percent in the total population.[12] HIV/AIDS could also have a major economic impact on Pacific Island nations. Estimates suggest that the cost of care is high, on the order of ten times the average expenditure on health care per capita and several times the national income per capita. Far larger are estimates of the economic value of years of work lost because of death from AIDS. In the mid-1990s these were estimated to be between F$30,000 and F$100,000 for Fiji and between 10,000K and 200,000K in PNG depending upon the individual's job (Ahlburg, Larsen, and Brown 1995).

Life expectancy is much higher in dependent territories, with 75 years in New Caledonia and French Polynesia in 2005 and 2006 respectively, with the predominantly Melanesian Northern and Loyalty Islands province of New Caledonia reaching 73. Life expectancy is also high in Guam, American Samoa, and NMI (at least 76 years). Territories have much more modern medical facilities and have IMR similar to developed countries with 5 per 1,000 in New Caledonia and 6.8 in French Polynesia (Bar, Baudchon, and Rallu 2004). Infant mortality is also low in Guam, American Samoa, and NMI, with rates below 10 per 1,000.

Migration

Migration from the Pacific has been dominated by Polynesians, principally from Samoa and Tonga, and Micronesians. Migration from Fiji has been relatively small although of long standing. But it has increased significantly in recent years in response to ethnic and political tensions (Brown et al. 2006). Tongans have migrated to New Zealand and the United States since the 1960s with the strength of the flow being sensitive to changes in labor and immigration policy. Tongans began to migrate to Australia in the 1970s with the end of the "White Australia" policy, and migration accelerated in the 1990s but then slowed with a tightening of immigration laws (Ahlburg 1991; Levin and Ahlburg 1993; Lee 2003). New Zealand, Australia, and the United States have also been the primary destination countries for Samoan migrants. In the early 1970s about half of Fijian migrants, principally Indo-Fijians, went

to Canada. In the late 1970s the United States became a favored destination and by the 1980s the United States and Canada received about two-thirds of all Fijian migrants.

The pattern of migration has undergone some changes in the Pacific from the late 1980s. Australia and New Zealand emerged as important host countries for Fijian migrants. Indo-Fijian emigration increased strongly after the 1987 and 2000 coups. Ethnic Fijians have started to migrate but to a much lesser extent, with average yearly negative net migration of 560 males and 450 females in 1996–2003—or rates of -0.26 percent and -0.22 percent for each sex, against -1.6 percent and -1.9 percent for Indo-Fijians. By the late 1990s about one-third of Fijian migrants went to the United States, one-third to Australia, 20 percent to New Zealand, and 10 percent to Canada (Narayan and Smyth 2006). In the Cook Islands, migration has increased, resulting in population declines in 1996–2001, with partial recovery in 2001–2006 according to provisional census results. A recent study of Tongan and Fijian migration found that 58 percent of Tongan households had at least one member living abroad (the average per household was 2.4 family members abroad). The respective numbers for Fiji were 35 percent (26 percent ethnic-Fijian, 43 percent Indo-Fijian) and 1.8 members per household. Fully 63 percent of Fijian migrants were in Australia or New Zealand and 18 percent in the United States. About two-thirds of Tongan migrants were in Australia or New Zealand and one-third in the United States (Jiminez 2007). Jiminez found that 36 percent of Fijian migrants had postsecondary education (45 percent for Indo-Fijians, 13 percent for ethnic-Fijians) and 14 percent of Tongan migrants had postsecondary education. These figures raise concerns about a continued "brain drain," at least from Fiji, where emigration of qualified teachers and nurses is frequent. Filipino migrant nurses are often required to fill the missing spots.

In Micronesia, RMI has witnessed a period of high emigration in the late 1990s, but emigration has now fallen to around 18 per 1,000 population. Emigration continues in FSM at about 15 per 1,000 population.[13] Kiribati is currently experiencing little emigration.

Palau is the only PIC with significant net immigration. Fiji receives migrants from most PICs due to USP and regional organizations, and the Cook Islands receive migrants working in the tourism industry, but both have negative net migration.

Net migration is low in French territories except Wallis and Futuna, with -0.4 percent annual net migration in 1996–2004 and fluctuating between -0.1 and 0.1 percent in French Polynesia for the past decades. Wallis and Futuna is affected by large-scale emigration to New Caledonia and mainland France. Net migration has picked up again in Guam but emigration is still high from American Samoa at 21 per 1,000 population and is expected to remain at that level. NMI experienced high immigration in the 1990s, but it declined in the 2000s. The cohorts aged 20–34 years, however, are double their expected size, consisting of working-age people working in factories.

Migration improves the economic position of the migrant and, because of remittances, the economic lot of the family that remains behind. Recent research has shown that the economic position of PIC migrants, primarily from Samoa, Tonga, Micronesia, and Fiji, improved in the 1980s despite unfavorable macroeconomic conditions, and improved further in the long economic upswing of the

1990s. Part of the improvement in the position of PIC migrants was due to increases in their human capital: education, work experience, and language skills. These gains allowed more PIC workers to acquire white-collar jobs and increase their earnings (Ahlburg and Song 2006). Not surprisingly, the poverty rate of Pacific Islanders fell from 1.57 times the U.S. rate in 1990 to 1.33 times the U.S. rate in 2000. Perhaps a better relative measure is a comparison with Native Hawaiians. In 1990, the poverty rate of Pacific Islanders was 58 percent higher than the rate for Hawaiian households. In 2000 it was only 15 percent higher.

A controversial view of migration is that educating sons and daughters for migration may be a desirable development strategy for small, isolated Pacific Island nations (Bertram 2006; Bertram and Waters 1985, 1986). The evidence suggests that migration plays a very important economic role in the lives of people living in Pacific Island nations. In her recent study of Tonga and Fiji, Jiminez (2007) found that 91 percent of Tongan and 42 percent of Fijian households received some type of remittance from a migrant overseas. The size of the average remittance received was large: US$3,067 in Tonga and $1,328 in Fiji. These figures underestimate the actual value of remittances received because churches, youth, cultural, and sporting groups also receive remittances. Remittances are equal to 62 percent of GDP in Tonga and 154 percent of the value of exports. The respective figures are 6.2 percent and 8.3 percent in Fiji (Brown et al. 2006). The estimates for Tonga are consistent with those estimated by Ahlburg (1991) for the 1970s and 1980s. Ahlburg estimated that remittances were equal to 40 percent of GDP in Samoa.

Remittances form a link between demography and economics. Remittances have an impact on poverty and income distribution. The impact depends upon the share of remittances in total income, the distribution of remittances, and where recipients are located in the overall distribution of income. Thus the impact can vary across countries or over time within a country. Early work in the Pacific by Connell (1981) found that remittances increased inequality, but later work by Ahlburg (1996) found that remittances decreased inequality in Tonga. Recent work by Jiminez (2007) found that the impact of remittances on inequality was sensitive to the measure of inequality employed. She found, however, that for four of the five measures of inequality she used, remittances increased inequality in Tonga and reduced it in Fiji. It is common for remittances to increase inequality early in the migration process as migrants tend to be from higher-income groups. As migration becomes more established, migrants from lower-income groups move overseas and their remittances improve the distribution of income. The results of Jiminez for Fiji are consistent with this story, but the results for Tonga suggest a more complex pattern in a country with a well-established history of migration. Jiminez also investigated the impact of remittances on poverty. She found that remittances decreased poverty in Tonga and Fiji and that the impact was greater in Tonga (where migration is more significant). In fact, in the absence of remittances, poverty would be greater in Tonga than in Fiji. After the receipt of remittances, poverty was less in Tonga than in Fiji. Very little work has focused on the impact of sending remittances on the poverty status of the sending (not the receiving) household. Barringer, Gardner, and Levin (1993) speculated that sending remittances may worsen the economic situation of the sending household. Ahlburg (2000) found that because many Pacific Island households live at or near the poverty line in the United States, the payment of the average level of remittances can force many of them into poverty and those already in poverty even deeper into poverty.

Population Growth

While natural population growth shows moderate differences between PICs, between 1.5 percent and 2.5 percent, consistent with the range of TFR levels, total population growth[14] is much more varied, including negative growth in the smaller nations with heavy out-migration, such as Niue, Tokelau, and the Cook Islands.[15] Migration also counterbalances most of the natural increase in Tonga, Samoa, FSM, and Wallis and Futuna, and to a lesser extent in RMI, Tuvalu, and Fiji. Western Melanesia and Kiribati[16] show total growth close to natural growth or even higher (see above). Growth appears to be higher than expected from HIES (household income and expenditure survey) data in Solomon Islands implying a population of just above 500,000 at end of 2006, whereas estimates based on the 1999 census were around 485,000. This was due to underenumeration in the 1999 census that took place during the so-called "Ethnic Conflict," or 1999–2000 crisis. The growth rate could reach 3.0 percent for the period 1986–2006 against estimates of 2.8 percent in 1986–1999.

In territories, New Caledonia has population growth of 1.3 percent and French Polynesia of 1.1 percent, but because of emigration from Wallis and Futuna the population grew by only 0.8 percent in the early 2000s (Bar, Baudchon, and Rallu 2004; Baudchon and Rallu 1999). Population growth in Guam and American Samoa has increased somewhat due to reduced out-migration (2.7 percent and 1.2 percent respectively). The impact of net immigration was much higher in NMI, leading to dramatic population growth. The rate of population growth was estimated to be 5 percent in 1995 but declined steeply afterward. Selective in-migration can also severely distort the age structure of the population and dependency ratios, as we shall see below.

Population projections show that population size should slowly increase in Polynesia, but prospects for growth are extremely high in PICs that have no or little migration outlet: Western Melanesia and to a lesser extent Kiribati, due to high population momentum. With current trends in TFR, Western Melanesia will probably grow well into the second half of the century. This would bring the population of Vanuatu, Solomon Islands, and PNG respectively to 280,000, 620,000, and 7.3 million by 2015, and 360,000, 800,000, and 9.9 million by 2030 (Hayes 2007). However, AIDS could result in slower population growth in PNG, with 7.2 million in 2015 and 9.4 million in 2030.[17] Given population momentum, the population of Solomon Islands will reach one million around 2055 or as soon as 2040 with slower fertility decline.

Age Structure and Prospects for a Demographic Bonus

Usually, rapid population growth directly translates into younger age structures, but in the Pacific many countries have age structures affected by emigration or, in the case of NMI, immigration, where the cohorts aged 20 to 34 years are double their expected size. In PICs with high and slowly declining fertility, dependency is primarily youth dependency (see Table 22.2). Proportions of elderly aged 65 and over remain below 5 percent in many countries and even around 3 percent in some. Even in high emigration countries the percentage of the population aged 65 and over is not much above 5 or 6 percent. Projections based on recent fertility trends show that aging will not be a significant policy issue for at least another decade or two. The age pyramids of Solomon Islands and Samoa clearly show large bases and small elderly populations, with a depletion of adults from age 20 due to migration in Samoa (Figure 22.2). Fiji is more advanced in the demographic transition; the basis of the age pyramid is starting to stabilize and adults aged 15 to 64 represent a higher share of the population while elderly remain below 5 percent.

The total dependency ratio[18] is below 50 only in Palau (35); it is 52 in Fiji (but Indo-Fijian dependency ratio is 39 while it is 60 for indigenous Fijian), and most other PICs show dependency ratios above 70 or even 80. The distinction between emigration countries with decades-long fertility declines and Western Melanesia with high fertility is veiled by the depletion of adult ages by emigration. Thus, Tonga and Samoa have similar dependency ratios (around 75) to Solomon Islands and Vanuatu. Dependency is stable or even slightly increasing in the Cook Islands and Tuvalu (Figure 22.3). Except in RMI and FSM, dependency is only declining slowly in the region, particularly in Western Melanesia. By comparison, in South, East, and Southeast Asia, where the fertility transition is more advanced (Mujahid 2006; Seetharam 2006), three countries have dependency ratios below 50 (China and Thailand 43, Singapore 39), four (Vietnam, Indonesia, Myanmar, and Brunei) are below or around 55, and only three are above 75 (Timor Leste, PR Lao, and Pakistan). This shows the delayed demographic transition process in Melanesia and part of Micronesia compared to Asia.

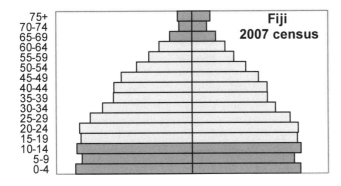

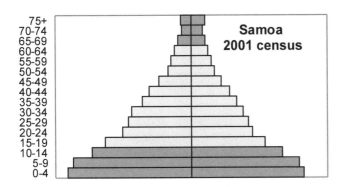

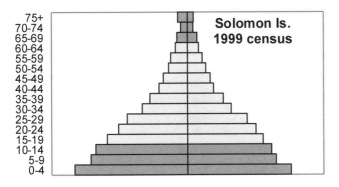

Figure 22.2. *Age/sex structures, Fiji, Samoa, and Solomon Islands (left males, right females).*

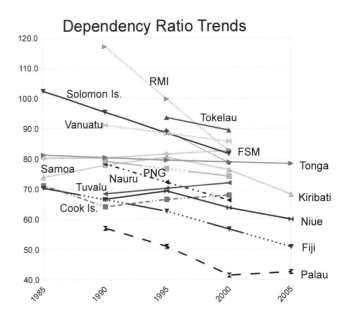

Figure 22.3. *Dependency ratios in the Pacific from mid-1980s to mid-2000s.*

Dependency ratios are much lower in territories as a result of immigration and more established fertility decline. New Caledonia and French Polynesia have dependency ratios just below 50, and even in emigration-affected Wallis and Futuna, rapid fertility decline has led to a dependency ratio of 64. Dependency is also rather high in American Samoa at around 67, but it is much lower at 52 in Guam, and exceedingly low (43) in NMI because of the influx of working-age adults.

Recent research has established a potential link between declining dependency and economic growth (Bloom and Canning 2001; Mason 2001; Lee, Mason, and Miller 2001; Birdsall, Kelley, and Sinding 2001; Ahlburg 2002). Increasing numbers of workers, relative to those not working, enter the labor market, which leads to an increase in the rate of economic growth. This favorable effect does not begin before dependency drops below 60, with ratios between 40 and 50 characterizing a strong "demographic bonus."[19] Prospects for such a strong demographic bonus are weak in the Pacific either because the demographic opportunity has not arisen (dependency ratios are still high) or because the economic, social, and political situation is unsupportive. We calculated population projections in two scenarios: slow and rapid fertility declines for Kiribati and Solomon Islands. Kiribati would reach dependency ratios under 50 between 2020 and 2030 according to respectively rapid and slow scenarios, and Solomon Islands would reach it between 2027 and 2040 (Rallu and Robertson 2009). Except for Fiji and Palau, the potential for a demographic bonus is still small and there are questions about the ability of PICs to translate favorable demographic change into a real economic bonus. Territories have undergone the demographic transition required but have not captured the economic bonus that Asian countries have captured. Economic, social, and political conditions would need to change to enable these countries and territories to capture the positive economic aspects of the demographic bonus.

Population and Development

General Context

Whether the demographic bonus, or "window of opportunity," translates into economic growth and development depends upon large cohorts entering the productive workforce, triggering savings and investment. The bonus, however, is not automatic. It relies upon countries having adequate investment policies, good governance and political stability, and supportive infrastructures making investment attractive to local and foreign investors (Williamson 2001). Many of these features are lacking in the Pacific.

Beyond the traditional adverse effects of smallness and remoteness, the current economic situation in PICs is one of high unemployment, specifically for youth (often hidden by large subsistence sectors), a low level of education in technical areas, and poor infrastructure: transport is a major problem in large Melanesian islands as well as for remote islands, electricity and telecommunications are expensive and not always reliable, and there is little to support economic development and attract new industries or services. Urban growth is often high (see below) and unmanageable given state resources, which leads to expanding slums and insecurity that impede social and economic development. Moreover, access to land is difficult, corruption is widespread, and social and political instability is frequent in Melanesia, including Fiji, as well as in Tonga. These issues are disincentives for foreign investors and a factor in the emigration of skilled and entrepreneurial locals.

Access to Cash Employment and Urban Drift

Youth unemployment rates are frequently between 30 percent (Tonga, Tuvalu, Nauru) and 60 percent (RMI), with Solomon Islands at 46 percent.[20] They are between 10 percent and 15 percent in Fiji, the Cook Islands, Palau, and Samoa (SPC/UN 2004). In most PICs, only 10 to 20 percent of those leaving school can find a job in the formal sector. The informal cash sector, however, is developing rapidly in urban areas and is a factor in urban drift. Data from Kiribati show that employment in the cash sector (both formal and informal excluding agriculture) unexpectedly increased by 29 percent between the 2000 and 2005 censuses.[21] Although urban unemployment is high, youth have twice the rate of cash employment in South Tarawa compared with the outer islands. Therefore, rural-urban migration remains important, particularly for women who have much less opportunity to work in the cash sector in rural areas. While the 2005 census data show that the urban growth rate has declined from 5.1 percent in 1995–2000 to 1.9 percent in 2000–2005,[22] it appears that some areas of South Tarawa still have growth rates above 4 percent and periurban areas in North Tarawa are growing at rates above 6 percent (Rallu 2009).

The percentage of the population living in urban areas was 51 percent in Fiji in 2007 and is above 50 percent in RMI, the Cook Islands, Palau, and Nauru. PNG, Solomon Islands, and Vanuatu are still predominantly rural with only 13 percent, 19 percent, and 26 percent of the population in urban areas.

In many PICs, except Fiji between 1986 and 1996, there has not been a reclassification of urban areas for several censuses, and urban growth may be underestimated. Urban growth seems to be declining in Fiji (with 1.5 percent in 1996–2007 against 2.6 percent in 1986–1996[23]) and in Kiribati (see above). Solomon Islands and Vanuatu have urban growth rates above 4 percent and still higher rates for informal settlements in periurban areas. Given the lack of rural development, urban growth is likely to remain high in these countries.

In Polynesia, urbanization remains limited because people do not need to move to town to work there. Tonga and Samoa have 32 percent and 22 percent of their populations in urban areas and urban growth rates around 1 percent. But, RMI, Kiribati, and Tuvalu have respectively 72 percent, 44 percent, and 51 percent of the population living in urban areas and urban growth rates between 1.5 and 2.7 percent, despite significant emigration from RMI. The pressure of urbanization on the atoll environment has direct implications for health, mostly in South Tarawa, Ebeye, and Majuro.

The size of the rural population is declining in Fiji at 0.5 percent per year (0.1 percent in 1996–2007). This is also the case in most outer islands region-wide, and it is becoming a concern as regards the sustainability of communities in outer islands of the Cook Islands, Tuvalu, Kiribati, Tonga, and to a lesser extent Lau (Fiji). The situation is very different in predominantly rural countries such as Solomon Islands, Vanuatu, and PNG, where most of the population growth in absolute numbers is still in rural areas. Declining or scattered populations in Melanesia and remote islands make it expensive to provide social services, which increases the difficulty of rural development.

Gender Issues

The position of women varies by country. Fijian women live under patriarchal systems and have subordinate social status (Asindkrah 2001). In contrast, in Tonga women enjoy a higher social status (Emberson-Bain 1998): the "*fahu*" system confers special rights to women but they are limited to a few areas of tradition. Gender equity has been achieved or almost so in primary education (except in Western Melanesia), and there are often more girls than boys in secondary education, but the number of girls in tertiary education remains well below that of boys. Interruptions of studies due to teen pregnancies, as well as other social factors, certainly play a role in this situation. Despite apparent educational parity, the share of women in the nonagricultural formal sector is often below 35 percent, except in the Cook Islands (45 percent), Tuvalu (43 percent), Palau (40 percent), Kiribati (39 percent), and Samoa (38 percent), and it is as low as 26 percent in Solomon Islands and 6 percent in PNG (SPC/UN 2004).[24] Moreover, the share of women declines in higher administration and in decision-making positions. PICs are at the bottom of all countries for the proportion of parliamentary seats held by women, with declines in recent elections. In most PICs less than 5 percent of legislators are female, except the Cook Islands, Samoa, Nauru, Niue, Tokelau, and the former parliament in Fiji, with figures between 5 and 10 percent. In Tonga, Solomon Islands, and PNG the figure is less than 1 percent. The social status of women affects their economic status in many ways, from differences in representation at various levels of the labor market to differences in social and reproductive rights. Gender-based violence is prevalent in many countries and becomes a social issue, aggravated in the context of increasing HIV prevalence.

As a consequence of gender inequity the usually positive role women play in poverty reduction and enhanced health care and education—including sexual and reproductive health—is muted in PICs.

MDG Attainment as a Proxy for Development Progress

An overall assessment of the level and dynamism of social and economic development in PICs can be obtained through an investigation of their progress toward attaining their Millennium Development Goals (MDG),[25] although data inadequacy makes such an investigation difficult. HIV and sexual-behavior-related indicators are usually missing or unreliable.[26] The contraceptive prevalence rate is often available, but a related indicator, unmet need for contraception, is usually not available. Minimum dietary consumption is also most often lacking, and while hunger is infrequent in the Pacific, malnutrition does exist. Historically, poverty data have been unavailable and poverty was considered nonexistent by Pacific governments because of family solidarity and plentiful island subsistence. The availability of data on poverty is improving as ADB and UNDP have conducted more frequent HIES. Only three countries, however, have two data points,[27] but comparability of the data is questionable. Income poverty has increased in Fiji, from a revised estimate of 29.2 percent in 1990–1991[28] to 34.4 percent of the population living under national (basic needs) poverty line in 2002–2003 (Abbott 2006). This does not translate into extreme poverty—only 11 percent of the population is under the food poverty line—but it implies poverty of opportunity, meaning difficulty in participating fully in social and economic life. Poverty in rural Fiji is higher than in urban areas (38 percent against 32 percent). Vanuatu and Solomon Islands have higher poverty in urban (33 percent) than in rural areas (between 15 and 20 percent) due to the lower cost of living and the large subsistence economy in rural areas. Tonga and Samoa have respectively 23 percent (2009) and 27 percent (2008) of their population living below national poverty lines. Estimates are higher in Micronesia (38 percent in FSM and around 50 percent in Kiribati and RMI) and PNG (30 percent). In large rural countries and outer islands, poverty of opportunity is widespread due to lack of rural development and is a major cause of migration to urban areas. Most HIESs show larger household size in the lowest income quintiles, indicating a risk of the reproduction of poverty across generations. Thus, PICs appear ill-prepared to tackle poverty, HIV/AIDS, and sexual and reproductive health issues that directly affect population growth and well-being.

Levels and trends in MDG indicators show that Polynesia, Fiji, and Palau have already achieved or are likely to achieve many of the targets in education, health (except HIV), and environment. Progress, though, has often recently stalled, mostly in child mortality (Fiji, the Cook Islands, and Palau) and maternal mortality, and important aspects of gender equity are low (see above). Micronesia (except Palau) struggles to reduce child mortality (between 30 and 60 per 1,000) and maternal mortality (with figures between 250 and 300 per 100,000 in Kiribati and FSM). Progress in education and environment (access to clean water and sanitation) remain slow. Gender equity is less favorable than in Polynesia. Poverty is higher and indications are that it is not decreasing.

Western Melanesia has unfavorable levels for most indicators and is unlikely to achieve most of the MDGs, although some progress appears to have taken place in reducing maternal mortality in Solomon Islands and infant mortality in Vanuatu, with increases in health services delivery in the latter. Recent rapid increases in primary enrollment in Solomon Islands appears to be partly a result of a policy to fund schools based on enrollment, resulting in reports of inflated figures by school principals. Gender equity is a major concern in this subregion, from primary education to labor force (only 26 percent female in nonagricultural wage/salary employment in Solomon Islands) and with little or no female representation in parliament.

PNG, Solomon Islands, and Vanuatu are the only PICs with population growth around 2.5 percent. They also have infant mortality rates twice the PIC average and maternal mortality rates three times the PIC average. These higher mortality rates are likely related to immunization rates that are nearly 20 percent below the PIC average and the percentage of births attended by skilled health personnel, which is 23 percent below average. Another contributing factor is inadequate access to clean water and sanitation, particularly in rural areas (52 percent and 29 percent below the PIC average respectively). These countries also have much lower levels of education and income and higher gender inequity. Their lower economic and social position relative to other PICs may be related to rapid population growth that hinders extension of service coverage, mostly in fast-growing informal periurban areas. Difficulty of access in rural areas is also an issue.

New Zealand and Hawai'i

New Zealand and Hawai'i have achieved the fertility transition, with fertility just below replacement level in New Zealand. Thus, natural growth is low (Table 22.1). Migration has been sluggish in Hawai'i, while it has increased in New Zealand, resulting in total growth of 1 percent. Low dependency ratios are a consequence of demographic transition. A large urban percentage of the population, high life expectancy, and low infant mortality are testimony to a high level of socioeconomic development. Maori, Hawaiian, and islanders life expectancy, however, may be lower than for the total population, but precise estimates are difficult to derive because of changes in ethnic reporting in censuses and at civil registration.

The population of Hawai'i is composed of 6.2 percent Native Hawaiians and 2.7 percent other Pacific Islanders, with Samoans representing nearly half of the latter. In New Zealand the Maori population increased from 11.9 percent in 1991 to 14.0 percent in 2006 due to higher fertility and younger age structure. The Pacific Island–born population increased from 2.9 percent in 1991 to 3.4 percent in 2006 (Bedford et al. 2006; Bedford 2005). Between the 2001 and 2006 censuses, the number of those born in the Pacific Islands increased by 18,800, or 3 percent yearly, to 135,850, and ethnic Pacific Islanders (including part islanders) reached 288,000.[29] Thus, more than 20 percent of the New Zealand population can claim full- or part-Maori or Pacific Islander origin, and most were born in New Zealand, with 20–25 percent of Niueans, Tokelauans, and Cook Islanders and about 40 percent of Samoans and Tongans born in their island "of origin." This is a result of a steady migration flow that is more than half a century old.

Table 22.2

Proportion (%) of Population by Large Age Groups and Dependency Ratio

	0–14	15–64	65+	Dependency ratio
American Samoa	35	60	5	67
Cook Islands	27	64	9	56
French Polynesia	25	68	7	47
Fiji	29	66	5	52
FSM	36	60	4	67
Guam	27	66	7	52
Kiribati	35	61	4	64
Marshall Islands	42	55	3	82
Nauru	35	63	2	59
New Caledonia	25	67	8	49
Niue	24	64	12	56
Northern Marianas	26	70	4	43
Palau	20	74	6	35
PNG	39	58	3	72
Samoa	37	58	5	72
Solomon Islands	40	57	3	75
Tokelau	41	53	6	89
Tonga	37	57	6	75
Tuvalu	32	62	6	61
Vanuatu	38	58	4	72
Wallis and Futuna	33	61	6	64
New Zealand	20	67	13	49
Hawai'i	19	67	14	49

Source: UNESCAP 2011.

Native people and Pacific migrants in both New Zealand and Hawai'i have lower educational attainment than other segments of the population, as do Maoris, but studies have shown that the economic integration of islanders in Hawai'i (Ahlburg and Song 2006) and New Zealand is improving and the economic gap between migrants and both Hawaiian natives and other sectors of the population has been declining.

Conclusion

In the last decade the Pacific has seen little progress in demographic processes. Fertility transition has been slow in Melanesia and part of Micronesia and is stalled in Polynesia, RMI and Nauru. The Cook Islands and Tuvalu have experienced fertility increases. Declines in infant mortality have been slow, and, unlike territories, no PIC reached below 10 per 1,000. Life expectancy has increased slowly or not at all because noncommunicable diseases have erased most of the benefits of reduced child mortality. While aging is not an urgent issue, dependency has declined very slowly, with a limited advance toward a demographic window of opportunity that could enhance development. Countries in Polynesia and Micronesia have migration- and remittance-based economies, and economic growth remains sluggish, while Melanesian countries have seen declines in GDP per capita for several years, with some recent improvement in a postconflict Solomon Islands and postcoup Fiji.

Social change has been hindered by strong traditional and religious groups and, unlike Asia (McNicoll 2006), state incentives to foster slower population growth, more rapid economic development, and pro-poor policies are weak. Empowerment of women is low and parliamentary representation of females is the lowest in the world. Women could play a critical role as agents of change but their role in economic and political life has been impeded.

Regionally, Western Melanesia is subjected to the most difficult population, economic, and social challenges. AusAID's recent Pacific 2020 report (AusAID 2006) mentions major concerns over the region's future. Micronesian countries also face various obstacles to achieving further demographic, social, and economic progress. While the overall situation is better in Polynesia, further progress is likely to be slow.

NOTES

1. The first edition of this chapter included a section on historical background. This has not been replicated here. The authors would however like to say that findings have brought more evidence of large population in the Pacific before European contact, specifically in Polynesia (Kirch and Rallu 2007).

2. TFR (Total Fertility Rate): The number of births a woman would have in her fertile life (from age 15 to 49) if age-specific fertility rates remained the same as in the current year.

3. Since the early 2000s, Ministry of Health data for births are nearly complete and have been used to estimate TFR by ethnic groups.

4. Western Melanesia is short for PNG, Solomon Islands, and Vanuatu, which moreover share very similar population trends and structures.

5. Natural growth rate is the difference between crude birth and death rates. Total or population growth rate includes natural growth and net migration, the difference between immigration and emigration.

6. This is mostly due to large numbers of female temporary immigrant workers.

7. CPR should be interpreted cautiously because contraceptives distributed by the private sector and NGOs and are not counted in Ministry of Health Statistics.

8. DHSs were conducted in RMI, Tuvalu, Solomon Islands, and Nauru in 2006–2007.

9. For instance, an indirect measure of life expectancy from census data is based on the question: "Is your father/mother still alive?" Since many residents enumerated in islands have their parents living in rim countries, life expectancy is based partly on individuals who do not reside on the islands.

10. Infant mortality is the ratio of deaths under 1 year of age to births in a given year.

11. Approximately the percentage of people in the population infected with HIV.

12. Projected prevalence is 5 percent by 2012, reducing life expectancy by between 4 and 5 years by 2015 (Hayes 2007).

13. For a historical discussion of Micronesian migration patterns see Nero and Rehuher (1993) and Rehuher (1993).

14. We use de facto or de jure population according to data provided by various PICs. The difference is only important for the Cook Islands, with a resident population of 14,990 against 18,027 including visitors (2001) and Tokelau with 1,151 against 1,466 "de jure usual residents" (2006); Niue has a resident population of 1,538 in 2006. It is minor for other countries and there is usually no change between censuses, so that trends are consistent.

15. The resident population of the Cook Islands declined by 3.7 percent yearly in 1996–2001, but it increased by 1.2 percent yearly in 2001–2006 (provisional). The Cook Islands migration varies greatly according to the local and New Zealand economic situations as Cook Islanders have New Zealand citizenship and migrate freely.

16. Kiribati has significant emigration in the form of seamen, with balanced emigration and return migration (quasi-nil net migration) for the 2000–2005 period.

17. Assuming HIV prevalence stabilizes at 5 percent from 2012.

18. Ratio of dependents: Children under 15 and elderly above 65 to 100 adult (15–64) population.

19. Such as the current situation in China and Thailand (43) and most Southeast Asian countries having ratios around or below 60.

20. Youth unemployment rates below 5 percent in Vanuatu and Kiribati are due to large subsistence sectors or so-called "village workers" and do not reflect the real situation. A question on "seeking paid job" was asked to all in the 2005 census. Including "village workers" seeking paid work with the unemployed lifts youth unemployment rate to 37 percent.

21. Actually, 6 percentage points of this increase are due to population change; the cash employment rate increased by only 23 percent (19 percent for males and 29 percent for females). It seems that a large part is due to the informal sector. The public sector, which represents now 53 percent of the cash sector, has grown by 17 percent, lower than other sectors.

22. Relocation of people to the Christmas Islands explains part of the reduction in urban growth.

23. Urban and periurban boundaries, however, were only partially revised for the 2007 census, while a major revision occurred for the 1996 census.

24. Figures have been corrected using census reports when necessary, specifically for Solomon Islands and Samoa.

25. The eight Millennium Development Goals are:

- Eradicate extreme poverty and hunger
- Achieve universal primary education
- Promote gender quality and empower women
- Reduce child mortality
- Improve mental health
- Combat HIV/AIDS, malaria, and other diseases
- Ensure environmental sustainability
- Develop a global partnership for development

26. Increased HIV testing in PNG has revealed a much higher prevalence than expected (reaching 1.6 percent) while in other PICs, real figures may be ten times as high as official figures.

27. Fiji, Samoa, and Kiribati. Due to errors in estimating the food poverty line in the 1997 Samoa HIES, trends are not reliable. Results of the second HIES in Kiribati are not yet available.

28. A previous estimate of 25 percent was based on a "revised" and lower poverty line. The previous figure of 29.2 percent is reinstated to reduce increase in poverty as shown from the 2002–2003 HIES.

29. Of which 131,000 were Samoans, 58,000 Cook Islanders, 50,500 Tongans, 22,500 Niueans, 6,800 Tokelauans, and 9,900 Fijians; there were also 2,600 Tuvaluans and 1,100 Kiribati.

BIBLIOGRAPHY

Abbott, D. 2006. *Analysis of the 2002/03 household income and expenditure survey, estimation of basic needs poverty lines and incidence of poverty in Fiji.* Suva: UNDP Pacific Centre.

Abbott, D., and S. Pollard. 2004. *Hardship and poverty in the Pacific.* Manila: Asian Development Bank.

Ahlburg, D. A. 1991. Remittances and their impact: A study of Tonga and Western Samoa. Pacific Policy Paper 7. Canberra: National Center for Development Studies.

———. 1996. Remittances and the income distribution in Tonga. *Population Research and Policy Review* 15: 391–400.

———. 2000. Poverty among Pacific Islanders in the U.S.: Incidence, change, and correlates. *Pacific Studies* 23(1–2): 51–74.

———. 2002. Does population matter? A review essay. *Population and Development Review* 28(2): 329–350.

Ahlburg, D. A., and H. J. Larson. 1995. Sexual activities in the Pacific and HIV/AIDS risk. *Pacific Health Dialog* 2(2): 103–106.

Ahlburg, D. A., H. J. Larson, and T. Brown. 1995. Health care costs of HIV/AIDS in the Pacific. *Pacific Health Dialog* 2(2): 14–19.

———. 1998. The potential demographic impact of HIV/AIDS in the Pacific. *Pacific Studies* 21(4): 67–81.

Ahlburg, D. A., and Y. N. Song. 2006. Changes in the economic fortunes of Pacific Islanders in the USA in the 1990s. *Asia Pacific Viewpoint* 47(1): 109–121.

Asindkrah, M. 2001. Patriarchal family ideology and female homicide victimization in Fiji. *Journal of Comparative Family Studies* 32(2): 283–301.

AusAID. 2006. *Pacific 2020, challenges and opportunities for growth.* Canberra: AusAID, Canberra. www.ausaid.gov.au/publications.

Bar L., G. Baudchon, and J. L. Rallu. 2004. Les dynamiques socio-démographiques dans les TOMs du Pacifique: vers un développement durablement assisté. *Espace, Populations, Sociétés* 2004–2, numéro spécial : *Regards vers l'outre-mer français à l'aube du 21ème siècle,* 373–386.

Barringer, H., R. Gardner, and M. Levin. 1993. *Asians and Pacific Islanders in the United States.* New York: Russell Sage Foundation.

Baudchon G., and J. L. Rallu. 1999. Changement démographique et social en Nouvelle Calédonie après les Accords Matignon. *Population* 3: 391–426.

Bedford, R. D. 2004. International migration, identity and development in Oceania: A synthesis of ideas. In *International migration: Prospects and policies,* ed. J. E. Taylor and D. S. Massey, 231–260. Oxford: Oxford University Press.

———. 2005. International migration and globalization: The transformation of New Zealand's migration system since the mid-1980s. In *Sovereignty under seige? Globalization and New Zealand,* ed. R. Patman and C. Rudd, 129–156. Critical Security Series. Aldershot: Ashgate Publishing Ltd.

Bedford, R. D., E. S. Ho, V. Krishnan, and B. Hong. 2006. The neighbourhood effect: The Pacific in Aotearoa and Australia. *Asian and Pacific Migration Journal* 16(2): 251–269.

Bertram, I. G. 2006. Beyond MIRAB: The political economy of small islands in the twenty-first century. *Asia and Pacific Viewpoint* 47(1).

Bertram, I. G., and R. F. Watters. 1985. The MIRAB economy in South Pacific microstates. *Pacific Viewpoint* 26(3): 497–519.

———. 1986. The MIRAB Process: Earlier analyses in context. *Pacific Viewpoint* 27(1): 47–59.

Birdsall, N., A. C. Kelley, and S. W. Sinding, eds. 2001. *Population matters: Demographic change, economic growth and poverty in the developing world.* Oxford: Oxford University Press.

Bloom, D., and D. Canning. 2001. Cumulative causality, economic growth, and the demographic transition. In *Population matters,* ed. N. Birdsall, A. C. Kelley, and S. W. Sinding, 165–197. Oxford: Oxford University Press.

Brown, R., and J. Connell. 1993. *Migration and remittances in Tonga and Western Samoa.* Bangkok: ILO.

Brown, R., J. Connell, E. V. Jiminez, and G. Leeves. 2006. Cents and sensibility: The economic benefits of remittances. In *World Bank, home and away: Expanding job opportunities for Pacific Islanders through labor mobility,* 46–99. Washington, D.C.: The World Bank.

Bryant, J. 2007. Theories of fertility decline and evidence from development indicators. *Population and Development Review* 33(1): 101–128.

Connell. J. 1981. Remittances and rural development: Migration, dependency and inequality in the South Pacific. In *Population mobility and development: Southeast Asia and the Pacific,* ed. G. W. Jones and H. V. Richter. Canberra: National Centre for Development Studies, Australian National University.

Economic and Social Commission for Asia and the Pacific (ESCAP). 2011. Population Data Sheet. http://www.unescap.org/publications/detail.asp?id=1465.

Emberson-Bain, A. 1998. *Women in Tonga.* Manila: Asian Development Bank.

ESCAP, UNDP, and ADB, 2005. *A future within reach: Reshaping institutions in a region of disparities to meet the millennium development goals in Asia and the Pacific.* New York: United Nations.

Hayes, G. 2007. The demographic impact of the HIV/AIDS epidemic in Papua-New Guinea, 1990–2030. *Asia Pacific Population Journal* 22(3): 11–30.

ICF International. 2013. Measure DHS: Demographic and health surveys. Calverton, Md.: ICF International. http://www.measuredhs.com/data/available-datasets.cfm.

Jimenez, E. V. 2007. The social protection role of remittances. PhD dissertation, University of Queensland, Australia.

Kirch, P. V., and J. L. Rallu, eds. 2007. *The growth and collapse of Pacific Island societies: Archaeological and demographic perspectives.* Honolulu: University of Hawai'i Press.

Lee, H. 2003. *Tongans overseas: Between two shores.* Honolulu: University of Hawai'i Press.

Lee, R. D., A. Mason, and T. Miller. 2001. Savings, wealth, and population. In *Population matters,* ed. N. Birdsall, A. C. Kelley, and S. W. Sinding, 137–164. Oxford: Oxford University Press.

Levin, M., and D. A. Ahlburg. 1993. Pacific Islanders in the U.S. census data. In *A World perspective on Pacific Islander migration: Australia, New Zealand and the USA,* ed. G. McCall and J. Connell, 95–144. Pacific Studies Monograph No. 6. Sydney: Center for South Pacific Studies, The University of New South Wales.

Mason, A. 2001. Population and economic growth in East Asia. In *Population change and economic development in East Asia: Challenges met, opportunities seized,* ed. A. Mason, 1–30. Stanford, Calif.: Stanford University Press.

———. 2006. Population ageing and demographic dividends: The time to act is now. *Asia Pacific Population Journal* 21(3): 7–16.

McNicoll, G. 2006. Policy lessons of the East Asian demographic transition. *Population and Development Review* 32(1): 1–26.

Minja, K. C., and J. Chen. 2006. Potential for reducing child and maternal mortality through reproductive and child health intervention programmes: An illustrative case study from India. *Asia Pacific Population Journal* 21(1): 13–44.

Mujahid, G. 2006. Population ageing in East and South-East Asia, 1950–2050: Implications for elderly care. *Asia Pacific Population Journal* 21(2): 25–44.

Narayan, P., and R. Smyth. 2006. What determines migration flows from low-income to high-income countries? An investigation of Fiji-US migration 1972–2001. *Contemporary Economic Policy* 24(2): 332–342.

Nero, K. L., and F. Rehuher. 1993. Workers and servants: The internationalization of Palauan households. Unpublished paper.

Pool, I., L. R. Wong, and E. Vilquin. 2006. *Age-structural transitions: Challenges for development.* Paris: CICRED.

Rallu, J. L. 2009. Urban drift, urban growth, urban youth. In *A new generation youth lifestyle – Influence and impact,* ed. M. Rao, 68–96. Hyderabad, India: Icfai University Press.

Rallu, J. L., and D. Ahlburg. 1999. Demography. In *The Pacific Islands: Environment & society,* ed. M. Rapaport, 258–269. Honolulu: Bess Press.

Rallu, J. L., and A. S. Robertson. 2009. The demographic window of opportunity in Pacific Island countries: Future prospects. In *Pacific,* 13–38. New York: UNESCAP. http://www.unescap.org/EPOC/pdf/Pacific%20Perspectives_ST_ESCAP_2551_S2_final.pdf.

Rehuher, F. 1993. Pursuing the dream: Historical perspectives on Micronesian movement patterns. In *A world perspective on Pacific Islander migration: Australia, New Zealand and the USA,* ed. G. McCall and J. Connell, Research in Pacific Studies Monograph No. 6. Kensington, New South Wales: Centre for South Pacific Studies, University of New South Wales.

Seetharam, K. S. 2006, Age-structure transition and development in Asia and the Pacific: Opportunities and challenges, *Asia Pacific Population Journal,* special issue, 65–86.

SPC/United Nations. 2004. *Pacific Islands Regional Millennium Development Goals report,* Noumea: SPC.

———. 2010. HIES (Household Income and Development Survey). Noumea: SPC. http://www.spc.int/prism/reports.

UNESCAP. 2011. 2011 ESCAP population data sheet. Bangkok: UNESCAP. http://www.unescap.org/publications/detail.asp?id=1465.

Williamson, J. G. 2001. Demographic change, economic growth, and inequality. In *Population matters,* ed. N. Birdsall, A. C. Kelley, and S. W. Sinding, 106–136. Oxford: Oxford University Press.

Mobility to Migration

John Connell and Moshe Rapaport

23

Since the earliest settlement of the Pacific Islands, mobility has been associated with both challenges and opportunities, as islanders have sought new homes or been displaced from older ones. This chapter provides a broad overview of mobility, beginning from oral traditions, followed by the historical transitions in mobility patterns among island communities in various parts of the Pacific. The movements of European settlers and associated labor migrants are then discussed, along with the displacements that ensued. We then consider contemporary migration, focusing on trends, rationales, and impact.

As emigration has evolved, small, vulnerable, and now mainly independent Pacific Island states have become irrevocably a peripheral and dependent part of a wider world. Contemporary patterns of migration have diversified and become both more selective and skilled, demographic structures have changed, and the restructuring of global and island economic landscapes present different development contexts. The life courses of island people, present or absent, are increasingly embedded in international ties, and island states have sought out new migration opportunities. About half a century of international migration from several parts of the Pacific, and especially from Polynesian states, has transformed the region. Island states, individuals, and various international agencies have attached new and increased significance to migration, remittance flows, return migration, and the role of the diaspora, in contexts where "conventional" development strategies have achieved limited success.

Mobility in History: Ancestral Journeys

The extent and time depth of oral tradition vary significantly across the Pacific Islands region. Oral traditions are most extensive in the case of large and culturally homogenous populations, hierarchical political systems, and societies where lineage and primogeniture were important. Genealogies and related traditions in Polynesia are especially well developed, reaching up to thirty-six generations in Tonga and even longer in Hawai'i and the Marquesas. Voyaging traditions can be recalled in New Zealand, where first colonization was relatively recent. In Melanesia, oral traditions generally span shorter periods, at least in terms of genealogy. Tradition foreshortens time, telescoping several generations into a single heroic figure or episode, while perceptions of historical truth are pragmatic, serving social and political ends.

Prior to European contact, travel was often difficult and hazardous, at least in those areas now known as Polynesia, where islands were small and far apart. The perils of open sea navigation and the dangers of warfare were both significant challenges, commemorated in narratives about the great founding journeys (Lacey 1985; Rapaport 1999), which provided a link to the ancestors, a legitimating charter, and validation of the rights to particular locations. Such founding journeys continued to around five hundred years ago with the settlement of the Chatham Islands, east of New Zealand, which completed the basic settlement of the Pacific Islands. A handful of small islands, now known as Henderson, Pitcairn, and Fanning, in eastern Polynesia, had been settled but already abandoned (Denoon 1997). In the western Pacific especially, the sea was no great barrier to human settlement, linking almost as much as dividing communities (Hau'ofa 1994; D'Arcy 2006), and beaches were places of exchange and trade.

In subsequent centuries voyages more commonly centered around trade and exchange. Such trading voyages were particularly characteristic of Melanesia, where resources varied more between islands and between coasts and inland areas. Beyond the Vitiaz Strait, between New Guinea and New Britain, pre-European exchanges involved obsidian, live pigs, dogs' teeth, bows and arrows, net bags, pottery, and taro in exchange for boars' tusks, live dogs, mats, disc beads, betel nut, red ochre, and sago. Other such networks included the Kula cycle between the islands of what is now Milne Bay, centered on the Trobriand Islands.

A long-distance exchange network (*sawei*) connected islanders on fifteen atolls in the Western Carolines, who voyaged more than a thousand kilometers to the high island of Yap with tribute of woven cloth, twine, and shell valuables to "partner/parents" and received countergifts of food and turmeric (Alkire 1978; Bellwood 1979). Only rarely did such trading journeys, here the most extensive trading networks in the pre-European era, involve anything other than temporary mobility, though marriage partners sometimes came from a distance.

Other journeys took people beyond their home areas but again only temporarily. Journeys of initiation occurred in parts of Melanesia. In the New Guinea highlands, young initiates journeyed to "secret" areas, experiencing seclusion, purification, fasting, trials, and transmission of ancient knowledge, often involving daring journeys to procure the necessary sacred plants and the appropriate chants (Lacey 1985). Men from Malakula, in central Vanuatu, would voyage once in a lifetime in pilgrimage to neighboring Aoba, conducting ceremonies and exchanges with local islanders (Bonnemaison 1994). Such distant journeys were relatively rare and lives were often severely circumscribed.

In Polynesia and Micronesia, journeys were sometimes longer. The *marae* (temple) of Taputapuatea on Raiatea, French Polynesia, attracted worshippers from a reputed radius of around 700 km. A highly respected group of entertainers, the *arioi*, traveled throughout the Society Islands providing songs, dances, athletics, and acting; recitations of poetry, history, and folklore; and even social critique of local *ari'i* (chiefs) (Luomala 1955).

There were also journeys of exile and refuge. In New Zealand, in at least some versions of traditional accounts, several ancestral voyaging canoes are said to have fled Hawaiki following warfare (originally ignited by either theft, insults, or land disputes). Disputes led to people joining adjacent tribal groups or moving away from home islands. Thus in the nineteenth century several Solomon Islands groups, such as the Rorovana, moved northward to resettle on Bougainville Island (Terrell and Irwin 1972). Such movements were often prompted by violence, food shortages, or other social problems, but they effectively ended with the start of the colonial era.

Traditional Mobility and Its Transformations

Throughout the Pacific, mobility patterns have altered significantly in postcontact times in response to pacification and the gradual emergence of commercial economies.

At contact, especially in Melanesia, mobility was usually highly localized. Among such subsistence cultures as the Tairora of highlands New Guinea, despite trade extending over hundreds of kilometers, mobility was limited to about ten kilometers, as men went out into the bush to hunt or trade with neighbors (Watson 1985). Similarly, in Tanna (Vanuatu) local population groups were linked to particular sacred places and to one or more *nakamal* (kavadrinking places). Beyond this, movements were usually short, infrequent, dangerous, and only for men. Access to the sea for inland groups was possible only after delicate negotiations and payment in pigs and women (Bonnemaison 1994). Among the Siwai of Bougainville, prior to European contact the population lived in small hamlets on the land of matrilineage elders called *mumis* (big men). Population movement occurred either for marriage or following the changing status of *mumis*; less frequently, entire hamlets were relocated, but few population movements, including marriages, were over much more than a kilometer or so (Connell 1985). Elsewhere, where cultures were more homogeneous over greater distances, settlement having been more recent, mobility was more widespread and enabled various long-distance ties such as those that bound the outer coral islands to Yap.

Termination of warfare, weakening of traditional power structures, establishment of missions, "modern" trade for goods such as sandalwood, and the establishment of plantations led to greater mobility, from the late nineteenth century, but not until the postwar years in such places of late contact as highlands New Guinea. At the same time pacification largely ended traditional tribute movements, such as *sawei*, while new commercial structures broke down

exchange relationships such as the Kula ring. Later movement was influenced by population growth, the reduction of available land in some cases, urbanization (see chapter 26), mining, and new needs for cash incomes.

Between the end of the nineteenth century and the end of World War II, circular migration to plantations became the dominant form of mobility throughout much of the western Pacific. In the nineteenth century a significant part of that migration was between countries, as islanders were "blackbirded" to the sugar plantations of Queensland and even to the mines of South America (Maude 1981; see below). While most returned from Australia to Melanesia, few of those who went to South America ever returned. That early phase of labor migration was effectively over by the start of the twentieth century. Migrations within the Pacific subsequently absorbed available local labor, but in Fiji Indians were introduced to work on the sugar plantations, and between 1879 and 1916 waves of new Indian settlers utterly transformed the population composition of Fiji.

In New Guinea, inducement for plantation labor was provided by an imposed head tax, from which contract laborers were exempt. Contracts were for three years, but work was hard and few signed on for a second contract. Return migration was assured in a classical form of "circular migration." Following World War II, plantation labor shortages led to reduction in hourly requirements and a tripling of the minimal wages. Returning plantation workers, however, increasingly began to undertake cash cropping on their own, engaging in short-term plantation work mainly in periods when crop sales were inadequate. After the labor frontier had exhausted the newly contacted parts of highlands New Guinea, the plantation era gradually drew to a close, as opportunities in home villages, but particularly in newly growing towns, became more attractive.

Settlement and Displacement

Among the most important long-term consequences of colonialism was the development of administrative centers and the establishment of a commercial economy, based on trade and plantations, that significantly transformed the population of several island groups. Consequent labor migration brought significant Asian populations into the Pacific Islands, most notably Chinese, Japanese, Koreans, and Filipinos in Hawai'i (359,000 by 1931); Indians in Fiji (62,000 by 1920); and smaller numbers of Asians in New Caledonia (from diverse sources, including Chinese, Vietnamese, and Javanese) and French Polynesia (Chinese). In the Northern Marianas, Asian migration is a more recent phenomenon, primarily from China and Southeast Asia. While numbers were smaller in Guam and the Northern Marianas and were mainly from the Philippines, they greatly transformed the indigenous population composition.

Extensive European settlement in the Pacific Islands and the associated influx of Asian migrant labor was generally most prominent in the larger islands, where commercial opportunities were greater. Small pockets of European settlement occurred throughout the Pacific, but the magnitude and impact of settlement were greatest in New Zealand, Hawai'i, and New Caledonia.

The influx of European settlers in New Zealand was intense (45,730 arrived in 1863 alone), the result of population increase in Britain and the frustration and poverty that accompanied the industrial revolution (Sinclair 1980). In other island groups the demographic influx was smaller, but the presence of even a few determined foreigners could have significant consequences. Planters such as Claus Spreckels, who used their capital to "get a toehold, then a foothold, then a near stranglehold" in the islands (Daws 1983), could cause considerable upheaval. Even a trickle of traders, missionaries, and planters, compounded with an influx of migrant labor, might have a significant impact. Emigrants came from all classes, but were most often the small cultivating classes, tenants, and laborers (Wilson, Moore, and Munro 1990).

Colonial settlement, assisted in some places by elements of "guns, germs, and steel" (Diamond 1997), led almost inevitably to displacement of indigenous populations. One of the largest such displacements occurred in New Caledonia. Between 1860 and 1894, more than forty thousand French prisoners were sent to the island, many of whom settled subsequently. In 1864, nickel ore was discovered; this along with settler demands for agricultural land and cattle ranching led to a policy of *cantonnement* (reserves) and considerable frontier violence. Indigenous Melanesians were relocated and confined to reservations comprising around 10 percent of the land on the main Grand Terre, giving rise to guerrilla wars in 1878 and 1917 (Connell 1987b). The subsequent nickel boom of the 1960s brought renewed migration to New Caledonia in a calculated phase of "demographic colonization" that left Melanesians a minority in their own island.

Elsewhere, islanders were displaced through individual purchases and government claims to "unused land." In Hawai'i during the 1840s, American advisors persuaded King Kamehameha III to effect the "Great Mahele," legislation transforming the land to individualized (and alienable) property ownership, of which commoners received less than 1 percent. Sugar planters and ranchers found it easy enough to purchase immense tracts from the king and land-rich chiefs. In New Zealand, overwhelming settler numbers and warfare with resentful Maori ended with the confiscation of 7.5 million hectares of land. Maori survivors "were pushed back into unwanted corners" (Oliver 1989). The commanding economic and political heights were taken by European migrants.

On several atolls and small islands, catastrophic displacement ensued during the Peruvian slave raids of 1862–1863, striking with the force of a great "tsunami" (Maude 1981). In many islands, only a fragment of the original community remained. An estimated 3,634 islanders were taken to Peru, the majority by deceit or kidnapping by sheer force, where they were sold and treated as slaves for plantation labor and domestic service at wealthy haciendas. Following political pressure, an attempt was made to repatriate 1,009 recruits, but because of neglect, disease, or being thrown overboard, only 157 reached the islands alive.

Ethnic diversity has created a volatile situation in island societies—particularly so in Fiji, site of four political coups. The indigenous Fijian population has only recently grown to more than half the population, and most coups have been directed at least in part against the assumed ascendancy of Indo-Fijians, many of whom have emigrated since 1987. In New Caledonia, native Kanaks (Melanesians) lost most of their land during the nineteenth century to French colonists and are now outnumbered by Europeans and other groups, including Vietnamese, Polynesians from Tahiti,

the Australs, and those from Wallis and Futuna. In Guam, the local Chamorro population is outnumbered by Anglo-Americans, especially military personnel, and Filipinos. In Hawai'i and New Zealand, native groups are minorities, but there are increasing demands for indigenous rights, including land return, cash payments, and some form of self-government.

Nuclear testing by the United States led to evacuation of four atolls in the Northern Marshalls. Inhabitants of Bikini were evacuated in 1946 to Rongerik, but due to inadequate resources there, they were later resettled on tiny Kili. Some islanders returned to Bikini in 1972 following an attempted cleanup but were re-evacuated six years later following evidence of nuclear toxicity, resulting in lawsuits and multimillion-dollar settlements by the United States. Enewetak Islanders were evacuated in 1947 to Ujelang; many returned in 1980 following a cleanup there, but parts of Enewetak remain unsafe. Rongelap and Utirik Islanders were evacuated in 1954 to Kwajalein; they were permitted to return subsequently, but many left again due to radiation exposure (Kiste 1974). Some now see the resettlement of Carteret Islanders to Bougainville and the pleas of other atoll dwellers to be relocated in the face of environmental changes that have been attributed to global warming, as in Tuvalu (Connell 2003), as further contemporary examples of the impact of alien forces on Pacific island populations.

Contemporary migration has continued to bring new migrants to the Pacific Islands, whether as miners, bureaucrats, or commercial venturers. While there have long been Chinatowns in most Pacific towns, a new wave of Chinese migrants, most from southern China, have become established in several countries, including Tonga, Fiji, and Solomon Islands. Their presence, especially their dominance of some parts of the commercial sector, has been resented, and the Honiara Chinatown was burned down in 2006. Smaller numbers of Indians, Filipinos, and others represent distinct population flows, and a regular flow of Europeans and others have come as miners, aid donors, missionaries, university lecturers, and so on. The island Pacific is now as cosmopolitan as it has ever been.

Migration and Modernity

Plantation migration brought no new skills to islanders who were already agriculturalists, and though other sources of cash employment existed in the early colonial era, they employed few people or lasted only briefly. Mines in Nauru and Banaba, which brought substantial migration from Tuvalu and Kiribati (and also China), and in New Caledonia, which brought workers from France and France's other Pacific territories, were rare exceptions. In Fiji and Papua New Guinea, mining had a longer but sporadic history (see chapter 31) until the 1970s brought in a new era of more modern, large-scale mining that offered substantial, highly attractive employment opportunities. The Panguna mine in Bougainville employed more than four thousand people, from the island itself and from distant parts of Papua New Guinea. Within a few years of its opening, mine workers were staying there for longer and longer periods, suggesting the slow emergence of an "urban-industrial proletariat," a decline in circular mobility, and long-term migration (Connell 1985). Simultaneously in Papua New Guinea and elsewhere, as the colonial era drew to a close in many places, more educated islanders were drawn into urban employment mainly in bureaucratic positions, and a phase of more rapid urbanization began, resulting in parallel forms of more permanent migration (chapter 26). In Polynesia especially, the first wave of contemporary international migration, mainly to New Zealand, began at the same time. In every place, migration was over longer distances, whether from mountain to coast or from a Polynesian island to a New Zealand or Hawaiian city.

In the blackbirding and plantation era of the nineteenth and early twentieth centuries almost all migration was return migration, and migrants were rarely away from their villages for more than two or three years, a classical pattern of return migration. As education increased and wages and salaries grew, urban and overseas opportunities became more attractive and migration gradually became more permanent. Intermarriage in towns between migrants from different areas, the birth and education of children in towns, and reduced use of indigenous languages there, all further encouraged a greater degree of urban permanence. Return migration declined in significance.

Return migration did occur where particularly attractive development opportunities existed in home areas, as in the Tuamotus when black pearl shell farming began, and in various parts of the Pacific where mining ventures have developed. By the 1980s, pearl farming had begun on some sixteen atolls in the Tuamotus, leading to waves of migration from Tahiti and population increases of up to 20 percent per year. Most of the migration was of "returning" migrants, including many who had been absent for two or three generations. While the migrants were generally welcomed, small quarrels inevitably ensued over access to land, associated lagoon space, and government-allocated pearl farming concessions, and opposition was particularly directed toward all pearl farmers lacking roots on the atoll or with questionable claims to local ancestry (Rapaport 1996, 1999). Similar disputes between established populations and newer arrivals have occurred at mine sites in the highlands of New Guinea over just who were local landowners and thus entitled to employment and compensation payments.

As return migration gave way to a more permanent migration, the slow but usually incomplete depopulation of small islands and remote mountainous areas became common and populations became more concentrated. Employment opportunities and services are concentrated in the urban centers; in small island states where manpower and capital are often limited, centralization is inevitable. The more educated have tended to migrate first, and migrants have left many rural areas to take advantage of superior urban educational and employment opportunities. Urbanization characterizes contemporary migration in the Pacific.

The existence of kin in urban areas is a major influence and support. Early migrants are beachheads for those who follow. Not only do they provide demonstrations, or create images, of an impressive lifestyle, they may also provide remittances (the visible monetary symbols of success), fares, and accommodation for new migrants to the city. Indeed, migration is often best seen "as an almost inevitable decision that they [villagers] will have to make sooner or later and once this view is accepted a sort of migration momentum develops" (Walsh 1982: 7). The spreading taste for commodities has influenced work habits, and for many in the Pacific, the largest cities and the metropolitan countries exercise a powerful allure, offer a sense of future, and simply validate

migration. The combination of growing urban permanency, high unemployment, and increased expectations has put considerable pressure on urban services (chapter 26).

As in other parts of the world, migration has led to significant changes in Pacific societies (Connell 1987a, 1990, 2008a), though it is rarely possible to separate those consequences that derive from migration and those that derive from the spread of capitalism and modernization (partly because migration itself derives to a large extent from economic disparities). Moreover, the demographic, economic, and social changes associated with migration differ from rural to urban areas, and from place to place, particularly in Melanesia, where substantial cultural divides exist even between adjacent areas. Impact differs in sending and receiving communities and over space and time.

As recently as the 1970s it was possible to examine the impact of the earliest phases of migration in remote Papua New Guinea highland communities, where migration to coastal plantations was the first significant source of both cash and social change. Income brought back by Ilakia Awa men, in the Eastern Highlands of Papua New Guinea, led to significant changes in local patterns of consumption. Returning migrants were perceived to be in a state of indebtedness, which required distribution of some portion of the savings. Parents and older siblings staked their claims on the basis of prior care for the migrant during the years of childhood, while the wider community reminded migrants of their obligations before they left home by mourning their departure and through gifts of food and magical protection items. New goods brought back with them, or purchased with the income they had earned, brought Western styles of dress, imported foods such as rice, and radios (Boyd 1990). In what was then an extremely remote location and where earnings were low, the new income could only boost consumption rather than transform the local economy.

Migration has had important effects on age structure and dependency ratios. Emigration is concentrated among young adults of both sexes and offsets natural increases in the more fertile age groups 20–24 and 25–29, causing "hourglass" age pyramids in island groups with high out-migration. Thus high fertility, low mortality, and out-migration of young adults combine to produce high dependency ratios (see Table 22.2). Equally, these migrants are often the more educated and skilled within island populations. In many places the loss of village leaders through migration has weakened village social organization and made collective activities such as environmental management more difficult to achieve. These trends can place a heavy burden on societies, such as that of Niue (Connell 2008) or of tiny islands such as Merir, in Palau (Osborne 1966), a rare example of an island that has been depopulated in the twentieth century.

Quantitative Comparisons

Pacific-wide demographic comparisons are subject to many problems, including varying census dates, assumptions, reliability, and definitions. With this important caution in mind, selected demographic trends relevant to migration will be presented (Table 23.1). Significant population declines (negative values for total annual growth rates) occurred in the Northern Marianas (-2.3 percent) and Tokelau (-0.9 percent). The magnitude of annual net migration

Table 23.1

Population Growth and Migration Rates, Pacific Islands

	Population (thousands)	Population density (per km²)	Rate of natural increase (percent)	Annual growth rate (percent)	Net migration rate (percent)	Urban population (thousands)	Urban growth rate (percent)	Net urban growth (percent)
Melanesia								
Fiji	852	47	1.2	0.5	-0.7	52	1.5	1
New Caledonia	252	13	1.0	1.3	0.3	67	2.6	1.3
PNG	7,014	15	2.2	2.2	0.0	13	2.3	0.1
Solomon Is.	552	19	2.6	2.6	0.0	19	4.3	1.7
Vanuatu	246	20	2.4	2.4	0.0	26	4.3	1.9
Micronesia								
FSM	102	146	1.9	0.4	-1.5	23	0.6	0.2
Guam	192	355	1.2	2.7	1.5	93	1.3	-1.4
Kiribati	103	127	2.0	1.8	-0.2	44	1.7	-0.1
Marshall Is.	55	304	2.5	0.7	-1.8	72	2.7	2
Nauru	10	476	2.1	2.1	0.0	100	0.3	-1.8
Northern Marianas	1.5	4	0.5	-2.3	-2.8	38	-1.4	0.9
Palau	21	47	0.6	0.6	0.0	84	1.8	1.2
Polynesia								
Am. Samoa	67	335	1.9	1.2	-0.7	93	2.1	0.9
Cook Is.	15.5	65	1.0	0.3	-0.7	76	2.0	1.7
Fr. Polynesia	274	78	1.1	1.1	0.0	57	1.7	0.6
Niue	4,405	16	0.8	0.9	0.1	86	1.0	0.1
Samoa	184	63	1.9	0.4	-1.5	22	1.3	0.9
Tokelau	1.1	100	2.4	-0.9	-3.3	na	na	na
Tonga	105	162	2.0	0.5	-1.5	34*	0.7	0.2
Tuvalu	11	374	1.4	0.5	-0.9	51	1.4	0.9
Wallis & Futuna	14.2	100	1.4	0.8	-0.6	na	na	na
New Zealand	64	140	1.5	-0.1	-1.6	91	2.1	2.2
Hawai'i	1,375	83	0.7	1.2	0.5	70	na	na

Source: Abstracted from Table 22.1, with the addition of a calculated column for net urban growth.

* Greater Nuku'alofa is considered urban; Nuku'alofa represents 23.2% of total population in 2006 with growth rate of 0.5% over 1996–2006 ; growth rate of suburban area is 1.7%.

is computed from the difference between the rates of population growth and natural increase. The highest out-migration rates (indicated by negative net migration rates) occur in the Northern Marianas and Tokelau (reflecting migration to the United States and New Zealand). The highest net in-migration flows occurred in Guam (reflecting employment opportunities related to the U.S. military base).

Table 23.2, based on international census data, shows the distribution of Pacific Island migrants in the United States, New Zealand, Australia, Canada, and other locations. The data were compiled by the Development Research Center at the University of Sussex (Development Research Center 2007). While the figures for some countries are based on assumptions and interpolation, and dated, they are the only region-wide data available. Niue and

Table 23.2

Pacific Island First-Generation Migrant Diasporas

	Census yr.	Diaspora (thousands)	Home resident (thousands)	Total (thousands)	Diaspora %	Resident in (thousands)					
						USA	NZ	AUS	CAN	Other P.I.	Other
Am. Samoa	2000	40.7	57.0	97.7	42	33.3	0.4	0.2	0.0	2.4	4.5
Cook Islands	2001	22.7	19.0	41.7	54	0.1	15.2	4.7	0.0	0.2	2.3
Fiji	1986	143.1	810.7	953.8	15	31.5	25.7	44.3	22.8	3.8	15.0
Fr. Polynesia	2002	3.5	236.1	239.6	1	0.0	0.5	0.3		2.3	0.4
Guam	2000	89.6	155.4	245.0	37	71.7	0.0	0.1	0.1	2.6	15.0
Kiribati	2000	3.7	90.7	94.4	4	1.0	0.5	0.4	0.0	1.2	0.5
Marshall Is.	1999	11.5	52.8	64.3	18	7.3	0.0	0.0	0.0	0.6	3.5
FSM	2000	24.6	107.1	131.7	19	7.5	0.0	0.0	0.0	10.0	7.1
Nauru	2000	1.0	12.0	13.0	8	0.1	0.2	0.5	0.0	0.1	0.2
New Caledonia	1996	1.8	213.2	215.0	1	0.0	0.2	1.1	0.0	0.4	0.2
Niue	2001	6.6	2.0	8.6	77	0.1	5.3	0.5	0.0	0.1	0.7
Norfolk Island	2001	0.4	1.9	2.3	16	0.0	0.1	0.2	0.0	0.0	0.0
Northern Marianas	2000	10.7	76.0	86.7	12	4.2	0.0	0.0	0.0	2.5	4.0
Palau	2000	12.8	19.7	32.5	39	2.3	0.0	0.0	0.0	2.7	7.8
PNG	1971	51.0	5,298.9	5,349.9	1	1.8	1.2	23.6	0.4	16.4	7.6
Samoa	2001	105.8	177.5	283.2	37	17.5	47.1	13.3	0.1	19.3	8.5
Solomon Is.	1999	4.2	418.7	423.0	1	0.2	0.5	1.3	0.0	1.4	0.8
Tokelau	1996	2.4	1.4	3.9	63	0.1	1.7	0.3	0.0	0.2	0.2
Tonga	1996	50.7	100.2	150.9	34	18.0	18.1	7.7	0.1	2.0	4.8
Tuvalu	2002	1.8	10.0	11.8	15	0.0	1.0	0.1	0.0	0.2	0.4
Vanuatu	1999	4.2	191.5	195.6	2	0.1	0.3	0.9	0.0	1.6	1.3
Wallis & Futuna	1999	7.0	15.0	22.0	32	0.0	0.0	0.0	0.0	6.2	0.7
New Zealand	2001	528.6	3,857.8	4,386.4	12	26.4		355.8	9.9	7.0	129.5

Source: Global Migrant Origin Database, Version 4, http://www.migrationdrc.org/research/typesofmigration/global_migrant_origin_database.html.

Note: The data may undercount Europeans born in French Polynesia and New Caledonia.

Tokelau had the largest proportionate diaspora population (77 percent and 63 percent of the "total populations," respectively), followed by the Cook Islands, American Samoa, Palau, Samoa, Guam, Tonga, and Wallis and Futuna. Low diasporic percentages are evident in French Polynesia, New Caledonia, Papua New Guinea, Solomon Islands, Vanuatu, and Kiribati.

The United States has by far the largest number of Pacific Island migrants, with the leading countries of origin including Guam, American Samoa, Fiji, New Zealand, Samoa, and Tonga. New Zealand follows, with primary migrants coming from Samoa, Fiji, the Cook Islands, and Tonga. Australia is third, with a very large migration from New Zealand, followed by migrants from Fiji, Papua New Guinea, and Samoa. Canada has large numbers of Fijian migrants, with very few from other Pacific islands.

Comparative data on internal migration are scarce. Walsh (1982) provides internal migration rates (defined as the percent of urban residents not born in the urban area—note that this is a proportion rather than an annual rate) for nine Pacific Island groups, based on censuses from 1976 to 1979. Highest values were found in Solomon Islands (97.3 percent), followed by Kiribati (77.7 percent), Tuvalu (67.2 percent), Fiji (50.3 percent), Samoa (43.3 percent), the Cook Islands (29.9 percent), and Tonga (20.6 percent).

The exceptionally high rate for the Solomons occurred because Honiara was a new town, having begun from a U.S. military base during World War II.

Net urban growth (in Table 22.1) is derived from the difference between urban and total population growth rates and provides an indicator of internal migration. This is only an approximation, as differential urban/rural rates of population increase and external migration can also affect relative growth rates (see Walsh 1987). The data suggest net rural-to-urban migration on most Pacific Islands, with highest rates in Solomon Islands, Vanuatu, the Cook Islands, and New Zealand. Negative rates occur in Guam and Nauru.

The New International Migration

Until the second half of the twentieth century, international migration from the Pacific Islands was rare, though some of the smaller Polynesian islands such as Niue were characterized by young men finding work on ships and regularly traveling to distant ports. Some never returned but settled in countries such as New Zealand. Nonetheless it was not until the 1960s that long-distance migration came to characterize the contemporary Pacific.

Since then, alongside urbanization, the main direction of migration has been out-migration to the metropolitan states of the Pacific Rim in response to relatively better economic prospects. Periodic deterioration of the economic situation of these host countries, passage of restrictive legislation on migration, and expulsions of overstayers in the 1970s (at least from New Zealand) only marginally reduced emigration from islands. The economic gap remains large, and illegal migration strategies were possible: entry with a short-term visa, settlement and job finding through relatives in the country, and subsequent application for residency or citizenship status.

Migration broadly followed colonial links, linking New Zealand to its former colony (Samoa) and its remaining dependent territories, and the United States with American Samoa and the Micronesian islands that were formerly part of the Trust Territory of the Pacific Islands (Palau, the Federated States of Micronesia, and the Marshall Islands). A third network is that between New Caledonia and the other French territories (Wallis and Futuna and French Polynesia). Relatively impoverished Kiribati and Tuvalu, previously under British administration, have experienced limited out-migration, with a distant colonial power, but have been dependent on temporary labor migration to Nauru (until quite recently) and employment on shipping lines.

International migration is primarily a Polynesian and more recently a Micronesian phenomenon. In parts of Polynesia, more people are resident overseas than in the home islands. This applies almost as much to island states with large populations (Tonga and Samoa) as to those with small populations (Niue, Tokelau, Wallis and Futuna, and the Cook Islands). In 1996 some 33 percent of Tongans and almost 40 percent of Samoans lived overseas. Migration from these countries in the 1980s was so great that absolute population declined, outweighing the effects of natural increase. While migration has continued, only the smallest states, such as Niue and the Cook Islands, now have declining populations (Connell 2005, 2006). For the smaller states, including the Cook Islands, American Samoa, Wallis and Futuna, Niue, Tokelau and Pitcairn,

dramatic migration has meant that a substantial majority of the ethnic population lives overseas. Niue, Tokelau, and the Cook Islands have experienced declining populations over the past quarter of a century, while it has long been forecast—incorrectly—that the smallest state, Pitcairn, may simply disappear as its population falls below what is sustainable (Connell 1988). Niue too is presently welcoming immigration from Tuvalu as its population has sharply declined in the recent context of cyclone Heta and a long term "culture of migration" (Connell 2008). Larger states, such as Samoa and Tonga, continue to experience very limited population growth as emigration has become something of a "safety valve" for high-population growth rates, but more obviously for at best slowly growing economies.

Most international migration, such as that from Tonga and Samoa and the smaller Polynesian states, is to New Zealand, the United States, and Australia. Fiji has experienced significant out-migration since the two coups in 1987 and a third in 2000, and in this century has provided the largest flows in the region, both to the "traditional" destinations of North America (including Canada), Australia, and New Zealand, but more recently to the Middle East. The Indo-Fijian population has declined significantly since the second half of the 1980s. After the former Trust Territory states signed compacts of free association with the United States, migration to the United States grew dramatically, especially from the Marshall Islands. Guam and the Northern Marianas (Saipan) have also received large numbers of Micronesians as well as large numbers of Asian migrants, but most Micronesians now move to Hawai'i and the mainland United States (Hess, Nero, and Burton 2001). Over time the United States has tended to become the preferred migration destination.

The Pacific Diaspora

Generally increasing migration numbers, greater permanence of migrants overseas, the emergence of second-generation Pacific Islanders overseas (Morton 2003), and declining populations in some smaller island states and islands have emphasized the shifting balance of island populations toward metropolitan states and the emergence of what has been described a Pacific diaspora (Connell 1991). Within the islands a parallel urbanization has continued (chapter 26). While the actual extent of overseas migration is impossible to measure and data on Pacific Islanders overseas can take little account of second- and third-generation islanders, for several states the demographic balance has firmly shifted away from the islands. Large urban centers in New Zealand, Australia, Hawai'i, and California have significant Pacific Island populations alongside various institutions, such as churches and sports clubs, associated with them. Auckland has a larger Polynesian population than any other urban center.

Guamanians and Samoans are some of the most numerous Pacific Rim immigrants, followed by Fijians (mainly Indo-Fijians), Tongans, Cook Islanders, and American Samoans. Perhaps more than any other group, Samoans have something of a global distribution. However, compared with populations in their home states, a substantial proportion of Micronesians, but above all Polynesians from smaller states, are also overseas. Contemporary trends emphasize that this moving is continuing. Four times as many

Niue-born live in New Zealand than in Niue, and those of Niuean descent are even more numerous there. Much the same is true of Tokelau. By contrast, and very differently from the blackbirding era of a century ago, few Melanesians are now overseas, and those who appear to have moved away are more likely to be Europeans born in the islands. International migration, and its absence, is thus largely a consequence of colonial histories and continuing political and economic relationships.

Growing populations overseas have emphasized "the end of insularity" (Nero 1997) and "the expanding worlds of Oceania" (Ward 1996), as new webs of relationships span island and metropolitan contexts and even beyond. Island incomes are increasingly derived from overseas, as remittances and aid, and growing pressures have been placed on metropolitan states to remove obstacles to further migration. Meanwhile, as is evident for Niue and Tonga (Morton 2003), "islanders" grow up in new contexts—islanders without islands—with more detached perceptions of what being an islander entails and a reduced likelihood of ever living or even visiting there. The lives of such new transnational populations have only a tangential relationship even to that of the grandparents, unfettered by complex ties to island places, but with new uncertainties about identity and belonging in places where they may be seen as minorities who belong elsewhere.

International migration flows have increasingly been of skilled workers. In recent years migration opportunities in metropolitan states have tended to decline and are increasingly targeted toward skilled migrants rather than family reunions. Structural changes within metropolitan states have meant that certain sectors, notably health, are short of skilled workers (Connell 2004), while there has also been a significant flow of teachers (Voigt-Graf 2003), engineers, IT workers, airline pilots, and others. Pacific Island nurses, usually entering the bottom levels of the "global health care chain," have migrated much greater distances, to the United Arab Emirates and beyond, as demand intensifies, and also to new destinations within the region, including the Marshall Islands and Palau (e.g., Rokoduru 2008; Connell 2004, 2009). Similarly, the globalization of sport has meant rugby players going beyond the "traditional" destinations of New Zealand and Australia to Japan and the United Kingdom. Newer patterns of emigration became particularly important in the mid-2000s, with migration to the Middle East, emphasizing the manner in which a new "outward urge" had resulted in highly paid overseas employment opportunities being firmly grasped, even in a threatening security and social context. By 2005, about 150 Fijian soldiers were deployed in Iraq, and others were in Iraq as members of the British army. Still more were peacekeepers in Solomon Islands (as they had earlier been in Bougainville). Many former Fijian soldiers were employed as security guards for private companies in the major Iraqi cities, and other Fijians were employed in support roles in Kuwait, covering engineering, mechanical, and IT employment. Smaller numbers of Tongans were in the Middle East, alongside soldiers from American territories (including the Compact states). Others were deployed as peacekeepers in Africa and elsewhere. Before the early 1980s, male migration had preceded female or family migration throughout the South Pacific. Minimal gender bias now exists in the numbers of Pacific Islanders migrating to the Pacific Rim, but preferences are shifting toward women (Voigt-Graf and Connell 2005).

Interest in migration has long been such that in Samoa, when prospects for emigration were particularly poor at the start of the 1980s, the "broken dreams" of potential migrants contributed to a significant rise in youth suicide (Macpherson and Macpherson 1987). The economic future of several states partly hinges on the continued flow of remittances, and hence on some continuity of migration. While this has become part of a "culture of migration" where emigration is normal, expected, and anticipated and an important element in household and national social and economic systems, its future depends on contexts and decisions largely made outside the Pacific Islands.

Legislative changes are critical for migration. In New Zealand, the relaxation of restrictive migration policies introduced in the 1970s (culminating in December 1986 with a visa waiver for stays of less than three months for Tongans, Samoans, Fijians, I-Kiribati, and Tuvaluans) led to a significant migration influx and was quickly changed. The reintroduction of restrictive migration policies in New Zealand and Australia resulted in negative net migration to New Zealand by Tongans and Samoans in 1990–1994 (Bedford 1992). Subsequently, more Samoans migrated to American Samoa in the hope of gaining entry to the United States.

Tightening of requirements in Australia and economic developments in New Zealand led to step-migration of Samoans to Australia. In 1986–1990, 74 percent of Samoan arrivals in Australia occurred through the Trans-Tasman Agreement between New Zealand and Australia. In contrast, most Fijian and Tongan immigrants in Australia came directly from their home islands. In this century, restrictions on migration to Australia, New Zealand, and the United States have increased as each of these countries have primarily sought skilled migrants.

As a response to domestic economic stagnation, island governments have put increasing pressure on the metropolitan countries to enable guest worker migration. In 2007 New Zealand implemented a new policy of allowing a quota of 5,000 guest workers from several island states to work in the agricultural industry, which is notoriously short of labor and where such a scheme had previously been effective (Levick and Bedford 1988). Continued pressure from island states resulted in Australia's introducing a scheme at the end of 2008 for 2,500 workers. Early guest workers have been able to earn significant sums of money from some seven months of work in New Zealand, which has been used for new forms of consumption, housing, and education (Hammond and Connell 2009). The success of these schemes has resulted in numbers expanding in New Zealand, a parallel scheme being developed in Australia, and the scheme being extended to other countries including Solomon Islands and Papua New Guinea.

A Rationale?

The primary motive for migration in the Pacific, as elsewhere, is economic improvement for migrants and their families, although political and environmental changes and cultural considerations also affect flows. This is as true of internal migration as of international migration. In most Pacific countries, earning power is increasingly concentrated among urban bureaucracies, while the absence of developed state mechanisms for effecting transfers of income (such as progressive taxation, unemployment benefits, and pension schemes) minimizes redistribution toward rural areas other than through personal remittances. Simply stated, in Port Vila, one of the most important reasons was "*long winem smal vatu from no gat rod long winim vatu long aelan*" ("to earn a little money since there's no way to earn money on the home island") (Mitchell 2000: 172). For many that is reason enough. Growing inequalities and rising expectations are the catalysts of increased migration.

Internationally, young adults find better-paying jobs overseas, and their families benefit from their remittances. To some extent migrants from a single extended family may be distributed in different countries, in what has been described as a "transnational corporation of kin" (Marcus 1981), which strategically allocates family labor to local and overseas destinations (and also different employment sectors) to maximize income opportunities, minimize risk, and benefit from resultant remittance flows. Much the same was true in the highlands of New Guinea decades earlier (Boyd 1990). This "insures" the family against economic crises and unemployment and enables the ease of possible return migration. Pressure on governments to address rapid population growth and job creation for young adults is reduced by migration and the associated remittances. The removal of many young, educated people from the population slows the pace of social change, partly because of limited return migration.

Migration decisions are usually shaped within a family context, as migrants leave to meet certain family expectations, the key one of which is usually financial support for kin. Migration has rarely been an individual decision to meet individual goals, nor has it been dictated by national interests (except perhaps in the case of Kiribati and Tuvalu). Migration is directed at improving both the living standards of those who remain at home and the lifestyle and income of the migrants; consequently "families deliberate carefully about which members would be most likely to do well overseas and be reliable in sending remittances" (Gailey 1992: 465). To an even greater extent than for internal migration (where health, education, and social reasons explain some part of migration), international migration is more evidently an economic phenomenon, though other factors—such as access to high-quality education and training—are necessarily involved.

Several analytical models have been proposed to explain migration, some based on structural economic and demographic dynamics and others emphasizing the motives of individual migrants. Some of these models originated as ways to explain circular migration, but they are also relevant to the study of migration in general, given that many migrants begin with short-term circulatory moves. The emphases of the various models are different, but they are not necessarily in conflict; each attempts to explain a different facet of migration behavior.

One model suggests a balancing between the centripetal power of kinship ties, social relationships, and village obligations and the centrifugal attractions of wage and salary employment and commercial, social, and administrative services (Chapman 1976). Movement is thus a way of rationalizing a territorial separation between social ties, goods, and services, all of which may be dispersed between several locales. The composition and relative power of these opposing forces change over an individual's lifetime as circular migration gives way to permanent settlement, or return to home, as urban centers grow and overseas populations expand.

Linked to this is the second model, centered around the idea of the "transnational corporation of kin," where migration is viewed as a collective decision by migrant family units (rather than an individual decision by migrants) and as a "rational allocation of labor units" with potential long-term benefit to migrants and the sending community (Bertram and Watters 1985). Movement of individuals occurs without severing significant links with the kin group of origin. Home kin provide long-term security and resources to help send and support migrants in the initial stages, while migrants reciprocate with remittances and help with visiting relatives and potential new migrants. In an age of electronic communication, contact between migrants and those who remain has become easier, with "cyber-Polys" connected in space (Morton 1999) and remittances transmitted electronically.

Dependency theory provides a third model for explaining migration, based on the structural factors at work. According to this model, linked to early studies by authors such as Shankman (1976) and Connell (1987a), Pacific Island migrants are characterized as "discontented, over-socialized victims of the global capitalist system wrenched from their islands and families by the destructive forces of monetization, individualism, and consumerism" (Hayes 1991). Migration is consequently seen as a further destructive force that undermines the culture, social system, self-reliance, and demographic balance of the home society. An extension of this model situates migration in demographic transition theory and has been termed the "multi-phasic demographic response theory" in the context of a "modified Malthusian framework" (Hayes 1992). Rising populations, especially in Melanesia, increase pressure on resources; rural populations respond either through absorption (agricultural intensification, though this is rarely available), reductions in fertility (through culturally available means), urbanization, and migration.

In practice, variants of these models occur in most places at the same time. There are both varied and fluctuating pressures to leave as economic, environmental, and other circumstances change and incentives arise to go to particular places, usually those where earlier migrants have already established residences. But this has become more complicated. Since independence, both the small island states of Tuvalu and Kiribati have trained men, and increasingly also women, for employment on overseas shipping lines, and in the present century there has been renewed recruitment of skilled workers, such as Fijian nurses to work in the United Arab Emirates and Fijian men as security guards in Iraq.

Remittances

Remittances play an increasingly important role, especially in the smaller island states. In many countries remittances form a significant part of disposable income, hence some twenty years ago the smaller island states (specifically initially Kiribati, Tokelau, the Cook Islands, and Tuvalu) were conceptualized as MIRAB states, where MIgration, Remittances, Aid, and the resultant largely urban Bureaucracy are central to the socioeconomic system (Bertram and Watters 1985). The notion of MIRAB is also applicable in larger states such as Samoa and Tonga, where remittances constitute some of the highest proportions of GNP of any country in the world; in both countries remittances are well over 50 percent of GNP per capita and in aggregate more than three times the total value of exports (Connell and Brown 2005). While the MIRAB acronym is disliked in the Pacific for cultural reasons and because of its implication of a "handout mentality," it nonetheless suggests the centrality of migration and remittances in the island states and has been largely unchallenged for two decades (Bertram 1999).

Remittances are particularly important in the smaller states of Polynesia and Micronesia and in the more remote islands of every state. On the coral atoll of Nanumea in Tuvalu, remittances grew from being about half of the island income in the 1970s and 1980s to some 75 percent in the 1990s, in large part because of the collapse of the world copra market (Chambers and Chambers 2001: 156). In Kiribati the 2000 census recorded that overseas remittances, primarily from seamen, were the primary source of income for as many as 30 percent of households in the urban center of South Tarawa, and in 2002 some 35 percent of all households in Tuvalu received remittances. In both countries these were usually the main source of income in the outer islands (Borovnik 2006). Similar situations occur in other small islands and island states, and the northern Micronesian states are now following this pattern (Connell and Brown 2005: 6).

Conventional wisdom suggests that remittances are overwhelmingly used for consumption, and inadequate amounts are directed toward investment. After debt repayment, new forms of consumption, housing and community goals (such as water tanks and churches), airfares, and education (an investment in social capital), remittances are used for various forms of investment, sometimes in the agricultural sector but more frequently in the service sector, and especially into stores and transport businesses. In Samoa and elsewhere, remittance money has constituted the start-up money for many shopkeepers and other small entrepreneurs. Half of all market vendors in Apia (Samoa), all of whom received remittances, claimed that some had been used as capital for the purchase of seeds, fertilizer, and tools to engage in food production for sale (Muliaina 2001: 28). Throughout Tonga the increased use of remittances for investment purposes, in fishing, agriculture, stores, and transport businesses, attests to the shift from consumption to investment (Faeamani 1995) as immediate consumption goals have been satisfied. Remittances contribute to valuable objectives such as human resource development and are a means of maintaining social networks and creating social capital (Grieco 2003). In several contexts, especially in smaller islands, education is highly valued, both in a general sense and for the strategic development of specific skills (for example, in health care) to create human capital for potential migration.

Conclusion

As emigration continues, small and vulnerable South Pacific states have irrevocably become a peripheral and dependent part of a wider world. Contemporary patterns of migration have diversified and become both more selective and skilled, demographic structures have changed, and the restructuring of global and island economic landscapes present different development contexts. The life courses of island people, present or absent, are increasingly embedded in international ties, and island states have sought out new migration opportunities. Island states, individuals, and various international

agencies have attached new and increased significance to migration, remittance flows, return migration, and the role of the diaspora, in contexts where "conventional" national development strategies have achieved limited success.

In this century alone there has been a spectacular increase in overseas migration from the Pacific, and in unmet demand for it, from individuals whose dreams might turn to dust, and from governments, who have put increased pressure on countries such as Australia to relax what are perceived to be overly restrictive and even unethical policies. After about thirty years of independence and disappointment over the challenges and fruits of development, there is a new outward urge that is currently spilling over into Melanesia and taking islanders to new destinations. Migration has become more complex, globalization has extended the number of destinations and brought longer migration chains, migration has become more selective, and part of that selectivity has favored the migration of women. The more remote and rural parts of the island states are even less likely to be perceived as favorable places of residence. Migration has extended global horizons, shifted from seemingly voluntary migration toward recruitment, with echoes of the nineteenth century, and complicated once simple models of change.

The extent of international migration, and growing demands for migration opportunities, are indicative of a region where the best economic opportunities are seen by many households to be overseas rather than in the islands themselves. For even relatively large states such as Samoa and Tonga there are now as many ethnic Samoans and Tongans overseas as there are at home. The future—a diasporic future—is perceived to be elsewhere. While the continuity of a population on Pitcairn emphasizes that the Pacific will not become the "earth's empty quarter" (Ward 1989), it will be increasingly dependent on migration opportunities in other parts of the world.

As short-term and short-distance mobility has gradually given way to long-term or permanent migration over vast distances beyond the metropolitan fringes of the Pacific, this has raised new questions over identity and belonging. Given the "anastomosing" pattern of contemporary migration in the Pacific Islands, in which remittances and trade flow through transnational household economies, Ward (1996) has suggested that the fundamental premises of nationhood and sovereignty may have to be examined. As members of transnational ethnic communities, Pacific Islanders have access—however limited this may sometimes be—to considerably more geographically extended resources and opportunities than ever (Ward 1996). Yet even in precontact times remarkably similar patterns of mobility existed, at least within Polynesia, as centuries ago early voyagers moved back and forth between Hawaiki and Aotearoa long before there were jet planes. Pacific mobility has a long and increasingly complex future.

BIBLIOGRAPHY

Alkire, W. H. 1978. *Coral islanders*. Arlington Heights, Ill.: AHM Publishing Corporation.

Bedford, R. D. 1992. International migration in the South Pacific region. In *International migration systems: A global approach*, ed. M. M. Kritz, L. L. Lim, and H. Zlotnik, 41–62. Oxford: Clarendon Press.

Bellwood, P. 1979. *Man's conquest of the Pacific: The prehistory of Southeast Asia and Oceania.* New York: Oxford University Press.

Bertram, G. 1999. The MIRAB model twelve years on. *The Contemporary Pacific* 11(1): 105–138.

Bertram, I. G., and R. F. Watters. 1985. The MIRAB economy in South Pacific microstates. *Pacific Viewpoint* 26: 497–519.

Bonnemaison, J. 1994. *The tree and the canoe. History and ethnogeography of Tanna.* Honolulu: University of Hawai'i Press.

Borovnik, M. 2006. Working overseas: Seafarers remittances and their distribution in Kiribati. *Asia Pacific Viewpoint* 47: 151–161.

Boyd, D. J. 1990. New wealth and old power: Circulation, remittances, and the control of inequality in an Eastern Highlands community, Papua New Guinea. In *Migration and development in the South Pacific,* ed. J. Connell, 97–106. Canberra: National Center for Development Studies, Research School of Pacific Studies, Australian National University.

Chambers, K., and A. Chambers. 2001. *Unity of heart: Culture and change in a Polynesian atoll society.* Prospect Heights, Ill.: Waveland Press.

Chapman, M. 1976. Tribal mobility as circulation: A Solomon Islands example of micro/macro linkages. In *Population at microscale,* ed. L. A. Kosinski and J. W. Webb, 127–142. Christchurch: New Zealand Geographical Society.

Connell, J. 1985. Copper, cocoa and cash: Terminal, temporary, and circular mobility in Siwai, North Solomons. In *Circulation in population movement: Substance and concepts from the Melanesian case,* ed. M. Chapman and R. M. Prothero, 119–148. London: Routledge and Kegan Paul.

———. 1987a. *Migration, employment and development in the South Pacific.* Noumea: South Pacific Commission.

———. 1987b. *New Caledonia or Kanaky. The political history of a French colony.* Canberra: Australian National University Pacific Research Monograph No. 16.

———. 1988. The end ever nigh: Contemporary population changes on Pitcairn Island. *GeoJournal* 16(2): 193–200.

———. 1990. Modernity and its discontents: Migration and change in the South Pacific. In *Migration and development in the South Pacific,* ed. J. Connell, 1–28. Canberra: National Center for Development Studies, Research School of Pacific Studies, Australian National University.

———. 1991. The new diaspora: Migration, social change, the South Pacific and Australia. *Asian Migrant* 4(4): 108–113.

———. 2003. Losing ground? Tuvalu, the greenhouse effect and the garbage can. *Asia Pacific Viewpoint* 44(2): 89–107.

———. 2004. The migration of skilled health workers: From the Pacific Islands to the worlds. *Asian and Pacific Migration Journal* 13(2): 155–177.

———. 2005. A nation in decline? Migration and emigration from the Cook Islands. *Asian and Pacific Migration Journal* 14(3): 327–350.

———. 2006. Migration, dependency and inequality in the Pacific: Old wine in bigger bottles? In *Globalisation and governance in the Pacific Islands,* ed. S. Firth, 59–106. Canberra: Australian National University E Press.

———. 2008. Niue: Embracing a culture of migration. *Journal of Ethnic and Migration Studies* 34(6): 1021–1040.

———. 2009. *The global health care chain: From the Pacific to the world.* New York: Routledge.

Connell, J., and R. Brown. 2004. The remittances of migrant Tongan and Samoan nurses in Australia. *Human Resources for Health* 2 (2): 1–21.

———. 2005. *Remittances in the Pacific: An overview.* Manila: Asian Development Bank.

D'Arcy, P. 2006. *The people of the sea: Environment, identity, and history in Oceania.* Honolulu: University of Hawai'i Press.

Daws, G. 1983. History. In *Atlas of Hawaii,* ed. R. W. Armstrong, 97–106. Honolulu: University of Hawai'i Press.

Denoon, D. 1997. Land, labour and independent development. In *The Cambridge History of the Pacific Islanders,* 152–184, ed. D. Denoon. Cambridge: Cambridge University Press.

Development Research Center. 2007. Global migrant origin database, updated March 2007, version 4. http://www.migrationdrc.org/research/typesofmigration/global_migrant_origin_database.html.

Diamond, J. 1997. *Guns, germs, and steel: The fates of human societies.* New York: W. W. Norton and Company.

Faeamani, S. 1995. The impact of remittances on rural development in Tongan villages. *Asian and Pacific Migration Journal* 4(1): 139–156.

Gailey, C. W. 1992. State formation, development and social change in Tonga. In *Social change in the Pacific Islands,* ed. A. Robillard, 322–345. London: Kegan Paul International.

Grieco, E. 2003. *The remittance behavior of immigrant households: Micronesians in Hawaii and Guam.* New York: LFB Scholarly Publishing.

Hammond, J., and J. Connell. 2009. The new blackbirds: Vanuatu guestworkers in New Zealand. *New Zealand Geographer* 65(3): 201–210.

Hau'ofa, E. 1994. Our sea of islands. *The Contemporary Pacific* 6: 147–161.

Hayes, G. R. 1991. The use of scientific models in the study of Polynesian migration. *Asian and Pacific Migration Journal* 1: 278–312.

Hess, J., K. Nero, and M. Burton. 2001. Creating options: Forming a Marshallese community in Orange County, California. *The Contemporary Pacific* 13(1): 89–121.

Kiste, R. 1974. *The Bikinians. A study of forced migration,* Menlo Park, Calif.: Cummings.

Lacey, R. 1982. Traditional trade. In *Atlas of Papua New Guinea,* ed. D. King and S. Ranck, 8–9. Port Moresby: University of Papua New Guinea.

———. 1985. Journeys and transformations: The process of innovation in Papua New Guinea. *Pacific Viewpoint* 26(1): 81–105.

Levick, W., and R. Bedford. 1988. Fiji labour migration to New Zealand in the 1980s. *New Zealand Geographer* 44(1): 14–21.

Luomala, K. 1955. *Voices on the wind: Polynesian myths and chants.* Honolulu: Bishop Museum Press.

Macpherson, C., and L. Macpherson. 1987. Toward an explanation of recent trends in suicide in Western Samoa. *Man* 22: 305–330.

Marcus, G. E. 1981. Power on the extreme periphery: The perspective of Tongan elites in the modern world system. *Pacific Viewpoint* 22: 48–64.

Maude, H. E. 1981. *Slavers in Paradise: The Peruvian slave trade in Polynesia, 1862–1864.* Stanford, Calif.: Stanford University Press.

Mitchell, J. 2000. Violence as continuity: Violence as rupture—narratives from an urban settlement in Vanuatu. In *Reflections on Violence in Melanesia,* ed. S. Dinnen and A. Ley, 189–209. Sydney and Canberra: Hawkins Press and Asia-Pacific Press.

Morton, H. 1999. Islanders in space: Tongans online. In *Small worlds, global lives: Islands and migration,* ed. R. King and J. Connell, 235–253. London: Pinter.

Morton, H. 2003. *Tongans overseas: Between two shores.* Honolulu: University of Hawai'i Press.

Muliaina, T. 2001. Remittances, the social system and development in Samoa. In *Current trends in South Pacific migration,* ed. V. Naidu, E. Vasta, and C. Hawksley, 20–40. Wollongong: Asia Pacific Migration Research Network Working Paper No. 7, Centre for Asia Pacific Social Transformation Studies.

Nero, K. 1997. The end of insularity. In *The Cambridge history of the Pacific Islanders,* ed. D. Denoon, 439–467. Cambridge: Cambridge University Press.

Oliver, D. 1989. *The Pacific Islands.* Honolulu: University of Hawai'i Press.

Osborne, D. 1966. *The archaeology of the Palau Islands.* Honolulu: Bishop Museum Bulletin No. 230.

Rapaport, M. 1996. Between two laws: Tenure regimes in the pearl islands. *The Contemporary Pacific* 8(1): 33–49.

———. 1999. Mobility. In *The Pacific Islands: Environment & society,* ed. M. Rapaport, 270–281. Honolulu: Bess Press.

Rokoduru, A. 2008. Transient greener pastures in managed temporary labour migration in the Pacific: Fiji nurses in the Marshall Islands. In *The international migration of health workers,* ed. J. Connell, 171–180. New York: Routledge.

Shankman, P. 1976. *Migration and underdevelopment: The case of Western Samoa.* Boulder, Colo.: Westview.

Sinclair, K. 1980. *A history of New Zealand.* London: Allen Lane.

Terrell, J., and G. Irvin. 1972. History and tradition in the Northern Solomons: An analytical study of the Torau migration to southern Bougainville in the 1860s. *Journal of the Polynesian Society* 81: 317–349.

Voigt-Graf, C. 2003. Fijian teachers on the move: Causes, implications and policies. *Asia Pacific Viewpoint* 44: 163–174.

Voigt-Graf, C., and J. Connell. 2005. Towards autonomy? Gendered migration in Pacific Island countries. In *Migration happens,* ed. K. Ferro and M. Wallner, 43–62, Vienna: Lit Verlag.

Walsh, A. C. 1982. *Migration, urbanization and development in South Pacific countries.* New York: ESCAP.

———. 1987. *Migration and urbanization in Papua New Guinea: The 1980 census.* Papua New Guinea Research Monograph No. 5. Port Moresby: National Statistics Office.

Ward, R. G. 1989. Earth's empty quarter? The Pacific Islands in a Pacific century. *Geographical Journal* 155: 235–246.

———. 1996. Expanding worlds of Oceania: Implications of migration. In *Contemporary migration in Oceania: Diaspora and network,* ed. K. Sudo and S. Yoshida, 179–196. Osaka: Japan Center for Area Studies.

Watson, J. B. 1985. The precontact northern Tairoroa: High mobility in a crowded field. In *Circulation in population movement: Substance and concepts from the Melanesian case,* ed. M. Chapman and R. M. Prothero, 15–38. London: Routledge and Kegan Paul.

Wilson, M., C. Moore, and D. Munro. 1990. Asian workers in the Pacific. In *Labour in the South Pacific,* ed. C. J. Moore, J. Leckie, and D. Munro, 78–107. Townsville: James Cook University of Queensland.

Health

Annette Sachs Robertson

24

Concept of Health in the Pacific

The World Health Organization (WHO) defines health as "a state of complete physical, mental and social well-being and not merely the absence of disease or infirmity" (WHO 1948). While broadening the definition beyond a biomedical construct to include psychological and social dimensions was considered an advance, this definition of well-being has been described as being closer to happiness than health, without practical value (Saracci 1997). Saracci proposes an alternative definition of health as "a condition of wellbeing free of disease or infirmity and a basic and universal human right." Distinguishing between health and happiness is critical especially with respect to rights—health being a universal human right and happiness being a subjective achievement. According to the WHO definition, any disturbance to happiness is perceived as a health problem. In the quest for happiness, the quest for health will become boundless, leading to an unlimited demand for health services. In trying to meet the demand for happiness of each person, there is a danger that inequity in distribution of limited resources will make equity in health difficult to attain (Saracci 1997).

In the Pacific, spiritual and cultural dimensions of well-being should also be considered in the context of a healthy community, family, and individual. For Pacific Island people a holistic, communal view of humanity and links to the environment and their spiritual ancestry have been fundamental considerations in their conceptualization of contemporary and past health models. In Samoa, two broad sets of belief about health and illness exist (Macpherson and Macpherson 1990). Beliefs about the relationships between human beings and the natural, social, and supernatural environment coexist with beliefs about the body's normal function and the nature and causes of its malfunctions. The former belief, the precontact medical paradigm, holds that *aitu* (spirits) displeasure with human conduct, is the primary cause of illness. Thus Samoans believed that spirits determined the human condition. Culture, health, and illness are intertwined, with cultural beliefs defining and often explaining health and illness and resulting in diverse responses. The Maori health model, known as *whare tapa whai*, has holistic communal frameworks based on social, cultural, and economic interconnectiveness and emphasizes Maori self-determination in health (Durie 1994; Bryder and Dow 2001; McCreanor and Nairn 2002).

In Palau, *uab* is the mystic and sacred phenomenon that has provided the framework of survival for their society through several millennia (Kuartei 2005). To Palauans, *uab* represents a sacred gift, which if violated will lead to unhealthy inhabitants. This sacredness of Palau, *chedolel* Belau, governs the behavior of Palauans including the proper use of environment and resources. Kuartei states that there was a reverence for all that nature had to offer and that exploitation would bring about discordance with ancestral and spiritual governance, which might then expose one to illness or wrongness with the spirit. Such rules apply not only to disposal of waste, environmental conservation, and nutrition, but also to the control of sexuality and sexual behaviors. He states the need to preserve, respect, and bring about a return of the *chedolel* Belau, which is still considered important in contemporary Palauan society.

The Pacific Island concept of health encompasses health of the community and the ecosystem in which the people live. Hence, solutions to the health problems of Pacific Island peoples is more than a medical paradigm utilizing just pharmaceutical and Western medicine, but encompasses allopathic and traditional medicine as well as spiritual healing, not unlike other indigenous peoples of the world (Stephens et al. 2005).

Effects of First Contact with Western Society

The Pacific Island people, prior to European contact, were not without disease. While a few historical reports by early explorers suggest that Pacific Islanders were "robust and healthy" . . . "living on healthy islands," there was a low recognition of medical conditions and expectations of what constituted healthy (Pollock and Finau 1999; Howe 1984). But despite the difficulty of retrospectively providing an accurate diagnosis, endemic but not fatal diseases, such as yaws, filariasis, and intestinal parasitism, were reported in Polynesia (Lange 1984; Robertson 1990). Malaria in inland New Guinea and Solomon Islands was also reported. Bligh recorded cancers, consumptions, fevers, fits, and scrofula (Pollock and Finau 1999; Howe 1984). Analysis of bones suggests that arthritis was present in some communities. High maternal and infant mortality were most likely accepted by ancient Pacific societies (Pollock and Finau 1999).

Anthropologists have long discussed the irregularity of the food supply in many islands. The feast-and-famine theory suggests that times of abundant food supply alternated with times of little food. The ability to utilize food efficiently during times of food shortage has been implicated in the emergence of noncommunicable diseases and underlies the thrifty genotype theory. Theoretical explanations suggest that in more recent times, where food is sufficient at all times, the thrifty genotype has left Pacific Islanders susceptible to obesity and diabetes and no longer provides a survival advantage (WHO 2002).

Initial contact between Pacific Island people and Europeans are recorded in the mid-1600s, when Tasman visited the islands, and later in the mid-1700s, when Cook landed on various islands. When international explorations, commerce, and trade occurred through shipping missions, it brought successive waves of epidemics to indigenous populations in the Pacific Islands. Disease transmission most likely initially occurred between sailors and local populations around the middle to late 1700s and 1800s. Cook's visit in 1778 introduced tuberculosis and STIs (sexually transmitted infections) to Hawai'i, while tuberculosis was introduced to Fiji in 1791 and to the Cook Islands in 1830 (Igler 2008). In the early 1800s, after the dismantling of traditional social structural systems, which led to changes in diet and lifestyle, Hawaiians were decimated by tuberculosis, measles, typhoid fever, and STIs (Igler 2008). Gonorrhea and syphilis resulted in infertility, contributing to the decrease in population (Robertson 1991). The transmission of STIs by shipping crew to local women through the exchange of sex for trade goods, also occurred in Tahiti, Marquesas, and other Pacific islands. Epidemics among such "virgin" populations resulted in debilitating sickness, increased sterility, and high infant mortality rates (Igler 2008). A missionary ship called *Messenger of Peace* introduced influenza to Samoa in 1830. In Fiji in 1875, a measles epidemic, which destroyed between one-quarter and one-third of the Fijian population within six months, resulted from a single case of measles being transmitted from Chief Cakobau subsequent to an official visit to New South Wales on HMS *Dido*. Similar effects of measles epidemics were felt in Solomon Islands and in New Hebrides. As transoceanic trade and missionary visits increased, the transmission of communicable diseases such as tuberculosis, smallpox, measles, influenza, and STIs increased among Pacific peoples, striking them hard and resulting, through successive waves of disease, in substantial declines in health and population (Robertson 1991).

Several populations were severely reduced in size as a result of this early contact. Rallu reports the effects of early contact in Polynesian and Melanesian communities, suggesting an early decline in population size as a result of disease, reduced fertility, and childbirth complications. A period of high mortality occurred in the late 1800s and early 1900s (Rallu 1990). Stabilization of the Marquesan population only occurred after mortality rates decreased and fecundity increased. Similarly, in Vanuatu, depopulation followed early European contact at the end of the 1800s, but later stabilized as survivors became immune and programs of health and sanitation were implemented (Pollock and Finau 1999; Rallu 1990).

The inability to provide an accurate picture of past disease patterns may be related to a lack of accurate assessments of disease and causes of death and to incomplete recording systems. A disease like dengue fever may have been clinically diagnosed as influenza (Lewis and Rapaport 1995).

Contemporary Indigenous Health in the Pacific

While the Pacific region consists of many diverse cultural groups with varying histories of colonial influences and social and political change, in general indigenous societies in the Pacific have been marginalized and disadvantaged in their overall care over the past century (Anderson et al. 2006). In Australia, New Zealand, Hawai'i, and parts of the Pacific Islands, indigenous peoples—Aborigines, Maoris, and Hawaiians—have poorer health status, as measured by disease patterns and mortality rates, than the general population (Stephens, Porter, and Nettleton 2006). Maori have poorer health and social outcomes than other New Zealanders. Little improvement over time has been seen in Maori life expectancies, resulting in disparities between Maoris and non-Maoris. Cardiovascular disease, cancer, respiratory disease, and injury are the major causes of death in both groups. Disparities in cause-specific mortality rates for both sexes and in all age groups exist between Maori and non-Maori populations (Anderson et al. 2006).

Unequal access to quality health care based on ethnicity contributes to differences in mortality and life expectancies in Pacific Island countries. Ethnicity is defined as a "complex construct that includes biology, history, cultural orientation and practice, language, religion and lifestyle," each with potential to influence health (Pearce, Foliaki, and Sporle 2004). Such disparities in access to health care services may be a result of lack of influence in national priority setting, or it may be due to physical isolation (Stephens et al. 2005). This is especially so where traditional lifestyles have been replaced with maladjustment to Westernization, resulting in urban/rural poverty, poor housing, and unhealthy lifestyles such as poor nutrition, alcoholism, and drug use. Higher proportions of Maori women than non-Maori women have unmet needs for general practitioner care. While Maoris have higher mortality from ischemic heart disease, coronary artery revascularization procedures were more common in non-Maori, non-Pacific ethnic groups (Anderson et al. 2006).

A similar situation is evident for the Kanaka Maoli (Native Hawaiians), who today have the highest incidence of morbidity and mortality and age-adjusted mortality—especially for heart disease, diabetes, and cancer—than any other ethnic group in Hawai'i (Anderson et al. 2006). Although steady gains are being made in life expectancies in other ethnic groups, the Kanaka Maoli continue to have the lowest life expectancies, with little improvement. While infant mortality rates have dropped substantially, the percentage of low birth-weight babies is increasing. The Kanaka Maoli have higher smoking rates, higher levels of obesity, and higher suicide rates, and a higher percentage live below the poverty line (Anderson et al. 2006)

The United Nations states that "access to comprehensive, community-based and culturally appropriate health care services, health education, adequate nutrition and housing should be ensured without discrimination" and with the full participation of indigenous people (Stephens, Porter, and Nettleton 2006). Health for indigenous peoples has been defined as "not merely absence of ill health, but also a state of spiritual, communal and ecosystem equilibrium and well-being." Systems of traditional medicine and allopathic practice should be nurtured and supported to ensure that indigenous people's needs are met and their health knowledge is preserved and valued.

Maori health can be improved through self-determination and recognition of cultural perceptions and health and sickness (Durie 1994). Models of well-being are about trials and discoveries of the past, the energies and initiatives of the present, and the priorities and plans for the future (Bryder and Dow 2001). In Fiji, the traditional women's association of natural medicine therapy, Wainimate, has produced a policy statement that reflects the traditional healers' points of view and is working toward a national traditional medicine policy in Fiji to safeguard older cultural practices including Fijian medicine (Kuridrani 2007). A study on traditional healers found the presence of healers in almost all villages studied, more female than male healers, more healers in the older age groups, lack of proper documentation of knowledge, and concerns about intellectual property rights. Such issues are currently being addressed by the government in an attempt to ensure that Western medicine and traditional healing are integrated into the national health care system.

Environment and Health Interactions

Most Pacific islands are geographically isolated and economically disadvantaged and have unique health challenges related to past colonial history, fragile ecosystems, and cultural factors. To deal with health problems in the Pacific Islands, one must address the complexities of economic development given the economies of scale, the management of the environment, and social maladjustments. This holistic perspective, which interlinks sociocultural and physical environment and health into an ecological entity, was embodied in the Yanuca Declaration on Health in the Pacific in the 21st Century at the meeting of health ministers of fourteen Pacific Island nations. The Yanuca Declaration defines healthy islands as "places where children are nurtured in body and mind, environments invite learning and leisure, people work and age in dignity, and ecological balance is a source of pride" (Nutbeam 1996; WHO 1995; Dever and Finau 1995).

An obvious effect of ecological imbalance in the Pacific, as manifest in the degradation of the environment and its deleterious impact on health, is evident in the Republic of the Marshall Islands, where nuclear weapon testing began in 1946. The testing continued until 1958 and resulted in nuclear tonnage equivalent to 7,200 Hiroshima blasts (Anderson et al. 2006). As a result of exposure to the radioactive fallout of the Bravo hydrogen bomb test undertaken in 1954, 250 people from Rongelap, Utirik, and Ailinginae atolls suffered acute radiation sickness. A high rate of thyroid cancers and other radiation-associated cancers have been reported in those exposed on Rongelap and Utirik. The populations of these two islands and Bikini were evacuated and relocated, leading to major social and economic changes, including an end to traditional subsistence living and fishing practices. Similar nuclear testing in French Polynesia by the French, and on Christmas Island by the British, has had effects on the lifestyles of local populations and on their landscape, resulting in significant changes in health and mobility.

People in the Pacific, particularly those residing on low-lying atolls, are particularly vulnerable to the effects of climate change. Experts of climate change predict increases in global average temperatures of between 1.4 and 5.8 degrees Celsius and associated increases in sea level by 2100 (Patz et al. 2005; McMichael, Woodruff, and Hales 2006). The interrelationships between population growth, climate change, and the need to prevent unwanted or unintended pregnancies is being debated (Guillebaud and Hayes 2008; Stott and Godlee 2006). In the Pacific, vulnerability to climate change is shaped by many factors. The impact of climate change depends upon the magnitude of the change in the environment, the vulnerability of the population, and the current status and capacity of the ecological system. Population density, particularly in small island states, and the subsequent abuse of natural marine and land resources in all islands are factors that impinge on a community's ability to withstand deleterious effects of natural disasters such as hurricanes, storms, tsunamis, and floods. The direct effects on health are most severely experienced by people occupying low-lying atolls and the coastal areas of volcanic islands, and marginalized social and economic groups. Atolls in Tuvalu, the Marshall Islands, Kiribati, and the Federated States of Micronesia are vulnerable to rising sea levels as a result of greenhouse gas emissions. Already there is evidence that a diminishing landmass due to rising sea levels is being experienced in some of these atolls. With the pressure of continued high fertility rates, the sustainable livelihood and health of the resident populations are major concerns of the governments.

Indirect effects of climate change on infectious diseases and noncommunicable diseases are also of concern in the Pacific. In Papua New Guinea (PNG)—a land rich in natural resources, where approximately six million people reside and geographic and cultural diversity is immense—there are substantial concerns about the effects of climate change for the population. PNG national statistics reveal already high cause-specific mortality rates and the highest maternal mortality and infant mortality rates in the Pacific. There are real concerns about the spread of endemic malaria from coastal areas of PNG to the densely populated highlands if temperatures rise and the insect and parasite populations move inland (Woodward, Hales, and Weinstein 1998). With the current state of the health care system, the lack of surveillance and control measures for vector-borne diseases, and an impoverished population, the population is vulnerable. Similar patterns of change for other mosquito-borne diseases such as dengue fever are expected with rising temperatures and increasing rain. On the other end of the spectrum, New Zealand, with its current temperate climate, may also become vulnerable to such mosquito-borne diseases as new ecological niches are created with rising temperatures (Woodward, Hales, and Weinstein 1998). Food-borne diseases are likely to increase with increasing ambient temperatures. Furthermore, with fluctuating climates, deaths from cardiovascular disease and respiratory illness due to extreme heat are likely to rise.

Pacific Island Populations in Transition

Pacific Island nations fall along various points in the continuum of demographic transition from high fertility and mortality to low fertility and mortality. In some countries of the Pacific, there is slow fertility transition with high dependency ratios, rapid population growth (unless it is reduced by emigration), and a substantial youth bulge, or increasing youth cohorts (Rallu and Robertson 2008; Haberkorn 2000; Haberkorn and Jorari 2007). High fertility is the cause of high natural growth (rates above 2 percent in Melanesia [except Fiji], FSM, RMI, and Nauru in Micronesia and Samoa, Tokelau, and Tonga in Polynesia) (Table 24.1).

The related epidemiological transition is characterized by a high incidence of infectious diseases associated with malnutrition and poor sanitation on the one end, to high prevalence of noncommunicable diseases or chronic and degenerative diseases related to lifestyle and urbanization on the other (Zimmet, Dowse, and Finch 1990; Pobutsky et al. 2005; Lewis and Rapaport 1995). The highest mortality and highest proportionate mortality from infectious diseases is observed in less developed Melanesian countries, like PNG, and resource-limited atolls, like Kiribati, while lower mortality is observed in more developed Guam and the European population of New Caledonia (Lewis and Rapaport 1995). Dietary and nutritional transition occurs concomitantly with the switch from a diet associated with malnutrition and nutritional deficiencies to a diet rich in saturated fats and refined sugars that result in obesity.

In most Pacific Island nations, the transitions from one state to the other have not occurred in such a straightforward and unambiguous manner. Multiple health transitions are occurring within the context of demographic, socioeconomic, and political change (Lewis and Rapaport 1995). While populations are still suffering from infectious diseases, noncommunicable disease epidemics have emerged in many societies. Thus the coexistence of diseases from both sides of the spectrum, or "double jeopardy," is placing enormous burdens on fragile health care systems in the Pacific. In Micronesia, measles, tuberculosis, hepatitis B, Hansen's disease, and STIs occur at relatively high frequencies, while chronic diseases such as diabetes and ischemic heart disease have emerged as major health concerns (Pobutksy et al. 2005). In other countries, leptospirosis, filariasis, and other infectious diseases persist in populations also experiencing the noncommunicable disease epidemic (Dean 2000, 2003; Ichimori and Crump 2005; Berlioz-Arthaud et al. 2007).

In Pacific Island nations where social change as a result of Westernization and globalization is occurring at a rapid pace, negative consequences—coronary heart disease, obesity, alcohol and drug abuse, motor vehicle accidents, and suicide—are being seen at an alarmingly increasing rate (Kermode and Tellai 2005). Analysis of life expectancies over the past two decades reveals that

Table 24.1

Demographic Estimates for Pacific Island Populations, 2004–2006

Country	Total pop. 2008 (000s) (1)	Pop. density (per sq km) 2008 (1)	% pop. urban (1)	Nat. growth rate % (1)	% pop. 15–24 (2)	% of pop. under 15 (2)	Total fertility rate (1)	Fertility rate 15–19 yrs (1)	Health as % of GDP (3)	Life expectancy M/F (1)
Cook Is.	15.5	66	72	1.2	18.0	30.8	2.8	68	2.3	68.0 / 74.3
FSM	110.4	158	22	2.1	23.1	38.0	4.0	48	7.8	67.4 / 68.0
Fiji	839.3	46	51	1.6	19.6	33.0	2.6	43	3	63.8 / 67.6
Kiribati	97.2	120	44	1.9	21.2	36.1	3.4	39	8.6	58.9 / 63.1
Marshall Is.	53.2	294	68	2.6	24.2	41.0	4.4	71	9.8	63.7 / 67.4
Nauru	10.2	484	100	2.4	22.1	36.6	4.0	93	7.5	52.5 / 58.2
Niue	1.5	6	36	0.7	16.0	25.9	2.6	28	7.7	67.0 / 76.0
Palau	20.3	46	64	0.5	14.7	22.6	2.0	29	9.2	66.3 / 72.8
PNG	6473.9	14	13	2.2	19.9	38.9	4.6	70	4.4	53.7 / 54.8
Samoa	179.6	61	21	2.1	19.8	41.0	4.6	45	5.8	70.1 / 75.5
Solomon Is.	517.5	18	16	2.6	19.9	40.4	4.8	72	5	60.6 / 61.6
Tokelau	1.2	98	0	1.7	16.3	36.4	4.5	43	na	67.8 / 70.4
Tonga	102.7	158	23	2.2	21.7	37.4	4.2	24	5.5	67.3 / 73.0
Tuvalu	9.7	374	47	1.2	17.8	33.6	3.7	40	5.4	61.7 / 65.1
Vanuatu	233.2	19	21	2.5	20.8	38.8	4.4	59	3.8	65.6 / 69.0

Sources: (1) SPC Datasheet 2008. (2) SPC Projections 2007. (3) CHIPS WHO WPRO 2005.

some Pacific countries display a plateau in life expectancy, likely due in part to the emergence of noncommunicable disease (Taylor and Lopez 2007).

Further complicating the situation are the variable life expectancies, the increased proportion of the population aging, and the relatively low level of physical activity (WHO 2002). Nauru, with the highest rates of noncommunicable diseases, has the lowest life expectancies for males (Table 24.1). This epidemiological stagnation was described by Lewis and Rapaport in 1995 and the situation has not changed over the past decade. The diversity in disease patterns and life expectancies within various socioeconomic and ethnic groups in societies in the Pacific adds another layer of complexity to this discussion of epidemiological transition. While differences exist within countries, mortality has declined over the past two decades in all Pacific Island countries, with the smallest changes in states, such as Guam and American Samoa, that already had relatively high life expectancy (Taylor and Lopez 2007). Thus, there is no single epidemiological transition in the Pacific (Lewis and Rapaport 1995; Taylor and Lopez 2007).

Lifestyle Factors: Diet, Exercise, and Obesity

A high prevalence of obesity and substantial increases since the 1970s are present in many Pacific Island countries (Ulijaszek 2005; WHO 2005a). Some scholars have argued that body mass index (BMI) is an inappropriate measure for Pacific Island people. There is recent evidence to suggest, however, that BMI and waist circumferences are indicators of health among island populations and that cutoff points for predicting chronic disease need further investigation (Novotny et al. 2007). As many countries do not have trend data, predictions as to whether these trends will increase must be viewed with caution. Analysis of trend data from Fiji suggests that obesity is increasing rapidly and will continue to increase in the future. The WHO report states that in the Pacific "the rate of increase is still astonishing compared to many other regions in the world" (WHO 2005a).

There are extremely high rates of obesity in males and females in many Polynesian countries and in some Micronesian countries (Figure 24.1). Of particular note are the rates of obesity in 2005 exceeding 80 percent in Nauru and rates exceeding 60 percent in the Cook Islands, the Federated States of Micronesia, and Tonga. More than 75 percent of adult male and female populations are overweight in the Polynesian countries and in the Federated States of Micronesia, Nauru, and Palau.

Dietary change, particularly an increase in energy intakes and energy densities in diets, and the evolution of more sedentary lifestyles are key factors in this epidemic of obesity. Consumption of imported fatty foods and meats are implicated. The emergence of obesity in many Pacific Island nations has also been attributed to increasing numbers of Pacific Island migrants in the United States, New Zealand, France, and Australia providing a basis for modernization by way of remittances and economic opportunity (Ulijaszek 2005).

Studies into the problem of obesity among Pacific Island communities are numerous. Yamada investigated the perceptions and attitudes toward obesity of Samoans themselves. Samoans reported that many aspects of culture promote overeating (Yamada 1999).

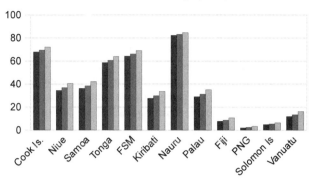

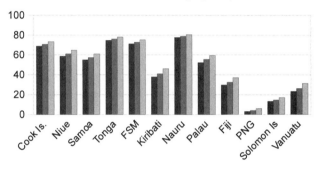

Figure 24.1. Prevalence of obesity estimates and projections for males and females, ages fifteen and above for selected Pacific Island countries.

These include the tolerance of obesity, food as an expression of love and respect, food as a focus of social interactions, and physical inactivity of high-status individuals. They suggested there was a need for the Samoan culture to de-emphasize food as a medium of exchange and expression of love and that the initiation of such change must come from Samoan leaders. Pollock reported eating as a symbolic act that is integrated with generosity and the social well-being of the group (Pollock, AhMu, and Carter 1989; Pollock 1992). A study undertaken in Tonga investigated why imported foods were increasingly consumed instead of traditional foods (Evans et al. 2001). Results revealed that eating imported foods was not related to food preferences or perceptions of nutritional value but instead related to cost and availability. Implications for the limited impact of health education interventions present challenges to health policy makers.

Alcohol, Drug, and Tobacco Use

Reports reveal that prior to European contact, the use of kava, betel nut, and wild plants with psychoactive properties was widespread and ritualized in many Pacific Island countries (Chen, Johnson, and Taufa 1999). But alcohol use in Pacific Island countries, including PNG, was not traditional, and marijuana use only emerged around the 1970s in PNG and other Pacific Island countries.

The abuse of alcohol, tobacco, illicit drugs, kava/*sakau*, or betel nut exists in varying degrees in most contemporary Pacific Island countries. A comparison of tobacco, alcohol, and illegal drug use among school students revealed relatively high prevalence rates, particularly among boys, in Tonga, Pohnpei, and Vanuatu (Smith et al. 2007). Rates of tobacco smoking range from 22 percent to 57 percent in males and from 0.6 percent to 51 percent in females in Pacific Island countries (Rasanathan and Tukuitonga 2007). These rates are generally higher than in Australia and New Zealand. Female smoking rates are particularly high in Nauru, Tokelau, French Polynesia, New Caledonia, and Kiribati. For youth, smoking rates range from 3 percent to 68 percent, with the highest rates reported in Palau, Northern Marianas, Guam, the Cook Islands, and American Samoa. While it appears that in some countries the rate of smoking in males has decreased in the past thirty years, the high rates in youth are of major concern.

The use of illicit drugs, particularly cannabis, is reported to be widespread in Fiji, Papua New Guinea, Samoa, Solomon Islands, Tonga, and Vanuatu (Devaney et al. 2006).

Alcohol consumption in Micronesia has caused significant social problems (Hezel 1981). In the Marshall Islands, there is evidence to suggest that substance abuse is worsening. It appears that substance abuse is contributing to emerging and re-emerging infections, like HIV/AIDS, sexually transmitted infections, and tuberculosis (RMI Epidemiological Working Group 2008).

Such patterns of behavior are associated with negative health consequences. Betel nut chewing is associated with the spread of respiratory infections, such as tuberculosis, and oral cancers. The consequences of kava use include dermopathy and sedation (Gounder 2006). The health consequences of smoking include cancers, cardiovascular disease, and lung disease (Khorram and Bruss 1999). The health consequences of excessive alcohol consumption include gastritis and duodenal cancers, pancreatitis, hepatitis, cirrhosis, cerebellar degeneration, heart and lung conditions, alcohol hallucinosis, psychosis, and vitamin deficiencies. Cannabis use is associated with impaired cognitive functions, psychosis, and chronic lung disease. These substances are associated with injuries and social problems including unemployment and crime, particularly in young males in some Pacific Island countries (Hezel 1981; Ravia 1999).

Noncommunicable Disease Epidemic: Cardiovascular Diseases, Diabetes, and Cancer

Poor diets—high in saturated fats, refined sugars, and salt and with limited amounts of fresh vegetables and fruit—limited physical activity, and tobacco use are considered the major causal factors of noncommunicable diseases, which include coronary heart disease, cardiovascular strokes, hypertension, obesity, diabetes, some forms of cancer, asthma, dental caries, and other conditions (WHO 2002; Strong et al. 2006; Ebrahim and Smeeth 2006). In the Pacific, the evolution of a noncommunicable disease epidemic has been attributed to urbanization and Westernization that has resulted in changed diets, lack of maintenance of ideal body weights, lack of exercise, and tobacco use (Coyne 1984; Robertson 1990). In a traditional PNG community, before socioeconomic change was experienced, there were low cholesterol levels, low salt intake, and a relative absence of diabetes, hypertension, cerebrovascular disease, and coronary artery disease (Lewis and Rapaport 1995).

Cardiovascular Disease

Cardiovascular diseases have been reported as the major cause of death in many Pacific Island countries, particularly in urban settings (Bloom 1987). Rising levels of heart disease and hypertension have been reported in Pacific Island urban communities (Fleming and Prior 1981; WHO 2002). Death rates from cardiovascular diseases and hypertension are predominantly in males but increasing incidence of hypertension in pregnancy is also being reported. Nauru, American Samoa, and Tonga have witnessed particularly high rates of hypertension and heart disease in the past few decades.

Diabetes

Diabetes is considered a major risk factor for coronary heart disease. In traditional societies of indigenous populations in the Pacific, diabetes was almost nonexistent. Diabetes is still less common in traditional societies living in the highlands of PNG than in urban dwellers of Port Moresby, whose prevalence rates now exceed 15 percent.

Over the past few decades, the prevalence of diabetes has increased in indigenous peoples of the Pacific Islands and in New Zealand (Foliaki and Pearce 2003). In Nauru, prior to compensation for phosphate mining, diabetes was not common, but by the middle of the twentieth century, as a result of relative affluence, changes in diet to predominantly imported foods, and a sedentary lifestyle, diabetes had increased substantially (Zimmet, Dows, and Finch 1990). At the beginning of the twenty-first century, approximately 80 percent of the adult male and female population is considered obese, and diabetes prevalence in Nauru exceeds 35 percent (Figure 24.1) (WHO 2002). Similar patterns of obesity and diabetes are also being observed in American Samoa and Tonga. Prevalence rates of diabetes in outpatients in the Marshall Islands are significantly higher than in the United States or worldwide, with age-adjusted prevalence rates in adult males thirty years or older reported to be approximately 27 percent (Yamada et al. 2004). While it would appear that the risk factors for diabetes are relatively well understood, prevention and control is not straightforward, and individual and population approaches are necessary (Foliaki and Pearce 2003).

Cancer

Although the etiology of most cancers is still being researched, a range of risk factors, including smoking, viral infections, obesity, diet, alcohol, hormonal factors, and genetics, have been implicated. While cancer registration systems are improving in some Pacific Island countries, cancer reports in the Pacific, which include lung, liver, prostate, breast, and cervical cancer, may be an underestimate of the population incidence.

The overall incidence of cancer in Pacific people living in New Zealand is similar to that of non-Maori and non–Pacific Island peoples, but disparities exist among various specific cancer (Dachs et al. 2008). Lung and cervical cancer are more common in Maoris and liver cancer more common in other Pacific Island people. Melanomas, prostate cancer, and colon cancer are less common in Maoris. Registration of diseases in Tonga revealed that Tongan women have higher incidences of liver and cervical cancer than Pacific women living in New Zealand. American Samoa has reported the major sites as breast, uterine, lung, prostate, and cervix, while Niue reports lung, stomach, and liver cancer in males and ovarian, uterine, and cervical cancer in women. In the Cook Islands, lung, stomach, and prostate cancer are reported in males and cervical, breast, and ovarian cancer in females (Dachs et al. 2008). The overall mortality patterns from cancer are higher in Maori and Pacific Island people than in non-Maori and non-Pacific people. Similarly, in Hawai'i, cancer survival is worse in Native Hawaiians than in Caucasian people living in Hawai'i.

Although cancer has emerged in Micronesia as a leading cause of morbidity and mortality, there is little population-based data documenting it (Katz et al. 2004). As cancer is the second leading cause of death in Guam, Northern Marianas, and the third leading cause in the Pohnpei and Chuuk states of the Federated States of Micronesia, there is need to increase public awareness, improve registration, and undertake more widespread detection and screening (Tseng, Omphroy, and Cruz et al. 2004; Tseng, Omphroy, and Songsong et al. 2004; Ichiho et al. 2004). Subsequent to nuclear

testing in the Marshall Islands, cancers of the thyroid have been reported in populations exposed to the nuclear fallout.

In Melanesia, particularly in PNG, there appear to be high rates of oral cancer, which is linked to betel nut chewing (Lewis and Rapaport 1995). In lower areas of PNG, elevated rates of lymphoma have been observed (Lewis and Rapaport 1995). In Vanuatu, cervical cancer screening and human papilloma virus studies reveal high levels of cervical cancer and cervical abnormalities in the population (Fotinatos et al. 2007).

Child Health

Nutritional Deficiencies

Despite economic progress, malnutrition in children is still reported in some Pacific Island countries. Estimates of the prevalence of underweight children under five years old vary in the Pacific, from approximately 2 percent or less in Samoa and Tonga, to 27 percent in the Marshall Islands (UNICEF 2008) (Table 24.2).

Estimates reveal that approximately 60 percent of Pacific children are anemic (UNICEF 2008). Such high prevalence has been attributed to the prevalence of malaria in Melanesian countries and parasitic infections. While breastfeeding was universal

Table 24.2

Infant and Child Health and Access Statistics in Selected Pacific Island Countries, 2004–2008

Country	Infant mortality rate (per 1,000 births) (1)	Under 5 mortality rate (per 1,000 live births) (2)	% 1 yr old immunized against measles (%) (3)	% underweight (>= −2 std deviations below mean weight for age) (3)	Pop. with improved access to drinking water— urban % (3)	Pop. with improved access to drinking water—rural % (4)	Pop. with improved sanitation— urban % (4)	Pop. with improved sanitation— rural % (4)
Cook Is	14.5	24.0	100	10	98	88	100	100
FSM	37.5		70	15	95	94	61	14
Fiji	18.8	22.0	100	8	43	51	99	98
Kiribati	52.0	69.0	60	13	77	53	59	22
Marshall Is	37	48.0	60	27	80	95	93	59
Nauru	42.3		96					
Niue	7.8		100					
Palau	20.0	29.0	98		79	94	96	52
PNG	64.0	88.0			88	32	67	41
Samoa	19.8	25.0	55	2	91	88	100	100
Solomon Is	66.0	73.0	70	21	94	65	98	18
Tokelau	38.0		0					
Tonga	19.0	17.0	99	2	100	100	98	96
Tuvalu	35.0	32.4	82		94	92	92	83
Vanuatu	25.0	33.0	98	23	85	52	78	42

Sources: (1) SPC Datasheet 2008. (2) SPC Pacific Regional MDG Report 2005. (3) UNICEF State of the Pacific Children 2008. (4) ADB database 2005.

in traditional Pacific societies and is actively promoted by baby-friendly hospitals and maternal and child health clinics, exclusive breastfeeding has declined (UNICEF 2008). Recent studies in the RMI have revealed high levels of childhood malnutrition with evidence of chronic malnutrition (RMI 2007).

There is some evidence that suggests that Vitamin A deficiency is a problem in some countries, including Kiribati and Solomon Islands. Cross-sectional studies revealed a prevalence of xerophthalmia in 15 percent of children six to seventy-two months old in Kiribati and 1.55 percent in Solomon Islands. Bitot's spots followed by night blindness were the more common clinical evidence of chronic Vitamin A deficiency. There were relatively negligible rates in the Cook Islands, Tuvalu, and Vanuatu (Schaumberg et al. 1995).

Infant and Child Mortality

Significant decreases in infant and child mortality have been observed in the past century. Over the past decade, however, infant mortality rates have tended to level off (UNICEF 2008). In some countries facing economic hardship and declining standards of health service delivery, infant mortality rates have increased. All countries with the exception of PNG, Kiribati, and Solomon Islands have infant mortality rates below 50 per 1,000 live births

(Table 24.2). In countries where a low percentage of the population has access to safe drinking water and sanitation, infant and child mortality rates tend to be higher. Many countries have measles immunization rates of one-year-old infants exceeding 90 percent. But immunization rates have fluctuated over the past five years in many countries and on average 20 percent of Pacific children were not immunized in 2005 (UNICEF 2003, 2004, 2005a, 2005b, 2005c, 2006a, 2008).

Women's Health

In all Pacific Island countries, life expectancy for females exceeds that of males (Table 24.1). In general, women face unique health situations that are reflected in their morbidity and mortality statistics, particularly related to maternal health. Furthermore, the roles and status of women vary widely across the Pacific, with the status of women being generally higher in Polynesian and Micronesian countries than in Melanesian countries (Lewis and Rapaport 1995).

As seen in Table 24.3, maternal mortality is higher in the Melanesian countries (Papua New Guinea, Solomon Islands, Vanuatu) and lowest or even extremely rare in some of the Polynesian (the Cook Islands, Niue, Samoa, Tuvalu) and Micronesian countries (Palau). Maternal mortality statistics in Papua New Guinea, Kiribati,

Table 24.3

Maternal Health Statistics for Selected Pacific Islands, 2004–2007

Country	Maternal mortality ratio (per 100,000 live births)	Proportion of births attended by skilled health personnel (%)	% of deliveries by Caesarean section	Unmet need for family planning	Contraceptive use among married women 15–49 any method (%)
Cook Is	0 deaths	98			43.8
FSM	317.0	88			56 (10)
Fiji	38	99	10.7 (11)	43–57 (14)	46 (11)
Kiribati	250 (2)	85			22 (2)
Marshall Is	73.8	90 (10)			35 (18)
Nauru					
Niue	0 deaths	100			
Palau	0 deaths	100			17.2
PNG	733 (3)	53 (3)	1.0 (1)	46 (15)	24.3 (3)
Samoa	27 (4)	90 (4)	7.4 (4)	20–53 (16)	30
Solomon Is	103 (5)	86 (8)	6 (8)		27 (8)
Tokelau					
Tonga	113 (6)	98.0 (6)	9.7 (12)		23 (6)
Tuvalu	1 death	98.0 (9)	7.5 (13)		22 (9)
Vanuatu	84 (7)	93.4 (7)	3.2 (7)	24 (17)	28

Sources: (1) Pacific Regional MDG Report 2005 and UNFPA updates based on MoH data. (2) Kiribati MDG Report 2007. (3) PNG DHS 2007. (4) UNFPA Samoa National EMOC/ FP Faculty Survey 2007. (5) UNFPA Solomon Islands National EMOC/ FP Faculty Survey 2007. (6) MOH Tonga. Ministry of Health National Statistics 2007. (7) UNFPA Vanuatu National EMOC/ FP Faculty Survey 2006. (8) SPC Solomon Islands DHS 2007. (9) SPC Tuvalu DHS 2007. (10) ICPD +10 Progress Report in the Pacific. UNFPA 2005. (11) MOH Fiji. Ministry of Health National Statistics 2007. (12) UNFPA Tonga National EMOC/ FP Faculty Survey 2005. (13) UNFPA Tuvalu National EMOC/ FP Faculty Survey 2007. (14) Fertility and Reproductive Health Survey, Fiji 1995 (range depicts age grouping). (15) PNG DHS 1996. (16) Fertility and Reproductive Health Survey, Samoa 1995 (range depicts age grouping). (17) House, Knowledge, Attitude and Practice Survey, Vanuatu 1999. (18) SPC Marshall Islands DHS 2007. (19) Pacific Regional MDG Report 2004.

and the Federated States of Micronesia are a cause for serious concern as the numbers are not decreasing, which also reflects declining standards of emergency obstetric care for women during and around childbirth. While maternal mortality ratio is an inappropriate statistic for small island states due to its stochastic variability related to unique events in small populations, it is evident that few maternal deaths have occurred in many countries (Robertson 2007). In the countries in which maternal mortality remains a major issue, the leading causes of death are postpartum hemorrhage, pre-eclampsia, obstructed labor, puerperal sepsis, and complications of unsafe abortion. Except PNG, in 2005 all Pacific Island countries reported percentages of births by skilled health attendants exceeding 85 percent (Table 24.3).

Family planning statistics are related to access to reproductive health care services, levels of education, and economic progress in the Pacific. In some countries that have high fertility rates (Kiribati, PNG, Solomon Islands, Tonga, and Vanuatu), contraceptive prevalence rates are below 30 percent. Underreporting of contraceptive usage complicates any assessment of trends and patterns.

As previously mentioned, adolescent fertility rates are high in many Pacific Island countries—Federated States of Micronesia, Kiribati, Republic of the Marshall Islands, Solomon Islands, Vanuatu. The consequences include high associated infant and maternal morbidity and often lost opportunities for education for the teenage girls. The high percentage of population under twenty-five years of age in these countries and the high rates of unprotected sexual activity in young people is a concern (Chung 1999; Burslem et al. 1997; UNICEF 2001; UNFPA 2002a, 2002b, 2002c, 2002d; Gold 2008).

High levels of violence against women have been reported in many Pacific Island countries (UNFPA 2003; Robertson and Hayes 2005). Such high levels of violence against women have been attributed to the relatively low status of women in society, rapid social change and urbanization, and increased alcohol abuse (Lewis and Rapaport 1995). Increased awareness and reporting is bringing the issue more into the public arena. Exceptionally high rates of rape, including gang rape, are reported in PNG. Rape and sexual abuse of young people is a public health issue in many countries, including Fiji, Kiribati, Solomon Islands, and Vanuatu (UNICEF 2006b; UNICEF 2008; Herbert 2007).

Emerging HIV Epidemic

While significant efforts at strengthening epidemiological surveillance, prevention, and treatment have occurred in the Pacific over the past five years, there is still limited data on the prevalence of HIV (Figure 24.2). The first case of HIV in the Pacific was reported in 1984, and to date HIV cases have been reported in all countries except Niue, Tokelau, and Pitcairn Islands (Sladden 2005).

To date, more than 90 percent of the cases in the Pacific have been reported from PNG. In PNG, the first case was detected in 1987. By 2002, the HIV prevalence among antenatal clients surpassed 1 percent at the Port Moresby General Hospital and a generalized epidemic was declared in 2004 (NAC PNG 2008). While a total of 18,484 people were diagnosed with HIV by the end of 2006, it is estimated that 46,275 people were living with HIV. Approximately 48 percent of these cases occurred in females and 46 percent

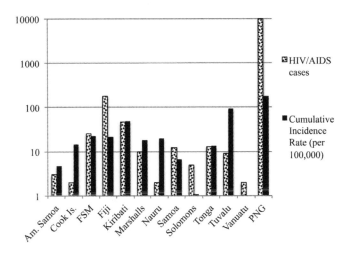

Figure 24.2. Cumulative incidence rate (per 100,000) and number of HIV cases in selected Pacific Island countries, 2005.

in males (6 percent sex unreported). Surveillance studies of antenatal women in PNG reveal that the percentage of pregnant women that were HIV-positive varied from 0 to 16.3 percent in 2006 (NAC PNG 2007; NAC PNG 2008). By the end of December 2007, the national HIV prevalence was projected to be 1.6 percent in the adult (fifteen to forty-nine years) population with a rural prevalence rate of 1.65 percent and an urban rate of 1.38 percent (NAC PNG 2008). The rural epidemic appears to be related to limited health services, limited transportation and communication, low levels of literacy, and cultural practices (Hammar 2007). Hayes estimated that by 2012 the prevalence of HIV would be 5 percent in PNG (Hayes 2007). Significant changes in life expectancies and demographic patterns are predicted with devastating health and economic impacts.

In other countries in the Pacific, while the absolute number of HIV cases is highest in Fiji, the cumulative incidence rate is highest in Kiribati and Tuvalu (exceeding 40 per 100,000 population) (Ministry of Health Fiji 2008; Gold 2008; Robertson 2007). In Fiji, the number of new cases per year has declined in the past year (Ministry of Health Fiji 2008). Caution in interpreting these statistics is recommended, however, as widespread confidential counseling and testing have not yet been fully implemented. The HIV cases detected in Kiribati and Tuvalu were imported by local seafarers subsequent to their return from travels to Asian countries and then spread to their families (WHO 2005b).

In most countries in the Pacific, the mode of spread of HIV has been predominantly heterosexual. However, perinatal transmission may be increasing in some countries, particularly Papua New Guinea (Sladden 2005; Robertson 2007).

While knowledge about HIV transmission appears to be increasing in some countries as a result of awareness campaigns, there are relatively high levels of early sexual debut and unprotected sex, and low levels of condom use among young people (Chung 1999; Corner et al. 2005; Jenkins 1997; WHO 2006). Given the high prevalence of STIs and the lack of adequate surveillance of HIV and STIs in many Pacific Island countries, halting or reversing the spread of HIV will only occur when effective interventions are strengthened among the population.

Reproductive Tract Infections: Sexually Transmitted Infections

Although widespread STI surveillance is not present in most Pacific Island countries, evidence suggests that there are high rates of STIs (WHO 2006). Second-generation surveillance studies revealed that the prevalence of chlamydia among pregnant women ranged from 6.4 percent in Solomon Islands to 29 percent in Fiji (WHO 2006). Chlamydia prevalence among pregnant women less than twenty-five years old was reported to be 20 percent or above in five countries (Fiji, Kiribati, Samoa, Tonga, and Vanuatu). Chlamydia prevalence rates in Fiji and Samoa among women aged less than twenty-five years (>30 percent) are considered to be among the highest in the world. Trichomonas vaginalis has been reported to be very high in Vanuatu (Fotinatos et al. 2008).

Mental Health

Pacific people view mental health as an intrinsic component of health. Traditional beliefs are that disturbed behavior is a manifestation of external spiritual forces, especially ancestral spirits possessing a person who has broken traditional taboos or offended the spirit (Ministry of Health New Zealand 2008).

In New Zealand, Pacific Islanders have a higher overall prevalence of mental disorders than the total New Zealand population as well as a low level of access to mental health services (Ministry of Health New Zealand 2008). Pacific Islanders who migrate to New Zealand at an early age have a higher prevalence of serious mental disorders than other migrants or New Zealand–born persons, and they have the lowest utilization rates of mental services (Ministry of Health New Zealand 2008).

Studies of suicide in Micronesia reveal an alarming number of suicides committed per year between 1960 and the mid-1980s (Hezel 1987, 1989). In Chuuk, the high incidence of suicides has been attributed to social change, cultural factors, and family conflict (Hezel 1984, 1987). In the Republic of the Marshall Islands, suicides have been decreasing in the past eight years. Among youth in 2007, 25.6 percent seriously contemplated suicide (RMI Epidemiological Working Group 2008).

The prevalence and burden of serious mental disorders has been increasing in some Pacific countries (Puamau 2006; Hezel and Wylie 1992). In Micronesia, prevalence rates of schizophrenia ranged from 16.7 per 1,000 population to 3.2 per 1,000 population (Hezel 1992). Chronic serious mental disorders were more common in males than females. Providing adequate prevention and treatment services for people with mental illnesses is still a long way off in Pacific Island countries.

Improving Health Care Systems

The need to improve health care systems to respond to changing patterns of illness, emerging infectious diseases, and noncommunicable diseases is critical in the twenty-first century. Several countries are experiencing plateaus or declines in their health statistics. With the generalized HIV epidemic in Papua New Guinea, major changes in population demographics and health status are occurring. The primary health care system, including government,

nongovernmental, and community elements, must be further strengthened to provide all people access to universal quality health care as a basic human right, in a manner that is culturally appropriate and sensitive. Finau has stated that failure of this approach to reach its maximum potential in the Pacific can be traced to a lack of vision, managerial problems, weak political commitment, and opposition of health professionals (Pollock and Finau 1999).

Harnessing traditional healers and natural medicine practitioners to complement existing services would be an important consideration. Given the bulging youth population, countries need to place more emphasis on addressing youth issues, particularly substance abuse and sexual and reproductive behavior. To move toward attaining the well-being of all Pacific people, greater partnerships are needed in-country and regionally to ensure that resources are utilized efficiently for maximal impact on health care systems.

BIBLIOGRAPHY

Anderson, I., et al. 2006. Indigenous health in Australia, New Zealand and the Pacific. *The Lancet* 367: 1775–1785.

Berlioz-Arthaud, A., T. Kiedrzynski, N. Singh, J. F. Yvon, G. Roualen, C. Coudert, and V. Uluiviti. 2007. Multi-centre survey of incidence and public health impact of leptospirosis in the Western Pacific. *Transactions of the Royal Society of Tropical Medicine and Hygiene* 101(7): 714–721.

Bloom, A. 1987. Health and nutrition in the Pacific: Problems and policy issues. In *Human resources development in the Pacific,* ed. C. Throsby, 53–88. Canberra: National Centre for Development Studies. Pacific Policy Papers No. 3.

Bryder, L., and D. Dow. 2001. Introduction: Maori health history: Past, present and future. *Health and History* 3: 3–12.

Burslem, F., O. Laohanpensang, J. Sauvarin, M. Young, and A. Larson. 1997. Naked wire and naked truths: A study of reproductive health risks faced by teenage girls in Honiara, Solomon Islands. *Pacific Health Dialog* 5(1): 8–15.

Chen, P., F. Johnson, and T. Taufa. 1999. *Societal and health aspects of psychoactive drug abuse in Papua New Guinea. Pacific Health Dialog* 6(1): 93–100.

Chung, M. 1999. Findings of the desk review of sexual behaviour research in Pacific Island countries. A report to the Task Force on Sexual Behaviour Research, Suva.

Corner, H., et al. 2005. Sexual health behaviors among Pacific Island youth in Vanuatu, Tonga and the Federated States of Micronesia. *Health Promotion Journal of Australia: Official Journal of Australian Association of Health Promotion Professionals* 16(2): 144–150.

Coyne, T. 1984. *The effect of urbanization and western diet on the health of Pacific Island populations.* Noumea: South Pacific Commission Technical Paper 186.

Dachs, G., M. Currie, F. McKenzie, M. Jeffreys, B. Cox, S. Foliaki, L. Marchand, and B. Robinson. 2008. Cancer disparities in indigenous Polynesian populations: Maori, native Hawaiians and Pacific peoples. *The Lancet* 9: 473–484.

Dean, M. 2000. Launching a lymphatic filariasis campaign in the Pacific Islands. *The Lancet* 356(9224): 143.

———. 2003. Pacific nations lead the way in fighting lymphatic filariasis. *The Lancet* 362(9399): 1906.

Devaney, M., G. Reid, S. Baldwin, N. Crofts, and R. Power. 2006. Illicit drug use and responses in six Pacific Island countries. *Drug and Alcohol Review* 25(4): 387–390.

Dever, G., and S. Finau. 1995. The Yanuca declaration: Pacific health in the twenty-first century. *Pacific Health Dialog* 2(2): 70–74.

Durie, M. 1994. *Whaiora: Maori health development.* Auckland: Oxford University Press.

Ebrahim, S., and L. Smeeth. 2006. Non-communicable diseases in low-income and middle-income countries: A priority or a distraction? *International Journal of Epidemiology* 34(5): 961–966.

Evans, M., et al. 2001. Globalisation, diet, and health: An example from Tonga. *Bulletin of World Health Organisation* 79(1) 856–862.

Fleming, C., and I. Prior. 1981. *Migration, adaptation and health in the Pacific.* Wellington: Wellington Postgraduate Medical Society.

Foliaki, S., and N. Pearce. 2003. Prevention and control of diabetes in Pacific people. *British Medical Journal* 327(23): 437–439.

Fotinatos, N., A. Warmington, T. Walker, and M. Pilbeam. 2007. Estimates for cervical abnormalities in Vanuatu. *Australian and New Zealand Journal of Public Health* 31(6): 571–575.

———. 2008. Trichomonas vaginalis in Vanuatu. *Australian Journal of Rural Health* 16(1): 23–27.

Gold, J. 2008. *Republic of Palau: Second generation HIV and STI surveillance surveys 2005-2007.* Pacific Regional HIV/AIDS Project and Centre for Epidemiology and Population Health Research, Burnet Institute.

Gounder, R. 2006. Kava consumption and its health effects. *Pacific Health Dialog* 13(2): 131–135.

Guillebaud, J., and P. Hayes. 2008. Editorials: Population growth and climate change. *BMJ* 337: a576.

Haberkorn, G. 2000. Fertility and mortality in the Pacific Islands. *Pacific Health Dialog* 2(1): 104–112.

Haberkorn, G., and A. Jorari. 2007. Availability, accessibility and utilization of Pacific Island demographic data—issues of data quality and user relevance. *Asia-Pacific Population Journal* 22(3): 75–93.

Hammar, L. 2007. Epilogue: Homegrown in PNG—rural responses to HIV and AIDS. *Oceania* 77(1) (March): 72–94.

Hayes, G. 2007. The demographic impact of the HIV/AIDS epidemic in Papua New Guinea, 1990-2030. *Asia-Pacific Population Journal* 22(3): 11–30.

Herbert, T. 2007. *Commercial sexual exploitation of children in the Solomon Islands: A report focusing on the presence of the logging industry in a remote region.* Solomon Islands: Christian Care Centre, Church of Melanesia.

Hezel, F. 1981. *Youth drinking in Micronesia. A report on the Working Seminar on Alcohol Use and Abuse among Micronesia Youth.* Kolonia, Ponape, November 12–14, 1981. Truk.

———. 1984. Cultural patterns in Trukese suicide. *Ethnology* 23(3): 193–206.

———. 1987. Truk suicide epidemic and social change. *Human Organization* 46: 283–296.

———. 1989. Suicide and the Micronesian family. *The Contemporary Pacific* 1(1): 43–74.

Hezel, F., and A. Wylie. 1992. Schizophrenia and chronic mental illness in Micronesia: An epidemiological survey. *ISLA: A Journal of Micronesian Studies* 1(2): 329–354.

Howe, K. 1984. *Where the waves fall.* Honolulu: University of Hawai'i Press.

Ichiho, H. M., V. Wong, J. Hedson, and W. J. David. 2004. Cancer in Pohnpei State, Federated States of Micronesia. *Pacific Health Dialog* 11(2): 44–49.

Ichimori, K., and A. Crump. 2005. Pacific collaboration to eliminate lymphatic filariasis. *Trends in Parasitology* 2(10): 441–444.

Igler, D. 2008. Diseased goods: Global exchanges in the eastern Pacific basin, 1770-1850. *American Historical Review* 109(3).

Jenkins, C. 1997. *Youth, sexuality and STD/HIV risk in the Pacific: Results of studies in four island nations.* Paper for the 4th International Congress on AIDS in Asia and the Pacific, Manila, 1–7.

Katz, A. R., N. A. Palafox, D. B. Johnson, S. Yamada, A. C. Ou, and J. S. Minami. 2004. Cancer epidemiology in the freely associated U.S.

Pacific Island jurisdictions: Challenges and methodological issues. *Pacific Health Dialog* 11(2): 84–87.

Kermode, S., and J. Tellei. 2005. A study of the effects of social change on health in the Republic of Palau. *Pacific Health Dialog* 12(1): 14–21.

Khorram, M. B., and J. B. Bruss. 1999. Smoking attributable mortality among the indigenous population of the Mariana Islands. *Pacific Health Dialog* 6(1): 45–51.

Kuartei, S. 2005. Environmental sacredness and health in Palau. *Pacific Health Dialog* 12(1): 92–95.

Kuridrani, L. 2007. Institutionalising traditional medicine in decision making: One woman's perspective. *Fiji Medical Journal* 26(2): 13–18.

Lange, R. 1984. Plagues and pestilence in Polynesia. *Bulletin of History of Medicine* 58: 325–346.

Lewis, N., and M. Rapaport. 1995. In a sea of change: Health transitions in the Pacific. *Health and Place* 1(4): 211–226.

Macpherson, C., and L. Macpherson. 1990. *Samoan medical belief and practice.* Auckland: University of Auckland Press.

McCreanor, T., and R. Nairn. 2002. Tauiwi general practitioners' talk about Maori health: Interpretative repertoires. *Journal of New Zealand Medical Association* 115(1167).

McMichael, A., R. Woodruff, and S. Hales. 2006. Climate change and human health: Present and future risks. *The Lancet* 367: 859–869.

Ministry of Health Fiji. 2008. *UNGASS progress report.* Reporting period: January 1, 2006–December 31, 2007.

Ministry of Health New Zealand. 2008. *Pacific peoples and mental health: A paper for the Pacific Health and Disability Action Plan review.* New Zealand Government.

NAC (National AIDS Council) PNG. 2007. *The 2007 Estimation Report on the HIV Epidemic in Papua New Guinea.*

———. 2008. *UNGASS 2008 Country Progress Report.* Reporting period: January 2006–December 2007.

Novotny, R., et al. 2007. BMI and waist circumference as indicators of health among Samoan women. *Obesity* 15: 1913–1917.

Nutbeam, D. 1996. Healthy islands—a truly ecological model of health promotion. *Health Promotion International* 11: 263–264.

Patz J., et al. 2005. Impact of regional climate change on human health. *Nature* 438: 310–317.

Pearce, N., S. Foliaki, and A. Sporle. 2004. Genetics, race, ethnicity and race. *British Medical Journal* 328: 1070–1072.

Pobutsky A., et al. 2005. Micronesian migrants in Hawaii: Health issues and culturally appropriate, community-based solutions. *Californian Journal of Health Promotion* 3(4): 59–72.

Pollock, N. 1992. *The roots remain.* Institute of Polynesian Studies and University of Hawai'i Press.

Pollock, N., A. AhMu, and A. Carter. 1989. Food and identity: Food preferences and diet of Samoans in Wellington, New Zealand. In *Migrations et identite Actes du Colloque, C.O. R. A. I. L.,* 3–4. Publications de L'Universite Francaise du Pacifique.

Pollock, N., and S. Finau. 1999. Health. In *Pacific Islands: Environment & society,* ed. M. Rapaport, 282. Honolulu: Bess Press.

Puamau, E. S. 2006. Utilisation review of first admission in 2002: St. Giles Psychiatric Hospital, Suva, Fiji. *Pacific Health Dialog* 13(2): 79–87.

Rallu, J. 1990. *Les populations oceaniennes aux XIXe et XXe siècles.* Institut National d'Etudes Demographiques. Travaux et Document, Cahier No. 18.

Rallu, J., and A. Robertson. 2008. *The demographic window of opportunity in Pacific Island countries: The impact of slow fertility transition.* UNESCAP.

Rasanathan, K., and C. F. Tukuitonga. 2007. Tobacco smoking prevalence in Pacific Island countries and territories: A review. *New Zealand Medical Journal* 120(1263).

Ravia, A. A. 1999. Alcohol related injuries in Yap. *Pacific Health Dialog* 6(1): 52–56.

RMI (Republic of Marshall Islands). 2007. *Demographic health survey.* Majuro: Marshall Islands.

RMI Epidemiological Working Group. 2008. *Substance abuse epidemiological profile 2008: Republic of Marshall Islands.* Majuro: Marshall Islands.

Robertson, A. 1990. Introduction. In *Food and nutrition in Fiji: A historical view,* vol. 1, ed. A. Jansen, S. Parkinson, and A. Robertson, 1–23. Suva: University of the South Pacific.

———. 1991. Morbidity and mortality. In *Food and nutrition in Fiji: A historical view,* vol. 2, ed. A. Jansen, S. Parkinson, and A. Robertson. 1–68. Suva: University of the South Pacific.

———. 2007. Current status of sexual and reproductive health: Prospects for achieving the programme of action of the international conference on population and development and the millennium development goals in the Pacific. *Asia-Pacific Population Journal* 3: 31–44.

Robertson, A., and G. Hayes. 2005. *ICPD+10: Progress in the Pacific.* United Nations Population Fund.

Saracci, R. 1997. The world health organization needs to reconsider its definition of health. *British Medical Journal* 314: 1409.

Schaumberg, D., M. Linehan, G. Hawley, J. O'Connor, M. Dreyfuss, and R. Semba. 1995. Vitamin A deficiency in the South Pacific. *Public Health* 109(5): 311–317.

Sladden, T. 2005. Twenty years of HIV surveillance in the Pacific—what do the data tell us and what do we still need to know? *Pacific Health Dialog* 12(2): 23–27.

Smith, B. J., P. Phongsavan, A. Bauman, D. Havea, and T. Chey. 2007. Comparison of tobacco, alcohol and illegal drug usage among school students in three Pacific Island societies. *Drug and Alcohol Dependence* 88(1): 9–18B.

Stephens, C., et al. 2005. Indigenous peoples' health—why are they behind everyone, everywhere? *The Lancet* 366: 10–13.

Stephens, C., J. Porter, and C. Nettleton. 2006. Disappearing, displaced and undervalued: A call for action for indigenous health worldwide. *The Lancet* 367: 2019–2028.

Stott, R., and F. Godlee. 2006. Editorials: What should we do about climate change? Health professionals need to act now, collectively and individually. *British Medical Journal* 333: 983–984.

Strong, K., et al. 2006. Preventing chronic disease: A priority for global health. *International Journal of Epidemiology* 34(5): 492–494.

Taylor, R., and A. Lopez. 2007. Differential mortality among Pacific Island countries and territories. *Asia-Pacific Population Journal* 22(3): 45–58.

Tseng, C. W., G. Omphroy, L. Cruz, C. L. Naval, and R. L. Haddock. 2004. Cancer in the territory of Guam. *Pacific Health Dialog* 11(2): 57–63.

Tseng, C. W., G. Omphroy, J. M. Songsong, and R. Shearer. 2004. Cancer in the Commonwealth of the Northern Marianas. *Pacific Health Dialog* 11(2): 23–29.

Ulijaszek, S. J. 2005. Modernisation, migration and nutritional health of Pacific Island populations. *Environmental Sciences* 12(3): 167–176.

UNFPA (United Nations Population Fund), Seniloli, K. 2002a. *Reproductive health knowledge and services in Samoa.* UNFPA Research Papers in Population and Reproductive Health, no. 1/2002.

———. 2002b. *Reproductive health knowledge and services in Cook Islands.* UNFPA Research Papers in Population and Reproductive Health, no. 4/2002.

———. 2002c. *Reproductive health knowledge and services in Kiribati.*

UNFPA Research Papers in Population and Reproductive Health, no. 5/2002.

———. 2002d. *Reproductive health knowledge and services in Kiribati.* UNFPA Research Papers in Population and Reproductive Health, no. 6/2002.

UNFPA (United Nations Population Fund), Secretariat of the Pacific Community. 2003. *The Samoa family health and safety study.* Noumea: Secretariat of the Pacific Community.

UNICEF Pacific. 2001. The state of health behaviour and lifestyle of Pacific youth: Pohnpei, FSM. Suva, Fiji: UNICEF Pacific Office.

———. 2003. *Republic of the Marshall Islands: A situational analysis of children, women and youth.* Suva, Fiji: UNICEF Pacific Office.

———. 2004. *Federated States of Micronesia: A situational analysis of children, women and youth.* Suva, Fiji: UNICEF Pacific Office.

———. 2005a. *Nauru: A situational analysis of children, women and youth.* Suva, Fiji: UNICEF Pacific Office.

———. 2005b. *Solomon Islands: A situational analysis of children, women and youth.* Suva, Fiji: UNICEF Pacific Office.

———. 2005c. *Vanuatu: A situational analysis of children, women and youth.* Suva, Fiji: UNICEF Pacific Office.

———. 2006a. *Samoa: A situational analysis of children, women and youth.* Suva, Fiji: UNICEF Pacific Office.

———. 2006b. *Commercial sexual exploitation of children (CSEC) and child sexual abuse (CSA) in the Pacific. A Regional Report.* Suva: UNICEF, 1–168.

———. 2008. *The state of Pacific children 2007.* Suva, Fiji: UNICEF Pacific.

WHO (World Health Organization). 1948. Preamble to the Constitution of the World Health Organization as adopted by the International Health Conference, New York, 19–22 June, 1946; signed on 22 July 1946 by the representatives of 61 States. Official Records of the World Health Organization 2: 100.

———. 1995. *Yanuca Island Declaration.* Manila: WHO, Regional Office for the Western Pacific.

———. 2002. *Globalization, diets and non-communicable diseases.* Geneva: World Health Organization, 1–78.

———. 2005a. *The SURF Report 2: Surveillance of chronic disease, risk factors; country level and comparable estimates.* Geneva: World Health Organization, 1–91.

———. 2005b. *Prevalence surveys of sexually transmitted infections among seafarers and women attending ante-natal clinics in Kiribati.* Manila: World Health Organization.

———. 2006. *Second generation surveillance surveys of HIV, other STIs and risk behaviours in six Pacific Island countries 2004–2005. World Health Organisation.* Secretariat of the Pacific Community, University of New South Wales, Global Fund.

Woodward, A., S. Hales, and P. Weinstein. 1998. Climate change and human health in the Asia Pacific region: Who will be most vulnerable? *Climate Research* 11: 31–38.

Yamada, S. 1999. Obesity in Samoans: A practice-based naturalistic inquiry. *Pacific Health Dialog* 6(1): 65–70.

Yamada, S., A. Dodd, T. Soe, T. H. Chen, and K. Bauman. 2004. Diabetes mellitus prevalence in out-patient Marshallese adults on Ebeye Island, Republic of the Marshall Islands. *Hawaii Medical Journal* 63(2): 45–51.

Zimmet, P., G. Dowse, and C. Finch. 1990. The epidemiology and natural history of NIDDM: Lessons from the South Pacific. *Diabetes/Metabolism Review* 6: 91–124.

Education

Ron Crocombe

25

From Closed to Open Learning Systems

Education had much in common throughout the Pacific when humans lived in small self-defending societies. It was largely learning by doing: an informal apprenticeship with parents or other relatives, supplemented by observing and imbibing the beliefs, values, traditions, and practices of the community. Where houses of learning taught skills to larger groups, these were usually families writ large, such as clans or lineages.

Specialized knowledge was often secret. Medicine, magic, religious esoterica, navigation, even techniques for catching octopus or barracuda, were secrets passed on by experts to selected children or other close relatives.

Knowledge was segregated by gender, by profession or craft, and in many societies by seniority or rank. Priests, craftsmen, and other experts trained some of their sons or nephews (but not usually all of either), and midwives, herbalists, and clothmakers their daughters and nieces.

From the 1800s, such closed knowledge systems came in contact with more open systems that emphasized imparting as much knowledge as possible to as many as possible, so much of the content of the closed systems was lost within a few generations. For this reason, among others, global knowledge swamped indigenous knowledge.

Some traditional knowledge that was lost is now being retrieved from the only places it survived—museums, books, archives, and other foreign records. Wallis Islanders abandoned tapa (bark) clothing for more convenient cottons, but in the 1970s they wanted it for new functions such as the tourist market. Nobody knew how to make it, but the anthropologist Edwin Burrows had recorded the techniques and patterns in 1932. His book was sent for and translated and the craft recommenced.

Some confidential knowledge is now being disseminated. Esoteric traditional medical skills are being recorded, published, and promoted as people realize that unless they are, they will be lost, as so much has been.

Mission Schools

Christian missions initiated formal education open to all and not based on kin. They blocked transmission of some traditional knowledge, but opened new windows. Protestants believed the Bible had to be read by each person, so they gave literacy top priority. For Catholics, only the priest could interpret the Bible to the masses. Thus, not until one hundred years after Catholic missionaries settled in Guam did the Spanish governor establish the first school for boys and another for girls, in 1771. Later, however, Catholic missions often did more for education than Protestants.

The first schools in the South Pacific were set up by the London Missionary Society in the Society Islands in the early 1800s. One of them evolved into the Pacific's first theological college. Its first major outreach was of Tahitian converts to the Cook Islands, where in 1839 Takamoa Theological College was founded to train missionaries to serve throughout the Pacific. They and others moved to Samoa, where Malua Theological College, founded in 1844, became the largest institution of higher education in the Islands outside Hawai'i and New Zealand. Both Malua and Takamoa still function. The American Board of Commissioners for Foreign Missions' seminary on Kosrae spread Christianity in eastern Micronesia.

Catholic, Anglican, Methodist, Presbyterian, Seventh-day Adventist, Latter-day Saints (Mormon), Assemblies of God, Pentecostal, and other missions followed, each establishing some schooling. Churches remain a major source of education from kindergarten to college.[1]

An enormous range of small colleges offer theological courses for adults. Most are associated with U.S.-derived churches of the new Christian right and appear to attract disproportionate numbers from more isolated islands with little secular education. This is the reverse of the situation last century, when religious education was regarded as the best.

Education Policies of Colonial Governments

Missions preceded colonial governments in most cases by several generations. After colonial administrations were set up, missions continued to provide most schools, but under government control. Standards were generally low and curricula oriented to religious indoctrination, despite such outstanding exceptions as Tupou College, set up by Dr. J. E. Moulton in Tonga in 1866, and Leulumoega High School in Samoa, set up by the London Missionary Society in 1890. Both still function.

Guam was a partial exception. The U.S. Navy took the island in 1898, deported the Spanish priests, and took over all education. By 1914 Guam had perhaps the best education in the Islands outside Hawai'i and New Zealand. High school began in 1917. The College of Guam, established in 1952, was the first postsecondary college in the Islands.

During the Japanese administration in Micronesia (1914 to 1944), mission schools were closed or marginalized, and military-related schools taught Japanese language, arithmetic, geography, filial piety, and obedience to authority. From 1923 three years of schooling were officially required for indigenous children, plus two years vocational training for the most promising, but those in isolated areas had no schooling. Like other colonial powers, Japan served its own nationals best, with eight years of separate schooling for Japanese children. A trade school opened in Palau in 1926 (Peattie 1988) and some Micronesian children were adopted by Japanese families and educated in Japan.

In the South Pacific, colonial governments slowly increased their role in education, mainly elementary until after World War II. As pressure for improvement mounted, major advances were made in the extent, level, and quality of schooling, at home and abroad.

Enclave Education: Military Bases, Mines, Forestry Camps, Resorts

Some of the best education developed in or near military bases of the United States in Guam and American Samoa, France in Tahiti, and Japan in Micronesia. Some were reserved for families of military personnel, but the military needs good public relations, so education was generally improved in surrounding communities also. Many mining enterprises in Papua New Guinea (PNG) today provide better education than government schools. Forestry camps, by contrast, tend to be high on promises and low on quality of education, as communities throughout West Papua, PNG, and Solomon Islands have found.

Independence and After: High Aspirations but Limited Resources

After independence, aid from the former colonial power usually increased, and other governments seeking influence also contributed. International agencies added a new dimension. Thus the training of most doctors in the Forum Islands countries is paid for by the World Health Organization (WHO) and foreign governments. Opportunities for higher education multiplied, with priority on replacing expatriate officials. They soon faced financial and other constraints, however, and some categories became oversupplied, especially those requiring a generalist college degree.

Because metropolitan powers have more money, staff, and infrastructure, standards rose more in territories of large powers than in independent nations. With average annual incomes around US$1,000 per person, independent Islands nations cannot spare much for education. Incomes in French Polynesia, Guam, Hawai'i, New Caledonia, New Zealand, and the Northern Marianas average ten to twenty times higher, and more resources enable better education. PNG in 2006 spent the world's second lowest amount on tertiary education.

Students from territories and associated states enjoy special rights in the metropolitan power. Those from Guam, American Samoa, and Northern Marianas have free access to U.S. institutions, scholarships, and other privileges; those from French Polynesia, New Caledonia, and Wallis and Futuna have similar privileges in France, as do Rapanui in Chile, Norfolk Islanders and the Torres Strait Islanders in Australia, and Tokelauans in New Zealand. Citizens of associated states (Federated States of Micronesia [FSM], the Marshall Islands, and Palau to the United States; the Cook Islands and Niue to New Zealand) have similar rights.

By contrast, students in independent nations seeking courses they cannot get at home need visas that cost time and money and are not necessarily granted. Also, most countries charge higher student fees for noncitizens.

Families who can afford it send their children abroad or to local private schools with better teachers and facilities, or they provide computers, books, travel, and other learning aids.

Mission schools a hundred years ago aimed to provide a fulfilling and useful rural education, but they failed for the same reason as educational planners doing the same thing today. It has always been popular to condemn rural schools as academic and urban-oriented, but teachers become models for the students. That model is to be paid a salary, go away for training, live in better-than-average housing, have better-than-average facilities, and know about the world beyond the village.

Good education is hard to attain in low-income nations. In most countries of Melanesia, many children receive no schooling (Mosley 1992). In Polynesia and Micronesia, education is almost universal, but it varies in quality and is particularly problematic on smaller, more isolated islands (Douglas 1994).

Commitment, Integrity, and Quality Are as Vital as Money

Money is not the only determinant of quality and quantity of education. Outstanding examples of high-quality education at low cost give inspiration and hope. In Micronesia, Catholics ran Xavier College and the Pohnpei Agriculture and Technical School (PATS), for students of all denominations. Only about 10 percent of Micronesians studied there, but their graduates include a high proportion of outstanding achievers in government and business.

The Seventh-day Adventist Church in FSM runs primary schools, staffed largely by volunteers from the United States, Canada, and Europe, that achieve academic levels two to three years ahead of government schools (on independent Stanford tests). Yet the Catholic and Seventh-day Adventist schools cost less than government schools at equivalent levels. A key issue is attracting staff with special patterns of motivation—for some this is religious, but for others it rests on other motivations.[2]

The family contribution is usually large. The Fiji government pays all teachers' salaries, but voluntary committees operate more than 90 percent of schools and vocational training centers and some teachers colleges. Parents contribute some cash and help with maintenance and equipment. The private input is increasing throughout the region. New Zealand in 1989 devolved funding, staff appointments, assessment, management, and maintenance from the government to 2,400 communities and reduced the Department of

Education from 2,500 staff members to 500. Several Islands nations drew on the New Zealand experience. Evaluations of that experience vary, but a specialist in the field says extensive devolution has been beneficial where the education system is highly professional and parents highly motivated. It is seldom successful where money, skill, and motivation are in short supply (Lex MacDonald, personal communication).

In the Marshall Islands in 1990, local governments on several atolls contracted Catholic sisters, the Seventh-day Adventist Church, or the Baha'i faith to operate their schools, and the government minister of education said the results were better. In PNG, Divine Word University and Pacific Adventist University offer bachelor's degrees in business studies, education, and other fields. Their graduates are in greater demand by business and government than those of government universities that cost several times more per student. As with schools that produce excellence, they draw their staff from many countries and can therefore select for higher skill and motivation than by recruiting from a small national pool. If excellence is a goal, localization on a small population base is inimical to it. But political pressures from staff in many institutions (seldom from students), trade unions, and governments result in priority to nationality over quality.

Regional institutions give priority in principle to staff of all member countries, but in practice the leverage favors nationals of the host country. Foreign governments aid less effective government institutions rather than higher-quality private ones—presumably because the aid aims to court the receiving governments rather than provide the best education for students and the nation. This is not to suggest that government education systems do not get quality staff, but some systems attract more than others, and money is far from the only factor determining who produces the best.

The success of church-based private schools refutes simplistic assumptions about "economies of scale" that are common among planners in Islands governments, donor governments, and international agencies. All the private institutions mentioned above are smaller, yet the unit cost is lower and quality higher.

Quality is also influenced by priorities in the home and community. In a rural area of PNG, "parents objected to a [school] fee increase from 5 to 7 kina. Yet the same parents . . . unthinkingly spend 20 kina on a carton of beer and hundreds on gambling" (Monsell-Davis 1993).

Quality and commitment are as important for students as they are for teachers. Too often it is assumed that persons who are not working effectively should be sent to take a course to impart a technical skill or information. But courses are a waste of time if students do not have integrity and motivation.

A UNDP conference in 1994 learned that islanders in Australian, New Zealand, and U.S. universities had a failure rate of 40 percent, whereas Asians in the same institutions had a failure rate of 2 percent. This is serious, as those sent abroad are better than average students, and almost all islanders had their secondary education in English, whereas most Asians did not. The vast difference seems to relate to the lower average quality of Islands educational institutions and to Islands students spending fewer hours studying. Ethnic Asian students from the Islands have a better record.

Education at Home: National and Territorial Institutions

Higher education began with theological colleges; much later came government and mission colleges for teachers and nurses. After World War II (and in a few cases before) the range exploded with colleges for agriculture, aviation, commerce, fisheries, forestry, marine, paramedical, police, and other topics.

Starting as a two-year college in 1952, the College of Guam became the University of Guam in 1968. In 1977, a separate College of Guam was established, offering two-year associate degrees and short courses. In addition, all citizens of Guam have free access to other U.S. institutions, and many go to the mainland. Levels of education on Guam, Saipan, and Hawai'i, and in the French territories, are higher than on independent Islands nations.

One argument for national institutions is that curricula will reflect national needs. What constitutes national needs, however, is much debated, and national institutions in small countries are more vulnerable to parochial politics than they are in larger countries, where multiple sources of information reduce the political significance of any one. The most important national need may be for quality and integrity in education, wherever it is obtained.

Nonformal Education

Voluntary and nongovernment organizations (NGOs) provide valuable training, usually short and specialized, in productive skills, small business management, community needs, parenting, family budgeting, youth development, first aid, and a host of other topics. Some countries have better employment prospects, but only one in five school leavers in Fiji is expected to get paid work, and one in twenty-five in PNG. In this context, nonformal education is often cheaper and more effective (Cole 1996).

Studies of rural training institutions in the region show that short courses, extension work, and block release (with formal study interspersed with time on the farm, and with outreach) are more effective than long-term institutionalized training. Training is most effective with mature, motivated trainees and trainers, and the latter tend to be more effective when working with voluntary agencies than with governments.[3]

Regionalism: The Host Eats Most of the Other People's Cake

More than thirty regional educational institutions exist: universities; professional, technical, and theological colleges; examinations boards; institutions for training youth leaders; community workers; broadcasting, police, and various others. All regional institutions have been set up on the initiative and at least partly at the expense of foreign donors—governmental, religious, or philanthropic. None covers the whole Islands region.

Regional education began in the theological colleges. Malua College in Samoa took students from both Samoas, Niue, Tokelau, Tuvalu, and Kiribati in the 1800s and early 1900s, and some from Melanesia. It has almost none from outside Samoa today—partly because Malua was so Samoa-centered that each country developed its own institution. American Samoa reluctantly established its own institution because Samoa dominated Malua despite heavy funding from American Samoa.

Theological students today study at national, regional, and international colleges in the Pacific and abroad. Catholic priests train in national seminaries, Pacific Regional Seminary in Fiji, Holy Spirit Seminary in PNG, and in metropolitan countries. Most Protestant churches have national theological colleges. Pacific Theological College (set up in Suva in 1966 with funds from the World Council of Churches and others) has good standards but depends on diminishing foreign funds. Seventh-day Adventist pastors are trained at the Pacific Adventist University in PNG. Pacific Bible College (Assemblies of God) and Ambassador College of Evangelism, both in Fiji, take students from several countries. University of the Nations in Hawai'i (Youth with a Mission) set up a campus in Tonga in 1994 for students of this region and beyond. Many islanders study theology in the United States, New Zealand, Australia, Europe, or the Philippines.

The first nonchurch regional college was the Central Medical School, initiated in 1928 by the Rockefeller Foundation to serve the Islands region. Rockefeller and the British, New Zealand, and Islands governments paid running costs. It provided equitably for participating countries until it was taken over by the government of Fiji as the Fiji School of Medicine. Aid agencies continued to contribute heavily to costs, equipment, staffing, and training as it was ostensibly "regional," but numbers accepted from other countries became nominal.[4]

The Community College of Micronesia, founded in 1970, offered two-year associate degrees, with graduates able to complete a bachelor's degree in U.S. universities. This and other institutions came together in 1978 as the College of Micronesia (COM). Tension arose because Pohnpei benefited disproportionately in student numbers, staffing, and other criteria. The regional college held together while the United States paid for it on the condition that it remain unified. Once the districts separated into countries in 1986, they preferred national solutions, and the regional system collapsed.

When Fiji was the headquarters of the British Empire in the Pacific, some students were sent from other British colonies to Queen Victoria School and other institutions in Fiji that were subsidized by Britain for all its colonies. One of these institutions, the Derrick Technical Institute, was taken over by the government of Fiji as the Fiji Institute of Technology, and jobs and staff training were reserved for Fiji citizens. By 1996 more than 98 percent of the students were from Fiji. This retarded technical education in other countries, so technicians from Fiji are employed all over the Pacific, and all other countries are short.

The first major intergovernmental educational exercise was a one-year course for women community development workers. Begun by the South Pacific Commission (SPC) in 1965, it trains one or two from each country each year. It has given about 1,200 women skills and the experience of living together as a multinational family. SPC has since provided short courses in fisheries, primary health care, statistics, etc.

UPNG and the PNG University of Technology began in 1966. They accept students from Solomon Islands and Vanuatu, and a few from beyond. PNG's law and order problems reduced their attractiveness to external scholars.

Sir Michael Somare, PNG's longest-serving prime minister and previously a staunch supporter of the university, said in the UPNG graduation address that "[t]he public is outraged at the number of students and teachers being killed on the campus and students being intimidated against doing studies, and lecturers lives being threatened to make them award degrees to non-performers" (*Uni Tavur,* March 22, 1996). He also noted that most university staff members were from India, Africa, or other places with which PNG had little trade, aid, political, media, or other relations, and he did not see their countries as models.

The largest regional educational entity is the University of the South Pacific (USP), set up in 1968 by the withdrawing colonial powers to provide for the eleven British and New Zealand territories (the Cook Islands, Fiji, Kiribati, Nauru, Niue, Samoa, Solomon Islands, Tokelau, Tonga, Tuvalu, and Vanuatu). The Marshall Islands joined in 1992. PNG, West Papua, and French and U.S. territories and associated states have their own university systems. In addition to USP there is a private University of Fiji and a government Fiji University of Science and Technology.

USP declares regularly that it cannot maintain standards with reducing ratios of staff and funds per student. The ratio of students to staff fell to 25 to 1 in 1996 from 15 to 1 four years earlier. Ratios have fallen further since, and are due for further falls due to financial constraints.

The hope that USP would provide equitably for the twelve countries did not materialize. The main campus is in Fiji, and Fiji interests have ensured that Fiji benefits at the expense of the other eleven countries—even though all the buildings in Fiji (but in many cases not those in other countries), most research, staff training, books and equipment, and a share of all salaries and running costs have always come from regional aid intended to serve all countries equitably. Of the scholarships given to junior staff for advanced study abroad, 85 percent have been given to Fiji citizens, mainly nonindigenous. Most who have equivalent prospects elsewhere emigrate.

Multinational agencies worldwide favor other multinational institutions, and donor governments see it in their political interest to centralize. It is administratively easier for them too, and some consider it cost-effective (though I doubt this). Donors request, largely cosmetically, that benefits of their aid be spread. The central response is to welcome this in principle but subvert it in practice. For example, donations will ostensibly be used for extension teaching, but it will not be pointed out that more than 90 percent of regional staff dealing with extension courses are Fiji citizens or that participation by people of other countries is nominal. Token beneficiaries are treated well, for their connivance or passivity is needed.

Most students from countries other than Fiji have been on scholarships that the foreign donors will not allow to be held elsewhere. Without that pressure, the institution would have been forced to treat the others equitably or ceased any significant regional role long ago.

Retention within the region after graduation is often cited as a reason for regional over metropolitan education, but little evidence supports this. Retention correlates with ethnicity more than with the place of education, with emigration much lower among indigenous than nonindigenous people. Few Fijians emigrate, but every Fiji Indian with access abroad does so. Only a small percentage of students from PNG, Solomon Islands, Vanuatu, Kiribati, or Nauru who have studied in metropolitan countries have stayed there. Tongans and Samoans, on the other hand, in many cases try to emigrate wherever there is an opportunity, irrespective of where they studied.

The only country for which I have precise data is the Cook Islands (using data compiled by the director of the USP center to 1986). It shows little difference in emigration between those educated at USP and those educated in metropolitan universities. Of USP graduates, 77 percent remained and 23 percent were in metropolitan countries. Of graduates from metropolitan universities, 73 percent worked in the Islands and 27 percent abroad. The Cook Islands is an important test case, because Cook Islanders have free access to New Zealand and Australia. Whereas emigration by graduates averaged 24 percent, that by nongraduates was much higher; 90 percent of Cook Islanders live abroad. There are more opportunities per capita to be a minister, head of a department, director, or other leading citizen in a small population than in a large one (and nationalism is an elite ideology for these reasons). The opposite applies to the unskilled, as wages are higher in industrialized countries. Fran Hezel tells me the same trends are apparent in Micronesia. The reason for higher graduate emigration from countries without free access is that recipient countries admit more graduates.

It is also a test case on quality. This is difficult to measure, but one indicator is the success of students. For the Cook Islands (again the only country for which I have measured data) in 2007, of the seven MPs with university degrees, only two got their degrees from USP, despite its having more resident graduates. No USP graduate had achieved head of a government instrumentality by 1998 except for one who after attaining a degree at USP got an MA in the United States and worked for years in Australia. Many graduates from metropolitan universities have been appointed at that level, including many at the same age levels as USP graduates. In 2007 only four such leaders were USP graduates but ten were graduates from elsewhere. The assumption that a regional university education is better suited to national needs than a metropolitan university education is thus probably false. Tonga's former minister for education (Dr. Kavaliku) advised me that Tonga's experience is similar, and an evaluation of externally financed higher education in Samoa identified the same problem.

Quality of staff depends on the effective size of the pool from which they are hired, salaries and conditions offered, academic freedom, and other factors. On these criteria, USP is better placed than most universities in the independent Pacific, but less well placed than metropolitan universities or universities in the United States or French Pacific with vastly larger pools to draw from. A disadvantage of the last two, however, is that they restrict recruitment to their own nationals more than USP or Australasian universities do.

Financial and other benefits, whether from member countries or from aid donors, pour overwhelmingly into the Fiji economy. The Fiji government pays an extra sum in nominal recognition of this inequity, but the income derived by Fiji from the university (in direct and indirect taxes and other benefits) is about the same as the total it pays for all its students there. The other countries pay but receive no economic benefits.

USP has been cost-effective because of deteriorating staff/student ratios and because real costs are much higher than revealed costs due to foreign aid for buildings, staff, equipment, staff training, research, and travel. Private universities in the region are less expensive still. The Pacific Adventist University and Divine Word University in PNG have much lower costs than the PNG government universities or USP, partly because of a different pattern of staff motivation from secular universities and partly because they require work input from students.

As with quality (to the extent quality correlates with cost), much depends on whether the external donors see it to their advantage to pay their money to regional or national institutions. Because the former colonial powers initiated and designed USP, paid for all its buildings and material assets, still pay part of its staff and other costs, and see it as serving their long-term political interest of holding the Pacific in a group they can more conveniently deal with, they will not allow their present allocations for university education to be used nationally (though most countries would prefer to) and will continue to force university education to be mainly Fiji-centered and for Fiji's benefit.

Curriculum is another debated issue. The goal of designing a curriculum suited to the countries and cultures of the region is compromised by the fact that few teaching staff, including citizens of a member country, belong to the indigenous majority, or to any but one of the twelve countries officially involved. Social science curricula have been determined more by staff preferences for competing theories from Europe and America than by Pacific realities.

Many unacknowledged processes ensure Fiji's dominance. Preference for citizens of "the region" in staff appointments gives overwhelming advantage to the host country, as applicants from other member countries require work permits, which are for a maximum of three years. Fiji seldom refuses work permits but has often achieved the same goal by not granting them and endlessly "considering" them. Permits can be revoked without explanation, spouses and children are not generally allowed to work, and there is a range of other overt and covert disincentives.

The official claim that it advertises worldwide and selects the best is not the practice. When a science lectureship was advertised for the extension center in one USP member country, a part Polynesian applicant had a first-class PhD, excellent publications, an award-winning science teaching film, several years of university teaching experience specializing in basic university science to Maori and Pacific students, and excellent references. Her appointment was recommended unanimously by the extension center staff and advisory committee. But she was rejected by Fiji decision makers, and a Fiji citizen with a bachelor's degree, no experience as a university lecturer, and no publications was appointed instead. The case is far from unique. These and other unofficial processes ensure unequal representation.

More than 70 percent of academic posts held by citizens of the member countries are held by Fiji citizens, mainly Indian, but the percentage on the main campus is higher. Most other regional staff are in subsidiary, nonteaching roles, especially in extension centers, where their tutoring is controlled by staff on the main campus. As many expatriate staff are short-term and not interested in (or are intimidated away from) university politics, and as most citizens of other member countries are outside Fiji, decision making rests overwhelmingly with Fiji staff.

Fiji had 43 percent of the population of the twelve-country university region in 2004, but 70 percent of the 10,179 full-time students.

These and other discriminatory processes caused gross disparity between Fiji and other member countries in educated manpower and employment in "regional" posts and international organizations that are concentrated in Fiji and subject to Fiji influence. "Regional" staff of Fiji-based institutions visiting other countries to provide courses, consultancies, and services are overwhelmingly Fiji citizens. This is not, as is often claimed, because Fiji had more students ready for university education when the university began. Lord Morris' survey when the university was founded showed that the highest proportions of students ready to enter higher education were from the Cook Islands, Niue, Samoa, and Tonga. Systematic manipulation has transferred the advantages to Fiji. Nor is it because others are not available. I have witnessed many instances where Fiji personnel have been sent by regional agencies even though better-qualified and more appropriate local nationals were available. This problem is not apparent with regional organizations based elsewhere, nor in church-related institutions.

International experience is valuable in today's interactive world. Having some education outside one's national milieu is beneficial. Such experience is greater at a regional than a national university, though it could be achieved by exchanges between national universities, particularly if they specialize. A regional university also increases knowledge and awareness of the region. Nevertheless, if going outside their own country, most students, parents, and governments prefer metropolitan universities to any within the region, whether regional or national. Islanders know the value of experience with the industrialized countries with which they deal much more (e.g., trade within the region is less than 2 percent) and which are the main sources of information, resources, opportunities, and influence.

Why have more countries not set up their own institutions? The main reason is that the power to set up them up lay in donor capital that initiated and financed them. Once they realized they were being exploited by the "regional" host, most member countries of USP tried in the 1980s to set up national institutions or to send their students elsewhere. Donors opposed it and would not allow the countries concerned to decide how to allocate the funds donors provide for higher education for each country. Regional higher education is more a product of major powers with interests in the region than of independent Islands nations.

The potential for some kinds of higher education on a regional basis was higher in this region than most places. Nevertheless, in forty years of experiments with various institutions, the same problem of disproportionate benefit to the host country at the cost of the rest is more serious today than before, despite repeated assurances that it is being overcome. Given the vested interests of donors, the host government, and most university staff, it is unlikely to change (Crocombe and Meleisea 1988).

Regional institutions are no less vulnerable to political influence than national ones. Fiji national politics has always impacted heavily on USP, more since Fiji's military coups of 1987, 2000, and 2006, and 1994, when harassment by Fiji students forced almost all students from Solomon Islands, Vanuatu, and PNG to flee to their own countries. Many Pacific Rim donor countries still see it

as in their geopolitical interest to promote Fiji-based regional over equitable regional, national, or international solutions. Solomon Islands, Vanuatu, and Kiribati students have fled UPNG due to discrimination there. While national and ethnic tensions are endemic at USP, tribal and provincial conflicts are serious at UPNG, with more killing, wounding, and intimidation on the campus than is publicly revealed.

The University of Guam accepts some students from other parts of Micronesia, but most Micronesians prefer universities in the mainland United States if they can find funds. PNG has four government universities and three private (all church-based). Samoa has the National University of Samoa, Tahiti has L'Université de la Polynésie Francaise, and New Caledonia has L'Université de la Nouvelle-Calédonie. In addition there are many tertiary colleges throughout the region.

Pacific Islanders use some of the sixteen universities in Hawai'i, but several times more islanders study in New Zealand. Distance learning from metropolitan universities is another major source of education. Many national theological colleges offer bachelor's and/or master's degrees.

The most recent development in higher education is the Australia Pacific Technical Training College. The greatest need for that is in PNG, which has 70 percent of the region's population, but it will be centered in Fiji to suit Australia's geopolitical interests. Another proposal is for a regional nursing college—mainly to enable islanders to get skilled work abroad.

As anywhere, it is difficult to retain the best-educated workers if they can earn much more abroad. As a senior Islands official complained to me recently, the most talented people work for aid agencies, or on aid projects, or for the regional or international bureaucracy, or are away for training, all of which promise higher rewards.

Education in Metropolitan Countries

Four Hawaiians were at a mission school in the United States in 1819 (Garrett 1988: 35), and the London Missionary Society sent a few Cook Islander, Samoan, and Tahitian scholars to England in the mid-1800s. In the 1800s some islanders were sent to Rome to train as priests, but that failed.

Governments were slow to act. The British policy of indirect rule through local chiefs led to Ratu (later Sir) Lala Sukuna of Fiji studying at Oxford University from 1913. From 1919 the United States financed some Guamanians to study on the mainland. New Zealand in the 1920s began taking some Cook Islands, Niue, and Samoa high school children. Some Micronesians went to middle schools in Japan in the 1930s.

After World War II, education abroad escalated, mainly financed by colonial governments in response to changes in the climate of world opinion. They sent thousands of Papua New Guineans and Nauruans to Australia; Samoans, Cook Islanders, Niueans, and Tokelauans to New Zealand; those from British colonies to New Zealand or Britain; Micronesians to the United States; those from French colonies to France; Easter Islanders to Chile; and West Papuans to Jakarta.

Although the trend was expected to slow down after independence and the establishment of more facilities in the Islands, the reverse happened. Demand for overseas education remains high. Former colonial powers and other interested governments and organizations continue to supply scholarships.[5]

The 1990s saw a growing diversity of sources, kinds, and locations of international education. Competition is intense. More than two thousand islanders applied for thirty-four scholarships for advanced studies at Australian universities in 1994. When high school and college students in FSM were asked their views, only 24 percent wanted to study anywhere in the Islands. The others wanted the United States or other major countries (Douglas 1994: 46). Few Islands institutions can yet provide the diversity or quality of education they can get on the Pacific Rim.

Private action to send students abroad before World War II was mainly by European and part European settlers and by Japanese in Micronesia. Today many children of indigenous and Asian business and professional people also study abroad, those from north of the equator in the United States and some in the Philippines, Japan, China, or Taiwan, and those from the South Pacific mainly in Australia or New Zealand and recently Asia. Students from Tahiti and New Caledonia go to France, but increasingly also to the United States, Australia, or New Zealand. China began in 2007 to offer two thousand scholarships to Pacific Islanders, and Taiwan and Japan increased their offers to match.

Scholarships from the newer churches are growing. Brigham Young University (a Mormon facility) has taught nearly four thousand islanders, not including those who live in the United States. University of the Nations, also in Hawai'i, and church-related colleges in New Zealand and Australia have more students from the Islands than ever. More families are sending their children abroad privately.[6]

In 1998, Central Queensland University opened a campus in Fiji for students from Asia, to be taught mainly by staff flying from Australia to present short, intensive sessions interspersed with distance studies with local tutors. Fiji's coups, Suva's crime, and the university's wavering academic standards left it with a fraction of the number it hoped to attract.

Learning at a Distance: The Field of Fastest Growth

Everywhere in the world, distance learning is growing faster than conventional systems. More than fifty thousand Pacific Islanders are currently enrolled in a course of distance learning. The biggest system is the PNG College of Distance Education, set up in 1953. It provides secondary-level courses to fifteen thousand adults throughout the nation. Some courses (e.g., business studies) are complete in themselves, while others prepare students for tertiary studies. The paucity of educational facilities in rural areas and even many towns make distance teaching vital.

The two largest university distance systems are UPNG and USP. Smaller systems include the Solomon Islands Distance Education Network, which links provincial centers with the College of Higher Education via a teleconference network. The Pacific Adventist University offers courses throughout the region, including French and American territories, but numbers are small. USP, UPNG, UOG, and other institutions offer regular summer schools.

Probably most distance education is religious, mainly by U.S.-derived churches of the new Christian right. Every Home for Christ claimed 7,246 students in correspondence courses in 1993 (Ernst 1994: 91); the Pacific Islands Bible School in American Samoa claims more than 5,000 students from central Polynesia and has another school in Saipan. At least two New Zealand colleges claim similar numbers from the Islands. These are a few of many religious organizations offering distance courses. Some now teach accounting, business studies, management, computing, and other topics as well as religious studies.

Monopolies in education are being challenged worldwide, and increasing numbers of Pacific students are using international distance systems.

Academic staff everywhere tend to give preference to students on campus over those at a distance. Students on campus give teachers the psychological stimulus of their presence. But this problem can be overcome, for graduates of the Open University in UK, which is entirely by distance, are rated more highly by employers than those of any conventional university.

Private firms also train staff by distance. Staff members of Air New Zealand take courses on their office computers in the Cook Islands, Fiji, New Caledonia, Samoa, Tahiti, and Tonga. They log on to the training program in Auckland, take the courses, receive automatic error correction, and sit for examinations without a spoken word or a piece of paper.

The Internet is becoming an important source of education, especially for higher-income homes in the Islands. Some institutions cooperate to present distance courses from abroad. Two men in Rarotonga got an MA in astronomy with an Australian university. Such examples are multiplying (Crocombe 1999).

Media play a growing role in public education. It is generally financed by advertising (most of that teaching de-ethicized consumerism). Television stations play children's educational material daily and some cultural and adult education programs, almost all of foreign origin. Radio is useful in adult education—especially in remote areas, as are newspapers in urban communities. Specialized pamphlets and newssheets continue to multiply.

This escalating process of self-learning is enhanced by the growing market in imported materials that supplement or replace formal courses—books, cassette tapes, video, film, and CD-ROM. The Pacific World Directory in Micronesia advertised more than a hundred books, each providing step-by-step instructions on how to set up a particular kind of business—from restaurants and laundries to transport and security services. In New Caledonia and French Polynesia one can buy on CD-ROM every course—from kindergarten to university—as taught in the schools and universities. Distance learning offers great hope, but interaction with a known teacher helps learning, and motivation is harder to maintain when studying alone.

Women: The Rapid Growth of Female Student Numbers

Formal education used to be primarily for males—and more so the higher the level. This is no longer the case in most of Polynesia and Micronesia, but it is in Melanesia. In PNG, 15 percent of boys reach secondary school, but only 10 percent of girls.[7]

The proportion of women in universities in French Polynesia, Guam, Hawai'i, and New Zealand has long exceeded 50 percent (as it does in Europe, the United States, and Japan). The proportion of female students at USP has grown from every country. The proportion declines as one moves west across the Pacific, but is growing everywhere. In PNG it was below 20 percent.[8]

Table 25.1

Percentage of Female Dtudents at USP by Country

Country	1985	1995	2001	2006
Cook Is	60	62	58	73
Fiji	41	44	50	56
Kiribati	47	50	55	56
Marshall Is	0	33	60	54
Nauru	0	37	64	69
Niue	11	62	70	75
Samoa	32	55	56	61
Solomon Is	18	20	25	32
Tokelau	20	56	50	63
Tonga	35	46	46	60
Tuvalu	48	41	53	60
Vanuatu	19	30	35	45

Female students often do better academically than male students. In the Cook Islands high schools, girls have had better average grades than boys since the 1980s.[9] Why? International media and new patterns of employment in which women hold jobs formerly seen as the prerogative of men make boys see their superiority threatened. An educational psychologist (Lex MacDonald) tells me of evidence to indicate that the shift is also associated with women now teaching at all levels, leaving boys without role models. They tend to react by stressing traditional male roles through aggressive sports, alcohol, drugs, and pseudo-rebellion.

As teachers and educational administrators, women are overrepresented at lower levels and underrepresented at higher levels.

Resistance to gender equality is highest in theological colleges. Reverend Fei Taule'ale'ausumai explained in 1999 how, after a long struggle, women were allowed to take courses at Malua, the largest theological college in Samoa. But a woman topped the classes, so the rules were changed so that both sexes could study the courses, but only men could sit for exams!

Curriculum: Local, National, Regional, and Universal

It is not a question of which curriculum, but of what mix of each. Culture is a more debated issue than in most industrialized countries. PNG has more than eight hundred indigenous languages, Vanuatu more than one hundred. Each language is associated with some differences of culture. Debate is constant on how much local culture, how much national culture, and how much other countries' cultures can be integrated into a curriculum with an ever-increasing range of other topics that students and parents demand.

Unaisi Nabobo-Baba (2007) of Fiji, Konai Helu-Thaman (2000), and Ana Taufe'theulungaki (2001), all highly experienced educators, make a strong case for learning through indigenous means of acquiring and transmitting knowledge. The rejection of colonial models is appropriate, but with current and future information flows and cultural influences coming from vastly more diverse sources, too much reliance on past forms of learning could also be a disadvantage.

Thaman (1997) has suggested ways to incorporate cultural elements in Pacific education. Achieving an acceptable balance between external educational models and indigenous cultures is a widespread goal, but local cultures receive more emphasis in rhetoric than in reality. More important than any existing model might be prioritizing analytical thinking, creative problem solving, and ethical action.

The indigenous component is constrained by a lack of resources to prepare the necessary books, films, and other materials. For tiny populations, this is an enormous expense. Vastly more is available on big countries and global issues, at lower cost owing to the larger market. Moreover, many students are keener to learn about the outside world and international knowledge than about their traditional cultures.

Pacific societies were subsistence-based, giving a better background for social studies or biology than mathematics or physics. Due to limited finance, staff, equipment, and interest, the sciences have not had priority. Universities were set up around the time of independence and the new governments gave priority to training administrators, teachers, accountants, and others to take over from expatriates. Foreign scientists and technologists are less of a threat to local power than foreign managers, so some political leaders prefer foreigners who depend on them, are kept out of the political process, and are easier to terminate for nonperformance or noncompliance.

Students too tended to see politicians and officials as the leading models who got limelight, power, pay, and perks. But now that the market for liberal arts graduates is saturated and governments are shrinking due to financial constraints, students take science, technology, and commerce more seriously.

Values are also an issue—with indigenous traditions, English-derived traditions, Christianity, capitalism, consumerism, and secular modern values being the main contenders for emphasis. Government-run universities and colleges give little consideration to ethics, which is basic to personal development. As a result, graduates understand their own rights and privileges better than their obligations to others. As Ketudat (1990: 25), a senior minister in the Thai government, observed, educational institutions must "create people who are both ethical and expert." Little consideration is given to what package of values may best equip students for life in the twenty-first century. Palau's curriculum gives "more stress to the value of work (self-sufficiency) and community service as an appropriate yardstick for achievement" (Eastly 1994: 58). How widely such principles are applied is hard to know, for formal education "does little to help them cope with their problems concerning love/honesty/self-respect/identity. We are too busy domesticating them."

Directions in the New Millennium

It is becoming accepted that too big a share of educational funds is spent on higher education for a few, and that better results would come from more emphasis on basic education and more integrating of education and work. Congressman Robert Underwood of Guam, himself Chamorro and a professional educator, said, "Too much higher education is paid baby-sitting for young adults, an escape from work" (personal communication, September 24, 1994). Part-time higher education spreads costs and opportunities more equitably.

Public and private sources of learning continue to grow in the Islands and the world. Most growth is in distance learning from many sources, and from books, DVDs, and Internet contacts.

Schools impart knowledge and develop personalities, but they also mobilize support for political and religious ideologies. Church schools reinforced their denominations, colonial government schools supported the colonial power, national governments used them for "nation building"—a formidable task in the multilanguage countries of Melanesia and multiracial countries like Fiji. Schools are also used in Tonga, Fiji, the Marshall Islands, and some other countries to legitimate and buttress aristocratic elites. In the Cook Islands, Vanuatu, and elsewhere, the education system has at times been used to reinforce the ruling political party. Now that the power of national governments is fading, indoctrination in consumerism grows as children are instructed to promote Coca-Cola, on which they depend for sports equipment, or banks that give them computers, or other sponsors.

Belonging to larger systems has benefits. One is the regular inspection by independent judges, with sanctions for the loss of accreditation if the institution does not meet the standards of the hundreds of institutions in that system. The University of Guam has been required to lift its standards more than once because it belongs to a North American accreditation system that forced it to upgrade facilities and faculty. Likewise, educational institutions in the French Pacific are part of a system serving sixty million people, providing a benchmark that must be maintained.

Accreditation need not be within a nation. The College of Micronesia, owned by the FSM government, joined a North American accreditation system that has lifted standards higher than they would be without it. Most students want their institutions and qualifications to meet internationally recognized standards.

As the level of education increases, so does the level of dependence on foreign money, staff, equipment, teaching materials, and ideas. That sounds bad. But if we change the word "foreign" to "international" or "global," and add appropriate local components, it seems to be the direction the world is going, not only the Pacific. New Zealand, with universities for 130 years, still appoints immigrants to 69 percents of university posts. It is a two-way process. Pacific Islanders are achieving senior academic posts in Pacific Rim universities, many of which also serve Pacific Islands students.

Vocational education is receiving more prominence. A Pacific-wide survey showed that the top priority was teacher training, the second small business, and third tourism/hospitality (Luteru and Pongi 1997: 8). Ten Pacific Islands nations and several territories operate marine training schools, some for service in their own waters, but most to help their people find work abroad. Kiribati's German-subsidized school prepares men to work on German merchant ships, and a Japanese-subsidized one trains men for Japanese tuna boats. Most countries train officers, engineers, and other specialists.

Illiteracy remains a problem, much of it hidden. Given the financial and other constraints, it is likely to be overcome only if voluntary groups (such as women's groups, church organizations, and youth movements), as well as business firms, are mobilized along with the media.

The World Bank coined the term "Pacific Paradox" to describe the fact that aid per person is higher in this region than anywhere else in the world, but growth is among the lowest. An important factor seems to have been that educational funds were used overwhelmingly to take the most promising young people in their most active and enterprising years (fifteen to twenty-four) and make them full-time dependents on scholarships at home or abroad. After years of training in total dependency, they were absorbed in nonproductive bureaucracies. It should be no surprise that economic growth stagnated or that they used their bureaucratic power to skew what resources there were in their favor, worsening the average lot of the rest of the population.

The Pacific is not alone in having lost faith in bureaucratic monopolies as sources of salvation. Existing education is not a good preparation for the challenges of today or tomorrow; as technologies evolve at great speed, philosophies change more slowly, and education systems more slowly still.

Higher education has been oriented too much to staffing the public service and churches, and too little to productivity, innovation, and action. Competition has been limited in the former two, and posts have in many cases been obtained and retained on criteria other than effectiveness. Despite acceptance of the ideology that learning should be continuous throughout life, resources remain concentrated on institutional learning as the continuation of school. There is a good case for children to start work when they finish high school and to integrate work with study from then on— if not earlier. The common expectation is that learning is for those who are lucky and receive a scholarship (whether due to talent or connections) for full-time study.

Research: Mostly Foreign, Military, and Commercial

Research is expensive. Results come slowly, so countries with little money give it low priority. On the other hand, massive funds are spent on weapons research. The United States experimented with atomic and nuclear bombs in Bikini, Enewetak, Kiritimati, and Malden, and still tests intercontinental ballistic missiles at Kwajalein Missile Range (the largest research institution in the region), which also has a role in Star Wars weapons research. France tested at Moruroa and Fangataufa until 1996. Britain tested at Kiritimati and Malden in the 1950s. The USSR had a fleet of research vessels in the region, much of it probably for military purposes. Much other research in the region has been strategically related, even where the connection is not apparent. Thus massive research on seabirds conducted by Bishop Museum and Smithsonian Institution was later found to be funded by the U.S. military project on spreading germs in biological warfare. Much U.S.-funded research on tropical insects and plants was likewise initiated by and for the U.S. military.

The next largest area of research is commercial. Japan, Germany, the United States, and other countries have spent hundreds of millions of dollars studying minerals on the Pacific seabed, as well as on land.

All other research in the Pacific is minuscule in cost, scale, and number of researchers compared with that of military and minerals. Most research is financed and undertaken from the Euro-American region and Japan. The largest nonmilitary research programs are French, mainly in New Caledonia and French Polynesia, in marine studies, geology, aquaculture, and social sciences.

The proportion of research by Pacific Islands scholars and institutions is small. Most of it is externally funded, associated with universities and regional organizations and probably a declining proportion of the growing total. For example, the studies that resulted in the book *Re-thinking Vanuatu Education Together* (Sanga et al. 2004) were funded by New Zealand and made by staff members of Vanuatu, New Zealand, and regional institutions. The Pacific Education series, including *Pacific Voices: Teacher Education on the Move* (Puamau and Pene 2007a) and *The Basics of Learning: Literacy and Numeracy in the Pacific* (Puamau and Pene 2007b), were funded by New Zealand and Europe and carried out by Pacific Islanders and expatriates. And Fiji's latest education review, *Learning Together: Directions for Education in the Fiji Islands* (Bacchus et al. 2000), was funded by governments in Fiji, Australia, Canada, and New Zealand and carried out by Fiji and international experts.

Even where local people have advantages of language, culture, and access, as in the social studies and medicine, the great majority is still foreign. In anthropology, where islanders have a great advantage over outsiders, the Association of Social Anthropologists in Oceania listed only 17 of its its 354 members as resident in the Pacific in 2004 (Brison and Leavitt 2004). Few professions give more than token encouragement to effective participation by Pacific Islanders. Asian scholars are a minority, but increasing.

Because research is generally expensive and the benefits slow to emerge, it has not been a high priority for Islands governments or institutions. This is understandable, but there is scope for action research integrated with teaching and for more research outside formal institutions.

NOTES

1. This chapter is adapted from one in *The South Pacific,* 2008, with the approval of the author.

For mission education, see Garrett 1988, 1992, 1997; Lovett 1899. For Guam, see Carano and Sanchez 1964; Rogers 1995. For Micronesia, see Hezel 1984. Detailed studies exist for individual countries and churches.

2. The Anglican Church's Selwyn College in Solomon Islands had less money per student than government colleges, but a better record in externally adjudicated examinations and in national sports than even the premier government college. Many similar examples could be cited.

3. For education and training by NGOs see, e.g., Bamford 1986; Crossley et al. 1987; Finau et al. 1984; Oliver 1976; Veramu 1994.

4. From its first graduation in 1930 until 1974 (the last to begin studies before Fiji's independence in 1970), 42 percent of graduates were from Fiji. Of those who began studies after Fiji's independence until 1978, 85 percent were from Fiji. From 1975 to 1990, 82 percent were from Fiji.

5. Students from FSM, the Marshall Islands, and Palau have access to U.S. institutions and scholarships. Australia and New Zealand grant thousands of scholarships to islanders to study in those countries and in national and regional institutions in the Islands. Other aid comes from other governments and UN agencies. The Asian Development Bank offers scholarships to fourteen top universities in Australia, Hawai'i, Hong Kong, India, Japan, New Zealand, the Philippines, Singapore, and Thailand.

6. Two of the most popular localities abroad are New Zealand and Hawai'i high schools, polytechnics, and universities. The number of Pacific Islands students in Australia, New Zealand, and the United States exceeds twenty thousand. Perhaps one-quarter of them will return home; the others have found a new home.

7. In 2002 in PNG, 56 percent of the students in primary schools were male and 44 percent female; at secondary school 60 percent male, 40 percent female; at technical colleges 71 percent male, 29 percent female. In Solomon Islands in 2005 primary schools were nearly balanced (47 percent to 53 percent), but by senior secondary 40 percent, and college 25 percent. These figures are a big improvement on earlier years.

8. The proportion of women graduates at USP is likewise growing, and in 2006 women exceeded men by 50.5 percent to 49.5 percent, but 65 percent of MA and PhD graduates were men.

9. Tereora College chooses students on merit from all schools and offers the main pre-university program in the nation. From 1986 to 1996, 61 percent of girls but only 39 percent of boys qualified (Harry Ivaiti, principal, personal communication). All the Cook Islands high schools report a similar pattern.

BIBLIOGRAPHY

Bacchus, K., et al. 2000. *Learning together: Directions for education in the Fiji Islands.* Suva: Fiji Islands Education Commission.

Bamford, G. 1986. *Training the majority: Guidelines for the rural Pacific.* Suva: University of the South Pacific.

Brison, K., and S. Leavitt. 2004. *ASAO Newsletter #120.* December 2004. Retrieved from http://www.asao.org/pacific/newsletters/NL120.pdf. Accessed on February 25, 2012.

Carano, P., and P. Sanchez. 1964. *A complete history of Guam.* Rutland, Vt.: Tuttle.

Cole, R. 1996. *Pacific 2010. Challenging the future.* National Center for Development Studies. Canberra: Australian National University.

Crocombe, M. 1999. New trends in distance education in the Pacific. In *Distance education in the South Pacific. Nets and voyages,* ed. R. Guy, T. Tosuge, and R. Hayakawa. Suva: Institute of Pacific Studies, University of the South Pacific.

Crocombe, R., and M. Meleisea. 1988. *Pacific universities: Achievements, problems, and prospects.* Suva: Institute of Pacific Studies, University of the South Pacific.

Crossley, M., et al. 1987. *Pacific perspectives on non-formal education.* Port Moresby: University of Papua New Guinea.

Douglas, N. 1994. Education in the Pacific Islands today. *Pacific Magazine,* July–Aug., 43–70; Sept.–Oct., 40–64.

Eastly, M. 1994. Education in the Pacific Islands today: Palau. *Pacific Magazine,* Sept.–Oct., 58–60.

Ernst, M. 1994. *Winds of change: Rapidly growing religious movements in the Pacific Islands.* Suva: Pacific Council of Churches.

Finau, P., et al. 1984. *Education for rural development.* Suva: University of the South Pacific.

Garrett, J. 1988. *To live among the stars: Christian origins in Oceania.* Suva: University of the South Pacific.

———. 1992. *Footsteps in the sea: Christianity in Oceania to World War II.* Suva: University of the South Pacific.

———. 1997. *Where nets were cast: Christianity in Oceania since World War II.* Suva: University of the South Pacific.

Helu-Thaman, K. 2000. *Towards culturally democratic teacher education.* Suva: University of the South Pacific.

Hezel, F. X., S.J. 1984. Schools in Micronesia prior to American administration. *Pacific Studies* 8(1): 95–111.

Ketudat, S. 1990. *The middle path for the future of Thailand. Technology in harmony with culture and environment.* Chiang Mai: Chiang Mai University.

Lovett, R. 1899. *The history of the London Missionary Society 1795–1895.* London: Frowde.

Luteru, P., and S. Pongi. 1997. *Summary outcome of National Strategic Planning seminars and position papers.* Suva: University of the South Pacific.

Monsell-Davis, M. 1993. Education and rural development. In *Modern Papua New Guinea society,* ed. Laura Zimmer. Bathurst: Crawford House.

Moseley, L., et al. 1992. *A survey of literacy and language.* Honiara: Solomon Islands National Literacy Committee.

Nabobo-Baba, U. 2007. *Knowing and learning: An indigenous Fijian approach.* Suva: University of the South Pacific.

Oliver, D. 1976. *Rural youth.* Suva: YMCA.

Peattie, M. R. 1988. *Nanyo. The rise and fall of the Japanese in Micronesia 1855–1945.* Honolulu: University of Hawai‘i Press.

Pene, F., A. Taufe‘ulungaki, and C. Benson. 2002. *Tree of opportunity: Rethinking Pacific education.* Suva: University of the South Pacific.

Puamau, P., and F. Pene. 2007a. *Pacific voices: Teacher education on the move.* Suva: University of the South Pacific.

———. 2007b. *The basics of learning: Literacy and numeracy in the Pacific.* Suva: University of the South Pacific.

Rogers, R. F. 1995. *Destiny's landfall: A history of Guam.* Honolulu: University of Hawai‘i Press.

Sanga, K., J. Niroa, K. Malai, and L. Crowl, eds. 2004. *Re-thinking Vanuatu education together.* Vila: Ministry of Education.

Taufe‘ulungaki, A. 2001. *Vernacular languages and classroom interactions in the Pacific.* Suva: University of the South Pacific.

Thaman, K. H. 1997. Reclaiming a place: Towards a Pacific concept of education for cultural development. *Journal of the Polynesian Society* 106(2): 119–130.

Veramu. J. 1994. *Adult and community education in the South Pacific.* Bonn: Institut fur Internationale Zusammerabeit.

Urban Challenges

Donovan Storey and John Connell

26

In almost all Pacific Island countries a significant demographic, economic, and cultural transformation is taking place as urban populations are growing faster than total populations. Indeed, if Papua New Guinea is excluded, more than half of all Pacific Islanders live in urban areas, reflecting a global watershed heralded by the United Nations in 2007. In some countries—such as the atoll states of Kiribati and the Marshall Islands—this growth has resulted in exceptionally high population densities, comparable with those in the most highly populated Asian cities. In larger states, such as Fiji, the majority population now lives in cities and towns. And where urban areas still account for a minority of people, such as Papua New Guinea, Solomon Islands, and Vanuatu, urban growth rates are among the highest in the Asian Pacific, foreshadowing a late though inevitable urban revolution. Though migration still drives much of this growth, it is significant that an increasing share is generated by birth rates of second- and third-generation urban citizens, indicating the permanent shift of many Pacific Islanders from "traditional" rural societies to urban centers and contradicting the still held view that migration is temporary and urban challenges can be met through rural development. Unmistakably the Pacific faces an urban future, but what kind of future will this be?

The recognition of these urban realities, by both Pacific Islanders as well as outsiders, has been slow and this has arguably weakened effective responses. Emerging problems of poverty, urban management, environmental degradation, and security are evident throughout the region, yet they have received limited policy attention. As the president of Fiji, Sir Ratu Kamisese Mara (1994: 9), warned more than a decade ago:

> It does not require any great genius to figure out the consequences of this urban drift. Quite apart from the basic strains placed on limited infrastructure, we have seen an erosion of cultural values, growing unemployment and the attendant restlessness, increased crime and other ills which plague large urban centers. But in our case we have the additional constraints of limited resources, small land areas, isolation caused by distance and the consequences of the great social and cultural changes wrought by the new realities that our traditional ethos was not equipped to handle.

All these changes are now widespread in the Pacific, but alongside these problems many cities remain and will continue to be key centers of economic growth, tertiary education, and technological change.

Demographic Transformation

The movement of people within and between islands has intensified in volume, increased in distance, and become more complex in pattern and purpose since the conclusion of the Second World War. The shift of Pacific Islanders from rural to urban locales has also become more permanent. With the development of modern transportation, the continued stagnation of rural economic development, and the increasing significance of urban economies in globalizing spaces, the opportunity for and logic of migration has increased in a region that has historically been characterized by high mobility. Whereas in the past migration tended to be circular or repetitive—often seasonal and usually over short distances—permanent and relatively long-distance migration has in recent years become a more general feature. Throughout the Pacific there are a number of general trends in population movement, although not all are necessarily present. First, international migration extends beyond the region; second, small islands are being depopulated as people move to large islands; third, mountain populations are moving to lowlands, usually along the coast; and fourth, urban populations are continuing to grow. In the past quarter of a century these trends have intensified and been accentuated to the extent that it is no longer possible to regard the Pacific as characterized by rural populations. Within and even more so on the fringes of the Pacific, urban islander populations have grown substantially (Table 26.1).

The rationale for urbanization and increased population concentrations is consistent throughout the Pacific: employment opportunities and services (especially education and health) are concentrated in the urban centers. In small island states, where the labor force and capital are often limited, this urban concentration is inevitable to some extent; hence rural-to-urban migration follows. Urbanization is proportionally least in Melanesia—though towns and cities are larger—since modernization has been belated. Yet even in Kiribati and Tuvalu, urbanization has become significant and development problems have resulted. Almost everywhere, urbanization has been accompanied by rapid population growth

Table 26.1

Urbanization in the Pacific Islands

	Urban population, last census (percent)	Total growth rate (percent)	Urban growth rate (percent)
Melanesia			
Fiji	52	0.5	1.5
New Caledonia	67	1.3	2.6
Papua New Guinea	13	2.2	2.3
Solomon Islands	19	2.6	4.3
Vanuatu	26	2.4	4.3
Micronesia			
FSM	23	0.4	0.6
Guam	93	2.7	1.3
Kiribati	44	1.8	1.7
Marshall Islands	72	0.7	2.7
Nauru	100	2.1	0.3
Northern Marianas	91	-0.1	2.1
Palau	84	0.6	1.8
Polynesia			
American Samoa	93	1.2	2.1
Cook Islands	76	0.3	2.0
French Polynesia	57	1.1	1.7
Niue	38	-2.3	-1.4
Samoa	22	0.4	1.3
Tokelau	na	-0.9	na
Tonga	34	0.5	0.7
Tuvalu	51	0.5	1.4
Wallis and Futuna		0.8	na
New Zealand	86	0.9	1.0
Hawai'i	70	1.2	na

Source: See Table 22.1.

respective populations of Suva (Figure 26.1) and Noumea are estimated to be 250,000 and 160,000. Even official statistics may hide the real growth of cities. While Port Moresby's official population (based on the 2000 census) is recorded as 254,158, this excludes a high number of periurban and informal settlements. It is estimated by most government planning agencies in Port Moresby that the city's current actual population lies closer to 500,000 than official projections of a little over 350,000. Such urban undercounts exist in many other Pacific Island countries and have serious implications for infrastructure and service provision to rapidly growing urban populations.

Figure 26.1. *Modern urban facade, Suva (photo DS).*

Belated urbanization was in large part a result of deliberate efforts to deny indigenous populations access to what were essentially European urban enclaves. In the prewar years, urbanization was officially discouraged in the colonial Pacific, and towns were primarily European trading and administrative centers. Legacies of segregationist attitudes still linger in contemporary urban settings, evident in elite and government hostility to squatter/informal settlements and the informal sector, and also through the denial of services and infrastructure to those not seen as "belonging" to the modern city (Connell 2003; Storey 2003). Rapid urban expansion mainly followed postwar and, later, postindependence expansion in government activity and spending, and with it came a boom in bureaucratic job opportunities for the educated elite and skilled workers. Over time, more and more of this service sector employment became located in the urban areas.

As postcolonial migration restrictions declined (a reflection of the relaxation of colonial policies as well as the emergence of weak states) and labor demands increased, towns and cities grew and their populations became more permanent. Factors discouraging permanence of the urban population, including the lack of social security and insecure land tenure, were steadily offset by economic criteria such as higher urban wages and an actual decline of income-earning opportunities in some rural areas.

Circular or return migration has become less important, and rural-to-urban migration is progressively more permanent or at least long-term. As children are born in towns this stability is

(heightened through the limited impact of family planning), with the result that natural increase has become as important an influence on urban growth as rural-to-urban migration.

While urbanization in the Pacific has been historically late, recent growth has been remarkable. As late as 1960 only Suva and Noumea within the colonial Pacific had populations of over 25,000; hence the expansion of urbanization is a dramatic and very recent change in the history of the South Pacific. For Melanesia on the eve of independence, cities were still described as "still essentially communities of migrants" (Brookfield with Hart 1971: 384). Today the enhanced, while, increasingly, migrants prefer or at least become used to urban rather than rural life. A quarter of the children born in the large Papua New Guinea towns of Port Moresby (Figure 26.2) and Lae, for example, have never visited their "home" villages and, if they were to do so, would find acceptance there difficult (Connell 1997). It is in this context, above all, that the towns of the South Pacific are increasingly becoming more like those in other parts of the world, as second, third, and further generations of urban dwellers emerge with at best only tenuous ties to rural areas. This is significant not merely for the breakdown of traditional social organization that it implies but because it effectively ensures that these second- (or more) generation migrants are destined to remain and raise families in urban areas, despite popular and government rhetoric that continues to maintain the rural links of migrants.

Figure 26.2. Modern urban facade, Port Moresby (photo DS).

Access to land is a crucial influence on the duration of urban residence, and individual ownership of land has resulted in considerable urban permanency and marked differences between social groups in the intention to remain in town. In Fiji, for indigenous Fijians urban centers are regarded as locations of employment and modern amenities, and rural communities primarily as locations that offer opportunities for a better social and cultural life and the chance of a peaceful retirement. Indo-Fijians are more permanent urban residents because of their involvement in commerce and their inability to secure permanent rural land tenure. In general, those most likely to remain in urban areas are migrants from remote places where income-earning opportunities are few. Where rising expectations are combined with increasing pressure on rural resources and static job opportunities in the formal sector, migration from rural areas is more likely to be permanent either in Pacific urban areas or in the cities of metropolitan nations on the Pacific Rim.

Land and Housing

A distinctive form of urbanization has appeared in the Pacific associated with the rights, and the lack of rights, of residents to land in urban areas. Cities and towns are characterized by rapidly

growing uncontrolled fringes of periurban customary land, settlements on marginal lands—such as swamps and hillsides—beyond the reaches of the formal housing sector, and pockets of traditional villages swallowed up in the expanding modern town. Only in New Zealand and Hawai'i, and to a lesser extent Noumea, Suva, Port Moresby, Papeete, and Hagatna (Guam), are there extensive tracts of modern suburban low-density development. Otherwise, new offices and tourist establishments and the expensive dwellings of the elite (still largely expatriate in parts of the region) coexist uneasily with low-income suburbs and place huge demands on poorly developed networks of infrastructure and services. This complex and increasingly differentiated townscape is seldom under the jurisdiction of a single municipal authority and rarely are service providers (even state-owned) expected or compelled to extend provision to informal settlements or residential areas located on customary land beyond urban administrative boundaries. Management problems are visible in environmental degradation, traffic, and housing problems. Social and physical variations within towns reflect the availability and provision of housing. Within the towns enormous differences in residential standards occur.

In almost all Pacific Island countries urban land is saturated and all new development is taking place outside the formal city boundaries and therefore beyond the institutional and legal scope of authorities and planning (Figure 26.3). Pacific cities are spreading and developing on a mix of government/crown, freehold, and customary land, weakening the authority and even relevance of much urban planning (where it exists) and resulting in ad hoc development of urban areas. While land reform to increase access and affordability is critical for many towns and cities, the likelihood of this occurring is unlikely, given continued sensitivities over land tenure and the relative strength of customary landowners compared with weak urban institutions. Though land is also the most likely area of conflict in urban areas, there are few evident alternatives.

In Kiribati, outside of small pockets of state-owned land, urban land is privately held and government is reluctant to confront owners and traditional leaders over the way it is used. Where formal leasing occurs it has been overwhelmed and replaced with

Figure 26.3. Land for sale, Port Vila (photo DS).

informal agreements. Even in South Tarawa, where 60 percent of land is in government ownership, most development is taking place on private or traditional land as the use of government land is contested between the Land Management Department and the two town councils of South Tarawa. Population growth is also placing severe stress in South Tarawa. Land is being degraded, water tables polluted and exhausted, and foreshores have eroded to the point that they offer little resistance to tidal surges (Storey and Hunter 2010). Recent trends have seen an increasing landless population and pressure on reforming land tenure to prevent these trends as well as ameliorate overcrowding.

Throughout the urban Pacific, traditional tenure has not avoided the commodification of land and spiraling costs—and has probably accelerated these trends. Management and codification of land is spread across local and national agencies, and coordination between them is often weak. This is made more complicated through landowners retaining "veto" rights. As a result, uncontrolled squatting makes planning difficult and occupies remaining public space. While there are existing powers open to governments to appropriate land for the public good, these powers are rarely if ever used, largely a result of the perceived (and likely) political repercussions.

Where it occurs, formal subdivision or registration of land is proving too slow, too expensive, and too bureaucratic in the face of rapid and escalating demand. This is resulting in the growing prevalence of informal leasing throughout the Pacific. While this is satisfying basic access to land, such informal agreements between landowners (in many instances there are several) and "squatters" are prone to change and can result in conflict. Essential legal protection, especially for renters, is absent, hence conditions and payments are uneven and subject to contestation. In Fiji and Vanuatu more recent migrants to informal settlements complain of being harassed by those claiming to be indigenous owners of the land demanding rental or other payments in kind. There is little evidence of any formal or written agreements over squatting or renting on customary land, and this situation often opens the door for potential abuse and vulnerability. In some cases traditional landowners do not allow squatters to have their own gardens, for fear of competition at local markets or due to the lack of available garden space. Similarly, custom landowners often resist squatter attempts to improve the quality of their temporary housing for fear that it will be seen as permanent.

As population pressure increases in periurban and customary areas, land tenure systems will need to be addressed, as will the role of traditional landowners. The case for wholesale privatization of customary land remains politically and culturally untenable and so more innovative solutions need to be found. In Port Moresby, strategies that seek to mobilize customary land for housing and investment while also providing greater security and recognition of customary ownership have provided an example of finding a middle ground between tenure security and the traditional rights of land custodians (Chand and Yala 2007). Similar middle ground has also been sought through temporary housing (THAs, or "leaf housing") in Solomon Islands, where migrants are provided temporary squatting rights though without formal and permanent tenure security. While providing a breathing space in the absence of the creation of alternative formal housing options, THAs have in effect become

permanent settlements, though without access to electricity and water supplies or formal inclusion in the city proper (Talbot and Ronnie 2007). Vanuatu, where options for formal urban expansion are limited by customary land and landowners and which is leading to greater conflict, also provides a strong case for the need to more effectively address land issues to enable more rational urban growth while identifying a continuing role for traditional systems (Storey 2005). Successful examples in the region of this, though, are hard to find.

Land tenure shapes the pattern and availability of affordable and secure housing. Housing is often a barometer of people's income, their level of security, and their access to resources (including land). Although informal settlements (Figure 26.4) do not always house the very poor, the fact that Pacific middle classes have few alternatives but to live in poor-quality housing areas is an indication of the low incomes and high relative cost of living in many Pacific Island towns and cities. A great majority of migrants to cities in the region now build their own houses outside formal legal regulations. The "autonomous" growth of the region's cities outside formal planning and management may meet immediate shelter needs but does little in the way of providing a model of sustainable urban development.

Figure 26.4. Informal settlement, Port Vila (photo DS).

Although state-provided housing (Figure 26.5) has been pursued in many Pacific Island countries, it has long proved inadequate. A Fiji Housing Association report estimated that since the 1970s some 70 percent of applicants were unable to afford repayments on low-income housing that conformed to legal requirements (UNESCAP 1999). This has meant a recent explosion in informal settlements as the only viable shelter alternative for migrants and the urban poor. Though informal settlements in the Pacific have a long history, considerable recent growth has been evident throughout the region, though with specific drivers. In Fiji the expiration of Indo-Fijian land leases and poor economic performance resulted in Suva's squatter population alone increasing from 51,925 in 2001 to 82,000 in 2004. The number of squatter settlements nationally was estimated to be 182. The Ministry of Local Government, Housing, Squatter Settlement and Environment (MLGHSSE) and the Asian Development Bank have estimated that since 1998 some 70 to 80 percent of new land developments around urban areas have been

Figure 26.5. Public housing estate, Suva (photo DS).

through informal agreements and some 80 percent of new housing stock has been built independently of official planning authorities. In essence Fiji's booming urban areas are being developed autonomously, outside the control and authorization of government and planners, and this same trend is evident in several other Pacific Island countries.

Burgeoning informal settlements are the destination of Indo-Fijian cane farmers who have no customary rights to land, but also of Fijians moving to cities to further their opportunities, even when they have access to rural land. Increasingly these settlements consist of makeshift shelters with no water supply and sporadic access to electricity and are increasingly characterized by overcrowding, leading UNESCAP to note that "there is a need for governments to take a more proactive approach with squatter settlements particularly in promoting a greater understanding of rights and services" (UNESCAP/POC 2002: 30). Yet while governments are loath to relax building codes and regulations in informal settlements, the creation of affordable formal housing by government and nongovernment institutions is woefully inadequate. Government housing authorities have generally failed to provide affordable housing for those outside of relatively well-off groups. In 2006 Fiji Housing Authority (FHA) houses were typically priced between F$12,000 and 15,000, with mortgages offered at 5 to 6 percent, beyond the scope of the majority of many living in informal settlements with family incomes of F$100/week. Even NGOs struggle to make any serious impact on demand. As an example, the Housing Assistance and Relief Trust (HART) estimated that it built sixty new apartments in Fiji in 2002, and Habitat for Humanity has finished twenty-nine houses in Vanuatu over the period from 2001 to 2005. In effect these are little more than demonstration houses. Vanuatu faces similar problems of informal settlements providing essentially the only affordable housing for the vast majority of the population in Port Vila and Luganville for many Ni-Vanuatu. With the demise of the expensive housing schemes of the National Housing Corporation (which only managed to build a total of forty-nine houses), Vanuatu has no national scheme to provide affordable housing for low- and middle-income families. Similar state-provided housing failures are evident throughout the Pacific.

With formal housing outside the reach of many, increased pressure is evident in informal settlements. The settlement of Blacksands, north of Port Vila, experienced a 47 percent growth in population from 1997 to 2000 alone. In atoll states such as Kiribati, crowding is a particularly pressing problem. With more than one thousand homes in South Tarawa accommodating ten or more people, communicable diseases and stress are common afflictions. The Kiribati Housing Corporation (KHC), which has built a large number of formal houses in South Tarawa (numbering around 1,216 in 2003), caters primarily to civil servants, and many houses are currently in various states of disrepair (Eritai 2003: 27). In some parts of South Tarawa (e.g., Betio), one-third of all households are squatting. The KHC has recently estimated that at least 1,038 additional houses are required in South Tarawa, but that they cannot provide them (Eritai 2003: 73). Increasingly, informal settlements are being built within family compounds, leading to higher population densities and less open space for recreation, gardens, or access. Informal housing is also spreading onto water reserves and closer to coastlines, leading to degraded environments and threatened watersheds (Storey and Hunter 2010). The prevalence of informal housing is compounded by the absence of realistic building codes and any viable alternative to meet needs. This scenario applies to some extent throughout the Pacific, but environmental pressures are especially acute in the densely populated atolls of Kiribati and the Marshall Islands.

Renters in all three case studies, but especially in Vanuatu and Fiji, are uniformly overrepresented in categories indicating extreme poverty and vulnerability. In the case of Tagabe Bridge Settlement, Port Vila, several family members or friends share one room in a six- to eight-room block and typically pay between 8,000 and 15,000 Vatu a month to someone who, in turn, leases land from a customary landowner. Those renting on customary land often have the least protection in terms of legal redress for their housing conditions or tenancy, but such housing offers affordable and flexible access. They are also more likely to have insecure living status and conditions, constantly moving from settlement to settlement to avoid paying high rents, which are volatile and rarely subject to negotiation. Their vulnerability and poverty is obvious. While it is difficult to estimate the number of renters, it does appear to be increasing. In some parts of periurban Port Vila almost 80 percent of people rent (Figure 26.6) and a rentier/landlord class is clearly emerging within many poor settlements.

Figure 26.6. Informal rental housing, Port Vila (photo DS).

In terms of availability, affordability, and responsiveness, Pacific land and shelter strategies are struggling to match needs. There is a clear growth of periurban and informal settlements on indigenous land, which is resulting in ad hoc development. It appears that in the next generation, unless more effective responses and institutions are put in place, informal settlements on indigenous land will become the dominant form of new urban growth, and this will make infrastructure and service needs difficult to address, as well as ensuring that land and housing access continues to be a potential source of conflict.

Inequality, Poverty, and Urban Livelihoods

The economies of Pacific Island states and territories are constrained by various factors linked to their small size. These include remoteness and isolation, diseconomies of scale, scarce natural and human resources, and vulnerability to external shocks and natural hazards. Their urban economies are similarly limited (see chapter 27). All towns have administrative and service sectors—the principal reasons for their establishment—and these are often the only real contemporary economic functions in the smaller centers.

In the transition from colonial towns, urban economies diversified, but the manufacturing sector is small throughout the Pacific. Where manufacturing industries have developed, such as the garment industry in Fiji, they have proven to be uncompetitive and have relied in large part on favorable tariff arrangements and low wages (Storey 2006). These have proved ephemeral. Similarly, employment in the Northern Marianas has been dominated by clothes production because of tariff-free entry to the mainland American market, but recent years have seen significant closures. Most of the remaining workforce, who are paid minimum wages below American norms, are Asian women migrants. Industrial employment otherwise accounts for only a small proportion of the urban workforce. Among the indigenous population, urban unemployment levels are high.

Most manufacturing activities involve the processing of local agricultural and fisheries produce, and, with the exception of fish canneries in Papua New Guinea, Fiji, and American Samoa, these are of limited extent. Although breweries have recently been constructed in the Marshall Islands, Tonga, and Vanuatu, the phase of import substitution has largely passed; hence there has been a declining rate of urban job creation. Beyond food processing, industrial activity centers on the small-scale production of wood and metal products and on engineering.

Most urban economies are dominated by national governments because of the significance of the public sector, even in areas such as fisheries. Efforts to privatize and to increase competition are being made throughout the region, but the effects on urban unemployment have usually been negative; hence the struggle for jobs is a constant urban preoccupation. In many towns and cities urban employment remains dependent on the bureaucracy and service sector. The former is generally privileged, its higher wages and better job security and fringe benefits (though eroding) ensuring that it is the most sought after area of employment, second only to being a politician. In recent years public sector employment has stabilized and contracted, posing problems for urban economies. In those countries where tourism is important, many tourism facilities are in, or close to, the urban areas—as in Honolulu, Noumea, Papeete, Port Vila, and Rarotonga—and this labor-intensive industry employs a substantial proportion of the urban workforce (Lea 1996). Otherwise, urban employment is dominated by the visible evidence of retailing and other tertiary services.

The combination of migration, growing urban permanence, few new urban employment opportunities, and the lack of industrialization has resulted in the growing significance of the informal sector as a source of livelihood—though governments have been slow to recognize its role in employment creation and poverty alleviation (Connell 2003). In some of the larger cities—particularly Port Moresby and Suva—one of the most visible elements of the informal sector is marketing, though crime and prostitution are becoming increasingly visible. While the informal sector is constrained through restrictive legislation (especially on food sellers), small markets, and limited skills, employment creation is more likely than in the highly competitive and small formal sector. As an example, formal-sector employment in Kiribati is estimated at only 21 percent of adults, and often these individuals have to support large households (ADB 2002). Only around one-quarter of the two thousand annual school leavers can hope to find full employment. Even formal-sector employment does not guarantee escaping income poverty. Most urban poor families do have at least one income earner in the formal sector, but low wages and young dependents typically mean that household income remains below the poverty line. While employment creation is an important part of poverty reduction, wages are also a key issue. In Fiji in the mid-1990s as many as 47 percent of people employed full-time lived below the poverty line and two-thirds of these were women. Similar proportions exist elsewhere.

In the absence of well-paid formal-sector employment, secondary/informal sources of income have taken on a greater importance for many urban families. At present between 35 and 50 percent of Fiji's urban population and more than 60 percent of urban Ni-Vanuatu work in the informal sector, and a high proportion of these are women. The options for formal employment-generating industries are limited in a liberalized global trade environment. Governments in the past, however, have been reluctant to legitimize informal-sector work despite its critical role in job creation and poverty reduction. Fiji and Papua New Guinea have recently relaxed some laws on self-employment, but there is more to be done in the region in using informal-sector employment as a basis of income and business opportunity. In the future the informal sector will be the most important and accessible entry point into business and income generation for the poor, providing a critical source of employment generation and enterprise (Figure 26.7).

Detailed studies on the informal sector in recent years have been rare, but one that examined several urban centers in Fiji raised some interesting trends and opportunities as well as identifying impediments facing the sector. In Fiji the informal sector plays an increasingly important role in employment creation and labor absorption (Reddy, Naitu, and Mohanty 2003). The informal sector accounted for more than 50 percent of jobs in 2002, up from an estimated 37 percent in 1996. The principal occupations of those interviewed were vegetable sellers, couriers, fish sellers, BBQ operators, and "shoe shine boys." Most operations were run by women, had been established for more than a year, and operated six days a

Figure 26.7. *The informal sector is an important source of food as well as employment, especially for women (photo DS).*

Figure 26.8. *Betel nut and cigarettes for sale, Port Moresby (photo DS).*

week and ten hours a day. Most were family operations operating in public spaces, and a considerable number were "rural" or peri-urban workers who traveled into town to sell goods, indicating the strong inward/outward flow of labor and capital that characterizes Pacific towns and cities. The informal sectors in large cities such as Port Vila and Port Moresby are similar (Connell 1997: 204–207). Despite significant support from urban and national governments, many small urban businesses have been developed by women using microfinance. In Port Vila most small urban stores and market vendors have only been able to develop through such support.

Urban residents, many of them self-employed, purchase a substantial proportion of their food (and other goods) in the markets (Figure 26.8). In larger towns middlemen link urban markets with rural production. In most towns the formal sector workforce is youthful. Access to urban employment, even in the public service, is influenced by kinship ties, and in the larger island groups many enterprises are dominated by workers from a particular language group or region, a circumstance that may reduce productivity.

Consequently, there are few adequate measures of employment in use in the region. In the larger towns it is apparent however that unemployment is increasing. In the early 1990s a third of the population of Port Moresby was searching for work, with most of the unemployed being in the fifteen through nineteen age group, many of them with little or no education (Connell 1997: 196). Various estimates suggest that unemployment levels are frequently above 10 percent and that many urban households do not include wage and salary earners, but rely on distant kin or on subsistence production on the edge of town. The extent of urban unemployment has contributed to social disorganization (Connell 2008).

Limited opportunities to make an income to adequately support households and kin, and increasing competition for the employment opportunities that do exist, are a significant influence on urban poverty. Again, there have been few consistent attempts to measure urban poverty in the Pacific other than in Fiji, but the increased extent of begging and crime in some countries suggests that poverty is of growing significance, especially in the larger towns. Poverty is resulting from, and manifested in, increasing urban populations, a lack of employment opportunities, the

absence of effective safety nets, and limited access to land and quality housing (Storey 2010). The popular and romantic view of an urban safety net provided by the extended family, ensuring through redistribution that kin are never hungry or destitute, is no longer valid (Monsell-Davis 1993). In squatter settlements especially, hunger and poverty are no longer unusual, nor is the sight of families picking through municipal garbage sites for food.

By the early 1990s more than a third of the households living in urban settlements in Fiji were considered to be poor, compared with less than half that proportion a decade earlier (Bryant-Tokelau 1995: 110). Poverty is equally apparent in squatter settlements elsewhere, some of which have deteriorated into urban slums, even in Papeete and Noumea, where economies are relatively developed. A further consequence of difficult urban conditions is the growth of suicide and domestic violence, though neither are exclusively urban phenomena, and the increase in the number of female-headed households that follows on the heels of family breakdown and social disorganization.

Clearly, there are highly vulnerable and poor populations emerging in and around cities throughout the Pacific. Analysis of Vanuatu's 1998 Household and Income Expenditure Survey (HIES) indicated that while income poverty was more widespread in rural areas, levels of "extreme poverty" were overrepresented in urban areas. Young couples in their twenties with children, female-headed households, and those renting were particularly vulnerable, even though the majority of these households had at least one source of income (Government of Vanuatu 2002: 22). When asked to prioritize their needs, the most common responses were finding a house to rent, access to finance, having land to live on, having access to education, having adequate toilet facilities, finding a way to start a business, transportation, and accessing electricity (Government of Vanuatu 2002: 63–65). Clearly in urban Vanuatu, as elsewhere in the region, many basic urban needs remain unmet.

Though based on small samples, a number of recent surveys from the United Nations Economic and Social Commission for Asia and the Pacific (UNESCAP), the Ecumenical Center for Research, Education and Advocacy (ECREA), and academics in Fiji have pointed to the following trends. First, approximately

80 percent of those living in informal settlements in Suva fall below the "poverty line" (although this is an estimated figure); second, average incomes in settlements were between $90 and $100/week, even though at least one adult was working full-time and most families had a second source of income; third, urban poverty is increasing with migration and growth. In 1997 urban poverty was estimated at 27.6 percent of the population, in 2002 29.3 percent of urban households fell below the poverty line, and figures released in 2006 estimate that between one-quarter and one-third of urban populations continue to live below the poverty line. Again, these data point to the considerable extent of urban poverty, even in a country that has experienced positive economic growth for much of the past three decades.

Urban poverty in the region's microstates is also related to low incomes and high rates of migration, which in turn have resulted in overcrowding. In South Tarawa those living below the poverty line had a household average of 11.7 persons compared to families above the poverty line with 7.7 persons/household (ADB 2002: 68). One indicator of poverty and vulnerability on Tarawa is the comparative lack of food security. As a reflection of the lack of space, but also knowledge and essential tools, I-Kiribati on Tarawa are increasingly dependent on the monetary economy and imported food.

Although there is a need for more quantitative research on urban poverty, poverty cannot be adequately measured through statistics alone. In Fiji, despite its relatively high level of economic and human development, findings from the 2002 participatory assessment on hardship indicated increased poverty, especially chronic poverty, in the city's growing urban squatter settlements. But the poor expressed equal concerns about urban unemployment, governance, declining standards in the delivery of basic services, and a lack of economic opportunities.

A qualitative research project in the late 1990s gives some insight into the lives and expectations of Vanuatu's urban youth. More than one thousand young people between the ages of thirteen to twenty-five years were interviewed in settlements and in public places around Port Vila, resulting in a book and video *Kilim Taem* (Killing time) documenting their lives. The report found that half of youth were born in Port Vila and almost one-third had never been back to their "home" island, and the majority had not attended secondary school. Among this group many felt that they had "failed" the system without getting the necessary skills to find good work and felt that employment was their main problem. A large proportion of responses indicated they would like to start their own business; many felt that learning *kastom* (and church) offered some security and a sense of belonging, thus making "killing time" more bearable; youths were unaware of basic health and sexual reproduction issues; and young people lacked information and knowledge about facilities and opportunities available to them (Mitchell 2004). In small part some of these needs have recently been met by NGOs, which have developed sporting facilities, health clinics, and training courses for youth, but by their own admission, they still only meet the needs of a small number of Port Vila's youth. Broadly what is true of youth in Port Vila is relevant elsewhere in the region, as school leavers fail to find formal-sector jobs and experience frustration, often leading to increasing levels of alienation and problems of urban crime (Figure 26.9).

Figure 26.9. A city behind wire, Port Moresby (photo DS).

In almost all Pacific Island countries urban poverty is a growing problem. It is also poorly measured and understood but constitutes both an absolute poverty in terms of lack of adequate incomes and thus food and housing, but also a poverty of opportunity. The concerns of the poor go beyond income and encompass the desire to have access to urban infrastructure and services, notably water, sanitation, and electricity, and to be able to have a say in urban affairs. While the poor demand more services and infrastructure, however, they can rarely pay for them. The growth in urban poverty is likely to become the most important development in the Pacific over the coming decade and threatens progress toward the Millennium Development Goals (MDGs). Adequately responding to urban poverty requires an understanding based on holistic and multidimensional indicators. Urban poverty is more than just insufficient income, but also includes lack of services, poor living conditions, difficulty in meeting basic needs, and a lack of representation in the decision-making process. Rarely do studies, particularly official data, capture the multidimensional nature of urban poverty or adequately represent the voices of the urban poor.

The Urban Environment

Pacific urban cities are increasingly unhealthy and dangerous places to live, a trend noted almost two decades ago (Bryant 1993). Although progress has been made in terms of health facilities and awareness, some Pacific cities, particularly the microstate capitals Majuro (the Marshall Islands) and South Tarawa, face periodic threats of cholera and other water-borne diseases. Infant mortality rates, often as a result of diarrhea, continue to remain high in microstates such as Kiribati, as do communicable diseases, in large part aggravated by overcrowding. Pacific cities are invariably close to water sources and the continued health of rivers, lagoons, and the sea is critical for human well-being. Most water pollution is organic, though more hazardous forms of industrial water pollution may pose a greater threat in the future.

South Tarawa remains particularly vulnerable to environmental degradation (Storey and Hunter 2010). The entire population of Tarawa is under constant threat of epidemics, and diarrhea remains common. An Asian Development Bank project to draw water from a fresh lens source in North Tarawa is now under threat from population growth expanding into these reserves. At present, projects on developing stable sources of potable water and dealing with sewage and sanitation are being driven by donors, but eventually government will be required to take greater responsibility for this infrastructure and provision. Some officials describe the environment around South Tarawa as like "sitting on a time bomb" in terms of living standards and the impact on the environment. The key environmental issues faced in Tarawa are considerable and include groundwater depletion; increased salinity and pollution from sewage and animal excreta (around one-third of South Tarawa's population use beaches as toilets); marine life and seawater contamination from human and solid waste; overfishing of reefs and lagoons; nondegradable waste disposal; coastal erosion, beach mining, and deforestation eliminating sources of food, medicine, and habitat and increasing the vulnerability of coastlines; and breakdown of traditional subsistence production, resulting in poor nutrition and health-related problems (ADB 2002: 28).

South Tarawa may have a reticulated sewage system, but this is not available to a growing number of informal settlements and therefore has not solved problems of open defecation. Most sewage and solid waste continues to be disposed of along the waterfront and green belts, and water catchments have been replaced with housing. One recent survey has documented that residents in squatter settlements on South Tarawa were more likely to dump solid waste, use the beach as a toilet, and use dirty water for drinking as a result of being cut off from infrastructure and services. Water and sanitation facilities are only provided to those on public land (predominantly housing corporation homes), and "private" households are required to pay for their own connections. The majority of these cannot or choose not to pay for this service and end up dependent on wells and rainwater and basic toilets or squatting on the beach. Given that almost all new housing stock in Tarawa is now informal and "illegal," and treated as such by authorities, this is cause for concern. Water quality is a significant problem, as is the defoliation of the atolls to make way for housing. Lagoon pollution, in part exacerbated by the closing of the lagoon for causeways, is of increasing concern and threatens public health. The garbage collection system has only been partially successful. Much of the urban area is still plagued by garbage and the country still does not have legislation to deal with solid waste management or pollution of the lagoon. Similar circumstances are also emerging in Funafuti (Tuvalu) and in the Marshall Islands, causing repeated environmental management problems.

Environmental stress is not restricted to microstates. In the mid-1990s only about 40 percent of Fiji's urban population had adequate access to water, proper sanitation facilities, and waste collection services (World Bank 2000: 8). Even facilities that are in place are poorly maintained and depend upon aid budgets. The growth of periurban and informal settlements will make more extensive provision difficult. Levels of solid waste creation per capita are increasing in many of the region's cities, but the machinery of collection and disposal is rarely keeping pace. A UNESCAP/POC study of informal settlements in Nasinu (Suva) showed that only 19 percent of households had their garbage collected while 52 percent of households either burned or buried their garbage. Fully one-fifth of households reportedly threw their garbage into a nearby river

or dumped it on nearby land. The study consequently warned that environmental and health conditions in informal settlements were degraded and deteriorating with growing populations (UNESCAP/POC 2002: 20). In addition to such well-known environmental threats, Suva now faces an increased problem of hazardous waste disposal and air pollution.

Similar trends are also found in urban Vanuatu. The Port Vila Municipal Council does not collect any solid waste from informal areas, which constitute the largest and fastest-growing areas around Port Vila. Informal settlements depend on shared pit toilets, sometimes very close to watercourses and subject to flooding. There is no public service provider for sanitation and there are no sanitation master plans for either Port Vila or smaller towns. A lack of infrastructure provision in periurban areas in Vanuatu means that households depend upon rainwater and wells, which are increasingly susceptible to contamination (pollution of the aquifer, leptospirosis, and vector-borne diseases in rainwater) (Government of Vanuatu 2002: 25). Without positive intervention, environmental conditions in informal settlements will deteriorate and threaten the health of residents and ultimately environmental and health conditions in the wider urban area.

The rapid spread of cities into agricultural hinterlands is also creating a wider urban footprint, with resulting environmental impacts. One example of this is the impact of periurban areas on the Tagabe catchment area, which covers twenty-five square kilometers to the immediate north of Port Vila and is a key source of water for the city. It is now under significant pressure from rural runoff, industrial wastewater, and informal settlements, but authority for the river is divided between Efate, the Port Vila Municipal Council, and a number of customary landowners. The catchment is under threat from a range of developments, but solutions, if they are to be effective, require interaction between formal and customary institutions. Though there is movement to create this consensus, dealing with pollution and use of the catchment is a complex and time-consuming process, especially with divided ownership (ADB 2004: ch. 6). Often pressures on peripheral areas result from the extension of urban food gardens, hunting, and firewood collection.

As urban lifestyles change and consumerism increases, the amount of inorganic waste and per capita waste generation is increasingly putting coastal and fragile ecosystems under pressure. The capacity to collect, sort, and dispose of solid waste is stretched thin in many urban areas. In the Marshall Islands, the Majuro Atoll Waste Company actually declared a state of emergency in May 2008 due to the shortage of waste bins and the lack of financial resources to service urban centers and safely dispose of waste. Dealing with these issues will require both technical knowledge and materials in the form of planning and infrastructure, but equally so traditional authorities have an important role to play. An example of this is also found in the Marshall Islands where *alaps* (traditional land managers) have been encouraged to develop their own approaches to managing and enforcing controls over waste in their areas (ADB 2004: 31). The role of traditional leaders is also applicable to the servicing of periurban areas in growing Melanesian and Polynesian cities.

Despite such threats, levels of environmental awareness in urban areas are low, though recent concerns over climate change have undoubtedly focused more attention on vulnerabilities.

Perhaps this only reflects the attitudes of constituents. In a recent survey, more than one-third of people in Kiribati identified the sea as an acceptable place to dispose of waste, while almost one-third of Tarawa residents did not recognize that waste was a problem. An estimated one-fifth of Suva's residents also dump their garbage in waterways or in other public spaces and see this as an acceptable use of vacant land.

Urban Management

Throughout the Pacific serious questions challenge the efficiency and effectiveness of urban agencies in their response to the important and pressing issues facing the region's cities. In part this is because urban areas straddle modern and traditional authority, which is most evident in conflicts over land and resource management (Chung and Hill 2002). Both Jones (2003) and Storey (2005) have suggested that urban governance will be one of the most important issues facing Pacific Island countries this century. Clearly authorities are struggling to cope with the patterns and rates of urban development with respect to the resources at their disposal. This has partly to do with the diffuse nature of urban development, but it also concerns issues of governance. The end result is that many of the decisions about urban development and growth that are being made occur outside the policy and legal apparatus of the state.

While limits to the authority of institutions in part explain their weakness, many key agencies working on urban issues in the Pacific lack the necessary skilled staff to work effectively. This applies to those working in formal government structures and also to traditional authorities. Throughout the Pacific there is a lack of qualified urban specialists. There is a clear and urgent need for increased training of planners and professionals if more consistent urban policies and more effective practices are to develop.

While one response is to strengthen government agencies to deal better with urbanization, there is also a strong case for better equipping indigenous leaders and institutions to deal with decisions relating to land, urban development, and informal settlements. Community-based planning does have potential in the Pacific. In Palau, traditional authorities play the role of "advisors" to the more formal system. Community consultation and participation in urban planning have been adopted in Kiribati and Samoa (Jones and Lea 2007). Efforts to include disparate ethnic populations and the poor and marginalized are critical in building relationships and involving all urban citizens in decision making and planning. Moreover, in looking at towns through a more strongly indigenous lens we may see urban places and issues quite differently, as well as potentially identify a wider array of potential solutions and their champions. As one example, the Malvatamauri (National Council of Chiefs) in Vanuatu has recently encouraged chiefs to take part in training courses to raise their level of awareness and capacity in development issues. It has also encouraged the creation of an urban council of chiefs (Figure 26.10) to act as advisors on periurban land and social issues and to play a more proactive role in urban governance in general, providing a positive example of capacity building in this area.

No single institution or agency (whether government, donor, or NGO) has the capacity to comprehensively address the needs of

Figure 26.10. Port Vila's urban chiefs (photo DS).

urban development in the region. This implies the need for strong communication and effective linkages. But relationships between key institutions are characterized by the absence of coordination and a lack of interinstitutional awareness and communication. A recent University of the South Pacific initiative that involved bringing together government departments to talk about urban housing concluded that a panoply of initiatives existed but were divided into various ministries with limited knowledge and interaction between them. Also noted were the predominance of top-down solutions and a lack of community consultation. Few residents are aware of what is provided by government welfare agencies, NGOs, and other support agencies.

The coordination of urban planning is further complicated by the growth of urban settlements on customary lands. Chung and Hill (2002: 47) have noted that "Vanuatu currently has no specific national planning policies or strategies for managing present and future urban growth, and little capacity either in the public or private sector for this task." Typically, while those within town boundaries are under the jurisdiction of a municipal authority, periurban populations are the responsibility of provincial government. Both levels of government remain hampered by a lack of financial and human capacity.

Nevertheless, it is through local rather than central government that stronger relationships with communities are more likely to be forged. In recent years there has been an increased focus on the role of local government in playing a more important role between the state and civil society in the Pacific. There is much work to do, however, before decentralization to local authorities results in anything more effective than what central government may offer. Local government has struggled to build effective relationships with communities and has not always demonstrated any greater capacity or willingness to meet the needs of urban populations. Moreover, urban populations generally have a low level of understanding of local government. Despite the need and potential for a greater role, local governments have a weak resource base, lack human and financial resources, and are rarely able to act autonomously of the central government.

Even in countries where there have been concerted efforts to deal with urban problems alongside urban management, success has been limited. Thus in Kiribati, despite a series of attempts at more effective urban planning, concern has been expressed about the long-term commitment to change. With regard to urban planning and land, actual implementation of plans has been weak given their implied and actual confrontation of traditional leadership and landownership patterns. Capacity-building efforts, primarily in urban land administration in the late 1990s, were considered a success but questions remain over the sustainability of the gains (Jones and Lea 2007). Many initiatives have simply been overwhelmed by the day-to-day focus on survival and the lack of effective ongoing administration. A further difficulty that urban management faces is that while cities are places where power resides, rarely is political power and legitimacy *derived* from the city. There remains an urgent need to create effective partnerships that transcend "modern" and "traditional" structures if cities are to not become chaotic, sprawling places that are impossible to manage. Ultimately, harmonious urban life demands urban and national economies that generate adequate incomes to enable and sustain proper infrastructure provision, but also balanced development between urban and rural areas.

Toward an Uncertain Urban Future

The Pacific faces an uncertain urban future. Social disorganization and crime increasingly result from inequalities and have grown in concert with the increasing size of urban populations. In Papeete, Nukuʻalofa, and Honiara, there have been riots over inadequate urban employment and quality of life. Security concerns among the elite are prevalent in Port Moresby and accentuate topographical divisions in the city, with the better-off occupying the higher ground. In this way neocolonial towns have begun to revert to something akin to the segregated colonial outposts of the past, with an increasing separation of the elite from the poor (Connell and Lea 1994). It would be misleading to suggest that the situation characterizing Port Moresby is found everywhere in the urban Pacific, but increases in poverty, crime, and periodic unrest can be seen in towns and cities as diverse as Lae, Nukuʻalofa, and Suva. Social and economic divisions are more apparent and are usually spatially demarcated; urban unemployment, along with social disorganization and crime, has risen, alongside the growing visibility of the informal sector; and urban management has failed to cope (Goddard 2005). Even in the small towns, urban service provision is fragmented among numerous activities. Tension between landowners and migrants exists in the face of land shortages, and bureaucratic ineptitude and political corruption have contributed to division. In the failure to effectively deal with urban futures and in the absence of opportunities for growing populations, in both rural and urban areas, the Pacific is likely to encounter greater political instability and social insecurity in the decades to come.

Yet urbanization has many positive characteristics, and urban areas are increasingly vital to the region's future prosperity and development. Urban life enables individuals to obtain higher education and technical training and gain access to limited amounts of skilled employment and good housing. Migration may also reduce population pressure on scarce rural resources, increase access to more affordable infrastructure and services (especially in atoll economies), and, through remittances, lead to an improved quality of life in rural areas. Cities are centers of political and economic power and remain important symbols of nationhood and places of cultural diversity as well as economic opportunity and social development.

It is not inevitable that urbanization should be unmanageable and that problems should worsen. Strategies that emphasize integrated rural development and stress both economic advancement and social services will be important. As more children are born in town and remain there, however, long-term urban policies and visions need to emerge. As long as urban employment appears more prestigious and city life is perceived as being of higher quality than rural life, population pressures in urban areas will increase. The social, economic, and environmental future of the region depends to a great extent on how successfully these problems can be solved.

Although new attempts are being made in several countries to formulate coherent urban policy, present approaches toward the management of urbanization are still generally piecemeal and directed toward individual projects and particular towns. Coordination is conspicuous by its absence, a situation directly reflecting the condition of urban government across the region. The future of urban management is also bound up with the ability of urban authorities to become more self-sufficient. The potential for achieving this self-sufficiency depends on income-generating capacity, but taxes and fees are difficult to collect and funding for urban development is hard to obtain. Solutions materialize in episodic and expensive responses to crisis conditions without reference to the wider context of urban service provision. Urban management is often crisis management rather than good housekeeping. This does not augur well for a sustainable urban structure and function. Future towns and cities in the island Pacific are likely to be much larger and more difficult to manage than they are today.

BIBLIOGRAPHY

ADB (Asian Development Bank). 2002. *Kiribati: Monetization in an atoll society.* Manila: Asian Development Bank.

———. 2004. *Pacific region environmental strategy 2005–2009.* Manila: Asian Development Bank.

Brookfield, H. C., with D. Hart. 1971. *Melanesia: A geographical interpretation of an island world.* London: Methuen.

Bryant, J. 1993. *Urban poverty and the environment in the South Pacific.* Armidale, N.S.W.: University of New England.

Bryant-Tokelau, J. 1995. The myth exploded: Urban poverty in the Pacific. *Environment and Urbanization* 7(2): 109–129.

Chand S., and C. Yala. 2007. Improving access to land within settlements in Port Moresby. Working Paper 07–04, Crawford School of Economics and Development: Australian National University.

Chung, M., and D. Hill. 2002. Urban informal settlements in Vanuatu: Challenge for sustainable development. Report prepared for the Pacific Islands Forum Secretariat and UNESCAP, Suva.

Connell, J. 1997. *Papua New Guinea: The struggle for development.* London: Routledge.

———. 2003. Regulation of space in the contemporary postcolonial Pacific city: Port Moresby and Suva. *Asia-Pacific Viewpoint* 43(3): 243–257.

———. 2008. Poverty, migration and economic resilience in small island developing states. In *Small states and the pillars of economic resilience,* ed. L. Briguglio, G. Cordina, N. Farrugia, and C. Vigilance. Valletta: University of Malta.

Connell, J., and J. P. Lea. 1994. Cities of parts, cities apart? Changing places in modern Melanesia. *The Contemporary Pacific* 6(2): 267–309.

———. 2002. *Urbanisation in the Pacific: Towards sustainable development.* London: Routledge.

Eritai, R. M. 2003. Impact of urbanization on the growth and patterns of housing in South Tarawa, Kiribati. MA thesis, University of the South Pacific, Suva.

Goddard, M. 2005. *The unseen city: Anthropological perspectives on Port Moresby, Papua New Guinea.* Canberra: Pandanus Books.

Government of the Republic of Vanuatu. 2002. *Vanuatu poverty survey: Analysis report.* Port Vila: Vanuatu Statistics Office.

Jones, P. 2003. Urban development in the Pacific—issues paper. Pacific workshop on managing the transition from village to city: Pacific Urban Agenda. UNESCAP/POC, Nadi, December 1–4.

Jones, P., and J. P. Lea. 2007. What has happened to urban reform in the Island Pacific? Some lessons from Kiribati and Samoa. *Pacific Affairs* 80(3): 473–491.

Lea, J. P., 1996. Tourism, realpolitik and development in the South Pacific. In *Tourism, crime and international security issues,* ed. A. Pizam and Y. Mansfeld, 123–142. Chichester: Wiley.

Mara, R. 1994. *The Pacific Islands in the year 2010: A vision from within.* Honolulu: East-West Center.

Mitchell, J., 2004. "Killing Time" in a postcolonial town: Young people and settlements in Port Vila, Vanuatu. In *Globalization and Culture Change in the Pacific Islands,* ed. V. Lockwood, 358–376. Upper Saddle River, N.J.: Prentice-Hall.

Monsell-Davis, M. 1993. Urban exchange: Safety-net or disincentive? Wantoks and relatives in the urban Pacific. *Cultural Anthropology* 16(2): 45–66.

Reddy, M., V. Naidu, and M. Mohanty. 2003. The urban informal sector in Fiji: Results from a survey. *Fijian Studies* 1(1): 127–154.

Secretariat of the Pacific Community (SPC). 2011. Pacific Island populations: Estimates and projections of demographic indicators for selected years. http://www.spc.int/sdp/index.php?option=com_docman&task=doc_download&gid=344&Itemid=42&lang=en.

Storey, D. 2003. The peri-urban Pacific: From exclusive to inclusive cities. *Asia-Pacific Viewpoint* 43(3): 259–279.

———. 2005. Urban governance in Pacific Island countries: Advancing an overdue agenda. State Society and Governance in Melanesia Project Discussion Paper 2005/7. Canberra: Australian National University.

———. 2006. End of the line? Globalisation and Fiji's garment industry. In *Globalisation and governance in the Pacific Islands,* ed. S. Firth, 217–238. Canberra: Australian National University E-Press.

———. 2010. *Urban poverty in Papua New Guinea.* Port Moresby: National Research Institute.

Storey, D., and S. Hunter. 2010. Kiribati: An environmental 'perfect storm.' *Australian Geographer* 41(2): 167–181.

Talbot, J., and B. Ronnie. 2007. Postcolonial town planning in Commonwealth nations. *The Round Table: The Commonwealth Journal of International Affairs* 96(3): 319–329.

UNESCAP. 1999. *Managing the transition from the village to the city in the South Pacific.* New York: United Nations.

UNESCAP/POC. 2002. Squatter settlement assessment Nasinu. Phase II Report. Suva.

World Bank. 2000. *Cities, seas, and storms: Managing change in Pacific Island economies.* Vol. II, *Managing Pacific towns.* Washington D.C.: World Bank.

Economy

Pacific Island economies are constrained by factors of scale, distance, limited resources, and the vicissitudes of global political economy. Substantive development has occurred in New Zealand, Hawai'i, and, to a lesser extent, the large, resource-rich islands in Melanesia. Most island economies remain partially dependent on external aid and/or remittances. Topics covered in this section include economy, agriculture, logging, ocean resources, mining, tourism, communications, and development.

Pacific Island Economies

Geoff Bertram

27

Pacific Island economies are small and isolated, but for the most part they are not poor by the usual standards of world poverty. Environmentally deprived areas of Papua New Guinea are a partial exception (Booth 1995: 208; World Bank 1999; Allen, Bourke, and Gibson 2005). Provision of basic needs has seldom been under threat for the indigenous populations of the islands, and living standards across much of the region continue to be underwritten by official transfers and private remittances, while rising earnings from tourism (Milne 2005; Taylor, Hardner, and Stewart 2006) and fisheries (Gillett et al. 2001) have transformed several of the region's economies. There is considerable geographic mobility of individuals, which makes migration a central issue for economic policy and ensures that most of the region's labor markets are open, with wages in the islands indexed (at a discount) to wage rates obtainable in the outside world. It is limited migration outlets, rather than natural resource constraints, that locate Papua New Guinea and Solomon Islands at the bottom of the human development scale in the region (UNDP 1999: 16–19).

Smallness brings with it relative insignificance on the global scale. In 2005 Melanesia, Micronesia, and Polynesia excluding Papua New Guinea and Hawai'i had a combined population of 3.2 million, only 0.05 percent of the world population of 6.5 billion. Adding in those two larger entities brings the total to 9.9 million, still only 0.15 percent of the world total (United Nations 2005: tables 1, 3, and 5). Including New Zealand as part of the island Pacific adds another 4 million people.

Almost all the Pacific islands have at some stage in the past century been colonies, associated territories, or integrated parts of larger industrialized countries. A significant number continue to operate as subnational jurisdictions. Hawai'i, Guam, Northern Marianas, and American Samoa are fully under U.S. rule; New Caledonia, French Polynesia, and Wallis and Futuna are parts of France; Easter Island and the Galapagos are included within Chile and Ecuador respectively; Tokelau remains part of New Zealand despite continual pressure from Wellington to force "decolonization."

A number of other entities are politically associated, more or less closely, with metropolitan patrons. These ongoing linkages provide institutional resources of great value to the island economies: reliable aid flows, opportunities for migration and maintenance of diasporas, and concessional access to services and markets available from the metropolitan economies (Bertram 2004, 2006). Rallu

and Ahlberg (chapter 22 in this volume) observe that "territories" have significantly longer life expectancy than independent island states, due partly to far better medical facilities.

Trade flows, capital flows, asset ownership, official languages, government structures, and currencies in use have been determined over the past century by the existence of eight main spheres of influence—British, French, U.S., Australian, New Zealand, Chilean, Japanese, and German, the last two of which became absorbed by the others during and after the two world wars of the century. A revival of Japanese influence, in the context of rapidly increasing linkages between the island Pacific and the East Asian economies in general, was evident in the early 1990s. Since then rivalry between Mainland China and Taiwan for influence in the region has brought a rapidly increasing role for Chinese aid and trade, along with rising political tensions.

The ongoing importance of close links between individual island economies and their out-of-region metropolitan patrons—mainly former colonial powers—is evident in Table 27.1, which provides basic background data.

Of the twenty-six entities apart from New Zealand listed in Table 27.1, only nine (Papua New Guinea, Samoa, Fiji, Kiribati, Solomon Islands, Tonga, Vanuatu, Nauru, and Tuvalu) are independent nation-states, only six (Papua New Guinea, Samoa, Fiji, Solomon Islands, Tonga, and Vanuatu) have their own currencies, and only nine (Papua New Guinea, Samoa, Fiji, Solomon Islands, Tonga, Vanuatu, the Marshall Islands, Federated States of Micronesia, and Kiribati) are members of the World Bank and IMF. This accounts for the weak representation of the region in most major international databases, a gap only partly filled by the Asian Development Bank and the PRISM online statistical network.

The internationalization of markets for goods, services, and factors of production over the past three or four decades was less of a change for Pacific Islanders than for the inhabitants of most of the world's developing countries, because of the Pacific's pre-existing freedom of trade and capital flows and its long history of labor migration both within the region and to metropolitan economies.

Industrialization and export-led growth are the exception, not the rule, in the region. Repeated attempts by aid donors and local governments to trigger such growth have produced boom-bust cycles of investment, but not sustainable industrial economies. The past half-century's economic development in most of the island

Table 27.1

Background Data on Twenty-Seven Pacific Economies ca. 2005

Territory	Population ca. 2005	Political classification	Currency	Per capita GNI/GDP US$, purchasing-power parity
U.S. Pacific				
Hawai'i	1,285,498	Integrated	US$	50,322
Guam	169,000	Integrated	US$	15,000
Northern Marianas	69,221	Integrated	US$	12,500
FSM	107,008	Associated	US$	2,390
Palau	19,907	Associated	US$	7,990
Marshall Islands	50,848	Associated	US$	2,900
American Samoa	66,000	Integrated	US$	5,800
Total	1,767,482			
French Pacific				
French Polynesia	255,000	Integrated	Pacific franc	16,070
New Caledonia	230,789	Integrated	Pacific franc	14,020
Wallis and Futuna	14,944	Integrated	Pacific franc	3,800
Total	500,733			
Australian Pacific				
Papua New Guinea	5,190,786	Sovereign	Kina	740
Kiribati	92,533	Sovereign	Australian $	1,240
Solomon Islands	471,000	Sovereign	Solomons $	690
Vanuatu	186,678	Sovereign	Vatu	1,690
Nauru	9,919	Sovereign	Australian $	5,828
Tuvalu	9,561	Sovereign	Australian $	2,516
Norfolk Island	2,523	Integrated	Australian $	
Total	5,963,000			
New Zealand Pacific				
New Zealand	3,820,749	Sovereign	NZ$	26,750
Samoa	183,000	Sovereign	Tala	2,270
Cook Islands	20,000	Associated	NZ$	9,100
Niue	1,788	Associated	NZ$	5,800
Tokelau	1,537	Integrated	NZ$	1,000
Pitcairn Island	66	Integrated	NZ$	na
Total	4,027,140			
Independent Central Pacific				
Fiji	842,000	Sovereign	Fiji $	3,720
Tonga	101,134	Sovereign	Pa'anga	2,250
Total	943,134			
South American Pacific				
Easter Island	3,791	Integrated	Chilean peso	na
Galapagos Islands	30,000	Integrated	US$	2,989
Total	33,791			
GRAND TOTAL	13,235,280			
Excluding Hawai'i, New Zealand, PNG	2,938,247			

Sources: Population from United Nations 2005 (Hawai'i from US Bureau of Census). Income data from World Bank "World Development Indicators," *CIA World Factbook,* Asian Development Bank Key Indicators of Member Countries, and Taylor et al. 2006.

Pacific has been founded upon the modern infrastructure installed prior to and during decolonization, and the growth and maintenance of living standards has been import-led, funded from a diverse range of sources. It has been the quest for means to finance rising imports without incurring unsustainable indebtedness that has dictated the various economies' structural evolution, including the establishment of large diasporas of migrant workers.

Output, Trade, and the Balance of Payments

Prosperity versus Independence

The usual benchmark statistics used to rank economies in the world scene are Gross Domestic Product (GDP) per head,[1] the Gross National Income (GNI)[2] measure now promoted by the World Bank, and the United Nations' Human Development Index (HDI).[3] Of the 177 countries in the Human Development Index database at http://hdr.undp.org/en/statistics/, only six (or seven including New Zealand) are Pacific Island economies, although a 1999 study (UNDP 1999) calculated HDIs for fourteen Pacific countries on a cross-section basis for that one year. Coverage of the region's GDP and GNI in the World Development Indicators database is better but still incomplete. For only some of the Pacific Island economies are reliable output or income data available on a consistent basis over time. In any case, for many of the smaller ones the statistical concepts underlying GDP and GNI are less applicable than for large developing economies because of the importance of sources of income (remittances, aid, and other transfers) that are not counted and the extent to which modern-sector economic activity has moved offshore to the neighboring metropolitan economies. Nevertheless, the data on GDP and the balance of payments do have a story to tell.

The first outstanding fact to emerge is that with the exception of New Zealand (a rich country that is better classified as part of the metropolitan Pacific Rim economy), the GDP per head of island economies listed in Table 27.1 is inversely related to their degree of political independence. Table 27.2 shows that the collective per capita GDP per head of fully sovereign island territories is only 3 percent that of politically integrated territories. Exclusion of sovereign Papua New Guinea raises this only to 7 percent. Exclusion also of Hawai'i, the largest and highest-income nonsovereign territory, raises the figure to 18 percent. Only tiny Tokelau, fully integrated with very low estimated GDP per head, breaks the pattern.

Table 27.2

Per Capita GDP/GNI by Political Status 2005: US Dollars

	All	Excl PNG	Excl PNG and Hawai'i
Sovereign nations*	1,193	2,433	2,433
In free association	3,782	3,782	3,782
Integrated	35,793	35,793	13,466
Region average	9,052	19,282	5,673

Source: Table 27.1.
* Excluding New Zealand.

Armstrong et al. (1998), Bertram (2004), and Sampson (2005: 7) find strong statistical evidence that nonsovereign status is positive for the level of per capita GDP. Sampson found, however, no significant effect of sovereignty status on the growth rate, and a negative effect on growth of being a small state, after controlling for sovereignty. Higher incomes, in other words, are explained by past, not current, economic growth.

While the data in Table 27.2 show a correlation between political integration and late-twentieth-century relative prosperity, they do not prove causality: has political integration led to relative economic prosperity, or is it just that poorer territories were more likely to be decolonized? The cases of French Polynesia and the Federated States of Micronesia—both extremely resource-poor but with relatively high incomes because of official transfer payments—provide support for the first hypothesis. Kiribati, decolonized by Britain in the year its phosphate resource was exhausted, gives some credibility to the second. Papua New Guinea, with rich mineral resources but very low incomes and failing growth as a sovereign nation-state, lends some credence to the idea that the transition from colony status to sovereign independence places a drag on economic development (Connell 1997; Manning 2005). The difficulties encountered at the beginning of the twenty-first century by the sovereign nation-states Nauru and Solomon Islands (Connell 2006a, 2006b) point the same way.

Provisionally, it seems reasonable to regard political connections as more a source than a consequence of economic welfare. This proposition—that in the Pacific relative wealth flows from "dependency," and relative hardship from independence—has seemed paradoxical to many social scientists familiar with the larger developing economies of Latin America and Asia. It is nevertheless a feature of small island economies not only in the Pacific but also in the Caribbean and Atlantic and Indian oceans (Baldacchino and Milne 2000; Bertram and Poirine 2007).

Slow Growth

A second main fact about Pacific Island economies is that across the region, economic growth as measured by GDP during the past three decades has been slow and often outpaced by population growth, so that per capita incomes have been flat or have even fallen slightly according to the official statistics.

Data on the growth rates of output and incomes in Pacific Island economies are patchy and unreliable, but they generally indicate slow growth rates relative to other regions of the world and a tendency for growth rates to have fallen since the 1970s. Fichera (2005: 46) reports annual growth rates of real GDP for nine Pacific small-island economies from 1995 through 2004 as only 1.7 percent, falling to 1.6 percent per annum in the last three years of the period. Allowing for population growth, this implies stagnation of per capita domestic output.

Faal (2007: 16) reports Papua New Guinea's growth of real GDP falling from 5.5 percent from 1960 to 1975 to 2.3 percent from 1975 to 2004 and less than 1 percent from 1996 to 2004, and estimates that per capita GDP in 2004 was below the level of the early 1970s (2007: 20). Sugden and Tevi (2004) trace decades of weak growth performance in Vanuatu.

Sampson (2005) in a major cross-country statistical study of 177 countries, including eight small-island Pacific economies, found that being located in the Pacific had a significant negative effect on growth in the period from 1995 to 2003. This was replicated by Gibson (2007), who found evidence that while remoteness per se may have contributed to slow growth and while there is some evidence of regional contagion effects (whereby an economy with slow-growing neighbors will itself grow more slowly than would otherwise be the case), an important factor inhibiting growth seems also to have been the prevalence of market power[4] in the transport and communications sectors, reflected in higher air fares and costs of money transfers, communications, and freight, relative to other regions of the world economy. Money transfer costs were the focus of an earlier study by Gibson, McKenzie, and Rohorua (2006), who found that remitting money from New Zealand to Tonga cost between 19 and 31 percent of the amount sent, which was "between 2.5 and 3 times as expensive as transfers from the United States to Mexico, and approximately twice as expensive on average as bank transfers to a wide variety of countries from the United States and United Kingdom including countries with similar volumes of remittances as Tonga" (2006: 121). Such evidence of high margins indicates a substantial deadweight burden of market power potentially holding back economic growth based on remittance finance.

The region-wide pattern of slow output growth is common across a wide variety of income levels, political regimes, and trade orientations. It represents a significant slowdown compared with the rapid material progress of the region up until the early 1980s and is attributable directly to the end of a period in which government was a strongly growing "leading sector" for the island economies.

From the Second World War until the late 1970s, with the international political spotlight focused on issues of development and decolonization, the dominant metropolitan powers (particularly the United States, Britain, France, and New Zealand) financed and organized the project of extending to their island dependencies many of the attributes of their own welfare states, especially in the fields of education, health, and public works. But once the dependent territories had been raised to levels of material welfare consistent with the desire of the metropolitan governments to emerge with credibility from the decolonization era, the impetus of state expansion slackened (except in French Polynesia, where the nuclear testing program resulted in a continuing economic boom through the 1980s [Poirine 1994a]). Decolonization was usually followed by a drop or leveling off in the amount of ongoing aid funding provided by former metropolitan powers, and a corresponding loss of the previous momentum of public-sector expenditure.

The era of government-led growth left a valuable legacy of physical infrastructure (roads, ports, energy and telecommunications systems, public buildings, education and health) and economies with employment heavily concentrated in the externally financed public sector. As public expenditure leveled off, however, there was no subsequent takeoff of private-sector-led growth in GDP except in Fiji, where sugar, tourism, and manufacturing provided high-linkage export sectors. In most island economies, private investment has remained concentrated in nontraded goods and services such as commerce, construction, transport, communications, and financial services. Because local markets are small, the growth potential of these sectors is limited, and hence investment opportunities are limited.

Low growth of GDP is not due to any lack of finance for investment. The Pacific Islands do not have a "savings gap"; on the contrary, a common theme in the literature on island finance is the existence of excess liquidity due to the shortage of bankable projects (Nagai 1996). It is lack of profitable investment opportunities, due partly to small scale and geographical isolation, that limits the possibilities for orthodox textbook growth models based on large-country experience.

A third fact is the lack of economic integration, as usually understood, among the Pacific Island economies. Trade statistics show the Pacific to be the least integrated region in the world, with trade between the island states amounting to less than 2 percent of their total exports (McGregor, Sturton, and Halapua 1992: 20–21). Each island economy trades mainly with bilateral partners outside the region, with former or actual metropolitan patrons as the preferred trading partners. Only in nontradeable economic activities—government, education, scientific research, transport, communications—is there a tendency toward integration among the island states.

Financing Imports

A fourth major feature of the region is its unusual combination of very large trade deficits with a generally healthy current account on the balance of payments. Figure 27.1 plots for seventeen Pacific Island economies the balance of trade in goods and services over the three decades to 2004. This balance, sometimes termed the "commercial balance," is calculated by adding together all of a territory's foreign-exchange earnings from the sale of exported goods and services including tourism, transport, and communications and subtracting all foreign-exchange payments for imported goods and services, including services such as transport and insurance that enter into the cost of imported goods. This gives a measure of the extent to which the sale of local output on world markets enables an economy to pay for its import needs.

For purposes of cross-country comparison, the data for each economy have been averaged for each five-year period between 1975 and 2004 and expressed as a percentage of merchandise imports (that is, imports of goods, excluding services purchased overseas). Only minerals-rich Papua New Guinea has consistently shown a positive commercial balance over the past fifteen years. The remainder show deficits ranging from around 10 to 20 percent of imports (Hawai'i, Solomons, American Samoa, Fiji) to 80 percent or more (Tuvalu, French Polynesia, Federated States of Micronesia).

Because of the open nature of these economies, the trade deficits are large relative to GDP. Across the six countries surveyed in detail by the World Bank in 1991 (Fiji, Papua New Guinea, Vanuatu, Kiribati, Western Samoa, and Tonga [World Bank 1991: 12]), exports averaged 55 percent of GDP and imports averaged 67 percent, so that their collective commercial deficit was 12 percent of GDP—a very high ratio by international standards.

Some possible classifications suggest themselves in Figure 27.1. Melanesia and Hawai'i, with larger landmasses and populations, have relatively "strong" commercial balances (small trade deficits). Small-island Polynesia and Micronesia have conspicuously

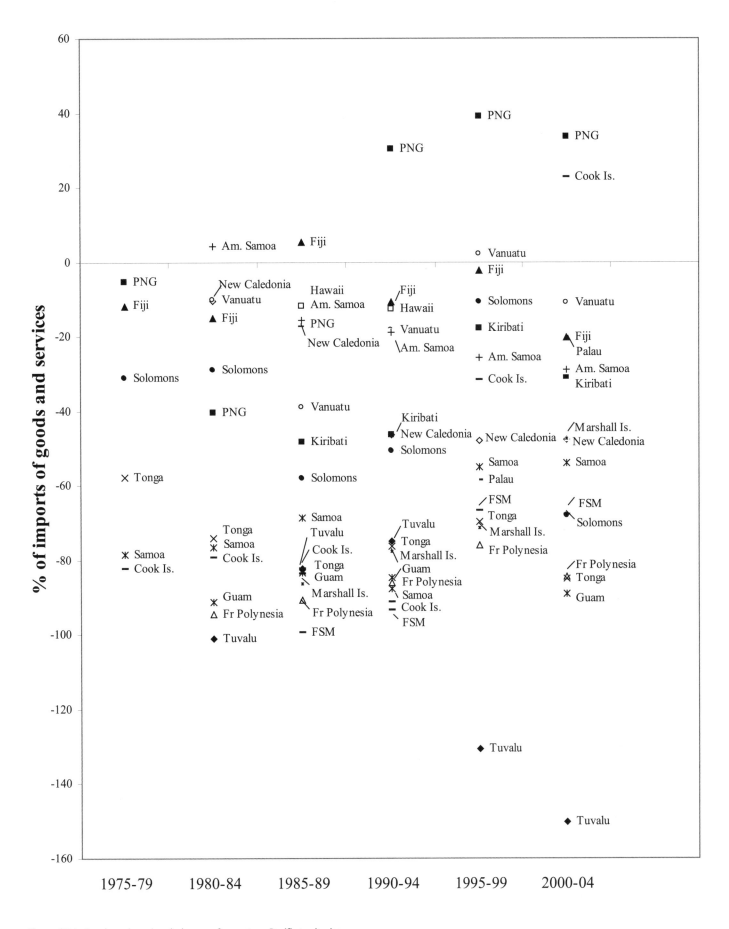

Figure 27.1. Goods and services balances of seventeen Pacific territories.

large deficits, with the exception of the Cook Islands since 2000, where a tourism boom (included in services exports) has triggered a transition out of MIRAB[5] status. Many of the Polynesian and Micronesian microstates shown in Figure 27.1 have commercial deficits between 50 and 150 percent of imports, which means that more than half the imports to those economies are financed either by current transfers (repatriated overseas earnings, private remittances, and official aid) or by capital inflow (borrowing plus direct foreign investment).

These two possible means of financing trade deficits have radically different implications for economic sustainability. Economies with trade deficits financed by capital inflows face rising overseas indebtedness over time, but Pacific Island economies have kept their overseas debt at modest and declining levels. A 1996 World Bank study (World Bank 1996: 240–241) classified the degree of indebtedness of 210 economies, including thirteen Pacific Island economies. No Pacific Island states were among the 53 "severely indebted low and middle income" economies. Only two (Samoa and Papua New Guinea) appeared among the 31 "moderately indebted" countries. The other eleven Pacific economies covered were ranked "less indebted" or had no classifiable external debt.

As Figure 27.2 shows, the level of public overseas indebtedness in Pacific small-island economies for which data are readily available was generally below half of GNI in 2005–2006, following a decade-long downward trend. (The total debt figure for Samoa since 2000 has been inflated by short-term debt associated with the country's Offshore Finance Center; excluding this, Samoa's external debt matches the trend in the other countries of the region).

It is, therefore, not capital inflow that has funded the large trade deficits seen in Figure 27.1. It is current-account transfer payments into the island economies. These transfers come from three main sources. First is the payment of interest and dividends on financial assets held overseas—income from overseas investments such as Kiribati's Revenue Equalisation Reserve Fund (RERF) and Tuvalu's Trust Fund. Second is the flow of remittances sent home by migrants living and working in metropolitan economies such as Australia, New Zealand, the United States, and Canada, or employed as seamen by international shipping lines (Kiribati and Tuvalu) and as peacekeeping troops by the UN (Fiji). Third is official aid provided in the form of "unrequited transfers" for which no repayment is required, so that island governments' budgets can be funded with no need for large-scale borrowing.

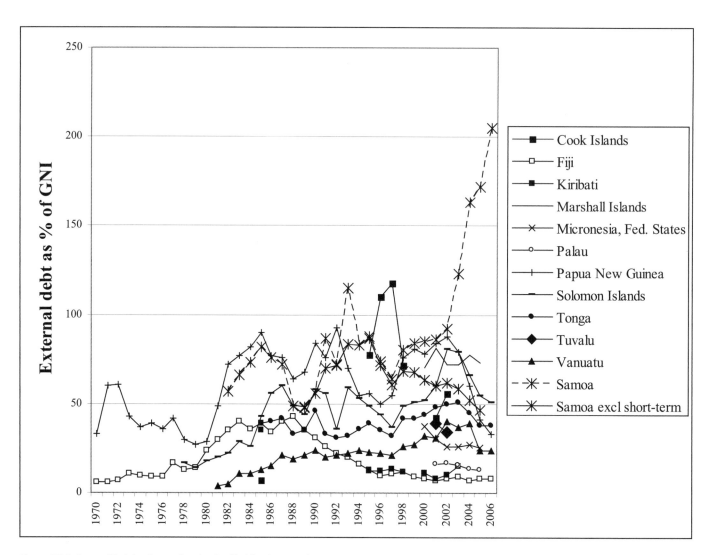

Figure 27.2. *External indebtedness of twelve Pacific Island economies.*

Table 27.3 demonstrates the various ways in which Pacific island economies maintain strong current accounts in their balance of payments despite having generally large commercial deficits. Only two of the twelve countries in Table 27.3 have strong trade balances. Fiji, as already seen in Figure 27.1, is an economy that does not have a significant trade deficit, and so pays its way on the basis of export earnings. Papua New Guinea is the largest single aid recipient in the region, reflecting its low income and large population, but aid funding is only about 10 percent of export earnings and serves mainly to offset the outflow of dividends, interest, and repatriated earnings. (Private remittances flow out from Papua New Guinea because of the large number of expatriates employed there. The small number of Papuan migrants overseas means that remittances in the other direction are small.)

The Federated States of Micronesia, the Marshall Islands, Tuvalu, and Solomon Islands all have heavy commercial deficits financed by large official transfers. French Polynesia (not included in Table 27.3) also funds its commercial deficit in this way. These economies can be described as aid-driven. In contrast, Tonga and Western Samoa rely mainly on private remittances to fund their

Table 27.3

Financing of the Current Account in Thirteen Pacific Island Economies: US$ million annual averages

Country	Exports: goods & services	Imports: goods & services	Commercial balance	Interest, dividends, etc.	Remittances	Official transfers	Current account balance
American Samoa							
1985–89	292.33	337.67	-45.33	na	na	na	na
1990–93	331.5	390	-58.5	na	na	na	na
1995–99	353.70	473.14	-119.44	na	na	na	na
2000–05	391.44	549.68	-158.24	na	na	na	na
Cook Islands							
1985–89	20.43	29.66	-9.23	na	na	na	na
1990–92	25.85	50.37	-24.52	na	na	na	na
1995–99	59.08	55.84	3.24	na	1.33	8.07	3.24
2000–04	92.54	79.80	12.75	na	1.30	5.07	12.75
Federated States of Micronesia							
1985–89	16.83	83.74	-66.91	d	6.53	113.75	53.36
1990–94	43.32	154.14	-110.82	d	2.4	114.93	8.42
1995–99	56.12	148.14	-92.02	d	1.80	86.18	-4.50
2000–04	54.38	176.70	-122.33	7.50	-0.63	101.10	-15.70
Fiji							
1985–89	581.46	565.78	15.68	-25.22	-10.42	24.04	4.04
1990–94	905.08	922.84	-17.76	-13.7	8.28	34.32	11.14
1995–99	1,113.42	1,129.40	-15.98	-69.18	12.78	92.50	-36.10
2000–04	1,100.44	1,300.63	-200.18				-133.92
Kiribati							
1985–89	20.42	41.41	-20.99	7.43[a]	2.1	19.67	8.21
1990–94	29.18	62.76	-33.58	19.94[b]	7.08	25.38	14.48
1995–99	12.16	57.75	-45.59	30.26[b]	10.90	17.97	3.83
2000–04	11.60	70.19	-58.59	33.22[b]	13.95	17.38	-4.64
Marshall Islands							
1985–89	22.26	57.96	-35.7	d	6.01	52.8	23.1
1990–94	35.14	78.61	-43.46	d	5.68	64.12	26.34
1995–99	38.52	80.04	-41.52	d	0.54	42.14	1.16
2000–04	60.00	96.46	-36.46	d	-10.42	51.44	8.38

Table 27.3. (continued)

Country	Exports: goods & services	Imports: goods & services	Commercial balance	Interest, dividends, etc.	Remittances	Official transfers	Current account balance
Palau							
1995–99	66.20	144.90	-78.70				
2000–04	66.20	115.51	-49.31	5.48	-19.74	22.12	-14.91
Papua New Guinea							
1985–89	1,303.74	1,494.34	-190.6	-150.3	-5.96	100.18	110.88
1990–94	2,256.36	1,867.98	388.38	-305.22	-10.95	4.70	76.35
1995–99	2,555.39	1,867.39	688.00	-351.64	-5.96	100.18	110.88
2000–04	2,285.60	1,926.53	359.07	-311.07	-10.95	4.70	76.35
Solomon Islands							
1985–89	92.6	137.34	-44.74	-7.18	-0.54	26.77	-25.69
1990–92	116.09	167.25	-51.16	-8.06	3.06	35.4	-20.77
1995–99	213.86	234.23	-20.36	-8.75	-8.77	34.35	2.92
2000–04	94.19	153.55	-59.37	-2.57	-3.91	49.88	-46.45
Tonga							
1985–89	24.99	57.05	-32.07	3.23	21.57	5.65	-1.61
1990–93	33.26	74.33	-41.07	3.25	30.7	6.95	-0.17
1995–99					35.60		-10.80
2000–04	39.92	113.54	-73.62	6.79	55.50	4.70	-8.13
Tuvalu							
1985–89	4.35	7.86	-3.52		c	3.53	0.02
1990–93	6.55	10.54	-3.99		c	6.17	2.18
1995–99	5.44	15.76	-10.32	10.41	-0.90	6.51	0.35
2000–04	4.44	23.41	-18.96	15.10	-0.91	6.53	-1.57
Vanuatu							
1985–89	51.1	84.82	-33.72	-0.45	6.84	25.81	-1.52
1990–94	86.43	100.11	-13.68	-24.52	11.16	15.58	-11.26
1995–99	128.84	127.40	1.44	-15.31	-37.25	31.15	-21.43
2000–04	141.58	151.81	-10.24	-9.74	-19.52	23.72	-26.96
Samoa							
1985–89	32.85	71.01	-38.16	0.08	32.41	12.92	7.25
1990–94	42.6	113.03	-70.43	2.61	33.37	13.78	-21.36
1995–99	76.40	129.39	-53.00	1.72	35.38	24.49	6.41
2000–04	106.74	197.33	-90.59	-16.52	56.56	16.90	-17.04

Sources: IMF *Balance of Payments Yearbook* and *International Financial Statistics*; United Nations *Statistical Yearbook 1994*; Asian Development Bank *Key Indicators of Developing Asian and Pacific Countries*; UNCTAD *Handbook of International Trade Statistics*; country statistical office websites.

a   Reserve Equalization Reserve Fund income
b   RERF income plus fishery royalties
c   All transfers included in aid column
d   Included in export and import data

trade deficits; in both these economies remittance flows are on a par with export earnings, and aid provides a top-up. These economies can be described as driven by migration and remittances.

A third funding pattern is that of Kiribati, with its large inflow of dividends and interest from offshore financial assets (RERF) and fishery royalties (Purfield 2005). (Nauru until the 1990s had an even stronger role for investment income in its current account and received only a trickle of aid; the loss of its reserve assets through mismanagement and exhaustion of all but the smallest residual phosphate deposits has converted this former high-income enclave into an impoverished "failed state" [Connell 2006a].) These economies can be described as rent-driven.

Island Economies and Economic Development Theory

The theoretical literature on so-called "microstates" and their economic status has burgeoned in recent years (Baldacchino and Milne 2000; Bertram 2006; Bertram and Poirine 2007; Briguglio et al. 2005; McElroy and Pearce 2006; Sampson 2005; Winters and Martins 2004). The debate can be traced back to the end of the 1950s, when the newly established field of development economics turned its attention to the issue of whether the size of a nation-state influenced its economic development. Two books of collected papers from that period (Robinson 1960; Benedict 1967) set the framework for most work until the 1980s and presented a puzzle that still lies at the heart of the microstate literature. This can be stated in the following terms.

Modernization theories predict that small size should be a handicap for growth and development. A recent careful theoretical analysis by Winters and Martins (2004) considers the consequences of small scale for an economy's ability to sustain a successful export trade on the basis of comparative advantage, and strongly suggests that at least some small island economies will prove nonviable (Winters 2005: 101) Yet the world's very smallest autonomous political units are not located at the bottom of the development ladder, nor is there any robust statistical evidence that small size correlates with low standards of living (Milner and Westaway 1993; Armstrong and Read 2000, 2002, 2006; Baldacchino and Milne 2000).

Theoretical interpretation of these empirical regularities is clearly important for policymaking purposes. By the early 1990s the literature on growth, trade, and migration in the Pacific Islands could be characterized in terms of the emergence of two competing paradigms (Hayes 1991). The dominant mainstream paradigm regarded the observed economic success of island microstates as an anomaly (Briguglio et al. 2005) and prescribed a "big push" to promote investment, output, and commodity exports; otherwise, the paradigm suggests, in the long run the theoretical disadvantages of smallness and isolation must assert themselves.

MIRAB, SITE, and PROFIT Economies

An alternative paradigm is built around the idea that the mainstream theory should be revised to recognize the validity of multiple possible paths to develop and secure material welfare, with island economies serving as exemplars of a wide range of options (Bertram and Poirine 2007). This paradigm originally took shape in the MIRAB model of Bertram and Watters (1985), but has since extended to include small-island tourism economies ("SITEs"—see McElroy 2006) and a wide-ranging set of small states and subnational jurisdictions exercising what Baldacchino and Milne (2000) have termed the "resourcefulness of jurisdiction," leading to the emergence of a category of small-island economies classed as "PROFITs" (Bertram 2006; Baldacchino 2006). The charts in Figure 27.2 and Table 27.3 highlight the ability of small-island economies to sustain living standards significantly above GDP per capita, often by taking advantage of their special circumstances to generate nontraditional income flows.

In MIRAB, SITE, and PROFIT economies the indigenous population maximizes its material well-being by means of globalization and a willingness to seize opportunities as they arise. Subsistence production from land, most of which remains unalienated under customary tenure, puts a floor under living standards by providing for basic needs and possibly also for some modest cash sales of produce to urban or export markets. But it is the release of family members and family savings from village agriculture and fishing, and their outward movement not merely to other sectors but to other islands and other countries, that opens one way to securing higher incomes and wealth. Another is the allocation of effort and ingenuity to negotiating deals, and designing legal and regulatory regimes, to cash in on the willingness of rich-country inhabitants and governments to pay for access to geographic and/or institutional attributes of small islands. Where aid flows are secured, employment in the government sector puts cash into the hands of all households with members engaged in such employment. In the 1990s the public sector accounted for 70 percent of paid employment in Kiribati, 69 percent in Tuvalu, 48 percent in Solomon Islands, and 46 percent in the Federated States of Micronesia (Gillett et al. 2001: 22).

The scale of migrant remittances into the small-island Pacific is substantial, possibly on the order of US$350–400 million annually across three million people, though the distribution is uneven. Browne (2006) estimates total remittance inflows of US$336 million into Fiji, Kiribati, Micronesia, Samoa, and Tonga during 2004, offset only slightly by $12 million of outflows from the Marshall Islands and Palau. Tonga, Samoa, Kiribati, and Vanuatu all appear in the IMF's list of the twenty countries with the highest remittances-to-GDP ratios in the 2005 *World Economic Survey*.

Luthria et al. (2006: 51–52) estimate that one-third of households in Fiji, and 60 percent in Tonga, had at least one overseas migrant. Forty-three percent of Fijian households and 90 percent of Tongan households were reported to be in receipt of remittances. Remittance flows into Fiji in 2004 were estimated as US$130 million and growing rapidly (they were reported as little more than $30 million in 2002). Surveyed households in Tonga received $3,067 each per year in 2004, and Fijian households US$1,328 per year (Luthria et al. 2006: 61). Econometric analysis of the survey data indicated that remittances contributed positively to savings in both economies, more so in Fiji than in Tonga (Luthria et al. 2006: 78), and that remittances had a major effect in reducing income disparities, with the lowest-income quintile of the population securing dramatic increases in disposable incomes (more than 600 percent in Tonga, 82 percent in Fiji [Luthria et al. 2006: 84]).

Offsetting the large remittance inflow to Fiji has been a reverse flow of emigrant capital transfers out of Fiji following each of the coups. Gani (2005) estimated that following the first political crisis in 1987, about US$40 million annually flowed out over the subsequent twelve years.

In Tuvalu, Boland and Dollery (2007: 112) have assembled remittance data from 1986 to 2003 showing a consistent annual inflow of about AU$4 million. Since 1996 remittances have been running at more than 15 percent of GDP, with a peak of 24 percent in 1998.

Outside the New Zealand sphere of influence where it was formulated (Tokelau, Niue, pre-1995 Cook Islands) the MIRAB model has been applied to French Polynesia (Poirine 1994b, 1995; Blanchet 1996), the Federated States of Micronesia (Cameron 1991; Gaffaney 1995; Hezel and Levin 1996), the other small U.S.-associated former Pacific Trust territories, Tonga and Western Samoa, Chile's Pacific outpost of Easter Island (Rapanui), outlying islands of Papua New Guinea and Solomon Islands (Hayes 1993; Friesen 1993), Tuvalu, and Kiribati. Boland and Dollery (2006, 2007) argue that Tuvalu has become a full-fledged MIRAB economy, with remittances (largely from seafarers, but with likely future increases from the growing migrant diaspora in New Zealand) accounting for more than 15 percent of GDP since 1996 and large (though volatile) rental incomes garnered by the government from fishing and telecommunications licenses, philatelic sales, and an investment passport scheme.

The rise of tourism earnings (effectively rents on local landscapes and climate) in economies such as the Cook Islands, Samoa, Vanuatu, and Easter Island—expanding on earlier development in French Polynesia, Hawai'i, Guam, and the Northern Marianas—has recently made tourism a leading sector in several economies, for which the acronym SITEs has been coined by McElroy (2006). Tourism has proved an escape route from MIRAB status for the Cook Islands (Milne 2005) and Norfolk Island (Treadgold 1999).

The more diffuse PROFIT economies (Baldacchino 2006) rely upon institutional innovation to generate rent incomes. Using jurisdictional autonomy (often as subnational rather than sovereign jurisdictions), small-island authorities have experimented with offshore financial centers (Vanuatu and Samoa) and rents from the country's Internet domain and postage stamps (Tuvalu—see Connell 2003). They have introduced institutional changes and regional agreements to increase their share of tuna fishery revenues (Gillett et al. 2001). In several cases they have commanded "geo-strategic rents" (Poirine 1998) from hosting military bases. In the early 2000s Nauru provided a detention center for illegal migrants intercepted by Australia.

Limitations of Tradeable Goods Production

The "industrialization" approach to Pacific Island development lays heavy emphasis on export promotion and private investment, both of which have poor track records in the region over the past half-century with the exceptions of New Zealand and Fiji and possibly, more recently, clothing manufacturing based on migrant Asian workers in the Northern Marianas.

The most important sector producing tradeable goods over the past two decades has been tuna fishing and canning. This sector is 90 percent dominated by operators from outside the region, and the activity takes place offshore, which means that only a fraction of the industry's added value appears in GDP statistics because most of the revenues from sale of the product on world markets do not accrue directly to the island economies. Gillett et al. (2001: ix–xi) report that the value of the tuna catch in the Pacific Islands region increased from about $375 million in 1982 to $1.2 billion in 1993 and $1.9 billion in 1998, equivalent to 11 percent of the combined GDP of all the countries in the region, but benefits to the island economies were limited to royalties, wages, and some local expenditures by the fleets. Governments in the region were estimated to have received $60.3 million in access fees for foreign fishing activity in 1999, just over 3 percent of the catch value. Petersen (2006) similarly estimated royalties as 3 to 4 percent of the catch value. These revenues were unevenly distributed across countries relative to their home economies. Parris and Grafton (2006: 271) show the Federated States of Micronesia, Kiribati, the Marshall Islands, and Solomon Islands as having the largest ratios of fishery rents to GNI. Turning to wages, in 2000, 10,000 Pacific Islanders were directly employed on fishing vessels—mainly in Kiribati, Solomon Islands, and PNG (Gillett et al. 2001: 20)—and total employment directly and indirectly supported by the fishing industry was estimated at between 29,000 and 43,000, between 8 and 11 percent of total wage employment in the region (Gillett et al. 2001: 19). This made fisheries the largest private-sector employer in several island economies.

By 2000 the region had enjoyed most of the limited economic growth potential from tuna fishing. Conservation of stocks places a limit on further increases in catches; forward linkages into processing and canning are fully developed and the cannery sector is mature with five large plants. There may remain scope to increase the fiscal contribution from access rental payments by hard bargaining, but there is no prospect that tuna fisheries can provide any further impulse for accelerated industrial growth. Other candidates to fill the role in an orthodox growth model are not to be found. This leaves the way open for the sort of nonorthodox growth and development strategies canvassed by the alternative, bottom-up paradigm of small-island economic development.

For larger island states, development success hinges on success in production of tradeable goods, because the small-state strategies of the MIRAB, SITE, and PROFIT models run into political resistance above a certain scale. To sustain living standards above subsistence, large-island economies require either strong per capita export performance or the sort of financial transfers associated with subnational status. Those that lack the opportunity to become politically integrated have, of necessity, been forced to attempt an orthodox transition from staple exports to modernization. This is the situation for much of Melanesia, given neighboring Australia's lack of interest in political integration and constraints on per capita aid availability. Only Fiji has been successful in making the transition; the other independent Melanesian states (Vanuatu, Papua New Guinea, and Solomon Islands) have struggled to establish any sustainable economic dynamic and remain dependent on export sectors with limited backward and forward linkages. New Caledonia, in contrast, exhibits the material benefits of its political integration with France (note its GDP per capita figure in Table 27.1 compared with the rest of Melanesia). The largest Polynesian island economy, Hawai'i, enjoys U.S. living standards.

New Zealand

New Zealand and Hawai'i are different in size and character from the small-island Pacific. Both are high-income postindustrial economies that host migrant diasporas and are the source of transfer payments to the smaller, less-developed islands. Their relative prosperity and historically strong growth performance have gone together with the establishment of large "settler" populations ethnically and culturally transplanted from outside the Pacific. They have highly skilled labor forces and an autonomous capitalist dynamic. This brief discussion will focus on the economy of New Zealand.

By the last decade of the nineteenth century, New Zealand was already among the world's top three or four economies in terms of real income per head, a status from which it has since slipped, but to which it was originally driven by a particular combination of circumstances, of which two deserve special mention.

First was the high degree of political integration with Great Britain, of which New Zealand was at that time still a colony. The special political access New Zealand enjoyed in British government circles remained formidably effective through the Great Depression of the 1930s (when at the 1932 Ottawa Conference New Zealand secured imperial preference for its agricultural exports at the expense of South American export economies) and on into the 1970s. At that point the political linkage failed in the face of Britain's entry to Europe, and a pronounced slowdown in New Zealand's growth performance has been evident in the subsequent four decades.

Second, as part of the high-income legacy of colonialism in settler colonies, a very open and fluid labor market caused real wage rates in New Zealand to be indexed to rates initially in Britain and in the other "settler capitalisms" of Australia, South Africa, Chile, Uruguay, Argentina, and the west coast of the United States (Denoon 1983). (The same process probably applied to Hawai'i, which is not included in Denoon's study.) After British migration to New Zealand slowed down after the 1960s, a close migration nexus continued to bind together the New Zealand and Australian labor markets, with large numbers of New Zealand–born workers resident in Australia on a long-term basis. This extreme openness of the labor market renders closed-economy modernization models as inapplicable to New Zealand economic history as they are today to most other Pacific Island economies.

The lesson of New Zealand is not, therefore, that growth can be induced by independence, but rather that economic prosperity can be secured under conditions of dependence and that a transition to greater autonomy may involve some economic loss. Hawai'i's experience points in the same direction.

Migrant Diasporas

Economic development is conventionally defined in terms of the output produced by the resident population of a territory. For many Pacific Islanders, however, development means capitalizing on economic opportunities across a wider international arena. The migrant can access income-earning opportunities, investment opportunities, and educational and lifestyle opportunities that are not available in the home territory and that could be provided there only at unwarranted cost. Wherever they are not restrained by legal barriers, Pacific Islanders are geographically mobile in pursuit of economic opportunity.

A feature of many of the small-island economies, especially those of Polynesia, therefore, is that a significant proportion of their home-born population reside and work away from their home islands. Correspondingly, an important feature of the economies of larger regional economies such as New Zealand and Hawai'i is the presence of large communities of migrants who retain strong ties with their home communities. Other Pacific Rim economies such as Australia, California, and British Columbia also have substantial Pacific Islander communities living and working there.

Table 27.4 shows the geographic distribution of 600,000 people born in the island Pacific (excluding New Zealand) who were recorded in censuses as living in a country other than their place of birth at the year 2000. (The table shows in addition the New Zealand first-generation diaspora (mainly in Australia) which comprised another 529,000 individuals.) Since the data is only for place of birth and omits second-generation descendants of migrants who, despite having been born in the host country, identify themselves as part of the diaspora of their family's country of origin, the figures are lower bound.

Of the twenty-three places of birth in Table 27.4, three have more than half of their locally born population living abroad, and nine have more than one-third. The United States, New Zealand, Australia, and Canada are the main host economies, and there is also evidence of considerable movement within the Pacific Island region.

Hayes (1991: 3–9) assembled figures from a range of sources to construct an estimate of the geographic distribution of several Polynesian ethnic groups about 1986. Of his total of 500,000 ethnic Polynesians excluding the indigenous peoples of New Zealand, Hawai'i, and French Polynesia, nearly 40 percent were resident in the three main metropolitan destinations New Zealand, Australia, and the United States (including Hawai'i). The proportion of these ethnic Polynesians resident outside their homelands in 1986 ranged from 22 percent for Tongans to 78 percent for Niueans. By 2000 (Table 27.4) the Tongan ratio had risen to 34 percent while the Niuean ratio remained at 77 percent.

Ahlburg and Levin (1990: chapter 1) found that of 83,000 islands-born migrants living in the United States in 1980, about 27,500 were from Polynesia. The other two significant migrant communities were Guamanians (36,782) and Fijians (mainly Indo-Fijians) (7,538). Relative to the home populations, thus, more than one-third of Guam's indigenous population was living in the metropolitan United States in the early 1980s. The corresponding figure in Table 27.4 is 29 percent, but as already noted this place-of-birth data understates the true diaspora. Fijian-born migrants in the United States, New Zealand, Australia, and Canada totaled more than 33,000 in 1980; by 2000 this number had grown to 124,000 (Table 27.4).

Ahlburg (1996a: 8–10) notes that in the 1990s the Federated States of Micronesia, Guam, Palau, and the Northern Marianas all became major host countries for in-migrants from Asia while the migration of Micronesians themselves continued, resulting in an increasingly complex and dynamic demographic picture in that part of the Pacific. Within Micronesia, large-scale migration movements from smaller to larger islands have reproduced internally the wider pattern of movement; Hezel and Levin (1996: 95) estimated

Table 27.4

Pacific Island First-Generation Migrant Diasporas

	Diaspora (thousands)	Home resident (thousands)	Total (thousands)	Diaspora %	Resident in (thousands)					
					USA	NZ	AUS	CAN	Other Pacific islands	Other
American Samoa	40.7	57.0	97.7	42	33.3	0.4	0.2	0.0	2.4	4.5
Cook Islands	22.7	19.0	41.7	54	0.1	15.2	4.7	0.0	0.2	2.3
Fiji	143.1	810.7	953.8	15	31.5	25.7	44.3	22.8	3.8	15.0
French Polynesia	3.5	236.1	239.6	1	0.0	0.5	0.3		2.3	0.4
Guam	89.6	155.4	245.0	37	71.7	0.0	0.1	0.1	2.6	15.0
Kiribati	3.7	90.7	94.4	4	1.0	0.5	0.4	0.0	1.2	0.5
Marshall Islands	11.5	52.8	64.3	18	7.3	0.0	0.0	0.0	0.6	3.5
Micronesia, Federated States of	24.6	107.1	131.7	19	7.5	0.0	0.0	0.0	10.0	7.1
Nauru	1.0	12.0	13.0	8	0.1	0.2	0.5	0.0	0.1	0.2
New Caledonia	1.8	213.2	215.0	1	0.0	0.2	1.1	0.0	0.4	0.2
New Zealand	528.6	3,857.8	4,386.4	12	26.4		355.8	9.9	7.0	129.5
Niue	6.6	2.0	8.6	77	0.1	5.3	0.5	0.0	0.1	0.7
Norfolk Island	0.4	1.9	2.3	16	0.0	0.1	0.2	0.0	0.0	0.0
Northern Mariana Islands	10.7	76.0	86.7	12	4.2	0.0	0.0	0.0	2.5	4.0
Palau	12.8	19.7	32.5	39	2.3	0.0	0.0	0.0	2.7	7.8
Papua New Guinea	51.0	5,298.9	5,349.9	1	1.8	1.2	23.6	0.4	16.4	7.6
Samoa	105.8	177.5	283.2	37	17.5	47.1	13.3	0.1	19.3	8.5
Solomon Islands	4.2	418.7	423.0	1	0.2	0.5	1.3	0.0	1.4	0.8
Tokelau	2.4	1.4	3.9	63	0.1	1.7	0.3	0.0	0.2	0.2
Tonga	50.7	100.2	150.9	34	18.0	18.1	7.7	0.1	2.0	4.8
Tuvalu	1.8	10.0	11.8	15	0.0	1.0	0.1	0.0	0.2	0.4
Vanuatu	4.2	191.5	195.6	2	0.1	0.3	0.9	0.0	1.6	1.3
Wallis and Futuna	7.0	15.0	22.0	32	0.0	0.0	0.0	0.0	6.2	0.7
TOTALS	1,128.4	11,924.6	13,053	540	223.2	118	455.3	33.4	83.2	215.0

Source: http://www.migrationdrc.org/research/typesofmigration/Global_Migrant_Origin_Database_Version_4.xls.

6,330 citizens of the Federated States of Micronesia residing in Guam in 1994, and a further 2,420 in the Northern Marianas—a total of nearly 10 percent of the FSM population. The figures for 2000 were 6,983 in Guam and 2,697 in the Northern Marianas.

The diaspora of each islander community remains important as a source of remittance income and of potential employment opportunities for the home residents. Migrants have colonized selected economic sectors and residential neighborhoods of major Pacific Rim cities such as Auckland, Sydney, and Los Angeles, and as their numbers have grown the links between standards of living in those metropolitan economies and the feasible expectations of island residents have been reinforced and multiplied, effectively indexing many of the economic parameters of the islands to the economies of their larger patrons.

The typical Pacific migrant does not become separated from the home community simply by virtue of migration. On the contrary, migrants exhibit strong tendencies to retain close ties with their home kin groups and to maintain patterns of return visiting and remittances in cash and kind, which continue to bind them to their places of origin and to enable kin groups to live and earn on the international, rather than the national, stage.

Economic development for islander communities, thus, is not restricted to economic development of island territories. Economic research on these globalized communities really began with Marcus (1981), but has progressed rapidly since (Loomis 1990; Ahlburg and Levin 1990; Ahlburg 1996b; Brown 1995; Brown, Foster, and Connell 1995; Brown 1997). One outstanding point to emerge is the sustainability of migrant remittances. Many writers have predicted that remittance effort by migrants should tend to decline over time as ties to the home community wither away; but the evidence from the Pacific Islands does not support this prediction. As Connell and Brown (1995: 17–18) remark,

> what is striking in every case, and well-documented in the case of Tongans and Cook Islanders overseas, is just how long and at what levels remittances are maintained, with only slight evidence of the anticipated decay. From their econometric analysis of recent cross-sectional data from a survey among Tongan migrants in Brisbane, Walker and Brown found that while the propensity to remit was negatively related to the age of the migrant, it was positively related to the migrant's length of absence from home.

Macroeconomic Management

To evaluate problems of macroeconomic management in small-island economies one must begin from a model of the very small open economy with free capital mobility, a fixed exchange rate, and an open labor market. The goals government can pursue within this framework are limited. On the demand side, fiscal policy and remittance flows set the level of domestic activity and incomes, with the money supply adjusting passively. Fiscal crowding out mechanisms are not operative, since the interest rate is externally fixed and the domestic price level is set by the purchasing power of the externally issued or pegged currency. Crowding out occurs through the real-exchange-rate-driven profit squeeze on tradeable goods production.

Limited Dualism

As in most developing countries, the central microeconomic issues in the Pacific Islands arise out of the interplay between small-scale local production and consumption systems and the forces of the wider market. The dualism that has characterized twentieth-century developing economies in Latin America, Africa, and Asia is, however, muted in the Pacific (except for Papua New Guinea, where the gap between primitive and modern remains stark, and large segments of the precapitalist economy remain relatively little modified).

In most of the Pacific, the modern and neotraditional economies are integrated rather than separate, and tend to become more rather than less integrated over time. Modern activities involve fully monetized transactions in the context of formal markets for labor and goods, together with the deployment of relatively advanced technology. Neotraditional activities include nonmonetary transactions mediated by networks of social relationships, and deployment of economic resources on the basis of a combination of market and nonmarket calculations. Again with the exception of PNG, the technological level of the two sectors is not diverging over time. Village fishing is done from motorboats with nylon lines and nets; people and goods are transported in the village sector by motorbikes, cars, and bicycles; radio and television penetration of the village sector is high. Most important, and associated with high literacy rates in most island economies, intersectoral labor mobility is high and most kin groups have individual members at each end of the modern-neotraditional spectrum.

One result of this interpenetration of the two poles of the developing economy is that the modern sector in most Pacific Island states has a distinctive flavor attributable to the incomplete proletarianization of the labor force. Wage workers have other dimensions to their economic lives as members of village-based kin groups, with access to land and a variety of life opportunities. Possibilities for exploiting a captive labor force are limited both externally by migration opportunities (especially in Polynesia and Micronesia) and internally by the scope for involution offered by the neotraditional village economy. The fluidity of the labor market, indeed, is probably the defining characteristic of Pacific Island economies that most clearly sets them apart from their continental counterparts.

Fundamental to this flexibility is the persistence of "traditional" land tenure, with most cultivable land retained in family ownership and used for subsistence agriculture (including production of foodstuffs for exchange). Commercial plantation agriculture, mainly for copra and sugar, has existed in the region since the late nineteenth century, but it has never become a sufficiently dominant rural sector to dissolve the integrity of smallholder subsistence cultivation. On the contrary, outside Hawaiʻi, both copra and sugar production have tended to slide back toward small-scale cultivation due to an apparent lack of scale economies under Pacific Island conditions.

The high degree of labor market flexibility puts a perennial squeeze on the rate of profit in capitalist enterprises. Hemmed in from above by fixed or semifixed nominal exchange rates and high transport costs, the private sector capitalist can obtain no relief from below by downward pressure on the real wage, because labor costs are indexed to opportunity costs of labor at the involution and migration thresholds.[6] Not surprisingly, private sector entrepreneurship encounters substantial obstacles within the island economies (see, for example, the case studies in Fairbairn 1988) and succeeds best when it modifies capitalist rationality to fit the demands of customary practices and traditions (Fairbairn 1988: 273). The most talented entrepreneurs from Pacific Island communities are drawn out to the metropolitan economies around the rim of the Pacific where there are wider opportunities for profitable enterprise and investment. Vancouver, Los Angeles, Auckland, and Sydney contain a growing number of successful Pacific Islander–owned businesses—a pattern foreshadowed in Marcus' (1981) study of the outward movement of Tongan economic activity.

Conclusion

This chapter has traversed a range of economic issues that define a substantial research agenda for economists working in the Pacific region. The rapidly improving statistical coverage of Pacific Islanders' economic activities, due both to major database development by international agencies and to a growing body of census material and questionnaire research on the migrant communities, has opened the way for a new round of empirically grounded theoretical work on the characteristics and history of economic development in these globalized, flexible, and much-underestimated economic systems.

NOTES

1. GDP is the market value of output produced within a country or territorial unit in a period (usually a year).

2. GNI (formerly GNP) is a country's GDP plus income received from assets owned abroad, minus income paid to overseas investors in the local economy. In the Pacific, major sources of income from abroad are remittances and aid, which keep people's disposable incomes in many island economies above GDP per capita. These two sources of income are excluded from GNI as well as from GDP.

3. The HDI combines GDP with measures of life expectancy, literacy, and educational attainment.

4. Market power is the degree of monopoly in a market, reflected in the ability of suppliers to charge prices that include a large markup on cost, securing larger profits than could be gained under competitive conditions.

5. An acronym for economies that are driven by migrant remittances and aid flows spent by a large public sector (bureaucracy). The term was coined by Bertram and Watters (1985).

6. Trigger points in wage rates below which workers either go back to the village (involute) or move to other locations (migration).

BIBLIOGRAPHY

Ahlburg, D. 1991. *Remittances and their impact: A study of Tonga and Western Samoa.* Pacific Policy Papers No. 7, Center for Development Studies. Canberra: Australian National University.

———. 1996a. *Demographic and social change in the island nations of the Pacific.* Asia-Pacific population research report No. 7. Honolulu: East-West Center.

———. 1996b. Remittances and income distribution in Tonga. *Population Research and Policy Review* 15(4): 391–400.

Ahlburg, D., and M. J. Levin. 1990. *The northeast passage: A study of Pacific Islander migration to American Samoa and the United States.* Pacific research monograph No. 23. Canberra: Australian National University.

Aldrich, R. 1993. *France and the South Pacific since 1940.* Honolulu: University of Hawai'i Press.

Allen, B., R. M. Bourke, and J. Gibson. 2005. Poor rural places in Papua New Guinea. *Asia Pacific Viewpoint* 46(2): 201–217.

Armstrong, H., R. J. De Kervenoael, X. Li, and R. Read. 1998. A comparison of the economic performance of different microstates and between microstates and larger countries. *World Development* 26(4): 639–656.

Armstrong, H.W., and R. Read. 2000. Comparing the economic performance of dependent territories and sovereign micro-states. *Economic Development and Cultural Change* 48: 285–306.

———. 2002. The phantom of liberty? Economic growth and the vulnerability of small states. *Journal of International Development* 14(3): 435–458.

———. 2006. Geographical "handicaps" and small states: Some implications for the Pacific from a global perspective. *Asia Pacific Viewpoint* 47(1): 79–92.

Asian Development Bank. 1994. *Key indicators of developing Asian and Pacific countries 1994,* vol. 25. Manila: Asian Development Bank.

Asian Development Bank Office of Pacific Operations. 1995. *Cook Islands: Economic performance, issues and strategies.* Manila: Asian Development Bank.

Baldacchino, G. 2006. Innovative development strategies from nonsovereign island jurisdictions? A global review of economic policy and governance practices. *World Development* 34(5): 852–867.

Baldacchino, G., and D. Milne. eds. 2000. *Lessons from the political economy of small islands: The resourcefulness of jurisdiction.* Basingstoke: Macmillan.

Benedict, B., ed. 1967. *Problems of smaller territories.* London: Athlone Press.

Bertram, G. 1986. "Sustainable development" in Pacific micro-economies. *World Development* 14(7): 809–822.

———. 1987. The political economy of decolonization and nationhood in small Pacific societies. In *Class and culture in the South Pacific,* ed. A. Hooper et al. Suva: Institute of Pacific Studies.

———. 1993. Sustainability, aid, and material welfare in small South Pacific island economies, 1900–1990. *World Development* 21(2): 247–258.

———. 1998. The MIRAB model twelve years on. *The Contemporary Pacific* 11(1): 105–138.

———. 2004. On the convergence of small island economies with their metropolitan patrons. *World Development* 32(2): 343–364.

———. 2006. Introduction: The MIRAB model in the twenty-first century. *Asia Pacific Viewpoint* 47(1): 1–14.

Bertram, G., and B. Poirine. 2007. Island political economy. In *A world of islands,* ed. G. Baldacchino, 325–377. Charlottetown: Institute of Island Studies, University of Prince Edward Island.

Bertram, G., and R. F. Watters. 1985. The MIRAB economy in South Pacific microstates. *Pacific Viewpoint* 26(3): 852–867.

———. 1986. The MIRAB process: Some earlier analysis and context. *Pacific Viewpoint* 27(1): 47–57.

Blanchet, G. 1985. *L'Économie de la Polynésie Française de 1960 à 1980.* Tahiti: ORSTOM Travaux et Documents 195.

———. 1996. Quel avenir pour la Polynésie Française? *Journal de la Société des Océanistes* 102(1): 31–46.

Boland, S., and B. Dollery. 2006. The value and viability of sovereignty conferred rights in MIRAB economies: The case of Tuvalu. *Pacific Economic Bulletin* 21(2): 140–154.

———. 2007. The economic significance of migration and remittances in Tuvalu. *Pacific Economic Bulletin* 22(1): 102–114.

Booth, A. 1995. Development challenges in a poor Pacific economy: The case of Papua New Guinea. *Pacific Affairs* 68(2): 207–230.

Borovnik, M. 2006. Working overseas: Seafarers' remittances and their distribution in Kiribati. *Asia Pacific Viewpoint* 47(1): 151–162.

Briguglio, L. 1995. Small island developing states and their economic vulnerabilities. *World Development* 23(9): 1615–1632.

Briguglio, L., G. Cordina, N. Farugia, and S. Vella. 2005. Conceptualising and measuring economic resilience. In *Pacific Islands regional integration and governance,* ed. S. Chand. Canberra: Australian National University Press.

Brookfield, H. C. 1972. *Colonialism, development and independence: The case of Melanesian islands in the South Pacific.* Cambridge: Cambridge University Press.

Brown, R. P. C. 1994. Migrants' remittances, savings and investment in the South Pacific. *International Labor Review* 133(3): 1–19.

——. 1995. Hidden foreign exchange flows: Estimating unofficial remittances to Tonga and Western Samoa. *Asian and Pacific Migration Journal* 4(1): 35–54.

——. 1997. Estimating remittance functions for Pacific Island migrants. *World Development* 24(4): 613–626.

Brown, R. P. C., J. Foster, and J. Connell. 1995. Remittances, savings, and policy formation in Pacific Island states. *Asian Pacific Migration Journal* 4(1): 169–185.

Browne, C. 2006. Remittances and migration. In *Pacific Island economies,* ch. 5. Washington D.C.: International Monetary Fund.

Browne, C., and D. Scott. 1989. *Economic development in seven Pacific Island countries.* Washington D.C.: International Monetary Fund.

Cameron, J. 1991. Economic development options for the Federated States of Micronesia at independence. *Pacific Studies* 14(4): 35–70.

Campbell, I. C. 1992. An historical perspective on aid and dependency in Tonga. *Pacific Studies* 15(3): 59–75.

Connell, J. 1987. *Migration, employment and development in the South Pacific.* Noumea: South Pacific Commission.

——. 1988. *Sovereignty and survival: Island microstates in the Third World.* Sydney: University of Sydney research monograph 3.

——. 1997. *Papua New Guinea: The struggle for development.* London: Routledge.

——. 2003. Losing ground? Tuvalu, the greenhouse effect and the garbage can. *Asia Pacific Viewpoint* 44(2): 90–107.

——. 2006a. Nauru: The first Pacific failed state? *The Round Table* 95: 47–63.

——. 2006b. 'Saving the Solomons': A new geopolitics in the 'arc of instability'? *Geographical Research* 44 (2): 111–122.

Connell, J., and R. P. C. Brown. 1995. Migration and remittances in the South Pacific: Towards new perspectives. *Asian and Pacific Migration Journal* 4(1): 1–34.

——. 2005. *Migration and remittances: A Pacific perspective.* Manila: Asian Development Bank.

D'Arcy, P. 2006. The role of the tuna fishery in the economy of Federated States of Micronesia. *Pacific Economic Bulletin* 21(3): 75–97.

Denoon, D. 1983. *Settler capitalism: The dynamics of dependent development in the Southern Hemisphere.* Oxford: Clarendon Press.

Faal, E. 2007. Growth, investment and productivity in Papua New Guinea. *Pacific Economic Bulletin* 22(1): 16–38.

Fairbairn, T. I. J., ed. 1988. *Island entrepreneurs: Problems and performances in the Pacific.* Honolulu: East-West Center.

Fairbairn, T. I. J., and D. Worrell. 1996. *South Pacific and Caribbean island economies.* Brisbane: Foundation for Development Cooperation.

Fichera, V. 2005. The Pacific Islands and the East Caribbean currency union: A comparative review. In C. Browne, *Pacific Island economies.* Washington D.C.: International Monetary Fund.

Fleming, E. M., and J. B. Hardaker. 1995. *Pacific 2010: Strategies for Polynesian agricultural development.* Canberra: Australian National University National Center for Development Studies.

Fleming, E. M., J. B. Hardaker, and J. Delforce. 1991. Smallholder agricultural economy at the crossroads: Policy priorities for sustained agricultural development in South Pacific Island nations. *Journal de la Société des Océanistes* 92–93(1&2): 119–126.

Flinn, J. 1992. *Diplomas and thatch houses: Asserting tradition in a changing Micronesia.* Ann Arbor: University of Michigan Press.

Foster, J. 1995. The relationship between remittances and savings in small Pacific Island states: Some econometric evidence. *Asia Pacific Migration Journal* 4(1): 117–138.

Fraenkel, J. 2006. Beyond MIRAB: Do aid and remittances crowd out export growth in Pacific microeconomies? *Asia Pacific Viewpoint* 47(1): 15–30.

Friberg, E., K. Schaefer, and L. Holen. 2006. US economic assistance to two Micronesian nations: Aid impact, dependency, and migration. *Asia Pacific Viewpoint* 47(1): 123–134.

Friesen, W. 1993. Melanesian economy on the periphery: Migration and village economy in Choiseul. *Pacific Viewpoint* 34(2): 193–214.

Gaffaney, T. J. 1995. Linking colonization and decolonization: The case of Micronesia. *Pacific Studies* 18(2): 23–59.

Gani, A. 2005. Fiji's emigrant transfers and potential macroeconomic effects. *Pacific Economic Bulletin* 20(2): 117–128.

Gibson, J. 2007. Is remoteness a cause of slow growth in the Pacific? A spatial-econometric analysis. *Pacific Economic Bulletin* 22(1): 93–101.

Gibson, J., D. J. McKenzie, and H. Rohorua. 2006. How cost-elastic are remittances? Estimates from Tongan migrants in New Zealand. *Pacific Economic Bulletin* 21(1): 112–128.

Gillett, R., M. McCoy, L. Rodwell, and J. Tamate. 2001. *Tuna: A key economic resource in the Pacific Islands.* Manila: Asian Development Bank.

Hardaker, J. B., ed. 1975. *The subsistence sector in the South Pacific.* Suva: University of the South Pacific.

Hardaker, J. B., and E. M. Fleming. 1994. *Pacific 2010: Strategies for Melanesian agriculture for 2010: Tough choices.* Canberra: Australian National University National Center for Development Studies.

Hayes, G. 1991. Migration, metascience, and development policy in island Polynesia. *The Contemporary Pacific* 3(1): 1–58.

——. 1992. Polynesian migration and the demographic transition: A missing dimension of recent theoretical models. *Pacific Viewpoint* 33(1): 1–35.

——. 1993. "MIRAB" processes and development on small Pacific Islands: A case study from the southern Massim, Papua New Guinea. *Pacific Viewpoint* 34(2): 153–178.

Hezel, F. X., and M. J. Levin. 1996. New trends in Micronesian migration: Migration to Guam and the Marianas, 1900–1993. *Pacific Studies* 19(1): 91–114.

Hezel, F. X., and T. B. McGrath. 1989. The great flight northward: FSM migration to Guam and the Northern Mariana Islands. *Pacific Studies* 13(1): 47–64.

Hooper, A., S. Britton, R. Crocombe, J. Huntsman, and C. Macpherson, eds. 1987. *Class and culture in the South Pacific.* Suva: University of the South Pacific.

——. 1993. The MIRAB transition in Fakaofo, Tokelau. *Pacific Viewpoint* 4(2): 241–264.

James, K. 1991. Migration and remittances: A Tongan village perspective. *Pacific Viewpoint* 32(1): 1–23.

——. 1993. The rhetoric and reality of change and development in small Pacific communities. *Pacific Viewpoint* 34(2): 135–152.

Kakazu, H. 1994. *Sustainable development of small island economies.* Boulder, Colo.: Westview Press.

Kim, I., E. Sidgwick, and M.-H. Duprat. 1995. *Kiribati: Recent economic developments.* Washington D.C.: IMF staff country report 95/117.

Laplagne, P., M. Treadgold, and J. Baldry. 2001. A model of aid impact in some South Pacific microstates. *World Development* 29(2): 365–383.

Lee, H. 2004. 'Second-generation' Tongan transnationalism: Hope for the future? *Asia Pacific Viewpoint* 45(2): 235–254.

Lewis, W. A. 1954. Economic development with unlimited supplies of labor. *The Manchester School.*

Loomis, T. 1990. Cook Island remittances: Volumes, determinants and uses. In *Migration and development in the South Pacific,* ed. John Connell. Pacific Research Monograph No. 24, Center for Development Studies. Canberra: Australian National University.

Luthria, M., R. Duncan, R. Brown, P. Mares, and N. Maclellan. 2006. *At home and away: Expanding job opportunities for Pacific Islanders through labor mobility.* Sydney: World Bank.

Manning, M. 2005. Papua New Guinea thirty years on. *Pacific Economic Bulletin* 20(1): 145–158.

Marcus, G. 1981. Power on the extreme periphery: The perspective of Tongan elites in the modern world system. *Pacific Viewpoint* 22(1): 48–64.

Marsters, E., N. Lewis, and W. Friesen. 2006. Pacific flows: The fluidity of remittances in the Cook Islands. *Asia Pacific Viewpoint* 47(1): 31–44.

Mayo, L. W. 1988. U.S. administration and prospects for economic self-sufficiency: A comparison of Guam and select areas of Micronesia. *Pacific Studies* 11(2): 53–75.

McElroy, J. 2006. Small island tourist economies across the life cycle. *Asia Pacific Viewpoint* 47(1): 61–78.

McElroy, J., and K. B. Pearce. 2006. The advantages of political affiliation: Dependent and independent small-island profiles. *The Round Table* 95(386): 529–539.

McElroy, J., and K. Sanborn. 2005. The propensity for dependence in small Caribbean and Pacific islands. *Bank of Valleta Review* 31 (Spring): 1–16.

McGregor, A., M. Sturton, and S. Halapua. 1992. *Private sector development: Policies and programs for the Pacific Islands.* Honolulu: East-West Center, University of Hawaiʻi.

Milne, S. 1992. Tourism and development in South Pacific microstates. *Annals of Tourism Research* 19: 191–212.

———. 2005. *The economic impact of tourism in SPTO member countries: Final report prepared for South Pacific Tourism Organisation,* August. http://csrs2.aut.ac.nz/NZTRI/nztrinew/documents/Pacific_Economic_Impact_Report.pdf.

Milner, C., and T. Westaway. 1993. Country size and the medium-term growth process: Some cross-country evidence. *World Development* 21(2): 203–211.

Nagai, S. 1996. Background paper on monetary control instruments in the South Pacific. IMF Staff country report 96/76. Washington D.C.: International Monetary Fund.

Ogden, M. R. 1989. The paradox of Pacific development. *Development Policy Review* 7: 361–373.

Parris, H., and R. Q. Grafton. 2006. Can tuna promote sustainable development in the Pacific? *Journal of Environment and Development* 15(3): 269–296.

Peterson, E. H. 2006. *Institutional economics and fisheries management.* Cheltenham: Edward Elgar.

Poirine, B. 1992. *Tahiti: du melting pot a l'explosion?* Paris: Editions L'Harmattan.

———. 1994a. *Tahiti: la fin du paradis?* Tahiti: Imprimeries STP Multipress.

———. 1994b. Rent, emigration and unemployment in small islands: The MIRAB model and the French overseas departments and territories. *World Development* 22(12): 1997–2010.

———. 1995. *Les petites économies insulaires: théories et stratégies de développement.* Paris: Editions l'Harmattan.

———. 1996. La contribution de la substitution d'importation à la croissance dans les Dom-Tom. *Revue française d'économie* 11(4): 167–190.

———. 1998. Should we hate or love MIRAB? *The Contemporary Pacific* 10(1): 65–105.

Purfield, C. 2005. *Managing revenue volatility in a small island economy: The case of Kiribati.* IMF Working Paper 05/154.

Rapaport, M. 1995. Pearl farming in the Tuamotus: Atoll development and its consequences. *Pacific Studies* 18(3): 1–26.

Robinson, E. A. G., ed. 1960. *Economic consequences of the size of nations.* London: Macmillan.

Rostow, W. W. 1960. *The stages of economic growth: A non-Communist manifesto.* Cambridge: Cambridge University Press.

Sampson, T. 2005. *Notes on the economic performance of small states 1995–2003.* Working Paper No. 2, Asian Development Bank-Commonwealth Secretariat Joint Report to the Pacific Islands Forum Secretariat. Suva: Forum Secretariat. http://www.adb.org/Documents/Reports/Pacific-Regionalism/vol3/wp02.pdf.

Shand, R. T., ed. 1980. *The island economies of the Pacific and Indian Oceans: Anatomy of development.* Development Studies Center monograph No 23. Canberra: Australian National University.

Streeten, P. 1993. The special problems of small countries. *World Development* 21(2): 197–202.

Sugden, A., and O. Tevi. 2004. Vanuatu's search for growth. *Pacific Economic Bulletin* 19(3): 1–21.

Taylor, J. E., J. Hardner, and M. Stewart. 2006. Ecotourism and economic growth in the Galapagos: An island economy-wide analysis. Department of Agricultural & Resource Economics, UCD. ARE Working Papers. Paper 06–001. http://repositories.cdlib.org/are/arewp/06–001.

Tisdell, C., and T. I. J. Fairbairn. 1984. Subsistence economies and unsustainable development and trade: Some simple theory. *Journal of Development Studies* 20(2): 227–241.

Treadgold, M. L. 1999. Breaking out of the MIRAB mould: Historical evidence from Norfolk Island. *Asia Pacific Viewpoint* 40(3): 235–249.

United Nations. 1995. *UN statistical yearbook 1994.* New York: United Nations.

———. 2005. *Demographic yearbook 2005.* New York: United Nations.

UNDP (United Nations Development Program). 1999. *Pacific human development report—creating opportunities.* Suva: UNDP.

Walker, A. M., and R. P. C. Brown. 1995. From consumption to savings? Interpreting Tongan and Western Samoan survey data on remittances. *Asian and Pacific Migration Journal* 4(1): 89–116.

Winters, L. A. 2005. Small economies in a globalizing world: The policy challenges ahead. *Pacific Economic Bulletin* 20(3): 94–102.

Winters, L. A., and P. Martins. 2004. When comparative advantage is not enough: Business costs in small remote economies. *World Trade Review* 3(3): 347–383.

World Bank. 1991. *Pacific Island economies: Towards higher growth in the 1990s.* Washington D.C.: World Bank.

———. 1996. *World development report 1996.* New York: Oxford University Press.

———. 1999. *Papua New Guinea: Poverty and access to public services.* Washington D.C.: World Bank.

Agriculture

Harley I. Manner and Randolph R. Thaman

28

The environments where agriculture is practiced in the Pacific Islands range from frost-prone but gardened mountain slopes at 2,600 m in Papua New Guinea through temperate-latitude New Zealand to tiny atoll islets lying scarcely above the reach of the waves in the always warm equatorial ocean. A comparable dissimilarity exists in rainfall—from virtual desert to constantly humid—and in soils, with some young volcanic and alluvial soils being highly fertile, whereas on atoll islets the only natural soil material may be no more than rough, highly alkaline coral rubble.

Traditional Pacific Island agriculturalists adapted to this wide range of conditions with an even wider range of agronomic techniques and crop combinations, which enabled food production on all but the most barren islets or at the highest elevations of the larger islands. Outside of Hawai'i, Guam, and New Zealand, the majority of today's Pacific Island families still work the land with a wide variety of agricultural practices that continue to provide many of their daily needs, a significant portion of their cash income, and the economic and cultural foundation of a relatively benign and bountiful existence.

We gratefully acknowledge the input of Bill Clarke, coauthor of the first edition of this chapter.

Origins

No longer is indigenous Pacific agriculture seen to be the result of a simple transfer into the islands of an agriculture developed outside the region—with Southeast Asia commonly believed to be the hearth. Although many domesticated and wild plants and animals of Southeast Asian origin and domestication were transferred to New Guinea and beyond to the insular Pacific without significant change (certain species of yam, for instance), it can now be argued that the peoples who settled Western Melanesia thirty to forty thousand years ago gradually developed their own distinctive indigenous agricultural and land-use systems and domesticated a variety of plants, including sago, one type of *Colocasia* taro, *Canarium* nut, one kind of banana, sugar cane, kava, the pandanus nut of high-elevation New Guinea, several fruit trees, and other plants (Clarke 1994; Yen 1990). The earliest dates for agriculture in New Guinea can be traced back to at least nine thousand years ago (Bayliss-Smith and Golson 1992).

Brief mention must also be made of the sweet potato, which originated neither in Melanesia nor Asia but in the American tropics. The widespread presence of the sweet potato in indigenous (pre-European-contact) Pacific agriculture—where it became extremely important in places such as Highland New Guinea and New Zealand—has been explained by various theories of prehistoric migration or as the result of Spanish and Portuguese introductions during the fifteenth and sixteenth centuries. Recent archeological evidence from Mangaia in the Cook Islands of the crop's presence there around 1000 CE (Hather and Kirch 1991), together with linguistic evidence, supports earlier assumptions of its pre-European introduction into central Polynesia from the east, directly from tropical America (Scaglion and Soto 1994; Yen 1974).

Based on crop plants and associated wild plants (e.g., indigenous or naturalized exotic weeds, trees, and fallow vegetation) from these three sources—the Pacific Islands themselves, Southeast Asia, and tropical America—a range of indigenous Pacific forms of agriculture evolved in response to varying environmental conditions, local agronomic innovations, the levels of available labor supply and basic demand for food that depend on population dynamics, and the diversity of deep cultural attributes often assigned to food and food production, as exemplified, for instance, by the "uneconomic" effort and attention put into growing the highly esteemed greater yams (*Dioscorea alata*) (e.g., Bonnemaison 1994: 172–176).

Production Systems

One way to classify agriculture is to subdivide it on the basis of the purposes and the socioeconomic organization of production. Such a classification of Pacific Island production systems, or "modes of production," has been provided by Ward (1980) and Yen (1980). The oldest of these is the integral subsistence system, in which virtually all the requirements of the community are produced locally, cash cropping is absent, and the producers and consumers are the same set of people. The integral subsistence system is now rare in its pure form and would be found, if at all, only in the remoter parts of the island of New Guinea. Elsewhere, it has given way to mixed subsistence–cash cropping, which began shortly after the coming of the first permanent European settlers. Under this system, islanders added introduced commercial crops to their traditional inventory of crops so as to have at least some access to the expanding economy based on money.

The plantation or estate production system was introduced by Europeans in the last century. Foreign-owned and foreign-managed, plantation production was directed almost entirely toward export crops. Unlike in traditional agriculture, the units of production were large and monocropping predominated. Spatially, coconut palms quickly became the major plantation crop across the coastal lands of most Pacific islands. Although plantations remain important in parts of the Pacific, they are no longer a favored form of production. Because independent Pacific Island governments and their people see foreign-owned plantations as a remnant of colonial exploitation, the balance of ownership has shifted toward individual nationals or groups of nationals.

The most recently emerged system of production involves a "plantation mode of management." The economies of scale claimed for plantations are achieved through the aggregation of smallholder production under centralized marketing and management control. The most outstanding example of this approach is the sugar industry of Fiji. With the collapse in the second decade of the twentieth century of the indentured labor scheme, whereby Indians had been brought to Fiji to work on plantations, the industry converted to a system of smallholder tenant farmers. General direction is provided by the sugar millers (now the Fiji Sugar Corporation [FSC], a largely government-owned enterprise), with the FSC providing economies of scale in credit facilities, research, extension, and transportation as well as some agronomic inputs and large-scale processing.

Modern privately owned or controlled commercial farms and pastoral properties now exist in Hawai'i, New Zealand, Fiji, and Papua New Guinea, and to a lesser extent in some other island countries. These enterprises vary in size and include, for example, the vast cattle ranches and sugar plantations of Hawai'i, the extensive sheep runs of New Zealand, market-garden plots and small-scale ginger or pineapple farms in Fiji, and the coffee groves of indigenous capitalists in the Papua New Guinean highlands.

Traditional and Semitraditional Agriculture

Traditional (subsistence) and semitraditional agriculture in the Pacific can be classified in accordance with the methods of cultivation and land use (e.g., Kirch 1991; Manner 1993; Falanruw 1993, 1994; Brookfield with Hart 1971). Expectably, classifications vary depending on criteria used or the region treated, but they all suggest the Pacific-wide distribution of five cultivation systems and animal husbandry (which also may involve crop production). Each cultivation system has its specific cultivation techniques, cropping frequency, crop inventory, and other features. The six traditional systems are not, of course, necessarily spatially segregated. Often most or all six of them are or were found on a single community's landholding. The six systems are:

(1) shifting cultivation in forest or bush, sometimes alternating with tree gardens or agroforests;

(2) arboriculture (tree gardens or mature fallow forests) and agroforests;

(3) water control: irrigation and drainage, including wetland taro systems and drainage for sweet potatoes;

(4) intensive dry-field, open-canopy cultivation, including cultivation systems in fern and grass savannas;

(5) houseyard gardens; and

(6) animal husbandry.

Shifting Cultivation

Shifting cultivation—also called swidden and slash-and-burn cultivation—is often held to be the archetypal form of traditional agriculture in the tropics (Figures 28.1 and 28.2). In the Pacific Islands, it is found on almost all high islands and raised limestone islands where at least some secondary forest or productive grassland-savanna remains. As Brookfield with Hart (1971: 116) notes for Melanesia, all the more technically elaborate forms of agriculture exist within an integument of shifting cultivation, coupled with the extensive use of wild foods. Simple though shifting cultivation may be technically, it can be very sophisticated, biologically as well as

Figure 28.1. A six-month-old slash and burn garden (swidden) on 'Upolu, Samoa. The cultivated plants are banana (Musa spp.), edible hibiscus, true taro (Colocasia esculenta), and kava (Piper methysticum). The trees in the background, Leucaena leucocephala, were recently defoliated by a psyllid fly outbreak (photo HIM).

Figure 28.2. A bush fallow subsistence garden at Buma, Kwara'ae District, Malaita, Solomon Islands. Cultivated plants in the photo are sweet potato, pineapple, Alocasia macrorhiza taro, and yams (Dioscorea spp.) climbing on poles. Colocasia taro is no longer grown here because of Phytophtora colocasiae disease (photo HIM).

intellectually, in that its management often involves a manipulation not only of a diversity of annual or near-annual crop plants but also of the intervening forest fallow.

More specifically, cultivating crops for a few years in forest clearings and then leaving the land to revert to forest fallow for a longer period suppresses weeds, crop pests, and diseases and renews the soil with organic matter and nutrients. The cultivators, through selective weeding and planting, thereby encourage some tree species and discourage others so that a highly useful tree-garden fallow results. What to the inexperienced eye looks like spontaneous secondary forest proves to be a human-created swidden-fallow agroforest (e.g., Clarke 1971: 80–82, 136–139; Thaman 1993a: 63–84). Case examples of shifting cultivation in the Pacific include Clarke (1971) for Papua New Guinea, in Melanesia; Falanruw (1993, 1994) for Yap, in Micronesia; and Kirch (1978, 1994) for Uvea and Futuna, in Polynesia.

Arboriculture and Agroforestry

A distinguishing characteristic of the earliest agriculture of the Western Melanesian region is the presence of arboriculture—the culture of trees, domesticated following a history of use during a pre-agricultural hunting-gathering stage dating back well beyond 10,000 years BP (Yen 1996). Archeological evidence for arboriculture at least 3,500 years ago comes from the Mussau Islands, north of New Ireland, where tree species included coconut, two or three species of pandanus, the "Tahitian chestnut" (*Inocarpus fagifer*), the *Canarium* "almond" (*Canarium* spp.), the vi-apple (*Spondias dulcis*), and several hardwoods prized for carving (Kirch 1989). Many of these trees and others such as breadfruit—which perhaps also has origins in Western Melanesia (Ragone 1991: 205)—were transported Pacific-wide, carried by voyaging colonist-cultivators, begetting the rich and beautiful tree groves and orchards that typify Pacific villages and landscapes almost everywhere (Clarke and Thaman 1993; Falanruw 1994; Thaman 1993a; Walter 1994).

In Micronesia, tree gardens still are one of the most conspicuous vegetation formations, a relatively permanent system of land use that provides a wide range of subsistence needs. In its simplest form, the tree gardens consisted of a canopy of timber, food, medicinal, and other multipurpose trees, with an understory of useful annual and perennial plants. It was also a habitat for wild and domesticated animals and a source of many culturally valued items, including traditional medicines, building materials, and firewood. Tree garden composition and structure vary greatly with habitat and island. Along the coast and on atolls, they are relatively simple, dominated by coconuts together with other salt-tolerant species. Farther inland and on the higher slopes, the structure and species composition of these mixed forests are more complex and diverse, with breadfruit (*Artocarpus altilis* and *Artocarpus mariannensis*) the dominant tree species. A detailed description of agroforestry on Pohnpei has been provided by Raynor and Fownes (1993).

Water Control: Irrigation and Drainage

Of the three main tuber- or corm-bearing starchy staples that dominated indigenous Pacific cultivation systems—aroids (the taro family), several species of yams, and the sweet potato—the taros are the most water-tolerant (Figure 28.3). Yams grow only under dryland conditions and require a dry season. The sweet potato, which tolerates a greater range of soil type and climate than yams, grows well in fertile swampland soils if provided with adequate drainage. Massive systems of ditches to provide drainage for sweet potatoes were constructed in the swamplands of highland New Guinea (e.g., Barrau 1958). On a smaller scale, sweet potatoes and sometimes yams were planted in mounds, ridges, or ditched beds to provide better drainage as well as to loosen heavy soils. Throwing ditch spoil onto the bed maintained fertility. In some places, the contrasting moisture tolerances of taro compared with yams and sweet potatoes were complementary, with taro grown in the pits excavated to make mounds or ridges for the other two crops.

Figure 28.3. *Hydroponic cultivation of* Colocasia *and* Cyrtosperma *taro on Falalop Islet, Ulithi Atoll, Yap. Growing taro in these tanks lessens the damage to taro from saltwater intrusion of the freshwater lens and storm wave surges (photo HIM).*

Widespread across the Pacific were a variety of techniques for irrigating true taro (*Colocasia esculenta*). True taro is also planted in dryland shifting gardens and given moderately high rainfall, but it yields better, more permanently, and with greater freedom from weeds and some insect pests when grown in water (Spriggs 1990). Irrigation techniques included the use of natural ponds, the construction of small dams to pond a stream, the erection of bamboo aqueducts to carry trickles of water to hillside sites, making taro "islets" in swampy areas (Manner 1994), and the construction of extensive canal systems for elaborate hillside terrace systems, such as those of New Caledonia, Fiji, and Hawai'i (Barrau 1958, 1961; Handy, Handy, and Pukui 1972; Kuhlken 1994; Kirch 1977, 1991, 1994). In Palau, *Colocasia* taro was the traditional prestige staple, with many myths and rituals associated with its cultivation. The taro swamps were labor intensive, with fields being visited daily and green manures added to the soil to improve fertility, and were traditionally said to be the "mother of life" (McKnight and Obak 1960).

The other traditional aroid that was particularly subject to irrigation is the giant swamp taro *Cyrtosperma chamissonis*. Not of great importance in Polynesia except on coral atolls, *Cyrtosperma* taro was present in Melanesia in coastal swamps from northern New Guinea to Fiji, where it was a significant traditional staple in the densely populated Rewa Delta on the island of Viti Levu. *Cyrtosperma* came to be of greatest importance on coral atolls (Small 1972). In those harsh agricultural environments almost without soil, often with low rainfall, giant swamp taro was capable of producing sustained yields of staple food. A pit was excavated to reach the freshwater lens, and soil was created by adding composted leaves of *Guettarda speciosa, Tournefortia argentea,* breadfruit, and several other trees, as well as seaweed, pumice, and other materials (Thaman 1990b). The "seed" corm is planted together with the compost of leaves in a bottomless basket that reaches below the water level in the pit. The pit continues to be composted at least four times a year until harvest, two or three years after planting. Some varieties, grown mainly for prestige and ceremonies, may be cultivated for ten to fifteen years.

Rice, also grown in pond fields (paddies), is traditionally grown for subsistence among ethnic Indians in Fiji, and formerly by Chamorros in the Marianas (although whether rice was introduced to the Marianas prior to European contact is uncertain).

Intensive Dry-Field, Open-Canopy Cultivation

Given a choice between practicing shifting cultivation in the forest or cultivating in open grasslands, tropical cultivators worldwide will generally choose to cut the forest and garden for the newly cleared land because, compared with grassland soils, forest soils are relatively more fertile, more friable, and freer of pathogens and pertinacious weeds. But as the human population grows and the density of shifting gardens increases, the forest inevitably diminishes until, if the pressure continues, it is replaced by grass-fernland-scrub complexes. In dry-field, open-canopy cultivation, the polycultural richness of species and varieties found in forest-fallow shifting gardens usually declines sharply, with many fewer crops planted and crop segregation becoming the rule. Fallow times also diminish, often being shorter than or equal to the cultivation period. Tillage, which requires labor, almost always increases compared with the minimum of soil working and disturbance typically associated with shifting gardens in the forest.

In Yap, in the Federated States of Micronesia, the savannas of the interior are known as the *tayid* or *ted* (Hunter-Anderson 1991). Here, sweet potatoes are grown in a manner similar to those grown in extensive open fields in ditched and sometimes mounded beds in the Eastern Highlands of Papua New Guinea. The Yapese ditched beds, or *milai* (Mueller 1917), are rectangular and surrounded by ditches closed at the ends. The beds are prepared by slashing the grass cover or merely flattening it with a layer of grass cut from around the perimeter of the bed. Blocks of soil and grass are dug up around the perimeter of the garden bed and placed upside down on the bed, and then covered with a layer of soil excavated from the ditches (Falanruw 1993; Hunter-Anderson 1991). Soil accumulations in the ditches are also added to the mound. Other vegetative litter from the surrounding area may be added. Clumps of clay soil from the ditch bottoms are sometimes piled around the perimeter of the garden bed to reduce erosion.

Dry-field-intensive systems like that described for Yap were widely spread across the Pacific, for instance, in Hawai'i, New Zealand, and isolated, treeless Easter Island (Handy, Handy, and Pukui 1972; Leach 1984; Metraux 1940: 151–152). Such systems are assumed to have developed out of a process of intensification from shifting cultivation (Clarke 1966; Kirch 1991: 120–121; 1994). Such a developmental sequence has been demonstrated archeologically for the Kohala Field System on the island of Hawai'i (Rosendahl 1972; Tuggle and Griffin 1973; Kirch 1994). When the Polynesian Maori reached temperate-latitude New Zealand, they developed special techniques to produce dryland sweet potatoes as a staple under the nontropical conditions. In many islands, following European contact and the decline of indigenous populations and changes in the economy and settlement patterns, the intensive dry-field systems have undergone disintensification or fallen wholly out of use, a process that also happened to most irrigated taro terraces—and to many excavated pit gardens in atoll Micronesia.

Houseyard Gardens

Houseyard gardens, which may also be named kitchen gardens, dooryard gardens, or backyard gardens, were traditionally present throughout Oceania and remain of great significance today (Landauer and Brazil 1990). Such gardens contain a wide assemblage of trees, shrubs, herbaceous plants, and vines that contribute a wide variety of products, including staple foods, fruits, spices, medicines, stimulants, ornamentation, shade, and perfumes (Thaman 1990a). Often disregarded in assessments of agriculture, houseyard gardens are important spatially, nutritionally, and aesthetically. Today, a walk through any Pacific Island town or village immediately reveals the wealth of productive beauty created by the ubiquitous plantings of mangoes, breadfruit, coconuts, citrus, bananas, hibiscus, *Cordyline* and *Codiaemum,* the annatto tree, betel nut in places where that habit prevails, fig species, bamboo, soursop, lemongrass, peppers, sugar cane, the paper mulberry, trees and shrubs with edible leaves or colorful leaves, plants with fragrant bark or flowers, taros and yams, cassava, beans, cabbages, and much, much more.

Thaman (1993b) points out that people in towns also make great use of undeveloped or idle lands for planting in addition to their home gardens. In Port Moresby, more than one-third of all households were found to have gardens on idle land. On the urbanized Suva Peninsula in Fiji, it was estimated that approximately 5 sq km (more than 70 percent) of the undeveloped area was under this type of cultivation. Thaman (1993b: 150) also notes how the gardens vary from house to house:

> Whereas some households have only a few scattered fruit-trees and vegetables, many cultivate food crops on over 50 per cent of their allotments. . . . [I]n some cases in Nuku'alofa, up to 75 per cent of 500–1,000 sq m allotments were under food cultivation, mainly root crops such as taro, tannia, and cassava, amongst *Musa* spp. and scattered trees. Trees become increasingly dominant in long-settled areas, as cash incomes increase, soils decline in fertility, and tree seedlings mature and increasingly shade garden areas.

Animal Husbandry

The Pacific's pre-European domestic animals were only three, the pig, dog, and chicken, all of Southeast Asian ancestry (although the cassowary, native to New Guinea, was tamed to some extent). All three were not present everywhere. The pig and dog were absent from Easter Island, the pig and chicken were absent from New Zealand, and one or another were absent from various atolls, indicating either a failure of initial dispersal or a failure to survive in harsh environments. Generally, the dog and chicken occupied a scavenging or foraging niche and were not important agriculturally. The pig was often of great significance, as communities devoted more and more effort to building up herds for ceremonies and presentations until a large part of food production, especially of sweet potatoes, was directed toward the pigs.

Waddell (1972) reported that up to 63 percent of the weight of the tubers harvested by a group in the Papua New Guinea Highlands was fed to their pigs (also see Brookfield with Hart 1971: 87). A demand for food for pigs at this level requires a considerable expansion or intensification of agriculture. The increasing numbers of marauding pigs cause increased damage to gardens. Caring for and feeding the animals brings a disproportionate increase in women's work, at least in Melanesia. In many forested areas, feral pigs remain an important food resource and are highly esteemed.

Since European contact, other domestic animals, notably horses, cattle, and goats, have been introduced to most larger South Pacific islands but to few atolls. Where cattle have been introduced, they have sometimes caused considerable dislocation to cultivation systems (Grossman 1981).

The Dynamic Character of Pacific Agriculture

The cultivation systems described above suggest that there is great variation in approaches to agriculture from place to place in the Pacific. In practice, these systems often occurred very close together in a diverse mosaic, the parts of which shifted frequently. Figure 28.4 attempts to show schematically the sort [...] that results from such a mixture. This is a landscape [...] cultural biodiversity, containing a wide range of dom[...] quasi-domesticated plants, varied in what and when t[...] has an amorphous spatial organization that conceals [...] ity designed for producing and maintaining the rich [...] sector of rural communities. It is difficult to assess i[...] yield and productivity, so that where it survives, the eco[...] nutritional significance of such diverse production system[...] undervalued.

Such landscapes came into being through incremental additions and long-term experimentation with trees and annual plants and with different methods of cultivation—that is, evolution over many generations of villagers (Clarke and Thaman 1997). Because the evolution took place on many isolated islands or in separate valleys of the larger islands and because each set of gardeners had a different history, arrived with a different stock of plants, and carried out their experimentation in different environments under different densities of population, diverse subsistence production systems developed. There was, however—with the exception of the processing of sago starch from wild or semiwild trees in the swamplands of New Guinea—a common dependence on horticulturally produced high-starch staple foods (taros, sweet potatoes, yams, bananas, and breadfruit), an absence of grains, and an animal protein supplementation to the diet gained by some combination of hunting, pig husbandry, and fishing.

In the history of changes in Pacific agriculture the process of agricultural intensification has long been significant (see Brookfield 1984). Briefly, intensification refers to the increasing application of labor (such as by mulching or by more thorough weeding) or the products of labor (such as agricultural terracing or the construction of drainage ditches) to land in order to increase output of crop from a given area of land over time. In various forms, intensification occurs widely in the Pacific, often mixed with low-input, low-intensity systems such as long-fallow shifting cultivation. Intensification, which often leads to a diminishing return of harvest per unit of labor—even while the yield per hectare increases—is not carried out solely because of population pressure. For example, an increased yield may be desired for presentations of large high-prestige yams or taro or to feed an increasing pig herd needed for purely [cere]mo[ni]al reasons. Building terraces may also have the purpose of [prevent]ing soil erosion on steep slopes.

[At the] other end of the spectrum is a process of agricultural [disintensifi]cation. Disintensification may be defined as the aban[donment o]f intensive agricultural practices and the reduction in [amounts] of labor devoted to agriculture. Sweet potatoes, *Cyr[tosperma ch]amissonis* taro, and the introduced tropical American [cassava] (Figure 28.5) require less labor for their production

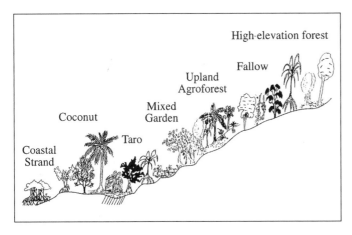

Figure 28.4. Model of Pacific Islands polyculture.

Figure 28.5. Cassava or tapioca cultivation under coconuts on Rotuma, Fiji. One citrus tree is also present. Cassava is replacing taro as a staple crop in many islands because it is easy to grow and has high yields (photo HIM).

than yams and true *Colocasia esculenta* taro and are more tolerant of inferior environments. In the highlands of Papua New Guinea, cash-cropping, employment opportunities and store-bought foods, Christianity, the reduction or abandonment of pig raising, and the greater reliance on cassava and higher yielding varieties of sweet potatoes have resulted in a disintensification or reduction of labor input in agriculture (Umezaki et al. 2000; Boyd 2001).

In many Micronesian atolls, *Cyrtosperma* has replaced taro as the dominant aroid because it is reputedly more tolerant of salt than *Colocasia esculenta,* produces larger corms, and is longer-lived. On many atolls, *Colocasia* taro is no longer grown or persists as an insignificant crop. In some parts of Fiji and other island groups, particularly in urban areas, cassava has replaced yams and taro as the staple food because it requires less work and produces more on infertile soils (Thaman and Thomas 1985).

Abandonment of taro patches has also occurred in response to changes in the socioeconomic conditions of the Pacific Islands. Since the mid-1800s, the development of the copra plantations and a cash economy in many atolls led to the abandonment of many taro pits as people grew coconuts for cash. On many atolls, up to 70 percent of the total land area was converted to coconut woodlands (Hatheway 1953). In the mid-1950s on Kapingamarangi Atoll, 57 percent of the land area was dominated by coconuts, 27.5 percent was under coconuts and breadfruit, 6.6 percent under breadfruit, and only 9 percent in *Cyrtosperma* taro pits (Wiens 1956). In Island Melanesia and coastal New Guinea the extensive abandonment of taro in favor of sweet potato was the result mainly of virus disease spreading among taro since the 1950s (Tim Bayliss-Smith, personal communication).

A process called agrodeforestation (Thaman 1992) is currently diminishing the richness of the humanized forests that make up so much of the Pacific landscapes. Reasons for this include the growing significance of imported foods, but also the ignorance among the younger generation of the ecological, economic, and cultural importance of trees. Many trees are not being replaced or protected by a present generation that commonly knows neither the vernacular names nor the uses of such species.

Akin to agrodeforestation is the process of simplification going on in agriculture generally (Ward 1986). Even though many new crops have been introduced into Pacific agricultural systems over the past century, the net effect has been to reduce the diversity of species, cultivars, and methods that characterized traditional agriculture. Some of the most significant introductions have been the native American crops *Xanthosoma* taro, cassava, or manioc (*Manihot esculenta*), white potato, maize, and the peanut. The reasons for the rapid adoption of these crops are many. Some of them fill in what were gaps in food production—maize, for instance, becoming ready for harvest earlier than the root crops. *Xanthosoma* taro and cassava require less labor and grow better on infertile soils than taro or yams and can be left in the ground until needed.

Several fruit trees—mangoes, oranges, and others—have also been valuable introductions, supplementing the diet with additional energy and important micronutrients. The same is true of a wide variety of vegetables. High-yielding cultivars of traditional crops, such as bananas and sweet potatoes, also have been introduced. These have spread widely, replacing the many traditional cultivars.

Commercial Agriculture

The history of commercial export agriculture in the tropical Pacific Islands is that of export agriculture everywhere in the tropical world: success and setback, boom and collapse, enthusiasm and disenchantment. Commercial agriculture (Figures 28.6 through 28.8) remains important in the increasingly monetized Pacific Island economies, and although many governments see tourism as their countries' economic support in the future, almost all still say that export agriculture must be further developed and diversified, particularly in Vanuatu, Solomon Islands, Tonga, Samoa, and Papua New Guinea, where most people still rely on agriculture for their livelihood.

Figure 28.6. Commercial dryland taro (Colocasia esculenta*) cultivation near Talafofo, Guam. Agricultural production has not kept pace with the island's economic growth. Despite efforts by the government to increase food production, Guam imports 90 percent of its foods, and agriculture remains the smallest economic sector (photo HIM).*

The production of many long-term export items has declined in recent years, most significantly copra, but also cacao, bananas, and specialty crops such as oranges and pineapples from the Cook Islands. The reasons are many, including persistently low commodity prices, cyclones, disease, poor marketing, transportation delays, storage problems, and a disinclination on the part of farmers to increase crop output and improve its quality. Since smallholders predominate in the agriculture of the tropical Pacific, the question becomes how to vitalize smallholder agriculture so as to expand food production, employment, and incomes. The issue of management was mentioned above in the description of the "plantation mode of management," whereby smallholder producers receive the economies of scale of centralized processing, marketing, and agronomic advice (Ward and Proctor 1980).

Another aspect of farmer success or failure is motivation. Are Pacific farmers enjoying such "subsistence affluence" that they are not motivated to work hard for cash? Certainly people sometimes have target sums for particular expenses and will work hard, for example, to produce copra until achieving their goal and then stop. Basically, agricultural labor is not rewarding enough to make people want to engage in it as a full-time occupation. A common outcome of government and aid schemes in the Pacific to intensify, improve, and increase smallholder commercial production is that people accept the seed money and the subsidies to plant or experiment with manufactured, external inputs but drop the enterprise when these monies stop (Asian Development Bank 1996a: ch. III). A related aspect is that Pacific land-tenure systems militate against the granting of loans for agriculture because the individual farmers do not hold title to the land.

On the other hand, most rural people in the tropical Pacific Islands have access to land and enjoy the security of subsistence production and the ability to produce tubers, tree crops, and pigs or cattle to meet kinship obligations for presentations at weddings or funerals or welcoming celebrations. This approach to the use of land and labor can be seen as efficient and practical, even if it does not lead to maximum commercial production. To some extent, Pacific Island governments and aid agencies are coming to realize the value of subsistence production. A recent assessment of the Vanuatu economy noted that more than 80 percent of the people rely on subsistence agriculture for their livelihood (Fallon 1994: 37). An Asian Development Bank (1996b: 3) review of Fiji's agricultural sector noted similarly that the contribution to GDP of subsistence crops grown in the country was similar to that of sugar, the country's main agricultural product.

Figure 28.7. Sugar cane agriculture near Sigatoka, Fiji. Most sugar cane is grown on small plots, often less than six hectares in area, and mostly by manual labor. Infrastructural support—seed, fertilizer, and technical expertise—for small cane farmers in Fiji is provided by the Fiji Sugar Corporation. Sugar is the backbone of the Fijian economy (photo HIM).

In export agriculture there is a growing focus in ministries and departments of agriculture on niche products suitable as Pacific export crops—that is, specialized, high-quality, high-priced products. Current and potential niche products include ginger, spices, and kava from Fiji; vanilla and off-season high-quality vegetables such as squash (butter pumpkin) from Tonga; coffee, kava, and currently an expansion of squash production from Vanuatu; flowers, mangoes, and asparagus from Samoa; kava, betel nut (*Areca cathecu*), and *Piper betle* leaves from the Federated States of Micronesia (FSM 2006); *noni* (*Morinda citrifolia*) from Palau and many other Pacific islands; and *Eucheuma* seaweed from Kiribati, from where coconut products have previously been the only significant agricultural export. Large-scale production of some crops remains important, such as the estate production of palm oil in Solomon Islands, the smallholder "umbrella" management system of sugar production in Fiji, and the coffee and tea of Papua New Guinea.

Even major crops, however, can quickly disappear from exports. For example, after two severe tropical cyclones (hurricanes) badly damaged Samoa's agricultural output in the early 1990s, in 1993 a fungal leaf blight (*Phytophthora colocasiae*) virtually wiped out the production of taro, a crop that was the favored staple food of Samoans and had during the 1980s and into the 1990s become the country's major export crop (worth over US$2 million), supplying the demand for the food among the islander-immigrant population in New Zealand. Research and development of *Phytophthora*-resistant and *Pythium* ssp. corm-rot-tolerant varieties of taro has been met with both success and controversy. Strong opposition by Hawaiian activists because of cultural reasons against licensing and royalty sales of three patented hybrid strains of *Colocasia* taro resulted in the abandonment (terminal disclaimer) of the patents in 2006 (Ostrander and Gaines 2006). The new varieties have been offered to the public without licensing and royalty sales restrictions.

Figure 28.8. Commercial intercropping of pineapples and Colocasia *taro near Pago Pago, American Samoa. Plastic and organic mulches are used for moisture conservation and weed control (photo HIM).*

In a related controversy, genetic engineering research aimed at developing *Phytophthora*-resistant taro led to the introduction of a bill in the Hawai'i legislature that would place a ten-year moratorium (from July 1, 2007 to June 30, 2017) on such research (State of Hawaii Senate 2007). Legislative action on the bill has been deferred. Natural disasters and disease outbreaks (many of which are at least partly culturally induced) encourage island governments to seek further export diversification, including the niche products mentioned above. Table 28.1 provides recent data showing the major export products from the tropical Pacific Islands. Export data from Hawai'i and New Zealand are presented for comparative purposes. As suggested above, it is best to consider this information as a slice in time. In later years, the situation may well be quite different.

One crop of great importance spatially, if not always economically, is the coconut palm. Once a major export crop and significant industry, coconuts have been planted in immense numbers covering the coastal areas of most Pacific islands since the Europeans came. Although copra continues to be the main commodity export from Vanuatu and, generally, the only cash crop available to the inhabitants of the outer islands of Kiribati, the Federated States of Micronesia, the Marshall Islands, and Tuvalu, coconut products are now generally in decline, except again for a few specialized products

Table 28.1

Pacific Island Agricultural and Marine Exports for the Year 2004 (Data in Million US$)

	Palm products	Coffee	Cocoa	Vanilla	Coconut oil	Tea	Copra	Sugar/ molasses	Hides	Fruit/ juice	Crude organics	Taro	Beverages
Am. Samoa													
Cook Islands										2.21	0.32		
FSM							0.17			0.09			
Fiji								108.8			5.4	11.1	30.4
Fr. Polynesia				2.5	3.0					13.2	2.9		1.5
Guam (2003)													
Kiribati							1.8						
Marshall Is.					1.40		0.02						
Nauru													
New Caledonia									0.3		0.6		0.1
Niue										0.07		0.25	
Norfolk (2000–01)													
CNMI (2000)													
Palau													
PNG	152.4	88.1	67.7	31.7	25.1	7.1	5.3		3.4				
Pitcairn Island													
Samoa					1.5		0.1			1.8	0.1	0.4	
Solomon Islands	15.8		7.0		7.3		8.2				1.0		
Tokelau													
Tonga				0.7						0.3	1.3		
Tuvalu							0.01						
Vanuatu			1.4		11.5		4.8		0.3		0.8		
Wallis and Futuna													
Hawai'i								94.1		46.4			
New Zealand										850.2			

Notes and Sources:

* Value of fish and marine produce are not included in the total agricultural exports.

† Total exports may not equal the sum of agricultural (or marine) exports, as the table does not list all exports individually.

Unless noted below, the source for most data is from FAO 2006. Value of exports and commodity data for American Samoa, Northern Mariana Islands, and Guam are from Daniel 2007. Commodity data for Palau is from ADB 2007.

Value of fish and marine produce and wood and wood produce are from Daniel 2007.

Commodity data and value of agricultural export for the FSM is from Table 3.1.A., FSM 2006. Value of total exports for the FSM is from FAO 2006. Wood products and fish data for Solomon Islands is from ADB 2007.

Dairy products	Prepared food	Fresh vegetables	Meat	Wool	Flour	Marine products	Wood products	Kava	Miscellaneous	Total agricultural exports*	Total exports†
						402					446
	0.02								0.01	2.55	14.58
						10.26		0.13	0.38	0.79	32.0
					5.6		27.91		21.6	212.8	678.6
	0.1					4.23			3.3	25.2	198.2
											43.3
						0.38				1.8	8.0
										8.5	1.4
											40.00
	0.2	0.7	0.6		0.2	27.77			0.1	3.4	1,000.0
		0.02							0.01	0.35	0.35
											1.48
											1,000
						8.85					
									4.3	401.2	2,555.6
											0.022
	1.0								0.6	5.6	14.7
						17.62	62.5		2.5	41.9	116.4
		0.1								14.3	31.8
										0.01	1.46
			2.6						0.6	22.1	24.2
											0.048
			15.8						3.4	499.7	
2,991	329		2,674	336						10,031	19,830

Value of wood and wood products for Fiji is for 2005. Value for fish for Fr. Polynesia is for 2005. Value for fish and marine produce for Kiribati is for 2002.

Data for Hawai'i is estimated and compiled from National Agricultural Statistics Service 2013 and represents exports to the mainland USA and foreign countries. Meat includes livestock.

Misc. includes for Cook Islands—roots and tubers (0.01); Fiji—ginger (4.0), pastry (7.4), macaroni (5.9), and breakfast cereals (4.3); French Polynesia—beer (1.3) and rice (2.0); FSM—betel nuts (0.35), piper leaves (0.006), root crops (0.017), and other farm produce (0.011); Hawai'i—ornamentals (6.5), tree nuts (10.9),and others (minor seed oils, beverages other than juices, feeds and fodder, wine, vegetable products, etc., [286.1]); Niue—honey (0.01); PNG—rubber; Samoa—beer (0.1), desiccated coconut (0.3), and coconuts (0.2); Solomon Islands—palm kernels (2.5), tobacco products, coconuts, and copra cake (0.0); Tonga—pumpkin, gourd, and squash (10.6), cassava (0.4), coconuts (0.1), roots and tubers (0.9), and yams (0.1); Vanuatu—cheese (0.3), pastry (0.2), and ice cream and ice (0.1).

such as high-quality coconut soaps, a coconut cheese from Fiji, and coconut cream. There is also the suggestion that simply processed coconut oil could provide a substitute for diesel fuel (Morton 1993). Otherwise, the millions of often senile and poorly tended trees are the despair of development planners, who forget the food use of coconuts. What Brookfield (1985: 117) describes for Fiji would be applicable across the Pacific:

> In the coconut regions almost every cooked meal employs coconut milk (*lolo*) derived by grating the meat and straining the product. Data collected in the rural areas show that families with good stands of palms might consume about 600 nuts/capita/yr, and a reasonable estimate of average consumption might lie between 300 and 400. . . . Actual consumption varies greatly, but on certain islands it may absorb nuts equivalent to from ten to thirty per cent of normal copra production.

With regard to modern animal husbandry, in many countries there is now battery production of chickens (for meat and eggs) and pigs, based on imported or partly locally produced feeds and on improved imported poultry and pig breeds. In some countries, such as Papua New Guinea, New Caledonia, Vanuatu, and Fiji, large-scale cattle ranching based on improved breeds and pasture, for both local and export sale, has been successful.

Agriculture in Hawai'i and New Zealand

In Hawai'i, traditional agriculture, dependent on extensive culvert-fed irrigated taro systems and dryland agriculture of sweet potatoes (Kirch 1985b, see also the discussion above on traditional agriculture), went into a long-term decline by the mid-nineteenth century, a consequence of depopulation, land alienation, and commercial cultivation of sugar and pineapple. Sugar and pineapple (together with large-scale cattle grazing) continue to dominate the agricultural sector, but they are losing ground, pineapple to cheaper foreign production, and sugar to a combination of low prices, competition from other sources of sweetening, and sugar lands' being priced out of the market by land-use changes from agricultural to urban. As the acreage used for plantation agriculture declines, smaller-scale diversified production has gained ground. Macadamia nuts have been a marked success. Other crops include papaya, flowers, bananas, passion fruit, coffee, vegetables, avocados, and guavas (Daws 1968; Armstrong 1983).

A high-value crop that does not enter the official statistics is *pakalolo* (marijuana or *Cannabis sativa*), which is grown widely, concealed in sugar cane fields, state forests, and other public lands, as well as in backyards and greenhouses. Estimates have placed its turnover above that of any other crop, another example of the success of niche marketing. Illegal cropping of marijuana is also known to be important in Fiji and Papua New Guinea and, most likely, many other Pacific islands.

Agricultural transformation in New Zealand was equally dramatic. Precontact societies were dependent on the cultivation of sweet potatoes and flax and, in suitable locations, taro, yams, and other crops. Here too, depopulation and land alienation led to a decline of traditional agriculture. Much of the landscape was transformed by the late nineteenth century into an enormous pasture land of native grasses or introduced alien grasses and clovers upon which grazed huge numbers of sheep and cattle. Farming landscapes continue to change as crops fail or succeed and as the modern trend toward a decrease in the number of farms and an increase in the size of individual farms takes place. Market gardening dominates in the Auckland vicinity, supplying the country's largest, and growing, urban market. Orchards of citrus, Chinese gooseberry (kiwifruit), apples, peaches, apricots, or fields of corn, beans, and other vegetables are scattered from north to south according to the suitability of climate and soils and access to land, transport, and processing.

Recent changes in New Zealand agriculture include a decline in sheep numbers (down from seventy million in 1983 to fifty million in 1993) because of the withdrawal, with economic restructuring, of agricultural support in the form of fertilizer subsidies and minimum prices, especially in the face of a depressed international market for sheep meat. Beef and dairy cattle numbers, on the other hand, have increased. The recent success of the New Zealand wine industry has gained the country much notice overseas as growers have concentrated on premium varieties in demand in export markets. Mention may also be made of the remarkably extensive afforestation efforts that have taken place in New Zealand, leading to the largest planted forests in the world, composed of exotic conifers, especially radiata pine (Britton, Le Heron, and Pawson 1992; Cumberland and Whitelaw 1970; Le Heron and Pawson 1996).

Sustainability Issues

The agroforests, humanized woodlands, and polycultural gardens of traditional Pacific agricultural systems were all protective of the soil, imitating natural forest. Intensive agriculture on irrigated terraces or the mulched ditched systems acted to lessen erosion and maintain soil fertility. This is not to say that the early agriculturalists were "in harmony" with their environments. At times, like all settlers in new environments, they caused considerable damage—such as by felling forest on steep slopes or by the indiscriminate use of fire—but then made mitigating adjustments, such as developing swampland agriculture, terraces, and agroforests that sustained their agriculture for centuries or millennia (Clarke 1994: 15, 16).

Compared to modernized systems of agriculture, traditional agricultural systems are characterized by high species and cultivar diversity. Altieri (1999) has suggested that biodiversity performs key ecological services and functions that lead to sustainability. During this millennium, however, there are few studies that demonstrate the direct and indirect contributions of diversity to sustainability of Pacific Island agricultural systems or that explain how biodiversity defines the ecological or biophysical interactions that maintain or enhance the productivity and viability of these systems (Manner 2008). Furthermore, Falanruw (1994) has suggested that the sustainability of traditional agricultural systems requires an intact ecosystem and one that is not stressed beyond its tolerance limits. Thus, research and in particular the long-term ecological monitoring of traditional agricultural systems is needed to determine the limits of tolerance in order to ensure their sustainability. A second priority of research in traditional agriculture is the need to record and document the existing ethnoecological knowledge and practice because rapid socioeconomic changes are quickly changing the value and practice of traditional agriculture. In Palau, for example, a country with approximately 20,900 residents in 2007, more than 6,800 people (or about 32 percent of the population) are foreign nationals on work permits (U.S. Department of State 2008). Thus, today, one can usually find a Bangladeshi, Taiwan Chinese, or Filipino male laboring in the Palauan *mesei* (taro swamp), whereas formerly it was the singular domain of the Palauan woman. As few young women today want to work in the *mesei,* the values and accumulated knowledge of this system are surely in jeopardy.

Over the past several decades in the tropical Pacific Islands an environmental threat has been the great expansion in area of land in agricultural use. The causes of the expansion come from several directions. First is the rapid population growth in some countries (notably Solomon Islands, Vanuatu, and Papua New Guinea) where shifting cultivation is practiced. Such growth leads quickly to a shortened fallow period, which in turn leads to loss of forest biodiversity, agrodeforestation, soil degradation, and declining yields. Another cause is the increase in cash cropping and the development of pastures for cattle. Both these ventures "freeze" what is often the best and flattest land in the community into permanent uses, forcing shifting gardens to be concentrated on steeper, poorer land, bringing soil degradation and erosion. Frazer (1987: ii) noted in his long-term study of a community on Malaita Island in Solomon Islands that between 1971 and 1985 the area of tree crops doubled, production of cocoa tripled, and copra production quadrupled. This resulted in land shortages, a reduction in bush fallow periods, declines in crop yields, and land degradation. On Pohnpei Island, the cultivation of *sakau* for cash and export, and traditional agroforestry, has resulted in the decline of the upland forest area from 42 percent in 1975, to 15 percent in 1995, in turn jeopardizing its biotic diversity and ecological functions (Merlin and Raynor 2005).

Nor is the Pacific free of polluting agricultural chemicals, with Samoa, for instance, known as a heavy user of weedicides (Fairbairn 1993). Thaman, in his paper "The Poisoning of Paradise" (1984), chronicles the indiscriminate and careless use of pesticides from Hawai'i to Papua New Guinea. In the countries and territories of the Pacific Islands, there is only limited control over the imports of pesticides; some of the pesticides in use have been banned as too dangerous for use in the countries where they were produced.

Pacific Islanders do not generally use fertilizers to the extent that some developed countries do, but on atoll islets, even frugal use of fertilizer can lead to dangerous contamination of the underground freshwater supply. On larger islands, fertilizer runoff has been a significant contributor to eutrophication and clogging of waterways with aquatic weeds. On any Pacific island with a high percentage of coastal area and adjoining reef relative to land area, agricultural chemicals and soil erosion pose a particular threat because of their rapid flow-on effects on the productivity of coasts and reef.

Avoiding degradation in the face of the pressures for an expansion of area under agriculture and an increase in local and export production will require far more attention to sustainability requirements. One approach is to use lands that have already been cleared, farming them more intensively using traditional subsistence and agroforestry practices (Thistlethwaite and Davis 1996; Clarke and Thaman 1997). This approach would maintain marginal lands under protective forest as well as counter the loss of managed biodiversity as crop species and varieties succumb to the uniformity that characterizes market-directed production (Yen 1980: 86–87). There are, however, difficulties in putting this prescription into practice.

Governments are less interested in agriculture than in alternative cash-earning ventures such as mines in Papua New Guinea, logging and fisheries in Solomon Islands, offshore financing in Vanuatu, industrialization in Fiji, and tourism wherever it seems at all possible. Even if sustainable intensification were given serious policy consideration, national institutional capacities are inadequate to the task of providing the information on degradation necessary for environmental planning. Nor are there agencies now capable of monitoring trends or enforcing practices that would lead to sustainability. Further, intensification requires additional inputs, either in the form of imported chemicals or human labor. The first are expensive and can be environmentally damaging; the second is often difficult to mobilize because agricultural effort, if directed toward many of the traditional cash crops, has such a low priority among Pacific Islanders. As Penelope Schoeffel argues (Asian Development Bank 1996a: 69):

> In most Pacific island countries the return on a full day of work by an individual on cocoa or copra or coffee will barely cover the cost of 1 kg rice and a can of mackerel—hardly enough to feed a family for a day. Understandably, when a day's labor purchases so little and does not feed a family, smallholders turn their attention away from cash crops and concentrate on subsistence activities that ensure their survival.

If niche products are found that bring good prices, many farmers will be ready to incur environmental degradation for the sake of temporary profit. Possibilities for reasonable returns and more organized environmental management exist under centralized forms of management, such as the organization of smallholder producers in the Fiji sugar industry, but under centralization, the primary motivation may remain export production, not conservation (Clarke and Morrison 1987).

Conclusion

Despite the problematic situation described here, there are possibilities for a more cheerful outlook. Both authors of this chapter have in the course of recent research had the pleasure of walking in durable, beautiful, and productive gardens created by today's Pacific Islanders in all three of the Pacific's major cultural divisions: Polynesia, Micronesia, and Melanesia. These are not the integral subsistence systems described earlier in this chapter. All contain some production for cash as well as subsistence, and all their creators have interests other than agriculture, but the gardens themselves possess some of the components of sustainability evolved early on in Pacific agriculture—such as polycultural diversity and continued production without the need for external inputs. Certainly, a return to the independence of the integral subsistence way of life that existed in the Pacific's past is unlikely (Yen 1980: 88). But there is the possibility and challenge for Pacific men and women who work the soil and tend the trees to evolve hybrid systems that combine commercial and subsistence agriculture and that will endure productively to meet the needs of future generations.

BIBLIOGRAPHY

Altieri, M. A. 1999. The ecological role of biodiversity in agroecosystems. *Agriculture, Ecosystems and Environment* 74: 19–31.

Armstrong, R. W., ed. 1983. *Atlas of Hawaii.* Honolulu: University of Hawai'i Press.

Asian Development Bank (ADB). 1996a. *Sociocultural issues and economic development in the Pacific Islands.* Manila: Asian Development Bank.

———. 1996b. *Fiji agriculture sector review: A strategy for growth and diversification.* Manila: Asian Development Bank.

———. 2007. *Key indicators 2007,* vol. 38. Manila: Asian Development Bank. http://www.adb.org/Documents/Books/Key_Indicators/2007 /pdf/Key-Indicators-2007.pdf. Accessed August 3, 2007.

Barrau, J. 1958. *Subsistence agriculture in Melanesia.* Honolulu: Bernice P. Bishop Museum Bulletin 219.

———. 1961. *Subsistence agriculture in Polynesia and Micronesia.* Honolulu: Bernice P. Bishop Museum Bulletin 223.

Bayliss-Smith, T., and J. Golson. 1992. A Colocasian revolution in the New Guinea Highlands? Insights from Phase 4 at Kuk. *Archaeology in Oceania* 27: 1–21.

Bonnemaison, J. 1994. *The tree and the canoe: History and ethnogeography of Tanna.* Honolulu: University of Hawai'i Press.

Boyd, D. J. 2001. Life without pigs: Recent subsistence changes among the Irakia Awa, Papua New Guinea. *Human Ecology* 29(3): 259–282.

Britton, S., R. Le Heron, and E. Pawson, eds. 1992. *Changing places in New Zealand: A geography of restructuring.* Christchurch: New Zealand Geographical Society.

Brookfield, H. C. 1984. Intensification revisited. *Pacific Viewpoint* 25(1): 15–44.

———. 1985. An historical and prospective analysis of the coconut districts. In *Land, cane and coconuts: Papers on the rural economy of Fiji,* ed. H. C. Brookfield, 111–247. Department of Human Geography Publication HG/17. Canberra: Research School of Pacific Studies, Australian National University.

Brookfield, H. C., with D. Hart. 1971. *Melanesia: A geographical interpretation of an island world.* London: Methuen.

Clarke, W. C. 1966. From extensive to intensive shifting cultivation: A succession from New Guinea. *Ethnology* 5: 347–359.

———. 1971. *Place and people: An ecology of a New Guinean community.* Berkeley: University of California Press.

———. 1994. Traditional land use and agriculture in the Pacific Islands. In *Land use and agriculture,* vol. II of *Science of Pacific Island peoples,* ed. J. Morrison, P. Geraghty, and Linda Crowl, 11–37. Suva: Institute of Pacific Studies, University of the South Pacific.

Clarke, W. C., and J. Morrison. 1987. Land mismanagement and the development imperative in Fiji. In *Land degradation and society,* ed. P. Blaikie and H. C. Brookfield, 176–185. London: Methuen.

Clarke, W. C., and R. R. Thaman, eds. 1993. *Agroforestry in the Pacific Islands: Systems for sustainability.* Tokyo: United Nations University Press.

———. 1997. Incremental agroforestry: Enriching Pacific landscapes. *The Contemporary Pacific* 9(1): 121–148.

Connell, J. 1994. Beyond the reef: Migration and agriculture in Micronesia. *Isla: A Journal of Micronesian Studies* 2(1): 83–101.

Cumberland, K., and J. Whitelaw. 1970. *New Zealand.* London: Longman.

Daniel, L., ed. 2007. *The Far East and Australasia 2007.* 38th ed. Europa Regional Surveys of the World. London and New York: Routledge.

Daws, G. 1968. *Shoal of time: A history of the Hawaiian Islands.* New York: Macmillan.

Doty, M. S. 1954. Part 1. Floristic and ecological notes on Raroia. *Atoll Research Bulletin* 33: 1–41.

Fairbairn, T. I. J. 1993. *Western Samoa's census of agriculture: Major features and implication for development.* Pacific Studies Monograph

No. 7. Sydney: Centre for South Pacific Studies, University of New South Wales.

Falanruw, M. V. C. 1993. Micronesian agroforestry: Evidence from the past, implications for the future. In *Proceedings of the workshop on research methodologies and applications for Pacific Islands agroforestry,* technical coordinators B. Raynor and R. Bay, 37–41. General Technical Report PSW-GTR-140. Pacific Southwest Research Station, US Forest Service.

———. 1994. Food production and ecosystem management on Yap. *Isla: A Journal of Micronesian Studies* 2(1): 5–22.

Fallon, J. 1994. *The Vanuatu economy: Creating conditions for sustained and broad based development.* Canberra: Australian International Development Assistance Bureau.

Food and Agriculture Organization of the United Nations (FAO). 2006. *Compendium of food and agricultural indicators 2006.* The Statistics Division, Rome, Italy. http://www.fao.org/ES/ess/compendium_2006 /default.asp. Accessed September 24, 2007.

Frazer, I. 1987. *Growth and change in village agriculture: Manakwai, North Malaita.* Occasional Paper 11, South Pacific Smallholder Project. Armidale, N.S.W.: University of New England.

FSM (Federated States of Micronesia). 2006. *International trade publication: Federated States of Micronesia, 2004.* Palikir, Pohnpei: Dept. of Economic Affairs, FSM National Government.

Grossman, L. 1981. The cultural ecology of economic development. *Annals of the Association of American Geographers* 71(2): 220–236.

Handy, E. S. C., E. G. Handy, and M. Pukui. 1972. *Native planters in old Hawaii: Their life, lore and environment.* Honolulu: Bernice P. Bishop Museum Bulletin 233.

Hather, J., and P. V. Kirch. 1991. Prehistoric sweet potato (Ipomoea batatas) from Mangaia Island, Central Polynesia. *Antiquity* 65: 887–893.

Hatheway, W. H. 1953. The land vegetation of Arno Atoll, Marshall Islands. *Atoll Research Bulletin* 16: 1–68.

Hunter-Anderson, R. 1991. A review of traditional Micronesian high island horticulture in Belau, Yap, Chuuk, Pohnpei, and Kosrae. *Micronesica* 24(1): 1–56.

Kirch, P. V. 1977. Valley agricultural systems in prehistoric Hawaii: An archaeological consideration. *Asian Perspectives* 20: 246–280.

———. 1978. Indigenous agriculture on Uvea (western Polynesia). *Economic Botany* 32: 157–181.

———. 1985a. Intensive agriculture in prehistoric Hawaii: The wet and the dry. In *Prehistoric intensive agriculture in the tropics,* ed. I. S. Farrington, 435–454. BAR International Series 232.

———. 1985b. *Feathered gods and fishhooks.* Honolulu: University of Hawai'i Press.

———. 1989. Second millennium B.C. arboriculture in Melanesia: Archaeological evidence from the Mussau Islands. *Economic Botany* 43: 225–240.

———. 1991. Polynesian agricultural systems. In *Islands, plants, and Polynesians: An introduction to Polynesian ethnobotany,* ed. P. A. Cox and S. A. Banack 113–133. Portland, Ore.: Dioscorides Press.

———. 1994. *The wet and the dry: Irrigation and agricultural intensification in Polynesia.* Chicago: University of Chicago Press.

Kuhlken, R. 1994. *Tuatua ni Nakauvadra: A Fijian irrigated taro agrosystem.* In *Land use and agriculture,* vol. II, *Science of Pacific Island peoples,* ed. J. Morrison, P. Geraghty, and Linda Crowl, 51–62. Suva: Institute of Pacific Studies, University of the South Pacific.

Landauer, K., and M. Brazil, eds. 1990. *Tropical home gardens.* Tokyo: United Nations University Press.

Leach, H. 1984. *1,000 years of gardening in New Zealand.* Wellington: A. H. and A. W. Reed.

Le Heron, R., and E. Pawson, eds. 1996. *Changing places: New Zealand in the nineties.* Auckland: Longman Paul.

Manner, H. I. 1993. A review of traditional agroforestry in Micronesia. In *Proceedings of the workshop on research methodologies and applications for Pacific Islands agroforestry,* technical coordinators B. Raynor and R. Bay, 32–36. General Technical Report PSW-GTR-140. Pacific Southwest Research Station, US Forest Service.

——. 1994. The taro islets (maa) of Puluwat Atoll. In *Land use and agriculture,* vol. II, *Science of Pacific Island peoples,* ed. J. Morrison, P. Geraghty, and Linda Crowl, 77–87. Suva: Institute of Pacific Studies, University of the South Pacific.

——. 2008. Directions for long-term research in traditional agricultural systems of Micronesia and the Pacific Islands. *Micronesica* 40(1/2): 63–86.

Marten, K. D. 1985. Forestry in Melanesia and some Pacific Islands. In *Environment and resources in the Pacific,* 115–128. UNEP Regional Seas Reports and Studies No. 69. Geneva: UNEP.

Massal, E., and J. Barrau. 1956. *Food plants of the South Seas.* Technical Paper 94. Noumea: South Pacific Commission.

McKnight, R. K., and A. Obak. 1960. *Taro cultivation in the Palau District. In Taro cultivation practices and beliefs. Part I. The Western Carolines.* Anthropological Working Papers, No. 6. Guam: Staff Anthropologist, Trust Territory of the Pacific Islands.

Merlin, M. and W. (B). Raynor. 2005. Kava cultivation, native species conservation, and integrated watershed resource management on Pohnpei Island. *Pacific Science* 59(2): 241–260.

Metraux, A. 1940. *Ethnology of Easter Island.* Honolulu: Bernice P. Bishop Museum Bulletin 160.

Morton, B. 1993. Coconut power. *Pacific Islands Monthly* 63(12): 37.

Mueller, W. 1917. Yap. In *Ergebnisse der Sudsee Expedition.* II Ethnographie: Band 2, ed. G. Thilenius. Hamburg: L. Friederichsen & Co.

National Agricultural Statistics Service. 2013. Hawaii agricultural exports, January 13, 2013. USDA in cooperation with Department of Agriculture, State of Hawaii. http://www.nass.usda.gov/Statistics_by_State/Hawaii/Publications/Miscellaneous/exports.pdf. Accessed January 18, 2013.

Ostrander, G. K., and J. Gaines. 2006. Memorandum of terminal disclaimers for taro cultivars (pa'akala, pa'lehua, and paukea [sic]). University of Hawai'i at Manoa, Honolulu, June 20, 2006.

Paulson, D. 1994. Understanding tropical deforestation: The case of Western Samoa. *Environmental Conservation* 21(4): 326–332.

Ragone, D. 1991. Ethnobotany of breadfruit in Polynesia. In *Islands, plants, and Polynesians: An introduction to Polynesian ethnobotany,* ed. P. A. Cox and S. A. Banack, 203–220. Portland, Ore.: Dioscorides Press.

Raynor, B., and J. Fownes. 1993. An indigenous Pacific Island agroforestry system. In *Proceedings of the workshop on research methodologies and applications for Pacific Islands agroforestry,* technical coordinators B. Raynor and R. Bay, 42–58. General Technical Report PSW-GTR-140. Pacific Southwest Research Station, US Forest Service.

Rosendahl, P. H. 1972. Aboriginal agriculture and residence patterns in upland Lapakahi, Island of Hawaii. PhD dissertation, University of Hawai'i, Honolulu.

Scaglion, R., and K. A. Soto. 1994. A prehistoric introduction of the sweet potato in New Guinea? In *Migration and transformations: Regional perspectives on New Guinea,* ed. A. Strathern and G. Sturzenhofecker, 257–294. Pittsburgh: ASAO Monograph No. 15.

Schoeffel, P. 1994. Where are all the farmers? Agriculture, land tenure and development in the Pacific Islands. In *Land issues in the Pacific,* ed. R. Crocombe and M. Meleisea, 35–42. Suva: Institute of Pacific Studies, University of the South Pacific.

Small, A. C. 1972. *Atoll agriculture in the Gilbert and Ellice islands.* Tarawa: Department of Agriculture.

Spriggs, M. 1981. Vegetable kingdoms: Taro irrigation and Pacific prehistory. PhD dissertation, Australian National University, Canberra.

——. 1990. Why irrigation matters in Pacific prehistory. In *Pacific production systems: Approaches to economic prehistory,* ed. D. E. Yen and J. M. J. Mummery, 174–189. Canberra: Department of Prehistory, Research School of Pacific Studies, Australian National University.

State of Hawaii Senate. 2007. SB 958. Genetically modified organisms; taro; moratorium. The Senate, Twenty-fourth Legislature, State of Hawaii.

Thaman, R. R. 1984. The poisoning of paradise: Pesticides, people, environmental pollution and increasing dependency in the Pacific Islands. *South Pacific Forum* 1(2): 165–200.

——. 1990a. Mixed home gardening in the Pacific Islands: Present status and future prospects. In *Tropical home gardens,* ed. K. Landauer and M. Brazil, 41–65. Tokyo: United Nations University Press.

——. 1990b. Kiribati agroforestry: Trees, people and the atoll environment. *Atoll Research Bulletin* 333: 1–29.

——. 1992. Agrodeforestation as a major threat to sustainable development. Box 19.4 in *Environment and development: A Pacific Island perspective,* ed. R. Thistlethwaite and G. Votaw, 194–195. Manila/Apia: Asian Development Bank/South Pacific Regional Environment Programme.

——. 1993a. Fijian agroforestry at Namosi and Matainasau. In *Agroforestry in the Pacific Islands: Systems for sustainability,* ed. W. C. Clarke and R. R. Thaman, 63–84. Tokyo: United Nations University Press.

——. 1993b. Pacific Island urban agroforestry. In *Agroforestry in the Pacific Islands: Systems for sustainability,* ed. W. C. Clarke and R. R. Thaman, 145–156. Tokyo: United Nations University Press.

Thaman, R. R., and P. M. Thomas. 1985. Cassava and change in Pacific Island food systems. In *Food energy in tropical ecosystems,* ed. D. J. Cattle and K. H. Schwerin, 191–228. New York: Gordon and Breach.

Thistlethwaite, R., and D. Davis. 1996. *A sustainable future for Melanesia? Natural resources, population and development.* Canberra: National Centre for Development Studies.

Thistlethwaite, R., and G. Votaw, eds. 1992. *Environment and development: A Pacific Island perspective,* ed. R. Thistlethwaite and G. Votaw. Manila/Apia: Asian Development Bank/South Pacific Regional Environment Programme.

Tuggle, H., and P. Griffin. 1973. Lapakahi, Hawaii: Archaeological studies. *Asian and Pacific Archaeology* Series 5. Honolulu: Social Science Research Institute, University of Hawai'i.

Umezaki, M., Y. Kuchikura, T. Yamauchi, and R. Ohtsuka. 2000. Impact of population pressure on food production: An analysis of land use change and subsistence pattern in the Tari Basin in Papua New Guinea. *Human Ecology* 28(3): 359–381.

U.S. Department of State. 2008. *2007 Country reports on human rights practices—Palau.* 11 March 2008. UNHCR Refworld. url: http://www.unhcr.org/cgi-bin/texis/vtx/ refworld/rwmain?docid =47d92c7ec. Accessed April 3, 2008.

Waddell, E. 1972. *The mound builders: Agricultural practices, environment, and society in the Central Highlands of New Guinea.* Seattle: University of Washington Press.

Walter, A. 1994. Knowledge for survival: Traditional tree farming in Vanuatu. In *Fauna, flora, food and medicine,* vol. III of *Science of Pacific Island peoples,* ed. J. Morrison, P. Geraghty, and Linda Crowl, 189–200. Suva: Institute of Pacific Studies, University of the South Pacific.

Ward, R. G. 1980. Agricultural options for the Pacific Islands. In *The island states of the Pacific and Indian oceans: Anatomy of development,* ed. R. T. Shand, 23–39. Canberra: Development Studies Centre Monograph No. 23, Australian National University.

——. 1986. Reflections on Pacific Island agriculture in the late 20th century. *Journal of Pacific History* 21(4): 217–226.

Ward, R. G., and A. Proctor, eds. 1980. South Pacific agriculture: Choices and constraints. *South Pacific agricultural survey 1979.* Manila/Canberra: Asian Development Bank/Australian National University.

Wiens, H. J. 1956. The geography of Kapingamarangi Atoll in the Eastern Carolines. *Atoll Research Bulletin* 48: 1–93.

Yen, D. E. 1974. *The sweet potato and Oceania: An essay in ethnobotany.* Honolulu: Bernice P. Bishop Museum Bulletin 236.

———. 1980. Pacific production systems. In *South Pacific agriculture: Choices and constraints. South Pacific agricultural survey 1979*, ed. R. G. Ward and A. Proctor, 73–106. Manila/Canberra: Asian Development Bank/Australian National University.

———. 1990. Environment, agriculture and the colonisation of the Pacific. In *Pacific production systems: Approaches to economic prehistory*, ed. D. E. Yen and J. M. F. Mummery, 258–277. Canberra: Department of Prehistory, Research School of Pacific Studies, Australian National University.

———. 1991. Polynesian cultigens and cultivars: The questions of origins. In *Islands, plants, and Polynesians: An introduction to Polynesian ethnobotany*, ed. P. A. Cox and S. A. Banack, 67–95. Portland, Ore.: Dioscorides Press.

———. 1996. Melanesian arboriculture: Historical perspectives with emphasis on the genus Canarium. In *South Pacific indigenous nuts*, ed. M. L. Stevens, R. M. Bourke, and B. R. Evans, 36–44. ACIAR Proceedings No. 69. Canberra: Australian Centre for International Agricultural Research.

Logging

Colin Filer

29

According to the Oxford English Dictionary, "logging" is "the work of cutting and preparing forest timber." In current political debate, however, "logging" sounds like an activity that causes lots of unnecessary environmental damage, whereas "forestry" lacks these negative connotations, and "forest management" sounds quite benign. When people talk about "logging in the Pacific," the sort of thing that comes to mind is an image of bulldozers trashing the native forests of New Guinea or other parts of island Melanesia. But the indigenous people of the region have been "cutting and preparing forest timber" wherever they have encountered forests, and much of the commercial logging that goes on today involves the harvesting of timber from cultivated tree plantations. An assessment of logging in the region therefore needs to consider what sort of forest has been logged, for what purpose, with what technology, and with what economic, social, and environmental impact.

One general point to be made at the outset is that logging (timber cutting) has only rarely been the primary cause of deforestation in any part of the Pacific Island region, although it has recently become the main cause of what is nowadays called "forest degradation" in those parts of Melanesia where native forests still abound. The harvesting of timber from cultivated tree plantations only counts as an act of deforestation if the harvest is followed by conversion to another form of land use, and the "scientific" management of natural or native forests is based on the idea that periodic timber harvests are compatible with the maintenance of a permanent forest estate. The "selective" logging of native forests may have many negative environmental impacts, but deforestation has generally occurred when deforested land has greater economic value to its owners than land that is still covered by trees.

There have been two key moments in the historical transformation of regional logging practices (and forest management practices more generally) since the original settlement of the region in prehistoric times. The first was the introduction of European or Western populations, production systems, and resource management regimes at various points in the nineteenth century; the second was the globalization of the timber trade and the concomitant rise of international forest protection campaigns over the past thirty years or so. This does not mean that the history of logging (or forest management) is identical in all parts of the region; it just means that we can now divide the region into three parts by reference to the way their forests (and their forest industries) were affected by these changes. Most of the land in the "New Guinea region"—which is here taken to include Solomon Islands and what are now the Indonesian provinces of Papua and West Papua, as well as Papua New Guinea—was still covered by dense and diverse primary forests in 1980, and the logging of these forests has been a significant and highly contentious economic activity in the most recent period of history. New Zealand is the only other country in the region in which the export of timber and wood products plays a major role in the national economy, but this industry is largely based on the management of tree plantations that have almost entirely replaced native forests as a source of timber. In the rest of the Pacific Island region, neither of these two forms of industrial activity is of major economic significance, and logging has rarely if ever provided the raw material for an export industry.

Forest Ecosystems and Indigenous Production Systems

Indigenous people have been logging the islands of the Pacific region for thousands of years. If they had not done so, they would not have been able to build the canoes in which they sailed across the ocean and settled so many of the islands. They also cut down big trees in order to make house posts, wooden statues, musical instruments, and a range of other artifacts. And they cleared whole areas of forest to make more space for cultivating food crops, although this activity would not fit our definition of "logging" because the trees were normally cleared by burning or the timber was burned after the trees had been felled.

Prehistorians and ecologists continue to debate the relative influence of human agency and the forces of nature in changing the quantity and quality of forest cover in different parts of the region before the advent of European observers. At one extreme lies the sad story of Easter Island, where the Rapanui people apparently contrived to remove every single tree, including several species of hardwood, in the few centuries between their own arrival and that of European seafarers in the early eighteenth century (Bahn and Flenley 1992). At the other extreme we have evidence of people chopping, slashing, and burning the forests of New Guinea for thousands of years without endangering the basis of their own subsistence (Groube 1989; Haberle, Hope, and van der Kaars 2001; Hope 2007). This has sometimes been construed as the effect of a "cultural" difference between Polynesians and Melanesians (or between Austronesians and non-Austronesian "Papuans"). For example, Flannery (1994: 258) has linked "the unique Polynesian lifestyle and the Polynesian preference for small islands" with a "great passion . . . to discover new, virginal lands, overexploit them briefly, then move on"—a strategy that only worked so long as there was somewhere else to go. But another well-known commentator on the Easter Island story has made the equally pertinent observation that:

> When one chops trees down in a wet hot place like the New Guinea lowlands, within a year new trees 20 feet tall have sprung up on the same site. . . . Hence regrowth can keep pace with moderate rates of cutting on wet hot islands, leaving the island in a steady state of being largely tree-covered (Diamond 2005: 116).

Diamond goes on to list a number of other factors, aside from rainfall and temperature, that have made the natural forest ecosystems of the region more or less vulnerable to degradation by human beings armed with firesticks and stone axes. In crude terms, it seems clear that small islands with poor soils are more vulnerable than large islands with better soils or a wider range of terrestrial ecosystems. What Pacific Islanders have made of their environment depends as much on the environment itself as on the culture and technology they have applied to it (Kirch and Hunt 1997). If Maori settlers managed to remove more than a third of New Zealand's forest cover in much the same time that it took for the Rapanui people to deforest the whole of Easter Island, this was partly because their "Polynesian" production system was ill-adapted to this new environment, and partly because the temperate forests of New Zealand did not have the resilience or regenerative capacity of a Melanesian tropical rain forest (Anderson 2002).

The indigenous people of the New Guinea region are sometimes called "forest people" because of an assumption that native forests supplied most of their basic needs. If this assumption were correct, one might expect the defense of local custom and traditional production systems to entail an automatic opposition to industrial logging operations on customary land. But matters are not quite so simple. The first professional forester to survey the forests in the former Territory of Papua found it hard to ascribe the existence of many underpopulated grassland areas

> to any other reason but that a large population existed in the past, and it has migrated to other parts of the territory for various causes, possibly the most urgent being that it had exhausted the land, created the grass, and could no longer farm it. If any population remains, it is always sufficient to maintain the grass lands, for a couple of boys going hunting will set the whole countryside on fire (Lane-Poole 1925: 35).

On the other hand, the same author thought he had discovered at least one group of indigenous people

> who, though individually apparently low in the scale of civilization, had evolved a social system of living in communities that might well be called towns instead of villages, so peopled were they, and who had already shown a greater forethought and longer view than the young white democracies of

civilized lands, in the matter of assuring a future supply of wood for unborn generations (Lane-Poole 1925: 48).

By the 1950s, colonial forestry officials in the combined Territory of Papua and New Guinea had realized that much of its forest was a "mosaic or patchwork quilt" constructed through the process of shifting cultivation and other forms of human disturbance (Womersley and McAdam 1957: 21). A study of aerial photographs taken in the early 1970s found that 20 to 25 percent of Papua New Guinea's surface area was still covered by this sort of "secondary" forest (Hammermaster and Saunders 1995). This does not mean, however, that the "primary" forest that still covered more than 60 percent of the surface area, and which has now become the target of commercial logging companies, existed in a uniform state of "climax." On the contrary, most of the native forests of the New Guinea region as a whole have been shaped by different cycles of human and natural disturbance over a long period of time (Johns 1990; Whitmore 1990; Bayliss-Smith, Hviding, and Whitmore 2003). The important point is that indigenous production systems can destroy, create, degrade, or enrich these forests in many different ways, but there is little evidence that indigenous people ever wanted to preserve entire forest ecosystems in a stable state.

Sawmills, Plantations, and Forest Departments

As people of European descent began to establish their own settlements and trading posts across the region during the nineteenth century, they discovered some tree species the economic value of which made it worthwhile to ship their timbers overseas. The most notable of these was the sandalwood traded out of Hawai'i and Fiji between 1810 and 1830 (Culliney 1988; Qalo 1993), and later from New Caledonia and the New Hebrides (now Vanuatu) between 1830 and 1865 (Shineberg 1967). The intensive harvesting of sandalwood to feed the Chinese market and firewood to feed American whaling ships has been blamed for the wholesale destruction of the Hawaiian lowland native forests and the decimation of the Hawaiian native population before the middle of the century (Culliney 1988; Cuddihy and Stone 1990). The kauri forests on the North Island of New Zealand supplied high-value building timbers to the neighboring colonies of Australia throughout the second half of the nineteenth century, but this resource was also nearing exhaustion by the time the government imposed an export ban after the First World War (Roche 1987, 2002; Wynn 2002). In all parts of the region, most of the timber harvested by colonial settlers was processed and consumed within the boundaries of each colonial territory, and the size of the harvest mainly reflected the size of the invading population.

New Zealand in the second half of the nineteenth century has been described as a "wooden world" in which British farmers and sawmillers were engaged in a "symbiotic relationship" that reduced the extent of native forest cover by half between 1840 and 1900 (Roche 2002; Wynn 2002). Once any valuable timber species had been harvested, the rest of the forest was typically set alight to make way for new farms and pastures. The same pattern was repeated throughout the Pacific Island region, where the sawmill became an integral component of the new plantation economy, and the profits to be made by colonial settlers from the cultivation of different agricultural commodities largely determined the size of the commercial log harvest and the rate of native forest clearance (Jonas 1985; Qalo 1993; Bennett 2000). The rate of native forest clearance by colonial settlers then determined the point in time at which colonial policy makers began to worry about the prospect of a future timber shortage and the loss of other forest ecosystem services.

The New Zealand government took the lead in 1874 by passing legislation that provided for the appointment of a conservator of forests. The first man appointed to this position (Captain Inches Campbell Walker) argued that the colony's native forests could meet future timber demands if they were scientifically managed in a rotational system on land leased from the Crown (Roche 1987). His advice fell on deaf ears, however, and although it was repeated by other "scientific foresters" during and after the First World War, the prevailing view was that New Zealand's prospective "timber famine" could only be avoided by a program of reforestation with fast-growing exotic species such as eucalypts and pines. By 1923, the newly established State Forest Service was planning to expand the area of state-run pine plantations from 13,000 acres to 300,000 acres by 1935, on the grounds that almost 600,000 acres would eventually be needed to meet future domestic timber demand. In practice, the Forest Service consistently exceeded its own planting targets in the decades that followed, and by the end of the 1970s, 44,000 hectares (about 109,000 acres) were being added to the total area of timber plantations each year—half planted by the government and half by private investors (Kirkland and Berg 1997). It was only after the Second World War that the harvest of exotic plantation sawlogs began to exceed the harvest from New Zealand's native forests, but by that time, the Forest Service was already under attack from conservationists for reviving plans to harvest native forest timber on a "sustainable" (rotational) basis (Roche 2002).

The rapid expansion of plantation forestry in New Zealand was not matched in any other part of the Pacific Island region with the partial exception of Fiji (Qalo 1993), but forest management became the province of a specialized government agency in most of the larger colonial territories. The officials in these forestry departments or divisions were expected to apply the principles of economics and ecology to the formulation of policies and plans for the allocation of land between four types of forest—native forests to be protected for one reason or another; native forests that could be cleared for other forms of land use; native forests from which timber could be harvested at periodic intervals; and timber plantations developed through a program of reforestation. The way forestry officials dealt with these tasks depended on the ways native forests had already been exploited or protected, the quality and extent of the remaining native forest cover, and the division of forested land between state, private, and customary ownership. But their activities were also typically constrained by the political subordination of the forestry sector to the agricultural sector.

The political power of the farming lobby and private landed interests caused particular problems for the "scientific" management of native forests in New Zealand and Hawai'i (Culliney 1988; Kirkland and Berg 1997). But in the tropical colonies, the problem lay not so much in the political power of white planters or plantation companies as in the colonial policy of protecting indigenous property rights and farming systems (Qalo 1993; Bennett 2000). In Papua New Guinea, for example, there were only limited areas of alienated land available for the development of timber plantations, and colonial state foresters were obliged to construct most of their plans around the purchase of temporary timber harvesting rights from customary landowners (Womersley and McAdam 1957). When the World Bank castigated the Australian colonial administration for the slow pace of economic development in the 1960s, the Department of Forests made a big effort to sell some of these "Timber Rights Purchases" to foreign investors, but they only made one major catch—a Japanese woodchipping project. Their lack of success was partly due to the diversity and unfamiliarity of the native timber resource, and partly to the fact that the Indonesian government was able to offer larger and more lucrative timber concessions with far fewer restrictions on their exploitation (Jonas 1985; Lamb 1990).

When Papua New Guinea (PNG) achieved independence in 1975, state-owned timber plantations accounted for roughly 120,000 hectares of alienated land (Lamb 1990), and state-owned national parks less than 8,000 hectares (King and Hughes 1998), while New Zealand, with a comparable surface area, had 670,000 hectares of "state forests" and an equivalent area of national parks before its State Forest Service was established in 1919 (Roche 2002). In 1975, 97 percent of PNG's surface area, and 99 percent of its native forests, remained under customary ownership, even if the state had managed to secure the timber harvesting rights to more than a million hectares of this customary land (White 1977). At a seminar held on the eve of PNG's independence, a pair of Australian environmentalists complained about the overwhelming commitment on the part of forest services to the interests of big wood-based industry, which interests dictated the large-scale mass production forestry and the heavy-handed, capital-intensive, factory-style operations that are so destructive of forest values (Routley and Routley 1977: 376).

These sentiments were typical of the way environmentalists were now beginning to question the role of state forest departments in the "scientific" management of native forests throughout the Pacific Island region (and the rest of the world as well). Indeed, it could be argued that this was the point in time when a new constellation of political and economic interests first took shape in the forestry sector. But despite the signs of a new alliance between the forces of indigenous nationalism and Western environmentalism, the fact remains that the logging industry was still making a very small contribution to PNG's national economy at this juncture, and if it had not been for the economically marginal Japanese woodchipping project, forest policy would not have been a major political issue. As in other parts of the region, another decade would have to pass before the economic realities pushed the policy debate to a new level.

Transformation of the Regional Timber Trade

For most of the twentieth century, the organization of the regional timber trade reflected the political relationship between Western metropolitan powers and their colonial dependencies. For example, one British company was responsible for three-quarters of the logs exported from (state-owned) native forests in Solomon Islands during the 1960s and 1970s (Frazer 1997), Australia consumed most of PNG's timber exports during the final period of colonial administration (Jonas 1985), and where domestic supplies were insufficient to meet the demand for processed wood products in the smaller island territories, the deficit was normally met by exports from New Zealand or the United States. The initial round of Japanese investment in logging the native forests of Southeast Asia and the New Guinea region in the 1970s was only the harbinger of a much bigger shift in the patterns of trade and investment in the last two decades of the century. One of the key elements of this transformation was the emergence of a group of ethnic Chinese timber barons from Malaysia and Indonesia who controlled the expansion of logging operations to meet the growth in demand for tropical forest timbers, first from Japan and later from mainland China (Dauvergne 1997, 2001).

The recent expansion of PNG's large-scale logging industry is well documented by the Swiss company engaged to monitor the country's raw log exports. Here there is evidence of a "double boom" in which the volume of log exports almost reached three million cubic meters in 1994, fell by almost two-thirds as a result of the Asian financial crisis in 1997, and then climbed back toward its earlier peak. The same general pattern is evident in the rest of the New Guinea region—and in many other tropical countries that still contained large volumes of commercially accessible native forest in 1980. In Solomon Islands, log exports (from native forests) reached an initial peak of almost three-quarters of a million cubic meters in 1996 (Dauvergne 1999), and a new peak of almost one and a half million in 2007 (CBSI 2008). The pattern is fairly clear but not so well documented in (West) Papua because a major part of the log harvest is "exported" to processing facilities in other parts of Indonesia, and an unknown portion is smuggled out of the province (EIA/Telapak 2005; Cannon 2007; IMOF 2007).

In 1994, at the peak of the first timber boom, raw logs accounted for 98 percent of the value of all forest products exported from PNG, and those forest products accounted for 19 percent of the value of the country's total exports. In 2007, raw logs accounted for 90 percent of the value of all forest product exports, but forest products accounted for less than 5 percent of total export values. Most of the increase in the proportion of processed exports was due to the construction of a large veneer factory by Rimbunan Hijau, the company responsible for more than half of the country's total log harvest (ITS Global 2007). The reason for the relative decline in the value of exports from the forestry sector is the recent boom in the prices of oil, copper, and gold, which together accounted for nearly 80 percent of PNG's total export earnings in 2007 (BPNG 2008).

By way of contrast, the logging industry's contribution to the total export earnings of Solomon Islands has risen from around 50 percent to around 70 percent over the period since 1994 (Bond 2006). Nowhere else in the Pacific Island region do we find this degree of economic dependence on the logging industry. In 2007, New Zealand exported more than six million cubic meters of logs and poles—four times the volume of logs exported from Solomon Islands and twice the volume exported from PNG—and their combined value (around NZ$600 million) was only 20 percent of the total value of all forest product exports (around NZ$3 billion) (NZMAF 2008), yet forest products have accounted for only 10 percent of New Zealand's total export earnings in recent years (Curtin 2005). In other parts of the region, the contribution of the logging industry to export earnings has been limited by the imposition of log export bans to protect the remaining native forests (as in the case of Vanuatu), or problems in the management of exotic timber plantations developed as a substitute for native forests (as in the case of Fiji), or the limited availability of timber from either of these two sources (as in the case of Samoa) (Paulson 1994; Ward 1995; Brown 1997; Regenvanu, Wyatt, and Tacconi 1997; Hammond 2002; Bond 2006).

In 1994, 65 percent of PNG's log exports went to Japan, 26 percent to South Korea, and only 2 percent to China; in 2007, 83 percent went to China, 5 percent to Japan, and 2 percent to South Korea. This dramatic change reflects China's recent emergence as the world's largest importer of industrial roundwood, a major exporter and importer of wood-based panels, the second largest importer of paper and paperboard, and the largest exporter of secondary processed wood products such as wooden furniture (FAO 2007: 90).

The "mixed tropical" logs from PNG that once ended up in cheap and disposable Japanese plywood (Light 1997) are now more likely to end up in the furniture that China exports to the rest of the world. A similar, though much less dramatic, change is evident in the destination of the "logs and poles" exported from New Zealand. Between 2002 and 2007, the Chinese share rose from 17 to 21 percent, while the Japanese share fell from 18 to 14 percent and the larger South Korean share from 56 to 52 percent. But the market for New Zealand's processed forest products looks rather different: 26 percent (by value) went to Australia, 18 percent to Japan, and 14 percent each to the United States and China (NZMAF 2008).

What now distinguishes debate about the economics of logging in New Zealand and the New Guinea region is not the size and eventual fate of the log harvest but its environmental, political, and social costs. When the New Zealand Forest Service proposed to log the native beech forests of the South Island in the 1970s, environmentalists formed a Native Forest Action Council, which got 340,000 people to sign a petition to the national parliament (the Maruia Declaration) demanding an end to all such activity. Protection of native forests then became one plank in the Labor Party's successful election campaign of 1984, the responsibility for protecting them was transferred to the new Department of Conservation, the management of state timber plantations was privatized, and the Forest Service was abolished (Kirkland and Berg 1997). Since then, native forests have accounted for less than 2 percent of New Zealand's total log harvest, and political debate about the costs and benefits of plantation forestry has been subsumed in the wider debate about land use planning. The New Guinea region has thus become the focus for recent debate about the social and environmental costs of logging native forests.

Environmental Costs of Logging Native Forests

Just over 10 percent of PNG's land area is currently included in large-scale logging concessions (ITTO 2007), while 25 percent of (West) Papuan territory has been designated as "production forest" (IMOF 2005), and logging companies are active in nearly all the commercially accessible forest areas of Solomon Islands, which cover roughly half of the country's total surface area. Given the current rate of harvest, it is reasonable to predict that the native forests of Solomon Islands will have been "logged out" within a few years

(Bond 2006). Even in Vanuatu, logging companies were licensed to harvest a volume of native forest timber that was far in excess of the "sustainable yield" until a new forest policy was brought into effect in 1997 (Regenvanu, Wyatt, and Tacconi 1997; Wyatt, Bartlett, and Mathias 1999).

In PNG, the annual log harvest from native forests has never exceeded the estimate of "sustainable yield" that was made when a new forest policy was devised in 1990 (PNGMOF 1991). This estimate, however, was based on the assumption that commercially accessible areas of native forest would yield a constant volume of merchantable logs on a forty-year cutting cycle, which is only five years longer than the cutting cycle originally adopted for New Zealand's fast-growing pine plantations (Kirkland and Berg 1997). This assumption has been repeatedly questioned on the grounds that it underestimates the diversity of native forest types and overestimates the capacity of many (if not most) of these different types of forest to recover from the damage caused by large-scale "selective" logging operations (Barnett 1992; Nadarajah 1994; Hammermaster and Saunders 1995). A study of various sites in PNG found that 40 to 70 percent of the trees in a logged-over forest are killed or fatally damaged by such operations (Cameron and Vigus 1993).

For reasons such as these, a recent report has suggested that 83 percent of PNG's commercially accessible forest area will have disappeared or been damaged beyond repair by 2021—only six years after a similar fate is expected to befall the native forests of Solomon Islands (Shearman et al. 2008). However, this prediction errs on the side of excessive pessimism because it overestimates the rate of deforestation in recent decades and underestimates the rate of regrowth in forests degraded by logging operations. An earlier study showed that 6.6 percent of PNG's total forest area had been subjected to some form of selective logging, but not permanently converted to other forms of land use, between 1975 and 1996. An additional 1.2 percent had been logged and then cleared, while 3.2 percent had been cleared without first being logged (see Table 29.1). Much of the damage would obviously have been caused by the first log export boom that peaked in 1994, but there is no evidence to show that the extent of the damage and destruction caused by a given quantum of log exports has grown since that time.

Another recent study has found that logging companies in PNG are removing the commercial timber resource at a higher rate than they ought to because the government has overestimated the available forest area and timber volumes in its own inventories (Keenan et al. 2005). This again throws doubt on the sustainability of the timber yield that can be obtained under the official harvesting cycle, which has now been set at thirty-five years. The question then is whether economic factors will intervene to discourage logging companies from even attempting a second cut when merchantable timber yields are likely to be very poor. If it is true that "logging companies do not seek to acquire concessions logged 30 years ago but only concessions offering primary forest" (Shearman et al. 2008: 52), a second cut may only make economic sense if the PNG government implements its occasional threat to impose a log export ban or create additional incentives for the development of industrial timber processing operations (Bird et al. 2007c).

PNG's forest policy framework contains a variety of rules and regulations that are meant to minimize the extent of environmental damage as a result of selective logging operations. These have not

Table 29.1

Contribution of Logging to Deforestation in PNG, 1975–1996

	Area (km²)	% 1975
Gross forest area in 1975	293,175	100.0
Forest logged and regenerating by 1996	19,223	6.6
Forest logged then cleared by 1996	3,476	1.2
Forest cleared but not logged by 1996	9,397	3.2
Gross forest area remaining in 1996	261,079	89.1

Source: McAlpine and Quigley 1998.

been effective because they overestimate the capacity of government officials to keep the industry in line and make effective use of the "reforestation levy" the government imposes on the logging industry (Filer 1998; Bird et al. 2007a; ITTO 2007). It can be argued that customary ownership of native forests adds a further disincentive for logging companies and local landowners alike to implement better management plans because there can be no security of title under customary tenure (Lea 2005; Curtin and Lea 2006). The central government has less control over the allocation of logging concessions in Solomon Islands than it does in PNG, and selective logging operations on customary land seem to cause much the same level of environmental damage in both countries (Louman and Nicholls 1994; Lindemalm and Rogers 2001). But the evidence from (West) Papua (and other parts of Indonesia) suggests that state ownership of native forests may well produce environmental outcomes that are even worse (Cannon 2007).

Environmentalists who oppose the logging of native forests are also opposed to definitions of "sustainability" that are essentially concerned with the maintenance of timber yields. From their point of view, logging is unsustainable if it causes a long-term reduction in the biodiversity values of native forests, even if those values partially reflect a prior history of human and natural disturbance (Johns 1990, 1992). It is also unsustainable if it damages the capacity of native forest ecosystems to provide other "services" to human consumers, like watershed protection or carbon sequestration, or if it causes lasting damage to adjoining ecosystems, like the pollution of rivers or reefs (Louman 1997; Carothers and Cortesi 1998). These additional forms of damage, however, have not been well documented in those parts of the Pacific Island region where native forests are still being logged on a significant scale, and claims are sometimes based on evidence obtained from other parts of the world (Shearman et al. 2008).

Political and Social Costs of Logging Native Forests

Environmentalists have supplemented their attacks on the large-scale logging industry with charges that it does as much damage to national political systems and local social systems as it does to native forest ecosystems. The origin of such accusations in the New Guinea region can be traced back to a judicial inquiry (the Barnett Inquiry) set up by the PNG government in 1987 to investigate what the judge in charge of it later described as the "heavy odour of corruption, fraud and scandal arising from the timber industry" (Barnett 1992: 97). The findings of this inquiry prompted Senator Al Gore to declare that the forests of PNG were "being destroyed so quickly that they will be completely gone in less than 10 years," while the logging companies were "cheating the indigenous peoples, robbing them of their homes, their culture, and the basic sustenance of their lives" (Filer 1998: 96). The inquiry's findings also led to a major overhaul of the governance framework for PNG's forestry sector. It removed the right of customary landowners (or their political leaders) to make "private dealings" with logging companies, and it centralized the process of "resource acquisition and allocation" in the hands of a National Forest Board and National Forest Service designed to operate independently of ministerial control. Some critics of the logging industry then began to question the exclusion of local communities from this new form of centralized bureaucratic control (Brunton 1996; Taylor 1997; Montagu 2001), yet it did seem to set PNG's forest management regime apart from the networks of patronage and corruption that still controlled the allocation timber harvesting rights in (West) Papua and Solomon Islands (Frazer 1997; Dauvergne 1998).

Perhaps this was only an illusion. Some critics now claim that the logging industry responded to PNG's new management regime through a process of internal consolidation that soon placed more than half of PNG's logging concessions in the hands of one Malaysian company—Rimbunan Hijau—and this one company then used its economic and political power to subvert the institutions established under the new National Forest Policy. This company now stands accused of bribery and corruption on a grand scale, the abuse of its own workers, intimidation of political opponents, the organization of black markets in sex, guns, drugs, pornography, and endangered species of wildlife, and even provision of support to Islamic terrorists in (West) Papua (Greenpeace 2004, 2005; ACF and CELCOR 2006; Chesterfield 2006). The company's initial response to such accusations was to set up a national newspaper that broadcast good news about the economic and social benefits of the logging industry (Wood 1999), but as the accusations broadened and intensified, it has more recently engaged an Australian consulting firm to produce a more detailed academic record of these benefits and a simultaneous attack on what is now portrayed as an unholly alliance of Western environmentalists with some of the Western governments represented on the board of the World Bank (ITS Global 2006a, 2006b, 2006c, 2006d, 2007).

It is true that the World Bank played an important but controversial role in helping the PNG government to implement the recommendations of the Barnett Inquiry in 1989. After the World Bank abandoned its role in PNG's forest policy process in 2005, it published a paper claiming that "illegal logging" now accounts for 70 percent of the log harvest in PNG and 70 to 80 percent of the log harvest in Indonesia (World Bank 2006). No specific body of evidence is presented to support these claims, but in the PNG case, the claim appears to be based on the findings of an independent forestry review team that received funding from the World Bank to examine the compliance of various logging operations with national government regulations (Forest Trends 2006). Critics of PNG's logging industry have since been debating whether 70 percent should really be 80 or 90 percent (Schloenhardt 2008), while its defenders say that all major logging operations are legal because they take place on concessions properly granted by the state, log exports are monitored by an independent firm of auditors, and log export taxes are duly paid to the government treasury (ITS Global 2006c). The point that tends to get lost in this argument is that measurement of an industry's failure to comply with a set of government regulations partly reflects the complexity of the regulations themselves and the level of investment made in the investigation of compliance (Filer 2000). In this respect there are still major differences between PNG and the two neighboring jurisdictions of the New Guinea region, precisely because PNG's regime of centralized bureaucratic control has made it easier to document the appearance of illegality.

In Solomon Islands, where the logging industry is more disorganized and less well regulated but accounts for a far bigger share of national income in a much smaller political community, it makes more sense to treat the national political cycle and the recent crisis of governance as a partial effect of "private deals" between Asian loggers and indigenous politicians (Bennett 2000; Wairiu 2007). But this should not lead us to assume that rural villagers are simply excluded and expropriated in a resource allocation process controlled and corrupted by members of an urban political elite. As in other parts of Melanesia, the costs and benefits of commercial logging are also negotiated and redistributed within rural village communities in ways that do not necessarily conform to Western ideas about the contest between "conservation" and "development," and in ways that also vary from place to place and time to time (Hviding 2003; Scales 2003). In one part of the country, for example, a history of sporadic engagement and disengagement between local villagers and foreign loggers eventually led to the development of an indigenous form of plantation forestry by a micronationalist Christian sect (Hviding and Bayliss-Smith 2000; Makim 2002).

A range of local social impacts and political responses has also been documented in different parts of PNG. Perhaps the most typical pattern is one in which local villagers start out with a pressing desire for "development," are thus persuaded to let the government convert their forests into a logging concession, but later get into arguments over the distribution and consumption of a benefit package that fails to meet their earlier expectations (De'Ath 1980; Mullins and Flaherty 1995; Filer 1996; Wood 1996; Sagir 1997). But there are also variations on this theme. The Barnett Inquiry found many cases of trickery and deception in the resource acquisition process, which meant that most local villagers had little or no choice in the matter, and that is why the resulting policy reforms insisted on the formal consent of "incorporated land groups" (Holzknecht 1997). In some cases, the bureaucratic complexity of the resource allocation process initiated by those same reforms caused local disillusionment and conflict to erupt before logging had even started (Wood 1997). In other cases, long-standing rivalries between neighboring communities were translated into a contest over the choice between logging and forest conservation (Barker 2002). This choice may also reflect a contest between Christianity and local "custom" (Schieffelin 1997; Brunois 1999), or be modified by the active intervention of environmental organizations offering an alternative type of benefit package (Henderson 1997), but when loggers and conservationists contend for the hearts and minds of rural villagers, the latter can sometimes opt to play both ends against the middle (McCallum and Sekhran 1997). And when local landowner decide that logging has not lived up to their expectations, they may either take direct action against the operators (Leedom 1997; Majid Cooke 1997) or else take their cases to court (Nen 1997; Bird et al. 2007b).

Al Gore's vision of the destructive impact of large-scale logging operations on indigenous society and culture is widely shared by Western environmentalists, but it tends to assume that logging must damage the livelihoods of "rain forest peoples" because it is known to degrade the forests on which those livelihoods are thought to be dependent. Evidence from Vanuatu should serve to remind us that Melanesian villagers are not necessarily disadvantaged by the selective logging of primary forests because their subsistence needs are mainly met from the secondary forest fallows that result from the practice of shifting cultivation (Tacconi 1995; Regenvanu, Wyatt, and Tacconi 1997). If anything, their need to extract timber from primary forests has been diminishing with the advent of new construction materials: canoe trees lose most of their value when the labor cost of carving canoes outweighs the purchase price of a fiberglass banana boat. Indeed, evidence from other parts of the Pacific Island region suggests that local farmers are even losing the interest and capacity to cultivate some of the tree species that were once significant components of indigenous "agroforestry" systems (Clarke and Thaman 1993, 1997). But even where the cycle of shifting cultivation retains its traditional form, it is not hard to see how rural villagers might regard selective logging operations in primary forests as a similar type of activity (Hviding and Bayliss-Smith 2000; Bayliss-Smith, Hviding, and Whitmore 2003), and their attitude to commercial logging will then have more to do with perceptions of economic gain than perceptions of environmental loss.

BIBLIOGRAPHY

ACF (Australian Conservation Foundation) and CELCOR (Centre for Environmental Law and Community Rights). 2006. *Bulldozing progress: Human rights abuses and corruption in Papua New Guinea's large scale logging industry.* Melbourne and Port Moresby: ACF and CELCOR.

Anderson, A. 2002. A fragile plenty: Pre-European Maori and the New Zealand environment. In *Environmental histories of New Zealand,* ed. E. Pawson and T. Brooking, 19–34. South Melbourne: Oxford University Press.

Bahn, P., and J. Flenley. 1992. *Easter Island, earth island.* London: Thames and Hudson.

Barker, J. 2002. Missionaries, environmentalists, and the Maisin, Papua New Guinea. Canberra: Australian National University, State, Society & Governance in Melanesia Project (Discussion Paper 2002/3).

Barnett, T. E. 1992. Legal and administrative problems of forestry in Papua New Guinea. In *Resources, development and politics in the Pacific Islands,* ed. S. Henningham and R. J. May, 90–118. Bathurst, N.S.W.: Crawford House Press.

Bayliss-Smith, T., E. Hviding, and T. C. Whitmore. 2003. Rainforest composition and histories of human disturbance in Solomon Islands. *Ambio* 32: 346–352.

Bennett, J. A. 2000. *Pacific forest: A history of resource control and contest in Solomon Islands, c. 1800–1997.* Cambridge: White Horse Press.

Bird, N., A. Wells, F. van Helden, and R. Turia. 2007a. *What can be learnt from the past? A history of the forestry sector in Papua New Guinea.* Papua New Guinea Forest Studies 1. London: Overseas Development Institute.

———. 2007b. *The current legal and institutional framework of the forest sector in Papua New Guinea.* Papua New Guinea Forest Studies 2. London: Overseas Development Institute.

———. 2007c. *Issues and opportunities for the forest sector in Papua New Guinea.* Papua New Guinea Forest Studies 3. London: Overseas Development Institute.

Bond, A. 2006. *Pacific 2020 background paper: Forestry.* Canberra: AusAID.

BPNG (Bank of Papua New Guinea). 2008. *Quarterly economic bulletin, March 2008.* Port Moresby: BPNG.

Brown, C. 1997. *Regional study: the South Pacific.* Asia-Pacific Forestry Sector Outlook Study Working Paper APFSOS/WP/01. Rome: UN Food and Agriculture Organization.

Brunois, F. 1999. In paradise, the forest is open and covered in flowers. In *Expecting the day of wrath: Versions of the millennium in Papua New Guinea,* ed. C. Kocher Schmid, 111–130. Monograph 36. Boroko: National Research Institute.

Brunton, B. 1996. A quarter of next to nothing: Participation and responsibility with forestry resources. In *From Rio to Rai: Environment and development in Papua New Guinea up to 2000 and beyond,* vol. 3: *A quarter of next to nothing,* ed. D. Gladman, D. Mowbray, and J. Duguman, 109–130. Port Moresby: University of Papua New Guinea Press.

Cameron, A. L., and T. Vigus. 1993. *Papua New Guinea volume and growth study: Regeneration and growth of the tropical moist forest in Papua New Guinea and the implications for future harvests.* Brisbane: Commonwealth Scientific and Industrial Research Organisation, Division of Wildlife and Ecology (for the World Bank).

Cannon, J. B. 2007. Natural resource economics of Papua. In *The ecology of Papua,* ed. A. J. Marshall and B. M. Beehler, 1167–1195. Singapore: Periplus Editions.

Carothers, A., and L. Cortesi. 1998. *Sustaining Papua New Guinea's natural heritage: An analysis of the Papua New Guinea National Forest Plan.* Suva: Greenpeace and WWF.

CBSI (Central Bank of Solomon Islands). 2008. *Annual report 2007.* Honiara: CBSI.

Chesterfield, N. 2006. *Terror-razing the forest: Guns, corruption, illegal logging, JI & the Indonesian military in Papua New Guinea.* Windsor, Vic.: Nick Chesterfield.

Clarke, W. C., and R. R. Thaman, eds. 1993. *Agroforestry in the Pacific Islands: Systems for sustainability.* Tokyo: United Nations University Press.

———. 1997. Incremental agroforestry: Enriching Pacific landscapes. *The Contemporary Pacific* 9(1): 121–148.

Cuddihy, L. W., and C. P. Stone. 1990. *Alteration of native Hawaiian vegetation: Effects of humans, their activities and introductions.* Honolulu: University of Hawai'i, Cooperative National Park Resource Studies Unit.

Culliney, J. L. 1988. *Islands in a far sea: Nature and man in Hawaii.* San Francisco: Sierra Club.

Curtin, T. 2005. Forestry and economic development in Papua New Guinea. *South Pacific Journal of Philosophy and Culture* 8: 105–117.

Curtin, T., and D. Lea. 2006. Land titling and socioeconomic development in the South Pacific. *Pacific Economic Bulletin* 21(1): 153–180.

Dauvergne, P. 1997. *Shadows in the forest: Japan and the politics of timber in Southeast Asia.* Cambridge, Mass.: MIT Press.

———. 1998. Weak states and the environment in Indonesia and the Solomon Islands. In *Weak and strong states in Asia-Pacific societies,* ed. P. Dauvergne, 135–157. St Leonards, N.S.W.: Allen & Unwin.

———. 1999. Corporate power in the forests of the Solomon Islands. *Pacific Affairs* 71(4): 524–546.

———. 2001. *Loggers and degradation in the Asia-Pacific: Corporations and environmental management.* Cambridge: Cambridge University Press.

De'Ath, C. 1980. *The throwaway people: Social impact of the Gogol*

Timber Project, Madang Province. Monograph 13. Boroko: Institute of Applied Social and Economic Research.

Diamond, J. 2005. *Collapse: How societies choose to fail or survive.* London: Allen Lane.

EIA (Environmental Investigation Agency)/Telapak. 2005. *The last frontier: Illegal logging in Papua and China's massive timber theft.* London/Jakarta: EIA/Telapak.

FAO (Food and Agriculture Organization of the United Nations). 2007. *State of the world's forests 2007.* Rome: FAO.

Filer, C. 1996. The social context of renewable resource depletion in Papua New Guinea. In *Resources, nations and indigenous peoples: Case studies from Australasia, Melanesia and Southeast Asia,* ed. R. Howitt, 289–299. Melbourne: Oxford University Press.

———. 1998. *Loggers, donors and resource owners.* Policy That Works for Forests and People, Papua New Guinea Country Study. London: International Institute for Environment and Development in association with the National Research Institute.

———. 2000. *The thin green line: World Bank leverage and forest policy reform in Papua New Guinea.* Port Moresby and Canberra: National Research Institute and Australian National University.

Flannery, T. F. 1994. *The future eaters: An ecological history of the Australasian lands and people.* Sydney: Reed New Holland.

Forest Trends. 2006. *Logging, legality and livelihoods in Papua New Guinea: Synthesis of official assessments of the large-scale logging industry.* 2 volumes. Jakarta: Forest Trends.

Frazer, I. 1997. The struggle for control of Solomon Island forests. *The Contemporary Pacific* 9(1): 39–72.

Greenpeace. 2004. *The untouchables: Rimbunan Hijau's world of forest crime & political patronage.* Amsterdam: Greenpeace International.

———. 2005. *Partners in crime: The UK timber trade, Chinese sweatshops and Malaysian robber barons in Papua New Guinea's rainforests.* Amsterdam: Greenpeace International.

Groube, L. 1989. The taming of the rain forests: A model for late Pleistocene forest exploitation in New Guinea. In *Foraging and farming: The evolution of plant exploitation,* ed. D. R. Harris and G. C. Hillman, 292–304. London: Unwin Hyman.

Haberle, S. G., G. S. Hope, and S. van der Kaars 2001. Biomass burning in Indonesia and Papua New Guinea: Natural and human induced fire events in the fossil record. *Palaeogeography Palaeoclimatology Palaeoecology* 171(3/4): 259–268.

Hammermaster, E. T., and J. C. Saunders. 1995. *Forest resources and vegetation mapping of Papua New Guinea.* Canberra: Australian Agency for International Development, PNG Resource Information System (Publication 4).

Hammond, D. 2002. *Hardwood programmes in Fiji, Solomon Islands and Papua New Guinea.* Rome: UN Food and Agriculture Organization, Forest Resources Development Service (Forest Plantations Working Paper 21).

Henderson, M. 1997. Forest futures for Papua New Guinea: Logging or community forestry? In *Environment and development in the Pacific Islands,* ed. B. Burt and C. Clerk, 45–68. Canberra: Australian National University, National Centre for Development Studies (Pacific Policy Paper 25).

Holzknecht, H. 1997. Problems of articulation and representation in resource development: The case of forestry in Papua New Guinea. *Anthropological Forum* 7(4): 549–573.

Hope, G. S. 2007. The history of human impact on New Guinea. In *The ecology of Papua,* ed. A. J. Marshall and B. M. Beehler, 1087–1097. Singapore: Periplus Editions.

Hviding, E. 2003. Contested rainforests, NGOs, and projects of desire in Solomon Islands. *International Social Science Journal* 178: 539–554.

Hviding, E., and T. Bayliss-Smith 2000. *Islands of rainforest: Agroforestry, logging and eco-tourism in Solomon Islands.* Aldershot: Ashgate.

IMOF (Indonesian Ministry of Forestry). 2005. *Forest statistics of Indonesia 2004.* Jakarta: IMOF.

ITS Global 2006a. *The economic importance of the forestry industry to Papua New Guinea.* Melbourne: ITS Global for Rimbunan Hijau (PNG) Group.

———. 2006b. *Masalai i Tokaut and Rimbunan Hijau Watch: A political and deceptive campaign against Rimbunan Hijau.* Melbourne: ITS Global for Rimbunan Hijau (PNG) Group.

———. 2006c. *Whatever it takes: Greenpeace's anti-forestry campaign in Papua New Guinea.* Melbourne: ITS Global for Rimbunan Hijau (PNG) Group.

———. 2006d. *The World Bank and forestry in PNG.* Melbourne: ITS Global for Rimbunan Hijau (PNG) Group.

———. 2007. *The economic contribution of Rimbunan Hijau's forestry operations in Papua New Guinea.* Melbourne: ITS Global for Rimbunan Hijau (PNG) Group.

ITTO (International Tropical Timber Organization). 2007. *Achieving the ITTO objective 2000 and sustainable forest management in Papua New Guinea: Report of the diagnostic mission.* Port Moresby: ITTO.

Johns, R. J. 1990. The illusionary concept of the climax. In *The plant diversity of Malesia,* ed. P. Baas, K. Kalkman, and R. Geesink, 13–146. Dordrecht: Kluwer Academic Publishers.

———. 1992. The influence of deforestation and selective logging operations on plant diversity in Papua New Guinea. In *Tropical deforestation and species extinction,* ed. T. C. Whitmore and J. A. Sayer, 143–147. London: Chapman & Hall.

Jonas, W. J. 1985. The commercial timber industry in colonial Papua New Guinea. *Journal of Pacific Studies* 8(2): 45–60.

Keenan, R. J., V. Ambia, C. Brack, I. Frakes, A. Gerrand, M. Golman, H. Holzknecht, K. Lavong, N. Sam, J. K. Vanclay, and C. Yosi. 2005. Improved timber inventory and strategic forest planning in Papua New Guinea. Canberra and Lae: Bureau of Rural Sciences and Forest Research Institute.

King, B., and P. J. Hughes. 1998. Protected areas in Papua New Guinea. In *Modern Papua New Guinea,* ed. L. Zimmer-Tamakoshi, 383–405. Kirksville, Mo.: Thomas Jefferson University Press.

Kirch, P. V., and T. L. Hunt, eds. 1997. *Historical ecology in the Pacific Islands: Prehistoric environmental and landscape change.* New Haven, Conn.: Yale University Press.

Kirkland, A., and P. Berg 1997. *A century of state-honed enterprise: 100 years of state plantation forestry in New Zealand.* Auckland: Profile Books.

Lamb, D. 1990. *Exploiting the tropical rain forest: An account of pulpwood logging in Papua New Guinea.* Paris: UNESCO and Parthenon Publishing (Man and the Biosphere Series, Volume 3).

Lane-Poole, C. E. 1925. *The forest resources of the territories of Papua and New Guinea.* Melbourne: Report to the Parliament of the Commonwealth of Australia.

Lea, D. 2005. The PNG forest industry, incorporated entities and environmental protection. *Pacific Economic Bulletin* 20(1): 168–177.

Leedom, J. M. 1997. "Private dealings": A social history of the Hawain Local Forest Area, East Sepik Province. In *The political economy of forest management in Papua New Guinea,* ed. C. Filer, 35–66. Monograph 32. London and Boroko, PNG: International Institute for Environment and Development and National Research Institute.

Light, A. 1997. The politics of large-scale timber consumption in Japan. In *The political economy of forest management in Papua New Guinea,* ed. C. Filer, 293–310. Monograph 32. London and Boroko, PNG: International Institute for Environment and Development and National Research Institute.

Lindemalm, F., and H. M. Rogers. 2001. Impacts of conventional logging and portable sawmill logging operations on tree diversity in East New Britain, Papua New Guinea. *Australian Forestry* 64(1): 26–31.

Louman, B. 1997. Biophysical parameters for sustainable utilisation of Papua New Guinea's forests. In *The political economy of forest management in Papua New Guinea,* ed. C. Filer, 333–352. Monograph 32.

London and Boroko, PNG: International Institute for Environment and Development and National Research Institute.

Louman, B., and S. Nicholls. 1994. Forestry in Papua New Guinea. In *Papua New Guinea country study on biological diversity,* ed. N. Sekhran and S. Miller, 155–168. Port Moresby: Department of Environment and Conservation.

Majid Cooke, F. 1997. Where do the raw logs go? Contractors, traders, and landowners in Lak. In *The political economy of forest management in Papua New Guinea,* ed. C. Filer, 109–129. Monograph 32. London and Boroko (PNG): International Institute for Environment and Development and National Research Institute.

Makim, A. 2002. *Globalisation, community development, and Melanesia: The North New Georgia Sustainable Social Forestry and Rural Development Project.* Discussion Paper 2002/1. Canberra: Australian National University, State, Society & Governance in Melanesia Project.

McAlpine, J., and J. Quigley 1998. *Forest resources of Papua New Guinea: Summary statistics from the forest inventory mapping (fim) system.* Coffey MPW Pty Ltd for the Australian Agency for International Development and the Papua New Guinea National Forest Service.

McCallum, R., and N. Sekhran 1997. *Race for the rainforest: Evaluating lessons from an integrated conservation and development "experiment" in New Ireland, Papua New Guinea.* Port Moresby: PNG Biodiversity Conservation and Resource Management Programme.

Montagu, A. S. 2001. Reforming forest planning and management in Papua New Guinea, 1991–94: Losing people in the process. *Journal of Environmental Planning and Management* 44(5): 649–662.

Mullins, M., and M. Flaherty 1995. Customary landowner involvement in the Kumil Timber Project, Papua New Guinea. *Geoforum* 26: 89–105.

Nadarajah, T. 1994. The sustainability of Papua New Guinea's forest resource. Discussion Paper 76. Boroko, PNG: National Research Institute.

Nen, T. 1997. The invisible developer: The landowners' dilemma in the Buhem-Mongi TRP area. In *The political economy of forest management in Papua New Guinea,* ed. C. Filer, 67–83. Monograph 32. London and Boroko, PNG: International Institute for Environment and Development and National Research Institute.

NZMAF (New Zealand Ministry of Agriculture and Forestry). 2008. Annual forestry export statistics. Wellington: NZMAF.

Paulson, D. 1994. Understanding tropical deforestation: The case of Western Samoa. *Environment and Conservation* 21: 326–352.

PNGMOF (PNG Ministry of Forests). 1991. *National forest policy.* Hohola: PNGMOF.

Qalo, R. R. 1993. Indigenous politics in the governance of Fiji: The case of forestry. PhD thesis, Australian National University, Canberra.

Regenvanu, R., S. W. Wyatt, and L. Tacconi. 1997. Changing forestry regimes in Vanuatu: Is sustainable management possible? *The Contemporary Pacific* 9(1): 73–96.

Roche, M. M. 1987. *Forest policy in New Zealand: An historical geography 1840–1919.* Palmerston North: Dunmore Press.

———. 2002. The state as conservationist, 1920–60: "Wise use" of forests, lands, and water. In *Environmental histories of New Zealand,* ed. E. Pawson and T. Brooking, 183–189. South Melbourne: Oxford University Press.

Routley, R., and V. Routley. 1977. Destructive forestry in Australia and Melanesia. In *The Melanesian environment: Papers presented at the Ninth Waigani Seminar,* ed. J. H. Winslow, 374–397. Canberra: Australian National University Press.

Sagir, B. F. 1997. Living with logging and broken promises: Madang Timbers in the Madang North Coast. In *The political economy of forest management in Papua New Guinea,* ed. C. Filer, 130–146.

Monograph 32. London and Boroko, PNG: International Institute for Environment and Development and National Research Institute.

Scales, I. A. 2003. The social forest: Landowners, development conflict and the state in Solomon Islands. PhD thesis, Australian National University Canberra.

Schieffelin, E. L. 1997. History and the fate of forests on the Papuan Plateau. *Anthropological Forum* 7(4): 575–597.

Schloenhardt, A. 2008. *The illegal trade in timber and timber products in the Asia-Pacific region.* Research and Public Policy Series 89. Canberra: Australian Institute of Criminology.

Shearman, P. L., J. E. Bryan, J. Ash, P. Hunnam, B. Mackey, and B. Lokes. 2008. *The state of the forests of Papua New Guinea: Mapping the extent and condition of forest cover and measuring the drivers of forest change in the period 1972–2002.* Port Moresby: University of Papua New Guinea.

Shineberg, D. 1967. *They came for sandalwood: A study of the sandalwood trade in the South-West Pacific 1830–1865.* Melbourne: Melbourne University Press.

Tacconi, L. 1995. The process of forest conservation in Vanuatu: A study in ecological economics. PhD thesis, University of New South Wales Sydney.

Taylor, R. 1997. The state versus custom: Regulating Papua New Guinea's timber industry. In *The political economy of forest management in Papua New Guinea,* ed. C. Filer, 249–268. Monograph 32. London and Boroko, PNG: International Institute for Environment and Development and National Research Institute.

Wairiu, M. 2007. History of the forestry industry in Solomon Islands: The case of Guadalcanal. *Journal of Pacific History* 42: 233–246.

Ward, R. G. 1995. Deforestation in Western Samoa. *Pacific Viewpoint* 36: 73–93.

White, K. J. 1977. Constraints on developing forest industries in Papua New Guinea. In *The Melanesian environment: Papers presented at the ninth waigani seminar,* ed. J. H. Winslow, 398–406. Canberra: Australian National University Press.

Whitmore, T. C. 1990. *An introduction to tropical rain forests.* Oxford: Clarendon Press.

Womersley, J. S., and J. B. McAdam. 1957. *The forests and forest conditions in the territories of Papua and New Guinea.* Port Moresby: Government Printer.

Wood, M. 1996. Logs, long socks and the "tree leaf" people: An analysis of a timber project in the Western Province of Papua New Guinea. *Social Analysis* 38: 83–119.

———. 1997. The Makapa Timber Rights Purchase: A study in project failure in the post-Barnett era. In *The political economy of forest management in Papua New Guinea,* ed. C. Filer, 84–108. Monograph 32. London and Boroko, PNG: International Institute for Environment and Development and National Research Institute.

———. 1999. Rimbunan Hijau versus the World Bank and Australian miners: Print media representations of forestry policy conflict in Papua New Guinea. *Australian Journal of Anthropology* 10(2): 177–191.

World Bank. 2006. Strengthening forest law enforcement and governance: Addressing a systemic constraint to sustainable development. Washington, D.C.: World Bank.

Wyatt, S., A. Bartlett, and A. Mathias. 1999. Developing a forest policy in a small nation: The Vanuatu National Forest Policy. *International Forestry Review* 1(2): 102–108.

Wynn, G. 2002. Destruction under the guise of improvement? The forest, 1840–1920. In *Environmental histories of New Zealand,* ed. E. Pawson and T. Brooking, 100–116. South Melbourne: Oxford University Press.

Ocean Resources

Vina Ram-Bidesi

30

The twenty-two developing states and territories of the Pacific Islands region consist of only about 551,390 km² of land with about 9.5 million people spread across 30 million km² of ocean (as shown in Figure 30.1). The region therefore comprises mainly ocean, which accounts for 98 percent of the total area and extends thousands of kilometers from north to south of the equator. The islands are linked and controlled by the oceanic environment.

The dependence of the Pacific Island countries upon the ocean resources has been a vital part of their cultural, social, and economic development. The coastal and marine ecosystems of the region are extremely important habitats for sustaining the livelihoods by providing food and nutritional security. With limited arable land and poor soils in the low-lying islands, the reliance on marine resources is extremely important. As the population increases, this dependence becomes even more critical. The ocean is seen as the "lifeline" that "provides the greatest opportunities for economic development" (SPREP 2002). Economic activities such as fisheries, tourism, and trade are highly dependent on the marine environment. On the other hand, the economies and environments of many of the island countries are extremely fragile not only in relation to the global economy but also because of their vulnerability to a wide range of environmental factors. Natural disasters such as cyclones, floods, drought, increasing amounts of waste and pollution, and overexploitation of resources pose major threats to realizing the ocean's potential.

This chapter will consider Pacific Island ocean resources according to their distinctive uses and will highlight some threats and challenges to the future sustainability of these valued resources.

Ocean Environments

Marine ecosystems include those that are associated with seafloor, known as benthic, and those that are in open water, called planktonic and/or pelagic. The major abiotic factor within these marine ecosystems is light, which distinguishes shallow ecosystems (coral reefs in the tropics) from deep-water ecosystems (Lobban and Schefter 1997). The harvestable productivity is largely dependent on the rich upwelling systems of the continental margins of the ocean. Most of the islands rise steeply from the deep ocean floor and have little shelf area, with the exception of Papua New Guinea and New Zealand. As a result, most Pacific Island countries lack the broad shallow shelves characteristic of continental margins and major island archipelagoes like those found in Southeast Asia and the Caribbean. It is common to find depths of 3,000 m within 2 km of shore (Adams, Dalzell, and Ledua 1999). Coral reefs characteristically surround the islands either close to shore (fringing reefs) or further offshore (barrier reefs), in which case a coastal lagoon is enclosed. Mangrove forests often border the inshore waters, especially around the larger islands, and provide habitat for the juveniles of many important food fish.

Coral dominates the nearshore substrate of geologically young island groups like Hawai'i, the Marquesas, Vanuatu, and the Northern Marianas where reef building hermatypic coral structures are not well developed and barrier reefs uncommon.

A primary feature of the central equatorial Pacific is a strong divergent equatorial upwelling called the cold tongue, which is favorable to the development of a large zonal band with high levels of primary production (Lehodey 2001). Contiguous to the cold tongue is the western Pacific warm pool, characterized by warmer water with lower levels of primary productivity.

Despite its low primary productivity rates, the western equatorial Pacific warm pool supplies the largest proportion of tuna catch in the Pacific Ocean and contributes approximately 40 percent of the world's annual tuna supply (Lehodey 2001: 441). The pool's boundaries are dynamic, moving in response to oceanographic features. The warm pool can undergo spectacular displacements of more than 40° of longitude (nearly 4,000 km) in less than six months as part of the El Niño/La Niña phenomenon (Lehodey 1997). Tuna abundance and yields are displaced east-west by the same phenomena. The geographic locations of catches of purse seine fleet can be predicted in advance based on the east-west movement of the 29° C isotherm and variation in the Southern Oscillation Index (a measure of the difference in barometric pressure between the eastern and western Pacific Rim) (Lehodey 1997).

In contrast to animal populations that are dispersed in the open ocean, tropical reefs are highly productive. Many Pacific islands are surrounded by barrier reefs, almost all have fringing reefs, and the surface area of some islands consists entirely of reefs in the form of atolls (Adams, Dalzell, and Ledua 1999: 367). Coral reefs are home to more than a quarter of all known marine fish species and have been termed the "rainforests of the marine world" (Bryant et al. 1998; United Nations 2000: 103). Coral reef

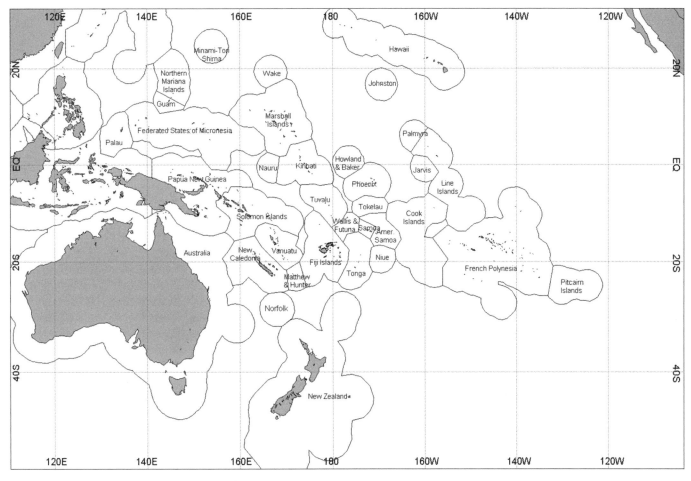

Figure 30.1. *Pacific Island 200-mile zones (SPC n.d.).*

systems provide a useful indicator of marine biodiversity and eco-logical health. About 40 percent of global coral reefs are found in the Pacific region (United Nations 2000: 103). Barrier reefs around New Caledonia, the Western Province in Solomon Islands, the Great Astrolabe, and Great Sea Reef in Fiji are examples of areas of high species diversity. The extensive coral reefs of the Pacific Islands consist of seventy coral genera supporting more than four thousand fish species, thirty mangrove species, and a range of rep-tiles, marine mammals, and seabirds (SPC 2008b: 1).

Mangroves are important habitats in the coastal areas of the western Pacific, although mangroves are not found naturally east-ward of Samoa, in line with the general decline in natural species biodiversity from west to east across the Pacific (Adams, Dalzell, and Ledua 1999). The South Pacific subregion provides about two million hectares of mangroves or about 10 percent of the total man-grove areas in the world (United Nations 2000: 102).

Seagrasses are common features of shallow marine ecosystems and, like mangroves, are particularly significant as "nursery habi-tat" for the juveniles of many of the living resources that are impor-tant food sources for humans. The generic richness of seagrass beds is centered in the Indo–West Pacific region, while species diversity is highest in the area defined by Indonesia, Borneo, Papua New Guinea, and Northern Australia (United Nations 2000: 103). In the western Pacific, seagrass beds exist due to the sheltering effect of the extensive barrier reefs.

Direct and Indirect Uses of the Ocean Resources

Pacific Ocean resources have direct and indirect uses and can be either extractive or nonextractive. Resources can also be catego-rized as living, such as fish and marine plants, or non-living, such as oil, gas, and minerals.

Fisheries Resources

Fisheries resources discussed are either coastal or offshore. While the major emphasis is on developing smaller island countries of the Pacific, a brief note will be made on the more developed fisher-ies of New Zealand and Hawai'i, where the scale of operations and management systems is similar to fisheries in developed countries. In New Zealand, the value of harvests from wild fisheries ranges from $1.2 to $1.5 billion per annum, of which aquaculture con-tributes about $200 million per annum (New Zealand Ministry of Fisheries 2008). Seventy percent of the fish is taken from deep water, and management of most important commercial fisheries is under the quota management system. For example, there are 129 species separated into 96 groupings that are managed under the quota management system, with an estimated quota value of NZ$3.8 billion (New Zealand Ministry of Fisheries 2008). Likewise in Hawai'i, fisheries are predominantly commercial, having a var-ied fishing fleet that targets offshore tuna and pelagic and bottom fishes. The scale of commercialization can be seen, for example, from a report that stated that nine bottom fishers in the northern Hawaiian Islands fishing in federal waters brought in a catch worth around US$1.5 million each per annum (McAvoy 2005).

Coastal Fisheries

In most Pacific islands, coastal fisheries are characterized as artisanal and subsistence fishing carried out in the lagoons, on the mud flats, reefs and outer shelves, and in offshore areas extending to a distance where small vessels can operate. The dispersed nature of the islands, the informal types of fishing activities, and the limited resources of governments makes any assessment of the coastal fisheries difficult. The production estimates are typically guess estimates produced by agricultural censuses, household surveys, or nutritional statistics (Visser 1997). While recent estimates are almost nonexistent, some figures have been available from the mid-1990s for subsistence fisheries. Estimates of annual nominal per capita fish consumption based on domestic fish production and population figures range from 7 to 40 kg or a mean of 23 kg for Melanesia, while in Polynesia and Micronesia, the ranges are 6 to

121 kg and 4 to 170 kg with means of 60 and 63 kg, respectively (Dalzell, Adams, and Polunin 1996). According to FAO data, fish (of which the vast majority is from coastal areas) represents 38.7 percent of the total animal protein intake in the Pacific Islands region, much greater than the world average of 16.1 percent (FAO 2005). Table 30.1 shows the relative importance of coastal fisheries in the Pacific Islands in terms of catch per capita.

Estimates show that as much as 83 percent of the coastal households of Solomon Islands, 35 percent of the rural households of Vanuatu, 99 percent of the rural households of Kiribati, 87 percent of the households in the Marshall Islands, and half the rural households in Upolu Samoa fish primarily for local consumption (World Bank 1995). Besides providing a source of food and nutritional security, subsistence fisheries also play an important role in national economies through import substitution. It is further estimated that some Pacific Island countries would have to spend an additional US$7 to 18 million a year for imported protein substitutes if subsistence fisheries did not exist (World Bank 1995). According to a report in 2000, the value of annual subsistence production of finfish and shellfish in protein equivalent was US$6.7 million in Fiji, US$18 million in Kiribati, US$13.9 million

Table 30.1

The Relative Importance of Coastal Fisheries in the Pacific Islands

Country	Land area (km²)	EEZ area (km²)	EEZ area/ land area	Population	GDP/capita (US $)	Total coastal fish (tonnes)	Coastal fish catch/capita (kg)
Am. Samoa	199	390,000	1,959.8	66,107	6,995	267	4.0
Cook Islands	237	1,830,000	7,721.5	15,537	8,553	875	56.3
FSM	701	2,978,000	4,248.2	110,443	2,183	10,000	90.5
Fiji	18,272	1,290,000	70.6	839,324	3,175	30,920	36.8
Guam	541	218,000	403.0	178,980	22,661	590	3.3
Hawai'i (USA)	16,641	2,381,000	143.1	1,262,840	49,563	13,424	10.6
Kiribati	811	3,550,000	4,377.3	97,231	653	16,000	164.6
Marshall Is.	181	2,131,000	11,733.5	53,236	2,851	3,244	60.9
Nauru	21	320,000	15,238.1	10,163	2,807	425	41.8
Niue	259	390,000	1,505.8	1,549	5,828	206	133.0
CNMI	457	1,823,000	3,989.1	62,969	12,638	2,966	47.1
N. Caledonia	18,576	1,740,000	93.7	246,614	29,898	3,481	14.1
Palau	444	629,000	1,416.7	20,279	8,423	2,115	104.3
PNG	462,840	3,120,000	6.7	6,473,910	991	31,500	4.9
Pitcairn Is.	5	800,000	160,000	66	-	8	121.2
Fr. Polynesia	3,521	5,030,000	1,428.5	263,267	22,472	6,043	23.0
Samoa	2,935	120,000	40.9	179,645	2,872	7,169	39.9
Solomon Is.	28,370	1,340,000	47.2	517,455	753	16,200	31.3
Tokelau	12	290,000	24,166.7	1,170	-	191	163.2
Tonga	650	700,000	1,076.9	102,724	2,319	7,036	68.5
Tuvalu	26	900,000	34,615.4	9,729	1,831	1,100	113.1
Vanuatu	12,190	680,000	55.8	233,026	2,127	2,930	12.6
Wallis & Futuna	142	300,000	2,112.7	15,472	-	917	59.3

Source: Adams et. al (1999); (FAO) 2005; Gillett & Lightfoot (2001); Gillett (2009); Gillett (2011); SPC 2008; http://www.st.nmfs.noaa.gov/st1/fus/fus09/02_commercial2009.pdf; http://hawaii.gov./dbedt/info/economic/databook/2008-individual/ 2008.

in Solomon Islands, and US$14.7 million in Vanuatu (World Bank 2000). In Papua New Guinea, the catch of subsistence coastal fisheries was estimated to be around 26,000 tonnes (mt) per year with a sale value of 60 million kina and the catch of artisanal/commercial coastal fisheries at 5,500 mt/year. Estimates indicated that 250,000 people participated in coastal subsistence fisheries (Gillett Preston and Associates 2000). Of the rural households engaged in fishing, 60 percent were subsistence fishers. The estimated subsistence production in Fiji in 2002 was 18,400 mt with a value of US$7.1 million, or an import substitution value of US$9.2 million (Fiji Fisheries Department 2005). Artisanal catch of 6,871 mt in the local market was valued at F$26.6 million while exports of inshore fisheries was valued at F$26 million, consisting largely of aquarium products (Fiji Fisheries Department 2005).

A more recent study attempted to value the contribution of small-scale nonpelagic fisheries to GDP in two American territories (American Samoa and Northern Marianas) by reconstructing the production and consumption patterns based on earlier estimates. The study concluded that between 1982 and 2002, the small-scale nonpelagic fisheries alone may have contributed approximately US$54.7 million to the GDP of American Samoa and Northern

Mariana Islands (Zeller, Booth, and Pauly 2007). This was 5.1 times the value of subsistence assessed by official statistics.

Table 30.2 shows the annual volume and value of commercial and subsistence production of coastal fisheries. The table indicates that the value and volume of subsistence catch far outweighs the commercial coastal catch. The value of subsistence fisheries to food security can be gauged by how much Pacific Island governments would have to pay for imported substitutes if these fisheries ceased to exist. An interesting feature of this fishery is that the most active fishers are generally women, children, and youth.

Subsistence fishing also plays a significant social role in the Pacific communities as fishing activities have been interwoven into the daily lives of people for generations. Subsistence fishing, commonly regulated by local custom, contributes to preservation of cultural traditions and helps maintain social cohesion of coastal communities.

Pacific Island countries do not export many varieties of coastal fisheries products. The principal exports include dried sea cucumber (bêche-de-mer), trochus, pearls and aquarium fish, coral, and live rock and seaweeds, most of which are targeted at specific niche markets.

Table 30.2

Annual Volume and Value of Commercial and Subsistence Coastal Fisheries

Country	Coastal commercial (t)	Coastal commercial ($)	Coastal subsistence (t)	Coastal subsistence ($)
American Samoa	35	166,000	120	478,000
Cook Islands	133	1,029,412	267	1,250,000
Federated States of Micronesia	2,800	7,560,000	9,800	15,732,000
Fiji	9,500	33,750,000	17,400	33,812,500
French Polynesia	4,002	23,004,598	2,880	13,208,276
Guam	44	195,000	70	217,000
Kiribati	7,000	18,487,395	13,700	28,571,429
Marshall Islands	950	2,900,000	2,800	4,312,000
Niue	10	58,824	140	617,647
Nauru	200	840,336	450	661,345
New Caledonia	1,350	8,689,655	3,500	15,770,115
Northern Marianas	231	950,000	220	631,700
Palau	865	2,843,000	1,250	2,511,000
Papua New Guinea	5,700	27,027,027	30,000	35,472,973
Pitcairn Islands	5	37,500	7	36,765
Samoa	4,129	19,557,592	4,495	14,903,842
Solomon Islands	3,250	3,307,190	15,000	10,980,392
Tokelau	0	0	375	711,397
Tonga	3,700	11,287,129	2,800	6,182,178
Tuvalu	226	616,526	989	2,232,686
Vanuatu	538	2,176,923	2,830	5,740,385
Wallis & Futuna	121	1,206,897	840	6,333,333
TOTAL	44,789	165,691,002	109,933	200,366,961

Source: Gillett 2009.

Dried sea cucumber exports date back to the early days of European contact and is found throughout the tropical Pacific. About thirty-six species of sea cucumbers (Holothuroidea) are currently exploited in the region, primarily for export to Asia. Villagers can process sea cucumber into a nonperishable product that can be stored for extended periods until transport becomes available (Foale 2008). Figure 30.2 shows the drying of bêche-de-mer destined for export. The fishery is characterized by a boom-and-bust cycle of intense exploitation followed by a sharp fall in the abundance, then a dormant period in which the resource is able to recover. For example, in Papua New Guinea, Solomon Islands, and Fiji, production increased in the late 1980s and early 1990s but declined due to overfishing by use of underwater fishing gear and equipment.

Figure 30.2. *Drying of sea cucumber (photo VRB).*

Although the natural range of *Trochus niloticus* is limited to the western part of the Pacific, it has been transplanted to almost all Pacific Island countries. The annual harvest of *Trochus niloticus* in the region in recent years has been estimated at 2,300 metric tons with an export value of about US$15 million (FAO 2005). It is an important fishery because it requires low technology and equipment and because shells may be stored for long periods prior to shipment to market. In several remote Pacific Island countries, trochus provides an important source of cash income at the village level, especially since the demise of the copra industry. In Fiji, trochus is semiprocessed into button blanks, which not only adds value but also reduces the transport costs considerably. On the island of Aiututaki in the Cook Islands, trochus harvesting is managed through a quota system that allows harvesting for a limited number of days within a year.

In most of the Pacific Islands, finfish found in relatively shallow water (<50 m) are the basis of much of the commercial fisheries. About three hundred species representing thirty to fifty fish families make up the majority of the catch (FAO 2005). Yields in the region have been estimated to be between 5 and 50 kg per hectare per year (Wright and Hill 1993). Commercial export of shallow-water reef fish is not a major industry; most of the overseas

shipments of these fish are in the form of passenger baggage by Pacific Islanders during visits to Guam, Hawai'i, Australia, and New Zealand.

Snappers and groupers are found on slopes of one to four hundred meters depth of most Pacific islands. Because they receive a high price in overseas markets, deep-slope snappers and groupers have been the subject of considerable interest in the 1970s and 1980s. One of the major objectives was to ease fishing pressure in the inshore areas by diverting fishing efforts to outer reef slopes. The aggregating nature of the fish stocks, however, led to their increased vulnerability to fishing pressure on the seamounts, consequently reducing the scale of fishing in the region.

Another valuable export product that is gaining much attention is black lip pearl shells (*Pinctada margaritifera*), cultivated primarily from wild stocks. In the wild they are found attached to coral reefs in depths of five to sixty meters. In the past, divers collected the pearl oysters, and the shells (mother-of-pearl) were exported to be made into products such as buttons. But these days, black-lipped oysters are more valuable if kept alive and cultured for their black pearls.

Black pearls are a major contributor of foreign exchange in the Cook Islands and French Polynesia, and they also contribute to export revenue in Fiji. The Marshall Islands, Solomon Islands, and Tonga are currently involved in trial operations. In the Cook Islands in 2007, there were about 110 pearl farms on Manihiki, and 1.5 million adult oysters were being cultured (SPC 2008c). On Penrhyn there were about 100 pearl farms and about 200,000 cultured oysters, with annual production valued at NZ$5 million. The true figures, however, may be much higher; the Ministry of Marine Resources estimated that it is probably more than NZ$10 million (SPC 2008c). Black pearls account for about 85 percent of the export industry, and the economic value of the industry is second only to tourism.

Aquarium fish collectors target a large number of species, with the major families being butterfly fish (Chaetodontidae), damselfish (Pomacentridae), surgeonfish (Acanthuridae), and angelfish (Pomacanthidae). The relatively recently established aquarium fish industries in Kiribati and the Marshall Islands account for 78 percent and 95 percent of all fishery exports from those countries respectively. Aquarium trade exports from Solomon Islands accounts for about 4 percent of the total international coral trade (Lal and Kinch 2005: 6). Almost seventy species of live coral are regularly exported from Solomon Islands, together with nineteen species of dead coral (Lal and Kinch 2005: 9). Maintaining the quality is of utmost importance for fetching the optimum price. Figure 30.3 shows the special packaging boxes for aquarium fish and live corals.

While seafood remains an important source of protein for the Pacific Islands, catches of many important species that are easily accessible have been declining in some islands over the years. In the few islands where data is collected continuously, the recorded decline has sometimes been dramatic. In Guam, for example, catch rates have been reduced by 70 percent over the past 15 years (King et al 2003: 1). The major reasons for decline include overexploitation, shift from subsistence to commercial fishing, use of overly efficient and destructive methods, and environmental degradation (King et al. 2003: 1).

Figure 30.3. *The special packaging materials required to ensure that quality is maintained (photo VRB).*

Offshore

For centuries, tuna has provided an important source of food for Pacific Island people and has shaped their rich maritime culture. The fishery ranges from small-scale artisanal operations in the coastal areas to large-scale industrial purse seine, longline, and pole-and-line operations in the exclusive economic zones (EEZs) of Pacific Island countries and on the high seas. It is estimated that the Western and Central Pacific region meets about 60 percent of global tuna demand for canning and 30 percent of the tuna for the high-value Japanese sashimi market and is ranked as having the largest tuna resource in the world (Gillett et al. 2001). Figure 30.4 distinguishes the western Central Pacific from the eastern Central Pacific (SPC 2011).

The economic importance of tuna to the Pacific Islands region has been highlighted in a number of studies (Gillett et al. 2001; Gillett and Lightfoot, 2001; Ram-Bidesi 2003; Reid 2006). Tuna provides an important source of employment, income, and source of foreign exchange to island economies. Access revenue from foreign fishing vessels is also an important source of government revenue for a number of smaller island countries such as Kiribati, Tuvalu, the Marshall Islands, and the Federated States of Micronesia. Tuna is a major export commodity for countries that have established shore-based processing such as Fiji, Solomon Islands, Papua New Guinea, and American Samoa. Direct employment in the tuna industry includes crewing opportunities, shore-based processing, and administration and management work, while indirect employment includes port services, research, and monitoring and surveillance activities. Indirect employment is also created in related industries such as gear manufacture, fuel, food, hotel, and hospitality. The more labor-intensive the activities are, the more spin-offs are likely to arise. To create greater employment opportunities, many of the Pacific Island countries over the years have formulated development policies that aim to increase benefits to the local economy from the tuna resources.

In 2007, the total annual catch in the Western and Central Pacific was approximately 2.4 million tonnes, with a catch value of US$3.8 billion, which accounted for 55 percent of the total global tuna catch (Hampton 2008). Figure 30.5 shows the catch trends. Total annual catches increased steadily during the 1980s through the expansion of the purse seine fleet, followed by a relatively stable period in the 1990s and again with increase in catches.

The purse seine fishery contributed 1,818,255 mt (75 percent) of the total catch, while pole-and-line methods contributed 171,597 mt (7 percent), longline fishing 248,589 mt (10 percent) and remaining 7 percent by troll gear and artisanal gears (SPC 2011: 95). The four main target species are skipjack tuna (*Katsuwonus pelamis*), yellowfin (*Thunnus albacares*), bigeye (*T. obesus*), and albacore (*T. alalunga*). Table 30.3 shows catch by gear type, while Table 30.4 shows the catch by species. The purse seine fishery targets skipjack but also records significant amounts of juvenile yellowfin and bigeye. The longline fishery targets adult bigeye, yellowfin, and albacore, whereas the target species for pole-and-line fishing is skipjack.

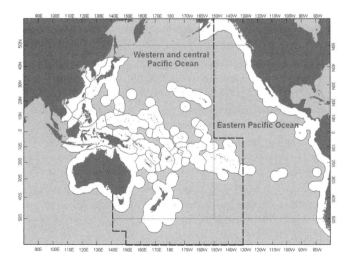

Figure 30.4. *The boundaries of the Western and Central Pacific Ocean Area (SPC n.d.).*

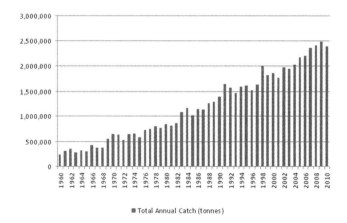

Figure 30.5. *Regional Tuna Catch in the Western and Central Pacific Fisheries Convention Area (Source: SPC 2011).*

Table 30.3

Tuna Catch by Gear Type in Western and Central Pacific Fisheries Region (Tonnes)

	Longline	Pole and line	Purse seine	Troll	Other	TOTAL
Year						
1970	141,360	409,754	16,222	50	69,633	637,019
1975	164,049	279,663	27,686	646	111,669	583,713
1980	227,707	395,746	113,266	1,489	102,645	840,853
1985	172,886	293,206	403,252	3,468	144,604	1,017,416
1990	181,591	250,390	773,730	7,219	196,934	1,409,864
1995	207,042	297,106	939,172	23,585	150,516	1,617,421
2000	217,465	261,937	1,191,103	25,845	184,693	1,881,043
2005	223,146	213,055	1,582,426	13,293	148,021	2,179,941
2010	248,589	171,597	1,818,255	9,988	172,684	2,414,692

Source: SPC 2011.

Table 30.4

Tuna Catch by Species in Western and Central Pacific Region (Tonnes)

	Albacore	Bigeye	Skipjack	Yellowfin	TOTAL
Year					
1970	74,350	40,102	423,348	99,216	637,016
1975	84,651	69,523	288,220	141,319	583,713
1980	95,156	72,948	455,747	217,002	840,853
1985	77,060	92,270	573,931	274,155	1,017,416
1990	63,872	131,723	850,180	364,089	1,409,864
1995	91,750	118,247	1,001,299	406,125	1,617,421
2000	101,161	156,097	1,142,508	481,277	1,881,043
2005	101,170	152,052	1,331,657	595,062	2,179,941
2010	126,017	125,757	1,610,578	558,761	2,421,113

Source: SPC 2011.

Skipjack and yellowfin catch by purse seine vessels are destined for canning either in the region or in canneries in Southeast Asia. Longline-caught bigeye and yellowfin are exported fresh or frozen to sashimi markets in Japan and the United States. Albacore has been used as "premium white meat" for canning, but it is increasingly being exported as fresh for sashimi.

Table 30.5 shows the catch by vessel flag. Historically, the majority of the purse seine catch has been by vessels from Japan, Korea, Chinese-Taipei, and the United States. In 1995, there were 145 purse seine vessels but these declined to 110 in 2007 (Williams and Terawasi 2008: 2). Conversely, there has been an increase in the number of vessels flagged by Pacific Island countries. In the overall Western and Central Pacific Convention Area, the fishing fleet consists of many smaller vessels in the Indonesian and Philippines domestic fisheries and a variety of other domestic and foreign vessels, including several relatively new distant-water entrants such as China, New Zealand, and Spain (Williams and Terawasi 2008: 3).

Skipjack tuna is a fast-growing species that has high resilience to fishing pressure and can support annual catches at the current level of 1.7 million tonnes. The current impact of the fishing represents a depletion of the adult biomass in equatorial waters of around 40 percent from unexploited levels. As this depletion is below the maximum sustainable yield, the stocks are considered to be in a healthy state (Hampton 2008).

Bigeye tuna is a slow-growing species that takes three to four years to mature. Significant exploitation of juveniles occurs in the purse seine fishery on floating fish aggregating devices and in the domestic fisheries of the Philippines and Indonesia (Hampton 2008). This has a subsequent impact on the adult population, which is the target of the longline fishery. Scientific assessment by the Secretariat of the Pacific Community (SPC) has indicated that there is overfishing of bigeye. Advice from the Western and Central Pacific Fisheries Commission (WCPFC) Scientific Committee is that fishing for bigeye tuna in the Western and Central Pacific must be reduced by 30 percent so that fishing can return to the average of 2003–2006 levels (Hampton 2008).

The yellowfin tuna is mostly harvested in the western equatorial region of the Western and Central Pacific by purse seine vessels

Table 30.5

Tuna Catch by Flagged Vessels in the Western and Central Pacific Ocean (Tonnes)

Country	1970	1980	1990	2000	2010
Australia	100	117	6,983	6,997	2,566
Belize	-	-	-	270	127
Canada	-	-	235	351	-
China	-	-	453	6,244	78,734
Cook Islands	-	-	-	335	3,058
Ecuador	-	-	-	3,992	8,451
El Salvador	-	-	-	-	6,824
Federated States of Micronesia	-	-	-	21,688	23,802
Fiji	-	2,496	3,830	9,660	10,060
French Polynesia	-	936	2,109	6,833	6,192
Indonesia	17,600	61,795	142,237	284,310	320,726
Japan	505,452	522,844	471,098	498,958	417,017
Kiribati	-	1,812	2,407	14,726	38,787
Republic of Korea	16,927	46,096	204,399	207,498	300,057
Marshall Islands	-	-	-	7,560	57,225
Nauru	-	-	-	11	4
New Caledonia	-	-	1,730	1,662	2,488
New Zealand	50	1,519	7,120	18,918	26,939
Niue	-	-	-	-	110
Palau	8,082	6,576	88	240	-
Papua New Guinea	2,428	33,994	-	68,818	208,253
Philippines	52,000	77,505	202,214	234,519	285,594
Russia	-	-	2,126	-	-
Samoa	-	-	-	5,389	3,090
Solomon Islands	-	23,241	26,612	12,929	24,785
Spain	-	-	-	12,896	29,485
Chinese Taipei	33,887	48,323	164,640	279,197	247,623
Tonga	-	-	192	1,161	128
Tokelau	-	-	-	-	4
Tuvalu	-	-	90	-	10,582
USA	493	13,483	171,301	135,410	256,872
Vanuatu	-	-	-	37,545	38,861
Vietnam	-	-	-	-	11,958
Eastern Pacific (NEI)	-	114	-	2,925	709
TOTAL	637,019	840,851	1,409,864	1,881,042	2,421,111

Source: SPC 2011.

and domestic fisheries of Philippines and Indonesia (Hampton 2008). Recent stock assessments indicate that stock is at least fully exploited and that there is a 50 percent chance that overfishing is occurring (Hampton 2008). In the case of albacore fishing, the Scientific Committee has advised that there should not be any further expansion of catch or effort, given that assessments show a depletion of adult biomass of around 60 percent (Hampton 2008).

Under the United Nations Fish Stocks Agreement (1995), cooperation between coastal states and distant-water fishing nations (DWFNs) is mandated to ensure the compatibility of conservation and management between EEZs and high seas because of the biological unity of the highly migratory fish stocks. In September 2000, the coastal states and DWFNs fishing in the Western and Central Pacific adopted the Convention on the Management and Conservation of Highly Migratory Fish Stocks in the Western and Central Pacific. The objective of the convention is to ensure, through effective management, the long-term conservation and sustainable use of highly migratory fish stocks based on the principles outlined in the Law of the Sea Convention (1982) and the United Nations Fish Stocks Agreement (1995).

The convention has led to the establishment of the Western and Central Pacific Fisheries Commission (WCPFC) in 2004. The commission has a permanent secretariat based in Pohnpei, FSM. It has two technical subcommittees, one dealing with compliance and the other with scientific issues. Conservation and management measures of the commission are legally binding and apply to all members in the convention area as shown in Figure 30.4. Some of the decisions of the commission include the need to reduce incidental catches of seabirds, reducing overcapacity, reducing the catch of nontarget species, and reducing the impact of fishing on sea turtles.

Nonliving Resources

Like fisheries resources, the nonliving resources can also be categorized as coastal and oceanic.

Coastal Nonliving Resources

In all Pacific Island countries, beach and lagoon sand and gravel are extracted for use as aggregates in construction activities. The demand for aggregate has been increasing alongside increase in population growth, urbanization, and housing development. The highly bulky granular materials have low unit value and are extracted close to the construction site. In Majuro, aggregate is obtained onshore, from beach mining, and near shore from dredging and reef blasting (McKenzie, Woodruff, and McClennen 2006: 9). In Majuro, 68 percent of the households surveyed collected aggregate from beaches for private use and the total annual household demand for aggregate was estimated to be approximately 10,587 m³ per year (McKenzie, Woodruff, and McClennen 2006: 9). In Kiribati, the government, businesses, families, and donor-funded projects require aggregates to build homes, renovate buildings, construct seawall, and reclaim land (Greer Consulting 2007). The majority of the aggregates used to meet the demands are from beaches and coastal flats around Tarawa.

Dredging lagoons has been an important source of coral sand for the cement factory in Fiji. An assessment system under a tribunal exists in Fiji for compensating users toward the loss or diminution of fisheries resources when extraction takes place in the *qoliqoli,* or customary fishing rights areas.

There is continued use of hard boulders for lining septic tanks for private sewage systems in urban areas and for constructing seawalls and garden landscaping. This has raised environmental concerns in many island countries because of the potential harmful effects on reefs and marine organisms.

Oceanic Nonliving Resources

Polymetallic nodules containing nickel, copper, cobalt, and manganese have long been considered the prime economic mineral resource in the deep sea. These nodules have been known for more than a hundred years to exist on the deep ocean bed in the Pacific in depths of 4000 to 6000 m (Adams, Dalzell, and Ledua 1999: 378). Considerable effort and resources have been put into prospecting

and developing methods of recovery. Since 1972, research interest in marine minerals within the South Pacific has been coordinated through the South Pacific Applied Geoscience Commission (SOPAC).

Demand for metals in countries like China and India and technological advances in the oil and gas industry have enabled extraction of hydrocarbons from depths of more than ten thousand feet and have led to renewed interest in mining manganese nodules. In the Pacific Ocean, research and exploratory studies have identified five areas that contain abundant nodules: the Carion-Clipperton Fracture Zone between Hawai'i and California, Central Southwestern Pacific Basin, Northeast-Pacific Musicians Seamount area, the Southern Ocean around 60° S latitude, and the Northern Peru Basin (Ghee and Valencia 1990; Kojima 2001). The central part of the Penrhyn Basin between the Cook Islands and Kiribati west of the Southern Line Islands has been identified as having the highest potential (Tiffin 1988). In recent years mining companies have approached the Cook Islands government to conduct exploratory work within its EEZ. Rising fuel prices, uncertainty over ownership, and environmental problems relating to collection and processing of nodules could remain key obstacles to the mining of manganese nodules.

Polymetallic crusts or manganese crusts have a chemical composition similar to manganese nodules, but the cobalt content is three to five times higher than that of nodules (Kojima 2001). They are abundant on seamounts at depths of around 800 to 2400 m in the Western and Central Pacific such as in the waters of the Marshall Islands, the Federated States of Micronesia, and Kiribati (Ghee and Valencia 1990).

Minerals such as copper, gold, zinc, and silver could be extracted from massive seafloor sulfide deposits. Polymetallic sulfide deposits in the Pacific Islands have been found in the north of Fiji Basin, Lau Basin (Tonga), Eastern and Central Manus and Conical Seamount (Papua New Guinea) (International Seabed Authority 2006). Mining massive polymetallic sulfide deposits is likely to be viable when there are high gold and base-metal grades present, sites are located close to land, and water depths are less than 2,000 m. Most of the deposits located in the southwest Pacific therefore may be economical in the near future (SOPAC 2008). Nautilus Minerals Limited, which has exploration licenses for several sites in the southwest Pacific, is currently developing the technology to mine deep-sea polymetallic sulfide deposits (Magick 2008). Neptune Mining, which discovered two hydrothermally inactive seafloor sulfide zones on the Rumble II West seamount north of New Zealand in the Kermadec area, has been granted tenements in New Zealand, Papua New Guinea, the Federated States of Micronesia, and Vanuatu (*Fiji Times* 2008).

In November 2007, Nautilus Minerals was granted sixteen offshore exploration licenses covering about 88,000 km² in which there are also occurrences of polymetallic sulfide (SOPAC 2008), to begin deep-sea mining of polymetallic sulfide deposits in the Manus Basin, located in Papua New Guinea's territorial sea. Korea has also secured rights to develop mineral resources in a 20,000 km² area within Tonga's EEZ in which mineral deposits are estimated around nine million tons and which include minerals such as gold, copper, silver, and zinc (Pacnews 2008a, 2008b).

Although exploration studies on hydrocarbons by SOPAC so far have revealed the presence of more deep sedimentary basins in island arc countries such as Solomon Islands and Vanuatu, no petroleum accumulations have yet been discovered (SOPAC 2008). The Bligh Water Basin and Bau Waters Basin in Fiji have geological features similar to those of Southeast Asia, where major reserves of oil and gas have been discovered (SOPAC 2008). While drilling activities between 1969 and 1987 revealed the presence of rock capable of generating oil and gas, no commercial reserves were discovered (SOPAC 2008). The main factors that determine the economics of an oil field are the price of oil, the size of the oil field, well productivity, well depth, and water depth (Rodd and van Meurs 1993).

Nonextractive Uses

Tourism in the Pacific is one of the fastest-growing industries, and most countries see their white sandy beaches, coral reefs, and lagoon-based resources as the prime attraction. A study by South Pacific Travel (formerly the South Pacific Tourism Organisation) in 2005 estimated that a total of US$1.75 billion was spent by tourists across its thirteen Pacific Island member countries (Pacific Islands Forum 2008). Tourism is a major contributor to GDP in the Cook Islands and is the main source of foreign exchange in Fiji. It is also of economic importance to Hawai'i, Guam, and the Northern Mariana Islands. Most hotels and resorts are strategically located along the coastal areas to take advantage of coastal and ocean-based activities such as snorkeling, diving, surfing, kayaking, and whale watching.

The Pacific Islands region has a high diversity of cetaceans (whales, dolphins, and porpoises). It contains important breeding, calving, and feeding grounds and provides the migratory pathways for many species. In 2005, tourists and Pacific Islanders made more than 110,700 visits to watch whales and dolphins and spent an estimated US$21,011,873 (IFAW 2008). Countries with the strongest growth in whale watching are Guam and French Polynesia, whereas New Caledonia and Tonga have continued sustained growth (IFAW 2008). Whale watching is also a big business in New Zealand, where the total expenditure in 2004 was estimated to be NZ$72,338,157 (IFAW 2005).

Tourists are also attracted to the deep blue seas of the Pacific region to dive among the sea turtles, dolphins, sharks, rays, and whales among the World War II wrecks and reef areas.

Surfing is another major water sport that not only draws tourists but also attracts competitive sporting events. For example, famous Hawaiian wave swells, generated from October to March from deep lows tracking across the North Pacific, can be anywhere from ten to thirty feet. Surfing spots are also found in New Zealand, the Cook Islands, American Samoa, Fiji, French Polynesia, and New Caledonia.

Certain spots along Fiji's wide reef expanse are protected sites, such as the "Shark Reef," a hard coral reef off the coast of the largest island Viti Levu, which is a habitat of many culturally significant shark populations. Shark feeding has been a major tourist attraction in the area for the past seven years (waidroka.com).

Besides receiving direct benefits such as food, people derive other benefits from marine ecosystems, such as protection from natural hazards, carbon capture, potential pharmaceutical ingredients and genetic materials, nursery grounds, and so on. Human well-being depends on these "ecosystem services," so maintaining the ecological integrity of the ecosystems is critical for human well-being. Establishing and maintaining marine protected areas are the most plausible way to preserve the pristine ecosystems and the best way to provide protection for endangered species.

In order to preserve the unique, rare, and pristine environment, the Kiribati government, together with the New England Aquarium and Conservation International, established the Phoenix Islands Protected Area, which at 410,500 km^2 is currently the largest marine protected area (MPA) in the world today. This MPA contains deep-sea habitats, eight atolls, and two submerged reef systems (phoenixislands.org). More than 120 species of coral and 514 species of reef fish have been identified so far, and the area also includes a sanctuary for seabird aggregation (phoenixislands.org). The MPA is financed through an endowment fund that will assist in compensating the people of Kiribati for the loss of fishing license revenue and pay surveillance and management costs.

In addition to the Phoenix Island Marine Protected Area, leaders of Palau, FSM, the Marshall Islands, Guam, and the Northern Marianas made a commitment at the Conference of Parties under the United Nations Convention on Biological Diversity in March 2006 to conserve 30 percent of their nearshore marine and 20 percent of their terrestrial resources across Micronesia. This initiative is known as the "Micronesia Challenge" and covers an area of 6.7 million km^2, representing 5 percent of the Pacific Ocean. The leaders hope that this can assist in protecting 66 currently identified threatened species, 10 percent of the global total reef area, and 462 coral species (*Pacific Magazine* 2008).

Other Uses

While aspects of mariculture and aquaculture have been briefly discussed under coastal fisheries, they can easily be considered as another use of ocean resources because of their growing importance in the global food supply. Aquaculture continues to grow more rapidly than all other animal food-producing sectors (FAO 2007: 16). In the Pacific Islands that are surrounded by sheltered bays and lagoons, aquaculture is seen as having the potential to cultivate new commodities, as a means of stock enhancement, and way to rehabilitate reefs and lagoons. Table 30.6 gives a summary of the various species that are currently being cultivated in the Pacific Island region.

Most of the production in the smaller island countries is relatively small-scale or still at an experimental stage. Notable commercial cultivation is that of pearls, seaweeds, tilapia, giant clams, shrimps, and freshwater prawns. About sixty tonnes of freshwater prawns were produced in Fiji in 2006 (Fiji Fisheries Department 2008). These were targeted at the growing hotel and tourism industry and mostly sold domestically. Kiribati has had a regular production of *Eucheuma* since 1986, although annual production is declining after reaching a peak of 11,174 tons in 2000 (FAO 2005). Access to markets has been a major factor for the *Eucheuma* and is probably the reason the industry has not had a full takeoff even though there are several suitable sites for cultivation. While the potential for aquaculture exists, there are several environmental and institutional factors that need to be considered. The availability of seed and feed; marine tenure systems; biological risk factors such

Table 30.6

Cultivation of Aquaculture Commodities in the Pacific Islands Region

Commodity	Countries cultivating
Barramundi	French Polynesia, Papua New Guinea
Carp	Fiji, Papua New Guinea
Clams (*Anadara*, bear paw, nei)	Fiji, Palau, Samoa, Tonga, Micronesia
Crocodile	Papua New Guinea
Freshwater prawns	Fiji, French Polynesia
Giant clam (crocus, elongate, fluted, smooth, nei)	Palau, Samoa, Tonga, Cook Islands, Solomon Islands, Marshall Islands, Fiji, Micronesia, French Polynesia
Hard coral/ Live rock	Fiji, Tonga, Vanuatu, Marshall Islands, Micronesia
Marine fish nei	French Polynesia
Marine shrimps (blue, banana, tiger, whiteleg)	French Polynesia, New Caledonia, Vanuatu, Fiji, Cook Islands, Solomon islands, Papua New Guinea, Guam, Northern Marianas
Milkfish	Guam, Kiribati. Micronesia, Palau, Tuvalu, Cook Islands, French Polynesia, Nauru
Mullet (flathead, grey, nei)	Fiji, Guam
Mussel (green, Sea nei)	New Zealand, French Polynesia, Fiji
Oysters (mangrove cupped, Pacific, nei)	New Zealand, Papua New Guinea, New Caledonia
Pearl Oysters (blacklip, nei)	French Polynesia, Cook Islands, Fiji, Papua New Guinea, Marshall Islands, Micronesia
Seaweed (elkhorn, seamoss, Eucheuma, Zanzibar weed)	Tonga, Fiji, Solomon Islands, Kiribati, Micronesia
Southern crayfish	New Caledonia
Spinefoot (rabbitfish)	Fiji
Sponge	Micronesia
Tilapia	Fiji, Papua New Guinea, Vanuatu, Samoa, American Samoa, Guam, French Polynesia
Trout and salmon	New Zealand, Papua New Guinea

Source: Adapted from FAO 2005; Hamberg Consulting in association with Nautilus Consultants 2011.

as diseases and competition; and natural disasters in the fragile island coastal ecosystems are just some of the considerations.

In the broader sense of how the ocean impacts Pacific Islanders, it is also important to consider their dependence on ocean-based trade and the seafaring lifestyle that supports their social and economic needs. Shipping facilitates exports and contributes to economic growth and trade opportunities. Many of the countries are highly dependent on imports of food, fuel, and manufactured items. Bulky export commodities such timber, copper ores and concentrates, palm oil, sugar, and so on are transported by ocean-based tankers and container ships.

Many Pacific Islanders also work on foreign vessels as seafarers and send money back to their families. In Tuvalu, for example, remittances are approximately 30 percent of the gross national product (Clark 2003). Papua New Guinea, Solomon Islands, Fiji, Samoa, Tonga, and the Marshall Islands also have a number of seafarers on foreign vessels, and remittances are also important means of alternative livelihood.

Threats to Ocean Resources

While seafood remains an important source of protein for the Pacific Islands, catches of most accessible stocks have been declining over the years. In islands where data is collected routinely, the recorded decline has been dramatic; in Guam, for example, catch rates have declined by 70 percent over the past fifteen years (King et al. 2003: 1). In a survey carried out by the Secretariat of the Pacific Community, the declines in fisheries catches have been attributed to overexploitation, shift from subsistence to commercial operations, use of overly efficient and destructive fishing methods, and environmental degradation (King et al. 2003: 1). Chemical and traditional poisons, fish drives, use of scuba gear and underwater torches, small mesh sizes of nets, and uncontrolled fishing have led to the degradation of marine ecosystems. A number of reports have raised concerns about the sustainability of coastal fisheries resources (see, for example, Thistlethwait and Votaw 1992; Dalzell and Schug 2002). Targeting large predatory species for the live reef fish market has generated particular concern due to the ease with which most fish can be caught. Groupers are particularly vulnerable, as they aggregate to spawn in reef areas. Johannes et al. (1999) noted that grouper spawning aggregations have been fished to near extinction in many places in the Pacific Islands such as Palau, the Cook Islands, and French Polynesia.

For a number of Pacific islands, even the most distant or highest point of land is close to the sea, and activity on land often has significant effects on the marine resources. Urbanization leads to destruction of mangroves and beaches. Pollution from industries, settlements, harbors, and ports contributes to fouling of the nearshore and reef areas that reduces the productivity of areas that support fishing activities, as well as posing risks for human health. Improper disposal of sewage and domestic solid waste have been one of the major environmental problems of urbanization. Increased flow of nutrients often leads to eutrophication and eventual fish kills. Sedimentation due to deforestation, mining, and changes to land use also contribute to loss of coral cover.

Use of large and technologically efficient fishing vessels with limited controls on fishing have also led to overexploitation of important tuna resources. Figures 30.6 and 30.7 provide an illustration of the relative technologies used in inshore and oceanic fisheries. Figure 30.6 shows tuna vessels in port, while Figure 30.7 shows typical small-scale artisanal vessels. Many countries initially issued licenses to foreign fishing vessels in order to raise revenue, but they did not use adequate and sound scientific data on which to base their fishing limits. This problem has been further exacerbated by increased fishing pressure by distant-water fishing vessels fishing in the high seas and high seas pockets over the years. Even if Pacific Island countries were to manage the tuna fisheries effectively in their regulated zones, management would be undermined by this uncontrolled fishing on the high seas, since tunas are highly migratory and move between EEZs and high seas.

With limited sources of revenues, many governments in the Pacific Islands have given priority to their short-term economic needs by issuing more licenses than recommended by scientific advisors. This has led to the overexploitation of important tuna resources such as the bigeye and yellowfin tuna.

The vast distances between islands also makes monitoring and surveillance work both logistically difficult and expensive. Consequently, the Western and Central Pacific region, which has the world's largest tuna resources, attracts illegal fishers and vessel operators from around the world. Commonly known as illegal, unreported, and unregulated (IUU) fishing, it has become a major concern for the Pacific Islands region that could undermine the sustainability of the important tuna resources. A recent Greenpeace study shows that European-owned and/or operated purse seine vessels with Ecuadorian, Venezuelan, and Netherland Antilles flags licensed to fish in the Eastern Pacific were involved in IUU fishing in the Western and Central Pacific (Greenpeace 2007). The report further states that eleven Latin American– and Netherland Antilles–flagged vessels have been observed and some arrested for illegally fishing in the EEZ of Jarvis, Howard and Baker, Kiribati, the Cook Islands, and French Polynesia (Greenpeace 2007). Illegal fishing costs millions of dollars in lost revenues—in Papua New Guinea alone, an estimated US$18 million was lost as a result of purse seine and longline vessels underreporting and illegally fishing in their EEZ.

Figure 30.6. Tuna vessels in port (photo JS).

Figure 30.7. Artisanal vessels in port (photo VRB).

"Fishing down the food web" can lead to diverse impacts on the biodiversity of the oceans. Loss of biodiversity can have a disastrous effect on the supply of seafood. There are also concerns about the nonselective nature of tuna fisheries that increases the mortality of sharks, turtles, and other billfishes.

Beach mining has been a problem particularly in the low coralline islands or atolls which have critical shortages of suitable construction grade sand and aggregate for infrastructure development. This not only destroys the habitats of marine organisms but also increases the islands' vulnerability to storm surges and coastal flooding.

Sustainability and Management Issues

The very existence of many Pacific Island communities depends on the continued health of their marine environment and its resources. Intensive fishing associated with population increase and the use of efficient fishing technologies pose major threats to the sustainability of both coastal and oceanic fisheries resources. Command-and-control fisheries governance based on legislative control such as catch limits, seasonal closures, and size limits are effective only where there is a strong monitoring and enforcement capability.

Considering the nature of coastal-based subsistence and artisanal fishing operations and with limited government enforcement capabilities, community-based resource management systems that incorporate stakeholder participation are seen to be more effective. In the Pacific Islands, a number of case studies show that participatory fisheries governance is most successful where social and cultural ties remain strong (see, for example, Kuemlangan 2004). This is recognized as an effective approach in the recently developed strategic plan for regional coastal fisheries, which states that "community empowerment [is] to be responsible for sustainable fisheries management within the boundaries of its traditional fishing grounds" (SPC 2008b: 2). By empowering community self-management of fisheries regulations, customary marine tenure has the potential to provide a cost-effective means to enforce fisheries management measures. Helping to enhance the stewardship of the resources partially or fully resolves the problem of open access, which is often blamed for excess fishing capacity. Figure 30.8 shows rehabilitation of a mangrove area under a community project in Fiji.

Figure 30.8. *Mangrove replanting for rehabilitation (photo VRB).*

In order to manage the coastal resources, therefore, there is a need to strengthen and revive the traditional marine tenure and resource allocation mechanisms. This is most effectively done through partnerships and collaborative efforts between countries, governments, scientists, and other stakeholders. Through the use of scientific information and traditional knowledge, effective resource-management measures and best practices could be identified and adopted by the local communities. The locally managed marine areas (LMMA) approach in Fiji is an example of such a collaborative approach, where scientific studies are used to determine the *tabu,* or protected areas.

Ideally the protected zones, or *tabu,* within a particular area should enable the preservation of habitats that play a key role in early life stages of coastal and marine species. Conservation strategies should provide protected areas the needed support so that they can maintain the replenishment of populations in the wider marine and coastal environment (United Nations 2000).

The main management issue facing the oceanic fisheries is the current overexploitation of bigeye and possibly yellowfin tuna due to increased fishing capacity in the Western and Central Pacific region. Scientific advice suggests that there should be a reduction in fishing of bigeye tuna, a reduction in purse seine fishing that uses floating objects and FADs that increase fishing mortality of juvenile yellowfin, and a reduction in fishing activities in Indonesia and Philippines waters, which provide the breeding ground for tuna that eventually migrate southward (Hampton 2008).

While management measures have been agreed upon by the Western and Central Pacific Fisheries Commission members, limited action has been taken so far because some members are still interested in fulfilling their short-term economic interests.

A number of Pacific Islands countries face the dilemma of choosing between their social and economic development aspirations and revenue from expanded fishing. The highly migratory tuna requires an effective enforcement mechanism to ensure that illegal fishing is eliminated. There is a need for a more genuine and committed approach to regional and international cooperation among the coastal states themselves and with the distant-water fishing nations. Innovative cooperative approaches will need to be identified sooner rather than later to ensure the long-term sustainability of the tuna stocks. There are several commission decisions and resolutions that require implementation at the national level, such as the regional vessel monitoring and data-reporting requirements aimed at improving the basis for management decisions.

While deriving economic benefits from the seabed seems a near reality, seabed mining raises the fundamental problem of boundary delimitation. Countries with overlapping boundaries must enter into negotiations with neighboring countries for an agreement on shared boundaries before declaring their maritime boundaries. There are a number of shared boundaries in the Pacific Islands region that are yet to be negotiated.

Realizing the ocean's potential as well as dealing with the accompanying threats requires a further strengthening of the institutional approaches to the management of marine and coastal resources through better coordination among countries and national government sectors and departments. A cooperative network of departmental, local, national, and regional management together with active participation of civil society is necessary. The need for cooperative and coordinated approaches between the Pacific Islands countries and the Pacific Rim countries is a critical factor because of the transboundary nature of the ocean resources, whether it is harvesting fisheries resources or conducting seabed mining.

BIBLIOGRAPHY

Adams, T., P. Dalzell, and E. Ledua. 1999. Ocean resources. In *The Pacific Islands: Environment & society,* ed. M. Rapaport. Honolulu: Bess Press.

Anthony, J. M. 1990. Conflict over natural resources in South East Asia and the Pacific. In *Natural resources of South East Asia,* ed. L. T. Ghee and M. J. Valencia. London: Oxford University Press.

Bryant, D., et al. 1998. *Reefs at risk in the world: A map-based indicator of threats to the world's coral reefs.* Washington, D.C.: World Resources Institute.

Clark, P. 2003. *Economic tracer study for Pacific Island seafoods' expenditure.* Suva: Secretariat of the Pacific Community.

Dalzell, P., T. Adams, and N. Polunin. 1996. Coastal fisheries in the Pacific Islands. *Oceanography and Marine Biology* 34: 395–531.

Dalzell, P., and D. M. Schug. 2002. *Issues for community-based sustainable resource management and conservation: Considerations for the strategic action programme for the international waters of the Pacific small island developing states.* Vol. 4, Synopsis of information relating to sustainable coastal fisheries. Technical Report 2002/4. Apia, Samoa: South Pacific Regional Environment Programme.

Ecological Values. 2008. www.phoenixislands.org. Accessed November 23, 2008.

FAO. 2005. *Review of the state of world marine fishery resources.* FAO Technical Paper 457, Fisheries Resources Division. Rome: FAO.

———. 2007. *State of world fisheries and aquaculture 2006.* Rome: FAO.

Fiji Fisheries Department. 2005. Annual Report 2002.

———. 2008. Annual Report 2006.

Fiji Times. 2008. Managing our seabed for the future. September 4, 2008.

Fiji Waidroka Bay Surf. 2008. http://waidroka.com/pages.cfm/beqa-shark-dive. Accessed November 22, 2008.

Foale, S. 2008. Appraising the resilience of trochus and other nearshore artisanal fisheries in the Western Pacific. *SPC Trochus Information Bulletin,* July 14, 2008

Ghee, L. T., and M. J. Valencia, eds. 1990. *Conflict over natural resources in South East Asia and the Pacific.* Singapore: United Nations University Press.

Gillett, R. 2004. *Tuna for tomorrow? Some of the science behind an important fishery in the Pacific Islands.* Manila: Asian Development Bank and Secretariat of the Pacific Community.

———. 2009. *Fisheries in the economies of the Pacific Island countries and territories.* Manila: Asian Development Bank.

———. 2011. Fisheries of the Pacific Islands: Regional and National Information. RAP Publication 2011/03. FAO Regional Office for Asia and the Pacific, Bangkok, Thailand.

Gillett, R., and C. Lightfoot. 2001. *The contribution of fisheries to economies of Pacific Island countries.* Manila: Asian Development Bank.

Gillett, R., L. McCoy, L. Rodwell, and J. Tamate. 2001. *Tuna: A key economic resource in the Pacific Islands.* Manila: Asian Development Bank.

Gillett Preston and Associates Inc. 2000. Report of the Feasibility Study on the 8th EDF Rural Coastal Fisheries Development Programme in Papua New Guinea. November 3, 2000.

Greenpeace. 2007. *Fishing business: Stolen Pacific tuna in the European market.* Amsterdam: Greenpeace.

Greer Consulting Service. 2007. *Report of economic analysis of aggregate mining on Tarawa.* Kiribati Technical Report. March 2007. Suva: South Pacific Applied Geoscience Commission.

Hamberg Consulting in association with Nautilus Consultants. 2011. *Opportunities for the development of the Pacific Islands' mariculture sector: Report to the Secretariat of the Pacific Community.* Noumea: Secretariat of the Pacific Community.

Hampton, J. 2008. *Update on tuna fisheries, 1/2008.* Noumea: Secretariat of the Pacific Community.

IFAW (International Fund for Animal Welfare). 2005. *The growth of the New Zealand whale watching industry.* Surry Hills, N.S.W.: IFAW.

———. 2008. *Pacific Islands whale watch tourism: A region-wide review of Activity.* Surry Hills, N.S.W.: IFAW.

International Seabed Authority. 2006. *Workshop on mining of cobalt-rich ferromanganese crusts and polymetallic sulphides. Technological and economic considerations.* Background Paper by Secretariat. July 31–August 4, 2006, Kingston, Jamaica: International Seabed Authority.

Johannes, R. E., L. Squire, T. Graham, Y. Sadovy, and H. Renguul. 1999. *Spawning aggregations of groupers (Serranidae) in Palau.* The Nature Conservancy Marine Research Series Publication No. 1.

King, M., U. Fa'asili, S. Fakahau, and A. Vunisea. 2003. *A strategic plan for fisheries management and sustainable coastal fisheries in Pacific Islands.* Noumea: Secretariat of the Pacific Community.

Kojima, K. 2001. Overview of offshore minerals in the SOPAC region. Paper presented at Marine Scientific Research in the Pacific Region workshop: Issues and Challenges, February 27–March 1, 2001. Port Moresby.

Kuemlangan, B. 2004. *Creating legal space for community-based fisheries and customary marine tenure in the Pacific: Issues and opportunities.* FIP/FCR7. Rome: Food and Agriculture Organization of the United Nations.

Lal, P., and J. Kinch. 2005. *Financial assessment of marine trade of corals in the Solomon Islands.* Apia: SPREP.

Lehodey, P. 1997. *The impact of ENSO on surface tuna habitat in Western and Central Pacific Ocean.* 12th standing committee on tuna and billfish, June 16–23, 1999, Tahiti. Noumea: Secretariat of the Pacific Community.

———. 2001. The pelagic ecosystem of the tropical Pacific Ocean: Dynamic spatial modeling and biological consequences of ENSO. *Progress in Oceanography* 49: 439–468.

Lobban, C. S., and M. Schefter. 1997. *Tropical Pacific Island environments.* Mangilao: University of Guam Press.

Magick, S. 2008. Riches from the sea: Nautilus minerals charts new territory in deep sea exploration. *Pacific Magazine,* February 28, 2008.

McAvoy, A. 2005. Commercial catches threaten Hawaiian fish. Associated Press, October 25, 2005.

McKenzie, E., A. Woodruff, and C. McClennen. 2006. Economic assessment of the true cost of aggregate mining in Majuro Atoll, Republic of the Marshall Islands. SOPAC Technical Report No. 383, October 2006.

Network of Aquaculture Centre in Asia-Pacific. 2005. *Regional review on aquaculture development. Asia and the Pacific.* FAO Fisheries Circular No 1017/3. Rome: FAO.

New Zealand Ministry of Fisheries. 2008. http://www.fish.govt.nz/en-nz/commercial/default.htm. Accessed November 22, 2008.

NOAA Fisheries, Office of Science and Technology. Fisheries of the United States 2009. http://www.st.nmfs.noaa.gov/st1/fus/fus09/02-commercial2009pdf. Accessed February 9, 2013.

Pacific Islands Forum. 2008. Pacific Island Forum Post-Forum Dialogue Plenary Statement on Tourism. July 11, 2008. http//www.South-Pacific travel/news/press/ppac08.pdf. Accessed November 23, 2008.

Pacific Magazine. 2008. Micronesian challenge gets $1m donation. September 3, 2008.

PacNews. 2008a. Korea wins mining rights from Tonga. Thursday, April 3, 2008.

———. 2008b. Seabed mining likely to begin soon in Tonga. Monday, March 24, 2008.

Ram-Bidesi, V. 2003. An analysis of the domestication of the tuna industry in the Pacific Islands. PhD thesis. University of Wollongong.

Reid, C. 2006. Economic implications and trade-offs in achieving maximum sustainable yield for bigeye and yellowfin tuna in the Western and central Pacific. *Pacific Economic Bulletin* 21(3): 31–45.

Rodd, J. A., and P. van Meurs. 1993. Economic analysis of offshore petroleum prospects for SOPAC member countries. SOPAC Technical Report 145.

SOPAC (South Pacific Applied Geoscience Commission). 2008. Economic analysis of maritime boundaries in the Pacific Island countries. Draft report.

SPC (Secretariat of the Pacific Community). 2008a. *Pocket Statistical Summary.* New Caledonia.

———. 2008b. *Pacific Islands regional coastal fisheries management policy and strategic action (Apia policy) 2008–2013.* Noumea: Secretariat of the Pacific Community.

———. 2008c. Cultured pearl industry in the Cook Islands. http:// www.spc.int/Coastalfish/Countries/CookIslands/MMR/2/Pearl .htm. Accessed December 29, 2008.

———. 2011. *Western and Central Pacific Fisheries Commission tuna fishery yearbook 2010*. Noumea: Secretariat of the Pacific Community.

SPREP (South Pacific Regional Environment Programme). 2002. Pacific Islands regional ocean policy. 13sm/Official WG4. 13th SPREP Meeting, July 21–24, 2002.

State of Hawaii Databook. 2008. http://hawaii.gov/dbedt/info/economic /databook/2008-individual. Accessed February 9, 2013.

Thistlethwait, R., and G. Votaw. 1992. *Environment and development: A Pacific Island perspective*. Manila: Asian Development Bank.

Tiffin, D. L. 1988. Seabed resources and maritime boundaries in the Southwest Pacific. CCOP/SOPAC Miscellaneous Report 49.

United Nations. 2000. *State of the environment in Asia and the Pacific*. Economic and Social Commission for Asia and the Pacific. New York: United Nations.

Visser, T. A. M. 1997. Status of fisheries statistics in the South Pacific region. Regional Office of Asia and the Pacific. RAP Publication 1997/30.

Western and Central Pacific Fisheries Commission (WCPFC). 2006. *Summary Report. Scientific Committee Second Regular Session. 7–18 August 2006,* Manila: WCPFC.

Williams, P., and P. Terawasi. 2008. *Overview of tuna fisheries in the Western and Central Pacific Ocean including economic conditions—2007.* WCPFC-SC4-2008/GN WP-1, August 11–22, Port Moresby, Papua New Guinea: Western and Central Pacific Fisheries Commission.

World Bank. 1995. *Pacific Island economies: Building a resilient economic base for the 21st century.* East Asia Pacific Region, Report No. 13803—EAP. Washington, D.C.: World Bank.

———. 2000. *Cities, seas and storms: Managing change in the Pacific Island economies.* Vol. 1, Summary Report. Washington D.C.: World Bank.

Wright, A., and L. Hill, eds. 1993. *Nearshore marine resources of the South Pacific.* Suva: Institute of Pacific Studies.

Zeller, D., S. Booth, and D. Pauly. 2007. Fisheries contribution to gross domestic product: Understanding small-scale fisheries in the Pacific. *Marine Resource Economics* 21: 355–374.

Mining

Glenn Banks

31

This chapter addresses the exploitation of minerals and petroleum hydrocarbons in the island Pacific, extending from Papua Province in Indonesia to New Zealand. The discussion tends to focus on mining because in terms of investment, economic contribution, areal extent, and particularly social and environmental change it has generally had, to date at least, a greater impact than oil and gas production. In the decade since the first edition of this book was published, there have been dramatic changes in the global mining industry and mining operations in the Pacific, as well in the extent of the literature on mining and oil extraction in the region. Given the breadth of this literature, as well as the size and complexity of the industry and the issues that it raises, this review can be little more than introductory. The historical development of mining in the region, covered in the earlier edition, is excluded here to provide more scope to discuss contemporary and future developments. I am grateful to Frank McShane for his kind review and input to the first edition of this chapter.

Digging Deeper: Mining as a Development Dilemma?

As in other parts of the world, Pacific Island states have often found a rich mineral endowment to be a mixed blessing. Papua New Guinea has been disrupted by a separatist uprising and civil war associated with the Panguna copper mine on Bougainville (May and Spriggs 1990); the oil-rich Southern Highlands Province descended into chaos from the late 1990s (Haley and May 2007); the spectacular Mount Kare gold rush of 1987–1989 made global headlines; and the Ok Tedi mine attracted international attention regarding the environmental effects of its mine waste (Banks and Ballard 1997). In the 1990s Fiji was troubled by poor labor relations and revenue sharing at its Emperor (Vatukoula) gold mine (Emberson-Bain 1994a), then the mine abruptly closed in 2006 only to reopen in 2009, the country's other smaller mines closed, and all the while the Namosi copper deposit has seen a number of potential investors come and go over the past twenty years (McShane 1994). The controversial Freeport mine in Papua Province, Indonesia, has been the center of international scrutiny over long-standing human rights and environmental abuses (Ballard and Banks 2009). Nauru has witnessed a protracted battle in the international courts over compensation for environmental damage caused by phosphate mining (Weeramentry 1992; Connell 2006). In New Caledonia mines have been a target for Kanak separatist resistance (Howard 1988) and concerns over their environmental and social impact (Pascal et al. 2008; Horowitz 2004; Le Meur 2009). New Zealand has seen historically prolonged legal battles by Maori for the recognition of their land and resource rights in the Hauraki gold mining area (Williams 2003), the Tainui tribal lands in the North Island coal mining areas (Mahutu 1992), and most recently the national foreshore and seabed (Bargh 2006). These high-profile, contentious, and significant issues, among others, warrant a critical appraisal of the mining industry's role in Pacific Island development.

Early inquiries into mining in the region focused on the macroeconomic characteristics of mining development and analysis of the political economy of mining, raising questions about resource ownership and management and in particular the role of the state in minerals development (Howard 1988; Henningham and May 1992). The 1990s saw a much-needed analysis of local-scale social and economic dynamics and an increased emphasis on the environmental practices of mining companies and the issue of sustainability (see Denoon et al. 1995). The embroiling of mining operations in local and regional conflicts and the dynamics of the industry in terms of commodity prices and corporate structures in the early years of the twenty-first century have reshaped the mining map of the Pacific. The response by the global mining industry to these challenges (through initiatives such as the Mining, Minerals and Sustainable Development [MMSD] project) has again shifted the configuration of the corporate-community-state relationships in the region.

The following sections offer some perspectives on these issues. First, a summary of the major mineral deposits in the region is presented. A discussion of the macroeconomic implications of mining and the links to resource conflicts is followed by consideration of the politics of resource ownership and the local-scale effects of mining on traditional communities and the environment. Finally, the future of mining in the region and the relevance of corporate responsibility, stewardship, community participation, and the concept of sustainable development for the future of the industry in the Pacific is discussed. What emerges clearly is the dilemma created by mining, often encouraged by host countries and some communities but often introducing unanticipated consequences.

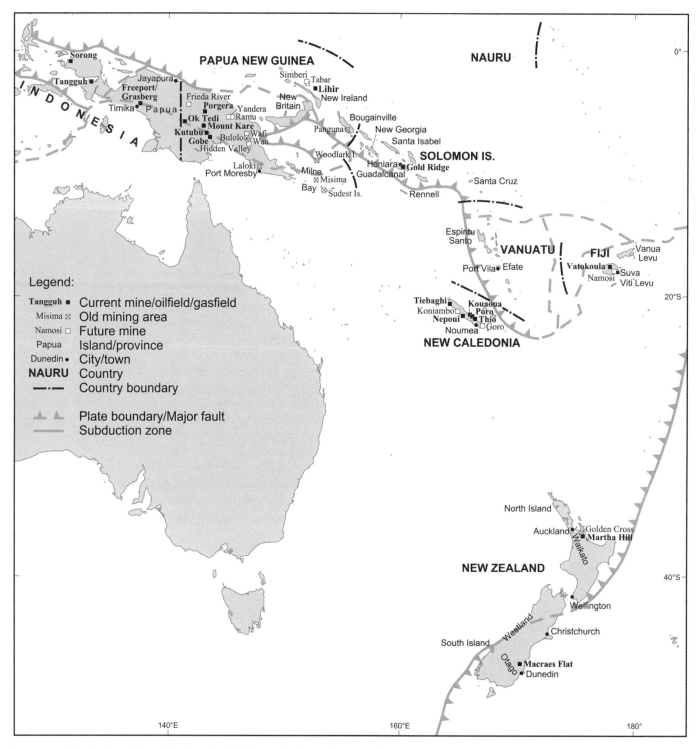

Figure 31.1. *The location of the major mineral and oil deposits in the southwest Pacific Islands.*

Where Are the Resources?

The islands in the southwest Pacific with rich mineral endowments are part of the Melanesian island arc that marks the meeting point of the Indo-Australian and the Pacific tectonic plates. The geology of arc terrains is known to favor mineral formation; accordingly many of the high volcanic islands are sources of base and precious metals, particularly gold, silver, and copper. The locations of current mine production and exploration are shown on the map above (Figure 31.1).

Papua New Guinea has substantial deposits of gold, silver, and copper, which are currently extracted at several "world class" mines (Table 31.1). The Ok Tedi mine (Figure 31.2) for example produced 160,000 tonnes of copper and 486,000 ounces of gold in 2010. Porgera remains a major gold producer, with production of more than 500,000 ounces of gold in 2010, while the Lihir gold mine in

New Ireland Province, where production started in 1997, produced 800,000 ounces of gold. There are smaller although still sizeable gold projects at Tolukuma (near Port Moresby), Simberi (New Ireland), Sinivit (East New Britain), and Kainantu (in Eastern Highlands Province). Small-scale, mostly alluvial gold mining occurs in a number of sites, with around fifty thousand people earning a living from this (Crispin 2003). Oil is produced from the Kutubu, Moran, and Gobe oil fields while natural gas is produced from the Hides gas field. A refinery, established close to Port Moresby, means Papua New Guinea supplies a significant proportion of its own oil needs. Long-standing plans to develop large onshore and offshore gas deposits in the Gulf and Southern Highlands Provinces, after barely advancing in the past decade, have rapidly crystalized, with current plans for the US$15 billion ExxonMobil operation seeing production beginning in 2014.

Figure 31.2. *Ok Tedi mine, Papua New Guinea (photo GB).*

Exploration projects continue to attract investors in Papua New Guinea, particularly with the recent boom in commodity prices, driven in large part by Chinese demand for industrial metals. By 2010 agreements had been finalized and advanced construction was under way at the US$800 million Ramu Nickel project in Madang Province, with the Chinese Metallurgical Construction Group (MCC) holding 85 percent of the project. Hidden Valley, a gold complex in Morobe Province jointly owned by Australian Newcrest Mining and South African–based Harmony Gold Mining, began production in 2010 and produced more than 200,000 ounces of gold in 2011. Exploration, planning, and construction work was at various stages in relation to other large copper and/ or gold deposits at Freida/Nena (East Sepik Province), Wafi-Golpu (Morobe), and Yandera (Madang) (Wu 2007a).

There are currently two large gold producers in New Zealand, Macraes Flat in Central Otago, and Martha Hill in Waihi in the Bay of Plenty. These two mines between them produced 13.4 of the 16.2 tonnes of gold produced in 2008, with a total value of over NZ$600 million. Alluvial mining is still significant in New Zealand, with the bulk of the alluvial gold produced in 2010 coming from the West Coast of the South Island. Coal mining, for export and domestic consumption, is a significant industry in New Zealand, with $1.2 billion worth of coal mined in 2007, more than 40 percent of which was exported. This was produced from four underground and twenty-two open-pit coal mines, concentrated in the Waikato, West Coast, and Southland. The production of aggregate remained

Table 31.1

Comparative Mineral Production Statistics for Selected Countries

	1992	2010
Copper, metal content (000 tons)		
Papua New Guinea (Ok Tedi)	193.4	160
Australia	331.5	900
USA	1,778.80	1,120
World	9,320.00	16,200.00
Gold, metal content (tons)		
Papua New Guinea	68.3	60
New Zealand	10.5	13.5
Fiji (Emperor)	3.7	1.9
South Africa	609.3	190
Australia	233.8	255
World	2,250.00	2,500.00
Nickel, metal content (000 tons)		
New Caledonia	100	138
Canada	188	155
Australia	55	139
Russia	257	265
World	900	1,550
Coal (000 tons)		
New Zealand	2,979.70	5,300.00

Source: Adapted from USGS 2007 and 2011; MED 2007.

a significant part of the economy, with the extraction of 13 million tonnes of sand and rock for roads alone worth NZ$133 million (MED 2009).

Fiji has produced gold from the underground Emperor mine at Vatukoula for more than seventy years. Increasing costs, labor relations, and concern with political events led to the closure of the mine in late 2006. The property was sold in 2008 and reopened in 2009 under its new UK-based owner, River Diamonds Ltd. A number of other mineral occurrences are known (including the large Namosi copper/gold deposit currently being explored by Japanese investors), but their development has been stalled largely by political uncertainty.

New Caledonia was the world's fifth largest producer of nickel in 2006 (Wu 2007b). Société Le Nickel (SLN) has mines at Nepoui-Kopeto, Poro, Kouaoua, Thio, Tiebaghi, and Etoile du Nord, while the two other major companies, Société Minière du Sud Pacifique (SMSP) and Société des Mine de la Tontouta (SMT), operated another six laterite (limonite) nickel mines across the island. Vale Inco, a Canadian-based subsidiary of Brazilian-based Companhia Vale do Rio Doce (Vale), is developing a US$3.2 billion laterite nickel mine at Goro, with limited production beginning in 2009 leading to full production in 2013. Japanese interests hold a significant share of the project, with the two New Caledonian provinces also both holding equity in the project. In late 2007 Swiss-based Xstrata announced the development of the Koniambo nickel-cobalt mine in North Province, with the majority partner being Société Minière du Sud Pacifique, the development arm of the North Province. Full production is due to begin from the US$5 billion investment in 2012. SMSP is a joint venture partner in the development. These developments will keep New Caledonia among the most significant global nickel producers for many decades.

Freeport McMoRan, an American multinational, operates one of the largest copper/gold mines in the world in Papua Province, Indonesia. In 2008 the mine produced 68.5 tonnes of gold and more than 540,000 tonnes of copper (more than the entire Papua New Guinea industry). Elsewhere in Papua, the long-standing oil industry in Sorong is about to be joined by a massive new natural gas operation at Bintuni Bay in West Papua at the western end of the island.

The Gold Ridge gold mine on Guadalcanal in Solomon Islands opened in 1997 and by 1999 was producing 3.5 tons of gold a year. It was closed by the ethnic and political conflict that erupted in 2000. A small Australian miner, Allied Gold, reopened the mine in 2011. There were also small alluvial deposits being worked at Chovohio. Low-grade nickel deposits are reported from other islands (Government of Solomon Islands 1993). By the start of the twenty-first century, Nauru's phosphate production had effectively ended—production in 2001 was a mere 250,000 tonnes, down from its peak of 2.3 million tonnes in 1974 (Connell 2006: 54), although production apparently increased again in 2008.

Elsewhere in the Pacific there is a lot of interest in the offshore areas around Papua New Guinea, Vanuatu, Fiji, Tonga, and New Zealand, both as hydrocarbon reservoirs (although apart from New Zealand they have failed to produce any major finds to date) and as a potential source of high-grade deep-sea mineral nodes. The most advanced of the latter is the Solwara gold and base metal project operated by Nautilus Minerals off the coast of New Britain Province in Papua New Guinea, which expects to commence production in 2013. And in late 2007 Neptune Minerals was granted ten prospecting licenses covering 914 km² in the exclusive economic zone (EEZ) of Vanuatu to explore for commercial, high-grade, seabed mineral deposits.

It is a sign of changes in broader political and economic patterns that whereas the industry in the region used to be dominated by Australian, Canadian, and UK-based multinationals, much of the recent interest and investment has come from Asia—China, Japan, and Korea in particular. This highlights the changing patterns of industrial growth and demand, particularly in terms of the drive for base metals such as nickel and copper.

Issues in Mineral Extraction

Mining and the Economy

Where minerals have formed a significant part of the national economy, they have generally been a central component of the formal economy and a key sector in terms of planning for economic development in the respective nation. In short, a minerals endowment

Table 31.2

Mining's Contribution to Some Pacific Island Economies

	1990	2000	2007
Fiji			
Mining contribution to GDP (%)*	0.2	1.5	0.01
Contribution to export earnings (%)*	12.5	9.2	0.3
Persons employed†	1660	1724	-
Papua New Guinea			
Mining and petroleum contribution to GDP (%)	14.7	28.8	26.5
Contribution to exports earnings (%)‡	67	77.4	78.6
New Zealand			
Mining and petroleum contribution to GDP (%)§	1.2	1.3	0.9
Contribution to export earnings (%)§	3	3.3	5.1

Sources:
* Reserve Bank of Fiji 1994, 2008
† UN 1994, PNG Department of Treasury 2008
‡ Bank of Papua New Guinea 1995, 2008
§ New Zealand Yearbook 1996; NZ Statistics, 2001, 2008, includes mineral fuels and precious metals.

is regarded as a potential source or driver of broader-based growth for economic development. Table 31.2 indicates the contribution of minerals production to the economies of some Pacific Island countries in recent years using several common indicators.

Important in the case of both Fiji and Papua New Guinea, mining has been a significant contributor to export earnings but generally contributed much less to GDP. Elsewhere, but not included in the table, are New Caledonia, where nickel contributed 11 percent of GDP and 94 percent of export earnings in 2006 (David et al 2010), and Nauru, where until its exhaustion at the turn of the twenty-first century, phosphate accounted for virtually all the island's economic production. Within Papua Province, the PT Freeport Indonesia has a similar economic presence, accounting for the bulk of exports (90 percent) and a significant component of GDP (50 percent) (Ballard and Banks 2009). But while a large minerals endowment can be a desirable national resource, recent history shows that in economic terms it poses several management challenges.

New Zealand is clearly different in this regard from other Pacific Island cases. Mining is a relatively limited component of the formal economy and is much more integrated in the economic structure of the country. Much of the coal mined (almost 50 percent) is used in energy production within New Zealand, particularly in industrial uses such as steel making. Likewise, the sand and gravel mined is used internally for maintenance of the road network. This is in sharp contrast to the rest of the Pacific, where mineral extraction is primarily directed at export. As a result, much of the discussion below does not apply to New Zealand.

Papua New Guinea provides an example of the dilemmas that may stem from strong growth in the minerals sector. From independence in 1975 the government encouraged commercial exploitation of minerals and oil with attractive investment incentives. When a new government took office in 1992, increased minerals revenues were used to introduce tax cuts, and government spending rose, which increased the budget deficit. With the fiscal deficit at 8 percent of GDP, domestic public debt at 30 percent of GDP, and facing insolvency, the government devalued the kina in 1994. Devaluation led to a capital flight and loss of confidence in the economy. This triggered effectively a decade of economic and political uncertainty that stalled mineral exploration and new investment. Accumulated funds derived from the sector were plundered to pay off external debt in the late 1990s. The relative stability of the Somare government from 2002 combined with the rapid rise in commodity process has led to a significant increase in exploration and mining investment. Enhanced government revenues, derived in significant part from this commodity boom, have produced significant government budget surpluses and allowed for the repayment of external debt that resulted from previous excess (Government of Papua New Guinea 2008).

Clearly, economic management of the minerals sector raises several questions for Pacific Island states. First, how can the maximum share of profits be obtained from mining by national governments without dissuading the foreign corporate investment the industry requires? The design and subsequent reshaping of fiscal regimes is both critical to government attempts to secure what they regard as a reasonable share of mineral rents, and to investor interest and confidence in the country. The role of state equity in mining operations as a means of ensuring a fair return to the country from these mineral assets remains contentious and open to changes in policy decisions—after selling off state mining assets from the late 1990s, Papua New Guinea recently re-established a state vehicle (Petromin PNG Holdings) to try and maximize country ownership and economic gains from the sector. Second, what can be done to stabilize minerals revenues that vary due to fluctuations of minerals commodity prices on the world market, or due to changes in both the rate of mining and the grade of ore being mined? This has potentially severe implications for states when they receive a resource windfall for a short period of time. The Papua New Guinea government received a significant boost in its internal revenue over the period from 2006 to 2008 due to enhanced commodity prices (to the extent that these flows made up more than 50 percent of all internal revenue), but was still actively engaged in trying to prudently plan for reduced revenues in future years. Third, what alternatives remain when minerals are exhausted? All the policy decisions that arise from these questions are made under conditions of high risk and uncertainty that generally pertain in the minerals sector (see Nankani 1980; Daniel 1992; Auty 1993, 1995).

Management of the mining sector is complicated by the tendency of mines to act as enclaves in isolation from the local economy (Emerson 1982). Foreign mining corporations are generally obliged to source both specialized technology and skilled labor overseas as these do not exist in-country. The increase in foreign exchange that accompanies increased exports of minerals may lead to rises in the real exchange rate and a relative decline in the competitiveness of the nonminerals sectors, a situation described as "Dutch disease" after the economic effects of the North Sea oil boom on the Dutch economy (Auty 1995). A profitable minerals sector can lead to demands for increased wages, which, in the absence of strong wage restraint policies, bring higher salaries, particularly in mining. Politically and economically powerful local elites, supported through legitimate and sometime illegitimate resource rents, further shape economic patterns through their increasing consumption of foreign imports, shifting the trade balance and squeezing domestic industry. As consumption increases, wage restraint becomes more difficult, particularly with the entry of highly paid expatriate mine workers. The public sector also grows as new jobs are created because new capacity to monitor and evaluate the mining industry is required (Auty 1993). Fiscal control, and the control over corruption, typically suffer during resource booms.

The net effect of mining enclaves is to create a dual economy in which the minerals sector enjoys preferential fiscal arrangements while manufacturing, agricultural, and service sectors decline. The reorientation of the economy toward the minerals sector can create a dependency on minerals exports, characterized by initially rapid growth and spending as the minerals revenues are absorbed and economic collapse when minerals revenues fall through decreased production or declining commodity prices. The underperformance of developing country economies based on minerals as opposed to those with no mineral endowment has been such a common feature that the term "resource curse" has been applied to the phenomena (Gelb and Associates 1988; Auty 1993, 1995). More recently the links between resource-dependent, export-oriented economies such as Papua New Guinea and Solomon Islands and the outbreak of civil conflict has led to these countries being incorporated into a global discourse whereby this resource dependence is itself regarded as a key factor contributing to the conflict (see Collier and Hoeffler 2004; Banks 2008 for a counterview).

Several mechanisms are available to the government for control of minerals projects and their revenue arrangements. The most important of these is that while the mining codes lay down the statutory conditions for mining practice, in reality these can often be just a starting point for the negotiation of individual project agreements. Such agreements typically reflect the spirit of minerals policy and the mining code, but they must also reflect differences in ore bodies, the economic objectives of the government, and changing conditions of national and international trade, among other things. One of the potentially most far-reaching changes to minerals agreements has been the incorporation of renegotiation clauses, which allow contract review after specific periods of time so that new mining and trade conditions can be taken into account.

The Politics of Resource Ownership

In most parts of the Pacific, prior to the arrival of Europeans, the notion that anyone other than the landowner could possess the rights to resources on or under that land was a foreign one. Ownership of these resources, like other natural resources (see chapter 16) was communal, and, subject to certain rules, all members of the clan had access to the resources of the land.

The arrival of the European powers and prospectors introduced new mineral ownership regimes, which vested the ownership of precious mineral resources with the Crown or the state. These new regimes were based on the mineral laws that applied in the home country of the colonial power (in Papua New Guinea's case, on the Queensland mining ordinance).

This fundamental difference in notions of rights to resources, and the enforcement by the colonial powers and postcolonial governments of their own versions, has been implicated in all the major mineral resource conflict issues in the Pacific. The establishment of the Bougainville mine in the late 1960s saw continued conflicts between the administration and the local communities over the rights to mineral resources and access to land (Bedford and Mamak 1977). Since independence, there has been a gradual shift in many parts of the Pacific toward local participation in and control over mineral developments. To an extent this represents the acknowledgment by the governments that the legal regimes relating to minerals do not reflect the realities of ownership in the Pacific context. Development of the Porgera mine (Figure 31.3) in 1989 saw a significant change in this trend when the Papua New Guinea government included the Porgera landowners, the provincial government, and the mine developers in negotiations over the project (West 1992).

Figure 31.3. Porgera mine, Papua New Guinea (photo GB).

The outcome of this process was a much greater proportion of the mine's benefits going to the local community in the form of royalties, equity, and government infrastructure and services (Filer 1999). In the past two decades this trend has intensified. Policy changes in Papua New Guinea now see all the royalties (currently set at 1.25 percent of the value of production) from new large mines go to local communities, along with an option to purchase a carried 5 percent shareholding in the development and their integral involvement in development negotiations. Another direction is signaled by developments in the Kanak-dominated Northern Province of New Caledonia, where in 1990 an ailing nickel mine was purchased by the new provincial investment company. After five years the mine had increased production tenfold and accounted for more than half of New Caledonia's nickel output, and the company, SMSP, is currently the second largest New Caledonia nickel

producer. Profits have been reinvested in new capital and a range of diversifications—agriculture, aquaculture, and hotels (Keith-Reid 1996: 46). Increasingly these forms of local equity, control, and ownership amount to a de facto sovereignty over resources, one that is subverting legal categories and definitions and leading to outcomes more in line with traditional notions of resource ownership.

Such developments also reshape the relationship between these communities and their respective national governments. In Papua New Guinea the legitimacy of the national government is questioned in many rural areas, which have seen a decline in health and education services over the past twenty years. As a result, when they are involved in negotiations over a mine development, local communities are both eager to see an improvement in these services and reluctant to rely on the rhetoric of government alone. Mine developments since the 1990s have therefore seen communities enter into contracts with the government and the mining company for the delivery of health and other services (see, for example, Imbun 1994). While this has resulted in some improvements in infrastructure and services for these mining areas, the lack of will and capacity of the government to fulfill its commitments is a constant source of concern for communities and companies.

Finally, in parts of the Pacific where specific groups have an identity distinct from the broader national culture (such as the Kanak of New Caledonia, the Bougainvilleans within Papua New Guinea, Papuans within Indonesia, and the Maori in Aotearoa/New Zealand), these groups are able to use disputes over resource sovereignty as a focal point for their claims to greater self-determination. In these situations, questions of resource ownership become entangled with the discourses of nationalism and international geopolitics (Howitt, Connell, and Hirsh 1996: 1). On New Caledonia, nickel mining is a central tool in the official policy of economic "rebalancing" between the wealthy South and the Kanak-dominated Northern Province. The politics of the PT Freeport Indonesia mine in Papua Province are closely linked to broader questions of Papuan autonomy and separatism. In New Zealand, resource ownership questions are inextricably enmeshed with Maori claims for land and reparations under the Treaty of Waitangi (Barclay-Kerr 1991; Williams 2003). Decisions over mineral resource developments in the Pacific have become intensely political for communities. On the one hand, rights to the wealth under their land, which most still believe they hold, are abruptly taken from them by the minerals laws of the country. On the other, they are able to use the mineral development as a strong bargaining chip in securing access to better infrastructure, services, material wealth, and redress for past wrongs. The outcomes of these processes for local communities are not always, however, what they anticipate.

Social, Cultural, and Economic Impacts: Local-Scale Effects

Mining clearly brings changes to traditional economies, demographic structures, polities, and social organization that have far-reaching implications for the integrity and identity of local groups in the locality of a mine (Filer 1990; Connell and Howitt 1991). These changes are the subject of a now substantial literature that includes nuanced anthropological studies of the ways communities across the Pacific understand and respond to the intrusion of large-scale mining operations (see, for example, edited collections by Filer [1999], Rumsey and Weiner [2001], Imbun and McGavin [2001], and special issues of *Social Analysis* [1998] and *The Contemporary Pacific* [2006]). For most traditional Pacific societies, land is inalienable, communal, intricately bound into social networks, and of spiritual and cultural importance. Land lies at the heart of social, cultural, and economic structures. Its loss may mean reduced areas for subsistence gardening and a shift from self-sufficiency to dependence on imported foods and a monied economy; loss of economic resources, particularly for those who work the land under traditional agreements but are not part of landowning clans eligible for compensation; rural-urban migration for those who cannot find alternatives to subsistence agriculture locally, and the breakdown of traditional family structures centered on sharing land and working on it together (Connell and Howitt 1991; Emberson-Bain 1994b). The most traumatic circumstance of land loss has been expropriation under colonial rule as happened in Banaba, Bougainville, New Caledonia, and New Zealand. Equally, compensation and royalty payments for land occupation and damage have brought their own dilemmas (Bedford and Mamak 1977; Filer 1990; Gerritsen and MacIntyre 1991; Connell 1992; Macintyre and Foale 2002). Indeed it can be argued that the monetary benefits of mining bring as much disruption and conflict as the direct costs. Internecine rivalry may lead to community conflict as local elites compete to increase their wealth and power through control of compensation monies and lucrative business spin-offs from a mine. Clan leaders who fail to accumulate and disburse the new forms of wealth may lose respect, power, and influence. Massive migration into areas around mining operations can be especially damaging in terms of local identity, claims to ownership, and environmental stresses (Jorgensen 1997).

Where mining has come to remote rural areas, the locus of social activity becomes the "mining town" (Figure 31.4). Initially, the town comprises housing compounds, local shops, a health center (Figure 31.5), and perhaps a school. Yet invariably these settlements attract a migrant population of hopeful people, both from surrounding villages and farther afield, looking for access to benefits from the project. The growth of such settlements is hard to avoid even when mine workers are segregated from the resident rural community. Piecemeal dwellings spring up around the core; often poorly serviced, they become centers for prostitution, alcoholism, petty crime, and violence (Polier 1994; Hyndman 1994; Emberson-Bain 1994b). Health problems including malnutrition among children may surface. Cross-cultural tension is often high, particularly in the context of labor relations (Imbun 2002).

Critically, the last decade has linked the large-scale mines in the region to human rights abuses. Communities at Freeport, Porgera, and other sites have been subjected to extrajudicial killings by state or corporate security forces, and there are widespread allegations of other abuses: rape, assaults, and more generalized threats of violence and loss of rights such as the right to a healthy environment (Human Rights Watch 2011). The details of these situations are often complex: at Porgera, the effects of migration, informal mining by migrants and locals within the open pit and waste dumps, and the crowded, high-consumption living conditions immediately adjacent to the mine operation, provide a potent

Figure 31.4. Suyan Mining Camp, Porgera 1994 (photo GB).

Figure 31.5. New hospital, Porgera (photo GB).

cocktail that regularly descends into chaos and violence—without any external intervention. But the bottom line is that mine and state security are often implicated in episodic violence and people are injured or killed. This does much fundamental damage to the building of relationships of trust between the companies and the surrounding communities.

Arguably the greatest social and economic impact falls on women (Figure 31.6). Absentee partners working at the mine may mean increased workloads for women, who may be denied access to salaried work at the project (Jorgensen 2006). Alternatively, women may only be eligible for low-paying work considered unsuitable for men (Emberson-Bain 1994b). Communal activity is replaced with individual rent-seeking activity and the competition for benefits. Women fare worse in this process, losing the labor and emotional support of the extended family. Alcohol may consume a large part of the family income, and violence toward women is common. Teenage pregnancy and rape are other common symptoms of women's marginalization in mining towns (Pollock 1996; Bonnell 1999). Meanwhile, few of the other benefits such as business loans have been available to women because men control most avenues of commerce. A recent statement from a Women and Mining Network meeting in Madang reiterated many of these points and called for women to be involved in decision making over whether or not mining could proceed (Pacific Region International Women and Mining Network 2007).

Figure 31.6. Women's Association meeting, Porgera (photo GB).

In discussing these local-scale impacts of mining, three additional points are worthy of note. First, these impacts have often been recognized by developers, and attempts, in various forms, are usually made to address them. The boomtown phenomena are ameliorated by "fly-in, fly-out" policies that avoid the establishment of a town at the mine site; community liaison officers are appointed to address community concerns; funds are established for community development; employment preference is often given to local community members. As will be discussed below, these efforts are typically not as far-reaching (or as altruistic) as they could be. Second, reification of the "traditional village" is misplaced. Traditional societies do not all exist in an absence of social dilemma, political maneuvering, economic inequality, or the marginalization of women. The metamorphosis of traditional structures was not invented by the mining industry; it is part and parcel of the changes such villages are exposed to. Third, as Emberson-Bain (1994b) points out, the community opposition to mining and its impacts takes different paths where the mine is the raison d'être for a settlement in previously uninhabited rural areas and where settlement existed prior to mining. At Vatukoula in Fiji, for example, the focus of attention has not been compensation for land access, but wage ceilings, the hierarchical employment structure that favors expatriates, appalling living conditions, and the mine's fiscal agreements with the government, which benefited expatriate investors at the expense of local workers (Emberson-Bain 1994a).

Most corporations and governments, through the various agreements, have sought to channel sustainable benefits, not just cash, to the local level through the use of support grants, business programs, infrastructural development programs, and community infrastructure grants, among others (Stephens 1995; Imbun 1994; Gilberthorpe and Banks 2012). More recently, there has been an increase in the involvement of women in mining projects (Bonnell 1995). Yet the expertise and commitment of mining corporations to the soft skills has been questioned. Burton (1999) and Filer, Banks, and Burton (2008) maintain that despite the rhetoric aimed at addressing social impacts, what materializes is often a piecemeal effort at addressing immediate problems with little coordinated long-term planning. Disputes and long-standing grievances that continue to dog all the major Pacific resource sites demonstrate that a rational, monetized approach is unlikely to capture the deeply culturally embedded (and often, from a Western perspective, hopelessly unrealistic) expectations and aspirations of the affected communities.

Environmental Aspects

A large-scale mine such as the Panguna mine on Bougainville, the Ok Tedi mine, or the Freeport mine in Papua processes more than 80,000 tonnes of ore per day (much more in Freeport's case). Of this amount only the 1 or 2 percent copper and small quantities of gold are extracted, and the rest (known as tailing) must be disposed of, along with often even larger quantities of waste rock that is shifted to gain access to the ore (Figure 31.7). The disposal of both the tailings and the waste rock requires land, river, or ocean dumping sites. While the large-scale copper/gold deposits rely primarily on mechanical processes to recover ore, gold mining in the region has often utilized chemical processes (involving mercury or cyanide) in the gold-recovery process (Hughes and Sullivan 1992; Sisto 1999).

Figure 31.7. Tailings from Freeport mine, West Papua, Indonesia (photo GB).

Pacific Island environments are certainly sensitive to these forms of disruption, although there are also many factors inherent within these tropical systems that work to reduce these impacts. These include the dynamic nature of the physical systems (with high rainfall, steep relief, and high natural erosion rates—the Ok Tedi catchment, for example, experienced a massive landslide in 1989 that added more sediment to the river system over a short period than the mine delivered over several years) and the rapid recovery of many of the environments to disturbance. Evidence from the past ten years, though, shows that the sheer scale of damage at Ok Tedi and Freeport (Figure 31.8), and the concentrations of particularly copper in the tailing, means the effects will persist for decades, even centuries (Paull et al. 2006; World Bank 2000).

The large scale open-pit mines bring a range of environmental effects. The most obvious and significant impacts are in the immediate mine area. Land is permanently disturbed and lost for open-pit mines. On Bougainville a mountain became a pit more than 200 m deep—similar processes are underway at Ok Tedi, Porgera, Freeport, and in New Caledonia. On Nauru, a century of phosphate mining consumed two-thirds of the area of the island, turning it into an unusable wasteland with few prospects for rehabilitation (Dupon 1989; Weeramentry 1992; Connell 2006). In addition, land is required for the mine's supporting infrastructure—processing plant, workshops, offices, accommodation, and township etc.

Figure 31.8. *Open pit Freeport mine, West Papua (photo GB).*

Land is also required for waste dumps, some of which are dispersed by natural erosion into river systems. Where river systems are used for waste disposal, this can cause flooding and inundation in downstream areas—Ok Tedi mine waste has covered more than 1,500 km² of rain forest and riverbank gardens in the lower Ok Tedi area, more than 100 km downstream from the mine (World Bank 2000). This damage sparked the high-profile lawsuit and subsequent exit of BHP from the mine operation (Banks and Ballard 1997; Kirsch 2008). The environmental damage is often inflected through cultural lenses and worked into broader community understandings of social and environmental change. Issues of equity can then arise as those downstream communities most affected rarely receive the same level of attention or compensation as communities located adjacent to the mine operation (Jorgensen 2006; Banks 2002).

Despite the insidious presence of various heavy metals in most tailing, the most significant impact on the ecology of the affected river systems appears to be physical, due to the vastly higher sediment loads produced by the mines. The Ok Tedi River prior to the mine, for example, carried an average of 30 million tonnes of sediment annually. The mine trebled this, and added 40 percent to the sediment load carried by the Fly River, into which the Ok Tedi flowed. This had the effect of rendering the Ok Tedi river biologically dead and affecting the biology of the middle Fly River (World Bank 2000). Similar effects have been recorded on New Caledonia (Dupon 1986; Winslow 1993, Pascal et al. 2008). Ocean disposal of tailings such as occurred at Misima and continues at Lihir in Papua New Guinea appears to be a more environmentally acceptable solution, particularly where the sediment is delivered at depth to steep ocean slopes. The longer-term impacts of this method of disposal in tropical environments are, however, still unclear at this stage (Brewer et al. 2007).

New Zealand has a long history of environmentally destructive mining. Large parts of the Central Otago provide a stark reminder of the long-term damage that can be done by large dredging operations. At the other extreme, the tailings dam at the Golden Cross mine on the Coromandel Peninsula began to move during 1996, threatening to spill tailings into the downstream environment. This illustrates that in the wrong circumstances not even best practice technologies can provide complete protection from the environmental risks associated with mining.

Generally, the environmental protection legislation within most Pacific islands is poor (Hughes and Sullivan 1989). Papua New Guinea's environmental legislation is probably the most comprehensive, but the capacity of the government to regulate the environmental performance of the mines is limited. The Department of Environment and Conservation, for example, is underresourced and finds it hard to attract and retain quality graduates. Critics also point out that the government in Papua New Guinea has a significant financial stake in the mines through equity holding and taxation receipts, and this sets up a potential conflict of interest with their role as environmental regulators (Rosenbaum 1993; Hughes and Sullivan 1989).

Increasingly the transnational mining companies face pressure to provide enhanced environmental management and performance. International court action against BHP by Papua New Guinean landowners at Ok Tedi highlighted the growing sensitivity to and power of communities in relation to environmental issues and the new avenues they are able to pursue to seek remedies (Banks and Ballard 1997; Kirsch 2008). Court action against Britain, Australia, and New Zealand by Nauru for environmental damage caused during the colonial period (like the Ok Tedi lawsuit, settled out of court) shows that polluters may be held responsible for environmental damage that occurred at some time in the past. This principle has also been supported by a number of other international torts against mining multinationals, including Freeport and Bougainville Copper, even though these cases themselves did not succeed. Likewise, multinational mining companies face increasing scrutiny and pressure for better environmental practice from lobby groups based in their home countries. Mining Watch Canada and the Australian-based Mineral Policy Institute, for example, regularly highlight perceived social and environmental abuses in the Pacific perpetrated by multinationals from their respective countries, and this can translate into shareholder pressure on the corporation (Emel 2002). Several of the multinational operators in the region (including Rio Tinto and Barrick) have activist websites devoted to monitoring their activities.

The industry response to this pressure has been a general improvement of standards, more research into improved environmental management, and, to be cynical, glossier brochures. Instances of specific breaches of environmental requirements and conditions are rare: the central issue is that these regulations and requirements permit environmental practices (such as riverine disposal of tailings) that are not permitted in most other parts of the world. This may not itself be an issue if it can be shown that the "environmental best practice" employed reflects the culture, priorities, and geographic context of the country where they are operating (Nelson 1996). Hence environmental "trade-offs" that see sustainable development benefits accrue to host countries and communities may be justified in some instances, but this decision is rarely an uncontested process: in the Ok Tedi case the Papua New Guinea government believes the development benefits outweigh the massive environmental damage, even though the World Bank felt otherwise (World Bank 2000). And a cynical manipulation of the "trade-off" rhetoric can be used by corporations and governments to justify actions that often bring few benefits to those most affected.

The Future

There is no doubt that mining will be an integral part of the future development path of the region. With increasing demand driving higher commodity prices, exploration is intensifying in Papua New Guinea and elsewhere in the Pacific. New Caledonia's nickel reserves are anticipated to last well into the later part of this century. The Papua New Guinea oil and gas industry is set for a massive expansion and promising oil seeps have also been located in Bligh Sound and off the shores of Fiji and Tonga. The economic potential of the Pacific's mineral-rich deep ocean nodules is also likely to be unlocked over the next few decades.

Leon Davis, the former chief executive of Con Rio-Tinto Australia (CRA), said more than a decade ago that part of the challenge of mining in the twenty-first century will be "re-capturing the public mandate that we in the mining industry have partially lost" (Davis 1995). This mandate (which one suspects may not have existed among local groups in much of the non-industrialized world) eroded when it became apparent that sections of the host societies derived few benefits from the mining projects on their doorsteps. Environmental strategies, particularly for waste disposal, have been questionable at best, and there is increasing disillusion among Pacific people about whether mining can deliver on its developmental promises: public confidence in mining as a development panacea has diluted considerably.

Following the Rio Summit of 1992, the rhetoric of "sustainable development" has been incorporated into the policy statements of most governments and mining companies mindful of their public image. Yet what does sustainability mean in the context of an industry based on extracting minerals at the lowest cost and over a finite time span? Robert Solow (1993: 163) states that the term is an "injunction to preserve productive capacity for the indefinite future, [while] society as a whole replaces used up resources with something else." A framework for achieving this has been suggested by Auty (1995), who maintains that sustainable minerals-driven development requires pragmatic, prudent, and orthodox economic policies, substitution of alternative wealth-generating assets for when the ore is depleted, and incentives to curb environmental degradation. The MMSD project, a two-year global project (corporately funded, in part to recapture some of the public mandate Davis talked of) came to a similar, albeit broader, set of conclusions. Some of the mechanisms for achieving these objectives are dealt with in brief below.

Managing Mineral Wealth

The Pacific has seen a number of attempts at the long-term management of mineral revenues, most of which have failed. Nauru is an extreme case (Connell 2006), but other instruments, such as the Mineral Resources Stabilisation Fund in Papua New Guinea, have also failed to provide stable, sustainable, resource-derived revenue flows. The key at the national level remains finding a way to translate nonrenewable resource wealth into long-term development. Recent government policies in Papua New Guinea aim to use 30 percent of windfall revenues from the sector (defined as revenues in excess of 4 percent of GDP) to repay public debt and the remaining 70 percent to bring forward planned spending on the rehabilitation, maintenance, and enhancement of public infrastructure: roads, schools, hospitals, and the like (Government of Papua New Guinea 2008). This blend of debt repayment (a form of investment) and developmental spending appears to be a model that offers a pragmatic and prudent approach to the translation of mineral wealth into sustainable benefits. The problem, of course, is the realization of these benefits in contexts where governance and capacity is poor.

Environmental Management

Environmental management of such a visible industry (Freeport, Ok Tedi, and Lihir are easily viewed on Google Earth these days) is crucial to its public profile and reputation. There is no doubt that evolving technologies and practices have improved environmental management in the mining sector. As noted earlier, though, there are limits to the effectiveness of these regimes when the fundamental issue is the enormous scale of the impacts. Future developments in environmental management will center around three central players—state, corporation, and community—each of which has different approaches, tools, and agendas. Policy and regulation that can be exercised through the minerals agreements and the mining code to promote environmental "best practice" will continue to be critical, as will the capacity and will of nation-states in the Pacific to enforce their own statutes. In a similar fashion, governments may opt for command-and-control regulations that control emission standards (the amount of pollution discharged), quality standards (which focus on the quality of the receiving environment), and process and product standards (ISO14001, for example). Alternatively, economic incentives such as reduced taxes for reduced pollution output can be applied. Liability, environmental litigation, and financial penalties can also be used as economic disincentives to pollution. Given their relatively novel status in many parts of the world, though, it is unlikely that such approaches will become widespread in the Pacific in the short term.

Corporate environmental policies and practices have evolved considerably in the past decade and will no doubt continue to do so in the future. Despite the well-documented limitations of relying on corporate social responsibility to improve practice, and the formidable environmental legacy issues the reputation of the industry has to overcome, self-initiated corporate changes (albeit often under external duress or at least pressure) will be critical to improving practices in the region, simply because of the continuing unwillingness or incapacity of the state to do so.

And finally, in tandem with the state and corporate trajectories outlined above, it is inevitable that existing levels of community involvement in environmental management will increase. Not only does this reflect trends elsewhere (O'Faircheallaigh 2007), but there is now acceptance by corporations and states that inclusive approaches are more likely to result in more secure and stable long-term partnerships and hence longer-term profit-making mining operations. Community participation provides greater legitimacy and acceptance of the decisions that are made, and local knowledge of ecological conditions and traditional interactions with these ecosystems in the Pacific can enhance the understanding by others of these systems. This has been done poorly in the past, ensuring that there is considerable distrust and suspicion (often well-founded as noted above) of the environmental effects of the mining operations by local communities. Working with international environmental NGOs has led to the environmental concerns of affected communities being aired in a global context, although again the outcomes are not always predictable (Kirsch 2008).

Community Participation

Satisfying community aspirations for involvement in decision making has been the slowest of the "soft skills" to evolve in the mining industry. Labonne (1996: 113) remarked that community involvement has to be enforceable through contracts that guarantee information access, economic sustainability, the prioritizing of sustainable technologies, and a range of implementation mechanisms including inspection agreements, external audits of health, safety, and environmental conditions, and enforcement provisions for arbitration, dispute resolution, and penalties. Even today, few community agreements would meet such standards (O'Faircheallaigh 2007).

Several UN charters recognize the community's "right to know," the "power to act," and the "principle of subsidiarity" enunciated in the Agenda 21 of the 1992 Rio Summit, which states that decisions must be made as close as possible to the level at which they impact (Labonne 1996). Many of these principles have since been included in the Berlin Guidelines on Mining and the Environment (United Nations 1992) and became central pillars of the MMSD project findings (MMSD 2002). The MMSD project concluded that subsidiarity, best practice, capacity building, and collective efforts were critical to the industry moving forward in terms of its relationships with local communities; interestingly some of the examples of such practices used in the MMSD report came from the Pacific region, most notably the Development Forum concept from Papua New Guinea.

Corporate Social Responsibility

Many Pacific Island countries are still refining policy and incorporating these cutting-edge concepts into practice, and many are unable to effectively implement policy due to a lack of capacity and resources. In this case, mining corporations may be asked to assume many of the responsibilities of government in determining "best practice" in environmental performance and monitoring. "Good neighbor" policies involving communication with and accountability to local communities (Figure 31.9) have been the industry's response to its critics' calls for sustainability in mining. The result has been increased involvement by mining companies in community affairs, funding of business development cooperatives, the setting up of trust funds, and encouraging community organization. The boundaries and effectiveness of this "corporate social responsibility" are, though, unclear and vary markedly depending on the company and the context (see Banks 2006; Filer, Banks, and Burton 2008; Gilberthorpe and Banks 2012).

Mining corporations have to balance the often conflicting objectives of Pacific Islands governments and local peoples for development, the demands of shareholders for low-cost, high-profit minerals production, and the demands of others for minimal environmental and social impact. Achieving the environmental

Figure 31.9. Company meeting with community, Porgera (photo GB).

and social standards demanded by stakeholders involves a reassessment of the paradigms that have governed the industry in the past, internalizing many social and environmental costs, which may in turn mean reduced short-term profit in exchange for greater long-term security. Grassroots awareness of the vulnerability of minerals projects to delays forced by community protest, the potency of international media attention, and the financial costs of ignoring these issues (A$500 million in the case of Ok Tedi) have now focused stakeholder attentions on the local dimensions of minerals development. The challenge is to include communities in all stages of planning and development; the dilemma is how this objective can be achieved in a planning process that is still capital-driven and rooted in formal Western knowledge–based ideas of development, which may not be shared by Pacific Islanders.

BIBLIOGRAPHY

Auty, R. M. 1993. *Sustaining development in minerals economies: The resource curse thesis.* London: Routledge.
———. 1995. Achieving sustainable minerals driven development. Keynote speech. In *Mining and mineral resource issues in Asia Pacific: Prospects for the 21st century. Proceedings, 1–3 November 1995,* ed. D. Denoon, et al., 3–11. Canberra: Australian National University.
Ballard, C., and G. Banks. 2009. Between a rock and a hard place: Corporate strategy at the Freeport Mine in Papua, 2001–2006. In *Development and environment in eastern Indonesia,* ed. B. Resosudarmo and F. Jotzo, 174–177. Singapore: ISAS.
Bank of Papua New Guinea. 1995. *Quarterly economic bulletin.* March. Port Moresby: Bank of Papua New Guinea.
Banks, G. 2002. Mining and environment in Melanesia: Contemporary debates reviewed. *The Contemporary Pacific* 14(1): 39–67.
———. 2006. Mining, social change and corporate social responsibility: Drawing lines in the Papua New Guinea mud. In *Globalisation, governance and the Pacific Islands,* ed. S. Firth, 259–274. Canberra: ANU E Press. Available online at http://epress.anu.edu.au/ssgm/global_gov/pdf_instructions.html.
———. 2008. Understanding "resource" conflicts in Papua New Guinea. *Asia-Pacific Viewpoint* 49(1): 23–34.
Banks, G., and C. Ballard, eds. 1997. *The Ok Tedi settlement: Issues, outcomes and implications.* Pacific Policy Paper No. 27. Canberra: Resource Management in Asia-Pacific and National Centre for Development Studies.

Barclay-Kerr, K. 1991. Conflict over Waikato coal: Maori land rights. In *Mining and indigenous peoples in Australasia*, ed. J. Connell and R. Howitt, 183–195. Sydney: Sydney University Press.

Bargh, M. 2006. Changing the game plan: The Foreshore and Seabed Act and constitutional change. *Kotuitui: New Zealand Journal of Social Sciences Online* 1: 1, 13–24.

Bedford, R., and A. Mamak. 1977. *Compensating for development: The Bougainville case*. Christchurch: Bougainville Special Publication No. 2, Department of Geography, University of Canterbury.

Bonnell. S. 1995. Women and mining: From project victims to project beneficiaries. In *Mining and mineral resource issues in Asia Pacific: Prospects for the 21st century. Proceedings, 1–3 November 1995*, ed. D. Denoon, et al., 162–166. Canberra: Australian National University.

———. 1999. Social change in the Porgera Valley. In *Dilemmas of development: The social and economic impact of the Porgera gold mine 1989–1994*, ed. C. Filer, 19–87. Pacific Policy Paper 34, Resource Management in Asia Pacific Project, and National Research Institute Special Publication. Canberra and Port Moresby: Asia-Pacific Press.

Brewer, D. T., D. A. Milton, G. C. Fry, D. M. Denis, D. S. Heales, W. N. Venables. 2007. Impacts of gold mine waste disposal on deepwater fish in a pristine tropical marine system. *Marine Pollution Bulletin* 54: 309–321.

Burton, J. 1995. What is best practice?: Social issues and the culture of the corporation in Papua New Guinea. In *Mining and mineral resource issues in Asia Pacific: Prospects for the 21st century. Proceedings, 1–3 November 1995*, ed. D. Denoon, et al., 129–134. Canberra: Australian National University.

———. 1999. Evidence of the "new competencies"? In *Dilemmas of development: The social and economic impact of the Porgera gold mine 1989–1994*, ed. C. Filer, 280–301. Pacific Policy Paper 34, Resource Management in Asia Pacific Project, and National Research Institute Special Publication. Canberra and Port Moresby: Asia-Pacific Press.

Collier, P., and A. Hoeffler. 2004. Greed and grievance in civil wars. *Oxford Economic Papers* 56: 563–595.

Connell, J. 1992. "Logic is a capitalist cover-up": Compensation and crises in Bougainville, Papua New Guinea. In *Resources, development and politics in the Pacific Islands*, ed. S. Henningham and R. J. May, 30–54. Bathurst, Australia: Crawford House Press.

———. 2006. Nauru: The first failed Pacific state? *The Round Table* 95(383): 47–63.

Connell, J., and R. Howitt. 1991. Mining, dispossession and development. In *Mining and indigenous peoples in Australasia*, ed. J. Connell and R. Howitt, 1–17. Sydney: Sydney University Press.

Crispin, G. 2003. Environmental management in small scale mining in PNG. *Journal of Cleaner Production* 7(2): 175–183.

Daniel, P. 1992. Economic policy in minerals exporting countries: What have we learned? In *Mineral wealth and economic development*, ed. J. E. Tilton, 81–121. John M. Olin Distinguished Lectures in Mineral Economics. Washington, D.C.: Resources for the Future.

David, G., M. Leopold, P. Dumas, J. Ferraris, J. Herrenschmidt, and G. Fontenelle. 2010. Integrated coastal zone management perspectives to ensure the sustainability of coral reefs in New Caledonia. *Marine Pollution Bulletin* 61: 323–334.

Davis, L. 1995. The new competencies in mining. Speech to the Australian Institute of Company Directors, Melbourne, October 3.

Denoon, D., C. Ballard, G. Banks, and P. Hancock, eds. 1995. *Mining and mineral resource issues in Asia Pacific: Prospects for the 21st century. Proceedings, 1–3 November 1995*. Canberra: Australian National University.

Dupon, J. F. 1986. *The effects of mining on the environments of high islands: A case study of nickel mining in New Caledonia*. Noumea: South Pacific Regional Environment Program, Environmental Case Studies. No 1.

———. 1989. *Pacific phosphate islands versus the mining industry: An unequal struggle*. Noumea: South Pacific Regional Environment Program, Environmental Case Studies, No. 4.

Emberson-Bain, A. 1994a. *Labour and gold in Fiji*. Cambridge: Cambridge University Press.

———. 1994b. De-romancing the stones: Gender, environment and mining in the Pacific. In *Sustainable development or malignant growth: Perspectives of Pacific Island women*, ed. Atu Emberson-Bain, 91–110. Suva: Marama Publications.

Emel, Jody. 2002. An inquiry into the green disciplining of capital. *Environment and Planning A* 34: 827–843.

Emerson, C. 1982. Mining enclaves and taxation. *World Development* 10(7): 561–571.

Filer, C. 1990. The Bougainville rebellion, the mining industry and the process of social disintegration in Papua New Guinea. *Canberra Anthropology* 13(1): 1–39.

———. ed. 1999. *Dilemmas of development: The social and economic impact of the Porgera gold mine 1989–1994*. Canberra and Port Moresby: Asia-Pacific Press, Pacific Policy Paper 34, Resource Management in Asia Pacific Project, and National Research Institute Special Publication 24.

Filer, C., G. Banks, and J. Burton. 2008. The fragmentation of responsibilities in the Melanesian mining sector. In *Earth matters: Indigenous people, the extractive industries and corporate social responsibility*, ed. C. O'Faircheallaigh and S. Ali, 163–179. Sheffield: Greenleaf.

Gelb, A., and Associates. 1988. *Oil windfalls: Blessing or curse?* Washington D.C.: World Bank Research Publication.

Gerritsen, R., and M. MacIntyre 1991. Dilemmas of distribution: The Misima gold mine, Papua New Guinea. In *Mining and indigenous peoples in Australasia*, ed. J. Connell and R. Howitt, 34–53. Sydney: Sydney University Press.

Gilberthorpe, E., and G. Banks. 2012. Development on whose terms? CSR discourse and social realities in Papua New Guinea's extractive industries sector. *Resources Policy* 37(2): 185–193.

Government of Papua New Guinea. 2008. *Medium term fiscal strategy, 2008–2012*. Waigani: Government of Papua New Guinea.

Government of Solomon Islands. 1993. *Solomon Islands national environment management strategy*. Honiara: Government of Solomon Islands.

Haley, N., and R. May, eds. 2007. *Conflict and resource development in the Southern Highlands of Papua New Guinea*. Canberra: Studies in State and Society in the Pacific, No. 3, State, Society and Governance in Melanesia Program, Australian National University.

Henningham, S., and R. J. May, eds. 1992. *Resources, development and politics in the Pacific Islands*. Bathurst, Australia: Crawford House Press.

Horowitz, L. S. 2004. Toward a viable independence? The Koniambo Project and the political economy of mining in New Caledonia. *The Contemporary Pacific* 16(2): 287–319.

Howard, M. 1988. *The impact of the international mining industry on native peoples*. Sydney: Transnational Corporations Research Project, University of Sydney.

Howitt, R., J. Connell, and P. Hirsh. 1996. Resources nations and indigenous peoples. In *Resources nations and indigenous peoples: Case studies from Australasia, Melanesia and Southeast Asia*, ed. R. Howitt, J. Connell, and P. Hirsh, 1–30. Melbourne: Oxford University Press.

Hughes, P., and M. Sullivan. 1989. Environmental impact assessment in Papua New Guinea: Lessons for the wider Pacific region. *Pacific Viewpoint* 30(1): 34–55.

———. 1992. *The environmental effects of mining and petroleum production in Papua New Guinea*. Port Moresby: University of Papua New Guinea Press.

Human Rights Watch. 2011. *Gold's costly dividend: Human rights impacts of Papua New Guinea's Porgera Gold Mine*. New York: Human Rights Watch.

Hyndman, D. 1994. *Ancestral rainforests and the mountains of gold: Indigenous peoples and mining in Papua New Guinea.* Boulder, Colo.: Westview Press.

Imbun, B. Y. 1994. Who said mining companies take and do not give?: The mining companies' role of social responsibility in Papua New Guinea. *TaimLain: A Journal of Contemporary Melanesian Studies* 2(1): 27–42.

———. 2002. *Industrial and employment relations in the Papua New Guinea mining industry.* Waigani: University of Papua New Guinea Press.

———. 2007. Cannot manage without the 'Significant Other': Mining, corporate social responsibility and local communities in Papua New Guinea. *Journal of Business Ethics* 73: 177–192.

Imbun, B., and P. A. McGavin. 2001. *Mining in Papua New Guinea: Analysis and policy implications.* Waigani: University of Papua New Guinea Press.

Jorgensen, D. 1997. Who and what is a landowner? Mythology and marking the ground in a Papua New Guinea mining project. *Anthropological Forum* 7(4): 599–628.

———. 2006. Hinterland history: The Ok Tedi mine and its cultural consequences in Telefolmin. *The Contemporary Pacific* 18(2): 233–263.

Keith-Reid, R. 1996. The mine that's getting the Kanaks into business. *Islands Business* (April): 46.

Kirsch, S. 2008. Indigenous movement and the risks of counter-globalisation: Tracking the campaign against Papua New Guinea's Ok Tedi mine. *American Ethnologist* 34(2): 303–321.

Labonne, B. 1996. Community and minerals resources: From adversarial confrontation to social development through participation, accountability and sustainability. In *Mining and mineral resource issues in Asia Pacific: Prospects for the 21st century. Proceedings, 1–3 November 1995,* ed. D. Denoon, et al., 111–116. Canberra: Australian National University.

Le Meur, P.-Y. 2009. Operateurs miniers, gouvernementalite et politique des ressources a Thio, Nouvelle-Caledonie. *Proceedings of 11th Pacific Science Inter-Congress.* Pacific Science Association: Hawai'i. Available online at: http://webistem.com/psi2009/output_directory/cd1/Data/articles/000166.pdf.

Macintyre, M., and S. Foale. 2002. Politicised ecology: Local responses to mining in Papua New Guinea. Resource Management in Asia-Pacific Working Paper No. 33, Resource Management in Asia-Pacific Program, RSPAS, Australian National University. Available online at http://hdl.handle.net/1885/41853.

Mahuta, R. T. 1992. Maori land and resource issues in New Zealand. In *Resources, development and politics in the Pacific Islands,* ed. S. Henningham and R. J. May, 195–205. Bathurst, Australia: Crawford House Press.

May, R. J., and M. Spriggs, eds. 1990. *The Bougainville crisis.* Bathurst, Australia: Crawford House Press.

McShane, F. 1994. The proposed Namosi Copper Mine (Fiji) in the context of regional mining practice. In *The margin fades: Geographical itineraries in a world of islands,* ed. E. Waddell and P. Nunn, 167–188. Suva: Institute of Pacific Studies, University of the South Pacific.

MED (Ministry of Economic Development). 2009. Facts and figures, available online at http://www.crownminerals.govt.nz/cms/minerals/facts-and-figures.

MMSD (Mining, Minerals and Sustainable Development Project). 2002. *Breaking new ground: Mining, minerals and sustainable development.* London: Earthscan.

Nankani, G. 1980. Developing problems of non-fuel mineral exporting countries. *Finance and Development* 17(1): 6–10.

Nelson, R. 1996. Establishing off-shore environmental performance criteria. In *Mining and mineral resource issues in Asia Pacific: Prospects for the 21st century. Proceedings, 1–3 November 1995,* ed. D. Denoon, et al., 185–190. Canberra: Australian National University.

O'Faircheallaigh, C. 2007. Environmental agreements, EIA follow-up and aboriginal participation in environmental management: The Canadian experience. *Environmental Impact Assessment Review* 274: 319–342.

Pacific Region International Women and Mining Network. 2007. Statement of the Pacific region international women and mining network meeting, Madang, Papua New Guinea, October 24–26, 2007. Available online at http://www.oxfam.org.au/campaigns/mining/docs/Statement-of-the-Pacific-Region-RIMM-meeting-October-2007.pdf.

Pascal, M., B. Richer de Forges, H. Le Guyader, and D. Simberloff. 2008. Mining and other threats to the New Caledonia biodiversity hotspot. *Conservation Biology* 222: 498–499.

Paull, D., G. Banks, C. Ballard, and D. Gillieson. 2006. Monitoring the environmental impact of mining in remote locations through remotely sensed data. *GeoCarto International* 21(1): 1–9.

Polier, N. 1994. A view from the "cyanide room": Politics and culture in a mining town in Papua New Guinea. *Identities* 1(1): 63–84.

Pollock, N. 1996. Impact of mining on Nauruan women. *Natural Resources Forum* 20(2): 123–134.

Reserve Bank of Fiji. 1994, 2008. *Quarterly Review.* Suva: Government Publishers.

Rosenbaum, H. 1993. Ok Tedi: Undermining PNG's future? *Habitat Australia* (November): 39–44.

Rumsey, A., and J. Weiner, eds. 2001. *Mining and indigenous lifeworlds in Australia and Papua New Guinea.* Adelaide: Crawford House.

Sisto, N. 1999. *An introduction to metal mining: Economic and environmental issues in the South Pacific.* Suva: School of Social and Economic Development, University of the South Pacific.

Stephens, A. 1995. Social planning through business and infrastructural development. In *Mining and mineral resource issues in Asia Pacific: Prospects for the 21st century. Proceedings, 1–3 November 1995,* ed. D. Denoon, et al., 122–128. Canberra: Australian National University.

Solow, R. 1993. An almost practical step towards sustainability. *Resource Policy* (September): 162–172.

United Nations. 1992. *Mining and the environment: The Berlin guidelines.* London: Mining Journal Books.

———. 1994. *Statistical yearbook for Asia and the Pacific.* Paris: United Nations Publications E/CN, Ser. A.

United States Geological Survey. 2007. *2006 Minerals Yearbook.* Washington, D.C.: United States Geological Survey.

Weeramentry, C. 1992. *Nauru: Environmental damage under international trusteeship.* Oxford: Oxford University Press.

West, R. 1992. *Development forum and benefit package: A Papua New Guinea initiative.* Port Moresby: Institute of National Affairs Working Paper 16.

Williams, D. 2003. Gold, the case of mines (1568) and the Waitangi Tribunal. *Australian Journal of Legal History* 7: 157–175.

Winslow, D. 1993. Mining and the environment in New Caledonia: The case of Thio. In *Asia's Environmental Crisis,* ed. M. Howard, 111–134. Boulder, Colo.: Westview Press.

World Bank. 2000. Report on Ok Tedi Mining Ltd. Mine waste management project risk assessment and supporting documents. Report to Government of Papua New Guinea, January 2000.

Wu, J. 2007a. The mineral industry of Papua New Guinea. In *United States Geological Survey, 2006 Minerals Yearbook.* US Department of the Interior and US Geological Survey, 23.1–23.5.

———. 2007b. The mineral industry of New Caledonia. In *United States Geological Survey, 2006 Minerals Yearbook.* US Department of the Interior and US Geological Survey, 16.1–16.2.

Tourism

Simon Milne

32

Any attempt to understand the economic, cultural, and environmental dynamics of the Pacific region must take into account the role of tourism (ADB 1996, 2006; AusAID 2006). Governments throughout the Pacific have, almost without exception, turned to the industry as a source of potentially sustainable economic development (Fagence 1999; Harrison 2004; UNESCAP 2008). While the cultural and environmental resources upon which the industry depends are vulnerable to uncontrolled tourism development (Connell and Rugendyke 2008), they can also potentially benefit from tourism—sustained, and perhaps enhanced, by the money and awareness that the industry brings (SPTO 2003a, TRIP 2007).

Tourism is a complex industry, an industry that not only links local communities to global economic systems, but also provides the additional dimension of direct interpersonal interaction between resident and tourist (Milne 1997; Milne and Ateljevic 2001). The challenge for the people of the Pacific is how to manage and develop this industry in such a way that it can be a sustainable source of livelihood for future generations and not degrade their quality of life and the natural and cultural resources upon which it depends (Craig-Smith and Fagence 1994; SPTO 2003a; TRIP 2007).

The focus of this chapter is on identifying and discussing the key issues that presently prevent tourism in the region from reaching its potential as a tool to achieve local economic development. The chapter begins with a brief overview of the size and nature of the tourism industry in the Pacific—highlighting the important differences that exist between a range of nascent and developing industries and those that have reached more mature phases of development.

A number of pressing issues that face the industry in the region are then highlighted: transport access; human resource development and availability; the use of, and potential for, information technology; the need for economic linkage development, especially with the agriculture sector; the impact of regional instability and tensions over land use and ownership; and global climate change and local environmental degradation. While this list is clearly not a comprehensive coverage of all the issues facing Pacific tourism, it certainly includes some of the most pressing.

Pacific Island Tourism—An Overview

While tourism is now a dominant feature in many of the Pacific economies discussed in this book, it is important to highlight the fact that tourist flows, and related benefits, are not spread evenly through the region. Fagence (1999), in an earlier edition of this volume, identifies tourism "honey pots" in the Pacific, including Hawai'i, New Zealand, Guam, Fiji, and Tahiti. These are all tourism destinations that have grown considerably in the past two or three decades and now dominate tourist arrival statistics for the Pacific (Table 32.1).

While it is always difficult to categorize "stages" of tourism development, regional tourism industries can be categorized in the following way (Milne 2006):

- Large-scale: Hawai'i, New Zealand, Guam
- Advanced: Fiji, the Cook Islands, French Polynesia, New Caledonia
- Developing: Vanuatu, Samoa, Tonga, Federated States of Micronesia
- Nascent: Kiribati, PNG, Solomon Islands, Tuvalu, Niue, the Marshall Islands

Among the large-scale group, Guam benefits from its proximity to the large tourism market of Japan and other important markets such as Taiwan and Korea. Hawai'i has a long association with inbound Japanese tourism and visitors from the mainland United States. New Zealand maintains its pattern of visitation from Australia, the United States, Japan, and the United Kingdom.

The advanced group includes the largest destination among the Melanesian nations—Fiji. The Fijian tourism industry is a key element of the national economy (Rao 2002). In the north of the country where dwindling European Union subsidies and expiring land leases have had a negative impact on agriculture (especially sugar cane), tourism can provide a particularly important source of economic development (ADB 2006: 75–78). The Cook Islands have grown their tourism industry from very small beginnings in the 1970s and 1980s; visitor numbers now far outstrip the resident population (Levinson and Milne 2004). French Polynesia continues to build on its North American, European, and Australasian

Table 32.1

Background Data on Pacific Island Tourism

Territory	Tourist arrivals	Year	Major markets: No 1 / No 2 / No 3
American Samoa	7.762	2006	USA / New Zealand / Australia
Cook Islands	97,019	2007	New Zealand / Australia / USA
Fed. States of Micronesia	13,345	2006	USA / Japan / Europe
Fiji	539,255	2007	Australia / New Zealand / USA
French Polynesia	218,241	2007	USA / Japan / Australia / Europe / New Zealand
Guam	967,579	2004	Japan / USA / Micronesia
Kiribati	4,709	2007	Australia / Fiji / New Zealand
Marshall Islands	2,727	2005	USA / Pacific Island countries /Japan
New Caledonia	103,363	2007	Japan / Australia / New Zealand
Niue	3,463	2007	New Zealand / Australia / USA
Northern Marianas	389,345	2007	Japan / Korea / China
Palau	84,566	2007	Japan / Taiwan / Korea
Papua New Guinea	104,122	2007	Australia / USA / Japan
Samoa	122,250	2007	New Zealand / American Samoa / Australia
Solomon Islands	13,748	2007	Australia / Papua New Guinea / USA
Tonga	46,040	2007	New Zealand / Australia / USA
Tuvalu	1,130	2007	Fiji / Australia / New Zealand
Vanuatu	81,345	2007	Australia / New Zealand / New Caledonia
Wallis and Futuna	5,304	2006	New Caledonia / France / Fr. Polynesia
Hawai'i	7,368,048	2007	USA / Japan / Canada
New Zealand	2,479,796	2007	Australia / United Kingdom / USA

visitors. New Caledonia is far less dependent on tourism than its counterpart—with the industry coming a distant second behind mining, the industry relies heavily on the New Zealand and Australian markets (d'Hauteserre 2005; Treloar and Hall 2005c: 226).

The developing group features some of the fastest-growing industries and others that show considerable, if unrealized, potential. Samoa stands out as the success story of the 1990s—with strong but controlled growth of the industry and considerable investment in new resorts and local enterprise (Milne 2004c; Scheyvens 2008). The Vanuatu industry is also well-positioned for further growth—especially in some of its less-developed outer islands (Gay 2007; Slatter 2006). Both Tonga and the Federated States of Micronesia have yet to successfully grow tourism in a sustained fashion but have the infrastructure to support further development (Harkness 2001; Milne 2004b; Treloar and Hall 2005b: 184–185).

The final, nascent group of nations are made up of industries that have struggled to develop—although in some cases (Papua New Guinea, Solomons) there are plenty of environmental, cultural, and labor resources to support an industry (Gay 2008; Yamashita 2003: 129–130). For Kiribati, Tuvalu, Niue, and the Marshall Islands the constraints are more to do with lack of size (both physical and demographic) and relative isolation. In many cases there is simply not the population and/or natural resource base to support anything other than a small tourism industry.

The Pacific region is a diverse one and the tourist destinations outlined above all attempt to market their unique features.

Nevertheless there are certain commonalities shared by many of the nations marketing their tourism products (Fagence 1999; Harrison 2004; Treloar and Hall 2005a): a focus on marine and beach-based activities; untouched, unhurried, uncrowded; the ability to get away and experience something new and different—including new cultures and peoples.

Fagence (1999) notes four elements of cultural distinctiveness that attract overseas visitors to the Pacific Islands: community or social systems; traditions, customs, and behavior; artifacts, crafts, and art forms; and "the Pacific Way." There is also a growing awareness of the role that health, wellness, and traditional foods can play in developing the visitor experience (Milne 2006).

The tourism industry now represents a major source of foreign exchange earnings in many of the nations and territories in the region. Recent reviews of the current state of tourism in the South Pacific have highlighted that tourism is an important supplement to traditional economies, natural resource extraction, and donor funding/remittance flows (Milne 2005b; for link to MIRAB see Bertram 1999, 2006; and Apostolopoulus and Gayle 2002).

The tourism sector has for some time featured strongly in national government and/or state/provincial government policies (Wilkinson 1989; Craig-Smith and Fagence 1994; SPTO 2003a; Milne 2006). In the less-developed parts of the region, international donor agency policy initiatives are often focused on generating income and increasing employment creation (Adams 2002; AusAID 2006; World Bank 2005). A problem remains, however, in generating opportunities for local people to take part in the ownership and management of the industry (Milne 2005a).

Many of the Pacific Island countries are embarking upon development programs that emphasize and incorporate ecotourism or sustainable tourism development principles (Fagence 1995; Milne 2006). The core objectives of these strategies can be summarized as:

- Promote strong economic growth through sustainable tourism development. Minimize degradation of the physical environment.
- Generate substantial foreign exchange, local income, and employment. Reduce negative economic impacts (leakages) while maximizing the socioeconomic contribution of the industry.
- Promote balanced regional tourism development, reducing imbalances in regional tourism development.
- Promote greater participation/involvement of local people and create livelihood opportunities and develop skills. Enhance public awareness of tourism.
- Sustain local cultures/customary practices—limiting sociocultural impacts while increasing appropriate, culturally focused tourism.
- Promote greater community awareness of tourism benefits.
- Build a cooperative tourism sector in which businesses and other key stakeholders network and link with each other to enhance product offerings and build visitor experience.
- Develop human resources at both the front-line and managerial/ownership levels.
- Improve infrastructure and access—with a focus on air transport, cruise shipping, and telecommunications.
- Create an enabling institutional framework—with a focus on developing greater awareness among governments of the vital role that tourism plays.

While there are clearly variations in the range and type of issues dealt with in tourism strategic plans in the region, there is no doubt that the overall tenets of sustainable development and enhancing visitor yield (not just arrival statistics) have increasingly become the standard throughout the region. This is mirrored in the only regional tourism strategy currently in place, the SPTO Tourism Strategy for the South and Central Pacific 2003–13 (SPTO 2003a). A recent review of the strategy, which involved consultation throughout the region, revealed that the specific strategic areas (human resource development, small business development and assistance, investment facilitation, planning resource development, marketing, and market research) continue to be seen as vital and relevant to stakeholders in the region. Nevertheless there is strong feeling that environment, transport and communications, and culture should be added as areas of strategic focus (Milne 2006).

Critical Issues in Pacific Tourism

If the tourism industries are to develop in a way that will meet the strategic objectives listed above, it is vital that certain challenges be addressed. Several issues influence the ability of the region's tourism

industries to act as tools for sustainable economic development. The challenges differ from place to place, depending in part on the sophistication and size of the industry that has developed and the human and natural resources that can be allocated to the industry.

International and Domestic Transport Linkages

The access to, and reliability of, international and domestic air and sea transport is a perennial issue for the tourism industry in the region (Britton and Kissling 1984; Duval 2005; Taumoepeau 2008). Suffice to say that island nations with robust and competitive international connections (including cruise links), and solid domestic transport networks, have a major competitive advantage over those that do not (SPTO 2003a, 2003b; Taumoepeau 2008).

The international airline industry is one of the most competitive in the world. These pressures have increased in recent years with rising fuel prices and additional concerns about terrorism. The past two decades have seen many Pacific airline carriers cease operations because of a mixture of competitive pressures, limited demand, and poor management (Taumoepeau 2008). The impact of such failures on small island nations in the region is usually dramatic.

The Tongan government invested considerable public money into its "Royal Tongan" airline between 1985 and 2004, when it ceased operations. The airline provided important links to New Zealand and Australia as well as some international connections to the United States. The airline leased a Boeing 757 for international routes and also operated smaller turboprop planes to the domestic destinations of Haʻapai, Eua, and Vavaʻu from its main base in Nukuʻalofa. When the airline closed in 2004, several hundred passengers were left stranded at international terminals, and the domestic sector in Tonga fell into disarray (Milne 2004b). The impacts on the local tourism industry were considerable: international service from the major market of New Zealand was forced to rely solely on Air New Zealand. Domestic services took some time to fully recover from the closure, and this had a negative impact on government attempts to spread the benefits of tourism to outlying areas.

A further important issue for the tourism industry in the less-developed nations of the region is the lack of adequate runways and facilities and difficulties in maintaining and upgrading aircraft (Taumoepeau 2008). An example of these problems can be drawn from Solomon Islands, where many of the airport runways and facilities in more than twenty airline destinations throughout the country, including the Honiara domestic airport terminal, are poorly maintained and equipped (Gay 2008). Because of the poor conditions, some of these runways are often closed temporarily by the civil aviation authority, causing cancellation or rerouting of domestic flights. The impact of such constraints on Solomon Islands' tourism can be seen from the following comment drawn from a recent post on the online travel blog "Thorntree":

[T]he domestic planes are small, and often overbooked. Also, depending on the condition of the smaller airfields, planes often get cancelled without warning. So make sure you have insurance which will pay if a scheduled service is cancelled. Also, allow at least a week after your last internal flight to anywhere far from Honiara before your international flight out—I have been delayed that long.

More advanced nations also face pressures. Air New Zealand has relied on public-sector funds to survive in the past. The Fijian carrier Air Pacific has been forced to reduce some long-haul flights. Even more dramatically, Aloha Airlines of Hawai'i ceased operations in 2008 (Blair 2008). While the impact of losing an airline like Aloha is less dramatic for Hawai'i than, for example, Royal Tongan's demise was for Tonga, the repercussions are nevertheless significant. The demise of the airline led to the loss of nearly two thousand jobs. Although not a major long-haul operator, Aloha was an important carrier within the state and its closure reduced competition on domestic routes (Blair 2008). The closure of charter airlines has also had an impact on Hawai'i, with the Canadian-based Harmony Airlines ceasing operations in April 2007 and reducing seat capacity to the west coast of Canada by nearly 25 percent (Segal 2007).

The cruise sector is highly competitive and shows signs of continued ownership concentration at the global scale (SPTO 2003b; Butler 2004; Douglas and Douglas 2006). It appears that two cruise product models are most likely to thrive in the future: (i) larger "escape palaces" that rely on economies of scale and a proven, largely standardized formula for core mass markets; and (ii) specialized boutique vessels that take advantage of a vessel's flexibility to provide different, unique, and "authentic" experiences. Both of these growth categories are of importance to the Pacific (SPTO 2003b).

The cruise industry has grown in significance throughout the region—with strong "hubs" existing in the major tourism centers—led by Hawai'i (Douglas and Douglas 2006). Fiji's cruise industry is centered around the Port of Denaru, for shorter local cruises, and Suva, which is an important port of call for larger vessels. Both Fiji and French Polynesia have competitive advantages in terms of infrastructure, port facilities, and adequate flight connections to base ports (SPTO 2003b).

A number of South Pacific nations are attempting to tap into the cruise market but are hampered by a lack of proper passenger-friendly facilities at ports. In many cases the attractive option of smaller cruises within island chains is hampered by the lack of facilities on outer islands. Most important there is a clear need for effective strategies to be put in place to improve community preparedness for, and awareness of, cruise ships (SPTO 2003b).

Vanuatu is trying to develop its relatively small cruise industry (Gay 2007). The nation has two major ports of call, Port Vila on Efate and Luganville on Espiritu Santo. Cruise ships also call at "Mystery Island," where supplies are brought in for the passengers to enjoy a beach and bathing experience in a remote setting (Cleverdon 2004; Gay 2007). Day visitors (cruise ship visitors) have been a highly volatile segment for much of the past twenty years, with major fluctuations in visitor numbers. In recent years numbers have ranged from 38,000 (2004) to 86,000 (2006). Espiritu Santo alone received thirteen cruise ships in 2006 but then expected only eight in 2007 (Gay 2007). Data on the economic value of cruise ships to the Vanuatu economy is limited (SPTO 2003b) and highlights a data gap that is mirrored throughout the region. There is no doubt, however, that the increasing number of cruise ships visiting remote locations injects relatively significant amounts of cash. Inflows of cash can bring tensions however; in recent years there have been some disagreements between cruise ship operators and local landholders over the amount of compensation to be paid for use of custom-owned resources (Gay 2007).

Human Resource Development

While tourism hubs such as New Zealand, Fiji, Hawai'i, and Guam have developed publicly funded tourism and hospitality programs that meet the evolving needs of the industry and also have a range of private-sector training alternatives, many nations in the region have limited educational resources (Craig-Smith 2005; Milne 2005a). For some nations, most notably the Cook Islands and Niue, limited population size is the major challenge faced when it comes to finding labor (SPTO 2003a, UNESCAP 2008: 75–76). For other nations such as Solomon Islands, Vanuatu, Kiribati, and Papua New Guinea, the problems lie more in a limited skills base rather than a lack of available workers (Milne 2005a; EC 2006).

It is in the area of tourism education and training that international donor agencies have made a big impact on the region's tourism sector. During the 1980s and 1990s the European Union's Pacific Region Tourism Development Program funded in-country training, using primarily outside trainers on intensive visits, and the program was evaluated highly by fund recipients (Cleverdon, Milne, and Goodwin 2003). In recent years donor funding has shifted away from bringing trainers into countries to undertake short programs and toward the establishment of lasting regional education hubs (EC 2006; AusAID 2006). The Australian government has funded the Australia-Pacific Technical College (APTC), which aims to deliver vocational training across the Pacific to a standard accredited in Australia.

APTC has recently established a tourism program in Port Vila, Vanuatu. The European Union has also committed major in-country funding to tourism education—with the main focus on the Vanuatu Tourism Education and Training program (VATET), based at the Vanuatu Institute of Technology (EC 2006). A full working restaurant and training center has been established and the focus in the long term is to have students attending the facility from around the region.

It is essential that education move beyond the labor needs of the industry itself. An additional component of the VATET project is tourism awareness, which is closely linked to the rural training program. A number of tourism awareness tools were produced as part of a "Tourism Toolkit" and were distributed among the different training agencies and training providers in the country to achieve maximum impact (EC 2006).

The skills gaps that afflict many destinations in the region not only exist at the level of waiters, cleaners, and front office workers—they also represent a constraint at the level of entrepreneurs, business owners, and planners (Holden, Bale, and Holden 2004). The region is replete with entrepreneurial ideas and small tourism businesses that wish to expand and build their market presence. Challenges related to skills and education, limited access to finance, and high startup and operating costs often prevent small tourism enterprises (STE) from developing effectively (Holden, Bale, and Holden 2004; Milne 2005a). In several nations skills shortages necessitate the hiring of expatriate middle and upper management staff.

A recent study of the training needs of those who own and manage small tourism businesses in the South Pacific Islands identified the following core areas of skills development: marketing; management (HR, accounting, finance); information technology use and application; business and environment; developing cultural and "sense of place" aspects of business; networking and alliance development; and an improved understanding of how the tourism industry "works." The report concluded that current training providers are not able to satisfy entirely the current demand for training from the owners and managers of tourism businesses in the region—identifying a critical gap between high-end, often longer duration university courses and courses on business startup (Milne 2005a).

Information Technology

It has not been easy in the past for small island nations in the region to reach the "elusive tourist" (Milne 1996). Limited marketing budgets, a wide array of competing destinations, and an increasingly experienced and "picky" consumer make it difficult to create and sustain a profitable industry. Several commentators argue that even if a nation is successful in reaching the consumer, the benefits to the local economy will be reduced by the very nature of marketing and travel distribution channels themselves and the colonial structures that underlie links between Pacific islands and the global economy (Britton 1982; d'Hautesserre 2005). The traditional marketing channels steer visitors toward the types of operations with large marketing budgets and the ability to link into integrated travel package structures. Thus many small, local businesses are excluded from the core areas of the tourism industry. This in turn can bring negative social and environmental consequences for the host nation (Milne 1997).

Information and communication technologies (ICT), and especially the Internet, represent an important alternative or addition to the traditional system outlined above (Milne, Mason, and Hasse 2004). The Internet has enabled small tourism enterprises and remote destinations around the world to gain a footing in the international marketplace. The Internet has not only changed the business model of many tourism enterprises throughout the Pacific region but has also opened up interesting opportunities for participatory planning and enhanced visitor experiences (Pene and Doorne 2004; Levinson and Milne 2004).

The potential of the Internet to assist in the sustainable development of tourism is not yet being tapped in many remote parts of the region because of limited access and high costs (UNESCAP 2008: 74). While the Internet offers the potential for greater local input into, and control over, the image creation and marketing process, research highlights a number of less positive outcomes. As Levinson and Milne (2004) show in the case of the Cook Islands, the bulk of the websites are often developed and maintained overseas. Local levels of information technology acumen must be enhanced if the notion of control is to be extended to the local development and upgrading of sites. Many websites remain as virtual brochures with limited interactivity and e-commerce and very few links to other features of the destination.

In simple terms there is only so much that can be done to throw off the difficulties associated with small size, isolation, and limited marketing budgets. While the Internet can, and will, play a role in enhancing the ability of small destinations and operators to reach the elusive tourist, they will doubtless have to rely on a mixed array of marketing tools—that borrow from both the traditional and new (Milne, Mason, and Hasse 2004).

The impact of ICT goes beyond simple marketing. It can help strengthen networks and communications, build community initiative, integrate the local business community in social networks, and link to broader issues of sustainability (Loader, Hague, and Eagle 2000). Policy makers are increasingly aware of the importance of information technologies in enabling economic development by facilitating collaborative activity, especially network formation. In the more advanced tourism nations in the Pacific, technology is also being seen as a tool to enhance the planning, development, and broader competitiveness of the industry (UNESCAP 2008: 74–75; Milne et al. 2008).

The current New Zealand tourism strategy, like many others in the region, emphasizes the importance of web-based marketing tools in increasing visitor numbers and in particular in reaching the high yield "interactive" traveler who is willing to spend money on authentic natural and cultural experiences (Milne et al. 2008). The strategy also focuses on the role technology can play in the dissemination of information and the creation of networks that enhance STE performance. Local and regional governments are also focused on increasing the use of ICT as a tool to achieve greater economic benefits from tourism. A key focus of much of this policy is on breaking down the competitively focused, individualistic character of the nation's small businesses and on getting tourism operators to engage in networks and clusters (Milne et al. 2008).

Tourism in the islands of the Pacific is not just about sun, sand, and sea. For a growing number of visitors it is about people and culture as well (SPTO 2003a). Learning about community and hearing local stories helps visitors create a sense of place—and encourages them to stay longer and spend more money. With cultural features now a growing component of tourism strategies around the region, it is essential that communities have the ability not only to work in the industry but also to be actively involved in the planning and development of the sector (Doorne 2004; Hasse and Milne 2005). Much of the region is still characterized by low levels of community involvement in tourism planning and development. Poor community understanding of tourism, exacerbated by limited mechanisms to engage local people in tourism development processes, can lead to conflict at a later date (Milne 2006; Pene and Doorne 2004).

There are clearly opportunities for ICT to play a role in overcoming some of these difficulties. Doorne (2004) has shown how geographical information systems can play a role in assisting Fijian communities to have more effective input into tourism development and planning. Milne et al. (2008) have revealed the important role that ICT, and specifically community-controlled and community-developed websites, can play in enhancing interstakeholder communication and in building a closer networking of tourism operators. At present, though, the ability of ICT to enhance the sustainable development outcomes of tourism remains hampered by access, cost, and skills issues (UNESCAP 2008: 74).

Building Economic Linkages

While nations throughout the region are benefitting from the tourism industry, there is no question that the economic potential of the industry is not being met (Milne 2005b). The direct flows of money from visitors to the businesses that make up the hotel industry are vital to income and job creation, but so are the indirect flows between the tourism sector and surrounding sectors of the economy. These economic linkages are vital as they assist in spreading the benefits of the tourism sector and help to build the yield that is central to many tourism strategies in the region.

A particularly important sector to foster links with is agriculture (Torres and Momsen 2004; Berno 2006; UNESCAP 2008). Agriculture is a vital part of the economy (subsistence and cash) and culture of virtually all the nations in the region—and tourism, if well-managed, can be an effective tool to help grow and sustain the sector. The use of local food is a vital component of developing visitor experience and creating a sense of authenticity and "place" (Richards 2002). Some of the positive outcomes of the links between tourism and agriculture that have been highlighted in the literature include stimulation of new agricultural development, increased profitability of agricultural production, creation of new market opportunities, the provision of increased or supplementary income for farmers, and opportunities for economic diversification (Torres and Momsen 2004; Berno 2006; Mason and Milne 2007).

In addition to links with traditional farming there are other areas of linkage that can be developed. While difficult to manage in tropical climates, hydroponics offers potential for the production of vegetables demanded by the tourism sector—such as lettuce. There is also, of course, the opportunity to develop "agri-tourism," with the farming sector becoming part of the tourist experience—in some cases through farm stays but more commonly through farm visits and educational excursions.

Unfortunately, linkages to local agriculture can be hindered by problems of supply and quality and a general lack of communication between farmers and the tourism industry. Nevertheless, increased fuel and imported food prices, together with an increasing desire among visitors to try local fare, is providing an important incentive to boost consumption of local foods (Milne 2005b; Gay 2008).

Regional Instability and Land Tensions

The Pacific Islands generally have a well-deserved reputation for safety and stable democratic governance. In recent decades, however, an increasing number of political and ethnic "hotspots" have emerged and in some cases have led to outbursts of anger and violence that have hurt the tourism industry badly (Harrison 2004: 6–7). On rare occasions the industry itself has been targeted (though not, to date, the tourists). Whatever the cause or outcome of the violence, the government travel advisories and media coverage that almost inevitably follow in source markets like Australia and New Zealand will have a negative impact on the tourism sector. The mid-1990s saw Tahitian demonstrators rioting on the streets of Papeete, the main passenger terminal at the international airport gutted, and parts of the city set on fire (Shenon 1995). The impact on tourism was dramatic and immediate, although the industry did recover as relative calm returned following the banning of the nuclear tests that had triggered the unrest. The relatively large Fijian tourism industry has also been buffeted by a series of military coups, the most recent of which occurred in late 2006. In general the visitor numbers take one to two years to recover, but what takes longer to recover is the confidence of local businesspeople and potential foreign investors (Rao 2002; Harrison 2004).

Smaller, less resilient tourism sectors can be hit even harder by political unrest. The 2006 riots in Tonga largely destroyed the downtown shopping area of Nukualofa and severely shook the confidence of the local tourism sector. The case of Solomon Islands also shows the impact of such events (Gay 2008). The Solomon Islands tourism industry has been hit by ongoing ethnic and political unrest, with the most recent events seeing riots in Honiara in 2006. While the number of visitors in 2007 was 13,700, representing considerable growth from 2002 (4,000), it must be remembered that the figure was still well below the peak of 18,000 in 1998, before ethnic tensions turned into violent confrontation (Table 32.2). To make matters worse for the struggling industry, in April 2007 a series of earthquakes triggered a tsunami—swamping coastlines of the Western Province of the nation, where several resorts are located.

Table 32.2

Solomon Islands Arrival Statistics 1997–2008

Year	Total arrivals	Defining events
1997	15,390	
1998	17,586	
1999	9,208	Ethnic Tensions
2000	6,100	
2001	5,760	
2002	4,445	
2003	6,565	RAMSI (June)
2004	11,116	
2005	12,533	
2006	11,482	Riots (April)
2007	13,748	Tsunami (April)
2008	16,000	

Source: Gay, in press.

Sometimes tourism is not just the indirect victim of unrest—it can also be the direct cause. The issue of land and tourism development is particularly complex throughout the region, land is central to people's lives and traditions, and many people reside in rural areas on custom land (Doorne 2004). Nearly 90 percent of land in Solomon Islands is custom-owned, and the rest is alienated. Because of population pressures and unclear titles, land reform is pressing, yet for cultural reasons and to ensure political stability it cannot take the form of a move to private freehold ownership (Gay 2008). Recent reports and past research (Gay 2007, 2008; Slatter 2006; de Burlo 1989) provide numerous examples of tensions in Solomon Islands and Vanuatu that exist over the tourist industry's use of custom-owned terrestrial or marine resources. Similar issues of industry encroachment on traditional lands and resources can be seen throughout the region—from protests and conflict over the use of foreshore areas for commercial gain in New Zealand (Bargh 2006) to concerns over lagoon and land rights in Fiji (Doorne 2004).

It is clear that there needs to be improved awareness and understanding of land-related issues between stakeholders throughout the region. For tourism operators it is particularly important to make sure benefits flow back to the community—not just in monetary terms but also through upskilling, infrastructure investment, and other mechanisms. At the same time, awareness and understanding of the tourism industry is vital if landowners and community groups are to interact effectively with the tourism industry and participate as active agents in the development process (Milne 2006).

Global Climate Change and the Environment

Discussions of economic linkages, STE performance, and land tenure are of limited significance to some Pacific islands when compared to the pressures exerted by global warming (UNESCAP 2008: 31–38; TRIP 2007; Becken and Hay 2007). Vulnerability to sea rise and intensifying cyclonic activity varies across the region—with low-lying atolls being particularly at risk. For nations such as Tuvalu, sea-level rise sounds the death knell for a nation, not just for tourism (Mimura 1999; Guldberg and Timmerman 2000; Church, White, and Hunter 2006).

Tuvalu, which consists of four reef islands and five true atolls, none of which is over 4.6 meters above sea level, is extremely vulnerable to the sea-level rises and warming that would be associated with global climate change (Church, White, and Hunter 2006). Several outer islands in the main lagoon of Funafuti are losing their vegetation cover as waves breach fringing reefs that are, in many cases, becoming bleached by high water temperatures. Beachhead erosion is also occurring because of the use of sand for building materials; demands for wood fuel have led to excessive clearance of forest undergrowth. At the same time the Crown of Thorns starfish has caused considerable damage to coral reefs (Government of Tuvalu 2008).

Population pressures continue to place strains on the marine resource base—especially in the main settlement of Funafuti. The marine resources of Funafuti lagoon, as well as seabirds and coconut crabs found on the surrounding islets, have always been an important source of food for the local population. Over the past twenty years, however, these resources have declined due to overharvesting and damage to nearshore reefs from fishing nets and pollution. Septic tank systems are in place in most areas and can overload in densely populated areas. In effect the northern end of the main island has become a dumping zone, and leaching and runoff into the lagoon is now becoming a concern. The establishment of a marine conservation area near Funafuti is an attempt to reduce some of these impacts (Government of Tuvalu 2008).

Perhaps the most poignant dimension to Tuvalu's plight is that the very force that is destroying the nation is, at the same time, a sudden source of curiosity for the world's journalists and hardened travelers. The Tuvalu Tourism Office (personal communication) points out that peak visitor flows to the nation now occur around the time of king tides, with journalists and photographers coming to see firsthand the reality of global warming.

Another of the smaller nations in the Pacific, Niue, represents a stark physical contrast to Tuvalu. Commonly known as the "Rock of Polynesia," Niue is an isolated island located east of Tonga, southeast of Western Samoa, west of Rarotonga, and 2,400 km northeast of New Zealand. The single island is 260 square kilometers in size and is one of the largest raised coral atolls in the world—with twenty-five-meter cliffs encircling the shoreline. The island's upraised coral makeup creates an exciting rugged coastline and reef that provide a range of marine tourism and terrestrial experiences. Despite Niue's relative height above sea level, the tourism industry there has been severely disrupted by a series of cyclones since the late 1980s—with storm surges destroying buildings and infrastructure (Milne 1992b, 2004a; Barker 2000). Since the last cyclone in 2004 the bulk of the tourism industry on the island has relocated to higher, inland areas of the island.

Like many of the more developed tourism destinations in the region, Fiji is facing the challenge of managing a large tourism industry in a fashion that is environmentally sustainable and is also in keeping with the needs and wishes of host communities (Doorne 2004). Nowhere are these tensions more keenly felt than in the marine environment and coastal areas (Levett and McNally 2003). The mixed tourism and residential development at Denaru provides a good example of the rapid changes in coastal geography associated with increasing reclamation driven by tourism and urbanization. The Denaru development is on a low-lying coastal area and has had a major impact on mangroves. Such low-lying developments are also prone to flooding during cyclone activity or sea-level rise.

Any growth in tourism within the Pacific region will create the potential for increased environmental degradation in the offshore and coastal zones. Coastal development represents a moderate to severe threat around many tourism sites and can result in the destruction of coral reefs, lagoons, seagrass beds, and beaches (TRIP 2007, SPREP 2008). There are real concerns about depletion or loss of species and shortages of groundwater and surface water as a result of developments. The collection of corals and mollusks for the souvenir trade has also been identified as a marine threat driven by the expansion of tourism. The disposal of solid waste is also resulting in the deterioration of aesthetics, alteration of coastal habitats, and damage to coastal and marine life. Beach litter has become a growing problem in many areas. A lack of adequate waste disposal regulations, inadequate enforcement, and limited public awareness frustrate control of this problem (TRIP 2007; SPREP 2008).

Toward Sustainable Tourism?

In the first edition of this volume, Fagence (1999) asked the important question of whether tourist benefits can be balanced with environmental sustainability and the concerns of indigenous cultures. He also expressed concerns that changes in numbers of international visitors and shifts in demand, together with perennial problems of transportation and product development and supply, would cause tourism in the Pacific region to have an uncertain future.

The ten or so years that have elapsed since Fagence's chapter was written have seen the industry grow in many instances, but also suffer some setbacks. A range of internal and external pressures have indeed forced a period of uncertainty upon the Pacific tourism industry and those who depend on it. There have been considerable regional fluctuations in arrival numbers in many parts of the Pacific.

Nevertheless, enthusiasm for tourism development remains undiminished and strong throughout the region. Many Pacific Island governments and donor agencies around the region have adopted development approaches that place a strategic focus on more sustainable and "yield driven" forms of tourism (Milne 2006). Policy makers throughout the Pacific are embracing concepts of "ecotourism," "pro-poor tourism," and "green tourism" (SPTO 2003a; TRIP 2007). The emphasis is on creating a tourism industry that brings more benefit for host populations, sustains environment and culture, and does not degrade local quality of life.

While it is too early, and in some cases too difficult due to data deficiencies, to measure the overall success of these sustainable, yield-driven approaches to tourism development, this chapter has shown that there are a number of important issues that place constraints on the ability of such strategies to succeed. This chapter has outlined some of the more important constraints, but it cannot hope to address the full range of the challenges that face the peoples of the Pacific as they try to maximize the potential of this important industry to assist them in achieving sustainable livelihood options.

The overall prognosis for tourism in the region remains relatively positive. The most important positive sign for the future is that the region's focus is now very much on sustainability and yield. To support this emphasis, though, it is essential that the quality and timeliness of data relating to the nature and impact of tourism in many Pacific Island nations be improved and standardized, and that more research is focused on the sector. A focus on timely and robust research is essential if the region is to truly measure and enhance tourism's ability to achieve the strategic objectives set for it.

BIBLIOGRAPHY

Adams, P. 2002. *Towards a strategy for the Pacific Islands region.* Wellington: New Zealand Agency for International Development (NZAID).

ADB (Asian Development Bank). 1996. *Strategy for the Pacific: Policies and programs for sustainable growth.* Pacific Studies Series. Manila: Asian Development Bank.

———. 2006. *Asian development outlook 2006.* Manila: Asian Development Bank.

Apostolopoulos, Y., and D. J. Gayle. 2002. From MIRAB to TOURAB? Searching for sustainable development in the maritime Caribbean, Pacific, and Mediterranean. In *Island tourism and sustainable development, Caribbean, Pacific and Mediterranean experience,* ed. Y. Apostolopoulos and D. J. Gayle, 3–14. Westport, Conn.: Praeger.

AusAID. 2006. *Pacific 2020: Challenges and opportunities for growth.* Canberra: Commonwealth of Australia.

Bargh, M. 2006. Changing the game plan: The Foreshore and Seabed Act and constitutional change. *Kōtuitui: New Zealand Journal of Social Sciences Online.* www.royalsociety.org.nz/site/publish/journals/kotuitui/2006/02.aspx.

Barker, J. C. 2000. Hurricanes and socio-economic development on Niue island. *Asia Pacific Viewpoint* 41(2): 191–205.

Becken, S., and Hay, J. 2007. *Tourism and climate change—risks and opportunities.* Clevedon: Channel View Publications.

Berno, T. 2006. Bridging agriculture and sustainable tourism to enhance sustainability. In *Sustainable development policy and administration,* ed. G. M. Mudacumura, D. Mebratu, and M. S. Haque, 207–224. Boca Raton, Fla.: CRC Press, Taylor and Francis Group.

Bertram, G. 1999. The MIRAB model twelve years on. *The Contemporary Pacific* 11(1): 105–138.

———. 2006. Introduction: The MIRAB model in the twenty-first century. *Asia Pacific Viewpoint* 47(1): 1–13.

Blair, C. 2008. Judge won't stop Aloha Airlines closure. *Pacific Business News* (Honolulu), March 31.

Britton, S. G. 1982. The political economy of tourism in the Third World. *Annals of Tourism Research* 9(1): 331–358.

Britton, S. G., and C. C. Kissling. 1984. Aviation and development constraints in South Pacific microstates. In *Transport and communication in Pacific microstates: Issues in organisation and management,* ed. C. C. Kissling, 79–96. Suva: The Institute of Pacific Studies of the University of the South Pacific.

Butler, M. 2004. *Worldwide cruise ship activity.* Madrid: World Tourism Organization.

Church, J., N. White, and J. Hunter. 2006. Sea-level rise at tropical Pacific and Indian Ocean islands. *Global and Planetary Change* 53(3): 155–168.

Cleverdon, R. 2004. *Vanuatu investment profile.* Proinvest Profit in the Pacific Program. Brussels: European Union.

Cleverdon, R., S. Milne, and H. Goodwin. 2003. *Pacific Regional Tourism Development Programme final evaluation,* Project Number: 7.Acp.Rpr.787/8.Acp.Rpa.13. Brussels: European Union.

Connell, J., and B. Rugendyke. 2008. Tourism and local people in the Asia-Pacific region. In *Villages and visitors in the Asia Pacific,* ed. J. Connell and B. Rugendyke, 1–40: London: Routledge.

Craig-Smith, S. 2005. Tourism education in Oceania. In *Oceania: A tourism handbook,* ed. C. Cooper and C. M. Hall, 362–379. Clevedon: Channel View Publications.

Craig-Smith, S., and M. Fagence. 1994. A critique of tourism planning in the Pacific. *Progress in Tourism, Recreation and Hospitality Management* 6: 92–110.

de Burlo, C. 1989. Land alienation, land tenure, and tourism in Vanuatu. *Geojournal* 19(3): 317–321.

d'Hauteserre, A. M. 2004. Postcolonialism, colonialism, and tourism. In *A Companion to Tourism,* ed. A. Lew, C. M. Hall, and A. Williams, 235–245. Oxford: Blackwell.

———. 2005. Customary practices and tourism development in the French Pacific. In *Oceania: A tourism handbook,* ed. C. Cooper and C. M. Hall, 308–320. Clevedon: Channel View Publications.

Doorne, S. 2004. *Community integrated tourism development in the South Pacific,* Working Paper (JICA). Suva: University of the South Pacific.

Douglas, N., and N. Douglas. 2006. Paradise and other ports of call: Cruising in the Pacific Islands. In *Cruise ship tourism,* ed. R. Dowling, 184–194. Wallingford: CABI.

Duval, D. 2005. Tourism and air transport in Oceania. In *Oceania: A tourism handbook,* ed. C. Cooper and C. M. Hall, 321–334. Clevedon: Channel View Publications.

EC (European Commission). 2006. *Evaluation of the Vanuatu tourism education and training project (VATET),* 9.ACP.VA.11 Loc No: 2006/128536 Framework Contract Beneficiaries—Lot 9. Brussels: European Commission.

Fagence, M. 1995. Changing paradigms of orthodoxy: The case of spatial models in tourism planning. *Les Cahiers du Tourisme.* Aix-en-Provence: Centre Des Hautes Etudes Touristiques.

———. 1999. Tourism. In *The Pacific Islands: Environment & society,* ed. M. Rapaport, 394–403. Honolulu: Bess Press.

Gay, D. 2007. *Diagnostic trade integration study (DTIS)—Vanuatu.* New York/Vila: UNDP.

———. 2008. *Diagnostic trade integration study (DTIS)—Solomon Islands.* New York/Vila: UNDP.

Government of Tuvalu. 2008. Funafuti Conservation Area. www.timelesstuvalu.com.

Guldberg, H., and A. Timmerman. 2000. *Pacific in peril: Biological, economic and social impacts of climate change on Pacific coral reefs.* London: Greenpeace.

Harkness, L. 2001. Recent economic developments in the Kingdom of Tonga. *Pacific Economic Bulletin* 16(1): 19–43.

Harrison, D. 2004. Tourism in Pacific islands. *The Journal of Pacific Studies* 26(1/2): 1–28.

Hasse, J., and S. Milne. 2005. Participatory approaches and geographical information systems (PAGIS) in tourism planning. *Tourism Geographies* 7(3): 272–289.

Holden, P., M. Bale, and S. Holden. 2004. *Swimming against the tide? An assessment of the private sector in the Pacific.* Manila: Asian Development Bank.

Levett, R., and R. McNally. 2003. *A strategic assessment of Fiji's tourism development plan.* Suva: World Wildlife Fund.

Levinson, J., and S. Milne. 2004. From brochures to the internet: Tourism, marketing & development in the Cook Islands. *Journal of Pacific Studies* 26(1/2): 175–198.

Loader, B. D., B. Hague, and D. Eagle. 2000. Embedding the net. In *Community informatics: Enabling community uses of information and communications technology,* ed. M. Gurstein, 81–103. Hershey, Pa.: Idea Group Publishing.

Mason, D., and S. Milne. 2006. Generating agri-tourism options in the Caribbean: A cost effective model. In *Caribbean tourism: More than sun, sand and sea,* ed. C. Jayawardena, 61–75. Kingston, Jamaica: Ian Randle Publishers.

Milne, S. 1992a. Tourism and development in South Pacific microstates. *Annals of Tourism Research* 19(2): 191–212.

———. 1992b. Tourism development in Niue. *Annals of Tourism Research* 19(3): 565–569.

———. 1996. Travel distribution technologies and the marketing of Pacific microstates. In *Pacific tourism,* ed. C. M. Hall and S. Page, 109–129. London: Thomson International Press.

———. 1997. Tourism, dependency and South Pacific microstates, beyond the vicious cycle? In *Island tourism, trends and prospects,* ed. D. G. Lockhart and D. Drakakis-Smith, 281–301. London: Pinter.

———. 2004a. *National tourism investment profile: Niue.* Proinvest Profit in the Pacific Program. Brussels: European Union.

———. 2004b. *National tourism investment profile: Tonga.* Proinvest Profit in the Pacific Program. Brussels: European Union.

———. 2004c. *National tourism investment profile: Samoa.* Proinvest Profit in the Pacific Program. Brussels: European Union.

———. 2005a. *The training needs of South Pacific tourism small and medium enterprise owners & managers—2005.* Suva: South Pacific Tourism Organisation.

———. 2005b. *The economic impact of tourism in SPTO member nations.* Suva: South Pacific Tourism Organisation.

———. 2006. *Review of the SPTO South and Central Pacific Regional Tourism Strategy.* 2003–2013 EU REIP 5.1. Suva: South Pacific Tourism Organisation.

Milne, S., and I. Ateljevic. 2001. Tourism, economic development and the global-local nexus: Theory embracing complexity. *Tourism Geographies* 3(4): 369–393.

Milne, S., V. Clark, U. Speidel, C. Nodder, and N. Dobbin. 2008. Information technology & tourism enterprise collaboration: Cases from rural New Zealand. In *Handbook of research on electronic collaboration & organizational synergy,* ed. J. Salmon and L. Wilson, 651–663. Hershey, Pa.: IGI Publishing.

Milne, S., D. Mason, and J. Hasse. 2004. Tourism, information technology and development: Revolution or reinforcement? In *A companion to tourism geography,* ed. C. M. Hall, A. Lew, and A. Williams, 184–195. Oxford: Blackwell.

Mimura, N. 1999. Vulnerability of island countries in the South Pacific to sea level rise and climate change. *Climate Research* 12: 137–143.

Pene, C., and S. Doorne. 2004. GIS as a planning support tool for community integrated tourism development. *Pacific Islands GIS & RS News,* November 2004: 14–15.

Rao, M. 2002. Challenges and issues for tourism in the South Pacific island states: The case of the Fiji islands. *Tourism Economics* 8(4): 401–429.

Richards, G. 2002. Gastronomy: An essential ingredient in tourism production and consumption. In *Tourism and Gastronomy,* ed. A. Hjalager and G. Richards, 1–20. London: Routledge.

Scheyvens, R. 2008. On the beach: Small scale tourism in Samoa. In *Villages and visitors in the Asia Pacific,* ed. J. Connell and B. Rugendyke, 131–147. London: Routledge.

Segal, D. 2007. Airline closure hurts visitors from Canada. *Honolulu Star-Bulletin,* March 28.

Shenon, P. 1995. Tahiti's antinuclear protests turn violent. *New York Times,* September 8.

Slatter, C. 2006. *The con/dominion of Vanuatu: Paying the price of investment & land liberalisation—a case study of the Vanuatu tourism industry.* Wellington: Oxfam.

SPREP (South Pacific Region Environmental Program). 2008. *Pollution,* available at www.sidsnet.org/pacific/sprep/topic/pollution.

SPTO (South Pacific Tourism Organisation). 2003a. *Regional tourism strategy for the South and Central Pacific—2003–2013.* Suva: South Pacific Tourism Organisation.

———. 2003b. *South and Central Pacific cruise shipping.* Suva: South Pacific Tourism Organisation.

Taumoepeau, S. 2008. South Pacific. In *Aviation and tourism—implications for leisure travel,* ed. A. Graham, A. Papatheodorou, and P. Forsyth, 323–331. Aldershot: Ashgate.

Torres, R., and J. H. Momsen. 2004. Challenges and potential for linking tourism and agriculture to achieve pro-poor tourism objectives. *Progress in Development Studies* 4(4): 294–318.

Treloar, P., and C. M. Hall. 2005a. Introduction to the Pacific. In *Oceania: A tourism handbook,* ed. C. Cooper and C. M. Hall, 165–172. Clevedon: Channel View Publications.

———. 2005b. The Federated States of Micronesia. In *Oceania: A tourism handbook,* ed. C. Cooper and C. M. Hall, 184–190. Clevedon: Channel View Publications.

———. 2005c. New Caledonia. In *Oceania: A tourism handbook,* ed. C. Cooper and C. M. Hall, 225–228. Clevedon: Channel View Publications.

TRIP Consultants. 2007. *South Pacific action strategy in green tourism.* Suva: South Pacific Tourism Organisation.

UNESCAP. 2008. *Economic and social survey of Asia and the Pacific: Sustainable growth and sharing prosperity.* New York: United Nations.

Wilkinson, P. 1989. Strategies for tourism in microstates. *Annals of Tourism Research* 16(2): 153–177.

World Bank. 2005. *Regional engagement framework for Pacific Islands.* World Bank Report No. 32261-EAP. Washington, D.C.: World Bank.

Yamashita, S. 2003. *Bali and beyond, explorations in the anthropology of tourism.* Oxford: Berghahn Books.

Communications

Michael R. Ogden

33

Economic development, trade, delivery of education and health services and general improvement in the quality of life of Pacific islanders are all based on the infrastructure required to communicate.

—GREG URWIN, SECRETARY GENERAL, PACIFIC ISLANDS FORUM SECRETARIAT, 2007

Despite the incredible diversity among Pacific Island countries and territories (PICTs), most gained their political independence, or right to self-governance, prior to the development of modern telecommunication satellites, fiber-optic cables, cellular telephony, or Internet-based information and communication technologies (ICTs). Yet the past few decades have borne witness to the global transformative capabilities of telecoms/ICTs.[1] This is just as true for PICTs as for any other country in the world. It is therefore not surprising that the establishment of communications infrastructure in the Pacific Islands has been a priority for many decades (cf. Ogden & Jussawalla 1994; SPFS 1998; ITU 2001; PIFS 2002a, 2005). The result is that most PICTs now have access to a comprehensive range of communication services, including broadcast radio and television, fixed line and cellular mobile telephony, and more recently, Internet services. Thus,

> [on] the streets of Port Moresby and Kokopo today, sellers of prepaid mobile phone cards compete for space with betel nut sellers while the betel nut sellers order fresh supplies on their new, cheap mobile phones. In cafes in central Suva and Apia, students research papers and apply for jobs through broadband wireless Internet; people of all ages call their relatives overseas via the Internet. Most importantly, there is growing awareness among the region's leaders, business community, and the public at large of the potential benefits of more affordable, reliable and accessible telecoms/information and communications technologies (ICT) infrastructure and services and its [sic] contribution to economic and social development. (World Bank 2008: 2)

Although great strides have been made to bridge the "access gap," the buildout of telecom/ICT infrastructures in the region remains inadequate (especially for broadband services) while pent-up demand is high. This "digital divide"[2] has become problematic for the majority of Pacific Islanders living in rural areas and outer islands where the processes of communication remain costly, inefficient, and uncertain (AusAID 2008; Spenemann 2004; Ogden 1995). "While many rural people lack a more efficient means to communicate, they also lack access to information—on market conditions, government policies, healthcare, education, business opportunities—compounding their isolation" (World Bank 2008: 2), exacerbating urban-rural disparities. Recognizing the uneven distribution and access issues that have plagued Pacific Islands communications development efforts, the Pacific Islands Forum member countries have set an ambitious goal: "ICTs for every Pacific Islander" (PIFS 2002b). The objective is that by connecting people and places, telecoms/ICTs can play a vital role as key enablers in national, regional, and global development. Challenges of scale, institutional capacity, and isolation notwithstanding, Pacific Island leaders are committed and believe telecoms/ICTs hold enormous promise for the future.

From Slit Gongs to Satellites

Precontact indigenous communication systems were primarily oral and limited by the proximity and mobility of islander populations. Oratory, chant, storytelling, and gossip were, however, augmented by carved wooden drums (Figure 33.1) or wind instruments used

Figure 33.1. *Fijian slit gong or* lali *(photo MO).*

to announce ceremonial activities and regulate daily routine. European and American missionaries introduced Western-style "mass" media into these indigenous communication micronetworks in the early 1800s. Increasing European activity in the mid-1800s also led colonial administrations into the publishing business, while commercial media appeared with the influx of colonists and merchant capital during the 1870s.

Early Developments in Communication

From the arrival of the missionaries, exchanging letters with home was the only means of staying in touch with the world. Letters were most often sent collect and took months to be delivered, while incoming mail was even less reliable. In 1874, with postal services established in most Pacific Island colonies and the proliferation of steamship routes enhancing international mail services, the Universal Postal Union was formed. The basic treaty, the Universal Postal Convention, regulated the exchange of international mail and has been carefully tended and modified as circumstances warranted (Sinclair 1984), up to the present.

The first reliable electronic communication links across the Pacific were undersea telegraphic cables. The Pacific cable, completed October 31, 1902 (Figure 33.2), connected Asia and Australia/New Zealand with North America and "island-hopped" its way across the Pacific, making landfall at only a few geographically strategic colonial centers (Fanning in the Line Islands, Fiji, and Norfolk Island). In 1903–1904, a second Pacific telegraph cable connected

the United States with the Philippines, China, and Japan—it too "island-hopped" from the Philippines to Guam, Midway, and Hawai'i before making landfall in San Francisco (Burns 2008). Outside of important administrative or business communications, however, the international postal system remained the main mechanism of overseas communications for many years.

The first radiotelegraph connection inaugurated across the Pacific was between San Francisco and Hawai'i in 1912. But the real watershed of telecommunications services in the Pacific occurred in the late 1920s with the widespread propagation of high-frequency (HF) radio technology. By 1927, Australia was connecting with England by HF radio links via Fiji and Canada. Likewise, New Zealand established a radiotelegraph connection with its colonial offices in Apia 1927; the service was extended to Rarotonga by 1930. Indeed, until the Japanese bombing of Pearl Harbor in 1941, a large and growing network of HF radiotelegraph communications was expanding hand-in-hand with the newfound strategic and political importance of the Pacific Island territories (Figure 33.2).

Soon after World War II, "push-to-talk" HF radiotelephone links quickly became the most economical means of maintaining contact with metropolitan governments, colonial administrations, and provincial offices (Davey 1984). Yet despite these improvements, few outer islands or rural villages had access to such technology. Most Pacific Islanders still relied on the postal service or negotiated delivery of handwritten notes with passing vehicles or boats to relatives in urban centers, and vice versa.

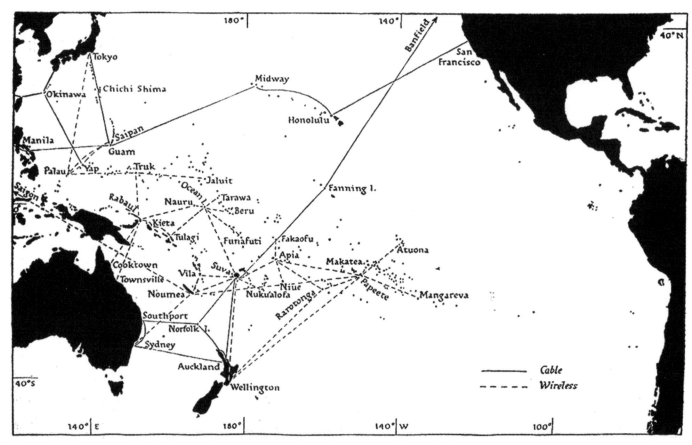

Figure 33.2. Telegraph and HF radio ("wireless") communications, circa 1939. Source: Pacific Islands [Geographical Handbook Series]. Great Britain Admiralty, Naval Intelligence Division, 1943–1945. Retrieved September 11, 2008, from http://www.lib.utexas.edu/maps/historical/pacific_islands_1943_1945.html.

Modern Communication Developments

HAW-1 became the first undersea telephone cable in the Pacific in 1957—linking Hawai'i with the west coast of the United States—but it was not until the 1960s that transoceanic telephone cables (COMPAC in 1963 and SEACOM-2 in 1964) connected North America with Asia, Australia, and New Zealand. Following historical precedents, only the islands along the routing path of the undersea cables were fortunate enough to have land-based relay stations; namely, Hawai'i, Guam, Fiji, and Papua New Guinea. Not

until the 1990s—with advancements in fiber optics—did changes in the deployment and routing of undersea cables benefit other PICTs (Table 33.1).

The first geosynchronous satellite to be placed into commercial service was INTELSAT's "Early Bird" (Intelsat I, 1965), with a total traffic capacity of 240 telephone circuits or one television transmission. From this humble beginning to the present, a proliferation of satellites (each subsequent generation having far greater capacity and longer operational life than its predecessor) was being put into service for global communications.

Table 33.1

Trans-Pacific Communication Cables

Cable system	Short name	In-service	Use	Capacity Gb/sec.	Length (km)	Routing
Hontua Tahiti–Hawai'i	Hontua	2010	Future	320	4650	Tahiti, French Polynesia, HI
Pacific Rim Cable Hawai'i–Am. Samoa	HAS	2009	Future	.56	3701	HI, Am. Samoa (PacRim East redeployed)
Pipe–Pacific Cable 1	PPC-1	2009	Future	1920	6900	Australia, Guam
Telstra Sydney–Hawai'i Cable		2008	Future	1260	9000	Sydney, Australia, HI
East Asia Crossing	EAC	2008	Future	2560	2558	Philippines, Guam
Asia–America Gateway	AAG	2008	Future	1280	20000	SE Asia, Philippines, Guam, HI, CA
Gondwana I		2008	In use	20	2200	Australia New Caledonia (incl. Loyalty Is.)
Australia–Papua New Guinea 2	APNG-2	2006	In use	0.56	1800	Australia, PNG (PacRim West redeployed)
VSNL Pacific	VSNL-Transpac	2003	In use	5120	24192	Japan, Guam, HI, OR, CA
Japan–US Cable	Japan-US	2001	In use	640	21000	Japan, HI, CA
Southern Cross Cable Network	Southern Cross	2001 2008	In use upgrade	480 +860	30500	Australia, New Zealand, CA, OR, HI, Fiji
Australia–Japan Cable	AJC	2000 2008	In use upgrade	640 +120	12700	Australia, Guam, Japan
China–US Cable Network	CUCN	2000	In use	80	30000	CA, OR, Guam, Japan, Korea, Taiwan, China
Guam–Philippines	G-P	1999	In use	20	3600	Guam, Philippines
MTC Mariana–Guam Cable	MTC	1997	In use	3732	240	Guam, N. Marianas (Rota, Tinian, Saipan)
Palau Interisland System	PII	1996	In use	5?	200?	Palau (domestic)
Trans-Pacific Cable #5	TPC-5	1996	In use	10	24593	OR, CA, HI, Guam, Japan
Pacific Rim West Cable	PacRim West	1995	Reused	0.56	7062	Australia, Guam
Pacific Rim East Cable	PacRim East	1995	Reused	0.56	7855	HI, New Zealand
Tasman 2		1995	In use	1	2195	Australia, New Zealand
Micronesian Interisland System	MIC	1993	In use	0.622	240	Guam, Marianas (Rota, Tinian, Saipan)
Marshall Islands Inter-Island		1992	In use	14.4	232	Kwajalein, Marshall Is. (domestic)

Sources: UNESCAP 2008, Appendix A; World Bank 2008.

Early on, satellites put into orbit over the Pacific Ocean facilitated greater communications, providing robust and flexible coverage for the entire Pacific hemisphere; something earlier undersea cable efforts could not match. It was not until 1976, however, when smaller and thus cheaper earth stations were allowed access to the global satellite network—and at reduced rates—that PICTs saw much benefit from satellite communications (Figure 33.3). As a result, PICTs initiated the phased introduction of satellite operations using the smaller (and cheaper) Intelsat Standard B configuration. In 1984, Kiribati was the last Pacific Islands country to be provided with a Standard B earth station, while even smaller earth stations (Standard D and F) brought affordable satellite communications to even the smallest

and most remote of PICTs by the beginning of the twenty-first century (Table 33.2).

Whereas satellite coverage for PICTs is essentially complete for C-band-based telecommunications, it has not, however, turned out to be the hoped-for communications panacea. C-band has a relatively low bandwidth, thus making communication services slow and expensive compared to modern alternatives (e.g., Ku/Ka-Bands or fiber-optic cable). This has proven to be a significant handicap. An "information society" demands bandwidth—lots of it! It is anticipated that international bandwidth capacity will need to increase substantially over the next few years, driven primarily by greater Internet use. Projections indicate that in most PICTs the potential demand for international bandwidth will increase

Table 33.2

Satellite Communications Infrastructure

Country/ territory	Stations		Satellite provider	Installation/operator
	Dom	Int'l		
American Samoa	1	1	Intelsat New Skies	Standard A (Pago Pago) *Operator:* Am. Samoa Telecommunications Authority (statutory corp., limited competition).
Cook Islands	10	1	Intelsat New Skies	Standard B (Rarotonga), 10 Standard F3 (domestic); 1 USPNet* 4.6-meter downlink. *Operator:* Telecom Cook Is., Ltd. (joint venture; 40% govt. & 60% Telecom NZ, monopoly).
Federated States of Micronesia (FSM)	4	1	Intelsat	Standard A (Pohnpei); Standard B (Chuuk, Kosrae & Yap) & Standard F1 (Ulithi). *Operator:* FSM Telecom Corporation (statutory corporation, monopoly).
Fiji	287?	1	Intelsat	Standard A (Suva); 11-meter VSAT hub (Yaqara) for VT SAT network (Telecom Fiji, domestic); USPNet 7.6-meter Hub up/downlink. *Operator:* Fintel (private; 49% Cable & Wireless & 51% govt. holding co., monopoly).
French Polynesia	41	1	Intelsat New Skies	Standard A; Polysat domestic VSAT system; Ku-band Tahiti Nui Satellite (direct to home) Internet & TV to all 118 islands. *Operator:* Office des Postes et Télécommunications de Polynésie Française (statutory corporation, limited competition).
Guam	—	2	Intelsat	Standard A *Operator:* GTA TeleGuam (private, TeleGuam Holdings LLC, full competition).
Kiribati	na	2	Intelsat	Standard B Intelsat DAMA (Bairiki & Kiritimati); USPNet 4.6-meter downlink (Tarawa). *Operator:* Telecom Services Kiribati, Ltd. (corporatized, monopoly).
Marshall Islands	na	2	Intelsat New Skies	Standard A (Majuro), Standard F3 (Ebeye); USPNet 4.6-meter downlink. *Operator:* Marshall Is. Telecom Authority (private; 25% govt. & 75% private citizens, monopoly).
Nauru	—	1	Intelsat	Standard B (Yaren District); USPNet 4.6-meter downlink. *Operator:* Department of Communications (government monopoly).
New Caledonia	1	4	Intelsat Panamsat[†] Teleglobe	Standard A (Noumea, 1 at Goro Nickel mine); 1 domestic Ku Band VSAT (Petit Borendi). *Operator:* Office des Postes et Télécommunications de Nouvelle-Calédonie (government agency, monopoly).
Niue	—	1	Intelsat	Standard B (Alofi, or F2, variously reported); USPNet 4.6-meter downlink. *Operator:* Telecom Niue (corporatized, monopoly).

Country/ territory	Stations		Satellite provider	Installation/operator
	Dom	Int'l		
Northern Marianas, Commonwealth of	—	2	Intelsat	Standard B (Saipan & Tinian); F1 Vista for N. Marianas College (non-common carrier). *Operator:* Micronesian Telecoms Corporation, owned by Prospector Holdings (Philippines) & DBA Pacific Telecommunications, Inc. (private, full competition).
Palau, Republic of	—	2	Intelsat Telstar	Standard B (Koror, or Standard A, variously reported); Standard F1 (Koror, Internet). *Operator:* Palau National Communications Corp. (statutory corporation, monopoly).
Papua New Guinea	27	3	Intelsat Aussat Asiasat Palapa	Standard A (Port Moresby), 7-meter Optus antennas (Port Moresby & Lae); 11-meter DOMSAT hub (Port Moresby) & 26 remote terminals; 21 VSAT nodes in academic/research PNGARNET, hub in Hong Kong. *Operator:* Telecom PNG, Ltd. (corporatized, monopoly).
Pitcairn Islands	—	1	Inmarsat	Small Radome for Planet 1 Inmarsat Mini-M satellite system, international relay via British Telecom earth station in New Zealand, telephony & limited Internet. *Operator:* Pitcairn Island Administration (government monopoly).
Samoa	—	2	Intelsat New Skies	Standard A (Apia), Standard F1 (Apia, Internet); USPNet 6-meter Mini-Hub up/downlink. *Operator:* SamoaTel (private; 40% government, 27.5% National Bank Provident Fund, 22.5% Bank of Samoa, 10% Samoa Life Insurance, monopoly).
Solomon Islands	6	1	Intelsat New Skies Panamsat†	Standard B (Honiara); Standard F3 Domsat hub (Honiara), Standard F2 (Gizo & Auki); Standard F1 (Taro, Munda & Auki); USPNet 4.6-meter downlink. *Operator:* Solomon Telecom Company (private; 51% Solomon Provident Fund, 41.9% Cable & Wireless, 7.1% Investment Corp. of Solomon Is., monopoly).
Tokelau	—	3	Intelsat	Standard F1 (Fakaofo, Nukunonu & Atafa) DAMA Net, Telstra Hub in Aust., telephone & Internet (2003); USPNet 4.6-meter downlink. *Operator:* TeleTok, Telecommunications Tokelau Corporation (statutory corp., monopoly).
Tonga	5	1	Intelsat	Standard A (Tongatapu, or Standard B, variously reported); Domsat network, 3 Intelsat IDR, 2 smaller centers using Intelsat; USPNet 4.6-meter downlink. *Operator:* Tonga Communications Corporation (corporatized, monopoly).
Tuvalu	8	1	Intelsat New Skies	Standard F3 (Funafuti), Standard F1 (8 other islands, domestic); USPNet 4.6-meter downlink. *Operator:* Tuvalu Communications Corp. (statutory corporation, monopoly).
Vanuatu	na	2	Intelsat New Skies	Standard A (Port Vila); Standard F2 (Port Vila, Internet); reportedly using Yaqara, Fiji VSAT hub for rural/remote connectivity; USPNet 4.6-meter mini-hub up/downlink. *Operator:* Telecom Vanuatu, Ltd. (private; 34% government, 33% Cable & Wireless, 33% France Cable & Radio, monopoly).
Wallis & Futuna	—	1	Intelsat? New Skies?	Standard F1, 3.7-meter VSAT terminal (Wallis). *Operator:* Service Des Postes et Télécommunications (& France Cable & Radio, monopoly).

Sources: UNESCAP 2008, Appendix A; World Bank 2008; CIA 2008; World Bank 2006b; PIFS 2002a.

* USPNet is a closed satellite network used exclusively by the University of the South Pacific (USP) for distance education. The network consists of twelve earth stations, one for each USP Campus or Center.

† In 2006, Intelsat acquired Panamsat for US$6.4 billion, making Panamsat a wholly owned subsidiary and Intelsat the largest provider of fixed satellite services worldwide.

Figure 33.3. Satellite earth station, Majuro, Republic of the Marshall Islands (photo MO).

between 50 and 200 percent over the next five years, representing a huge cost burden (Network Strategies 2007). Unfortunately, "the recent revolution in cost-effective satellite broadband, coupled with great improvements in terminal performance/cost, has not yet substantially benefited the Pacific" (UNESCAP 2008: 4).

The newest generations of fiber-optic undersea cables can deliver large amounts of bandwidth at nearly the speed of light. Unfortunately, they remain primarily an expensive, high-traffic, point-to-point solution ill-suited to the small and dispersed populations of PICTs. As first-generation trans-Pacific fiber-optic cables installed in the mid-1990s became overburdened, however, newer and higher-capacity cables were installed to replace them. Such "retirements" occurred long before the cables were technically unserviceable, thus presenting an unexpected opportunity for PICTs (UNESCAP 2008). Beginning in 2006, several "dark" cables were redeployed to meet the demand for higher bandwidth in the Pacific Islands. Thus a portion of the former PacRim East cable was used to interconnect Australia and Papua New Guinea (Table 33.1). Likewise, the redeployment of PacRim West connected Hawai'i with American Samoa in 2009. Furthermore, several undersea cable projects using cheaper, state-of-the-art fiber optics are also either under way or under consideration (Table 33.1). But despite these developments—and given the distances involved and the comparatively low traffic volumes within PICTs—the costs and benefits of any new undersea cable infrastructure require careful consideration (World Bank 2008).

Developing a Pacific Information Society

For governments and regional policy makers in PICTs, understanding how telecoms/ICTs—including their pervasiveness, connectivity, and utilization—can further economic and social development has become a primary focus of attention (PIFS 2005, 2006). An examination of select telecom/ICT capability indicators as determined by the ITU (ITU 2007b) provides a "snapshot" (Table 33.3) of the pervasiveness and connectivity of telephone subscribers (both fixed and mobile) and telephone densities (number of telephones per 100 population) for twenty-two PICTs. Whereas these indicators have greatly improved since the mid-1990s, when only two Pacific Island nations exceeded 20 percent telephone penetration with a regional average of only 2.1 percent (ITU 1993; Cutler 1994; Ogden and Jussawalla 1994), telephone penetration rates still remain low (ITU 2007a). Presently, only six of the twenty-two PICTs exceed 20 percent fixed-line telephone penetration (nine for mobile), while—surprisingly—the average for the entire Pacific Islands region increased nearly tenfold (18.26 percent for fixed, 24.07 percent for mobile). But these aggregate numbers belie regional disparities. Papua New Guinea, with the largest population and greatest land area, has the lowest fixed-line teledensity at just below 1 percent, while Niue, a single-island nation with one of the smallest populations, has the highest fixed-line teledensity with more than 57 percent.

Furthermore, although PICT urban teledensities range from about 20 to 60 percent (still low by global standards), when household sizes and social patterns are taken into consideration, nearly every urban resident has access to telecommunication services. Rural teledensities, though, range from one-half to one-tenth of those in urban areas (PIFS 2003). In response, most governments have put into place policies and targets to extend at least "basic" services to rural and remote locations. Domestic and interisland connectivity is gradually improving in some countries (notably Fiji, Samoa, Vanuatu, and Tonga) as operators seek to increase their capacity by upgrading microwave links and even rolling out fiber-optic cables. Still, network capacity is generally considered to be inadequate to meet present—let alone future—demand (World Bank 2008).

Mobile cellular telephones are now a common sight in urban centers throughout the Pacific, more so now because of the conversion of first-generation analog systems to GSM[3] networks. Efforts are also under way to introduce higher-speed "third generation" (3G) and 3G+ mobile broadband services. According to the World Bank (2008), since its introduction in the early 1990s, mobile cellular telephony has seen rapid growth, particularly in countries that permit competition (Figure 33.4).

Mobile cellular systems have likewise extended phone services beyond the reach of the traditional fixed-line telephone system (Kami 2005), and the introduction of prepaid cellular has resulted in mobile subscribers now exceeding the number of fixed-line subscribers in nearly half of the PICTs (Table 33.3). Rural and outer islands' mobile cellular services are still a challenge despite improvements in technology. Yet innovative approaches to mobile telephone connectivity in rural and outer island areas are being deployed. The Republic of Nauru recently implemented a hybrid network that provides local and international voice and data services at broadband speeds (Oceanic Broadband Solutions 2008). In Wallis and Futuna, an overseas territory of France, the installation of a turnkey high-speed Internet and voice-over-IP service provides connectivity for ten thousand residents and businesses on the island. Prepaid, Bluetooth-enabled WiFi phones are rented at

Table 33.3

Pacific Islands Fixed-Line and Mobile Telephones 2007[1]

Country/territory	Main (fixed) telephone lines		Mobile cellular telephones	
	Total subscribers	*Per 100 inhabitants*	*Total subscribers*	*Per 100 inhabitants*
American Samoa	10,400	16.70	2,200	3.63
Cook Islands[2] (2002)	6,200	50.00	1,500	12.00
FSM	8,700	7.83	27,400	24.69
Fiji	108,400	12.92	437,000	52.10
French Polynesia	53,600	20.65	174,800	66.54
Guam	65,500	40.45	98,000	59.39
Kiribati	4,000	4.30	700	0.75
Marshall Islands	4,500	8.27	700	0.86
Nauru[2] (2002)	1,900	16.52	1,500	13.04
New Caledonia	60,200	24.91	176,400	72.96
Niue[2] (2002)	1,100	57.89	400	21.05
Northern Marianas[2] (2000)	21,000	30.33	20,500[1]	27.301
Palau, Republic of[2] (2002)	6,700	34.89	1,000	5.20
Papua New Guinea	60,000	0.95	300,000	4.74
Pitcairn Islands[2] (2004)	1*	2.12	—	—
Samoa	19,500	10.89	86,000	45.98
Solomon Islands	7,600	1.55	10,900	2.20
Tokelau[2] (2002)	300	20.96	—	—
Tonga	21,000	20.96	46,500	46.37
Tuvalu[2] (2005)	900	2.57	1,300	11.17
Vanuatu	8,800	3.90	26,000	11.50
Wallis & Futuna[2] (2002)	1,900	12.19	—	—

Sources: [1]ITU 2007b; [2]CIA 2008.

* Pitcairn Islands, a British overseas territory, with a total population of 47, used to have 17 telephone subscribers sharing one party line. In 2006, thanks to British government funding, all homes now have a private telephone and fast Internet connection as well as live television broadcasts.

low cost to the public while IP desk phones and company PBXs are used in the businesses and connected to the network using wireless antennas (Apex Broadband 2008).

The Internet has undoubtedly diffused faster than almost any other technical innovation in modern times, and Pacific Islanders—though relatively slow in initial adoption—have proven to be just as adroit in Internet usage as their counterparts in more developed countries. The number of Internet users (Table 33.4) is difficult to assess and compare. The most reliable metric has been the number of host computers permanently connected to the Internet. This is tracked at a global level and reported for all top-level domains (i.e., country codes). According to Internet Systems Consortium, Inc. (http://www.isc.org/), the number of global Internet domain hosts has grown from zero in 1991 to over 732.7 million as of January 2010. There is not necessarily any correlation, however, between a host's domain name and where it is actually located. This accounts for the disproportionately large number of Internet hosts reported for Niue, Tonga, Tuvalu, and Tokelau. These figures are the result of an innovative approach to the sale of the .nu, .to, .tv, and .tk domain

names (respectively) and are not an accurate reflection of Internet infrastructure in these countries. For example, Tuvalu—with perhaps one of the most exploitable domain assignments, .tv—partnered with Verisign to license its domain name. Unfortunately, revenues from the deal have fallen short of projections and failed to make a significant impact on the island (Whittle 2007).

Internet subscriber numbers listed in Table 33.4 refer to the number of dial-up, leased line and broadband Internet subscribers, while the Internet user numbers are based on nationally reported data. Although Internet usage in the Pacific is not uniform, there are some interesting surprises. Whereas only five PICTs have Internet densities greater than 20 per 100 inhabitants (the Cook Islands, French Polynesia, Guam, New Caledonia, and Niue), Niue stands out. Using funds generated by registrations of the .nu domain, the Internet Users Society–Niue, a private, nonprofit, nongovernment charitable foundation, built the world's first nationwide WiFi Internet access service, all at no cost to the public or the local government (http://www.niue.nu/). This solar-powered, free WiFi Internet service may account for an Internet user density of nearly

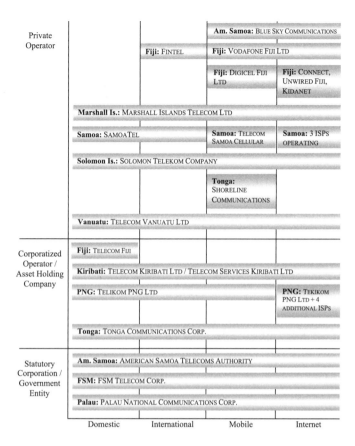

	Domestic	International	Mobile	Internet
Private Operator			**Am. Samoa:** Blue Sky Communications	
	Fiji: Fintel	**Fiji:** Vodafone Fiji Ltd		
		Fiji: Digicel Fiji Ltd	**Fiji:** Connect, Unwired Fiji, Kidanet	
	Marshall Is.: Marshall Islands Telecom Ltd			
	Samoa: Samoatel		**Samoa:** Telecom Samoa Cellular	**Samoa:** 3 ISPs operating
	Solomon Is.: Solomon Telekom Company			
			Tonga: Shoreline Communications	
	Vanuatu: Telecom Vanuatu Ltd			
Corporatized Operator / Asset Holding Company	**Fiji:** Telecom Fiji			
	Kiribati: Telecom Kiribati Ltd / Telecom Services Kiribati Ltd			
	PNG: Telikom PNG Ltd			**PNG:** Tekikom PNG Ltd + 4 additional ISPs
	Tonga: Tonga Communications Corp.			
Statutory Corporation / Government Entity	**Am. Samoa:** American Samoa Telecoms Authority			
	FSM: FSM Telecom Corp.			
	Palau: Palau National Communications Corp.			

Figure 33.4. Institutional arrangements in Pacific telecommunications, 2008. Source: World Bank (2008), UNESCAP (2008).34.5: CocoNET Wireless website.

21 per 100 inhabitants. Likewise, in Tuvalu, an Internet user density of 10.67 means that every eighth member of the population is a registered user, while in French Polynesia the rate is 28.54, or nearly one registered user for every three individuals. Outer island and rural connectivity to the Internet remains a major challenge for most PICTs. As a result, Internet access is still limited to urban and periurban areas, although some countries have flat fee dial-up access to the Internet from anywhere in the country, allowing cost-effective Internet access for some rural subscribers (Kami 2005). Reliable Internet links for rural areas beyond provincial centers, though, are still a challenge. The same can be said for most distant islands communities.

Of course, the Internet is of little use if computers are not available to access it, and computer ownership has proven to be a substantial barrier in most PICTs. In 2007, One Laptop Per Child Oceania Project (OLPC Oceania) was launched with the stated goal of providing low-cost laptops to every child in the Pacific Islands by 2015. Niue became the first nation to reach 100 percent distribution when five hundred of the little green XO laptops were distributed to primary and high school students in August 2008 (One Laptop . . . 2008). A related activity in the region includes implementation of the satellite-based Pacific Rural Internet Connectivity System (PACRICS), a project providing low-cost, reliable, and easy-to-use broadband VSAT technology that allows rural and remote Pacific Island communities to connect to the Internet. PACRICS, together with the OLPC Oceania initiative, address issues of both

Internet access and use to meet primarily educational goals—thus, "every PACRICS site is an OLPC [Oceania] Hub" (http://www.pacrics.net/). Initial participating countries include Solomon Islands, Tonga, Kiribati, Vanuatu, and Papua New Guinea; other PICTs are expected to participate later in the project's cycle. This initiative, launched at the 2007 Pacific Islands Forum Leaders meeting in Tonga, responds to a call in the *Pacific Plan Digital Strategy* by island leaders to bridge the digital and communication divide between the urban and rural and remote areas in the Pacific Islands (http://wiki.laptop.org/go/OLPC_Oceania).

The Mass Media

Historically, there have been—and continue to be—three kinds of media in the Pacific Islands: mission or church-owned or directed, government-owned or directed, and commercial (Cass 2004). A full accounting of media's development under church, state, and private-sector ownership and operation is beyond the scope of this chapter. Suffice it to say that even though circulations have been comparatively low and/or radio broadcasts geographically limited, church media have remained important given their role in preserving local languages and their historical function as the home of the Pacific's first indigenous journalists, printers, and broadcasters (Cass 2004). State-owned media emerged when the governments of the newly independent PICTs inherited media outlets established by departing colonial administrations—mostly public service broadcast (PSB) radio stations (Seward 1999). Private-sector media are generally descended from newspapers that were established during the colonial period to serve the needs of expatriate populations. Those private media companies that survived the transition to independence have, for the most part, remained in the hands of outside interests (Cass 2004).

Today, the greatest number of mainstream media outlets (newspapers, magazines, and radio and television stations) exist in countries with the largest expatriate populations. For the English-speaking Pacific (outside of Hawai'i and Guam), this is Fiji and Papua New Guinea (PNG). Small markets like the Federated States of Micronesia (FSM), Kiribati, Palau, Nauru, the Republic of the Marshall Islands (RMI), and Tuvalu have a limited range of media outlets. Even a medium-sized country like Solomon Islands has only five mainstream news-producing media sources. A notable exception, however, is Tonga. "With an estimated population of only 108,000, Tonga has 11 weekly, fortnightly [biweekly] or monthly newspapers, some of which are produced by church organisations [*sic*], one PSB service (radio and television), four commercial radio stations, one commercial television station and one pay television service" (AusAID 2005: 13).

Technologies like the fax machine dramatically increased the timely and comprehensive coverage and sharing of news throughout the region. Likewise, developments in computer technologies such as desktop publishing and e-mail further enhanced regional information flow. No doubt, increased access to telecom/ICTs has also contributed to the proliferation (or sustained existence) of the mass media in the Pacific. Today most of the major media outlets in the PICTs have their own websites serving the information needs of resident and nonresident islanders. Still, in the majority of PICTs, local news programs are largely urban sourced and produced. This

Table 33.4

Pacific Islands Internet and Broadband 2007[1]

Country/ territory	Country code	Internet hosts	Internet subscribers		Internet users		Broadband subscribers	
			Total	per 100 inhabitants	Total	per 100 inhabit.	Total	per 100 inhabit.
American Samoa	.as	1,124	na	—	na	—	na	—
Cook Islands[2]	.ck	1,479	na	—	3,600	29.33	na	—
FSM	.fm	866[3]	1,300	1.16	15,000	13.50	43	0.04
Fiji	.fj	12,592[3]	13,300	1.57	80,000	9.36	8,500	0.99
French Polynesia	.pf	14,059	25,200	9.59	75,000	28.54	23,400	8.91
Guam	.gu	37	na	—	65,000	38.46	2,700	1.56
Kiribati	.ki	41	na	—	2,000	1.81	—	—
Marshall Islands	.mh	3	700	1.29	2,200	3.48	—	—
Nauru[2]	.nr	53	—	—	300	2.17	—	—
New Caledonia	.nc	15,487[3]	21,000	8.90	80,000	33.20	20,300	8.40
Niue[2] (2002)	.nu	382,599[3]	—	—	900*	20.77	—	—
N. Marianas[2] (2003)	.mp	5	—	—	10,000	11.54	—	—
Palau, Republic of[2]	.pw	1	na	—	na	—	—	—
PNG2 (2006)	.pg	2,436	—	—	110,000	1.83	—	—
Pitcairn Is.[2] (2004)	.pn	9	—	—	—	—	—	—
Samoa[2]	.ws	11,307[3]	—	—	8,000	3.68	87	0.04
Solomon Islands	.sb	3,141	1,900	0.40	8,000	1.37	1,000	0.17
Tokelau[2]	.tk	273[3]	na	—	na [†]	—	—	—
Tonga	.to	18,653	3,700	3.11	8,400	7.05	928	0.78
Tuvalu[2]	.tv[‡]	56,209[3]	na	—	1,300	10.67	—	—
Vanuatu	.vu	1,010	1,600	0.74	17,000	7.52	1,000	0.44
Wallis & Futuna[2] (2002)	.wf	1	na	—	900	5.91	—	—

Sources [1]ITU 2007b; [2]CIA 2008; [3]ISC 2008.

*Originally a dial-up e-mail only service in 1997, Niue now enjoys nearly island-wide free WiFi services thanks to the Internet Users Society–Niue; a U.S. incorporated, private charitable foundation locally managed in Niue that uses revenue from the registration of the .nu domain to develop and fund free broadband Internet services.

[†]Tokelau has invested revenue from the sale of services using their .tk domain to fund ICT infrastructure including high-speed satellite Internet services that enable residents to stream live radio and TV content as well as use IP telephony (e.g., Skype).

[‡]In 2000, Tuvalu negotiated a 12-year deal with DotTV to sell access to Tuvalu's .tv domain. In 2002 DotTV was bought by VeriSign which partnered with Demand Media to market .tv as the preferred domain for online video sites.

is the result of a combination of factors—the use of English or French as well as limitations with distribution and/or transmission to rural areas and outer islands (AusAID 2005).

Relatively small market size, diversity of languages, relatively low rates of literacy, and difficulties in distribution (IPI 2006) have all impacted media development and practice in the region. Furthermore, in the past ten years the media in PICTs have faced a range of challenges affecting their development and operations. Internal strife, state control, and the chronic problems of poor working conditions have been some of the key issues (Harris 2004; Layton 1995). Indeed, although PICTs' respective governments give assent to Western principles of good governance—including the "watchdog" role of journalism—when a crisis erupts, island governments tend to selectively invoke "tradition" or the "Pacific Way" to criticize or even silence the media. Sensitive to such criticisms, Pacific Island journalists have not rejected the cultural norms they grew up with. Cultural mechanisms are being deliberately appropriated by island journalists—as a type of "Pacific-style journalism"—in order to protect and develop the free flow of information in their societies (Layton 1995). Despite this, "[journalists] have been threatened with physical violence, newspaper offices and television studios have been burned down or trashed by mobs, and politicians have threatened to impose regulatory control" (Harris 2004).

As a result of political and popular pressure, media councils have been established in Papua New Guinea, Solomon Islands, Fiji, and Tonga (Papoutsaki and Harris 2008). While the establishment of media councils in the region can be seen as a positive development, media practitioners have cautioned that they should remain independent of government control. Likewise, some constitutional protections for the media and freedom of expression do exist—although the scope of such protections varies considerably between PICTs (AusAID 2005). For example, "Niue is the only country that makes no reference at all to the principle of freedom of expression in its Constitution, whereas . . . [others, such as PNG and Fiji] make extensive and detailed provision for freedom of the press and the freedom of people to communicate and receive communications" (AusAID 2005: 40). Perhaps it was best said by Cass (2004: 104) when he stated in the conclusion to his article on Pacific media ownership that:

> If there is a *fa'a Pasifika,* or Pacific Way, a means of finding a way to move forward and become stronger by accommodation and adaptation, then there is also Pacific journalism. It is not yet fully developed, but its outlines are distinct and, while endangered from time to time by repressive social structures and authoritarian governments, it is strong enough to survive.

With the emergence of "Pacific-style journalism" came the development of professional regional associations. In 2007, senior journalists from media outlets across Micronesia formulated the Micronesian Media Association (MMA) to promote professional development, facilitate the exchange of regional news, and provide mutual support to members. The MMA membership includes regional newspapers, television stations, radio stations, magazines, and regional websites from the CNMI, Guam, Palau, FSM, RMI, Kiribati, and Nauru (Regional Journalists . . . 2007). The longest-running media organization, however, is the Pacific Islands News Association (PINA), a nongovernmental organization representing the majority of regional media outlets that traces its roots back to the Fiji Press Club in 1972. In November 2004, PINA and the Pacific Islands Broadcasting Association (PIBA, established in 1988) agreed to merge their organizational operations. According to the organization's website, "PINA is the main professional association of the Pacific Islands news media. It links radio and TV stations, newspapers, magazines, online services, national associations of news media practitioners and journalism schools in 23 Pacific Island countries and territories" (http://www.pinanius.com/).

Newspapers

Today, there is great variety among the print media, ranging from the fortnightly FSM not-for-profit newspaper the *Kaselehlie Press,* with two journalists and an editor, to the *PNG Post-Courier,* published five days a week, with forty-two journalists on staff (AusAID 2005). Nearly all PICTs have at least one locally published newspaper, and eleven have two or more competing papers, along with a variety of specialist periodicals. In addition, major news magazines are available: *Islands Business, Pacific Islands Monthly,* and *The Review,* published in Fiji; *PNG Business* from Papua New Guinea, and *Guam Business News* from Guam, while the magazine *Matangi*

Tonga has been distributed widely to Tongans living and working overseas, particularly in New Zealand (Cass 2004).

The biggest newspapers are dailies located in the major English-speaking markets: the *Papua New Guinea Post-Courier,* the *Fiji Times,* the *Pacific Daily News* on Guam, and Hawai'i's *Honolulu Star-Advertiser*—a merger of the two major daily newspapers, the *Honolulu Advertiser* and the *Honolulu Star-Bulletin* in June 2010—has held steady as the largest English-language newspaper in circulation in the Pacific Islands (Pacific Business News 2011). Dailies in the French territories are also sizable in regional terms: *La Dépêche de Tahiti, Les Nouvelles de Tahiti,* and *Les Nouvelles Calédonnienes* are, respectively, the largest and most notable French-language newspapers in the region.

Foreign-based media corporations own all seven major dailies in the region, and it has been argued that the major international media players are in the Pacific primarily to keep the competition out (Cass 2004). The Gannett Corporation has owned the *Pacific Daily News* on Guam since 1970, while the Victoria, British Columbia–based Black Press Ltd., through its Oahu Publications, Inc., subsidiary, owns and manages the *Honolulu Star-Advertiser*.[4] In 1986, Rupert Murdoch's News (South Pacific) Ltd. took over a majority share of the *Herald* and *Weekly Times* titles in Papua New Guinea and Fiji (respectively), and through subsequent mergers and consolidations, controlled majority shares in the *PNG Post-Courier* and The *Fiji Times* (along with Fiji's local-language weeklies *Nai Lalakai* and *Shanti Dut*). In 2010, however, Commodore Frank Bainimarama's government issued a media decree restricting foreign media ownership and forced the sale of Murdoch's controlling interest in the *Fiji Times* to the Suva-based conglomerate Motibhai (ABC News 2010). Robert Hersant's Groupe Pacifique Presse Communication has owned *Les Nouvelles Calédonnienes, Les Nouvelles de Tahiti,* and *La Dépêche de Tahiti* since the late 1980s.

Some of the best newspapers in the region, however, have been quite small. For example, in 2007, the coveted PINA Media Freedom Award went to Tavake Fusimalohi, the embattled editor of a small pro-democracy newspaper in Tonga, the *Kele'a* (3,500 monthly). Among the more vibrant of small-island presses, the Cook Islands support one daily newspaper (the former government-owned *Cook Islands News,* privatized in 1989, has a circulation of 2,000) and two weeklies with a combined circulation of 2,600 (the *Cook Islands Herald* and the *Cook Islands Independent,* both owned by the Pitt Media Group). Other microstate newspapers include the government-run weekly newspaper *Te Uekera* (2,000) in Kiribati (competing, since 2000, with the country's first independent weekly newspaper, *The Kiribati Newstar,* with a circulation of 2,000), Nauru's biweekly *Naoero Bulletin* (500 copies published in English), which contains mainly government announcements and news, and in Niue, the privately owned biweekly *Niue Star* (founded by a Niue politician, with a circulation of approximately 800). Niue is also home to the *Niue News,* a privately owned, weekly online news service (http://www.niuenews.nu/). Perhaps the smallest of island presses—with a local subscriber base of only 47—the biweekly *Pitcairn Miscellany* also sells subscriptions on its website (principally for "off-islanders"), which is updated monthly and claims more than 1,000 readers worldwide (http://www.miscellany.pn/).

Weekly newspapers are important in the regional media economy; in fact, weekly circulation is nearly twice that of dailies (excluding Hawai'i) and represents one out of three newspaper copies in the region (Layton 1992). For example, originally a private weekly paper called the *Port Vila Presse*, the *Independent* (1,000) is published weekly in English, French, and Bislama, the three main languages in Vanuatu. In Samoa, the *Savali Weekly* (500) publishes in English and Samoan, and the *Savali Samoa* (3,000 monthly) in Samoan only; although the papers are funded by the Samoan government and are distributed free, both must still compete for advertising revenue (AusAID 2005). Church and nongovernment organizations publish most of the smaller weeklies and monthlies, such as the *Ko'e Tohi Fanongonongo* in Tonga, a monthly newspaper produced by the Wesleyan Church. The Catholic Church in Kiribati publishes a monthly newspaper called *Te Itoi ni Kiribati* (2,300) in the indigenous language, while the Protestant Church in Kiribati publishes the weekly *Te Mauri* (2,500). In Tahiti, *Ve'a Porotetani* (5,000) is a monthly newspaper published by the Protestant Church of French Polynesia. Finally, the church-owned but secularly oriented Tok Pisin–language weekly *Wantok Niuspepa* (10,000) has a significant periurban and rural circulation in Papua New Guinea.

Broadcast Radio

Radio ownership is fairly standard in all of the PICTs, with most countries reporting at least one radio per family (Cass 2004). Thus, radio—predominantly broadcasting in the local languages—remains the dominant medium for receiving news, information, and entertainment in the Pacific Islands.

National PSB organizations in the Pacific Islands are uniquely placed to provide a range of programming to address a diversity of audience interests and cultural requirements. Their capacity to produce a mix of spoken-word formats and to provide access to the airwaves for government and other interest groups, and their mandate to serve all demographic and cultural groups, underscores the unique role of PSB radio stations. While commercial media can be an important source of news and information, the dominance of their music formats, combined with the need to target specific, profitable audiences, limits their public service capacity (AusAID 2005).

Almost all PICTs have maintained nearly continuous operation of at least one national PSB organization or government radio station since their initial establishment under former colonial administrations. Beginning in the late 1980s, though, there was increasing pressure from island governments for their respective PSB stations to become government-owned corporations (Seward 1999). Thus throughout the 1990s—due in large measure to contracting economies—far less funding was being allocated to government-owned media organizations. This meant that in the smaller states, PSB radio facilities almost ceased to function (Cass 2004). Stations that previously received government underwriting were forced to seek commercial advertising and sponsorship to maintain broadcasting services in an increasingly competitive market. The PSB stations in Fiji, Kiribati, Niue, PNG, Samoa, Solomon Islands, Tonga, Tuvalu, and Vanuatu all became government-owned corporations (AusAID 2005). In Nauru, Palau, and RMI, the PSB radio stations remain part of a government department, but they are starting to chafe under government program restrictions.

On the other hand, the larger media markets in the Pacific support a vibrant and competitive broadcast radio environment that provides a variety of music, entertainment, and news programs. For example, both PNG and Fiji have long radio broadcasting histories, with the first government information radio station commencing in 1933 in PNG, followed two years later by Fiji. Presently, the Fiji Broadcast Corporation, Ltd. (FBCL)—a government-owned statutory company—operates a network of six radio stations, two in each of the three major languages: Radio Fiji One and Naba Dua Ena Sere FM (Fijian), Radio Fiji Two and Radio Mirchi (Hindustani), Radio Fiji Gold and 2Day FM (English). The FBCL publishes its broadcast news online (http://www.radiofiji.com.fj) and is also considering establishing public service television (AusAID 2005). Coexisting in this rich broadcast environment are two religious radio stations and six private radio stations, five of which are owned by Communications Fiji Limited (CFL). CFL also has a popular subscription-based website (http://www.fijivillage.com) that contains news, music, and sports. French Polynesia and New Caledonia both have independent radio stations reflecting the views of indigenous nationalists, in addition to the Radio France d'Outre-mer network and commercial stations.

International and interregional broadcast news and information in English within the Pacific has been received primarily via the British Broadcasting Corporation, Voice of America, Radio Australia, and Radio New Zealand, International—although the overseas broadcasts from France are important in the French-speaking Pacific. Radio Australia, however, stands out as the most received international broadcast service (IBS), primarily because it has the strongest signal targeting the Pacific region and maintains correspondents in the islands (Ogden and Hailey 1988). It should also be noted that few Pacific Islanders possess shortwave radio receivers and therefore rely instead on the rebroadcast of IBS news and information services via local radio stations (Ogden and Hailey 1988).

Video and Television

Prior to the introduction of broadcast television, videotape technology held prominence in the Pacific Islands—perhaps softening the market for television's eventual arrival (Ogden 1993). Whereas television reception has primarily been concentrated in the urban and periurban areas, videotape systems spread rapidly throughout the Pacific Islands. Most of this expansion has been in combination with the expansion of electrification into rural and outer island areas. Furthermore, in the Cook Islands, the introduction of broadcast television actually increased the video market by 33 percent, because people purchased both television sets and VCRs (Varan 1993). The increasing availability and ubiquity of the "mom and pop" video rental shops likewise fueled video's diffusion and acceptance. Where television and/or video systems are not present in rural areas, it is more likely due to poor reception or lack of power rather than purely economic reasons (Ogden 1993).

Until the mid-1980s, only seven Pacific Island states had television services, all of them either territories of France or the United States (Bentley, Schultz, and Hermanson 1993). Likewise, high television usage also occurs in countries with close historic ties to New Zealand (Cass 2004). Outside the U.S. and French territories television developed far more slowly, but by the late 1980s the pace had substantially quickened. Improved satellite as well as terrestrial delivery systems removed impediments to the establishment of national television services; remoteness from capital cities, rugged terrain, and small, isolated rural populations were no longer proving to be barriers (Stewart, Horsfield, and Cook 1993).

In 1984, the Kingdom of Tonga initiated terrestrial transmission with two free-to-air channels. One was primarily focused on entertainment, the other was owned and operated by an interdenominational Christian organization, and both featured U.S. programming (Bentley, Hermanson, and Rao 1993). In 1986, Niue launched its free-to-air broadcast of *TV Niue* with mainly overseas, family-oriented programs and some local news content (twice a week, simulcast on radio), as well as coverage of important local events. Papua New Guinea also began television transmissions in 1986 with two licensed broadcasters, EMTV, a national free-to-air television station, and NTN (Niugini Television Network). "By 1987 both of these foreign owned [broadcasters] had commercial . . . transmissions servicing the greater Port Moresby area with approximately 8 hours of programming each day. Within the year, however, the NTN service closed down" (Thomas, Khushu, and Rutstein 1993: 10). Broadcasting in both English and Tok Pisin, EMTV's service (claiming to reach 400,000 to 500,000 viewers) now extends, by simultaneous relay, to six provincial centers, and by tape relay to another.

In 1989, Elijah Communications Ltd. launched the Cook Islands Television service in Rarotonga, broadcasting entertainment and religious programs as well as local and international news and Australia Broadcasting Corporation's Asia Pacific programs airing from 11:00 p.m. to 9:00 a.m. Unique to the Cook Islands broadcast environment, there are seven community television stations on the outer islands of Mangaia, Mauke, Mitiaro, Atiu, Manihiki, Pukapuka, and Tongareva—each owned by the respective Island Councils (AusAID 2005). Aitutaki Television, Ltd., is a separate commercial station privately owned and funded through advertising sales, telethons, and commercial sponsorship.

In 1991, both Nauru and Fiji initiated broadcast television services. Fiji One is a free-to-air broadcast service predominantly available in urban and periurban areas, whereas SKY Fiji (a pay TV service initiated in 1996) effectively gives Fiji TV 100 percent national coverage. In 2005, SKY Pacific extended this pay TV service throughout the Pacific region.

In 1992, Solomon Islands (two channels, one relays international content from Australia's Asia Pacific service, while Trinity TV broadcasts videotapes of overseas religious programs) and Vanuatu (government-owned Television Blong Vanuatu; the service has no live component nor any local content) launched their domestic television services (Thomas, Khushu, and Rutstein 1993). The Samoa Broadcasting Corporation began free-to-air broadcasting in 1993, airing predominantly foreign programming during the day, daily local news, some entertainment filmed during national days and a locally produced program called *Lali*—a TV adaptation of bulletins, birthdays, and funeral notices from radio interspersed with presenters' commentary (AusAID 2005). Kiribati was the last to begin television transmissions commencing in 2004, operated by Telecom Services Kiribati, Ltd., a government-owned statutory corporation. Currently it televises Australian Broadcasting Corporation's Asia Pacific service, CNN, and occasional local programming (AusAID 2005). Today, only the microstates of Tuvalu and Tokelau are without a broadcast television facility of some kind.

Television broadcasts are almost invariably in English or French, with some content produced in the local language(s), but the amount of purely local language material is small. Indeed, the bulk of Pacific Island television transmissions contain programming ranging from 80 to 100 percent foreign (Bentley 2002). The main providers of this programming are the United States, the United Kingdom, France, Australia, and New Zealand, but it is not unusual to see programs made in Japan, Singapore, Korea, Israel, India, Philippines, and China also on the schedule (Bentley 2002). This has, of course, raised concerns in the Pacific Islands over "indigenous" content—or rather the lack thereof. Indeed, the rapid push for TV service from "outside," along with a perceived lack of government regulatory commitment compounded by insufficient funding and inadequate training, has been blamed for constraining the potential of indigenous television production from the very beginning. The newer Pacific television stations have had time to reflect on this and have responded by emphasizing the importance of local content appropriate to the social, economic, political, and cultural interests of their countries (Molnar 1993). In fact, many Pacific Island TV stations stress their intent to produce local material. A UNESCO survey in the early 1990s, however, found local production levels averaged only about 5 to 10 percent—consisting primarily of local news, cultural or official events, and sports (Bentley 1993). A follow-up study conducted in 2002 illustrated that local television program production has not improved much, ranging from 0 to 20 percent. Only Tonga-TV and PNG's EMTV report local programming levels approaching 50 percent (Bentley 2002), and in both cases this represents either deliberate corporate planning or significant changes in company policy. One of the problems confronting those who want to make local language programs is that effective program exchanges can only be made in English or French—to take advantage of economies of scale in production, programs cannot be made in a local language if they are to be regionally shared (Cass 2004). Furthermore, foreign-made programs often have the highest ratings. It has been speculated that one reason for the incursion of Australia and New Zealand broadcasters into the Pacific Islands is due to the limited size of their own respective domestic markets and the desire to promote exports of their programming (Stewart, Horsfield, and Cook 1993).

With few exceptions, television has remained concentrated in the urban centers of the Pacific Islands. A UNESCO-sponsored study of television in the Pacific Islands, however, found that broadcast TV existed in nineteen of twenty-two PICTs surveyed (Bentley 2002). Despite the relatively small populations and limited economies of the region, many PICTs are close to a television "saturation point." The number of televisions per capita in the region range from American Samoa and New Caledonia with 1.4 persons per television set, to Solomon Islands with 174 persons per television set and a regional average of 40 persons per television set (CIA 2008)—even Tuvalu, which presently lacks television services, reportedly has more than four hundred television sets on Funafuti. With twenty-four-hour availability and with multichannel options now available, it would appear that the medium is very popular and the general public is willing to meet the costs (Bentley 2002). Concerns now being raised were perhaps best expressed in 1989 by Ratu Inoke Kubuabola, then Fiji's minister for information, broadcasting, television, and telecommunications, during his opening address at the Pacific Regional TV Meeting when he stated, "[T]he introduction of television services in the Pacific Islands will be, for most of us, a new industry. A development which I believe may have greater impact on the community than any other single development in our history." The overall extent of this impact has yet to be made fully manifest.

Pacific Islands Film

Films made on or about the Pacific Islands tend to be primarily "ethnographic" and do not of themselves constitute a "national cinema," nor do they display enough unity of purpose even to be categorized into a "regional cinema." The most obvious reason for this, of course, is that Pacific film production has, since its inception, remained something that outsiders do—despite the emergence of a small number of islanders working in the field (Douglas 1994). Furthermore, the long tradition of film production in the Pacific, which began in Hawai'i shortly after the birth of cinema itself with the 1913 production of two one-reel films (*Hawaiian Love* and *The Shark God*), has tended to be dominated by Western sensibilities of filmmaking and exotic myths of the South Seas.

The first film to be labeled a "documentary," *Moana: A Romance of the Golden Age* (1925), by Robert Flaherty, used Samoa as its locale. This film has been described as a milestone in Pacific and ethnographic film (Douglas 1994: 5). Likewise, Robert Gardner established a name for himself in the Pacific with his first feature-length ethnographic film, *Dead Birds* (1964), an evocative portrait of the Dani people of the Baliem Valley in West Papua. More recently, and along the same path blazed by Gardner, filmmakers like Dennis O'Rourke (*The Shark Callers of Kontu*, 1982; *Yap: How Did You Know We'd Like TV?* 1982; *Half Life*, 1986; *Cannibal Tours*, 1988) as well as Bob Connolly and Robin Anderson (*First Contact*, 1983; *Joe Leahy's Neighbours*, 1989; *Black Harvest*, 1992) have presented some of the strongest and most sympathetic images of the Pacific Islands (Douglas 1994). It is perhaps telling that in the "open-ended discourse" presented in the films produced by these independent filmmakers, there has been a blurring of the long-held distinction between documentary and narrative, calling attention to the act of "myth making" most Pacific films engender.

But far more typical of the film industry has been the use of Pacific Islands as backdrops and islanders as "set dressings" to embellish essentially Western narrative preoccupations. The few indigenous filmmakers in the region have never really taken up this issue, nor has any sense of a "Pacific Island genre" emerged to counterbalance the enthusiastically embraced myth of the "exotic" propagated by Hollywood.

A few feature "films"—shot on video—have been produced in Papua New Guinea, among the more notable being *Tukana: Husat i Asua?* (1984), screenplay written by Albert Toro; *Cowboy and Maria in Town* (1992); and *Tinpis Run* (1991), the first "film" directed by Albert Toro. Likewise, the Fiji National Video Centre was at one time a source of locally produced videos prior to its absorption into Fiji's national television service. More recently,

Pacific Islanders in Communication (PIC), founded in Honolulu in 1991, has made significant strides in promoting "the development of [U.S.] public broadcast programming that enhances public recognition of and appreciation for Pacific Islander history, culture, and society" (http://www.piccom.org/). For the most part, however, the main source of indigenously produced feature films about Polynesia has been New Zealand. Most of these films, like *Utu* (1983), *Ngati* (1987), and *Once Were Warriors* (1994), are dark, albeit realistic, portrayals of dispossessed Maori living on the fringes of pakeha (white) society (Howard 2006). Even the immensely popular *Whale Rider* (2002) presents itself as a refounding myth, seesawing between archetype and innocence. Hereniko points out that "the image of the Pacific Islander with multiple identities, straddling traditional and modern worlds successfully, is one that doesn't exist yet in film or video" (Hereniko 1999a: 1–2). Ginsburg supports this sentiment in her treatise on indigenous media when she observes that the analysis of indigenous films and videos should focus less on the formal qualities of the media as text and more on the cultural mediations that occur. "This requires examining how indigenous media are situated in relevant discursive fields in order to understand how this work gets positioned by those practicing it and by those in the dominant culture with some interest in it" (Ginsburg 1995: 259). Perhaps, to paraphrase Maori filmmaker Barry Barclay, director of the internationally acclaimed Maori film *Ngati* (1987), we will get to know what a Pacific Islander film is when islanders get a chance to make more films.

Likely the first feature-length film written, directed, and coproduced by a Pacific Islander is Vilsoni Hereniko's *The Land Has Eyes* (2004), set on the Polynesian island of Rotuma with Rotumans making up most of the characters in the film (Howard 2006) (Figure 33.5). The film debuted at the Sundance Film Festival in 2004 and was screened three times to sold-out audiences before going on to other prestigious film festivals around the world (http://www.thelandhaseyes.com/). Hereniko's "freshman film" eventually became the first film to be submitted by Fiji for an Academy Award. Despite the critical accolades and enthusiastic receptions the film received from film festival audiences in the West, however, it was the reactions and opinions of Hereniko's fellow Rotumans and other Pacific Islanders that mattered most. When screened on Rotuma, the residents often responded to the film with deep emotions, moved by scenes that resonated with their own experiences growing up or living on the island (Howard 2006). The film also resonated with other Pacific Islanders as well; "Polynesian moviegoers from Samoa, Hawai'i, and New Zealand . . . responded with equal enthusiasm, often thanking Vilsoni for representing 'us' [Pacific Islanders] in such a splendid manner" (Howard 2006: 88). Kaleikipio'ema Brown of the Ka'iwakiloumoku Hawaiian Cultural Center at the University of Hawai'i, cited by Howard, stated that, "You will not, in years to come, be able to carry on an intelligent conversation about indigenous filmmaking in the Pacific if you haven't seen *The Land Has Eyes*. Hereniko's 'film for Rotuma' is every bit as important as *Once Were Warriors* and *Whale Rider*. Maybe more so" (Howard 2006: 89). There is little doubt that *The Land Has Eyes* is a major critical milestone in Pacific Islanders' quest to gain control of the way they are represented in the media. After all, as Hereniko himself has stated, "cultural identity is process, not product" (Hereniko 1999b: 138), and this film is an important step in that process.

Figure 33.5. *Cinematographer Paul Atkins shoots the canoe scene with Mareko Veu for* The Land Has Eyes *(photo VH).*

"ICTs for Every Pacific Islander"

There are five main categories of online indigenous content produced within the Pacific region. Most common are news sites, including previously discussed newspapers, broadcasting companies, and online magazines, such as *Fiji Live* (http://www.fijilive.com/). Also common are portal sites and directories that attempt to provide comprehensive information on a country, such as *Planet Tonga* (http://www.planet-tonga.com/) or the more business-oriented *Papua New Guinea Tourism and Business Directory* (http://www.pngbd.com/). Many of these news, portal, and directory sites are targeted at, and supported by, the large Pacific Islander diasporas. There are also an increasing number of Pacific Island government sites, typically containing directories and official documents. Recently, a growing number of Pacific Island online retailers have also emerged on the Internet. Finally, there are regional sites, frequently hosted by intergovernmental organizations like the Secretariat of the Pacific Community (http://www.spc.int/corp/), that contain a wide range of information including documentation of development projects in many sectors and links to regional resources and contacts.

Presently, only anecdotal evidence of ICT usage patterns among Pacific Islanders exists. One survey in Solomon Islands reported that about half of the regular users of the public Internet café in Honiara used e-mail to keep in touch with friends and family abroad, about one-quarter were students looking for educational information, and one-quarter were business and professional users maintaining contacts and working collaboratively (Chand et al. 2005). For young Tokelau Islanders, the Internet opens up a whole new world. The majority use the Internet to research school projects or access information that is not in the school library, but most of the time they access social networking sites. For one young Tokelauan, "It [Bebo] means I can keep in touch with my extended family, even though I haven't met some of them" (Whittle 2007). In fact, according to *Internet World Stats* (http://www.internetworld stats.com/), Internet penetration into the Pacific Islands seems to be growing in lockstep with the increasing popularity of social networking sites. Thus, from 2000 to 2008 the Marshall Islands' Internet use increased 340 percent, FSM's Internet use increased 700 percent, and Guam's Internet use increased 1,200 percent (Noto 2008).

Still, PICTs—in their drive to embrace modern telecoms/ICTs—face a significant number of constraints. It is obvious that limited infrastructure (particularly in rural areas), the high cost of equipment and services, insufficient bandwidth, shortage of skilled ICT workforce and/or a computer-literate population, lack of awareness about the benefits of ICTs to meet development needs, lag in introducing the latest technologies, and the outdated nature or absence of sufficient regulatory frameworks at the national level (PIFS 2005) are all major barriers to increased use of ICTs. These obstacles, of course, are not confined to PICTs. The international discourse on telecoms/ICTs lists the same obstacles to ICT development in most countries of the world. The Pacific Islands, however, suffer from extremes of some of these obstacles, which must be overcome if PICTs are to realize the goal of "ICTs for every Pacific Islander" (PIFS 2002b). Affordability remains a paramount barrier, particularly for purchasing a computer. Although import taxes on computers are being eliminated and prices have fallen, the cost of an entry-level computer is still steep for most islanders. But a large and growing part of the population of the Pacific region is becoming aware of what telecoms/ICTs can do, and they know that the Internet can link them to the world. Large segments of PICTs' populations likewise have access to broadband services; they use 3G wireless cell phones and state-of-the-art computer technologies at work. Because of the isolation of the islands and their distance from major trading centers, Pacific Islanders are continually forced to find better means of communicating.

In the Wellington Declaration, promulgated at the 2006 Forum ICT ministerial meeting, PICT leaders recognized that telecoms/ICTs are not an end in themselves. Yes, they can play a key role as the basis for sustainable economic development while at the same time promoting and enhancing good governance, social cohesion, cultural enrichment, and environmental conservation (PIFS 2006). Indeed, PICTs stand to benefit enormously from the effective use of ICTs. Unfortunately, technology also has the potential to aggravate underlying inequalities that may further widen the digital divide between and within PICTs as well as with the more developed countries. Likewise, it is important for island governments and civil groups to remain vigilant in order to ensure that telecoms/ICTs do not play a corrosive role in island society but instead empower Pacific Islanders to preserve their culture. Indeed, telecoms/ICTs offer as many opportunities to erode indigenous language, traditions, and history as they do opportunities to preserve and strengthen them. As Pacific Island nations begin to overhaul and expand existing telecoms/ICTs systems and services to meet the stated goal of "ICTs for every Pacific Islander" (PIFS 2002b) and the demands of a nascent Pacific information society, it becomes even more of an imperative that inequalities do not become codified for the next generation.

NOTES

1. Much of the literature on communication technology and development makes a distinction between telecommunications technologies (primarily carrier networks; the satellites, fiber-optic, and cellular

wireless infrastructures that facilitate voice, video, and data transmissions) and ICTs (digital user services focused on Internet-based modes of communication including e-mail, World Wide Web, wikis, and blogs as well as broadband voice, data, and "converging" media services), but it must be recognized that the latter cannot easily exist without the former. Therefore, the moniker "telecoms/ICTs" is purposefully used here to highlight this symbiotic relationship and to underscore the coequal importance of both carrier networks and user services in an information society.

2. For clarity and brevity, the "digital divide" is used here to represent both the tangible and intangible manifestations of inequalities in access to information, communication infrastructure (including the traditional media), and education, and in the legal protection of information and/or communication rights at the global, regional, and/or national/local level.

3. Groupe Spéciale Mobile, anglicized to mean Global System for Mobile communications, is the most popular digital cellular standard in the world. Third-generation mobile cellular telephone standard, or 3G, supersedes GSM and enables network operators to offer users a wider range of broadband services (like high-speed Internet) while achieving greater network capacity.

4. In 1971 the *Star-Bulletin* and its share of the Hawaii Newspaper Agency were sold to the Gannett Corporation, publishers of *USA Today*. In 1993, Gannett sold the *Star-Bulletin* to Liberty Newspapers and bought its previous competitor, *The Honolulu Advertiser* (Brislin 1996). In 2001, Canada-based Black Press, Ltd., purchased the *Star-Bulletin* from Liberty Newspapers and later that year purchased the *MidWeek* newspaper, whose presses were expanded to handle production of the *Star-Bulletin*. Under the ownership of Black Press, Ltd., the *Star-Bulletin* rolled out a morning edition and a Sunday edition, beginning independent head-to-head competition against the *Advertiser* for the first time since 1962 (*About the Honolulu Star-Bulletin* 2008). In June 2010, Oahu Publications, Inc., wholly owned and administered by Black Press, Ltd., purchased the *Honolulu Advertiser* and merged the two previous daily newspaper competitors into Hawai'i's only remaining daily, the *Honolulu Star-Advertiser* (http://www.staradvertiser.com/about/Star_Advertiser_Contact_Information.html?id=95588574).

BIBLIOGRAPHY

ABC News. 2010. News Limited sells Fiji Times newspaper. Retrieved March 21, 2010, from http://www.abc.net.au/news/2010-09-15/news-limited-sells-fiji-times-newspaper/2261730. September 15.

About the Honolulu Star-Bulletin. 2008. Retrieved October 10, 2008, from http://www.starbulletin.com/about/.

Aoki, D., ed. 1994. *Moving images of the Pacific Islands: A guide to films and videos.* Occasional Paper 38. Honolulu: Center for Pacific Islands Studies.

Apex Broadband. 2008. *South Pacific Ocean–Wallis Island Chamber of Commerce.* Retrieved September 16, 2008, from http://www.tonywaters.co.uk/Wallis%20Island%20Case%20Study.pdf.

AusAID (Australian Agency for International Development). 2005. *Informing citizens: Opportunities for media and communications in the Pacific.* Canberra: Pacific Media and Communications Facility.

——. 2008. *Pacific economic survey 2008: Connecting the region.* Canberra: Commonwealth of Australia. http://www.caslon.com.au/austelecomsprofile1.htm. Retrieved August 28, 2008, from http://www.pacificsurvey.org/site/.

Bentley, J. 1993. *How local is our TV?* Pacific Islands News Association Conference, Suva, Fiji, July 10–13.

——. 2002. *Pacific Islands television report.* New York: UNESCO. Retrieved August 18, 2008, from http://portal.unesco.org/ci/en/files/8153/11858921141bentley_report.pdf/bentley_report.pdf.

Bentley, J., D. Hermanson, and V. V. Rao. 1993. *Pacific Regional television survey project: Polynesia report.* New York: UNESCO. Retrieved August 18, 2008, from http://unesdoc.unesco.org/images/0013/001377/137721eo.pdf.

Bentley, J., A. Schultz, and D. Hermanson. 1993. *Pacific regional television survey project: Micronesia report.* New York: UNESCO. Retrieved August 18, 2008, from http://unesdoc.unesco.org/images/0013/001377/137720eo.pdf.

Brislin, T. 1996. *Hawaii journalism history.* Retrieved August 20, 2008, from http://www2.hawaii.edu/~tbrislin/jourhist.html

Burns, B. 2008. *The Commercial Pacific Cable Company. History of the Atlantic cable and undersea communications.* Retrieved September 12, 2008, from http://www.atlantic-cable.com/CableCos/ComPacCable/index.htm.

Cass, P. 2004. Media ownership in the Pacific: Inherited colonial commercial model but remarkably diverse. *Pacific Journalism Review* 10(2): 82–110.

CIA (Central Intelligence Agency). 2008. *World fact book, 2008.* Washington, D.C.: Central Intelligence Agency. Retrieved August 27, 2008, from https://www.cia.gov/library/publications/the-world-factbook/index.html.

Chand, A., D. Lemming, E. Stork, A. Agassi, and R. Biliki. 2005. *The impact of ICT on rural development in Solomon Islands: The PFnet case.* Suva, Fiji: ICT Capacity Building at USP Project, University of the South Pacific. Retrieved August 20, 2008, from http://www.peoplefirst.net.sb/Downloads/PFnet_JICA_USP_Research_Final_Report.pdf.

Cutler, T. 1994. *Telecommunications: The Pacific link.* A Green Paper report for the Pacific Forum on the development of the telecommunications sector in the region. Melbourne: Cutler and Company.

Davey, G. 1984. Telecommunications development in the South Pacific region. In *Transport and communications for Pacific microstates: Issues in organization and management,* ed. C. Kissling, 15–24. Suva, Fiji: Institute of Pacific Studies, University of the South Pacific.

Douglas, N. 1994. Electric shadows in the South Seas: The Pacific Islands in films—A survey. In *Moving images of the Pacific Islands: A guide to films and videos.* Occasional Paper 38, ed. D. Aoki, 3–19. Honolulu: Center for Pacific Islands Studies.

Ginsburg, F. 1995. Mediating culture: Indigenous media, ethnographic film and the production of identity. In *Fields of vision: Essays in film studies, visual anthropology, and photography,* ed. L. Devereaux and R. Hillman, 256–291. Berkeley: University of California Press.

Harris, U.S. 2004. The role of media in reporting conflicts. Economies for Peace and Security (EPS) Policy Brief. Retrieved August 27, 2008, from http://www.epsusa.org/publications/policybriefs/harris.pdf.

Hereniko, V. 1999a. Representations of Pacific Islanders in film and video. *Documentary Box* 14: 18–20.

——. 1999b. Representations of cultural identity. In *Inside out: Literature, cultural politics, and identity in the New Pacific,* ed. V. Hereniko and R. Wilson, 137–166. New York: Rowman & Littlefield.

Howard, A. 2006. Presenting Rotuma to the world: The making of the film *The Land Has Eyes. Visual Anthropology Review* 22(1): 74–96.

IPI (International Press Institute). 2006. *World press freedom review: Overview of Australasia and Oceania.* Retrieved September 4, 2008, from http://www.freemedia.at/cms/ipi/freedom_detail.html?ctxid=CH0056&docid=CMS1177330958008.

ISC (Internet Systems Consortium). 2010. *ISC Internet domain survey.* Retrieved March 14, 2010, from http://www.isc.org/solutions/survey.

ITU (International Telecommunication Union). 1993. *Asia-Pacific telecommunications indicators.* Geneva: ITU, United Nations.

———. 2001. Pacific Islands Telecommunications Association (PITA), Pacific Report. Report to the Asia and Pacific Regional Preparatory Meeting for the World Telecommunication Development Conference (WTDC-02), Bali, Indonesia, April 2001.

———. 2007a. *Measuring the information society ICT opportunity index and world telecommunication/ICT indicators.* Geneva: ITU.

———. 2007b. World telecommunication/ICT indicators. *ICT Statistics Database.* Retrieved August 27, 2008, from http://www.itu.int/ITU-D/ICTEYE/~indicators/Indicators.asp.

Kami, T. 2005. *Feasibility study for an information society program for the African, Caribbean and Pacific (ACP) countries. ANNEX VI: Regional Report–Pacific.* Washington, D.C.: The World Bank. Retrieved September 11, 2008, from http://www.infodev.org/en/Document.102.aspx.

Keesing, R. 1989. Creating the past: Custom and identity in the contemporary Pacific. *The Contemporary Pacific* 1(1–2): 19–42.

Kubuabola, R. I. 1989. Opening address. In *Report of the Pacific regional TV meeting* (November 27–December 1, 1989), 46–48. Suva, Fiji: Asia-Pacific Broadcast Union and South Pacific Commission.

Layton, S. 1992. *The contemporary Pacific Islands press.* Brisbane: University of Queensland Department of Journalism.

———. 1995. Introduction. *Pacific Islands Communication Journal* 16(2): 1–5.

Molnar, H. 1993. Video and television training in the South Pacific: A regional approach. *Pacific Islands Communication Journal* 16(1): 125–142.

Network Strategies. 2007. *Final report: Satellite services in the Pacific—perspectives from the region.* Department of Broadband, Communications and the Digital Economy, Commonwealth of Australia. Retrieved September 4, 2008, from http://www.dbcde.gov.au/_data/assets/pdf_file/0004/83821/final_report.pdf.

Noto, D. 2008. Pacific islands move towards online networking. *Pacific Islands Report,* September 15. Retrieved December 18, 2008, from http://pidp.eastwestcenter.org/pireport/2008/September/09-24-rl.htm.

Oceanic Broadband Solutions. 2008. *Nauru government case study.* Retrieved September 16, 2008, from http://www.oceanicbroadband.com/nauru.html.

Ogden, M. R. 1993. Foreign influences, local choices: The social impact of television in Micronesia. *Pacific Islands Communication Journal* 16(1): 7–27.

———. 1995. Pacific Islands, information technology and universal access: It's not just about wires. *Development Bulletin* 35 (October) (Special Issue: Information technology and development): 19–22.

Ogden, M. R., and J. Hailey. 1988. International broadcast services to isolated audiences: The role of Radio Australia during the Fiji crisis. *Media Asia* 15(1): 22–25, 41.

Ogden, M. R., and M. Jussawalla. 1994. Telecommunications and IT in Pacific Islands development. *Asian Journal of Communication* 4(2) (Special Issue): 1–32.

One laptop for every Niuean child. 2008. *BBC News,* August 22. Retrieved August 27, 2008, from http://news.bbc.co.uk/go/pr/fr/-/1/hi/technology/7576573.stm.

Pacific Business News. 2011. Honolulu Star-Advertiser's circulation holds steady. November 1. Retrieved February 25, 2012, from http://www.bizjournals.com/pacific/news/2011/11/01/honolulu-star-advertisers-circulation.html.

PIFS (Pacific Islands Forum Secretariat, formerly SPFS). 2002a. *Pacific ICT capacity and prospects.* Working paper. Retrieved August 20, 2008, from http://www.forumsec.org.fj/UserFiles/File/ICTsurveyreport2002.pdf.

———. 2002b. *Pacific Islands information and communication technologies policy and strategic plan* (PIIPP). Suva, Fiji: PIFS. Retrieved August 20, 2008, from http://www.forumsec.org.fj/UserFiles/File/PIIPP_Final.pdf.

———. 2003. *Pacific Islands: Pacific Islands input to the World Summit on the Information Society* WSIS/PC-3/CONTR/91-E. Retrieved August 29, 2008, from http://www.itu.int/dms_pub/itu-s/md/03/wsispc3/c/S03-WSISPC3-C-0091!!PDF-E.pdf.

———. 2005. *The Pacific plan for strengthening regional cooperation and integration: Pacific regional digital strategy.* Retrieved on August 20, 2008, from http://www.forumsec.org.fj/UserFiles/File/Regional_Digital_Strategy.pdf.

———. 2006. *Wellington declaration.* Forum Information and Communications Technologies Ministerial Meeting. Retrieved on August 20, 2008, from http://www.forumsec.org.fj/UserFiles/File/Wellington_Declaration.pdf.

Papoutsaki, E., and U. S. Harris. 2008. Unpacking "Islandness" in South Pacific islands communication. In *South Pacific islands communications: Regional perspectives, local issues,* ed. E. Papoutsaki and U. S. Harris, 1–12. Singapore: Asian Media Information and Communication Center.

Regional Journalists form Micronesian media group. 2007. *Saipan Tribune,* September 26. Retrieved September 4, 2008, from http://www.saipantribune.com/newsstory.aspx?cat=1&newsID=72699.

Robie, D. 2005. South Pacific notions of the fourth estate: A collision of media models, culture and values. *Media Asia* 32(2): 86–94.

Seward, R. 1999. *Radio happy isles: Media and politics at play in the Pacific.* Honolulu: University of Hawai'i Press.

Sinclair, J. 1984. *Uniting a nation: The postal and telecommunication services of Papua New Guinea.* Melbourne: Oxford University Press.

Spennemann, D. 2004. A digital library and archive the Marshall Islands: Experiences and challenges. *Australian Library Journal* 53(3). Retrieved from http://alia.org.au/publishing/alj.53.3/full.text/spennemann.html.

SPFS (South Pacific Forum Secretariat, now PIFS). 1998. *Pacific Islands involvement in the global information infrastructure.* Suva, Fiji: South Pacific Forum Secretariat.

Stewart, J., B. Horsfield, and P. Cook. 1993. Television and dependency: A case study of policy making in Fiji and Papua New Guinea. *The Contemporary Pacific* 5(2): 333–363.

Sullivan, J., and J. E. Morris. 1996. The development of Internet in the South Pacific. *Pacific Telecommunications Profile* 3(2): 455–457.

Thomas, W., O. P. Khushu, and D. Rutstein. 1993. *Pacific Regional Television Survey project: Melanesia report.* New York: UNESCO. Retrieved August 18, 2008, from http://unesdoc.unesco.org/images/0013/001376/137689eo.pdf.

UNESCAP (United Nations Economic and Social Commission for Asia and the Pacific). 2008. *Enhancing Pacific connectivity: The current situation, opportunities for progress.* New York: United Nations. Retrieved August 29, 2008, from http://www.unescap.org/icstd/research/pacific-connectivity.asp.

Varan, D. 1993. Introducing television: Seven lessons from the Cook Islands. *Pacific Islands Communication Journal* 16(1): 29–61.

Whittle, S. 2007. Putting an island in touch with the world. *The Guardian,* October 25. Retrieved August 31, 2008, from http://www.guardian.co.uk/technology/2007/oct/25/internet.guardianweeklytechnologysection/print.

World Bank. 2006. *The Pacific infrastructure challenge: A review of obstacles and opportunities for improving performance in Pacific Islands.* Washington, D.C.: The World Bank. Retrieved August 21, 2008, from http://siteresources.worldbank.org/INTPACIFICISLANDS/Resources/PacificReportFinal.pdf.

———. 2008. *Telecommunications in the Pacific: Background paper for Pacific economic survey 2008.* Retrieved August 29, 2008, from http://www.pacificsurvey.org/UserFiles/PS-BackgroundPaper-Telco.pdf.

Development Prospects

Donovan Storey and David Abbott

34

Since the first edition of *The Pacific Islands: Environment & Society,* much of the region has undergone profound political, economic, and social change. There have been political crises in Solomon Islands and Fiji and even social discord evidenced in Tonga. In Tuvalu, Vanuatu, and the Marshall Islands, governments have been under increasing pressure to perform essential service and infrastructure functions in the face of severe fiscal challenges. Fiji, once the most diverse and robust economy in the South Pacific, with a booming tourist market, manufacturing and service industries, and mining and agricultural exports, has in a generation become an economy and society increasingly dependent on migration and remittances. In effect, Fiji is becoming a twenty-first century MIRAB economy. Solomon Islands underwent a political meltdown in 2000 and required international intervention to stabilize its situation. Papua New Guinea, the region's largest state, has achieved better economic growth but questions remain over sharing the benefits of its mineral boom (Duncan 2007).

Connell (2007) has recently reminded both "insiders" and "outsiders" that development in the region has always been a struggle. The "idyllic" portrayal of remote and distant islands forms an uneasy tension with the reality of distant, relatively poor, global outliers confronting tensions of social change and transition. "Development," in its narrowest blueprint formulation, has never been a comfortable bedfellow in the Pacific, including the colonial and postcolonial experience of indigenous nations in Hawai'i and Aotearoa/New Zealand. The failure of imported development models and policies to either take root or gather political support is manifest in the clamor for greater migration opportunities and in social and political discord within an increasing number of states (including those in "peaceful Polynesia"). The region confronts looming environmental tipping points (created by both external factors and domestic impacts of pollution on fragile microstates) and a growing disenchantment arising in the region's depopulating rural areas and urban informal settlements.

Pacific Islanders, however, have never been passive in the face of change. Indeed adaptation, resilience, and making the most out of livelihood opportunities is evident throughout the region, in the form of vibrant informal sectors, subsistence farming, continuity of intergenerational migration and remittance flows, and the politics of aid, recently evidenced in the trading off of loyalties to Taiwan and mainland China (Crocombe 2007). Resistance, opportunity,

and hybridity are manifested in the continued resilience of cultural systems and norms. This final chapter examines the limitations of development efforts in a range of countries, showing growing hardship, poverty, and deteriorating human development indicators (especially in Melanesia), but it also explores the potential benefits from globalization and development.

"Failed" Economies and Their Consequences

In aggregate, Pacific Island economies have performed relatively poorly in recent years. According to the *Asian Development Outlook (ADO) 2008,* the average growth rate across the region in 2006 was only 2.3 percent, down from a previous estimate of 3.3 percent. In both 2007 and 2008 forecasts were revised downward as economies struggled to grow and sustain livelihoods and meet the expectations of increasing populations. These rates of growth for PICs (Pacific Island countries) compare with an average 6.0 percent per annum in Southeast Asia over the 2005–2007 period, and even higher rates in South Asia and East Asia. Pacific countries are therefore being left behind.

In many countries, per capita growth rates are either very low or even negative, while populations and expectations continue to grow. Even this data is skewed toward formal-sector employment and traded goods and services. Yet a high proportion of urban populations (especially youth and women) work in the informal sector at much lower levels of income. In rural areas people still rely greatly on growing their own food. Subsistence production is estimated to contribute between 40 and 100 percent of rural food needs across the region, but periurban and urban gardens also contribute up to half of urban food consumption in some countries.

Almost all development trends in the Pacific over the past two decades suggest that poverty and hardship are likely to be increasing. Even in countries such as Papua New Guinea (PNG) that have enjoyed high rates of growth, the benefits of growth are not necessarily being spread evenly. Growing levels of inequality seem to be most likely in countries where urbanization is increasing and where the rural agricultural sector is in decline.

Notwithstanding the low rates of growth overall, and reflecting the diversity in the countries of the region, there has been both good and bad news in recent years. For example Palau, Vanuatu, and the Cook Islands benefited from rising numbers of tourists.

Conversely, Fiji has struggled to attract tourists in the aftermath of the 2006 military takeover and the collapse of its garment industry following the end of favorable tariff agreements in 2005 (Storey 2006). The continued state of political uncertainty is having an adverse impact on business confidence, exacerbated by weakness in the sugar sector. Tonga struggled to recover from the riots of 2006 and experienced reductions in earnings from tourism, squash exports, and remittances. In Solomon Islands postconflict recovery has seen gradual expansion in economic activity and increased employment and exports, though this has tended to concentrate economic activity and employment on Guadalcanal. Centralization is increasingly apparent throughout much of the island Pacific, including the concentration of Maori and Pacific Islanders in the urban areas of Aotearoa/New Zealand and Hawai'i.

Even where gains have been made, Pacific Island countries are facing increasing inflation (which averaged 5.0 percent across the region in 2008), food import costs, and costs in transportation and power—driven in great part by the escalating price of oil. In recent years there has been a sharp increase in the cost of rice, flour, and other essential foods, which has affected the ability of consumers to meet the costs of basic needs. This is especially true in urban centers where access to homegrown foods is limited. The significantly greater reliance on home production in rural households, and thus their greater degree of food security, is illustrated in Figure 34.1.

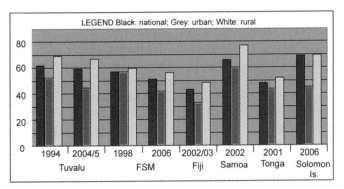

Figure 34.1. *The proportion of food in total expenditure of low-income households.*

For many commentators the past two decades have seen a gradual loss of earlier development gains by Pacific Island countries and even a weakening in national security and sovereignty as a result. Donald Denoon has characterized Papua New Guinea's independence as a "trial separation"; such is the level of continued dependence on Australia (Denoon 2005). Similar sentiments can also be found regarding Solomon Islands, which has arguably become more dependent on the regional community (especially Australia) since 2000. For many PICs, remittances from migrant and temporary overseas workers are seen as a panacea for the failure of domestic policies to create investment and employment opportunities. Remittances have become one of the primary sources of income for many households in Fiji, having risen in value from F\$50 million in 1999 to F\$320 million in 2006. In recent years there have been demands that Australia and New Zealand allow greater migrant access to offset the poor performance of national economies and the lack of opportunities for island populations. The New Zealand Recognized Seasonal Employer Scheme, initiated in

2007, has had an impact on remittance flows to Vanuatu, Tuvalu, Kiribati, Samoa, and Tonga. While these new opportunities do provide a safety valve and source of seasonal income for families and communities who are able to participate, they are offset by loss of skills and (especially) male labor. There are numerous unintended social consequences relating to absent families and spouses, both for those left at home as well as those away, that have yet to be fully investigated and understood. There are also inconsistencies in administrative policies toward rural areas and outer islands. Governments are concerned over the depopulation and changing demographics of the rural areas and are encouraging more investment, but at the same time are encouraging working-age people to leave for overseas opportunities.

Commentators also argue that this "easy money" is a disincentive for young people to actively look for work. In Tonga and Tuvalu, remittances equivalent to 48 percent and 38 percent of GDP in 2002 respectively were the most important source of foreign exchange revenues and an important source of income for many families. In Kiribati and Samoa, where remittances were equivalent to 12 percent of GDP in 2001 and 21 percent of GDP in 2002, this source of income was also extremely important to many individual households. Still, remittances have supported small business development and helped to pay for school fees, health care, and services (often erroneously measured as "consumption") (Walker and Brown 1995). Building financial literacy skills and providing financial services to recipient communities is regarded as essential if the benefits of remittances are not to be wasted.

Globalization, Development, and the Pacific Islands

As is the case with other contemporary states and societies, globalization limits the opportunities for development but also opens up new windows. In the short term at least, Firth sees this readjustment as bringing more economic, social, and political disruptions to the region than benefits (Firth 2007). More and more people are becoming reliant on having cash to meet their basic needs. Though prevalent at independence, a traditional subsistence, noncash lifestyle is now almost impossible for most Pacific Islanders. The trend toward cash societies has hastened a greater individualism, leading in turn to a broadening of horizons and a narrowing and weakening of ties among family members. These trends, and the erosion of cultural safety nets, have been evident for some time (Monsell-Davis 1993). The failure of Pacific economies to "take off" makes it essential to minimize the adverse impacts of global linkages and monetization on the poor and most disadvantaged and to maximize the positive benefits for economies as a whole.

Government policies, especially fiscal policy, public sector reforms, and broader economic strategy, are contributing to the monetization of Pacific Island economies and the consequent pressure on household finances. Reforms are often double-edged. In a number of countries economic reforms have contributed directly to the hardship and poverty that are reportedly being experienced by many households. Yet they are essential in keeping economies afloat and are an important factor in maintaining aid flows from regional donors and international development banks. Foster (2005) sees the relationship between globalization and Pacific

Islanders as a series of "negotiations" over identity, livelihoods, representation, and relationships. These are occurring as much within state boundaries as they are outside, and they are as evident in the experiences of Maori and indigenous Hawaiians as they are among Pacific Islanders.

Globalization is not the sole underlying cause of growing poverty and hardship. Increasing flows of people, trade, and services have also presented opportunities and challenges. National strategies need to be developed to meet those challenges and take advantage of change. The various Trust and Reserve Funds in the region benefited from the rapid rise in share prices between 2002 and late 2007. Booming international trade has kept the market for Pacific seafarers buoyant (Borovnik 2007). Tourism has been boosted by instability elsewhere in the world and greater competition in Pacific air transport. The creation of new employment opportunities in the global security industry, in sports, in caregiving, and in other temporary labor schemes are all advantages of global labor flows. It may be argued as well that Pacific Islanders, through migration and the creation of "transnational corporations of kin" (Bertram and Watters 1985), have successfully adapted to global flows and opportunities and that globalization is an important part of modern "islander" identity.

The monetization of traditional, subsistence-based societies brings with it changes that are often uncomfortable. Access to services, education, and infrastructure is becoming unaffordable for a growing proportion of Pacific Islanders. This is most evident in the explosion of informal and periurban settlements in and around many towns and cities (see chapter 26). Increases in user charges for government services, particularly for health and education, pose a particular burden on low-income households. Even where education is nominally free, there are frequently additional costs imposed by schools for books, materials, and building and maintenance funds because of funding cutbacks and budgetary constraints. Introducing improved transport and communication services raises demand and the need to pay for them. Promoting the private sector increases the availability of goods and services and also the need for money with which to purchase them.

The changes brought about by access to and dependence on cash incomes are manifest in outer island and rural areas. Dependency ratios are rising as elderly family members are being left to care for grandchildren when the younger generation moves to the urban centers or overseas. The population pyramid charts for many small island states illustrate this clearly. Thus the elderly, less commonly being cared for in the traditional ways, are becoming increasingly burdened with additional responsibilities. It is also seen in the attitude of youth who are no longer generally satisfied with the prospect of a traditional Pacific subsistence lifestyle.

The result of this monetization is that even families in remote rural or outer island villages have to find cash for everyday needs, be it for school fees, utilities, newly essential store goods, social obligations, "bride price," or church donations. Where social obligations could once have been met with woven mats, traditional food, or other home-produced items, there is now an ever-increasing need to make cash for purchased contributions (ADB 2002). How to meet these needs and spread the opportunities and benefits of globalization in the context of faltering national economies poses a great challenge to the region's leaders.

Poverty and Hardship

Until recently poverty was not considered a serious issue in most PICs. Pacific societies have long been seen as a traditional culture of caring for, and sharing with, family, clan, or community, resulting in the continuing belief that poverty cannot and should not be a part of normal life. The suggestion that there might be poverty in some form (Table 34.1) is not, therefore, something many governments or people in the region have been prepared to accept (Storey, Bullock, and Overton 2005). While Pacific Island people might not be well off in financial or material terms, their strong family and community ties have traditionally provided social safety nets for the most disadvantaged and vulnerable.

Table 34.1

Poverty Head Counts in the Pacific

Country	Year	National	Urban	Rural
Cook Islands	2005/06	28.4	30.5	23.6
Fiji Islands	1990/91	25.5	27.6	22.4
	2002/03	34.4	31.8	38.1
Kiribati	1996	50.0	51.0	50.0
Marshall Islands	1999	20.0	na	na
FSM	1998	27.9	29.5	32.9
	2005	29.9	33.9	28.7
Palau	2006	24.9	26.2	28.9
Papua New Guinea	1996	37.5	na	na
Samoa	2002	20.3	23.3	17.9
Solomon Islands	2005/06	22.7	32.2	18.8
Tonga	2002	22.3	23.6	22.8
Tuvalu	1994	24.4	32.4	23.6
	2005	21.2	27.6	17.5
Vanuatu	2006	15.9	32.8	10.8

Source: ADB 2004 and 2008; UNDP estimates.

Poverty in the Pacific Island context does not generally mean hunger or destitution, but rather the continuous struggle to meet essential daily/weekly living expenses, particularly those that require cash payments. Families constantly have to make choices between the competing demands for expenditures on food and basic needs. Trade-offs are made between paying one bill or another, between food or school fees. Households are therefore facing hardship on a daily basis. They struggle to pay bills and to purchase adequate and nutritious food. They borrow regularly from "loan sharks" who charge high rates of interest for small unsecured loans to meet family commitments and community obligations. They are thus frequently, and occasionally constantly, in debt.

The UNDP Human Development Report (2011) provides data on only six developing PICs (Table 34.2). Tonga, Samoa, and Fiji are ranked 90th, 99th, and 100th (of 187 countries) in the Human Development Index (HDI). The three Melanesian countries of Vanuatu, Solomon Islands, and PNG are ranked 125th, 142nd, and 153rd respectively. In all six countries these rankings fell from their levels just a few years earlier. Trends in human development indices over the past decade have notably been stagnant or in decline.

Table 34.2

Selected Human Development Index Trends

	GDP per capita (PPP US$) 2011	HDI 2006	HDI 2011	HDI rank x/187 countries (2011)
Fiji Islands	4,145	.743	.688	100
Papua New Guinea	2,271	.514	.466	153
Samoa	3,931	.760	.688	99
Solomon Islands	1,782	.591	.510	142
Tonga	4,186	.774	.704	90
Vanuatu	3,950	.686	.617	125
New Zealand	23,737	.944	.908	5

Source: UNDP 2011.

Although generalizations can be misleading given the diversity among PICs, the overall trend in the progress toward achieving the MDGs (the United Nations' Millennium Development Goals) is that the Polynesian countries have been performing relatively well; the Micronesian countries of the North Pacific have been struggling to maintain gains; and in some of the Melanesian countries, notably those that have been impacted by natural disasters or where there has been conflict or civil/political tension, a reversal of earlier development progress is being witnessed. The result is that many countries are off track to achieve at least five or more of the eight MDGs, ranging across a number of indicators (reduction in child mortality, access to water and sanitation, reduction in maternal mortality, gender equality in education, universal primary education) and extending to a broad spectrum of states, such as the Federated States of Micronesia, Kiribati, Papua New Guinea, Fiji, and Vanuatu.

The latest available national poverty estimates suggest that approximately one in four households across the region has a per capita income below the respective national poverty line (Table 34.1, above). The figures also suggest that with a couple of exceptions, hardship and poverty are equally felt by urban and rural families alike, though the causes and policy objectives for each may be different. This contrasts with most other developing countries in the Asia-Pacific region, where rural poverty tends to be higher than that experienced in the urban centers. It suggests that while on the one hand the traditional subsistence lifestyle of the Pacific helps to underpin a minimum standard of living in the rural areas, the lack of overall economic growth in the economy as a whole and the urban areas in particular is not enabling urban dwellers to improve their standards of living above the basic minimum. Even these "orthodox" forms of data are unlikely to capture the true extent and experience of poverty in the region, encompassing loss of land, a breakdown of family life, and the lack of power to change one's life.

Levels of inequality are on the rise. The level of inequality in income or consumption across the Pacific can be seen in the share of income/consumption that is attributable to the highest and lowest quintiles. Consistently across the region, the lowest quintile enjoys less than 10 percent of income/consumption whereas the top quintile has around 40 percent.

Urban drift, leading to higher levels of unemployment and growing numbers of people living in squatter settlements and substandard housing conditions, results in a deteriorating social environment. Many of the poor live in low-quality housing without proper access to water, sanitation, and other basic services. Poor housing conditions lead to poor health, poor employment prospects, and poor education. Children frequently miss school through ill health or because school fees have not been paid. Adults are often poorly educated and unable to get anything but the lowest-paid and often casual employment, if even that is available. The cycle of poverty can therefore be perpetuated.

Increasing urbanization is placing ever-greater burdens on urban infrastructure, basic services, and environmental health. Greater resource allocation is necessary to meet the demands of urban areas. As a consequence there is growing inequity in access to basic services between the urban and rural areas, exacerbating the desire to move to where services are perceived to be better. Nevertheless, poor first- or second-generation migrants living in urban informal settlements or on customary land may be as isolated from services and improved infrastructure as rural communities.

Food security is an emerging problem in a number of countries. In those countries that have well-established local market systems and short supply lines from the growing areas to the urban centers (e.g., Vanuatu, Samoa, Solomon Islands, Fiji), the supply of produce can respond quickly to changes in demand. But in those countries that do not have good local markets, such as most of the atoll nations, the price shocks can have significant impact. The urban dwellers in Tuvalu, Kiribati, FSM, and RMI, as well as those in Nauru (around 30 to 40 percent of national populations) are likely to be most affected. In Fiji there are concerns about lowest-income groups in the main urban centers who have little or no access to their own production or the cash needed to buy local produce or imports. The relatively high levels of poverty in Honiara and Port Vila, where there are large squatter settlements, suggest that there will be many among these households that are feeling the impact of price rises.

Whether they are on the atolls, in the highlands, or in the urban centers—those who are likely to experience the greatest degrees of hardship and poverty are the young, the old, the infirm, those who have no source of regular income, or those with no access to adequate land on which to grow food for consumption and/or sale (Abbott and Pollard 2004). Weakening food security and the declining contribution of subsistence agriculture to national income are serious emerging issues throughout the region.

Meeting Basic Needs: A Case of Doing More with Less

Weak fiscal situations and poorly defined budget priorities compound development problems. Budget allocations are not necessarily responsive to the needs of the poorest and most disadvantaged, and most are not focused on the need to achieve the MDG targets at the aggregate level. Increasingly, NGOs such as Wan Smol

Bag Theatre (Vanuatu), the Solomon Islands Development Trust (SIDT), Ecumenical Centre for Research, Education and Advocacy (ECREA) (Fiji), and Foundation for the South Pacific International (FSPI) fill the gaps and meet the needs of those left out of formal-sector employment and the limited social welfare assistance that is available.

The Asian Development Bank (2005) has made explicit links between declining governance standards, poor economic performance, and the struggle of a number of countries to meet the MDGs. High rates of population growth, particularly in the Melanesian and some Micronesian countries, make it difficult to achieve real per capita increases in income and are putting pressure on government budgets. The high proportion of youth in the populations of many countries is leading to a weakening of the overall social environment, rising problems of crime (notably in urban PNG), emerging problems in mental health, and a vulnerability to STDs, especially HIV/AIDS (Jourdan 2008; UNICEF 2005).

Lack of employment opportunities, particularly among youth, together with the growing numbers of people engaged in temporary labor mobility, both domestically and internationally, are becoming critical human development policy issues for many countries. The agenda of decent work for all is therefore relevant to PICs, as well as to indigenous and Pacific Island populations in Aotearoa/New Zealand, who remain disproportionately in low-wage and low-skill employment and overrepresented in unemployment and other government benefits. Despite gains in human development and economic opportunity over the past decade, Gibbs has argued that "on average, Maori people [continue to] experience significantly poorer educational outcomes, higher unemployment, lower levels of income, lower rates of home ownership, and poorer health than Pakeha (New Zealanders of European descent)" (Gibbs 2005: 1369). The positive and negative impacts particularly on those—often the elderly, women, and children—left behind, in both rural and urban environments, is adding to the complexity of modernizing and monetizing Pacific Island countries and meeting the human development needs of the most vulnerable. Growing inequality and a poverty of opportunity is becoming more visible in a number of countries. The increasing reliance on remittances together with the monetization of society is heightening the need for better financial literacy and more opportunities for financial inclusion. Banking and financial inclusion are now recognized as key catalysts for rural economic prosperity.

Many disadvantaged groups do not have access to basic services such as telephone, electricity, financial services, and basic goods. Lack of access to markets and poor knowledge of finance marginalizes income opportunities for rural communities. Geographic impediments, inefficient state-owned enterprises, and state-supported monopolies have historically obstructed the private sector (where it exists on any meaningful scale) from delivering services effectively. New ideas and partnerships, such as those in Asia that link local government with the informal sector, private sector, and communities in service and infrastructure provision, need to be explored (Hasan 2006). To do so will also require new forms of governance and innovative practices that look beyond standard solutions (Storey 2005). Simply put, many Pacific Island countries will need to do more with less in the coming decades.

For some authors, thinking outside the square necessitates a considerable change in the way development is conceived and practiced in the region. Writers such as Epeli Hau'ofa (1993) and William Clarke (1990) have long criticized the negativity in much practitioner and academic policy discourse that has perpetuated a sense of hopelessness and nihilism in Pacific studies. They instead present alternative visions of a region that should actively engage and adapt to change, often in the face of considerable odds. Gegeo (1998) has gone as far as to outline indigenous epistemologies of development in Malaita (Solomon Islands), locating these in concepts of a "good life" in opposition to outside development (or "bisnis"), which is seen as existing without values. Huffer and Qalo (2004) have explored how indigenous governance systems may be grafted onto foreign ideas of good governance, to the ultimate benefit of both donors and Pacific Islanders. Some recent attempts have demonstrated the practical applications of hybridity, in the form of urban village courts in Papua New Guinea (Goddard 2000), land mobilization that balances the needs of both customary owners and development in Melanesia (AusAID 2008), governance structures that fuse traditional and modern systems (Tuvalu, Vanuatu, the Marshall Islands), and attempts to create "custom economies" (Vanuatu). Examples of how indigenous business principles can work in modern capitalist enterprises exist throughout the Pacific (Huffer and Qalo 2004), including the region's "periphery" (e.g., the *iwi* of Ngai Tahu in Aotearoa/New Zealand maintains its own investment company, which returned a net surplus of NZ$80 million to shareholders in 2006/7).

Though this provides a brief list and a set of examples that are not without their problems and limitations, it is important to note that Pacific Islanders are not passive in the face of change. Far from being "historical artifacts," cultural systems can and do play a role in development that could be more effectively utilized in meeting the basic needs of a greater number, in contrast to the redistributive failures of many modern postcolonial states and economies.

Pro-Poor Policies

There are a number of complex development-related constraints and challenges confronting PIC governments in the early twenty-first century. These include weak fiscal situations; a lack of domestic resources and productive investment, in part driven by a poor and unstable policy environment; the impact of global forces, such as oil, food, and commodity price increases; high levels of domestic rural/urban migration and external labor mobility (which both strengthens and weakens domestic and national economies); increasing inequality, as well as gender disparities and youth unemployment; the growing threat of HIV/AIDS, other STDs, and drug abuse; insecurity, political instability, and crime; climate change; and domestic environmental degradation.

These problems directly affect the ability, capacity, and commitment of PIC governments and regional bodies to implement the policy initiatives for improving human development, reducing hardship and poverty, and attaining the MDGs. The impacts of these various challenges are having profound effects on the likely long-term sustainability of some small island states, and they present formidable obstacles to the formulation of policy agendas for human development in the Pacific Island region.

So what can be done to create a more equitable and inclusive region, one that enjoys high economic growth and human development in the twenty-first century? Poverty reduction and hardship alleviation interventions aimed at pro-poor growth and achieving the MDGs need to be adapted to particular circumstances, with due attention to the identified priorities and needs of those who are most disadvantaged (Abbott 2007). A one-size-fits-all policy approach needs to be avoided. A more consultative and participatory conceptual framework for setting and implementing development priorities and strategies nationally and regionally are important ends and means.

Governments need to have clearer policy priorities and targets (e.g., localized MDGs) within the context of their national development strategies and to allocate resources more effectively to achieve the targeted goals. Institutions and governance standards need to be strengthened in line with regional and international commitments (e.g., Paris and Pacific Principles of Aid Effectiveness, Forum Principles of Accountability). Pacific governments and development partners together must strive to implement their commitments in order to deliver better development outcomes to the people of the region.

Growth is a necessary but not sufficient condition for poverty reduction and development across the Pacific region. If inequality is to be reduced, the patterns of growth are important, as are the redistributive benefits. Growth and opportunity must occur in the sectors in which the poor and low-income groups are more likely to be involved, namely agriculture, fisheries, construction, personal services, small-scale manufacturing, and informal activities. Notwithstanding the lure of overseas migration, the rural sector in particular must be made more attractive to the younger generation if the viability of the smaller states is to be secured. Policies must therefore serve to reduce inequality, and the rate of growth of per capita incomes of the poor need to rise faster that average incomes over the whole population. Policy should focus on increasing the capabilities of the poorest so that current patterns of deprivation and hardship do not become intergenerational and result in a region characterized by endemic poverty, inequality, and instability, but rather a model of sustainable and equitable small-island development to the world.

BIBLIOGRAPHY

Abbott, D. 2007. Poverty and pro-poor policies for Pacific Island countries. *Asia-Pacific Population Journal* 22(3): 59–74.

Abbott, D., and V. Pollard. 2004. Hardship and poverty in the Pacific. Manila: Asian Development Bank Pacific Department.

ADB (Asian Development Bank). 2002. *Priorities of the people: Hardship in Samoa.* Manila: Pacific Department.

———. 2004. *Hardship and poverty in the Pacific: Strengthening poverty analysis and strategies.* Manila: Pacific Department.

———. 2005. *Remittances in the Pacific: An overview.* Manila: Pacific Studies Series.

———. 2008. *Asian development outlook 2008.* Manila.

Asian Development Bank and Government of Vanuatu. 2008. *The Vanuatu poverty report card: 2006.* Port Vila, Vanuatu.

AusAID. 2008. *Making land work.* Canberra: Commonwealth of Australia.

Bertram, G., and R. Watters. 1986. The MIRAB process in South Pacific microstates. *Pacific Viewpoint* 26(2): 497–519.

Borovnik, M. 2007. Labor circulation and changes among seafarers' families and communities in Kiribati. *Asian and Pacific Migration Journal* 16(2): 225–249.

Clarke, W. C., 1990. Learning from the past: Traditional knowledge and sustainable development. *The Contemporary Pacific* 2(2): 233–253.

Connell, J. 2007. Islands, idylls and the detours of development. *Singapore Journal of Tropical Geography* 28: 116–135.

Crocombe, R. 2007. *Asia in the Pacific: Replacing the West.* Suva: Institute of Pacific Studies, University of the South Pacific.

Denoon, D. A. 2005. *A trial separation: Australia and the decolonisation of Papua New Guinea.* Canberra: Pandanus Books.

Duncan, R. 2007. Papua New Guinea economic survey: Fiscal discipline needed. *Pacific Economic Bulletin* 22(1): 1–15.

Firth, S. 2007. Pacific Islands trade, labor, and security in an era of globalization. *The Contemporary Pacific* 19(1): 111–135.

Foster, R. J. 2005. Negotiating globalization: Contemporary Pacific perspectives. *Ethnohistory* 52(1): 167–177.

Gegeo, D. 1998. Indigenous knowledge and empowerment: Rural development examined from within. *The Contemporary Pacific* 10(2): 289–315.

Gibbs, M. 2005. The right to development and indigenous peoples: Lessons from New Zealand. *World Development* 33(8): 1365–1378.

Goddard, M. 2000. Three urban village courts in Papua New Guinea: Some comparative observations on dispute settlement. In *Reflections on violence in Melanesia,* ed. S. Dinnen and A. Ley, 241–253. Canberra: Hawkens Press and Asia Pacific Press.

Hasan. A. 2006. Orangi Pilot Project: The expansion of work beyond Orangi and the mapping of informal settlements and infrastructure. *Environment and Urbanization* 18(2): 451–480.

Hau'ofa, E. 1993. Our sea of islands. In *A new Oceania: Rediscovering our sea of islands,* ed. E. Waddell, V. Naidu, and E. Hau'ofa, 147–161. Suva: University of the South Pacific.

Huffer, E., and R. Qalo. 2004. Have we been thinking upside-down? The contemporary emergence of Pacific theoretical thought. *The Contemporary Pacific* 16(1): 87–116.

Jourdan, C. 2008. *Youth and mental health in Solomon Islands: A situational analysis.* Suva: Foundation of the South Pacific International.

Monsell-Davis, M. 1993. Urban exchange: Safety-net or disincentive? Wantoks and relatives in the urban Pacific. *Cultural Anthropology* 16(2): 45–66.

Storey, D. 2005. *Urban governance in Pacific Island countries: Advancing an overdue agenda.* State Society and Governance in Melanesia Project Discussion Paper 2005/7. Canberra: Australian National University.

———. 2006. End of the line? Globalisation and Fiji's garment industry. In *Globalisation and governance in the Pacific Islands,* ed. S. Firth, 217–238. Canberra: Australian National University E Press.

Storey, D., H. Bulloch, and J. Overton. 2005. The poverty consensus: Some limitations of the "popular agenda." *Progress in Development Studies* 5(1): 30–44.

UNDP (United Nations Development Programme). 2011. *Human development report 2011.* New York: Palgrave Macmillan.

UNICEF (United Nations Children's Fund). 2005. *The state of Pacific youth report 2005.* Suva: UNICEF.

Walker, A., and R. Brown. 1995. From consumption to savings? Interpreting Tongan and Western Samoan sample survey data on remittances. *Asian and Pacific Migration Journal* 4: 89–116.

ATLAS

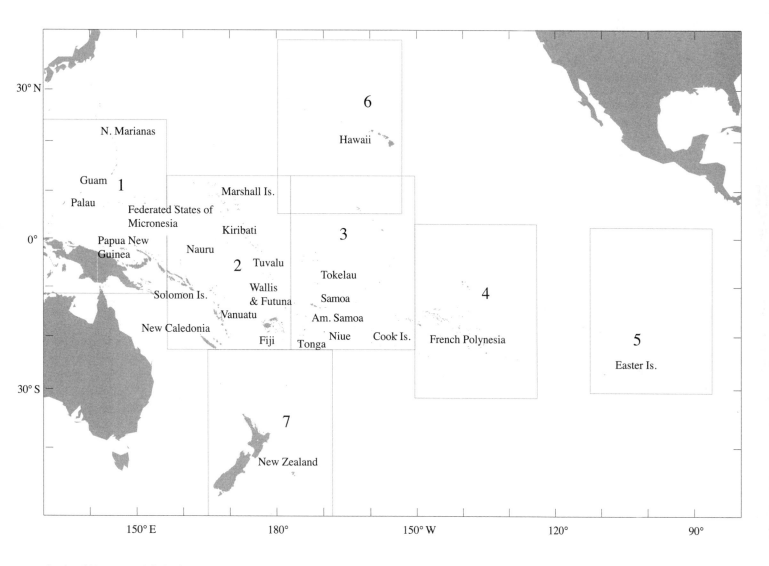

Sectional Maps. *Copyright by the United States Government. No copyright claimed under Title 17 U.S.S. Series 1150 Edition 3 DMA. Prepared and published under the direction of the Department of Defense by the Defense Mapping Agency.*

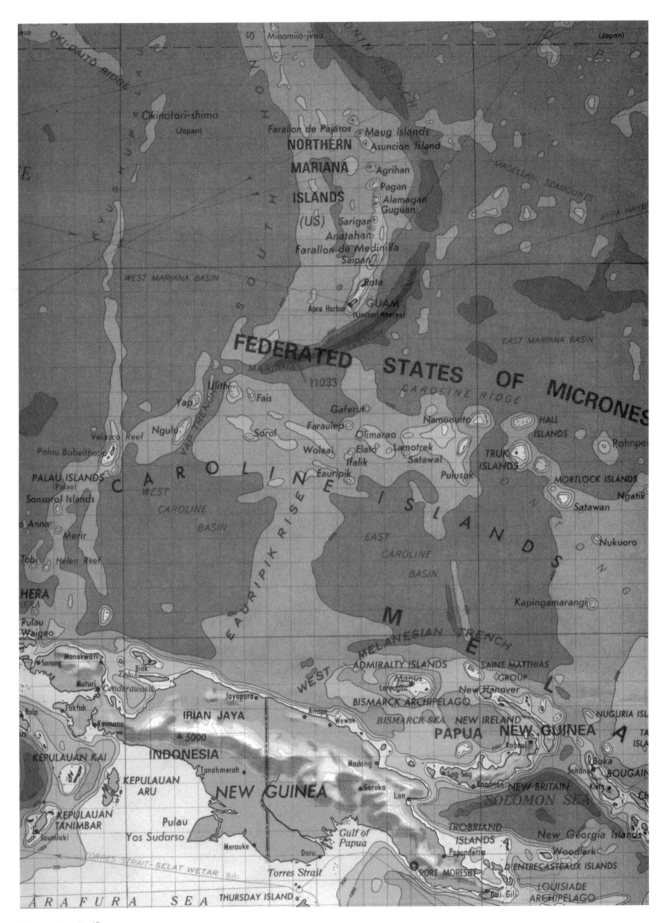

Map 1. West Pacific

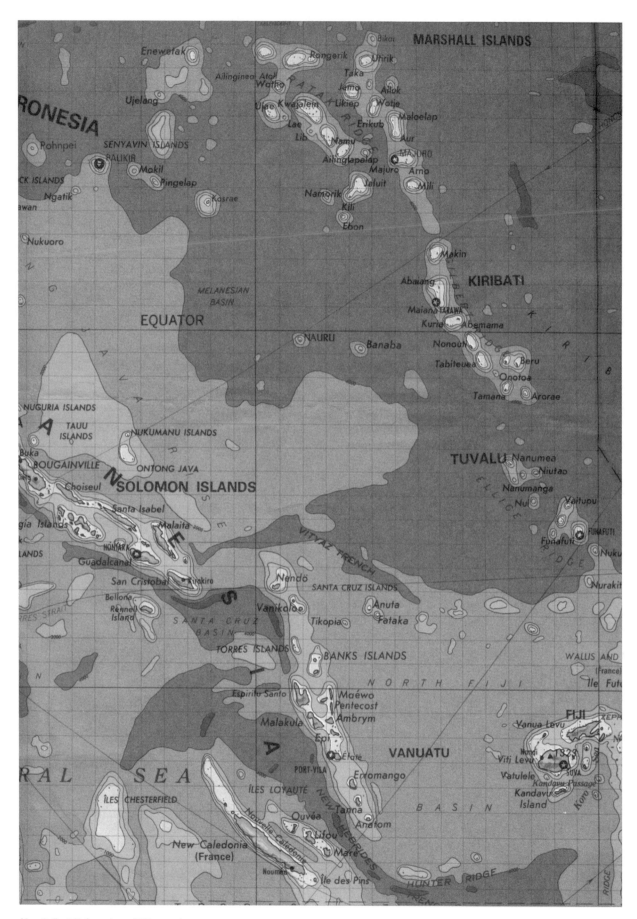

Map 2. *East Melanesia and Micronesia*

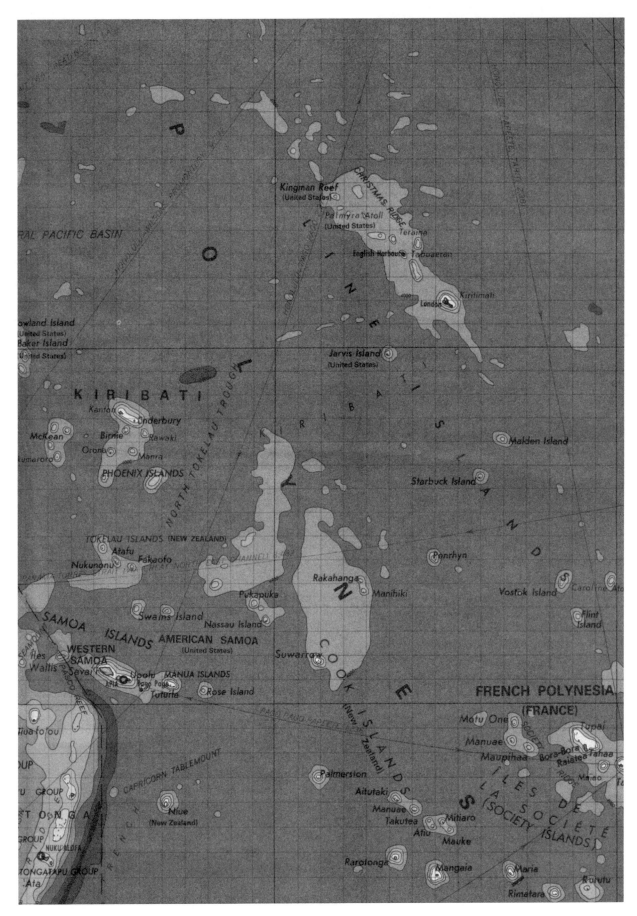

Map 3. *Central Pacific*

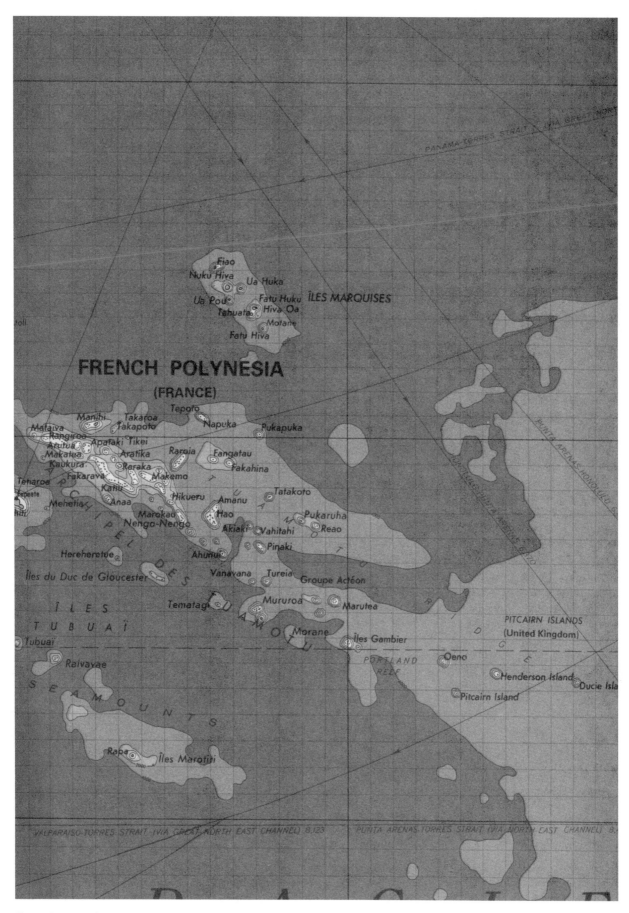

Map 4. *Eastern Polynesia*

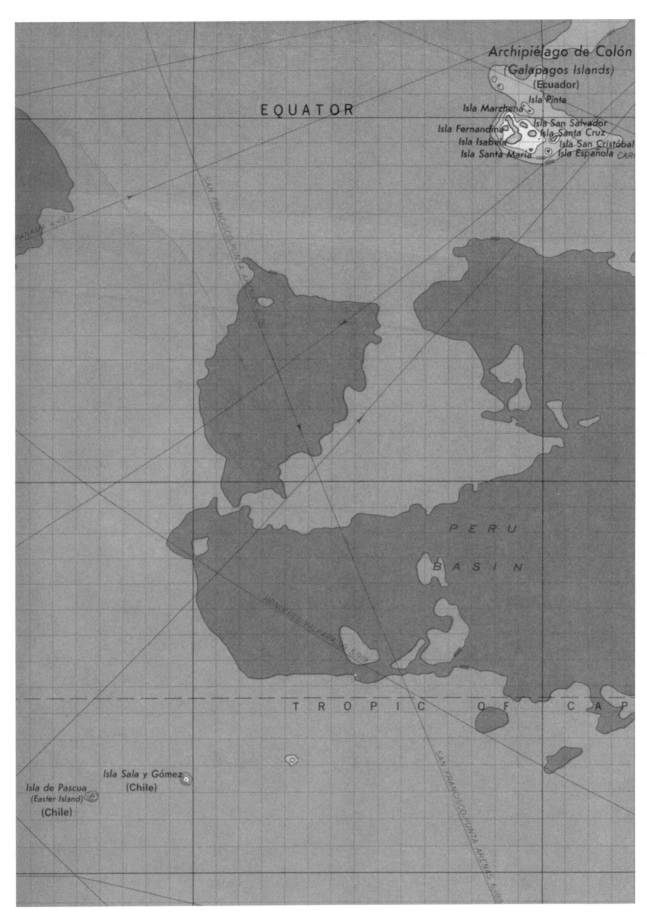

Map 5. *East Pacific*

Map 6. Hawai‘i

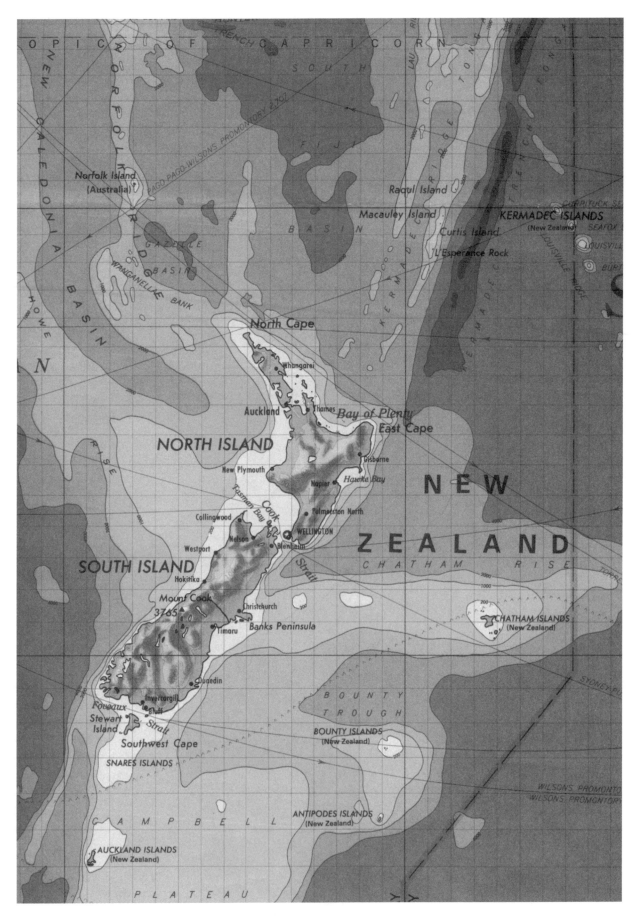

Map 7. *New Zealand*

ISLAND GAZETTEER

Note: Abbreviated list. For geographic coordinates of other locations see references:

Bryan, E. H. 1943. *Guide to Pacific Islands.* Honolulu: Fourteenth Naval District Intelligence Office.
Getty Information Institute (GII). 1998. Thesaurus of geographic names. http://www.gii.getty.edu/tgn_browser/index.html.
Motteler, L. S. 1986. *Pacific Island names.* Honolulu: Bishop Museum Press.

Abbreviations used:

Am.Sam.	American Samoa	Marq.	Marquesas Islands
Aus.	Austral Islands	Moala	Moala Group
Banks	Banks Islands	N.Sol.	North Solomon Islands
Bis.	Bismarck Archipelago	NC.out.	New Caledonia outliers
Chuuk	State of Chuuk	NG.group	New Guinea Group
CI	Cook Islands	NWHI	Northwestern Hawaiian Islands
D'Ent.	D'Entrecasteaux Islands	Pal.out.	Palau outliers
Epac.	East Pacific outliers	Phoe.	Phoenix Islands
Fi.out	Fiji Outliers	PNG	Papua New Guinea
FP	French Polynesia	Pohnpei	State of Pohnpei
FSM	Federated States of Micronesia	Ralik	Ralik Chain
Gal.	Galápagos Islands	Ratak	Ratak Chain
Gam.	Gambier Islands	S.Cruz	Santa Cruz
Gil.	Gilbert Islands	SI	Solomon Islands
Ha'ap.	Ha'apai Group	Soc.	Society Islands
Haw.	Hawai'i	Sol.out.	Solomon Island outliers
J.Fer.	Juan Fernandez Islands	Sol.Sea	Solomon Sea Islands
Kad.	Kadavu Group	Tor.	Torres Islands
Kir.	Kiribati	Tuam.	Tuamotu Archipelago
Lau	Lau Islands	USadm.	U.S.–administered Pacific Islands
Line	Line Islands	Va.L.	Vanua Levu Group
Lom.	Lomaiviti Group	Van.	Vanuatu
Lou.	Louisiade Archipelago	Vi.L.	Viti Levu Group
Loy.	Loyalty Islands	W&F	Wallis and Futuna
Mar.	Northern Mariana Islands	Yap	State of Yap

ISLAND	GROUP	LATITUDE	LONGITUDE
Abaiang	Gil., Kir.	1°50′N	173°02′E
Abemama	Gil., Kir.	0°21′N	173°51′E
Agakauitai	Gam., FP	23°10′S	136°01′W
Agrihan	Mar.	18°46′N	145°40′E
Aguijan	Mar.	14°51′N	145°34′E
Ahe	Tuam., FP	14°30′S	146°17′W
Ahunui	Tuam., FP	19°40′S	140°25′W
Ailinginae	Ralik, MI	11°08′N	166°30′E

ISLAND	GROUP	LATITUDE	LONGITUDE
Ailinglaplap	Ralik, MI	7°25′N	168°45′E
Ailuk	Ratak, MI	10°20′N	169°57′E
Aitutaki	CI	18°52′S	159°45′W
Aiwa	Lau, Fiji	18°19′S	178°43′W
Akamaru	Gam., FP	23°11′S	134°54′W
Akiaki	Gam., FP	18°30′S	139°14′W
Alamagan	Mar.	17°36′N	145°50′E
Alcester	Sol.Sea, PNG	9°28′S	152°28′E

ISLAND	GROUP	LATITUDE	LONGITUDE
Alexander Selkirk	J.Fer.	33°45'S	80°45'W
Alim	Bis., PNG	2°55'S	147°05'E
'Alofi	W&F	14°19'S	178°02'W
Amanu	Tuam., FP	17°48'S	140°45'W
Ambitle	Bis., PNG	4°10'S	153°35'E
Ambrym	Van.	16°15'S	168°09'E
Anaa	Tuam., FP	17°25'S	145°30'W
Anatahan	Mar.	16°21'N	145°40'E
Anatom	Van.	20°12'S	169°46'E
Aniwa	Van.	19°17'S	169°34'E
Ant	Pohnpei, FSM	6°54'N	157°58'E
Anuanuraro	Tuam., FP	20°28'S	143°33'W
Anuanurunga	Tuam., FP	20°38'S	143°19'W
Anuta	S.Cruz, SI	11°35'S	169°51'E
Aoba	Van.	15°23'S	167°50'E
Apataki	Tuam., FP	15°25'S	146°20'W
Apolima	Samoa	13°49'S	172°07'W
Aranuka	Gil., Kir.	0°10'N	173°38'E
Aratika	Tuam., FP	15°33'S	145°30'W
Arnavon	SI	7°24'S	158°00'E
Arno	Ratak, MI	7°05'N	171°42'E
Arorae	Gil., Kir.	2°39'S	176°55'E
Art	NC Group, NC	19°44'S	163°39'E
Arutua	Tuam., FP	15°10'S	146°45'W
Asuncion	Mar.	19°40'N	145°24'E
'Ata	Tonga	22°20'S	176°12'W
Atafu	Tokelau	8°32'S	172°31'W
Atiu	CI	20°02'S	158°07'W
Aua	Bis., PNG	1°25'S	143°05'E
Aukena	Gam., FP	23°08S	134°54'W
'Aunu'u	Am.Sam.	14°16'S	170°35'W
Aur	Ratak, MI	8°15'N	171°05'E
Avea	Lau, Fiji	17°11'S	178°55'W
Awin	Bis., PNG	1°40'S	144°05'E
Babase	Bis., PNG	4°00'S	153°40'E
Babeldaob	Palau	7°30'N	134°34'E
Bacon	Lau, Fiji	18°01'S	178°28'W
Bagaman	Lou., PNG	11°10'S	152°40'E
Bagbag	NG.group, PNG	4°50'S	146°15'E
Bakawari	N.Sol., PNG	6°15'S	155°35'E
Baker	USadm.	0°13'N	176°28'W
Baltra	Gal.	0°26'S	90°16'W
Baluan	Bis., PNG	2°30'S	147°15'E
Balum	Bis., PNG	4°00'S	153°40'E
Bam	NG.group, PNG	3°40'S	144°50'E

ISLAND	GROUP	LATITUDE	LONGITUDE
Banaba (Ocean)	Gil., Kir.	0°52'S	169°55'E
Basilaki	Lou., PNG	10°35'S	151°00'E
Bat	Bis., PNG	2°50'S	146°15'E
Batiki	Lom., Fiji	17°47'S	179°08'E
Beautemps-Beaupré	Loy., NC	20°24'S	166°10'E
Bellona	Sol.out., SI	11°18'S	159°48'E
Beqa	Vi.L., Fiji	18°24'S	178°07'E
Beru	Gil., Kir.	1°20'S	176°00'E
Bikar	Ratak, MI	12°15'N	170°05'E
Bikini	Ralik, MI	11°35'N	165°23'E
Bipi	Sol.Sea, PNG	2°05'S	146°25'E
Birnie	Phoe., Kir.	3°35'S	171°31'W
Blup Blup	NG.group, PNG	3°30'S	144°35'E
Boang	Bis., PNG	3°25'S	153°15'E
Bokaak (Pokak)	Ratak, MI	14°35'N	168°58'E
Bora-Bora	Soc., FP	16°30'S	151°45'W
Bougainville	N.Sol., PNG	6°10'S	155°10'E
Buka	N.Sol., PNG	5°20'S	154°38'E
Butaritari	Gil., Kir.	3°05'N	172°50'E
Caroline	Line, Kir.	10°00'S	150°14'W
Choiseul	SI	7°S	157°E
Chuuk (Truk)	Chuuk, FSM	7°20'N	151°45'E
Cicia	Lau, Fiji	17°45'S	179°20'W
Cikobia	Va.L., Fiji	15°45'S	179°56'W
Clipperton	EPac.	10°18'N	109°13'W
Cocos	EPac.	5°32'N	87°00'W
Crown	NG.group, PNG	5°10'S	146°55'E
Culpepper	Gal.	1°39'N	92°00'W
Dobu	D'Ent., PNG	9°47'S	150°53'E
Dublon	Chuuk, FSM	7°23'N	151°52'E
Ducie	Pitcairn	24°40'S	124°48'W
Duke of York	Bis., PNG	4°10'S	152°25'E
Easter (Rapa Nui)	EPac.	27°06'S	109°22'W
Eauripik	Yap, FSM	6°41.5'N	143°3'E
Ebon	Ralik, MI	4°38'N	168°43'E
Efate	Van.	17°40'S	168°23'E
Egum	Sol.Sea, PNG	9°25'S	152°00'E
Eiao	Marq., FP	8°00'S	140°41'W
Elato	Yap, FSM	7°30'N	146°10'E
Eloaua	Bis., PNG	1°40'S	149°40'E
Emae	Van.	17°04'S	168°23'E
Emirau	Bis., PNG	1°40'S	145°55'E
Enderbury	Phoe., Kir.	3°08'S	171°05'W
Enewetak	Ralik, MI	11°30'N	162°15'E
Eot	Chuuk, FSM	7°23'N	151°44'E

ISLAND	GROUP	LATITUDE	LONGITUDE
Epi	Van.	16°44'S	168°17'E
Erikub	Ratak, MI	9°08'N	170°00'E
Erromango	Van.	18°48'S	169°05'E
Espa	angoGal.	1°2'S	89°40'W
Espiritu Santo	Van.	15°20'S	166°55'E
Etal	Chuuk, FSM	5°35'N	153°34'E
'Eua	Tonga	21°20'S	174°57'W
Ewose	Van.	16°57'S	168°35'E
Faaite	Tuam., FP	16°44'S	145°15'W
Fais	Yap, FSM	9°46'N	140°31'E
Fakahina	Tuam., FP	15°59'S	140°07'W
Fakaofo	Tokelau	9°23'S	171°15'W
Fakarava	Tuam., FP	16°15'S	145°32'W
Fanapanges	Chuuk, FSM	7°21'N	151°40'E
Fangatau	Tuam., FP	15°49'S	140°51'W
Fangataufa	Tuam., FP	22°15'S	138°42'W
Farallon de Medinilla	Mar.	16°01'N	146°05'E
Farallon de Pajaros	Mar.	20°32'N	144°54'E
Faraulep	Yap, FSM	8°36'N	144°33'E
Fatu Hiva	Marq., FP	10°26'S	18°38'W
Fatu Huku	Marq., FP	9°27'S	138°55'W
Fayu	Chuuk, FSM	8°34'N	151°22'E
Fefan	Chuuk, FSM	7°20'N	151°51'E
Fergusson	D'Ent., PNG	9°30'S	150°40'E
Fernandina	Gal.	0°25'S	91°30'W
Flint	Line, Kir.	11°26'S	151°48'W
Floreana	Gal.	1°20'S	90°25'W
Foa	Ha'ap., Tonga	19°45'S	174°17'W
Fonuafo'ou	Ha'ap., Tonga	20°19'S	175°25'W
Fulanga	Lau, Fiji	19°07'S	178°35'W
Funafuti	Tuvalu	8°31'S	179°08'E
Futuna	W&F	14°16'S	178°08'W
Futuna (Erronan)	Van.	19°32'S	170°10.5'E
Gaferut	Yap, FSM	9°14'N	145°23'E
Gagil Tamil	Yap, FSM	9°32'N	138°10'E
Garove	Bis., PNG	4°40'S	149°30'E
Gau	Lom., Fiji	18°02'S	179°18'E
Gawa	Sol.Sea, PNG	9°00'S	151°55'E
Ghizo (Gizo)	SI	8°04'S	156°48'E
Goodenough	D'Ent., PNG	9°24'S	150°15'E
Guadalcanal	SI	9°40'S	160°20'E
Guam	Guam	13°25'N	144°45'E
Guguan	Mar.	17°19'N	145°51'E
Ha'ano	Ha'ap., Tonga	19°40'S	174°17'W
Hao	Tuam., FP	18°10'S	140°55'W

ISLAND	GROUP	LATITUDE	LONGITUDE
Haraiki	Tuam., FP	17°28'S	143°32'W
Hatutaa	Marq., FP	7°56'S	140°34'W
Hawai'i	Haw.	19°40'N	155°30'W
Henderson	Pitcairn	24°22'S	130°05'W
Hereheretue	Tuam., FP	19°53'S	145°05'W
Hikueru	Tuam., FP	17°36'S	142°40'W
Hiti	Tuam., FP	16°42'S	144°08'W
Hiu	Tor., Van.	13°09'S	166°34'E
Hiva Oa	Marq., FP	9°45'S	139°00'W
Howland	USadm.	0°48'N	176°38'W
Huahine	Soc., FP	16°45'S	151°00'W
Hunga Tonga	Ha'ap., Tonga	20°33'S	175°23'W
Hunter	NC.out., NC	22°24'S	172°94'E
Huon	NC Group, NC	18°03'S	162°58'E
Ifalik	Yap, FSM	7°15'N	144°27'E
Isabela	Gal.	0°30'S	91°10'W
Jabwot	Ralik, MI	7°45'N	168°59'E
Jaluit	Ralik, MI	6°00'N	169°35'E
Jarvis	Line, USadm.	0°23'S	160°02'W
Jemo	Ratak, MI	10°08'N	169°32'E
Johnston	USadm.	16°45'N	169°30'W
Kadavu	Vi.L., Fiji	19°01'S	178°12'E
Kaho'olawe	Haw.	20°33'N	156°37'W
Kaileuna	Sol.Sea, PNG	8°30'S	150°55'E
Kairiru	NG.group, PNG	3°20'S	143°30'E
Kamaka	Gam., FP	23°15'S	134°57'W
Kaniet	Bis., PNG	0°50'S	135°30'E
Kanton (Canton)	Phoe., Kir.	2°50'S	171°43'W
Kao	Ha'ap., Tonga	19°40'S	175°02'W
Kapingamarangi	Pohnpei, FSM	1°03'N	154°46'E
Karkar	NG.group, PNG	4°40'S	146°00'E
Katiu	Tuam., FP	16°25'S	144°20'W
Kaua'i	Haw.	22°N	159°30'W
Kauehi	Tuam., FP	15°50'S	145°10'W
Kaukura	Tuam., FP	15°40'S	146°40'W
Ka'ula	Haw.	21°39'N	160°33'W
Kili	Ralik, MI	5°39'N	169°07'E
Kiritimati	Line, Kir.	1°55'N	157°20'W
Kiriwina	Sol.Sea, PNG	8°40'S	151°05'E
Kitava	Sol.Sea, PNG	8°36'S	151°20'E
Koil	NG.group, PNG	3°20'S	144°10'E
Kolombangara	SI	8°S	157°05'E
Koro	Lom., Fiji	17°16'S	179°23'E
Kosrae	Kosrae, FSM	5°20'N	162°59'E
Kure	NWHI, Haw.	28°25'N	178°25'W

ISLAND	GROUP	LATITUDE	LONGITUDE
Kuria	Gil., Kir.	0°14′N	173°28′E
Kwaiawata	Sol.Sea, PNG	8°55′S	151°50′E
Kwajalein	Ralik, MI	9°05′N	167°20′E
Lae	Ralik, MI	8°56′N	166°15′E
Lakeba	Lau, Fiji	18°13′S	178°43′W
Lamotrek	Yap, FSM	7°30′N	146°20′E
Lāna'i	Haw.	20°50′N	156°55′W
Late	Vava'u, Tonga	18°48′S	174°39′W
Lavongai	Bis., PNG	2°32′S	150°15′E
Laysan	NWHI, Haw.	25°46′N	171°44′W
Lehua	Haw.	22°01N	160°06′W
Lib	Ralik, MI	8°19′N	167°24′E
Lifou	Loy., NC	21°00′S	167°15′E
Lifuka	Ha'ap., Tonga	19°48′S	174°21′W
Lihir	Bis., PNG	3°15′S	152°39′E
Likiep	Ratak , MI	9°55′N	169°08′E
Liot	Bis., PNG	1°25′S	144°30′E
Lisianski	NWHI, Haw.	26°04′N	173°58′W
Lolobau	Bis., PNG	4°55′S	151°10′E
Long	NG.group, PNG	5°20′S	147°05′E
Losap	Chuuk, FSM	6°52′N	152°42′E
Lou	Bis., PNG	2°25′S	147°20′E
Luf	Bis., PNG	1°35′S	145°05′E
Lukunor	Chuuk, FSM	5°31′N	153°46′E
Maap	Yap, FSM	9°35′N	138°11′W
Madau	Sol.Sea, PNG	9°00′S	152°25′E
Maewo	Van.	15°10′S	168°10′E
Mahotani	Marq., FP	10°S	138°39′W
Mahur	Bis., PNG	2°45′S	152°40′E
Maia	Soc., FP	17°37′S	150°37′W
Maiana	Gil., Kir.	1°00′N	173°01′E
Maiao	Soc., FP	17°37′S	150°37′W
Majuro	Ratak, MI	7°07′N	171°12′E
Makaroa	Gam., FP	23°13′S	134°58′W
Makatea	Tuam., FP	15°50′S	148°13′W
Makemo	Tuam., FP	16°35′S	143°40′W
Makin	Gil., Kir.	3°16′N	172°58′E
Makogai	Lom., Fiji	17°27′S	178°57′E
Malaita	SI	9°S	161°E
Malakula	Van.	16°15′S	167°30′E
Malden	Line, Kir.	4°03′S	154°59′W
Malendok	Bis., PNG	3°30′S	153°15′E
Mali	Bis., PNG	3°10′S	152°40′E
Maloelap	Ratak , MI	8°45′N	171°00′E
Malpelo	EPac.	4°N	81°15′W

ISLAND	GROUP	LATITUDE	LONGITUDE
Malum	N.Sol., PNG	3°10′S°	154°25′E
Manam	NG.group, PNG	4°05′S	145°05′E
Mangaia	CI	21°55′S	157°55′W
Mangareva	Gam., FP	23°07′S	134°57′W
Manihi	Tuam., FP	14°26′S	145°55′W
Manihiki	CI	10°23′S	161°01′W
Manono	Samoa	13°50′S	172°05′W
Manra (Sydney)	Phoe., Kir.	4°27′S	171°16′W
Manu	Bis., PNG	1°20′S	143°35′E
Manuae	CI	19°21′S	158°56′W
Manuae	Soc., FP	16°30′S	154°40′W
Manuhangi	Tuam., FP	19°11′S	141°15′W
Manui	Gam., FP	23°14′S	134°56′W
Manus	Bis., PNG	2°05′S	147°E
Marakei	Gil., Kir.	2°00′N	173°20′E
Marchena	Gal.	0°21′N	90°30′W
Maré	Loy., NC	21°30′S	168°00′E
Maria	Tuam., FP	22°01′S	136°10′W
Marokau	Tuam., FP	18°03′S	142°17′W
Maron	Bis., PNG	1°35′S	145°00′E
Marotiri Nui	Aus., FP	27°55′S	143°26′W
Marutea North	Tuam., FP	17°00′S	143°10′W
Marutea South	Tuam., FP	21°30′S	135°30′W
Masahet	Bis., PNG	3°00′S	152°40′E
Mataiva	Tuam., FP	14°54′S	148°40′W
Matthew	NC.out., NC	22°20′S	171°19′E
Matuku	Ha'ap., Tonga	19°10′S	179°45′E
Matureivavao	Tuam., FP	21°46′S	136°25′W
Maui	Haw.	20°50′N	156°25′W
Mauke	CI	20°09′S	157°23′W
Maupihaa	Soc., FP	16°49′S	153°57′W
Maupiti	Soc., FP	16°26′S	152°15′W
Mbuke	Bis., PNG	2°25′S	146°50′E
McKean	Phoe., Kir.	3°36′S	174°08′W
Mehetia	Soc., FP	17°53′S	148°06′W
Mejit	Ratak, MI	10°17′N	170°53′E
Mere Lava	Banks, Van.	14°26′S	167°58′E
Merig	Banks, Van.	14°17′S	167°48′E
Merir	Pal.out., Palau	4°19′N	132°19′E
Midway	USadm.	28°13′N	177°23′W
Mili	Ratak, MI	6°08′N	171°57′E
Misima	Lou., PNG	10°40′S	152°43′E
Mitiaro	CI	19°49′S	157°43′W
Moala	Moala, Fiji	18°36′S	179°53′E
Moce	Lau, Fiji	18°39′S	178°31′W

ISLAND	GROUP	LATITUDE	LONGITUDE
Moen	Chuuk, FSM	7°26'N	151°52'E
Mohotani	Marq., FP	10°S	138°39'W
Mole	Bis., PNG	2°50'S	146°25'E
Moloka'i	Haw.	21°08'N	157°W
Molokini	Haw.	20°38'N	156°29'W
Moorea	Soc., FP	17°30'S	149°50'W
Morane	Tuam., FP	23°07'S	137°07'W
Moruroa	Tuam., FP	21°50'S	138°55'W
Mota	Banks, Van.	13°49'S	167°42'E
Mota Lava	Banks, Van.	13°40'S	167°40'E
Mota Lava (Valua)	Banks, Van.	13°40'S	167°40'E
Motu Iti	Marq., FP	16°16'S	151°49'W
Motu One	Marq., FP	7°53'S	140°23'W
Motu One	Soc., FP	15°50'S	154°30'W
Motutunga	Tuam., FP	17°05'S	144°22'W
Murilo	Chuuk, FSM	8°40'N	152°11'E
Muschu	NG.group, PNG	3°25'S	143°30'E
Mussau	Bis., PNG	1°25'S	149°37'E
Muwo	Sol.Sea, PNG	8°45'S	151°00'E
Muyua (Woodlark)	Sol.Sea, PNG	9°10'S	152°45'E
Mwokil	Pohnpei, FSM	6°40'N	159°46'E
Nairai	Lom., Fiji	17°49'S	179°24'E
Nama	Chuuk, FSM	7°00'N	152°35'E
Namoluk	Chuuk, FSM	5°55'N	153°08'E
Namonuito	Chuuk, FSM	8°45'N	150°05'E
Namorik	Ralik, MI	5°35'N	168°07'E
Namu	Ralik, MI	8°00'N	168°10'E
Nanumanga	Tuvalu	6°18'S	176°21'E
Nanumea	Tuvalu	5°39'S	176°08'E
Napuka	Tuam., FP	14°09'S	141°15'W
Narage	Bis., PNG	4°30'S	149°05'E
Nasai	Sol.Sea, PNG	9°10'S	152°40'E
Nassau	CI	11°33'S	165°25'W
Nauna	Bis., PNG	2°15'S	148°10'E
Nauru	Nauru	0°32'S	166°55'E
Nayau	Lau, Fiji	17°58'S	179°03'W
NC	NC Group, NC	21°28'S	164°40'E
Necker	NWHI, Haw.	23°35'N	164°42'W
Nendö	S.Cruz, SI	10°46'S	165°55'E
Nengonengo	Tuam., FP	18°50'S	141°47'W
Neoch	Chuuk, FSM	7°02'N	151°55'E
New Britain	Bis., PNG	4°10'S	6°20'E
New Georgia	SI	8°15'S	157°35'E
New Ireland	Bis., PNG	3°30'S	152°E
Ngcheangel	Palau	8°03'N	134°43'E

ISLAND	GROUP	LATITUDE	LONGITUDE
Ngeaur	Palau	6°54'N	134°09'E
Ngemlis	Palau	7°07'N	134°15'E
Ngeruktabel	Palau	7°15'N	134°25'E
Ngetik	Pohnpei, FSM	5°50'N	157°15'E
Ngulu	Yap, FSM	8°27'N	137°29'E
Niau	Tuam., FP	16°10'S	146°20'W
Nihiru	Tuam., FP	16°43'S	142°50'W
Nihoa	NWHI, Haw.	23°03'N	161°55'W
Ni'ihau	Haw.	21°55'N	160°10'W
Nikumaroro (Gardner)	Phoe., Kir.	4°40'S	174°32'W
Nikunau	Gil., Kir.	1°21'S	176°28'E
Niningo	Bis., PNG	1°15'S	144°15'E
Nissan	N.Sol., PNG	4°30'S	154°10'E
Niuafo'ou	Tonga	15°35'S	175°38'W
Niuatoputapu	Tonga	15°58'S	173°48'W
Niue	Niue	19°00'S	169°50'W
Niulakita	Tuvalu	10°45'S	179°30'E
Niutao	Tuvalu	6°06'S	177°16'E
Nomuka	Ha'ap., Tonga	20°27'S	174°46'W
Nomwin	Chuuk, FSM	8°31'N	151°47'E
Nonouti	Gil., Kir.	0°40'S	174°20'E
Normanby	D'Ent., PNG	10°00'S	151°00'E
Nuakata	Lou., PNG	10°15'S	151°00'E
Nuguria	N.Sol., PNG	3°15'S	154°40'E
Nui	Tuvalu	7°16'S	177°10'E
Nuku Hiva	Marq., FP	8°52'S	140°05'W
Nukufetau	Tuvalu	8°00'S	178°29'E
Nukulaelae	Tuvalu	9°22'S	179°51'E
Nukumanu	N.Sol., PNG	4°32'S	159°26'E
Nukunonu	Tokelau	9°10'S	171°53'W
Nukuoro	Pohnpei, FSM	3°51'N	154°58'E
Nukutavake	Tuam., FP	19°16'S	138°51'W
Nukutipipi	Tuam., FP	20°42'S	143°03'W
Nupani	S.Cruz, SI	10°21'S	166°17'E
O'ahu	Haw.	21°30'N	158°W
Oeno	Pitcairn	23°56'S	130°44'W
Ofu	Am.Sam.	14°11'S	169°41'W
Olimarao	Yap, FSM	7°41'N	145°52'E
Olosenga	Am.Sam.	14°11'S	169°39'W
Oneata	Lau, Fiji	18°24'S°	178°29'W
Ono	Kad., Fiji	18°54'S	178°29'E
Ono-i-lau	Lau, Fiji	20°40'S	178°43'W
Onotoa	Gil., Kir.	1°50'S	175°33'E
Ontong Java	Sol.out., SI	5°20'S	159°30'E
Oreor (Koror)	Palau	7°20'N	134°30'E

ISLAND	GROUP	LATITUDE	LONGITUDE
Oroluk	Pohnpei, FSM	7°32'N	155°18'E
Orona (Hull)	Phoe., Kir.	4°29'S	170°43'W
Ouen	NC Group, NC	22°26'S	166°49'E
Ouvéa	Loy., NC	20°35'S	166°30'E
Ovalau	Vi.L., Fiji	17°41'S	178°47'E
Pagan	Mar.	18°07'N	145°46'E
Pak	Bis., PNG	2°05'S	147°35'E
Pakin	Pohnpei, FSM	7°03'N	157°48'E
Palmerston	CI	18°04'S	163°10'W
Palmyra	Line, USadm.	5°52'N	162°06'W
Panaeati	Lou., PNG	10°40'S	152°20'E
Panatinane	Lou., PNG	11°15'S	153°10'E
Panawina	Lou., PNG	11°10'S	153°00'E
Paraoa	Tuam., FP	19°09'S	140°43'W
Peleliu (Beliliou)	Palau	7°00'N	134°15'E
Pelelun	Bis., PNG	1°05'S	144°25'E
Penrhyn	CI	9°00'S	158°03'W
Pentecost	Van.	15°45'S	168°12'E
Pikelot	Yap, FSM	8°05'N	147°38'E
Pinaki	Tuam., FP	19°22'S	138°42'W
Pines	NC Group, NC	22°39'S	167°28'E
Pingelap	Pohnpei, FSM	6°13'N	160°46'E
Pinipel	N.Sol., PNG	4°25'S	154°05'E
Pinta	Gal.	0°35'N	90°45'W
Pitcairn	Pitcairn	25°04'S	130°05'W
Pohnpei	Pohnpei, FSM	6°52'N	158°14'E
Pott	NC Group, NC	19°35'S	163°36'E
Pukapuka	CI	10°55'S	165°50'W
Pukapuka	Tuam., FP	14°56'S	138°45'W
Pukarua	Tuam., FP	18°20'S	137°02'W
Pulap	Chuuk, FSM	7°35'N	149°25'E
Pulo Anna	Pal.out., Palau	4°40'N	131°58'E
Pulusuk	Chuuk, FSM	6°41'N	149°19'E
Puluwat	Chuuk, FSM	7°21'N	149°11'E
Qamea	Va.L., Fiji	16°45'S	179°46'W
Rabi	Va.L., Fiji	16°31'S°	179°59'W
Raiatea	Soc., FP	16°50'S	151°25'W
Raivavae	Aus., FP	23°52'S	147°40'W
Rakahanga	CI	10°02'S	161°06'W
Rambutyo	Bis., PNG	2°20'S	147°50'E
Rangiroa	Tuam., FP	15°05'S	147°40W
Ranongga	SI	8°05'S	156°35'E
Rapa	Aus., FP	27°36'S	144°18'W
Raraka	Tuam., FP	16°10'S	144°50'W
Raroia	Tuam., FP	16°05'S	142°23'W

ISLAND	GROUP	LATITUDE	LONGITUDE
Rarotonga	CI	21°14'S	159°46'W
Rat	Bis., PNG	2°55'S	146°20'E
Ravahere	Tuam., FP	18°13'S	142°10'W
Rawaki (Phoenix)	Phoe., Kir.	3°43'S	170°43'W
Reao	Tuam., FP	18°30'S	136°20'W
Reitoru	Tuam., FP	17°48'S	143°06'W
Rekareka	Tuam., FP	16°49'S	141°55'W
Rendova	SI	8°34'S	157°20'E
Rennell	Sol.out., SI	11°32'S	160°10'E
Rimatara	Aus., FP	22°38'S	152°45'W
Robinson Crusoe	J.Fer.	33°38'S	78°50'W
Romonum	Chuuk, FSM	7°25'N	151°40'E
Rongelap	Ralik, MI	11°20'N	166°50'E
Rongrik	Ralik, MI	11°20'N	167°27'E
Rose	Am.Sam.	14°33'S	168°09'W
Rossel	Lou., PNG	11°22'S	154°10'E
Rota	Mar.	14°09'N	145°12'E
Rotuma	Fi.out., Fiji	12°30'S	175°52'E
Rumung	Yap, FSM	9°37'N	138°10'E
Rururu	Aus., FP	22°26'S	151°20'W
Sae	Bis., PNG	0°40'S	145°15'E
Saipan	Mar.	15°10'N	145°45'E
Sakar	NG.group, PNG	5°25'S	148°05'E
Sala-y-Gomez	EPac.	26°28'S	105°28'W
Samarai	Lou., PNG	10°35'S	150°35'E
San Ambrosio	EPac.	26°21'S	79°52'W
San Cristobal	Gal.	0°50'S	89°30'W
San Cristobal	SI	10°35'S	161°45'E
San Felix	EPac.	26°17'S	80°05'W
Sanaroa	D'Ent., PNG	9°40'S	151°00'E
Sandy	NC.out., NC	19°10'S	159°57'E
Santa Cruz	Gal.	0°35'S	90°25'W
Santa Fe	Gal.	0°50'S	90°04'W
Santa Isabel	SI	8°S	159°E
Santa Maria (Gaua)	Banks, Van.	14°20'S	167°28'E
Santiago	Gal.	0°15'S	90°45'W
Sariba	Lou., PNG	10°35'S	140°40'E
Sarigan	Mar.	16°42'N	145°47'E
Satawal	Yap, FSM	7°21'N	147°02'E
Satawan	Chuuk, FSM	5°23'N	153°35'E
Savai'i	Samoa	13°40'S	172°30'W
Savo	SI	9°08'S	159°48'E
Shortland	SI	7°03'S	155°48'E
Sideia	Lou., PNG	10°35'S	150°50'E
Siis	Chuuk, FSM	7°18'N	1551°49'E

ISLAND	GROUP	LATITUDE	LONGITUDE
Sikaiana	Sol.out., SI	8°22'S	162°40'W
Simberi	Bis., PNG	2°35'S	152°E
Sonsorol	Pal.out., Palau	5°20'N	132°13'E
Sorol	Yap, FSM	8°08'N	140°23'E
Starbuck	Line, Kir.	5°37'S	153°53'W
Sudest (Tagula)	Lou., PNG	11°30'S	153°30'E
Sumasuma	Bis., PNG	1°30'S	144°05'E
Surprise	NC Group, NC	18°29'S	163°07'E
Suwarrow	CI	13°15'S	163°05'W
Swains	Am.Sam.	11°03'S	171°05'W
Tabar	Bis., PNG	2°55'S	152°E
Tabiteuea	Gil., Kir.	1°25'S	174°50'E
Tabuaeran (Fanning)	Line, Kir.	3°54'N	159°23'W
Taenga	Tuam., FP	16°19'S	143°06'W
Tafahi	Tonga	15°51'S	173°44'W
Tahaa	Soc., FP	16°38'S	151°28'W
Tahanea	Tuam., FP	16°56'S	144°47'W
Tahiti	Soc., FP	17°38'S	149°25'W
Tahuata	Marq., FP	9°55'S	139°05'W
Taiaro	Tuam., FP	15°44'S	144°37'W
Taiof	N.Sol., PNG	5°35'S	154°40'E
Taka	Ratak, MI	11°08'N	168°38'E
Takapoto	Tuam., FP	14°36'S	145°12'W
Takaroa	Tuam., FP	14°27'S	144°55'W
Takume	Tuam., FP	15°45'S	142°10'W
Takuu	N.Sol., PNG	4°50'S	157°05'E
Tamana	Gil., Kir.	2°32'S	175°58'E
Tanna	Van.	19°30'S	169°20'E
Taravai	Gam., FP	23°09'S	136°01'W
Tarawa	Gil., Kir.	1°30'N	173°00'E
Tarawai	NG.group, PNG	3°15'S	143°20'E
Tatakoto	Tuam., FP	17°20'S	138°22'W
Tatau	Bis., PNG	2°0'S	151°55'E
Ta'u	Am.Sam.	14°14'S	169°28'W
Tauere	Tuam., FP	17°22'S	141°28'W
Taveuni	Va.L., Fiji	16°50'S	179°58'W
Tefa	Bis., PNG	3°35'S	153°10'E
Tegua	Tor., Van.	13°14'S	166°36'E
Tekokota	Tuam., FP	17°19'S	142°37'W
Tematangi	Tuam., FP	21°40'S	140°40'W
Temoe	Gam., FP	23°20'S	134°30'W
Tenararo	Tuam., FP	21°19'S	136°46'W
Tenarunga	Tuam., FP	21°19'S	136°33'W
Tench	Bis., PNG	1°40'S	150°40'E
Tepoto North	Tuam., FP	14°05'S	141°24'W

ISLAND	GROUP	LATITUDE	LONGITUDE
Tepoto South	Tuam., FP	16°48'S	144°17'W
Teraina (Washington)	Line, Kir.	4°43'N	160°26'W
Tetepare	SI	8°44'S	157°33'E
Tetiaroa	Soc., FP	17°05'S	149°32'W
Tikehau	Tuam., FP	15°00'S	148°10'W
Tikei	Tuam., FP	14°54'S	144°32'W
Tikopia	S.Cruz, SI	12°18'S	168°49'E
Tinian	Mar.	15°00'N	145°38'E
Toau	Tuam., FP	15°52'S	146°W
Tobi	Pal.out., Palau	3°00'N	131°10.5'E
Tofua	Ha'ap., Tonga	19°43'S	175°03'W
Toga	Tor., Van.	13°26'S	166°41'E
Toku	Tonga	18°09'S	174°09'W
Tol	Chuuk, FSM	7°21'N	151°38'E
Tolokiwa	NG.group, PNG	5°20'S	147°35'E
Tongariki	Van.	17°00'S	168°38'E
Tongatapu	Tonga	21°10'S	175°10'W
Tongoa	Van.	16°54'S	168°34'E
Totoya	Moala, Fiji	18°57'S	179°51'W
Tower	Gal.	0°20'N	89°57'W
Tuanake	Tuam., FP	16°40'S	144°14'W
Tubuai	Aus., FP	23°23'S	149°26'W
Tulun (Kilinilau)	N.Sol., PNG	4°44'S	155°24'E
Tupai	Soc., FP	16°16'S	151°49'W
Tureia	Tuam., FP	20°46'S	138°31'W
Tutuila	Am.Sam.	14°18'S	170°42'W
Tuvana-i-Colo	Lau, Fiji	21°02'S	178°50'W
Tuvana-i-Ra	Lau, Fiji	21°00'S	178°44'W
Ua Huka	Marq., FP	8°54'S	139°32'W
Ua Pou	Marq., FP	9°24'S	140°03'W
Udot	Chuuk, FSM	7°23'N	151°43'E
Ujae	Ralik, MI	9°04'N	165°38'E
Ujelang	Ralik, MI	9°50'N	160°55'E
Uki Ni Masi (Ugi)	SI	10°15'S	161°44'E
Ulithi	Yap, FSM	9°56'N	139°40'E
Ulu	Bis., PNG	4°15'S	152°25'E
Uman	Chuuk, FSM	7°18'N	151°53'E
Umboi	NG.group, PNG	5°29'S	147°48'E
Unea	Bis., PNG	4°55'S	149°10'E
Uoleva	Ha'ap., Tonga	19°51'S	174°25'W
'Upolu	Samoa	13°55'S	171°45'W
Ureparapara	Banks, Van.	13°31'S	167°20'E
Utrik	Ratak, MI	11°15'N	169°48'E
Utupua	S.Cruz, SI	11°19'S	166°33'E
'Uvea (Wallis)	W&F	13°18'S	176°10'W

ISLAND	GROUP	LATITUDE	LONGITUDE
Vahanga	Tuam., FP	21°20'S	136°39'W
Vahitahi	Tuam., FP	18°44'S	138°52'W
Vairaatea	Tuam., FP	19°18'S	139°19'W
Vaitupu	Tuvalu	7°28'S	178°41'E
Vakuta	Sol.Sea, PNG	8°50'S	151°10'E
Vanavana	Tuam., FP	20°37'S	139°08'W
Vangunu	SI	8°40'S	158°00'E
Vanikolo	S.Cruz, SI	11°40'S	166°54'E
Vanua Balavu	Lau, Fiji	17°15'S	178°59'W
Vanua Lava	Banks, Van.	13°48'S	167°26'E
Vanua Levu	Va.L., Fiji	16°09'S	179°57'E
Vatoa	Lau, Fiji	19°50'S	178°13'W
Vatulele	Vi.L., Fiji	18°33'S	177°38'E
Vava'u	Vava'u, Tonga	18°35'S	174°00'W
Vella Lavella	SI	7°45'S	156°40'E
Viti Levu	Vi.L., Fiji	17°50'S	178°00'E
Vokeo	NG.group, PNG	3°15'S	144°05'E

ISLAND	GROUP	LATITUDE	LONGITUDE
Vonavona	SI	8°15'S	157°15'E
Vostok	Line, Kir.	10°06'S	152°23'W
Wake	USadm.	19°17'N	166°35'E
Walis	NG.group, PNG	3°15'S	143°20'E
Walpole	NC.out., NC	22°38'S	168°56'E
Wamea	D'Ent., PNG	9°15'S	150°55'E
Watom	Bis., PNG	4°10'S	152°05'E
Wawiwa	D'Ent., PNG	9°20'S	150°45'E
Wenman	Gal.	1°23'N	91°49'W
West Fayu	Yap, FSM	8°05'N	146°44'E
Woleai	Yap, FSM	7°21'N	143°53'E
Wotho	Ralik, MI	10°07'N	165°58'E
Wotje	Ratak, MI	9°28'N	170°00'E
Wuvulu	Bis., PNG	1°45'S	142°45'E
Yap	Yap, FSM	9°31'N	138°08'E
Yeina	Lou., PNG	11°20'S	153°25'E

CONTRIBUTORS

David Abbott is a Pacific development consultant and was until recently the regional macroeconomic and poverty-reduction advisor with UNDP's Pacific Centre based in Fiji, providing policy analysis and advisory support to all fifteen PICs. David has more than thirty years of experience in development economics in the Pacific Islands and is one of the leaders in poverty analysis and research in the Pacific Islands.

Dennis Ahlburg is president and professor of economics, Trinity University. He has held visiting appointments at the Australian National University, the Program on Population at the East-West Center, and the Centre for Population Studies at the London School of Hygiene and Tropical Medicine. He has published widely on various economic and demographic aspects of the Pacific Islands, including the impact of population growth on economic development, determinants and consequences of migration and remittance flows, poverty, job creation, and the economic and demographic impact of HIV/AIDS.

Glenn Banks is an associate professor in development studies at Massey University, New Zealand. He completed his PhD from the Australian National University with a dissertation on the Porgera gold mine in Papua New Guinea in 1997 and has continued to work as a researcher and consultant on the mining industry until the present. His research interests include community involvement in large-scale resource developments, development in the Pacific, and mining in the developing world. He has published a number of books and journal papers on community social and economic issues around large-scale mining, resource conflicts, and corporate social responsibility in the minerals sector.

John Barker is professor of anthropology at the University of British Columbia. His has undertaken research in Papua New Guinea and among First Nations peoples in British Columbia on religion, politics, and cultural change. His edited books include the widely read *Christianity in Oceania: Ethnographic Perspectives* (University Press of America, 1990) and *The Anthropology of Morality in Melanesia and Beyond* (Ashgate, 2007). He also wrote *Ancestral Lines: The Maisin of Papua New Guinea and the Fate of the Rainforest* (University of Toronto Press, 2008).

Geoff Bertram is senior associate at the Institute for Governance Studies, Victoria University of Wellington. He is a graduate of Victoria University with a DPhil. in economics from the University of Oxford. He has published extensively on development issues in small-island jurisdictions and has served on the editorial boards of *World Development, Asia Pacific Viewpoint,* and *Island Studies Journal.* His other research areas include Peruvian and New Zealand economic history, the economics of climate change, energy economics, and regulation of natural monopolies.

David A. Chappell is associate professor of Pacific Islands history at the University of Hawai'i at Mānoa. He has published articles in scholarly journals such as the *Journal of Pacific History, The Contemporary Pacific,* and *Pacific Studies,* as well as in the *Samoan News, Pacific Islands Monthly,* and *Islands Business.* In 1997, he published *Double Ghosts: Oceanian Voyagers on Euroamerican Ships* (M. E. Sharpe, 1997). He has also taught history courses in the Marshall Islands and American Samoa. His recent work has focused on nationalist politics in New Caledonia, with a book forthcoming from the Pacific Islands Manuscripts Series of UH Press.

John Connell is professor of geography at the University of Sydney. He worked from 1974 to 1976 in Bougainville on issues of rural development, and in Nouméa from 1981 to 1983 as coordinator of the joint SPC/ILO project on Migration, Employment, and Development in the South Pacific. He has written more than a dozen books, mainly on the Pacific, including two on New Caledonia, and several on Pacific urbanization with John Lea. He wrote *Papua New Guinea: The Struggle for Development* (Routledge, 1997) and *The Global Health Care Chain: From the Pacific to the World* (Routledge 2009).

Ron Crocombe (1929–2009) was professor of Pacific Studies of the University of the South Pacific from 1969 to 1989. In 1976, he founded the university's Institute of Pacific Studies and was director through 1985. He was director of the New Guinea Research Unit of the Australian National University from 1965 to 1969. He authored or coauthored and edited forty books, seventeen of them dealing with land tenure and/or rural development in the Pacific. Others deal with social and cultural policy, higher education, politics, and international relations in the Pacific region.

Julie Cupples teaches human geography at the University of Edinburgh. She carries out research in both New Zealand and Latin America and has published widely on gender, development, the construction of citizenship, disaster management, and environmental risk.

Derrick Depledge is a consulting hydrogeologist and engineering geologist with an MSc from Imperial College in London. He has been working in the Pacific since 1989 on various major water and sanitation projects in Solomon Islands, Vanuatu, Fiji, and Kiribati and has visited many of the other island nations in both the South and North Pacific. His publications include subjects as varied as the water resources of urban areas in Vanuatu, sanitation for small islands, and geothermal resources of the South Pacific. He delivered a keynote paper on the water resources of the Pacific at an Asian Development Bank workshop.

Colin Filer holds a PhD in social anthropology from the University of Cambridge. He has taught at the Universities of Glasgow and Papua New Guinea and was projects manager for the University of Papua New Guinea's consulting company from 1991 to 1994, when he left the university to join the PNG National Research Institute as head of the Social and Environmental Studies Division. Since 2001, he has been the convenor of the Resource Management in Asia-Pacific Program at the Australian National University.

Gerard J. Fryer is a geophysicist at the Pacific Tsunami Warning Center and affiliate faculty member at Hawai'i Institute of Geophysics and Planetology at the University of Hawai'i at Mānoa.

Patricia Fryer is planetary scientist (senior researcher) at Hawai'i Institute of Geophysics and Planetology at the University of Hawai'i at Mānoa. Her expertise is in convergent plate margin processes. Her work includes twenty-seven marine geology research cruises; fieldwork on land in Papua New Guinea, the Mariana island arc system, and central California; and three books edited and sixty refereed publications.

Brenden S. Holland is a member of the faculty in the Center for Conservation Research and Training at the University of Hawai'i at Mānoa. Dr. Holland studies biodiversity and diversification of tropical island species, specializing in phylogeography and conservation genetics of endemic invertebrate radiations in the marine and terrestrial environment. He has field experience on a number of tropical Pacific Island archipelagoes and Pacific Rim countries and holds a doctoral degree from Texas A&M University.

E. Alison Kay (1928–2008) was professor of zoology emeritus at the University of Hawai'i. She had degrees from Mills College and Cambridge University, and a PhD from the University of Hawai'i. She was author of *Hawaiian Marine Shells and Shells of Hawaii* (with Olive Schoenberg Dole) and editor of *A Natural History of the Hawaiian Islands: Selected Readings*. Her articles include papers on the Cypraeidae of the Indo-Pacific, Cenozoic phylogeny and biogeography, Darwin's biogeography and the oceanic islands of the central Pacific, and biogeography of the Pacific. Dr. Kay was associate editor of the *Hawaiian Journal of History* and Fellow of the American Association for the Advancement of Science and of the Linnean Society of London. She was named Scientist of the Year by ARCS Hawai'i in 1998.

David M. Kennedy is a geologist who specializes in the response of coastal and marine systems to climate and environmental change. He particularly focuses on the Quaternary period, researching estuarine, coral reef, and rocky coast environments. He completed his doctoral study at the University of Wollongong, Australia, under the guidance of Professor Colin Woodroffe following undergraduate studies at the University of Sydney, Australia. After a postdoctoral research position at Wollongong he was based at Victoria University of Wellington, New Zealand. He is currently a senior lecturer in the Department of Resource Management and Geography at the University of Melbourne, Australia.

Lamont Lindstrom is Kendall Professor and Chair of Anthropology at the University of Tulsa. He has published a number of studies of Pacific cultures, including *Knowledge and Power in a South Pacific Society*

(Smithsonian Institution Press, 1990) and *Cargo Cult: Strange Stories of Desire From Melanesia and Beyond* (University of Hawai'i Press, 1993). He has also edited several volumes of Pacific scholarship with Geoffrey M. White, including *Chiefs Today: Traditional Pacific Leadership and the Postcolonial State* (Stanford University Press, 1998).

Rick Lumpkin is a research oceanographer at NOAA's Atlantic Oceanographic and Meteorological Laboratory in Miami, Florida, where he also directs the Global Drifter Program. He received his PhD from the University of Hawai'i School of Ocean and Earth Science and Technology in 1998. His dissertation examined the impact of the Hawaiian Islands on the ocean currents of the North Pacific.

Harley I. Manner is emeritus professor of geography and Micronesian Studies, former chair of the Micronesian Studies Program, and chair of the Division of Social/Behavioral Sciences at the University of Guam. He holds BA, MA, and PhD. degrees in geography from the University of Hawai'i at Mānoa and also taught at Bucknell University, Yale, and the University of the South Pacific in Suva, Fiji. Dr. Manner has conducted fieldwork in Fiji, Guam, the Federated States of Micronesia, Nauru, Palau, Papua New Guinea, and many other Pacific islands. His research specializations include traditional agroforestry systems, ethnobotany, and tropical ecology. He is the Micronesian Coordinator for PABITRA (Pacific Asia Biodiversity Transect Network) and now studies coastal erosion and the cultural ecology of small, remote islands.

Selina Tusitala Marsh is of Samoan, Tuvalu, English, and French descent. She was the first person of Pacific Island descent to receive a PhD from the English Department at the University of Auckland, where she now teaches New Zealand and Pacific literature. She is a performance poet, part of the Pasifika Poets Collective who premiered their poetry show "Polynation" at the Queensland Poetry Festival (2008). Her first collection of poetry, *Fast talkin' PI* (2009), won the national Best First Book award. She coordinates Pasifika Poetry Web, a sister site of Auckland University's New Zealand Electronic Poetry Centre (www.nzepc.auckland.ac/pasifika).

Nancy McDowell is professor emeritus of anthropology at Beloit College. Her major interests are in Melanesian conceptual systems, particularly the place of exchange in such schemes, and with contemporary millenarian movements in the United States. Her fieldwork in the Sepik region of Papua New Guinea began in 1973 and continued intermittently until 2001. She served as the director of the Reproductive Decision-Making Project at the Institute for Social and Economic Research (PNG) in 1981, which resulted in an edited volume. She is also the author of a monograph on the Mundugumor, using the field notes of Margaret Mead as well as her own familiarity with the region. She was the secretary of the American Ethnological Society, chair of the board of the Association of Social Anthropology in Oceania, and has published numerous articles and reviews.

Hamish A. McGowan is reader in climatology at the University of Queensland, Brisbane, Australia. He received his PhD in 1995 from the University of Canterbury, Christchurch, New Zealand. His research interests, on which he has published widely, center on Earth's surface— atmosphere interactions, interregional transport of aerosols, coastal meteorology, and the palaeoclimate of eastern and north Australia.

Simon Milne is professor of tourism at Auckland University of Technology, where he directs the New Zealand Tourism Research Institute. Simon completed his PhD in economic geography at Cambridge in 1989 and taught at McGill University, Montreal, until 1998. He has conducted research on South Pacific tourism since 1985, focusing on economic impacts, labor markets, small- and medium-enterprise performance, and sustainable tourism strategy development. He has worked for both the UNDP and EU in the region.

R. John Morrison is BHP Professor of Environmental Science at the University of Wollongong, where he has worked since 1992. Originally trained as a chemist, he has spent much of his working life in developing countries (two years in East Africa, and almost twenty in the Pacific Islands), where he has applied his scientific expertise to addressing environmental issues, particularly land and water management. He has ongoing research interests in Pacific Island environmental issues, particularly lagoons, estuaries, land-water interactions, atolls, and waste management.

Dieter Mueller-Dombois is emeritus professor in the Botany Department, University of Hawai‘i. He wrote *Aims and Methods of Vegetation Ecology* (Wiley & Sons, 1974) with Professor Heinz Ellenberg, a first synthesis of European and Anglo-American approaches to vegetation science. In the 1970s, he was the scientific coordinator of the Hawai‘i contribution to the International Biological Program (IBP). This collaborative research effort culminated in the book *Island Ecosystems* (Hutchinson Ross Publications, IBP Synthesis Series 15, 1981). With F. R. Fosberg he wrote *Vegetation of the Tropical Pacific Islands* (Springer Ecological Studies 132, 1998).

Stephen G. Nelson is professor emeritus of marine biology at the University of Guam and a senior research scientist at the Environmental Research Laboratory of the University of Arizona, Tucson. He received a PhD in ecology from the University of California-Davis in 1976. From 1977 until 1997 he was a member of the faculty of the Marine Laboratory at the University of Guam, including two three-year stints as director of the laboratory.

Patrick D. Nunn is head of the School of Behavioural, Cognitive and Social Sciences at the University of New England and formerly professor of oceanic geoscience at the University of the South Pacific, Fiji. He has carried out research in many Pacific Island countries and in 1994 published *Oceanic Islands* (Blackwell), a book that recounts the physical development of islands. In 1998 his monograph *Pacific Island Landscapes* (Institute of Pacific Studies, University of the South Pacific) appeared, and in 1999 his book *Environmental Change in the Pacific Basin* (Wiley) appeared. His most recent books are *Climate, Environment and Society in the Pacific during the Last Millennium* (Elsevier, 2007) and *Vanished Islands and Hidden Continents of the Pacific* (University of Hawai‘i Press, 2008). In March 2003, Nunn was awarded the Gregory Medal of the Pacific Science Association for "outstanding service to science in the Pacific."

Michael R. Ogden is professor and director of film and video studies at Central Washington University. Dr. Ogden has more than twenty-five years of research and consulting experience in the Pacific Islands, focusing on issues of communication and media development, technology impact, and documentary film production. He has previously been affiliated with the University of the South Pacific, the East-West Center, and the University of Hawai‘i Center for Pacific Island Studies. He has produced several documentaries on traditional cultural revival and published many journal articles and book chapters dealing with the challenges of development in Pacific Island microstates and the impact of information and communication technologies on indigenous peoples.

Andrew Pawley is emeritus professor of linguistics at the Research School of Pacific and Asian Studies, Australian National University. He has done linguistic fieldwork among communities in Papua New Guinea, Fiji, and Samoa and has published extensively on the languages and history of the Austronesian- and Papuan-speaking peoples of the Pacific Islands. Before joining the Australian National University in 1990 he taught at the University of Auckland, the University of Papua New Guinea, and the University of Hawai‘i at Mānoa.

Jean Louis Rallu has been a demographer at INED (National Institute for Population Studies) since 1977. He worked for ORSTOM (Institute for Development and Cooperation) at the University of the South Pacific in Suva, Fiji, from 1992 to 1994. His interests are in fertility analysis in developed and developing countries, population and migration in Asia and Pacific, and the historical demography of the South Pacific. He published *Les Populations Océaniennes aux 19e et 20e Siècles* (INED, 1990) and *Population, Migration et Développement dans le Pacifique Sud* (UNESCO-MOST, 1997).

Vina Ram-Bidesi is a senior lecturer in marine studies at the University of the South Pacific in Suva, Fiji. She also works closely with the International Ocean Institute–Operational Centre for the Pacific Islands on training programs in ocean resources management. Her research interests are in tuna industry development and economics of community-based resource management. Her publications are on varied topics relating to social and economic aspects of Pacific Island fisheries such as gender issues, trade, industry development, and resource management.

Moshe Rapaport is lecturer in geography and environmental studies based at the University of Hawai‘i–West Hawai‘i Center in Kealakekua, Hawai‘i. His doctoral dissertation concerned socioeconomic aspects of pearl farming in the Tuamotu Archipelago, based on research in Takaroa Atoll, French Polynesia (1990–1991). His research has appeared in *Atoll Research Bulletin, Ocean Yearbook, Journal of Pacific History, Island Studies Journal,* and other publications.

Annette Sachs Robertson is the deputy director/deputy representative and formerly technical advisor in Health Systems and Reproductive Health at the United Nations Population Fund (UNFPA) Pacific Sub-Regional Office. She completed her Doctorate of Science at Harvard School of Public Health and undertook her medical training at the Fiji School of Medicine. She has held faculty positions at the Bahrain University Faculty of Medicine, Fiji School of Medicine, and the University of Hawai‘i's Pacific Basin Medical Officers Training Program. Her research interests include the health of the Pacific Island people, particularly reproductive health and family planning. She is also the abstract editor of the *Pacific Health Dialog.*

Richard Scaglion is UCIS Research Professor of Anthropology at the University of Pittsburgh. His primary interests are Melanesia, comparative Austronesia, and the anthropology of law. Dr. Scaglion has conducted long-term field research with the Abelam people, beginning in 1974. He is the former director of customary law development for the Law Reform Commission of Papua New Guinea and has been a Visiting Fellow at the Australian National University, the University of Hawai'i, and the East-West Center. He is editor of *Homicide Compensation in Papua New Guinea* and *Customary Law in Papua New Guinea,* and author or editor of numerous books and articles about Pacific cultures.

Donovan Storey is currently Chief of the Sustainable Urban Development Section, Environment Division at the United Nations Economic and Social Commission for Asia and the Pacific (UNESCAP). At the time of writing he was a senior lecturer in development planning at the University of Queensland, Brisbane, Australia, with a focus on urban governance, management, and informal settlements in developing countries, especially the Pacific Islands. He has worked and researched in the Asia-Pacific region for twenty years, concentrating on housing, livelihoods, community development, environment, urban poverty, and urban safety and violence.

Andrew P. Sturman is professor in geography at the University of Canterbury, New Zealand. He has extensive teaching and research interests at the university level in weather and climate, particularly in New Zealand, Australia, and the southwest Pacific. His systematic interests include synoptic, mesoscale, and local weather and climate, as well as applications to environmental issues such as air pollution, agriculture, and wind energy. Since 1997, his research has been funded in New Zealand by national funding awards (including the Marsden Fund and the Foundation for Research Science and Technology) and he is the leader of an active atmospheric research group at the University of Canterbury. In 2003, he was awarded the inaugural Edward Kidson Medal for research excellence in meteorology and climatology. His publications include *The Physical Environment: A New Zealand Perspective* (Oxford University Press, 2001) and *The Weather and Climate of Australia and New Zealand* (Oxford University Press, 1996 and 2006), as well as more than ninety national and international publications.

Lynne D. Talley is professor at the Scripps Institution of Oceanography, University of California, San Diego. She is a fellow of the American Meteorological Society, American Geophysical Union, Oceanography Society, and American Academy of Arts and Sciences. She has published extensively regarding large-scale ocean circulation, water properties, heat transport, and ocean variability, and is the lead author of *Descriptive Physical Oceanography: an Introduction (Sixth Edition).*

James P. Terry is associate professor in physical geography at the National University of Singapore. He is also adjunct professor and former head of the School of Geography at the University of the South Pacific, where he worked from 1996 to 2008. He is currently the chair of the International Council for Science (ICSU) steering group on natural hazards in the Asia-Pacific region. He has published on many aspects of island physical geography, including climatic extremes, tropical hydrology and geomorphology, water resources, natural hazards, soil erosion, and island geoscience.

Randolph R. Thaman is professor of Pacific Islands biogeography at the University of the South Pacific, Suva, Fiji, where he has taught for twenty-five years. He is coauthor with William C. Clarke of *Pacific Islands Agroforestry: Systems for Sustainability* and has authored numerous other works on Pacific Islands biogeography, sustainable development, food systems, and community-based biodiversity conservation.

Frank R. Thomas is senior lecturer and Pacific Studies Postgraduate Chair at the University of the South Pacific and former staff archaeologist for the Republic of the Marshall Islands Historic Preservation Office. His main research interests include historical ecology, particularly in atoll settings; human behavioral ecology; island archaeology; cultural heritage management; and traditional ecological knowledge. He is coeditor (with James Terry) of *The Marshall Islands: Environment, History and Society in the Atolls* (Faculty of Islands and Oceans, USP).

Caroline Vercoe is a senior lecturer in the Art History Department at the University of Auckland. She teaches courses in Pacific Art, Postcolonial Theory, and Contemporary New Zealand Art. She has published essays relating to Pacific art and visual culture, stereotypes and representation, and performance art in a number of journals including the *Journal of Pacific History, The Journal of New Zealand Art History,* and *Art Asia Pacific,* and in books including *Pacific Art Niu Sila: Pacific Heritage in the Arts* (Te Papa Press), *Paradise Now? Contemporary Art from the Pacific* (Asia Society Museum), and *The Bodies That Were Not Ours and Other Writings* (Routledge). Her writing also features in the London-based Digital Archive of the Institute of International Visual Art. Her doctorate focused on American performance art that deals with issues of race and gender.

Terence Wesley-Smith is the director and graduate chair at the Center for Pacific Island Studies at the University of Hawai'i at Mānoa. He writes and teaches about contemporary issues in Oceania, with a particular interest in mining, development, and the war in Bougainville. He is editor of *The Contemporary Pacific: A Journal of Island Affairs* and recently directed a collaborative research and instructional project funded by the Ford Foundation called Moving Cultures: Remaking Asia-Pacific Studies. The project explored new ways of doing "area studies" and focused on transnational flows of capital, labor, and tourists from Asia into the Republic of Palau.

Paul Wolffram lectures in film production at Victoria University of Wellington. His doctoral fieldwork among the Lak people of Southern New Ireland, Papua New Guinea, focuses on the music and dance practices associated with the region's extensive mortuary rites. He is an ethnomusicologist and ethnographic filmmaker and has produced and directed films on Pacific communities in Fiji, Papua New Guinea, and New Zealand.

INDEX

NOTES

1. Page numbers in boldface type include illustrations.

2. The method for referencing endnotes is shown by the following example: 169n9 (page 169, note 9).

3. Variant spellings and place-name usages are provided in parentheses.

4. Considerable variation exists with regard to nomenclature, spelling, and diacritics. The terms listed below should not be regarded as the single "correct" version.

ABBREVIATIONS OF ISLAND GROUPS

CI   Cook Islands
FP   French Polynesia
FSM   Federated States of Micronesia
MI   Marshall Islands
NC   New Caledonia
NZ   New Zealand
PNG   Papua New Guinea
SI   Solomon Islands
WP   West Papua

A

abn, 159
"AD 1300 event," 56
adaptive shifts, 85, 87, 88
Admiralty Islands, PNG, 126, **424**
adoption, 176, 192, 195, 211–212
age grades, 256
age/sex structures, 268, **269**, 290
aging, 263, 269, 272, 311
agriculture, 341–351; commercial, **346**, **347**, 348, 349, 350; crop disease, 347; crop yields, 351; dynamics of, 345–346; hydroponics, 397; origins of, 341; polyculture, **345**; precontact, 128–130; production systems, 341; and sustainability, 350–351; traditional, 341–345; women's roles in, 198–199. *See also* food
agriculture and marine exports, 348

agrodeforestation, 346
ahu ula, 241
airlines, 198, 394, 395
aitu, 229
Aitutaki, CI, 73, 75, 212, **426**
alcohol consumption, 178, 291–292
algae, 110, 113. *See also* kelp; plankton
algal ridges, 47
Alpine deserts, **101**
Alpine Fault, NZ, **34**, 37, **43**
altimetry, 20
altitudinal zonation, 101, 105
American Samoa, 87, 142, 143, **426**
amphidromes, 21
amphitheater-headed valleys, 45, 50
Anaa, Tumotus, FP, 54, **427**
Anatahan, Northern Mariana Islands, 46, **424**
Andesite Line, 40
Angaur, Palau, 198
angin tem air, 255
annexations, 140–141
anticyclones, **4**, **5**
Anuta, SI, 173, **425**
Aoba (Ambae), Vanuatu, 179, 208, 276
'Apia, Samoa, 77, 140, 141, **426**
apologies, 177
aquaculture and mariculture, 343, 373–374, 375
aquatic ecosystems, 190–122; classification of, 119; continental shelf and slope, **116**, 117; coral reef, 113, **114**, **115**; deep sea, **118**; fresh water, **109**, 110; kelp, **115**, 116; mangrove, **111**, 112; nutrient flux, **114**, **118**; pelagic, **117**, 118; seagrass meadow, **112**, 113; zonation, **109**, **111**, **115**
aquifers, 71–72
arboriculture, 126, 342, 343
arc of instability, 147
ariki (ali'i), 132, 149
arioi, 276
Arno, MI, 96, **425**
aroha, 230
aroids, 343–344
art, 236–246; ceramics, 237; clothing, 243; featherwork, 241; fiber arts, **239**, 243; galleries, **244**, **245**, 246; kula, 241; masks, **239**, **240**; ornaments, 241;

prehistoric, 237; and ritual, 237–238; scarification, 243; tattoos, 243–244; woodcarving, **239**, 241
Asians: in fisheries, 370–371; Japanese colonialism, 142; land rights of, 199; languages, 165; in logging, 358; migrants, 125–126, 276–277; as minorities, 143, 179; in tourism, 393–394; in war, 142
assimilation, 159. *See also* ethnicity; identity
associations: anthropologists, 308; healers, 289; literary, 228; media, 410; religious, 221; women, **386**
Atiu, CI, 53, **104**, 214, 220, **426**
atmospheric circulation, 1–4
atmospheric convection, 1
atmospheric convergence, 2, **4**
atmospheric pressure, 1, **2**, **3**, 46
atmospheric subsidence, 2, 4, 5
atolls: agriculture on, 343–344; biota of, **95**, 96; geomorphology of, 52; and island life cycle, **37**, **51**; urbanization on, 314, 317–318
Auckland, NZ, **8**, **13**, 43, 77, 232, 281, 350, **430**
Australia: aid, 154, 192; ANZUS, 142; blackbirding, 276; colonial period, 140, 141, 151; currents, 26; drought, 31; language affinities, 166; mangroves, 96; migration to, 77, 267, 282, 284, 334; monotremes, 105; monsoons, 4; peacekeeping operations, 147, 153, 177; Pleistocene occupation, 125, 126, 128, 165; Tasman lows, 7; tides, 21; tsunamis, 55
Austral Islands, FP, 88, **426**, **427**
Austronesian language family, 160–162; cognate sets, 161
Austronesians, 148, 166–169, 202–203
authority: and art, 236; aviation, 394; colonial, 141, 149, 243, 300; communication, 404; educated class, 230; international, 197; missionaries, 219, 220, 221; municipal, 312, 314, 318, 319, 320; precontact, 130; state, 207; symbolic, 140; traditional, 179, 194, 202–203, 205, 319; transitional, 207–208, 211

B

Baliem Valley, WP, 128, 413
bamboo, 250
Banaba, Kiribati, **252, 255, 425**
Banks Peninsula, NZ, **43, 430**
Ba River, Fiji, 73
barrier reefs, 22, 38, 364, 365
Bau, Fiji, 373
beachboys, 188
beachcombers, 139
beach mining, 372
bêche-de-mer, 368
Bellona, SI, **126**, 256, **425**
benthos, 116–117
betel nuts, 293
Betio, Tarawa, Kiribati, 72, 314
big men, 178, 184, 205, 208. *See also* chiefs
big women, 184
Bikini, MI, 142, 187, 277, 289
biodiversity, 83, 84, 85, 86, 87, 89, 90
biogeography, 83–94; and adaptive shifts,
    87–88; boundaries, **84, 111, 125**;
    distribution patterns, 86–87; East
    Pacific barrier, 87; and endemism, 85;
    and extinctions, 89, 91; human impact
    on, 90–91; island biota, 84–85; marine
    biota, 85–86; molecular approaches,
    83; progression rule, 88; source areas,
    90; and speciation, **88, 89**, 90; and
    vicariance, 89–90
biologic productivity: continental shelves,
    116; coral reefs, 55, 114; high elevations,
    105; kelp, 115, 116; mangrove, 97;
    nekton, 118; and El Niño, 14; ocean,
    112; plankton, 25, 117; rain forests, 98;
    seagrass meadows, 113; soil, 59, 68;
    wetlands, 110
birds, 104–105; adaptive radiation, 85; and
    dance, 254; as dispersal agents, 84,
    85, 86, 96; exotics, 99; extinctions, 91,
    102; as food, 398; lineages, 88; and
    music, 249; origins, 90; penguins, 116;
    precontact, 129, 134, 241
Bird's Head, WP, 164
birth, 176, 183, 216–217, 241, 243, 294–295.
    See also fertility
births attended by skilled health personnel,
    294
Bismarck Archipelago, PNG, **424**; karst,
    104; languages, 160, 166; Lapita sites,
    126–127, 167; obsidian trade, 130; plate
    subduction, 40, 50
blackbirding, 140, 276
black markets, 360
body art, 238–239, 243
bogs, 99
Bonriki, Tarawa, Kiribati, 72
boom growth: agriculture, 346; aid-related,
    311, 325; fishing, 368; health-related,
    194; independence, 311; logging, 358,
    359; mining, 143, 277, 381, 383, 386;
    nuclear testing, 328; tourism, 330, 417

Bougainville, PNG, **424**; changing mobility
    patterns, 276; gender relations, 187,
    188; landowner rights, 198; languages,
    160; mercenaries, 153; mining, 48, 384;
    ore formation, 40; secessionism, 142,
    144, 153, 177, 179; settlement, 165
brass bands, 257
breadfruit, 127, 139, 168, 193, 343, 346
Britain: aid, 328; colonialism, 140, 141;
    "condominium" arrangement, 140;
    decolonization, 150, 152, 327, 328;
    nuclear tests, 142, 307; phosphate
    exploitation, 387
broadband connectivity, 401, 406, 408, 414
Bua, Fiji, 198
Buka, PNG, 126, **424**
bullroarers, 251
bureaucracy, 143, 152, 198, 283, 304, 315,
    338

C

calabashes, 251
cancer, 292–293
canoes: in contemporary art, 244; in film,
    414; in kula trade, 241; and language
    diversity, 164; Proto-Oceanic canoe
    terms, 168; in song, 249; voyaging, 167;
    and warfare, **242**
capital flight, 383
capital flows, 328–333, 337–338
capitalism, 138, 178–179
cardiovascular disease, 292
cargo cults, 141, 219–220
Caroline Islands, FSM, **424**; colonial rule,
    140–141; mangroves, 97; missionaries,
    218; *sawei* network, 275; settlement,
    127, 167; social stratification, 148. *See
    also* Chuuk; Kosrae; Pohnpei; Yap
carrying capacity, 131
cash cropping, 341–342
catastrophic events, 55
catchment, fresh water, 74
caves, 52, 159
ceramics, 132–133, 148–149
cetaceans, 373
Chamorros: agriculture, 244; demography,
    277; history, 138, 139, 145; language,
    160, 167; law, 211, 212
Chatham Islands, NZ, 22, 129, 275, **430**
chedolel Belau, 287
chiefly rights, 192
chiefs, 132–133, 139–141, 148, 215
China: aid, 325, 417; Austronesian dispersal,
    167; migrants, 276, 277; minerals
    market, 382; timber market, 358
Chinatown, 277
Christchurch, NZ, **74**, 233, **430**
Chuuk (Truk), FSM, 142, 177, 178, 296, **424**
circulation, atmosphere, 1, **2**
circulation, demographic, 194, 275–276, 310
circulation, oceanic, 25–29
circumcision, 178. *See also* initiation rites

"civilizing" mission, 138, 149, 218
class, 149, 179–180, 208, 314. *See also*
    hierarchy
climate, 1–18; atmospheric circulation,
    global, 1–4; climographs, **13**; Köppen
    map, **11**; regional patterns, 10–11; and
    soils, 60; weather systems, 6–10
climate change, anthropogenic, 16, **17**; and
    atoll populations, 145, 277, 289; and
    coral reefs, 115; and gender, 188–189;
    and groundwater, 72, 78; and health,
    289; and rainfall, 71; sea-level change,
    31; and tourism, 398
climate change, natural, 39, **45**, 47–48, 126,
    133
clothing, 241, 243, 299, 334
cloud cover, 11, 23
cloud forest, 99
coal, 379
coasts: embayment, 47; human colonization,
    128; recession and progradation, 53;
    sea-level changes, 48, 56; sea surface
    temperatures, 24; soils, 60, 61; strand
    ecosystems, 95–96, 99; subsidence, 47;
    uplift, 39; wave attack, 52; winds, 8. *See
    also* aquatic ecosystems
coconuts: chiefly *tabu*s, 215; copra, 194, 347,
    350; in poetry, 228; precontact, 128; salt
    tolerance, 343; as taro replacement, 346
coevolution, 88, 105
colonial education, 299–300
colonialism: gender aspects of, 187–188;
    and governments, 148–150; and
    mineral rights, 383–384; narratives of,
    227; resistance to, 140–142. *See also*
    decolonization
colonization, by islanders, 126–127, 166–169
colonization, by natural biota, 86–87
commercial balance, 328–329
commodification, 176, 313
commodity prices, 346–347, 379, 381, 383,
    388, 421
communications, 401–415; broadcast radio,
    411; early developments, **402, 403, 405,
    406**; Internet, 406–408; mass media,
    408–410; newspapers, 410–411; positive
    and negative aspects of, 401; traditional,
    401, 402; video and television, 411, **412**
community participation, 379, 388, 389
Compact of Free Association, 142, 143, 144,
    145, 150, 154n3, 281
company contracts, 276, 384, 389
compensation: for environmental damage,
    142, 379, 387; for land use, 196;
    for mining, 278, 386; for radio
    transmission, 198; and warfare, 193
conquest rights, 192
conservation, 56, 106–107, 134, 119, 373, 387
consumerism, 283, 306, 318
continental islands, **42, 43**
continental shelves and slopes, 20, 116–117,
    372–373

contraceptive use, 266, 273n6, 294
controls on landform development, 45–49
Cook Islands, **426**; deforestation, 134; education, 299, 303, 306; geology, 39, 47; hymns, 257; *makatea* forests, 104; *makatea* islands, **53**; migrants, 244, 267; missionaries, 219; pearl farming, 368; taro swamps, **53**; television and video, 411; tourism, 330, 392; tropical cyclones, 72; water supply, 71, 73, 74
cooperatives, 141, 142, 184, 220, 389
copper, 379
copra, 346
coral reefs: bleaching, 115, 398; distribution of, 46, 114, 364; ecosystems, 113–115; and island aging, 38–39; and uplift, 47, 51. *See also* atolls; limestone; *makatea* islands
Coral Sea, 7, 26, **425**
Coriolis effect, 1, 27
Coromandel Peninsula, NZ, 387
corporations: domination by, 143; and local elites, 179; logging, 356, 357, 358, 359, 360; mining, 141, 372, 379, 381, 383, 386, 387, 389, 410; public, 314, 318, 342, 367, 404, 405, 411, 412
corruption: and colonialism, 229; and indigenous elites, 230, 231; and logging, 360; and mining, 383; and political stability, 147
cosmologies, 215–216
costumes, 249, 251, **252–256**
countries and territories, political classification, 144, 326
coups, 143, 267, 277
courts, 194, 205–207
craters, 46, 96, **101**
crime: and demography, 421; and inequality, 320; and mining, 385; in Port Moresby, 143; and poverty, 316; and substance abuse, 292; in Suva, 305; and unemployment, 317; and urbanization, 310
crude birth rate, 264
crude death rate, 264
cruise ships, 395
crustaceans, 250
cultural misunderstandings, 139, 195–196
cultural resilience: agriculture, 350–351; art, 244–246; climate change, 17; colonization strategies, 128; conservation, 106; dance, 237; history, 145; journalism, 410; land rights, 199; language, 159; law, 209–211; literature, 231; livelihood, 417; magic, 216; migration, 419; music, 251, 256–258; state-making, 151–153; *wantok*, 176; women, 188
culture: beliefs, 287; contact, 125, 138; criminal, 188; and deforestation, 360; education, 306; and the environment,

248–249, 356; and film, 413; food, 291; and gender, 182, 183; and imperialism, 228; inheritance, 198; intangible elements, 165; and Internet, 414; land rights, 193; Lapita, 167, 244; maritime, 369; material, 236; migration, 281, 282, 283; musical, 249, 250, 251, 258; myths, 139; national, 384; political, 154; politics, 209; popular, 153; and religion, 217, 219, 220, 222; and self-determination, 384; textile arts, 237; tools, 242; youth, 245. *See also* cultural misunderstandings; cultural resilience; custom; Pacific Way
currency, 177, 326, 337
currents, 20, 21, 25, 26, 27
current transfers, 330
custom (*kastam/kastom*): beachcombers, 139; and class relationships, 179; cultural losses, 138; and development, 420, 421; and the economy, 333, 338; and fisheries, 367, 372, 376; indigenous rights, 143; land tenure, 176, 192, 193, 194, 195, 196, 197, 198, 199; law, 202, 203, 204, 205, 206, 207, 209, 210, 211, 212; and logging, 356, 357, 359, 360; marriage, 177; and modernity, 145, 153; and national consensus, 142; in poetry, 231; and religion, 214, 220, 221; and tourism, 394, 395, 397, 399; and urbanization, 312, 313, 314, 315, 318, 319, 142, 152, 209, 231, 317
customization, 78

D

dams, 110
dance, 252–255; competitions, 255
dance, regional styles: Banaban, 254, **255**; Enga, **253**; Lak, **253**; Maisin, **217**; Tahiti, 254; Tokelau, 254; Tongan, **254**; Yap, 254
Darwin Point, 39
death: dances, **253**; and music, 255; rituals, 176, 183, 216, 237, 238, 239, 253. *See also* mortality
debt: colonial period, 141; loan sharks, 419; overseas, 145, 330, 383, 388; traditional concepts, 278
decentralization, 319
decolonization, 142–144, 150–151, 231. *See also* nationalism
deficits: commerce, 328, 330, 331, 333, 358, 383; energy, 1; soil moisture, 66; water, 60
deforestation, 48, 128, 355
deliveries by Caesarian section, 294. *See also* birth
democracy, 143, 147, 152, 154, 397, 410
Demographic and Health Surveys (DHS), 263, 264, 266, 273
demographic bonus, 270
demographic transition, 263, **269**, 270, 283

demography, 263–273; age structures, 268, **269**; boom growth, 311; contemporary, 272; depopulation, 288; and development, 270–271; enumeration methods, 273n14; forecasts, 281; historical background, 288. *See also* demographic transition; epidemiological transition; ethnicity; fertility; migration; mortality
denationalization, 152
dengue, 289
dependency: and capitalism, 138; and colonialism, 141; and foreign aid, 307; and migration, 283; and mining reliance, 383; and neocolonialism, 143; and wealth, 327
dependency ratios, 268–270, 272, 273n18
depopulation, 138–139, 288
depth zonation (marine biota), 116–117
desalination, 75
development, 142–143, 417–422; ad hoc, 312, 315; basic needs, 420–421; booms and collapses, 346; concept, 417; and demographic bonus, 270–271; "failed economies," 417; food security, **418**; and gender, 189, 270–271; globalization, 418–419; poverty, 419–420. *See also* economic development; infrastructure
diabetes, 292
diadromy, 110, 111
Diamond Head, O'ahu, HI, **36**, 39
diasporas, 280, 281–282, 335–337. *See also* first-generation migratory diasporas; migratory transnationalism
diet, 291. *See also* foods
digital divide, 415n2
disease. *See* morbidity
disintensification, 345–346
disparities: in communication, 406; economic, 278; ethnic, 288; regional, 406; urban/rural, 401
dispersal (biota), **86**, 87, 88, 114
displacement, 276–277
dispossession. *See* land alienation
dispute resolution, 177, 203–205, 208, 389
distance education, 305
Dobu, D'Entrecasteaux Islands, PNG, 184, **424**
domestic abuse, 178, 187, 188, 316
domestication, 126, 127, 133, 341
doomsday predictions, 147
drosopholid flies, 85
drought, 15, 16
drug abuse, 291–292
drums, 250
dryfield agriculture, 344
drylands, 99
dual economy, 337–338
Ducie, Pitcairn, 79, **427**
Duke of York Islands, PNG, 257
Dunedin, NZ, 11, **13**, **430**
"Dutch disease," 383

E

earthquakes: and lithospheric uplift, 54; on plate boundaries, 50; and plate tectonics, 35, **37**; and tsunamis, 22–23

Easter Island/Rapa Nui, **428**; arid landforms, 46; calderas, 48; environmental impact, 133–134, 355, 356; and midocean ridge, 39; *moai* statues, 132; social stratification, 148

East Pacific Barrier, 87

East Pacific Rise, 27, **34**, 35, 39

Ebeye, MI, 75, 270

ecological succession: on Nauru, 106–107; in secondary forests, 100; speciation, 88; in volcanic ecosystems, 103; wetlands, 97

economic development: and agriculture, 350–351; and communications, 401; and demography, 270–271; failed economies, 417; and fisheries, 375–376; and forestry, 357–358; and mining, 388–389; prospects, 417–422; slow growth, 327; theory of, 333–334; and tourism, 398–399; in towns, 319–320

economic involution, 337

economy, 325–340; balance of payments, 328, **329**, 330–333; currency, 337; current account, 331–332; currency, 337; development theories, 333–334; dualism, 337–338; indebtedness, **330**; indicators of, 331, 332; macroeconomics, 337–338; and migration, 335–336; models, 333–334; and modernization, 333, 337–338; neotraditional, 337; output, 327–328; and political status, 326; regional integration, 327; success stories, 335. *See also* aid; economic development; economic involution; remittances; trade; trust funds

ecosystem conversion, 95, 99, 133

ecstatic experience, 255

education, 299–308; closed and open systems, 299; under colonial rule, 299–300; distance learning, 305; efficiency, 300–301; enclave schools, 300; financing, 300; in metropolitan countries, 304–305; mission schools, 299; national institutions, 301; in the new millennium, 307; nonformal, 301; and regionalism, 301–304; research, 307–308; of women, 305–306

educational curricula, 303, 306

Efate, Vanuatu, 318, 395, **425**

egalitarianism, 207–208

Ekman transport, 27

elites: colonial period, 141; local, 383, 385; postcolonial, 142, 143, 144, 179, 208, 209, 231; precontact, 130, 131, 218; urban, 311, 312, 320, 360

e-mail, 244, 408, 409, 414, 415

Emperor Seamounts, 88, 89

employment, 270, 273n21; and agriculture, 346; and alcoholism, 189; and development, 417, 418, 419, 420, 421; and the economy, 328, 333, 334, 337; and education, 301, 304, 306; and fisheries, 369; and gender, 187; and kinship, 176; and migration, 277–278, 279, 281, 282, 283; and mining, 386; and tourism, 393, 394; and urbanization, 310, 312, 315, 316, 317, 320

endemism, 85, 86, 89. *See also* biogeography

energy balance, atmospheric, 1

energy production: *See* geothermal energy; hydroelectric power; oil

Enewetak, MI, 277, 307, **425**

entrepreneurs, 180, 195, 270, 284, 338

environmental hazards. *See* drought; earthquakes; flooding; sea-level changes; storms; tornadoes; tropical cyclones; tsunamis; volcanoes; wind

environmental impact: agriculture, 62, 66–68, 90, 134, 351; climate change, 16, 289; coral reefs, 16–17, 115; deforestation, 48, 134, 356, 357, 359; erosion, 16; economic costs, 90–91; erosion, 16; exotic introductions, 90, 111; extinctions, 90, 91; fisheries, 370, 372, 374, 375; and gender, 188–189; habitat destruction, 90; humans vs. nonhuman causes, 55–56; landforms, 55–56; logging, 358–359; mangroves, 111, 112, 398; mining, 48, 386–387; nuclear testing, 289; overharvesting, 90; pollution, 90; precontact, 47, 55–56, 90, 128, 133–134, 356; seagrasses, 113; sea levels, 16–17; soil, 62, 66–68; terrestrial ecosystems, 105, **106**, **107**; tipping points, 417; tsunamis, 22, 55; urban growth, 314, 318, 420; water, 16, 76, 78, 79; wetlands, 111

environmental resilience, 356

epidemics, 77, 140, 288, 290, 317. *See also* mortality

epidemiological transition, 290–291

epiphytes, 99

equivalence, 178. *See also* hierarchy

erosion: and agriculture, 350–351; and island dissection, 46–47; and island life cycle, 38–39; and logging, 359; and mining, 386–387; rates of, 53–54; and sediment flows, 64–66

Espiritu Santo, Vanuatu, 71, 395, **425**

ethnicity: perspectives on, 179–180; politics of, 151

Etoile du Nord, NC, 381

'Eua, Tonga, 71, 394

Eucheuma, 373

evapotranspiration, 1, 29, 70–71

exchange: precontact, 130–131, 167, 249; tokens, 173, 176–177, 178, 179. *See also* trade

exchange rate, 337

exclusive economic zone (EEZ), 143, 197, 369, 382

exile: precontact, 276; postcontact, 142

exotic introductions (biota): ecosystem disruption, 90–91, 102; as habitat for native species, 104–105; precontact, 128–130; recovery in maquis, 102–103; and species turnover, 90–91. *See also* extinctions

exoticism, 187, 219, 232, 236

exploration: by Europeans, 138–139; by Pacific Islanders, 127–128

exports: agricultural, 346–350; economic role of, 333; minerals, 372–373; total, 332; tuna, 369–372

extended families, 175–176. *See also* kinship

external debt as percentage of GNI, 330

extinctions, 91, 133

F

Facebook, 233, 244, 245

fahu, 270

Fais, FSM, 104, 173, **424**

Fakaofo, Tokelau, **56**, **426**

fallow periods, 100, 193, 345–346

family planning, 263, 294–295

"fatal impact," 138

fatele, 254

Federated States of Micronesia, **424**; agriculture, 347, 348, 349; communications, 404, 407, 408, 409, 410, 414; demography, 263, 264, 272; economy, 326, 337; education, 300, 305, 307, 308; fisheries, 366, 372, 373; health, 266, 271, 290, 293, 294; migration, 267, 268, 279, 280; poverty, 419; urbanization, 311, 420. *See also* Chuuk (Truk); Kosrae; Pohnpei; Yap

feeder clouds, **8**

femininity, 242

fertility, **263**, 264–266

Fiji, **425**; airspace rights, 198; cassava cultivation, 345, 346; coup, 152; emigration, 276, 281; erosion, 48, 66; ethnic divisions, 143, 222, 231, 267; feather trade, 238; flooding, 49; fortification, 133; health, 289, 295, 296; housing, 313; informal sector, 315; informal settlements, 314; infrastructure, 318; land rights, 197; literature, 232, 246; microplate, 35; mining, 379, 386; poverty, 316, 317, 419, 420; rainfall, **9**; rain forest, 98; reefs, 22; remittances, 334; soil impoverishment, 66–68; storytelling, 174; sugar industry, 342; *talasiqa* savannas, 101; *taukei* protests, 141; tourism, 418; University of the South Pacific, 302; uplift, 46, 51; urbanization, 312; water supply, 75, 78

films and videos, 232–233, 411–414

financing of the current account, 331

fire: and erosion, 133–134; and grasslands, 61–62, 97, 99–101, 356; and settlement dating, 55–56

first-generation migrant diasporas, 336
fiscal policy, 337–338
fisheries. *See* ocean resources
fishing quotas, 365
fishing songs, 249
flightlessness, 85
flooding, 5, 31, 48–49, 71
floodplains, 49, 73, 101
flutes, 250
Fly River, PNG, 51, 110, 387
fog drip, 99
fono, 141, 206, 212
Fonuafoʻou, Tonga, 46, **426**
food, postcontact: agriculture, 341–350;
  aquaculture, 373; and diabetes, 292;
  diet, 291; and exchange, 176, 177;
  fisheries, 365–372; food-borne diseases,
  289; imports, 291, 292, 385, 397;
  import substitution, 366, 397; informal
  sector, 316; junk food, 145; and land
  rights, 192, 193, 197; and obesity,
  291; offerings, 214; and poverty, 271,
  273n27, 317; resource depletion, 368,
  398; in ritual, 215, 216, 217; security,
  420; subsistence production, 341–346,
  366, 417; tradeoffs, 419; and women,
  185, 187, 189. *See also* nutrition
food, precontact: in chiefdoms, 133; and
  deforestation, 355; feast-and-famine
  theory, 288; food plants, 126–127;
  intensification of production, 129;
  in Near Oceania, 128; in New Zealand,
  129; and ocean voyaging, 126; Proto-
  Oceanic terms, 168; in Remote Oceania,
  128–129; storage, 132; and storms, 249;
  surpluses, 148
food webs, 114, 375. *See also* nutrition
forcing, ocean circulation: anthropogenic,
  31; natural, 27–29
foreign aid, 327–333, 333–334
forestry. *See* logging
fortifications, 132
fossils, 88, 89, 91
founding journeys, 275
France: aid, 143, 334; "condominium"
  arrangement, 140; and migration, 267;
  New Caledonia, 150, 177, 198; nuclear
  tests, 142
Freeport, WP, 379, **380**, 382, 384, 386, 387
French Frigate Shoals, Northwestern
  Hawaiian Islands, **114**, **429**
French Polynesia, **426**, **427**; colonial
  administration, 149; distance learning,
  305; hymns, 257; independence
  movement, 177; indigenous literature,
  225; lagoon rights, 197; nuclear testing,
  143, 328; political status, 150; religious
  pilgrimages, 276; undermining of
  traditional leadership, 149; water
  supply, 74, 75
freshwater lens, 53, 71, **72**
fronts: atmospheric, **7**; oceanic, 25

fuel prices, 372, 394, 397
Funafuti, Tuvalu, 31, 75, 398, 412, **425**

G
Galápagos Islands, **428**; adaptive shifts, 85,
  88; biodiversity, 85, 87; climate, 47;
  extinctions, 91; mangroves, 111
gangs, 177, 180, 188
gender, 182–189; concepts of, 182; and
  development, 270–271; and education,
  187; and environment, 189; *fahu*
  system, 270; and health, 187, 294;
  masculinity, 188; Melanesia, 183–184;
  Micronesia, 185–186; and politics,
  186; Polynesia, 184–185; seminal
  anthropological work, 182–183, 189n1;
  sexual antagonism, 183; and violence,
  187–188. *See also* marriage
genealogical descent, 175–176, 204
genealogy: and art, 242; and dance, 237, 254;
  and rank, 148, 178, 184, 204, 255; and
  social organization, 133
genetic engineering, 347
geologic time scale, 47
geology, 34–44; atolls, 52; continental
  islands, 42–43, 50–51; island arcs,
  39–41, 50; islands of mixed lithology,
  52–53; limestone islands, 50–51;
  marginal seas and backarc basins,
  41–42; midplate islands, 37–39, 49–50;
  plate tectonics, **34**, 36–37; seafloor
  spreading, 39
geomorphology. *See* landforms
geostrategic rents, 143, 334
geostrophic transport, 27, 28
geothermal energy, 72, 114
ghosts, 216. *See also* spiritual beings
Gilbert Islands, Kiribati, 140, 148, 149, **425**
gisaro, 249
glaciation, 48, 50, 51
globalization: and aid, 153–154; and
  development, 418–419; and health,
  290–291; indigenous appropriation,
  248; and migration, 282; and trade, 355
global warming. *See* climate change
gods: creation narratives, 240; new, 218; and
  ritual, 216, 217, 241, 250, 255
gold, 380–382
Gold Ridge, Guadalcanal, SI, **380**, 382
Gondwana, 38, 41, 42, 43, 50; relicts (biota)
  of, 90, 101, 102
Goroka, PNG, 179, 183, **424**
governments. *See* nationalism; politics; states
grasslands, 61–62, 100–101
Great Mahele, 140, 277
great men, 148
greenhouse gas emissions, 16
gross domestic product, 326, 327–328, 338n1
gross national income, 327, 338n2
groundwater, 71–72
Guadalcanal, SI, 73, 142, 144, 153, 177, 188,
  418, **425**

Guam, **424**; agriculture, 346; annexation,
  140, 141; climate, **13**; colonial
  encounters, 138, 139, 149; ecosystems,
  100, 101, 104; education, 300, 301, 307;
  fertility decline, 266; geologic uplift,
  40; mangroves, **97**; missionaries, 299;
  oil spill, 112; reefs, 113; tree snakes,
  91; tropical cyclones, 4, 6; U.S. military
  presence, 187; water supply, 73, 77
guano, 45, 62, 96
guerrilla movements, 151
Gulf of Papua, 116, 219, **424**
guyots, 38, 46
gyres, 25–29

H
Haʻapai, Tonga, **126**, 394
Hadley cell, 1, **2**
haka, 249
Hagatna, Guam, 312
Haleakalā, Maui, HI, 88, **101**
Haleʻiwa, Oʻahu, HI, 21
halophytes, 95
hanai, 176
Hansen's disease (leprosy), 290
hapuu, 175
harmonies, 255
hau, 149
Hauraki, NZ, 379
Hawaiʻi (Big Island), **8**, 10, 54, 101, 103,
  129–130, **429**
Hawaiʻi (Hawaiian Islands), **429**; activism,
  143; agriculture, 347; annexation, 141;
  art, 246; beachboys, 188; carving, 242;
  chiefs, 133, 185, 215; family relations,
  175, 176, 177; feathered cloaks, 241;
  fisheries, 365–366; fishponds, 130;
  hula, 250; indigenous health, 288,
  293; kapa, 243; landslides, **38**; literature,
  226; music, 251, 257, 258; "mystery"
  islands, 128; El Niño–Southern
  Oscillation, 15; ocean temperature, **23**;
  orographic rainfall, **8**; post-erosional
  volcanism, 39; sandalwood trade, 356;
  surfing, 373; tectonics, **39**, 47, 54; tides,
  21; tsunamis, **22**; vog, 10; water supply,
  75, 79
Hawaiian biota: adaptive shifts, 87–88;
  colonization sequence, 86; dispersal, 87;
  endemism, 86; extinctions, 91; flightless
  birds, 85; high-altitude ecosystems, 101;
  marine ecosystems, 114, 116; origins,
  90; speciation, **88**; tree snails, **85**;
  volcanic ecosystems, 103
Hawaiians (*Kanaka Maoli*): art, 246;
  demography, 272; education, 272;
  health, 288, 293; *hoʻoponopono,*
  177; identity, 410; kinship, 175;
  language revival, 145; literature, 226;
  missionaries, 218, 304; poverty, 268;
  whaling, 139
Hawaiki, 276

health, 287–296; alcohol, drug, and tobacco use, 291–292; cancer, 292–293; cardiovascular disease, 292; child health, 293–294; concepts of, 287; contemporary indigenous health, 288–289; diabetes, 292; diseases of modernization, 292; effects of contact, 287–288; environmental health, 289; epidemiological transition, 289–291; health care systems, 296; HIV, **295**; infectious disease, 76, 77, 287, 288, 290, 296; lifestyle factors, 291; mental health, 296; obesity, **291**; sexually transmitted disease, 296; women's, 294–295
health expenditures as percent of GDP, 290
heat flux, ocean, **29**
hegemony, 228
heiau, 132. *See also* temples
height anomalies (ocean), **14**
heliphytes, 100
Henderson Island, Pitcairn, 39, 87, 88, 104, 130, **427**
herbivory, 87, 110
heroes, 275
hiapo, 243
hierarchy: contemporary, 178; and law, 202–206; precontact, 132–133, 148. *See also* class
higher education, 301
Hikurangi Trench, **42**
Hilo, Hawai'i, 11, **13**, 22, **429**
hip-hop, 249
historiography, 138
history (postcontact), 125–137; beachcombers, 139; colonialism, 140–141; decolonization, 142–144; explorers, 138–139; missionaries, 139–140; resistance to colonialism, 141–142; traders, 139–141
history (precontact), 138–146; communication, 401–402; environmental impact, **133**, 134; exchange, **130**, 131; intensification of production, 129, 130; population growth, **131**; ritual sites, **133**; settlement sequence, **126**, 127, 128; sociopolitical evolution, **132**, 133; subsistence, 128, **129**; warfare, 131, **132**
hiva hahaka, 255
HIV/AIDS, 267, 295
Hiva Oa, Marquesas, FP, 22, **427**
Hokitika, NZ, 11, **13**, **430**
Honiara, SI, 75, 76, 177, 281, 394, 397, 414, 420, **425**
Honolulu, Hawai'i, **13**, 141, 410, 415, 413, **429**
ho'oponopono, 177
hot spots, **37**
houseyard gardens, 344
housing: precontact, 127–128; and ritual, 132, 256; squatter settlements, 312–315; in towns, 317–319

hula, 250
human development index, 327, 338n3, 419, 420
humidity, 4, 70
humification, 63
Huon Peninsula, PNG, 39, 45, 54, **126**
hurricanes. *See* tropical cyclones
hydrocarbon deposits, 372–373
hydroelectric power, 74
hydrothermal vents, 118, 372
hymns (*himene/imene*), 256, 257

I
identity: and colonialism, 227–228; multicultural, 233; personal, 172–175
'ie toga, 238
Ifalik (Ifaluk), FSM, 174, 216, **424**
ifoga, 177
illegal drug use, 292
illiteracy, 307
imports: colonial period, 140, 141; postcolonial, 193, 327, 328, 330, 346, 351, 374, 383, 420; precontact, 130; total, 332
improved access to drinking water and sanitation, 293
indigenous minorities. *See* Chamorros; Hawaiians; Kanaks; Maori
indigenous rights, 196, 209, 277, 383–384
individualism, 173, 283, 418
Indo-Australian Plate, **34**, 35, 42, 43, 47, 72
Indonesia: affinity with Austronesian languages, 160, 162, 167; diversity center, 86, 365; and island settlement, 125; mining, 382, 384; timber market, 358, 360; warm pool, 16, 29, 31. *See also* West Papua
Indo-West Pacific, 87
inequality, 420, 421, 422; gender, 186, 187, 189; and remittances, 268; social relations, 178; in towns, 315, 417
infant mortality, 264, 288, 289, 293, 294, 317; precontact, 287; water-related, 76–77
infant mortality rate, 265, 266, 267, 271, 272, 273n10, 293
infectious disease, 76, 77, 287, 288, 290, 296
infertility, 288
infiltration capacity, 64–65
infiltration galleries, 74, **75**
inflation, 196, 418
infrastructure: airports, 394; communications, 401–409; and flooding, 48–49; housing, 312–315; tourism, 393–396; and towns, 315–318; water and sanitation, 74–75. *See also* air traffic; energy; transportation
inheritance rights, 192–193, 198
initiation rites, 183–184, 217–218, 242, 275
insectivory, 87, 110
intensification of production, agricultural, 129–130, 345–346

International Law of the Sea Convention, 197, 371–372
Internet, 407–408, 414; in art, 244, 245; domain name sales, 334; and education, 305, 307; and literature, 233; and music, 258; and religion, 221, 414; and tourism, 396
Internet penetration rates, 409
intertropical convergence zone, **2**, **4**
inversions, temperature, 4, **5**, 6, 101
investment, private: and aid, 154; Asian, 358, 382; cycles, 325; and demography, 198; island economies, 328, 330, 333, 334; and migration, 335; and mining, 383, 384; in Pacific Rim countries, 338; and remittances, 284
ipomoean revolution, 148
ipwin pohn warawar, 337
irrigation, 73, 78–79, 132–133, 343–344
island arcs, 39, 40, **41**, 50
islands: classification of, 37–43, 49–53
iwi, 175

J
Japan: aid, 307; colonialism, 141, 142, 196, 219, 300; mining investments, 381, 382; sashimi market, 369, 370; scholarships, 305; timber market, 193, 357, 358; tourism market, 393
joking relations, 176

K
Kaho'olawe, Hawai'i, 143, **429**
Kanaks: agriculture, 193; demography, 277; history, 140, 143, 145; independence movements, 150, 151, 221; law, 211; literature, 225; mining, 379, 384; music, 258. *See also* New Caledonia
kaneka, 258
Kāne'ohe Bay, HI, 79
Kanton (Canton) Island, Phoenix Islands, Kiribati, 11, **13**, 96, **426**
kapa haka, 251
Kapingamarangi, FSM, 346, **424**
kapkap, 239
karanga, **252**, 258
karst, 47, 51, 72, 103–104
Kaua'i, Hawai'i, 53, 86, 87, 88, **429**
kauri, 85, 90, 102, 103, 356
kava (sakau): and chiefly titles, 204; in dispute settlement, 177; effects, 292; *nakamals*, 276; as niche product, 193
kawana, 207
kawanatanga, 207
kelp, 112, **115**, 116, 119
Kermadec Islands, 98, 129, 372, **430**
Kīlauea, Hawai'i, **103**
Kili, MI, 277, **425**
Kilu, PNG, 128
kinship, 132, 175–176, 283, 316, 347. *See also* marriage
kipuka, 87, 103

Kiribati, **425**; aquarium fisheries, 368; dance, 255; employment, 315; exports, 347; housing, 314; imports, 317; land 195, 312; marriage law, 199; overseas investment, 330; remitances, 284, 333; seasons, 11, 45; waste disposal, 319; water supply, 72, 73, 74, 75, 76, 77

Kiritimati (Christmas Island), Line Islands, Kiribati, 75, **77**, 196, 307, **426**

knowledge, traditional: agriculture, 128–129, 342–246; art, 236, 244, 246; conservation, 318–319, 388; education, 299, 306; environment, 186–189, 376; genealogy and tenure, 193; governance, 421; health, 289; language, 159; law, 211–212; leadership, 146–148; music and dance, 251, 255, 257; ownership of, viii; personhood, 173; seafaring, 275–276; spirituality, 217–221; stories, 227–228; sustainability, 350–351

koloa, 237

Kolombagara, SI, **98**

Kona, HI, 9

Kona storms, 7

konohiki, 149

Koʻolau Range, Oʻahu, 38

Koronovia, Fiji, 61

Koror, Palau, **13**

Kosipe, PNG, **126**, 128

Kosrae, FSM, 97, 11, 299, **424**

Kuk, PNG, 61, 126

kula, 183

kundu, 250

Kutubu, PNG, 381

Kwajalein, MI, 142, 277, 307, **425**

L

labor: and agriculture, 344, 345, 351; and class, 179; and gender, 184–185, 242; historical aspects of, 132, 140–142; market, 335, 337–338; and migration, 194, 226, 267, 276–277; and mining, 385; and tenure, 193, 198; and tourism, 395; and towns, 310–311, 315–316

Lae, PNG, 312, 320, **424**

lagoon rights, 193, 197, 278, 397

lakalaka, 237

Lakeba, Fiji, 101

Lake Karapiro, NZ, 74

lakes, 71, 72, 74, 110

laments, 249

Lānaʻi, Hawaiʻi, 38

land. *See* agriculture; tenure

land alienation: and contemporary tenure, 176, 195–196; history of, 140; and logging, 357; and mining, 385; and poverty, 420; and resettlement, 142, 277; and tourism, 397

land area, 264

landform dissection, 46, 47, 52, 103

landforms: development of, 45–49; human impact on, 48–49, 55–56; rates of

change, 53–54; varieties of, 49–53. *See also* geology

landlessness, 195, 313

land reclamation, 48, 398

land reform, 199, 312, 397

landslides, **38**

Langa Langa Lagoon, SI, 48

language families, 159–165

languages, 159–169; Asian, 165; Austronesian (Malayo-Polynesian), 160, **161**, **162**, 166–169; diversity of, 164, 165; hybrid, 165; non-Austronesian, 162, **163**, 164, 166; Oceanic, **162**

Lapita, NC, **126**

Lapita culture: art, 237, 243, 244; expansion, 126–128; language, 167; settlement sites, 126;

latitudinal zonation: aquatic, 115–116; terrestrial, 101–102

Lau Basin, 372

Lau Islands, Fiji, 46

lava, 37, 38, 39, 103

law, 202–212; and authority, 202–203; and conflict management, 205–206; contemporary, 205–207; customary systems, compared, 211–212; and legal centralism, 208; legal interactionism, 208; and legal pluralism, 202; local, 205, **206**, 207–209; and succession, **204**, 205; traditional, 194, 202–205

leadership: and gender, 186; and language, 148; and law, 203, 205, 207–208; and performance, 256; and politics, 152; and religion, 221; and social relations, 178; and tenure, 197–198; in towns, 320. *See also* big men; chiefs; hierarchy

lexical reconstructions, 166, 167, 169n10, 170

life expectancy: contributing factors, 266–267; gender differences, 265; and indigenous minorities, 271–273; indirect measure, 263, 266, 273n8, 290

Lifuka, Tonga, 133

Lihir, PNG, 189, **380**, 387, 388

limestone: and agriculture, 342; archaeological aspects, 130; forests, 103–104; islands, 46, 47, 51, 52–53; in reefs, 113–114; soils, 59, 61, 62; and water supply, 71, 72, 75. *See also* karst

linear island chains, 37–39, 49–50

Line Islands, Kiribati and the United States, 86, 196, 254, 372, 402, **426**

literacy: and communication, 409; and development, 418, 421; in education, 299, 307, 308; and health, 295; indigenous, 226, 229

literature, 225–233; anthologies, 232; colonial transformations of, 227–228; and custom, 231; and decolonization, 228–230; film, 232–233; indigenous renaissance, 226–227; novelists, 227; personal, 231; playwrights, 233; poets, 225–229; stereotypes, 227

lithospheric subsidence, 38, 39, 47, 50, 54

litter layer, 159

livestock, 194, 277, 342, 344, 345, 350–351

living standards, 283, 318, 325, 327, 333, 334, 420

loans, 183, 347, 385, 419

logging, 355–361; environmental costs, 358–359; indigenous productions systems, 355–356; political and social costs, 359–361; postcontact forestry, 356–357; regional timber trade, 357–358

longlining, 369, 370, 375

Lord Howe Island, **36**, 38, 39

Lord Howe Rise, 41

Losap, FSM, 97

lotu, 257

Lou Island, PNG, **127**, **130**

Loyalty Islands, NC, 39, 54, 104, 266, 267, **425**

luakini, 132

M

Maasina Rule, 142

Macrae's Flat, NZ, 381

macroeconomics, 267–268, 337, 379

Madang, PNG, 163, 219, 381, 385, **424**

Madang Province, PNG, 164, 381

magic: and education, 299; and migration, 278; and music, 257; and religion, 214, 216, 219

magma, 35, 37, 39, 40, 42

magmatic intrusion, 42

mahiole, 241

Maiana, Kiribati, 197, **425**

Majuro, MI, **13**, 71, 74, 75, 270, 317, 318, 372, **425**

Mākaha Valley, Oʻahu, Hawaiʻi, 132

makatea, 46

Makatea, Tuamotus, FP, 51, 52, 104, **427**

makatea islands: biota, 103, 104; geology, 46, 51, 52, 53

malagan images, 238, 239

Malaita, SI, 39, 48, 141, 142, 153, 177, **342**, 351, 421, **425**

Malakula, Vanuatu, 276, **425**

malaria: and demography, 97; environmental aspects, 76, 77; health, 287, 289, 293

Malesia, 102

malnutrition, 293–294

Malthusianism, 283

malu, 243

mana: in art, 242; and gender, 185; and leadership, 140, 178, 207; in literature, 230; in music, 255; publication, 227, 229; and religion, 215, 221

Mangaia, CI, 103, 130, 133, **134**, 341, **426**

Mangareva, FP, 127, **427**

mangroves: 96–97, 102, 104, **111**, 112

Manihiki, CI, 368, 412, **426**

mantle convection, 37

mantle upwelling and downwelling, 35, 37

manufacturing: contemporary, 315, 328, 334, 369, 383, 417; and gender, 187; nineteenth-century, 140; precontact, 131; in tradition, 243

Manus Basin, 372

Manus Island, PNG, 126, 197, 216, 219, **424**

Maori: agriculture, 344; art, 242, 244; Christianity, 219, 221; creation stories, 217; deforestation, 356; demography, 271, 272; education, 272; filmmaking, 232, 413; grievances, 143; health, 288, 289, 292, 293; identity, 179, 419; kinship, 175; language revival, 145; law, 206, 207, 209, 212; literature, 230; mining, 379, 384; music, 250, 251, 252, 257, 258; rights, 198, 199; social status, 421; stereotypes, 227; Treaty of Waitangi, 140; urbanization, 418; warfare, 193, 196, 277. See also New Zealand

marae: on atolls, 133; and dance, 249; and gender, 185; and migration, 276; and music, 250; and religion, 217. See also temples

Maré, NC, 54, **425**

Marginal Polynesia, 128

marginal seas, 41, **42**

Mariana Islands, **424**; arc volcanism, 40; backarc basins, 42; colonialism, 138, 139, 149; exclusive economic zone, 197; fisheries, 367; hydrothermal vent, 118; inheritance, 198–199; language, 161; population decline, 278; precontact foods, 111. See also Northern Marianas

Mariana Trench, **34**, **42**

Mariana Trough, **42**

marijuana, 291, 350

marine protected areas, 373

maritime continent, 2

marketing: agricultural, 342, 346, 350; historical aspects, 141; literary, 225; tourism, 394, 395, 396; in towns, 315. See also economy; trade

market power, 338n4

Markham River, PNG, 100, 101

Marquesas, FP, **427**; efficacy of biotic dispersal, 87, 91; gender relations, 185; genealogies, 275; polyandry, 185; reef development, 22, 54; settlement, 167; tattoos, 243; volcanism, 37, 46; war club, 242

marriage: cultural differences, 183–185; and domestic violence, 178, 187; as exchange, 176–177; intermarriage, 167; and kinship, 175; in oral tradition, 275; and politics, 139; polygamy, 175, 204, 210; rituals, 216; and tenure, 192. See also gender; kinship

Marshall Islands, **425**; atomic tests, 142; cancer, 293; chiefs, 179, 205; fertility transition, 263; mangroves, 97; nutritional deficiency, 293; parochial education, 301; Pisonia forests, 62, 96;

religious celebrations, 214; settlement, 167; substance abuse, 292; support networks, 131; urban crowding, 310, 311, 314; water supply, 74, 75, 317

marshes, 97, 111

marsupials, 105, 128

masks: as art, 238, 240, 241; in rituals, 219

mass media. See communications

mass wasting, 54

matai, 140

Matainasau, Viti Levu, 49

maternal mortality, 294–295

maternal mortality ratio, 294

Matignon Accords, 150

mats, 177, 237, 238, 239, 241

Mauke, CI, 89, 412, **426**

Maui, Hawai'i, 101, 103, **429**

Mauna Loa, Hawai'i, **36**, 38, 101

measles, 288

media. See communications

medicine. See health

Mekeo, PNG, 216

melodies, 249

men's house, 219

menstruation, 176, 183, 185

mental health, 141, 273, 287, 296, 421

mercenaries, 153

mesei, 351

microstates: communications, 412; deficits, 330; development theory, 333; environmental stress, 318; poverty, 317; tipping points, 417

midocean ridges, 35, 37, 39, 40

Midway Atoll, Northwestern Hawaiian Islands, 89, 402, **429**

migration, 275–284; circular, 276; and economy, 333, 335–337; and identity, 226; illegal, 281; immigrant needs for land, 196; impact, 278; internal, 280–281; international, 281–282; and modernity, 277–278; motives for, 282–283; policies of, 282; quantitative comparisons, 278–281; return, 278; and tenure, 210; theoretical models, 283. See also displacement; mobility

milai, 344

military. See colonialism; coups

military bases, 104, 142, 187, 279, 281, 300, 334

Millennium Development Goals (MDG), 263, 266, 271, 273n25, 420, 421, 422

Milne Bay, PNG, 162, 275, **380**

mineral production, 381

mining, 379–391; and culture, 384, **385**, **386**; deep sea deposits, 372; and economy, 382–383; and environment, 48, **386**, **387**; and gender, 189; land rights, 198, 383–384; locations, **380**; major mines, 380, **381**, 382; management, 388, **389**; political aspects of, 383, **384**; resource exhaustion, 333, 382; towns, 316, 317; trends, 382

mining contribution to the economy, 381

minorities. See Asians; Chamorros; Hawaiians; Kanaks; Maori

MIRAB economies, 143, 283–284, 333–334, 338n5

Misima, PNG, 387

missionaries: colonial period, 139, 140, 216, 218–220, 299; today, 221. See also religion

Mitiaro, CI, 71, 412, **426**

moa, 85, 90, 105, 133

moai, 132

mobility: contemporary, 277–278; postcontact, 194, 276; precontact, 128, 134, 275–276; settlement and displacement, 276–277. See also migration

modekngei, 141

modernity, 145, 180, 231, 258, 277

modernization: and economy, 333, 334, 335; in literature, 229, 230, 231; migration, 278; and millennialism, 141; theory, 333; and urbanization, 310

moka, 238

Mokil, FSM, 97, **425**

Moloka'i, Hawai'i, **38**, 85, 99, 111, **429**

monetization, 283, 419

money. See currency

money supply, 337

monsoons, 2, 4, 6, 48, 31, 46, 50

Moorea, Society Islands, FP, 91, **426**

Mopir Island, PNG, 130

morbidity: postcontact, 76, 288–296; precontact, 287–288. See also health

Morobe Province, PNG, 162, 166, 381

mortality, 266–267; archaeology, 132; Bougainville crisis, 153; and chiefly succession, 204; combat, 139; indigenous, 288; infants and children, 76–77, 267, 271; introduced diseases, 138; and land rights, 194; precontact, 131, 132, 287; at sea, 128, 249; sexual competition, 193; tsunamis, 22; water-borne diseases, 76. See also death; health

Moruroa (Mururoa), FP, 54, 307, **427**

motu, 52, 55, 95–96

Mount Hagen, PNG, 174, 182

Mount Kare, PNG, 379

Mount Nanalaud, Pohnpei, 97

movies. See films and videos

multiple ownership, 192

music, 248, 255–258; contemporary, 257–258; and the environment, 248–250; instruments, **250**, **251**, **252**, **256**; modern, 249, **250**, 256–258; traditional, 255–256

Mussau Island, PNG, **130**, 131, 160, 343

N

Nadi (Nandi), Fiji, 60, 64, 381, 382, **425**

nakamal, 276

nakwiari, 176

Namosi, Fiji, 379, **380**, 381

Nan Madol, Pohnpei, **133**

nationalism, 152, 303, 384. *See also* decolonization

nation building, 142–144, 151–153

natural growth rate (NGR), 266, 268, 271, 273n5, 290

Nauru, **425**; compensation for environmental damage, 379, 387; detention center, 334; ecological succession, **106**, **107**; health problems, 145, 266, 291; investment losses, 333; phosphate mining, 382, 386; resource conflict, 151; soil recovery, **62**; tilapia cultivation, 111; wartime relocation, 142; water supply, 73, 75, 76

Nausori, Fiji, **13**

naval bases, 140

ndat, 240

neotraditional economy, 337

Nepoui, NC, **380**, 381

net migration rate (NMR), 264

New Britain, PNG, **424**; archaeology, 126, 127, 128, **130**, 165; dance, 240, 251; hymns, 257; language, 162, 164; minerals, 39, 382; mourning and memorial ceremonies, 216; suicide, 184

New Caledonia, **425**; animal husbandry, 176; conifers, 99; floods, 73; impact of contact, 238; independence movement, 150, 221; indigenous reserves, 277; Lapita site, 126; literature, 225; maquis, **102**, 103; migration network, 281; mining pollution, 387; music, 258; *niaouli* savannas, 97, 100; nickel mining, 381–382; oceanic overthrust, 105; reptile diversity, 105; university education, 304, 305, 308

New Georgia, SI, 242, **424**

New Guinea, island of, **26**, **424**

New Guinea Highlands: changes in forest cover, 48; class formation, 179; dance, 253; disintensification, 346; global warming and malaria, 289; languages, 160, 163; male–female antagonism, 183; mass wasting, 54; mobility, 275, 276, 278, 283; oil resources, 379; Pleistocene sites, 126; sweet potato cultivation, 344

New Guinea peoples: Abelam, 204; Arapesh, 182; Chambri, 182; Dani, 160; Ekagi, 160; Enga, 160; Jale, 205; Kalam, 159; Kaluli, 249; Koitabu, 193; Kuma, 183; Lak, 253; Maisin, 215; Melpa, 160; Motu, 193; Mundugumor, 182; Nduindui, 184; Orokaiva, 184; Rorovana, 276; Tairora, 276; Tolai, 198

New Ireland, PNG, **424**; archaeology, 126, 128, **130**, 165; dance, **253**; funerary rites, 238; gold mining, 381; languages, 160, 162, 184; *malagan* carvings and masks, 238, 239

newspapers, 410–411; in art, 246; and education, 305; and logging, 360

New Zealand (Aotearoa), **430**; agriculture, 129, 344, 350; artists, 244; atmospheric pressure systems, 4, **7**; biologic diversity, 85; carving, 240; coastal recession and progradation, 53; continental shelf fisheries, 116–117; demography, 271–272; earthquakes, **37**; faulting, 37; fauna, 105; film, 413; fisheries, 365; gender issues, 186; geological evolution, 41, **42**, **43**; hot springs, 75; hydropower, 74; indigenous health, 288; indigenous poverty, 421; kelp ecosystems, 115–116; literature, 230–233; mining, 379, 381, 382; moa extinction, 133; mobility, 267, 276, 278, 282; music, **251**, **252**, 258; oceanography, 30; orographic effects, 8–9, 46; prophets, 219; sea breezes, 8; settler capitalism, 335; shoreline zonation, 115; snowfall, 10; streams, 110; terrestrial ecosystems, 101–102; timber industry, 355, 356–357, 358; tornadoes, 10; tourism, 373, 392, 394, 396; uplift, 47, 54; volcanism, 35, 36; Waitangi Tribunal, 207; water supply, 70, 71, 73, 74; youth, 188

ngatu, 236

ngwayé kundi, 205

niaouli, 97

niche products, 347, 351

nickel, 277, 381–388

La Niña, 14, **15**

El Niño–Southern Oscillation (ENSO), **14**, **15**, 19, **30**, 31, 70

Niua Group, Tonga, 39

Niuatoputapu, Tonga, **126**, 127

Niue, **426**; brain drain, 278; cancer, 293; coral terraces, **36**, 39; extinction and recolonization, 89; *hiapo,* 243; Internet, 408; karst, 51; literature, 231; migrant communities, 244, 282; monthly rainfall, 71; soils, 60, 61; tourism, 398; water, **72**, 73, 76

Niutao, Tuvalu, 52, **425**

Nombe, PNG, **126**

nongovernmental organizations: and development, 420–421; and education, 301; and gender, 186; and housing, 314; and mining, 389; and urbanization, 319; and youth, 317

Non-Trans-New Guinea languages, 164

Norfolk Island, Australia, 98, 334, **430**

Northern Marianas, Commonwealth of, **424**; archaeology, **133**; demography, 276, 277; employment, 315, 334; health, 292, 293; history, 143, 150; migration, 276, 281, 335; political status, 154; tenure, 196, 197, 198. *See also* Mariana Islands

North Island, NZ, **430**; coal mining, 379; deforestation, 48; kauri forests, 356; mangroves, 111; plate convergence, 35, 43; precontact subsistence, 129; snow, 10; water, 73

Northwestern Hawaiian Islands, 114, **429**

Noumea, NC, **13**, 150, 316, **425**

Noumea Accords, 150

nuclear testing: and displacement, 277; and economy, 328; health consequences of, 289, 293; history of, 142; protests against, 142, 143, 397; research, 307

Nukuʻalofa, Tonga, 239, 343, 397, **426**

Nuku Hiva, Marquesas, FP, **46**, **427**

Nukulaelae, Tuvalu, 208, **425**

number of indigenous languages by country, 160

nutrient cycling: in aquatic ecosystems, 109–119; in rain forests, 98; in soils, 63

nutrition, 291, 366

O

Oʻahu, Hawaiʻi, **429**; land reclamation, 48; landslides, 38; leeward scrub, **99**; *pali,* **50**; rain forest, 99; stratification, 132; subsistence, 130; surf, 20; tides, 21; tree snails, 85, 87; tsunami, 22, 38; volcanism, 39; water, 71, 78

obesity, 291

obsidian exchange, **130**

ocean floor upthrusting, 39

Oceania, **vii**; concept of, 145, 225; insularity, 138, 282; Melanesia, Micronesia, and Polynesia, viii, 169, 237; Near/Remote, **125**, **126**; pan-Pacific identity, 231

Oceanic language subgroups, 162, 169n7

oceanography, 19–33; cold tongue, 23, 355; currents, **25**, **26**, **27**, **28**; eddies, 26, 27; salinity, **24–25**; temperature, 23, **24**, **29**; tides, 20, **21**; tsunamis, 21, **22**; warm pool, 23, 29, 31, 364; waves, 19, **20**

ocean pressure, 27–29

ocean resources, 364–376; aquaculture and mariculture, 373, 374, **375**; aquarium fish, 368, **369**; bêche-de-mer (trepang, or sea cucumber), 368; black pearls, 368; coastal, 366, 367, **368**; deep slope fish, 368; environments, 364–365; exclusive economic zones, **365**, **369**; gear, 368, 370; hydrocarbons, 372–373; longlining, 369, 370, 375; minerals, 372; nonextractive uses, 373; offshore, **369**, 370, 371, 372; open sea rights, 197; stock decline, 368; sustainability, 375, **376**; threats, 374–375; trawling, 117; tuna, 364, 369–372

ocean upwelling and downwelling: and ecosystems, 112, 113, 114, 116, 117; Ekman transport, 27–29; endo-upwelling, 113; and nutrients, 25; and temperature, 23, 24

offshore financial assets, 330, 333

ʻohana, 175

oil: industry, 381, 382, 383; spills, 112, 116, 117

Ok Ningi, PNG, 51, 54
Ok Tedi, PNG, 51
Ontong Java, SI, 37, 55, 56, 185, **425**
oral traditions: in education, 299; as literary
    canon, 225, 232; and memory, 192, 367;
    and scientific approaches, 138; and
    voyaging, 275; and warfare, 133
ore formation, 39, 40
ori, 254
ornaments (body), 127, 238
orographic effects, **8, 9, 50**
Oro Province, PNG, 215, 243
Otago, NZ, 43, 381, 387
Otago Peninsula, **43**
overharvesting, 91, 111, 368, 374, 398

P
Pacific Plate, **34,** 35; arc volcanism, 40;
    earthquakes, 43; and geothermal
    waters, 72; and hot spots, 88; island age
    progressions, 39; movement, 38, 39, 46;
    subduction, 42; subsidence, 47
Pacific Way (*Fa'a Pasifika*), 393, 409, 410
Pago Pago, American Samoa, 141, 347, **426**
pahu, 250
Palau (Belau), **424**; agriculture, 343, 347,
    351; alcohol, 178; antinuclear clause,
    143; *chedolel Belau,* 287; education,
    306; endangered marine species, 375;
    fertility transition, 263; geology, 42;
    immigration, 267; invasive species,
    106; limestone forests, 104; literature,
    226; mangroves, 112; marine diversity,
    86; marine protected areas, 373;
    megapodes, 85; *Modekngei* movement,
    141; Ngermeskang River, **109**; reefs,
    113; urbanization, 319
paleodemography, 131
pali (cliffs), O'ahu, 50
Pamwak, PNG, **126,** 128
pandanus: in costume, 249; dispersal, 128;
    language, 166; limestone forest, 103,
    104; littoral forest, 96; New Guinea
    Highlands, 166; nuts, 341, 343; swamps,
    97. *See also* mats
Panguna, Bougainville, PNG, 153, 277, 379,
    380, 386
Papeete, Tahiti, FP, 175, 312, 316, 320, 397,
    427
Papua New Guinea, **424**; agriculture, 346;
    ancestral spirits, 216; arson, 196; art,
    246; birds of paradise, **105**; business
    elite, 179; Christianity, 221; climate
    change, 16, 289; coastal fisheries, 365;
    concepts of self, 174; cultural diversity,
    220; dance, **253**; deforestation, 48;
    economy, 328; employment, 346; gender
    roles, 182, 187, 189, 242; geologic uplift,
    39, 45, 54; grasslands, 100; health, 295;
    high-altitude ecosystems, 101; impact
    of contact, 238; karst, 51; kula ring, 241;
    land rights, 195, 198; landforms, **51;**

languages, 202; literature, 226, 227, 410;
    marine rights, 197; mining, 39, 48, 277,
    372, 384, 387, 380, 381; missionaries,
    218; mobility, 278; music, **250, 251;**
    nation making, 153; oil refinery, 381;
    overfishing, 368; pigs, 217, 345; post-
    independence period, 418; rain forests,
    97, 99, 104; religious rites, 215; river
    flows, 71; river sediments, 51, 65; "rules
    of behavior," 204; seafloor rifting, 39;
    singing, 249, 256; string bands, 258;
    swamps, 97; timber industry, 357;
    tok pisin, 165; traditional knowledge,
    193; urbanization, 310, 312; village
    courts, 205, 206, 208, 209; warfare, 193;
    weather, 8, 10; youth, 177
Papuanization, 148
Papuan languages, 162–164, 169n9
Papuans (Non-Austronesians), 148, 165–166,
    203
par-nga-but, **254**
pasinja meri, 184
paua, 240
peace: gender differences, 188; international
    initiatives, 144, 153, 282, 330; and law,
    206; movements, 218, 219; rituals, 217
pearl farming, 197, 278
Pearl Harbor, Hawai'i, 142, 402
pe'a tatau, 237
pedogenesis, 60–63
pelagic ecosystems, 117–118
Pentecost, Vanuatu, 209, **425**
peoples. *See* Chamorros; Hawaiians;
    *individual countries and territories, and
    locations within these regions;* Kanaks;
    Maori; New Guinea peoples
personal boundaries, 196–198
personhood, 173–175. *See also* social
    relations
perspectives: anthropological, 182;
    geographic, 186; holistic, 289;
    indigenous, 125, 226; legal, 208; local,
    248; musical, 256
phase lines, 21
phosphate: and biota, 103–104, 106; colonial
    exploitation, 141; cycling, 114, 117;
    exhaustion, 144; geology, 45, 47, 51, 52;
    and soils, 62, 67; toxicity, 75
photic zone, 25, 113, 117, 118, 119
phreatophytes, 96
pidgin, 165, 229
pigs: as brideprice, 183; as cause of disputes,
    193, 208; ecosystem disruption, 91, 99,
    106; in exchange, 148, 173; feral, 345;
    and mobility, 276; in ritual, 217; and
    women's work, 182
pilgrimages, 275–276
Pinzón Island, GI, 31
Pio, SI, 104
Pitcairn Island, **427**; communications, 180;
    geology, 39; language, 165; law, 212;
    newspaper, 410; precontact settlement,

130, 275; prospects, 281, 284
plankton, 87, 114–117
planning: communication, 408; community
    involvement, 144, 318, 389; family, 263,
    294, 295; fisheries, 376; governance,
    147; land use, 351, 357, 358; mining,
    382, 383, 386; top-down, 143; tourism,
    396; urban, 312, 313, 314, 319, 320;
    water resources, 78, 79
plantation labor, 140, 179, 276
plantation mode of management, 342
plantation owners, 277
plantations: and dispossession, 141, 196; and
    logging, 356–359; and migration, 276,
    278; and pidgin, 165; as production
    system, 342, 346
plate boundaries, 35, 72
plate tectonics, **35,** 46, 88, 127
Pleistocene settlement sites, 126
Pohnpei, FSM, **424**; agroforestry, 343, 351;
    beachcombers, 139; chiefly succession,
    203, 204; cloud forest, **99**; College
    of Micronesia, 302; colonialism,
    141; conservation, 106; kinship, 175;
    mangroves, 97; Nan Madol, 133; poetry,
    226; social stratification, 148; water
    policy, 75
political boundaries, colonial period, 149
political integration, 150–151
politics, 147–153; colonial state, 148–150;
    during decolonization, 150–151;
    doomsday scenarios, 147–148; gender
    aspects of, 186; globalization, 153–154;
    precontact power relations, 148; state
    and nation building, 151
pollen record, 48, 61, 102, 133
pollution: agriculture-related, 351; of coastal
    ecosystems, 375, 398; and development,
    417; gender aspects of, 183, 184, 185,
    188, 189; mining-related, 145, 387, 388;
    of reefs, 113, 116; of rivers, 76; sewage,
    78; in towns, 317, 318; of wells, 74
polymetallic crusts and nodules, 372
Polynesian Triangle, 128, 160
pondfields, 104, **129,** 343–344
population density, 264
population growth, 268–270; and
    agriculture, 345; on atolls, 313; and
    ecosystems, 100; and migration, 281;
    and policy, 283; precontact, 56, 131;
    and urbanization, 313, 320; and water
    supplies, 77–78. *See also* demography;
    family planning
Porgera, PNG, **380,** 384, 385
Port Moresby, PNG, **424**; bridewealth,
    177; census, 311; climate, **13**; crime,
    143, **317**; diabetes, 292; epidemics,
    77; health, 295; houseyard gardens,
    344; income disparity, 320; informal
    economic sector, 315, **316**; migrants,
    312, 313; mobile phones, 401; town
    center, **312**; writers' workshop, 226

Port Vila, Vanuatu, 72, **425**; affordable housing, **314**; informal sector, 316; informal settlement, **313**; kinship, 173; national library, 227; newspaper, 311; poverty, 420; remittances, 283; sanitation, 318; tourism, 395; "urban chiefs," **319**; water supply, 75, 77, 78; youth, 317

postal services, 180, 402. *See also* e-mail; Facebook; Internet

pottery. *See* ceramics; Lapita

poverty, 271, 273nn27–28, 419–420; basic needs provision, 420–421; impact of remittances, 268; policies, 421–422; in towns, 314–317. *See also* economic development; Millennium Development Goals

poverty head counts, 419

power. See *mana*

power bands, 257

precipitation, 2, **11**, **12**; and ecosystems, 101, 102; and landscapes, 45, 46, 47, 50; and oceans, 23–29; and soils, 61; and water supply, 70, 73

prehistory. *See* history (precontact)

priestly specialization, 217

primogeniture, 185, 204, 275

privacy, 174

private sector, 337, 338, 419, 421

profit squeeze, 337

progradation rates (coasts), 53

proletarianization, 337

prophetic movements, 219

prosperity (economic), 327

Proto-Oceanic communities, 132, 175

Proto-Oceanic languages, 162, 167, 169nn7–8

proto-states, 149

public domain, 197

public service: aid dependence, 143; broadcasts, 408, 413; staffing, 307; and urbanization, 316, 318

Pukapuka, CI, 72, 148, 185, 225, **426**

Pukarua, Tuamotus, FP, **133**, **427**

Puluwat, FSM, **96**, 97, 161

puraka, 193

Purari River, PNG, 51, 71, 110

purchasing-power parity, 326, 337

purse-seining, 364, 369, 370, 375, 376

putorino, 252

R

ra'atira, 254

Rabaul, New Britain, PNG, 76, 141, **424**

race, 149, 227, 229, 231. *See also* ethnicity; representation

radio, 411; and education, 305; and globalization, 337; history, 402; indigenous involvement, 226; and indigenous rights, 198; and literature, 226; and music, 258; and social relations, 180

radioactivity (soil), 61. *See also* nuclear tests

Raiatea, FP, 276, **426**

rainfall, 11, 70, 71. *See also* precipitation

rain forests: lowland, 97–98; montane, 98–99

rain shadow, 9

Ramu River, PNG, 101, 110, 164

ranching. *See* livestock

rangatira, 207

rangatiratanga, 207

Rano Kao, Easter Island, 48

Rapa, Austral Islands, FP, **132**, **427**

Rapa Nui. *See* Easter Island

rape, 187, 295, 385

rap music, 257

Rarotonga, CI, 47, 52, 74, 85, 238, 305, **426**

raskols, 177

rate of natural increase (RNI), 264, 265, 268, 281, 311

ravine forests, **100**

reefs. *See* coral reefs

reforestation, 357, 359

refugee rights, 192

regional cooperation: conservation, 371, 376; cooperative intervention, 154; political, 145, 147

regional studies, vii–viii

relatedness. *See* kinship

religion, 214–222; and activism, 221–222; cargo cults, 220; cosmology, 216; and life cycle, 216–217; magic and sorcery, 214, 216, 219; and nationalism, 221–222; postcontact, 218, 219, **220**; power and knowledge in, 217–218; power encounters, 219; prayer, **215**, 217, 257; prophetic movements, 141, 219; rituals, 216–217; spirits, 216; traditional, 215–218; traditionalism, 220–221. *See also* missionaries

religious conversion, 139, 211, 218, 219, 236, 238

remittances: and banking, 421; comparative data, 331–332; and demography, 268; and investment, 283–284; theory of, 333–334. *See also* MIRAB

representation: by islanders, 220; in literature, 227–233; in music, 249; by Westerners, 187. *See also* identity; race

resourcefulness of jurisdiction, 333

resource management: agriculture, 350–351; climate, 17; competition, 132; coral reefs, 115; corporations, 179, 387, 389; and the economy, 337, 382–383; forests, 106–107, 355, 357, 359, 360; and gender, 189, 198; indigenous rights, 207, 379; landscape, 56; land tenure, 313; local control and ownership, 289, 383, 384; mangroves, 111; and migration, 278; mineral resources, 333, 379, 388–389; ocean resources, 365–366, 371, 375–376; pollution, 318–319; precontact, 128; soil, 63, 66, 68; tourism, 394, 397; water, 78, 79

return migrants, 140, 197, 276, 277, 278, 283, 311

rice, 63, 73, 127, 167, 168, 344

rift zones, 37

riots, 147, 320, 397, 418

rituals: and art, 238; contemporary fusions of, 141, 219; and dance, 252–255; and education, 296; and gender, 176, 183, 184, 185; and life cycle, 148, 177; and music, 249; in religion, 216–218

rivers: comparative data, 71; ecosystem features, 97, 100, 101, 109, 110; flooding, 48, 73; management, 78; native rights, 199; pollution, 75, 317, 359; remediation, 77; sediment yields, 51, **65**; use, 74

Rock Islands, Palau, 104

rock types, 40

roles, social, 172–173

Rongelap, MI, 277, 289

Rotorua, NZ, 43, 75

Rotuma, Fiji, 160, 345, 413

Ruapehu, Mount, NZ, **36**, 43

runoff, 51, 65, 70–71, 111, 113, 318, 351

S

sacred, concepts of: activities, 257; entities, 215; houses, 256; masks and carvings, 219; persons, 215; plants, 275; rules, 287; sites, 185, 249, 276, 288. See also *heiau; marae; tapu*

sago, 97, 127, 128, 168, 240, 249, 275, 345

Sahulland (Sahul), 125

Saipan, Northern Mariana Islands, 143, 281, 301, 305, **424**

saline intrusion, 76

salinity, ocean, 24–25

salt water: uses, 75

Samoa, **426**; adolescence, 182, 231; agriculture, 342, 351; art, 245; battered women, 187; Christianity, 140; colonialism, 140, 141; corruption, 230; debt, 330; democratic reforms, 143; diaspora, 272, 281, 282; dispute resolution, 177; education, 301, 302, 304; endangered species, 91; endemism, 85; health, 287, 288, 296; independence, 142, 150; land rights, 192, 196; localism, 151, 152; Mau rebellion, 199; motto, 221; parental discipline, 178; personhood, 173, 174; poetry, 233; rainfall, 4, **9**; remittances, 284; Samoan Passage, 27; stereotypes, 228; tourism, 393; traditional hierarchy, 179; tropical cyclones, 347; water supply, 75, 77

San Cristobal, SI, 104, 126, 162, **425**

sanitation, 76–77, 293

Santa Cruz Islands, SI, 60, 126, 127, 169, **425**

satellites: communications, 403; weather, 20

Savai'i, Samoa, **9**, 60, 62, 71, 206, **426**

savannas, 100–101. *See also* grasslands

savings gap, 328

sawei, 275, 276
scarification, 243
scholarships, 300, 302, 305, 307, 308
Schrader Ranges, PNG, 159
seabirds, 104, 307, 373, 398
sea breezes, **8**
sea encroachment (lateral inundation), 53, 54
seafarers: and disease transmission, 295; as employment, 419; precontact, 126, 202; remittances, 334
seafaring, 126–128, 275–276; dances, **254**; motives, 276
sea-floor ridges, 25, 26, 27
sea-floor spreading, 34, 35, 41–42
seafood, 366, 367
seagrasses, 112–113
sea-level changes: effect of greenhouse gases on, 31, 31–32; and extinctions, 91; and geomorphology, 38–39, 45, 48, 52, 55; and human colonization, 126, 127, 128; Huon reef record of, 39, **45**; and soil, 61
seamounts, 37–38
secessionism, 142, 144, 179
secondary ecosystems, 100
secret sites, 275
secret societies, 251, 256
sediment flows: comparative measurements, 51, 65; impact on wetlands, 76–77; and mangroves, 111–112
seeder clouds, **8**
self-alienation, 228, 231
senescence, 103
Sepik River, PNG: cargo cults, 219; catchment area, 71; customary law, 204, 206; flute players, **256**; initiation ceremonies, 216; languages, 162, 164; sacred secrets, 184; savannas, 100, 101
settlement. *See* colonialism; colonization; housing; urbanization
settlements, informal: hostility by governments and elites, 311; infrastructure needs, 77, 314; land registration problems, 313; poverty, 316, 317, 420
settlements, periurban: communications, 411, 412; housing, 313, 314, 315, 318, 319; subsistence, 417
settler colonies, 140, 149, 151, 218, 335
sex, premarital, 266
sexuality: as commerce, 139, 185; control of, 287; in dance, 252, 255; family roles, 176; freedom, 185; notions of pollution, 183; and sexual maturity, 216. *See also* gender
sexually transmitted infections (STI), 288
shantytowns. *See* settlements, informal
shells, 250
shifting cultivation, 100, 342–343, 344, 345, 351, 356, 361
shrimp farms, 112

siblings: bonds, 176; domestic violence, 178; returning migrants, 278
Sigatoka, Fiji, 64, **126**, 347
slave raids, 277
slavery, 178
slit drums, 250, **251**
Snake River, PNG, 100, 101
snowfall, 10, 101
social relations, 172–180; class, 178–179; dispute resolution, **177**; equivalence, 178; ethnicity, 179–180; exchange, 173, **176**, **177**; hierarchy, 178; identity, 172; kinship, 175–176; personhood, 173–175; relatedness, 176; role, 172–173; violence, 177, 178
social stratification. *See* hierarchy
Society Islands, FP, **426**; *arioi*, 276; chiefly systems, 148; colonialism, 140; emergence of coastal plains, 48; endemism, 86, 88; feathers, 240; geologic subsidence, 50; missionaries, 299; quilts, 243
sociopolitical evolution, 132–133
soil, 59–69; acid, 63, **64**; and agriculture, 66–68; carbonate, 64; Cation Exchange Capacity, 66; chemistry, 63–64; degradation, 67, **68**; erosion, 64–66; formation, 62, **63**, **64**; hydrology, 61; management, 63–64; moisture, 60; nutrients, 63; parent material, 60–61; radioactivity, 61; recovery, **62**; and relief, 61; texture, 60; types, 59–60; use, 63–64; and vegetation, 61
solar radiation, 1
solidarity: clan, 238; education, 301–304; family, 271; men, 183; musical encouragement, 258; national, 151; women, 185
Solomon Islands, **425**; agriculture, 342, 351; ancestral shrines, 219; artificial islands, 48; centralization, 418; demography, 263, 266, 268, 269; education, 305, 308; emerged reefs, **50**; employment, 270, 333, 334; explorers, 139; flooding, 50, 73; housing, 313; infectious disease, 76, 77, 296; Internet use, 414; law, 210; logging, 189, 357, 359, 360; marine exports, 368; mining, 382; money, traditional, 177; music, **251**; oil palm plantations, 63, 347; poets, 231; political instability, 153, 154; priestly authority, 221; rain forest, 98, 99; resistance to colonialism, 141; singing, 256; strikes, 179; tourism, 394, 397; urbanization, 177, 270; water supply, 74; women, 188, 271
song: arrivals and departures, 249; conciliatory, 205; contemporary, 257–258; and the environment, 249; European, 257; hymns, 257; in literature, 229, 231, 232; lyrics, 255–256; performance, 254; styles, 256. See also *arioi; music*

sorcery, 218. *See also* magic
Southern Alps, NZ, **9**, 10, 11, 43, 46
Southern Oscillation Index (SOI), **15**, 73, 364
South Island, NZ, **430**; colonialism, 207; conservation, 358; geology, 43; gold, 381; kelp ecosystems, 115; orographic rainfall, 9, 46; river flows, 71; snowfall, 10; subsistence, 129; temperate ecosystems, 102
South Pacific Convergence Zone (SPCZ), 2, **4**, 5, 9, 25
sovereignty. *See* nationalism
speciation, 83, **88**, **89**, 90
spiritual beings, 217, 218
squatter settlements. *See* settlements, informal
Star Mountains, WP, 10
states: colonial, 148–150; contemporary, 151–153
status marking, 178, 237, 244
status rivalry, 131–132, 185,
stereotypes: of gender, 188; of islanders, 214; of leadership, 207; in literature, 227, 228, 229
Stewart Island, NZ, 207, **430**
stick dance, **252**
storms, 7, 8, 9, 10; constructive role on atolls, 52, 55; and floods, 73; and health, 289; interisland community assistance, 249; and ocean waves, 19; in ritual, 255
storytelling, 228, 232, 401
stratification, social, 132–133, 148, 185. *See also* hierarchy
streams: as ecosystems, **109**, 110, 111; and erosion, 49; floods, 73; hydrology, 71; management of, 78; in song, 249
string bands, 257
subduction: backarc basins, 41; island arcs, 39–40; in New Zealand, 42; process, 35–37
subsistence: agricultural, 342; fisheries, 367; and neotraditional village economy, 337; precontact, 128–130. *See also* shifting cultivation
subsistence affluence, 346
sugar: impact on soil, 66–68; plantations, 342, 347, 350; precontact, 127, 168
suicide: "broken dreams," 282; in Melanesia, 178, 184; in Micronesia, 296; in New Zealand, 288; as revenge, 184
Sundaland (Sunda), 125
supertyphoons, 6
surf, 20
surface water, 71
surfing, 168, 373
sustainability: and agriculture, 350–351; and economy, 330; and fisheries, 374–376; and island futures, 145; logging, 357–359; and mining, 383, 388; and tourism, 392, 396, 398. *See also* conservation
Suva, Fiji, **425**; crime, 305, 315; earthquake,

22; houseyard gardens, 344; housing, 313, **314**, 317; literature, 225, 232; pollution, 318; rainfall, 60, 64, 71; tourism, 395; town center, **311**; University of the South Pacific, 229, 302; waste disposal, 319; youth, 231

swamps: as cultural barriers, 164; mangrove ecosystems, 97, 111; as site of ancestors, 215; and taro, 343

sweet potato: cultivation, 343, 346; origins, 341; precontact, 127, 128, 129, 130

symbiosis, coral reefs, 113

T

Tabuaeran (Fanning), Line Islands, Kiribati, 275, 402, **426**

Tahauku Bay, Hiva Oa, 22

Tahiti, FP, **426**, **427**; chiefs, 133, 149, 218; climate, **13**; coastal plain, **48**; colonialism, 140; dance, 254; education, 305; endemism, 85, 87, 88; extinctions, 91; feathered cloaks, 241; gender relations, 184; hymns, 257; invasive species, 100; literature, 225; lithospheric loading, 51; missionaries, 139; nationalism, 143; religious movements, 219; rituals, 217; urbanization, 179; water supply, 73, 75; wedding ceremonies, 243

Talafofo, Guam, 97, 346

Talasea, New Britain, PNG, **130**

talasiqa, 101

Tanna, Vanuatu, **425**; circumcision, 178; Jon Frum Movement, 219, 221; knowledge and power, 217; marriage, 177, 178; missionaries, 141; *nakamal*, 276; *nakwiari* dance cycle, 176; secession movements, 142; thermal groundwater, 75

taonga, 207

Taongi, MI, 96

tapa, 237, 238, 240, 243

tapu (kapu/tabu): concept, 185, 215; in fisheries, 376; in Hawai'i, 139

Taputapuatea, Raiatea, FP, 276

Tarawa, Kiribati, **425**; beach mining, 372; climate, **13**, 45; environmental stress, 313, 318; groundwater, **72**; landlessness, 313, 314; land sales, 195; octopus exports, 197; poverty, 317; remittances, 284; sewage, 75, 319; soil moisture, 64; urban growth, 270; water use, 73

taro: commerical production, 346, 350, 351; cult, 219; cultivation, 343–344, 345–346; as ecosystems, 104; origins, 341; precontact, 126–130, 168; rights to, 193, 197–198

Taro cult, 219

Tasman Sea: currents, 26, 30; low-pressure systems, 7; tectonics, 38, 39, 41, 42

tattoos (*tatau*): application, 255; as art, 237, 238, 243, 244; in ritual, 217

Taukei, 141

Taupo, Lake, NZ, **36**, 43

taupou, 185

Tauranga Harbor, NZ, 53

Taveuni, Fiji, 60, 61, 62

taxes: under colonial rule, 141; contemporary, 143, 151; difficulty of collection, 320; export taxes, 360; import taxes, 414; reduction, 388

tayid, 344

teen pregnancy, 271

tekoteko, 240

Telefomin, PNG, 128

telegraphic cables, 402

telephone penetration rates, 407

telephones, mobile, 401, 406, 407

telephone systems, 403–407

television, 411–413; in education, 305; and globalization, 337; historical aspects, 411–413; impact of, 221, 337; and literature, 245; and religion, 221

temperature: aquatic ecosystems, 115, 117, 118, 356; atmospheric, 10, **11**, 43; global warming, 16–17, 398; and health, 289; long-term, 45; El Niño–Southern Oscillation, 14–15, 30–31; ocean, 23, **24**, 29, 30; and soil, 62–63; in terrestrial ecosystems, 98, 102, 105; thermal groundwater, 72; and voyaging, 133

temples, 132, 133, 218, 241, 276

tenure, 192–199; and absenteeism, 197, 199; and air space, 198; and chiefs, 195, 196, 197, 198; codification of, 194, 313; contemporary, 193–194; land reform, 312; leases, 196, 197, 313, 314, 392; marine, 197; and mineral rights, 198; and minorities, 199; registration, 194–195, 313; solutions, 199; traditional precedents for, 192–193; water, 193; women, 198–199. *See also* land alienation

tephra, 40, 61

terracing, 65, 129, 345

terrestrial ecosystems, 95–108; bogs, 99; controls on, **105**, 106; dryland, 99; fauna in, 104, **105**; high-altitude, **101**; high-latitude, 101–102; leeward, **99**, 100; limestone, 103, **104**; lowland rain forest, 97–**98**; mangrove, **96**, 97; Massenerhebung's effect, 99; montane forest, 98, **99**; profile diagrams of, **95**, **98**; savanna, **100**, 101; secondary, **100**; strand, **95**, 96; ultramafic maquis, **102**, 103; volcanic, **103**; wetland, 97; zonation, **105**

thermocline, **14**, 23, 24, 25

Thio, NC, **380**, 381

thunderstorms, 9, **10**

thyroid cancer, 289

tides, 20, **21**

Tiebaghi, NC, **380**, 381

tiekepe, 337

tifaifai (tivaevae), 243

Tikopia, SI, 39, 185, 215, 249, **425**

Tinian, Northern Mariana Islands, **133**

titles: ceremonies, 237; customary law, 211–212; and descent, 203–204; gender aspects, 185, 189, 198; *matai*, 152, 178, 179, 205, 206

toa, 132

tobacco use, 288, 292

Tokelau, **56**, 249, 254, 255, 327, **426**

Tonga, **426**; agriculture, 347; brass bands, 257; chiefs, 185; dance, 254; diaspora, 338; diet, 291; exclusive economic zone, 372; fine mats, 238, **239**; genealogies, 275; geology, 39, 43, 46, 47, 51; kinship, 176; *koloa*, 237; land ownership, 193, 194; limestone forests, 104; migrants, 267; monarchy, 205; music, **251**, 255; pro-democracy movement, 152; resistance to colonialism, 141, 149; riots, 147; soil, 61; tapa, 243; tourism, 394, 395, 397; water, 71, 76; weddings, 216

Tongatapu, Tonga, 39, **47**, 61, 130, **426**

tornadoes, 10

total coastal fisheries catch and value, 367

total fertility rate, 263, 266, 268, 272n2, 290

total growth rate, population, 265

total resident population, 264, 290, 326

total tuna fisheries catch, 369, 370, 371

tourism, 392–399; advertising, 396; arrivals, 393; categories, 392–393; and climate change, 398; cruise industry, 395; development strategies, 394; economic linkages, 396–397; and the economy, 334; human resource development, 394–395; origins, 393; and political instability, 397–398; and sustainability, 398–399; transport linkages, 394–395

towns. *See* urbanization

trade: balance of payments, 328–333; colonial period, 139, 140, 141; timber, 357–358. *See also* economy; exchange

trade partnerships, 275

trade winds: driving force, 4; location, 1, **2**; and El Niño, 14; and ocean waves, 20; and precipitation, 9, 46; and rainshadow effects, 99; seasonal shifts, 4; and upwelling, 29

transnationalism: corporations, 387; migratory diaspora, 145, 283–284, 419; political instability, 154

Trans–New Guinea languages, 163–164; cognate sets, 163; geographical distribution, 166

transportation: economic costs of, 328, 337, 368, 418; galleon trade, 139; precontact interaction spheres, 130

Treaty of Waitangi, 140, 207, 384

trenches, geologic, 34, 37, 39, 40, 41

Trobriand Islands, PNG, **424**; chiefly authority, 203; descent, 175; hierarchy, 183; *kula* exchange, 177, 275; sexual relations, 184; spiritual knowledge, 217

trophic relationships, 109–110, 118

tropical cyclones, **5**, **6**; and agriculture, 347; and frequency of flooding, **6**; genesis of, 5; and global warming, 16; and El Niño, **15**; and reef islets, **55**, **56**; and tourism, 398

tropical depressions, 7

troughs, low-pressure. *See* pressure, atmospheric

troughs, sea-floor, 42

Truk. *See* Chuuk

trust funds, 143, 330

Trust Territory, 142, 154, 281

tsunamis, **22**, 23, 38, 55, 397

Tuamotu Archipelago, FP, **427**; *barachois,* **52**; interatoll voyages, 215; lithospheric loading, 51; nuclear tests, 142; pearl farming, 197, 278; pearl trade, 139; precontact ritual sites, 133; precontact trade, 130; rubble rampart, **56**

tuberculosis, 288

Tuka Cult, 218

tuna, 334, 364, 369–372

Tutuila, American Samoa, 130, **426**

Tuvalu, **425**; codification of land customs, 194, 212; health, 295; income, 143, 197, 283, 330, 333, 350, 369, 407; inundation rate, 54; relocation, 277; remittances, 284, 334; sanitation, 318; sea level rise, 17, 398; seasons, 11; soil, 64; urbanization, 310; water supply, 73, 75

typhoons. *See* tropical cyclones

U

uab, 287

Ujelang, MI, 214, 277, **425**

ukulele, 257

Ulithi, FSM, **343**, **424**

ultramafic maquis, 102–103, 106

United States: colonialism, 140, 141; Compact of Free Association, 143; decolonization, 154n2; disaporic communities, 258, 335; migration to, 196, 267, 280, 281, 282; mineral exploration, 308; nuclear tests, 142, 277, 307; overseas education, 300, 302, 303, 304; remittances, 328; sashimi market, 370; tourism market, 392

universities, 225–229, 301–306

uplift, lithospheric, 35, 54; at hot spots, 39; of island arcs, 40, 50; islands of mixed lithology, 52; of limestone islands, 51

ʻUpolu, Samoa, **9**, 61, 206, 342, 366, **426**

urban growth rate, 265

urbanization, 310–321; affordability, 313, 314; comparative growth rates, 311; crime, 315; demographic influx, 270, 310; employment, 315–316; future,

320; increasing permanence, 311–312; informal settlements, 312–314; land rights, 313; management, 319–320; minorities, 275; pollution, 317–319; poverty, 316–317

urban population (percent of total), 264, 290

Utrik (Utirik), MI, 134, **425**

V

Vairaatea, Tuamotus, FP, **52**, **129**

Vanua Levu, Fiji, 61, 66, 67, 68, 101, **425**

Vanuatu, **425**; agriculture, 347, 351; cancer, 293; colonial rule, 152; depopulation, 288; ecosystems, 85, 97, 98, 99, 103; esoteric knowledge, 217; geology, **41**, 47, 54; health, 296; inheritance changes, 198; kinship, 175, 176, 177; land alienation, 195; land diving, 209; law, 202, 208, 209, 210; logging, 358, 359, 361; naming, 174; national library, 227; patriarchy, 231; pilgrimages, 276; poverty, 316; reclamation of alienated land, 196; religion, 219, 221, 227; sanitation, 318; slit drums, 250; tourism, 393, 395; urban land shortage, 313, 314; urban planning, 319; volcanic succession, 40–41; water, 73, 74, 77, 78; youth, 273, 317

Vatukoula, Fiji, 379, **380**, 381, 386

Vatulele, Fiji, 54, **425**

Vatu Vara, Fiji, 62

Vavaʻu, Tonga, **47**, **126**, 394

vicariance, 83, 89, 90

violence: colonial, 149, 277; domestic, 178, 316; explorers, 138; and gender, 187–188, 271, 295; toward journalists, 409; mining, 385; postcolonial, 150, 151, 152, 177; and religion, 216; and seafaring, 276; suicide, 178; and tourism, 397; youth, 177. *See also* suicide; warfare

Vitiaz Strait, 275

Viti Levu, Fiji, **425**; agriculture, 63; climate, **9**, 46, 71; erosion, **48**, **49**, 54, 64; rain forest, **98**; shark feeding, 373; *talasiqa* savannas, 101; tsunami, 22; water supply, 73

volcanic ash, 16, 37, 39, 40

volcanic life cycles, 40

volcanoes: atmospheric effects of, 10, 16; ecosystems, 85, 103, 104; as hazard, 10; hot spots, 37–39; island arcs, 39–40; and soils, 59, 60, 61, 62, 63; spreading centers, 39; varieties, **36**; vog, **10**; and water supply, 76

voyaging. *See* seafaring

W

wages: under colonial rule, 141, 142, 276; economic policy, 325; multinationals, 143; postcolonial, 276, 278; in towns, 315

Waikīkī, Honolulu, Hawaiʻi, 48

Waimea, Oʻahu, Hawaiʻi, 53, 54

Wairarapa, NZ, 48

Waitangi Tribunal, 206, 207, 212

Walker circulation, **2**, **14**

Wallacea, 125

Wallace-Huxley Line, 125

Wallis (ʻUvea) and Futuna, 140, 143, 205, 281, 284, 299, **425**

wantok groups, 176, 411

warfare: armor, 241; and art, 238, 243, 244; in colonial period, 140, 177, 277; and gender, 183, 184, 185; and land rights, 193, 194, 195; and music, 256; pacification, 276; precontact, 131–132, 133; reasons for, 132, 177–178; and research, 307; and ritual, 217; shields, 246; theories of, 132. *See also* colonialism; fortifications; violence

waste management. *See* sanitation

water, 70–80; access statistics, 293; allocation of, 78–79; catchment of, 74; chemistry, 76; and disease, 76; droughts, 73; floods, 72–73; importation of, 75; impoundment of, 75; metering of, 75; policy, 75; politics, 78–79; pollution of, 76–77; purification of, 77; quality of, 75–77; rights to, 193; and seafaring, 275, 276; sources of, 70, 71, **72**; table, 72; technology, 74–75; use of, 73–74. *See also* precipitation; sanitation

waterfalls, 249

watersheds: as boundaries, 197; ecosystems, 97, 103, 106, 110; and logging, 359; management, 78, 101, 115

Watom Island, PNG, **126**, **130**

Wau, PNG, 141

waves, 19, **20**

weapons: and gender, 188; precontact, 131; testing, 142, 307

weather, local, 7–10; synoptic-scale, 4–7. *See also* cyclones, tropical; precipitation; storms

weathering, 46, 54, 60, 61, 62, 63

weddings, 216, 243

welcome songs, 249

Wellington, NZ, 43, **430**

wells, 74–75, 77

westerly winds, 1, **2**

West Papua (Irian Jaya), **424**; agriculture, 128; Dani people, 160; glaciers, 10; guerrilla war, 151; Islamic influence, 199; languages, 164; mining, 386; natural gas industry, 382; opposition to migrants, 196

West Sepik Province, PNG, 164

wetlands, 97

whaanau, 175

whaling, 139, 356

whare, 244

whenua, 230

Willaumez Peninsula, PNG, 162

winds: anabatic and katabatic, 8, 10; global, 1–4; as hazard, 5; local, 8; tropical cyclones, 5–7; trades, 4; westerlies, 7

windward/leeward division: ecological significance, 99; erosion differences, 46, 47; orographic effect, 9; precontact settlement, 129; and soil, 60, 63

Witu (Vitu) Islands, PNG, 39

wok meri, 183

Woleai, FSM, 97, **424**

women. *See* gender

women in education, 305–306

wood carving: and arboriculture, 343; canoes, 241; contemporary art, 244; gender aspects, 242; musical instruments, 250; precontact, 237; and ritual, 219; Tangaroa myths, 240

World War I, 141, 149

World War II: cargo cults, 219; and communication, 402; and education, 301, 304; Japanese repatriation, 196; and music, 258; and tourism, 373; as turning point in Pacific history, 141, 142, 244; and wages, 276

World Wide Web, 233, 415

Y

yams: cultivation, 343; precontact, 129; and tenure, 193; in tradition, 341

Yanuca, Fiji, **126**, 289

Yap, FSM, **424**; agriculture, 343, 344; biodiversity, 86; dance, 254; geologic uplift, 40; *sawei*, 131, 249, 275, 276; settlement, 127, 167; social stratification, 148; stone money, 177

Yapen Island, PNG, 164

youth: dance, 217; demographic bulge, 289, 296, 421; employment, 270, 273n20; gangs, 177; in literature, 231; music, 245, 258; organizations, 302; rejection of tradition, 419; sexual and reproductive health services, 266; smoking, 292; suicide, 282; in towns, 317; violence, 178

Production Notes for RAPAPORT / *The Pacific Islands*

Interior designed by University of Hawai'i Press production staff
    with display type in Meta and text type in Minion Pro.

Printing and binding by Sheridan Books
Printed on 60# House White, 444 ppi